BizTalk

Susie Adams, Clifford R. Cannon, Dilip Hardas, Cuneyt Havlioglu, Akhtar Hossein, Charles Kaiman, Tom Lake, Bill Martschenko, Rand Morimoto, Robert Oikawa, Rick Pearson, Kevin Price, Stephen Tranchida, and Larrry Wall

SAMS

Unleashed

BizTalk Unleashed

International Standard Book Number: 0-672-32176-9

Library of Congress Catalog Card Number: 2001097282

Printed in the United States of America

First Printing: March 2001

05 04 03 02 4 3 2 1

Trademarks

All terms mentioned in this book that are known to be trademarks or service marks have been appropriately capitalized. Sams Publishing cannot attest to the accuracy of this information. Use of a term in this book should not be regarded as affecting the validity of any trademark or service mark.

Warning and Disclaimer

Every effort has been made to make this book as complete and as accurate as possible, but no warranty or fitness is implied. The information provided is on an "as is" basis. The authors and the publisher shall have neither liability nor responsibility to any person or entity with respect to any loss or damages arising from the information contained in this book.

Executive Editor
Rochelle J. Kronzek

Development Editor
Songlin Qiu

Managing Editor
Matt Purcell

Project Editors
Christina Smith
Rebecca Martin

Copy Editor
Geneil Breeze

Indexer
D&G Limited, LLC

Proofreader
D&G Limited, LLC

Technical Editor
Larry Wall

Team Coordinator
Pamalee Nelson

Media Developer
Dan Scherf

Interior Designer
Gary Adair

Cover Designer
Aren Howell

Page Layout
D&G Limited, LLC

Contents at a Glance

Contents

About the Author

Susie Adams has been in the computer industry for 15 years. She has been a contributing author on several books including Microsoft Press's *Microsoft Visual InterDev 6.0 Enterprise Developer's Workshop*, Sams Publishing's *Visual InterDev Unleashed*, and several industry journals. She also regularly speaks on Microsoft distributed Web application development topics at industry conferences including Microsoft Tech Ed and VBITS. As a Senior Technology Specialist at Microsoft Corporation, Susie focuses on the evangelism of Microsoft distributed Web solutions, which include COM+, BizTalk, .NET, Visual Studio .NET, and .NET Web Services. Prior to working for Microsoft, Susie was a consultant with several large and small consulting companies specializing in Internet application design and development. In her spare time, she enjoys sports; her friends ; her dogs Willie, Moxie, and Ethel; and playing at the beach.

Dilip Hardas is a Systems Architect at Omicron Consulting's XMLabs in Philadelphia. He enjoys harnessing computing technologies to create effective business solutions, working with Microsoft products and technologies along with open and standards-based systems incorporating XML and Internet technologies. Dilip has shepherded projects and teams, integrating relevant technologies, from inception to delivery. Dilip's interests cover distributed computing systems—not only in their design for robustness, security, and performance but also their application in an increasingly connected world.

Prior to Omicron, Dilip worked for Digital Equipment Corp., Tektronix, and DCM Data Products. He holds a B.Tech degree in Electrical Engineering from IIT Delhi (India) and an M.S. degree in Computer Science from SUNY Buffalo. He is a member of the ACM, IEEE, and AAAI.

Akhtar Hossein is a Senior Consultant at Microsoft, based out of Houston, Texas. His expertise is in architecting and implementing EAI and B2B integration of applications and business processes both within and across organizational boundaries. Akhtar has been involved with BizTalk Server since the Technical Preview version and has been instrumental in implementing EAI solutions for his customers at Clear Channel, Tyco Flow Controls, Compaq, Dell, and others.

Akhtar received his Master's degree in Computer Science in 1989 and has more than 10 years experience in designing and developing software. Akhtar's bachelor's degree is in Civil Engineering, and he has worked as an engineer in the design and construction of process engineering plants in Indonesia and Singapore. Akhtar has traveled extensively and is fluent in five languages. His passion is technology.

Clifford R. Cannon, MCDBA, MCSD, MCSE, MCT, is a Principal Software Architect at InterKnowlogy, LLC (`www.interknowlogy.com`), a Microsoft Certified Partner company.

InterKnowlogy has completed several BizTalk Server projects for units within Microsoft Corporation itself, in addition to developing a major BizTalk and HIPAA consulting practice for customer companies. During more than 20 years of computing experience in medical imaging, computer-aided drug design, and distributed database and financial transaction systems, Cliff has developed three principles for success: rapid and flexible development; attention to customer needs and economic sense; and built-in performance and reliability. He has designed and delivered advanced training courses on BizTalk Server 2002 and has contributed to several database integration and application security projects employing all aspects of BizTalk Server.

Rand Morimoto, MCSE, has been in the computer industry for more than 20 years and as a Premier level member of the National Speaker Association (NSA) is world-renowned for public speaking and authoring books on networking technologies, communication, and security. As president and a senior consultant for Convergent Computing, a San Francisco area based consulting firm, Rand leads the e-business, e-communications, security, and Enterprise Application Integration (EAI) practice of the business. Each year, Rand travels to dozens of countries to speak at conferences and conventions on subjects ranging from electronic commerce, mergers and acquisitions, e-Outsourcing, B2B internetworking, Internet security, and electronic messaging. Rand is also an advisor to the White House, setting domestic policy on electronic commerce and communications.

Kevin Price is a Senior Systems Architect, who has been working with BizTalk since its beta inception, specializing in the securing of information and platform scalability. Kevin has both architecture and hands-on experience using technologies including ASP, Crypto API, JSP, Java, COM/DCOM, VB, C++, .Net, and numerous other technologies related to the Internet and/or the Microsoft-based toolset. Kevin also served as the technical lead responsible for the development and implementation of solutions including supervising teams of multiple developers. Kevin performed consulting engagements with customers to determine their strategic IT direction including both infrastructure and application development and integration. Kevin has been designing Internet-based applications for more than seven years and has also authored chapters for *.NET Framework Security*, 067232184X, also published by Sams Publishing.

Stephen Tranchida is an architect of distributed systems working for Omicron Consulting in Philadelphia. He has been working on application integration challenges for more than 10 years. Stephen is currently in charge of developing an enterprise-class Web portal using Windows DNA 2000 and featuring XML and BizTalk Server. He has consulted for Microsoft on special projects and is the coauthor of *Understanding BizTalk*.

Bill Martschenko is a software architect using COM, XML, XSL, Web Services, BizTalk, and .NET. He is currently Chief Technology Officer at NetEdge Software, which provides BizTalk and Internet products and services.

Rick Pearson is a Lead Software Developer for Applied Research Associates. His experience with BizTalk began at Stingray Software with a project that integrated CORBA and J2EE into BizTalk Orchestration. He became (a little too) familiar with the BizTalk Messaging Configuration object model while creating a series of administrative Web Services for the same project. Although this is Rick's first contribution to a book, he is not new to technical authorship. While at Stingray, he compiled and wrote the first printed User's and Programmer's Guides for Objective Grid. When he isn't writing code, Rick enjoys spending time with his wife, family, and friends.

Tom Lake is a Software Test Engineer at Microsoft, working on BizTalk Server in Redmond, Washington. He has been working on the product since just before the release of BizTalk Server 2000. During the product cycle for BizTalk Server 2002, he worked on testing the new BizTalk replication driver for Application Center 2000.

Rob Oikawa, M.D., MCSE, MCSD, MCT. Since joining Microsoft in 1997, Rob has focused on Web commerce in the manufacturing industry and healthcare domains where most recently he served as Principal Consultant with Microsoft Consulting Services Healthcare. As Microsoft HIPAA Team Chief Instructor, he led the Microsoft Consulting Services team involved with delivery of the service readiness offering for the Microsoft BizTalk Accelerator for HIPAA, first of the Microsoft Solution Offerings, and has worked closely with the Microsoft BizTalk Server Product team in Early Adopter customer deployments with the product since its inception.

Rob received his M.D. from Johns Hopkins in 1979 and pursued post-doctoral work in Biomedical Engineering at Johns Hopkins developing real-time physiology laboratory control and analysis systems. For five years, he worked as an Interventional Cardiologist, returning to software engineering in 1992. In addition to his, M.D., Rob holds a Master's degree in the History of Medicine (1981) from the Johns Hopkins University and an A.B. from the University of Michigan (1974) in Philosophy and Classics. He holds the MCSD, MCSE, and MCT certifications and is a Microsoft Solutions Framework instructor for Application Development, Infrastructure Deployment, and Enterprise Architecture.

Cuneyt E. Havlioglu has been working at Microsoft Corporation for more than three years. He is a Program Manager in the BizTalk Server team managing the BizTalk Accelerator for RosettaNet design and development efforts. Before joining the BizTalk team, he was part of the Microsoft Exchange and BackOffice teams, working on several topics including collaboration applications development and application migration. Prior to joining Microsoft, Cuneyt worked for a financial institution focusing on remote transaction processing solutions. Cuneyt holds an Advanced Computer Science Master's degree from the University of Manchester, UK, where he focused on artificial intelligence, multiprocessor computing, object-oriented programming, and visualization techniques. Outside work, Cuneyt is a sailor in the summer, living with the idea of a year-long dream voyage in the Mediterranean seas, and a snowboarder in the winter, enjoying the beautiful northwest slopes.

Charlie Kaiman has more than eight years experience working with XML and various Internet-related technologies. His early contributions include building SGML and XML applications for the U.S. Congress, and consulting on B2B initiatives with cXML and BizTalk. He has also spoken at numerous conferences, including eGov 2000, on the impact that XML will have on the future of application development. More recently, he has been developing knowledge management solutions for various federal organizations, using .NET and XML. When not focusing on the next breakthrough technologies, he enjoys setting up ski trips out west, playing rugby, and reading those old philosophy books that he never actually understood in college.

Larry Wall has been developing with Visual C++, MFC, Visual Basic, and all the other assorted Microsoft tools since the days of the Windows SDK. For the past few years, he has been architecting and delivering Windows DNA applications and has been heavily involved with BizTalk since its pre-beta delivery at PDC 2000. He is a Microsoft Certified Solution Developer, Microsoft Certified Database Administrator, and a Microsoft Certified Systems Engineer. He is currently the Manager of Microsoft Solutions at Synapse Technology in Charlotte, North Carolina.

Dedication

To my family, friends, and Shas for putting up with my laptop and cell phone, which were on endlessly during the weekends, trips to the beach, and Thanksgiving, even when I promised they wouldn't be.

—Susie Adams

This book is dedicated to my gorgeous wife, Shiuly, and to our children, energetic daughter, Karishma, (10 yrs) and mischievous son, Amir, (7 yrs).

—Akhtar Hossain

To Hannah, Sawyer, and Finn for keeping me laughing everyday.

—Kevin Price

For my wonderful wife, Erin.

—Rick Pearson

This book is dedicated to my fiancé Patricia, who will become my wife on December 27, 2001, in Negril, Jamaica.

—Tom Lake

Thank you to my lovely and patient wife, Ginny, and my children, Evan and Elissa.

—Larry Wall

Acknowledgments

Susie Adams: It would be difficult to say that authoring this book was an effortless and challenge-free process. The challenges began with obtaining approval to write the book and concluded with the daunting task of locating authors in the eleventh hour to tackle some of the most challenging chapters. Many people and resources have gone into making this a successful endeavor. First and foremost I'd like to thank my management at Microsoft for standing by me during the lengthy approval process. I'd also like to thank the BizTalk product team—in particular Nagender Vedula, John Ballard, Scott Woodgate, and Bryan Nylin—for building an awesome product, giving me the support and assistance I needed when scavenging for authors, and answering my questions. It goes without saying that the Sams publication staff deserves much of the kudos and thanks for the completion of this book. In particular, I would like to acknowledge Shelley Kronzek, the Executive Editor for this project, Songlin Qiu, the Development Editor, and Christina Smith, the Project Editor. Without their help and patience, this could not have happened.

I'd like to specifically acknowledge Larry Wall, the Technical Editor who gave up many weekends, missed Thanksgiving dinner, and even worked while hanging Christmas lights! Of course, none of this would be possible without the tremendous efforts of the other coauthors (thank goodness!) on this project: Larry Wall, Akhtar Hossain, Dilip Hardas, Rand Morimoto, Stephen Tranchida, Kevin Price, Rob Oikawa, Bill Martschenko, Cuneyt Havlioglu, Rick Pearson, Charlie Kaiman, Cliff Cannon, and Tom Lake. I commend and thank each of them for their dedication in helping to make this a book a success.

Akhtar Hossein: I want to thank my Managing Consultant, Robyn Pierce, for believing in me and giving me the chance to implement my first BizTalk project. I am grateful to my customers for their strong support and encouragement at Clear Channel (Steve Solomon and Henry Dwrefs), at Tyco Flow Controls (Doug Snyder and Jeff Lynch), at Compaq (Ravnish Luthra and Reza Wajih), and at Dell (Greg Hansen and Manohar Rao). I am also grateful to Sams Publishing for giving me this opportunity and all the editors for tolerating my awful slipped schedules and delays.

Kevin Price: Thanks to Susie Adams for getting me involved; Scot Johnson at i3solutions; Shelley, Pamalee, Songlin, and all at Sams Publishing for keeping things going; and my wife—for not hiding the keyboard.

Rand Morimoto: I want to thank my wife, Kim, and our two children, Kelly and Andrew, for their patience and support as I had my head down at my computer to do the writing for this book.

Rick Pearson: I would like to thank Bill for suggesting me on this project and Susie and Shelley for giving me the chance to do it. I would also like to thank the entire Sams team for guiding me through the process. I would especially like to thank Erin for being so understanding during those late nights and marathon weekends.

Tom Lake: I would like to thank Mahendra Agrawal for encouraging me to apply for the position with BizTalk Server. I am also grateful to all the excellent people on the BizTalk Server team who I work with. Without them we would not have such a wonderful product.

Tell Us What You Think!

As the reader of this book, *you* are our most important critic and commentator. We value your opinion and want to know what we're doing right, what we could do better, what areas you'd like to see us publish in, and any other words of wisdom you're willing to pass our way.

As an executive editor for Sams Publishing, I welcome your comments. You can fax, e-mail, or write me directly to let me know what you did or didn't like about this book—as well as what we can do to make our books stronger.

Please note that I cannot help you with technical problems related to the topic of this book, and that due to the high volume of mail I receive, I might not be able to reply to every message.

When you write, please be sure to include this book's title and authors' names as well as your name and phone or fax number. I will carefully review your comments and share them with the authors and editors who worked on the book.

Fax: 317-581-4770

E-mail: `feedback@samspublishing.com`

Mail: Rochelle J. Kronzek
Executive Editor
Sams Publishing
201 West 103rd Street
Indianapolis, IN 46290 USA

Introduction

Integrating a company's internal applications has traditionally been difficult. Integrating them with external customers, suppliers, or other applications has been even more difficult. Microsoft BizTalk Server 2002 helps alleviate many of these integration challenges in both the enterprise and Internet environments. BizTalk Server 2002 unites enterprise application integration (EAI) and business-to-business (B2B) integration and helps orchestrate business processes for internal applications as well as cross-company business processes.

If you are reading this book, you are probably involved in process integration at some level. Maybe you are responsible for integrating an internal system with other internal applications. Perhaps you have been asked to integrate your Web-based commerce application with your back-end legacy manufacturing system. BizTalk Server's strong support for industry standard data formats and transport protocols including XML, CSV, EDI, HTTP, HTTPS, SMTP, SSL, S/MIME, and x509v3 certificates makes it a powerful tool in a developer's integration toolbox.

Instead of just skimming the surface of what BizTalk Server has to offer, this book provides an overarching view of how BizTalk Server impacts the traditionally difficult application integration tasks developers face.

Who Is This Book's Intended Audience?

This book is intended for both intermediate and advanced users who already know something about BizTalk Server but are still unsure of its various intricacies, technical complexities, and implementation details. The book begins with a brief introduction to BizTalk Server and its related technologies; however, most chapters deal with the more challenging aspects of developing an application that employs one or more of BizTalk Server's application services. Detailed information and example code is given on the new BizTalk 2002 features as well as the correlation of BizTalk Messaging and Orchestration services, the integration of .NET, and the RosettaNet and HIPPA BizTalk Server accelerators.

What Do You Need to Know Prior to Reading This Book?

This book is intended to augment a developer's knowledge of specific BizTalk server topics; therefore, this book assumes a basic knowledge of BizTalk Server and its capabilities. It is also helpful to have some knowledge about Microsoft development tools and languages including Visual Studio 6, Visual Studio .NET, and Visual Basic. Many examples include application code written using one or more of each.

What Will You Learn from This Book?

This book covers a wide range of implementation and development tools, techniques, and technologies for use with BizTalk Server. You will learn everything from the basic foundation and history of XML to how to create, transform, process, and configure BizTalk server specifications, maps, and BizTalk Messaging.

What Software Will You Need to Complete the Examples Provided with This Book?

Each chapter in the book minimally requires the use of the developer version of BizTalk Server 2000. At the time of the writing of this book, BizTalk Server 2002 was in release candidate status, and as such most of the chapters have been tested and discuss BizTalk Server 2002 features and functionality. The two accelerator chapters require either BizTalk Server 2000 or BizTalk Server 2002 with service pack 1 for each of the accelerators. From a developer perspective, Visual Studio 6.0, including Visual Basic and Visual C++ are required as well as the PDC 2001 or better version of Visual Studio .NET for the two chapters discussing the integration of .NET.

How This Book Is Organized

This book is divided into the following parts:

- **Part I. Setting the Stage for BizTalk Server:** This part briefly introduces the basic concepts fundamental to the BizTalk Server product, including the business problems addressed by BizTalk Server's services and a quick introduction to XML and XML programming concepts. It then concludes with an introductory chapter on BizTalk Server.

- **Part II. BizTalk Server Messaging:** This part discusses BizTalk Server Messaging services and its associated tools. It begins with an introduction to the BizTalk Editor and BizTalk Mapper. Both the Mapper and Editor chapter include step-by-step examples on how to create BizTalk Server specifications and maps. After you've mastered the tools, we move on to an introduction to BizTalk Messaging Services and the configuration of BizTalk Messaging properties, including the use of the BizTalk Messaging Desk.
- **Part III. BizTalk Server Orchestration:** Part III introduces and then discusses BizTalk Server Orchestration in detail. It begins with an introduction to business process workflow concepts and the BizTalk Orchestration Designer. It then walks through a step-by-step explanation of how to create and run a BizTalk Orchestration schedule.
- **Part IV. Advanced BizTalk Server Topics:** This part includes content on advanced BizTalk Messaging and Orchestration topics including BizTalk Messaging and Orchestration correlation and the integration of .NET and .NET Web Services.
- **Part V. Extending BizTalk Server:** This part discusses how to extend the capabilities of BizTalk Messaging using Application Integration Components and the BizTalk configuration object model. It concludes with a detailed discussion on how to create custom BizTalk serializers and parsers.
- **Part VI. BizTalk Server Administration:** This part addresses how to install, deploy, and manage BizTalk Server applications and services.
- **Part VII. Line of Business Adapters and Industry Toolkits:** This part discusses two BizTalk Server accelerators, HIPPA and RosettaNet. It introduces the concepts surrounding the standards and then explains in detail how to install and build applications that use them.
- **Part VIII. Appendixes:** This book includes two appendixes. The first discusses XML and its associated technologies. The second serves as a reference to the BizTalk Server Editor document properties.

What's on the Sams Web Site for This Book

The associated code files described in this book are available on the Sams Web site at `http://www.samspublishing.com/`. Enter this book's ISBN in the Search box and click Search. When the book's title is displayed, click the title to go to a page where you can download all the code in a chapter-by-chapter zip file format.

Conventions Used in This Book

The following typographic conventions are used in this book:

- Code lines, commands, statements, variables, and any text you type or see onscreen appears in a `mono` typeface. **`Bold mono`** typeface is often used to represent the user's input.
- Placeholders in syntax descriptions appear in an *`italic mono`* typeface. Replace the placeholder with the actual filename, parameter, or whatever element it represents.
- *Italics* highlight technical terms when they're being defined.
- The ➥ icon is used before a line of code that is really a continuation of the preceding line. Sometimes a line of code is too long to fit as a single line on the page. If you see ➥ before a line of code, remember that it's part of the line immediately preceding it.
- The book also contains Notes, Tips, and Cautions to help you spot important or useful information more quickly. Some of these are shortcuts to help you work more efficiently.

Setting the Stage for BizTalk Server

PART I

IN THIS PART

CHAPTER 1

Motivation and Uses for BizTalk Server

by Rand Morimoto

In This Chapter

As the opening chapter of this book, instead of stepping you through the basic features and functions of the BizTalk Server product, this chapter shares ways that organizations around the world have implemented BizTalk to improve their internal and external business processes. Unlike traditional case studies that tell you about great solutions implemented by various companies but then fall short of telling you how to actually implement the solutions yourself, this chapter introduces you to creative business-improving scenarios and then refers you to parts and chapters later in this book that actually step you through the implementation of these technologies and solutions in your own environment.

From this chapter, you will gain a significantly broader perspective of what BizTalk Server can do to fulfill the business requirements of virtually any organization that needs to exchange data between multiple systems. BizTalk Server is a powerful tool that can help an organization overcome its traditional challenges of business-to-business, application-to-application, and enterprise application integration needs.

BizTalk as an Enabler, Not Just a Product

When you opened this book, you probably already knew that BizTalk Server is a Microsoft server-based application that helps organizations simplify their business-to-business transaction processes through a series of data translation tools. But you might not be aware of all that BizTalk does that extends far beyond the basic functionality of simple data mapping between two or more systems. BizTalk Server enables an organization to simplify its transaction-based communications to business partners while providing the tools necessary for more efficient internal enterprise application integration. When fully leveraged, a BizTalk Server implementation is an enabler that helps an organization simplify the process and improve the throughput of data and information between business partners, as well as improve the integration of business applications within an organization. This in turn decreases transaction costs while it improves business efficiency, which ultimately serves to make the organization more competitive in its core business activities.

Facilitating Business-to-Business (B2B) Communications

Although the common perception of BizTalk Server is that it is a business-to-business gateway, effectively a replacement of EDI gateway systems, BizTalk has the capability of doing much more. In the area of business-to-business (B2B) transactions, an organization typically needs the capability to transfer and synchronize information not just with one business partner but with several different organizations as shown in Figure 1.1. This frequently requires the flexibility of supporting numerous different transaction formats to meet the various B2B communication needs.

FIGURE 1.1
BizTalk Server in a B2B environment.

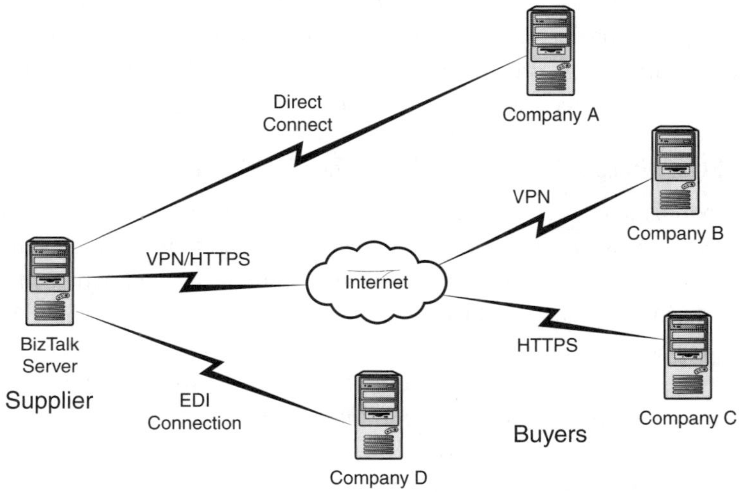

Not only are the transactional formats different between business partners, but also the type of B2B communications can vary in function and complexity. Some organizations may need to exchange purchase order information, whereas other organizations may need to exchange entire inventory and pricing data. These different interpretations of what B2B communications is creates the need to have different types of solutions fulfilled by as few systems as possible.

BizTalk Server is such a system that provides the capability for multiple organizations with varying needs to exchange data in areas such as automated procurement, product catalog exchange, business-to-business portal, and embedded forms Data Submission. These common B2B uses of BizTalk Server are highlighted in the following sections.

Automated Procurement

Automated procurement is the common use of current Electronic Data Interchange (EDI) transactions, where orders are placed electronically between business partners. BizTalk Server supports traditional EDI transaction formats (such as ANSI X12 and UN/EDIFACT), or more flexible XML-based automated procedure processes can be created between business partners to facilitate B2B transaction processing. It is through agreed on send and receive formats that organizations can transact electronic business.

Product Catalog Exchange

Another common B2B communication process involves the exchange of product catalogs. This might be as simple as exchanging a simple part number and price list or as complex as exchanging entire inventory availability information and detailed client data. Typically in a product catalog exchange, large sets of data are transferred, and depending on the type of business, the information may be updated weekly, daily, or even near real-time. As just-in-time order and fulfillment processing becomes common in B2B transactions, the need to have accurate and current information becomes important.

Business-to-Business (B2B) Portals

B2B portals have become popular in the past couple of years as a hybrid method of having both a local copy of product catalog information as well as links to real-time availability information. Because inventory availability can change frequently for organizations building products on demand, or in high transactional industries, having real-time access to inventory availability becomes important between trading partners. However, complete real-time solutions that require a Web-based transactional look-up system are typically slow or prone to Internet-induced delays and have been found to be unpopular among busy purchasing agents. B2B portals provide the best of both worlds where part number, product description, product details, and other relatively static information is exchanged in a Product Catalog Business to Business Exchange process; however, the dynamically changing information, such as price and availability, either is automatically updated in real-time or requires a simple query/request.

The end result is the fastest access to the most up-to-date information exchange between business partners. BizTalk Server can be configured to support the product catalog exchanges, and an XML script can be written to automatically query and update the dynamic portions of information that needs to be requested.

Embedded Forms Data Submission

Another common B2B transaction process is one where forms data is electronically exchanged between business partners. Traditionally, forms data is entered on paper and then the data is entered into a database system. There are various methods of data input. With direct entry, information is keyed right into the database directly. Information also can be captured and queued on one system and then transacted in a batch process to the database system. BizTalk Server can facilitate the batch processing of information by having information captured by one system and dumped into a BizTalk Server either record by record or batched as a series of data into a system. In either case, BizTalk Server simplifies the exchange of information between trading partners because proprietary gateway and transaction systems do not need to be built for each business partner.

Because BizTalk Server supports multiple transaction formats, when multiple partners need to submit and consolidate information to a single source, a common BizTalk Server can accept the information in a variety of different input formats to the common system.

Providing Enterprise Application Integration (EAI)

Although BizTalk Server can provide a variety of B2B transaction processes, as noted in the previous section, the product can also provide internal Enterprise Application Integration (EAI). For years, organizations have been challenged with integrating business applications, and typically an organization would have data entered manually into multiple systems. Manual data entry is not only a tedious task, but it is also prone to typographical errors and delays in data transaction. The EAI capabilities of BizTalk Server, shown in Figure 1.2, allow disparate internal business systems, such as an accounting and finance system, to seamlessly communicate with customer relationship management, point of sale, and manufacturing or production line systems.

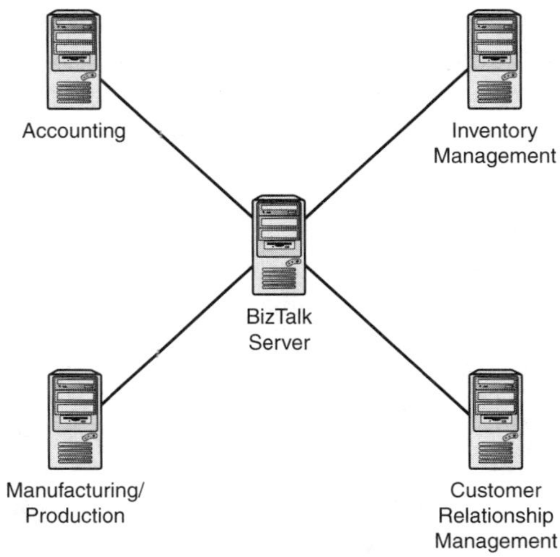

FIGURE 1.2
BizTalk Server in an EAI environment.

BizTalk Server is used several ways in an enterprise application integrated environment. Some solutions include business process integration, back-end supply chain integration, and consolidation of information. These various methods are highlighted in the following sections.

Business Process Integration

Instead of trying to find an "all-in-one" system that provides an organization with customer relationship tools, sales force automation tools, finance, general ledger, inventory management, cost accounting, and other business modules, using BizTalk Server provides a method for application-to-application transactions to simplify business process integration functionality. Most organizations find that the "all-in-one" solutions do not exist, are expensive, or are a combination of overpriced and mediocre functionality. As an EAI enablement tool, BizTalk Server either links existing business process applications together or allows an organization to acquire best of breed solutions and then link core data between the applications.

Back-end Supply Chain Integration

As organizations provide electronic commerce access for transactional order processing (either business to business, or business to consumer), the organization has to automate its back-end supply chain processes so that it provides scalability to transactional events. Many organizations accept orders over the Internet; however, the simple form entry system accepts the order that then needs to be manually keyed in to a point of sale or order processing system. Although an organization may set up a fully electronic commerce front-end system for clients to look up product information, price, and availability, the front-end e-commerce system needs to be tightly tied in to the accounting and order processing system on the back-end.

BizTalk Server provides the link between the front-end and back-end system through application-to-application integration support, thus providing a way for an organization to minimize the double entry or manual entry processes created by accepting business online.

Consolidation of Information

Another common use of BizTalk Server in an application-to-application environment is sharing internal data between applications rather than having islands of independent information as is traditional for many organizations. Instead of having a separate customer list for e-mail, order processing, and billing and accounting, BizTalk Server can be set up to share common data between the back-end systems. This might be as simple as sharing organization data, such as billing addresses and contact information, or it can be as complex as completely integrating customer data along with order data within the transactional information.

When successfully integrated, an organization can minimize the time it spends manually entering or re-entering information between systems, and it helps the organization scale its order processing capabilities by transferring information between systems automatically through a BizTalk Server system.

BizTalk Server Solves Business Needs

BizTalk Server solves several business needs and helps an organization stay in business. In any business model, efficiency allows the organization to decrease overhead costs and thus provides the organization the capability to operate more profitably than other less-efficient organizations. When competition or market conditions force prices to fall, anything that the organization can do to improve its efficiency and lower its costs will help the organization remain profitable.

Additionally, BizTalk Server can improve the response times on transactions and communications, improve relationships, and decrease transaction costs so that the organization can grow its market size and customer base without extending excessive costs to achieve the growth. BizTalk Server enables an organization to meet the business challenges of growth without exponentially increasing overhead costs and inefficiencies.

Providing Tools to Exchange Disparate Information

BizTalk Server is a single server system that accepts various data inputs and transmits various data outputs both in a common XML-based format or through the support of standard transaction formats such as EDI or HTTP. Chapter 3, "Overview of BizTalk Server," provides an introduction to the graphical mapping tool included with the BizTalk Server software that helps an organization map data fields for information exchange. With the graphical tool, an organization can take proprietary input data (or structured common information data) and map fields between the input and the output system.

Through the inclusion of integrated security technologies built-in to Windows 2000 and BizTalk Server, transacted communications is secured to ensure privacy and data integrity.

Improving the Speed of Data Interchange

When mapped, information can be exchanged automatically between business trading partners, and there is no need for double or multiple manual entry of information. Additionally, there is no need for scheduled exports or imports or datasets nor is there a need to go through a third-party communication provider, such as a Value-Added Network (VAN) commonly used in EDI transactions. By mapping information directly between business partners, organizations can set up a direct connection over a private telecommunication connection (such as a lease line), or the organization can set up a server-to-server dial-up communication link, or even set up a virtual private network over the Internet to directly connect business partners for communications.

By improving the method and process of communications between business partners, an organization can increase the speed of data interchange. This efficiency translates not only to faster transaction processing, but also means fewer levels of double entry, conversion scripts, and other transactional communication systems that can induce corruption of data and transactional delays in information processing.

Creating Transaction Standards

Another benefit of BizTalk Server is its use of standards. BizTalk Server uses industry standard XML and SOAP to link messaging formats between business partner systems, or it can use existing standards, such as EDI ANSI X12 or HTTP. The biggest drawback in most B2B integrated solutions is the dependence on a proprietary gateway that links the information between business systems. Although the proprietary system fulfills the need to integrate two systems, it provides no scalability or cross-integration with other systems; therefore, a gateway or proprietary communication system must be purchased, configured, and supported between every business application.

Additional transaction standards supported by BizTalk Server include HTTPS, SMTP, and MSMQ. These formats enable secured transaction processing, Internet-based system-to-system communication, and message transaction queuing and logging, respectively.

Security is of great importance as organizations share information between business partners over traditionally unsecured communication links, such as the Internet. With public key integration built in to the Windows 2000/BizTalk Server 2002 environment, secured PKI transactions can ensure both privacy as well as integrity of information between trading partners.

Building B2B transactions on industry standards not only provides ease of development and product integration, but also provides a common communication transport mechanism between business partners. Many organizations set up business systems and then the communication links are delayed as security officers for the business trading organizations scrutinize the desired opening of firewall "ports" between sites to share information. When proprietary systems are built, they frequently use proprietary communication systems. However, because BizTalk Server uses standards, such as SMTP, PKI, HTTP, and HTTPS, most internetworking infrastructures already support those data formats to pass through firewalls. Simply add a BizTalk Server to the firewall filter list, and the BizTalk Server system will be able to share information with a trading partner.

Decreasing the Cost of Transactions

All organizations want to decrease their cost of transactions, and BizTalk Server can minimize costs because of its use of off-the-shelf Microsoft/Intel technologies over existing Internet-based connection links. Unlike traditional EDI systems that require transactions to be conducted through a Value Added Network (VAN), typically over dedicated lease line or frame relay connections (or slow dial-through systems), BizTalk Server can provide communications with a business partner directly over the Internet. For a more secure connection, the trading partners can set up a Virtual Private Network (VPN) that would create a dedicated tunnel over the Internet to facilitate B2B communications.

As noted earlier, because transactions are automated, the entry costs (both in terms of manual data entry, as well as the cost of incurring typographical errors when information is manually entered) impact efficiencies and typically increase the cost of transactions. With the automated system built-in to BizTalk Server, entry costs decrease due to the elimination of manual data entry systems and the costs associated with entry errors.

Finally, because BizTalk Server runs on a single off-the-shelf Microsoft/Intel platform computer system, the cost of purchasing and maintaining proprietary specialized communication devices is greatly minimized.

Increasing Market Share and Business Opportunities

As an organization leverages the capabilities of BizTalk Server, it also lowers its costs and increases its flexibility on communication standards that ultimately increase the organization's capability to establish more business partnerships and conduct more B2B transactions. This increase in market share and business opportunities, through the use of standards and Internet communications, also provides the organization the capability to expand its reach to new geographies with little increase in transaction overhead. Typically as an organization increases its market reach, it linearly if not exponentially increases its overhead in incremental cost of doing business in the larger geography.

Enabling Marketplace Competitiveness

When properly implemented and integrated into external as well as internal business and application environments, BizTalk Server makes an organization more easily accessible to more businesses and people than before. The lowering of costs and the increase in market share enables the organization to attract more business opportunities and thus creates an economy of scale that improves marketplace competitiveness.

Additionally, the lower cost of transactions means that scalability costs are more likely to be linear than exponential thus increasing business without a commensurate increase in transaction overhead costs. Because BizTalk provides a single source for both external and internal B2B and application-sharing functionally, the use of the technology can also help an organization scale down its operation or increase its growth depending on the organization's needs. Many times, an organization loses a client and is forced to make drastic cuts in overhead allocated to manage and maintain the infrastructure needed to support the business the client transactions used to require. However, with BizTalk Server, because a single server can provide a host of services to multiple business partners, it enables the organization to decrease its market share dynamically while retaining the same support mechanisms and resources because system components and operational overhead have already been taken into account with the implementation of BizTalk Server.

Improving Business Relationships

As an organization lowers its costs, improves its response times, provides more flexibility on the input and output format of information, uses a host of industry standards, and has the capability to make input/output changes quickly, the end result leads to an improvement in business services and business relations with its clientele. Customer service is built on quality, reliability, competitive costs, and fast response time, all the business relationship and business value proposition tasks of an organization.

BizTalk Server's Role in Other Data Exchange Needs

Although BizTalk Server can help organizations solve their business needs, there are many data transactions within an organization or between organizations that are not necessarily going to be facilitated better by BizTalk. Using the right tool for the right job is important in ensuring the successful implementation of the solution.

What Would You Use if BizTalk Server Did Not Exist

For organizations just beginning to build their B2B and EAI environments, having a solution like BizTalk Server makes sense as an immediate B2B/EAI solution.

However, for organizations already using some type of business solution, the issue relative to conversion becomes important to know what BizTalk Server can and cannot do.

Some typical B2B business transaction systems used in place of BizTalk Server include customized Electronic Data Interchange (EDI) solutions, Direct Point-to-Point Connected Transactions systems, Custom APIs configurations, HTTP Web-based Direct Entry solutions, File Transfer Protocol (FTP) procedures, and Fax/Mail Data Entry systems. All these traditional technologies are discussed in the following sections.

Electronic Data Interchange (EDI)

EDI is a system that provides a set series of parameters that organizations can use to electronically exchange data with each other. Several EDI templates define field names that an organization would agree on that need to be exchanged, such as part number, description, quantity, unit price, extended price, and so on. Two or more organizations would agree on which fields to exchange.

After the fields are agreed on, the organization would set up or contract with a VAN that is the intermediary that accepts incoming EDI information and transports the information to the agreed on destination. Both the sending and receiving organizations acknowledge their transmissions as well as receive confirmations of the completed transaction.

EDI is frequently implemented on the BizTalk Server to provide an interim standard for communications between two existing business trading partners. However, after an XML-based transfer script is set up, the organizations could change from communicating via the VAN of EDI data to conducting business transactions over a secured connection on the Internet directly to each other. In practice, BizTalk Server does not necessarily replace EDI altogether, but rather organizations using EDI can implement BizTalk Server and send transactions over nonproprietary Internet standard transports or VANs, and eliminate costly EDI translators.

Direct Point-to-Point Connected Transactions

Organizations that want to ensure a higher level of security or organizations where the transmit and receive software does not have built-in security safeguards may find that it requires a point-to-point connection between them and their business partners. From an internetworking perspective, the connection may be a dedicated lease line or a frame relay line. However, in any case, the connection links two or more organizations by the way of a physical connection to and from the sites.

A direct connected transaction link has the advantage of scaling transmission speed and throughput based on the needs (and the budget) of the organization. Because the connection is typically paid for on a flat monthly fee as opposed to a per-session or per-packet of transmitted data like a VAN or other proprietary connection, an organization can use 56 KB, 256 KB, half-T1 (768 KB), full-T1 (1.54 MB), or faster link speeds 24 hours a day, 7 days a week. This availability in communication bandwidth provides the organization a significant amount of flexibility in transmitting or even streaming large sets of data between sites.

The reason an organization using this solution may choose to standardize on a BizTalk Server type solution is the cost of connected link. Although connection to a single business partner within a few miles of the host organization may only cost $300–$500 per month, lease lines become expensive over long distances ($1000–$5000 per month domestically, $3000–$15,000 per month internationally). Also, the cost of a lease line connection is charged "per site," so an organization that wants to connect to 100 locations will pay 10 times more than the cost of connecting to just 10 locations. This linear cost becomes extremely expensive as the organization expands its market share and market reach.

Custom APIs

After an organization selects a method of transmission, the format of communication between sites needs to be determined. One method is creating custom programming scripts using the Application Programmer Interface (API) published by the application software of the two organizations' software programs. An organization can conceivably have a custom application written that provides the sending party and the receiving party a method of exchanging information.

Writing custom API applications between trading parties or internal to an organization has been a necessity in most cases in the past where applications have had few options for exporting or importing information across disparate systems. However, because every system requires a custom application to be written, it becomes expensive, and it can take weeks or months to connect the organizations' systems.

By standardizing on a system like BizTalk Server that has tools to exchange information between business partners, it is much faster to interconnect systems.

HTTP Web-Based Direct Entry

In the past two to three years, organizations have provided their business partners with Web-based look-up and entry tools so that users can gain real-time access to price, availability, and other information. However, although these solutions provide direct access to information, performance is limited to the speed of the site-to-site connection. When multiple users in a single site want to access information stored on a server hosted in another site, user access has no performance gains because each session is independent of the other. All the Web-based direct entry system does is offload the entry process from the supplier to the buyer. Suppliers typically want to burden the customer the least to provide valuable customer service and to retain the business from that customer, so Web-based direct entry systems do little to improve customer satisfaction.

For organizations that have high activity of information look-up between business partners, having a dedicated system extract and transmit information between the business partners allows for a local copy of data to be stored on the LAN of the trading partner. This transfer of selected information using a BizTalk Server can drastically minimize the amount of time a user might normally take to access her existing Web-based solution.

File Transfer Protocol (FTP)

The file transfer protocol (FTP) is a common method for organizations to exchange information. One organization sets up an FTP server and provides a logon and password to the other organizations to send or receive files. The files could be updated product catalog information stored in a data file, it could be raw data prepared to be imported directly into a database, or the information could be a scanned image file or other document file containing purchase order type information. FTP transfers can be automated to allow the transfer of information to occur automatically at set times.

FTP does nothing to facilitate the management or synchronization of data with the data file, so if just a few of the objects in a dataset change, the entire data file needs to be FTP transferred rather than just a few objects. This greatly extends the amount of information that needs to be exchanged on a regular basis, whereas a system that exchanges data at the field level can make sure that the most current fields of information are updated regularly.

Fax/Mail with Manual Data Entry

The last common data exchange process used in business transactions is one where information is manually written or printed onto a form and faxed or mailed to another location where it is then manually keyed in to the database system. This process obviously has no electronic data exchange mechanism built-in and has the potential for data entry errors or other errors induced by a manual system.

When Is BizTalk Server Not the Right Solution?

Because BizTalk Server provides seamless system-to-system data interchange functionality, it is common to believe that BizTalk Server will provide virtually any type of data interchange service for an organization. There are, however, other tools that more commonly and more appropriately provide the data interchange tasks for specific functions much better. This includes using tools such as electronic messaging (e-mail) systems, file replication tools, or database system specific replication tools.

Ad Hoc Message Communications

For the ad hoc exchange of information between partners or business organizations that includes unformatted text or information frequently stored in different file formats, configurations, or settings, e-mail is frequently a better system to allow this form of data interchange. Most B2B interchange systems expect information exchanged between trading partners to be formatted in similar formats so that the information can be properly parsed with automated scripts properly extracting the right information from the data transfer.

XML- and SOAP-based transaction scripts can be created to analyze a file and extract specific sets of data from the file. Additionally, scripts can be created to even analyze the file format itself and apply an appropriate filter to the file. However, there are limitations in file format filters and data parsing filters that should be applied to an automated process before automated errors are induced to the system. To maintain better accuracy in the exchange of data, the more structured the transfer file format and content is, the better chance the system has to extract the right information from the exchange.

Data File Transfers

When an organization needs to replicate large sets of files between locations and not look specifically at the data contained within the files but rather just look at the time and date stamp of the file for relative changes to the file itself, the organization is more likely better off with a file replication tool, not a B2B interchange tool such as BizTalk Server. BizTalk Server can be configured to analyze entire file sets and exchange the information between servers and locations; however, BizTalk is better suited to taking structured data and transacting the information between locations.

Database-to-Database Replication

For most database systems, a built-in database replication process is either included or available for the database to analyze information within the database and synchronize the parts of the database that require duplication. Because BizTalk Server does not have the built-in tools to look into a database and analyze specific changed data content, it will not efficiently manage the replication of database content. An integrated replication tool for a specific database system keeps track of transactions sent and received between databases, handles duplicate records between datasets, handles aging and data conflicts, and typically has a roll back or roll forward mechanism to ensure that database information remains consistent.

BizTalk Server Scenarios

To better understand how BizTalk Server can help an organization leverage the capabilities of the product, this section presents several scenarios noting how BizTalk Server can be implemented to improve data transaction interchange. Seven different scenarios are given with the first four (automated procurement, product catalog exchange, B2B portals, and embedded forms data submission) focused on B2B transaction scenarios, and the last three (business process integration, back-end supply chain integration, and consolidation of information) focused on internal EAI scenarios.

Automated Procurement

In this first scenario, two organizations want to automate their procurement system on B2B transactions. Currently, the organizations use a combination of manual fax forms that contain purchase order information that is then manually entered into the order processing system, and the organizations exchange information over a Web-based data entry system. The buyer does not like the Web-based data entry system because it takes a lot of time and effort to manually key in similar orders, and when the Internet is slow, there are considerable delays in accessing and entering information. The buyer prefers to continue to process the information in his local purchase order system, print the purchase order, fax it to the supplier, and have a customer service representative contact him with a confirmation of the order receipt and processing.

The supplier created the Web-based data entry system to cut costs by having the buyer enter the information directly into the order processing system. Although the concept sounded great when it was being developed, the supplier realized that although organizations want to occasionally look up current price and availability information or they want to check on the status of an existing order, buyers rarely want to actually key in their own order information. This is primarily due to the fact that the buyer is already keying the information in his own purchase order transaction system. So for the buyer to enter it into the supplier's system over the Web creates a double entry system that burdens the buyer.

The solution in this scenario was to install BizTalk Server and have information extracted straight from the buyer's purchase order creation system and securely transfer the information to the supplier's order entry system, as shown in Figure 1.3. The automation built-in to this system requires the buyer to enter the information only once. That information is then parsed to create a transaction ticket that is transferred to the supplier's system that is automatically processed in the supplier's order entry. The automated structure eliminates entry errors, decreases the transaction time to process the information, and allows both the buyer and the supplier to see real-time transaction reports.

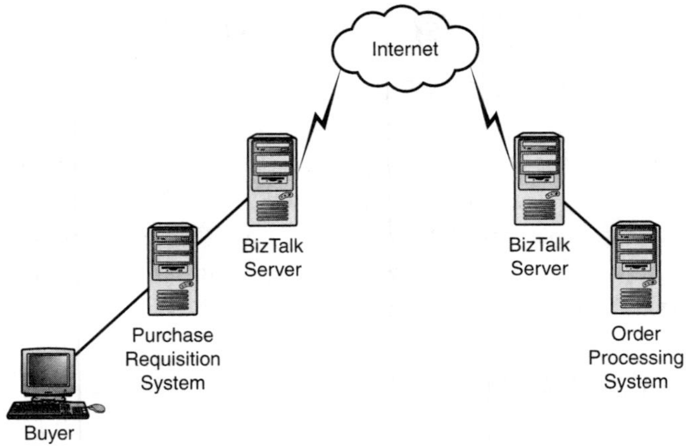

FIGURE 1.3
Using BizTalk Server in an automated procurement process.

Because all the transactions are now automated, the buyer can get order confirmations much faster than before. Additionally, because there is only a single entry of the information into the buyer's own purchase requisition system, both the buyer and the seller do not need to re-enter the information, thus creating a faster transaction system for scaling additional orders into the system. The buyer can now drastically increase purchase volumes without having to increase the time spent to process the orders beyond basic entry. The supplier can scale up or scale down transactions to this client and to other clients without adding personnel to process the orders because they are automatically handled by BizTalk Server.

Overall, both buyer and seller can lower their transaction costs, improve transaction times, and minimize errors introduced to the system. This scenario is created and implemented through the use of BizTalk Server Messaging, which is detailed in Part II, "BizTalk Server Messaging."

Product Catalog Exchange

In this scenario, an organization wants to receive the latest part number, price, and product description catalog of its major supplier. Today, the catalog is provided in both a printed form that is mailed each month as well as an electronic copy that is available for download weekly. The challenge to this process is that the information is frequently out-of-date, and it requires the buyer to manually download the updated catalog. Furthermore, when the buyer wants to select an item, the individual must enter the information into the purchase requisition system, which has created an occasional data entry error in the past.

The better solution for these organizations was to set up a BizTalk Server system in each location and have the price, part number, and description information parsed for any changes and automatically extracted and sent to the buyer's BizTalk Server. The buyer's BizTalk Server translates the information and formats the data to be imported directly into the buyer's requisition system. Because the information only processes modified data, the amount of information transferred regularly is minimal. Because the information is updated regularly, the buyer's requisition system has the most current set of part numbers, pricing, and descriptions readily available for requisitions to be created immediately. Any changes are automatically reflected in the buyer's system.

Because the supplier's part numbers are used all the way from requisition through order processing, there are no longer any errors caused by the mistyping of information. Additionally, because the information is automatically updated, there is no longer the need for either the buyer or the seller to create product catalogs, create download catalogs, or manually update information. This has a huge benefit to the buyer by minimizing interaction time to acquire up-to-date information, and it greatly improves the transaction time because outdated part numbers and incorrect price information are no longer introduced to the system. Both organizations have been able to decrease their cost per transaction, and the supplier has even been able to replicate the process for several other organizations wanting updated price, product description, and part number information provided in real-time.

B2B Portals

Although the previous scenario provides a way to exchange part number, product description, and price information updated regularly, it fails to provide up-to-date product availability information. As an extension to the previous scenario, after the product catalog exchange was working perfectly, the same two organizations wanted to eliminate a manual step that required the buyer to call to check on availability of the products being ordered. Because most products are regularly available, the buyer can assume that any order placed would typically be filled; however, certain items are purchased in quantity on an irregular basis and frequently need to be special ordered. Although this is limited to a certain list of products on a random basis, the buyer wants the ability to check availability on a real-time.

The solution was to extend the product catalog exchange system to include a B2B portal add-in that links availability information to the regularly updated price, part number, and detailed description information. The first revision of the solution allowed the buyer to click on a link that then sent a query to the supplier's system that displayed product availability in 2 to 3 seconds. Because the buyer was really only interested in the availability of certain parts on any given order, the portal look-up to the information provided the desired results of having real-time access to product availability information.

However, over time, the buyer wanted to see availability on all items being purchased and wanted to have not only the ability to one-click request current availability, but also to have product availability automatically appear onscreen for all items desired for purchase. This requires an automated portal processing system that takes the queued-up order and automatically requests the parts availability information to be sent to the buyer's system. After the modification was added to the system, within 3 to 4 seconds, all order requisition information had the corresponding current availability information for parts displayed onscreen.

The buyer now has all the information desired including price, part number, detailed product description, and product availability data. The supplier does not have to provide a full-time customer service representative to export data files and relay availability information. Instead, the mundane tasks are automated, providing faster access to more accurate information. Rather than eliminate the customer service position, the supplier trained the customer service representative to provide more specific service information to the buyer, follow up on transactions, and improve other customer support tasks for the client. This enables the supplier to provide new services that ultimately improve the communications and relationship, thus improving relations with the buyer.

This solution is built on application integration components that are plugged in to BizTalk Server that extend BizTalk Server beyond just data transfers but also into portal information access, scripted queries, and updates to information. This solution to BizTalk Server can be found in Part IV, "Advanced BizTalk Server Topics," which is specific to Web Services integration, as well as in Part V, "Extending BizTalk Server," which discusses application integration components.

Embedded Forms Data Submission

In this scenario, an organization accepts orders from buyers in a variety of formats, including orders written on paper and mailed and orders printed on forms and faxed. Other information is manually entered over both a Web-based and a custom entry form system directly into the supplier's business system. However, as the organization began to grow, the amount of time and resources required to process the information grew. Additionally, because the organization's business is seasonal, the constant hiring for the holidays and then reducing personnel after the holidays was a human resources nightmare.

The organization needed the capability to have orders automatically submitted into the order processing system. However, because the buyers used many different systems, it was not going to be easy to create a system that extracts information manually from each system and transfers the transactions system-by-system. The solution required a process flexible enough to allow for the processing of information from a variety of different sources and centrally consolidate the information for order acceptance.

The solution was built on BizTalk Server. The BizTalk Mapping tool was used to create data maps between each buyer's system to BizTalk Server using a number of input formats including HTTP, HTTPS, EDI, and XML. With the new system, buyers enter the information once into their own purchase requisition systems, and an export file is then created that securely sends the information to the supplier's BizTalk Server. The supplier's BizTalk Server processes the information and automatically transacts the data in the supplier's order processing system. Within minutes, the buyer is notified that that the order has been processed and accepted.

The advantage of this system is the capability for the supplier to accept the input from a variety of different sources. It also does not require the buyers to convert their systems or use special forms to enter information. All the data entry forms and individual system processes were automated, minimizing entry errors and decreasing the time and effort it took to process the orders. Forms were replaced almost altogether as the processing of information was automated.

This solution is based on the BizTalk Mapper covered in detail in Chapter 5, "The BizTalk Mapper," as well as in the Part II, "BizTalk Server Messaging."

Business Process Integration

Business process integration is critical to organizations wanting to simplify their internal application-to-application communication. This scenario took an organization that, like most organizations, had its back-end processes completely unlinked. The organization frequently required double and multiple manual entry of the same information from the point-of-sale system, to the general accounting system, to the organization's customer relationship management system, to the order fulfillment system. Users were constantly cutting and pasting information between systems; in fact, the organization did a study and determined that each employee spent an average of 52 minutes each day entering information or cutting/pasting information that had already been entered into another system.

The solution was to integrate all the organization's applications so that common information was transferred automatically between systems. The organization did not want to create custom gateways between each system because the applications being used were expected to be updated or replaced over the next year or two anyway. So the organization installed BizTalk Server and created data maps between its various business applications.

This EAI initiative focused not on making the accounting system tie directly to the customer relationship system, and the customer relationship system tie directly to the product fulfillment system, and so forth. Instead, each application was configured to communicate with a single centralized BizTalk Server system, as shown in Figure 1.4. Each dataset was mapped using BizTalk Mapper into a common data exchange format. After each system was able to successfully communicate with BizTalk Server, information was transmitted to BizTalk Server in a common format and then communicated with several other systems automatically. A single entry system provided multiple sets of data being distributed out of the BizTalk Server system.

FIGURE 1.4
Using BizTalk Server in a business process integration system.

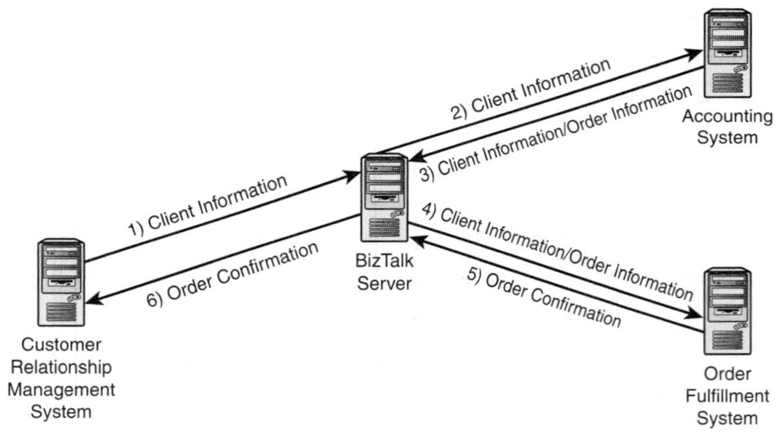

In addition to minimizing cut-and-paste manual processes, the organization is also able to monitor transaction logs to better track information distribution, and the organization is able to throttle and schedule transaction processing that did not have real-time demands to a time when processing power was idle. The system is able to ensure consistency of data interchange, and it minimizes the chance of typos or other entry errors being introduced into the data stream.

This solution is based on several BizTalk technologies, including BizTalk Mapper covered in Chapter 5, as well as the information covered in detail in Part VII, "Line of Business Adapters and Industry Toolkits."

Back-end Supply Chain Integration

When many organizations think of extending their business to facilitate an external e-commerce presence on the Internet, they frequently forget to take into account the effort needed to integrate the e-business system into their existing order processing and transaction systems. This scenario highlights the challenges and the solution implemented by one organization that integrated its existing internal accounting and inventory management system with a new e-commerce system.

This scenario involves a traditional e-commerce system that accepts business-to-consumer orders on a Microsoft Commerce Server 2000 system. A Web-based front-end enables consumers to enter information that is then tracked and forwarded on to the organization's back-end system. This is where the challenges arose—trying to integrate an existing accounting and inventory system with the new e-commerce system.

The organization found that there was no direct gateway product that transferred e-commerce information into the order processing system, nor was there a seamless way to get inventory information out of the inventory management system into a viewable mode available for the e-commerce system. The organization set up a Microsoft SQL Server that served as the depository for inventory, pricing, and order information, as shown in Figure 1.5. The BizTalk Mapper was used to get extracted information out of the inventory management system and into the SQL Server. The e-commerce system was linked to the SQL Server and gave external customers a view of the most current price and availability information that was updated on the system.

FIGURE 1.5
Using BizTalk Server as a supply chain integration tool.

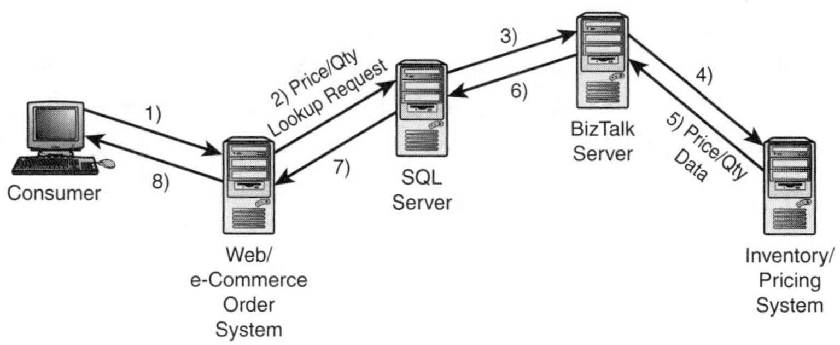

When an e-commerce order was entered, the information was sent to the SQL Server where the temporary transaction was held. The information was then processed by the BizTalk Server that mapped the transaction into the organization's existing order processing system. Because the information was now directly accepted by the order processing system, the organization had an automated method of getting information from the e-commerce system directly into the order processing system. Confirmation information was then processed and sent back to BizTalk Server. This system mapped the data to update the e-commerce system where the transaction was accepted with updated status information.

In this example, instead of replacing its accounting and inventory management system or creating a manual bridge between its old and new systems, EAP allowed the organization to integrate its business systems. BizTalk Server facilitated more than just a manual bridge but actually an automated system that linked the external with the internal system.

Key to this solution is the integration of BizTalk Server with Commerce Server 2002, covered in Chapter 25, "Integrating BizTalk with Server Accelerator for Ressetta.NET." Also important in this solution is the integration of BizTalk Server with other .NET technologies covered in Part IV and Part VII.

Consolidation of Information

This last scenario involves BizTalk Server where it helped an organization integrate several different business application systems that were eventually consolidated into common applications across business units. The organization had more than 20 different applications where customer data, product information, inventory data, and other critical business information reside. The variation in systems was brought on by several recent mergers and acquisitions of the organization.

Each user had to open several specialized applications to simply view a full list of customers and company products and services. BizTalk Server helped the organization by using the BizTalk Mapper that allowed the mapping of information between systems and ultimately the exchange of key information between systems. This included the connecting of inventory management and accounting systems, centralization of price and availability look-up information, the creation of a transaction database system, and the provision of a centralized look-up of information.

All the systems extracted core data and mapped the information to be stored in a SQL Server. The SQL Server became the centralized depository of the transacted data. Several data maps were created to link the information between the various systems, and because there were more than 20 different applications in use, the maps became extensive as the correlation of critical data necessitated a complex network of informational links.

BizTalk Server was able to accept the information and simplify the organization's integration of data between and within the applications. This solution was built on BizTalk Mapper also covered in Part III, "BizTalk Server Orchestration."

Summary

BizTalk Server provides organizations that need to exchange data, both externally with business partners as well as internally within the enterprise, a solution to transfer information. As organizations strive to lower costs and improve efficiencies, BizTalk Server provides the flexibility an organization needs to support existing data interchange standards such as EDI or HTTP while moving to standards that can lower costs and improve data interchange compatibility.

The scenarios highlighted in this chapter provide an overview of the various ways BizTalk Server can help an organization meet its goals of improving communications, and the balance of this book focuses on directly implementing the technologies introduced.

CHAPTER 2

XML and Related Technologies

by Charlie Kaiman

In This Chapter

XML is not just about documents. XML is not just about data. XML is about both. It is becoming more important that developers learn this fact. Data is no longer limited to the world of relational databases such as SQL Server and Oracle.

The "winners" in the development market will be those who can ascertain the best way to integrate the two—relational data and object-oriented data—into a functional application.

So why put a chapter on XML in a book about BizTalk Server? The answer is because BizTalk Server relies heavily on XML technologies for everything from data transformation to workflow orchestration. XML is not only a format that BizTalk utilizes at the application level, but BizTalk Server also relies on XML technologies for performing its own native functions. The bottom line is that to understand BizTalk Server and how it fits into Microsoft's .NET Framework, you are going to need to know a little bit about XML-related technologies. And this chapter is devoted to getting you started. Specifically, it covers the following:

- Information on XML and related technologies
- Parsing XML with the DOM, SAX, and .NET
- XSLT and XPath
- XML applications, frameworks, and protocols
- XML and BizTalk Server

The Fundamentals of XML Technologies

This section covers the fundamentals of XML and how markup technologies will revolutionize the way we build business applications for a long time to come.

XML Background

Let's begin with a short history lesson about where XML began and then discuss where it will take us. A few years back (the late 1960s), some IBM scientists were interested in ways to abstract the data in their documents from their proprietary formatting codes. In other words, they wanted to separate their precious data from the proprietary codes normally dispersed throughout the data in the document. They also wanted a document that could add context to their data—that is, add meaning to the document. More important, they wanted computer programs to be able to interpret a document as well as any human being could.

One way to accomplish this is with the use of metadata. *Metadata* is data used to describe information or put information into a proper context. For instance, if I wanted you to understand the string "Washington," it might help if I were to add some context to it. How about if I prefaced it with another string, "George." That might put things in a better perspective for you, right? If, instead, I added the string "D.C." to the end of the original string, it would bring about an entirely different connotation. However, the same does not hold true for a computer application. Even though our minds can decipher what is meant when we read the words, "George Washington," or "Washington, D.C.," any computer application would be hard-pressed to make sense of it.

XML has an answer to this problem. XML adds context to data in a standard, ubiquitous way, so that applications can interpret contextual data in the same way that humans were meant to interpret it. For instance, if we wrap the string "George Washington" in XML, it might look something like this:

```
<President country="US" lineage="1">George Washington</President>
```

Now, not only would a human being be able to determine that George Washington was the first President of the United States, but a computer application could also come to the same conclusion using a minimal amount of programming.

So what does this have to do with BizTalk? Let's think about that for a minute. At the core, BizTalk is a business document router and business process/application integration server. Ask yourself this question: Would BizTalk be of any value to the enterprise if it could process only Microsoft Word documents or SQL Server calls? No, it wouldn't, because not everyone uses Microsoft Word and SQL Server to share and store data. Therefore, Microsoft needed to come up with a way to share and store information using standard, nonproprietary formats that everyone could agree to use. XML is quickly becoming the syntax for defining those formats. The argument goes, if it is in XML format, then an application should be able to interpret and process the data.

But there's more to the story than just semantics. BizTalk also adds value to your enterprise because it does not confine you to proprietary transports, such as COM, DCOM, or IIOP. In fact, to be successful, Microsoft needed to create a server that would provide the underlying plumbing and tools necessary to integrate applications regardless of their platform or how the data is stored. It would need to be able to communicate using standard Internet protocols and data formats as well as proprietary and/or legacy protocols and data formats. This standardization requirement led to the development of something known as the Simple Object Access Protocol, or SOAP. We will discuss SOAP later in this chapter, but for now, it is only important to understand that SOAP was designed as an open format for accessing data over the Internet.

Would BizTalk be of any value if it could only route documents using proprietary transports such as COM, DCOM, or IIOP? Absolutely not. To be successful, Microsoft needed to create a server that would provide the underlying plumbing and tools necessary to integrate applications regardless of where they lived or how they store their data. It would need to be able to communicate using standard Internet protocols and data formats as well as proprietary and/or legacy protocols and data formats. The server would also need to define a standard format for describing documents.

When developing BizTalk Server, Microsoft needed to find a way to aggregate data in a standard format that was both ubiquitous and robust enough to be useful but not proprietary or required. Microsoft couldn't "own" or require the use of the format because then not everyone would use it. Microsoft's answer was XML. XML could be used to describe not only the contents of the document and the data inside it but also routing parameters and data types. But the best thing about it was that everyone was willing to work with XML. Sun, IBM, Microsoft—as unbelievable as it might seem—all agreed on something. That something was (and is) XML.

Microsoft realized that although the movement towards XML, for most, seems inevitable, it's not going to happen over night. Most integration solutions need to include access to legacy applications using legacy data formats and legacy protocols. With that in mind, BizTalk utilizes a number of XML-related technologies to help bridge the XML-to-legacy application gap as well as facilitate the entrance into an XML-centric world. If BizTalk was going to be successful, it needed to use the power of XML without requiring the developer to know how to use it. To accommodate this requirement, Microsoft built an engine that is XML-centric and an XML framework to help standardize the way messages are formatted and transported. So Microsoft designed a server that can accept any type of flat file document and translate it to any other flat file document. Internally, it parses the inbound document into its XML representation, applies an XSLT style sheet to transform it into its outbound XML document (also known as *mapping*), and then serializes it into its native format for transport. It also made sure that the server supports most all of the standard Internet protocols including HTTP, HTTPs, SMTP, and proprietary protocols such as COM.

Note

In later chapters we will discuss how BizTalk accomplishes these tasks in great detail but hopefully this gives you a glimpse at the role XML plays in the BizTalk Server environment.

Now that you know a little about how BizTalk the server uses XML, let's talk a little about XML in general. In the perfect XML world, when an application needs to pass data to another application that it knows nothing about, it requires a standard way to do it and a self-describing format so that the application on the other side can be told how to handle it.

The BizTalk Framework is a specification that aims at identifying itself to systems that are ambiguous at the time of design or indefinable altogether. By enveloping documents in an XML "wrapper" that conforms to the BizTalk Framework spec, you are enabling disparate systems that are BizTalk compliant to process those documents correctly. This is because the BizTalk compliant application can parse the BizTalk message and strip out the necessary information it needs to process the message.

Listing 2.1 shows a BizTalk Framework 2.0 message and illustrates how this works.

LISTING 2.1 BizTalk 2.0 Purchase Order

```
<SOAP-ENV:Envelope
xmlns:SOAP-ENV="http://schemas.xmlsoap.org/soap/envelope/"
xmlns:xsi="http://www.w3.org/1999/XMLSchema-instance">
<SOAP-ENV:Header>
<eps:endpoints SOAP-ENV:mustUnderstand="1"
xmlns:eps="http://schemas.biztalk.org/btf-2-0/endpoints"
xmlns:agr="http://www.trading-agreements.org/types/">
<eps:to>
<eps:address xsi:type="agr:organization">Big Books, Inc.</eps:address>
</eps:to>
<eps:from>
<eps:address xsi:type="agr:organization">Book Lovers Book Store</eps:address>
</eps:from>
</eps:endpoints>
<prop:properties SOAP-ENV:mustUnderstand="1"
xmlns:prop="http://schemas.biztalk.org/btf-2-0/properties">
<prop:identity>uuid:74b9f5d0-33fb-4a81-b02b-5b760641c1d6</prop:identity>
<prop:sentAt>2000-05-14T03:00:00+08:00</prop:sentAt>
<prop:expiresAt>2000-05-15T04:00:00+08:00</prop:expiresAt>
<prop:topic>http://electrocommerce.org/purchase_order/</prop:topic>
</prop:properties>
</SOAP-ENV:Header>
<SOAP-ENV:Body>
<po:PurchaseOrder xmlns:po="http://electrocommerce.org/purchase_order/">
<po:Title>BizTalk Unleashed</po:Title>
</po:PurchaseOrder>
</SOAP-ENV:Body>
</SOAP-ENV:Envelope>
```

Listing 2.1 describes data being sent to Big Books, Inc from Book Lover's Book Store. Without getting into too much detail, let's think about the vital data that is trying to be conveyed here.

You need to go all the way down to lines `<po:PurchaseOrder xmlns:po="http://electrocommerce.org/purchase_order/">` through `</po:PurchaseOrder>` from Listing 2.1 to really understand what this message is all about. It's a purchase order for your book, *BizTalk Unleashed*. Everything else you see is metadata that **could** be used by BizTalk Server to figure out where this document needs to go, where it is from, and how it should get there. The purchase order information is the meat, but the metadata contains information that ensures the safe and secure handling of the meat.

Now imagine trying to share this information with another company, without using XML. How would you do it? Would you send the data in an Excel spreadsheet? But what if the company doesn't own the Microsoft Excel software? It won't be able to process the data. How about a simple text document? The problem with that is that the receiving application would have to be deliberately programmed to process the message to know intrinsically what to do with it. But then, even if the application could interpret the message, you would still have to get everyone to agree on the message format. Seem familiar? Are you really ready for that kind of an administrative nightmare once again? Probably not. In this case, a human being would have to read the message and then manually enter the data into the application. With BizTalk messaging, the human being is bypassed, which means that the time and effort associated with such a transaction is minimized—as is the chance for human error fouling the process. Using XML, you have an open format that everyone has agreed to use to exchange data.

The goal of this chapter is for you to see how XML can be used to convey important information about data in a programmatically accessible fashion, making it perfect for business-to-business (B2B) processing and enterprise application integration (EAI). But what is XML exactly? XML architects prefer to think of XML as more of a family of technologies than as a single entity. For instance, learning XSLT would be useless without a rudimentary understanding of XML because XSLT is most often used to transform XML documents into another format. So, as you will now see, each member of the XML family is firmly tied to one or more of the other members.

XML 1.0

The XML 1.0 specification defines the syntax for defining your own Markup Language. For instance, SOAP uses XML syntax to define how it will be expressed. HTML uses a similar syntax, but one described by the SGML (Standard Generalized Markup Language) specification, the precursor to XML. SGML is a much more robust language than XML, but that is exactly why it is not as useful in defining Web-based languages. It is simply too heavy—there are too many rules. XML is a slimmed-down version of SGML that will define application languages for many years to come.

A typical XML document is made up of many nodes. Each node can represent items in a document such as elements, attributes, and text. There are other types of nodes, but for the sake of simplicity, we will deal with only these three. It might help to think of an XML document in terms of a tree structure, much like the directory structure in the Windows Explorer. Each folder could be likened to an element, with additional folders (elements) inside. These are known as *container* or *parent* elements. Each file inside a folder could be considered an element as well (for example, a text element), and the statistics relating to that file would be regarded as being *attributes* of the file.

Schemas are used to define the structure of an XML document but are not required by most applications. Some typical schema languages are Document Type Definitions (DTD), XML Data-Reduced (XDR) schemas, and the W3C Schema (XSD) language. If a schema defines an XML document, and that document can be verified against the schema, it is said to be "valid." Validity is generally not required; however, an XML document is required to be well-formed. This is to say that it conforms to a basic tree structure, uses quotes around attribute values, and is sensitive to case—meaning that if you open an element in ALL CAPS, make sure that you close the element in ALL CAPS as well.

When you parse—or process—an XML document, the purpose is generally to ascertain the value of one of those particular nodes. In addition to this, it is possible that you want to update or delete the value of a particular node in the XML document. Next, you will take a look at some standard ways to parse through an XML document.

Processing XML with the DOM, SAX, .NET, XSLT, and XPath

So you have XML, as a syntax, for defining the format of business documents. However, that is not enough; you need other technologies to work with the business documents created using XML. These technologies are DOM, SAX, .NET, XSLT, and XPath.

The Document Object Model (DOM)

You might want to use the DOM (Document Object Model) to place an XML document in memory and manipulate it programmatically. Using the DOM, you can load an XML purchase order into memory and use a program to establish what the purchase order is for, who it needs to go to, where it should be billed, and so on.

The importance of the DOM makes it necessary to look at an example. In this case, we will build an XML document using the DOM and pass it to another ASP (Active Server Page) using the XMLHTTP object available via the MSXML3 parser (see Listing 2.2). This is just a sample of the JavaScript used to manipulate the DOM. To see a working example of this in an actual HTML document, see Listing 2.3:

Note

First, Listing 2.2 is a client-side application that only works with IE 5.0 (and above) with the MSXML parser installed.

Second, Listing 2.2 uses the 3.0 version of the MSXML parser. If you are using an earlier version and choose not to upgrade, simply replace every instance of the `("Msxml2.DOMDocument.3.0")` and `("Msxml2.XMLHTTP")` object references with the `("Msxml.DOMDocument")` and `("Msxml.XMLHTTP")` objects, respectively. The latest MSXML parser is free, and it is simple to install. It is available at `http://msdn.microsoft.com/xml/general/xmlparser.asp`.

LISTING 2.2 Parsing XML using the DOM

```
function buildXML() {
var oXmlDocument = new ActiveXObject("Msxml2.DOMDocument.3.0");
var oXmlRoot = oXmlDocument.createElement("PurchaseOrder");
oXmlDocument.appendChild(oXmlRoot);
var oShipTo = oXmlDocument.createElement("ShipTo");
oXmlRoot.appendChild(oShipTo);
oShipTo.text = "'Wild Meadow Tea Company,' 555 Wellington Way, New City,
➥VA, 55555";
var oBillTo = oXmlDocument.createElement("BillTo");
oXmlRoot.appendChild(oBillTo);
oBillTo.text = "'Wild Meadow Tea Company,' 555 Wellington Way, New City,
➥VA, 55555";
var oItems = oXmlDocument.createElement("Items");
oXmlRoot.appendChild(oItems);
var oItem = oXmlDocument.createElement("Item");
oItems.appendChild(oItem);
oItem.setAttribute("name", "1 Case Chai Tea");
var oHTTP = new ActiveXObject("Msxml2.XMLHTTP");
oHTTP.open ("POST", "http://myServer/application/processXML.asp", false);
oHTTP.send (oXmlDocument.xml);}
```

In the second line of Listing 2.2, we instantiate the ActiveX object. Two models are available for parsing: the rental-threaded model (which we are using in this code sample) and the free-threaded model. The rental-threaded model is optimal when you don't expect to have more than one person accessing the document at any one time. The free-threaded model is best when multiple users are expected to access the XML enabled application simultaneously.

When you find yourself loading an XML document into memory, you may want to use the `async` method. This method—when set to false—declares that the processing should be done synchronously, as opposed to asynchronously. It would be issued directly under the second line of Listing 2.2 and look like this:

```
oXmlDocument.async = false;
```


The result is that the script will not continue processing until the entire XML document has been loaded into memory. Because we are creating a document in memory, it is not necessary to call the method. Just remember that errors will occur if processing is continued without a completely downloaded XML instance, simply because you won't have a complete document to process. Once the document is completely downloaded, parsing can continue.

Note

You can use the `readyState` property to manage asynchronous downloads, but that is beyond the scope of this sample. You can read more about that in the MSXML SDK available from Microsoft.

In the code snippet below, the `createElement` method is used to generate an element in the DOM. Once generated, the element needs to be appended to the correct parent node. You do this by referencing the parent node object and using the `appendChild` method. The element is then populated—that is, text is added, using the `text` method on the newly created element object.

```
var oShipTo = oXmlDocument.createElement("ShipTo");
oXmlRoot.appendChild(oShipTo);
oShipTo.text = "'Wild Meadow Tea Company,' 555 Wellington Way, New City,
➥VA, 55555";
```

Another useful method is the `setAttribute` method. Whenever you need to add an attribute to an element, you can use this method. The following code from Listing 2.2 shows this example.

```
    oItem.setAttribute("name", "1 Case Chai Tea");
```

Some other things that you might want to do with the DOM is delete parts of the XML document or manipulate them and save them back to the server. Another method is available, should you decide to save the XML, and that is the save method. You can even save the document to a URL by using the following syntax:

```
oXmlDocument.save("http://myServer/application/folder/myFile.xml");
```

This saves the DOM document named myFile.xml to a folder named folder.

However, if you want to process the XML document after it is on the server, instead of just saving it to a local directory, you probably will want to use the XMLHTTP object. In the following code snippet (from Listing 2.2), the first line instantiates the XMLHTTP object on the client and provides a way to send an XML document to the server to be processed by an ASP page.

```
var oHTTP = new ActiveXObject("Msxml2.XMLHTTP");
    oHTTP.open ("POST", "http://myServer/application/processXML.asp", false);
    oHTTP.send (oXmlDocument.xml);
```

The open method enables you to define whether this is an HTTP POST or GET to the server. The method requires the HTTP method, a URL to the application, and a true or false parameter to dictate whether this is an asynchronous transmission. The send method is used to initiate the transmission and deliver the XML to the application.

Look at the same code now, with a few more methods in place, to see how the whole process might work (see Listing 2.3). In this case, Wild Meadow Tea Company is requesting a few items from ACME Tea Company. The idea is that a procurement officer at Wild Meadow will submit the order online and receive a response from ACME regarding the receipt of the order.

LISTING 2.3 Generating XML with the DOM

```
<html>
<head>
<script>
function buildXML() {
var oXmlDocument = new ActiveXObject("Msxml2.DOMDocument.3.0");
oXmlDocument.async = false;
var oXmlRoot = oXmlDocument.createElement("PurchaseOrder");
oXmlDocument.appendChild(oXmlRoot);
var oShipTo = oXmlDocument.createElement("ShipTo");
oXmlRoot.appendChild(oShipTo);
oShipTo.text = "'Wild Meadow Tea Company,' 555 Wellington " +
"Way, New City, VA, 55555";
var oBillTo = oXmlDocument.createElement("BillTo");
oXmlRoot.appendChild(oBillTo);
oBillTo.text = "'Wild Meadow Tea Company,' 555 Wellington " +
"Way, New City, VA, 55555";
var oItems = oXmlDocument.createElement("Items");
```

LISTING 2.3 continued

```
oXmlRoot.appendChild(oItems);
var oItem = oXmlDocument.createElement("Item");
oItems.appendChild(oItem);
var oItemName = oItem.setAttribute("name", document.all("item").value);
var oHTTP = new ActiveXObject("Msxml2.XMLHTTP");
oHTTP.open ("POST", "http://localhost/listing2_4.asp", false);
oHTTP.send (oXmlDocument.xml);
alert (oHTTP.responseText);
}
</script>
</head>
<body>
<h1>Online Tea Order</h1>
<input type="text" name="item" />
<input type="button" value="Submit Order" onclick="buildXML();" />
</body>
</html>
```

Notice in Listing 2.3 that the purchase order is being built dynamically using the DOM. The structure of the XML is created using methods such as `createElement`, `setAttribute`, and `appendChild`. Then text is added to those elements by way of the *text* property. However, in the case of attributes, notice that the *value* of the attribute is added as the second parameter in the `setAttribute` method. The first parameter in this method represents the *name* of the attribute, whereas the second—as stated before—represents the value of that attribute.

When this file is submitted, using the `buildXML()` function and the `XMLHTTP` object, the following ASP page (shown in Listing 2.4) processes the request and responds with an acknowledgment message:

LISTING 2.4 Server-Side Response to XML POST

```
<%@ Language = "JavaScript" %>
<%
var oXmlDocument = Server.CreateObject("Msxml2.FreeThreadedDOMDocument.3.0");
oXmlDocument.async = false;
oXmlDocument.load(Request);
var err = oXmlDocument.parseError;
if (err.errorCode != 0) {
Response.Write ("There was an error processing your order. Please try again!");
} else {
 Response.Write ("Your order has been received.  Thank you!");

}
%>
```

Notice that the XML request is being captured by the `Request` object in the ASP page. To load the document, all you need to do—when receiving a `POST`—is use the `load` method, as shown here:

```
oXmlDocument.load(Request);
```

From there, you can process the document as required by the business rules. Using BizTalk Server, these rules will be enforced by the components integrated with BizTalk and defined by the visual tools that come as part of the BizTalk package.

This has given you a good feel for the DOM and how to process XML in a simple but efficient manner. The following section describes another XML processor called SAX, the Simple API for XML. However, we will not go into much detail with regards to SAX because it appears that Microsoft may be developing an improved API to be used within the .NET framework.

SAX

Another technology that you might want to use to access particular pieces of an XML business document is SAX (Simple API for XML). SAX is a great way to parse—or process—an XML document without having to load it into memory.

> **Note**
>
> The DOM requires an XML instance to be loaded into memory. When working with large XML documents, this can overburden the application and cause slow results at best. SAX is an event-driven parser that does not require the XML document to be loaded into memory, and thus is optimal for bigger jobs requiring the parsing of larger XML documents.

SAX is an event-driven parser that looks for particular pieces of the XML document—that is, nodes. When it finds what it is looking for, SAX processes it. However, SAX is not capable of manipulating a document in the same fashion as the DOM, so people typically use the DOM if they want to manipulate an XML document, and SAX if they want to simply find what they are looking for in the XML and pass it off to another process.

> **Note**
>
> If you are going to be working with Microsoft's .NET technology, you're going to encounter a few alternative parsing technologies. The DOM will remain, but

SAX may become obsolete given that Microsoft has developed another event-driven parser that uses a "pull" model rather than the SAX-related "push" model. Because of this fact, we will leave SAX for now and discuss the .NET model in greater depth.

XML Parsing in .NET

It comes as no surprise for most of you to learn that XML is a core technology in the Microsoft .NET framework, but just how this technology is implemented might still be a mystery. The good thing is that what you just learned about the DOM was not a waste of time. The .NET framework uses the DOM to provide access to data in XML documents and additional classes to read, write, and navigate through those documents. The DOM is also used to map XML to relational data in ADO.NET. We will look at an example of how XML is processed using the DOM in the `System.Xml` namespace; but before we do, it is important to understand an important aspect of .NET XML parsing.

As mentioned previously, the DOM is great for manipulating smaller XML instances, but when it comes to larger data sets, an event-driven parser that doesn't require you to load XML into memory is an absolute necessity. So, with .NET comes a new set of classes to build on the innovative ideas that SAX brought us, called `XmlReader` and `XmlWriter`.

These new classes are both easy to learn and functional. But don't take my word for it; let's take a look at some code. Listing 2.5 is a C# code sample that searches for a Purchase Order number and alerts you when it finds the correct one.

LISTING 2.5 Using `XmlTextReader`

```
using System;
using System.IO;
using System.Xml;
public class Test2 {
public static void Main() {
Test2 tester = new Test2();
}
public Test2() {
StringReader stream = null;
XmlTextReader reader = null;
try {
String sXmlDoc = "<?xml version=\"1.0\"?>" +
"<PurchaseOrders>" +
"<PurchaseOrder number='2023'>" +
"<Items><Item name='1 Box Chai Tea' /></Items>" +
"</PurchaseOrder>" +
```

LISTING 2.5 continued

```
"<PurchaseOrder number='2024'>" +
"<Items><Item name='4 Boxes Ginkgo Tea' /></Items>" +
"</PurchaseOrder>" +
"<PurchaseOrder number='2025'>" +
"<Items><Item name='10 Boxes Ginseng Tea' /></Items>" +
"</PurchaseOrder>" +
"<PurchaseOrder number='2026'>" +
"<Items><Item name='1 Box Green Tea' /></Items>" +
"</PurchaseOrder>" +
"<PurchaseOrder number='2027'>" +
"<Items><Item name='1 Box Black Tea' /></Items>" +
"</PurchaseOrder>" +
"</PurchaseOrders>";
stream = new StringReader(sXmlDoc);
reader = new XmlTextReader(stream);
Console.WriteLine("Parsing . . .");
while (reader.Read()) {
String qs = reader.GetAttribute("number");
if (qs != null) {
if (qs == "2026") {
Console.WriteLine("=====================================\n");
Console.WriteLine("Your purchase order number {0} has been found:\n", qs);
reader.MoveToElement();
Console.WriteLine("Current PO Data Goes Here...\n");
Console.WriteLine("=====================================");
} else {
Console.WriteLine ("Purchase Order Number: {0}", qs);
}
}
}
}
catch (Exception e) {
Console.WriteLine("###Exception: {0}", e.ToString());
}
}
}
```

The code in Listing 2.5 is simple really, and even if you don't know C#, you can at least get a feel for how you can parse XML in .NET. Realize that this is not the only way we could have done this, but just one of the many possible ways to use .NET to parse an XML document. Let's get into the code.

For the purposes of this section, ignore the lines from `using System` through `try {`. At line, `String sXmlDoc = "<?xml version=\"1.0\"?>" +`, notice that we are generating some XML syntax and throwing it into a string object called "`stream`" in `stream = new StringReader(sXmlDoc);`. The `XmlTextReader` parses this object and looks for a

Purchase Order number that corresponds with the search criteria. This query string could easily be submitted through some type of form to get the matching Purchase Order back, but for this sample we just hard-code it in.

To compile the code, use the following statement at the command line. Remember to run it from the same location as your code:

```
csc /r:System.Xml.dll listing2_5.cs
```

When the parser stumbles on the correct Purchase Order number, it alerts us and passes the entire Purchase Order node off to our processing application. This passing off of the node is not shown but would not be difficult to implement using either the DOM or the `XmlTextWriter` class. The output of this program is shown in Listing 2.6.

LISTING 2.6 Result of the `XmlTextReader` Example

```
Parsing . . .
Purchase Order Number: 2023
Purchase Order Number: 2024
Purchase Order Number: 2025
===============================================

Your purchase order number 2026 has been found:

Current PO Data Goes Here..

===============================================
Purchase Order Number: 2027
```

The great thing about this type of processing is that each independent XML node is parsed and forgotten. There is no need to persist the data in memory because the data is no longer required by the application.

You have looked at three different models for parsing XML, but what if you needed to format the XML data into an open format such as HTML or Wireless Markup Language (WML)—, or even a proprietary format such as PDF? XSLT may be your answer, and the next section shows you why.

XSLT and XPath

Apart from parsing an XML document, there is also the need to format and query XML data. You may have heard of XSLT and Xpath mentioned in this context before. *XSLT* (eXtensible Stylesheet Language for Transformations) is a language that can be used to format and transform XML.

For example, say that you have an XML file that needs to be viewed by two types of devices, a standard PC using a Web browser and a wireless device such as a cell phone or PDA. To accomplish this, you could write two XSLT style sheets—one to transform the XML into HTML and the other to transform it into WML (Wireless Markup Language).

Typically, XSLT is used in accordance with CSS (cascading style sheets). In such cases, XSLT is used to define the structure of the HTML, and CSS takes care of the actual formatting—for example, font sizes, coloration, and so on.

XPath can be used within an XSLT file to extract precise pieces of XML data required by the application. *XPath* can be thought of as SQL for XML. It is a query language that enables developers to pinpoint the exact path to data in an XML document that an application requires for processing.

Here we look at a sample of how XSLT and XPath can be used to transform XML into HTML. Listing 2.7 is an example of how a news agency might store its data as XML.

LISTING 2.7 XML News Document

```
<?xml version="1.0"?>
<TodaysNews date="20010313">
<Story id="001" title="Techs Rally, But Still A Uncertain Market">
<div>
<p>Technology stocks rebounded in late morning trading on Tuesday as investors
prowled the market in search of bargains, but blue chips slipped as tension
ran high on Wall Street, a day after a gut-wrenching selloff.</p>
p>"The underlying force in this market is the economic slowdown: How long and
how deep?" said Peter Coolidge, managing director of equity trading at Brean
Murray &amp; Co. "It's going to be tough going until the market gets a handle
on that. There will be bumps up along the way, but that's all there will be in
an otherwise down-trending market."</p>
</div>
</Story>
<Story id="002" title="Smithsonian Has Donor for George Washington Portrait">
<div>
<p>The Smithsonian Institution said Tuesday a single donor had come forward to
enable it to buy a famous portrait of President George Washington whose British
owner had demanded $20 million for the painting.</p>
<p>The portrait, painted by Gilbert Stuart in 1796, has been on loan to the
Smithsonian's National Portrait Gallery in Washington from flamboyant British
aristocrat Lord Dalmeny.</p>
</div>
</Story>
</TodaysNews>
```

Now we will build an XSLT file that can be used to transform this document into HTML. Let's look at the entire XSLT file first (see Listing 2.8) and then break it apart and investigate the style sheet line-by-line.

LISTING 2.8 XSLT: XML to HTML

```
<?xml version="1.0"?>
<xsl:stylesheet version="1.0" xmlns:xsl="http://www.w3.org/1999/XSL/Transform">
<xsl:template match="/">
<html>
<head>
<title>Today's News</title>
</head>
<body>
<h3>Today's News</h3>
<h4>
<script language="JavaScript"><![CDATA[
var sDate = "]]><xsl:value-of select="TodaysNews/@date" /><![CDATA[";
var sYear = sDate.substring(0,4);
var sMonth = sDate.substring(4,6);
var sDay = sDate.substring(6,8);
document.write(sMonth + "/" + sDay + "/" + sYear);
]]></script>
</h4>
<xsl:for-each select="TodaysNews/Story">
<h5><xsl:value-of select="@title" /></h5>
<xsl:copy-of select="div" />
</xsl:for-each>
</body>
</html>
</xsl:template>
</xsl:stylesheet>
```

If you are new to XSLT, have no fear. Doing basic XML manipulation using the syntax is simple. Don't get me wrong; XSLT can get complex, but we'll just deal with the basic syntax for now.

The first thing to realize is that XSLT is an XML-based language. The style sheet declaration (`<xsl:stylesheet version="1.0" xmlns:xsl="http://www.w3.org/1999/XSL/Transform">`) tells the processing application that this particular XSLT conforms to the 1999 specification of XSL for Transformations. You can think of this as a form of versioning for XSLT documents.

The line `<xsl:template match="/">` defines an XSLT template. A *template* defines a reusable instance for generating output in whatever format you choose. You only see one template in this document, but you can create as many as you want, depending on the number of nodes in your document. In the case of this document, the template corresponds to the root node of the XML document. This means that for each root node that the XSLT encounters (there is only one root node in every XML document—remember the root node is the top element in an XML document), the instructions between the `<xsl:template select="/">` and the `</xsl:template>` tags must be processed.

Within the template are a number of HTML elements and attributes, but you will also find certain XSL elements interspersed throughout the tags. To account for this, XML uses *namespaces* to differentiate between different XML *vocabularies* (see the special section on namespaces later in the chapter). In this case, the `xsl:` prefix denotes that the tag is an XSLT element and should be processed as such by the XSLT processor. In some cases, an XSLT processor and an XML parser will be separate components; however, the MSXML3 parser does both XML and XSLT processing.

An interesting thing occurs in the line (`<script language="JavaScript"><![CDATA[`. You should notice something called a `CDATA` section, which is delimited by the `<![CDATA" and "]]>` structures. The CDATA structure tells the parser to skip over these "Character Data" sections and not process them in any way. That is why you see the end of the `CDATA` section `var sDate = "]]><xsl:value-of select="TodaysNews/@date" /><![CDATA[";`, allowing the `value-of` tag to be processed and the value inserted into the JavaScript. As soon as the XSLT tag is parsed, we begin the `CDATA` section again until the script section is complete. The only thing the `<xsl:value-of />` tag does is extract the data from a particular node. You define the node by inserting an XPath statement into the `select` node. For instance:

```
<xsl:value-of select="TodaysNews/@date" />
```

This statement extracts the value of the `date` attribute in the `TodaysNews` element. In the preceding sample, the value of the `date` attribute is 20010313. We extract that value using the XPath statement and use the JavaScript substring method to break the date apart into a more recognizable format—for example, 03/13/2001.

The first line in the following code snippet (from Listing 2.8) introduces the `for-each` element in XSLT. The purpose of this element is to loop through a particular element list. In this case, we are looping through every instance of the `story` node. Every time the processor runs across another `<Story>` tag, the processor executes the following rules:

```
<xsl:for-each select="TodaysNews/Story">
 <h5><xsl:value-of select="@title" /></h5>
 <xsl:copy-of select="div" />
</xsl:for-each>
```

The value of the `title` attribute is inserted into an `<h5>` element and the entire contents of the XML `<div>` tag are copied straight to the HTML output. This direct copy is done via the `copy-of` XSLT element. In this case, not only is the text in the XML `<div>` tag copied to the HTML output, but the XML `<p>` tags are also copied. This way, there is no need to reformat the contents under the `<div>` tag because they can be transferred directly to the HTML output in a clean, concise manner.

It's worth mentioning, though, that this only works for an HTML transformation. Imagine, for example, that you are transforming the XML into WML for display on a wireless device. The WML specification does not allow for `<div>` tags. Therefore, an XSLT document that is going to be used to transform this XML into WML would need to do something else with the XML `<div>` tag. For instance, you might change the XML `<div>` to a WML `<p>` tag, using the following XSLT:

```
<xsl:template select="div">
 <p><xsl:value-of select="node()" /></p>
</xsl:template>
```

You would need to call this script from somewhere within the root XSLT template, using the `<xsl:apply-templates>` element. But after you do, this code extracts the value of the XML `<div>` tag and includes all its text and child nodes into a WML `<p>` element. If all this seems a bit confusing (especially if you have not worked with WML), don't worry. After some practice, it will all become much more clear to you. Remember, XSLT is only in version 1.0, so this is a great time to get started with it before it becomes much more complicated.

With these six parts of the XML family—XML 1.0, DOM, SAX, .NET, XSLT, and XPath—you can accomplish almost any task required of an XML application. Using your programming language of choice—for example, JavaScript, Perl, Java, C++, Visual Basic, C#, Python, and so on, all you need to do is find the right parser for the job. The MSXML3 parser is an excellent processor, and Microsoft has done an outstanding job at making this parser conform to W3C standards; however, other excellent ones are available that have been hand-crafted by the XML community to work with every language you can think of. The Java community has perhaps the best arsenal of XML processors on the market, but if you are a Microsoft developer—like me—I highly recommend MSXML 3.0.

XML Frameworks, Applications, and Protocols

Now that we have discussed XML to some degree, let's talk a bit about the BizTalk Framework and other related initiatives, such as ebXML, cXML, RosettaNet, and UDDI. But before doing so, it is important that you understand SOAP (Simple Object Access

Protocol) because it, frankly, has had the greatest influence on the BizTalk Framework to date and is likely to influence many other initiatives as well.

Introduction to SOAP

At the most fundamental level, Simple Object Access Protocol (SOAP) is an XML-based language used to perform Remote Procedure Calls (RPC) over the Internet. Using SOAP, you can invoke an object on a Unix box in California, for example, from the Windows NT development machine running in your office in Virginia.

Let's say that your corporate intranet is running on your server, which is an NT machine with IIS installed, and all your applications are built using ASP 3.0 and VB 6. Now imagine that a user requests a weather update from your intranet. The user is going to assume that the `weatherUpdata.asp` page is extracting the information from some local data source and feeding her the information; but, she would be wrong! Instead, the Weather application is a SOAP-compliant interface that links to a Unix-based, SOAP service (also known as a *Web Service*).

When a user makes a request to your Web server by issuing a `POST` with some basic information—for example, a ZIP Code—an ASP script accepts the request and invokes a VB component, which *wraps* the request parameters—that is, the ZIP Code—in a SOAP request. The VB component passes a SOAP-compliant message (we will discuss some of the requirements of SOAP v1.1 a bit later, but for now, it is important to understand the theory) over HTTP(S) to the Unix box in California. The Unix box is running Apache, which receives the XML message and parses out the SOAP request. The SOAP message tells the server which method to use—ergo which object to invoke—and passes off the required parameters—in this case, the ZIP Code. The Unix box, which is a Weather Service application, looks up the ZIP Code in a database and feeds the respective weather information back to the Apache Web Server. The weather information is then wrapped up into a SOAP response, sent back to the IIS box and VB component, parsed, and passed on to the original `weatherUpdate.asp` page to be viewed by the user in her browser as HTML. The result is a real-time weather service that uses logic from the source application to provide the necessary data via the Internet.

Some people might wonder what the difference is between this kind of distributed model and a more traditional model in the form of Remote Procedure Call (RPC). The primary difference is that a SOAP application—or Web Service—must be compliant with the SOAP standard and most often will use HTTP as its transport protocol. However, other protocols can be used. HTTP is just the most common.

Another way to think of it is that instead of making a request with a browser, a Web server will be capable of brokering those requests for you and managing the presentation of the material independent of where that data lives. That way, there is no need for a person to keep track of a hundred different Web sites. Your corporate portal or favorite Web portal will be responsible for aggregating specific information for you, and making it presentable. Let's talk now about how this can be accomplished.

Understanding the SOAP v1.1 Specification

First, there is the SOAP v1.1 specification. SOAP consists of three independent parts:

- The SOAP envelope construct defines an overall framework for expressing what is in a message, who should deal with it, and whether it is optional or mandatory.
- The SOAP encoding rules define a serialization mechanism that can be used to exchange instances of application-defined data types.
- The SOAP RPC representation defines a convention that can be used to represent remote procedure calls and responses.

A SOAP message is an XML document that consists of a mandatory SOAP envelope, an optional SOAP header, and a mandatory SOAP body.

Namespaces

Before we continue, it is important that we discuss something in XML called *namespaces*. For the sake of simplicity, Namespaces are unique identifiers that are qualified by use of a Uniform Resource Indicator (URI) and are important in creating XML elements and attributes. For instance, if I wanted to create an XML document for tracking my favorite books and post it to the Web, I would probably want to create my own namespace. Here's why. Look at this HTML:

```
<html>
<head>
<title>My Favorite Books</title>
</head>
<body>
</body>
</html>
```

Now look at my XML document:

```
<books>
<book id="1">
<title>Hunt for Red October</title>
<author>Tom Clancy</author>
</book>
...
</books>
```

You might have noticed something—besides my obvious lack of culture when it comes to book choices (I can't help it though, Clancy writes great books)—there is a duplication of the element `<title>` in the HTML and the XML. So how is the application to know that one means the title of my book, whereas the other is the title of the HTML document? By the use of namespaces. Thus, you would use the following format to add my XML to the HTML document:

```
<html xmlns="http://www.w3.org/1999/xhtml"
➥xmlns:b="http://myFavoriteBooks.org">
<head>
<title>My Favorite Books</title>
</head>
<body>
<b:books>
<b:book b:id="1">
<b:title>Hunt for Red October</title>
<b:author>Tom Clancy</author>
</b:book>
...
</b:Books>
</body>
</html>
```

The first line of code declares the default namespace with the XHTML namespace. Therefore, every element and attribute in the document, without a namespace prefix attached to it, is an XHTML element or attribute. Likewise, my XML "books" document has a namespace, but I must have a prefix attached to each element and attribute for it to be recognized by the application as a part of the "book" dataset. There is more to the story, but that should help you to understand enough about namespaces to get through the SOAP specification. To find out more about namespaces, go to `http://www.w3.org/TR/REC-xml-names/` at the W3C Web site.

The *SOAP Envelope* defines the overall framework for the message. It does this by qualifying itself through use of the SOAP Envelope namespace. Following is an example of how a SOAP Envelope looks:

```
<SOAP-ENV:Envelope xmlns:SOAP-ENV="http://schemas.xmlsoap.org/soap/envelope/">
<SOAP-ENV:Header>
<SOAP-ENV:Body>
...
</SOAP-ENV:body>
</SOAP-ENV:Header>
</SOAP-ENV:Envelope>
```

The SOAP Envelope should be thought of as the entire SOAP message, of which the header and body are subparts.

The *SOAP Header* is where information about the message is expected to exist. Typical examples of header entries are authentication, transaction management, payment, and so on. The header is not required by the SOAP specification.

Finally, we arrive at the SOAP Body, where the core of the message exists. It encompasses the parameters, for instance, that will be required by the object that is going to be invoked by the request. Listing 2.9 shows a copy of a message we might send to receive weather information for our area.

LISTING 2.9 SOAP Request for Weather Update

```
<SOAP-ENV:Envelope
xmlns:SOAP-ENV="http://schemas.xmlsoap.org/soap/envelope/"
xmlns:xsi="http://www.w3.org/1999/XMLSchema-instance"
xmlns:xsd="http://www.w3.org/1999/XMLSchema">
<SOAP-ENV:Body>
<ns1:getTemp
xmlns:ns1="http://ourlocalweatherstation.org"
SOAP-ENV:encodingStyle="http://schemas.xmlsoap.org/soap/encoding/">
<zipcode xsi:type="xsd:string">94041</zipcode>
</ns1:getTemp>
</SOAP-ENV:Body>
</SOAP-ENV:Envelope>
```

In Listing 2.9, you see an element called `<nsl:getTemp>`. Ignoring the namespace, and focusing on the element name `getTemp`, that looks like it could be the name of a method, doesn't it? That's because it is a method name! In this case, the method is requesting the temperature for the area matching the 94041 ZIP Code, as defined in the body of the SOAP message.

Also notice that in addition to the namespaces talked about earlier, there is an additional namespace, `xsi`. This namespace is an XML schema qualifier that allows you to introduce data typing into the application. As you can see in `<zipcode xsi:type="xsd:string">94041</zipcode>` of the previous listing, the ZIP Code is being typed as a string. This becomes more valuable as the application grows in complexity.

Listing 2.10 is the response to our Weather request. It is a response to a request from a server that says, "I need to know the temperature for this particular ZIP Code." The reply, as seen in Listing 2.10, is 68.0 degrees.

LISTING 2.10 SOAP Response to Weather Update

```
<SOAP-ENV:Envelope
 xmlns:SOAP-ENV="http://schemas.xmlsoap.org/soap/envelope/"
 xmlns:xsi="http://www.w3.org/1999/XMLSchema-instance"
 xmlns:xsd="http://www.w3.org/1999/XMLSchema">
<SOAP-ENV:Body>
<ns1:getTempResponse
 xmlns:ns1=" http://ourlocalweatherstation.org"
  SOAP-ENV:encodingStyle="http://schemas.xmlsoap.org/soap/encoding/">
<return xsi:type="xsd:float">68.0</return>
</ns1:getTempResponse>
</SOAP-ENV:Body>
</SOAP-ENV:Envelope>
```

Only a few things are worth looking at in this SOAP response because it is so similar to the request. The first thing you should notice is that the method name has changed to indicate that this is a response to the original message, thus you have `<nsl:getTempResponse>`. Also notice that in `<return xsi:type="xsd:float"> 68.0</return>`, the node name has changed from `<zipcode>` to `<return>`, and the data type value is now a `float` with a node value of 68 degrees. To process the response to our request, all we would need to do is parse the XML, retrieve the temperature information, and then apply it to the application logic.

This is only a quick introduction to SOAP, but it gives you enough of a taste to understand how the BizTalk Framework uses the SOAP 1.1 specification later on in the chapter and throughout the book. For more information on SOAP, visit the W3C site at `http://www.w3.org/TR/SOAP/`.

ebXML, cXML, and RosettaNet

Without a doubt, SOAP is going to play a key role in XML-based messaging for years to come. Although the W3C is hard at work on a specification to expand on SOAP, the foundation has clearly been set. However, SOAP by itself, is nothing more than a messaging protocol. Along with the message routing rules must come standards for interoperability in terms of the messages themselves, schemas, repositories, and discovery tools. More than a handful of companies—and even the United Nations—are in the process of developing entire frameworks around these standards, and we will discuss some of them now.

ebXML (Electronic Business XML Initiative)

Perhaps the most influential framework—apart from Microsoft's own BizTalk initiative—is ebXML (Electronic Business XML). Depending on who you ask, the ebXML standard has perhaps the strongest chance of becoming the perennial leader in the B2B realm. With the largest amount of international support, ebXML is a joint venture casted by the United Nations Body for Trade Facilitation and Electronic Business (UN/CEFACT) and the Organization for the Advancement of Structured Information Standards (OASIS). Together, these two bodies are seeking to standardize business specifications as defined by the XML syntax.

The goal of the Electronic Business XML initiative is to develop a technical framework that enables XML to be used in a consistent manner for the exchange of all electronic business data—for example, purchase orders, invoices, acknowledgments, financial reporting, and so on. A primary objective of ebXML is to lower the barrier of entry to electronic business to facilitate trade, particularly with respect to small- and medium-sized enterprises (SMEs) and developing nations.

It should first be understood that this is not "revolutionary" technology. In fact, for the past 25 years, companies have been exchanging information with each other electronically, based on Electronic Data Interchange (EDI) standards. Unfortunately, EDI currently requires significant technical expertise and deploys tightly coupled, inflexible architectures. Although it is possible to deploy EDI applications on public networks, they are most often deployed on expensive dedicated networks to conduct business with each other. The ebXML initiative looks to correct this problem by decreasing the cost for entry into the Internet-based marketplace.

The ebXML framework consists of 11 separate project teams, working in cooperation to realize the goals of the initiative. They are

- Business Process Methodology
- Core Components
- ebXML Requirements
- Marketing, Awareness, and Education
- Registry and Repository
- Technical Architecture
- Technical Coordination and Support
- Transport/Routing and Packaging
- Proof of Concept
- ebXML Trading Partner
- TA-Security

One thing we haven't mentioned yet is the need for repositories. *Repositories* offer public and private parties a searchable, Web-accessible location to which they can publish their XML schemas. For instance, if Company X is a publishing company and required its authors to format their books in a particular XML format, Company X might save the XML schema representing the necessary book format to an XML repository. At the time of this writing, there are two major XML schema repositories: XML.org and BizTalk.org. It is likely that the ebXML initiative will either use XML.org in some way as its preferred repository or build a comparable repository customized to its particular needs.

Is ebXML at odds with BizTalk? Concerns about this were put to rest in mid-February 2001 when UN/CEFACT and OASIS announced that plans were underway to integrate SOAP 1.1 and SOAP with attachments specifications into the ebXML messaging specification. This landmark event makes it clear that the goal behind these standards is true interoperability. There will always be money to be made in proprietary systems that build on these systems, but if the infrastructure is unstable, then applications built on those standards will be inefficient. By adopting SOAP, you can rest assured that ebXML and BizTalk will be able to operate interdependently among one another.

For more information on ebXML, visit `http://www.ebXML.org` on the Web.

cXML (Commerce XML)

While we wait for the ebXML framework to come to fruition, another initiative called cXML (Commerce XML) has achieved actual results in a production environment. The cXML specification was developed by Ariba and uses XML for describing

- Business catalogs
- Purchase orders
- A "punch-out" process

Business catalogs and purchase orders are nothing new to most companies. cXML simply enables these documents to be exchanged in a uniform fashion over the Internet using XML as the document syntax. In this way, applications can be written using an open, nonproprietary API to extract information from these documents and to share them in a consistent manner.

Punch-out, on the other hand, offers us a unique way to enhance the way buyers procure goods from their business partners. Simply, cXML punch-out enables a procurement officer to click a link in the office's intranet, or otherwise punch-out-enabled site, and "punch out" to his distribution partner or manufacturer's procurement site. The punch-out usually occurs by opening another browser window, thereby maintaining state on the original punch-out browser.

The user then shops around on the procurement site, browsing for items that he wants to purchase. When the user is ready to buy, he clicks a "purchase" button—or something similar such as a "buy" button. Regardless, the procurement site wraps the shopping cart in cXML-compliant syntax and then sends it via HTTP(S) to the original punch-out site. The server from which the user initially punched out then processes the cXML shopping cart it received and enters it—for instance—into an internal purchase request (see Figure 2.1).

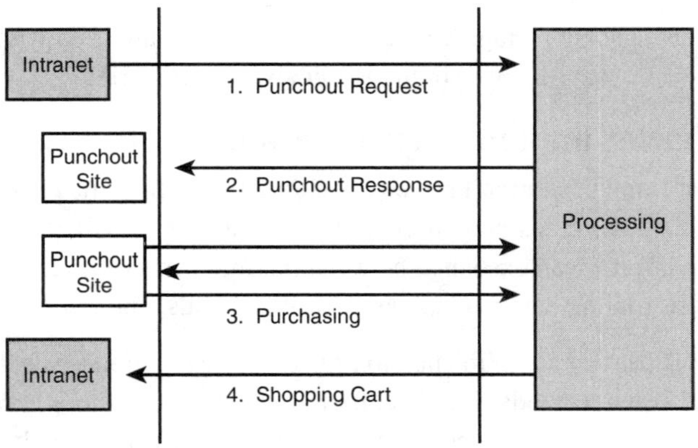

FIGURE 2.1
The cXML punch-out process.

As with SOAP, cXML is not a complete solution but can be thought of as more of a partial solution to help automate the integration process between business partners.

RosettaNet

We'll use a metaphor to assist in the understanding of what RosettaNet is about. The story goes that the name comes from the "Rosetta Stone," which was an ancient carving with a message that was done in three languages. This was a huge revelation leading to the understanding of hieroglyphics—which is, in a sense, the goal of RosettaNet. To break language barriers when it comes to doing business over the Net by enabling everyone to speak the same language.

Developed with the collaboration and expertise of leading high-tech companies, RosettaNet standards offer a robust nonproprietary solution, encompassing data dictionaries, implementation framework, and business message schemas and process specifications for e-business standardization. RosettaNet standards include the RosettaNet Business Dictionary, RosettaNet Technical Dictionaries, RosettaNet Implementation Framework (RNIF), and RosettaNet Partner Interface Processes (PIP).

The goal for the RosettaNet Business and Technical Dictionaries is to reduce confusion in the procurement process due to each company's uniquely defined taxonomies—that is, business terminologies. The RosettaNet Business Dictionary designates the properties for defining business transactions between trading partners, and RosettaNet Technical Dictionaries provide properties for defining products and services.

For instance, in your electronic business documents, do you semantically define a purchase order as a `<purchaseOrder>`, a `<purchaseorder>`, or a `<PurchaseOrder>`? Perhaps it is something entirely different, such as an `<orderRequest>`. Regardless, RosettaNet-compliant applications, due to XML's cap-sensitivity and strict adherence to semantics, require that everyone use the same language to define, for instance, a purchase order using this `<PurchaseOrder>` tag. All the possible tags that are used within RosettaNet-compliant messages can be found in the RosettaNet Dictionaries.

The RosettaNet Implementation Framework

The RosettaNet Implementation Framework (RNIF) Core Specification provides exchange protocols for quick and efficient implementation of RosettaNet standards. The RNIF specifies information exchange between trading-partner servers using XML, covering the transport, routing, and packaging; security; signals; and trading partner agreement.

The RNIF specification can be likened to SOAP. However, unlike SOAP, it is complex at first glance and is not a standard that is officially recognized among groups such as the W3C. It would be very nice indeed to see the RNIF specification evolve to a more SOAP-like standard than the current less-familiar syntax.

RosettaNet Partner Interface Processes

A key product of the RosettaNet effort is the set of *Partner Interface Processes* (PIPs), which are specialized XML-based dialog that define how business processes are conducted between trading partners. The PIPs define processes for a range of business activities, such as inventory, pricing, sales management, order handling, product configuration, and shipping. Each PIP specification includes a business document with the vocabulary and a business process with the choreography of the message dialog. PIPs apply to the following core processes:

- Administration
- Partner, Product, and Service Review
- Product Introduction
- Order Management
- Inventory Management
- Marketing Information Management
- Service and Support
- Manufacturing

Each of these initiatives exhibits a relatively noncomplex way for companies to conduct business online to lower the costs associated with commercial transactions. RosettaNet, ebXML, and cXML each share many of the same qualities, but each has a different goal.

As you will see, the BizTalk Framework seeks to solve the same problems that these initiatives do.

The bad news then—if there is any bad news—is that companies must go through a bit of effort to see which initiative is most suited to resolving their particular business requirements. The good news is that all these initiatives, because of their adherence to open standards such as XML and SOAP, will most likely be able to communicate with each other without the need for expensive systems or extensive programming "glue." The moral of the story then is to implement whatever types of systems and coding languages work for you internally and are capable of providing you the access you need to interface with others—and let them interface with your systems—in an open format that enables the simple, efficient, and secure exchange of business data.

UDDI

Now that you have taken a close look at some of the more popular B2B frameworks, you need to examine another piece of the puzzle that will play a large role in making online business processing a reality.

Introduction to UDDI

UDDI (Universal Description, Discovery, and Integration) is a set of specifications that define a way to publish and discover information about a Web Service.

> **Note**
>
> Before continuing, let's discuss what Web Services are. *Web Services* are Web components that can be invoked over the Internet using an XML language (SOAP) to be integrated into back-end systems. Using SOAP, a client application might make a request to a server, which in turn requests the data from another server over the Web, thereby creating a truly distributed application framework. Some will be small services—for example, a service that calculates the cost of shipping a package of a certain size or weight according to a specific carrier; others will be larger services—for example, an entity that enables companies to do all their corporate procurement via a single, online service. SOAP was discussed earlier, so this should sound familiar because most Web Services will be based solely on the SOAP specification.

UDDI basically takes an approach that relies on a distributed registry of businesses—think of an online White Pages—and their Web Service descriptions when applicable. The services are revealed in a common XML language that an application can process to find a best possible match for its business need. This common language is not SOAP, but a UDDI-specific XML grammar. Just remember that SOAP is used as a transport protocol, but the message itself can be of any type. In this case, the SOAP message encloses the necessary parameters required by the UDDI services.

The bottom line is that the UDDI business registry can be used for

- Establishing whether a given partner has a particular Web Service that can be used
- Finding companies in a given industry with a particular set of generic or bundled services
- Locating information about how a partner or intended partner has exposed a Web Service to learn the technical details required to interact with the service

Building with UDDI

So you are the CEO of ACME, and you build widgets. You are going to provide a Web Service that allows business partners to send a request for more widgets when their inventory gets low. You service thousands of customers and can't contact each one individually, so you decide to "advertise" your company's Web Service on UDDI. That way, as more of your partners decide to participate in eCommerce activities, they can simply "subscribe" to your service via UDDI.

The first step is for companies to sign up with UDDI. The information that businesses can register includes several kinds of simple data that help others determine the answers to questions such as "who, what, where, and how?" Corporate information such as company name, business identifiers (D&B, D-U-N-S, and so on), and specific contact information answers the "Who?" question. The "What?" question requires the classification of products and industry codes, in addition to the details about the Web Services that will be made available. Answering the question "Where?" is a matter of registering a unique address—for example, URL, e-mail, or other—through which a particular Web Service is accessed. Technically, the "Where?" question resolves to something referred to as *binding information*. In the design specs, the node name is *bindingTemplate*. This leads us to the "How?" question. The registrant issues references to specifications that can be used as models for how a particular software package or technical interface will function. These references are regarded as *tModels* in the UDDI documentation.

After you have registered your company, ACME, other companies will be able to find you based on a defined set of parameters. You will now see one way UDDI can be used by a potential business partner to find your Web Service to purchase widgets online.

XZY, Inc., is looking for someone who will allow them to purchase widgets online via an automated process that they have built in-house. When inventory drops below 10,000, they would like their system to automatically purchase a certain number of widgets based on business rules programmed into the system.

Because XYZ is looking for a particular company that can provide this type of service, it goes to the UDDI registry. When you, as CEO of ACME, defined your company's services, the UDDI registry saved your settings and propagated them throughout the UDDI distributed network. Now companies such as XZY, Inc., can use a format similar to the following to locate different companies with the types of services that you offer. Sure, this means more competition to you—potentially—but it is also a way for you to market yourself for free (because basic UDDI services are free of charge). Here is how XYZ, Inc., would search for a company to buy widgets from. The following UDDI message would be wrapped in a SOAP call to the UDDI registry:


```
<find_service
businessKey="uuid_key"
generic="1.0"
maxRows="20"
xmlns="urn:uddi-org:api">
<findQualifiers>
<findQualifier>sortByNameAsc</findQualifier>
</findQualifiers>
<name>Purchase Widget</name>
</find_service>
```

By issuing this command, XYZ, Inc., gets back a *service list* that includes all the services that match the request and the companies that provide those services, which in this case, is any service that provides for the purchasing of widgets online. XYZ, Inc., needs to parse the SOAP reply to extract the information it is looking for. This means that the same application responsible for sending the <find_service> request to UDDI should be able to process the <serviceList> reply that comes back.

Hopefully this explanation of UDDI has cleared up any confusion you might have had about its usefulness in the world of Web Services. For more information, visit the UDDI.org Web site at `http://www.uddi.org`.

BizTalk Framework 2.0

We have looked at XML technologies and the applications that have been developed around them. We've investigated XML frameworks for messaging and B2B, and also learned a bit about B2B registries and repositories. So now it is time to talk explicitly about how the BizTalk Framework 2.0 can be used to facilitate the efficient, secure exchange of your business products and services.

Introduction to BizTalk Framework 2.0

At the most rudimentary level, the BizTalk Framework provides a set of basic mechanisms required for most business-to-business electronic exchanges. The goal of this framework is to

- Give a general overview of the BizTalk Framework architecture, including the BizTalk document and message semantics
- Provide a detailed set of specifications for constructing BizTalk documents and messages
- Provide necessary insight into ways of securing BizTalk documents and messages over a number of Internet-standard transports and transfer protocols

> **Note**
>
> It is expected that other specifications and standards conforming to XML, SOAP, and the BizTalk Framework will be developed for more specific needs.

The BizTalk Framework specification was devised to define messaging interaction between BizTalk Framework 2.0 Compliant servers, referred to as *BFC servers*. It is important that you realize up-front that a BFC server is not necessarily a Microsoft BizTalk server. A BFC server can be any product—on any platform—that conforms to the BizTalk Framework 2.0 specification. The following list describes the different pieces that come together to form the BizTalk Framework:

- BizTalk Framework Compliant (BFC) server—A BFC server is represented by the set of services providing the message-processing functionality defined in the BizTalk Framework specifications.
- Application—An application is the line-of-business system where the business data and/or logic are stored and executed. An application also includes any additional adapters that may be required to emit or consume business documents (see the following item) and communicate with a BFC server.
- Business document—A business document is a well-formed XML document containing business data. This data may represent a purchase order, invoice, sales forecast, or any other business information. One or more business documents form the body of a BizTalk document. (Following is an example of a simple business document—in this case a PO—which will be processed by BizTalk Server and a variable number of other applications.)

```
<po:PurchaseOrder xmlns:po="http://electrocommerce.org/purchase_order/">

<po:Title>BizTalk Server Unleashed</po:Title>
</po:PurchaseOrder>
```

Note

The BizTalk Framework does not delegate the structure and formatting of the business document. This is an entirely open process, carried out by the business entities involved. A business document is not to be confused with a BizTalk document.

Always remember that BizTalk Server and other applications are just ways of processing a business document. The business document represents the data ultimately required by end users. Listing 2.11 is a more robust sample of a BizTalk document with BizTalk Framework semantics included. The actual business document, starting with the element `<po:PurchaseOrder>`, is encased in the `<SOAP:ENV:Body>` element, near the end of the message.

LISTING 2.11 BizTalk 2.0 Message

```
<SOAP-ENV:Envelope
xmlns:SOAP-ENV="http://schemas.xmlsoap.org/soap/envelope/"
xmlns:xsi="http://www.w3.org/1999/XMLSchema-instance">
<SOAP-ENV:Header>
<eps:endpoints SOAP-ENV:mustUnderstand="1"
xmlns:eps="http://schemas.biztalk.org/btf-2-0/endpoints"
xmlns:agr="http://www.trading-agreements.org/types/">
<eps:to>
<eps:address xsi:type="agr:department">Book Orders</eps:address>
</eps:to>
<eps:from>
<eps:address xsi:type="agr:organization">Book Lovers</eps:address>
</eps:from>
</eps:endpoints>
<prop:properties SOAP-ENV:mustUnderstand="1"
xmlns:prop="http://schemas.biztalk.org/btf-2-0/properties">
<prop:identity>uuid:74b9f5d0-33fb-4a81-b02b-5b760641c1d6</prop:identity>
<prop:sentAt>2000-05-14T03:00:00+08:00</prop:sentAt>
<prop:expiresAt>2000-05-15T04:00:00+08:00</prop:expiresAt>
<prop:topic>http://electrocommerce.org/purchase_order/</prop:topic>
</prop:properties>
</SOAP-ENV:Header>
<SOAP-ENV:Body>
<po:PurchaseOrder xmlns:po="http://electrocommerce.org/purchase_order/">
```

LISTING 2.11 continued

```
<po:Title>BizTalk Server Unleashed</po:Title>
</po:PurchaseOrder>
</SOAP-ENV:Body>
</SOAP-ENV:Envelope>
```

A *BizTalk document* is a SOAP 1.1 message in which the body of the message contains the business documents, and the header contains BizTalk-specific header entries for enhanced message-handling semantics. Following are some concepts that apply directly to BizTalk documents, and how they are interpreted by BizTalk Framework compliant (BFC) servers. We will look at a number of concepts and then follow up with an example of how each works within the framework.

We will begin with the concept of document lifetime. The *lifetime* is the time period during which a document is meaningful. A document must not be sent, accepted, processed, or acknowledged beyond its lifetime. Listing 2.12 is an example of how a business document's lifetime is set within the context of the message itself.

LISTING 2.12 BizTalk 2.0 Lifetime Parameters

```
<prop:sentAt>2000-05-14T03:00:00+08:00</prop:sentAt>
<prop:expiresAt>2000-05-15T04:00:00+08:00</prop:expiresAt>
```

Another concept worth noting is the document identity. *Identity* is a universally unique token used to identify a document. Listing 2.13 is an example of how a business document will identify itself.

LISTING 2.13 BizTalk 2.0 Identity Parameter

```
<prop:identity>uuid:74b9f5d0-33fb-4a81-b02b-5b760641c1d6</prop:identity>
```

An *acceptance* is the act of being accepted for delivery by a receiver. A received document is accepted if it is recognized as being intended for an endpoint served by the receiver, including documents that are copies or duplicates of previously received documents (based on the identity). Acceptance does not mean that all header entries and the body have been inspected and their contents verified for any specific purpose.

Idempotence—a word few of us probably have encountered before—represents the capability of a document to be transmitted and accepted more than once with the same effect as being transmitted and accepted once.

Note

BizTalk Framework includes end-to-end protocols that prescribe certain receipts to be sent by the receiver to ensure delivery semantics in some cases. These receipts are first-class BizTalk documents with a prescribed syntax. Two different kinds of receipts are defined in this specification:

- A *delivery receipt* is a receipt to acknowledge that the receiver accepted a given document for delivery.
- A *commitment receipt* is a receipt to acknowledge that, in addition to being accepted, a given document has been inspected at the destination endpoint, all header entries marked `must Understand="1"` have been understood, the correctness of their contents as well as the contents of the body have been verified, and there is a commitment to process the document. If all these criteria have been accomplished, then the commitment receipt is sent.

A *BizTalk message* is the unit of wire-level interchange between BFC servers. BizTalk messages are used to send BizTalk documents, and any related files, between BFC servers. A BizTalk message must always contain a primary BizTalk document that defines the semantics of the message within the BizTalk Framework. It may in addition contain one or more attachments, including well-formed XML documents, some of which may themselves be BizTalk documents. BizTalk documents carried as attachments are treated just like any other XML documents and have no special significance in regard to the semantics of the BizTalk message. The structure of a BizTalk message depends on the transport being used to carry the message and often includes transport-specific headers.

The actual interchange of BizTalk messages between BFC servers presupposes a communication mechanism that is used to carry messages physically from the source to the destination business entity. The term *transport* refers to this mechanism. Transports used in this context vary widely in their characteristics, ranging from simple datagram and file transfer protocols to transfer protocols such as HTTP and SMTP, and sophisticated, message-oriented middleware. This specification does not differentiate between transports based on their capabilities. Transport characteristics affect only the transport bindings.

An *endpoint* is a BizTalk Framework compliant source or the destination of a BizTalk message. Listing 2.14 is an example of a BizTalk endpoint being defined.

LISTING 2.14 BizTalk 2.0 Endpoints

```
<eps:endpoints SOAP-ENV:mustUnderstand="1"
xmlns:eps="http://schemas.biztalk.org/btf-2-0/endpoints"
xmlns:agr="http://www.trading-agreements.org/types/">
<eps:to>
<eps:address xsi:type="agr:department">Book Orders</eps:address>
</eps:to>
<eps:from>
<eps:address xsi:type="agr:organization">Book Lovers</eps:address>
</eps:from>
</eps:endpoints>
```

> **Note**
>
> The *address* is the location of an endpoint, resolvable in context for the purposes of message transport and delivery.

Attachments are generally non-XML files or other related information that are not transmitted as a business document within the body of the BizTalk document. These may be related images, large compressed files, or any other information format or content that is not an appropriate business document. Attachments may be carried within the BizTalk message enclosing the BizTalk document, or they may be external to the message and simply referenced within the document.

Another interesting point is that the BizTalk Framework 2.0 does not follow a traditional *major* and *minor* versioning model. Instead, the version is implied by a namespace URI reference used to qualify BizTalk-specific elements. For instance, note in the namespace URI shown here that there is a `btf-2-0` reference. This string is going to change as an application evolves to handle the newer versions of the specification:

```
< ... xmlns:eps="http://schemas.biztalk.org/btf-2-0/endpoints">
```

The next version might look like this:

```
< ... xmlns:eps="http://schemas.biztalk.org/btf-3-0/endpoints">
```

> **Note**
>
> If an application is missing a particular versioning URI—or if it is ill-formed for some reason—the BFC server must respond with something referred to as a `SOAP-ENV:mustUnderstand` fault. The `mustUnderstand` attribute is a SOAP-specific attribute that defines which entries in a SOAP header are required.

This section gave you some insight into the semantics behind the BizTalk Framework. Now let's discuss the implementation layers of the framework.

The BizTalk logical implementation model consists of three layers. The first is the application layer. Applications will speak with other applications, whether they are external to the enterprise and outside the firewall, or inside the enterprise—for example, EAI or A2A. The application uses the BFC server for both sending and receiving business documents, but the application itself is responsible for the actual creation, evolution, and eventual destruction (or archiving) of the business document(s), including any attachments. Figure 2.2 is an example of how the BizTalk message flow works:

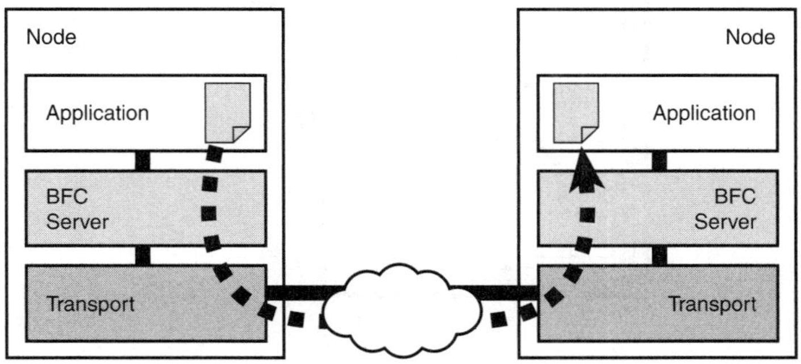

FIGURE 2.2
BizTalk message Flow.

The amount of work that the application is going to have to do to process a business document depends on the type of BFC server you are working with. If you are using Microsoft BizTalk Server as your BFC server, you can be confident that your application will be doing a minimal amount of work, when compared to the use of a "home-grown," third-party BFC server. The goal of the BFC server is to use information contained in the BizTags to determine the correct transport-specific destination address. The server then hands the message to the transport layer for transmission to the destination BFC server.

Structuring BizTalk Messages

In general, the body of the SOAP message constituting a BizTalk document contains several related business documents, and the header of the SOAP message contains several BizTalk-specific (and potentially other) header entries.

Figure 2.3 depicts the structure of a typical BizTalk document. First, you have the envelope, with two child elements:

- Header
- Body

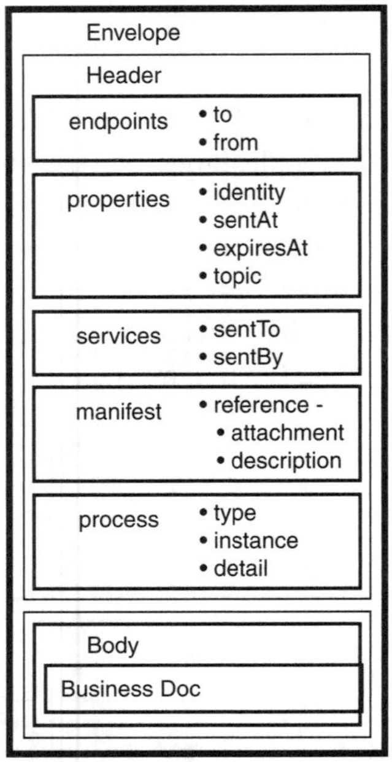

FIGURE 2.3
A SOAP message.

The header contains

- Endpoints—Mandatory
- Properties—Mandatory
- Services—Optional
- Manifest—Optional
- Process—Optional

The endpoints define the source and destination organizations. Properties provide information regarding the document's identity and the times of transmission. The source nodes enable the source organization to specify details about delivering the document reliably. The manifest is responsible primarily for document catalog information, whereas the process tag is responsible for persisting the process-management data and providing a processing context for the BizTalk document.

Note

The purpose of these elements will be discussed in later chapters regarding the routing and acknowledgement of receipts, but for now, it is important to understand that this is one of several places where information about self-routing can be stored. Remember, with XML documents, the business document itself is just a piece of the pie, the metadata surrounding the document is just as vital. BizTalk documents make effective use of this metadata to inform BFC servers about everything they might need to effectively route and service the document.

Not only is the BizTalk Framework effective at sending and routing documents, but the Framework also has extensive documentation regarding other features such as reliable delivery (that is, return receipts), sending documents with attachments (for example, pictures, binary files, and so on), security (for example, SSL, S/MIME, and detached signature mode), and transport bindings (for example, HTTP and SMTP). All these play an important role in making the BizTalk Framework a both efficient and secure document transport possibility that can only positively affect the future of business processing.

Summary

We have covered a lot of territory, from parsing XML and discovering Web Services via UDDI, to talking about the United Nations solution for B2B (ebXML) and Microsoft's own BizTalk Framework.

The goal of this chapter was to give you an overall understanding of XML: where it came from, what people are doing with it now, and where it is going from a business perspective. XML is bound to touch every aspect of computing in one way or another, but its impact on the business-to-business and enterprise-level sectors will be nothing less than profound. We urge you to read more on the subject. For more information, here are some links that you might find useful:

Robin Cover's SGML/XML Pages: `http://www.coverpages.org/`

Microsoft's XML Pages: `http://msdn.microsoft.com/xml/`

Microsoft BizTalk Page: `http://microsoft.com/biztalk/`

Microsoft's SOAP Pages: `http://msdn.microsoft.com/soap/`

ebXML Initiative: `http://www.ebXML.org/`

cXML: `http://www.cXML.org/`

Universal Description, Discovery, and Integration: `http://www.uddi.org/`

CHAPTER 3

Overview of BizTalk Server

by Rand Morimoto

IN THIS CHAPTER

Instead of listing the features and functions of the various technologies and tools built-in to the BizTalk Server product in a glossary/definition format, this chapter is organized chronologically by the process you follow to implement a BizTalk Server solution. Describing the BizTalk Server process flow involves defining goals and objectives of data interchange, modeling the business process, creating the specifications, and creating the maps, before finally confirming the trigger mechanisms and schedule for transaction processing.

In this chapter, BizTalk Orchestration is not purely defined, but instead illustrated how it relates to the business process model. And BizTalk Mapper is described in this chapter in terms of how it translates business processes into data interchange maps.

A BizTalk Server process flow starts with

1. Understanding the goals and objectives of the organizations that want to exchange information
2. Modeling the business process from start of the flow to completion
3. Agreeing on the specifications and parameters involved in the process
4. Creating the mapping between input and output data formats
5. Confirming the triggering mechanism to process the information
6. Completing the schedule for the transaction processes

When the process flow is followed, BizTalk Server can solve business information exchange challenges. The full process requires modeling business procedures, analyzing data communication formats, mapping formats, and properly configuring BizTalk Server. This chapter provides an overview of the sequential steps involved in the process and refers to the chapters throughout the balance of this book that highlight the steps in more detail.

Step 1: Determining the Interchange Goals and Objectives

Although BizTalk Server is an excellent solution for business to business (B2B) and Enterprise Application Integration (EAI), a successful implementation of BizTalk Server requires business analysis and goal setting to ensure that the solution meets the needs and objectives of the stakeholders of the project. This first step involves asking the right questions and gathering the information necessary to document the overall expectations for the project. A small amount of planning will go a long way in coming up with a complete end solution.

Who Understands the Interchange Goals and Objectives

When determining the interchange goals and objectives, it's important to understand who the project's stakeholders are who ultimately make the determination of whether the project is successful. Unlike many internetworking projects where the decision maker is frequently someone in the Information Technology (IT) department, for a BizTalk Server integrated solution, the decision maker is frequently the CFO, COO, or a Line of Business (LOB) manager. It is important to know who owns the results of the project. This individual or group of individuals will understand the overall goals and objectives for the data interchange needs of the project.

The stakeholders for the project also understand critical business factors necessary to know before and during the project. It is common that the stakeholder is also the person who would approve the budget and get personnel resources allocated to support the implementation and ongoing maintenance of the project.

Some stakeholders are hands-on and involved right from the beginning of the project and throughout the entire length of the project. These stakeholders will be directly informed on the project, process, and tasks to make decisions on budget and project engagement firsthand. Other stakeholders assign the information gathering and analysis tasks to someone else and only request that a final report be prepared and submitted for review. The stakeholder will typically still be the individual responsible for making the final decision, but others will be in a position of influencing the final decision. Their report and recommendation to the stakeholder would be biased by their opinion of the solution. In the cases where there are both stakeholder(s) and influencer(s), multiple individuals would need to be involved in the goal and objective definition process.

What Are the Interchange Goals and Objectives

With the stakeholder(s) and decision maker(s) identified, the goals and objectives for the project need to be understood. Determining the goals and objectives might be as simple as asking a single individual, or it might require a group meeting to come to a consensus. The data interchange goals and objectives vary from project to project. There are typically business goals and objectives, technical goals and objectives, and operational goals and objectives.

After the goals and objectives are understood, they should be written down to create a documented functional specification. This functional specification should then be approved and "signed off" by the stakeholders of the project to get a confirmation of their understanding of the goals and objectives of the project.

Business Goals and Objectives

The business goals and objectives for a data interchange project are those that impact or influence business processes. Examples of business goals and objectives would include

- Publish a part number and description catalog every week with updated information.
- Automate order processing and acknowledgement confirmation procedures.
- Decrease overall costs by automating order and transaction processing.
- Improve response time by eliminating manual processes with automated processes.
- Enhance transaction scalability by streamlining automated processes.

Technical Goals and Objectives

The technical goals and objectives for a data interchange project are those that impact or influence IT operational processes. An example of technical goals and objectives would include

- The consolidation of EDI and HTTP transaction systems into a single server system
- Improving logging and tracking of transactional information so that weekly reports can be created
- Standardizing the development language to be XML-based

Operational Goals and Objectives

The operational goals and objectives for a data interchange project are those that impact or influence timelines, budget, or operational processes. An example of operational goals and objectives would include

- The completion of the implementation of the project before the start of the next fiscal year
- The completion of the planning, programming, prototyping, testing, and implementation of the project for under $100,000
- The redeployment of idle personnel from a completed project to a new project

What Information Needs to Be Exchanged

With the stakeholders identified and the business, technical, and operational goals documented, the organization needs to define specifically what needs to be exchanged. This includes identifying the input format of the information coming into the BizTalk Server (such as EDI, HTTP, HTTPS) and the output format of the data being exchanged.

Also during the information gathering step, determining what applications will be involved and the transaction formats supported by the application need to be identified. There's a difference in how the BizTalk Server is configured and managed when two inventory control systems are connected versus the connectivity between a customer relationship management (CRM) application and an inventory control system. Each system has a defined format and method of communications.

There are several expectations for any implementation, whether it is an expectation of time, budget, scope of work, ongoing maintenance, or support arrangements to name a few. These expectations tend to drive behavior.

What Is the Need for Scalability and Integration

Finally, when determining the interchange goals and objectives, understanding the need for scalability of the BizTalk Server solution helps the organization plan the infrastructure needed to support the implementation. This involves planning and budgeting for multiple servers to support the demand for system transactions, or it might involve having multiple servers provide for a failover/fault tolerance system. An analysis of the needs and expectations of the stakeholders should assist in determining the type of programming needed to facilitate redundancy and performance metrics.

Additionally, an organization would want to know whether the BizTalk Server solution needs to integrate with an existing Windows environment or whether it would be tightly integrating with a non-Windows environment. An integration demand analysis would help the organization determine whether the tools available for development within a Windows-based environment are applicable and need to be acquired, or the support for multiple users can be identified and implemented in a native format or have non-Windows integration requirements.

Step 2: Modeling the Business Process

From the first step, we were able to interview the stakeholder(s) and/or the decision maker(s) to understand the business, technical, and operational goals and objectives of the organization. This information now needs to be modeled using the tools included with BizTalk Server to begin translating the process into code that can be run on the BizTalk Server.

This step involves identifying what needs to be processed, predicting what responses need to be returned, determining what events are sequential and what events trigger other events, and modeling the end-to-end information flow. This information is then entered in to a BizTalk Server tool called the BizTalk Orchestration Designer.

How to Describe the Business Processes

Key to the success of this step is translating the goals and objectives of the business into steps that can be followed methodically by the BizTalk Server. Effectively, a decision tree needs to be created where every yes/no or success/failure is identified, and appropriate loops are documented. If a group of planners is involved, this process may be done on a whiteboard.

If the organization already has a manual process that is desired to be automated, one big decision the organization needs to make is whether to mirror the existing process or rethink the entire process. Although an existing manual process might work fine, it might be laden with several steps that have no tie to any tangible function anymore. This might be a sign-off or verification process needed in a manual system but that can be bypassed in a fully automated system. It might be a process that involves checking or double-checking data entry information that might not be necessary in a single entry automated process. The business process steps need to be reviewed to determine whether they are necessary in an automated system.

Overview of BizTalk Orchestration

Unlike many IT-focused systems, BizTalk Server does not jump the organization straight from high-level business needs right into programming code. BizTalk Server includes a step called BizTalk Orchestration that allows an organization to define its business processes in a graphical format that can then be modeled and linked to more complex data processing models. This allows a separation between the definitions of a process and the implementation of the process. This enables different parts of the business process to be modeled by those who know the processes the best (the business-focused individuals). Those processes then are compared with the technical programmability parts of the process.

BizTalk Orchestration Designer

The tool that facilitates the modeling process is called the BizTalk Orchestration Designer. The tool is effectively a Visio modeling tool that provides a way for an organization to model its processes into a flowchart type drawing. This drawing is called an XLANG scheduling drawing. Most business managers understand the concept of BizTalk

Orchestration Designer because they are familiar with flowcharts and flowchart processing, so having this orchestration design step helps to ensure that the technical process mirrors the expected business goals and objectives.

> **Note**
>
> Although a business manager usually understands flowcharting and will be able to review the models created in the BizTalk Orchestration Designer, typically a technical expert would be involved in the actual creation of the BizTalk Orchestration Designer model.

BizTalk Orchestration and the BizTalk Orchestration Designer are covered in more detail in Chapter 9, "Introducing BizTalk Orchestration."

Some of the BizTalk Orchestration Designer process options include Action, Decision, While, Abort, Fork, and Join. These options enable different flow routines to occur.

Action

An Action defines a process that typically requires information to be manipulated. It might be an action step that runs the information through a filter, or it might be an action step that reformats data being processed.

Decision

A Decision defines a process where a yes/no, data query, or other information analysis is conducted, and the result determines which branch to follow to continue with the workflow. It may be determined that if a field is blank to have a branch that enables an action to fill the field with data. However, if the field is not blank, then a branch would allow the process to continue.

While

The While object allows a process to loop until a specific event occurs. This might be a process that continues until the end of the dataset is reached, or it might be a process that continues until a specific data record is reached. A branch can then be followed to a subsequent decision or action.

Abort

An Abort object identifies a step where the process needs to be terminated. In many cases, the abort becomes a fail-safe test that determines that the information received is malformed, signaling data corruption in the transmission or just that incorrect data was transmitted. This step can provide a way to stop a process from continuing with incorrect information.

Fork and Join

A Fork splits a process to conduct simultaneous tasks that can then be Joined later in the process. This is frequently a process that enables information to be gathered for decisions to be made. For example, a fork in a process can be created to go out and gather price and availability information from multiple vendors. This information can be gathered and processed simultaneously. From this fork, when the information has been analyzed, the system can join back together to continue with the process.

Step 3: Agreeing on Process Specifications and Parameters

After the models have been created and the processes defined and agreed on, the next step is to agree on the specifications and parameters for the information interchange. This step gets more involved in the technical data formats of the information.

Specifications are created and can be based on industry standards, such as XML, X12 EDI, SAP IDOC, or UN/EDIFACT, or the information can be structured simply as flat files, such as delimited, positional, or delimited and positional formats. From this data format and specifications the appropriate filters can be applied to the fields of input and output information.

The parameters of the data structure typically define what information to expect within the specification format. This could be as simple as knowing that the first fields in the dataset include name, address, and purchase order number, or the parameters might specify that the first fields in the dataset are raw order data such as quantity and agreed-on pricing. It is important to know the data format and the structure of the data so that the right information is automatically extracted and processed properly.

BizTalk Editor

The BizTalk Editor is a graphical tool that comes with BizTalk Server that helps with the creation, editing, and management of document specifications. It allows for the creation of these document specifications by defining the fields and records based on the needs of the organization using BizTalk Server. The specifications can be created by manually defining the records and fields in the BizTalk Editor tool, or by using any of the built-in specifications for the support of standards such as X12 EDI, UN/EDIFACT, XML Data-Reduced (XDR), and the like.

By defining or modeling the format of the document in the BizTalk Editor tool, the BizTalk Server can parse and serialize the output data regardless of the type or format of the information. Additionally, after the format has been defined, an instance of the data can be tested to verify that the specification is correct.

Although transparent to the user, BizTalk Server represents documents in an XML Schema Definition Language (XSDL) format. The document specifications define the attributes for the data, whether data fields are required or optional, whether the data values are fixed length or variable, and the like.

Simply, the BizTalk Editor is used to create and validate specifications to be used for reference purposes. After the specifications have been defined, data can be tested on the server to ensure that the specification is correct.

Step 4: Creating the Mapping Between Input and Output Data Formats

Although the BizTalk Editor can structure the information into common formats such as X12 EDI or UN/EDIFACT that can be read and processed by the system that understands the standard formats, many times information is received and needs to be translated into a different format. This mapping of input and output fields ensures that the right information is relayed to the destination.

The BizTalk Mapper is the tool included with BizTalk Server that provides the mapping between fields.

BizTalk Mapper

BizTalk Mapper allows the definition and the correlation of data between records and fields for one document specification, and the records and fields for another. The mapping of information from one input format to another goes through one of two different processes. The BizTalk Server can alter the schema of the information in a process that is said to transform the information, or the BizTalk Server can actually alter the data itself in a process that is said to be a translation of the information.

The transformation process used by the BizTalk Server is handled by script coding using *functoids*. A functoid is a reusable function built-in to the server engine that enables simple as well as complex structural manipulation between source and destination specifications. A transformation of information is common because input and output formats frequently do not match and need to be mapped so that fields from one format match the fields of the other format during the transformation process. A transformation process, although by definition means that the data is altered, does not necessarily mean that the information is deleted and replaced with completely different data, but that information is analyzed and modified for a new or different format.

An example of data transformation could be the replacement of a State definition such as Calif with a standard two-letter CA postal format, or a data label may be padded with extra spaces to keep the data format the same length such as keeping a field to eight total characters even if that means that several characters are spaces. BizTalk Mapper uses extensible style sheet language (XSL) to process the map transformation.

As an XSL generator, the BizTalk Mapper allows for both simple one-to-one mappings and more complex mappings using functoids. The graphical mappings defined in the editor are compiled down to XSL to be applied by the BizTalk Server engine at runtime to the inbound document. Inbound documents are parsed into XML representation of the information using the specifications defined in the BizTalk Editor. If mapping is required, the XSL is applied, and the document is serialized into the correct outbound format by the messaging engine using the outbound BizTalk Editor-generated specification.

Step 5: Configuring the Triggering Mechanisms to Process Information

After information is formatted with a common interchange format, the data needs to be transported between organizations or systems. The triggering mechanism that initiates the process to transport data is called BizTalk Messaging. BizTalk Messaging provides the capability to send data in a secure and reliable manner between systems. Because BizTalk is used for both external and internal data transport processes, the transport of information may be between external trading partners through a VPN tunnel over the Internet, or the transport of information may be between internal accounting and client management systems on a corporate LAN.

Overview of BizTalk Messaging

BizTalk Messaging takes information and transports it from a sender to a receiver. BizTalk Messaging is similar to a traditional e-mail system; however, an e-mail system assumes that a message comes in using a standard message format (such as SMTP) and transports it to a recipient using a standard (SMTP) message format. As highlighted in Chapter 1, "Motivation and Uses for BizTalk Server," BizTalk Messaging accepts data in a variety of incoming formats (such as EDI, HTTP, HTTPS, and so on), takes the programmed field map created in BizTalk Editor, and maps the data fields to an output format using BizTalk Mapper to create the transported BizTalk message.

BizTalk Messaging is covered in more detail in Chapter 6, "Introduction to BizTalk Messaging."

Data Stores

In a BizTalk Server environment, information is stored in data stores that are nothing more than SQL databases. The data stores hold the transaction data and more importantly the transaction logs. At any time, through the use of the document tracking utility built-in to BizTalk Server, reports can be generated using the data and log information to validate that information has been sent and received. The information can be verified to ensure accuracy, time stamps, and other critical confirmation of data transaction.

The Shared Queue (SQ) Database

One of the data stores in a BizTalk Server environment is the Shared Queue (SQ) database. The Shared Queue database is a SQL database shared by all servers in a BizTalk Server group. If there is only a single server in an organization, the Shared Queue tracks only one server. If there are multiple servers for a BizTalk Server group, all the queue information is stored and tracked on a single server.

The Shared Queue database also tracks checkpoints for data transactions. The checkpoint is a file that notes the transaction status of a BizTalk Server system. If one server in a group fails, other servers can take over the process tasks, such as receiving messages, posting messages to the work queue, and transporting messages to destination servers. In a way, the failover process facilitated by the checkpoints in the Shared Queue database creates a load balancing and built-in fault tolerance system for the BizTalk Server environment.

The BizTalk Messaging Management Database

Another SQL database critical to the operation of a BizTalk Server environment is the BizTalk Messaging Management database. The BizTalk Messaging Management database stores information related to server configurations, such as group and server settings and messaging configuration settings. The information in the database either is entered using the BizTalk Messaging Manager interface or is programmatically entered using an API. This database effectively stores the system configuration information for the server.

Send and Receive Architecture

As clarified throughout this chapter, BizTalk Server was built with variability so that there is flexibility on the process and data format to send and receive information from a variety of sources and destinations. The architecture enables disparate systems to communicate with each other, and the simplicity of message translation and transformation provides the capability to interconnect multiple systems with the same set of data.

Pass-Through Submission

One method of data transport is called *pass-through submission*. Pass-through submission allows data to bypass the parsing, decoding, decryption, transformation, and signature verification stages of a BizTalk Server process. Data is passed directly to the destination noted in the submission parameters. Pass-through submission is commonly used to transmit binary files, such as Word documents, applets, structured database files, and so on that do not require translation.

BizTalk Server Administration

For managing and administering the BizTalk Server environment, a BizTalk Server Administration tool is included. The BizTalk Administration tool is a Microsoft Management Console (MMC) snap-in that shows the Shared Queue databases on a BizTalk Server as a series of queues. Also within the administration tool, an administration can make modifications to the configuration of the server such as setting tracking information, group interaction, messaging transport, queue management, or database replication.

BizTalk Server Administration is covered in Part VI, "BizTalk Server Administration."

Step 6: Completing the Schedule for the Transaction Process

The first five steps of this process involved identifying the business, technical, and operational processes and then using BizTalk Orchestration to graphically represent the processes. The process continued with the creation of the specifications for the data and then mapping the information between trading partners and systems. This last step involves completing the XLANG schedule drawing by compiling it into an XLANG schedule that can be tested and then put into production.

Note

Not every application use of BizTalk Server requires the implementation of both Messaging and Orchestration services. Depending on the input and output format demands of the transaction, due to the overlap in functionality of these two services, an organization may find that only the Messaging or Orchestration service is required.

The BizTalk Orchestration XLANG Scheduler Engine

BizTalk Server comes with a service called the BizTalk Orchestration XLANG Scheduler Engine. This service controls the activation, execution, dehydration, and rehydration of an XLANG schedule. This process takes the final agreed-on business and technical process and puts it into a format that can be executed on the BizTalk Server.

The XLANG schedule defines the steps to be performed, the components that must be called, and the data that will pass through the BizTalk Server to fulfill the defined transaction process. When documents are sent from the XLANG schedule to the BizTalk Messaging Service, the name of a channel that will receive the documents must be defined. After the channel is defined, documents can pass from the BizTalk Messaging Service to the BizTalk Orchestration Service.

When in the BizTalk Orchestration Service, the document is either processed in XML format, or if the document is not in XML, the XLANG Scheduler Engine will need to embed the document in the engine's standard XML wrapper. When inside the XLANG schedule, the document can undergo any defined modifications. After processing the document, it can then be sent back to BizTalk Messaging or it can be sent out of the XLANG schedule to a private or public queue.

Schedule activation and execution are the processes that enable the schedule to be run and then ultimately be executed to process information. When schedules are unused, they are dehydrated and then dynamically rehydrated when needed. This dehydration/rehydration process minimizes the need to allocate resources of the BizTalk Server to processes that are unused, allowing for the optimization of the system to handle the needs of the transaction environment.

Summary

BizTalk Server is a powerful business transaction product that, when properly planned and implemented, is of help to organizations conducting B2B and EAI tasks. Several technologies are embedded, and several tools are included with the BizTalk Server product, including the BizTalk Orchestration Designer, Editor, Mapper, Messaging Manager, and Server Administration MMC utilities. This chapter introduced the tools and technologies and how they fit into a BizTalk process flow and provided references to more specific chapters throughout the book.

BizTalk Server Messaging

PART II

IN THIS PART

CHAPTER 4

The BizTalk Editor

By Susie Adams and Charlie Kaiman

In This Chapter

BizTalk Server Messaging guarantees the reliable delivery and transformation of structured documents between applications and organizations. To transform and route a document, the BizTalk Server Messaging engine parses it and then maps it into its desired outbound format. The parsing is accomplished by a BizTalk parser that's been developed specifically for that document type. The serialization of the document into its native format is handled by that document type's corresponding BizTalk serializer. The BizTalk Messaging engine associates inbound and outbound documents to their parsers and serializers using a BizTalk specification that describes the type and structure of the document.

The BizTalk Editor tool allows developers to create, manage, and edit specifications that define a structured document. A BizTalk specification is an XML Data Reduced (`XDR`) definition of a structured document, which provides a common vocabulary that is capable of handling the overlaps that commonly occur between syntactical, database, and conceptual data schemas. Specifications represent the structured data as XML regardless of their original format. When a document is received by the BizTalk Messaging Engine, the document is parsed by a BizTalk Server parser according to the properties of the records and fields contained in the specification. The resulting document is the XML representation of the original inbound document. The properties of the records and fields are represented as BizTalk Server-specific XML annotations in the XDR schema.

The BizTalk Mapper uses BizTalk specifications to create maps between inbound and outbound documents. A BizTalk map is an XLST style sheet that when applied to an inbound document transforms the document into an XML representation of the desired outbound document. The Messaging engine then uses a BizTalk serializer to read the outbound specification and serialize the XML document into its native outbound document format. This allows the BizTalk Messaging Engine to process documents based on any of the following document types:

- Well-formed XML
- XDR schemas
- Document type definitions (`DTDs`)
- Electronic data interchange (`EDI`) `X12` and `EDIFACT`
- Flat files, including delimited and/or positional files, SAP IDOCs
- Structured document formats

The BizTalk Editor allows you to create specifications starting with a blank specification or by importing an existing schema or well-formed XML document. You can import XDR schemas, well-formed XML documents, and `DTDs` documents. The BizTalk Server Editor also provides several templates that can be used as starting points for creating specifications for common document types, such as common XML purchase orders, `EDI X12`, and `EDIFACT` documents.

In this chapter, we will discuss how to create BizTalk specifications using the BizTalk Editor. Specifically, we will discuss how to create specifications for an XML document, a delimited flat file document, and a positional flat file document.

BizTalk Specifications

BizTalk Server is XML-centric underneath the hood. Every inbound document is parsed into its XML representation to make it easier to transform and then serialize it into its native outbound format. It uses the BizTalk Editor specification to parse and serialize the inbound and outbound documents. Simply put, a BizTalk specification is an XDR schema with XML annotations included. Just how many annotations are we talking about? Listing 4.1 displays an example of a bank transaction BizTalk XDR specification.

LISTING 4.1 A BizTalk Server XDR Specification—Bank Transaction

```
<?xml version="1.0"?>
<!-- Generated by using BizTalk Editor on Sat, Nov 17 2001 01:23:11 PM -->
<!-- Copyright (c) Microsoft Corporation. All rights reserved. -->
<Schema name="Transaction" b:BizTalkServerEditorTool_Version="1.5"
➥b:root_reference="Transaction" b:standard="XML"
➥xmlns="urn:schemas-microsoft-com:xml-data"
➥xmlns:b="urn:schemas-microsoft-com:BizTalkServer"
➥xmlns:d="urn:schemas-microsoft-com:datatypes">
<b:SelectionFields/>

<ElementType name="Type" content="textOnly" model="closed" d:type="string">
<b:FieldInfo/>
</ElementType><ElementType name="Transaction" content="eltOnly" model="closed">
<b:RecordInfo/>
<element type="Amount" maxOccurs="1" minOccurs="0"/>
<element type="Type" maxOccurs="1" minOccurs="0"/>
<element type="Facility" maxOccurs="1" minOccurs="0"/>
<element type="Location" maxOccurs="1" minOccurs="0"/>
</ElementType><ElementType name="Name" content="textOnly" model="closed"
➥d:type="string">
<b:FieldInfo/>
</ElementType><ElementType name="Location" content="eltOnly" model="closed">
<b:RecordInfo/>
<element type="Name" maxOccurs="1" minOccurs="0"/>
<element type="Address" maxOccurs="1" minOccurs="0"/>
</ElementType><ElementType name="Facility" content="textOnly" model="closed"
➥ d:type="string">
<b:FieldInfo/>
```

LISTING 4.1 continued

```
</ElementType><ElementType name="Amount" content="textOnly" model="closed"
➥d:type="float">
<b:FieldInfo/>
</ElementType><ElementType name="Address" content="textOnly" model="closed"
➥ d:type="string">
<b:FieldInfo/>
</ElementType></Schema>
```

The BizTalk specification, as you can see, has some BizTalk specific elements and attributes that need to be discussed. First, notice that a new namespace is defined by the URN `xmlns:b="urn:schemas-microsoft-com:BizTalkServer"`. Any elements prefaced with a `b:`, therefore, are assumed to be BizTalk-specific.

The lines immediately following that give three new attributes: `BizTalkServerEditorTool_Version`, `root_reference`, and `standard`. The purpose of the `BizTalkServerTool_Version` attribute is to classify the BizTalk Editor version used to build the schema. This could be important for future upgrades of the application that might require a later version of the BizTalk specification, for example.

The `root_reference` property defines the document element of this XML instance—in other words, the top element in this XML document, the element that encapsulates all the other data. In this case, the document element is `<Transactions>`. The `standard` attribute declares the format that is going to be used to express the data. In this instance, XML is used as the formatting type.

In addition to the attributes described previously, several elements are added to a traditional XDR schema. They are `SelectionFields`, `RecordInfo`, and `FieldInfo`. Because we are describing an XML document, the elements are empty; however, other formatting standards, such as comma-delimited files, require the data in these elements. The BizTalk Editor handles the annotation of the XDR schemas for us automatically requiring developers to have little or no knowledge of XDR or the supported BizTalk annotations. As a result, the remainder of the chapter focuses on the creation of the specifications using BizTalk Editor as opposed to physical characteristics of the XDR specifications created by the Editor.

Building Specifications Using the BizTalk Editor

In this section, we will build specifications that facilitate the delivery and transformation of bank transaction data between three banks, Sunset Bank, Bank of America, and

Fidelity. The application we will build is going to reside at Sunset Bank, whose internal systems expect to receive an XML transaction document. An example instance of the `Transaction.xml` XML document is displayed in Listing 4.2.

LISTING 4.2 The `TransactionInstance.XML` Document

```
<Transaction>
   <Account>1</Account>
   <Amount>500.00</Amount>
   <Type>Credit</Type>
   <Facility>Bank of America</Facility>
   <Location>
      <Name>Manassas</Name>
      <Address>6815 Stillbrooke Road</Address>
   </Location>
</Transaction>
```

Sunset Bank receives transaction data from two banks, Bank of America and Fidelity. Bank of America's internal systems export data to a CSV-delimited file and Fidelity's systems export their data to a positional flat file. To consume these input files, Sunset Bank's internal systems will need to transform both the CSV and positional flat file into the XML document format expected by their systems. To accomplish this, we will build three specifications: one that describes Sunset Bank's XML format, one that defines Fidelity's positional flat file format, and one that defines Bank of America's CSV transaction.

In the sections that follow you will learn how to build:

- A BizTalk specification based on an XML document.
- A BizTalk specification that describes a delimited flat file.
- A BizTalk specification that describes a positional flat file.

The Sunset Bank example in this chapter will walk through the steps required to create the specifications; however, the maps that would transform the documents into the Sunset Bank XML format are not discussed. The BizTalk Mapper is covered in detail in Chapter 5, "The BizTalk Mapper," of this book.

Building an XML BizTalk Specification

The first BizTalk specification we are going to build will define the Sunset Bank XML document.

Sunset bank requires an XML schema named `Transaction`.

To begin, open the BizTalk Editor and select File, New from the menu. In the New Document Specification dialog that appears, select the `Blank` specification option and click OK. A new blank XML specification appears in your BizTalk Editor window. Next, select the `Blank` Specification tag in the left-hand panel and right-click. In the pop-up menu that appears, select the Rename menu option and rename the root node of the document `Transaction`. The `Transaction` document will consist of element nodes as opposed to attribute nodes. We can configure the Editor to do this without having to manually declare each. To configure the BizTalk Editor options, select Tools, Options from the menu. In the BizTalk Editor Options dialog that appears, check the Create a New Field as an Element `Option` and click OK as displayed in Figure 4.1.

FIGURE 4.1
Setting the Editor options.

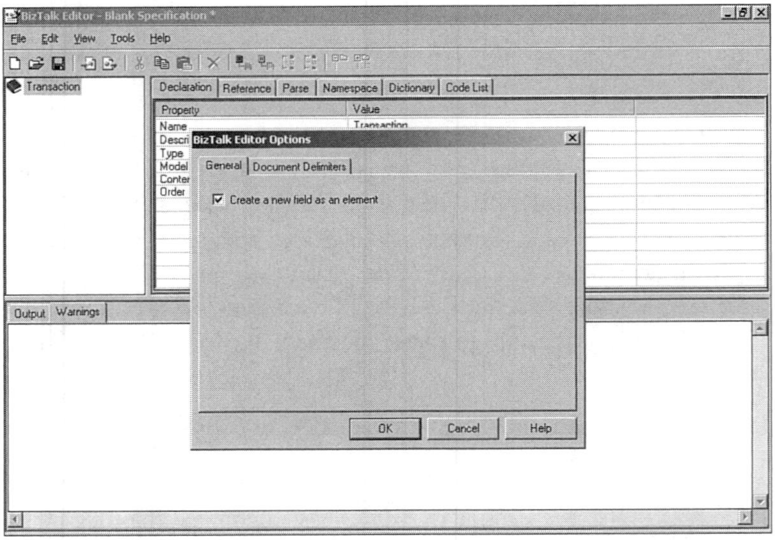

This XML document contains several elements and one record. The element names are `Account`, `Amount`, `Type`, and `Facility`. The record name is `Location` and consists of two elements, `Name` and `Address`. The XML specification for this document is displayed in Figure 4.2.

To add the elements and records to the BizTalk specification, select the `Transaction` root node in the left-hand panel and right-click. In the pop-up menu that appears, select the New Field menu option and name it `Account`. Then repeat the same steps, creating three additional fields, `Amount`, `Type`, and `Facility`. Next, select the `Transaction` root node, right-click, and select the New Record menu option. Name the new record `Location`. Then select the new location record in the left-hand panel and right-click.

In the pop-up menu that appears, select the New Field menu option and name the field `Name`. Then repeat the same steps to add a second field to the `Location` record named `Address`.

FIGURE 4.2
The `Transaction` *BizTalk specification.*

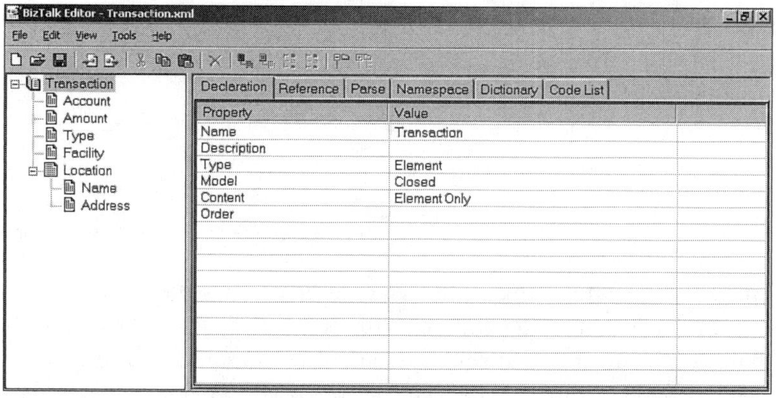

Next, we need to set the data type for each of the elements we created. To accomplish this, select each of the elements in the left-hand panel and navigate to the Declaration tab. Then select the `Data Type` property and configure the data types for each element as displayed in Table 4.1.

TABLE 4.1 The Data Types for the `Transaction` BizTalk Specification

Element Name	*Data Type*
`Account`	Number
`Amount`	Float
`Type`	String
`Facility`	String
`Name`	String
`Location`	String

Next, we need to set the `Location` record properties. To accomplish this, select the `Location` record in the left-hand panel and navigate to the Reference tab. Then, set the Minimum Occurrence property to 1 and Maximum Occurrence property to 1 as displayed in Figure 4.3.

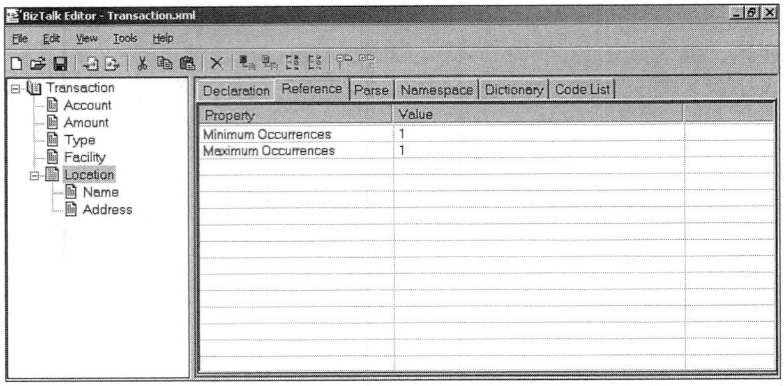

FIGURE 4.3
Setting the `Minimum` *and* `Maximum Occurrence` *properties.*

Finally we need to configure the required fields properties and restrict the length of the `Facility` element to 15 characters. To set the maximum length, select the `Facility` field in the left-hand panel and navigate to the Declaration tab. Locate the `Maximum Length` property and set it to 15. The `Transaction` XML schema only requires data in two elements, `Account` and `Amount`. To set these properties, select each individually in the left-hand panel and navigate to the Reference tab. Then, locate the `Required` property and set its value to `Yes`.

We are now ready to save and test our specification. The easiest way to test the specification is to select the Tools, Validate Instance option from the menu. If you don't have an instance of the document, you can have the Editor generate a native instance for you and then review its contents for accuracy. The Sunset Bank example located on the publisher's Web site has an instance of the document named `TransactionInstance.xml`. To test the `Transaction` specification, select Tools, Validate Instance from the menu. In the Validate Document Instance dialog that appears, navigate to the `TransactionInstance.xml` instance document and select it as displayed in Figure 4.4.

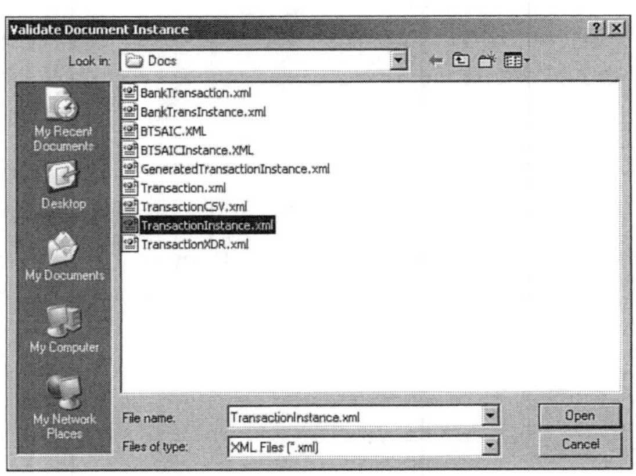

FIGURE 4.4
Validating the instance.

The `TransactionInstance.XML` document was displayed previously in Listing 4.2.

If the document had failed validation, a warning notifying you of the error would appear in the Warnings tab at the bottom of the Editor window. To demonstrate this, select the `Facility` field in the left-hand panel, reset its `Maximum Length` property to 10, and then test the validation of the `TransactionInstance.xml` document again. The `TransactionInstance.xml` document has a `Facility` name 15 characters in length and will therefore fail validation. The warning obtained is displayed in Figure 4.5.

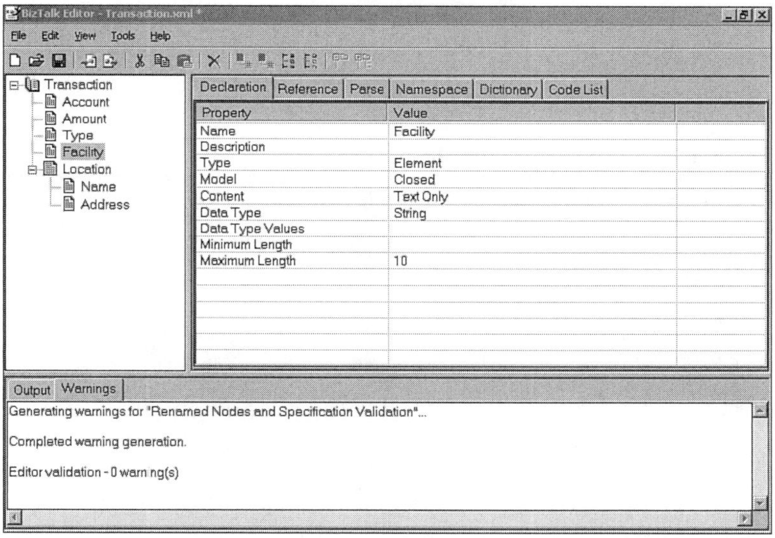

FIGURE 4.5
Validating the instance when it fails validation.

You can also have the BizTalk Editor generate an instance of the document for you. To accomplish this, select `Tools, Create XML Instance` from the menu. In the Create Document Instance As dialog that appears, name and save your instance file. The sample instance for the `Transaction` BizTalk specification we just created is displayed in Listing 4.3. Because the `Transaction` specification describes an XML document, the Create Native Instance menu option is unavailable on the Tools menu.

LISTING 4.3 The `Transaction` BizTalk Generated Instance

```
<Transaction><Account>1.</Account><Amount>1.0</Amount><Type>Type_1</Type>
➥<Facility>
➥Facility_1</Facility><Location><Name>Name_1</Name><Address>Address_1</Address>
➥</Location></Transaction>
```

In the next section, we will create a specification that contains the same transaction data; however, this time the transaction instance file and specification will describe the comma-delimited Bank of America data.

Building a Delimited Flat File Specification

The Bank of America transaction consists of data stored in a comma-delimited format with a carriage return line feed at the end of each record. This type of file is typically called a CSV delimited flat file. A delimited flat file is a term used to describe a file format in which a single character or pattern of characters is used to separate data into manageable pieces. Table 4.2 shows a list of common delimiters and their hexadecimal values.

TABLE 4.2 Common Delimiters and Hex Values

Common Delimiters	*Hex Value*
TAB	0x09
SPACE	0x20
LF	0xa
CR	0xd
*	0x2a
+	0x2b
,	0x2c
.	0x2e
;	0x3b
|	0x7c

Looking back at our scenario, the managers at Bank of America needed to come up with a good way to share account information. Due to time constraints and lack of IT infrastructure, they decided to go with a simple CSV format for transmitting account data. Listing 4.4 shows a sample flat file representing a Bank of America financial transaction.

LISTING 4.4 Bank of America's Transaction Data in Delimited Flat File Format

```
987890,-300
987890,-45.96
987890,-32.16
987890,2000
987890,-112.53
987891,3015
```

LISTING 4.4 continued

```
987891,-12.35
987891,-456.55
987891,-102.02
987891,-36.12
987891,110.5
```

Notice that the first column of data (prior to the comma delimiter) represents an account number, and the second column is the `+/-` value of the account transaction amount for that particular record. The specification we will create contains additional fields; however, only the account and transition amount are required.

Now that Bank of America has come up with a formatted standard for sharing its financial information, our goal is to be able to reformat the data into the Sunset Bank XML document format. To enable Sunset Bank to process the delimited document, we will need to create new BizTalk specifications to describe it and then a map to convert the contents of the file into the Sunset Bank XML transaction format.

To create the delimited specification, begin by opening the BizTalk Editor and selecting File, New from the menu. In the New Specification dialog that appears, select a Blank Specification and click OK. Next, select the `Blank Specification` root element displayed in the left panel and right-click. In the pop-up menu that appears, select the Rename menu option and rename the root object `Transaction`. The `Transaction` document will consist of element nodes as opposed to attribute nodes. To configure the Editor options to accommodate this, select Tools, Options from the menu. In the BizTalk Editor Options dialog that appears, check the Create a New Field as an Element option and click OK.

Next, select the `Transaction` root node and right-click. In the pop-up menu that appears, select the New Record menu option and name the new record `Transactions`. Adding a record denotes an important distinction between an XML document specification and its delimited counterpart. A delimited specification requires this subrecord to define the delimiters for each record in the file whereas an XML specification does not. In this example, the record delimiter is a carriage return line feed. If we didn't add this record, there would be no way to distinguish between the field and record delimiters for the file.

Next, we need to add five element fields beneath the `Transactions` record: `Account`, `Amount`, `Type`, `Facility`, `LocationName`, and `LocationAddress`. To accomplish this, select the `Transactions` record in the left-hand pane and right-click. In the pop-up menu that appears, select the New Field menu option and rename the field `Amount`. Repeat these steps four additional times for each of the remaining fields.

Next, as we did in the XML transaction example, we need to set the data type for each of the elements we created. To accomplish this, select each of the elements in the left-hand panel and navigate to the Declaration tab. Then select the Data Type property and configure the data types for each element as displayed in Table 4.3.

TABLE 4.3 The Data Types for the `Transaction` BizTalk Specification

Element Name	*Data Type*
`Account`	Number
`Amcunt`	Float
`Type`	String
`Facility`	String
`Name`	String
`Location`	String

We also need to configure the required field properties and restrict the length of the `Facility` element to 15 characters. To set the maximum length, select the `Facility` field in the left-hand panel and navigate to the Declaration tab. Locate the `Maximum Length` property and set it to 15. The `TransactionCSV` specification requires data in two elements—`Account` and `Amount`. To set these properties, select each individually in the left-hand panel and navigate to the Reference tab. Then locate the `Required` property and set its value to `Yes`.

Because the specification is describing a delimited file, we need to set several attributes to identify how the document is delimited. Let's begin by setting the document type, field, and record delimiters. First, select the root `Transaction` node in the left-hand panel and navigate to the Reference tab. Then, set the `Standard` property to `Custom` to denote a flat file specification type. Next, select the Parse tab and configure the properties as described in Table 4.4.

Note

You will be warned by a prompt when changing the `Standard` property that "`Changing the standard property might cause some properties to be cleared.`" Select Yes in this dialog to continue.

TABLE 4.4 The Properties for the Delimited Specification Root Node Parse Tab

Property	*Value*
`Structure`	`Delimited`
`Field Order`	`Postfix`
`Delimiter Type`	`Character`
`Delimiter Value`	`CR`
`Skip Carriage Return`	`No`

The `Structure` property denotes the physical structure of the specification, which in this case is `Delimited`. The `Field Order` property describes the location of the delimiters relative to one another. There are three `Field Order` property options: `Prefix`, `Postfix`, and `Infix`. `Prefix` describes delimiters that appear before each member in a series, *a*a*b*c. `Postfix` describes delimiters that appear after each member a*b*c*, and `Infix` delimiters appear between components a*a*b*c. In the Bank of America CSV file, the field delimiter should be configured as `Postfix` because each record is delimited with a carriage return, line feed with a carriage return, line feed after the last record. If the file does not have a carriage return, line feed after the last record, you would need to set this value to `Infix`.

> **Note**
>
> The line feed character is automatically ignored by the BizTalk Server flat file parser.

Finally, the `Delimiter Type` property should be set to `Character` with a `Delimiter Value` of `CR` and the `Skip Carriage Return` property should be set to `No`. The `Transaction` root node parse properties are displayed in Figure 4.6.

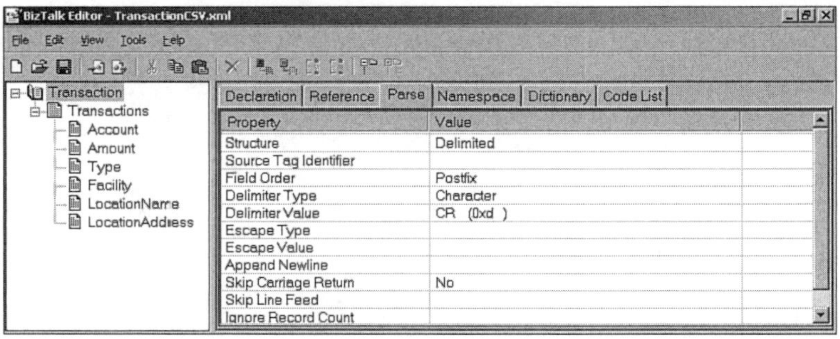

FIGURE 4.6
The root node parse properties.

Next, we need to configure the parse properties for the fields in the document by setting the parse properties on the `Transactions` record. To accomplish this, select the `Transactions` record node in the left-hand panel and navigate to the Parse tab. Then configure the parse properties as displayed in Figure 4.7.

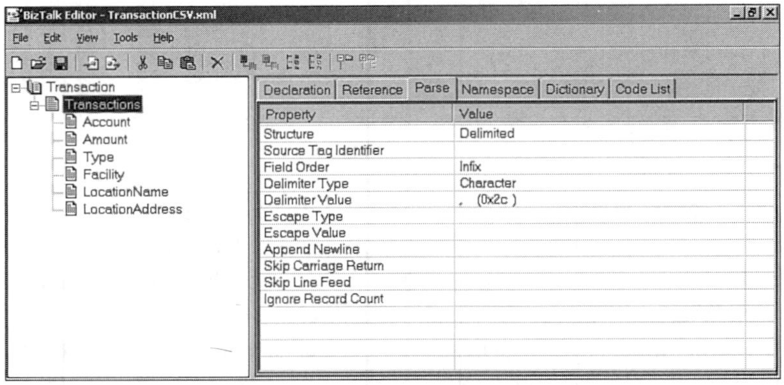

FIGURE 4.7
The `Transactions` *record parse properties.*

Again the `Structure` is Delimited, this time with a `Field Order` of `Infix`, a `Delimiter Type` of `Character`, and a `Delimiter Value` of ",".

We are now ready to save and test the `TransactionCSV.xml` BizTalk specification. To test the specification, select Tools, Validate Instance from the menu. In the dialog that appears, select the `.txt` file to validate. The publisher's Web site contains a copy of the `TransactionCSV.xml` specification as well as an instance of a `CSV` file with and without carriage returns at the end of the last record. Let's first validate the CSV sample file, `TransactionCSV.txt`, with carriage returns at the end of each line. Because we have set the record `Field` order to PostFix, the validate should successfully execute. Then, let's validate the specification again, but before we do, modify the specification's `Transaction` root node `Field Order` property setting to `Infix`. A warning message should appear as displayed in Figure 4.8, notifying you of the additional delimiter at the end of the file.

In the next section, we will build a positional BizTalk specification that defines the same transaction data.

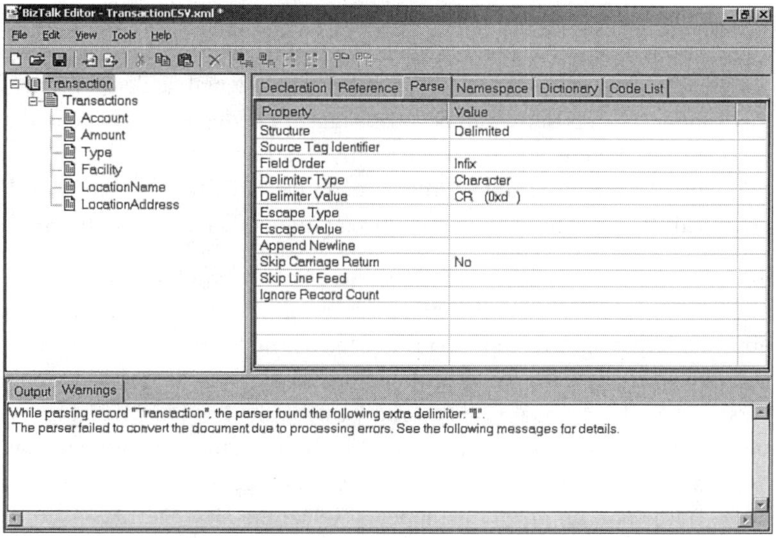

FIGURE 4.8
Testing the CSV specification with Field Order set to `Infix`.

Building a Positional Flat File Specification

Now assume that we want to do business with yet another bank, this time Fidelity. Fidelity uses a positional flat file to exchange financial data with its partners and customers. We (Sunset Bank) need to create a BizTalk specification to represent this flat file, so that it can be transformed by BizTalk Messaging into the XML format that our applications are designed to work with.

Here is an example of what a typical Fidelity positional transaction file will look like:

```
R987890-300xxxxxxx
R987890-45.96xxxxx
R987890-32.16xxxxx
R9878902000xxxxxxx
R987890-112.53xxxx
R9878913015xxxxxxx
R987891-12.35xxxxx
R987891-456.55xxxx
R987891-102.02xxxx
R987891-36.12xxxxx
R987891110.5xxxxxx
```

> **Note**
>
> The x's in the file denote blank space in the file in the real `TransactionPOS.txt` file.

Notice that there is an "R" in every transaction record. This character is a `Source Tag Identifier` used to represent the beginning of a new record. Each record contains a fixed-length account number field that is 6 characters in length and an 11-character amount field that supports (-+) positive and negative signs for deductions and credits to and from the account. The records are also delimited by a carriage return (CR), line feed (LF), just as in the Bank of America example. In this sense, the Fidelity document is both a positional and a delimited flat file. This is important to keep in mind as we build the BizTalk specification.

To create the `TransactionPOS.xml` specification, begin by opening the BizTalk Editor and selecting New, Blank Specification from the menu. In the blank specification that appears, select the `BlankSpecification` root node and right-click. In the pop-up menu that appears, select the Rename menu option and rename the root node `TransactionPOS`. Next, select the `TransactionPOS` root node in the left-hand panel and right-click. In the pop-up menu that appears, select the New Record menu option and name the new record `Transactions`. Then, select the `Transactions` record in the left-hand menu and right-click. In the pop-up menu that appears, select the New Record menu option and name the new subrecord `BankTransaction`.

Now, we are ready to add the fields for the specification. The Fidelity specification requires only two of the elements supported in the Bank of America specification, `Account` and `Amount`. To add the fields, select the `BankTransaction` record in the left-hand panel and right-click. In the pop-up menu that appears, select the New Field menu option and name the new field `Account`. The `Account` field data type should also be set to `Number` in that same property tab. Then repeat the same steps and add a second field named `Amount`, setting its data type to `Float`. The `TransactionPOS` specification should look as displayed in Figure 4.9. The fields in this case are denoted as attributes of the BankTransaction element. These could also be changed to elements with no effect on the outcome of this application.

FIGURE 4.9
The `TransactionPOS` *specification after the fields are added.*

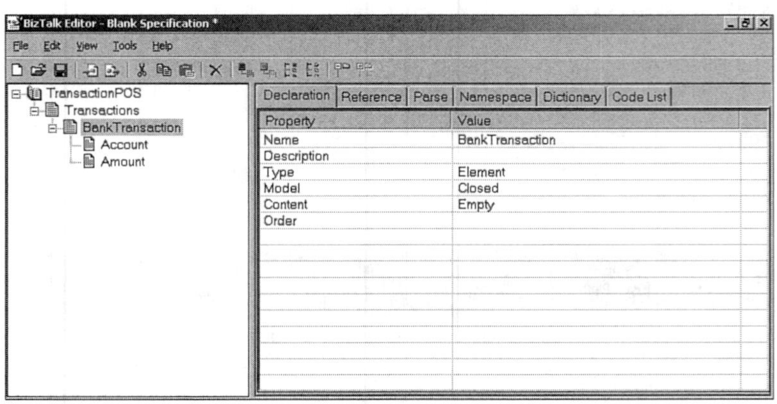

First, we need to set the `Standard` property to `Custom` on the `TransactionPOS` root node. This sets the document type for the document to flat file. To accomplish this, select the `TransactionPOS` root node in the left-hand panel and then navigate to the `Reference` tab. When you navigate off the Standard property that's been set to `Custom`, a pop-up dialog appears notifying you that changing this property might cause some properties to be cleared. Select Yes as displayed in Figure 4.10.

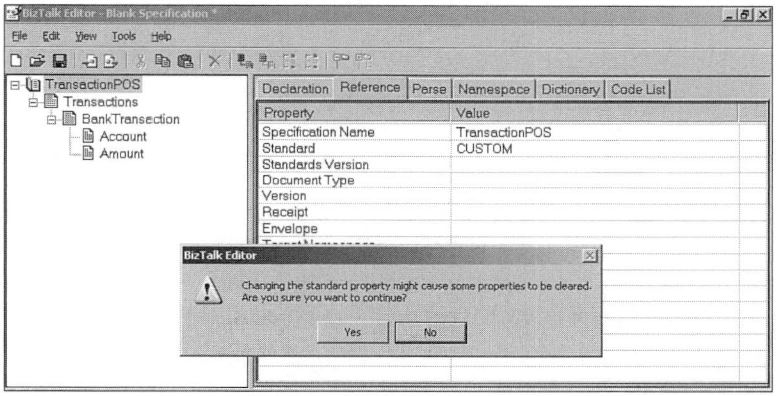

FIGURE 4.10
Setting the `TransactionPOS` *root node* `Standard` *to* `Custom`.

Then, we need to set the `Default Record Delimiter` property to `CR` in the same tab. The Reference tab for the `TransactionPOS` record should appear as displayed in Figure 4.11.

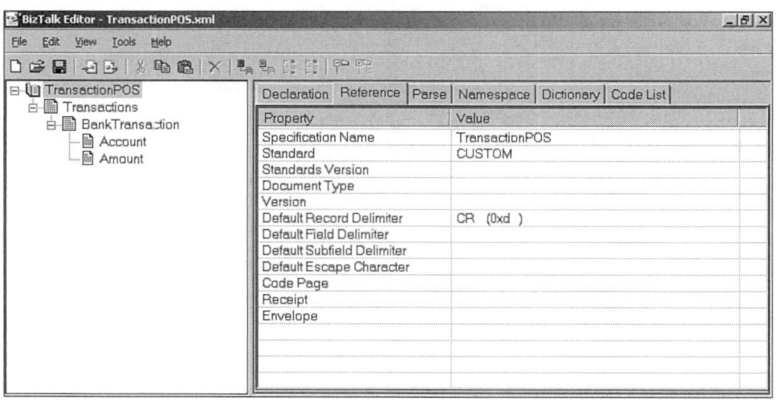

FIGURE 4.11
Setting the `TransactionPOS` *root node* `Standard` *to* `Custom`.

Next we need to set the Parse properties for the `TransactionPOS` record. Remember that this record denotes how the records in the file are delimited. In this case, the records are delimited by a CR, LF. To configure the properties, select the `TransactionPOS` root record in the left-hand panel and navigate to the Parse tab. Then set the properties as displayed in Table 4.5.

TABLE 4.5 The `TransactionPOS` Parse Properties

Property	*Value*
`Structure`	`Delimited`
`Field Order`	`Postfix`
`Delimiter Type`	`Default Record Delimiter`
`Append New Line`	`Yes`
`Skip Carriage Return`	`No`

The `Structure` is `Delimited`, and the `Field Order` is `Postfix` because a `CR LF` follows each record as well as the last record. The delimiter is set to the `Default Record Delimiter`, which was configured earlier as `CR` in the Reference tab. `LF CR` are automatically ignored unless they are explicitly specified in the `Skip Line Feed` and `Skip Carriage Return` properties. In this case, we want the `LF` to be skipped, so we don't need to set the property. The `Append New Line` property is set to ensure that an `LF` is placed at the end of each record when the BizTalk Messaging Engine uses the specification to serialize the outbound document. The Parse tab for the `TransactionPOS` root node appears as displayed in Figure 14.12.

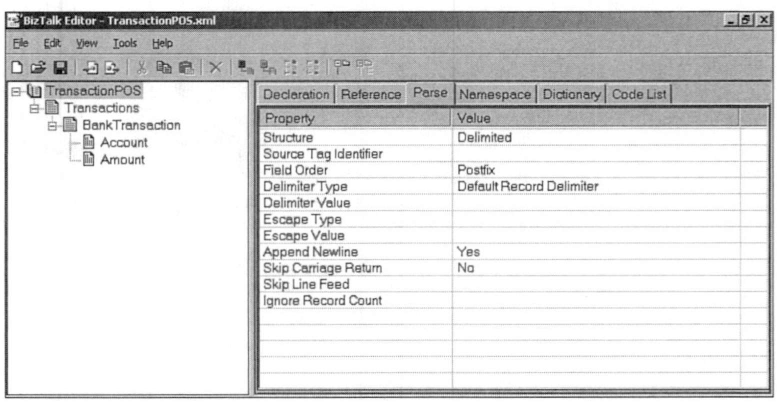

FIGURE 4.12
Setting the `TransactionPOS` *root node Parse properties.*

Next, we need to set the properties for the `Transactions` record. The `Transactions` record defines the properties for each record. This may seem a bit confusing to have two records that define how a single record is parsed; however, it is necessary when creating specifications for positional flat files that are also delimited. The `Source Tag`

`Identifier` in this case is the letter "R," and its positioning is `Infix` relative to the structure of the record. This subrecord is needed to differentiate between the `CR LF` record delimiters, which are `Postfix`, and the `Source Tag identifier` which is `Infix`.

To configure the properties, begin by selecting the `Transactions` record in the left-hand pane and navigating to the Reference tab to set the `Maximum Occurrences` value to `*`. This property denotes that the record can occur zero to many times. Next, navigate to the Parse tab on this same record and set the properties as defined in Table 4.6. The `Parse` properties are similar to those set on the `TransactionPOS` root node.

TABLE 4.6 The Transaction Parse Properties

Property	*Value*
`Structure`	`Delimited`
`Source Tag Identifier`	`R`
`Field Order`	`Infix`
`Delimiter Type`	`Default Record Delimiter`
`Skip Carriage Return`	`No`

In this case, the record is again delimited; however, this time we add a reference to the `Source Tag Identifier` "`R`," which is `Infix` relative to the records in the file. The `Delimiter Type` is again set to the `Default Record Delimiter CR`, and the `Skip Carriage Return` property is set to `No`. The `Transactions` Parse tab should appear as displayed in Figure 4.13.

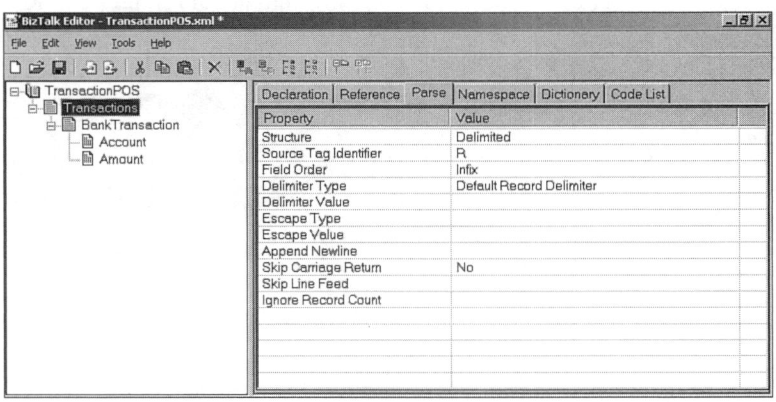

FIGURE 4.13
Setting the `Transactions` *node Parse properties.*

Next, we need to set the properties for the positional `BankTransaction` record and fields. To accomplish this, select the `BankTransaction` record in the left-hand panel and navigate to the `Reference` tab. Notice that the `Maximum Occurrences` property is set to `1` by default. Next, navigate to the Parse tab for the same record and set the `Structure` property to `Positional`. Again, when you navigate from the property, a warning appears notifying you that changing this property could result in the loss of some property values. Select OK when this message box appears. Then set the `Skip Carriage Return` to No. The Parse properties for the `BankTransaction` Parse tab should appear as displayed in Figure 4.14.

FIGURE 4.14
Setting the `BankTransaction` *node Parse properties.*

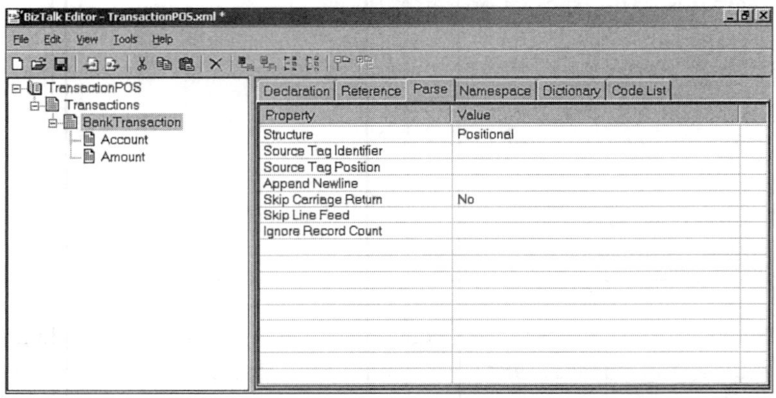

Finally we need to set the `Account` and `Amount` properties. Select the `Account` field in the left-hand panel and navigate to the Reference tab. Then set the `Required` property to `Yes`, the `Start Position` property to `1`, and the `End Position` property to `6` as displayed in Figure 4.15.

FIGURE 4.15
Setting the Account element reference properties.

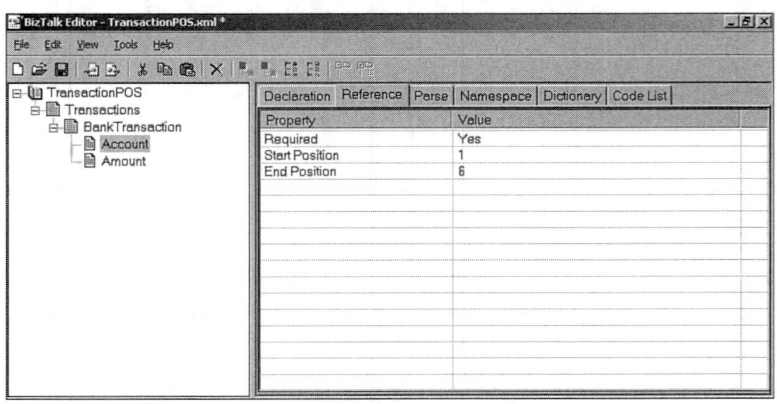

Then select the `Amount` field and set the `Required` property to `Yes`, the `Start Position` to `7`, and the `End Position` property to `18`. We are now ready to save and test the `TransactionPOS.xml` specification. The publisher's Web site contains a sample instance named `TransactionPOS.txt` to assist us with this task. The `TransactionPOS.txt` file consists of two records and is displayed in Listing 4.5.

LISTING 4.5 The `TransactionPOS.txt` File

```
R1      -300
R2      +500
```

To test the specification, select Tools, Validate Instance from the menu and select the `TransactionPOS.txt` example test file. The file should be parsed as displayed in Figure 4.16.

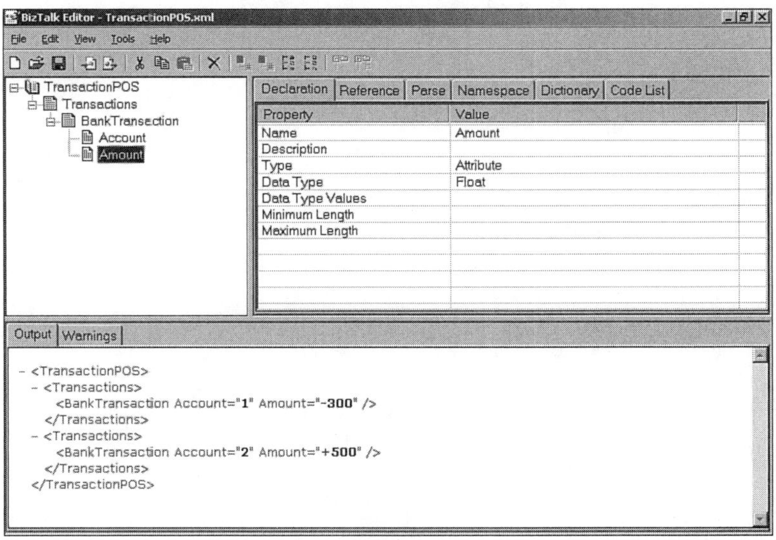

FIGURE 4.16
Testing the `TransactionPOS` *BizTalk specification.*

Voilá, we have created our BizTalk specification for a positional flat file that represents a data transmission from Fidelity.

Summary

BizTalk Server 2000 uses XML at its core, but as you can see, regardless of the file format the definition of the document structure is a snap. In the next chapter, you will learn how to use a BizTalk specification to map one specification to another. In other words, how to take a document generated using Fidelity's positional flat file format and transform it into the XML format that Sunset Bank's internal systems are designed to process.

CHAPTER 5

The BizTalk Mapper

By Clifford R. Cannon

In This Chapter

Microsoft BizTalk Server provides a standard gateway for sending and receiving documents across the Internet by providing a wide range of services that facilitate the transport and transformation of structured documents and that ensure the data integrity and security of those documents while in transit. To provide the transformation capabilities, BizTalk Server relies on the services of the BizTalk Mapper and an industry standard transformation language known as XSLT.

Maps are created using the BizTalk Mapper and can contain transformations between both industry standard documents such as XML, EDIFACT, or X12 and nonindustry standards such as delimited flat files, positional flat files, or delimited and positional flat files. To construct a map, you use two BizTalk specifications, one for the source specification and one for the destination specification. The Mapper then presents both the source and destination files side-by-side and lets you define the transformations by simply drawing lines between the records, fields, and functoids. A map can include simple value-copy translations, referred to as *links*, and complex structural manipulations, referred to as *functoids*. By combining these elements, you can easily map data between a source specification and a destination specification.

In this chapter, we will cover the following topics:

- The role of the BizTalk map in transforming data between documents
- How to create a BizTalk map to relate fields in the source document to fields in the destination document
- How to test a new or modified map, including testing with actual instances of the source document, and testing options
- A complete reference to the built-in functoids for data transformation

Transforming Data between Documents

To enable the use of the map by the BizTalk Messaging Engine, the map must be compiled into an Internet standard document called an Extensible Stylesheet Language Transformations (XSLT) file. XSLT is a language for transforming Extensible Markup Language (XML) documents from one XML schema into another. When the BizTalk Messaging Engine receives a document, it parses it into its XML representation using the BizTalk Editor specification that's been created for it. It then selects the channel(s) to execute and applies the BizTalk XSLT maps to the XML representation of the inbound document if required. The resulting outbound document is then serialized into its native format using an associated BizTalk serializer. Figure 5.1 depicts the general mapping process.

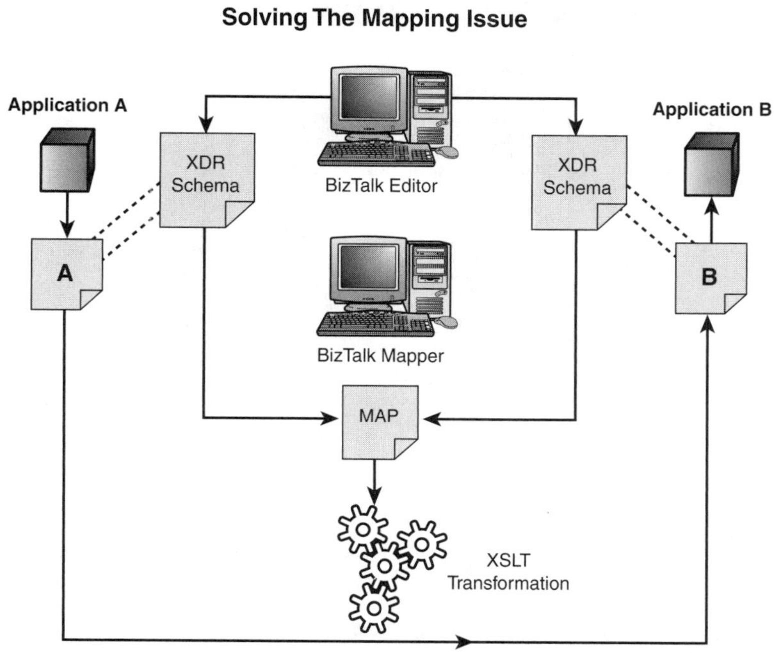

FIGURE 5.1
The general mapping process.

To facilitate the transformation of documents, you must first create an XML (XDR) representation of both the inbound and outbound documents using the BizTalk Editor. After you've created the specifications, you can then use the BizTalk Mapper to define the transformations between them. To accomplish this, you create a BizTalk *map* using the *BizTalk Mapper*, as shown in Figure 5.2.

Notice in the leftmost pane a document specification tree similar to what's displayed in the BizTalk Editor. That pane represents the source, or input, document. In the rightmost pane is a tree representing the destination, or output, document (right-justified and reverse-indented).

Strictly speaking, the left pane does not represent the actual input document structure but rather the XML structure of the source *interchange* after parsing of the input document according to its BizTalk specification. Similarly, the right pane represents the destination interchange before it is converted into the actual output document. Therefore, the BizTalk Mapper need not consider at all whether the input and output documents are XML, EDIFACT, ANSI X12, flat-delimited, or flat-positional files. The BizTalk Mapper always transforms data between well-formed XML interchange documents—vastly simplifying your task of constructing the mapping between documents.

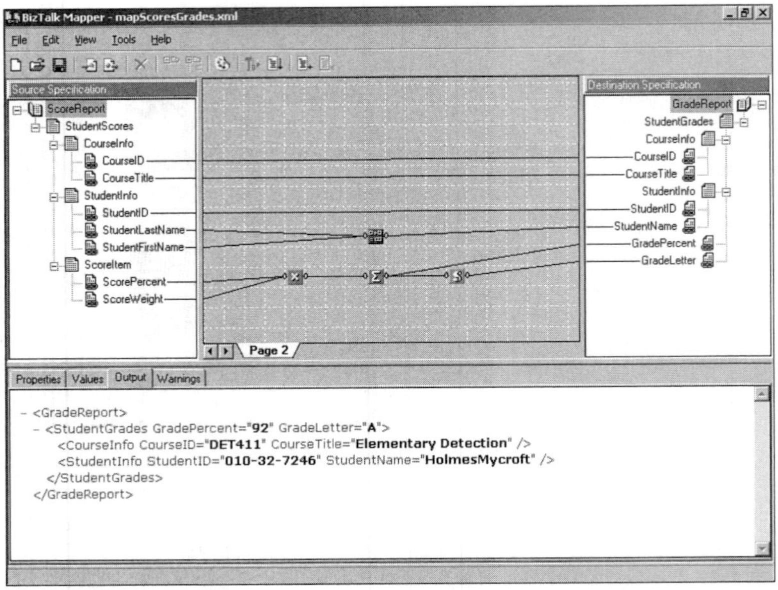

FIGURE 5.2
A completed map in the BizTalk Mapper.

The pane in the middle, the *mapping grid*, allows you to construct the mapping of the input document to the output document. Data can be copied from input fields to output fields and can also be routed through transformation objects that perform string, arithmetic, and many other functions on the input data to produce the fields needed for the output document. Because the mapping can become complex for complex documents, multiple pages of mapping can be created (as separate window tabs) to divide the map into more understandable individual pieces. Also note that the mapping is one way only, from left to right. If a reverse map is needed from the output format to the input format, a separate map must be created with the input and output exchanging positions.

The bottom pane (full width of the window) has several tabs for viewing document properties, entering sample field data to test the map, and viewing outputs and warnings from Mapper testing and compilation. We will cover each of those tabs at a natural point as we proceed.

To illustrate the capabilities of the BizTalk Mapper, we will use a scenario of student record interchange between applications used by a University Extension department. We will show how the information contained in class rosters, student grade reports, and other documents can be translated from one format to another using BizTalk specifications and maps.

Creating a New BizTalk Map

In this chapter, we will create a map between two BizTalk specifications, `specScoreReport.xml`, representing an XML input document, and `specGradeReport.xml`, representing an XML output document. `SpecScoreReport` contains a record for each test given during a single grading period. The `specGradeReport` file contains a single record that displays the student's cumulative grade as a result of those scores.

In the next several sections, we will walk through the steps required to create, test, and compile a map that transforms and accumulates the student's score into a semester CSV grade file.

Note

The BizTalk specifications and maps for this chapter can be downloaded from the publisher's Web site.

Choosing Source and Destination Specifications

To create a new map using the BizTalk Mapper, choose Start, Programs, Microsoft BizTalk Server 2002, BizTalk Mapper. Then choose File, New from the menu. Because a BizTalk map needs to reference both a source and a destination specification, a dialog appears immediately asking you to specify them (see Figure 5.3). You can choose specifications from a local file directory (on your machine or accessible by file share), a WebDAV file (Web Distributed Authoring and Versioning) location, or a template file provided by Microsoft. When you configure BizTalk Messaging, the file specifications are stored in a WebDAV repository, so in production situations you will usually create maps from files located in a WebDAV repository.

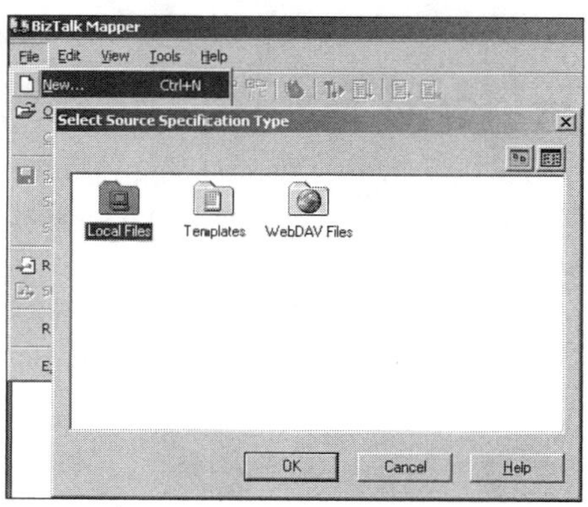

FIGURE 5.3
Choosing file specifications for a new map.

Examining Properties of Specification Records and Fields

Figure 5.4 shows source and destination specifications to map a document containing student scores for midterm exams, the final exam, homework, and so on, to a document containing the students' final grades expressed as a percentage and also as a letter grade. Note if we select the Properties tab in the bottom pane, we can select a record or field separately on both the left and right specification panes to examine (but not to modify) the properties of the selected record or field. In the example, note that the source `ScoreItem` record can appear zero or more times, whereas in the destination the `StudentInfo` record must appear exactly once.

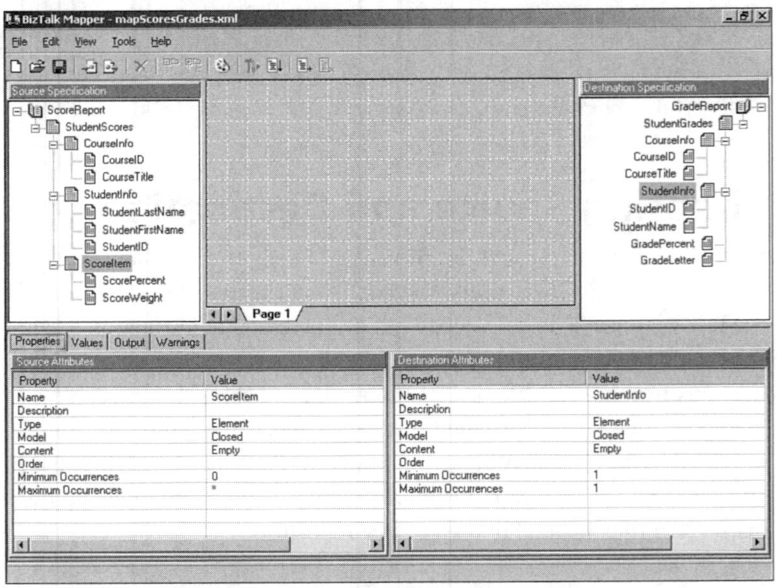

FIGURE 5.4
Record properties in BizTalk Mapper.

Linking Source Fields to Destination Fields

To copy the course ID from the source to the destination, simply click the `CourseID` field in the left pane and (holding down the mouse button) drag to `CourseID` in the right pane. When you release the mouse button, a *link* is drawn from the source field to the destination field. In the same manner, we link the source `CourseTitle` and `StudentID` fields to the corresponding fields in the destination specification (see Figure 5.5).

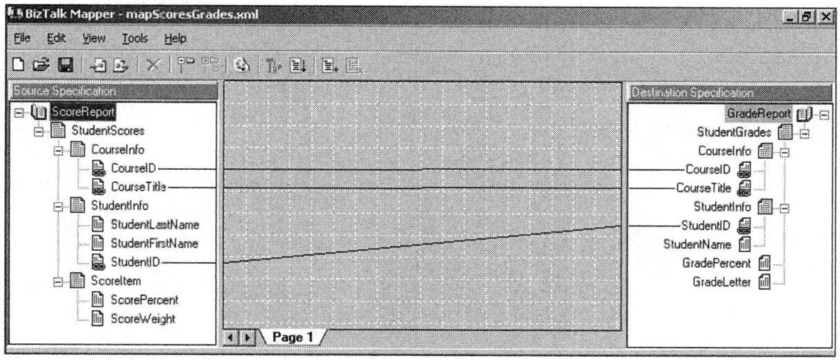

FIGURE 5.5
Linking fields in BizTalk Mapper.

Using Functoids to Transform Data

The student name cannot simply be copied from source to destination because the source uses separate first and last name fields, whereas the destination uses a single field. To combine the data from two separate fields into one field, we use a *functoid*, which simply refers to the embodiment of a mathematical, string, or other function (multiple input values, single output value) as a programming object.

To show the Functoid Palette, select View, Functoid Palette from the menu or click the yellow-background Palette icon on the toolbar. The String tab is displayed when the Palette is opened. Move the cursor arrow over the icons, reading the ToolTip text until you find the Concatenate functoid. Click and drag it to the *mapping grid*, the center pane between the two specification panes (see Figure 5.6).

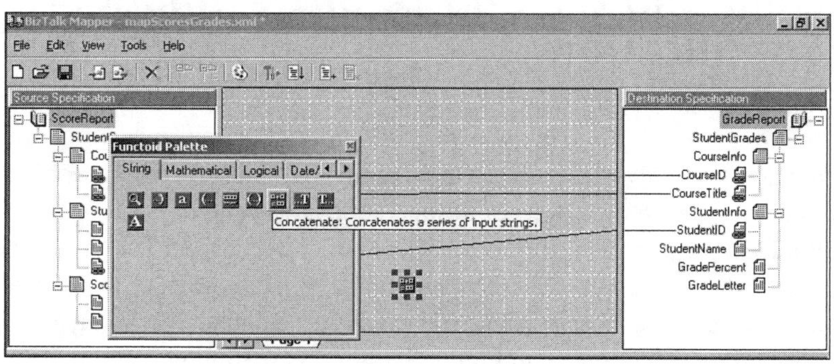

FIGURE 5.6
Adding a functoid to the mapping grid.

To transform the two separate name fields into a combined field, drag the `StudentLastName` field to the Concatenate functoid; then do the same for the `StudentFirstName` field. To copy the functoid result to the destination field, drag the functoid icon to the `StudentName` field. This result is not yet satisfactory because the last name and first name will be combined into a single string with no separation. To add punctuation between the names, double-click the functoid icon (or right-click and choose Properties), click the Insert New Parameter toolbar button, and enter a comma and a space (see Figure 5.7).

FIGURE 5.7

Input parameters of a functoid.

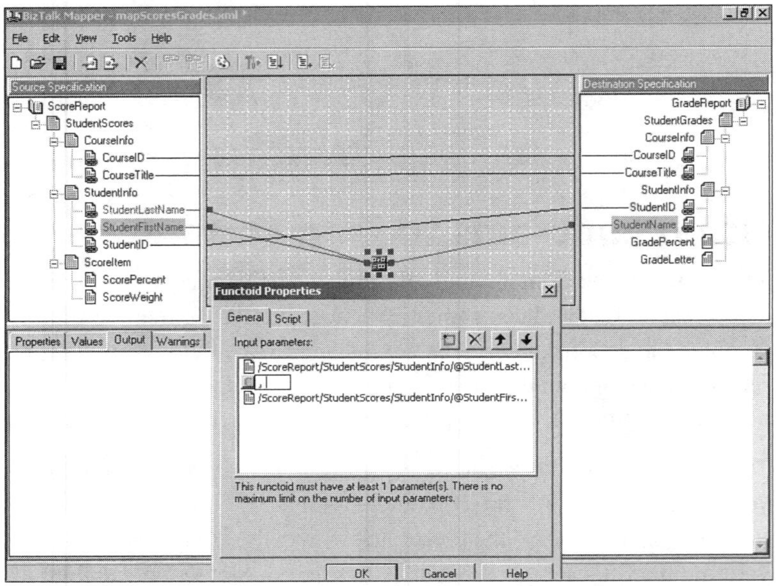

Updating the Source or Destination Specification

When you choose the source and destination specifications for a new map, those specifications are *copied* into the new map definition. Later changes to the specifications are not automatically incorporated into the map. To update either specification in the map, right-click the source (left) or destination (right) pane in BizTalk Mapper and choose Replace Specification. If our example Score Report specification were changed to place the `StudentID` field before the name fields, BizTalk Mapper would attempt to retain as many existing links as possible by matching field names from the old specification to the updated specification, as in Figure 5.8—compare to Figure 5.6 to see that the source fields have been reordered, but the links have been retained. The use of field name matching to maintain existing map links when a specification changes is a good reason to make record and field names easily distinguishable within the specification.

FIGURE 5.8
Updating the source specification.

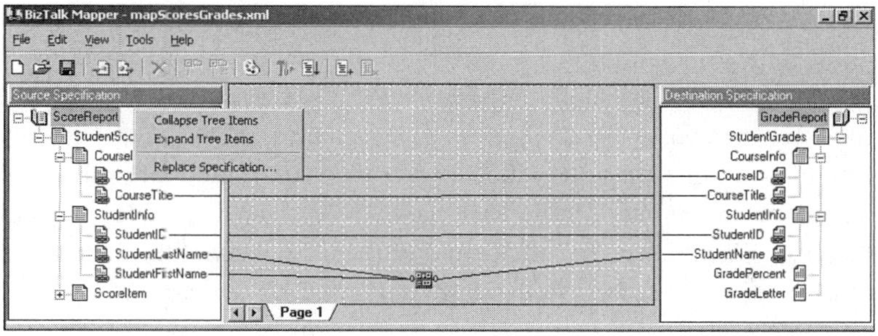

Adding a New Mapping Grid Page

A new feature of BizTalk Server 2002 is the capability to separate the map into several *pages*, accessible by tabs at the bottom of the mapping grid (see Figure 5.9). This is especially useful when complex source and destination specifications make it difficult to fit the entire map onto the grid pane so that it is both readable and all visible at once. Whether the map is simple or complex, it makes good sense to use a separate page for each logical coherent subunit of the mapping. In our scores to grades example, we used the first page to copy (or transform) the textual identifying data that appears in exactly-once records. Now we will use the second page to transform the numerical grading information that appears in zero-or-more-occurrences records.

FIGURE 5.9
Adding a new mapping grid page.

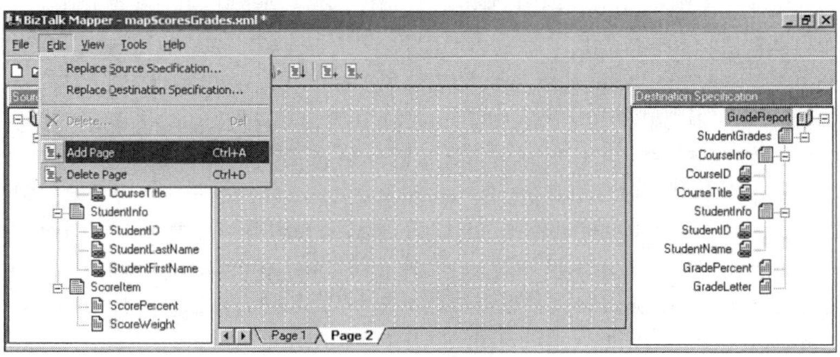

In Figure 5.10, the `ScorePercent` field in the `ScoreItem` records represents the percentage score (0 percent to 100 percent) achieved on individual components of a student's course grade: midterm exams, homework, final exams, and so on. The `ScoreWeight` field represents the weight given to each component (for example, 0.20 for a midterm, 0.4 for the final, and so on for a total of 1.0). Each `ScorePercent` should be multiplied by its `ScoreWeight`, and we have linked both fields to a Multiplication functoid to accomplish that in the mapping.

The next step illustrates that functoids cannot only link a source field to a destination field, but also functoids can be *cascaded* to perform a multistep transformation. In this case, we need to add up all the score x weight products to compute the student's total score for the course. To do that, we link the output of the Multiplication functoid to the Cumulative Sum functoid, which returns the sum of the input value iterated over all record instances that occur in each parent record (or the whole document, for top-level records). We can then link the output of the Cumulative Sum functoid (the weighted sum of all component scores) to the destination field `GradePercent`.

FIGURE 5.10
Cascading functoids and aggregating results.

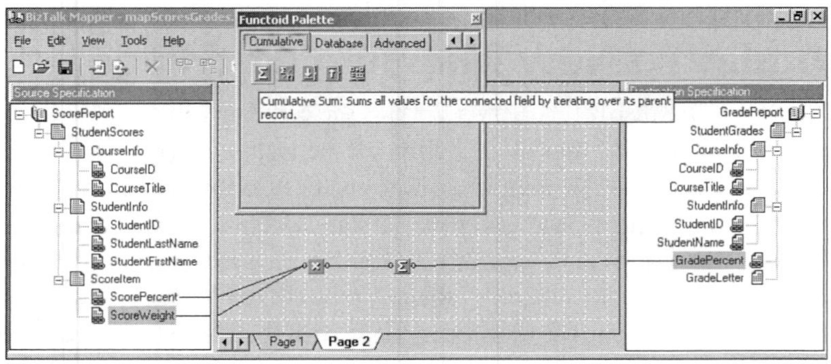

A design feature of BizTalk Mapper that does not become apparent until you cascade functoids is that all data flows are strictly *left to right* on the mapping grid. The Mapper enforces the direction of flow for functoids already linked by displaying red hatching when a cascaded functoid is selected for moving (see Figure 5.11). You cannot move the selected Multiplication functoid into the red-hatched area of the map grid because that would reverse the direction of data flow. When two functoids are not yet linked, it *is* possible to draw a link from the functoid more to the right side of the grid to the functoid more to the left. However, the data flow will still be from the left functoid to the right one: The direction in which you click and drag to draw the link does not matter. To avoid confusion, it might be best always to draw links from left to right as a mnemonic cue to the direction the data will be propagated during map execution.

The final item we need to supply to the destination is the `GradeLetter` field. There is no built-in functoid to compute an academic letter grade from a percentage, so we must make one of our own. An easy way to do that is with the Scripting functoid, which allows you to write a simple (or complex!) function in VBScript or (new for BizTalk 2002) in JScript. As Figure 5.12 shows, the Scripting functoid is on the Advanced tab of the Functoid Palette. You can add a Scripting functoid to the map just like any other and link it to its input and output fields (or functoids). To define the script to be executed (and to define how many and what type of parameters the functoid will expect), double-click the Scripting functoid to open the Properties dialog, click the Script tab, and choose the language to use (VBScript or JScript). A template function with a generic name will be added automatically to the script window, but because all functions in the map are in the same namespace, you should name your script function as specifically as possible.

FIGURE 5.11
Enforcing left-to-right data flow.

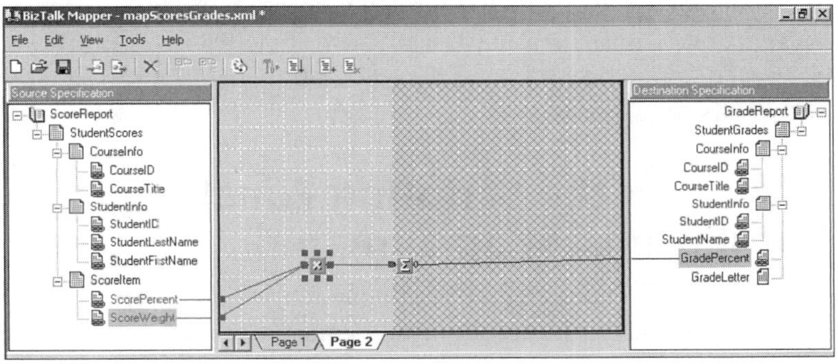

FIGURE 5.12
A custom Scripting functoid.

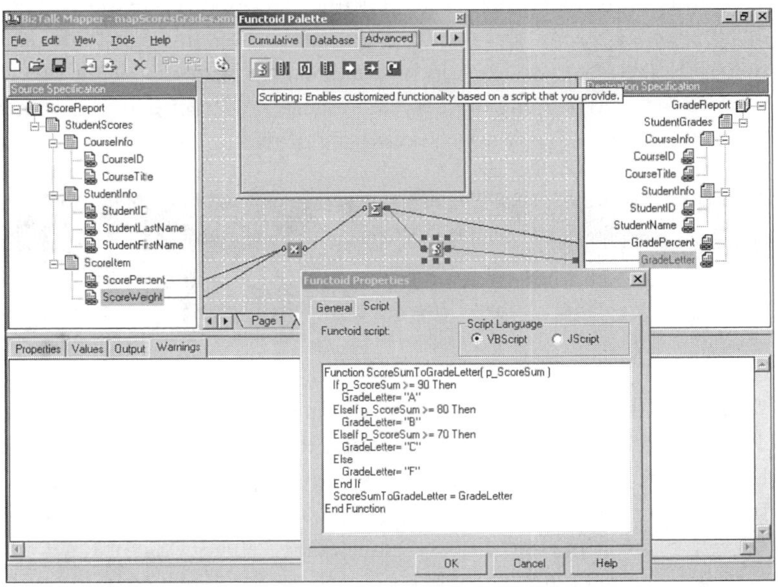

Note that a Scripting functoid can have as many input parameters as you want, but the script function *must* return a single, string-formatted result. Finally, any variables you declare outside the script function itself will become global variables that hold their values for the duration of the map execution. That can be useful for creating your own

Cumulative functoids; see the Properties, Script tab for the Cumulative Average functoid, which can be found by selecting the Cumulative tab, for a good example of how to use global variables.

For custom functoids too complex for scripting, or where a specialized action is not available and scripting is required, you can create and use functoids as COM+ components. A complete Visual Basic sample of a COM+ functoid is provided in `\Program Files\Microsoft BizTalk Server\SDK\Messaging Samples\SampleFunctoid`. To create a COM+ functoid using Visual C++ or C#.NET, go to BizTalk Server Documentation, Search tab, iFunctoid for full details on the component interface and special registration requirements.

Replacing the Scripting Functoid with a Database Lookup Functoid

In the previous section, we used a scripting functoid to convert the cumulative percentage into a letter grade for the `GradeLetter` element in the `GradeReport` schema. In many cases, you will need to perform a database lookup to extract the values for certain fields as opposed to script written in the functoid. To demonstrate this, we are going to modify the `mapScoresGrades.xml` map by deleting the Scripting functoid and adding two new functoids, the Database Lookup functoid and the Value Extractor functoid. The Database Lookup functoid is going to query a simple SQL Server database named `Grades` that contains a single table, `Grades`, consisting of two fields `GradeLetter` and `Percentage`.

Note

The source code to create the SQL Server table and add the required records as well as the map file are downloadable from the publisher's Web site.

To accomplish this, select the Page 2 tab in the grid and delete the Scripting functoid. Then, open the Functoid Palette, navigate to the Database tab, and drag the Database Lookup and Value Extractor functoids onto the grid. Next, connect the Cumulative Sum functoid to the Database Lookup functoid and the Database Lookup functoid to the Value Extractor functoid. Finally, connect the Value Extractor functoid to the `GradeLetter` field in the `GradeReport` schema as displayed in Figure 5.13.

The Database Lookup functoid performs a database lookup to find the appropriate record from the appropriate table. The output of the Database Lookup functoid can be connected only to the Value Extractor functoid. The Value Extractor functoid extracts the appropriate column name from the lookup record.

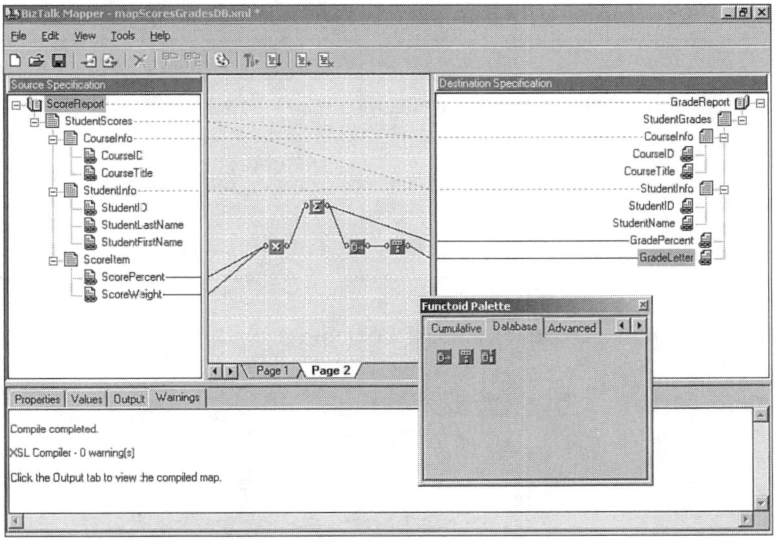

FIGURE 5.13
Adding the Database Lookup functoid.

The Database Lookup functoid requires four input parameters, in the following order:

- The lookup value
- The database connection string
- The table name
- The column name for the lookup value

The Value Extractor functoid requires two input parameters, in this order:

- The output from the Database Lookup functoid
- The column name to extract from the results

The Database Lookup and Value Extractor functoid parameters are displayed in Table 5.1.

TABLE 5.1 The Database Lookup and Value Extractor Functoid Properties

Functoid	*Parameter Name*	*Value*
Database Lookup	Lookup value	Link from Cumulative Sum functoid
Database Lookup	Database Connection String	`Provider=SQLOLEDB;server=(local);database=Grades;uid=sa;`
Database Lookup	Table Name	Grades

TABLE 5.1 continued

Functoid	*Parameter Name*	*Value*
Database Lookup	Column Name for the Lookup Value	Percentage
Value Extractor	Link to database lookup functoid	Link from Database Lookup functoid
Value Extractor	The column name	`GradeLetter`

Figure 5.14 displays the Database Lookup functoid properties.

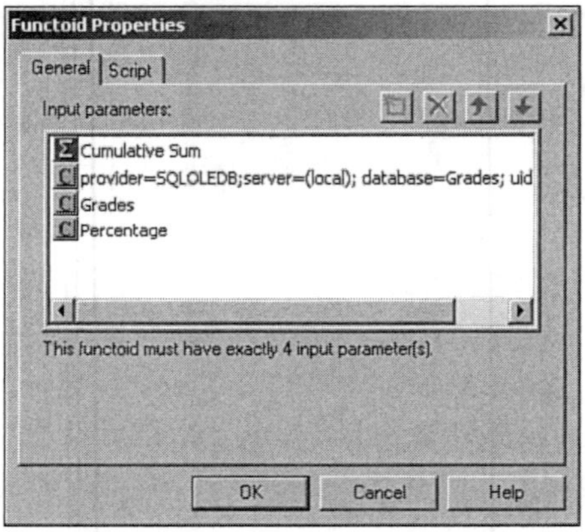

FIGURE 5.14
Database Lookup functoid properties.

Figure 5.15 displays the Value Extractor functoid properties.

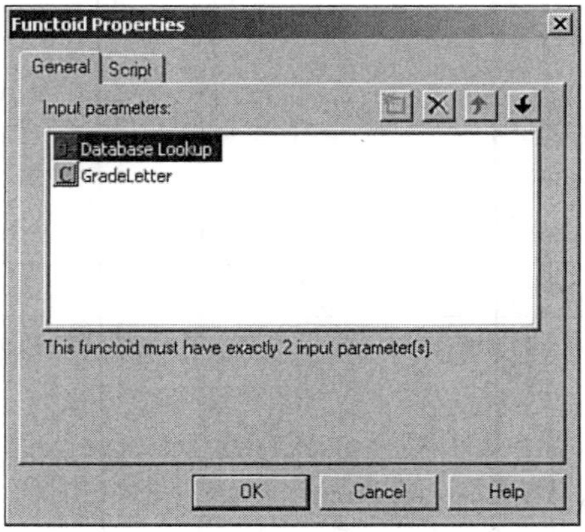

FIGURE 5.15
Value Extractor functoid properties.

We are now ready to test the map. Select Tools, Test Map, Generated XML to XML from the menu. Remember that the `ScorePercent` test value is set to 91. The output from the test should appear as displayed in Figure 5.16.

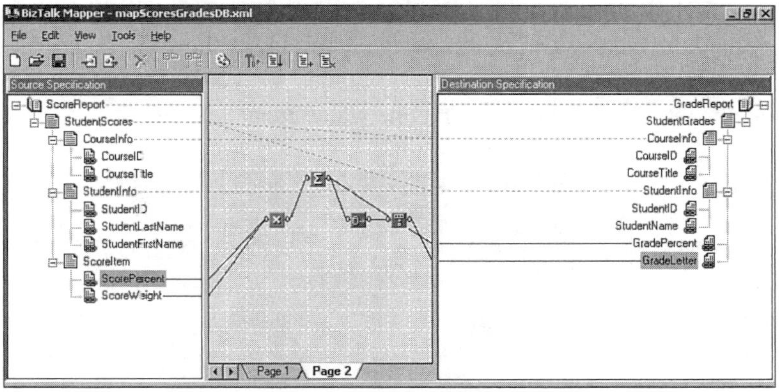

FIGURE 5.16
Output from map test with Database functoids.

You also have the ability to test the Database Lookup functoid using the Error Return functoid. The Error Return functoid outputs a string containing error information if there are errors (such as connection failures) at runtime when connected to the Database Lookup functoid. You can use the Error Return functoid to pass the error string to a designated field in the output document specification.

For example, if you need to connect to a named instance of SQL Server (syntax: `SERVERNAME\INSTANCENAME`), you will not be able to use (local) as the name of the SQL Server in the database connection string. If you forgot that and had trouble connecting to the database, the Error Return functoid could be connected (temporarily) to any string field in the output document with a large maximum length (or no maximum length). Testing the map would quickly give you the information you needed to correct the problem.

Testing the Map

After you create a map, or after you modify an existing map, you will want to unit-test it before incorporating the new or changed map into your BizTalk Server processes. The Mapper will first *compile* the map into an executable form and can detect a number of mapping errors at that stage. Then you can test the execution of the map with automatically generated field values, with field values you define, or with an actual instance of the source document. There are also a number of option settings for the Mapper that affect the process of map testing.

Compiling the Map

The first step in testing your completed map is to *compile* the specifications, links, and functoids into an XSLT script that actually performs the work specified by the map definition. To illustrate the error checking and reporting capability of BizTalk Mapper, we deleted the links to two of the destination fields as shown in Figure 5.17. Note that the compiler can detect which destination fields are required to have values in a valid output document. The compiler also reports which functoids are not connected to any output.

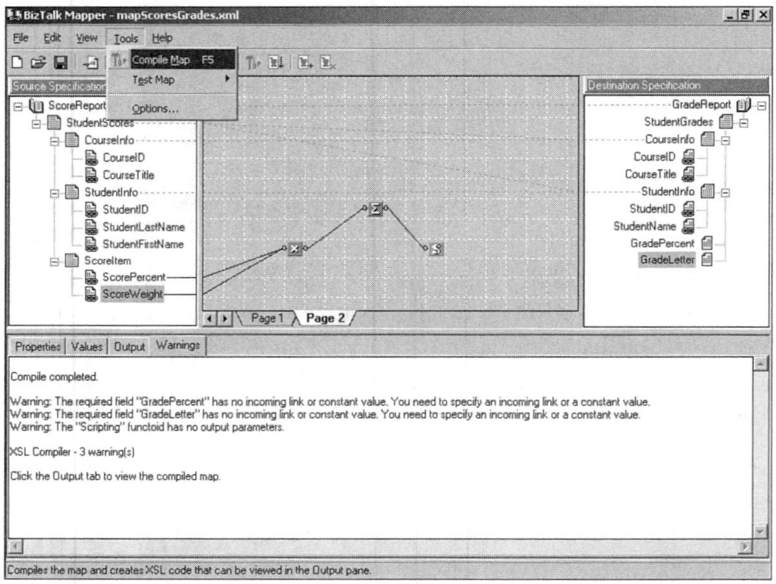

FIGURE 5.17
Compile errors in the Warnings tab.

Make it a habit to compile the map every time after adding a new functoid and linking it to its inputs and output. Compile warning messages are often specific enough to pinpoint a problem, but sometimes they are not. If you compile the map right after making a change, and a new warning appears, you already know where to look to find the problem—it must be something about the changes you made since your last successful map compilation.

Testing with Generated Data

When the map is compiling successfully, you can perform a simple test of the mapping process by choosing Tools, Test Map, Generated XML to XML (see Figure 5.18). Simulated values based on the source field name are provided as map inputs, and the resulting output interchange is displayed on the Output pane. (If you are working through these examples yourself, you will need to uncheck Tools, Options, Validate Content After Map Test to successfully execute the map. See the section "Testing and Validation Options" later in the chapter for details.) The grade percentage and letter don't look too good, of course, because the generated data are not realistic numbers for the corresponding input fields.

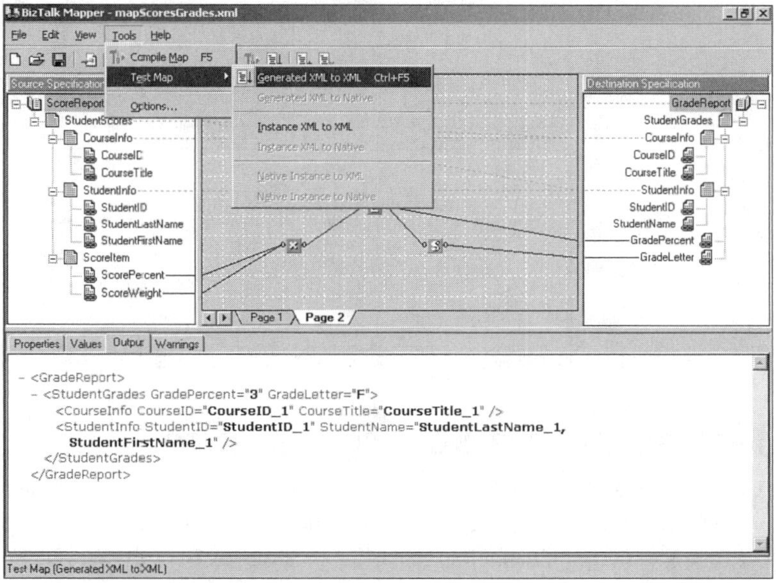

FIGURE 5.18
Testing the map with generated data.

Testing with Entered Values

To provide more realistic values for the input fields, click the Values tab (on the lower pane) and click each source field in turn to enter a single value to use for the Generated test. The Values tab can also be used to specify constant values for destination fields that are required to appear in the output specification but do not have corresponding source fields that can be linked to provide values using the map. To test with entered values, you still choose the menu item Tools, Test Map, Generated XML to XML (see Figure 5.19). As you can see, any entered values are used in place of the automatically generated `"FieldName_1"` strings. The entered values are stored with the map and can always be used for a quick test after any change to the completed map.

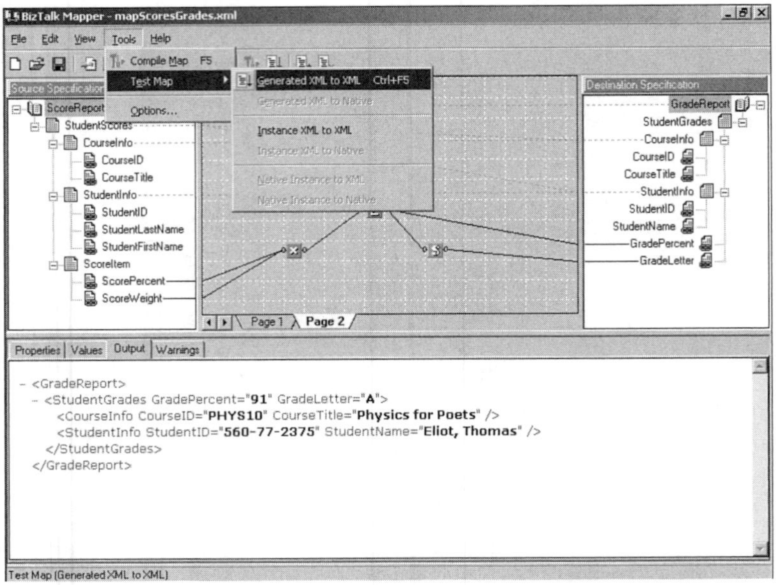

FIGURE 5.19
Testing with field data entered on the Values tab.

Testing with a Source Instance

A new and excellent feature of the Mapper for BizTalk 2002 is the capability to read and process an actual source document file in the Mapper itself, without having to set up a BizTalk Messaging Channel as in earlier versions of BizTalk Server. In addition, as you can see on the menu in Figure 5.20, the Mapper can read or write "Native" documents if the source or destination format is not XML. (Those options are grayed out as appropriate if the source or destination *is* an XML-format document). You can create a test instance entirely by hand, or you can use the BizTalk Editor to generate either an XML or a Native instance; then edit the attribute values as shown in Listing 5.1 to produce a suite of useful test instances. Of course, if you have *actual* examples of source documents, the map can now be tested against those examples directly in the Mapper application.

LISTING 5.1 A Source Instance Generated by BizTalk Editor, Edited with Test Values

```
<ScoreReport>
  <StudentScores>
    <CourseInfo CourseID="DET411" CourseTitle="Elementary Detection" />
    <StudentInfo StudentID="010-32-7246" StudentLastName="Holmes"
      StudentFirstName="Mycroft" />
    <ScoreItem ScorePercent="100" ScoreWeight="0.20" />
    <ScoreItem ScorePercent="90" ScoreWeight="0.20" />
    <ScoreItem ScorePercent="80" ScoreWeight="0.20" />
```

LISTING 5.1 continued

```
    <ScoreItem ScorePercent="95" ScoreWeight="0.40" />
  </StudentScores>
</ScoreReport>
```

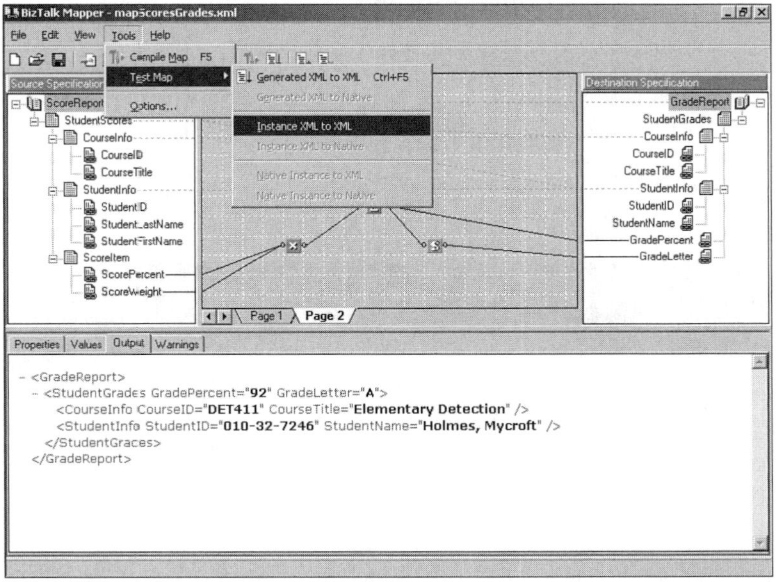

FIGURE 5.20
Testing the map with a source instance.

Testing and Validation Options

If you have been carrying out the preceding examples, you may already have encountered another new feature in the BizTalk 2002 Mapper: the capability to validate both incoming source test documents and the outgoing destination document resulting from the mapping. That is a terribly useful feature, especially for verifying that the output document fulfills the specification, but you don't always want it during initial testing of your map. One reason is that you may want to test a partial map, when you have mapped only a few fields—and not all the *required* output fields yet have values. To turn off validation temporarily, use the Tools, Options dialog (see Figure 5.21) and uncheck either or both of the Validate options as desired. Of course you will want to perform your final tests of the map with both validation options checked, so be sure to add that to your final-test checklist.

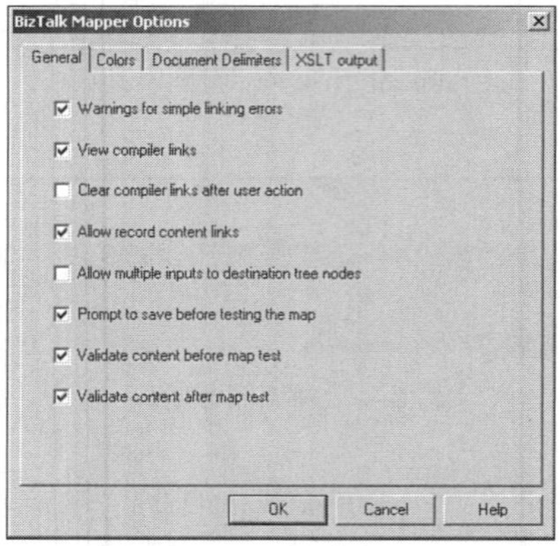

FIGURE 5.21
Source and destination validation options.

> **Note**
>
> To illustrate how simple it is to test and validate file types other than XML, the example code on the publisher's Web site contains a sample comma-delimited version of the Grade Report file named `specGradeReportCSV.xml`. It also contains a sample map file named `mapScoresGradesCSV.xml` that maps the inbound XML file to the CSV version.

Another option that affects testing (in a minor way) is Prompt to Save Before Testing the Map. When checked, that option offers to save any changes to the map file before beginning the test. Although that option is not as necessary as for a programming-language development environment—testing a BizTalk map is not likely to crash your machine—it is handy to have a reminder to save your map frequently, especially because the Mapper does not have an Undo function. However, all those Save changes dialogs can become a nuisance. Clearing the Prompt to save Before Testing the Map option stops the appearance of the Save dialog. Be aware that the Mapper does not automatically save the map *without* prompting; it simply *does not save* the map before beginning the test. You will need to save the map yourself at frequent intervals to guard your changes from being lost.

Guide to Built-In Functoids

One of the beauties of the Functoid Palette is the long ToolTip description of each icon, which makes it a quick matter to find the one you need for any given transformation. The help for functoids is fairly good as well, although it does lack precise details, such as whether record indices or string positions begin at 1 or at 0, or what value is returned by, for example, the String Find functoid if the string is *not* found. Help for functoids can be conveniently located in BizTalk Server Documentation, Index, String Functoids, Mathematical Functoids, Logical Functoids, and so on.

A good technique to determine *exactly* what most functoids do is to drag the functoid from the palette onto the mapping grid, double-click the functoid to open its Properties dialog, and click the Script tab (see Figure 5.22). You will be able to see (but not edit) the actual VBScript or JScript that would be added to the map file to execute the functoid. Reading the script allows you to know for certain the correct order of the input parameters and what values will be returned in cases such as empty input strings or search strings that are not matched.

FIGURE 5.22
Script properties of String Left functoid.

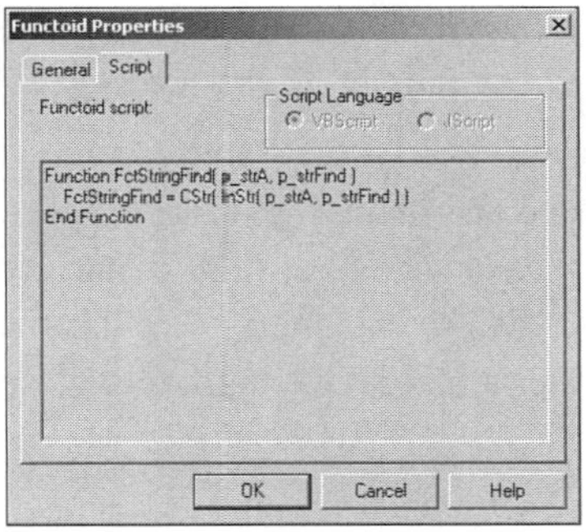

To give you an introduction and handy reference to all the built-in functoids, here is a list of the palette tabs and the functoids contained on each. Note that all functoids return a single, string-formatted value, even when the functoid value represents a number.

String Functoids

Here are the functoids to perform string manipulations such as concatenation, extraction, and case conversion (see Figure 5.23):

FIGURE 5.23
Functoid Palette, String tab.

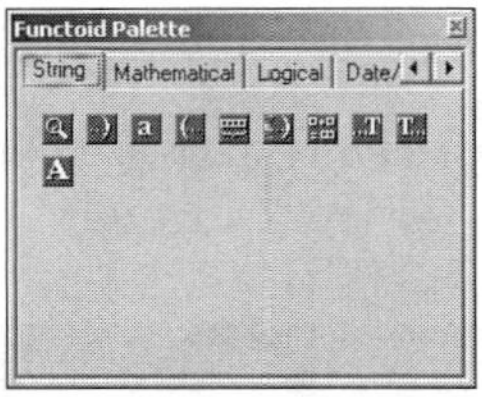

Here is a quick reference for each String functoid:

- String Find (2 Inputs)—Indicates the position at which second input string begins in first input string. First string position is 1. String not found returns 0.
- String Left (2 Inputs)—Extracts from beginning of first input string the number of characters specified by second input. First input shorter than specified number returns entire string. Second input negative number, or not a number, returns empty string.
- Lowercase (1 Input)—Converts all uppercase letters in input string to lowercase.
- String Right (2 Inputs)—Extracts from *end* of first input string the number of characters specified by second input. First input shorter than specified number returns entire string. Second input negative number, or not a number, returns empty string.
- String Length (1 Input)—Indicates the number of characters in string.
- String Extract (3 Inputs)—Returns portion of first input (string) starting from position specified by second input, up to and including position specified by third input. Empty string returned if either of second or third inputs is nonnumeric, if second input is negative or greater than string length, or if third input is less than second input. If third input is greater than string length, returns string from second input position to end.
- Concatenate (1 or more Inputs)—Concatenates inputs as strings, in the order specified. No upper limit on number of inputs. Note that you will often add constant parameters to this functoid to place spaces or punctuation between input strings. Can be used without a source link by adding at least one constant parameter, allowing this functoid to be a single-source for other functoids of complex strings such as database connection strings.
- String Left Trim (1 Input)—Removes leading spaces.
- String Right Trim (1 Input)—Removes trailing spaces.
- Uppercase (1 Input)—Converts all lowercase letters in input string to uppercase.

Mathematical Functoids

Here are the functoids to perform mathematical operations such as addition, subtraction, maximum value, or minimum value (see Figure 5.24):

Note

Mathematical functoids return an empty string if *any* of the inputs is nonnumeric.

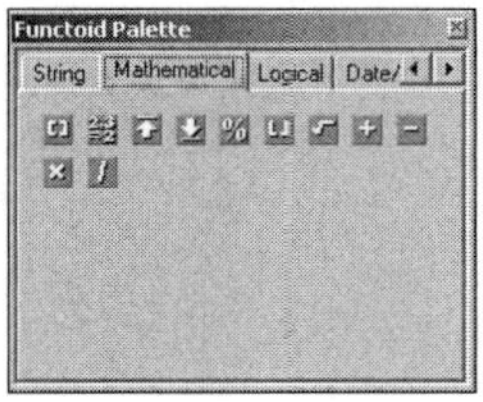

FIGURE 5.24
Functoid Palette, Mathematical tab.

Here is a quick reference for each Mathematical functoid:

- Absolute Value (1 Input)—Converts negative number input to positive number of equal magnitude; returns positive input number unchanged.
- Integer (1 Input)—Returns the closest integer less than or equal to number input. Note that this means a negative number input that is not an integer returns the next *lower* integer value.
- Maximum Value (1 or more Inputs)—Returns maximum value among all inputs.
- Minimum Value (1 or more Inputs)—Returns minimum value among all inputs.
- Modulo (2 Inputs)—Returns remainder after dividing first input by second input. Returns empty string if second input is zero.
- Round (2 Inputs)—Rounds a decimal-fraction number (first input) to a specified number of decimal places (second input). Number of places can be negative to round off to a multiple of 10, 100, and so on.
- Square Root (1 Input)—Returns empty string if number is negative.
- Addition (1 or more Inputs)—Indicates the sum of all inputs.
- Subtraction (1 or more Inputs)—Returns first input minus all subsequent inputs.
- Multiplication (1 or more Inputs)—Returns product of all inputs.
- Division (2 Inputs)—Returns first input divided by second input. Returns empty string if second input is zero.

Logical Functoids

Figure 5.25 shows the functoids that perform actions such as value comparison, type checking, or Boolean operations.

Note

Logical functoids return "true" or "false" as *case-sensitive* strings.

FIGURE 5.25
Functoid Palette, Logical tab.

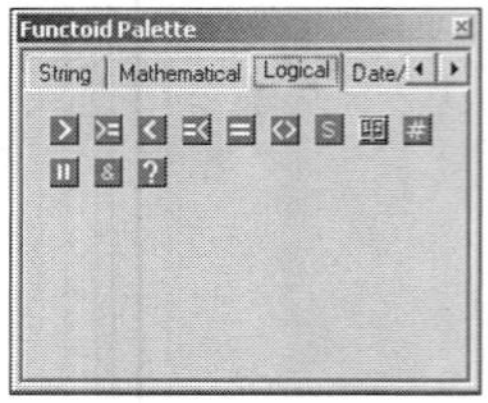

Here is a quick reference for each Logical functoid:

- Greater Than (2 Inputs)—Returns "true" if first input is greater than second input. If either input is nonnumeric, compares as strings.
- Greater Than or Equal To (2 Inputs)—Returns "true" if first input is greater than or equal to second input. If either input is nonnumeric, compares as strings.
- Less Than (2 Inputs)—Returns "true" if first input is less than second input. If either input is nonnumeric, compares as strings.
- Less Than or Equal To (2 Inputs)—Returns "true" if first input is less than or equal to second input. If either input is nonnumeric, compares as strings.
- Equal (2 Inputs)—Returns "true" if first input is equal to second input. If either input is "true" or "false" (not case-sensitive), comparison is made using the equivalent Boolean value. Otherwise, if either input is nonnumeric, compares as strings.
- Not Equal (2 Inputs)—Returns "true" if first input is not equal to second input. If either input is "true" or "false" (not case-sensitive), comparison is made using the equivalent Boolean value. Otherwise, if either input is nonnumeric, compares as strings.
- Logical String (1 Input)—Returns "true" if input is not an empty string. Note than most functoids (except Logical) return an empty string if their inputs are invalid, so this functoid can be used to test the output of other functoids.
- Logical Date (1 Input)—Returns "true" if input can be read as a date and/or time.
- Logical Numeric (1 Input)—Returns "true" if input can be read as a number.
- Logical OR (1 or more Inputs)—Returns "true" if *any* of the inputs is true. Any input that converts to Visual Basic Boolean True is treated as true.
- Logical AND (1 or more Inputs)—Returns "true" if *all* the inputs are true. Inputs that convert to Visual Basic Boolean True are treated as true.
- Logical Existence—Returns "true" if the input field or record is present in the source. Note that this is not the same as a field having an empty string value.

Date/Time Functoids

Here are the functoids to return the current date or time, or to add dates (see Figure 5.26):

FIGURE 5.26
Functoid Palette, Date/Time tab.

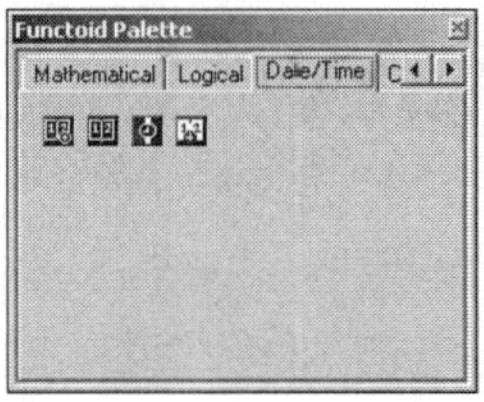

Here is a quick reference for each Date/Time functoid:

- Add Days (2 Inputs)—Adds second input (number of days), to first input (a date) and returns result in ISO 8601 format, *yyyy-mm-dd*. If first input is not a valid date, or second input is not numeric, returns empty string.
- Date (No Inputs)—Returns current local date in ISO 8601 format, *yyyy-mm-dd.*
- Time (No Inputs)—Returns current local time in ISO 8601 format, *hh:mm:ss.*
- Date and Time (No Inputs)— Returns current local date and time in ISO 8601 format, *yyyy-mm-dd*T*hh:mm:ss.*

Conversion Functoids

Here are the functoids to convert to and from character codes or to convert numeric radices (see Figure 5.27):

FIGURE 5.27
Functoid Palette, Conversion tab.

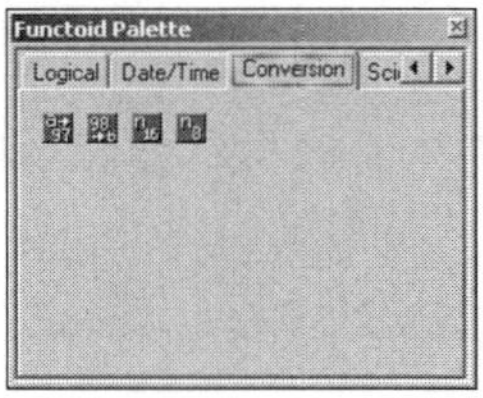

Here is a quick reference for each Conversion functoid:

- ASCII from Character (1 Input)—Returns ASCII (American Standard Code for Information Interchange) numeric code for the first character in the input string. If input is zero length string, returns empty string.

- Character from ASCII (1 Input)—Returns a one-character string corresponding to input ASCII code. If input is nonnumeric, or is not in the range of 1 to 127, returns empty string.
- Hexadecimal (1 Input)—Returns Base 16 representation of a decimal numeric input. Returns blank string if input is nonnumeric.
- Octal (1 Input)—Returns Base 8 representation of a decimal numeric input. Returns blank string if input is nonnumeric.

Scientific Functoids

Here are the functoids to perform advanced mathematical functions such as exponentiation, logarithms, and trigonometry (see Figure 5.28):

Note

Scientific functoids return an empty string if *any* of the inputs is nonnumeric.

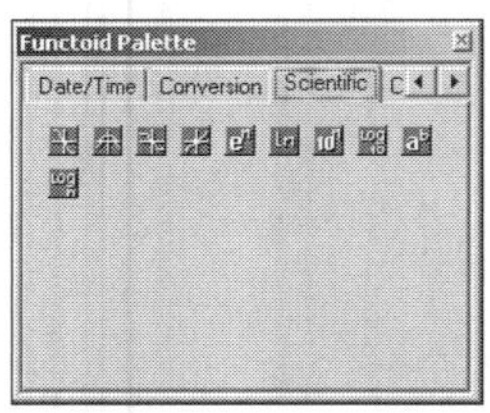

FIGURE 5.28
Functoid Palette, Scientific tab.

Here is a quick reference for each Scientific functoid:

- Arc Tangent (1 Input)—Returns angle whose tangent is the input value. Result in radians, in range –pi/2 to pi/2. To convert radians to degrees, multiply by 180/pi, and vice versa.
- Cosine (1 Input)—Cosine of input angle in radians.
- Sine (1 Input)—Sine of input angle in radians.
- Tangent (1 Input)—Tangent of input angle in radians.
- Natural Exponential Function (1 Input)—*e* raised to the power of the input.
- Natural Logarithm (1 Input)—Log base *e* of the input. If input is zero or negative, returns empty string.
- 10^X (1 Input)—10 raised to the power of X (the input).

- Common Logarithm (1 Input)—Log base 10 of the input. If input is zero or negative, returns empty string.
- X^Y (2 Inputs)—X (first input) raised to the power of Y (second input).
- Base-Specified Logarithm (2 Inputs)—Log base N (second input) of X (first input). Equivalent to natural log of X divided by natural log of N. If either input is zero or negative, or if second input is 1, returns empty string.

Cumulative Functoids

Cumulative functoids (see Figure 5.29) use global script variables (which retain their values for the life of the map execution) to calculate the sum, average, minimum value, and so on over all record instances in the source document that contain the input field.

Note

Nonnumeric values are ignored (except for Concatenate) but *are* counted for the divisor in Average.

FIGURE 5.29
Functoid Palette, Cumulative tab.

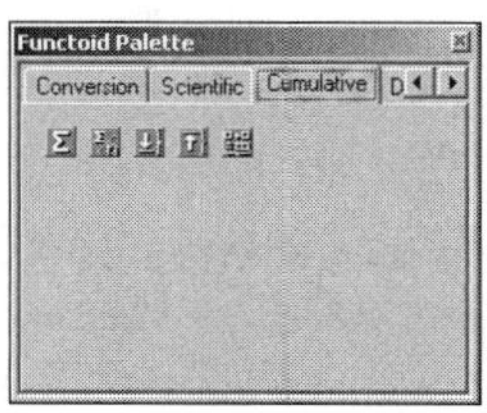

Here is a quick reference for each Cumulative functoid:

- Cumulative Sum (1 Input)— Returns sum of the input field over all records
- Cumulative Average (1 Input)—Returns average of the input field over all records
- Cumulative Minimum (1 Input)—Returns minimum value of the input field over all records
- Cumulative Maximum (1 Input)—Returns maximum value of the input field over all records
- Cumulative String—Returns concatenation of the input field over all records

Database Functoids

The Database functoids (see Figure 5.30) work cooperatively to query a database table for a record that contains a specified value in a specified column and then to return a value from another specified column in that record.

> **Note**
>
> The database connection is made only once and persists for the life of the map execution, but the query must be executed for each instance of the input value. Pay attention to the performance implication of executing one query for each value instance in the source document.

FIGURE 5.30
Functoid Palette, Database tab.

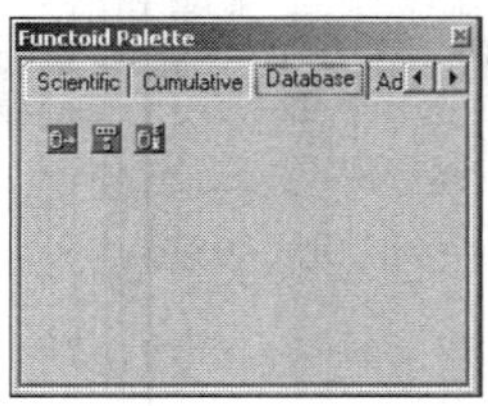

Here is a quick reference for each Database functoid:

- Database Lookup (4 Inputs)—Connects to the database using second input, queries table, and column specified by third and fourth inputs for value specified by first input. Normally, the table and column name will be constants in the functoid properties, whereas the value will be a linked source field or result of another functoid. Connection string may be a constant input to a separate Concatenate functoid (so the same connection string can be used by multiple Database Lookup functoids.
- Value Extractor (2 Inputs)—First input is a Database Lookup functoid; second input is a column name whose value in the looked-up recordset is to be returned. If recordset is empty, or column value is NULL, returns empty string. If query selected more than one record, only the value from the first record is returned.
- Error Return (1 Input)—Returns the ODBC error string, if any, for the Database Lookup functoid linked as its input. A separate functoid is needed to return the error string because each functoid can only return a single value.

Advanced Functoids

The Advanced functoids (see Figure 5.31) perform specialized actions such as allowing you to write your own custom functoid using script code, counting or picking out records in the source document, combining multiple source record types into a single destination record, or altering the schema complexity during transformation from source to destination. Specific help and examples for the Advanced functoids can be found in BizTalk Server Documentation, Index, Using the *[Name]* Functoid.

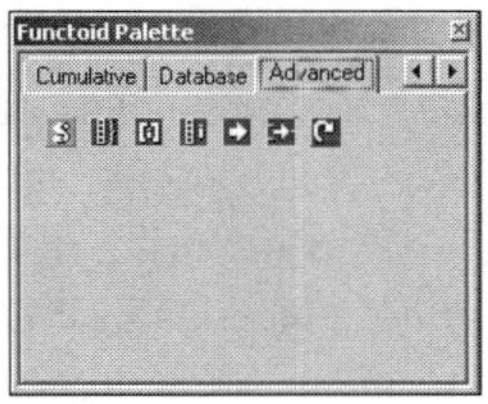

FIGURE 5.31
Functoid Palette, Advanced tab.

Here is a quick reference for each Advanced functoid:

- Scripting (Varying Inputs)—Contains your own custom script code. Number of inputs varies as required, but must return a single, string-formatted value. Code can be written in either VBScript or JScript.
- Record Count (1 Input)—Returns count of instances of a record in the source document. Input link must be a record.
- Index (2 or more Inputs)—Returns the value of the first input *only* for the record instance number(s) specified by the subsequent, index-number inputs. In the `ScoreReport` specification we have been using as an example, to return the `ScorePercent` field in the second `StudentScores` record in the document, in its nested third `ScoreItem` record, you would link the `ScorePercent` field to the Index functoid and then add 2 and 3 as constant inputs. An index input is required for each record level in the hierarchy containing the input field, not counting the document root node.
- Iteration (2 Inputs)—Returns the sequential number (starting at 1) of a record instance within its outer containing record (or document). Input must be a record.
- Value Mapping (2 Inputs)—Returns value of second input, if and only if first input is the string "true" (case-sensitive).
- Value Mapping (Flattening) (2 Inputs)—Same as Value Mapping, except that multiple input records (elements) are combined into multiple output fields (attributes), thereby reducing the number of levels in, or *flattening*, the output schema as compared to the input schema.
- Looping (1 or more Inputs)—Input link(s) and output link must be record specifications. Allows fields from multiple source record types to be linked to a single field under the linked destination record. Separate destination record(s) are created

for each source record regardless of record type. Equivalent to a `UNION SELECT` in a database query, in that it creates a single set of output records from multiple sets of input records.

Summary

BizTalk maps are central to the process of converting documents between different internal formats and provide powerful capabilities to combine, calculate, and otherwise transform data items in addition to complex reordering and restructuring of data fields and records between the source and destination documents. The BizTalk Mapper allows you to interact with the source and destination specifications to create a complete and correct mapping between them. The Mapper includes comprehensive unit-testing features, including verification that the map will produce a valid destination document, and enabling you to test the mapping of generated or entered source values, or to test actual instances of the source document. Finally, the Mapper comes with a large set of built-in data transformation functoids with which you should become familiar to maximize your effectiveness in creating mappings between documents.

CHAPTER 6

Introduction to BizTalk Messaging

By Charlie Kaiman

In This Chapter

Previous chapters have discussed how to define the structure of a business document using the BizTalk Editor, and you have seen how to map one document type to another using the BizTalk Mapper. Now it is time to learn how to tie them together using the BizTalk Messaging Engine.

At a very high level, the BizTalk Messaging Engine manages the various document specifications, maps, and processing instructions that tell BizTalk Server how to process a document—for example, how to get a purchase order from Company A's back-end to Company B's applications in an efficient manner. This chapter provides the information you need to understand the BizTalk Messaging process. Chapter 7, "Using the BizTalk Messaging Manager," discusses how to configure the BizTalk Messaging properties using the BizTalk management interface wizards.

The Fundamentals of Messaging

It might be confusing for some to understand how BizTalk Messaging is different from, say, Microsoft Exchange or some other typical e-mail application. The primary difference between the two is that Microsoft BizTalk Server can send and receive documents using multiple protocols and almost any document type imaginable, whereas applications such as Exchange expect a particular type of document to be delivered over a predetermined protocol—for example, SMTP. BizTalk Server 2002 offers more flexibility in that it can wait for data to be delivered from the Internet "cloud" and then, based on information in the document itself, determine how to process it. This is not to say that BizTalk can't take advantage of direct communication via the likes of Distributed COM (DCOM) or Microsoft Message Queues (MSMQ). However, BizTalk does not require a tightly coupled interface, which makes it appealing and important in an enterprise Business to Business (B2B) or Application to Application (A2A) solution.

BizTalk Server 2002 provides two ways to configure the properties required for the exchange of documents between trading partners (B2B) and enterprise applications (EAI/A2A). One way is to use the BizTalk Messaging Manager (see Chapter 7), which is a wizard-driven interface for configuring trading relationships between applications; the other is the BizTalk Messaging Configuration Object Model (see Chapter 19, "The BizTalk Messaging Configuration Object Model"), which enables developers to configure BizTalk Messaging solutions programmatically. Regardless of which method you choose, the ultimate goal is to configure the messaging engine to manage the exchange of business data between organizations and applications in those organizations.

Figure 6.1 shows an example of a basic message flow between two organizations, one of which is using BizTalk Messaging. Notice that the data sender is immersed in an Internet "cloud." In many cases, BizTalk Server Messaging receives data from an anonymous source and then makes processing decisions based on data contained within the document. BizTalk Server also can receive data via defined MSMQ queues or URLs, which help the server determine who is sending the data, what its purpose is, and where its final destination and document format should be.

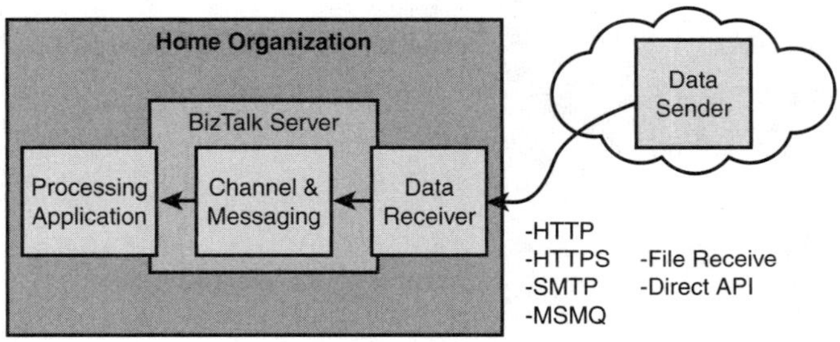

FIGURE 6.1
The basic BizTalk Messaging workflow.

BizTalk Server supports most standard Internet protocols including HTTP, HTTPS, SMTP, and the file system. To exchange data between two applications or organizations, both the sender and receiver must agree on the data formats they are exchanging. After you have identified the data formats that each expects, the sender simply needs to know where to send the data, a URL, e-mail address, or something similar. If you happen to be the data receiver, you need to know how to interpret that data and then architect and design your system to receive and process the documents in ways that are non-problematic for your organization and your business partners.

So let's talk about protocols. At the lowest level, BizTalk can accept documents from MSMQ, the file system, or the IInterchange COM interface. For instance, you could set up BizTalk Server to "sniff" a particular file location using the BizTalk Server receive functions. These receive functions monitor named queues or file locations for arriving documents and process them accordingly as specified by properties defined using the BizTalk Server Administration Console. You also could create an ASP Web site that would allow trading partners to POST their documents to you over HTTP or HTTPS. (We will do this in Chapter 7.) After the document is submitted to the correct URL, the ASP code invokes the IInterchange interface using the `submit` or `submitSync` methods, which causes the document to begin processing according to the configuration specified by the messaging engine.

The possibilities are great, and the configurations will vary to a large degree. Solutions will be made on a case-by-case basis, due to the many factors that make B2B and A2A so interesting.

BizTalk Messaging Mechanics

BizTalk Messaging requires the configuration of several properties that contain information that helps BizTalk Server process a document that's been submitted to the BizTalk Messaging Engine. This section discusses the new terms and properties encountered when configuring BizTalk Messaging. In particular, we will investigate the following topics:

- Organizations
- Document definitions
- Channels
- Messaging ports
- Envelopes
- Receipts
- Distribution lists

Organizations

BizTalk Server needs to know who to deliver a document to, and the application that receives the document typically insists on knowing who it is from. Therefore, BizTalk Server allows you to create organizations and applications.

An *organization* can represent a *home organization* or *trading partners*. A home organization represents your business, whereas trading partners represent each of the organizations with which you plan to exchange documents.

Note

Application-to-application integration is accomplished solely within the confines of the home organization, whereas B2B applications require the introduction of a trading partner organization. Therefore, applications can only be defined for the home organization.

The diagram shown in Figure 6.2 has one home organization and two separate trading partners. BizTalk Server is responsible for the B2B exchange between the home organization and its trading partners plus the A2A integration of applications in its enterprise. This example depicts a scenario in which Sunset Bank and Federal Central (the "trading partners") update Big Bank (the "home organization") with important information about one of Big Bank's clients, Jim Jones. In this case, Jim Jones has withdrawn money from both banks at different times throughout the day, and Big Bank is subsequently notified. In the world of Internet commerce, Jim can view Big Bank's Web Site via his wireless Web browser and see the effects of his transaction in real-time. The internal process involves the integration of the data sent from Big Bank's business partners with Big Bank's own Web Site.

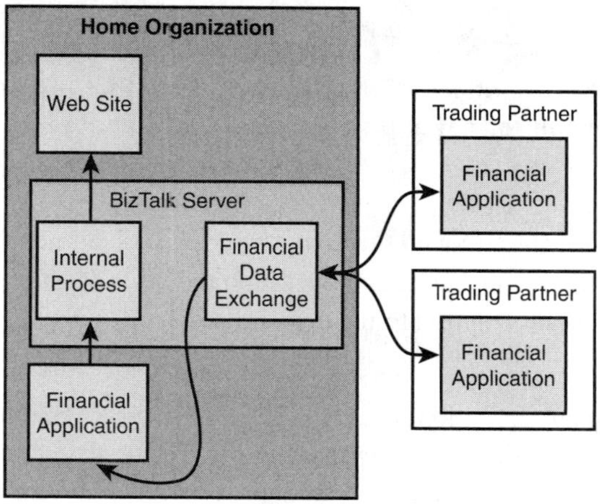

FIGURE 6.2
Financial transaction flow between organizations.

Home Organization

The BizTalk Messaging Manager generates the home organization automatically, and it cannot be deleted. However, you are free to rename the organization and modify its metadata known as *identifiers*. Identifiers are unique attributes used to assist in defining organizations to a more granular level. For instance, instead of just linking a name to a company, you can also reference a DUNS value, a telephone number, and so on. Each of these can be used to uniquely identify this particular organization within your applications. It is also possible to link applications to your home organization. It is important to understand that applications for internal processing can only be integrated within the home organization. In fact, you will only see the Applications tab when you are defining the home organization—that is, it is not available when defining trading partners.

Other Organizations

Apart from the capability to define application integration within an organization, creating an organization for trading partners is done the same way as defining the home organization. First you define the *organization name*, plus any *comments* you might want to add about the organization. All that is left to do is generate any additional identifiers, if required.

Document Definitions

A BizTalk Messaging Manager document definition is a pointer to a specification created by the BizTalk Editor and is referenced inside a *channel* to represent an inbound or outbound document. The same document specification can be used in any number of channels.

> **Note**
>
> You might recall from Chapter 4, "The BizTalk Editor," that a specification is how BizTalk defines the format and structure of a document.

Typically an inbound and an outbound document will not look alike. The inbound document might be a CSV file for instance, and the outbound, an XML file. In cases such as this, you need to incorporate a *map* into the application (see Chapter 5, "The BizTalk Mapper").

When creating a document definition in the BizTalk Messaging Manager, you have to give the definition a name. Use something that closely represents the purpose of the exchange and the specification it uses to avoid confusion down the road. After giving the definition a name, you have the option of selecting a document specification. If you choose to use one, then you need to browse its respective WebDAV directory and pick the correct specification.

Other configuration properties to take notice of include the *global tracking* properties. By choosing particular elements and attributes from a specification, you can track documents processed by BizTalk Messaging Services. Only *inbound* document fields are tracked by the database. A good example is a purchase order total. By tracking the amount in the `<total>` element, for example, you can determine the total amount for orders received from a particular trading partner over a certain period of time, or you can calculate the total received from all your business partners in the same amount of time and compare them statistically.

The final set of properties is related to EDI transactions only and is called the *selection criteria*. Selection criteria are a unique set of name-value pairs that enable BizTalk Server to select a document definition for an inbound X12 or EDIFACT document. Selection criteria are also used to create functional group header information in the envelope of outbound X12 or EDIFACT documents. Again, it is important to remember that the selection criteria features are only available when working with EDI-based documents.

Channels

A channel processes a document based on specific business rules and then passes the parsed document on to a *messaging port* or *distribution list* (each discussed later in the chapter). When the BizTalk Messaging Engine receives a document, the first thing it has to do is determine which channel or channels to execute. The engine needs to know the value of three properties to select a channel(s); the inbound document name, source name, and destination name. You can pass this information to the messaging engine in several different ways. It can be passed programmatically using parameters exposed by the IInterchange interface's `submit` or `submitsync` methods or by placing the metadata in fields defined in the body of the document, better known as a *self-routing document*.

These properties give you the capability to specify the channel by name, forcing the engine to execute that channel and only that channel, or to specify by document name, source name, and destination name. If you pass the document, source, and destination data explicitly, the messaging engine selects and executes any channel that fits that combination of criteria possibly causing the execution of multiple channels.

Channels can be defined to receive documents from a single source or declared as open. Open-source channels give you the ability to define a single channel that can accept the same document from multiple sources and then have the messaging engine deliver it to a single destination. You still need to specify a source at runtime either explicitly or in the document itself; however, the channel selection process will select an open channel based on the match of only two properties—the document type and destination—as opposed to all three. It is also possible to create more than one channel for each individual messaging port or distribution list causing the submission of multiple documents to be routed to a single destination.

A channel gives you the ability to customize the processing of your inbound document by setting multiple properties either programmatically (see Chapter 19) or by using the BizTalk Messaging Manager. The following sections discuss several of the properties and their designated tasks. Chapter 7 discusses how to use the BizTalk Messaging Manager wizards to define the values of the properties.

Source Organization or Application

The preceding paragraphs discussed the source property extensively. When defining a channel, your first task is to specify the source of the incoming document. A source can be defined as an organization—that is, a business partner—an internal application, or as open.

Note

If the source is an application, then you must first create the application for the home organization. Applications can be defined only for the home organization, and a home organization can have many applications.

It is also possible to assign a BizTalk Orchestration XLANG schedule as the source for your channel, allowing you to integrate the BizTalk Messaging Services with BizTalk Orchestration (see Chapter 16, "Correlation—Integrating BizTalk Server Messaging and Orchestration Services").

Apart from the BizTalk Messaging Manager, you can explicitly declare the source inside the document itself or within parameters supplied by the IInterchange interface methods.

Just remember that a channel is always created for a messaging port or a distribution list. The destination for the documents that you receive from the source of a channel is designated in the messaging port, or in the messaging ports of the distribution list, for which the channel is created and bound.

Inbound and Outbound Document Definitions

The next step is to specify inbound and outbound document definitions. If you recall, specification development was discussed in Chapter 4. Well, here is where we begin to integrate those specifications into BizTalk Messaging. The inbound document definition represents an incoming document from the source organization or application (or XLANG schedule). The outbound document definition represents the semantic format required by the receiving entity—that is, the destination, which can either be a business partner or an application (or an XLANG schedule). If the inbound document is formatted differently than the specified outbound document, you must specify a map for the channel to transform the inbound document into the outbound document.

Mapping

A BizTalk map uses XSLT to transform documents from one format to another. Maps are created using the BizTalk Mapper, discussed in Chapter 5. The BizTalk Server Messaging Engine uses BizTalk maps to transform the inbound document into the required outbound document format.

As stated earlier, it is possible to generate more than one channel for each messaging port or distribution list. For example, imagine that your organization receives financial data from ATM transactions that occur at two banks. When one of your clients uses either bank's ATM machine, the transaction is submitted via the Web to your application, thereby subtracting the amount from the client's existing bank account. In this case, you will have a channel for each bank, tied to a single messaging port. This gives you the flexibility to map two distinct inbound document formats, one for each bank, into a single outbound format by defining a different map for each channel bound to the destination port. In fact, for each additional bank you decide to accept transactions from, you simply need to create a channel for them and add that to the existing messaging port.

Tracking and Filtering properties

An interesting feature of the BizTalk Messaging Engine is its capability to track and log individual document fields to a SQL Server tracking database. This feature is only available for inbound documents. The fields are selected per inbound document/channel and are logged each time a document is processed by the channel. This data is easily accessible via a Web-based tracking interface provided out of the box or via custom queries to the SQL Server tracking database (see Chapter 8, "Document Tracking").

Another feature, known as a *channel filtering expression*, provides an additional way to define which channel(s) will be invoked when a document is received. When the server processes a document, the value of each of the specified fields is evaluated against the value of the channel filtering expression. If the expression is found to be true, the channel is invoked. If the expression is found to be false, the channel is not invoked. For example, if the channel filtering expression is created to look for a transaction of $500.00 or more, and the transaction is for a withdrawal of $550.00, the channel is invoked.

Document logging properties

BizTalk Server also gives you the capability to store a complete copy of the inbound or outbound documents. These documents can be stored in their native format, their XML format, or both.

> **Note**
>
> Having the ability to log a document XML version can be helpful in the debugging process. Remember that BizTalk Server is XML-centric. All inbound documents are parsed, upon submission, into XML and then serialized into their native format just prior to transport to their destination.

Other properties

Other properties that you can set within a channel include

- Configure receipts—You can request a receipt from the destination for a document that you send, and you can generate a receipt to the source for a document that you receive.
- Configure security properties—You can specify that the server verify the encryption and signature for an inbound document, or digitally sign the outbound document.
- Configure advanced properties—You can specify a group control number for documents with EDI formats, set the number and time interval that the server uses to resend documents, and override the transport component and envelope properties for the messaging port or distribution list.

Messaging Ports

Messaging ports are used to define a document's destination and consist of properties used to configure the BizTalk Messaging Engine to efficiently transport business documents to a specified destination via a designated transport protocol. A port must be bound to at least one channel and may be bound to multiple channels.

A messaging port consists of the following metadata:

- Destination
- Transport properties
- Envelope information
- Security properties

When you're designing a BizTalk Messaging architecture, an important thing to consider is the type of transaction you're going to implement (see Table 6.1). Is it an application-to-application integration task, for example, where you are trying to integrate one or more applications in your organization? Or is it more of a business-to-business type scenario, in which you need to integrate two disparate business applications living in two or more distinct organizations?

TABLE 6.1 Two Types of Messaging Ports

To an Application	
EAI/A2A (Application-to-Application)	Designate either an XLANG *schedule* or an application of the home organization as the destination.

TABLE 6.1 Two Types of Messaging Ports

To an Organization	
B2B (Business-to-Business)	Either designate a specific trading partner or declare an open destination.

After you decide on the type of application you are going to build, it makes it much simpler to choose the appropriate destination for the document and your business scenario.

Destination

A destination is an application or organization that receives and processes the business document. There are three fundamental destination types:

- Destination organizations
- Destination applications
- XLANG schedules

When choosing to port a message to an application, the application must be added to the home organization prior to creating the port. This is as simple as going to the Organizations link in the BizTalk Messaging Manager, finding your home organization, and adding the application's name to the wizard (see Chapter 7).

A messaging port to an organization can designate a destination organization (that is, trading partner), or it can be declared an *open messaging port*. Open messaging ports are ones in which the destination organization is not known until either the document is processed (that is, the destination is parsed from the message itself) or parameters from the `submit` or `submitSync` methods of the IInterchange interface are passed to BizTalk.

You can configure a messaging port for an XLANG schedule in several different ways. For one, you can configure the messaging port to activate a new instance of an XLANG schedule by specifying the path to the XLANG schedule (`.skx`) file and a reference to a schedule port. In this case, the messaging engine instantiates a new instance of the schedule and then passes the outbound document to the schedule port designated in the messaging port properties.

You can also configure a messaging port to send a document to an active XLANG schedule. In this case, the document is sent to an MSMQ queue monitored by the running XLANG schedule instance. The document must be self-routing (see Chapter 12, "Advanced BizTalk Messaging") and contain an MSMQ queue name in the transport property. This feature enables developers to take advantage of and integrate BizTalk Orchestration services into their BizTalk Messaging solutions. See Chapters 9, 10, 11, 13 and 16 for additional information on BizTalk Orchestration.

Transport Properties

Think of a transport property as a choice of vehicles to get your document from point A to point B. The transport services available to you are

- Application Integration Component (AIC)
- File
- HTTP
- HTTPS
- Loopback
- Message queuing
- SMTP

All the services have an address to which the document is sent for processing, except the loopback. The loopback transport is a special type of transport service that enables the synchronous return of data to the application from which it originated. The loopback transport is only available from ports bound to channels whose source is an application. The loopback transport is useful in situations that require the transformation of data during processing—for example, an XLANG schedule that requires the transformation of data. In this case, the transformed data is returned synchronously to the sending application, the XLANG schedule instance.

Envelope Information

An *envelope* provides additional information by adding BizTalk-specific metadata to the business document. The metadata is placed in either the header or the footer of the envelope, thereby making necessary routing information programmatically accessible to BizTalk via APIs or wizard-driven interfaces. The properties you specify in the envelope provide BizTalk's Messaging Engine with the properties it needs to either parse an inbound document or serialize an outbound document.

The BizTalk Messaging Engine natively supports XML documents and can recognize and parse inbound and outbound XML documents without an envelope.

Envelopes can be constructed using six generic formats:

- Reliable
- Custom XML
- ANSI X12
- UN/EDIFACT

- Flat file (i.e. delimited or positional)
- Custom

Reliable formats are those compliant with the BizTalk Framework 2.0 specification. That is to say that it has all the elements required as a BizTalk Framework document to route and parse documents correctly and is in XML format. A custom format, on the other hand, requires a custom parser or serializer to process inbound or outbound envelopes, respectively (see Chapter 18, "Creating Custom Serializers, Parsers, and Functoids"). Processing X12 or EDIFACT envelopes requires the identification of specific delimiters and also an *interchange control number*. These properties apply only to the envelopes selected for use with that particular messaging port. The delimiters and interchange control number are optional when working with custom formats. The basis for using them or not using them depends on the requirements built-in to your custom parser or serializer. Just remember that the format of an envelope that you select in a messaging port must agree with the format of the outbound document that it contains, and that the format of the outbound document is determined by the specification referred to in the outbound document definition of a channel. For example, if you choose an envelope with an EDI format for a messaging port, when you create a channel for that messaging port, you must select an outbound document definition that points to a specification that also has an EDI format.

Note

If you do not specify an envelope when creating a messaging port, the data is sent in XML format without any header.

Envelopes for Inbound Processing

The envelopes that you create to process inbound interchanges do not need to be selected in a messaging port to be used by the server but rather in the messaging channel. That being said, BizTalk Server *can* process an inbound document in X12 or EDIFACT without using an envelope defined using the BizTalk Messaging Manager. However, processing a flat file document does require the creation of an envelope; and the envelope must point to a local or Web-accessible location for validation of the message. The name of the envelope also is required when the document is submitted to BizTalk. When working with a flat file document, an envelope needs to be created.

Envelopes for Outbound Processing

When creating a messaging port in BizTalk Server 2002, you are given the option of selecting an envelope for the documents that are going to be processed by that port. If you decide to use an envelope, the format of the envelope must match the format of the documents referenced by the envelope itself. For instance, if your business document is in XML format, then you must choose an XML-formatted envelope (if you decide to use one at all).

If you decide to use custom XML as your format of choice for encapsulating your business data and you decide not to specify an envelope for a messaging port, the data will be sent using the reliable format—that is, envelopes compliant with the BizTalk Framework 2.0 specification.

As with inbound processing, the use of a custom format requires the integration of a custom serializer to get the data into your proprietary—or non-standardized—custom format.

Finally, if you are going to select an envelope with an EDI format, you must—as with inbound processing—specify an interchange control number and the required delimiters.

Note

For X12 and EDIFACT processing, the interchange control number is used to identify and track documents processed by the messaging port. The interchange control number is incremented with each use of the envelope and messaging port. Delimiters indicate the characters used to separate the records and fields of the envelope and the documents contained in the envelope. For envelopes with a custom format, an interchange control number and delimiters are optional.

Security Properties

Documents sent to a BizTalk Messaging port can be secured using three techniques:

- Encoding
- Encryption
- Digital signatures

BizTalk Server 2002 supports Multipurpose Internet Mail Extensions (MIME) encoding. Using MIME encoding, a programmer can

- Specify alternate content encoding mechanisms for each body part.
- Relate groups of multiple content parts within a message.
- Use character sets other than US-ASCII character sets in body parts and message header fields.
- Specify the intended disposition of a content part (for example, inline or attachment).

BizTalk Server 2002 also supports Secure Multipurpose Internet Mail Extensions (S/MIME) certificate-based public key encryption. Encryption can be applied to business data that you send to your trading partners. By using an encryption certificate to secure the data, you can ensure that only the intended recipient can access the information.

Note

For an open messaging port, the encryption security properties are disabled because the destination organization is unknown.

It is also important to know that BizTalk Server supports Secure Multipurpose Internet Mail Extensions (S/MIME) certificate-based public-key digital signing. Digital signing can be used to ensure the authenticity of the source of data, to ensure that the data has not been modified, and to prevent the source of the data from repudiating the message.

The security properties that you designate for a messaging port apply to all channels associated with that messaging port. If you have documents that need to be secured using a different encryption or that do not need to be encrypted, you need to create a separate messaging port with the appropriate security properties for those documents.

Note

For additional information on BizTalk security, see Chapter 22, "Security."

Receipts

Receipts are acknowledgements sent by a recipient back to the originating organization or application, announcing that the interchange has occurred successfully. Ultimately, the goal is to

- Configure a receiving server to generate a receipt and return it to the sender
- Make sure that the sender's application is able to handle the receipt
- Process it correctly

In the end, we have a device for tracking the status of a transaction and making it available for future reference.

There are two ways to process and handle receipts in BizTalk. The one you choose depends on the format that you are using for the business exchange. For exchanges that use the X12, EDIFACT, or custom parser—and require receipts—you can configure BizTalk Messaging Manager to use channels for processing receipts. For exchanges that use the XML parser, however, you have the option of using reliable messaging, which processes receipts automatically and guarantees the reliable delivery of data.

Processing Receipts Using Channels

If you are using X12, EDIFACT, or a custom syntax to format your document, then you can expect to use channel properties to control the processing of your receipts.

To use Messaging Services to send a message to a business partner and receive a verifiable receipt message, you need to create a channel and a messaging port to send a message to the proper destination and generate a specification for the receipt. Keep in mind that you have to set a timeout for the receipt and decide what actions to take when a receipt is not returned in a timely manner—for example, resend the message.

On the destination side, create a channel and messaging port for replying with the receipt prior to building the actual business document-processing page because when you design a messaging port, it will be necessary that you have the receipt information on hand to complete the process.

Processing Receipts Using Reliable Messaging

XML documents can facilitate the process of sending and receiving receipts through the use of reliable messaging. If you remember from the previous section on reliable messaging, all this means is that the messages are BizTalk Framework 2.0-compliant. In the header of the message will be a send-to address, to which a receipt should be submitted. For instance, if I were to send a document to my partner using reliable messaging, I would place a URL in the document header to explain where to send my receipt. This reply-to URL address is required for compliant interchanges.

Distribution Lists

We've discussed sending messages to a single destination, but what if you want to send a single message to multiple destinations? The answer is to use a distribution list. A distribution list is a collection of ports that share the same document types and configuration, thereby simplifying the task of sending several different organizations or applications the same data. Some good examples are price listings, catalog updates, newsletters, and even user guides. By submitting a document to BizTalk Server one time, you can be assured that it will reach each of the predefined organizations or applications safely and securely.

Create a messaging port for each of the business partners or applications that you want to share your data with. Then add these ports to a named distribution list.

> **Note**
>
> Open messaging ports cannot be added to a distribution list.

It is also possible to add future messaging ports to an existing distribution list, so don't feel as though you have to have all your partners in line, prior to designing your application.

BizTalk Server invokes those channels linked to the distribution list and not those associated with the respective messaging ports. This is why it is necessary to create at least one channel for each distribution list. You will, however, use the destination information in those messaging ports to define where those messages are going.

Just remember that distribution lists allow you to aggregate messaging ports for the exchange of data with multiple organizations and/or applications.

Summary

The goal of BizTalk Messaging is to streamline the process of data exchange. BizTalk Messaging provides the plumbing necessary to guarantee the reliable delivery and transformation of documents between organizations and applications in that organization.

Now that we have taken the opportunity to learn about the pieces that make up BizTalk Server Messaging, we will look at several examples of how to configure BizTalk Messaging using a real-world scenario. The next chapter presents an opportunity to build an application in which you will exchange financial data between two banking institutions.

CHAPTER 7

Using the BizTalk Messaging Manager

By Susie Adams and Charlie Kaiman

In This Chapter

In Chapter 6, "Introduction to BizTalk Messaging," you took a high-level look at BizTalk Server messaging and the services it provides. This chapter discusses how to use BizTalk Server's Messaging Manager and tools to configure BizTalk Server messaging.

In this chapter you will learn

- How to create an ASP application that can send a document in XML via HTTP using BizTalk Server
- To use that application to receive the file using the basic file and HTTP protocols
- To transform an XML document using a BizTalk map

The Business Scenario

The Web application we're going to build in this chapter will encapsulate a transaction and submit it to a trading partner who will process the transaction accordingly. Figure 7.1 depicts the type of application that we will build.

FIGURE 7.1
Application diagram.

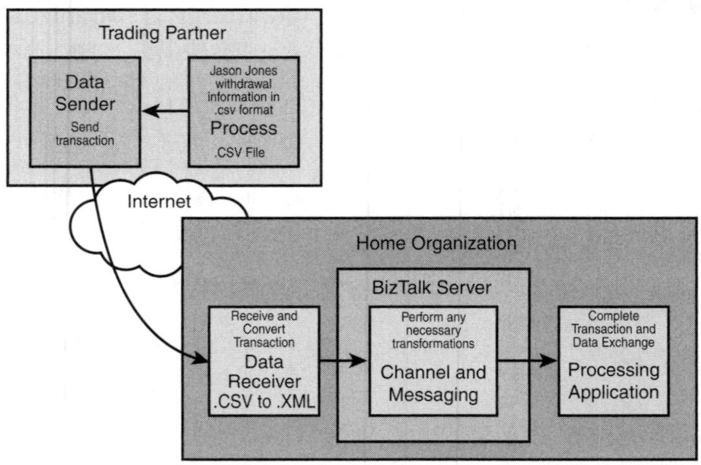

As the diagram shows, a process generates a business document as an XML document representing a financial transaction. The purpose of this document is to issue withdrawal notifications to Big Bank Co. For instance, when Jason Jones withdraws $50 from an ATM owned by Sunset Bank, Inc., Sunset Bank needs to notify Big Bank Co. of this transaction (because Mr. Jones is a member of Big Bank Co.). Listing 7.1 is an example of what an XML transaction being sent from Sunset Bank, Inc., might look like.

LISTING 7.1 Sample XML Transaction

```
<?xml version="1.0" encoding="UTF-8"?>
<Transactions>
 <Transaction id="ABC-001">
  <Account name="Jason Jones" number="xxx-77-xxx03" />
  <Amount>-51.50</Amount>
  <Type>ATM</Type>
  <Facility>Sunset Bank, Inc.</Facility>
  <Location>
   <Name>Sunset Bank, NW</Name>
  <Address>555 Western Blvd, CA  22222</Address>
 </Location>
 </Transaction>
</Transactions>
```

The transaction is simple. In the third line of code, the application applies a unique `id` to the transaction. The fourth line of code represents the account—that is, name and account number; whereas the fifth line tells how much is to be deducted from the account. Notice that an additional $1.50 is added to the initial $50 withdrawal. This represents a transaction fee that Sunset Bank charges for using its ATM. The rest of the document informs Big Bank Co. as to where the transaction was made.

In some cases, there will be a bulk notification to Big Bank Co., with multiple withdrawals (records) per transaction (file). This is okay because we could configure BizTalk to handle each type of transaction.

When the transaction at the member bank is complete, the member bank invokes a procedure to send the processed transaction data to Big Bank Co. When this occurs, the data is transported via HTTPS to an application, such as a SOAP Service, on Big Bank Co.'s servers. Upon receiving the document (a process discussed in more depth later in the chapter), the application forwards the message to BizTalk for processing. Actually, the only processing that likely will occur at this point is a transformation of the data into the necessary output format and some workflow activity. Other than that, BizTalk simply passes the formatted data off to the waiting application for processing. In this case, the application is some kind of financial application that processes ATM transactions for all its customer accounts. To demonstrate a similar scenario, the example code in this chapter is going to simulate the sending and receiving applications using ASP pages. The receiving company Big Bank is simply going to receive the inbound file, transform it into its required XML document format, and then save it to a local file directory.

The first thing we are going to do is imagine ourselves being in Big Bank Co.'s shoes. We have hundreds of business partners who are willing to pass along data to us so that our customers can take advantage of many ATMs across the nation. However, we need to make the integration process inexpensive and easy to accomplish. We are going to do this by allowing all our business partners to send us their data in whatever format they are comfortable with. We, in exchange for getting the data, will take care of the reformatting issues associated with the transaction. For instance, if they want to send us CSV files, that's fine, as long as we know what the format of the CSV files are beforehand. That way, we can set up the necessary map(s), using the BizTalk Mapper, to transform the CSV files into the XML that our application requires. Sunset Bank is going to make the process a little easier on us, however, because it is already sending us XML. The only thing we have to do then is take XML and turn it into an XML document that our application understands.

Note

For more information on XML, see Chapter 2, "XML and Related Technologies."

Now that we have an idea as to what we are building, let's get started on some coding!

Creating the Organizations and Applications

The first thing to do is create the *organizations*. Begin by opening the BizTalk Messaging Manager. You can do this by choosing Start, Programs, Microsoft BizTalk Server 2002, BizTalk Messaging Manager.

Note

You might get a message box at this point, depending on whether you just installed BizTalk Server. Click Cancel and follow the directions in the following paragraphs for creating a new home organization.

When the dialog opens, choose Organizations from the list of links under Search for Other Items and click Search Now. A list of available organizations appears in the righthand-panel (see Figure 7.2).

In the right pane, you see the home organization. Double-click Home Organization, and the Organization Properties dialog box opens, as shown in Figure 7.3.

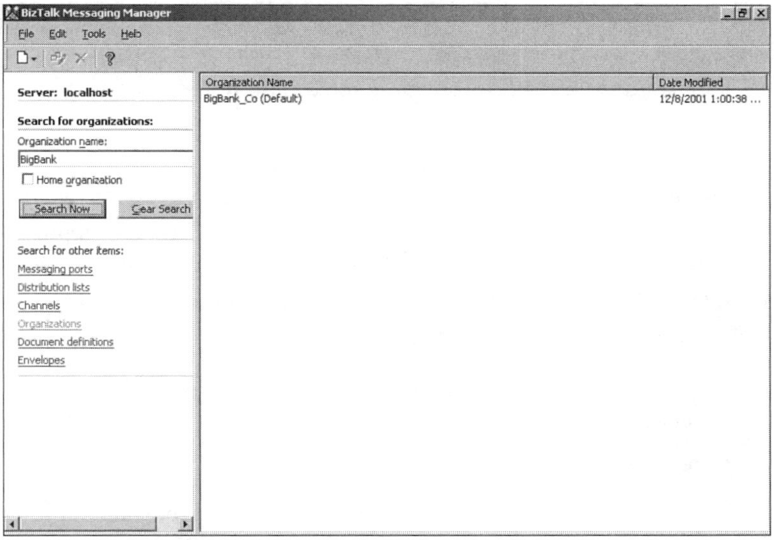

FIGURE 7.2
BizTalk development environment.

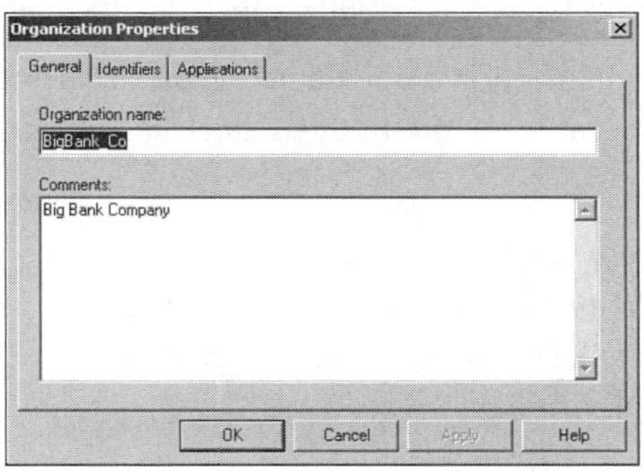

FIGURE 7.3
The Organization Properties dialog.

First, rename the home organization by entering **`BigBank_Co`** as the Organization Name. The Organization Properties dialog box contains two other tabs—Identifiers and Applications. The Identifiers tab allows you to assign multiple name/value pairs to identify your organization. The default value for your home organization is the organization name—that is, the one you just identified in the General tab, but you can add others.

The Applications tab is used to define applications that will be used as either the source or destination point for BizTalk Server. Applications are a logical versus physical distinction available to help you distinguish between applications exchanging data inside the home organization.

Note

You can define applications only for the home organization.

For instance, think of BizTalk Server as being used to integrate two disparate applications inside your organization, one to receive the data from an application to BizTalk (`sendData`) and another to receive the repurposed data and process it (`processData`). Both applications (`sendData` and `processData`) would need to be added to the Applications tab. In our example, however, we need to add two applications to this dialog box:

- `receiveTrans`
- `getTrans`

In this example, an ASP application, `receiveTrans.asp`, waits for a message from Sunset Bank, Inc. When a message is received (via HTTP), the `receiveTrans.asp` application submits it to BizTalk Server (you will see how this happens a bit later).

Next, we need to create a new organization named `SunSet_Bank`. To accomplish this, select File, New, Organization from the menu. In the dialog that appears, name the organization `SunSet_Bank` and then save it.

Before we continue, it should be noted that there is an ASP application running at Sunset Bank called `sendTrans.asp`. The purpose for `sendTrans.asp` ASP application is to send an XML transaction set to BigBank so that it can be properly processed. Figure 7.4 illustrates the basic flow for this application.

FIGURE 7.4
Transaction flow diagram.

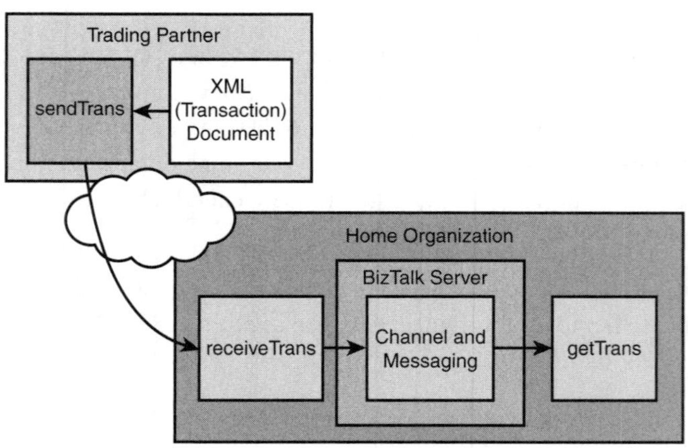

Defining Document Definitions and Maps

Before we can begin working with the *channels* and *ports*, we need to define the documents with which we are going to be dealing.

The document definitions in this example will be named:

- `SunsetBank.xml`
- `BigBank.xml`

The `SunsetBank` schema defines the document format that will be sent to Big Bank and subsequently submitted to BizTalk Server. Listing 7.2 shows this schema.

LISTING 7.2 `SunsetBank.xml`

```
<?xml version="1.0"?>
<Schema
  name="Transactions"
  b:BizTalkServerEditorTool_Version="1.0"
  b:root_reference="Transactions"
  b:standard="XML"
  xmlns="urn:schemas-microsoft-com:xml-data"
  xmlns:b="urn:schemas-microsoft-com:BizTalkServer"
  xmlns:d="urn:schemas-microsoft-com:datatypes">
<b:SelectionFields/>
<ElementType name="Type" content="textOnly" model="closed">
<b:FieldInfo/>
</ElementType><ElementType name="Transactions" content="eltOnly"_
➥ model="closed">
<b:RecordInfo/>
<element type="Transaction" maxOccurs="*" minOccurs="0"/>
</ElementType><ElementType name="Transaction" content="eltOnly" model="closed">
<b:RecordInfo/>
<AttributeType name="id">
<b:FieldInfo/></AttributeType>
<attribute type="id"/>
<element type="Account" maxOccurs="1" minOccurs="1"/>
<element type="Amount" maxOccurs="*" minOccurs="0"/>
<element type="Type" maxOccurs="*" minOccurs="0"/>
<element type="Facility" maxOccurs="*" minOccurs="0"/>
<element type="Location" maxOccurs="1" minOccurs="1"/>
</ElementType><ElementType name="Name" content="textOnly" model="closed">
<b:FieldInfo/>
</ElementType><ElementType name="Location" content="eltOnly" model="closed">
<b:RecordInfo/>
<element type="Name" maxOccurs="*" minOccurs="0"/>
```

LISTING 7.2 continued

```
<element type="Address" maxOccurs="*" minOccurs="0"/>
</ElementType><ElementType name="Facility" content="textOnly" model="closed">
<b:FieldInfo/>
</ElementType><ElementType name="Amount" content="textOnly" model="closed">
<b:FieldInfo/>
</ElementType><ElementType name="Address" content="textOnly" model="closed">
<b:FieldInfo/>
</ElementType><ElementType name="Account" content="empty" model="closed">
<b:RecordInfo/>
<AttributeType name="number">
<b:FieldInfo/></AttributeType>
<AttributeType name="name">
<b:FieldInfo/></AttributeType>
<attribute type="name"/>
<attribute type="number"/>
</ElementType>
</Schema>
```

Figure 7.5 shows what the previously listed schema looks like in the BizTalk Editor.

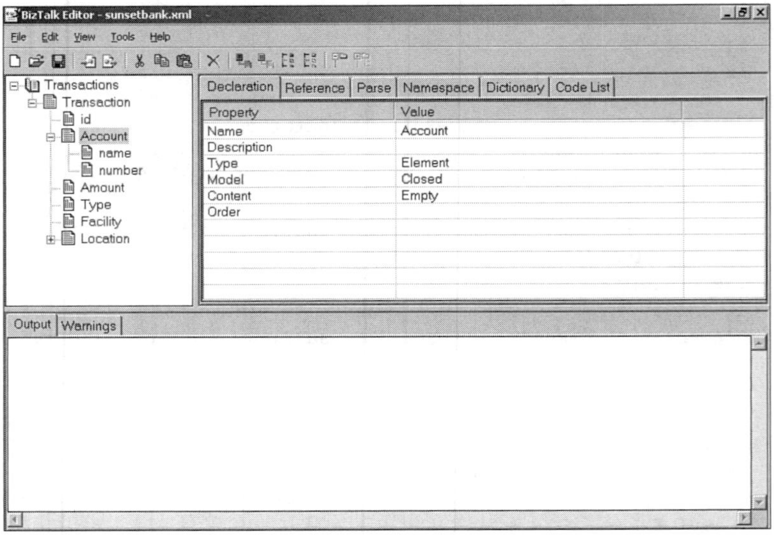

FIGURE 7.5
The `SunSetBank` *BizTalk specification.*

The `BigBank` schema, shown in Listing 7.3, defines the format that results from a BizTalk transformation on the Sunset Bank data and gets delivered to the `getTrans` ASP application.

LISTING 7.3 BigBank.xml

```
<?xml version="1.0"?>
<Schema
  name="Transactions"
  b:BizTalkServerEditorTool_Version="1.0"
  b:root_reference="Transactions"
  b:standard="XML"
  xmlns="urn:schemas-microsoft-com:xml-data"
  xmlns:b="urn:schemas-microsoft-com:BizTalkServer"
  xmlns:d="urn:schemas-microsoft-com:datatypes">
<b:SelectionFields/>
<ElementType name="Transactions" content="eltOnly" model="closed">
<b:RecordInfo/>
<element type="Transaction" maxOccurs="*" minOccurs="1"/>
</ElementType><ElementType name="Transaction" content="empty" model="closed">
<b:RecordInfo/>
<AttributeType name="id">
<b:FieldInfo/></AttributeType>
<AttributeType name="Amount">
<b:FieldInfo/></AttributeType>
<attribute type="id" required="no"/>
<attribute type="Amount" required="no"/>
</ElementType>
</Schema>
```


Figure 7.6 displays the `BigBank` schema in the BizTalk Editor. Both of these schema files should be saved to the WebDAV repository.

FIGURE 7.6
The `BigBank` *BizTalk specification.*

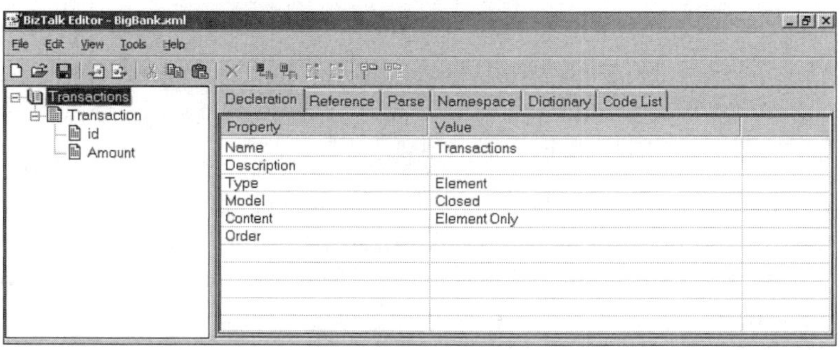

To add these specifications to BizTalk Server, go to the left pane in the BizTalk Messaging Manager and click on Document Definitions. Select the Search Now button to view a list of document definitions in the righthand pane.

From the menu, click File, New, Document Definition (or simply use Ctrl+D), and the New Document Definition dialog box opens, as shown in Figure 7.7. Now, name the document definition `SunsetBank`.

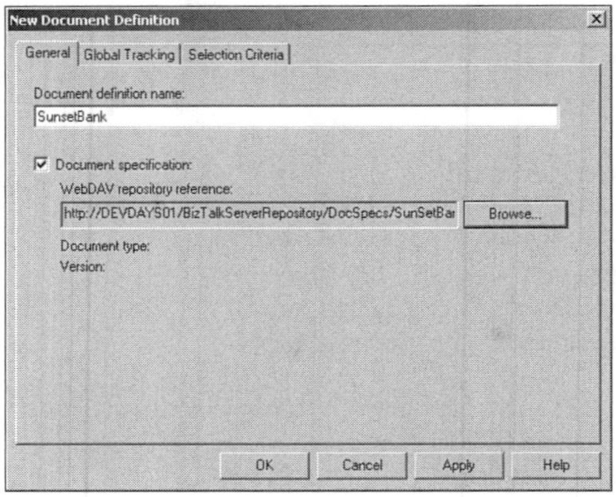

FIGURE 7.7
The Document Definition dialog.

Click the Document Specification check box and browse the WebDAV repository for your specification. You can put the specifications physically into the directories under BizTalk.

> **Note**
>
> If you haven't already created a specification, see Chapter 4, "The BizTalk Editor," for details on how to build a specification using BizTalk Editor. Another option is to copy the Sunset Bank specification given previously and insert it into WebDAV manually.

The last two tabs, Global Tracking and Selection Criteria, are optional at this point and will not be used for this example. However, these points will be covered later in Chapter 12, "Advanced BizTalk Messaging."

Click OK, and you see the document definition name populated in the right pane. Now, repeat these steps for the Big Bank Co. specification. Make sure that the name for your Big Bank document definition is `BigBank` and remember that BizTalk properties are case-sensitive.

Mapping the Document Definitions

There is one more step to take before getting into the process of generating channels and ports, and that is making sure that we have a map to transform the Sunset Bank and Sunrise Bank data into the Big Bank data format.

In Chapter 5, "The BizTalk Mapper," you learned how to map a specification from one format to another, so I am going to assume that you are comfortable with the process. Follow these steps for building your map:

1. Open BizTalk Mapper.
2. Choose File, New and select a Source Specification from WebDAV. Choose the `SunsetBank.xml` file.
3. Select `BigBank.xml` as your Destination Specification from WebDAV.

   You see both specifications on either side of the mapper. Drag items from the left (Sunset Bank) to the right (Big Bank) to define a model in which certain elements from Sunset Bank's XML equate to particular elements in the Big Bank XML document. For the purpose of this example, the only things we are going to map are the transaction `id` and the `Amount`. So, drag

   - The `id` node from the Sunset Bank specification over to the `id` node in the Big Bank specification
   - The `Amount` node from left-to-right in the same manner
4. Save (and compile) the map to WebDAV. Save the new map as `SunsetBanktoBigBank.xml`.

Figure 7.8 displays the map in the BizTalk Mapper.

Now that you have created and saved the map, you are ready to build a BizTalk Messaging port.

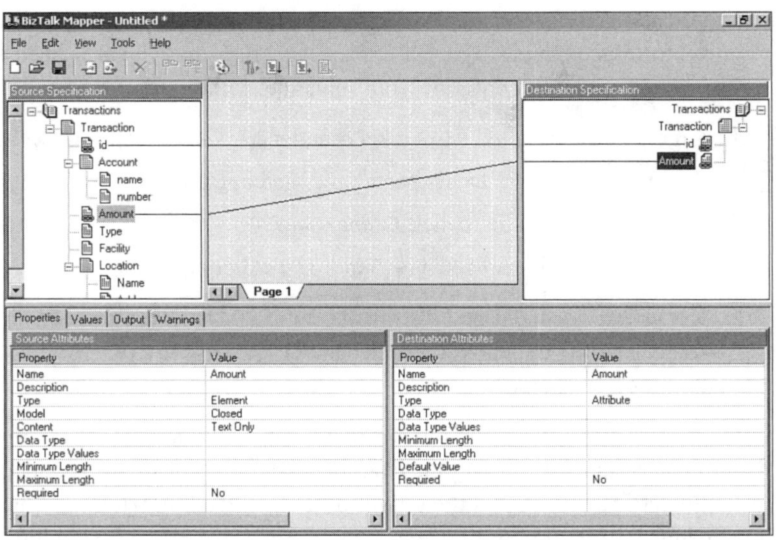

FIGURE 7.8
The BizTalk Mapper.

Creating the BizTalk Messaging Port

Let's recap what we have accomplished before we go on to build a messaging port in the BizTalk Server Messaging Manager. First, we renamed the home organization, added two applications, and created a sending member bank organization. Next, we designed both the inbound and outbound specifications to meet the criteria required by the application and then created documents in the BizTalk Messaging Manager to reference them. Then we created a map to transform the inbound document into the outbound document format.

> **Note**
>
> It might be confusing to think about creating the messaging port first and the channel last because the channel is the first component referenced by BizTalk. However, as you will see, when we are building the messaging port, the wizard asks whether we want to create a channel for this messaging port. We will reply "yes" to this and generate a channel at that time. Remember, a port describes the destination and must have at least one channel. It may also be referenced by many channels.

Now we are ready to create a messaging port to manage the delivery of data to the waiting application. Before we begin, we must set up the applications and directories required for this example. There are three ASP files that you will need to use for this sample application. To configure your machine, follow these steps:

1. Create a folder called `BigBank_Co` under *`drive`*`:\inetpub\wwwroot`.
2. Add two subfolders to `BigBank_Co` called `application` and `documents`.
3. Create another folder called `SunsetBank_Inc` under *`drive`*`:\inetpub\wwwroot`.
4. Add two subfolders to `SunsetBank_Inc` called `application` and `documents`.
5. Create two virtual directories using the IIS MMC that point to the `SunsetBank_Inc` folder and the `BigBank Co` folder under the `wwwroot` folder with the same names as the directory names.

In the next section, "Creating the BizTalk Channel," you will see code for the three files that are necessary for running the example. The ASP files will be added to their respective application folders, and the output of the application, which in this case is the XML documents, will be sent to the `document` folders (no need to do anything to this folder).

For the purposes of this example, it is important to make certain directories write-enabled. Using Windows Security, right-click on the `document` folders and choose Properties. On the Security tab, add the Internet Guest Account (for example, `WebServerName\IUSR_ WebServerName`) to the list of names and give this account Write access, in addition to its current defaults.

We are now ready to create the new port. To accomplish this, follow these steps:

1. Click on the Messaging Ports link in the left pane and then click on the Search Now button.
2. From the menu, choose File, New, Messaging Port, To an Application.

   Notice that we have a choice between building a port that goes To an Organization and one that goes To an Application. In this case, the document is coming from an organization, one of the member banks, and then being submitted to an internal application inside the `BigBank` organization. Therefore, as you will see, one of our choices in the wizard is to send this document to an application that we defined earlier in this chapter (see "Creating the Organizations and Applications"). After we have chosen to create a messaging port, the New Messaging Port dialog opens (see Figure 7.9).

FIGURE 7.9
The New Messaging Port dialog.

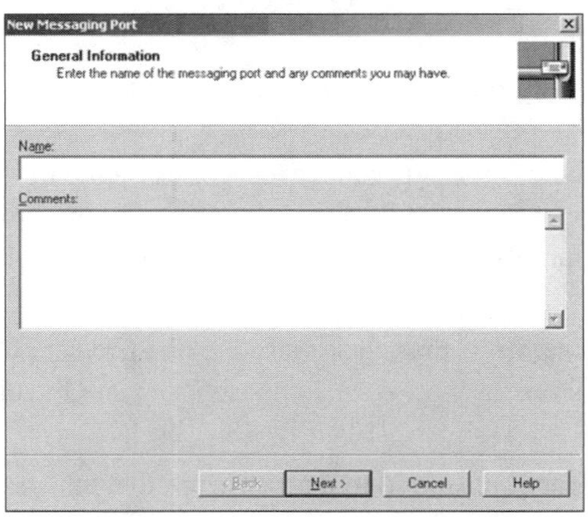

3. Name the port `SunsetBank_Inc to BigBank_Co via HTTP` and click Next.

   The Destination Application section allows you to define either an XLANG schedule to run against or a waiting application. Choose the default, which is an Application.

4. Click the Application radio button (which should be the default) and select `getTrans` from the choice of applications. This is the BizTalk application that BizTalk will submit the document to after it has finished processing it.
5. Choose a primary transport for the output document.
6. Click on Browse, within the context of the Primary Transport section and select HTTP as the transport type. Submit an Address for the application, which will be an ASP file—for example, `http://localhost/BigBank_Co/application/getTrans.asp`as displayed in Figure 7.10.

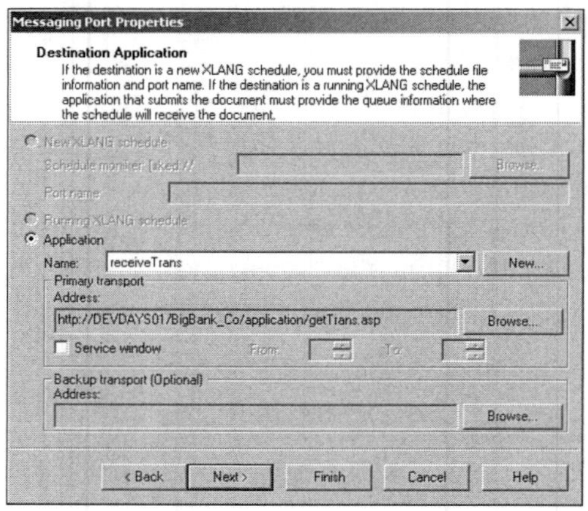

FIGURE 7.10
Selecting the port transport properties.

7. After you enter the address for `getTrans.asp`—for example, `http://localhost/BigBank_Co/application/getTrans.asp`—click Next. In the Envelope Information section, make sure that the default home organization identifier is selected and click Next.
8. In the Security Information section, make sure that the Create a Channel for this Messaging Port check box is checked and choose From an Organization as the Channel Type.
9. Click Finish, and you are transferred to a new wizard that allows you to create a new channel.

Creating the BizTalk Channel

When the Channel Wizard opens, enter a name for the channel in the Channel Properties section. Name this channel, `Transaction from SunsetBank_Inc to BigBank_Co via HTTP`, as shown in Figure 7.11. The next steps deal with creating the channel.

FIGURE 7.11
The Channel Properties dialog.

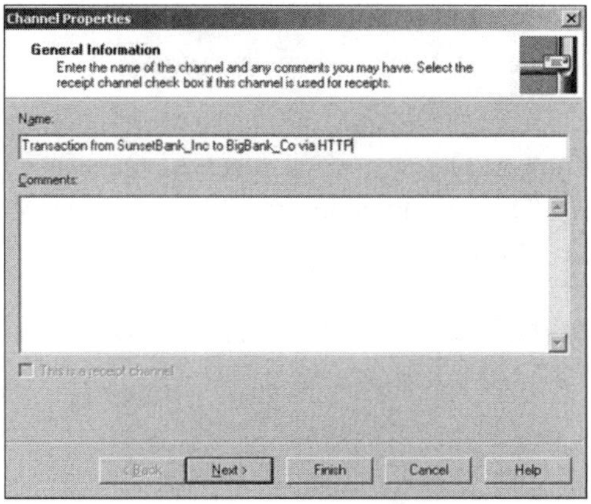

The Organization you are going to choose in the Source Organization section is Sunset Bank, so the Organization identifier will be Sunset Bank. At this point, we are not going to worry about receipts, so leave the other check boxes unchecked. Click Next.

Here is where the work we did earlier with document definitions and maps pays off. In the Inbound Document section, click Browse and select `SunsetBank` as your Inbound Document Definition Name, as displayed in Figure 7.12, and then click Next.

FIGURE 7.12
The Inbound Document Channel Properties dialog.

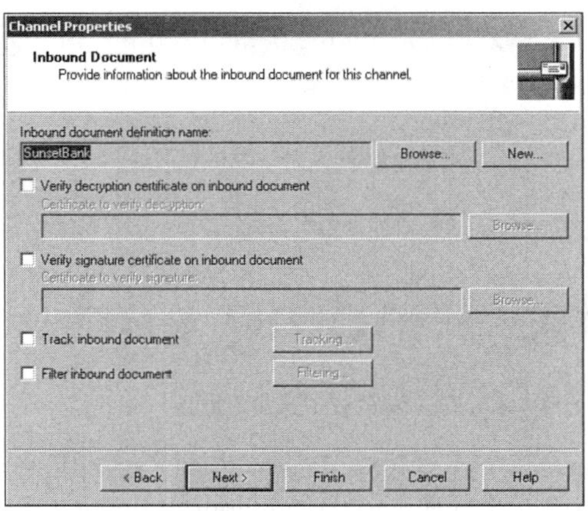

In the Outbound Document section, select `BigBank` as your Outbound Document Definition Name. Let's pause for a minute and figure out what we've just done. We've told BizTalk Server that the document coming into this channel will conform to the `SunsetBank` schema created earlier and that the output document will conform to the

`BigBank` schema. Now we need to tell BizTalk how to map the one to the other—that is, the Sunset Bank document to the Big Bank document format.

While still in the Outbound Document section, check the Map Inbound Document to Outbound Document check box and Browse to the location where you saved the map called `SunsetBanktoBigBank`. This should be located in your WebDAV directory. The Outbound Document Channel Properties dialog is displayed in Figure 7.13.

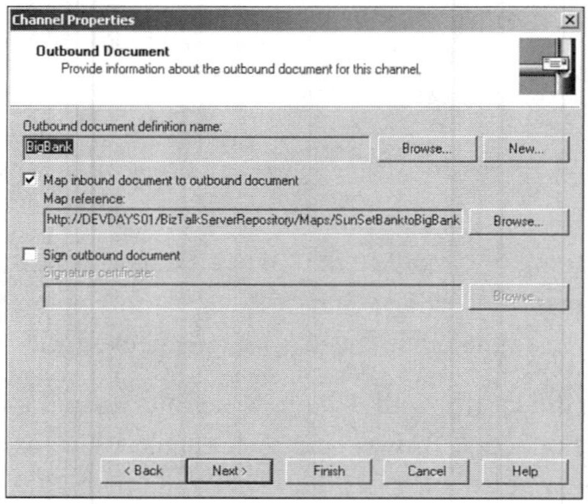

FIGURE 7.13
The Outbound Document Channel Properties dialog.

Continue moving through the wizard leaving the default settings through the remainder of the wizard steps. You can browse through them if you want to become more familiar with them or just click Finish. After you have created a messaging port, you can use it to create additional channels in the BizTalk Messaging Manager.

Congratulations! You are almost ready to submit a document to BizTalk Server 2002.

Creating the Sending and Receiving Applications

BizTalk Messaging is now ready to receive a document of a specific type from an application, transform it into another format, and pass it along to another application.

Now we need to modify and create the following three applications:

- Create an ASP application that will send the document from Sunset Bank, Inc., to Big Bank Co, `sendTrans.asp`.
- Modify the Big Bank Co.'s HTTP receive ASP page to receive the document coming from Sunset Bank, Inc., and submit it to BizTalk, `receiveTrans.asp`.

- Create the application that will receive the final document from BizTalk and process it according to ordinary business rules, `getTrans.asp`.

Working with the Code—`sendTrans.asp`

Let's begin. First, develop the ASP file that will send the XML file from Sunset Bank, Inc., to Big Bank Co. Call this ASP `sendTrans.asp` (see Listing 7.4).

LISTING 7.4 `sendTrans.asp`

```
  <%@ Language = "JavaScript" %>
  <%
  var xDoc = Server.CreateObject("Msxml2.FreeThreadedDOMDocument.3.0");
  xDoc.async = false;
  xDoc.load (Server.MapPath("../documents/sunsetbankinstance.xml"));
  var xHttp = Server.CreateCbject("Msxml2.XMLHTTP");
  xHttp.open ("POST", "http://localhost/BigBank_Co/application_
➥/receiveTrans.asp", false);
  xHttp.send (xDoc.xml);
  Response.Write (xHttp.responseText);
%>
```


Save this file to your `application` folder under `\SunsetBank_Inc`, in your `wwwroot` directory—for example, `c:\inetpub\wwwroot\SunsetBank_Inc\application\sendTrans.asp`. The primary purpose of this ASP file is to load an XML file representing financial data about transactions that occurred on a given day and submitting them via HTTP to an ASP file at Big Bank Co. In this application, the line, `xDoc.load (Server.MapPath("../documents/sunsetbankinstance.xml"));`loads the XML transaction (which will be reviewed next and can be manipulated in Notepad), whereas lines, `xHttp.open ("POST", "http://localhost/BigBank_Co/application/receiveTrans.asp", false);` and `xHttp.send (xDoc.xml);` are responsible for actually sending the document. The line, `Response.Write (xHttp.responseText);` asks that the response be sent back to the client with information regarding the success or failure of the transmission.

You need to save the following XML file as shown in Listing 7.5 to the `documents` folder under `\SunsetBanks_Inc`. This document, again, represents the actual data that you will be submitting to BizTalk Server. It can be manipulated in Notepad, if you want to manipulate the names, ids, account numbers, and so on. It is a basic syntax, but hopefully detailed enough to help you understand the inner workings of BizTalk.

LISTING 7.5 SunSetInstance.xml

```
<?xml version="1.0" encoding="utf-8" ?>
<Transactions>
<Transaction id="ABC-008">
<Account name="Jason Jones" number="159599" />
<Amount>-51.50</Amount>
<Type>ATM</Type>
<Facility>Sunset Bank, East</Facility>
<Location>
<Name>Sunset Bank</Name>
<Address>12121 Walker Dr., VA 55555</Address>
</Location>
</Transaction>
<Transaction id="ABC-009">
<Account name="Jane Smith" number="177589" />
<Amount>-12.50</Amount>
<Type>ATM</Type>
<Facility>Sunset Bank, East</Facility>
<Location>
<Name>Sunset Bank</Name>
<Address>12121 Walker Dr., VA 55555</Address>
</Location>
</Transaction>
</Transactions>
```

Again, the purpose of this document is simply to act as a data stream that will be sent from Sunset Bank to Big Bank.

Working with the Code—`receiveTrans.asp`

Now that we have an application that is sending data in XML to Big Bank, Inc., we need to modify the BizTalk HTTP receive ASP page that receives the data and submits it to BizTalk Server. This page ships with BizTalk and can be modified for each of our member banks. Listing 7.6 shows the code.

LISTING 7.6 receiveTrans.asp

```
<%@ Language = "JavaScript" %>
<%
var xmlTrans = Server.CreateObject("Msxml2.FreeThreadedDOMDocument.3.0");
xmlTrans.async = false;
xmlTrans.load (Request);
var strTrans = String(xmlTrans.xml);
var objInterchange = Server.CreateObject("BizTalk.Interchange");
```

LISTING 7.6 continued

```
  var strOpenType = "BIZTALK_OPENNESS_TYPE_NOTOPEN";
  var strHandle = objInterchange.submit (1, strTrans, "", "", "", +
      + "", "", "Transaction from SunsetBank_Inc to BigBank_Co via HTTP");
Response.Write ("Success: " + strHandle);
 %>
```

Save this file to your `application` folder under `\BigBank_Co`, in your `wwwroot` directory—for example, `c:\inetpub\wwwroot\BigBank_CO\application\receiveTrans.asp`.

In `receiveTrans.asp`, at line, `xmlTrans.load (Request);`, the XML document sent from `sendTrans.asp` is loaded into the DOM. The goal at this point is simply to take this XML and submit it to BizTalk. This occurs at the `var strHandle = objInterchange.submit (1, strTrans, "", "", "", + + "", "", "Transaction from SunsetBank_Inc to BigBank_Co via HTTP");` line. However, let's first look at the `var objInterchange = Server.CreateObject("BizTalk.Interchange");` line. Here we instantiate the `BizTalk.Interchange` object, which allows us to use a `submit` method to exchange documents with BizTalk Server. When we call the `submit` method, we have to supply a few parameters.

First is the `BIZTALK_OPENNESS_TYPE` enumeration. This value indicates whether the associated `BizTalkChannel` or `Port` objects are open. The enumeration values for the parameter are

- `BIZTALK_OPENNESS_TYPE_NOTOPEN`—This specifies that the instance of the `BizTalkPort` is not open.
- `BIZTALK_OPENNESS_TYPE_SOURCE`—Indicates that the source organization of the `BizTalkPort` is open.
- `BIZTALK_OPENNESS_TYPE_DESTINATION`—Specifies that the destination organization of this instance of the `BizTalkPort` is open.

In this case, we are passing the parameter that tells BizTalk Server that the associated `BizTalkPorts` cannot open. The next parameter represents the XML document as a string. This is the literal data that BizTalk has to preserve and pass along to the waiting application. Finally, we pass the name of the channel that processes the document. And that's it! From this point on, BizTalk Server handles the rest.

Of course, you can do more with this object, but this shows how easy it can be to get BizTalk working almost immediately in a B2B or A2A type solution.

This completes our assignment for getting data into BizTalk, and we have configured BizTalk to transform the data. Now we need to see how to get information out of BizTalk. It's really simple—which is the best part about all this.

Working with the Code—`getTrans.asp`

The final step in the application is to show you how to get data out of BizTalk and into your application. Listing 7.7 shows the code.

LISTING 7.7 `getTrans.asp`

```
<%@ Language = "JavaScript" %>
<%
var xRequest = Server.CreateObject("Msxml2.FreeThreadedDOMDocument.3.0");
xRequest.async = false;
xRequest.load (Request);
xRequest.save (Server.MapPath("../documents/test.xml"));
%>
```

Save this file to your `application` folder under `\BigBank_Co`, in your `wwwroot` directory—for example, `c:\inetpub\wwwroot\BigBank_CO\application\getTrans.asp`.

To run the application, browse to and run the `c:\inetpub\wwwroot\SunSetBank_Inc\application\sendTrans.asp` page using an Internet browser. If the application runs successfully, you should see an XML document named `text.xml` in the directory `c:\inetpub\wwwroot\BigBank_CO\documents`.

That's it. Again, you can make this infinitely more complex if you want, but the great part about this is its simplicity. All the files we are working with are even in the same working directory.

All we do here is accept the `request` object and the XML data and load it into the DOM. From this point on, we could

- Load the data into a SQL database.
- Parse out particular pieces of the XML, submit them in an e-mail to management, and save all the XML to the file system.
- Parse out the XML and send parts to another application, while saving the rest to a database.

Of course, all we are doing in Line 6 is saving the XML to the file server, but the possibilities are endless.

Summary

This chapter introduced you to BizTalk messaging. The items covered in this chapter are fundamental to building robust applications with BizTalk Server. This chapter covered the creation of several organizations as well as how to add document definitions and envelopes to the Messaging Manager. The chapter also discussed how to configure a messaging port to route data to an application or organization. We discussed building a channel to get data from a source application (or organization), transforming it into the necessary format, and passing it to the correct port. Finally, you learned how to pull all these components together using a simple ASP page.

In the next chapter, you will begin to learn more about BizTalk document tracking. In Chapter 12, you will learn how to integrate additional flat file formats into your BizTalk solutions. Congratulations, you are well on your way to building your first BizTalk solution.

CHAPTER 8

Document Tracking

by Stephen Tranchida

In This Chapter

Building an industrial strength distributed system can be a daunting task. The challenge is even greater when the system involves communication between organizations with different data models and different platforms. BizTalk Server enables you to build these types of systems using a loosely coupled architecture based on document interchanges.

The tasks of monitoring, analyzing, and debugging a system of document interchanges poses a unique set of challenges. The system must provide a means of tracking information as it moves from a source to a destination. The system should also keep a record of the transactions that get processed. These relatively simple features can be surprisingly difficult and expensive to build when dealing with a multitier distributed system. Fortunately, the architects of BizTalk Server recognized the importance of these features and provided a powerful and easy-to-use solution in the form of BizTalk Document Tracking.

This chapter covers the BizTalk Document Tracking system in depth. After explaining what you can do with document tracking, we'll take a high-level tour of the entire BizTalk Document Tracking System. Next, we anticipate that many readers have real-world application integration scenarios on the horizon that would benefit from BizTalk Document Tracking. With this in mind, we will explain how to properly plan for the use of BizTalk Document Tracking in the early stages of a development cycle. As you will see, there are some important scalability issues to consider when planning to use the document tracking system. Following the planning phase comes "the good stuff." We will cover how to configure and administer BizTalk Document Tracking through the various tools that expose tracking settings. After you know how to configure BizTalk Document Tracking, you will learn how to query and view tracking data using the tracking viewer provided with BizTalk Server. In case your system has some specialized tracking requirements, we will also cover how to build customized tracking solutions.

Understanding Document Tracking

Before discussing what you can do with document tracking, it is useful to have a conceptual understanding of how document tracking is implemented in BizTalk Server. The goal of this section is to provide a high-level introduction to the BizTalk Server Document Tracking System.

The Tracking Data Storage and Retrieval System

At the heart of BizTalk Document Tracking is a SQL Server database—called InterchangeDTA by default—where information about documents that have been processed by BizTalk Server is stored. As documents move through BizTalk Server, document data is stored to the InterchangeDTA database by the tracking engine.

All databases have two primary activities: data storage and data retrieval. Your document tracking tasks can therefore be summarized as follows:

- Configuring what document data goes into the InterchangeDTA database
- Configuring queries to retrieve tracking information from the InterchangeDTA database

Configuring the BizTalk Document Tracking system does not require that a single line of code be written. It is simply a matter of using the various graphical tools and dialog boxes provided by BizTalk Server. If you are disappointed by the lack of coding required, then you will be happy to hear that the BizTalk Document Tracking solution is wide open for extension. You can access the tracking database through Microsoft SQL Server Enterprise Manager in the same manner that you access any other SQL Server database. This means that you can design and write custom queries against the tracking database. BizTalk Server even exposes COM interfaces that allow you to configure and extend the tracking system. The topic of writing custom code for tracking is covered in "Developing Custom Tracking Solutions" later in this chapter.

What Is Stored by the Tracking System

The unit of work in BizTalk Server is the *interchange*. An interchange consists of the transmission of a document (or several documents packaged together) from one location to another. It should therefore come as no surprise that the primary job of BizTalk tracking is to capture information about interchanges. When the tools provided by BizTalk Server are used to query for tracking data, the result of these queries is always a set of interchanges.

At the highest level, BizTalk Server categorizes an interchange as either an inbound or outbound interchange. Inbound interchanges are documents that have been submitted to BizTalk Server for processing. Outbound interchanges are made up of documents that are leaving the BizTalk messaging system and are on their way to an external destination. The direction of an interchange (inbound or outbound) affects how it is logged by the tracking system.

BizTalk Server stores metadata about interchanges including the organizations involved, processing date and time stamps, and routing information. Specific field values within a document can be selected for tracking. Entire copies of documents can be maintained by the tracking database. If a document is transformed between formats during BizTalk Server processing, you can specify which of the formats to save for tracking purposes.

XML: The Key to BizTalk Document Tracking

You have already learned that all documents processed by BizTalk Server must contain well-formed XML. Documents may be submitted to BizTalk Server in formats other than XML, and documents may leave BizTalk Server in non-XML formats. Nevertheless, while the BizTalk Messaging Engine is processing a document, it requires the document to be in XML format.

There are many reasons why BizTalk Server mandates the use of XML within server boundaries. From the perspective of document tracking, the use of XML allows the tracking engine to parse documents and selectively extract data from the documents. Without having the documents in a standard format such as XML, there would be no way for BizTalk Server to understand enough about the documents to track data at the field level, and there would be no way for you to selectively configure which fields are tracked.

Document Processing Revisited

As mentioned earlier, BizTalk Server can retain entire copies of documents as they move through the server. To understand the capabilities of full document tracking, it is useful to review the stages that a non-XML document goes through during its journey through BizTalk Server.

When a document is submitted to BizTalk Server, it is placed in the work items queue. Placing inbound documents in a work items queue represents a form of load balancing, where the least busy server in your server group processes the inbound document. When the BizTalk Messaging Engine picks up the document, information about the inbound interchange is logged to the tracking database. One of the first steps in processing an inbound document is to check whether it is encrypted or encoded. BizTalk Document Tracking allows you to save MIME-encoded documents to the tracking database in their original format. This is a configurable option that you administer through the BizTalk Server Group properties.

> **Note**
>
> You learn how to configure tracking settings for an entire server group in the next section.

After the document's security requirements have been handled, the document is examined for routing data. If routing information is found in the document instance, this information is logged to the BizTalk Tracking database. Routing data may be specified in the document itself as well as in a receive function or through the parameters specified in `IInterchange::Submit()`. When routing data is specified in multiple locations, it is important to understand that the tracking engine will log the routing information specified in the document instance. The messaging engine may route the document based on the information specified in the receive function or the `IInterchange::Submit()` call, but the document's internal routing information is tracked.

A parser is then selected based on the metadata contained in the document's envelope. The job of a parser is to read the inbound document and transform it into XML format so that the BizTalk Messaging Engine can process the document. The parser may also save details about the inbound document to the tracking database.

Besides recording field-level data, you have the option to save the full document, in its original format, to the tracking database. After the document has been transformed into XML, BizTalk Server can once again save the entire inbound document (in its intermediate XML format) to the tracking database.

Tip

Having the inbound intermediate XML format saved to the tracking database can be useful for debugging, especially if you have written a custom parser that is not yet production ready.

Next, a channel is selected to process the document. Typical channel processing includes transforming the inbound document to another intermediate XML format. The resulting XML document complies with a BizTalk specification associated with the outbound document. BizTalk Server can save a copy of the outbound document, in XML format, to the tracking database.

The final steps are serialization and delivery. The outbound XML document is serialized to the native format expected by the recipient. After serialization has been completed, you may store the document in its native format to the tracking database. Routing information associated with the outbound interchange is logged for tracking purposes. For outbound interchanges, the tracking engine always logs the routing information contained in the channel.

As you can see, a lot of activity can be recorded by the document tracking engine during an interchange. BizTalk Document Tracking can be a valuable tool for understanding the stages that a document has passed through during its journey through BizTalk Server. Best of all, the logging details are fully configurable through a few simple dialog boxes.

Server Group Tracking Settings

BizTalk Server tracking settings can be configured at three basic levels:

- The server group level
- The document definition level
- The channel level

This section discusses the tracking settings that can be configured at the server group level. Later in the chapter, we will cover document definition and channel tracking settings.

Configuring the Document Tracking and Activity (DTA) Database

All servers in a BizTalk Server group share certain properties relating to the document tracking system. The most obvious of these properties is the tracking database itself. A server group shares one document tracking database that is specified as part of the server group properties.

Server groups are configured and managed through the BizTalk Server Administration tool, shown in Figure 8.1. The tool is located in the Microsoft BizTalk Server 2002 program group.

> **Tip**
>
> You can add the BizTalk Server Administration tool to an existing Microsoft Management Console file if the file is configured to allow authoring. If available, select the Add/Remove Snap-in option from the Console menu, click the Add button, and select Microsoft BizTalk Server Administration from the list of snap-ins.

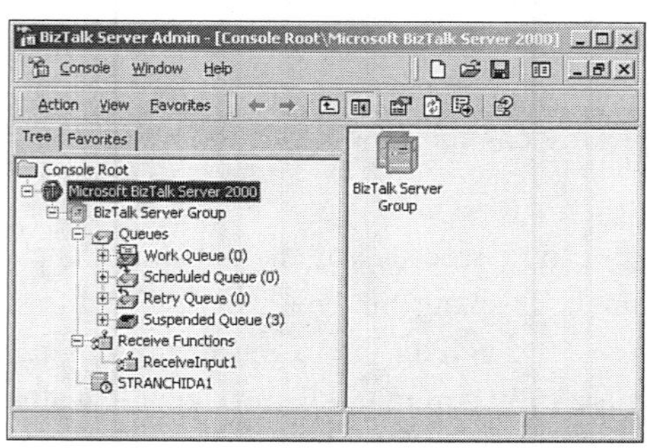

FIGURE 8.1
The BizTalk Server Administration tool.

To view the properties of a BizTalk Server group, right-click on the server group and select Properties. A dialog box appears with four tabs labeled General, Connection, Tracking, and Parsers. The first tab that is relevant to tracking is the Connection tab, displayed in Figure 8.2. This tab contains a group box labeled Tracking Database. Within this group box are controls for specifying the name, location, and security credentials for the document tracking database.

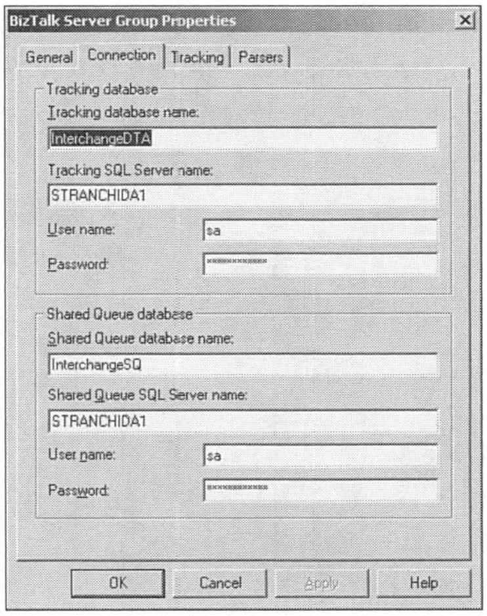

FIGURE 8.2
The Connection tab of the Server Group Properties dialog box.

Connection settings are intended to be configured during the initial setup of BizTalk Server. If you need to modify these settings, you should first stop all servers in the group. To stop a server, right-click on the server name under the BizTalk Server group and choose Stop. After you have finished editing the database connection information, restart each server by right-clicking on the server name and choosing Start.

Also be aware of the following issues when editing the tracking database server and name:

- The target database must already exist. The tracking database must be created *before* you attempt to change the database name in the Server Group Properties dialog box.
- When applying changes, a warning may appear stating that you need to shut down the BizTalk Server Interchange Application on all servers in the group before your changes will take effect. If you have already stopped all the servers in your group, then this warning can be safely ignored. When you restart the servers, the new tracking database settings will automatically take effect.

- BizTalk Server will not automatically transfer existing tracking data from the original database to the new database. To move the tracking database from one server to another, you must back it up, restore it on the new server, and then follow the previous instructions for changing the connection settings in the Server Group Properties dialog box.

Additional Server Group Tracking Settings

The Server Group Properties dialog box contains a Tracking tab. Clicking on this tab causes the screen shown in Figure 8.3 to be displayed. The tab contains four check boxes for configuring tracking settings at the server group level.

FIGURE 8.3
The Tracking tab of the Server Group Properties dialog box.

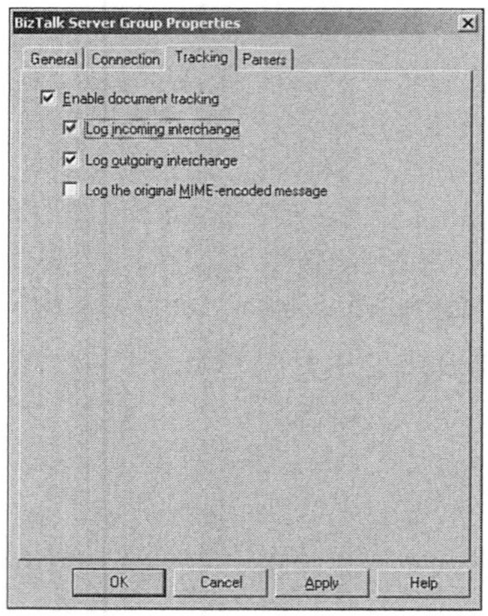

Enabling or Disabling Document Tracking

Although it is useful, document tracking adds overhead to BizTalk Server processing and can dramatically increase disk space requirements. Therefore, BizTalk Server allows you to enable or disable the entire tracking system through the Enable Document Tracking check box. Clearing this box means that tracking is turned off for the selected server group. When the Enable Document Tracking check box is cleared, all other check boxes on the Tracking tab become disabled.

> **Note**
>
> When you toggle tracking on or off, it is a good idea to restart the servers using the BizTalk Server Administration tool. Otherwise, it is possible that new settings may fail to take effect immediately.

Log Incoming/Outgoing Interchange Options

The Tracking configuration tab contains the Log Incoming Interchange and Log Outgoing Interchange check boxes. Despite their labels, these check boxes do not translate directly into turning inbound and outbound interchange logging on and off. Instead, they control whether full copies of inbound and outbound documents are stored in the tracking database. Enabling both options causes the tracking system to store full copies of inbound and outbound documents. You may need to adjust these settings if, for example, you expect large inbound documents but much smaller outbound documents. In this case, it might make sense to only retain copies of the outbound documents. BizTalk Server will still generate a record of the inbound interchange, but it won't save a copy of the document.

Logging MIME-Encoded Messages

BizTalk Server contains built-in support for MIME-encoded messages. MIME is a W3C-approved standard for including multiple objects in a single message and to represent the body of a message in character sets other than US-ASCII. The MIME specification is published as RFC-1521.

You can configure BizTalk Server Document Tracking so that MIME-encoded documents are stored to the tracking database in their original format before decoding takes place. This behavior is controlled through the Log the Original MIME-Encoded Message check box.

Planning to Use the Tracking System

At this point, you have gained an understanding of how the BizTalk Document Tracking System operates. The next step is to prepare for using it in a real-world system. This section presents some common usage scenarios for the document tracking system. You will learn that document tracking can fulfill some critical system requirements, such as record keeping, analysis, and even data recovery. On the other hand, you must also understand the impact of document tracking on system performance and scalability. We will discuss these issues and present some important information regarding document size constraints in the tracking system. Finally, we will reveal some steps that you can take when designing document specifications to facilitate field-level tracking of instance documents.

Usage Scenarios for Document Tracking

The BizTalk Server Document Tracking System is an invaluable tool for both developers and managers. Developers appreciate the value of document tracking for testing and debugging. Managers appreciate the tracking system because it often satisfies important business requirements for record keeping and auditing. The tracking system can help to resolve customer inquiries or disputes regarding "missing" documents. You can use the tracking system to satisfy contractual requirements, which may stipulate that copies of all transmitted data must be kept in an archive.

The tracking database can also be used to help analyze your business. For example, if your system is responsible for sending invoices, you can configure BizTalk Server to store the amount of each invoice transmitted to a customer. Armed with this information, you can write queries and build reports that calculate the total monetary value of invoices sent in a given time period to each customer.

There are also some less obvious ways to leverage document tracking. For instance, BizTalk Server allows you to submit documents programmatically using the `IInterchange::Submit()` API. When you submit documents in this fashion, there is no way for BizTalk Server to send the caller a response document, even if the caller explicitly requests a response. The good news is that a response document is actually generated and saved to the tracking database—it's just not delivered to the caller. You can save the submission handle returned by the call to `IInterchange::Submit()` and then use this handle to query the tracking database for the response document. This process can easily be automated by passing the submission handle to the API exposed by the tracking system.

The Effects of Tracking on Scalability and Performance

The critical factor in determining whether your system can take advantage of BizTalk Document Tracking is the anticipated size of documents to be processed by the server. Microsoft has stated that the maximum supported size of a document during any portion of an interchange is 20 MB. This is the threshold for BizTalk Server Document Tracking. If you anticipate having to process documents that exceed this size constraint, then you should disable document tracking in the server group properties.

Caution

Remember that BizTalk Server creates intermediate UNICODE XML representations of all files processed by the messaging engine. This UNICODE XML representation must also adhere to the 20 MB size constraint. Non-XML formats such as flatfiles and EDI files may double or even triple in size when transformed into a UNICODE XML format. This means that these documents should not exceed 7-10 MB in their native format.

Provided that your document sizes fall within the acceptable range, take steps to ensure that the tracking system does not become the major bottleneck of your system. Install the tracking database on a separate server from your other BizTalk databases and make sure that there is adequate disk space. You should also have an archiving strategy for the tracking database. Depending on the expected volume of interchanges, plan to move data from the primary tracking database to a permanent archive on a regular basis. Tracking database maintenance is discussed in "Maintaining the Tracking Database" later in this chapter.

Preparing BizTalk Specifications for Tracking

One of the first development tasks in a BizTalk Server system implementation is to define specifications for all documents that will pass through BizTalk Server. The vocabulary for these specifications is a superset of Microsoft's XML Data Reduced (XDR) schema dialect. From a programming perspective, an attractive feature of the XDR vocabulary is its capability to associate data types with elements and attributes. Disciplined programmers are well aware of the importance of strong data typing. Data type enforcement helps catch erroneous data and allows compilers to allocate the appropriate amount of memory for data. As it turns out, specifying data types in BizTalk document specifications is equally important to the document tracking system.

It is easy to understand why the document tracking system requires knowledge of data types. Tracking data is stored in an SQL Server database, and all fields in an SQL database expect a specific data type. When you assign a data type to a value in a BizTalk specification, the tracking engine can store that value in the proper database field.

Of course it is possible to convert a value found in a BizTalk document to a generic data type such as a string value. In fact, this is what happens in the tracking system when you do not specify data types in a specification. Typeless data selected for tracking is merged into an XML text field, which you must parse to extract a single field.

For each specification, BizTalk Server allows you to select up to two fields of the same data type for tracking in a strongly typed fashion. Additional fields of the same data type must be tracked together in an XML tree. Nevertheless, the specification writer may not know in advance which records will be tracked, so it is a good idea to specify data types for all fields in a specification.

The limitation of two fields per data type is a design choice based on the fact that a database field must be reserved for each strongly typed value. The tracking database reserves two fields per data type. Allowing more than two values of the same data type would require more database fields, which could be wasteful in terms of space.

Another limitation of strongly typed tracking is that the BizTalk Editor does not allow you to set data types on records (elements). You can only assign data types to fields (attributes). If you use the ActiveX Data Objects (ADO) library or SQL Server 2000 to turn recordsets into XML, fields are converted to attributes by default. Thankfully, you can strongly type these attributes using the BizTalk Editor.

Tip

XDR allows you to assign data types to either elements or attributes, it is only the BizTalk Editor that has the element constraint. This means that you can edit BizTalk specifications by hand to assign data types to elements.

Configuring Tracking in BizTalk Messaging Manager

Earlier you learned that BizTalk Document Tracking can be configured at three basic levels: the server group level, document definition level, and channel level. This section examines how to configure tracking at the document definition and channel levels.

Global Tracking Settings

When you create a specification using the BizTalk Editor (or by hand), you typically create a corresponding document definition in the BizTalk Messaging Manager. The abstraction of a document definition allows you to create multiple definitions that correspond to the same specification.

A set of properties associated with a document definition are used to control the behavior of document tracking. These properties are referred to as *global tracking settings* because they apply to every instance document processed by BizTalk Server that conforms to a particular document definition.

To configure global tracking settings, select the Global Tracking tab on the Document Definition Properties dialog box (see Figure 8.4).

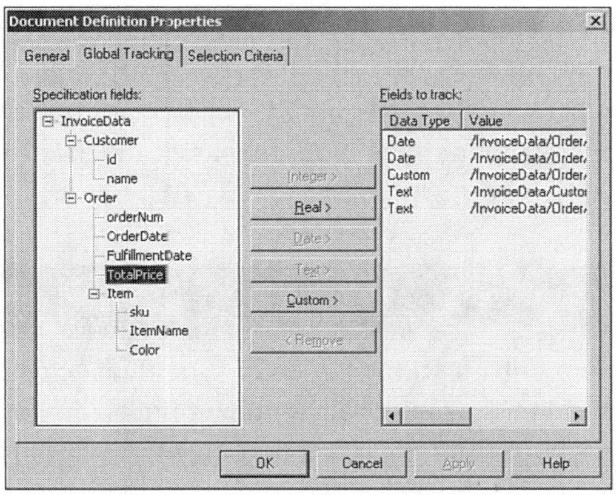

FIGURE 8.4
Configuring global tracking settings.

The Global Tracking tab contains two large view panes with option buttons in the middle. The view pane on the left is a tree view representing the document specification. You can use the tree view to navigate through a specification and select fields to track. The view on the right is a grid control containing the fields selected for tracking. The data type and XPath expression for each field are listed in this pane. No fields are selected for tracking by default.

To specify a field to be tracked, select the field from the tree view and click the button that corresponds to the data type of the selected field. This tells the tracking engine to save the field's value in a SQL Server field of the corresponding type. When you click the data type button, the field's type and XPath expression are added to the list on the right. To remove an entry from the list of tracked fields, simply select the row and click the Remove button.

Caution

A field's XPath expression cannot exceed 79 characters. If the XPath expression length exceeds this limit, it will be truncated and therefore not tracked. The 79-character limit applies only to fields tracked using a specific data type. Use the custom type (discussed later in this section) to track fields with long XPath expressions.

You may notice that after you have selected two fields of a particular data type for tracking, the button corresponding to that data type remains disabled, even if you select another field of the same data type. This is because you can only use a particular data type button to store a maximum of two fields to the tracking database. To select a third field of the same data type for tracking, you must use the Custom button.

When you choose a field for tracking via the Custom button, the value of this field is stored to the tracking database together will all other custom fields in the document as XML. Although you can select an unlimited number of fields for tracking in a custom fashion, keep in mind that it takes additional work to extract the data from the SQL Server field where it is stored.

Caution

There is a known problem with tracking fields of type `Number` using the `Integer` tracking type. The field value may exceed the maximum size allowed for an `Integer` value. If this happens, BizTalk Server generates a warning message. To avoid this issue, you may want to track large `Number` values using a custom field instead of an `Integer` field.

Channel Settings for Tracking

Tracking settings at the document definition level allow you to specify which fields are tracked in every document conforming to a particular specification—regardless of the processing that takes place on the document. Although useful, global tracking settings do not always provide enough control over document tracking. Consider the case of a large parts supplier receiving purchase orders via BizTalk Server. It is conceivable that the supplier does not carry a requested set of items. In these cases, the supplier forwards the purchase orders to an affiliate for fulfillment. The company wants to track the total monetary amount of each order forwarded to an affiliate. These types of scenarios require configuration of tracking settings at the channel level.

In the previous scenario, there would likely be distinct channels set up in BizTalk Messaging Manager for fulfilling a purchase order internally versus selecting an affiliate to fulfill the request. Each channel can have its own unique tracking settings.

Figure 8.5 shows the Channel Properties dialog box where tracking can be enabled or disabled for a channel. The dialog box is part of the Channel Wizard, which is used to create or edit a channel in BizTalk Messaging Manager.

FIGURE 8.5
Configuring tracking settings for a channel.

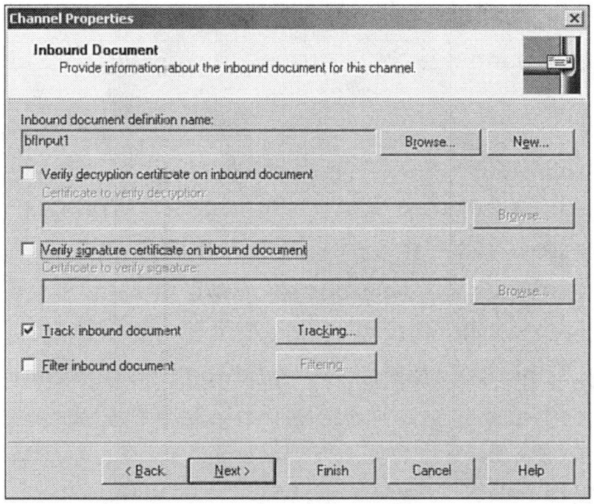

If you check the Track Inbound Document check box, then you will not be allowed to move forward or backward in the wizard without clicking on the Tracking button and selecting at least one field for tracking. When you click the Tracking button, the dialog box shown in Figure 8.6 opens. This dialog box is similar to the Global Tracking Settings dialog box (refer to Figure 8.4) except that an additional text box is displayed at the top. The additional text box is a read-only display of the global tracking settings that have been specified for the document definition.

FIGURE 8.6
Choosing fields to track for a channel.

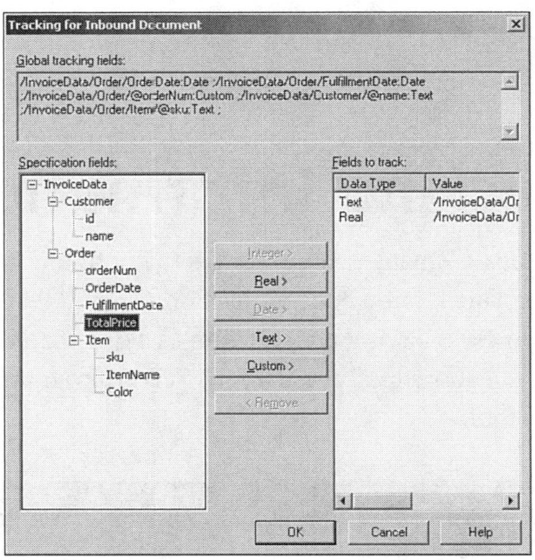

Tracking settings specified at the channel level override the settings specified at the document definition level. For example, if you have selected two text fields for tracking at the document definition level and select a third text field for tracking at the channel level, only the first text field specified at the document definition level will be tracked. The text field specified at the channel level overrides the second text field specified at the document definition level.

The field level channel settings provide a great deal of flexibility in tracking interchanges because they allow you to adjust tracking settings based on the processing that occurs on a document. BizTalk Server also offers this flexibility with regard to full document logging. The Channel Wizard provides a dialog box—shown in Figure 8.7—that allows you to adjust the document logging settings for a channel in a manner similar to the server group document logging settings. You can toggle inbound and outbound document logging for the native document formats and the intermediate XML representations.

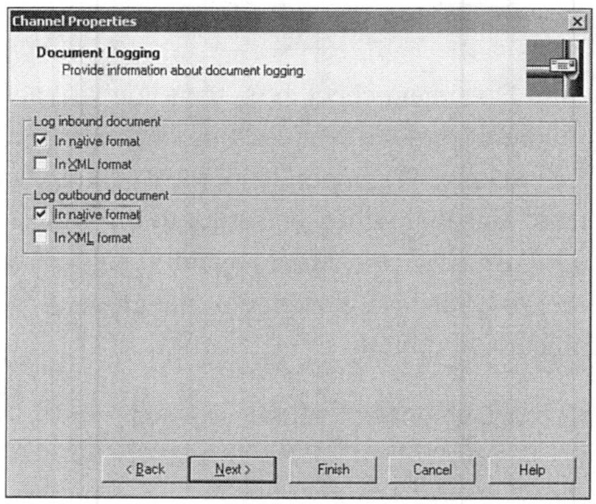

FIGURE 8.7
Document logging properties for a channel.

Viewing Tracking Information

Up to this point, we have discussed many different ways to configure the data that gets stored to the tracking system. This section concentrates on viewing that data. BizTalk Server provides an application for querying and viewing tracking data that you access via the BizTalk Document Tracking shortcut in the BizTalk Server program group. The following sections examine this tool.

> **Note**
>
> Throughout this section, we will often refer to the BizTalk Document Tracking application as the tracking data viewer.

You can build your own tracking data viewers using the COM interfaces for document tracking. The last section in this chapter covers programming with the tracking interfaces.

Overview of Tracking Tools

The tracking data viewer is a browser-based application driven by Microsoft Internet Information Server (IIS) and written using Active Server Pages (ASP). The tool requires Microsoft Internet Explorer version 5 or later. The browser-based interface offers the capability to query and view tracking data from remote locations without having to install a full-blown client application. As you will see, the tracking tool offers a rich user interface considering that it is browser-based. Microsoft has provided accessibility features, such as shortcut keys, for quick access to frequently used features.

Granting Permissions to Tracking Data

When you install BizTalk Server, a local user group named BizTalk Server Report Users is created. You must manually add users to this group to grant permission to the document tracking tool. To add users to the BizTalk Server Report Users group

1. Open the Computer Management console located in the Administrative Tools program group.
2. Under System Tools, expand the Local Users and Groups node and select the Groups folder. You should see a group called BizTalk Server Report Users.
3. Right-click on this group and select Add To Group. The dialog box shown in Figure 8.8 appears, allowing you to add and remove users from the group.

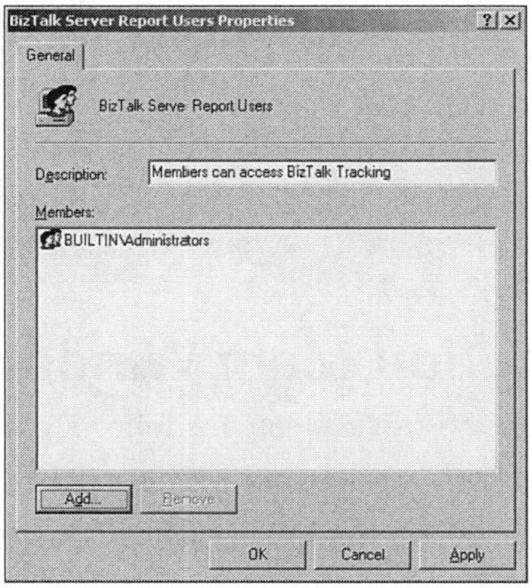

FIGURE 8.8
Granting permissions to the document tracking tool.

Running the Tracking Data Viewer for the First Time

When you launch the tracking data viewer for the first time, you may be prompted to allow installation of some components. The Document Tracking Application requires the Windows common controls and some specialized ActiveX controls. When all required components have been installed, the document tracking tool—shown in Figure 8.9—is displayed.

> **Note**
>
> The security features of Internet Explorer might trigger a message box to appear when opening or using the document tracking tool. The message asks whether you want to permit the Web page to access data on another domain. To avoid this message, add the URL for document tracking to the trusted sites list using Internet Explorer's security options.

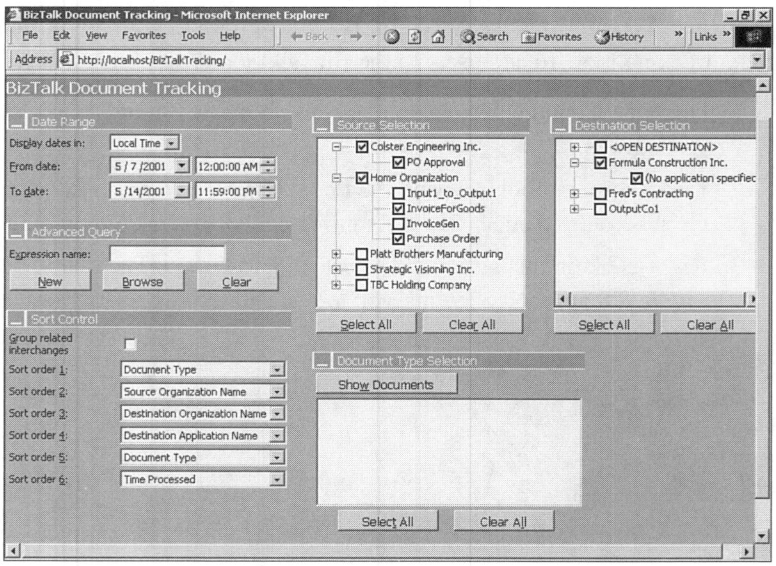

FIGURE 8.9
The BizTalk Server document tracking tool.

The Tracking Application Main Window

The "home page" for document tracking is divided into the following six areas (as shown in Figure 8.9), all of which are used to specify query parameters:

- Date Range—Allows the selection of a date range
- Source Selection—A list of organizations and associated applications that have been tracked during inbound interchanges

- Destination Selection—A list of organizations and associated applications that have been tracked during outbound interchanges
- Sort Control—Options for grouping and sorting the interchanges that are returned by the query
- Document Type Selection—A list of document types that have been tracked during interchanges
- Advanced Query—Advanced querying options

Tip

You can choose to show or hide each of the six groups of controls by clicking on the box next to the group heading.

The top-left portion of the page (shown in Figure 8.9) contains a set of controls for choosing a date/time range. Date/time values are saved to the tracking database in Universal Coordinated Time (UTC), also referred to as Greenwich Mean Time (GMT). When you search the tracking database for a particular time range, you need to specify whether your lower and upper date/time boundaries should be interpreted as local time or universal time. The Display Dates In drop-down list box is used for this purpose. This list box also controls the way that date/time values are displayed in the query results.

The Source Selection and Destination Selection controls are used to select the applications that you want to include in your search. For convenience, the application names are listed under their associated organizations.

Note

Remember that application names are specified as part of the Channel Wizard.

When an organization contains only one application, unchecking the application causes the associated organization to be unchecked, and vice versa. When an organization is not selected, checking it causes all applications for that organization to become checked. You can use the Select All and Clear All buttons as shortcuts for selecting or deselecting all applications in the list.

You can use the Sort Control options to specify how interchange results are grouped and sorted. You may specify up to six levels of sorting, with the following fields available at each level:

- Source Organization Name
- Source Application Name
- Destination Organization Name
- Destination Application Name
- Document Type
- Time Processed

Checking the Group Related Interchanges check box causes interchanges with the same properties to be listed consecutively. When grouping is enabled, the selected sorting options are applied within each group.

The Document Type Selection area displays a list of available documents that you can include in queries. The list is empty by default. To display all available documents, click the Show Documents button. After a document appears in the list, you may select it so that the query will retrieve documents of this type.

The final set of controls allows you to configure advanced queries. Because you are probably anxious to run some queries and examine the results, we will discuss advanced queries later in the chapter.

Running a Query and Viewing Results

When you have finished configuring query parameters, click the Query button to execute the search. A new Internet Explorer pop-up window similar to the one shown in Figure 8.10 appears with the query results.

The Query Results page holds a significant amount of information and functionality. The first thing to notice is that it scrolls horizontally to reveal many more fields than fit in the window space. The page displays 15 rows at a time, and each row represents an interchange processed by the BizTalk Server Messaging Engine. A record navigation control is provided in the bottom left portion of the page. Arrows with a line next to them allow you to jump to the first or last set of records in the resultset. Arrows without the line can be used to navigate forward or backward through the resultset, 15 rows at a time.

You can review the query parameters used to generate the resultset by clicking the box next to the Search Parameters label. This box toggles the search parameters display on or off as you click it (see Figure 8.11).

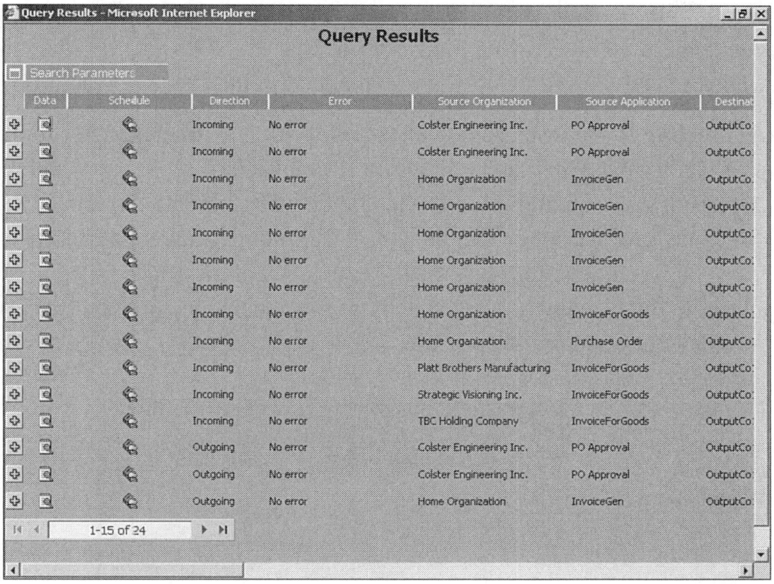

FIGURE 8.10
The Query Results page.

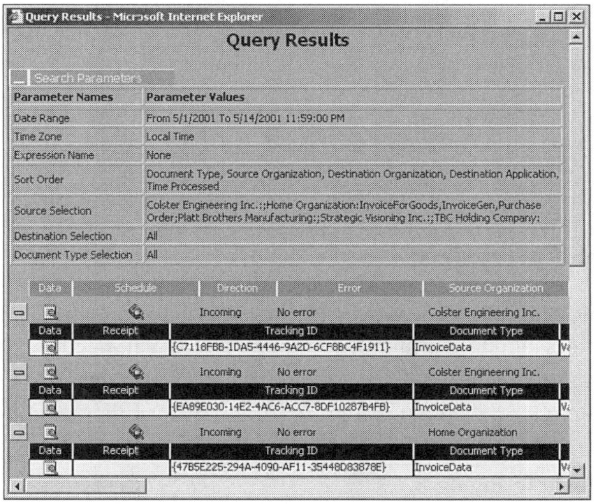

FIGURE 8.11
The Query Results page with search parameters showing.

Figure 8.11 also displays another feature of the Query Results page. Clicking on the plus sign at the left of each row causes the row to expand, displaying details about the document(s) involved in the interchange. The expanded portion of the row is itself a table of information. The table includes the unique tracking ID assigned to this document and any field values selected for tracking in the document definition or channel properties. If you configured any custom fields for tracking, the XML data containing the custom field values can be viewed by clicking on the icon in the Custom Search field.

A full copy of the instance document involved in an interchange can be viewed in native or XML format. Clicking on the Data icon launches a separate window that displays the document data and allows you to toggle between formats. Figure 8.12 shows this window. The Save As button can be used to store the document to disk as a file. This illustrates one technique for retrieving documents that may have failed to be delivered due to an error. You can always view a copy of the document using the tracking data viewer and save this copy as a standalone file.

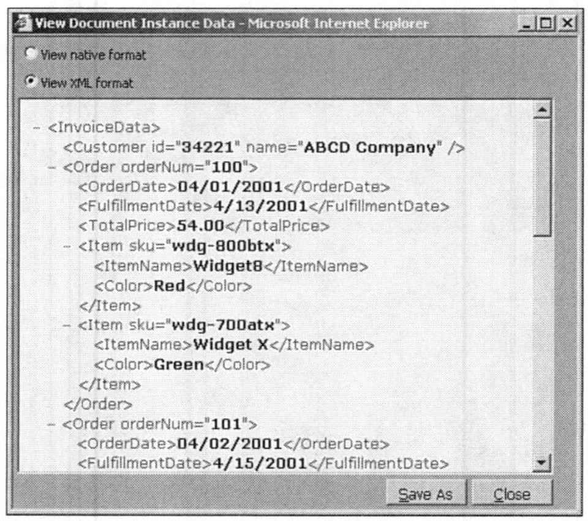

FIGURE 8.12
Viewing document instance data through the tracking tool.

Advanced Queries

The core set of query parameters offered by the document tracking tool allows you to perform basic filtering and sorting of tracking data. If you need to perform more advanced analysis, you need to use the Advanced Query Builder. The Document Tracking Tool main window contains a group of controls with a heading labeled Advanced Query. Clicking the New button or pressing Alt+N loads the Advanced Query Builder, shown in Figure 8.13.

The Advanced Query Builder allows you to select individual fields and perform logical operations on those fields using the Operators drop-down list box. The logical operations that you specify cause additional filtering to take place during the query. For example, you can configure a query to return only those interchanges where the total amount of a purchase order is greater than $5,000. The available operators are greater than (>), less than (<), equality (=), and inequality (`!=`). Comparison values are entered into the Value edit box. Comparison values must be constants that conform to the data type of the selected field. For example, if you try to compare the value of a real number field to a string constant, the Query Builder will display an error.

FIGURE 8.13
The Advanced Query Builder.

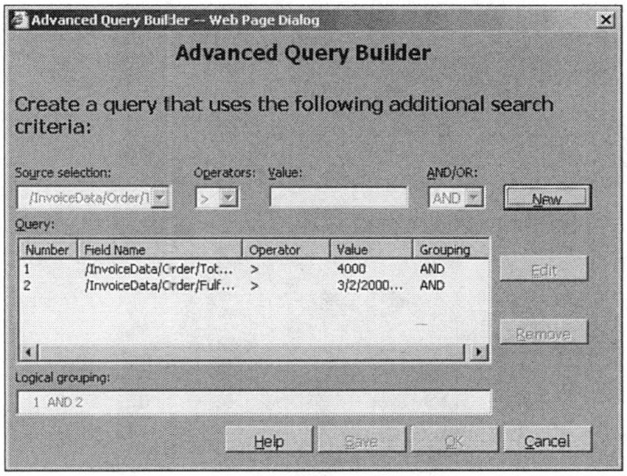

When you have finished selecting a field, logical operator, and constant value, click the Done button to add the clause to your query. You can specify multiple comparison clauses in the same query. Each clause is joined with the others using your choice of `AND`/`OR` operators. This allows the collective set of comparisons to evaluate to `True` or `False` when applied to an individual interchange.

Note

The entire set of comparisons specified for an advanced search is referred to as an *expression*.

The Logical Grouping box shows how the clauses are evaluated to come up with a single boolean value for the expression. To remove a clause from the expression, select the clause and click the Remove button.

Managing Advanced Queries

The BizTalk Server Document Tracking tool allows you to save advanced queries so that you are not forced to enter the same query expressions every time you need to execute a search. Clicking the Save button in the Advanced Query Builder window causes the dialog box shown in Figure 8.14 to appear, allowing you to specify a name for the query expression.

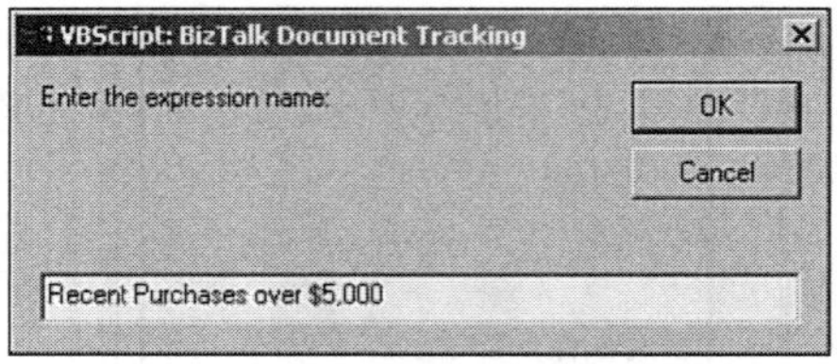

FIGURE 8.14
Assigning a name to an advanced query.

To retrieve the list of saved queries, click the Browse button in the Advanced Query section of the Document Tracking Tool main window. This invokes the screen shown in Figure 8.15, which allows you to manage saved queries.

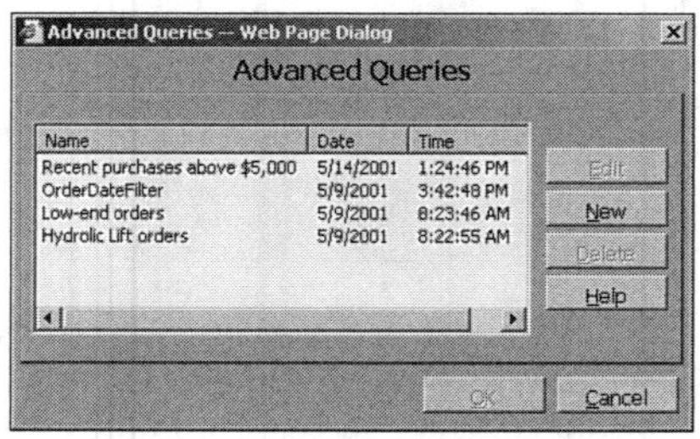

FIGURE 8.15
Managing saved queries.

Developing Custom Tracking Solutions

So far in this chapter you have been presented with a full tour of the document tracking system from the perspective of an end user. You are now armed with all the information that you need to perform the two primary tracking activities: configuring tracking settings and viewing tracking data. The remainder of this chapter introduces the topic of building customized tracking solutions using the infrastructure provided by BizTalk Server. We begin by covering the tracking database, including the core tables where interchange data, document data, and routing data is stored. Our database discussion also includes some tips on keeping the database size from growing too large. Finally, we discuss the COM interfaces that can be used to build custom tracking solutions and provide an example to complement the discussion.

The Document Tracking Database

The document tracking database ships with 23 tables and 49 stored procedures. Figure 8.16 shows the most important tables and their relationships with one another.

FIGURE 8.16
Core document tracking database tables.

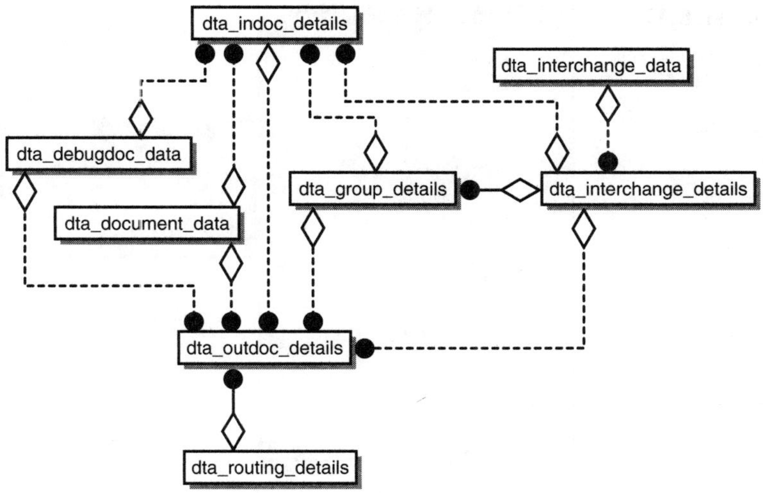

A solid black circle connected to a table name indicates a foreign key relationship. For example, the `dta_outdoc_details` table is showing six foreign keys. Its relationship to the `dta_document_data` table is one-to-one, whereas its other relationships are many-to-one.

A closer look at the core tables reveals the following three classes of information:

- Interchange data
- Document data
- Routing data

The tables associated with each type of information are introduced in the following sections.

Tables Containing Interchange Data

Interchange data is captured in two tables named `dta_interchange_data` and `dta_interchange_details` (shown in Figure 8.17). Both tables contain one record for every inbound and outbound interchange. Data specific to an interchange is stored in binary format in the `imgInterchangeData` field of `dta_interchange_data`. The `nBLOBType` field indicates the format of the data in the `imgInterchangeData` field. A value of one indicates that the data can be loaded using the MSXML `DOMDocument` object. `DTA_interchange_data` also contains the original filename submitted for inbound interchanges.

FIGURE 8.17
The dta_interchange_details *and* dta_interchange_data *tables.*

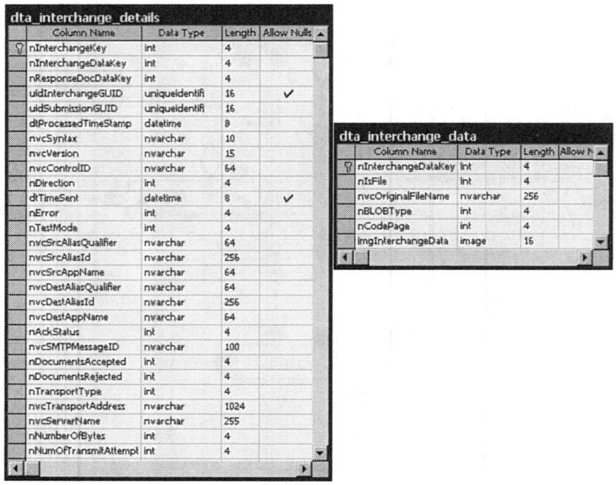

dta_interchange_details

Column Name	Data Type	Length	Allow Nulls
nInterchangeKey	int	4	
nInterchangeDataKey	int	4	
nResponseDocDataKey	int	4	
uidInterchangeGUID	uniqueidentifi	16	✓
uidSubmissionGUID	uniqueidentifi	16	
dtProcessedTimeStamp	datetime	8	
nvcSyntax	nvarchar	10	
nvcVersion	nvarchar	15	
nvcControlID	nvarchar	64	
nDirection	int	4	
dtTimeSent	datetime	8	✓
nError	int	4	
nTestMode	int	4	
nvcSrcAliasQualifier	nvarchar	64	
nvcSrcAliasId	nvarchar	256	
nvcSrcAppName	nvarchar	64	
nvcDestAliasQualifier	nvarchar	64	
nvcDestAliasId	nvarchar	256	
nvcDestAppName	nvarchar	64	
nAckStatus	int	4	
nvcSMTPMessageID	nvarchar	100	
nDocumentsAccepted	int	4	
nDocumentsRejected	int	4	
nTransportType	int	4	
nvcTransportAddress	nvarchar	1024	
nvcServerName	nvarchar	255	
nNumberOfBytes	int	4	
nNumOfTransmitAttempt	int	4	

dta_interchange_data

Column Name	Data Type	Length	Allow N
nInterchangeDataKey	int	4	
nIsFile	int	4	
nvcOriginalFileName	nvarchar	256	
nBLOBType	int	4	
nCodePage	int	4	
imgInterchangeData	image	16	

`DTA_interchange_details` identifies the direction of an interchange through the `nDirection` field. Zero indicates an outbound interchange, and one indicates an inbound interchange. The `DTA_interchange_details` table also includes date and time stamps for the interchange, information about the transmission protocol used, and any error information that may have been generated as a result of the interchange.

Tables Containing Document Data

The `dta_document_data` table serves as the master table for all instance document data. More specific information regarding inbound and outbound documents can be found in the `dta_indoc_details` and `dta_outdoc_details` tables, respectively. The `imgDocumentData` field of `dta_document_data` contains a full copy of documents processed by BizTalk Server. The `dta_outdoc_details` table contains two fields for each data type that may be present in a BizTalk specification. When you select specific fields for tracking using channel tracking settings, the values are stored to these fields. The `strCustomSearch` field stores all custom field values selected for tracking in a channel.

Tables Containing Routing Data

The `dta_routing_details` table (shown in Figure 8.18) serves as the central repository for routing information. The table captures the source and destination organization names, distribution list names, and channel and port references.

FIGURE 8.18
The `dta_routing_details` *table.*

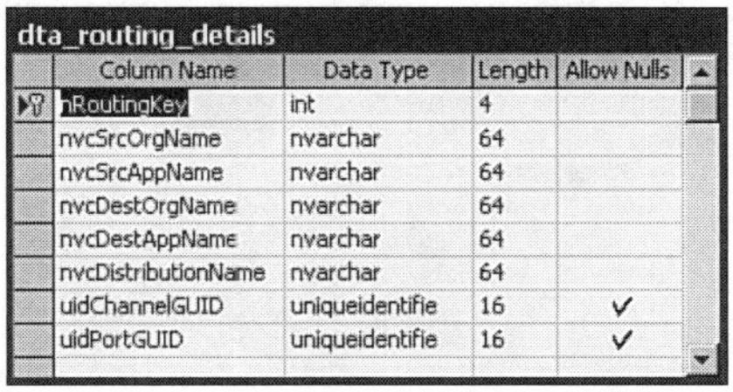

dta_routing_details

Column Name	Data Type	Length	Allow Nulls
nRoutingKey	int	4	
nvcSrcOrgName	nvarchar	64	
nvcSrcAppName	nvarchar	64	
nvcDestOrgName	nvarchar	64	
nvcDestAppName	nvarchar	64	
nvcDistributionName	nvarchar	64	
uidChannelGUID	uniqueidentifie	16	✓
uidPortGUID	uniqueidentifie	16	✓

Maintaining the Tracking Database

After you develop an understanding of the tracking database structure, consider developing an automated mechanism for purging the tracking database. One method of archiving the tracking database is to implement a SQL Server agent that runs at scheduled intervals. The agent can use SQL Server's data transformation services to transfer records from your production tracking database to an archive. After a set of records has been safely copied, you can delete them from the production database.

The BizTalk Server SDK includes a sample T-SQL script that sets up an agent for maintaining the tracking database. The script is called `DTA_SampleJobs.sql`, and it is located in the `\program files\Microsoft BizTalk Server\SDK\Messaging Samples\SQLServerAgentJobs` folder. Examining this script is an excellent way to gain a more in-depth understanding of the inner workings of the tracking database.

The Tracking System Component Object Model

The document tracking system exposes a core set of functionality through a Component Object Model (COM) interface called `IBizTalkTrackData`. This interface is exposed through a coclass called `BTSDocTracking`, which you can browse by using the OLE/COM Object Viewer included with Microsoft Visual Studio. The document tracking COM interface is implemented in `CISDTA.dll`, located in the `\Program Files\Microsoft BizTalk Server` folder.

`IBizTalkTrackData` contains three methods: `GetInterchanges()`, `GetInDocDetails()`, and `GetOutDocDetails()`. Figure 8.19 shows the syntax of these methods.

To make the `BTSDocTracking` class available in Visual Basic, add a reference to the Microsoft BizTalk Server Doc Tracking 1.0 Type Library. This allows you to instantiate the `BTSDocTracking` object within your project.

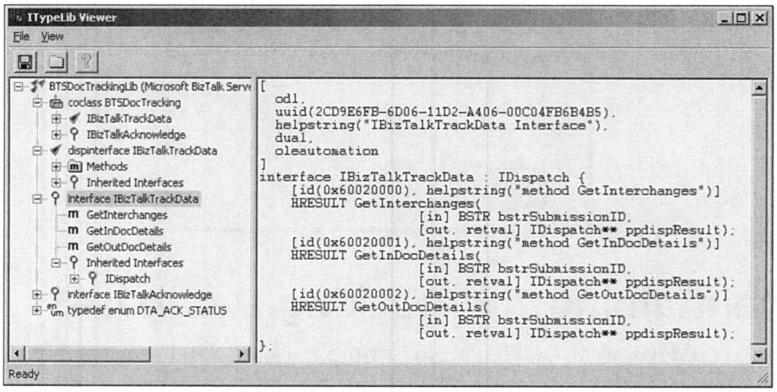

FIGURE 8.19
The `BTSDocTracking` *class and* `IBizTalkTrackData` *interface.*

All three of the methods in the `IBizTalkTrackData` interface require a submission ID to be passed as a parameter. A submission ID is returned when you initiate an interchange by calling the `IInterchange::Submit()` function. You can use this submission ID to retrieve tracking information for an interchange. You can also query the `dta_interchange_details` database for a list of submission IDs that have been tracked. Submission IDs are stored in the `uidSubmissionGUID` field.

Example: A Custom Tracking Solution

This book includes a useful application called `RouteTest` that can initiate a variety of interchanges using the BizTalk Server API. Chapter 12, "Advanced BizTalk Messaging," covers the `RouteTest` application in depth for the purposes of illustrating advanced messaging topics. In addition, the application contains a custom user interface for document tracking that demonstrates how to use the document tracking object model.

To install `RouteTest`, simply run the executable setup program located in the `\RouteTest\Setup` folder. The setup program installs the necessary application files and also automates the process of configuring BizTalk Messaging. After you have successfully run the setup program, run `RouteTest.exe` to launch the application.

Figure 8.20 shows the main window for `RouteTest`. You can initiate an interchange by choosing a scenario in the Routing Test list box and then clicking the Submit button. Each scenario represents a different type of interchange submission.

To use the document tracking portion of `RouteTest`, select Scenario 1 from the list of routing tests and click the Submit button. This submits an interchange to BizTalk Server and returns a submission identifier. The submission ID should be displayed in the results window. Next, click the Tracking button to view interchange and document details for the interchange just submitted. The results of making calls to the document tracking object model are displayed in the Interchange Tracking window (see Figure 8.21).

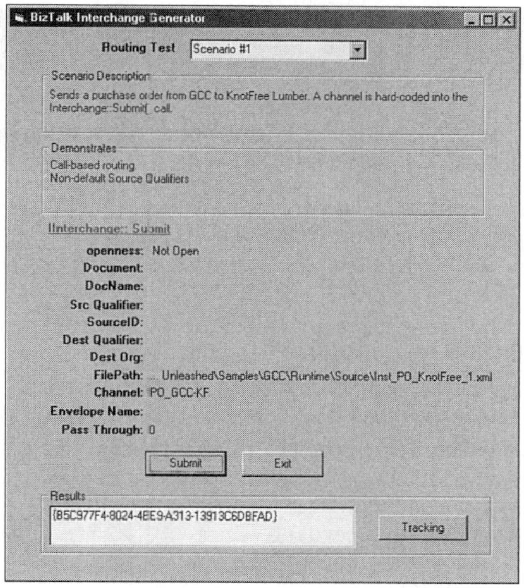

FIGURE 8.20
The `RouteTest` *application.*

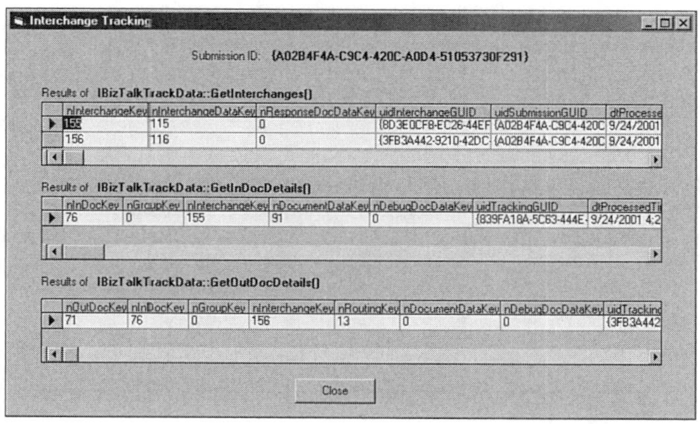

FIGURE 8.21
Viewing tracking data for an interchange using `RouteTest`.

Listing 8.1 shows the Visual Basic code for retrieving the tracking data. The code simply creates a new instance of the `BTSDocTracking` object and calls three methods in succession: `GetInterchanges()`, `GetInDocDetails()`, and `GetOutDocDetails()`. Each method uses the submission ID currently displayed in the `RouteTest` results window.

Note

The code is part of the `RouteTest` application that is used in Chapter 12. The code by itself is not a complete executable example, but it demonstrates how to use the `IBizTalkTrackData` interface in Visual Basic.

The file `Code08.bas` that contains the code for Listing 8.1 can be downloaded at the publisher's Web site.

LISTING 8.1 Using the Document Tracking API

```
Private Sub btnTracking_Click()
    Dim strSubHandle As String
    Dim oTracking As New BTSDocTrackingLib.BTSDocTracking
    Dim oRSInterchanges As ADODB.Recordset
    Dim oRSInDocDetails As ADODB.Recordset
    Dim oRSOutDocDetails As ADODB.Recordset
    Dim frmTracking As New frmTracking
    strSubHandle = ctlResults.Text

    ' Get tracking data
    Set oRSInterchanges = oTracking.GetInterchanges(strSubHandle)
    Set oRSInDocDetails = oTracking.GetInDocDetails(strSubHandle)
    Set oRSOutDocDetails = oTracking.GetOutDocDetails(strSubHandle)

    ' Display tracking data
    Set frmTracking.ctlInterchanges.DataSource = oRSInterchanges
    Set frmTracking.ctlInDocDetails.DataSource = oRSInDocDetails
    Set frmTracking.ctlOutDocDetails.DataSource = oRSOutDocDetails
    frmTracking.ctlSubmissionID.Caption = strSubHandle

    frmTracking.Show

End Sub
```

The methods of `IBizTalkTrackData` return ADO recordset objects, which can easily be displayed in a grid format using an ActiveX control. `RouteTest` uses the Microsoft `DataGrid` control and sets the `DataSource` property of the control to the ADO recordset returned by the tracking API calls.

Summary

BizTalk Server Document Tracking is an essential tool for monitoring and analyzing the activity of a BizTalk Server group. This chapter demonstrated how to configure what information is stored to the tracking database. As the administrator of a BizTalk Server group, you can configure the tracking system to store enough information to meet the specific requirements of your system. You can store entire copies of documents as they move through BizTalk Server, and you can choose individual document fields to save to the tracking database.

This chapter also covered the BizTalk Document Tracking tool in depth. The tracking tool enables you to perform searches based on a variety of parameters. The resulting set of interchanges contains detailed information, including full copies of inbound and outbound documents. These documents can be viewed in their native format or in XML format. You can even construct advanced queries and save those queries for future use.

Finally, you can customize and extend the tracking system. The tracking database and its stored procedures are available for you to leverage in a custom application. Microsoft provides a COM API that enables you to build custom viewers or analysis tools. Even the document tracking tool itself is provided as a set of Active Server Pages that you can reuse and extend.

All in all, BizTalk Document Tracking provides a rich solution for recording interchange activities. You will find it to be invaluable when developing application integration solutions with BizTalk Server.

BizTalk Server Orchestration

PART III

IN THIS PART

CHAPTER 9

Introducing BizTalk Orchestration

by Dilip Hardas

In This Chapter

This chapter introduces BizTalk Orchestration, a new technology from Microsoft for designing and implementing business process workflows.

The first part of this chapter provides a quick tour through BizTalk Orchestration, giving enough information up front for subsequent sections to fall into place. The second part describes the design aspects of BizTalk Orchestration—the components, implementation, and semantics of a process workflow drawing. Chapter 10, "Using the BizTalk Orchestration Designer," describes how to use the designer to build and run a BizTalk Orchestration business process.

In this chapter, you will learn what BizTalk Orchestration is, and what the terminology and concepts behind it are. You will understand the components of a process flow design and their function and operation. You will also see parts of the designer tool used to construct such designs.

What Is BizTalk Orchestration?

This section lays the groundwork for subsequent sections and chapters—that is, it covers enough material for you to recognize the connections between the terms and concepts that are inevitably intertwined. After all, we are talking about an integration framework.

Purpose

Traditionally, systems integration solutions have been, and continue to be to some extent, extensively hand-crafted and difficult to maintain. The systems integrator has had to contend with understanding and then translating an analyst's view of a business process into a working system.

Not only must the systems integrator comply with the logic of the business flow but also must address real systems issues, such as security, transactions, communication protocols, scalability, resource allocation, and so on.

BizTalk Server comes to the rescue by providing a system integration platform that leverages native services from the Windows platform, such as COM+ application services and messaging. This server platform is broadly segmented into two areas—BizTalk Messaging Services and BizTalk Orchestration Services. Although the entire BizTalk Server platform is intended to simplify systems integration efforts, BizTalk Orchestration Services, in particular, are useful for designing and implementing the business processes. Tools permit composition of business flows for an easy, evolutionary maintenance of the system.

Let's look at the features and the major pieces of BizTalk Orchestration.

Features

The design of a business process is captured in a BizTalk Orchestration drawing. This drawing is then compiled into a form that can be run by a runtime engine.

A BizTalk Orchestration drawing separates the definition of the business process from its implementation. This allows for a twofold benefit. The business analyst can focus on describing the workflow without being bogged down with implementation details, and the systems integrator can focus on implementation details, possibly reusing the implementation pieces even as workflows change.

With hooks into COM components, message queuing, and BizTalk Messaging Services, the BizTalk Orchestration workflows can communicate with other applications, without mandating compliance with any specific platform or custom protocols. This opens the door for truly any-to-any integration. The BizTalk Server ships with support for exchanging messages via SMTP, HTTP, HTTPS, MSMQ, and files. In addition, you can define your own components, called Application Integration Components (AICs), to process messages or have other applications post messages to BizTalk. Although the FTP protocol is not natively supported at this time, you can use either integrated third-party products (see the product Web site) or standalone third-party FTP services to deliver files to the file system.

With BizTalk Orchestration drawings, you can express the rich, dynamic interactions that exist between two organizations or applications. For example, a workflow action can bind to a specific remote application based on the execution history of a potentially long running business partner interchange.

Business processes can be easily refined, evolved, and assembled from simpler blocks—a clear advantage for maintainability.

The BizTalk Orchestration drawings allow you to express process concurrency and synchronization, branching, and error handling as part of your integration solution. Rich support for transactions, both long-lived and short-lived, also are included. A BizTalk Orchestration drawing is compiled before it is run by the runtime engine; this helps to detect simple design errors early on.

The BizTalk Orchestration engine supports *dehydration*. Dehydration gives the server a way to durably save the execution state of a workflow. By dehydrating workflows that are waiting and not performing any useful work and rehydrating them later only when the conditions are ready for them to continue, BizTalk Orchestration can support many workflows.

Terminology and Services

BizTalk Orchestration workflows are described using the *XLANG language*—a language developed specially to express components, flows, and structure of workflows. This language is based on the XML technology. The workflow expressed this way is called an *XLANG schedule*.

The XLANG schedule is an executable process; however, it needs a special service to execute it. This service is called the *XLANG scheduler engine* (or sometimes just the scheduler or the engine). When an XLANG schedule is run, the engine creates an instance of the schedule. Hence, many instances of an XLANG schedule may be running at a given time, each in a different state of execution.

The gamut of services needed to support the creation and running of an XLANG schedule, including the configuration and maintenance of the schedule are provided by BizTalk's Orchestration Services. One of the key features alluded to earlier is the engine's support for long-running business processes. A key capability of BizTalk Orchestration Services is dehydrating and rehydrating instances of XLANG schedules. This means that if the instance of a schedule is not performing any work, and is in a quiescent state waiting for an event, then the entire internal state of the schedule is automatically persisted to disk to conserve precious system resources. This is called dehydration of a schedule.

The reverse process is that of rehydration. Rehydration is performed when BizTalk Orchestration Services determine that conditions have changed to allow a dehydrated schedule to perform new work. This rehydration is also done automatically. When this occurs, a *new* schedule is created and its last-known state loaded from disk to conform to what it was at the time it was dehydrated.

Four implementation technologies are supported by BizTalk Orchestration. Two are component technologies, and two are messaging technologies. The components include COM or COM+ components built using any COM-aware Windows programming language and Windows Script Components. The messaging support is provided by Microsoft Message Queuing (MSMQ) and the BizTalk Messaging Services.

The XLANG schedules are designed using the BizTalk Orchestration Designer. The designer is used to construct XLANG schedule drawings. These drawings then are compiled into an XLANG schedule before they can be executed. The schedules must be debugged and tested before deployment. Configuration and monitoring tools for schedules are also available.

The Orchestration Persistence database stores the structure of XLANG schedules, the state of currently active schedule instances, and the state of dehydrated instances. The persistence database also contains the precise state of a schedule instance, both before and after a transaction. This facilitates the correct recovery from failures. Configuring the persistence database is covered in Chapter 11, "XLANG Orchestration Engine."

With this general introduction to BizTalk Orchestration, we can now jump into the topic of drawing an XLANG schedule.

XLANG Schedule Drawings—a Preview

The BizTalk Orchestration Designer is used to build an XLANG schedule drawing. The designer is really an extension of the Microsoft Visio 2000 drawing tool. Although this fact is only an implementation detail, we mention it to provide you an idea of what to expect in the designer. The designer provides specialized flowchart shapes and drawing sheets to enable you to express your business processes for use within BizTalk. Figure 9.1 shows a simple business process used in the tutorial that ships with the product. This schedule is located at `\Program Files\Microsoft BizTalk Server\Tutorial\Schedule\Solution\Buyer1.skv` and has been used at many points in the chapter to illustrate BizTalk Orchestration concepts. The BizTalk Orchestration Designer also works with Visio 2002 if you install BizTalk Server 2002 service pack 1a.

Error! Reference source not found. Figure 9.1 shows the Flowchart stencil window docked to the left and the Implementation stencil window docked to the right. Each stencil window displays shapes you can use within your XLANG schedule drawing. These shapes can be dragged onto the drawing surface. The shapes will be described in much more detail as you progress through the chapter.

The center panel shows the business process itself. The implementation is not visible, but you would see those things if you were to scroll to the right. The menu and the toolbars are at the top. The two toolbar buttons you will use often are the arrow button (shown pressed) and the Connector Tool next to it on the right. The page tabs are shown at the bottom; only part of one tab is visible.

An XLANG schedule drawing has four areas of focus. The first area is the business process itself, which the business analyst can first describe without paying too much attention to the implementation aspects for the process. Figure 9.1 showed an example of a business process using `Buyer1.skv` schedule.

The second area of focus defines the components used to implement this process allowing developers to bind the business process to its physical implementation details. Both these areas are displayed in the Business Process page in the designer and govern how messages flow in the schedule.

FIGURE 9.1
BizTalk Orchestration Designer.

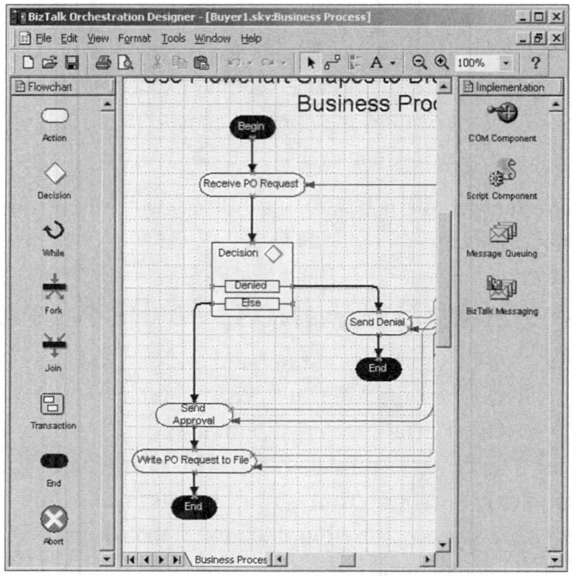

The third area focuses on the definition of the data elements that flow between the messages resulting from the business process. These data elements are displayed on the Data page of the schedule drawing. Finally, the last area is related to transaction management.

This area of handling transaction failures is important. Often, you want a set of actions to occur as a cohesive transactional unit. If one or more of the actions fails, you not only need the transaction to roll back, but you also need support for describing the compensation or failure handling business logic that should be executed. This business logic is displayed on separate pages in the schedule drawing. These pages are called On Failure of <*Transaction*> and Compensation for <*Transaction*>, where the <*Transaction*> token is replaced by the actual name of the transaction as defined on the main Business Process page.

All the other pages in an XLANG schedule drawing refer to the main Business Process page in the schedule.

> **Note**
>
> This chapter describes the first and last areas of focus on the business process and transactions. Chapter 10 covers the other two focus areas on implementation binding and data handling. Chapter 10 relies on the material covered in this chapter and provides details on BizTalk Orchestration.

Defining the Business Process

This section looks at the graphical vocabulary at your disposal to describe the business process in an XLANG schedule. The business process itself is shown on the left half of the Business Process page, with the related flowchart shapes displayed on the left panel. The right half of this page contains implementation shapes; these are described in Chapter 10. You can see this in a full view of the Business Process page, as shown in Figure 9.2. This is again from `\Program Files\Microsoft BizTalk Server\Tutorial\Schedule\Solution\Buyer1.skv`.

FIGURE 9.2
Sample business process.

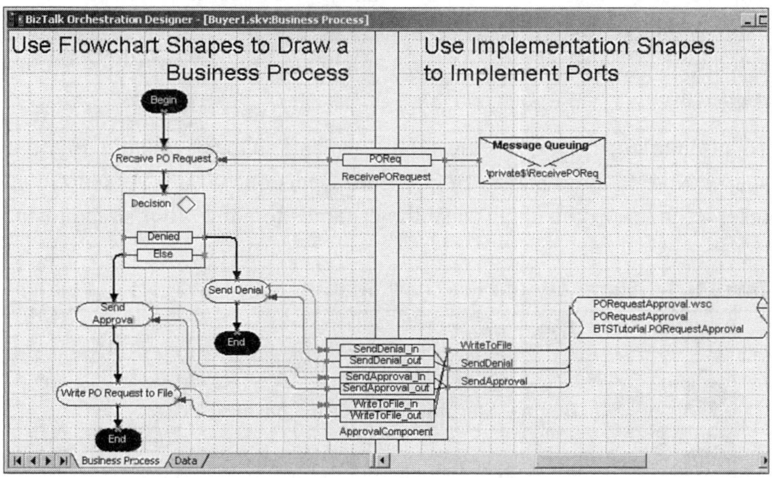

In Figure 9.2, the stencil panes, title, and menu bars all have been removed for clarity. This drawing, again, is from the tutorial provided with the product.

Flowchart Shapes Overview

Business processes are drawn as a flowchart. All business processes start with the Begin shape. There is exactly one Begin shape in an XLANG schedule drawing. You can add other shapes to the drawing and connect them to construct a flowchart rooted at the Begin shape. The connections between shapes denote a flow of control along that path. Each flow of control eventually terminates in either the `End` shape or the Abort shape. The `End` shape completes the process flow for that path. The Abort shape terminates a transaction and causes actions related to transaction failure to occur. This behavior is described in the "Transactions" section later in the chapter. Now, let's look at the shapes used to describe the process flow between these begin and end shapes.

The Action shape denotes a step in the process flow. You use an Action shape if you want to *do* something at this point in the process flow, and therefore you will bind this action to some implementation code later on. Chapter 10 covers this binding procedure in depth.

If you had no other shapes, you would be limited to defining just simple, sequential, business process flows. However, this is not the case. The Decision shape can be used to change the flow of control by using rules to test for data or status values. The `While` shape can be used to iterate a process flow. Many times business processes are not sequential; instead, parts of a process can occur in parallel. To exploit parallelism, you can use the Fork and Join shapes. Finally, you have the Transaction shape that is used to express the fact that the enclosed set of actions and process flows must occur as a transacted unit. A range of options are available to you to control the semantics of such a transaction.

To summarize, Table 9.1 shows the flowchart shapes available to you and describes each shape. Note that the names Begin, End, Decision, While, Fork, Join, and Abort are reserved names; you cannot use these names to name your shape instances.

TABLE 9.1 Summary of Flowchart Shapes

Shape	*Description*
	Begin—Starting point for the business process
	End—Termination point for any path in the business process
	Decision—Alternate pathways taken based on the value of an evaluated rule
	While—Repeated execution of a process flow pathway
	Fork—Concurrent execution of pathways
	Join—Rendezvous point for concurrent execution pathways
	Transaction—Enclosed actions treated as within a transaction boundary
	Abort—Force failure of an enclosing transaction
	Action—A processing step within a business process

At this point, it would be beneficial to review some elements of the Data page before diving into the details for the flowchart shapes. The Data page itself is covered in depth in Chapter 10. Figure 9.3 shows the data page from the `Buyer1.skv` schedule introduced in Figure 9.2 earlier.

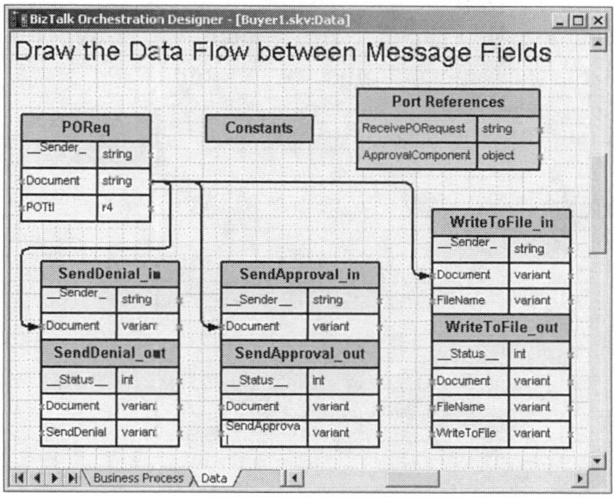

FIGURE 9.3
A sample Data page.

Figure 9.3 shows messages in the `Buyer1.skv` schedule. Note the message names, message fields, and arrows used to specify data flow between fields.

The Data page displays the messages used in the process flow. A message is associated with an action on the Business Process page. The messages are shown with the data fields that they contain. These fields have an associated data type. For incoming messages, the value of the field is populated by the sender; for outgoing messages, the value of the field must be populated by the XLANG schedule. Some message fields are provided as a standard part of BizTalk Orchestration Services; these fields are called *system fields*. The data values in any field can be used to construct rule expressions described in the "Rules" section later in the chapter. Special, built-in messages also are available on the data page, called *constants* and *port references*. With this rudimentary introduction to the Data page, you can now understand the rules in an XLANG schedule.

Rules

A *rule* is a VBScript expression that evaluates to `TRUE` or `FALSE`. Rules are used within a Decision shape or a While shape to control the process flow. A Decision can have many rules. A `While`, on the other hand, can have exactly one. To add or edit a rule, double-click on the rule or the shape in the designer.

A rule belongs to an XLANG drawing and not to the shape that uses it. In other words, you could define a rule and reuse it in multiple shapes on the same drawing (that is, on any page other than the Data page). If you update a rule in any shape, all instances of the rule also are updated.

Rules can be named and a description associated with them. The VBScript expressions used within a rule can include the Date and Time functions, along with constant values you define in the Constants message and other system fields.

Figure 9.4 shows the Rule properties dialog.

FIGURE 9.4

The Rule properties dialog.

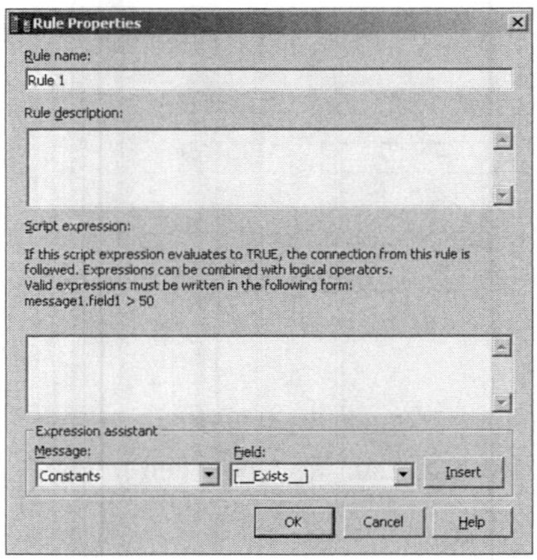

Figure 9.4 shows the default dialog displayed for configuring a rule. You can define a meaningful name for the rule and a short description of what it is intended for. The VBScript expression associated with the rule is constructed in the lower box. The expression assistant box lets you select specific fields from messages and insert them in the VBScript expression. (Unfortunately, the rule description and the expression do not show up as annotations in the drawing or in printouts.)

The following are examples of what sorts of VBScript expressions are allowed.

```
Msg1.Fld1 > 23 and Msg2.fld1 < 33
Message1.[__Exists__]
```

The rules need not be defined until you are ready to compile the schedule. During compilation, basic syntactical checks are conducted on the rule expression, but unfortunately these do not catch misspelled field names.

Flow Control

The Decision shape is used to express alternative paths of execution in a business process. The shape is used to define the flow of control in the schedule. You can use this shape to check the value of a message field and choose a specific path based on that value. This checking is done using rules.

The Decision shape can contain one or more rules in addition to the default clause Else. The rules in the Decision shape are evaluated sequentially. The first rule to evaluate to `TRUE` determines the path taken by the business process flow. The default rule clause, called Else, always evaluates to `TRUE` and is the path taken if all previous rules return `FALSE`.

Iteration

Iteration is the repeated execution of a set of actions until a desired outcome is achieved. The While shape is used to express such repetition in a business process. The repeated process, also called the `while` loop, continues until a rule stops the iteration. The rule is based on values of fields in the messages being processed by the schedule.

The While shape contains exactly one rule and a Continue clause. The business process you attach to the While shape's rule is called the body of the while loop. If the While rule evaluates to `TRUE`, the entire process, the body of the while loop, is executed, and control returns back to the While shape. An attempt to repeat the operation is then made based on the evaluation of the rule. If the rule evaluates to `FALSE`, no additional repetitions are attempted, and the control flows to the business process attached to the Continue clause.

Figure 9.5 illustrates the things described so far.

This process flow is from the `LineItems` XLANG sample provided with the SDK. It is at `\Program Files\Microsoft BizTalk Server\SDK\XLANG Samples\Iteration\LineItemsApp`, or a similar path, depending on your installation.

Figure 9.5 has been slightly rearranged, and the communication and implementation aspects have been hidden. Figure 9.5 shows a While loop with a rule called `ItemsRemaining`. The body of the While loop contains the entire process flow emanating from this rule and terminating in the sole End shape toward the bottom. The body of the While loop contains a Decision shape with three rules. The body of the While loop is repeatedly executed while the `ItemsRemaining` rule returns `TRUE`.

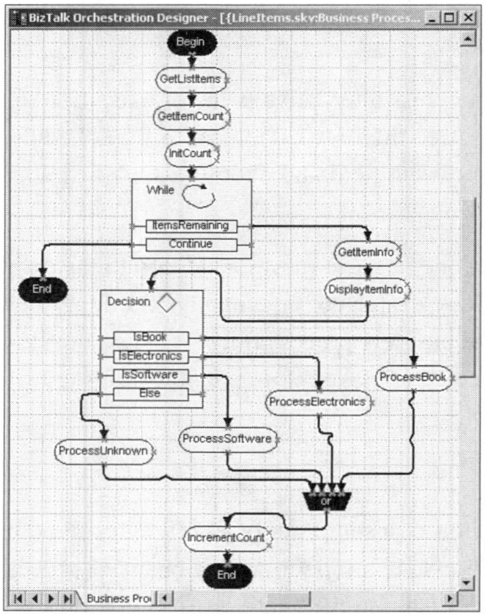

FIGURE 9.5
A business process with While and Decision shapes.

> **Note**
>
> The body of a While loop must conclude in a single End shape. You cannot have, for example, the process flow commingle with flows emanating from outside the body of the While shape.

Concurrency

Process concurrency is expressed using the Fork and Join shapes. As the names suggest, the Fork shape allows control to pass concurrently to multiple outgoing flows, and the Join shape is used to synchronize the resulting outgoing flows. The Join shape also may be used with the Decision shape to synchronize flows following the possible outcomes of a decision (refer to Figure 9.5).

At a Fork, the flow control can split at most 64 ways. The resulting flow can terminate either at an End shape or at a Join. All flows being synchronized at a Join must have emanated from a single Fork—that is, the Fork and Join shapes must be pair matched—except when Join is used with a Decision shape. As with Fork, Join too can synchronize at most 64 flows. Figure 9.6 shows a legal structure of Fork and Join shapes.

FIGURE 9.6
A legal combination of Fork and Join shapes.

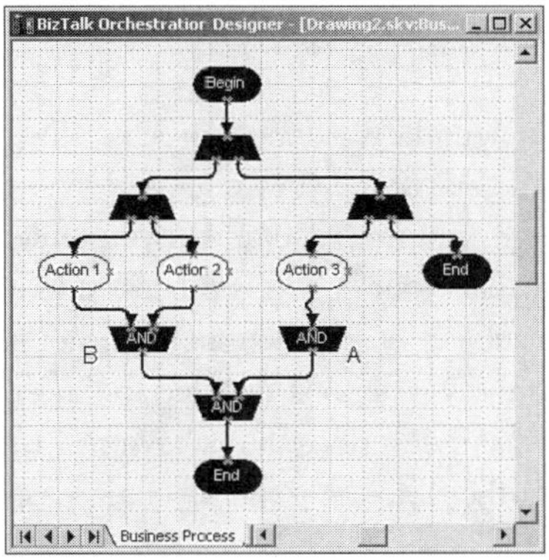

Figure 9.6 shows that each Fork shape is paired with a corresponding Join shape. You cannot remove the Join shape marked A just because there is only a single flow coming in. You also cannot remove the shape marked B hoping that the following Join can be used instead to synchronize all the flows.

There are two kinds of Joins: One is OR, and the other is AND. The type of the Join determines the kind of synchronization performed.

For an AND Join, the control does not flow out to the next shape until control reaches the Join from *all* flows coming in. For an OR Join, the control flows out immediately to the next shape as soon as control reaches it from *any* of the incoming flows.

The AND Join has fewer restrictions on its use. You can string multiple actions in the process flow leading up to this Join. Because all the concurrent incoming flows are guaranteed to have completed when the flow exits the AND Join, the actions following the Join can assume that the actions along the earlier concurrent pathways have completed—that the results of those actions are not indeterminate. Also, not all paths from a Fork need terminate at the AND Join; some may terminate in the End shape instead. However, none of this is true for the OR Join, which is described next.

For an OR Join, each flow segment reaching up to it can have exactly *one receive* action. This restriction does not apply if the flow is emanating from a Decision shape. The OR Join is satisfied when any one of the incoming flows completes; therefore, there is no guarantee about the state of other flows coming into the Join. The actions associated with those concurrent flows may or may not have completed. Note, however, that all actions leading up to the Join are attempted and are expected to execute.

Actions along parallel paths of execution (from a Fork) should never attempt to communicate messages. If you attempt this, you may get arbitrary behaviors or runtime failures with no indication of what went wrong—I don't know which option is worse.

Transactions

The Transaction shape is used to draw a boundary around a process flow fragment and then make assertions about the transacted behavior of the flow enclosed by the shape. The subject matter relating to transactions is large, and it is crucial that you understand the issues involved so that you can effectively translate your business process into a reliable and predictable XLANG schedule. Even if the subject of transactions were not new to you, it would be beneficial to augment your study with a book devoted to this subject matter. This section introduces the Transaction shape and describes the behavior of transactions in an XLANG schedule. Chapter 10 delves further into the implementation aspects for transactions in XLANG schedule.

Each Transaction shape provides a virtual Begin and a virtual End point for the business process that it encloses. The enclosed business process is called the *body of the transaction*. The business process outside the Transaction shape can treat the body of a transaction as if it were a single Action—that is, with a single path in and a single path out. The business process inside the Transaction shape is connected to these entry and exit points. The internal process flow cannot contain an End shape as a termination point; however, it may contain an Abort shape, in which case, the enclosing transaction is aborted—more on this later. However, an End shape may be present within a transaction to delimit the body of an enclosed While shape.

Transactions in an XLANG schedule are essentially of two types: long-running and short-lived. The BizTalk documentation mentions a third type called the timed transaction type; however, such a transaction type is a long-running transaction that is automatically aborted when the allotted time expires. The familiar database transaction falls in the short-lived category.

Short-Lived Transactions

Short-lived transactions have the familiar ACID properties of a transaction. An isolation level for such transactions can be specified by the programmer in the transaction configuration dialog. These types of transactions also are called *DTC style transactions* because they usually use the services of Microsoft Distributed Transaction Coordinator (MS DTC) to manage transactions that span multiple resource managers (such as databases). DTC uses the two-phase commit protocol to ensure that transactions are atomic and durable across all enlisted systems in the transaction—see more on these terms in the ACID sidebar later in the chapter.

You can specify that a short-lived transaction be re-attempted a certain number of times if it fails—the `Retry count` property of the Transaction shape. The time duration between retries also can be specified. This is done by setting the `Backoff time` property of the Transaction shape. These two properties are not available for long-lived transactions.

The backoff time is computed exponentially. For example, a backoff time of 10 seconds translates into retry intervals of 10, 10**2, 10**3, and so on. With a 10-second backoff time and 3 retries, the last retry occurs roughly 17 minutes later.

Figure 9.7 shows the default Transaction Properties dialog box.

FIGURE 9.7
The Transaction Properties dialog.

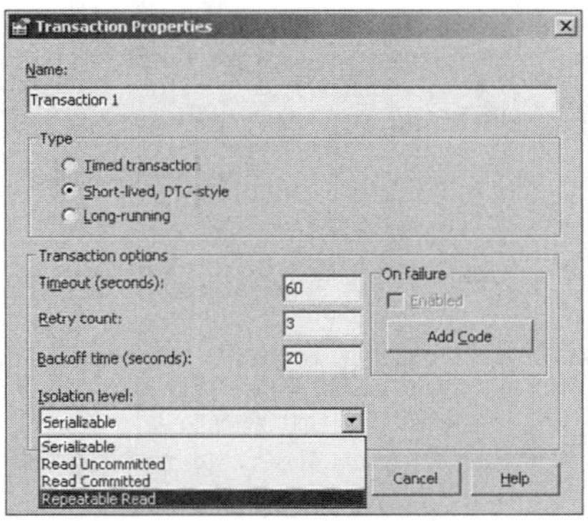

Figure 9.7 shows that a transaction can be named, and the transaction type can be specified. Based on the transaction type, you can set various options. The short-lived transaction is the default transaction type. We will discuss the isolation level and the handling of transaction failure a bit later. The sidebars later in the chapter discuss the ACID properties and isolation level of transactions.

ACID Attributes of Transactions

ACID stands for Atomic, Consistent, Isolated, and Durable. These are the desirable properties that make a transaction a useful abstraction.

A transaction is said to be Atomic because either all the work in a transaction is done or none of it is done. The transaction executes exactly once or not at all.

A transaction preserves the Consistency of data. A transaction should not break application data integrity constraints—for example, when transferring money between accounts, the amount withdrawn must not be more than the amount deposited. Integrity constraints are dictated by application domain.

A transaction is a unit of Isolation. The system should behave as if each transaction is the only transaction running on it at a time, even though in reality hundreds of transactions may be in progress at any given time. Also see the sidebar "Transaction Isolation."

A transaction is Durable. If a transaction completes, its effects cannot be lost despite system crashes. Conversely, if a transaction aborts, it can never be reattempted upon system recovery—whatever the final state, it is retained forever.

Transaction Isolation

Transaction isolation is a measure of what external data changes the transaction can "see." Database textbooks refer to three kinds of phenomena that can occur if a transaction is not isolated. These phenomena are *dirty reads*, *nonrepeatable reads*, and *phantoms*.

A dirty read occurs when a transaction reads data that has not been committed. In this case, the transaction is exposed to partial work of another transaction in progress, which may abort or further change the data during its lifetime.

A nonrepeatable read occurs when upon re-reading the same data (rows) the transaction sees different values. This happens when other transactions have committed and modified values for existing data (rows) already accessed by the current transaction.

A phantom occurs when the transaction sees a different set of data (rows) for the same search criteria used to access the current data. This happens when other transactions have added to the resultset (new rows) while the current transaction is in progress.

An application may have a different level of tolerance for such phenomena. The desirable isolation level is therefore dependent on the application. Four isolation levels are defined based on these phenomena.

At the *read-uncommitted* isolation level, all three phenomena are possible. No locks are used to coordinate data access.

At the *read-committed* isolation level, dirty reads are prevented, but two other phenomena can occur. For this isolation level, transactions must wait for all "write" locks to be released and use a "read" lock to access the data.

At the *repeatable read* isolation level, only phantoms can occur. This is like the read-committed isolation level, with the added requirement that "read" locks be held for the lifetime of the transaction.

Finally, at the *serializable* isolation level, none of these phenomena occur; the transaction is isolated. This is accomplished through higher level table or index locks.

Long-lived transactions shed all pretence of specifying any isolation because of the high cost of retaining long duration locks. Short-lived transactions need to lock resources for a short time, and hence the locking overhead is acceptable. For short-lived transactions, one selects the level of isolation that the application can tolerate. Lesser isolation leads to more concurrency and throughput performance.

Long-Running Transactions

Long-lived (or long-running) transactions sacrifice isolation for concurrency and scalability. By sacrificing isolation, the data as seen by actions within the long-running transaction may change as the transaction progresses because of other external actions. In return, the long-running transactions are unlikely to block (or deadlock) because they do not keep resources (like databases) locked for the duration of the transaction. This results in the higher concurrency.

For DTC style transactions, using locking and the two-phase commit protocol, you can implement application transactions to have the desirable ACID properties. Long-lived transactions do not have recourse to these mechanisms. Granted that long-lived transactions sacrifice isolation, how can they be implemented to exhibit the other attributes in ACID? There are no easy answers!

Let's take a step back to gain some perspective. When you define any transaction, you are effectively declaring that a set of application-specific actions be performed in a manner that complies with the ACID properties of transactions. For long-lived transactions, you are making a similar declaration (okay, pronouncing ACID without the "I" is not easy!). You are stating that all actions enclosed by the transaction shape should run as a unit; however, you are accepting the fact that the enclosed actions could be exposed to unqualified data from other transactions.

For long-lived transactions, therefore, the onus is on you to understand your application domain and then structure the process flow, actions, and transaction boundaries such that the data seen by actions is always appropriate in the context of your application.

To help you to accomplish this, two features are provided by BizTalk Orchestration. One is the capability to nest transactions within a long-lived transaction, and the other is the capability to define exception processing for transactions. Each is discussed in turn in the following sections.

Nested Transactions

You can define a long-lived transaction to contain other transactions and flowchart shapes. By nesting transactions in this manner, you can build application logic by composing larger units of work using smaller units of work. The term *unit of work* is used to highlight the fact that your application defines what is a unit of work, taking into consideration the atomicity and data consistency requirements of your application. However, the term is really a synonym for transaction.

Nested transactions have the following characteristics. The body of a long-lived transaction can contain other transactions, whether long-lived or short-lived. Any deeper nesting is not supported. The body of short-lived transaction cannot contain any nested transactions. However, this is not really a limitation. Short-lived transactions are intended to be just that, short and quick, and therefore they can hold onto resource locks without introducing concurrency problems.

Figure 9.8 shows a process flow involving nested transactions taken from the samples shipped with BizTalk. You can find this sample schedule at `\Program Files\Microsoft BizTalk Server\SDK\XLANG Samples\NestedTxns\NestedTxns.skv`, or a similar location depending on your installation. For clarity, the communication and implementation shapes have been hidden.

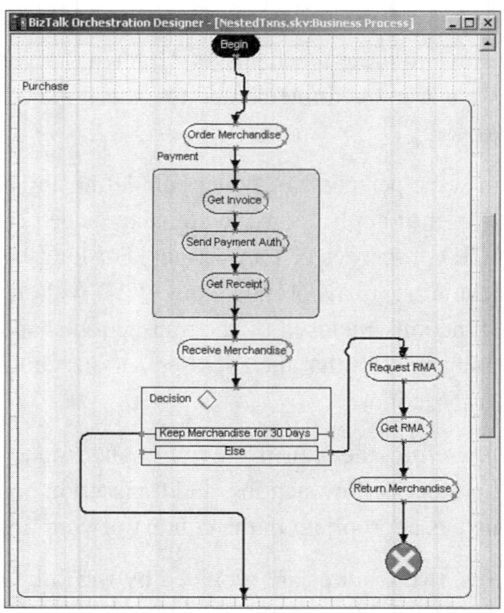

FIGURE 9.8
Nested transaction example.

Figure 9.8 shows an outer transaction, called Purchase. This is a long-running transaction. It is composed of many actions and a nested short-lived transaction called Payment. You can read up on the example in the SDK documentation, but the gist of the process flow is to order some merchandise, pay for it, and decide either to keep it or return it.

The three actions inside the Payment block are guarded by a DTC style transaction. The outer transaction, Purchase, may take a long time (days), and it has no such protection. However, it can treat Payment (the nested transaction) as if it were a single action. Note that the XLANG scheduler engine plays an important role in making sure that schedules themselves are durable and transaction aware. The engine is discussed in Chapter 11.

If a decision is made to return the merchandise, the process flow to the right ends in an Abort shape. Figure 9.9 shows the properties of the long-lived transaction and Figure 9.10 the properties of the short-lived transaction.

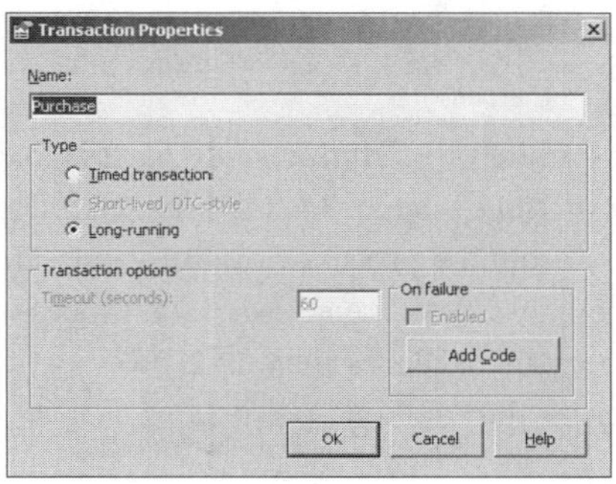

FIGURE 9.9
Properties of the long-lived transaction, Purchase.

Note that the long-running transaction has no timeout, and there is no option to specify isolation properties. Figure 9.10 shows the properties for the nested short-lived transaction.

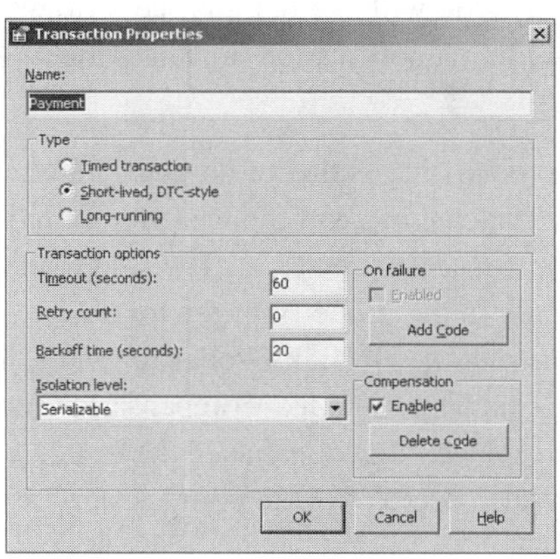

FIGURE 9.10
Properties of the short-lived transaction, Payment.

You already saw a property page for a short-lived transaction, so most of this should be familiar. We have not yet discussed the two groups you see there: On Failure and Compensation. These have to do with exception processing, discussed next.

Transaction Exception Processing

Exception processing allows you to specify an alternative process flow to execute if a transaction fails. There are two scenarios to consider, and there are two corresponding mechanisms for processing exceptions.

The first scenario is that of a transaction failing. The failing transaction can be of any type, whether nested or not. When you click the button Add Code in the group On Failure, you instruct the BizTalk Orchestration designer to add a new page to the process flow drawing. This page is called On Failure of <*Transaction*>, where the token <*Transaction*> is replaced by the actual name of the transaction. The page presents a fresh surface to draw a new business process, complete with a Begin shape to start off the process.

The process you define on the On Failure of <*Transaction*> page is executed in lieu of the process enclosed by the <*Transaction*> shape. This is important. Remember, that the transaction shape draws a boundary around a process flow fragment, and it provides virtual Begin and End points for the process flow it encloses. The process flow you define on the On Failure of <*Transaction*> page replaces the entire process flow inside the failed transaction, between its internal start and end points.

The goal of the failure handling process flow is *not* to reattempt the transaction—that is automatically done based on the configured retry count. You also do not need to attempt to undo the effects of the failed transaction—by definition there aren't any effects to undo; the transaction simply failed. Your goal here is to have your process flow recover from the failed transaction. Typically, you will attempt a process flow that is much more likely to succeed—for example, sending a notification message, logging the event, or making a manual intervention.

The second scenario for exception processing is that of an outer transaction failing, but the nested transaction succeeding. You cannot abort the nested transaction that committed! This is where the notion of compensation comes in. The Add Code button in the Compensation group is available only in the property pages for a nested transaction. When you click this button, you instruct the BizTalk Orchestration designer to add a new page to the process flow drawing. This page is called Compensation for <*Transaction*>, where the token <*Transaction*> is replaced by the name of the nested transaction that succeeded. On this page, you draw the process flow to compensate for the nested transaction that occurred and completed but now needs to be nullified. For example, on this page, you may define a process to reverse charges on an account, or authorize a service call.

If there were multiple nested transactions, you could define a compensatory process flow for each of them. When the outer transaction fails, each compensatory process flow for a successful nested transaction is executed. If the outer transaction has an On Failure of <*Transaction*> page defined, then all compensatory flows run before the process flow for the failed outer transaction. The order of execution of the compensatory flows is not specified.

Figure 9.11 shows the tabs for pages that would appear for the Payment and Purchase transactions showed earlier, assuming that a compensation process for Payment and failure handling process for Purchase are defined.

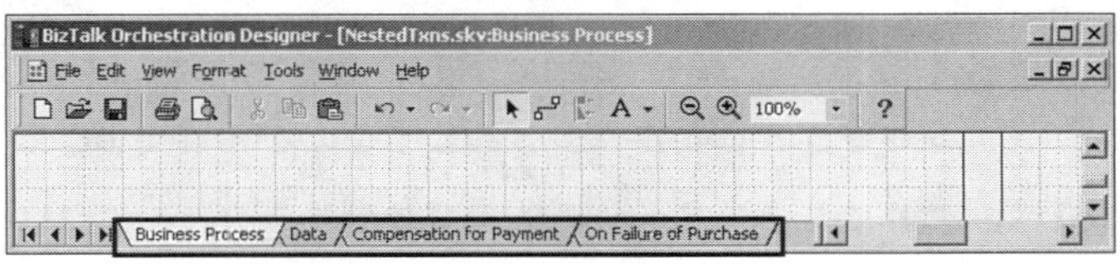

FIGURE 9.11
Page tabs for transaction exception handling at the bottom.

For completeness, Figure 9.12 shows the compensation process for the Payment transaction. It consists of a transaction to `ReverseCharges`. You can cogitate on whether the long-running Purchase transaction, as implemented, merits being called a transaction given the application it is written for. The point is that although long-running transactions do not support DTC style rigorous semantics, they are still useful.

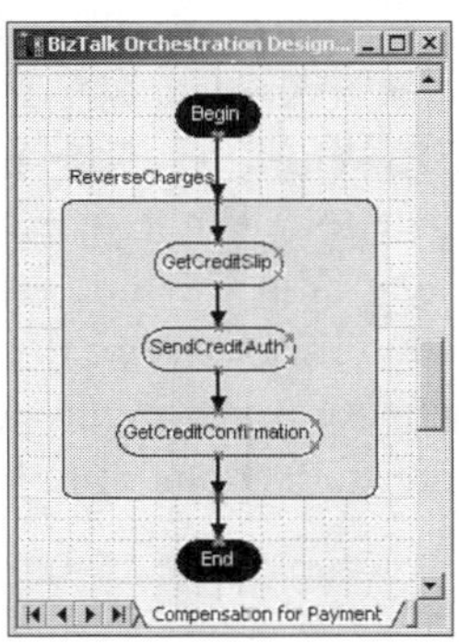

FIGURE 9.12
Compensation for Payment.

You may have noticed the Enabled check box on the property page of a transaction. If you don't check this box, the process flow on the corresponding page is not enabled.

This is useful when developing the compensation code. The actual process flow page is retained; it is removed only if you click the relabeled button Delete Code.

We discussed exception handling for transactions, but when does a transaction failure occur? Based on the material covered so far, a transaction fails when one of the following occurs:

- A transaction does not complete within timeout period, if specified.
- A transaction exhausts its allotted number of retries.
- The process flow within the transaction encounters the Abort shape.
- The DTC aborts a transaction.

Note

An outer transaction does not necessarily abort if a nested transaction aborts. Merely, the next action in the outer transaction is attempted. The outer transaction aborts if it encounters the Abort shape or runs out of its allotted time, if any.

We'll wrap up this section on transactions with a few additional comments. One of the issues covered in Chapter 10 is state management; however, it is important to draw attention to this in this section also. The following paragraphs address this further.

It is important to recover the state of the schedule prior to a failed transaction. It is also important that the state of a schedule be durable so that the effects of a committed transaction are not lost. The XLANG scheduler engine takes care of this.

For state, in the case of a While loop, BizTalk Orchestration allows you the option of retaining the state for each iteration of the body of a While loop. This is a property of the While shape. If you set the property to preserve state for a While loop, then the process flow on the On Failure of <*Transaction*> page or the Compensation for <*Transaction*> page is called for each successful execution of the While loop prior to the point of transaction failure. If you don't preserve the state, then these pages are invoked only once, for the last successful execution of the While loop prior to the point of failure.

The need to correctly manage schedule state and transaction context along with dehydration and rehydration of schedules results in behavior that you must understand when implementing schedules. There are subtle differences between a schedule and its rehydrated clone, but let's not get ahead of ourselves here; these issues are covered in subsequent chapters on BizTalk Orchestration.

Summary

This chapter introduced BizTalk Orchestration. We started from the motivation for BizTalk Orchestration and followed this with features, terminology, and services of BizTalk Orchestration.

Next the chapter went deeper into BizTalk Orchestration: how schedules are constructed using a Visio drawing tool, what the shapes mean, and how they are used. You learned about the different aspects of an XLANG schedule drawing. Four areas of focus were outlined. We have covered only two of these so far: describing a business process and onehandling transaction failures. We will cover the other two areas on how a business process is bound to an implementation and how you can specify the actual flow of data via message flows as the business process unfolds, in Chapter 10.

The chapter covered the vocabulary of shapes in defining the business process. The following shapes were described: Begin, End, Action, While, Decision, Transaction, Fork, Join and Abort. We also looked at Rules. Here we also covered the exception handling support for transactions, how the On Failure of *<Transaction>* and the Compensation for *<Transaction>* pages are created and used. In this discussion, we covered the concepts of how a business process flow is put together and described actual examples provided with the product.

CHAPTER 10

Using the BizTalk Orchestration Designer

by Dilip Hardas

In This Chapter

This chapter describes the usage of the BizTalk Orchestration Designer and builds on the concepts introduced in Chapter 9, "Introducing BizTalk Orchestration." Chapter 9 outlined four areas of focus, which, to recapitulate, were the business area, implementation area, data flows, and the handling of transaction failures. This chapter is devoted to the implementation of a BizTalk Orchestration schedule using the BizTalk Orchestration Designer. Of the four areas outlined, this chapter covers the second and third areas on implementation and data flows.

The BizTalk Orchestration Designer contains wizards that guide you through creating and configuring ports and message flows. This chapter describes these wizards and the numerous options available when designing XLANG schedules. In the course of describing the designer, we cover important details of how XLANG schedules are put together and operational implications of the choices available to you. The chapter discusses the elements before covering the wizards that configure those elements.

We start by describing the concept of business processes implementation. This is followed by the notion of ports and how these ports are used and bound to the underlying implementation. After describing ports, the messages flowing through the ports are covered. Next, the behavior of messages is described, followed by the options available for the management of state, transactions, and security. At this point of the narrative, there is enough background to cover the options provided by the port implementation wizards. The chapter concludes with the steps required to develop and run an XLANG schedule.

This chapter is a bit longer than Chapter 9; the subject matter covered here deals with many interrelated elements that have complex behaviors. Chapter 11, "XLANG Orchestration Engine," and Chapter 13, "Advanced BizTalk Orchestration," cover further Orchestration related topics.

Implementing Business Processes

This section shifts the focus from the business process itself to the technologies at your disposal to specify the implementation for the business process. The business process can be defined on all pages of the XLANG drawing, except the `Data` page. Stated another way, a business process can be described on pages labeled Business Process, On Failure of <*Transaction*>, and Compensation for <*Transaction*>.

In each of the pages containing a business process, the focus is on the right half of the page. A business process page is divided into two parts with a vertical pillar separating the two halves; this pillar is called the *separator bar*.

The process flow on the left of the separator bar (covered in Chapter 9) communicates with the implementation object on the right using *messages*. We briefly reviewed messages and the Data page in Chapter 9. A binding between an implementation shape on the right and an Action shape on the left is made via Port shapes located in the middle separator bar.

Caution

Chapter 6, "Introduction to BizTalk Messaging," and other chapters describing BizTalk Messaging Services also talk of "ports." The messaging port is conceptually similar to the port we talk of with XLANG schedules. However, these two creatures are entirely different beasts! Whenever we say "port," we mean the XLANG scheduler port described in this chapter. To refer to the other kind of port, we will use "messaging port."

Let's look at a specific example so that you can see concretely all the things we will discuss at length. The chosen example is the XLANG schedule drawing from the tutorial sample `Buyer1.skv` installed by default at `\Program Files\Microsoft BizTalk Server\Tutorial\Schedule\Solution\Buyer1.skv`. It is shown in Figure 10.1. The actual path to the sample depends on your installation. You may also open the drawing yourself, follow along the discussion, and explore different parts of the drawing.

A port is created when you drag an implementation shape from the stencil on to the drawing surface. A wizard specific to the implementation guides you through the configuration steps (these wizards are described in the section "Wizards for Port Implementations" later in the chapter). You can restart this wizard by double-clicking on the implementation object. Messages are created when you connect an Action shape with a port. Either an XML or a method communication wizard is started to guide you through the configuration steps (these wizards are described in the section "Defining Data Flow Through Messages" later in the chapter). You can restart the wizard by double-clicking on the connection between the action and the port.

When a schedule is compiled and run, a sequence of actions as described by the business process is performed. With each action, a message is either sent or received through a port. The XLANG schedule drawing pictorially shows the actions, messages, and ports and their interrelationships. This background should assist you to explore the sample shown in Figure 10.1.

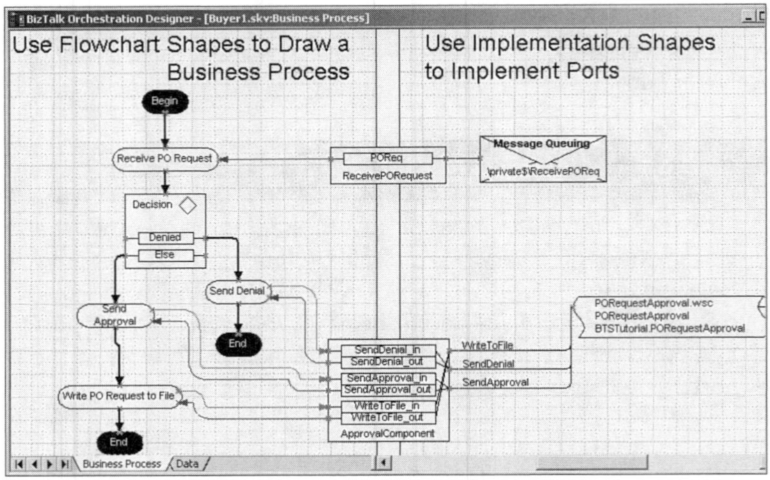

FIGURE 10.1
Sample schedule.

In Figure 10.1, the rectangular boxes sitting on the separator bar are ports. The ports are named `ReceivePORequest` and `ApprovalComponent`. The messages that flow through these ports are shown as rectangular boxes enclosed by the Port shape and are named as displayed in the box representing the Port shape. The port on the top has a single message associated with it, called `POReq`. The port on the bottom has three *message pairs* associated with it. The boxes representing message pairs are always grouped within the port shape. The names for the message pair contain tags `_in` and `_out` to differentiate the incoming and the outgoing messages. For example, the messages in the first message pair inside the `ApprovalComponent` port are called `SendDenial_in` and `SendDenial_out`, respectively. These messages are shown on the Data page (see Figure 10.2) where you specify the data flow.

The arrows connecting the message with the Action shape depict the direction of flow for the message. If you see the drawing in color, the red arrow is always going out from an Action shape, and the blue arrow is always going into an Action shape. The arrows indicate whether a message is flowing out of a schedule instance or into a schedule instance.

The shapes to the right of the separator bar represent the implementation bound to a port. Figure 10.1 shows two implementation shapes. The top shape is for an MSMQ queue named `.\private$\ReceivePOReq`. The lower shape is for a COM component built using the Windows Script Component technology. The shape contains three lines of annotation, the first one says that the component is implemented in the file `PORequestApproval.wsc`. The second line shows that the `PORequestApproval` interface is being used. The last line shows that it implements the ProgID of `BTSTutorial.PORequestApproval`. This interface used in the implementation exposes three functions shown to the left of the implementation shape. The functions exposed are named `WriteToFile`, `SendDenial`, and `SendApproval`.

The BizTalk Orchestration Designer creates a message definition when you connect an Action shape with a port. If the connected port represents a messaging-based implementation, like the MSMQ-based `ReceivePORequest` port on the top, then a single message is created, like the `POReq` message on top. In addition, the connection between the Action shape and port is a single arrow. On the other hand, if the connected port represents a COM component, like the script-based port `ApprovalComponent` at the bottom, then a message pair is created, like `SendDenial_in` and `SendDenial_out`. You will notice that the names for the messages in the message pair are derived from the function name associated with the message pair. The messages in the message pair are used for passing the function's arguments and its results. In this case, two arrows connect the Action and the port, one for each message in the message pair.

Message pair names may have an additional numeric suffix. This suffix is generated when two or more Action shapes call the same function on a component. The numeric suffix is used to disambiguate the messages and the calling context when calling the same named method at different points in an XLANG schedule. Note that such Action shapes that use the named method may lie on any process page (that is, any page other than the Data page) in the schedule.

A message pair is always used when communicating with a COM component. On the other hand, a single message is used when communicating with a port connected to an MSMQ queue or a BizTalk channel. The message pair represents the *call* and the *return* of a synchronous method call. The single message represents the asynchronous delivery or receipt of a message. The direction of the top arrow is significant where a pair of arrows connect an Action to a port. The top arrow indicates the origination of the method call. In the figure, all calls are shown to originate from the XLANG schedule instance. Later, in the section "Message Flow Behavior," you see calls originating from outside the schedule. In these situations, the top arrow goes from right to left and is colored blue when a call is initiated from outside a schedule.

When the schedule shown in Figure 10.1 runs, actions are executed starting from the Begin shape. As each action is executed, the associated messages are either received or sent. For example, the `Receive PO Request` action waits for the `POReq` message from the port `ReceivePORequest`. Some actions may not be executed—for example, only one of the actions `Send Denial` or `Send Approval` will execute. When an action is not performed, the associated message exchange does not occur.

Looking to the right of the separator bar and to the implementation shapes, there are two kinds of implementations. One kind uses the programmatic calls to COM-based components to exchange messages, and the other kind uses queue-based mechanisms implemented by messaging-based ports to exchange messages with XLANG schedules. The schedule described in Figure 10.1 shows one of each kind. A COM-based component may be a registered DLL or a script. A queuing-based component may be an MSMQ queue or a channel from BizTalk Messaging Services. Note that the messages here are the packets of data being exchanged as actions are executed within the XLANG schedule; these messages are not flowing through BizTalk messaging services.

A component is used in a schedule by calling a method that the component implements. From the discussion of Figure 10.1, you know that each component call involves a set of paired messages exchanged synchronously. One message represents incoming data (arguments) in the call; the other represents outgoing data (results) from the call return. You can implement a component using any language capable of authoring COM components; this includes Visual Basic, C++, or Windows Script Component technology (as shown in Figure 10.1).

A queue-based mechanism is used in a schedule by posting a message to it or by retrieving a message from it. This message exchange occurs asynchronously—the sender and the receiver of a message do not block one another when they exchange a message or a response. To implement such a port, you either use queues from MSMQ or use channels from BizTalk Messaging Services. A BizTalk channel, which is described in Chapter 6, is just like a queue when it comes to sending messages—although the actual feature set is extensive. Messages are received from BizTalk Messaging Services by an XLANG schedule via a port bound to a channel.

In the BizTalk Orchestration Designer, there are four shapes in the implementation stencil; each shape corresponds to a supported technology. Usually, this stencil pane docks to the right, but it may be docked to any edge or floated. These shapes are shown and briefly described in Table 10.1.

TABLE 10.1 Port Implementation Technologies

Shape	*Description*
	COM Component
	Script Component
	Message Queuing
	BizTalk Messaging

Now we'll round out the discussion of the tutorial example introduced in Figure 10.1. Figure 10.2 shows the Data page corresponding to the Business Process page shown in Figure 10.1. You might want to review the business process and ports described earlier.

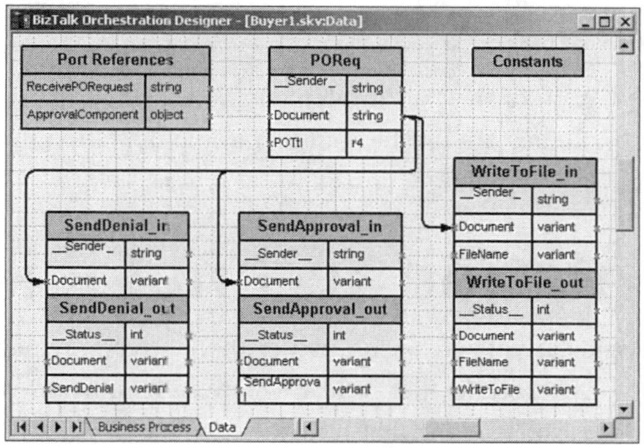

FIGURE 10.2
Messages and data flow in sample business process.

Figure 10.2 shows the messages automatically created when an Action shape was connected to a port on the Business Process page. The interconnections between the message shapes are not automatically created. Each rectangle represents a message or a message pair. You should be able to correlate each rectangle, other than the ones labeled Port References and Constants, with a message on the Business Process page. If you can see the color, the name of the message shows up inside a blue-gray heading in each rectangle. The table below the heading contains specific fields of the message. The shaded, yellow-orange fields are the system fields, and these are listed first. Note that the `__Sender__` field is always present in any incoming message. For message pairs, which represent COM method calls, the call return part of the message always contains the `__Status__` field, which contains the `HRESULT` for the call. The other fields inside the rectangle are specific to the message. Messages and fields are described further in the section "Defining Data Flow Through Messages."

The arrows connecting the message shapes show the possible movement of data among the messages. The data movement in Figure 10.2 is simple; the incoming document in the `Document` field of the `POReq` message can potentially be copied to any of the other messages associated with a method call. The actual movement of data is governed by the business process flow. The data movement does not occur until the action associated with the message flow is executed in the flow. Hence, depending on how the business process actually unfolds, either the `SendDenial_in` message field is populated with the document string or the `SendApproval_in` message field is populated, but not both.

There are no Constants in this drawing shown in Figure 10.2. The Port References are one each for the two ports implemented on the Business Process page.

The descriptions so far of the Business Process and the Data pages of the tutorial example should provide a good outline of all the basic pieces of a schedule as shown in the BizTalk Orchestration Designer.

We now return to review each of the port implementation technologies. In addition, later, we look at how the technologies are used to bind an implementation to a port and discuss further details about message handling.

Implementation Technologies

There are four technologies at your disposal; two of them are component based, described in the first two subsections that follow, whereas the other two are messaging based, described in the two subsections that follow.

COM+ Component

COM components are software components that conform to Microsoft's binary object model protocol standard. These components may be implemented using any of the supported languages on the Windows platform. COM+ is a powerful runtime environment for COM components that provides declarative transaction support, scalability, security, and other enterprise-level features.

The role of a COM+ component in a BizTalk XLANG schedule is to provide an opaque and efficient implementation of an irreducible yet reusable business function. A developer writing such components has access to the entire Win32 API and advanced language features for expressing and debugging business-relevant algorithms. An additional benefit is that these components are compiled, and hence their deployment and maintenance is more manageable.

The BizTalk Server product includes as part of the standard installation COM components that any program, including an XLANG schedule, can use. For example, the `IInterchange` method or the `Microsoft BizTalk Server Interchange 1.0 Type Library` can be used to submit documents to BizTalk Messaging Services.

Script Component

Windows scripting technology is a lightweight approach to writing COM components. These components have some of the same features of COM components described previously and can be installed in COM+ applications; however, there are some differences:

- Script components are vulnerable to tinkering, and this may be desirable if some aspects of an implementation are yet unclear and there is a need for this type of flexibility.
- Script components are more difficult to debug.
- The method calls are late bound, and there is no type enforcement, except possibly at runtime.
- A script component cannot contain an implementation for multiple classes nor can a class support multiple interfaces.
- All argument references used in a function call must be made by reference and not by value.
- Only function calls may be used; subroutines are not supported.

MSMQ Message Queuing

MSMQ message queuing provides a robust, scalable, and secure platform for sending messages between an XLANG schedule and another application. Unlike the COM+ and scripting components described previously, messaging facilitates loosely coupled asynchronous communication between applications, a desirable attribute when building scalable applications.

Message queues are persistent, fault tolerant, scalable, transactional, and secure. MSMQ message services are an important part of an overall application design. The XLANG schedule can directly address such MSMQ queues to integrate business processes with physically or temporally distant applications or components.

BizTalk Messaging

The BizTalk Messaging implementation shape provides access to a BizTalk Messaging channel. This Messaging shape allows an XLANG schedule instance to gain access to the reliable document delivery and transformation services provided by BizTalk Messaging. With this implementation technology, an XLANG schedule can post a document directly into a BizTalk channel, or vice versa, a BizTalk Messaging port can post a document directly into an XLANG schedule, starting a new instance of the schedule if necessary.

Ports

A *port* is a conduit used by a schedule instance to exchange messages. An action in the schedule communicates through a port. At a conceptual level, a port is a named endpoint for the delivery (or receipt) of a message from an attached implementation into (or out of) an XLANG schedule instance. This statement, however, is simplistic; it glosses over issues of synchronization, transactions, error handling, state, instantiation, naming, call semantics, and so on. Although a port is just a conduit for a message, its behavior is affected by the implementation behind the port. The rest of this chapter is devoted to looking at these issues more carefully. This section, however, attempts to provide a better conceptual understanding of ports. We begin at the process of creating a port. We will then work through use cases that motivate the issues raised here.

To create a port as an XLANG schedule designer, you usually pick an implementation shape from the stencil and drop it on the right half of a process flow page. When you do this, a wizard walks you through the necessary configuration steps needed for the specific implementation technology you selected. The wizards themselves are described in the section "Wizards for Port Implementations."

When designing the schedule, as an alternative to picking the implementation technology first, you can start instead with defining ports first; however, this works only for messaging-based implementations. You do this by right-clicking on the separator bar in a process flow page and selecting the Add New Port menu item. When created, these ports are unbound; however, you must subsequently bind these ports to an MSMQ queue or a BizTalk Messaging implementation before the schedule can be compiled and run. You may later proceed to bind Action shapes to these ports; however, the port properties are determined by the implementation you bind to the port eventually. Using an unbound port is useful when you want to proceed with designing your business process along with associated messages while deferring to select the messaging implementation. Communication through an unbound port is always asynchronous, and you must use the XML Communication Wizard to define the messages flowing through it.

A port can perform its function of exchanging messages only if the underlying implementation is available. For example, unless a COM component is instantiated, you cannot make method calls through the port; unless a queue or a channel exists, you cannot send or receive messages through the port. (In the special case of No Instantiation, you must have the type library of the COM component.) This may seem obvious but is something to keep in mind when a running schedule uses a port created by some other application or a schedule. We next look at a use case that motivates these instancing options.

At the time you design an XLANG schedule, you may possess all the information required to construct or specify the desired port implementation. In some cases, however, you need to communicate through a port instance that is available only at runtime and cannot be fully specified at design time. Such a port instance may be implemented, for example, by another application or even by a trading partner on a remote and inaccessible system. Figure 10.3 shows such a scenario in abstract. The `ScheduleA` and `ScheduleB` are reusing the business process defined by `ScheduleC`.

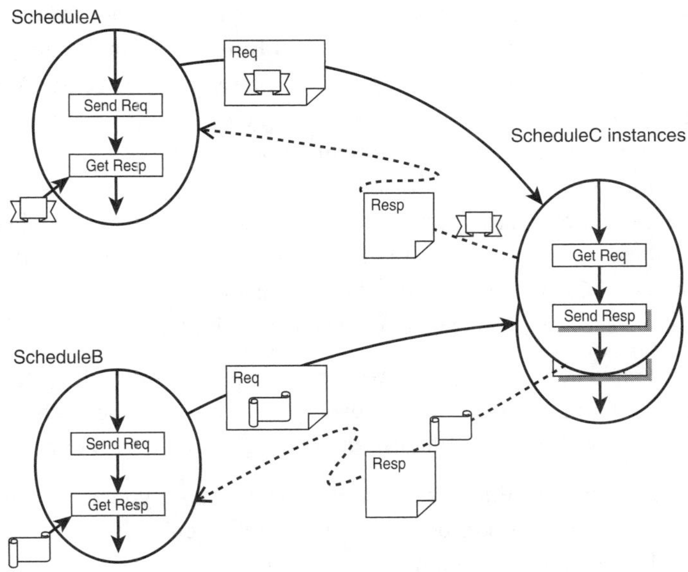

FIGURE 10.3
Using ports to integrate schedules.

Both schedules, A and B, are shown to contain just two steps: send a request to schedule C and then get a response from it. Both schedules, A and B, are unaware of each other's existence but use the same business process defined in schedule C: to get the request and send a response. Schedule C must maintain this isolation by sending the response back to the original requesting schedule. Schedule C does not know about schedules A and B; it merely processes the request sent by any schedule, like A or B. Therefore, when designing schedule C, you cannot hard-code the routing of messages; this routing must be resolved dynamically.

The `ScheduleC` is designed so that it can respond to ports on specific instances of running schedules, such as `ScheduleA` and `ScheduleB` shown in Figure 10.3. The schedules A and B may be two instances of the same schedule or an instance each of two different schedules; however, in each case, the running instance is sending a document to an instance of `ScheduleC`, shown by the solid arrows. The document sent to `ScheduleC` is called `Req`, and it contains a tag for the sender's port. The tags are shown by the ribbon shapes in the Figure 10.3. The `ScheduleC` is completely unaware of the sending schedule. It processes `Req` and generates a `Resp` document. This generated document is sent to the port identified by the tag in the `Req` document. This is shown by the dotted arrow. The action taken by the `ScheduleC` is identical in both cases; however, it ends up sending the document to different ports, each identified by the tag in the `Req` document.

This is a common trading partner document exchange scenario. There are many variations of this general scenario: schedules A and B may communicate with the same instance of C, or the entire business process represented by C (or by A or B) may be implemented by a trading partner without using the BizTalk Server. The important point is to note the mechanisms needed to integrate business processes. We need a way to generate a tag for a port that can be unambiguously resolved to a real port instance some time in the future, even after system failures. This notion of a tag applies to port references and dynamic ports, which are described next in the section "Port References and Dynamic Ports." Chapter 16, "Correlation—Integrating BizTalk Server Messaging and Orchestration Services," is devoted to correlation, alluded to in Figure 10.3.

Another example of when a port name is not adequate is multiple instances of the same schedule running in memory. Clearly, the design-time name for each port will be the same and will not serve to distinguish the ports. Now we return to port creation.

In an XLANG schedule drawing, when you create a port, you get to name it. However, this name is the static, design-time name that you assign and is not adequate as a tag that can be used as a name for a runtime instance of that port. For this, BizTalk Orchestration has the notion of port references.

When you choose an implementation technology for a port, by dragging a shape from the stencil to the drawing surface, you can specify at design time whether the XLANG Scheduler Engine should create the port instance object, or whether it should use a port that's already been created earlier. This is done by using a port reference. The ability to specify a port implementation that can be resolved at runtime is required to enable the scenario shown in Figure 10.3. To facilitate this, BizTalk Orchestration has the notion of static and dynamic ports.

Moving to other aspects of ports, the runtime behavior of messages passing through ports is also important to understand. When you bind an Action with a port, messages are defined; however, when the schedule runs, specific messages are created and flow through the ports. In the sections "Message Flow Behavior," "State Management," and "Transaction Support" and "Security" later in the chapter, we cover the runtime aspects of message flows, including concurrency in message flows, persistence relating to dehydration and rehydration, transactions, and security. All these issues are related to the runtime behavior of schedules, ports, and their underlying implementation.

To summarize, in the following sections we look at each of these items:

- Port names and references (See the next section "Port References and Dynamic Ports.")
- Static and dynamic ports (See the next section "Port References and Dynamic Ports.")

- Message schemas and data flow (See the section "Defining Data Flow Through Messages.")
- Synchronous versus asynchronous communication of messages, interplay of schedule instances and port instances (See the section "Message Flow Behavior.")
- State management for ports and schedules (See the section "State Management.")
- Transaction support in ports and schedules (See the section "Transaction Support.")
- Security mechanisms (See the section "Security.")

As promised, the next section discusses port references and dynamic ports.

Port References and Dynamic Ports

A port reference is a handle that can be passed into or out of an XLANG schedule instance. This handle represents a real port instance (not just a name), and its type depends on the technology used to implement the port. Whenever you add a port to an XLANG schedule drawing, a new port reference field is added to the Port References message on the Data page. This port reference can be passed around as a field inside a message.

If the port can be completely specified at design time, then at runtime the XLANG Scheduler Engine can connect to the actual object specified based entirely on the information provided at design time. The port instance is constructed a priori, or in some cases, by the engine. Such a port is called a *static port*. You can use the port reference field from the Port References message to pass out a reference to this static port for use by other schedule instances or applications. This port reference is, generally, an opaque handle to the other schedule instances or applications that receive it. However, on the originating system, where the reference was generated, it can be resolved back to the real port. This is related to the notion of the dynamic port described next.

If the port cannot be specified at design time—that is, the precise instance of the port is known only when the schedule runs—then the XLANG Scheduler Engine must acquire a reference to the port at runtime. Such a port is called a *dynamic port*. For dynamic ports to be successfully resolved at runtime, in the XLANG schedule design, you must populate the port reference field in the Port References message with a reference passed into the schedule. The passed reference is provided in a message by another schedule or application that has access to the underlying real port implementation. For the reference to be useful, it must arrive before the dynamic port is needed by the schedule at runtime.

Figures 10.4 and 10.5 are from another example provided with the product. This example is nominally at `\Program Files\Microsoft BizTalk Server\SDK\XLANG Samples\Dynamic Binding\Queue\QueueBindApp\QueueBind.skv`, or a similar place depending on your installation. Figure 10.4 is the business process page, and Figure 10.5 is the data page of `QueueBind.skv`. The schedule demonstrates the use of a dynamic port.

FIGURE 10.4
Example of dynamic port using MSMQ—Business Process.

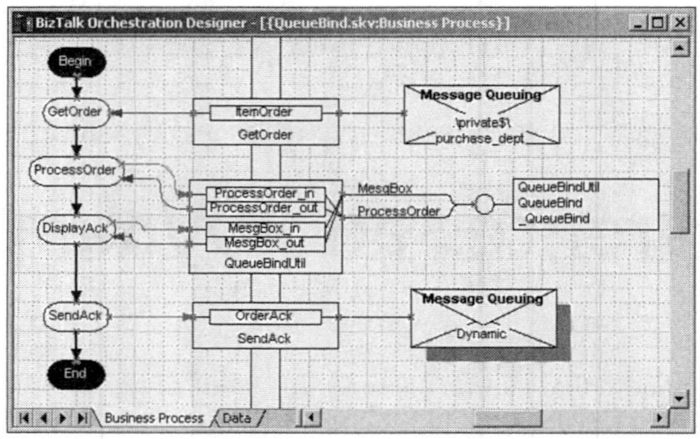

As with all examples supplied with the product, you can read more about such examples in a `readme` file supplied with the sample.

Figure 10.4 shows that the `QueueBind` XLANG schedule receives a message `ItemOrder`, via the `GetOrder` port connected to the `GetOrder` action, from an MSMQ queue called `.\private$\purchase_dept`. The received message contains a port reference to another MSMQ queue that must be used by this schedule to send a response. The next action, ProcessOrder, extracts this port reference and constructs the response document. The action `DisplayAck` is used to show the result of this operation, as part of the sample. The final step, `SendAck`, sends the constructed response to the port specified in the incoming document. Note that the `SendAck` port is a dynamic port using the MSMQ implementation technology. The port implementation box is shown with a light shadow under it. In Figure 10.5, note how the dynamic port reference is used on the Data page.

Figure 10.5 shows the Data page corresponding to the schedule shown in Figure 10.4. The `ItemOrder` is the incoming message. The `Document` field of this message is passed to the `ProcessOrder` method of the COM port `QueueBindUtil` using `ProcessOrder_in` message. The method returns the response document in the message `ProcessOrder_out`, in the `sOrderAck` field, and the MSMQ port reference in the `sQueuePath` field. Note that these fields are of the string type. The part that tells the XLANG Scheduler Engine how to resolve the dynamic port reference is the connection from the `sQueuePath` field of the `ProcessOrder_out` message to the `SendAck` field of the Port References message.

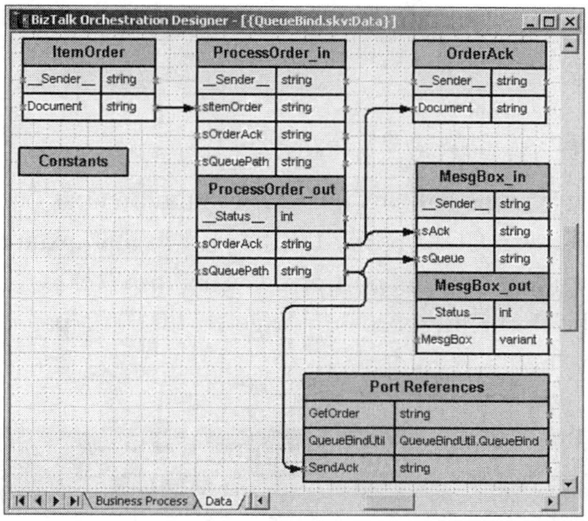

FIGURE 10.5
Example of dynamic port using MSMQ—Data.

A port reference must contain enough information for the application (in this example, the schedule) holding the reference to locate and access the real port instance (in this example, the MSMQ queue). This information varies based on the implementation technology. We look at each technology in turn to see what the port reference looks like.

A Port Using COM Components

For a port based on a COM component, the port reference is either an interface (for example, `IDispatch`) or a COM moniker that can be resolved to an interface. The interface is acquired by binding to the port object using an associated moniker class implementation. COM components bound to static ports are instantiated by the XLANG Scheduler Engine, which also creates the running schedule instance. The monikers for these static ports are available through the Port References message from within the running schedule instance. Therefore, on the Data page, you can use this moniker string to fill an outgoing message field. This outgoing message can be used later to retrieve the moniker and resolve it back to an interface of the COM component, which is, the port.

Alternatively, such monikers can be acquired through the engine's object model (described in Chapter 11). No matter how such a moniker is acquired, it can be subsequently resolved back to the ports either by using the moniker class `sked` or directly in the schedule drawing by binding to the Port References message to resolve a dynamic port. Note that the `sked` moniker class is also implemented by the XLANG Orchestration Engine.

An example of a port moniker for a static port bound to a COM component looks as follows:

```
sked://MyMachine!XLANG Scheduler/
➥{D1BD91F0-B480-410c-96ED-476E2BA12D91}/MyCOMPort
```

The XLANG Scheduler Engine instantiates the COM component as part of the running schedule instance and provides a COM proxy for the port in that instance. The moniker that is generated by the engine is for this port proxy. This moniker is accessible through the port-specific field in the Port References message on the Data page and is used to populate outgoing message fields, if so desired.

COM Primer on Monikers, Interfaces, and Proxies

Component Object Model (or COM) is an architecture that defines how objects interact. This interaction occurs over well-defined interfaces exposed by the objects and can occur within a single process or across processes or even across different machines. The remote interactions are covered by Distributed COM, or DCOM architecture. COM is a language-independent, binary specification for object interaction. It is the core of Microsoft's object framework.

A COM interface is a set of functions exposed by an object. The interface defines a "contract" between the object and its users. The interface is the only COM-supported mechanism for interacting with the object, and it is rigorously defined by COM. The interface consists of an array of methods (functions). The interface is identified by a globally unique interface ID (GUID).

COM provides many basic services as part of the framework. For example, you can create COM objects and inquire about the interfaces implemented by the objects. COM provides built-in support for managing object lifetimes, marshalling arguments between the caller and callee when an interface method is called, taking care of process and thread boundaries, enforcing access and rights control, and so on.

COM uses a proxy and stub mechanism to manage the marshalling of arguments when a method call is made. If the caller of an interface method is in a different context from the object that implements the interface, then COM must determine how to make the call. The different contexts may be due to threading, process, machine, or even security boundaries. COM constructs an interface proxy for the caller and a corresponding stub for the callee. These two objects make the interface method call appear to be a local function call. Of course, the method call will fail if arguments cannot be correctly marshalled across the differing contexts.

> A *moniker* is a name that uniquely identifies a COM object, usually a specific instance of a COM class. COM defines an `IMoniker` interface. This interface must be implemented by a moniker class, which is a class that knows how to resolve a name into a running COM object instance. The XLANG Scheduler Engine implements such a moniker class that knows how to translate names based on the `sked` prefix.

For a dynamic port using the COM technology, you must resolve this dynamic port by selecting a field in a message that contains a valid COM interface or a moniker for the real port that the dynamic port stands for. This message must be received before the dynamic port is accessed within the running schedule. The engine will acquire the COM interface to the real port (by resolving the moniker to an object instance, if necessary) before messages are sent in or out of the dynamic port.

Yet another kind of port is supported with COM components. This is called *No Instantiation*. This kind of port uses the method signature to construct a properly formed message, just like any other port connected to a COM component. However, what is different is the fact that the method and the COM component are never instantiated and called. See the section "Case 1: Application Calls a Method" for more information about this option.

A Port Using Message Queuing

For a static port connected to an MSMQ queue, the port-specific field in the Port References message contains the fully qualified path for the queue, as follows:

```
MyMachine\private$\QueuePrefix{373FEF8C-131B-4e39-97A2-ABABCFC14CB7}
```

The preceding example shows the path for a *per-instance queue*, as opposed to a *fixed queue* for all schedule instances. A per-instance queue contains a queue name prefix and a GUID to distinguish it from any other queue. If you need to, it is a good way of generating a unique endpoint for message delivery or receipt.

You can use a queue port reference to resolve a dynamic port connected to an MSMQ queue. You must connect a port reference that you get in a message to the field in the Port References message. The XLANG Scheduler Engine will locate the queue before sending or receiving messages through the dynamic port. See Figures 10.4 and 10.5 for examples.

A Port Using BizTalk Messaging

For a static port using the BizTalk Messaging Services, the port-specific field of the Port References message does contain a path for the BizTalk Messaging channel; however, the usage of this port reference is a bit different from other types of port implementations. For all other types of port implementations, the port reference is agnostic about the direction of message flow. For BizTalk Messaging-based ports, this is not so: You may only use the port reference of a receiving static port to resolve a sending dynamic port. Stated differently, dynamic ports that receive messages via BizTalk Messaging are not supported. Consequently, the port reference of a static port that sends messages cannot be used. See the section "BizTalk Messaging Binding Wizard" and Figure 10.19 for more information on how such a port is configured.

A port used to receive messages from BizTalk Messaging is always a static port. Such a port can optionally be used to activate the XLANG schedule. If used in this manner, the port cannot be used with multiple actions or with a single action in a loop. There can be at most one such port in a schedule. The port reference from this port cannot be used with any message.

A static port for receiving messages but not to activate the XLANG schedule does not have the previous restrictions—that is, you can use it in a loop and pass around its port reference so that others may send messages to it. However, the only protocol supported by BizTalk Messaging to post messages to an XLANG schedule port is HTTP. Figure 10.6 summarizes these statements.

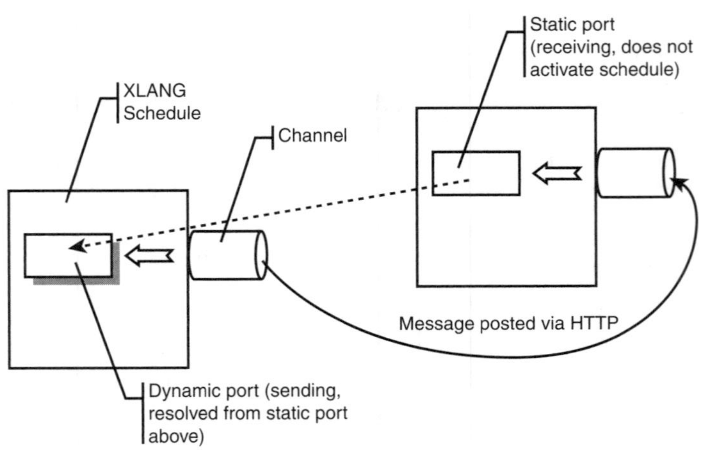

FIGURE 10.6
Use of dynamic ports with BizTalk Messaging.

Figure 10.6 shows a schedule on the left using a dynamic channel to send messages. The dynamic channel is resolved (shown using the dotted arrow) by using a reference to a static channel defined in a schedule as shown on the right. There could be any number of such schedules. The dynamic channel will direct the outgoing message to the referenced port using the provided HTTP URL. The schedule on the left must receive the port reference in some message before it must resolve the dynamic channel. Comparing Figure 10.6 to Figure 10.3, the schedule on the left is like schedule C that generates responses, whereas the schedule on the right is like A or B that makes the request.

We reviewed characteristics of a BizTalk Messaging-based static port. Figure 10.6 showed how a reference to the static port is used to resolve a dynamic port. Now we review other characteristics of BizTalk Messaging-based ports in an XLANG schedule.

A port used to send messages can be static or dynamic. As stated earlier, the port reference for a port that sends messages is not used. A static port directs the messages to a known preexisting channel.

For a dynamic port, the channel to send the message to is selected at runtime. To resolve the channel to use, you must have previously received a message containing the destination address (as shown in Figure 10.6). You must connect this to the port reference field in the Port References message on the Data page. How a dynamic channel is resolved is described later in the section "BizTalk Messaging Binding Wizard." This is an advanced topic and will be further dealt with in Chapter 16.

Note

Note that a dynamic channel is not the same as an open channel, which is a channel not associated with a specific source organization.

This concludes the conceptual material for ports and their binding to specific implementation technologies.

Defining Data Flow Through Messages

This section covers the behavior of data and message flows. A message definition is created when an Action shape is connected to a port. These message definitions appear on the Data page. We looked at an example of such a page earlier in Figure 10.2, and you should now be familiar with many of the concepts.

Two wizards in the BizTalk Orchestration Designer guide you through the process of defining a message. The XML Communication Wizard defines messages used for sending or receiving over messaging services, such as BizTalk Messaging and MSMQ queues. The Method Communication Wizard defines messages used in making calls to or receiving calls from COM components. The wizards consist of pages shown in succession. We will look at each of these wizards next.

XML Communication Wizard

The XML Communication Wizard has five pages. The first page is the Welcome to the XML Communication Wizard. On this page, you specify whether the message is to be sent or received. For a port using BizTalk Messaging Services, the direction of message flow is dictated by the port; you cannot change this. On this page, you can also specify a latency value if you are going to receive messages through this port. By default, this latency is 0 seconds, which is the time that the engine expects to wait for a message to arrive on the port. The default latency of 0 seconds means that the message is expected to arrive immediately. A latency of greater than 180 seconds causes a schedule instance to dehydrate immediately; a smaller value means that the schedule will never dehydrate (unless forcibly dehydrated; see Chapter 11 to see how this can be done).

The next page of the wizard is Message Information. On this page, you specify the name of the message to use. You can choose to create a new message or use an existing message for this communication action. Note that a message is the only way data is passed into or out of the schedule. If an Action is not executed, the corresponding message is not created. Multiple Actions can share a message going through any port connected to a messaging implementation.

The third page of the wizard is XML Translation Information. On this page, you select whether you want to send messages in XML. Although you have the option of passing non-XML messages, the XLANG Scheduler Engine uses XML natively for processing all messages. Therefore, to use a non-XML message, you must apply (or remove) an XML wrapper around the message before (or after) the engine processes the message. The engine automatically manages the wrapper after you define the wrapper as a constant on the Data page and make the appropriate connections. See the discussion of `StringData` in the section "System and Special Fields." Where possible, using XML messages is preferred because of the added flexibility of using XPath expressions; see the description for the last page of the wizard.

The next page is Message Type Information. On this page, you assign a message type `label`. The XLANG Scheduler Engine uses this label for message type identification. This label property can be used to optimize the performance of a schedule as follows. If the message type label does not match the XML root element of the message schema, then the engine examines the contents of the actual message and picks only those messages whose root elements are specified by the schema. On the other hand, if the label does match, no such filtering is done. This message label is particularly useful with MSMQ queues, where a label is associated with a message and a program can peek at a message in the queue without retrieving it. The property `Use instance id as message label` is used for correlation, described in Chapter 16. The message schema is specified on the next and final page of the wizard.

The last page of the wizard is Message Specification Information. This page is not shown if you chose to handle non-XML messages. On this page, you can optionally specify a document specification (built using the BizTalk editor) to validate the message or to pick apart the message fields. Figure 10.7 shows this page.

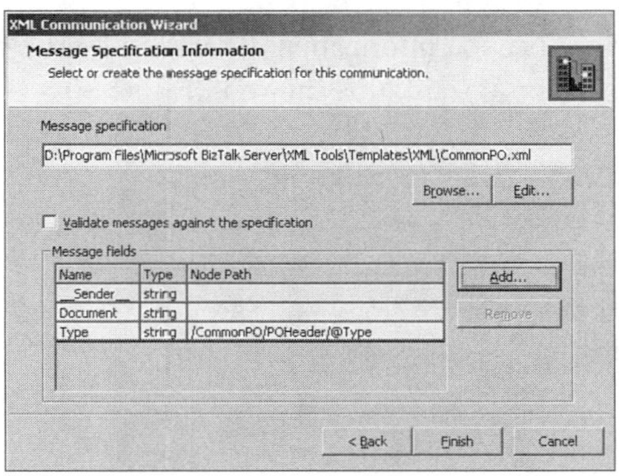

FIGURE 10.7
Adding message fields using the XML Communication Wizard.

Figure 10.7 shows that the `CommonPO.xml` message specification was selected. You can validate incoming messages against this specification by selecting the check box. Inside the Message Fields group, you can see the fields that will be available in the message on the Data page. The first two fields (`__Sender__` and `Document`) are always available. You can add more fields using XPath expressions to identify portions of the XML message. These fields can be used for building Rule expressions, or flowing the field to other messages in the schedule. Note that, if you pick apart fields like this, then, for an outgoing message, each field must be filled before the message can be sent.

The XPath expression must result in a scalar of an XLANG supported data type. You cannot select, for example, an XPath expression that results in an XML fragment as a message field.

Method Communication Wizard

The Method Communication Wizard has three pages. The Method Communication Wizard appears when you connect an action to a port using the COM component.

The first page, Welcome to the Method Communication Wizard, is functionally identical to the first page of the XML Communication Wizard. On this page, you specify whether the port is going to make an outgoing call or whether it is going to wait for an incoming call. As before, you can specify an expected latency period that governs how the schedule is dehydrated.

The second page is Message Information, as in the case of the XML Communication Wizard. On this page, you choose either to create a new message or reuse an existing message. You can reuse only the messages used for making or receiving method calls over the current port. You cannot share messages across ports.

The last page is Message Specification Information. It serves a similar purpose as the last page of the XML Communication Wizard. It is shown in Figure 10.8.

FIGURE 10.8
Specifying message fields using Method Communication Wizard.

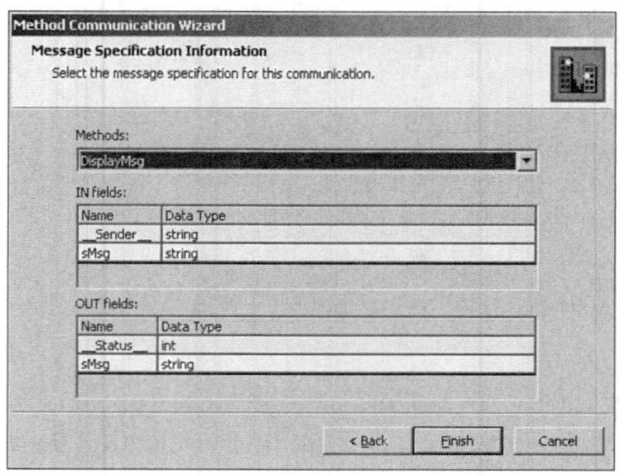

The message structure and the fields shown on the Data page are dictated by the method signature. The port represents a chosen interface of the COM component, and it can have many methods. You choose a specific method of this interface by picking it in the drop-down list box. The selected method determines the fields of the message. The selected fields are shown in the IN fields and the OUT fields portions of the wizard page.

For Visual Basic implementations, the IN fields contain all `ByVal` and `ByRef` parameters. The OUT fields contain only the `ByRef` parameters and function return values. For components implemented with scripting technology, all arguments are passed by reference, and therefore all arguments appear in both the IN and the OUT fields of the message.

For C/C++ implementations, the IN fields contain all `[in]` or `[in, out]` parameters as specified by the IDL. The OUT fields contain only the parameters with `[out]` or `[retval]` attributes.

If a field is present in both the IN and OUT parts of the message, then the IN part contains the pre-call, supplied, value, and the OUT part contains the post-call, returned, value. Recall that a message can either flow in from the port (a call into the schedule) or flow out (a call from the schedule). The IN fields are filled by the caller, and the OUT fields are filled by the callee to return the results.

Field Data Types

The following data types are supported in the message fields. The first column of Table 10.2 shows the data types denoted in the XLANG schedule; the other columns show corresponding data types in Automation and other languages.

TABLE 10.2 Data Types in an XLANG Schedule

XLANG	*Automation*	*Visual Basic*	*C*
Boolean	VT_BOOL	Boolean	VARIANT_BOOL
String	VT_BSTR	String	BSTR
Cy	VT_CY	Currency	CURRENCY
Date	VT_DATE	Date	Date
Dispatch	VT_DISPATCH	Object	IDispatch
Error	VT_ERROR		SCODE or HRESULT
I1	VT_I1		Signed char
I2	VT_I2	Integer	SHORT
I4	VT_I4	Long	LONG
Int	VT_INT		INT
R4	VT_R4	Single	FLOAT
R8	VT_R8	Double	DOUBLE
Ui1	VT_UI1	Byte	BYTE
Ui2	VT_UI2		USHORT
Ui4	VT_UI4		ULONG
Uint	VT_UINT		UINT
Unknown	VT_UNKNOWN	Object	IUnknown
Variant	VT_VARIANT	Variant	VARIANT

The data types of `Base64`, `Binary`, `ID`, `IDREF`, `IDREFS`, `Enumeration`, `i8`, and `ui8`, which are supported by BizTalk Messaging Services, are not supported by XLANG schedules.

Note that XLANG schedules can pass COM interface pointers via messages; however, only the supported interface types are passed.

System and Special Fields

In some examples earlier (for example, refer to Figure 10.2 or Figure 10.5), you saw messages with system-defined fields. These fields are provided by the XLANG implementation in addition to the fields required for message passing and method calls. Table 10.3 gives a summary of all such system or special fields.

TABLE 10.3 System and Special Fields

System Field	*Description*
`__Status__`	Returned status from a component. This is the `SCODE` or `HRESULT` and is included in the call return portion of a message pair.
`__Sender__`	Sender's authenticated identity as a `String` data type. The field is optionally checked by the receiver or callee of a message.
`Document`	The entire XML document as a `String` data type.
`StringData`	This is a special field defined when the document is not of XML form. The XLANG Scheduler Engine binds the non-XML document to this field. The non-XML document is wrapped as an element inside an XML wrapper. This wrapped entity, which is a well-formed XML document, is the preceding `Document` field.
	The wrapping XML fragment is an XLANG Scheduler Engine standard wrapper and is always `<?xml version="1.0" ?><StringData></StringData>`. The non-XML document is the value of the `StringData` element. To send non-XML messages, you must create a constant as the standard wrapper and connect it to the `Document` field of the outgoing message.
`__Exists__`	A test for whether a message exists.

Constants

The Constants message is a bag of named constant values for use within the Data page of the schedule. You can populate message fields with these values. Field values of the Constants message support additional data types that facilitate exchange of messages with the BizTalk Messaging Services. These additional data types are listed in Table 10.4.

TABLE 10.4 Additional Data Types for Constants

Data Type	*Description*
`Fixed Point` (14.4)	A data type useful for currency values. It can have at most 14 digits to the left of the decimal point and 4 digits to the right of the decimal point.
`Time`, `Time.tz`, `Date time`, and `Date time.tz`	These are four different data types. The format is a subset of the ISO 8601 format. `Time` has no date or time zone information. `Time.tz` is like `Time` but with time zone information. Similarly, for `Date time` and `Date time.tz`. Example: 2001-03-03T17:28:00-05:00
`URI`	Short form for Uniform Resource Identifier.
`UUID`	Short form for Universal Unique Identifier.

You can define constants of these data types and use them to plug in values in messages or parts of messages sent out by the schedule. The constants can also be used as part of Rule expressions.

Specifying Data Flow

After messages are created and displayed on the Data page, you can connect fields to show where data should flow. The arrow connecting the fields starts from the right of the source field to the left of the destination field. The movement of data, however, is tied to the actions being executed by the schedule—only those messages being sent or received by the action are populated with data flows.

A field can receive data from only one field; however, it can send data to many fields. The field providing data must have previously received data. In other words, a field is not valid unless a prior action caused it to be populated. You can check whether a message was received by using the `__Exists__` system field in a Rule.

Outgoing messages must have all their fields populated. The value of the field is not of consequence (it may be empty or null); it is important that the source of data needed to populate the field be specified in the drawing.

Message Flow Behavior

In this section, we review how messages flow into or out of a schedule through the ports. The XLANG Scheduler Engine, which hosts the schedule instance, manages the flow of messages in the running schedule. When an Action is performed, the running schedule intercepts messages that flow into or out of it, via a port. If the port is connected to a COM component, the schedule instance also holds (the proxy to) the component's interface needed for passing messages to it. Messages entering the schedule are captured as part of the schedule state; they are optionally parsed based on a schema, and the fields of the captured messages are available to populate outgoing messages or for use in Rule expressions within the schedule.

Some things are worth keeping in mind to understand the message flows. One is that the message flow occurs only in response to an Action being performed in the schedule. Another is that the schedule instance intercedes for an Action to deliver or receive a message to or from a port implementation. Finally, for a COM component, the schedule holds the interface required for passing messages to it. Having noted this, we look at two kinds of message exchange: synchronous and asynchronous.

As you know by now, an Action that communicates through a port connected to a COM component uses a message pair to communicate: one to make the method call request and pass arguments, and the other to receive the call response and return arguments. This is a synchronous exchange of messages. An Action that communicates through a port connected to a messaging service, on the other hand, uses a single message. This is an asynchronous action. For each of these two scenarios, the message sender can be the schedule or an outside application. Thus, there are four combinations to consider. These are depicted in Figure 10.9.

Figure 10.9 shows the two synchronous cases on top (cases 1 and 2), and the two asynchronous cases on the bottom (cases 3 and 4). The legend at the bottom describes the objects shown, and the arrows depict the flow of messages. Note that the port is just a logical endpoint for the delivery or receipt of messages; the message flow occurs when an Action is performed by the schedule instance. We look at each of these cases in the following sections.

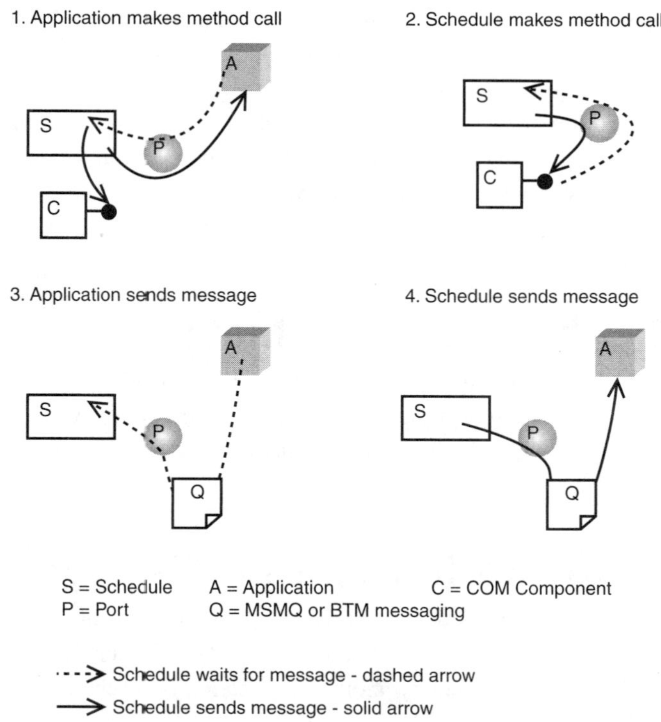

FIGURE 10.9
Message flow to or from a schedule.

Case 1: Application Calls a Method

This case is arguably the most nonintuitive of the three. In this case, an Action in the schedule is waiting for a method call from an application over a port bound to a COM component. In the schedule drawing, you see this as a message pair for a method call, with the blue arrow going into the Action shape on top of the red arrow depicting call return. When the application initiates the method call, the schedule intercepts the call request message and then forwards it to initiate the method call using the interface it holds for the COM component. It then again waits for the call to return from the component. When the call returns, it intercepts the returned message containing the returned parameters of the method call. Finally, it forwards the call return message to the application that initiated the call in the first place. Figure 10.9 shows these four steps using dashed and solid arrows.

The process is the same whether the port involved is static or dynamic. In either case, the schedule holds an interface to the COM component specified by the port, and messages are sent to the method on that interface.

One useful special case occurs when the application making the call merely wants to pass the call request message to the schedule and discards the call return message. That is, the application merely wants to provide some argument values. In this case, the schedule instance need not bother acquiring the COM interface in the first place! This is the case for No Instantiation when binding a COM implementation to a port. For a COM port binding, this is an additional option to Static or Dynamic in the wizard. You see this option when the port-binding wizards are described in the section "COM Component Binding Wizard."

Case 2: Schedule Calls a Method

In this case, an Action initiates a method call to a port bound to a COM component. The schedule passes the call request message by initiating the method call on the component's interface. The schedule then waits for the call response to come.

The next two cases are for asynchronous messaging.

Case 3: Application Sends a Message

This case is for an asynchronous receipt of a message. In this case, an Action waits for a message to arrive from a port connected to an MSMQ queue or BizTalk Messaging Services. The message is posted by another application or a schedule instance.

If the port is connected to BizTalk Messaging, the posted message may result in a new schedule being started. If the message is posted to an existing XLANG schedule, then it must be sent via the HTTP protocol for BizTalk Messaging to process it.

Case 4: Schedule Sends a Message

This case is for an asynchronous delivery of a message. In this case, an Action sends a message to a port connected to an MSMQ queue or BizTalk Messaging channel. The queue or the channel may be dynamic, but this does not alter the characteristics of the message flow.

Asynchronous and Synchronous Communication

Of the four cases shown in Figure 10.9, two showed synchronous exchange of messages, whereas the other two showed asynchronous exchange of messages.

Asynchronous communication, although arguably more difficult to use, is easy to understand. The sender just sends the message and forgets about it. The receiver waits until it gets a message. It is also more scalable because it provides loose coupling between the two communicating systems.

Synchronous communication, where the XLANG schedule calls a component, is akin to the normal programming paradigm of a function call. The XLANG schedule acquires an interface, possibly by instantiating the component, and makes the method call using the arguments described in the design of the schedule. This results in tight coupling between the interacting systems at the cost of concurrency.

Using asynchronous communication allows you to build robust and scalable solutions. In the real world, systems or applications that exchange documents do not reside on the same computing system. Different computing systems may encounter scheduled or unscheduled downtime, making the processes running on them unavailable. In addition, the network connectivity between the computing systems cannot be mandated. The connectivity may be disrupted due to operational reasons, or it may only be established at specific times. In such an environment, writing a tightly coupled solution is asking for trouble. The participating applications will interlock waiting for calls to return as every message is processed.

Asynchronous messaging allows one application to continue processing messages available to it and forwarding them to other applications without waiting for those applications to accept or process those messages. Typically, the messages get queued and wait until such time that the necessary communication channels become available or when the receiving application is able to process the message. The actual processing can be staggered to balance the load or prioritize the tasks.

State Management

An XLANG Scheduler Engine maintains the execution and messaging state of a schedule instance. This state must be correctly restored across system failures, in the presence of transactions, or when schedules are rehydrated. When a system recovers from a failure, the state of all the running schedules must be restored to some known point. If a transaction fails, the schedule must discard the changes caused by the failed transaction and restore the state prior to that transaction before continuing. When a schedule instance is dehydrated, the bulk of its state is saved to a database, with only some vestigial elements needed to detect any events that might trigger rehydration. Hence, state management is an important function of the XLANG Scheduler Engine.

If COM components are used in the schedule, then, clearly, the engine must know how the components themselves manage their state. This is not an issue for messaging services, which have their own persistence mechanisms and transport messages asynchronously—the schedule merely "fires and forgets" the message.

For a COM component, you can specify one of three options for how it handles state. The wizard used to set these options is described later in the section "COM Component Binding Wizard." The three options are

- Holds no state
- Holds state, but cannot persist it
- Holds state and can be asked to persist state on demand

Clearly, the first option where the component has no state to restore makes life easy for the engine. The XLANG schedules can be dehydrated or checkpointed prior to a transaction, without concern about how to deal with the internal state of the components. In this case, on restart, the engine can just discard the old component, create a brand-new component when the schedule next needs it, and use the new component to make method calls without concern for the component's internal computational state. This means that the instance of the component called may or may not be the one previously referenced in the schedule. If you passed an interface of this component to an application outside the schedule, that interface could be invalid some time later! However, not all is lost, at least within the schedule instance; the engine ensures that the references are updated when the schedule is rehydrated.

The second option, holding state but not being able to persist it, is not something you should aim for, if avoidable. This option provides for situations when you have no choice but to request the XLANG Scheduler Engine to try and hang on to the component (and its internal state). If the component is destroyed, its internal state goes with it. You may need to resort to this option—for example, when the component is communicating with legacy devices and the alternative of persisting its internal volatile state is unrealistic or impossible. In these situations, the XLANG Scheduler Engine keeps the component instance running. There is no automatic recovery available if the process hosting the component should die due to system failures.

The third option provides the more generalized solution. The XLANG Scheduler Engine can ask the component to checkpoint its state at any specific point in the process flow, or prior to dehydration. When checkpointed, the engine destroys the component object. The objects are re-created when necessary and asked to restore their saved state. The COM interfaces used for saving and restoring state are `IPersistStream` and `IPersistStreamInit`. If an object doesn't support both interfaces, it can not maintain state.

In Visual Basic, you implement these interfaces by setting class attributes to support persistence. When the class attribute is changed to `Persistable`, three new events are added to the class. These are `InitProperties`, `ReadProperties`, and `WriteProperties`. You must provide the proper implementation for these events.

Script components cannot implement the persistence interfaces, and hence you cannot specify the state options for such components.

The third option (and the first option) provides a scalable and robust solution. Note that state management is not an issue for messaging at all. The messaging systems provide their own persistence guarantees, the applications merely "fire and forget" messages.

We next look at how transactions are supported in the schedule.

Transaction Support

Recall from Chapter 9 that you can enclose a group of Actions within a Transaction shape. You can also declare the entire schedule as a transacted component by setting the properties of the Begin shape.

The XLANG Scheduler Engine manages the transactional integrity of a running schedule. This means that the effect of Actions enclosed by the Transaction either all occur or don't occur at all, and if they do occur, then the effects are never lost. The engine, therefore, checkpoints the entire state of the running schedule before and after a transaction. We looked at the state of the running schedule and how it is managed in the previous section "State Management." With transactions, when Actions enclosed by the transaction exchange messages through ports, the engine must coordinate the transaction state with the state in the port implementations. We now look at how transactions are used with each of the implementation technologies.

For messaging services, using transactions is simpler. MSMQ queues can be created as transactional, and you can optionally specify whether transactions are required when exchanging messages with the queue. MSMQ queues that are transactional use MSMQ transactions when exchanging messages. If you specify for the bound port that transactions are required, then the attached queue must be transactional, or else the engine will failfast the schedule. BizTalk Messaging queues are transactional. Due to the "fire-and-forget" nature of messaging, an action completes when the message is delivered or received. A transaction must make this action atomic and durable. Further coordination activity needed for the transaction, should it fail, is only to undo the delivery or receipt of a message. This simplicity is also related to the reduced isolation level supported by Messaging Services—for example, a message read by an uncommitted transaction is not seen on the queue by others, although it might reappear if the transaction aborts. The internal state of the messaging service is not of much concern for transaction management.

For COM components, using transactions effectively requires you to be aware of many options. These options, for example, allow you to use transaction-unaware components in your schedule and to control the isolation level at a fine granularity. The following transaction support is available for COM or script components that are installed. The wizard used to set these options is described later in the sections "COM Component Binding Wizard" and "Script Component Binding Wizard."

The following options are supported:

- Disabled—Applies to non-COM+ components. The component ignores COM transaction management.
- Not Supported—Applies to COM+ components. The component does not participate in transactions.
- Supported—Applies to COM+ components. If the XLANG Scheduler Engine has associated a transaction with the port, then the component can participate in that transaction context—the context flows through to the component. If no such transaction context is available, the component operates outside a transaction.
- Required—Applies to COM+ components. This is like the Supported option, except that if there is no transaction context available from the XLANG Scheduler Engine, the component creates a new one and operates within that context.
- Requires New—Applies to COM+ components. This states that the component always creates its own transaction context. This isolates the actions in the two contexts.

Notice that if a component is not installed in the COM+ environment, then from the point of view of the XLANG Scheduler Engine, transactions are disabled for it.

The default isolation level for COM+ configured components is serializable; however, you can specify a different isolation level as part of the Transaction properties, and this will override the COM+ setting. Note that, if a configured component calls a stored procedure, the isolation level and transaction context may be subverted by the stored procedure, causing unwanted behavior. Similarly, the transaction timeouts specified in the XLANG schedule override the default MSDTC settings.

See Chapter 9 for additional discussion of transactions and isolation levels. Chapter 9 also discusses the different kinds of transactions supported in an XLANG schedule. These are the short-lived DTC style transaction, long-lived transaction, and the timed transaction. The transaction attributes described in this section apply to the COM component and not to the XLANG transaction—they are primarily used with short-lived transactions.

Security

This section discusses security as it relates to ports and implementation technologies used in an XLANG schedule. As you already know, the schedule instance is created and managed by the XLANG Scheduler Engine. Both, the engine and the schedules are hosted as a COM+ application. Chapter 11 goes further into the details of this; however, the point is that, being COM+ applications, schedules abide by the native security mechanisms provided by Windows and COM+. These mechanisms consist of (among other things) access control based on role-based security and process identity. An application process that, for example, accesses a port on a running XLANG schedule must be appropriately authorized to do so. Chapter 11 describes these kinds of security issues relating to ports bound to COM components.

MSMQ queues have security settings that govern who can read or write messages from the queue. The identity of the COM+ application hosting the schedule must be included in the security settings for the queue; otherwise, the application or the schedule fails to post or receive messages from the queue.

BizTalk Messaging is itself implemented as a COM+ application, called `BizTalk Server Interchange Application`. Applications, including running schedule instances, that send messages to BizTalk Messaging must comply with the security settings for the COM+ application. This application provides the document submission API for BizTalk Messaging Services. Thus, a COM+ application that hosts an XLANG schedule must have appropriate rights to submit a document to BizTalk Messaging. Conversely, BizTalk Messaging Service must have adequate rights to create schedules or post messages to ports on the schedules. These rights are configured, for example, by assigning the Windows logon identity used by BizTalk Messaging service to the COM+ roles of the application that hosts the XLANG schedule.

Note

The default installation of BizTalk is not properly secured. You must enable security for BizTalk Messaging and populate COM+ roles that govern access to the XLANG Scheduler Engine and to messaging. For details, see Microsoft knowledge base article Q275849 on how to secure the BizTalk Server Messaging Service.

Not only schedules, but COM+ components also use the role-based security, hence schedules calling COM+ configured components must comply with the security settings for these components.

In addition to these built-in security features, which are automatically enforced, with XLANG schedules you have access to the message sender's authenticated identity in the XLANG schedule. This identity is provided as a field of a message on the Data page. This identity is of the `String` type and can be passed in messages. The data type is a `BSTR`, and it is a sequence of bytes representing a Windows 2000 SID. SID stands for a *Security Identifier*—a unique byte sequence assigned by Windows 2000 to identify a user or a group. (See the Platform SDK documentation on the structure of SIDs.)

The sender's identity is available when a message is received on ports connected to COM components or MSMQ queues (not from BizTalk Messaging Services). When you bind the port to its implementation, you can specify one of the following three options:

- Sender's identity is not required to receive a message.
- Sender's identity is optional. This identity can be accessed on the Data page, when available.
- Sender's identity is required; the XLANG Scheduler Engine will not accept a message from a sender whose identity cannot be established (authenticated).

The sender's identity is available in the Data page and may be logged or passed as a field in subsequent messages.

If the XLANG Scheduler Engine is unable to establish the identity of a message delivered by MSMQ, then it is posted to a dead letter queue. The queue is created if it is not present and is called `.\private$\<ApplicationName>.DeadLetter`, where the token `<ApplicationName>` is replaced by the name of the COM+ application hosting the schedule instance. The default host application is the XLANG Scheduler.

Wizards for Port Implementations

This section reviews the wizards used to specify the implementation options. The meaning of these options should now be much clearer.

There are four wizards used to bind an implementation to a port—one each for the technology used for binding. We cover each of these in turn here.

COM Component Binding Wizard

The COM Component Binding Wizard has six pages; some pages may not be shown, as described.

On the first page, you specify the port name. On the second page, Static or Dynamic Communication, you specify the instantiation options for the component (see Figure 10.10).

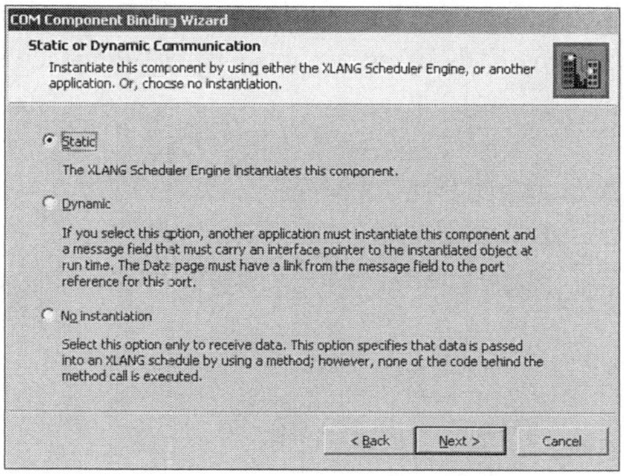

FIGURE 10.10
COM component instantiation options.

Figure 10.10 shows the three options of Static, Dynamic, and No Instantiation. The text provides a short description for each of these options. These concepts were discussed previously in the sections "Port References and Dynamic Ports," "A Port Using COM Components," and "Case 1: Application Calls a Method."

On the third page, Class Information, you choose a registered COM component or specify that the class instance be acquired through a moniker implementation (see Figure 10.11).

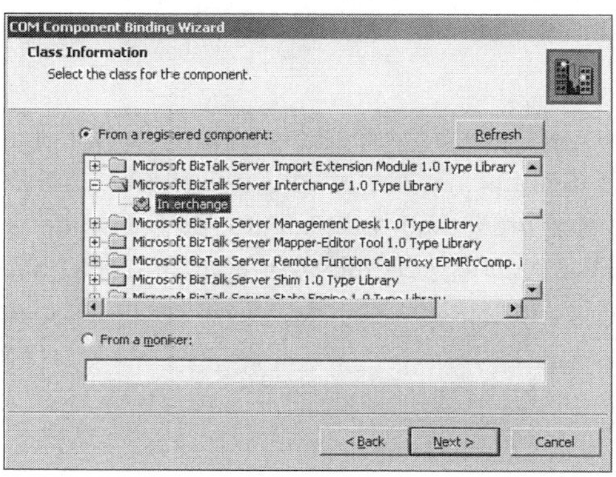

FIGURE 10.11
COM component class information.

Figure 10.11 shows the selection of the class with the name of Microsoft BizTalk Server Interchange 1.0 Type Library. The prog-id, BizTalk.Interchange.1, is not shown in Figure 10.11. If you select a moniker implementation to instantiate the class, then the class instance cannot be used with XLANG transactions.

On the fourth page, Interface Information, you choose the interface. If the class has only one interface, then this page does not appear. For components implemented using Visual Basic, class interfaces are shown with an underscore prefix.

On the fifth page, Method Information, you choose the methods that can be called through this port binding. The methods listed are those of the interface selected earlier. Figure 10.12 shows this page.

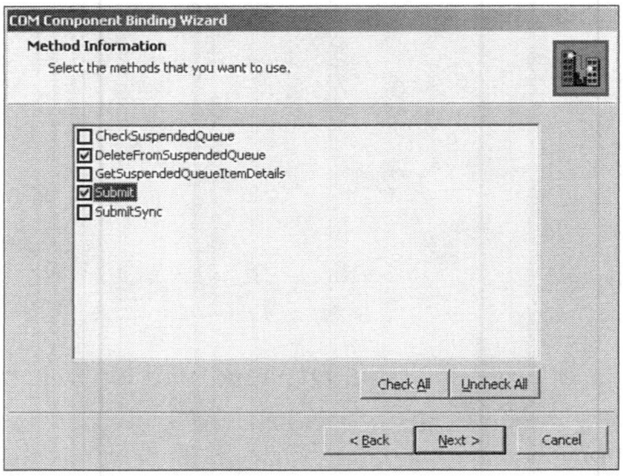

FIGURE 10.12
COM component method information.

Figure 10.12 shows that two methods have been selected. You must select at least one. Buttons are provided to select all methods or to deselect all methods. This page is not shown if the interface has only one method.

On the final page, Advanced Port Properties, as shown in Figure 10.13, you specify options for Security, Transaction Support, State Management Support, and Error Handling.

For security options, if you specify that the sender's identity is Optional, then the schedule requests the identity but continues to run, even if it is not available. If you specify that the sender's identity is Required, then if the identity is not available, the message is ignored. In an incoming call, the caller gets the error `E_ACCESSDENIED`. For the background on security options, see the section "Security" earlier in the chapter.

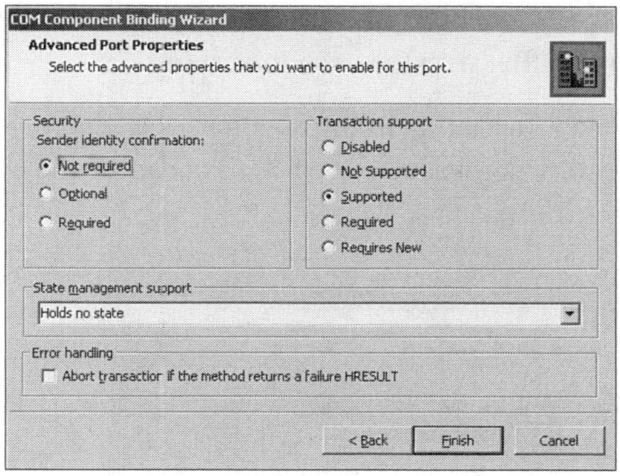

FIGURE 10.13
COM component advanced properties.

For transaction support options, select the appropriate option based on the component and business process. The transaction concepts were covered previously in the section "Transaction Support."

The state management options are chosen by selecting an item from the drop-down box. The choices are Holds No State, Holds State, But Doesn't Support Persistence, or Holds State, and Does Support Persistence. If you chose the last option, the component should implement the COM persistence interfaces. The state management concepts were covered previously in the section "State Management."

For error handling there is only one option: Abort Transaction if the Method Returns a Failure `HRESULT`. You can set this option only if the port is used in a transaction context in the schedule. The associated transaction is aborted if `HRESULT` denotes a failure. This option is useful for COM components not configured in COM+ or which do not natively support transactions. It works with all types of XLANG transactions.

We next look at the Script Component Binding Wizard.

Script Component Binding Wizard

The Script Component Binding Wizard is similar to the COM Component Binding Wizard, and it has six pages.

The first page is used to name the port. The second page specifies the instantiation options, as shown in Figure 10.10.

Instantiation concepts were covered previously in the sections "Port References and Dynamic Ports," "A Port Using COM Components," and "Case 1: Application Calls a Method."

On the third page, Specify the Script File, you can enter or browse to the path of the Windows Scripting Component file, with the `.wsc` extension.

On the fourth page, Component Instantiation Information, you specify whether the schedule should use a script file moniker or a prog-id to construct the component instance. Figure 10.14 shows this page.

FIGURE 10.14
Script Component instantiation information.

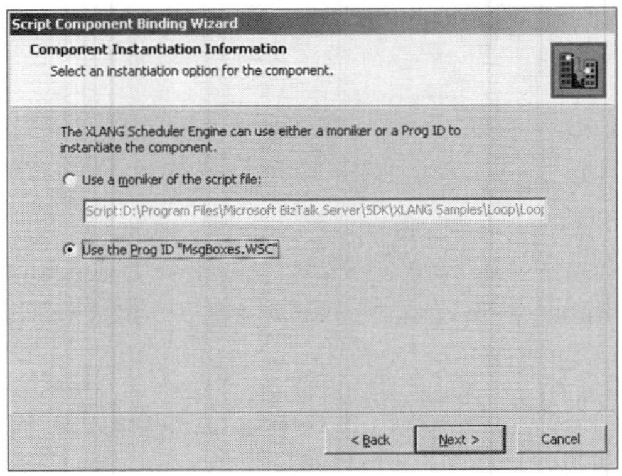

This page is akin to the class information for a COM component. This page is not shown if the schedule does not have to construct the component instance—that is, when you select either Dynamic or No Instantiation on the second page.

On the fifth page, Method Information, you select the method to use with this port binding. This page is similar to Figure 10.12 and is skipped if the script component has just one method.

The final page, Advanced Port Properties, is similar to Figure 10.13. One difference is that you cannot specify the state management options for scripting components—they cannot persist state.

> **Note**
>
> State management concepts were covered previously in the section "State Management"; refer to this section for the problems of not being able to persist state. The security and transaction concepts were covered previously in the sections "Security" and "Transaction Support," respectively.

Message Queuing Binding Wizard

This section covers the wizard for the MSMQ messaging technology. The Message Queuing Binding Wizard has four pages. Figure 10.15 shows the first page.

FIGURE 10.15
Message queuing—select or create a port.

On this first page, you can either create a new port and provide a name for it, or, if you have created unbound ports earlier (see the previous section "Ports"), then you can choose to use them with MSMQ.

The second page, Static or Dynamic Queue Information, is shown in Figure 10.16.

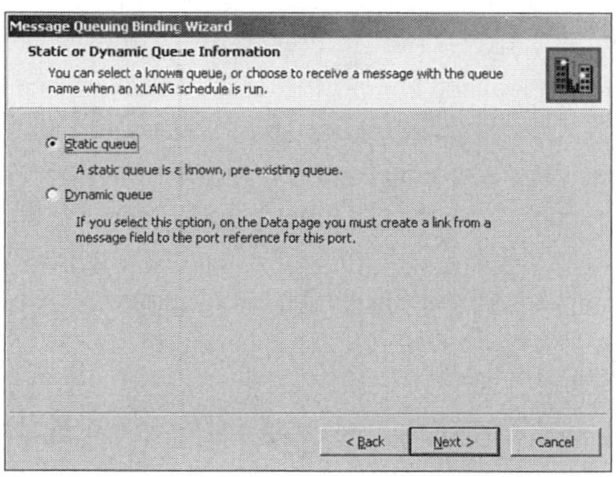

FIGURE 10.16
Message queuing—selecting preexisting or dynamic queue.

On this page, you choose to use a preexisting queue or a queue known only at runtime. If you choose the dynamic queue option, then you must identify how the schedule will get a reference to such a queue (at runtime) by connecting a link from a message field to the Port References message on the Data page. See the sections "Ports," "Port References and Dynamic Ports," "A Port Using Message Queuing," and "Defining Data Flow Through Messages" for more information.

The third page, Queue Information, is shown in Figure 10.17.

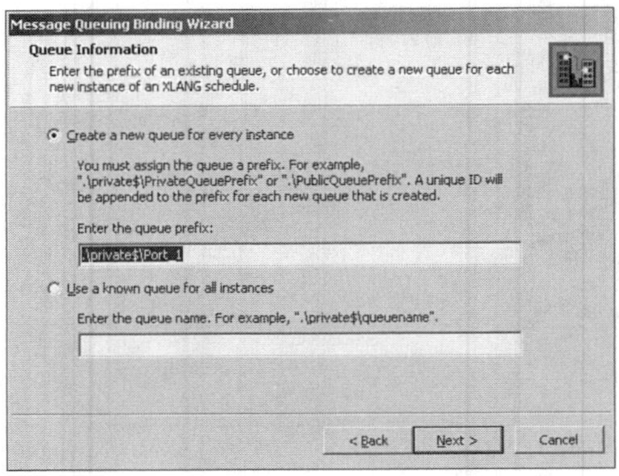

FIGURE 10.17
Message queueing—queue information.

On this page, you specify the queue you want to use. You have two options: create a new, uniquely named, queue for each instance of the schedule or create a known queue shared among all instances of the schedule. If a new queue is created for every schedule instance, the queue itself is uniquely named and created by the XLANG Scheduler Engine. The naming algorithm consists of appending a GUID to the name prefix you specify. Such a queue provides a useful port reference for getting back response document(s) to a specific schedule instance. The port reference can be used to resolve a dynamic port in another schedule later. In Figure 10.3, you could regard schedules A and B to be just two instances of the same schedule, and the dynamic port in schedule C can be resolved to the correct queue. If, instead, a known queue is used, then the queue must be created before the schedule instance is launched. If such a queue is used to resolve a dynamic port, then all responses will end up in the same queue.

The fourth, and the final, page is Advanced Port Properties, shown in Figure 10.18.

On this page, you have two sets of options to select: Security and Transaction Support.

Under the Security options, if you specify that the sender's identity is Not Required, then the `__Sender__` field for the received message is always blank. If you specify that the sender's identity is Optional, then the authenticated identity of the sender (if available) is provided in the `__Sender__` field. The value is the same as in the MSMQ message's `SenderID` property. If you specify that the sender's identity is Required, then the schedule receives the message only if the sender's authenticated identity is available.

Otherwise, the message is relegated to a dead letter queue, named after the COM+ application hosting the schedule, and an event is posted to the application event log. See also the previous section, "Security."

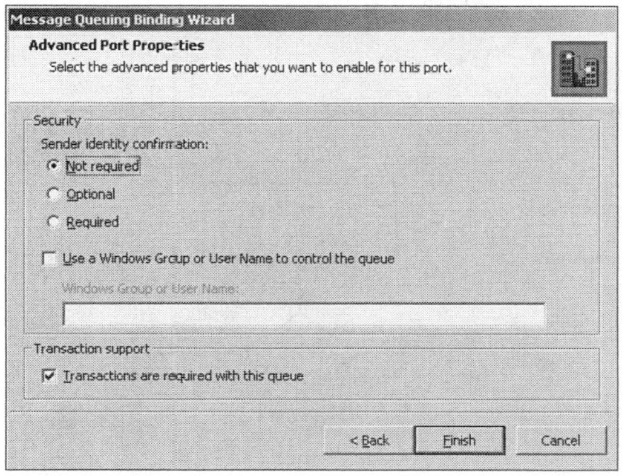

FIGURE 10.18
Message queuing—advanced port properties.

Under the Security options, you can also specify the Windows Group or User Name that should be used to post messages to the queue. These options are available only for a static queue.

In the Transaction Support area, you select whether Transactions Are Required with This Queue. If the queue is in fact not transactional, then, at runtime, the XLANG scheduler will fail-fast the schedule instance (that is, promptly destroy the instance).

BizTalk Messaging Binding Wizard

The BizTalk Messaging Binding Wizard has a different sequence of pages depending on whether messages are sent or received. The page sequence is shown in Figure 10.19. There are in all five pages; however, the actual pages shown depend on the choices made. These pages are described next.

On the first page, you specify the name of a new port or use an existing unbound port (see the section "Ports" earlier in the chapter). This page is shown in Figure 10.20.

On the next page, Communication Direction, you can choose to either send or receive messages. This page is shown in Figure 10.21.

As shown in Figure 10.19, the wizard pages shown next depend on whether you choose to send or receive documents. If you select to send messages, then the Static or Dynamic Channel Information page appears (see Figure 10.22). On this page, you can specify the name of a preexisting channel or a dynamic channel.

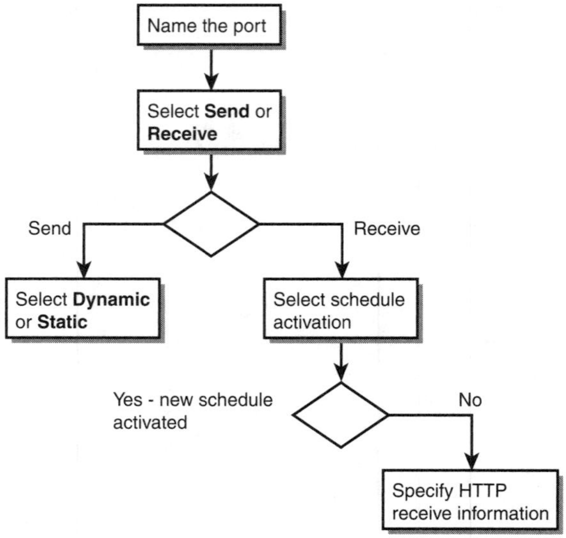

FIGURE 10.19
BizTalk Messaging wizard pages.

FIGURE 10.20
BizTalk Messaging—name the port.

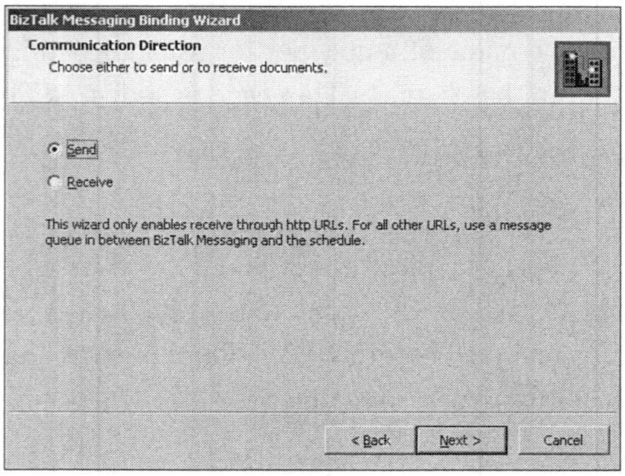

FIGURE 10.21
BizTalk Messaging—send or receive selection.

FIGURE 10.22
BizTalk Messaging—static of dynamic channel.

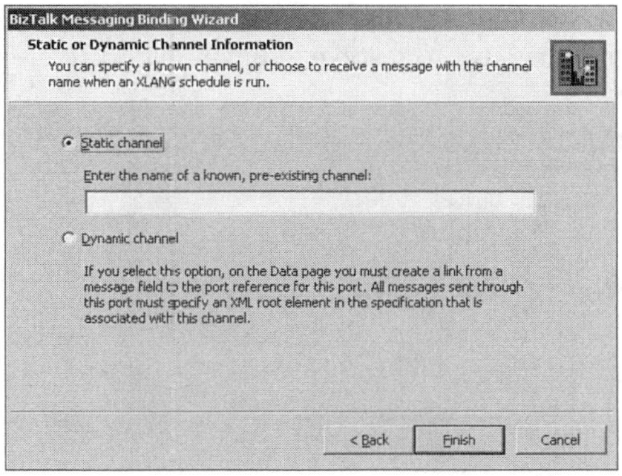

If you select Dynamic Channel, then the channel to deliver the message is determined at runtime. BizTalk Messaging Services already defines an algorithm for channel selection. Recall from Chapter 6 that this algorithm is a channel that is selected based on the triplet consisting of the source address, the destination address, and the document type.

The candidate channel must be configured with the XLANG schedule as its source and must be associated with an open messaging port. The destination address is specified at runtime. On the Data page, you choose a field in a received message and link it to the port reference for the dynamic channel. The field should contain a destination address for the open messaging port. The last leg of the triplet is the document type. You specify this when you use the XML Communication Wizard—the message flowing through the dynamic channel uses this document type.

There should be exactly one channel configured to meet the previous selection criteria. If this is not so, then the schedule instance will fail-fast and generate an application event-log entry. For additional discussion of dynamic channels, see the section "A Port Using BizTalk Messaging" earlier in the chapter.

This sequence of pages concludes the set of pages associated with the Send option. If you choose the Receive option instead, then the XLANG Schedule Activation Information page is displayed next, shown in Figure 10.23. See the sequence of pages in Figure 10.19.

On this page, you select whether the received message results in the activation of a new schedule instance. If you choose Yes, then there are restrictions on how this port can be used. These restrictions are

- Only one port in the schedule can be configured to activate the schedule.
- Only one message can be received. You cannot use this port to repetitively get multiple messages in a loop or use it in multiple actions to receive messages.

- You cannot forward a reference to this port via any message on the Data page. In other words, you cannot use this to resolve a dynamic port reference elsewhere.

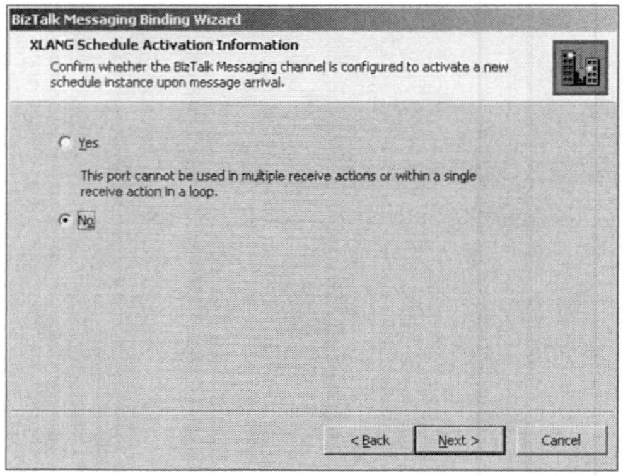

FIGURE 10.23
BizTalk Messaging—schedule activation.

There are no more steps to complete in the wizard at this point.

On the other hand, if you choose No—that is, the incoming message does not activate a new schedule—then you are presented with the page shown in Figure 10.24, Channel Information. Note the wizard page sequence shown in Figure 10.19 again to see what stage of the wizard you are at.

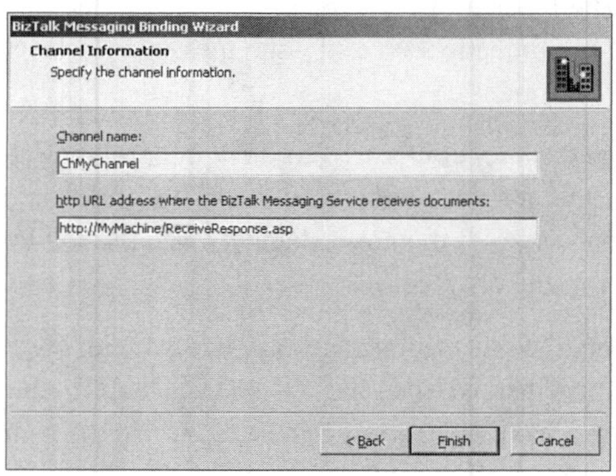

FIGURE 10.24
BizTalk Messaging—channel information.

On this page, you specify the channel that receives the incoming document over HTTP and the HTTP address where BizTalk Messaging Service receives the document. Recall from the section "A Port Using BizTalk Messaging," and also depicted in Figure 10.6, that HTTP is the only supported protocol to receive documents from a dynamic channel.

A sample ASP page, called `ReceiveResponse.asp`, is provided with the product for receiving documents over HTTP. This ASP page must be installed in an appropriately secured Web site. The sending dynamic channel constructs a URL of the following form to deliver the message:

```
https://MyMachine/ReceiveResponse.asp?channel=ChMyChannel&qpath=
➥MyMachine.MyDomain.com\private$\ChMyChannel{53E259E9-938C-4629-9E05-
6472A5CFE16D}
```

Note, in Figure 10.24, that the `ReceiveResponse.asp` page is accessed in the URL. The arguments in the URL specify the channel and the queue set up by the source XLANG schedule to receive the document.

The argument `channel` contains the name of the channel to receive the response document. You must create this channel. If this channel is not present, you get an application event log entry (from the XLANG Scheduler, with event category of `WFBinding`) stating that a valid open destination channel could not be found. This receiving channel can be used to validate and transform the incoming response document.

The argument `qpath` is treated as the destination identifier for document routing. Note that it is a per-schedule instance of an MSMQ queue, with the name constructed from the channel name and a GUID. This queue is created by the sending XLANG schedule as an endpoint to receive the response document. This queue is the target of the open destination port attached to the channel.

The system receiving the original document and generating the response does not have to run BizTalk Server. It merely posts the response, however generated, to the URL it receives embedded in the original document.

The server-side script `ReceiveResponse.asp` extracts the channel name and queue path information in the URL and uses this information to submit the document to BizTalk. The extracted channel and queue path are provided as routing information to BizTalk.

Note

See the BizTalk documentation for the `IInterchange::Submit` method for the arguments accepted by the method. Also see the code in the `ReceiveResponse.asp` provided with the product. See the section "A Port Using BizTalk Messaging" for more information about dynamic channels. As stated there, this is an advanced topic and will be discussed in detail in Chapter 16.

XLANG Schedule Development

Chapter 11 and Chapter 13 delve into the runtime for XLANG schedules and into advanced use cases. This section augments the rest of the chapter and describes only the basic concepts and techniques to develop and run XLANG schedules.

The general sequence of developing an XLANG schedule is to design it using the XLANG designer, compile it, and finally run the schedule and optionally monitor it. The compiled form of the schedule uses an XML syntax for the file format. The compiled schedule is run by the XLANG Scheduler Engine.

The XLANG Scheduler Engine runs in a COM+ application, which is set up at BizTalk install time. You may create additional COM+ applications to host XLANG schedule instances, although the engine still runs in the original application. These additional applications provide process isolation for the running schedules.

The development and runtime activities for using BizTalk Orchestration are covered next.

Development

During development, you will probably try out many configurations of your business process. You might have to try out different components and organization for queues and messaging channels, along with many rules appropriate for use in your business process. At some point, when you have designed at least the core parts of your schedule, you need to compile it. The process of compilation also performs a consistency and validity check on the schedule drawing. The orchestration drawing file has the extension `.skv`; the compiled file has the extension `.skx`. You compile the drawing by using the menu option File, Make <*DrawingName.skx*>. Figure 10.25 shows the menu bar with the Tools menu expanded, which is described next. The File menu is visible but is not shown expanded.

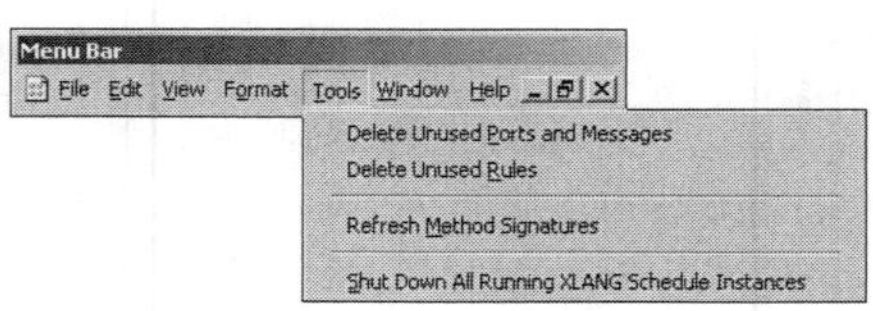

FIGURE 10.25
BizTalk Orchestration Designer menu bar and Tools menu.

When going through design gyrations, it is not unusual to have ports or messages that you thought you needed but don't anymore. The Tools menu can be used to remove unused (and probably unwanted) ports, messages, and rules from your drawing. This is done by using the menu options Delete Unused Ports and Messages and Delete Unused Rules. While designing the schedule, you may also update your components, adding new methods or arguments. The Tools menu item in the designer allows you to look for updated method signatures for the components used in your drawing. This is done by using the menu item Refresh Method Signatures.

The last menu item under the Tools menu is useful. The XLANG Scheduler Engine caches the schedules when it is running. If you were to modify a schedule and then rerun it, the engine would run the cached version of the schedule unless you restart the engine. Hence, if you modify a schedule, you should use this menu item to Shut Down All Running XLANG Schedule Instances.

Each schedule has a distinct identity. You can see this identity in the properties for the Begin shape in the form of a GUID. Every time you make modifications to your schedule, this GUID identity changes. You can use this identity to correlate your drawing (the `.skv` file) with the compiled schedule (the `.skx` file), which is an XML text file.

Figure 10.26 shows the viewing options in the designer.

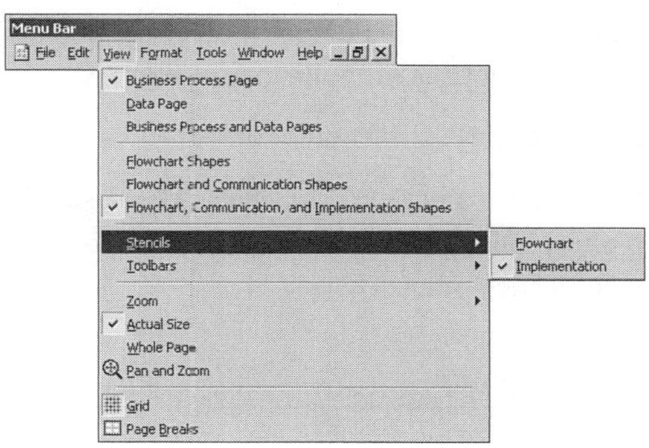

FIGURE 10.26
BizTalk Orchestration Designer viewing options.

By making appropriate selections on the menu, you can filter or augment the items you see in the designer. The first three menu options let you control which tabs are shown. You can switch between the Business Process or the Data tab by choosing the menu option or by clicking on the tab. You can optionally view both tabs at the same time—in this case, two windows are created and tiled horizontally to show each tab in its own window. The next set of menu options is used to filter the shapes shown on the drawing. You can optionally hide the ports or implementation shapes to reduce screen clutter depending on the task at hand. The stencils, too, can be hidden or shown. The stencil panes are normally docked; these can be optionally floated to free up more screen real estate for viewing. There is only one toolbar, and it cannot be changed.

The XLANG drawing can be zoomed using the toolbar buttons or zoom options, or you can use the menu options. The Pan and Zoom menu option opens a floating window containing a full page view in miniature with a marked rectangle depicting the area actually shown in the main window. You can drag the marked rectangle in the small floating window to pan and zoom in the main window. This is useful for navigating within a complex schedule where it might be necessary to zoom into specific areas of the schedule to work on it.

The remaining menu options allow you to display or hide the grid on the page and to show the page breaks if the schedule were to be printed.

Running XLANG Schedules: Using Monikers

This section describes how you run XLANG schedules. When BizTalk Orchestration is installed, it also installs the `sked` moniker class. This, in COM parlance, is a server that implements the `IMoniker` interface and provides the intelligence to bind names to object instances (see the side bar on this topic). The moniker class determines the structure of the name and how it is used to bind to an object instance. The `sked` moniker class provides this naming and binding service for the range of objects created by the XLANG Scheduler Engine. The moniker name has the following syntax:

```
Sked://[HostName][!GroupManager][/FilePath[/PortName]]
```

The optional components are enclosed in the `[]` brackets. The nested brackets indicate that the inner bracket is applicable only if the token in the outer bracket is specified. Table 10.5 describes the significance of each token.

TABLE 10.5 Schedule Moniker Syntax

Token	*Description*
`HostName`	You can specify the computer on which the object is to be created or is already running. If this token is missing, then the local computer is assumed by default.
`GroupManager`	This is the name of the COM+ application to use to host the object. If this token is missing, then the default application of XLANG Scheduler is assumed.

TABLE 10.5 continued

Token	*Description*
	If this and all subsequent tokens are missing, then a global object capable of enumerating currently defined group managers (COM+ applications) is instantiated. Note the `!` used to separate this token and host name.
`FilePath`	This is the path of the `.skx` file, which is the compiled XLANG schedule. If this token is missing, then a group manager object is created that represents that COM+ host application.
`PortName`	This is the name of the port bound to a COM component (not related to a messaging port) in the schedule. If this token is missing, then the schedule object is instantiated. If this token is present, then a COM proxy to the port is instantiated.

You can use the `sked` moniker class to instantiate a schedule. The following code fragment uses such a moniker to instantiate a schedule. This example starts the `ExampleSchedule.skx` schedule on the local system using the default group manager:

```
Dim oInst as COMRUNTIME.IWFWorkflowInstance
Set oInst = GetObject("sked:///C:\Temp\ExampleSchedule.skx")
```

The `COMRUNTIME` is a reference to the XLANG Scheduler Runtime Type Library. Of course, if you were to use VB Script, you wouldn't specify a type for `oInst` above.

Schedules may also be started by BizTalk Messaging on receipt of a message. To do this, a BizTalk messaging port must be appropriately configured to deliver the message to a new schedule instance. The messaging port references the schedule's port that will receive the message. See the section "BizTalk Messaging Binding Wizard" for information on setting up the port to receive messages. Also see Chapter 6 and Chapter 12, "Advanced BizTalk Messaging."

Another option to start schedules is to use the XLANG monitor described in the section "Monitoring" later in the chapter.

Stopping XLANG Schedules

This section looks briefly at using the COM+ facilities and the XLANG Event Monitor to manage schedules. XLANG schedules are run by the engine, which runs in a COM+ application. It is possible for you to use the COM+ management console to shut down the application and hence any schedules running in that application; however, it is not advisable to do so for many reasons.

To properly shut down running XLANG schedules, either use the assigned button to perform this task (the button is on the XLANG tab of the properties of the COM+ application hosting XLANG schedules; for details, see Chapter 11), or use the Tools menu in the XLANG Orchestration Designer (see the section "Development" earlier in the chapter).

Shutting down running schedules does not terminate them; instead, the schedules get dehydrated to the persistence database. You can rehydrate them by using the button provided on the XLANG property page of the COM+ application. Running schedules can be terminated using the XLANG Event Monitor.

If you shut down the COM+ application running XLANG schedules or kill the process some other way, it leaves components that are not in the COM+ application still running, and the schedule state will not be properly captured for restart.

Monitoring

To monitor the operation of the XLANG schedules, you can use the Microsoft Management Console (MMC), the BizTalk Tracking Database, or the XLANG Event Monitor.

The XLANG Scheduler Engine posts events to the Application Error Log. You can view this log in the system's event viewer through the MMC.

A tool, called the XLANG Event Monitor, is provided with the product. This tool is described further in Chapter 11. This tool hooks into the events raised by the XLANG Scheduler Engine and into the persistence database for the schedules. You can use this tool to see which schedules are running and their current progress. The XLANG Event Monitor can also be used for starting new XLANG schedule instances by using the Run menu and typing in the schedule's moniker.

Besides the event log, one useful technique is to write a small COM component that can display a message box or write to the debugger using the Win32 call `OutputDebugString`. You can use the system debug monitor, `DbMon`, that comes with the Platform SDK to view the output from your test component.

You can also have your components generate log files or monitor the effects of running your schedules by looking for files being created or written or looking for messages archived in the tracking database.

Summary

This chapter describes all the tools and wizards available to you with the BizTalk Orchestration Designer. More importantly, this chapter discusses the concepts you must understand to make meaningful choices when you do use these tools and wizards. This two-pronged approach should enable you to construct properly crafted XLANG schedules.

Having covered the business process drawing earlier in Chapter 9, we started with the implementation of the business process in this chapter. Chapter 9 outlined four areas of focus. This chapter is dedicated to the areas of business process implementation and data flows.

The chapter started with the description of what constitutes a business process implementation. We discussed the four supported implementation technologies. These are compiled COM+ components, script components, MSMQ message queuing, and BizTalk Messaging. This was followed by discussing the concept of ports and port references.

Port references are used to resolve dynamic ports. Each implementation technology has its own peculiarities in how port references and dynamic ports function. We delved into each in turn.

An Action in a running XLANG schedule results in the exchange of messages through ports. When an Action shape in a business process is connected to a port, these message definitions are created. We discussed the XML Communication Wizard and the Method Communication Wizard. These wizards guide the process of defining the messages.

As part of describing the messages in the schedule, we looked at the data types supported in the message and how data flows from field to field can be described in the schedule. Messages can be either synchronous or asynchronous; they can be externally initiated or schedule initiated. We looked at all these cases and what the key differences are.

The message flows associated with a running schedule have ramifications of state management, transaction management, and security. We first explored the issues conceptually and then looked at the port implementation wizards that assist in configuring the implementations correctly. We looked at the COM Component Binding Wizard, Script Component Binding Wizard, Message Queuing Binding Wizard, and BizTalk Messaging Binding Wizard in turn.

The chapter concluded with a review of the basics of developing and running XLANG schedules.

CHAPTER 11

XLANG Orchestration Engine

by Dilip Hardas

IN THIS CHAPTER

The XLANG Orchestration Engine controls the activation, execution, dehydration, and rehydration of running XLANG schedule instances. In Chapter 9, "Introducing BizTalk Orchestration," and Chapter 10, "Using the BizTalk Orchestration Designer," you learned how to create and compile BizTalk Orchestration schedules into an XML grammar named XLANG. In this chapter, you learn how the XLANG schedule created by the designer is processed.

When you install BizTalk Server 2002, several COM+ applications are created and configured, including one named the XLANG Scheduler. For a primer on COM+, see the sidebar. The XLANG Scheduler COM+ application hosts the default instance of the XLANG Scheduler Engine. To instantiate an instance of an XLANG schedule, you pass the moniker of an XLANG schedule to the XLANG Scheduler Engine. The engine instantiates the schedule instance and then begins to execute it. During the execution of the schedule, the engine may need to dehydrate or save the current state of the schedule. This occurs when the XLANG Scheduler Engine expects to wait for 3 or more minutes to receive a message. The engine, utilizing COM+ services, provides all the runtime services needed to execute the compiled XLANG schedule.

COM+ Primer for BizTalk Orchestration

COM+ is an evolution of COM—an acronym that stands for Component Object Model. COM+ provides component services such as security, transaction management, process isolation, thread allocation, concurrency, object pooling, and others to applications that you develop and deploy on the Windows 2000 system. A COM+ application is a group of COM components that share a common context (such as security and transaction) within COM+. This application is the primary unit of administration in COM+.

For BizTalk Orchestration, the COM+ applications used to host XLANG schedules are server applications, as opposed to library applications. In a server application, components run in a dedicated system process provided by COM+, whereas in a library application, the components run in the caller's process. Access to server applications, and the contained components and methods, is controlled by COM+ role-based security. The application process itself is run under a designated Windows logon identity. It is customary for this identity to be Interactive User during development, although this setting is unacceptable in a production situation.

Components in a COM+ application are called *configured components*, and these components can take advantage of COM+ services. With configured components, it is easier to build robust, scalable, and secure applications.

The XLANG Scheduler Engine is set up as one or more COM+ applications that can host running schedule instances. These applications can also contain configured components used by the running schedules. The components and schedules can be easily secured using COM+ security mechanisms. Short-lived XLANG transactions are integrated with COM+ transactions. COM+ events are used by tools that monitor schedule execution.

This chapter discusses the runtime behavior, programming model, and monitoring tools for the XLANG Orchestration Engine.

Specifically, you will learn:

- How XLANG schedules are run on the system
- What programmatic interfaces are supported to access these running schedules
- How to monitor these schedules in real-time and generate historical traces for troubleshooting
- How this information affects your design

You will recall from Chapter 9 that the XLANG Orchestration Engine implements a moniker class of the type `sked`. The chapter also described the moniker syntax supported by this moniker class and listed the corresponding objects provided by the class implementation. Later in this chapter, we will review each of these objects along with their properties and methods. Figure 11.1 is a pictorial summary of the runtime object model and the associated moniker syntax.

Figure 11.1 shows interfaces defined by `SkedCore.dll` (type library is called the `XLANG Scheduler Runtime Type Library`) and objects and collections implemented by `SkedsMgr.dll` (type library is called the `XLANG Scheduler - System Manager`). The figure also shows the key interfaces exposed by those objects. When you use these objects or interfaces in your programs, you can reference these type libraries.

Figure 11.1 shows the System Manager as the root of an object hierarchy. The COM class for the System Manager is called `SYSMGRLib.SysMgr`. The System Manager class is installed in the COM+ application named XLANG Scheduler. This is also the default host for running schedule instances and contains the default instance of the XLANG Scheduler Engine.

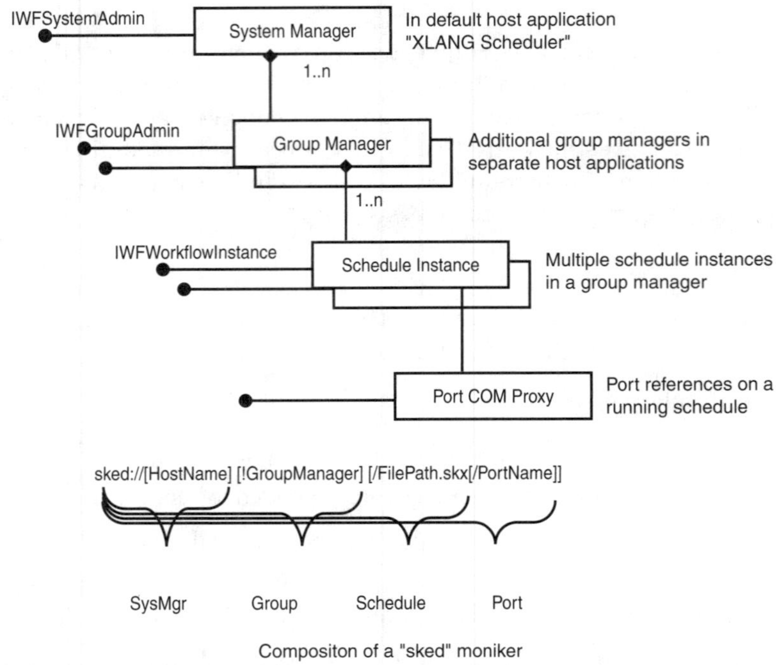

FIGURE 11.1
Objects exposed by XLANG Orchestration Engine.

There is a single instance of the System Manager root object on a server. This instance exposes a collection of group managers on that server. Each group manager represents a COM+ application on the server that can host the XLANG Scheduler Engine and run instances of XLANG schedules. Not all COM+ applications are enabled to run XLANG schedule instances and therefore are not group managers.

Each group manager instance exposes a collection of currently running schedule instances, and each instance in turn exposes port proxy objects for its COM bound ports. Although a group manager runs a single instance of the engine, it can run multiple instances of an XLANG schedule. Also, two instances of the same XLANG schedule can run in different group managers. Each running schedule is represented as a distinct object in the collection exposed by a group manager. Moreover, the engine provides access to ports bound to COM components in the schedule instance by exposing proxies for these ports. These proxies may be used by other applications wanting to communicate with the running schedule instance.

The System Manager class provides administrative access to all group managers on the server—that is, to all COM+ processes that can host the running XLANG schedule instances. Figure 11.1 also shows the composition of the `sked` moniker and relates it to the object hierarchy.

This chapter discusses all of this. First, you learn how the XLANG Scheduler Engine hosts schedules—that is, how schedule instances are managed, persisted, dehydrated, or rehydrated. Then, later in the chapter, you look at the details of objects exposed and the events generated by the engine and, finally, the tools used to monitor these events. The chapter also contains example code to use the runtime APIs described. Visual Basic 6.0 is used for the examples.

Orchestration Hosting Infrastructure

Let's look at the hosting infrastructure for running the XLANG schedules. This is provided by COM+ Services and by SQL Server 2000 database server.

Recall that the XLANG schedules embody long-running business processes; hence, running schedules must survive system restarts. Also, to support scalability, BizTalk Orchestration Services may dehydrate running XLANG schedules. These are schedules that have become quiescent and are now waiting for some event to occur before they can continue running. SQL Server 2000 provides the persistence database for saving the state of running schedules. COM+ application services provide the processes and the environment to run XLANG schedules. The following sections discuss each of these two areas.

COM+ Services

COM+ provides a number of services to components installed in a COM+ application. An XLANG schedule instance runs in the context of a COM+ application and takes advantage of the deployment and security configuration options as well as process isolation features of COM+. COM components referenced by an instance of a schedule leverage the object pooling, transaction management, just-in-time activation, and concurrency support services provided by COM+.

When BizTalk server is installed, a new XLANG tab is added to the properties page of all COM+ server applications (see Figure 11.2). COM+ applications that are activated as a library do not have this tab. The XLANG tab is used to configure the execution of the XLANG Scheduler Engine within that COM+ application. However, by default, the engine is enabled to run only within the XLANG Scheduler COM+ application, which is created when BizTalk is installed.

You can create new COM+ applications and enable them to host the XLANG Scheduler Engine and run schedule instances. Schedule instances running in two separate COM+ applications are isolated from each other because they run in separate processes. Also, the two COM+ applications can be secured differently.

When you develop a business process in an XLANG schedule, consider the deployment and security issues of running the schedule. These considerations will determine what COM+ applications you create, the configuration for these applications, your choice of databases, and security options. You may choose, for example, to dedicate a COM+ application to run schedules associated with a trading partner. This approach permits the business processes to be secured differently, based on the trading partner relationship, and to isolate them from each other, permitting you to, for example, shut down one process without affecting the other. Let's look at the configuration options in detail.

The default application to host XLANG schedules, as set up by the BizTalk Orchestration Services installation script, is a server application called XLANG Scheduler. By default, this server application uses the `Interactive User` identity to run the schedules (this identity is defined in the property pages of the COM+ application). The XLANG Scheduler application hosts the System Manager component that oversees all schedule activations on the server. Figure 11.2 shows the `XLANG` property page for the XLANG Scheduler COM+ application along with tabs for other pages.

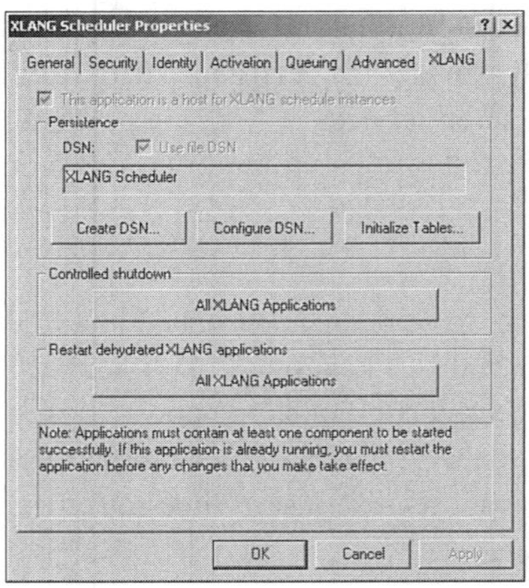

FIGURE 11.2
XLANG Scheduler Properties.

The check box on the top left in Figure 11.2 designates this application as an XLANG schedule host. It is grayed because changes to this application currently are disabled. The buttons and configuration settings shown on the XLANG tab of this property page are referenced throughout this chapter. Note the other tabs shown in Figure 11.2. Each tab serves a purpose; the default settings in tabs on `Security` and `Identity` usually need changes.

Access to the XLANG Scheduler application is controlled by COM+ role-based security. Hence, the object model described previously, exposed by the System Manager, is selectively available depending on the identity of the user or process accessing it.

The security roles defined for the XLANG Scheduler application are as follows:

- XLANG Schedule Creator—Allows a user to create XLANG schedule instances. By default, the Windows 2000 built-in group of `Everyone` is added to this role.
- XLANG Schedule User—Allows a user to interact with an XLANG schedule instance. By default, the Windows 2000 built-in group of `Everyone` is added to this role.
- XLANG Schedule Administrator—Allows a user to perform administrative tasks. By default, the Windows 2000 built-in group of `Administrators` is added to this role. The administrative tasks are related to tasks on the XLANG tab of the COM+ application property page, shown in Figure 11.2. They are
  - Declaring an application to be a host for XLANG schedules
  - Setting the persistence database configuration
  - Shutting down XLANG applications
  - Suspending, resuming, or terminating XLANG schedule instances
- XLANG Scheduler Application—Allows the XLANG Scheduler to interact with applications running with an identity included in this role. By default, the Windows 2000 built-in group of `Everyone` is added to this role. For example, another COM+ application running with an identity not in this role cannot use restricted features of the XLANG scheduler object model.

Figure 11.3 shows the Component Services administration console and the COM+ applications therein.

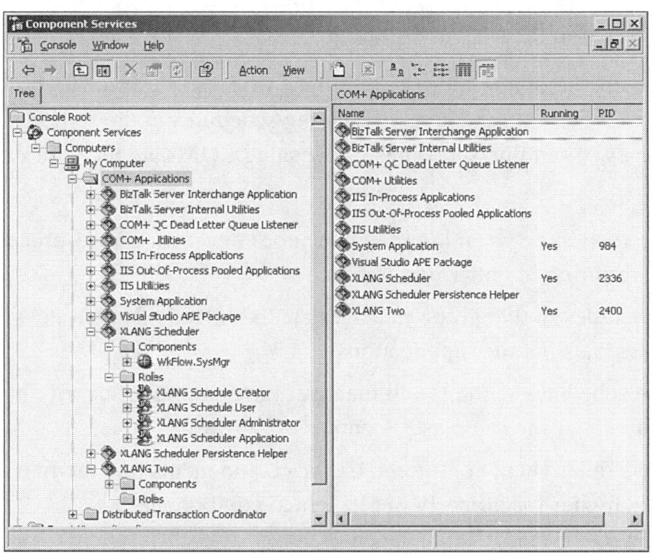

FIGURE 11.3
XLANG Group managers and security roles.

Figure 11.3 shows COM+ applications in the left pane and their `Status view` in the right pane. Two of these applications, XLANG Scheduler and XLANG Two, are group managers and are XLANG hosts. The left pane also shows the security roles for the XLANG Scheduler application. The installed component shown is `SysMgr` from the `SkedsMgr.dll`. The roles for XLANG Scheduler application are also shown. Note that roles are defined only for the default XLANG schedule host application, which also contains the `SysMgr`. The right pane shows three applications running. Besides the System Application, the other two are group managers. Note the process ID for the running group managers—this will show up in event traces discussed later in this chapter.

The security roles are used in many ways:

- Any user that you want to allow to kick start a schedule should be added to the XLANG Schedule Creator role. If an application starts a schedule instance, then the identity used by the application process should be part of this role.
- You can control who can interact with a running XLANG schedule instance by specifying users in the role XLANG Schedule User. Note that this level of control is in addition to other mechanisms available to you—for example, checking the sender's identity within the schedule or specifying access control on messaging queues or role-based security on COM+ configured components.
- You can restrict which users or application processes can access the XLANG Scheduler by controlling the membership of the XLANG Scheduler Application role.

If, at runtime, an access fails because of a role-based security violation, then an event log entry is generated in the system event log.

You have the choice of configuring multiple COM+ applications to host XLANG schedules. There are both pros and cons of running schedules in the same COM+ application. The advantages of running schedules in the same COM+ application or group manager are as follows:

- An interaction between the schedules does not incur out-of-process call overhead, hence resulting in better performance
- All schedules in that group manager can be selectively shut down, without affecting schedules in other applications
- All the schedules in the group manager have the same security profile. The schedules run under the same user identity
- The schedules share configured COM+ components and the likelihood of instance reuse is higher for properly implemented components

There are disadvantages, on the other hand, of running schedules in the same group manager. The advantages of running schedules in different COM+ applications or group managers are as follows:

- The schedules are part of different business processes and running them in separate processes isolates them from each other's failures
- A schedule has specific security needs, possibly because it interacts with outside organizations or other legacy applications with special configuration requirements Running it in a separate group manager allows customization of the security configuration.
- The business processes embodied in the schedule are still under development and the production applications must be isolated from the running and failures of these schedules Running the schedules under development in different group managers allows you to shut down schedules under development without affecting the production schedules.
- You can isolate the persistence database for schedules that run in separate group managers. You may want to do this possibly due to a business requirement for segregating the databases or servers.
- You want to make it easier to migrate the schedules to run on a different server some time in the future. At that point, you can create the group manager on the new server and point your references to this new server.

To create a group manager, you must first create a COM+ server application using the COM+ Application Install Wizard. To start this wizard, first start Component Services administration console, see Figure 11.3. Right-click on the COM+ Applications tree node and use the menu to create a new application. The wizard starts with the welcome page. The next page of the wizard is Install or Create a New Application. Choose to Create an Empty Application by clicking the button labeled as such. The wizard asks you to name the application. By default, a server application is created, which is what you want. On the next page of the wizard, you are asked to choose an application identity. By default, the identity is Interactive User, which is adequate for development purposes. You can change this identity later on the property page of a COM+ application. Clicking Next concludes the process of creating a COM+ application.

The COM+ application created is not yet a group manager; it cannot host the XLANG Scheduler Engine or run instances of XLANG schedules. To do this, you must go to the XLANG tab (refer to Figure 11.2) of the property page of the newly created COM+ application and check the box labeled This Application Is a Host to XLANG Schedule Instances. If, at this point, you decide to close the property pages for this COM+ application, then you will be prompted as shown in Figure 11.4.

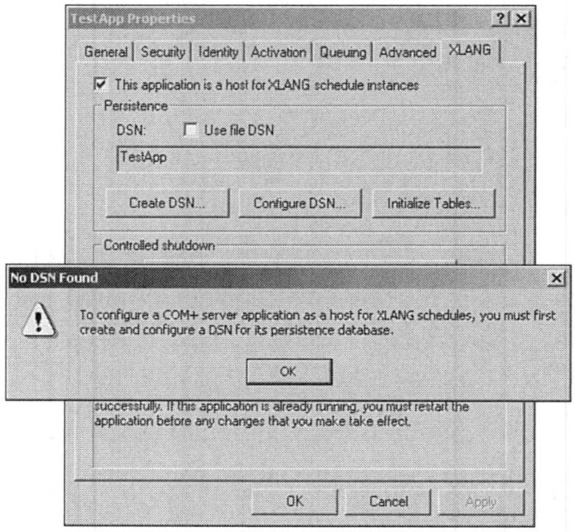

FIGURE 11.4
Creating the COM+ application for a group manager called TestApp.

The prompt reminds you that you must specify a persistence database for the engine to use before the COM+ application can become a group manager. We look at the persistence database in the next section and at the steps necessary to create and configure such a database.

> **Note**
>
> Any COM+ application that you create and designate as a host for an XLANG schedule must have at least one COM+ configured component installed.
>
> This component may be used by an application or by a running schedule. However, if there is no such component, then you must define a dummy component so that the COM+ application can be started and be an XLANG host.

> **Note**
>
> It's a good idea to change the default identity for the XLANG Scheduler application to be a service account.
>
> A service account is like any other user account with specific rights. Such an account must have the right to "Act as part of the operating system" and " Log on as a service". The default setting of Interactive User works fine for developers.

Not changing the identity in production or test systems could result in applications either not working, or working nondeterministically depending on who is currently the interactive user on the server machine(s). Failure to change the identity could also provide unintended privileged access if a system administrator happens to be logged on to the server.

It is recommended that you assign a specific user identity for each COM+ application instead of using the default identity of Interactive User. The identity you select is available to recipients of all messages posted by a schedule running in this group manager.

The name of the hosting COM+ application is used as the name of the group manager portion of the schedule moniker. Hence, by using the name of the COM+ application, in the moniker, you can designate which process should host the schedule instance. Here is an example of a valid moniker:

```
sked://MyMachine!XLANG Two/C:\Temp\ExampleSchedule.skx
```

This moniker refers to the group manager XLANG Two on the server called `MyMachine`. Chapter 10 covered the composition of `sked` monikers. You will also see additional moniker forms and moniker usage in subsequent sections.

Caution

Group manager names are case-sensitive and can contain spaces. Pay attention to moniker strings in this regard.

Persistence Databases

Another COM+ application that is installed by default is the **XLANG Scheduler Persistence Helper**, which provides database persistence services to running XLANG schedules. This is a `Library` application and, therefore, does not run in its own process. You can see this in the Component Services administration tool (refer to Figure 11.3). The persistence database stores the structure of the XLANG schedules being run, the dynamic state to track the progress of schedules being run, and a checkpoint state of all messages sent or received prior to dehydrating a schedule.

A persistence database is created when the default XLANG Scheduler application is created. This database is called XLANG; however, you could specify another name for a new database or bind to an existing database when BizTalk Orchestration Services are installed.

When you define a new application to host XLANG schedule instances, you must associate a database with this new application. The database you associate will be used to save the running XLANG schedule state when the schedule is dehydrated. You can choose to associate the default database or an existing database, or create a new database.

The database used by an XLANG hosting application is specified on the XLANG tab of the COM+ application's properties dialog box. The steps to associate a database are as follows:

1. Create the database using the SQL Server Enterprise Manager administration tool, unless you want to reuse an existing database.
2. Grant access rights to this database for the user identity that will be used to run the XLANG host application. You will need to grant permission to create tables and procedures in this database.
3. Create a data source name (DSN) to this database.

   Note that, for the default persistence database used by XLANG Scheduler, the BizTalk Orchestration Services always uses the Windows user identity for authentication instead of SQL Server authentication.

   Also, note that the name of the DSN must be identical to the name of the XLANG hosting application.

   Do not forget to check the Use File DSN check box, if in fact you use a file DSN. File DSNs are accessible from multiple servers in a group or a cluster using UNC path names. (UNC stands for universal naming convention, which defines a machine independent syntax for locating files).
4. Initialize the database, unless you are using an existing database. However, you can initialize an existing database, if in fact that is what you want to do. You initialize the database using the button on the XLANG tab of the group manager's property pages.

Note

Pay particular attention to the restrictions stated in step 3 on defining persistence database DSNs. Failing to properly configure the DSN and the persistence database will cause schedule persistence and dehydration to also fail.

To create a group manager, you must create a COM+ application and then enable it to host XLANG schedule instances. As part of enabling it to host running schedules, you must create a persistence database. This is what Figure 11.4 showed.

If you click the Create DSN button, you are reminded of items shown in Figure 11.5.

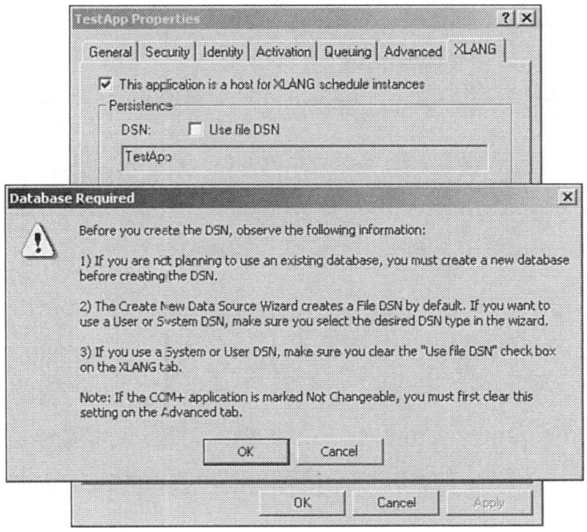

FIGURE 11.5
Creating a persistence database for a group manager called `TestApp`.

Clicking OK starts the Create New Data Source Wizard. Here you can create a file, user or system DSN. Select a SQL Server 2000 database server to host the database, and you should have created the database beforehand as described in the steps earlier. When the wizard for creating a DSN finishes, the wizard to configure the DSN is automatically started. Here you specify the database server, login information, and database name to use. Note that you could alternatively create and configure the DSN independently using standard administrative tools such as the ODBC Data Source Administrator. If you do this, you should update the DSN information by clicking the Configure DSN button. Remember to check the Use File DSN check box if in fact you use a file DSN.

At this point, you are ready to initialize the database for use by the XLANG Scheduler Engine. To do this, click the Initialize Tables button. Figure 11.6 shows the reminder when you do this.

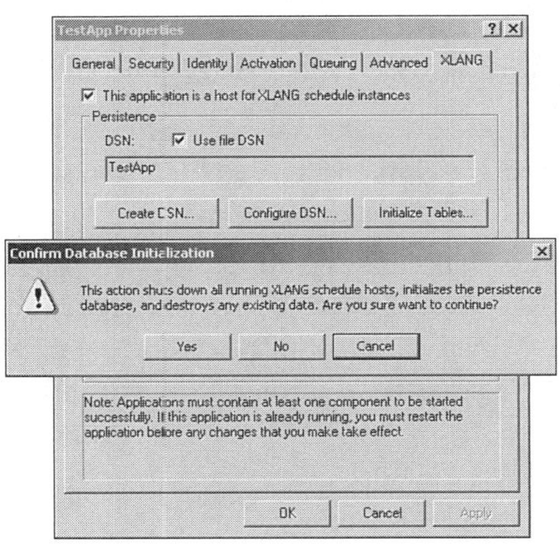

FIGURE 11.6
Initializing the persistence database for `TestApp`.

Click Yes to initialize the database. This adds the tables and stored procedures to the database as needed by the engine. Remember to add at least one COM component to the group manager as noted in the previous section.

At this point, you are good to go. You can run XLANG schedule instances in the XLANG hosting COM+ application you just configured, and the schedules will dehydrate to the associated database when they are quiescent.

If you look at the XLANG tab on the properties page of the hosting application, you will see a button designated for Controlled Shutdown. If it is the default application that you are looking at, XLANG Scheduler, then the button can shut down all XLANG instances on the *server* in a controlled manner. On a group manager that you create the button can be used to shut down all instances only in the current hosting application or group manager.

A controlled shutdown allows the XLANG Scheduler Engine to gracefully save the state of the schedule before stopping the application. You can later rehydrate all dehydrated XLANG schedules in all group managers by clicking the Restart Dehydrated XLANG Applications button on the XLANG properties page of the XLANG Scheduler application (refer to Figure 11.2). It is not a good idea to use the Component Services administration console to shut down a group manager because the state is not properly persisted when this brute force approach is taken. For example, if a schedule using per-instance MSMQ queues is shut down by force, you may get dangling MSMQ queues created by the engine.

Just as there were considerations for choosing to run schedules in the same group manager versus creating new group managers, there are reasons to choose the XLANG persistence databases used with each group manager. The size of the XLANG persistence database grows as schedules dehydrate and rehydrate. Different persistence databases can be secured separately. The network latency to the persistence database affects the speed of dehydration and rehydration. These observations suggest the following:

- Use different databases to isolate schedules used in different business processes. This way the business processes will not contend for disk resources, and they can be securely isolated using separate logon identities.
- Share a SQL Server to host all databases used for XLANG persistence. Having separate servers just adds unnecessary complexity. The chosen server should have low latency LAN connectivity to the other BTS servers hosting XLANG schedules. The server should also have fast disks and controllers, possibly with striping and mirroring built in.

- Use separate databases for different versions of schedules. For example, schedules being developed for a business process should have a separate database from the database used for the schedules for the production version of the business process.

The next section explores the object model exposed by the XLANG Scheduler Engine. The description covers all the properties and methods of each of the exposed objects. The format presents the signature immediately after the heading naming the property or method. This is followed by the description and usage. This format should make it easy to locate information quickly.

System Manager

The System Manager is the root object exposed by the engine. This COM+ component is configured in the XLANG Scheduler COM+ application, which is the default host for XLANG schedules.

In Visual Basic, this root object is referred to as `SYSMGRLib.SysMgr` when you add a reference to `skedsmgr.dll` nominally located at `\Program Files\Microsoft BizTalk Server\XLANG Scheduler\skedmgr.dll`. Note that this type library is called `XLANG Scheduler - System Manager` and is not listed among other BizTalk Server library references. Figure 11.7 shows the two type libraries of interest.

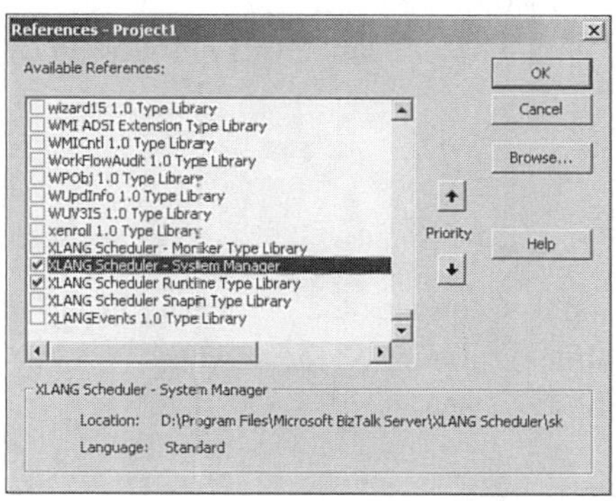

FIGURE 11.7
References for the XLANG Scheduler Engine.

The following code fragment shows how to get a reference to the System Manager:

```
Dim oMgr As SYSMGRLib.SysMgr
Set oMgr = GetObject("sked://")
```

The properties and methods of the System Manager are described in this section. Table 11.1 summarizes the properties, and Table 11.2 summarizes the methods of the System Manager.

TABLE 11.1 Properties of System Manager

Property	*Description*
`Count`	Number of group managers in server
`FullyQualifiedName`	Full moniker for the System Manager, with DNS style name of the server
`IsWorkflowHost`	True, if COM+ application is enabled for XLANG Scheduler Engine
`Item`	Reference to collection of group managers
`UseFileDSN`	Type of DSN used for the persistence database

TABLE 11.2 Methods of System Manager

Method	*Description*
`ShutdownAll`	Controlled shutdown of all group managers
`ShutdownApp`	Controlled shutdown of the named group manager
`StartUp`	Asynchronous rehydration of schedule instances
`TestAdminStatus`	Method to test access

Each property and method is described in the order listed in Tables 11.1 and 11.2. The property or method is identified with a bolded label; this is followed by a signature and description.

Property `Count`

```
Property Count As Long
```

The `Count` property returns a `Long` that contains the number of group managers (that is, XLANG hosting COM+ applications) running on the server.

This is a read-only property.

Property `FullyQualifiedName`

```
Property FullyQualifiedName As String
```

The `FullyQualifiedName` property returns a `String` that contains a moniker for the System Manager object. The moniker contains the fully articulated DNS style name, even though the local machine name is optional when you use the moniker to get a reference to the System Manager.

This is a read-only property.

Property IsWorkflowHost

```
Property IsWorkflowHost(varApplicationName As String) As Boolean
```

The `IsWorkflowHost` property controls whether the named COM+ application is an XLANG Scheduler Engine host. The returned value of the property is a `Boolean` indicating whether the named application is a host.

This is a read/write property. However, you cannot set this property on COM+ applications that have been marked `Disable changes`, in the Advanced tab of the property pages of the COM+ application. Also, this property cannot be set on the default XLANG Scheduler application.

Property Item

```
Property Item(name As String) As Unknown
```

The `Item` property is the default member of the System Manager object and returns a reference to a collection of running group managers. You also can get a reference to a specific group manager by using its name to index the collection. Code fragments that illustrate the usage are in the section "Group Manager" later in the chapter.

This is a read-only property.

Property UseFileDSN

```
Property UseFileDSN(varApplicationName As String) As Boolean
```

The `UseFileDSN` property controls whether the named COM+ application uses a file DSN to access the persistence database.

This is a read/write property; however, the changes in this property do not take effect until the application (group manager) is restarted.

Method ShutdownAll

```
Sub ShutdownAll()
```

This method performs a controlled shutdown of all XLANG hosting applications.

This is a synchronous call. When the call returns, all applications are shut down and the machine may be safely rebooted, for example.

Method ShutdownApp

```
Sub ShutdownApp(varApplicationName As String)
```

This method performs a controlled shutdown of the named XLANG host application. If called on the default host, XLANG Scheduler, then it is equivalent to calling the `ShutdownAll` method, and all applications are shut down.

Method **StartUp**

```
Sub StartUp()
```

This method starts up all configured XLANG host applications.

This is an asynchronous call. The rehydration process is initiated for schedules in each of the host applications; however, the call will return before the process is completed. See the "XLANG Event Monitor" section later in the chapter to see whether rehydration is complete.

Method **TestAdminStatus**

```
Sub TestAdminStatus()
```

A process can use this method to check whether the identity it is running under complies with the role membership as configured for the XLANG Schedule Administrator security role. This method is used internally by XLANG hosting COM+ applications (that is, group managers) that you configure and is not of much use to other applications.

Group Manager

This section looks at the object model exposed for XLANG hosting COM+ applications. You get a reference to this object as an item in the collection exposed by System Manager described previously. The object interface is used to stop, suspend, resume, and get information about a running schedule instances in the hosting application.

In Visual Basic, the type library for this object is available in `SkedCore.dll`, which is nominally located at `\Program Files\Microsoft BizTalk Server\XLANG Scheduler\SkedCore.dll`. This is the XLANG Scheduler Runtime Type Library. See Figure 11.7 for references.

The following code fragments show how to get a reference to the default group manager. This is the idiomatic use of the default property, `Item`, of the System Manager. In the code fragment, the collection of group managers exposed by the System Manager is being indexed by the name of the default group manager, which is XLANG Scheduler. You could substitute that with another name to access another group manager.

```
Dim oGrp As COMRUNTIME.IWFGroupAdmin
Set oGrp = oMgr("XLANG Scheduler")
```

The following fragment iterates through all running group managers on the system. This is the idiomatic enumeration of a collection in Visual Basic.

```
For Each oGrp in oMgr
    ' your code goes here…
Next
```

The following code fragment gets a reference to a group manager by asking COM to bind the moniker to the class implementation. The `GetObject` call results in resolving the moniker, activating the class server, and returning a reference to the group manager. In the example, the server name is missing and defaults to the local server. Note that the group manager's name is case-sensitive, and spaces are significant.

```
Set oGrp = GetObject("sked://!XLANG Scheduler")
```

The properties and methods of a group manager are described in this section. Table 11.3 summarizes the properties, and Table 11.4 summarizes the methods of a group manager.

TABLE 11.3 Properties of a Group Manager

Property	*Description*
`Count`	Number of running schedule instances
`FullyQualifiedName`	Moniker for the group manager
`IntanceIsResident`	True if schedule instance is in memory
`InstanceIsSuspended`	True if schedule instance is suspended
`Item`	Collection of running schedule instances
`Name`	Name of the group manager
`UseFileDSN`	True if group manager uses a file DSN

TABLE 11.4 Methods of a Group Manager

Method	*Description*
`ResumeInstance`	Resumes a previously suspended schedule instance
`Shutdown`	Controlled shutdown of the group manager
`StartUp`	Starts group manager and rehydrates its instances
`SuspendInstance`	Suspends a running schedule instance
`TerminateInstance`	Stops a schedule instance

Each property and method is described in the order listed in Tables 11.3 and 11.4. The property or method is identified with a bolded label; this is followed by a signature and a description.

Property `Count`

```
Property Count As Long
```

The `Count` property returns the number of running XLANG schedule instances in this group manager.

This is a read-only property.

Property `FullyQualifiedName`

```
Property FullyQualifiedName As String
```

The `FullyQualifiedName` property returns a `String` containing a moniker for the group manager. The moniker contains a full, DNS style, system name; hence, you can parse this moniker to extract the system name for this hosting application.

This is a read-only property

Property `InstanceIsResident`

```
Property InstanceIsResident(varParam As String) As Boolean
```

The property `InstanceIsResident` returns `True` if the named XLANG schedule instance is in memory or `False` if the instance is dehydrated.

The instance name specified in the `varParam` is a GUID assigned to it by the engine. This GUID is visible in the moniker assigned to a schedule instance—for example, the following is a valid moniker with the GUID identity of the running instance:

```
sked://MyMachine!XLANG Scheduler/{7DFE4B47-19EB-45a1-AE35-492886B4FF74}
```

This is a read-only property.

Property `InstanceIsSuspended`

```
Property InstanceIsSuspended(varParam As String) As Boolean
```

The property `InstanceIsSuspended` returns `True` if the named instance is suspended; `False` otherwise. The instance is identified by the GUID assigned to it. A suspended instance is still in memory and not dehydrated. A suspended instance cannot be within a short-lived transaction or any method call.

This is a read-only property. You must check this property before calling the `ResumeInstance` method.

Property `Item`

```
Property Item(name As String) As Unknown
```

The `Item` property is the default member of the group manager object and returns a reference to a collection of running schedule instances. You can get a reference to a specific running instance by using the GUID name for that instance as an index into the collection.

This is a read-only property.

Property `Name`

```
Property Name As String
```

The property `Name` returns the name of the group manager as a `String`. This is also the name of the COM+ application hosting the XLANG schedules.

This is a read-only property.

Property `UseFileDSN`

```
Property UseFileDSN As Boolean
```

The property `UseFileDSN` returns `True` if the group manager uses a file DSN to persist dehydrated schedules.

This is a read-only property. The value of the property is not necessarily the configured setting through the `SysMgr.UseFileDSN` property; instead, it is the setting at the time the group manager was launched.

Method `ResumeInstance`

```
Sub ResumeInstance(bInstanceId As String)
```

This method resumes a previously suspended schedule instance. The instance ID is the GUID assigned to it by the engine. Check whether a schedule is in fact suspended by getting the value of `InstanceIsSuspended` property first.

Method `Shutdown`

```
Sub Shutdown()
```

The `Shutdown` method dehydrates all running schedules to the database and then stops the group manager. Only schedules in the current group manager are affected.

When called, no new schedule activation requests are entertained until shutdown completes. This method should not be called by a component bound to a schedule; use an external application instead.

Method `Startup`

```
Sub Startup()
```

The `Startup` method rehydrates previously dehydrated schedule instances of this group manager. Microsoft recommends that you not use this method; use the `SysMgr.StartUp` method instead. This method is for internal use by the System Manager.

Method `SuspendInstance`

```
Sub SuspendInstance(bstrInstanceId As String)
```

The `SuspendInstance` method suspends the further execution of the specified running schedule in the current group manager.

This is a synchronous call. The call may block if the schedule is waiting for the completion of a method call or for a short-lived transaction to resolve.

Method `TerminateInstance`

```
Sub TerminateInstance(bstrInstanceId As String)
```

The `TerminateInstance` method stops the named schedule instance in the current group. A terminated schedule instance can never be restarted or resumed.

This is a synchronous call. The call may block if a component bound port is in the middle of a method call or if the schedule is waiting for a short-lived transaction to resolve.

Schedule Instance

This section looks at the interface exposed by the schedule instance object. You get a reference to this object either through the collection, exposed by the group manager, or through the corresponding moniker.

In Visual Basic, the type library for this object is in `SkedCore.dll`, the same as that for the group manager above.

The following code fragments show how to get a reference to a schedule instance. This is the idiomatic use of the default property, `Item`, of the group manager. The collection of instances exposed by the group manager is being indexed by the name of the instance, which is the GUID assigned to it by the XLANG Scheduler Engine:

```
Dim oInst As COMRUNTIME.IWFWorkflowInstance
Set oInst = oGrp("{7DFE4B47-19EB-45a1-AE35-492886B4FF74}")
```

The following fragment iterates through all running schedule instances in the group manager. This is the idiomatic enumeration of a collection in Visual Basic:

```
For Each oInst in oGrp
    ' your code goes here…
Next
```

The following code fragment gets a reference to a running instance by asking COM to bind the moniker to the referenced object. In the example, the group manager name is missing and defaults to the default host, XLANG Scheduler:

```
Set oInst = GetObject("sked:///{7DFE4B47-19EB-45a1-AE35-492886B4FF74}")
```

The properties and methods of a schedule instance are described in this section. Table 11.5 summarizes the properties, and Table 11.6 summarizes the methods of schedule instance.

TABLE 11.5 Properties of a Schedule Instance

Property	*Description*
`CompletionStatus`	Completion return code from the schedule instance
`FullPortName`	A fully qualified name of the port based on the implementation
`FullyQualifiedName`	A moniker for the schedule instance
`InstanceId`	GUID identity of the schedule instance
`IsCompleted`	True, if the schedule finished execution
`ModuleId`	GUID identity of the schedule itself
`ModuleName`	Name of the schedule
`ParentInstanceId`	GUID identity of the parent instance
`Port`	The `IUnknown` interface to the port COM proxy

TABLE 11.6 Methods of a Schedule Instance

Method	*Description*
`WaitForCompletion`	Call blocks until schedule completes

Each property and method is described in the order listed in Tables 11.5 and 11.6. The property or method is identified with a bolded label; this is followed by a signature and a description.

Property `CompletionStatus`

```
Property CompletionStatus As Long
```

The property `CompletionStatus` indicates whether the schedule instance was completely processed by the engine. The return code of '0' (zero) indicates successful completion. This code, however, does not indicate the success or failure of the embodied business process.

This is a read-only property.

Property `FullPortName`

```
Property FullPortName(varParam As String) As String
```

The property `FullPortName` returns a `String` that is a fully qualified name of the specified port. A port in a schedule can be bound to a component or to a messaging system. The name returned reflects the technology used in the binding. Thus, the name can be used to acquire a reference to the object from appropriate APIs of the system. For example, if the port is bound to MSMQ queue, then the name can be used to locate and use the queue using MSMQ APIs.

This is a read-only property.

Property `FullyQualifiedName`

```
Property FullyQualifiedName As String
```

The `FullyQualifiedName` property returns the moniker for the schedule instance. All optional fields of the moniker syntax are fully filled in in the returned string; hence, the returned string can be parsed to extract the system name, the group manager name, and instance GUID. As with any moniker, this string can be passed to another process or an application, which can then attempt to acquire a reference to this schedule instance.

This is a read-only property.

Property `InstanceId`

```
Property InstanceId As String
```

The `InstanceId` property returns a `String` containing the GUID identifier assigned to the running schedule instance by the engine.

This is a read-only property.

Property `IsCompleted`

```
Property IsCompleted As Boolean
```

The property `IsCompleted` returns `True` if the schedule instance has finished executing; `False` otherwise.

This is a read-only property.

See also the `CompletionStatus` property and the `WaitForCompletion` method of this object.

Property `ModuleId`

```
Property ModuleId As String
```

The property `ModuleId` returns a `String` containing the GUID of the XLANG schedule (that is, the `.skx` file created after compilation, also called the `module`), which is used to create this instance. This GUID is the same as the one you would see as a property of the `Begin` shape in your schedule drawing.

Note that this GUID keeps changing every time you make changes to your drawing. Hence, this is a way of determining which schedule is running in the instance under consideration. You can see this GUID as a property of the Begin shape in the schedule drawing. This property is also visible in the XLANG Event Monitor described later in the chapter. Two running schedules can have the same module name but different module Ids.

This is a read-only property.

Property `ModuleName`

```
Property ModuleName As String
```

The property `ModuleName` returns a string containing the name of the schedule the instance is derived from. The module name is based on the name of the compiled schedule's filename, the one with the `.skx` extension.

This is a read-only file.

Property `ParentInstanceID`

```
Property ParentInstanceID As String
```

The `ParentInstanceID` property returns the GUID instance ID of the parent XLANG schedule.

This is a read-only property. It returns `NULL` if the current schedule has no parent.

Property `Port`

```
Property Port(varParam As String) As Unknown
```

The `Port` property returns an interface to a COM proxy for the named port. You must specify a port name that exists in the schedule; otherwise, an error is generated. The returned interface is an `IUnknown interface`, hence you must QI `(query interface)` for the correct interface. In Visual Basic, you do this by declaring a variable of the correct type or by using a `Variant` data type to hold the returned interface. The following code shows this. Variable `oInst` is a running instance with a port named `"Port_1"`.

```
Dim oComp As MyProgID.MyClass
Set oComp = oInst.Port("Port_1")
oComp.MyMethod
```

This is a read-only property.

Method `WaitForCompletion`

```
Sub WaitForCompletion()
```

The method `WaitForCompletion` does not return until the current XLANG schedule instance completes executing.

Port COM Proxy

This section examines the interface exposed by the COM proxy for the Port object. You can acquire a reference to this object either through the `IWFWorkflowInstance.Port` property or through a port moniker string you have received from another application.

In Visual Basic, the type library for this object is `SkedCore.dll`, the same as that for the group manager and schedule instance earlier.

Through this COM proxy, you can `QI` for an interface implemented by the component for which this is a proxy. However, you can only QI for the interface actually used by the XLANG schedule. If the component has implemented other interfaces, the proxy does not expose them.

After you have a reference to the interface, and the port is set up to receive a message, then you can call a method on that interface. The method call is intercepted by the engine before passing the call to the component. This provides a mechanism to pass messages programmatically into a schedule.

The properties described in this section are those of the proxy itself and not of the interfaces of the component for which this object is the proxy.

The following code fragments illustrate how to get a reference to the port proxy and then how to use the proxy to make a method call on the component. In the following code, `oComp` is an interface of the COM component bound to `MyPort`:

```
Dim oPort As COMRUNTIME.IWFProxy
Set oPort = GetObject("sked:///{4607B374-C0BB-40F0-909D-355C1951F774}/MyPort")
Dim oComp As MyProgID.MyClass
Set oComp = oPort
oComp.MyMethod
```

The properties of a port COM proxy are described in this section. There are no methods for this object. Table 11.7 summarizes the properties a port proxy.

TABLE 11.7 Properties of Port COM Proxy

Property	*Description*
`FullyQualifiedName`	Moniker for the port instance
`WorkFlowInstance`	Interface of the schedule instance containing this port

Each property is described in the order listed in Table 11.7. The property is identified with a bolded label; this is followed by a signature and a description.

Property `FullyQualifiedName`

```
Property FullyQualifiedName As String
```

The property `FullyQualifiedName` returns a string (example below), which contains a moniker for the port instance for which this object is the proxy:

```
sked://MyMachine!XLANG Scheculer/{7F4BE554-1698-4FDE-9FFB-4B58C21EB033}/MyPort
```

The moniker can be used in a `GetObject` call to get a reference to the proxy as long as the schedule is not terminated.

This is a read-only property.

Property `WorkflowInstance`

```
Property WorkflowInstance As IWFWorkflowInstance
```

The property `WorkflowInstance` returns an interface to the XLANG schedule instance that has implemented the component for which object is the proxy. You would use this property to locate the schedule instance if you had an object reference to the proxy.

This is a read-only property.

Using the Object Model

This section demonstrates the use of the XLANG Scheduler Engine object model described in earlier sections.

The code example enumerates all the currently configured group managers. It locates and lists running schedule instances. It also locates instances derived from a schedule named `MySchedule`. The schedule `MySchedule` is assumed to contain a port called `MyPort`; the example prints the port name for this port.

The example is written in VB Script. You do not need to compile this script; you may run this script directly using the following command line in a command prompt window:

```
CSript ListSchedules.vbs
```

On the preceding command line, the name of the script file is `ListSchedules.vbs. This script file` contains the code shown in Listing 11.1. The code contains three object variables, `oMgr`, `oGrp`, and `oInst`. In VB Script, the variables cannot be data type specific; however, if you were to use a type-aware language, such as Visual Basic, the data types would be as follows:

```
Dim oMgr As SYSMGRLib.SysMgr
Dim oGrp As COMRUNTIME.IWFGroupAdmin
Dim oInst As COMRUNTIME.IWFWorkflowInstance
```

You can recognize the data types from the earlier description of the object model. The variable `oMgr` holds a reference to the System Manager object, the variable `oGrp` holds a reference to a group manager, and the variable `oInst` holds a reference to a running schedule instance. The script code is shown in Listing 11.1.

> **Note**
>
> You can also access this script in the `ListSchedules.vbs` file from the publisher's Web site.

LISTING 11.1 `ListSchedules.vbs` Script

```
Dim oMgr, oGrp, oInst
Set oMgr = GetObject("sked://")
WScript.Echo "System manager moniker = " & oMgr.FullyQualifiedName
WScript.Echo "Number of group managers = " & oMgr.Count
For Each oGrp In oMgr
```

LISTING 11.1 continued

```
    WScript.Echo "Group manager moniker = " & oGrp.FullyQualifiedName
    WScript.Echo "Name = " & oGrp.Name & ", number of instances = " &
➥CStr(oGrp.Count) & ", is workflow host = " & CStr
➥(oMgr.IsWorkflowHost(oGrp.Name))
For Each oInst In oGrp
        WScript.Echo "Schedule instance moniker = " & oInst.FullyQualifiedName
        WScript.Echo "Module name = " & oInst.ModuleName & ",
➥Module ID = " & oInst.ModuleId
        WScript.Echo "Instance ID = " & oInst.InstanceId
        If oInst.ModuleName = "MySchedule" Then
            WScript.Echo "MyPort port name = " & oInst.FullPortName("MyPort")
        End If
    Next
Next
```

The code first acquires a reference to the System Manager object using the moniker string `"sked://"`. The next two lines print the moniker for the System Manager and the number of configured group managers on the server.

The first `For` loop iterates through each of the group managers on the server. For each group manager, it displays the moniker, its name, and the number of instances running in it. It also shows whether the group manager is currently an XLANG Scheduler Engine host.

The second, inner, `For` loop iterates over all instances in the group manager selected in the outer loop. For each instance found, the script lists the moniker, the name, the module identity, and the instance identity. If the schedule name is recognized as `MySchedule`, the script also prints the full port name for the port `MyPort`.

Listing 11.2 shows the sample output from this script.

LISTING 11.2 Sample Output of the `ListSchedules.vbs` Script

```
System manager moniker = sked://bztk.bztkdom.omicron.com
Number of group managers = 3
Group manager moniker = sked://bztk.bztkdom.omicron.com!XLANG Scheduler
Name = XLANG Scheduler, number of instances = 2, is workflow host = True
Schedule instance moniker = sked://bztk.bztkdom.omicron.com!XLANG Scheduler/{CCE
➥5B532-5534-4329-B13A-58A7FF7C61F8}
Module name = SchedOne, Module ID = 77E34546-A1C9-4818-98D8-DC58F54C3597
Instance ID = {CCE5B532-5534-4329-B13A-58A7FF7C61F8}
Schedule instance moniker = sked://bztk.bztkdom.omicron.com!XLANG Scheduler/{453
➥095D9-92D3-4A6F-BF71-67621C8C0AEA}
Module name = MySchedule, Module ID = C65A7337-A07A-49A9-AEED-4C8295D5B967
Instance ID = {453095D9-92D3-4A6F-BF71-67621C8C0AEA}
```

LISTING 11.2 continued

```
MyPort port name = sked://bztk.bztkdom.omicron.com!XLANG Scheduler/{453095D9-92D
➥3-4A6F-BF71-67621C8C0AEA}/MyPort
Group manager moniker = sked://bztk.bztkdom.omicron.com!TestApp
Name = TestApp, number of instances = 1, is workflow host = True
Schedule instance moniker = sked://bztk.bztkdom.omicron.com!TestApp/{34DC7015-45
➥09-4720-BF53-AD2256DE5368}
Module name = SchedOne, Module ID = 77E34546-A1C9-4818-98D8-DC58F54C3597
Instance ID = {34DC7015-4509-4720-BF53-AD2256DE5368}
Group manager moniker = sked://bztk.bztkdom.omicron.com!XLANG Two
Name = XLANG Two, number of instances = 0, is workflow host = False
```

The sample output shows that there are three group managers; however, only two are enabled for hosting schedules. The group manager named XLANG Two is currently disabled from running schedule instances. The group manager XLANG Scheduler contains two running schedule instances. The modules associated with these instances are respectively `SchedOne` and `MySchedule`. The monikers are shown for the System Manager, the group managers, and the running schedule instances. The full port name for `MyPort` is also listed.

This wraps the discussion of the object model itself. We now look at the events generated when the engine runs.

Events

The XLANG Scheduler Engine generates COM+ events when running an XLANG schedule. These events are generated at various stages of execution of a schedule. BizTalk Server ships with one tool and a sample program to monitor these COM+ events and capture an execution trace. These tools are described in the following sections.

The XLANG Scheduler Engine also generates entries for the system event log when runtime errors occur. Figure 11.8 depicts how events can be filtered in the event log.

Using the Event Viewer administrative tool, you can select the `Application` event log in the tool and then use the right mouse menu to select a viewing option to filter the events shown. You will see the dialog shown in Figure 11.8 for setting the Filter options. Figure 11.8 shows that the display will be filtered to show only the XLANG Scheduler events. You can further choose to view just a specific category of the events, as shown in the drop-down list.

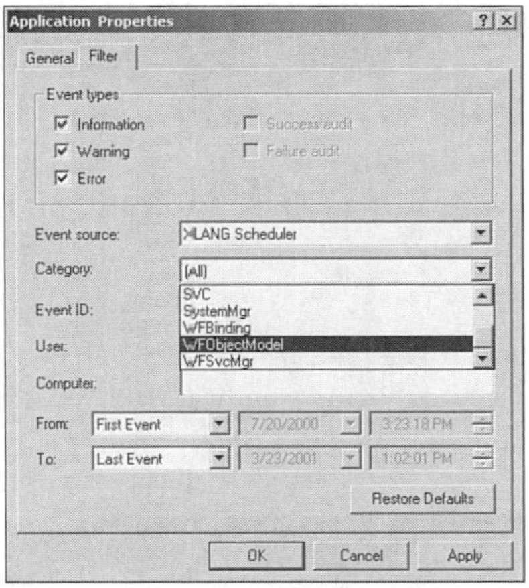

FIGURE 11.8
Filtering application events.

You can use both these capabilities to monitor the operation of your schedules. In addition, you can write custom components that monitor for specific events of interest and generate messages when such events occur. Other general-purpose system tools, such as the Performance Monitor and the Visual Studio development environment, will augment your monitoring capabilities.

XLANG Event Monitor

XLANG Event Monitor is a visual tool that displays current schedule execution activity and captures trace information for post-mortem review. This section describes the following capabilities of the monitor:

- The monitor can display schedule execution activity on multiple servers and group managers. You can select the event sources that you want to record.
- You can search for a specific schedule instance in the display by name.
- You can filter the events that you want to view. Event history and event details for each monitored schedule can be reviewed.
- You can selectively delete the trace data for a specific schedule execution.
- You can start and stop the recording as needed, and the captured trace can be saved to a file for later review.
- You can suspend, resume, or terminate a running schedule.
- You can manually start new schedules.

Tip

A shortcut to the XLANG Event Monitor is not installed under the usual Start, Programs, BizTalk Server 2002 Windows menu. You can create a shortcut to it by locating the program `XLANGMon.exe` in the following location (or a similar location depending on your installation):

```
" \Program Files\Microsoft BizTalk Server\SDK\XLANG Tools\XLANGMon.exe"
```

The documentation for the monitor is available as an HTML `Readme` file in the same directory. Note that the monitor is not a fully supported tool.

Note

Use Windows 2000 Service Pack 2 (or later); the service pack fixes some operational issues with the XLANG Event Monitor.

When you start the monitor, it immediately starts recording the activity of schedules. By default, it picks the local machine and the currently configured group managers on the local machine to start monitoring for running schedules. If the group managers on the local machine are not running, then these are started. Dehydrated schedules are rehydrated to monitor progress of all schedule instances. The rehydration, however, is usually only momentary, if in fact there is nothing for the schedules to do. In the activity recorded by the monitor, the prior execution history is not available for any schedule. This is true for the dehydrated schedules also, which are located but their prior history is not available.

Figure 11.9 shows various schedule instances in different states of execution. Two group managers are configured on the local machine. Under each group manager are two folders, one for running instances and the other for completed instances. An entry under either folder describes the state of an instance. This entry line consists of an icon (described later), the schedule name (also known as the module name), and the instance GUID (also known as the module ID).

The icon visually describes the state as follows:

- Green dot—Running schedule instance. (In Figure 11.9, see `ScheduleOne` in group manager `XLANG Two`.)
- Blue lines (as in a recorder pause button)—Suspended schedule instance. (In Figure 11.9, see `ScheduleOne` in the default group manager `XLANG Scheduler` under the `Running` folder.)

- Black dot—Successfully completed schedule instance. (In Figure 11.9, see `ScheduleThree` in the default group manager.)
- Red dot—Completed schedule instance, but with errors. (In Figure 11.9, see `ScheduleOne` in the default group manager, under the `Completed` folder.)
- Blue snowflake—Dehydrated schedule instance. (In Figure 11.9, see `ScheduleTwo` under the group manager `XLANG Two`.)

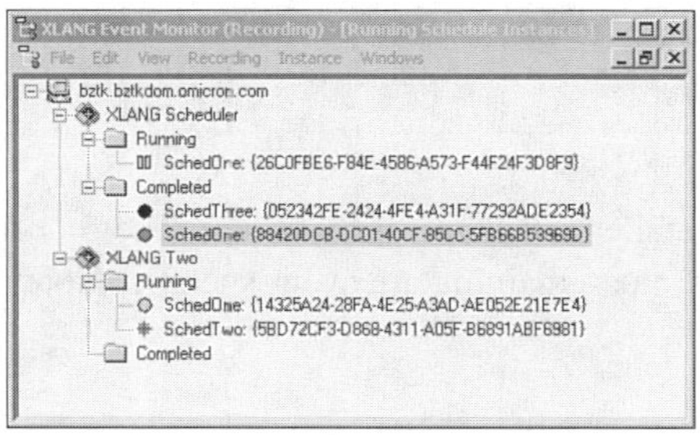

FIGURE 11.9
XLANG Event Monitor.

Note that only the running and suspended schedules consume nontrivial system resources. Dehydrated schedules consume minimal resources. A suspended schedule cannot be dehydrated; it will continue to hold on to precious system resources until its operation is either resumed or stopped.

Note

Successful completion of a schedule does not imply that the underlying business process completed correctly. For example, if errors occurred in the business process, the schedule may have (based on how it was designed) successfully recorded the failure without necessarily completing the business process.

In the XLANG Event Monitor you can double-click on a schedule instance entry to see all the recorded events for the schedule. For example, if you could double-click on the completed schedule `SchedThree` shown in Figure 11.9, you would see what's shown in Figure 11.10.

As you can see in Figure 11.10, the event window has been maximized. It is split into a top half and a bottom half. The top half contains a chronological list of events that occurred during the execution of the schedule. The event `ComSourceReturn` is highlighted. The other two columns list the shapes and messages from the process flow drawing.

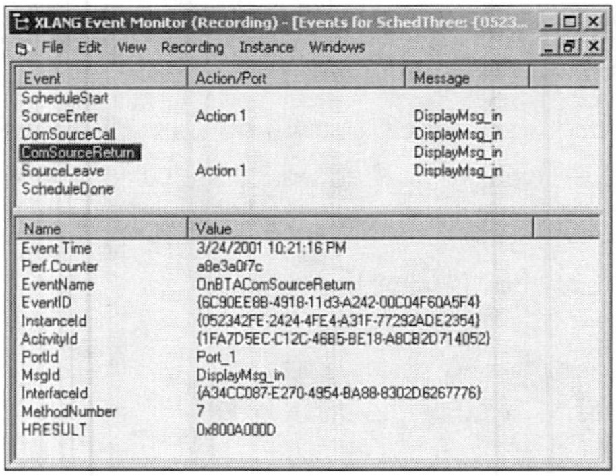

FIGURE 11.10
Events for schedule SchedThree.skv.

The bottom half contains the detailed attributes of this event. The first five attributes listed are common to all events; the remaining are event-specific. Note the following items:

- The `Event Time` is listed.
- The `EventName` is listed. This determines what event-specific properties are listed. The event shown is `OnBTAComSourceReturn`. This is a COM method call that originated from the XLANG schedule and is now returning. The `EventID` is a GUID identity for this event.
- The `InstanceID` is the same GUID as the schedule instance ID shown in Figure 11.9 for the `SchedThree` schedule.
- Other attributes (such as `ActivityId`, `PortId`, and others that follow) are specific to this event (`ComSourceReturn`) being that for a COM method call. If you select another method in the top pane, you will see a different set of attributes.
- Although not shown in Figure 11.10, the `ScheduleStart` and `ScheduleDone` events also list the `ModuleName`, which is the name of the compiled schedule file, and the `ModuleId`, which is the GUID identity that you would see as a property of your `Begin` shape in the visual drawing of your process flow. With this information, you know exactly which schedule ran.

You can correlate these events with what `SchedThree.skv` actually contains, shown in Figure 11.11.

The schedule shown in Figure 11.11 is simple. It consists of making a single call to a COM component, `TestXLANG`'s `Dbg` class. This class has a single interface with a single method, called `DisplayMsg`, which really does nothing. When the schedule is started, `Action 1` makes the call through `Port_1`, and the schedule terminates.

The events shown in Figure 11.10 were shown without filtering out any events.

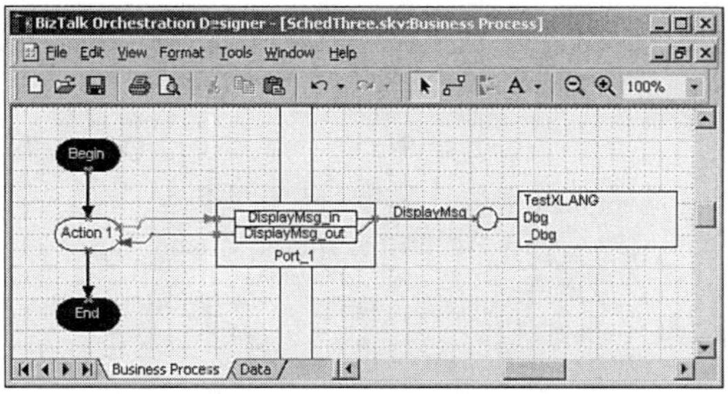

FIGURE 11.11
XLANG schedule `SchedThree.skv.`

You can filter what events are shown in the display, as shown in Figure 11.12.

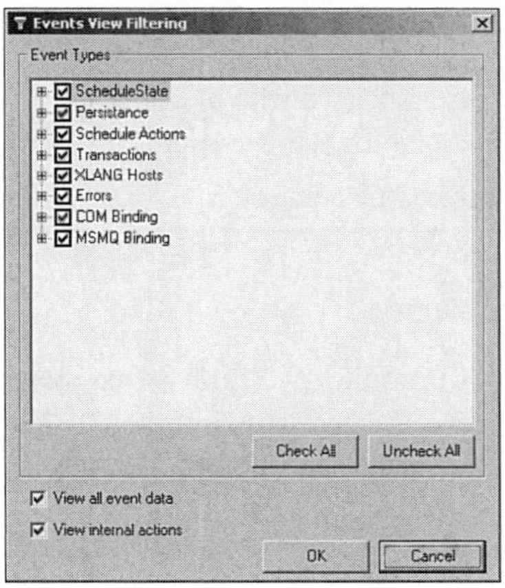

FIGURE 11.12
Events View filtering.

The full set of options is described in Table 11.8. If you check View All Event Data, then you also will see the event time and the event name. This event name can be logged into the BizTalk tracking database as described in the next section and viewed using BizTalk Document Tracking Web application.

TABLE 11.8 Filtering XLANG Events for Viewing

Event Category	*Events*
Schedule State	Events relating to starting, stopping, suspension, resumption, and completion of schedules.
Persistance (sic.)	Events relating to persistence to database, dehydration, and rehydration of schedules.
Schedule Actions	Events related to flow chart shapes as the schedule is being run. There is a separate event for a shape (or a port) that is being entered and exited.

TABLE 11.8 continued

Event Category	*Events*
Transactions	Events for both short-lived and long-lived transactions and for the transaction contexts.
XLANG Hosts	Events for the shutdown and startup of group managers.
Errors	Events associated with reported errors. (Also see the system event log.)
COM Binding	Events associated with the control flow of COM component method calls. The entry and exit of the method call can be traced, whether it is initiated by the schedule instance or by an external application. Not traced by default.
MSMQ Binding	Events associated with message delivery or receipt. Applies to both the BizTalk messaging and for MSMQ. Not traced by default.

You can control what event sources are captured.

If you want to change the event sources to monitor, you must first stop the current recording. Do this from the Recording menu. When stopped, the Event Sources menu is enabled. Figure 11.13 shows the dialog box for changing the event sources.

FIGURE 11.13
Select Event Sources.

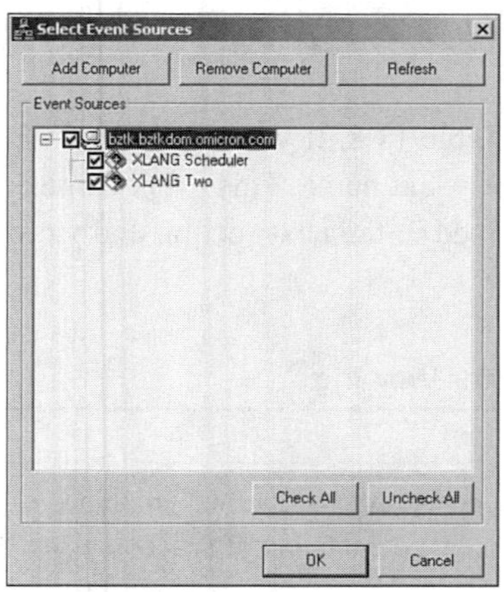

In the dialog box shown in Figure 11.13, you can add or remove servers and group managers to monitor. To start monitoring, you must start a new recording session; you cannot change your selections for the existing recording. However, you can save the old recording if necessary. You save a recording in the usual manner, using the File menu.

After capturing a lot of trace data, over some period, you may want to save event information for only a subset of the instances recorded. You can search for specific named instances using the Edit, Find menu command. You can also selectively delete trace histories of unwanted instances by first selecting an instance and then using the Delete Instance Data menu.

Tip

Use the XLANG monitor to see when a schedule is in fact dehydrated or not. The rehydration process completes asynchronously, whether it is initiated programmatically using the `SysMgr.StartUp` method or interactively using the XLANG tab of the group manager's properties. Hence, it may not be immediately apparent when the status of the schedule changes.

You can start new instances or suspend, resume, or terminate existing schedule instances from the Instance menu. The schedule instances can be run on any chosen group manager by first selecting the desired group manager folder in the display and then starting the new instance.

Before leaving this section, take a look at the execution trace for a less trivial schedule containing a `While` loop. This trace is generated from the sample provided with the SDK. The XLANG schedule is located at `\Program Files\Microsoft BizTalk Server\ SDK\XLANG Samples\Iteration\LineItemsApp\LineItems.skx`. You need to set up the sample as described in the readme file provided with the sample before running the schedule.

Figure 11.14 shows that the `LineItems` schedule instance ran to completion. The instance contained a `While` loop that executed eight times. Each execution of the body of a `While` loop is treated as a child subschedule. You can view the execution history for each of these executions by double-clicking on it. The last entry in the chain depicts that the `Rule` in the `While` shape returned `False`.

FIGURE 11.14
Event trace for a schedule with iteration.

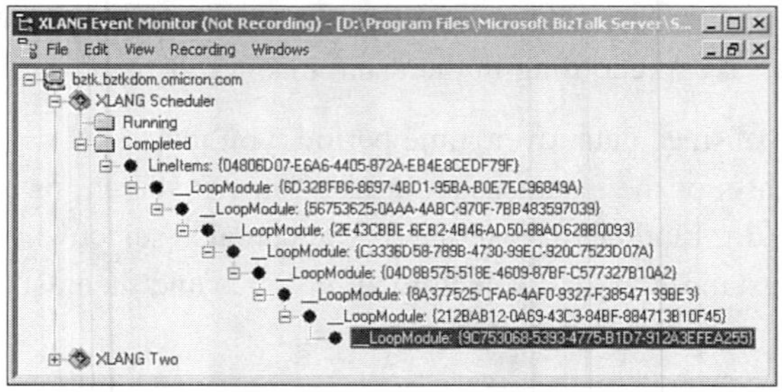

Tracking Events in the Tracking Database

You can also capture XLANG events in the tracking database. This is particularly useful when you want to correlate actions performed by an instance of an XLANG schedule on specific message instances flowing in and out of BizTalk Messaging Services. The BizTalk Document Tracking Web application allows you to query the database for document flows between organizations or applications. The XLANG events captured in the database can be viewed in relationship with the message flows displayed by the document tracking Web application.

This functionality of capturing tracking events is not part of the base installation of BizTalk Server. You must deploy a sample application called `WorkFlowAudit` to use this feature. This sample comes in two parts: one is a dynamic link library (DLL) that does the work of posting events raised by the scheduler into the database, and the other is a small graphical user interface (GUI) to start and stop this capture. The samples, along with the source code, are located at (or a similar location, depending on your installation):

```
\Program Files\Microsoft BizTalk Server\SDK\XLANG Samples\…
…\WorkFlowAudit\bin\WorkFlowAudit.dll
…\WorkFlowAuditClient\WorkFlowAuditClient.exe
```

To use this sample, you must first register the `WorkFlowAudit.dll`. Next, run the `WorkFlowAuditClient.exe` client application. The client application allows you to specify the database connection information, although the defaults are based on the current configuration. Now, you can start and stop the event capture using buttons on the client GUI.

Note

Event capture stops if you close the `WorkFlowAuditClient.exe` application. You would normally expect such a mechanism to be implemented as a background system process; however, it is currently provided as an interactive application.

The event data is captured into the tracking database tables `dta_wf_EventData` and `dta_wf_WorkFlowEvent`.Table 11.9 shows the structure of these tables.

TABLE 11.9 The `dta_wf_WorkFlowEvent` Database Table

Field	*Description*
`nWorkflowEventId`	Auto-incremented key field. Provides a link to the `dta_wf_EventData` rows.
`nvcEventId`	The event type. This is a GUID constant—an identity for the event.
`nvcEventName`	Event name. The event names that you will see are provided in Listing 11.3. All names begin with `OnBTA`.
`nProcessId`	The process ID of the group manager that hosted the schedule instance that generated the event.
`nvcApplicationId`	The GUID identity of the group manager (COM+ application).
`nvcInstanceId`	The GUID identity of the XLANG schedule instance. This is the identity visible in the XLANG Event Monitor.
`nEventTime`	UTC (Universal Coordinated Time) time of this event, as seconds elapsed since midnight, January 1, 1970.
`nEventSubTime`	Time offset in microseconds.
`nEventTick`	Value of the high-resolution performance counter at the time of the event.
`nvcServerName`	Server on which the event was detected.
`dtDateEntered`	Date and time of the event.

A row in `dta_wf_WorkFlowEvent` table denotes a single event. The detailed attributes of each such event are captured in `dt_wf_EventData`. This table contains multiple rows corresponding to an event, each row with a specific attribute of the event. Table 11.10 shows the `dt_wf_EventData` table.

TABLE 11.10 The `dta_wf_EventData` Database Table

Field	*Description*
`nEventDataId`	Auto-incremented key field.
`nWorkFlowEventId`	Foreign key to the parent event record in `dt_wf_WorkFlowEvent` table.
`nvcName`	Name of the event attribute.
	One particular attribute of interest is the `CorrelationID` attribute. Messaging events have such an attribute. The value of this attribute is a GUID, which is used to correlate with messages flowing through BizTalk Messaging Services.
`nvcValue`	The value of the attribute named in `nvcName`. This can be anything; however, for `CorrelationID`, it is a GUID.

The tables of the tracking database are documented as part of the BizTalk product documentation. You could, if you feel up to it, write SQL queries to mine specific data from the tracking database, for problem isolation, for example. The event names that you are likely to find are provided in Listing 11.3. You can see these event names in the XLANG Event Monitor.

LISTING 11.3 Event Names in Tracking Database

```
OnBTAAppError           OnBTACallEnter
OnBTACallLeave          OnBTACaseExecute
OnBTAComSinkCall        OnBTAComSinkReturn
OnBTAComSourceCall      OnBTAComSourceReturn
OnBTAConnectEnter       OnBTAConnectLeave
OnBTAContextAbort       OnBTAContextCompensate
OnBTAContextEnter       OnBTAContextLeave
OnBTADehydrated         OnBTAError
OnBTAMSMQDeliver        OnBTAMSMQReceive
OnBTAPartitionEnter     OnBTAPartitionLeave
OnBTAProxyEnter         OnBTAProxyLeave
OnBTARehydrated         OnBTAReturnEnter
OnBTAReturnLeave        OnBTAScheduleDone
OnBTAScheduleFailFast   OnBTASchedulePersist
OnBTAScheduleResume     OnBTAScheduleStart
OnBTAScheduleStop       OnBTAScheduleSuspend
OnBTAShutdown           OnBTASinkEnter
OnBTASinkLeave          OnBTASourceEnter
OnBTASourceLeave        OnBTAStartup
OnBTASwitchEnter        OnBTASwitchLeave
OnBTATaskEnter          OnBTATaskLeave
OnBTATransactionBegin   OnBTATransactionEnd
```

Although a deeper understanding of the tracking database is useful for design and troubleshooting, schedule development can be done using the XLANG Event Monitor and the document tracking Web application.

The BizTalk Document Tracking application is used to locate and view document interchange information recorded in the tracking database. The tracking application is described in Chapter 8, "Document Tracking." With the `WorkFlowAudit` sample described earlier, you can also add tracking information for document interchanges that flow between BizTalk Messaging and Orchestration Services. In the tracking application, you select the source, destination, and documents that you want to view tracking data for. You can also narrow your search to a specified time period.

After making your selections, you query the tracking database. The results of the query show the tracking information for document interchanges that occurred. You can look at the document or interchange actually handled in both the native and XML format. Along with this information, you can also view the events logged by the running XLANG schedule, the same information you saw in the XLANG Event Monitor but shown in relation to the document interchange. The events are shown in the tracking application with their name, attribute, and value. The events are shown in Listing 11.3.

Notes on Running XLANG Schedules

This section contains some notes on running and designing XLANG schedules. Also see Chapter 10 for using the Orchestration Designer and Chapter 13, "Advanced BizTalk Orchestration."

- Dehydrated schedules consume few precious system resources, such as CPU, memory, and semaphores. For an action that receives a message from an outside application, consider what wait time you want to assign. Any wait time less than 180 seconds causes the XLANG schedule to never dehydrate, unless the group manager is deliberately shut down. The default value is 0 seconds.
- Use components that can persist to disk, where possible. This allows the XLANG Scheduler Engine the flexibility to dehydrate the schedules when appropriate. If the components used by a schedule contain state and their state cannot be persisted to disk, then the schedule is unable to dehydrate.
- Consider collocating the group manager on the same server as the persistence database. Dehydration and rehydration are frequent operations, and you do not want to incur network latency for database access.

- Weigh the trade-off between running COM+ components in-process versus out-of-process. In-process gives you performance but trades it for stability.
- Don't get entangled in performance debates and optimization issues prematurely. First design and implement a process flow that incorporates the necessary business requirements while keeping the design simple. Then use the tools to evaluate the performance.
- Loosely coupled, asynchronous messaging is more scalable than synchronous calls. Use messaging where possible. Design COM components to return control quickly.
- The engine cannot dehydrate a running instance in the middle of a Distributed Transaction Controller (DTC) style transaction. However, it must persist the state before and after such a transaction. This (persistence) is an expensive operation; hence, it is beneficial to include as many actions as appropriate within a single transaction.

Summary

This chapter first described the hosting infrastructure for XLANG schedules, including how COM+ applications are set up to host XLANG schedules and how the persistence database is set up.

We next looked at the object model exposed by the XLANG Scheduler Engine. This included the root System Manager object and then the group manager, schedule instance, and the proxy for the XLANG port connected to a COM component. We covered all the properties and methods of these objects with code fragments on how to use them.

Next, we looked at the system event log followed by tools especially available to view and capture operational data from the running schedules. We looked at the XLANG Event Monitor and the WorkFlowAudit sample tool.

Finally, we reviewed some points to consider when running and designing schedules.

Chapters 9 and 10 provided mostly a static description of how XLANG schedules are constructed. This chapter described the dynamic, runtime behavior of the XLANG Scheduler Engine. The features described are useful for administering, monitoring, and troubleshooting the operation of XLANG schedules, and for building custom applications as part of an overall solution.

Advanced BizTalk Server Topics

PART IV

IN THIS PART

CHAPTER 12

Advanced BizTalk Messaging

By Susie Adams and Larry Wall

IN THIS CHAPTER

BizTalk Server messaging operations consist of receiving, processing, and delivering messages. In Chapter 6, "Introduction to BizTalk Messaging," you learned how to configure these operations by using the BizTalk Messaging Manager application. The techniques illustrated in Chapter 6 required some fundamental assumptions about message configurations. For example, it was assumed that the source organization, document formats, and destination organization were all fixed at design time. This assumption simplifies the configuration of channels, ports, document definitions, and envelopes. When the BizTalk Messaging system is configured with static information, it makes the task of routing documents simple. Unfortunately, static configurations also produce rigid operations that can only handle a specific set of inputs.

This chapter builds upon the lessons of Chapter 6 by covering more advanced topics in BizTalk Messaging. A major point of focus in this chapter is how to design messaging operations so that the routing of messages is determined at runtime. This type of design can produce more robust and reusable messaging configurations. Throughout this chapter we refer to the runtime determination of messaging operations as *dynamic routing*. Several different messaging elements can be configured to achieve dynamic routing, including the creation of *self-routing documents*.

Another assumption made during Chapter 6 is that messages are always delivered to a single location. In reality, you will often need to send messages to several destinations, with each destination playing a role in the overall business process. BizTalk Server facilitates the delivery of a message to multiple locations through a concept known as a *distribution list*. This chapter will demonstrate how distribution lists can be used to produce a richer set of interchanges.

The topics discussed in this chapter are reinforced with tangible examples that demonstrate each lesson. Prior to reading this chapter, we recommend that you install the `RouteTest` application that is downloadable from the publisher's Web site. We will open the chapter with a brief introduction to this application and walk through the steps necessary to install it. The scenarios implemented in the `RouteTest` application are referenced throughout this chapter.

In summary, the following topics are discussed in this chapter:

- Using the `IInterchange` interface to submit documents to BizTalk Server
- The `RouteTest` sample application
- Routing (with emphasis on dynamic routing)
- Distribution lists

Some topics in this chapter assume that you are familiar with the `IInterchange` interface exposed by BizTalk Server. The technique of *call-based routing*, for example, involves submitting documents via the `IInterchange` interface. In preparation for these advanced topics, we will discuss how to write COM+ applications that use the `IInterchange` interface to submit documents for either synchronous or asynchronous processing. The next section takes an in-depth look at the `IInterchange:Submit` interface and its parameters.

Submitting Documents Via the `IInterchange` Interface

Documents targeted for BizTalk Server must be transmitted to the server in some way. The appropriate submission method depends on the architecture of the source application and the requirements of the overall business process. You may choose from any of the following delivery protocols:

- HTTP—Hypertext Transport Protocol
- HTTPS—Secure HTTP
- MSMQ—Microsoft Messaging Queue
- SMTP—Simple Mail Transfer Protocol
- File—File-based transmissions
- COM/DCOM—Direct submissions via the Component Object Model or Distributed Component Object Model

With the exception of using COM/DCOM, the preceding approaches do not directly initiate BizTalk Server processing; they simply provide a means of transportation for messages. At some point during the submission process, the `IInterchange` interface must be employed. `IInterchange` may be used "behind the scenes" by BizTalk Server (this is how receive functions work), or it may be used directly by a source application.

`IInterchange` provides an API for submitting documents either synchronously or asynchronously. It also contains a set of methods for administering the suspended queue in case the document is rejected by BizTalk Server for some reason. A total of five methods are in the interface:

- `Submit()`
- `SubmitSync()`
- `CheckSuspendedQueue()`
- `GetSuspendedQueueItemDetails()`
- `DeleteFromSuspendedQueue()`

The following sections discuss how to use the `IInterchange` interface to initiate BizTalk Server processing.

Synchronous Versus Asynchronous Processing

`IInterchange::Submit()` creates and sends an interchange to BizTalk Server for asynchronous processing. This means that after the document has been placed in the work items queue, the calling program continues to execute, without waiting for the interchange to be processed. Alternatively, `IInterchange::SubmitSync()` sends a document to BizTalk Server and then waits for the interchange to finish processing before executing any subsequent code. The only major difference between the two methods is the fact that the `SubmitSync` method has the capability to return a response in addition to the interchange handle when executed. Because this is the only difference, we will focus on the `IInterchange::Submit()` method for the remainder of this section.

`IInterchange::Submit()` Parameters

One thing that makes `IInterchange::Submit()` so powerful (and challenging to master) is the seemingly endless combinations of parameters that the function will accept. Listing 12.1 shows the syntax of `IInterchange::Submit()`.

LISTING 12.1 `IInterchange::Submit()` Syntax

```
HRESULT Submit(
    BIZTALK_OPENNESS_TYPE lOpenness,
    BSTR Document,
    BSTR DocName,
    BSTR SourceQualifier,
    BSTR SourceID,
    BSTR DestQualifier,
    BSTR DestID,
    BSTR ChannelName,
    BSTR FilePath,
    BSTR EnvelopeName,
    long PassThrough,
    BSTR* SubmissionHandle
);
```

The following sections describe each parameter and the effects it can have on message processing. You may use this section both as a reference and to establish a foundation on which to build your understanding of advanced messaging topics.

The lOpenness Parameter

The first parameter, `lOpenness`, indicates whether the source and destination of an interchange are explicitly specified or open. The value of the `lOpenness` parameter must belong to the `BIZTALK_OPENNESS_TYPE` enumeration, which is documented in Table 12.1.

TABLE 12.1 `BIZTALK_OPENNESS_TYPE` Enumeration

Name	*Value*	*Description*
`BIZTALK_OPENNESS_TYPE_NOTOPEN`	1	Specifies that this instance of the object is not open
`BIZTALK_OPENNESS_TYPE_SOURCE`	2	Specifies that the source organization of this instance of the object is open
`BIZTALK_OPENNESS_TYPE_DESTINATION`	3	Specifies that the destination organization of this instance of the object is open

The value of `lOpenness` dictates whether messaging ports associated with an interchange can be configured as open. Open ports are discussed later in this chapter.

The `lOpenness` parameter also has implications on whether EDI formats are allowed in an interchange. If `BIZTALK_OPENNESS_TYPE_SOURCE` is used with an inbound EDI document, then the outbound document format cannot be EDI. If `BIZTALK_OPENNESS_TYPE_DESTINATION` is used, then the inbound document format cannot be EDI.

Identifying the Document Being Submitted

A document submitted to BizTalk Server for processing can be specified using the `Document` parameter or the `FilePath` parameter. If the `Document` parameter is used, you are expected to pass the pure bytes of the inbound document file. You cannot pass object pointers such as an XML DOM object or an ADO object using this parameter. If you specify a value for the `Document` parameter, then you cannot pass a value for `FilePath` parameter.

`FilePath` offers an alternative to submitting the document as a pure string. Using this parameter, you specify the path to the disk file that contains the document. The path value must be either a Uniform Resource Locator (URL), Universal Naming Convention (UNC) path, or a drive letter and disk path combination. URL and UNC formats eliminate the need to maintain a permanent network drive mapping on the BizTalk Servers if the input file resides on a remote machine.

> **Note**
>
> Remember that a URL specifies the location of a document by first indicating the protocol to use and then providing the IP Address or domain name and path to the document, such as `http://www.mcp.com/sams/`. In contrast, a UNC simply specifies the servername and path for a document, such as `\\MyServer\MySharename`. URLs and UNCs represent the two types of Universal Resource Identifiers (URIs).

Using the `FilePath` parameter may result in a slight performance penalty if the file resides on a remote machine because the document must be located and copied to the work items queue by BizTalk Server before control is returned to the calling program.

Identifying the Document Source and Destination

The document's source and destination are each specified via a pair of parameters that consist of a qualifier and an identifier. Listing 12.2 shows these parameters.

LISTING 12.2 Parameters for the Message Source and Destination

```
BSTR SourceQualifier,
BSTR SourceID,
BSTR DestQualifier,
BSTR DestID
```

The `SourceQualifier` indicates how the `SourceID` parameter is to be interpreted. Valid values come from the organization identifier qualifiers created when the user creates an alias for an organization. Qualifiers are entered in the BizTalk Messaging Manager with each organization identifier and allow you to specify as many unique identifiers for an organization as you want. Common qualifiers include the Data Universal Numbering System (DUNS) number, telephone number, and BizTalk. The default qualifier for all new organizations is Organization Name and refers to the name of the organization in the database. The `SourceID` contains the value of the qualifier of the source organization. For example, if the `SourceQualifier` parameter is Telephone, this value is the telephone number. If the `Openness` flag is set to `OpenSrc`, `SourceID` is interpreted as the source organization name. The `SourceID` parameter cannot be used if the `PassThrough` parameter is set to `TRUE`.

In the BizTalk Messaging Manager, you cannot save an organization identifier without entering a qualifier value. However, when using `IInterchange::Submit()`, you can specify an organization identifier and omit the qualifier. In this case, a default qualifier value of `OrganizationName` is automatically assumed by BizTalk Server.

Source and destination identifier/qualifier pairs have additional constraints when transmitting EDI data. When using the X12 format, the organization qualifier must be 2 characters or less, and the identifier itself must not exceed 15 characters. When using the `EDIFACT` format, the qualifier must be 4 characters or less, and the identifier value must be 35 characters or less. Both `X12` and `EDIFACT` formats do not allow the word "Organization" to be used as an identifier value.

You can omit the source organization and/or destination organization parameters completely from an `IInterchange::Submit()` call. In this case, BizTalk Server will attempt to determine this information by other means. This process—referred to as dynamic routing—is covered extensively later in this chapter.

Identifying the Document Format, `DocName`, `EnvelopeName` Parameters

The `DocName` and `EnvelopeName` parameters of `IInterchange::Submit()` enable BizTalk Server to understand the format of the documents being submitted. `DocName` refers to a document definition that has been configured in the BizTalk Messaging Manager. In most cases, a document definition points to an underlying BizTalk document specification, which defines the type and structure of a document. Under some circumstances, a document definition may not refer to an underlying document specification. In this case, the document submitted is not parsed or verified against a BizTalk specification, limiting the processing that can occur on the data. For example, you may want to transport a binary file, in which case you would want to pass a document through by setting the `PassThrough` parameter on the `Submit` method to `True`.

Envelopes are required when a non-XML message is being submitted to BizTalk Server. You can specify the envelope associated with a message by using the `EnvelopeName` parameter of `IInterchange::Submit()`. The name specified must match an envelope name that has been configured in BizTalk Messaging. Envelopes serve as a wrapper for business documents and describe the type of document being transmitted. Therefore, envelopes must point to a valid BizTalk specification configured in the Messaging system. Because many interchanges do not require envelopes, the `EnvelopeName` parameter is optional.

Specifying a Channel

`IInterchange::Submit()` allows you to explicitly specify the channel to use when processing a message. The `ChannelName` accepts a string value representing the name of a channel that has been configured in BizTalk Messaging. The technique of explicitly specifying a channel is one way to streamline the processing of a message because it allows BizTalk Server to bypass the "normal" channel selection process. The `ChannelName` parameter is optional unless the `PassThrough` parameter is set to `True`, in which case it is required.

For more information on how BizTalk Server decides what channel to invoke, see the section "The Channel Selection Process" later in this chapter.

Pass-Through Interchange Processing

As part of "standard" interchange processing, BizTalk Server can perform encoding, encryption, and digital signature verification on a document. There are times when you may want skip these processing steps and just have BizTalk Server Messaging route a document "as is" to its destination. This is the purpose of the `PassThrough` parameter in `IInterchange::Submit()`. Setting this parameter value to `True` adds protection against data corruption when you are submitting binary data that must be delivered exactly as it was submitted. By skipping the encoding process, for example, you ensure that BizTalk Server does not attempt to convert the input data to a `unicode` character set. Delivering binary images to a trading partner is one scenario where pass-through processing might be useful.

A value of `True` for the `PassThrough` parameter also imposes some rigid constraints on the other `IInterchange::Submit()` parameter values. You must specify `BIZTALK_OPENNESS_TYPE_NOTOPEN` for the `lOpenness` parameter, and you must pass a value in the `ChannelName` parameter. The specified channel is not permitted to apply mappings on the original input data. When you specify pass-through processing, you also must omit the `DocName`, `SourceQualifier`, `SourceID`, `DestQualifier`, `DestID`, and `FilePath` parameters. The delivery location for pass-through interchange data is confined to the address configured in the channel's associated port.

Information Returned by `IInterchange::Submit()`

When making asynchronous function calls, there is always the question of how to track the progress of the function invoked. The calling program will continue to execute, but at some point the caller may need to know whether the asynchronous process completed successfully. `IInterchange::Submit()` solves this issue by returning a "receipt" to the caller in the form of a submission handle. Armed with the submission handle, the calling program can query for the status of the interchange by presenting the handle to one of several BizTalk Server API functions. The submission handle uniquely identifies the interchange invoked as a result of an `IInterchange::Submit()` call. Listing 12.3 displays an example.

LISTING 12.3 Using the Submission Handle

```
Dim oInterchange As BTSInterchangeLib.Interchange
    Dim strRetVal As String
    Dim vSrcName as Variant
    Dim vDestName as Variant
    Dim vDocName as Variant
    Dim vReasonCode As Variant
    Dim vXMLDoc As Variant

        Set oInterchange = New BTSInterchangeLib.Interchange

        ' IInterchange::Submit() call
    'strRetVal contains the value of the submission handle that we will
➥ use to query  with
        strRetVal = oInterchange.Submit(BIZTALK_OPENNESS_TYPE_NOTOPEN, _
            "", _
            "", _
            "", _
            "", _
            "", _
            "", _
            "PO_GCC-KF, _
            "C:\RouteTest\Runtime\Source\Inst_PO_KnotFree_1.xml", _
            "", _
            0, )

    ' somewhere else in your code, you could check in the suspended
➥queue to see
    ' if the item was in the suspended queue or the reason that the
➥item was placed in
    ' the suspended queue
    ' If this item is not in the suspended queue, vReasonCode will be Null
     oInterchange.GetSuspendedQueueItemDetails _
        strRetVal, _
        vSrcName, _
        vDestName, _
        vDocName, _
        vReasonCode, _
        vXMLDoc


    ' For a list of 'reasons' why the document might fail, see the BizTalk
➥server
```

LISTING 12.3 continued

```
' online help 'CISReasonToQueue'
    If vReasonCode <> 0 Then
        MsgBox "Failure in submission. Reason code: " & vReasonCode
    End If


    Set oInterchange = Nothing
```

Submitting Messages from Remote Machines

`IInterchange::Submit()` allows application servers to initiate an interchange and then continue processing requests. To maximize the processing load that an application server needs to handle, it makes sense to have the capability to separate application servers from a BizTalk Server machine allowing the calling program to run on a different computer from the actual BizTalk Server(s).

To allow interchanges to be submitted from remote machines, you must create a Microsoft Installer Package (`.msi` file) on one of the BizTalk Server machines and run this installation package on all remote machines that will submit interchanges. To create the installation package, log in to the BizTalk Server machine directly and open the Microsoft Management Console snap-in for administering COM+ Services. A COM+ application named BizTalk Server Interchange Application should already be configured on the machine. Figure 12.1 shows the COM+ Services MMC.

FIGURE 12.1
The COM+ component services MMC.

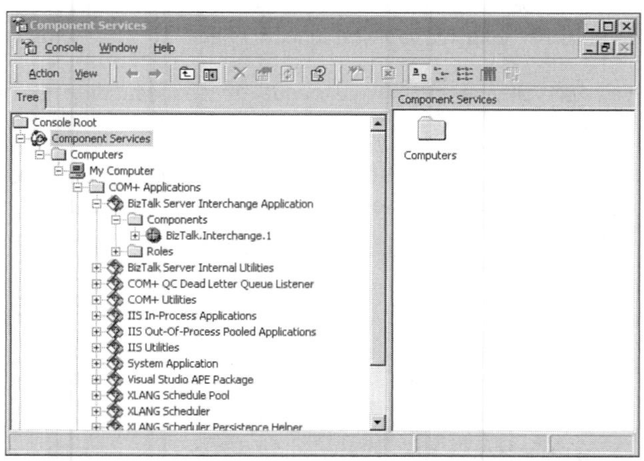

Select the application in the Explorer, right-click, and choose Export. This launches the COM+ Application Export Wizard. Clicking the Next button leads to the Application

Export Information dialog box shown in Figure 12.2. Enter the path for the `.msi` file to be created and select the Application Proxy radio button.

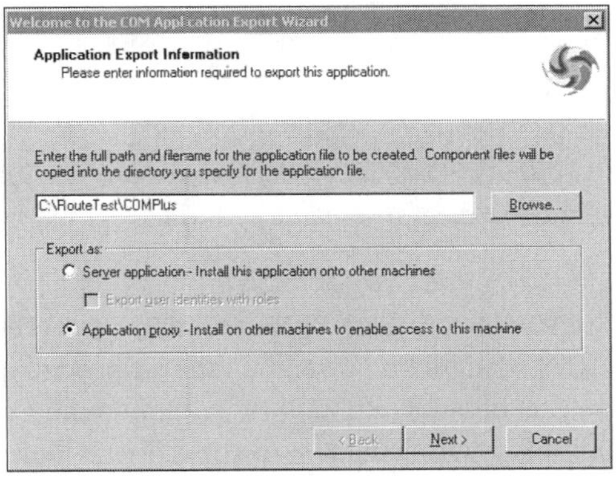

FIGURE 12.2
The COM+ Application Export Wizard.

Clicking the Next button on the Application Export Information dialog causes the installation files to be created at the location specified. The final screen of the wizard simply informs you that the export was successful. Click the Finish button to close the wizard.

After you successfully run the export wizard, you should see two files in the designated directory—an `.msi` file and a `.cab` file. Copy these files to the target machine(s) and run the installation program.

You may need to configure the COM+ identity of the BizTalk Server Interchange Application to successfully submit interchanges when there is no interactive user on the machine. To accomplish this, right-click on the BizTalk Server Interchange Application and choose Properties. Click on the Advanced Tab, and make sure that Disable Changes is unchecked. Finally, click on the Identity tab, select This User, and enter the credentials for the appropriate user account.

Administering the Suspended Queue

The Suspended queue contains work items that have failed processing for a variety of reasons, including parsing errors, serialization errors, failed transmissions, or the inability to find a channel configuration. You can retrieve or delete items from the queue using the `Interchange` interface.

To retrieve items from the suspended queue, you call the `CheckSuspendedQueue` method of the `IInterchange` interface. `CheckSuspendedQueue` retrieves a list of items in the suspended queue that meet the search criteria specified by the parameters of the method. This returns a list of handles that can subsequently be used to call the `DeleteFromSuspendedQueue` or the `GetSuspendedQueueItemDetails` method of the `IInterchange` interface. To process these items, you must get the item details associated with each item in the suspended queue by using `GetSuspendedQueueItemDetails`. `GetSuspendedQueueItemDetails` retrieves the details about an item in the suspended queue.

To remove items from the suspended queue, applications call `DeleteFromSuspendedQueue`. `DeleteFromSuspendedQueue` removes from the suspended queue a list of items that meet the search criteria specified by the parameters of the method.

One note of interest, the sixth parameter of the `GetSuspendedQueueItemDetails()` method contains the actual XML document passed into the suspended queue. If you retrieve this XML document, it is possible with a little programming expertise, to be able to programmatically resubmit this XML document to BizTalk and then delete the item from the suspended queue.

The `RouteTest` Application

The `RouteTest` example simulates the submittal of an XML purchase order for a company named General Construction Company (GCC) to a company named Knots Lumber. The XML purchase order created by GCC is submitted to a BizTalk server that's responsible for the transformation and transport of the XML document to Knots Lumber in Knots Lumber's XML purchase order format (slightly different from GCC's).

To simulate the purchase order system, we have written a Visual Basic 6.0 application that allows you to select from up to seven different scenarios that implement the `IInterchange::Submit()` method.

Each scenario specifies a different set of `IInterchange::Submit()` parameters to demonstrate the multiple BizTalk Messaging document routing possibilities. The `RouteTest` application consists of two forms and one class module that are described in the following sections. To run the application, you will also need to configure BizTalk Messaging document definitions, ports, and channels.

The `RouteTest` application is referenced throughout this chapter, and its setup is described in detail in the following section. The source code for the `RouteTest` application can be downloaded from the publisher's Web site.

The RouteTest Visual Basic Application

The `RouteTest` Visual Basic application consists of two forms and a class module. The forms and class module contents are described in detail in the following sections.

The frmRouteTest Visual Basic Form

The `frmRouteTest` form, shown in Figure 12.3, is used to select from a list of seven independent scenarios that demonstrate calling the `IInterchange::Submit()` method. Each scenario calls a method named `SubmitInterchange` that configures the `Interchange:Submit()` parameters at runtime.

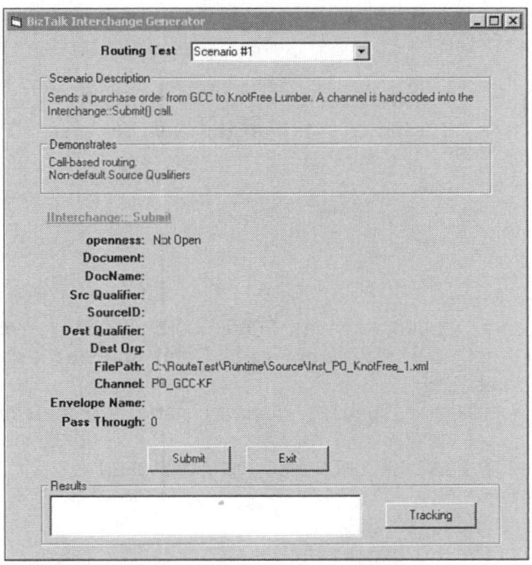

FIGURE 12.3
The `RouteTest` application.

Listing 12.4 shows the source code for the form.

LISTING 12.4 The `frmRouteTest.frm` Code

```
' ****************************************************************************
' FILE:  frmRouteTest.frm
' ****************************************************************************

Dim oParams As New CInterchangeParams

''''''''''''''''''''''''''''''''''''''''''''''''''''''''''''''''''''''''''''''
' SUB: Form_Load()
'
' Handle a change in the selected scenario
''''''''''''''''''''''''''''''''''''''''''''''''''''''''''''''''''''''''''''''
```

LISTING 12.4 continued

```
Private Sub ctlRouteTest_Click()
    Select Case ctlRouteTest.Text
        Case "Scenario #1"
            With oParams
                .Scenario = "Sends a purchase order from GCC to KnotFree Lumber
➥ A channel is hard-coded into the Interchange::Submit() call."
                .Lesson = "Call-based routing." + vbCrLf + "Non-default
➥Source Qualifiers"
                .Openness = BIZTALK_OPENNESS_TYPE_NOTOPEN
                .Document = ""
                .DocDef = ""
                .SrcQualifier = ""
                .SrcID = ""
                .DestQualifier = ""
                .DestID = ""
                .Channel = "PO_GCC-KF"
                .FilePath = "C:\RouteTest\Runtime\Source\Inst_PO_KnotFree_1.xml"
                .Envelope = ""
                .PassThrough = 0
                PopulateForm
            End With
        Case "Scenario #2"
            With oParams
                .Scenario = "*Demonstrates ERROR CONDITION* : A channel is
➥hard-coded into the Interchange::Submit() call, and Source/Destination
➥organizations are specified."
                .Lesson = "Cannot specify channel name AND source/destination
➥information."
                .Openness = BIZTALK_OPENNESS_TYPE_NOTOPEN
                .Document = ""
                .DocDef = "Spec_PO_GCC"
                .SrcQualifier = "OrganizationGCC"
                .SrcID = "GCC"
                .DestQualifier = "OrgKnotsLumber"
                .DestID = "KnotsLumber"
                .Channel = "PO_GCC-KF"
                .FilePath = "C:\Data\BizTalk Unleashed\Samples\RouteTest\
➥Runtime\Source\Inst_PO_KnotFree_1.xml"
                .Envelope = ""
                .PassThrough = 0
                PopulateForm
            End With
        Case "Scenario #3"
            With oParams
                .Scenario = "Purchase order sent from GCC to KnotFree Lumber.
➥ Source/Destination organizations and document definition specified
➥in Submit() call."
                .Lesson = "Demonstrates DYNAMIC ROUTING via
➥IInterchange::Submit()"
```

LISTING 12.4 continued

```
                .Openness = BIZTALK_OPENNESS_TYPE_NOTOPEN
                .Document = ""
                .DocDef = "Spec_PO_GCC"
                .SrcQualifier = "OrganizationGCC"
                .SrcID = "GCC"
                .DestQualifier = "OrgKnotsLumber"
                .DestID = "KnotsLumber"
                .Channel = ""
                .FilePath = "C:\RouteTest\Runtime\Source\Inst_PO_KnotFree_1.xml"
                .Envelope = ""
                .PassThrough = 0
                PopulateForm
            End With
        Case "Scenario #4"
            With oParams
                .Scenario = "Purchase order sent from GCC to KnotFree Lumber.
➥Destination organization and document definition specified in Submit()
➥call. lOpenness set to OPEN SOURCE"
                .Lesson = "*Demonstrates Open Source via
➥IInterchange::Submit()."
                .Openness = BIZTALK_OPENNESS_TYPE_SOURCE
                .Document = ""
                .DocDef = "Spec_PO_GCC"
                .SrcQualifier = ""
                .SrcID = ""
                .DestQualifier = "OrgKnotsLumber"
                .DestID = "KnotsLumber"
                .Channel = ""
                .FilePath = "C:\RouteTest\Runtime\Source\Inst_PO_KnotFree_1.xml"
                .Envelope = ""
                .PassThrough = 0
                PopulateForm
            End With
        Case "Scenario #5"
            With oParams
                .Scenario = "Purchase order sent from GCC to KnotFree Lumber.
➥Source/Destination organizations and document definition specified in
➥ Submit() call. lOpenness set to OPEN SOURCE"
                .Lesson = "*Demonstrates ERROR CONDITION* Cannot use
➥BIZTALK_OPENNESS_TYPE_SOURCE unless document contains routing
➥instructions."
                .Openness = BIZTALK_OPENNESS_TYPE_SOURCE
                .Document = ""
                .DocDef = ""
                .SrcQualifier = ""
                .SrcID = ""
                .DestQualifier = ""
                .DestID = ""
                .Channel = ""
```

LISTING 12.4 continued

```
                .FilePath = "C:\RouteTest\Runtime\Source\Inst_PO_KnotFree_1.xml"
                .Envelope = ""
                .PassThrough = 0
                PopulateForm
            End With
        Case "Scenario #6"
            With oParams
                .Scenario = "Purchase order sent from GCC to KnotFree Lumber.
➥Source/Destination organizations and document definition specified
➥in documnet."
                .Lesson = "Demonstrates Open Source Self Routing Document
➥and IInterchange::Submit()"
                .Openness = BIZTALK_OPENNESS_TYPE_SOURCE
                .Document = ""
                .DocDef = ""
                .SrcQualifier = ""
                .SrcID = ""
                .DestQualifier = ""
                .DestID = ""
                .Channel = ""
                .FilePath = "C:\RouteTest\Runtime\Source\Inst_PO_SelfRoute.xml"
                .Envelope = ""
                .PassThrough = 0
                PopulateForm
            End With
        Case "Scenario #7"
            With oParams
                .Scenario = "Purchase order sent from GCC to KnotFree Lumber.
➥Source/Destination organizations and document definition specified in
➥the document."
                .Lesson = "Demonstrates Self ROUTING Open Destination and
➥source in the document"
                .Openness = BIZTALK_OPENNESS_TYPE_DESTINATION
                .Document = ""
                .DocDef = ""
                .SrcQualifier = ""
                .SrcID = ""
                .DestQualifier = ""
                .DestID = ""
                .Channel = ""
                .FilePath = "C:\RouteTest\Runtime\Source\
➥Inst_PO_SelfRouteFile.xml"
                .Envelope = ""
                .PassThrough = 0
                PopulateForm
            End With
        Case Else
            MsgBox "Invalid Choice of Scenario"
            Exit Sub
```

LISTING 12.4 continued

```
    End Select
End Sub  ' ctlRouteTest_Click()

Private Sub PopulateForm()
    ctlScenario.Caption = oParams.Scenario
    ctlLesson.Caption = oParams.Lesson
    Select Case oParams.Openness
        Case BIZTALK_OPENNESS_TYPE_NOTOPEN
            ctlOpenness.Caption = "Not Open"
        Case BIZTALK_OPENNESS_TYPE_DESTINATION
            ctlOpenness.Caption = "Open Destination"
        Case BIZTALK_OPENNESS_TYPE_SOURCE
            ctlOpenness.Caption = "Open Source"
        Case Else
            ctlOpenness.Caption = "*Error"
    End Select
    ctlDocument.Caption = oParams.Document
    ctlDocDef.Caption = oParams.DocDef
    ctlSrcQualifier.Caption = oParams.SrcQualifier
    ctlSrcID.Caption = oParams.SrcID
    ctlDestQualifier.Caption = oParams.DestQualifier
    ctlDestID.Caption = oParams.DestID
    ctlChannel.Caption = oParams.Channel
    If Len(oParams.FilePath) > 60 Then
        ctlFilePath.Caption = "..." + Right(oParams.FilePath, 60)
    Else
        ctlFilePath.Caption = oParams.FilePath
    End If

    ctlEnvelope.Caption = oParams.Envelope
    ctlPassThrough.Caption = CStr(oParams.PassThrough)
End Sub

''''''''''''''''''''''''''''''''''''''''''''''''''''''''''''''''''''''''''''
' SUB: Form_Load()
'
' Initialize route test controls.
''''''''''''''''''''''''''''''''''''''''''''''''''''''''''''''''''''''''''''
Private Sub Form_Load()

    ' Load the scenario choices
    ctlRouteTest.AddItem "Scenario #1"
    ctlRouteTest.AddItem "Scenario #2"
    ctlRouteTest.AddItem "Scenario #3"
    ctlRouteTest.AddItem "Scenario #4"
    ctlRouteTest.AddItem "Scenario #5"
    ctlRouteTest.AddItem "Scenario #6"
    ctlRouteTest.AddItem "Scenario #7"
```

LISTING 12.4 continued

```
End Sub  ' Form_Load()

''''''''''''''''''''''''''''''''''''''''''''''''''''''''''''''''''''''''''''''''''''''''''''''
'  SUB:  SubmitInterchange()
''''''''''''''''''''''''''''''''''''''''''''''''''''''''''''''''''''''''''''''''''''''''''''''
Sub SubmitInterchange()

    ''''''''''''''''''''''''''''''''''''''''''''''''''''''''''''''''
    ' Submit the interchange
    ''''''''''''''''''''''''''''''''''''''''''''''''''''''''''''''''
    Dim oInterchange As BTSInterchangeLib.Interchange
    Set oInterchange = New BTSInterchangeLib.Interchange
    Dim strRetVal As String

    ' IInterchange::Submit() call
    strRetVal = oInterchange.Submit(oParams.Openness, _
            oParams.Document, _
            oParams.DocDef, _
            oParams.SrcQualifier, _
            oParams.SrcID, _
            oParams.DestQualifier, _
            oParams.DestID, _
            oParams.Channel, _
            oParams.FilePath, _
            oParams.Envelope, _
            oParams.PassThrough)

    Set oSubmit = Nothing

    ctlResults.Text = strRetVal

End Sub  ' SubmitInterchange()


Private Sub btnExit_Click()
    Unload Me
End Sub

Private Sub btnSubmit_Click()
    SubmitInterchange
End Sub

Private Sub lblScenario_Click()
End Sub

''''''''''''''''''''''''''''''''''''''''''''''''''''''''''''''''''''''''''''''''''''''''''''''
' SUB: btnTracking_Click()
'
```

LISTING 12.4 continued

```
' Display tracking data for interchange.
''''''''''''''''''''''''''''''''''''''''''''''''''''''''''''''''''''''''''''''''''''

Private Sub btnTracking_Click()
    Dim strSubHandle As String
    Dim oTracking As New BTSDocTrackingLib.BTSDocTracking
    Dim oRSInterchanges As ADODB.Recordset
    Dim oRSInDocDetails As ADODB.Recordset
    Dim oRSOutDocDetails As ADODB.Recordset
    Dim frmTracking As New frmTracking

    strSubHandle = ctlResults.Text

    ' Get tracking data
    Set oRSInterchanges = oTracking.GetInterchanges(strSubHandle)
    Set oRSInDocDetails = oTracking.GetInDocDetails(strSubHandle)
    Set oRSOutDocDetails = oTracking.GetOutDocDetails(strSubHandle)

    ' Display tracking data
    Set frmTracking.ctlInterchanges.DataSource = oRSInterchanges
    Set frmTracking.ctlInDocDetails.DataSource = oRSInDocDetails
    Set frmTracking.ctlOutDocDetails.DataSource = oRSOutDocDetails
    frmTracking.ctlSubmissionID.Caption = strSubHandle

    frmTracking.Show
End Sub  ' btnTracking_Click()
```


The `frmTracking` Visual Basic Form

The `frmTracking` form, shown in Figure 12.4, displays three grids reflecting the return values of three `IBizTalkTrackData` interface methods.

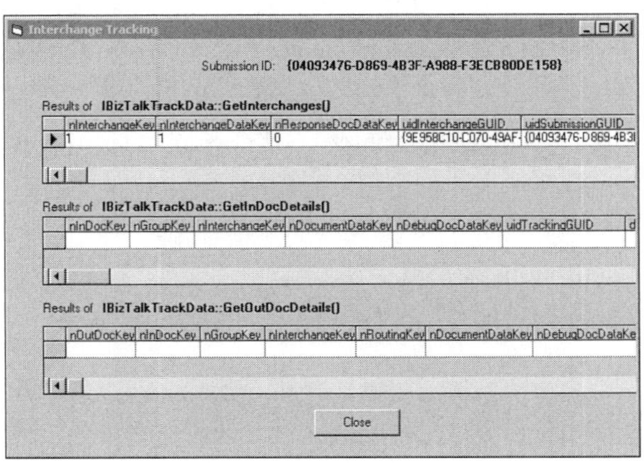

FIGURE 12.4
The `RouteTest` *Interchange Tracking screen.*

The `GetInterchanges` method returns an ADO record set that contains a list of interchanges for a `SubmissionHandle`. The `SubmissisonHandle` is returned from a call to the `IInterchange::Submit()` method and includes data from the tracking database. The `GetInDocDetails` method returns an ADO record set that contains specific information about the input document(s) again based on the `SubmissionHandle` returned from the `IInterchange::Submit()` method. The `GetOutDocDetails` method returns an ADO recordset that contains information about the output document(s) for the submission handle.

The `CInterchangeParams` Class Module

The `CInterchangeParams` class module is used to construct a parameter list for the `IInterchange::Submit` method call. The parameters are filled by the `frmRouteTests`' private subroutine `ctlRouteTest_Click()` whenever the user chooses a scenario. This parameter class object has its values extracted in the `SubmitInterchange` method when `IInterchange::Submit` is called.

Setting Up BizTalk Messaging

The `RouteTest` application processes purchase orders for a construction company named General Construction Company (GCC). GCC sends purchase orders to a lumber company named Knot Lumber. Both organizations accept XML purchase orders; however, the schemas are slightly different. To accommodate the Knot Lumber format, GCC has configured a BizTalk Server to process, transform, and route purchase orders to Knot Lumber. The `RouteTest` Visual Basic application simulates the GCC purchase order system that creates a purchase order and then submits it to BizTalk Server for transformation and transport. To keep the example simple, the Knot Lumber Company accepts the purchase order via the file transport protocol.

To run the sample `RouteTest` application, we need to configure BizTalk Messaging document definitions, ports, channels, and organizations. In the following section, we will

- Execute a script that copies the source code document specs and maps to the BizTalk repository.
- Create the document definitions and map.
- Create the organizations needed.
- Create a channel and port.

> **Note**
>
> Additional message ports and channels will be created throughout the chapter to demonstrate the different routing techniques available.

Table 12.2 shows a list of document definitions and organizations that we will set up in the next few steps.

TABLE 12.2 The Document and Organization Messaging Setup Details

Document Definitions:	Name: `Spec_PO_GCC` Reference: `<WebDAV>\Spec_PO_GCC.xml` Name: `Spec_PO_KF` Reference: `<WebDAV>\Spec_PO_KF.xml`
Organizations:	Name: Rename the Home Organization to General Construction Company Custom Name: `OrganizationGCC` Qualifier: `OrganizationGCC` Value: `GCC` Name: Knots Lumber Custom Name: `OrganizationKnotsLumber` Qualifier: `OrgKnotsLumber` Value: `KnotsLumber`
Port	Name: `PortFromGCCtoKnotsLumber` Destination Organization: Knots Lumber Primary Transport: File (to C:`\RouteTest\Runtime\Dest\KnotFree\PO.xml`)
Channel	Type: To an Application Name: `PO_GCC-KF` Source Application: `GCC App` Inbound Doc Spec: `Spec_PO_GCC` Outbound Doc Spec: `Spec_PO_KF` Map: `<WebDAV>\Map_PO_GCC-KFSelfRouting.xml`

Before we can configure BizTalk Messaging, we need to first create the document specifications and maps required to process the XML purchase order.

Copying the Document Specifications and Map

The document specification and maps needed for the `RouteTest` example have been created for you and can be downloaded from the publisher's Web site. There are two XML document specifications, `SPEC_PO_GCC.xml` and `SPEC_PO_KF.xml`, as shown in Figures 12.5 and 12.6.

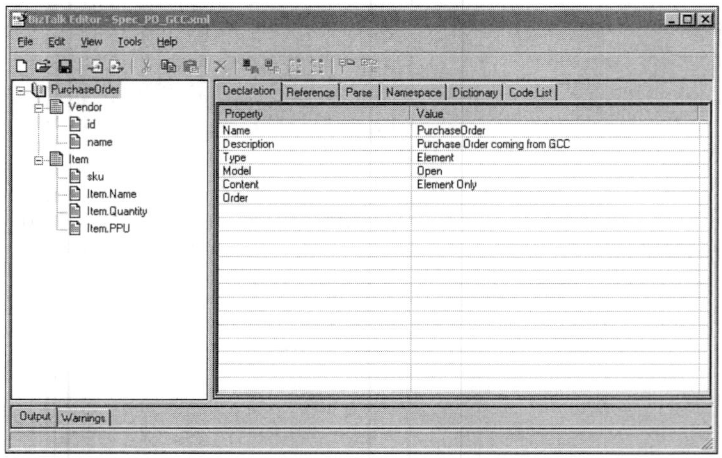

FIGURE 12.5
The `SPEC_PO_GCC` *General Construction Company XML purchase order specification.*

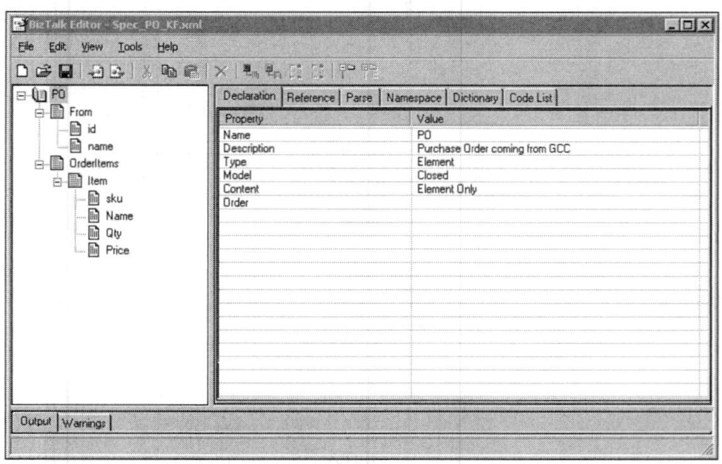

FIGURE 12.6
The `SPEC_PO_KF` *Knots Lumber XML purchase order specification.*

Because the specifications represent different XML purchase order documents, we need to create a map to transform the General Construction Company's purchase order into the Knot Lumber format. The map is named `MAP_PO_GCC-KFSelfRouting.xml` and is displayed in Figure 12.7.

FIGURE 12.7
The GCC to KF purchase order map.

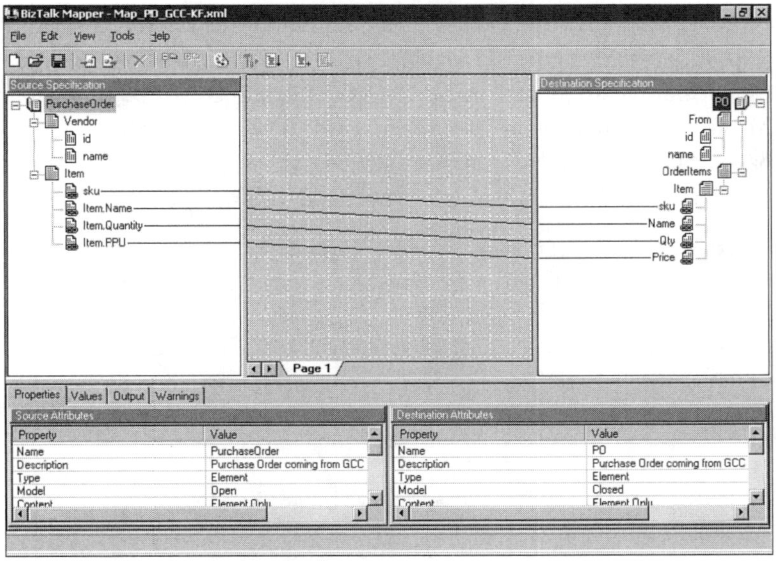

To run the example, download these documents as well as the `RouteTest` application source code from the publisher's Web site and unzip it onto your `C:` drive. This creates a directory with the associated source code named `RouteTest`. Then execute the VBScript file, `CopyDocSpecsAndMap.vbs`, located in the `C:\RouteTest` directory. This script places the document specifications and maps located in the `C:\RouteTest\Setup\Docs` and `C:\RouteTest\Setup\Maps` directory into your `:\Program Files\Microsoft BizTalk Server\BizTalk Server Repository\Docs` and `:\Program Files\Microsoft BizTalk Server\BizTalk Server Repository \Maps` directories.

Note

To ensure that the directory structure is set up correctly under `C:\RouteTest`, after you open the `12SampleRouteTest.zip`, make sure that when you extract the files you set the Extract To edit field to `C:\` and select the Use Folder Names check box.

If you unzip the source code into some other directory location, or if you have BizTalk installed on a hard drive other than the `C:` drive, you will need to manually edit the `CopyDocSpecsAndMap.vbs` file before you execute it.

Creating Document Definitions

Next, we need to create the document definitions for the purchase order specifications in the `RouteTest` example. To accomplish this, open the BizTalk 2002 Messaging Manager by selecting Start, Programs, Microsoft BizTalk Server 2002, BizTalk Messaging Manager from the menu. Then, click on the `Document Definitions` hyperlink in the left pane of the window. Now, click on the Search Now button. This displays all available document definitions in the right-hand pane.

To create a new document definition, select File, New, Document Definition from the menu. Figure 12.8 displays the New Document Definition dialog.

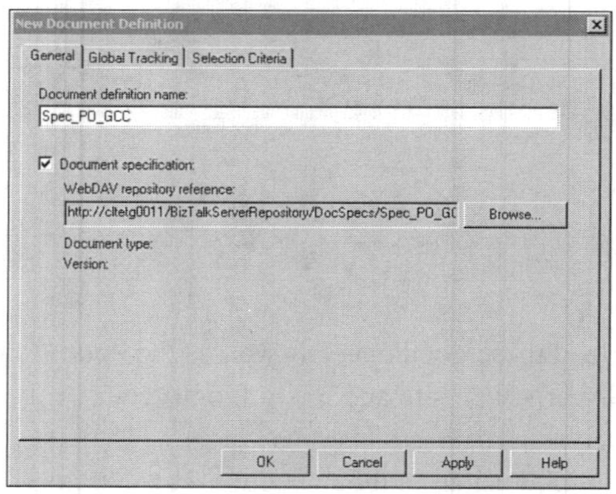

FIGURE 12.8
Creating a new document definition.

In the Document Definition Name edit field, type in the name **`Spec_PO_GCC`** and select the Document Specification check box. Now, select the Browse button. This will allow you to browse to your WebDAV server where you will find your document specification. Your WebDAV browser should look like Figure 12.9.

Select the document specification `Spec_PO_GCC.xml`, select Open, and then click OK. To create the second document definition, repeat the previous steps, but this time, the name of the document definition will be `Spec_PO_KF`, and the WebDAV document specification that it points to will be `Spec_PO_KF.xml`.

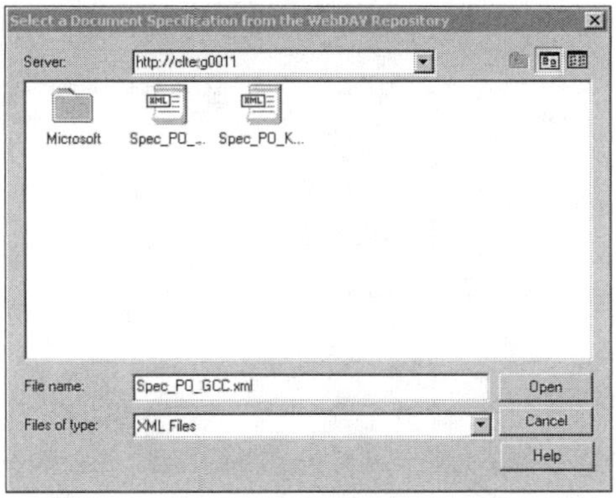

FIGURE 12.9
Choosing a document specification from WebDAV.

Creating the Organizations

The `RouteTest` application uses two organizations and one internal application. We will rename our default Home Organization to General Construction Company and create an application name for it. We will then create a new organization named Knots Lumber.

With the BizTalk Messaging Manager still open from the previous procedure, select the `Organizations` hyperlink in the left-hand pane and then select the Search Now button. A list of organizations will be displayed in the right pane. One of the organizations will have the name of an organization (probably Home Organization) and the word `(default)` in parentheses adjacent to it. This is your default home organization. Double-click on the Home Organization. This brings up the Organization Properties dialog. Change the name to General Construction Company. Next, click on the Identifiers tab. This is where you will set up your organizational names and identifiers. Figure 12.10 displays the Organization Properties dialog with the Identifiers tab selected.

Select the Add button. In the Custom edit field, enter the name **`OrganizationGCC`**. In the Qualifier field, enter the name **`OrganizationGCC`**. In the Value field enter the name **`GCC`**. Click OK when you have finished. Figure 12.11 shows the Identifiers Properties dialog.

Next, we have to create an internal application that represents our GCC organization. Select the Organization Properties Applications tab and then select the Add button. Figure 12.12 shows the New Application dialog. Enter the name **`GCC App`** and click OK. Click OK in the Organization Properties dialog box.

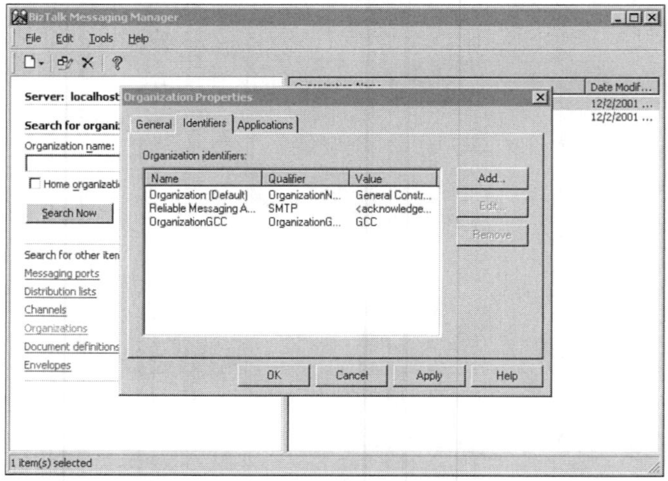

FIGURE 12.10
Adding an identifier to an organization.

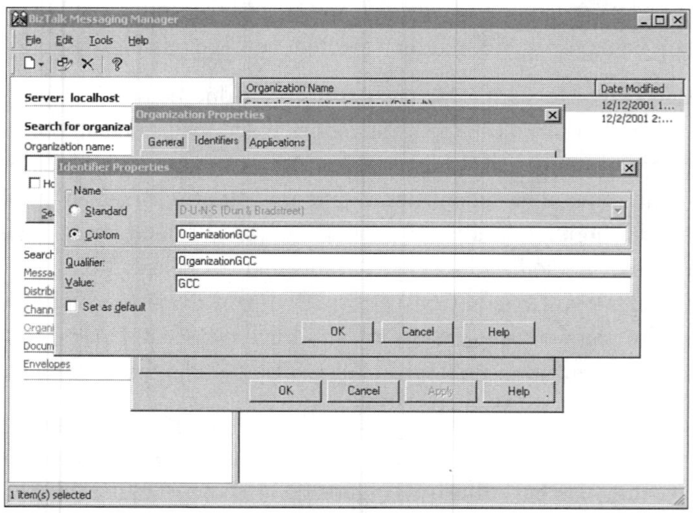

FIGURE 12.11
Adding Identifier properties.

Next, we will create a new organization, Knots Lumber. Select `File`, New, Organization from the menu. The New Organization dialog appears. In the Organization Name field, enter **Knots Lumber**. Click on the Identifiers tab. Here, we will set up the organizational names and identifiers specific to the Knots Lumber organization. Select Add. In the Custom field, enter **`OrganizationKnotsLumber`**. In the Qualifier field, enter **`OrgKnotsLumber`**. In the Value field enter **`KnotsLumber`**. Click OK when you are finished. Click OK in the New Organization dialog.

FIGURE 12.12
Adding an application to the Home Organization.

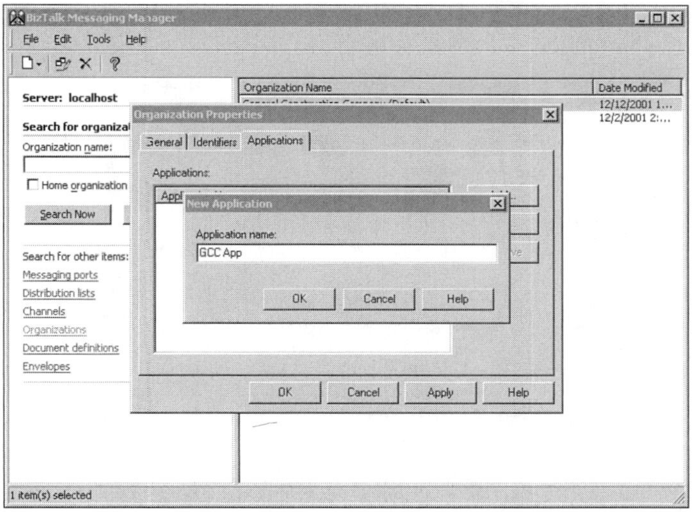

Now that we have configured the documents and organizations that are going to exchange purchase orders, we need to configure a port and channel to process them.

Creating the Messaging Port and Channel

The messaging port will be used to deliver our document to the Knots Lumber organization. To create the port, open the BizTalk Messaging Manager and select the `Messaging Ports` hyperlink. Then click the Search Now button. Select File, New, Messaging Port, To an Organization from the menu. The New Messaging Port window appears as shown in Figure 12.13.

FIGURE 12.13
The New Messaging Port Wizard.

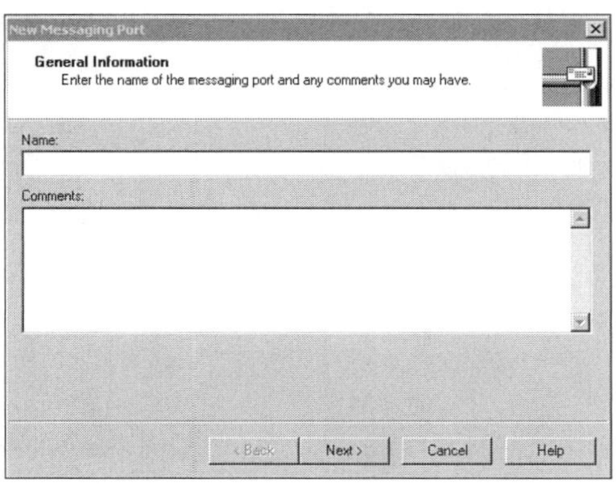

In the Name field, enter **`PortFromGCCtoKnotsLumber`** and then click Next. Next, select the Browse button located adjacent to the Organization Name field. Figure 12.14 shows the New Messaging Port Destination Organization window.

FIGURE 12.14
The New Messaging Port Wizard Destination Organization page.

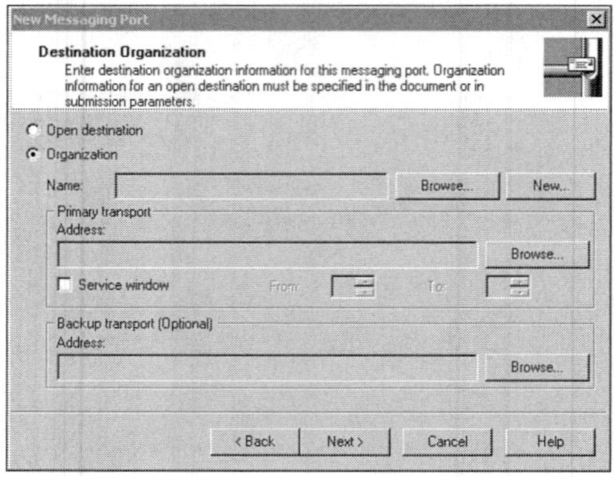

When the Browse button is selected, the Select an Organization dialog appears. Select the Knots Lumber organization and click OK. Figure 12.15 shows the Select an Organization dialog.

FIGURE 12.15
Selecting a destination organization.

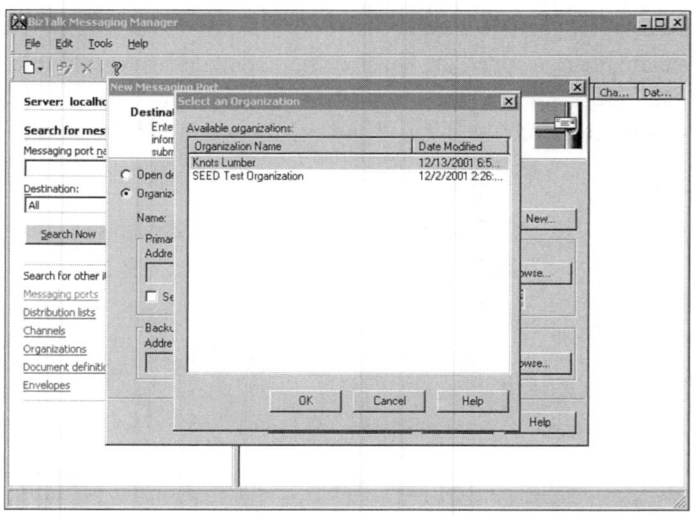

On the New Messaging Port Destination Organization window, select the Browse button located adjacent to the Primary Transport Address field. Figure 12.16 shows the Primary Transport dialog box. Select File from the Transport Type drop-down list and then enter the following string in the Address field **`file://C:\RouteTest\Runtime\Dest\KnotFree\PO.xml`**. It is important that you *do not* leave off the `file://` part of this string. Click OK.

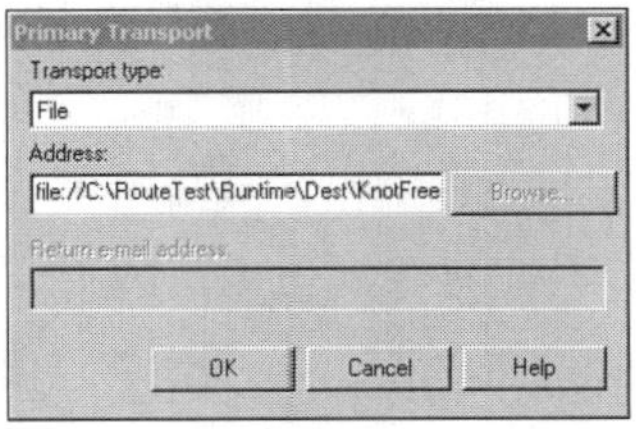

FIGURE 12.16
Setting up the primary transport.

By entering this pathname, we are telling the port to send our transformed document to the path and filename shown previously. Be sure to remember that if you run a document through the port more than once, it will append the data to the file that is already there. If there is no `PO.xml` file already there, one will be created.

Then click Next, accept the default settings on the Envelope Information page, and click Next again. On the Security Information page shown in Figure 12.17, the only change you need to make is in the Channel Type drop-down list. Select From an Application.

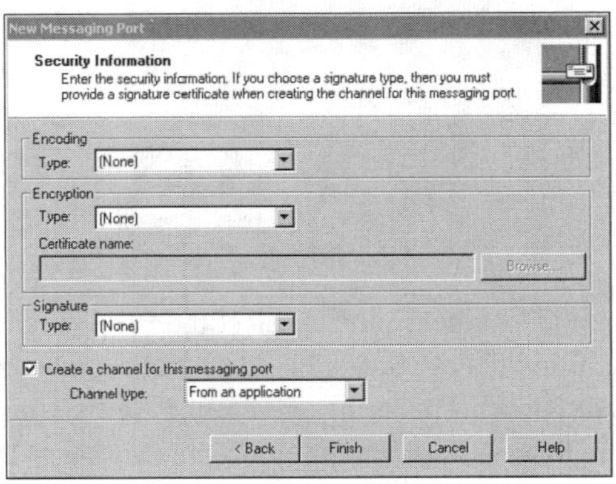

FIGURE 12.17
Selecting a channel from an application.

Click Finish. The New Channel Wizard first window appears as shown in Figure 12.18.

In the Name field, enter **`PO_GCC-KF`** and click Next.

The next screen is the New Channel, Source Application screen shown in Figure 12.19. If `GCC App` is not currently selected in the Application Name edit field, use the drop-down box to select it and click Next.

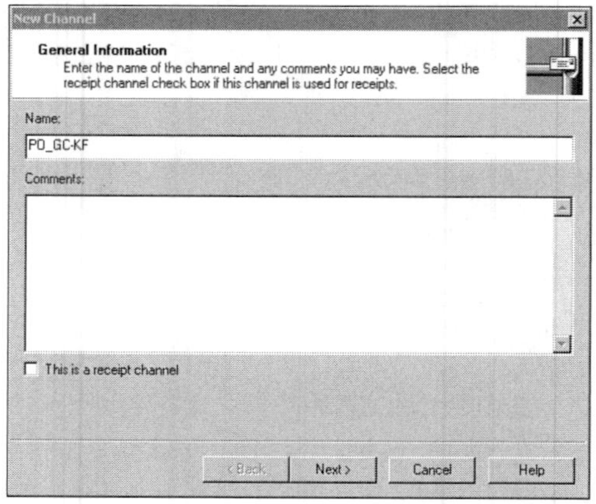

FIGURE 12.18
The New Channel Wizard.

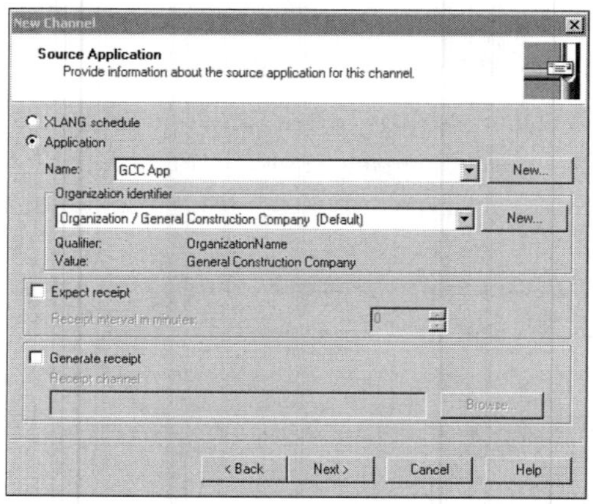

FIGURE 12.19
Selecting a source application.

On the New Channel, Inbound Document screen, select the Browse button. This opens the Select a Document Definition dialog. Select the `Spec_PO_GCC` document definition and then click OK. Then, click Next. This brings you to the New Channel Outbound Document screen. Select the Browse button adjacent to the Outbound Document Definition Name field and then, from the Select a Document Definition dialog, select the `Spec_PO_KF` definition. Click OK. Your New Channel Outbound Document screen should now look like Figure 12.20.

Notice how the Map Inbound Document to Outbound Document check box is automatically selected for you. This is because the New Channel Wizard recognized that your inbound document definition name on the previous screen is different from the outbound document definition name. Select the Browse button adjacent to the Map Reference edit field. Your WebDAV explorer screen appears. Select the map `Map_PO_GCC-KFSelfRouting.xml`, click Open, and click Next. On the Document Logging screen, deselect the Log Inbound Document In Native Format check box and click Next. On the Advanced Configuration screen, do not change any of the defaults and select Finish.

FIGURE 12.20
The outbound document definition selected.

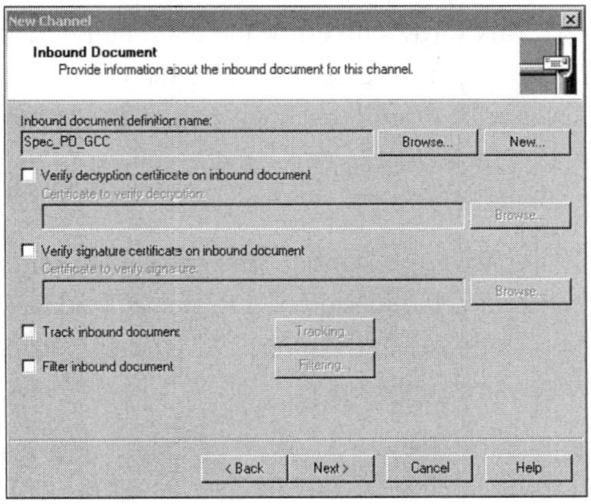

Running the `RouteTest` Example

Running the example is simple. To run the `RouteTest.vbp` application, open the `RouteTest.vbp` project using Visual Basic 6.0 and then select the Run menu option's Start menu option. The BizTalk Interchange Generator window appears. Then select a scenario in the drop-down list box and click Submit. The code will submit an XML purchase order named `Inst_PO_KnotFree_1.xml` to the BizTalk Server Messaging Engine. Listing 12.5 displays the `Inst_PO_KnotFree_1.xml` file.

LISTING 12.5 The `Inst_PO_KnotFree_1.xml` Purchase Order

```
<PurchaseOrder>
    <Vendor id="3005" name="Knotfree Lumber"/>
    <Item sku="1425A3X">
        <Item.Name>Pine 2x4x10</Item.Name>
        <Item.Quantity>75</Item.Quantity>
        <Item.PPU>1.20</Item.PPU>
    </Item>
    <Item sku="1847B2Z">
        <Item.Name>Cedar TG</Item.Name>
        <Item.Quantity>120</Item.Quantity>
        <Item.PPU>4.59</Item.PPU>
    </Item>
</PurchaseOrder>
```

This XML instance is used for every scenario except 6 and 7. The input documents for those scenarios are described in the "Dynamic Routing" section later in the chapter.

Before going into depth about the different scenarios available in the `RouteTest` application, let's first discuss how BizTalk Server handles error processing.

Any type of error that occurs when BizTalk is processing a document should be considered a serious error. When BizTalk throws an error, the document will more than likely be placed into the suspended queue. Regardless of where the document is put, unless you are specifically looking at the Application Event Viewer, you might never know that an error was raised. Therefore, it is important to consistently monitor this event viewer either programmatically or manually.

The scenarios represented in the Message Routing section display errors in a variety of fashions, some appear on the screen and require a response (bad news for a server product), others go to the Application Event Viewer. The descriptions of the scenarios will tell you where to expect to receive the error.

Although the `RouteTest` application doesn't cover all of them, to give you a better idea of just how many permutations are possible, Table 12.3 lists all possible permutations for the `IInterchange::Submit()` parameters critical to the routing process.

TABLE 12.3 Call-Based Routing Permutations

Id	lOpenness	DocName	SrcID	DestID	Channel	Valid
1	NOTOPEN	Empty	Empty	Empty	Empty	
2	NOTOPEN	Empty	Empty	Empty	Valid	Yes
3	NOTOPEN	Empty	Empty	Valid	Empty	
4	NOTOPEN	Empty	Empty	Valid	Valid	No
5	NOTOPEN	Empty	Valid	Empty	Empty	
6	NOTOPEN	Empty	Valid	Empty	Valid	No
7	NOTOPEN	Empty	Valid	Valid	Empty	
8	NOTOPEN	Empty	Valid	Valid	Valid	No
9	NOTOPEN	Valid	Empty	Empty	Empty	
10	NOTOPEN	Valid	Empty	Empty	Valid	No
11	NOTOPEN	Valid	Empty	Valid	Empty	
12	NOTOPEN	Valid	Empty	Valid	Valid	No
13	NOTOPEN	Valid	Valid	Empty	Empty	
14	NOTOPEN	Valid	Valid	Empty	Valid	No
15	NOTOPEN	Valid	Valid	Valid	Empty	
16	NOTOPEN	Valid	Valid	Valid	Valid	No

TABLE 12.3 continued

Id	lOpenness	DocName	SrcID	DestID	Channel	Valid
17	SOURCE	Empty	Empty	Empty	Empty	
18	SOURCE	Empty	Empty	Empty	Valid	
19	SOURCE	Empty	Empty	Valid	Empty	
20	SOURCE	Empty	Empty	Valid	Valid	
21	SOURCE	Empty	Valid	Empty	Empty	
22	SOURCE	Empty	Valid	Empty	Valid	
23	SOURCE	Empty	Valid	Valid	Empty	
24	SOURCE	Valid	Empty	Empty	Valid	
25	SOURCE	Valid	Empty	Empty	Empty	
26	SOURCE	Valid	Empty	Valid	Valid	
27	SOURCE	Valid	Valid	Empty	Empty	
28	SOURCE	Valid	Valid	Empty	Valid	
29	SOURCE	Valid	Valid	Valid	Empty	
30	DEST	Empty	Empty	Empty	Valid	
31	DEST	Empty	Empty	Empty	Empty	
32	DEST	Empty	Empty	Valid	Valid	
33	DEST	Empty	Empty	Valid	Empty	
34	DEST	Empty	Valid	Empty	Valid	
35	DEST	Empty	Valid	Valid	Empty	
36	DEST	Empty	Valid	Valid	Valid	
37	DEST	Valid	Empty	Empty	Empty	
38	DEST	Valid	Empty	Valid	Valid	
39	DEST	Valid	Empty	Valid	Empty	
40	DEST	Valid	Valid	Empty	Valid	
41	DEST	Valid	Valid	Valid	Empty	
42	DEST	Valid	Valid	Valid	Valid	

12 ADVANCED BIZTALK MESSAGING

Note

The permutations listed in Table 12.3 assume that the `PassThrough` parameter is set to `False`.

We have now successfully configured BizTalk Messaging for several of the `RouteTest` example scenarios. In the following sections we will discuss the different types of routing available.

Message Routing

One of the most important features of BizTalk Messaging is its capability to route messages between applications. It is logical to think of the path that a message takes from its source to its final destination as the *route* of travel. Although this may be conceptually correct, you need to understand the mechanics of how BizTalk Server processes messages to truly understand the routing process. This leads us to the formal definition of BizTalk Server routing: Routing is the process of selecting channels and associated ports to process a message.

In the following sections, we will examine how BizTalk Server goes about selecting a channel and port for message processing. We will then discuss the various ways that you can specify the parameters required for channel selection. Finally, we will focus on a particular type of message routing known as dynamic routing.

The Channel Selection Process

When a message arrives in BizTalk Server, an algorithm known as the channel selection process is invoked. Understanding the channel selection process is the key to mastering BizTalk Server routing. Channel configurations are stored in the BizTalk Messaging database, which is typically named `InterchangeBTM`. When a channel is not explicitly specified by the submitter of an interchange, BizTalk Server examines each channel stored in `InterchangeBTM` to determine whether the channel should be executed. This process is depicted in Figure 12.21.

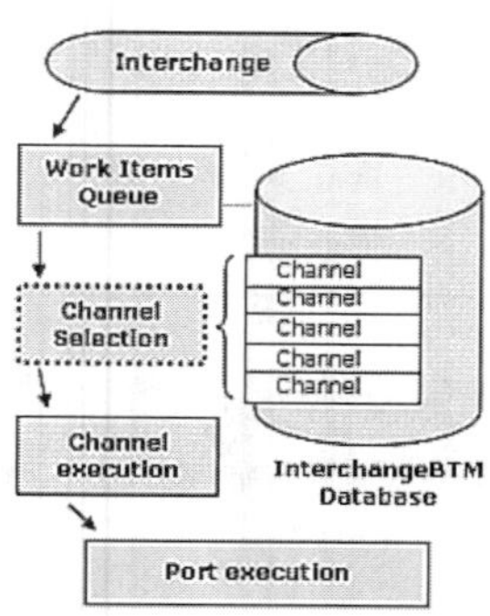

FIGURE 12.21
The channel selection process.

When a channel is not explicitly specified by the submitter of an interchange, there are three key pieces of information that BizTalk Server Messaging requires to select a channel:

- The source organization
- The destination organization
- The document definition for the message

By comparing these three inputs to each channel configuration in the `InterchangeBTM` database, BizTalk Messaging can select the proper channel to invoke.

Note

If more than one channel matches the combination of source organization, destination organization, and document definition, all the matching channels are executed. If no channels match, the interchange is moved to the suspended queue.

What makes BizTalk Server routing interesting is that the source organization, destination organization, and document definition can be specified using a variety of techniques. These techniques are examined later in this chapter.

Note

Throughout this chapter we refer to the combination of source organization, destination organization, and document definition as *routing instructions.*

BizTalk Server is flexible in its capability to extract routing instructions from an interchange. Each technique for specifying routing instructions has benefits and limitations, so it is important to understand all the available options. The following list summarizes the set of effective techniques for specifying routing information in BizTalk Server:

- Call-based routing
- Self-routing documents
- Custom receive functions

Call-based routing puts the onus on the submitter of the interchange to specify routing instructions as part of the submission call. Self-routing documents encapsulate routing instructions inside the document itself. Self-routing is discussed later as part of the more general topic of dynamic routing. Finally, custom receive functions allow you to specify routing instructions that apply to any message processed by the receive function. The following sections discuss each of these options in detail.

Call-Based Routing

Call-based routing refers to the placement of routing instructions inside the parameters of an `IInterchange::Submit()` (or `IInterchange::SubmitSync()`) function call. We've already discussed the `IInterchange::Submit()` parameters earlier in the chapter. This section covers how routing is affected by the various combinations of these parameters.

Call-based routing can be summarized as meaning one of two things: either the channel is explicitly specified or the `sourceId`, `destinationId`, and `docName` are explicitly specified. Other permutations of `IIntechange::Submit()` parameter values fall under the general technique of dynamic routing, discussed later in this chapter.

Explicitly Specifying a Channel Name

When a channel name is explicitly specified in an `IInterchange::Submit()` call, the channel is invoked regardless of the other parameters specified. There is nothing dynamic about this type of document submission. The caller is essentially saying "take this document and process it exactly as I tell you." The channel selection process is bypassed, and the named channel is invoked. Scenario 1 of the `RouteTest` application demonstrates this technique and is displayed in Figure 12.22.

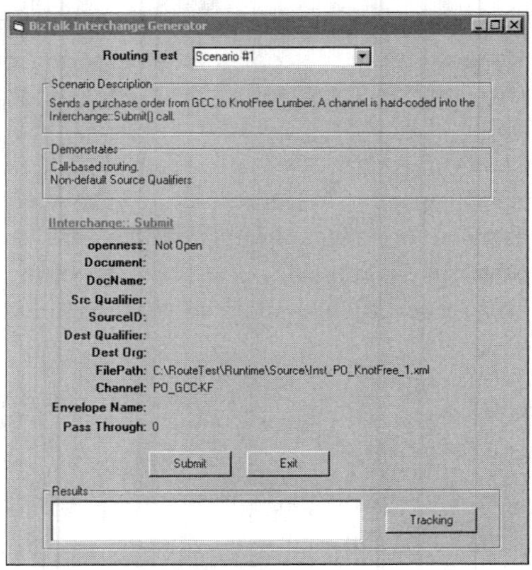

FIGURE 12.22
Scenario 1—channel specified in `submit` *call.*

To run the scenario, select `Scenario1` in the Routing Test drop-down list box and click the Submit button. If the scenario runs successfully, you will see an output document in the `\RouteTest\Runtime\Dest\KnotFree` directory named `PO.xml`.

BizTalk Server throws an error (shown in Figure 12.23) if any additional routing instructions are specified along with a channel name. This means that you must omit source, destination, and document information when specifying a channel. `Scenario2` in the `RouteTest` example demonstrates this.

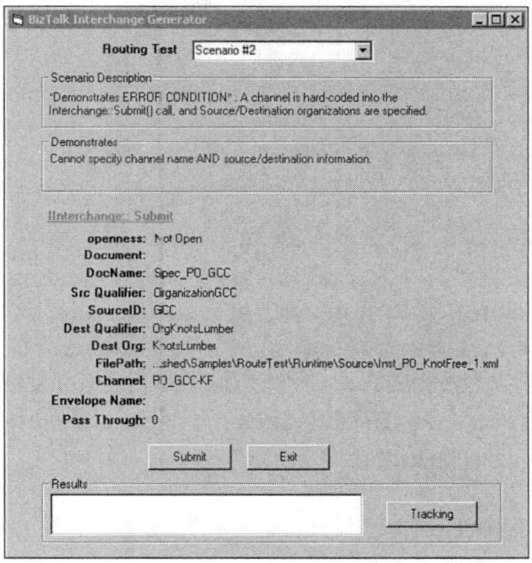

FIGURE 12.23
Error displayed when specifying routing information with a channel.

Figure 12.24 shows the error displayed when selecting the Submit button.

In the next section, we will discuss how to route the same input document using the `IInterchange::Submit` parameters.

Specifying Routing Instructions in `IInterchange::Submit()`

The steps presented in the BizTalk Messaging Manager Channel Wizard provide the ability to input a source organization, document definition, and destination organization. When you invoke `IInterchange::Submit()` by specifying values that match those specified in a channel, BizTalk Server automatically invokes that channel and any other channel that matches the criteria.

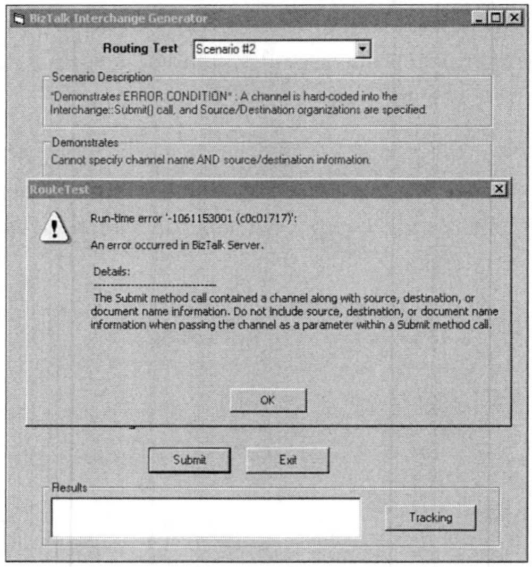

FIGURE 12.24
The Error dialog that appears for `Scenario2`.

Scenario 3, displayed in Figure 12.25, of the `RouteTest` application demonstrates this technique. The `ChannelName` parameter is left empty, but the values of `DocName`, `SourceQualifier`, `SourceID`, `DestQualifier`, and `DestID` match the values configured in the `PO_GCC-KF` channel. Therefore, BizTalk Server automatically invokes the *`PO_GCC_KF`* channel when this scenario is submitted.

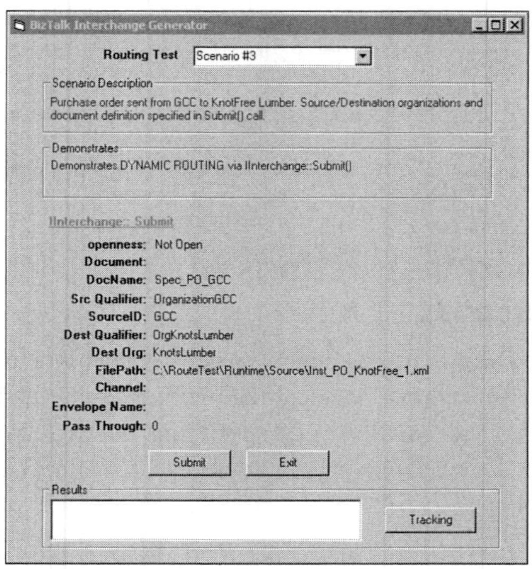

FIGURE 12.25
Scenario 3—Specifying routing instructions.

Again, if the scenario executes successfully, the `PO.xml` document appears in the `.\RouteTest\Runtime\Dest\KnotFree` directory.

If more than one channel had matched the source, destination, and document types provided in the submit method parameters, each channel would have been invoked. This feature gives you the ability to route a document to multiple business partners and applications with a single submit call. It also gives you the ability to map the inbound document to the multiple outbound document formats with a single submit. This may seem conceptually similar to a distribution list; however, distribution lists are a little different. Distribution lists allow you to specify multiple recipients for a single inbound document and outbound document combination. You cannot perform multiple transformations, one per recipient, as you can using the channel selection process. Distribution lists are discussed in detail later in this chapter.

> **Note**
>
> Direct routing between applications is not supported by BizTalk Server. Routing takes place between organizations, not between the applications inside an organization. Routing between applications can be accomplished indirectly by setting up different organizations for each application. You can simulate this by creating multiple channels with the same source organization but different application names. The channel selection process will occur based on the organization name, not the application name.

Now that we understand the role that the source organization, destination organization, and the document definition play in message routing, we will take a look at how these values can be "parameterized" using self-routing documents, a technique where routing instructions are placed within the actual documents submitted to BizTalk Server. Ports and channels can also be made more dynamic and reusable by configuring them as *open*. In the following section, we will discuss how to dynamically route documents using open ports and channels as well as self-routing documents.

Dynamic Routing

Business circumstances may arise that require the execution of the same core business process regardless of the source and destination addresses. For example, multiple departments in a company may need to send purchase orders to one or more of the same suppliers. Each of these transactions will likely have a similar workflow and document format. Therefore, it makes sense to programmatically implement the common workflow and have the specifics of each transaction be data driven. BizTalk's dynamic routing capabilities facilitate this as well as code reuse and process abstraction, two important attributes of a well-architected system.

Figure 12.26 shows how a document flows through the BizTalk Server Messaging Engine. Within this process flow are several elements that can be "parameterized" and targeted for reuse.

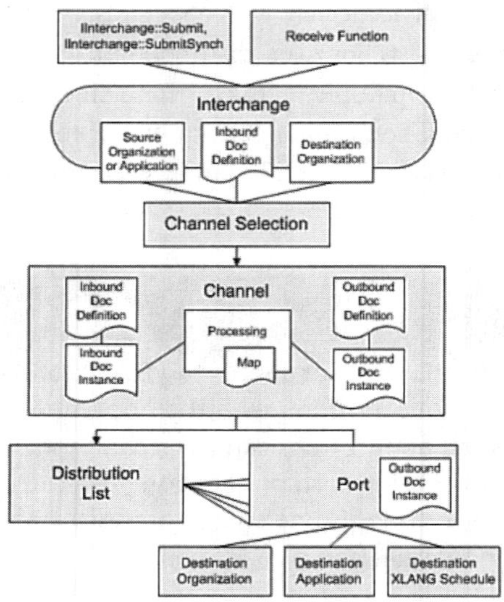

FIGURE 12.26
BizTalk Server document processing.

There are three ways to accomplish dynamic routing:

- Open source channels
- Open destination ports
- Self-routing documents

In the following sections, we will discuss each of these and then demonstrate how they work using the `RouteTest` sample application.

Open Source Channels

Open source channels allow you to specify the source organization at runtime programmatically using the `IInterchange` interface or inside a self-routing document. In this case, the channel selection process uses two of the three parameters, document and destination, to select the channel(s). The source organization value is not important because the channel selection process compares the two values to all channels and then selects those that are marked as open source and that have the same document and destination specified. This allows you to configure a single channel and port combination that can accept a document from multiple sources as opposed to having to construct a new channel for each source organization.

To demonstrate this concept, we have created a new channel that is connected to the same port we created earlier named `PortFromGCCtoKnotsLumber`. To create the new channel, open the BizTalk Messaging Manager, select the `Messaging Ports` hyperlink, and click Search. Select the `PortFromGCCtoKnotsLumber` port in the port list that appears and right-click. In the pop-up menu that appears, select the New Channel from an Organization option. In the dialog that appears, name the channel `FromGCCtoKnotsLumberOpenSource` as displayed in Figure 12.27.

FIGURE 12.27
Adding the open source channel.

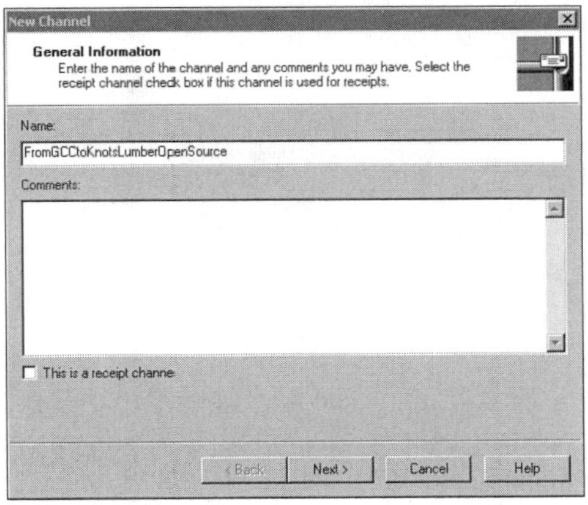

Click Next and in the Channel Properties, Source Organization dialog that appears, select the Open Source radio button as displayed in Figure 12.28; then click Next.

FIGURE 12.28
Setting the Open property.

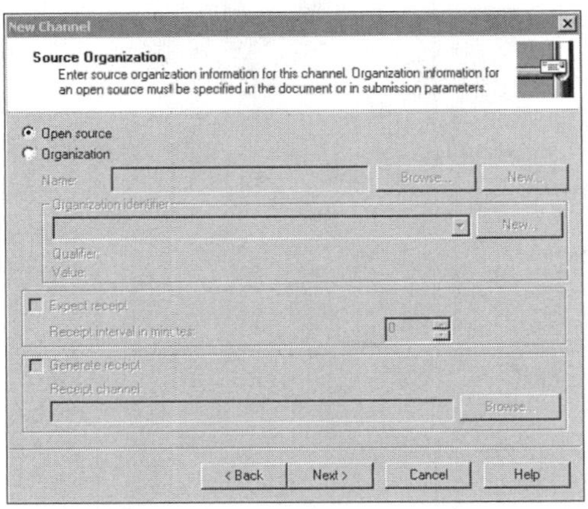

Next, set the inbound and outbound documents to the same values specified in the channel created earlier. The inbound document should be set to `SPEC_PO_GCC`, and the outbound document to `SPEC_PO_KF`. The outbound Channel Properties dialog prompts you for a map. Select the `Map_PO_GCC-KFSelfRoute.xml` map from the root `WebDav` directory as displayed in Figure 12.29.

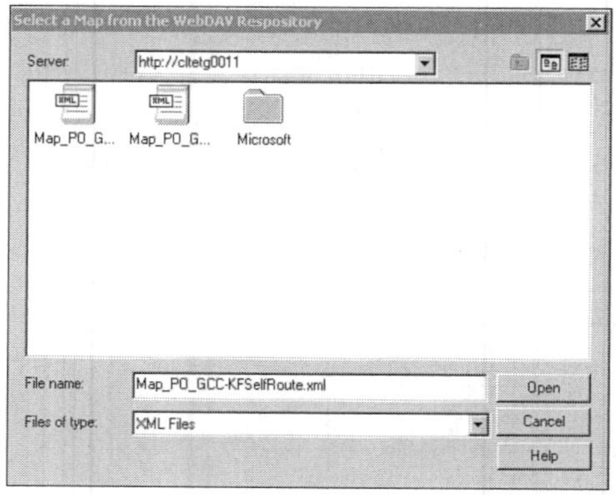

FIGURE 12.29
Setting the map for the open source channel.

Next, click Finish. We have now configured BizTalk Messaging for an open source channel.

In Scenario 4, displayed in Figure 12.30, of the `RouteTest` sample application, we demonstrate the use of the open channel by specifying the destination and document name values and not the channel name. We also specify the `lOpenness` parameter as Open Source.

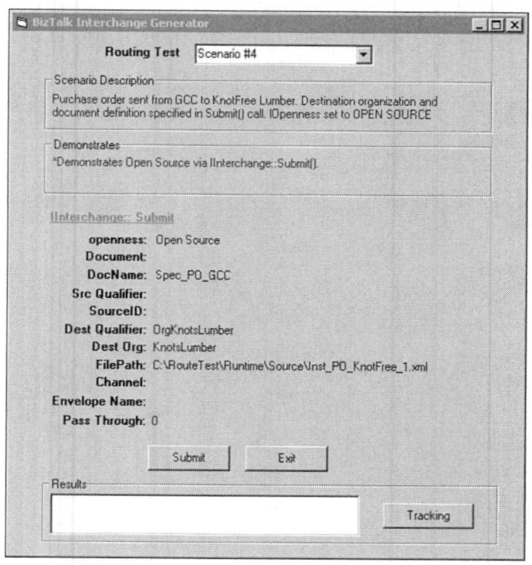

FIGURE 12.30
Scenario 4 of the `RouteTest` *application.*

If you do not specify the routing parameters programmatically or within the document itself, the document will fail the channel selection process and end up in the suspended queue. This is demonstrated in Scenario 5 of the `RouteTest` application and is shown in Figure 12.31.

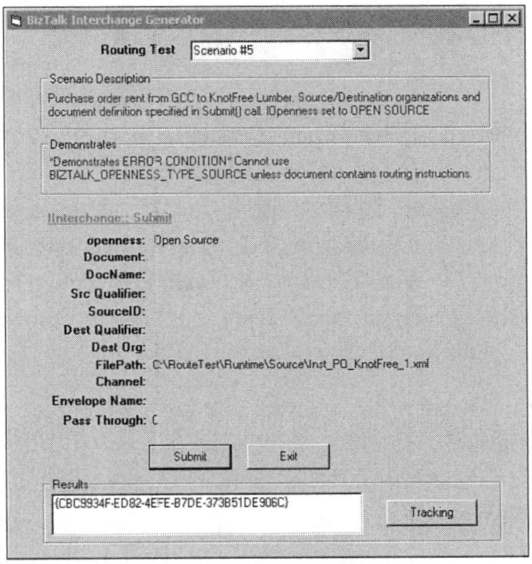

FIGURE 12.31
Scenario 5 of the `RouteTest` *application.*

In the next section, we will discuss the concept of open ports. An open port allows you to specify the destination as opposed to the source at runtime.

> **Note**
>
> A channel specified as an open channel cannot be created for a messaging port specified as an open messaging port.

Open Destination Ports

Open destination ports are similar to open source channels; however, they require the destination transport address to be either programmatically specified or available in the document that is submitted. In this case, the channel selection process uses the document name and source organization name to select the channel(s) to execute by comparing those values to channels that have the same values and that are bound to open ports. It then evaluates the transport information to know how to route the document. Thus, open ports give you the ability to construct a single port that represents multiple destinations.

Note

An open messaging port can be used to transport documents only to organizations, and the encryption security properties are disabled because the destination organization is unknown. To set the encryption properties, you need to specify a certificate from a specific, known destination organization.

When you declare a messaging port as an open messaging port, you cannot create channels for the messaging port that have an `X12` or `EDIFACT` outbound document definition. To build an `X12` or `EDIFACT` envelope, BizTalk server must have a source and a destination organization identifier. An open messaging port does not specify a destination organization identifier. In addition, the documents for an open messaging port must have the destination address within the document, but `X12` and `EDIFACT` documents do not contain this information.

When submitting a document to an open channel, you have the choice of submitting the destination information programmatically or within the document. If the destination information is provided in the document, the inbound document definition for that channel must reference a specification that is properly configured. If the submission parameters are used with the `IInterchange` interface, they override any destination and transport information contained within the document.

In many ways, the functionality of open ports may seem similar to the functionality achieved with a distribution list. There are, however, some major differences. An open messaging port differs from a distribution list in the following ways:

- With an open messaging port, each document from a channel results in only one document being delivered to only one destination. With a distribution list, each document from a channel can result in the document being delivered to multiple destinations.
- With an open messaging port, you do not have to change the properties of the messaging port to send information to a different trading partner organization. With a distribution list, you have to add a messaging port to send information to a different trading partner organization.

In our sample application, General Construction Company sends purchase orders to several different suppliers of raw materials, including KnotFree Lumber, Buzz Electrical Supplies, and Rigid Steel Company. Because each transaction is so similar, you can avoid having to write code for each potential supplier. Instead, you can make the process data driven by allowing BizTalk Server to route the purchase order based on either the contents of the order or by specifying an open destination port. The concept of self-routing documents will be covered in the next example. To demonstrate the ability to route a document using an open port, we need to create a new open port bound to a new channel. We cannot reuse a channel already created because a port can be bound to many channels, but a channel can be bound to one and only one port.

To create the new port, open the BizTalk Messaging Manager, select the `Port` hyperlink, and click Search. Then, right-click on the Port list and, in the pop-up menu that appears, select the New Messaging Port, To an Organization menu option. Name the new port `FromGCCtoKnotsLumberOpen` and click Next.

> **Note**
>
> Open ports cannot be created to an application.

In the New Messaging Port Destination Organization dialog that appears, select the Open Destination radio button as displayed in Figure 12.32 and click Next.

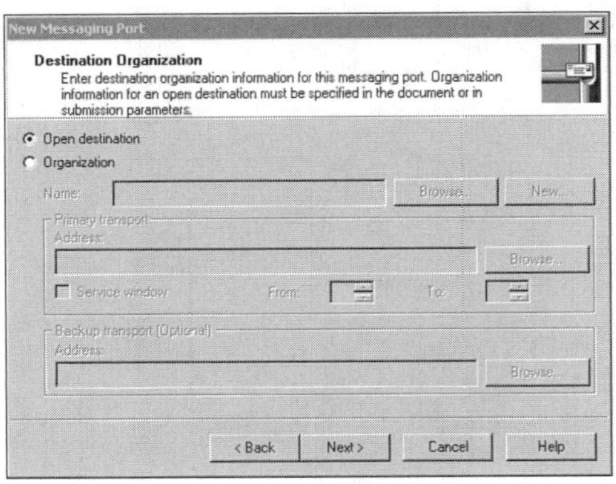

FIGURE 12.32
Creating the open port.

Then, keeping the default values in the Envelop Information dialog, click Next again. In the New Messaging Port Security Information dialog that appears, keep the default values as displayed in Figure 12.33 and click Finish.

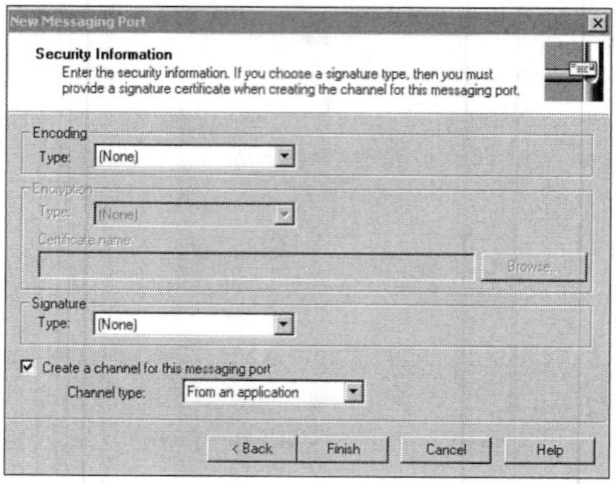

FIGURE 12.33
Creating a new channel for the open port.

In the New Channel dialog that appears, name the channel `FromGCCtoKnotsLumberOpenDest` and click Next. Then, in the Source Application dialog that appears, select the GCC App application and click Next. The source, destination, and map properties will be configured as they have been in the previous channels. The source document should be named `SPEC_PO_GCC`, the destination document should be named `Spec_PO_KF`, and the map, `Map_PO_GCC-KFSelfRoute.xml`, should be selected from the `WebDav` root as displayed in Figure 12.34.

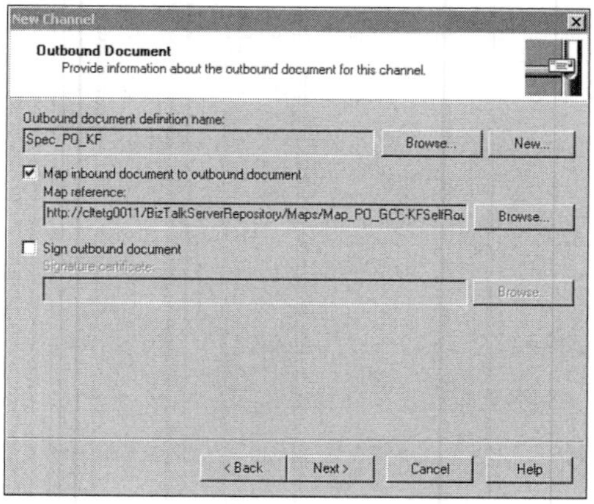

FIGURE 12.34
Selecting the map for the new open destination channel.

Next, click Finish allowing the remainder of the wizard steps to keep their default properties.

To test the configuration of the open port, we need to first learn a little about self-routing documents. In Scenario 7 of the `RouteTest` example, we will use the self-routing capabilities of BizTalk Server to execute the open port we just created.

Self-Routing Documents

Self-routing documents encapsulate all the information required by BizTalk Server to achieve dynamic routing. The source organization, destination organization, and document definition can each be discovered by BizTalk Server's Messaging Engine during the parsing of the document. Different types of documents have different ways of communicating routing instructions. Therefore, the location of routing instructions within a document is specified during the creation of its associated BizTalk specification in the BizTalk Editor using the Dictionary tab.

In the `RouteTest` examples, the GCC purchase order named `SPEC_PO_GCC` contains the routing instructions. The routing instructions are contained within the fields in the `RouteFields` record. To set the routing values, open the `SPEC_PO_GCC` specification and navigate to the Dictionary tab for the `RouteFields` fields. Then set the values as displayed in Figure 12.35.

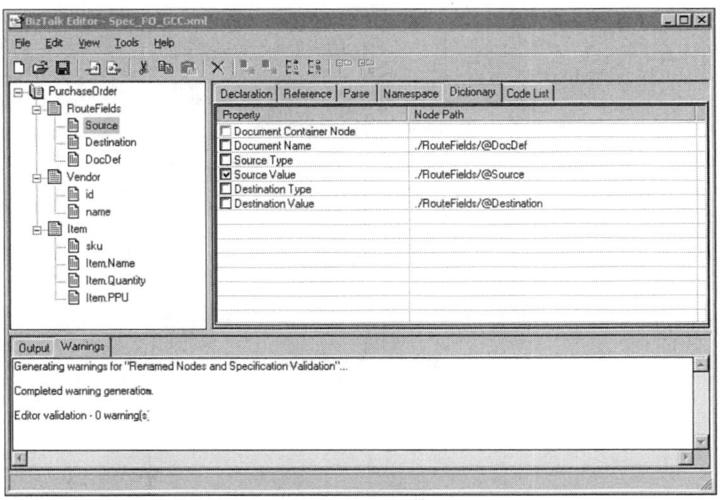

FIGURE 12.35
Dictionary tab of BizTalk Editor for the GCC purchase order.

In this case, we are going to use three fields in the XML document to represent the routing parameters. Each of the fields needs to be set in the Dictionary tab to their appropriate routing properties. The `Source` field in the `RouteFields` record is set equal to the `Source Value` in the Dictionary tab (refer to Figure 12.35). The `Destination` field is set to the `DestinationValue` property, as displayed in Figure 12.36, and the `DocDef` field is set to the `DocumentName` property, as shown in Figure 12.37.

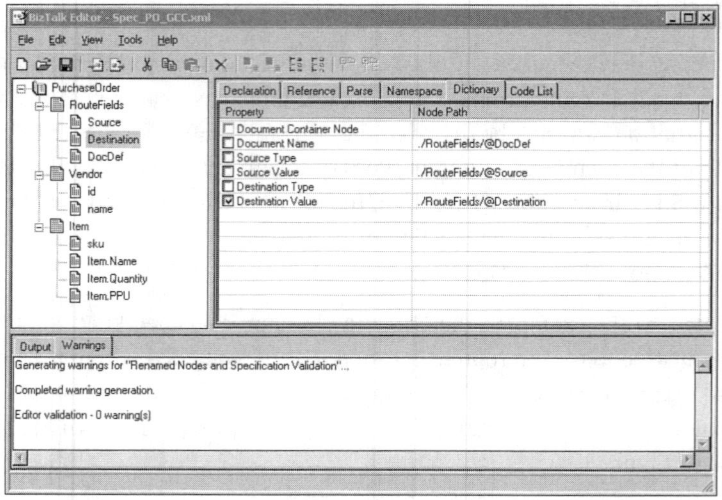

FIGURE 12.36
Setting the destination value in the Dictionary tab.

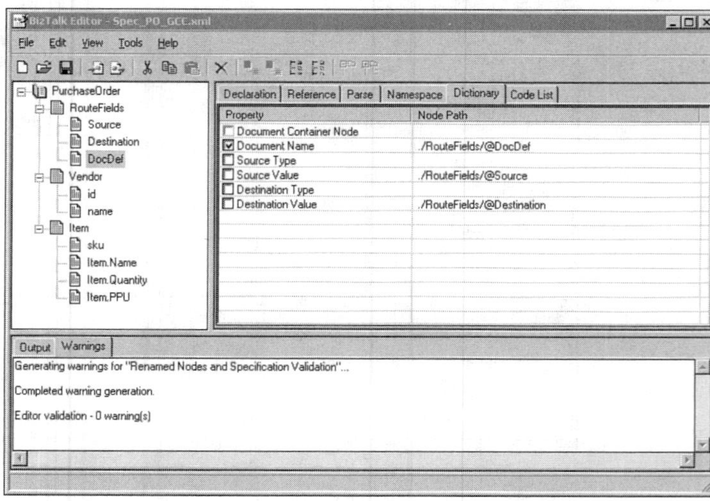

FIGURE 12.37
Setting the `DocDef` *property in the Dictionary tab.*

In the previous examples, the `RouteFields` were present in the XML purchase order schema, but no values were supplied for them in the XML purchase order instance. In Scenarios 6 and 7, we will specify routing parameters using two new example purchase order instance files, `Inst_PO_SelfRoute.xml`, displayed in Listing 12.6, and `Inst_PO_SelfRouteFile.xml`, shown in Listing 12.7.

LISTING 12.6 The `Inst_PO_SelfRouteFile.xml` File

```
<PurchaseOrder>
    <RouteFields Source="General Construction Company"
Destination="file://c:\routetest\runtime\dest\knotfree\POSelfRoute.xml"
➥DocDef="Spec_PO_GCC"></RouteFields>
    <Vendor id="3005" name="Knotfree Lumber"/>
    <Item sku="1425A3X">
        <Item.Name>Pine 2x4x10</Item.Name>
        <Item.Quantity>75</Item.Quantity>
        <Item.PPU>1.20</Item.PPU>
    </Item>
    <Item sku="1847B2Z">
        <Item.Name>Cedar TG</Item.Name>
        <Item.Quantity>120</Item.Quantity>
        <Item.PPU>4.59</Item.PPU>
    </Item>
</PurchaseOrder>
```


LISTING 12.7 The `Inst_PO_SelfRoute.xml` Purchase Order Instance

```
<PurchaseOrder>
    <RouteFields Source="General Construction Company" Destination="Knots
Lumber" DocDef="Spec_PO_GCC"></RouteFields>
    <Vendor id="3005" name="Knotfree Lumber"/>
    <Item sku="1425A3X">
        <Item.Name>Pine 2x4x10</Item.Name>
        <Item.Quantity>75</Item.Quantity>
        <Item.PPU>1.20</Item.PPU>
    </Item>
    <Item sku="1847B2Z">
         <Item.Name>Cedar TG</Item.Name>
         <Item.Quantity>120</Item.Quantity>
         <Item.PPU>4.59</Item.PPU>
    </Item>
</PurchaseOrder>
```

Two remaining scenarios demonstrate both the power of self-routing documents and that of open channels and ports. Scenario 6 demonstrates the capability to submit a self-routing document that contains the routing information required to select the open source channel. The only two parameters specified in the scenario are the `lOpenness` parameter, which is set to `True`, and the document name parameter, which now reads the `Inst_PO_SelfRouteFile.xml` document. Figure 12.38 displays Scenario 6.

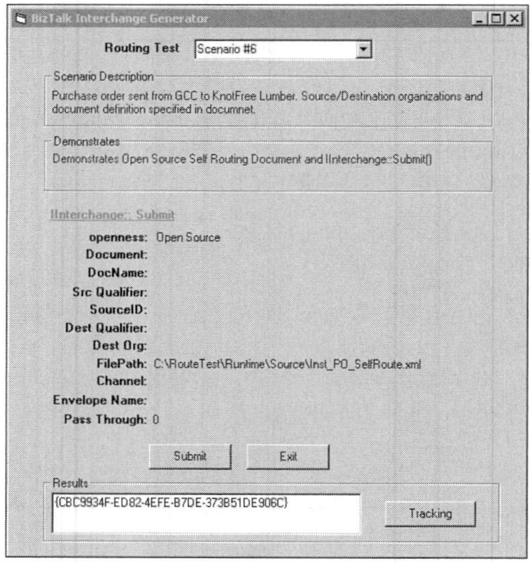

FIGURE 12.38
Scenario 6—Self-routing documents with the open source channel.

To run the scenario, select it in the Routing Test drop-down list box and click the Submit button. If the scenario runs successfully, you will see an output document in the `\RouteTest\Runtime\Dest\KnotFree` named `PO.xml`.

Scenario 7 of the Route Test example demonstrates the open port configured earlier and is displayed in Figure 12.39.

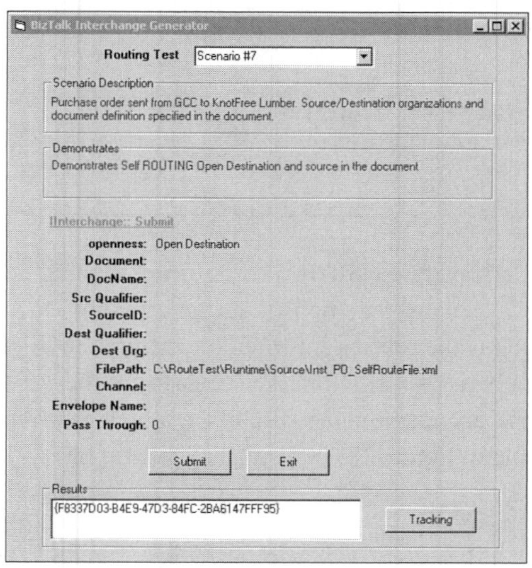

FIGURE 12.39
`RouteTest` *Scenario 7—Self-routing document example.*

Scenario 7 passes only two parameters to the `IInterchange::Submit()` method, `lOpenness`, which is set to Open Destination, and the name of the file to submit, which in this case is `Inst_PO_SelfRouteFile.xml`, displayed earlier in Listing 12.7. Note the `RouteFields` in the following code example. In this scenario, the `RouteFields` must contain the destination transport information if the channel selection process is to successfully execute a channel connected to an open port.

```
<RouteFields Source="General Construction Company" Destination="file://c:\
routetest\runtime\dest\knotfree\POSelfRoute.xml"
➥DocDef="Spec_PO_GCC"></RouteFields>
```


To run the example, select `Scenario7` in the drop-down list box and click the Submit button. If the scenario executes successfully, a file named `POSelfRoute.xml` should be placed in the `\RouteTest\Runtime\Dest\KnotFile` directory.

Each of the scenarios we have discussed assumes a programmatic submission of the instance document using the `IInterchange` interface. We also have the option of using a receive function. In the next section, we will discuss how to create and set the properties required to implement dynamic routing with a BizTalk receive function.

Configuring Receive Functions for Dynamic Routing

You can configure a single receive function that handles non-self-routing documents to receive a specific type of document from multiple sources better known as *open source scenario*. The location of the source organization, the destination organization, and the document definition information must be in the document or in parameters submitted along with the document.

For example, in the `RouteTest` open source `Scenario6`, we configured BizTalk messaging to receive an XML purchase order from multiple undefined sources using an open source channel and the `IInterchange::Submit` method. BizTalk Server parsed the document to read the document name and destination values to route the XML document.

We could also configure a receive function to accomplish the same results by setting the document definition and destination organization identifier properties in the receive function properties dialog. When BizTalk Server parses the document, it recognizes that the source is open and then combines this information with the parameters set in the receive function, to find the correct channel, and then processes the document.

To configure this example, open the BizTalk Administration console and navigate to the `Receive Functions` folder under the `BizTalk Server Group` as displayed in Figure 12.40.

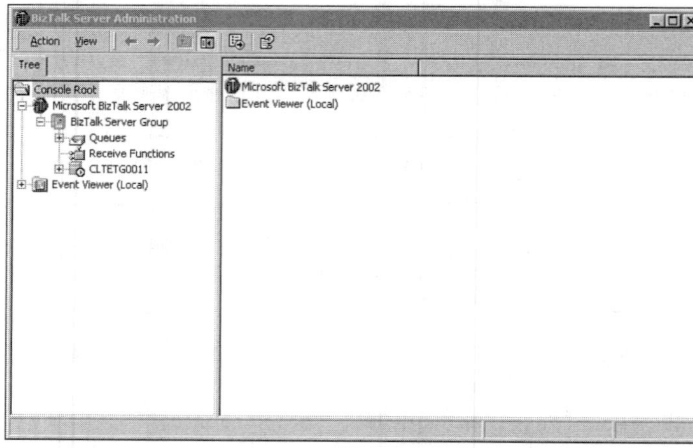

FIGURE 12.40
Configuring a receive function for dynamic routing.

Next, right-click on the `Receive Functions` folder, and in the pop-up menu that appears, select New, File Receive Function from the menu. In the Add a File Receive Function dialog that appears, configure the properties as displayed in Figure 12.41.

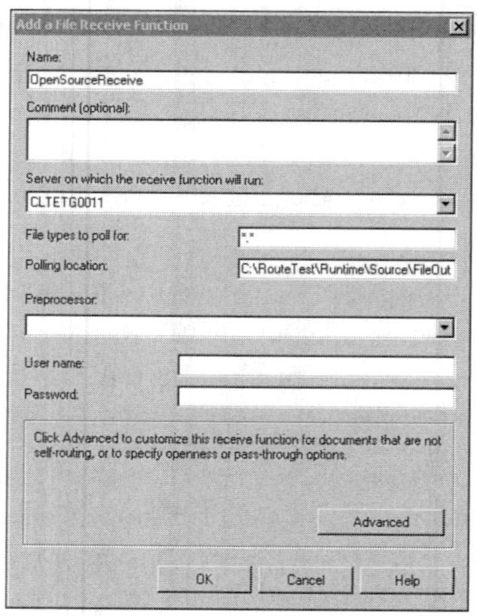

FIGURE 12.41
Configure the Add a File Receive Function dialog.

Next, select the Advanced tab. In the Advanced Receive Function Options dialog that appears, configure the properties as displayed in Figure 12.42.

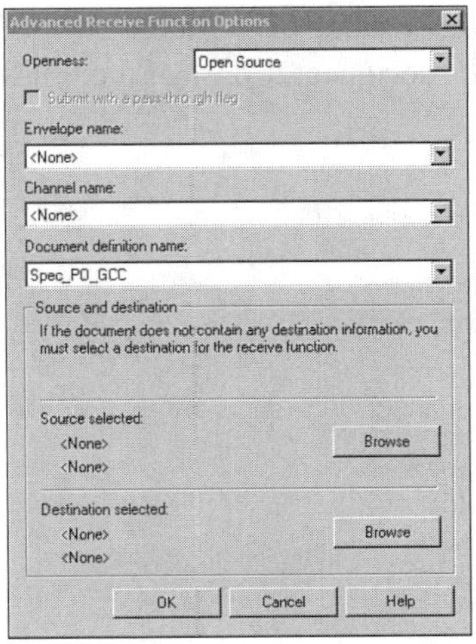

FIGURE 12.42
The Advanced tab properties on the file receive function.

We are now ready to run the `RouteTest` application. To run the application, make a copy of the `Inst_PO_KnotFree_1.xml` document from the `\RouteTest\Runtime\Source` directory and place it into the `\RouteTest\Runtime\Source\FileOut` directory. If the example executes successfully, you should see an instance of the `PO.xml` file located in the `\RouteTest\Runtime\Dest\KnotFree` directory.

Channel Filtering

BizTalk Messaging routes documents using the channel selection process. The channel selection process relies on the document name, source and destination values to select a channel, or group of channels to execute. To provide a more granular approach to channel selection, BizTalk Messaging also gives you the ability to apply a channel filter. Channel filtering enables a developer to build a filtering expression that facilitates content-based channel selection based on the value of a field or fields within the document. The `Expression` property contains an XPath expression that evaluates to a `Boolean` value. If the expression evaluates to true, the channel is used to process the document. Otherwise, the channel is not invoked to process the document.

> **Note**
>
> A channel filter is applied to only those documents that pass the normal channel selection process.

XPath expressions can be used to obtain the value of a specific element, attribute, or collection of these items within an XML document. Consider the following XML document:

```
<PurchaseOrder>
    <Vendor id="3005" name="Knotfree Lumber"/>
    <Item sku="1425A3X">
        <Item.Name>Pine 2x4x10</Item.Name>
        <Item.Quantity>75</Item.Quantity>
        <Item.PPU>1.20</Item.PPU>
    </Item>
    <Item sku="1847B2Z">
        <Item.Name>Cedar TG</Item.Name>
        <Item.Quantity>120</Item.Quantity>
        <Item.PPU>4.59</Item.PPU>
    </Item>
</PurchaseOrder>
```

Based on this document, the following XPath expression can be created to ensure that this channel only processes purchase orders that contain an item named `TG`:

```
myChannel.Expression = "/PurchaseOrder/Item/Name[@VALUE=""TG""]"
```

In the `RouteTest` example, we created three channels. Let's now modify the `PO_GCC-KF` channel to incorporate a channel filter. To accomplish this, open the BizTalk Server Messaging Manager, select the `Channels` hyperlink, and click Search Now. Then select the `PO_GCC-KF` channel in the channel list and right-click. In the pop-up menu that appears, select the Edit menu option and then navigate to the Channel Properties Inbound Document Wizard dialog as displayed in Figure 12.43.

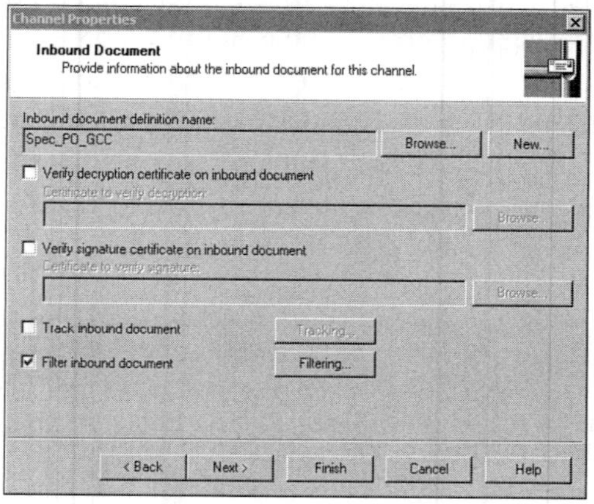

FIGURE 12.43
Setting the channel filtering option on a channel.

Next, check the Filter Inbound Document check box and select the Filtering button. In the Channel Filtering Expressions dialog that appears, navigate to the `Item` tree member and double-click to see its subfields. Then select the `Item.name` field and click the Add button as displayed in Figure 12.44.

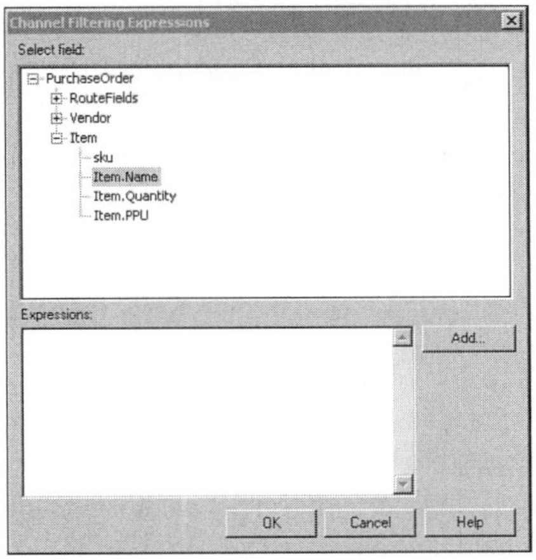

FIGURE 12.44
Creating the channel filter.

In the Expression Properties dialog that appears, enter the `TG` in the Value field as displayed in Figure 12.45 and click OK.

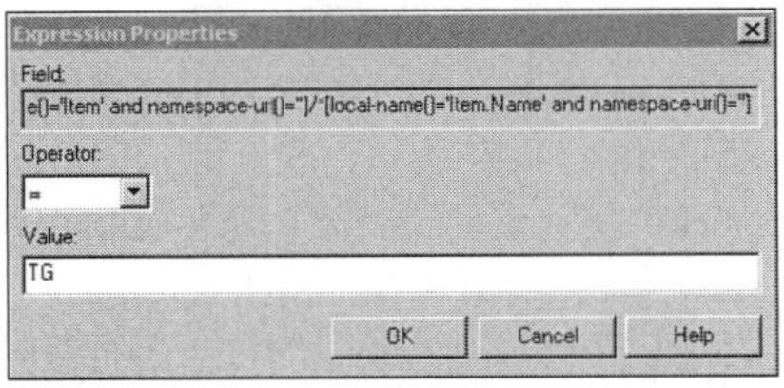

FIGURE 12.45
The channel expression properties.

Click OK again to save the filter and click Finish to save the modifications to the channel.

You have now successfully created a channel filter.

> **Note**
>
> The `RouteTest` example does not contain a scenario that tests this channel filter, but you can do so yourself by running `Scenario1` and modifying the `Inst_PO_KnotFree_1.xml` inbound document to contain items named `TG` and not named `TG`.

Distribution Lists

A *distribution list* is a group of messaging ports with which you can send the same document to several different trading partner organizations or internal applications. For example, you can send the same catalog, price list, or newsletter to several trading partner organizations by submitting the information only once to Microsoft BizTalk Server 2002.

You must first create a messaging port to each of the trading partner organizations or internal applications that you want to receive the data and then add the messaging ports to a distribution list. Open messaging ports cannot be added to a distribution list. You can create new messaging ports to additional trading partner organizations or internal applications and then add those messaging ports to an existing distribution list.

You must create at least one channel for each distribution list, or else the distribution list is not functional.

When BizTalk Server 2002 invokes a channel related to a distribution list, it invokes only the channel associated with the distribution list to process the data. None of the channels associated with the individual messaging ports in the distribution list are invoked. The server uses the properties of each messaging port successively to transport the data to the destinations specified in the messaging ports.

Again this may seem similar in nature to an open messaging port; however, there are some major differences. A distribution list differs from an open messaging port in the following ways:

- With a distribution list, each document from a channel can result in the document being delivered to multiple destinations. With an open messaging port, each document from a channel results in only one document being delivered to only one destination.
- With a distribution list, you have to add a messaging port to send information to a different trading partner organization. With an open messaging port, you do not have to change the properties of the messaging port to send information to a different organization.

Summary

This chapter focused on how to design and implement messaging operations that could route documents based on information determined at runtime. Throughout this chapter, we referred to the runtime determination of messaging operations as *dynamic routing*. You learned that several different messaging elements can be configured to achieve dynamic routing, including the creation of *self-routing documents*. You also learned that you have the ability to send messages to several destinations dynamically and that BizTalk Server facilitates the delivery of a message to multiple locations through a concept known as a *distribution list*.

CHAPTER 13

Advanced BizTalk Orchestration

by Dilip Hardas

In This Chapter

This chapter builds on your understanding of BizTalk Orchestration. It assumes that you understand the components of a BizTalk Orchestration schedule and how the schedule operates. This chapter focuses on the application of your knowledge and includes many examples.

In this chapter, you will see examples of concurrency, transactions, and dynamic ports. The examples have been chosen to demonstrate specific characteristics of the operation of schedules and not as elegant business solutions. The examples are developed along the following lines:

- Concurrency—Examples describe the use and behavior of the AND and OR Join shapes. In this first section, the construction of these examples is described with added detail for pedantic purposes.
- Transactions—Examples cover DTC style, short-lived transactions, long-lived transactions, and nested transactions.
- Iteration—The example describes how business processes can be designed that iterate. Interplay of iteration and transactions is shown.
- Dynamic ports—The example constructs an MSMQ-based dynamic port.

Although the preceding list provides the broad outline for the examples and the sections in this chapter, additional features of BizTalk Orchestration are discussed using these examples. These additional features are identified as appropriate in each section. The chapter concludes with considerations for development of BizTalk Orchestration Schedules.

Chapter 9, "Introducing BizTalk Orchestration," and Chapter 10, "Using the BizTalk Orchestration Designer," described the issues important in the design and operation of XLANG schedules. While describing the examples in this chapter, we will revisit these issues, listed below

- State management
- Dehydration and rehydration
- Transaction exception handling and compensation
- Security
- Use of port references and dynamic ports
- Data handling in schedules

Concurrency

The example schedules developed in this section are simple, yet these schedules show not only the use of Fork and Join shapes, but also some useful debugging and monitoring techniques. The steps to build and run these examples are described in detail; however, for examples in later sections, the basic steps or techniques covered here are skipped.

Although the examples in this section are designed to demonstrate the use of the OR and the AND Join shapes, the examples also serve to illustrate the following important points:

- Developing and using COM+ configured components in a schedule
- Using a COM component with No Instantiation option and verifying the component's behavior in a running schedule
- Using the BizTalk Orchestration Engine object model
- Building the business process, binding the port implementation, and constructing the data page associated with an XLANG schedule

We will construct two schedules and describe a third one briefly. The first schedule features the AND Join shape; the second one modifies this schedule to use the OR Join shape. The third schedule is an extension of the second which demonstrates how the ambiguity of execution paths can be resolved when an OR Join is used.

Using the AND Join Shape

We will first construct a simple schedule containing two actions that may be performed concurrently; however, in this example, both actions must complete before the schedule can complete its task. In the section "Using the OR Join Shape" later in the chapter, you will see a schedule that completes when either of the actions completes. The use of the Fork and Join shapes allows you to construct a business process with concurrently executing pathways. See Chapter 9 for the concepts behind using these shapes. The schedule also uses a COM component, called `AdvOrchUtil.CMsg`. This component has a single method to display a message box.

The section describes the schedule, provides detailed construction help, and finally describes how it is run and monitored. The schedule, after it is constructed, will look as shown in Figure 13.1. The schedule is called `Concur1.skv`.

Figure 13.1 shows that Action 1, through `Port_1`, is calling a method `ShowMsgBox` on an instance of `AdvOrchUtil.CMsg` class. The Action 2 is also calling the same method but over a different port and hence is using another instance of the class. This is necessary to keep the parallel process flows isolated from each other. For this example, the methods simply display a message dialog box.

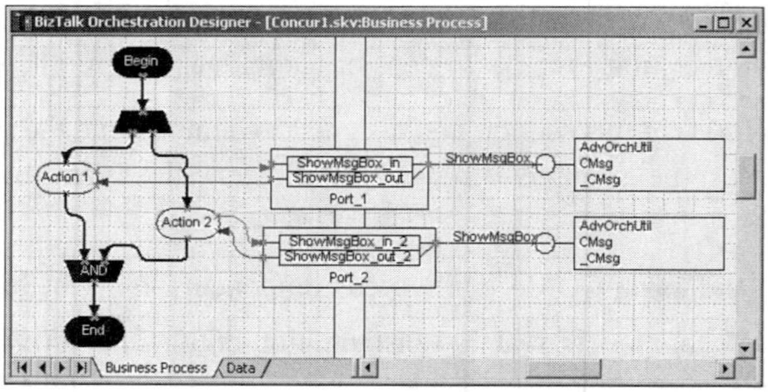

FIGURE 13.1
Example for AND Join: business process for `Concur1.skv`.

Later in this section, we will run the schedule, and you will see the two messages displayed. When the schedule runs, actions defined in the business process are performed. An action results in sending or receiving a message via a port connected to an implementation, in this case a COM component (see Chapter 10). The name of the message used is shown in the port. The contents of the message are determined by the Data page. This page looks as shown in Figure 13.2.

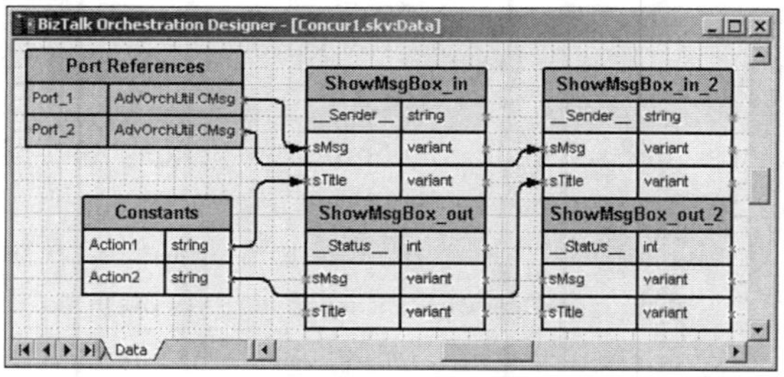

FIGURE 13.2
Example for AND Join: Data page for `Concur1.skv`.

Figure 13.2 shows that fields of the messages are populated by port references, and the message title is provided by a constant string. Port references are simply used as display strings here; their appropriate usage is described in the section "Dynamic Ports" later in this chapter. Now that we've described the schedule, let's start building it.

Creating the Concur1 XLANG Schedule

To construct this example, we can start by constructing the business process flow. Make sure that the Flowchart stencil is visible (it is not shown in Figure 13.1). Drag the Fork shape from the stencil onto the drawing surface to the left of the separator bar and place it under the Begin shape. Next drag two oval Action shapes onto the drawing surface and place them as shown. Finally, drag the Join shape and the End shape and place them as shown.

Use the connector tool to join these shapes as shown in Figure 13.1 (the connector tool is not shown in the figure; see Chapter 10). When you select the connector tool, the pointer icon changes to include the connector graphic under the arrow. As you move the arrow over the shapes, you will notice that a red rectangle pops up when the arrow is near a connection point. When you see this rectangle, you can click the mouse and drag the arrow to the destination connection point. At the destination, you see the red rectangle pop up again, indicating that it may be possible to terminate the connection there. Using this connector tool repeatedly, you can quickly complete the connections joining the flowchart shapes. These connections are depicted by heavy black arrows in Figure 13.1.

At this point, you can optionally save the interim XLANG schedule drawing as `Concur1.skv`.

Creating the `AdvOrchUtil.CMsg` Component

The next phase is to construct the `AdvOrchUtil.CMsg` class. To do this, we start Microsoft Visual Basic 6.0. Refer to a book on developing COM components using Visual Basic 6.0 or refer to the Visual Basic 6.0 product documentation. You do not have to use Visual Basic 6.0; you may use any other tool to create COM components—for example, the section "Dynamic Ports" later in the chapter has a sample on creating a script component.

In this example, we want to create an ActiveX DLL. After starting VB6 and choosing ActiveX DLL as the project type, rename the project `AdvOrchUtil` and the default class created by the project wizard `CMsg`. Currently for this class, we will go along with the default properties; however, we will modify the `MTSTransactionMode` to be `NoTransactions`. Listing 13.1 shows the full code listing for the class; however, let's discuss the design first.

The `AdvOrchUtil.CMsg` class has a single method called `ShowMsgBox`. This method takes two arguments, which it uses to show as the message and title of a message box. Another design goal for the class is to facilitate monitoring and testing the class.

Middle-tier components, such as this class, are notoriously difficult to test. Microsoft Visual Basic 6.0 provides a good emulation for COM+ services, yet there are situations when testing or monitoring requires a less intrusive approach. To keep tabs on the code execution of your components, you can generate traces to the application event log, or to a file or to the system debug output. Visual Basic 6.0 provides an easy mechanism of logging events to the application event log using the `App.LogEvent` call, although it does have some limitations compared to using the Win32 API directly. Here we will use a simple approach to post messages to the system debug output. To reiterate, do use the native debugging facilities of Visual Basic 6.0 IDE; however, we do not discuss the IDE here.

We will use the Debug Monitor utility available as `DbMon.exe`, and it comes with the Microsoft Platform SDK. The utility is also available with the other visual developer tools, such as Visual C++, and as code sample. The Platform SDK can be downloaded from the Microsoft developer Web site, although it is a large download.

The Debug Monitor runs in its own console window and displays messages sent to the system debug output via the Win32 function `OutputDebugString`. See additional documentation available on the Microsoft Developer Network (MSDN) about this system call and the DbMon utility.

Without further ado, Listing 13.1 shows the entire `AdvOrchUtil.CMsg` class.

LISTING 13.1 The `AdvOrchUtil.CMsg` Class

```
Option Explicit

Private Declare Sub OutputDebugString Lib "kernel32"
➥Alias "OutputDebugStringA" (ByVal lpOutputString As String)

Private Sub Trace(sMsg As String)
    OutputDebugString "AdvOrchUtil.CMsg: " & sMsg & vbCrLf
End Sub

Sub ShowMsgBox(ByRef sMsg As Variant, ByRef sTitle As Variant)
    Trace "ShowMsgBox(): Msg=" & CStr(sMsg) & " Title=" & CStr(sTitle)
    MsgBox CStr(sMsg), vbOKOnly, CStr(sTitle)
End Sub

Private Sub Class_Initialize()
    Trace "Class_Initialize()"
End Sub

Private Sub Class_Terminate()
    Trace "Class_Terminate()"
End Sub
```

At the head of Listing 13.1, there is a declaration for the Win32 call `OutputDebugString`—we are using the ANSI version for this example. The next procedure is used to generate the trace statements using the `OutputDebugString` API call. We prefix all strings with the class name so that the trace output can be properly interpreted. The sole public method of the class is `ShowMsgBox`, which takes two arguments by reference. We are using variants for testing so that numbers and other data types could also be shown if necessary. The next two procedures are private to the class, and these are called when the class is constructed or destroyed. We add trace statements to all the procedures so we can keep an eye on what is going on.

Now you are ready to save and compile the project. Figure 13.3 shows the project properties.

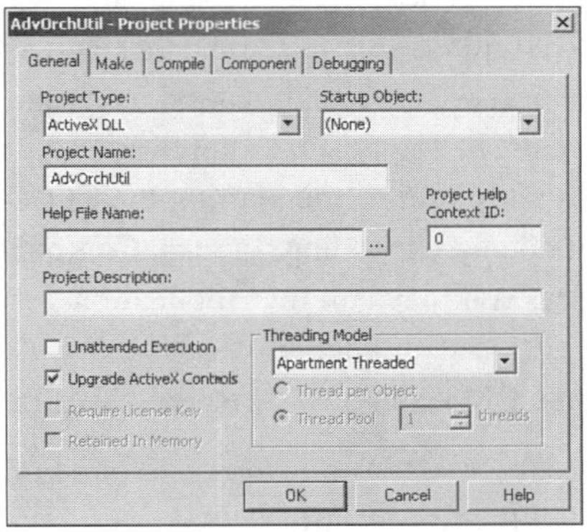

FIGURE 13.3
`AdvOrchUtil` *project properties.*

Using the Visual Basic 6.0 IDE, open the project properties dialog box by using the `Project` menu and selecting the `AdvOrchUtil` Properties. In the project properties dialog box, under the `General` tab shown in Figure 13.3, there are two check boxes of interest. For our testing, we will choose the defaults; however, consider checking off Unattended Execution and Retained In Memory for your production code. On the Component tab, compile the project with Binary Compatibility. You will need a reference type library or DLL, so first compile your project with No Compatibility and then switch to binary compatibility using the compiled DLL. The Compile tab has options to Create Symbolic Debug Info and to remove any optimization by checking off No Optimization. You will need to use these options if you choose to use debuggers other than the one integrated with the Visual Basic IDE.

Note

If you build your own `AdvOrchUtil.CMsg` and you download the sample from the Sams Web site, the type libraries for the two DLLs will be different. The sample schedule on the Web site will contain a reference to the downloaded DLL, not to your DLL. You have at least three options to avoid conflicts:

- Build the entire example all by yourself.
- Use the downloaded DLL as a reference type library to build a compatible DLL.
- Repair the schedule to use your component.

To do this, you must rerun the COM Component Binding Wizard and pick the correct component. You can verify the type library by using the menu Tools and Refresh Method Signatures in the BizTalk Orchestration Designer.

Configuring `AdvOrchUtil.CMsg` in COM+

After compiling the class, you could use it directly in the XLANG schedules; however, we will install the class in a COM+ application. For this example, we are not using any specific COM+ services; however we will be able to see the instance activations when the schedule runs. Therefore, create a new COM+ application using the Component Services administrative console. Create an empty server application by right-clicking on the COM+ Applications node of the console tree and starting the COM Application Install Wizard. You will reach this node by expanding, in turn, Component Services, Computers, and My Computer nodes. You may call this application TestCOM+ App. The application created is a server application with interactive user as its identity. See Chapter 10 for more background on COM+ and how it relates to BizTalk Orchestration.

Next, locate the TestCOM+ App under COM+ Applications. Expand this node and locate the Components node. You can install the `AdvOrchUtil.CMsg` class into COM+ in one of two ways. You can drag and drop the `AdvOrchUtil.dll` on the right pane of the administrative console, with the Components node selected on the tree in the left pane. Alternatively, you can right-click on the Components node and select the New Component menu item. Do this, and we will proceed to complete the XLANG schedule. Figure 13.4 later in the chapter shows the COM+ administrative console.

Using `AdvOrchUtil.CMsg` in the Schedule

Now go back to, or reopen the `Concur1.skv` schedule you were working on. Make sure that the Implementation stencil is now visible. Drag and drop the COM Component shape onto the drawing surface to the right of the separator bar and align it approximately with the elevation of Action 1. The COM Component Binding Wizard starts.

On the first page of the wizard, the default name of `Port_1` is fine. On the second page of the wizard, choose the Static instantiation option. On the third page, you have to locate the `AdvOrchUtil` class. Expand the tree node; locate and select the `CMsg` class. The class has only a single interface with a single method and hence the wizard skips to the sixth page where you can choose the Advanced Port Properties. The defaults are fine for now. (See Chapter 10 for details on the wizard.) Repeat this process for `Port_2`; see Figure 13.1 for port placement.

Now, with the connector tool, connect Action 1 to the `Port_1`. The Method Communication Wizard starts. On the first page, choose Initiate a Synchronous Method Call. You will be creating a new message based on the name of the only method of our class; the wizard therefore skips the second page. The last page shows the message and the fields that will be created on the Data page. Repeat this process by connecting Action 2 and `Port_2`.

Now shift your attention to the Data page, shown previously in Figure 13.2. There are two message pairs, corresponding to the two method calls, and a message each for Port References and Constants.

Double-click the Constants message. You see a dialog box showing Constants Message Properties. Click the Add button to add a new constant. Name the constant `Action1`, select the type as `string` (it is the default data type), and give it the value of "Action 1." Do the same for `Action2` and give the value of "Action 2." We use these strings for message box titles. The text message for the message box is taken from the Port References. As a side benefit of this example, we see the COM moniker strings that represent the two ports in our schedule. See Chapter 10 for the description of the wizards in the designer and on monikers used with BizTalk Orchestration.

Using the connector tool, connect the fields as shown previously in Figure 13.2. You are now ready to compile the schedule.

Tip

> When developing schedules, out of habit, I also use the Tools menu to remove any unused messages or rules and check whether the type information for any COM components has changed. Most importantly, however, I also use the Shutdown All Running XLANG Schedule Instances menu item. This is equivalent to safely shutting down schedules using the button on the XLANG tab of the property pages of the XLANG Scheduler COM+ application—the application that hosts the XLANG engine. This action removes any cached instances from the XLANG engine's database, which ensures that your newly compiled schedule runs rather than a stale cached version.

Compiling and Running the Schedule

To compile the schedule, choose File, Make XLANG Concur1.skx from the menu. Now we are ready to run the schedule.

Before running the schedule, get your tools in place. Start the DbMon, the XLANG Event Monitor, and the Component Services console, which should look as shown in Figure 13.4. The XLANG Event Monitor is described in Chapter 11, "XLANG Orchestration Engine."

Figure 13.4 shows the Status view for the components in the TestCOM+ App application. There is only one component there, and the column headings are for the runtime, dynamic metrics for this component.

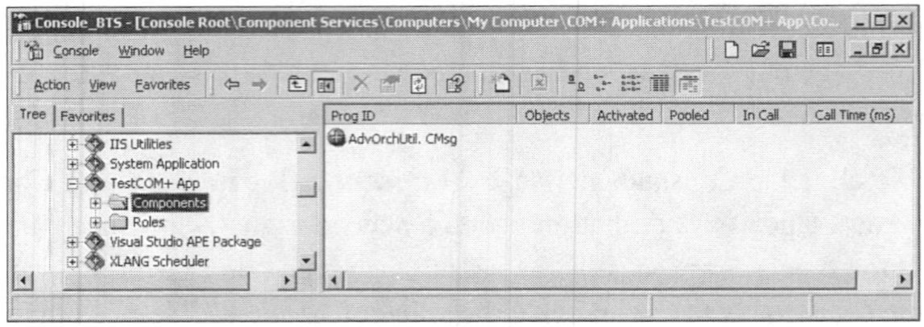

FIGURE 13.4
Component Services: TestCOM+ App Status view.

Run the schedule using the Instance and Run menu of the XLANG Event Monitor. First select the group manager in which you want to run the schedule and then, in the dialog box shown by the Run menu, type in the full path to the `Concur1.skx` schedule.

Note

The COM+ application `TestCOM+ App` is not a group manager, although you could configure it to be such. The sample output and the figures in this chapter demonstrate the use of a group manager named `XLANG Two`, which is not the default group manager. Components used by a schedule do not have to run in the same COM+ application. Chapter 11 describes the steps to create a new group manager.

An important point to recall from Chapter 11 is that for a new COM+ application to function as a group manager, you must not only create the persistence database, but you must also install at least one COM component, even if it serves no purpose.

When you run the schedule, you should see something like what is shown in Figure 13.5.

Figure 13.5 shows four windows in all. The first is the XLANG Event Monitor, followed by the two dialog message boxes displayed by the `AdvOrchUtil.CMsg` class, and finally the MMC console. The title in the dialog message box shows the action that is initiating the activity. The content of the message box is the port moniker for the port displaying the message. The port moniker is constructed using the instance ID of the running schedule. The XLANG Event Monitor shows the `Concur1` schedule running and the instance ID of that schedule. The Component Services console shows that two objects are constructed and activated and are within a method call. The method call time is atrocious because the dialog boxes are holding up the completion of the schedule. The sphere next to the `AdvOrchUtil.CMsg` component should also appear to be rotating—you will see the *plus* indentation on the sphere cyclically change.

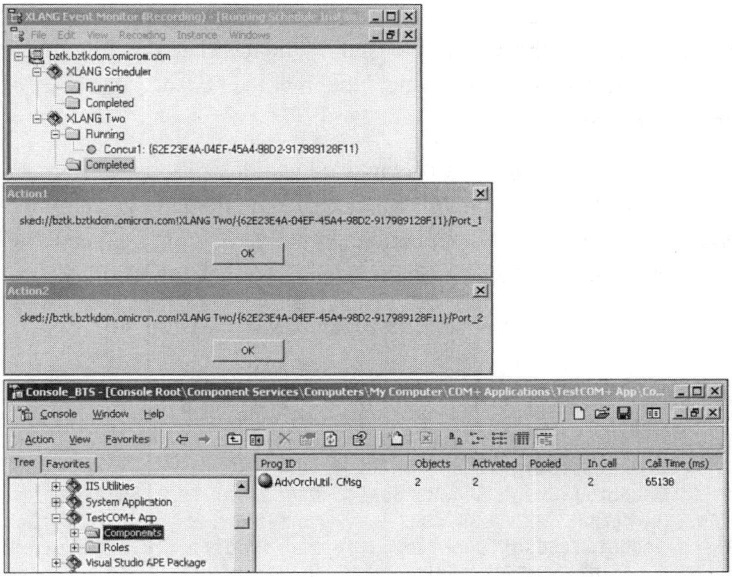

FIGURE 13.5
Running `Concur1.skx`.

If you double-click the `Concur1` running schedule instance in XLANG Event Monitor, you will see all the events for the schedule so far. In Figure 13.6, shows the display turned on for all the recorded events; this can be done from the View and Events Filter menus.

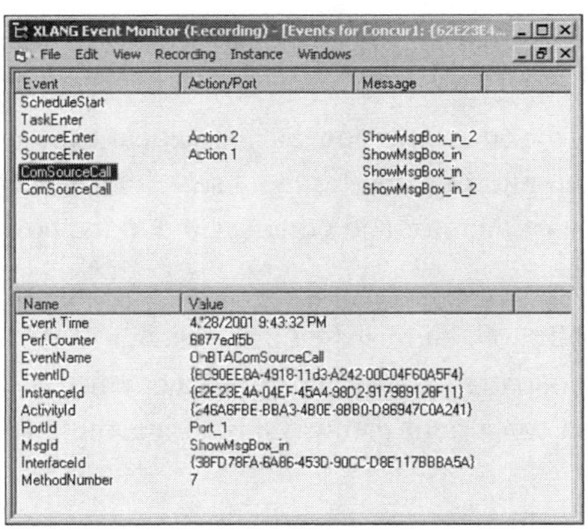

FIGURE 13.6
Events for `Concur1`.

Figure 13.6 shows, as expected, that both concurrent actions were initiated in the schedule. The middle column in the top pane names the actions executed; the right column shows the messages passed. The details for the highlighted event are shown in the lower pane. The event shown is that for a COM method call initiated by the XLANG schedule instance. Because both calls are blocked by the message box, the schedule has not progressed further, nor can it dehydrate. Note that the instance ID shown is the same as in Figure 13.5 earlier.

At this point, you can choose to acknowledge either of the message boxes. In the XLANG Event Monitor, you will notice that even though one action completes, the schedule still waits for the other action to complete. This is expected with the AND Join. When the remaining action is acknowledged, the schedule winds down and completes.

In the DbMon window, you will see something like Listing 13.2.

LISTING 13.2 DbMon Output for `Concur1.skx`

```
2188: AdvOrchUtil.CMsg: Class_Initialize()
2188: AdvOrchUtil.CMsg: Class_Initialize()
2188: AdvOrchUtil.CMsg: ShowMsgBox(): Msg=sked://bztk.bztkdom.omicron.com
➥!XLANG Two/{763573CE-CD65-4B86-9AA5-76A2E53C6D2B}/Port_1 Title=Action1
2188: AdvOrchUtil.CMsg: ShowMsgBox(): Msg=sked://bztk.bztkdom.omicron.com
➥!XLANG Two/{763573CE-CD65-4B86-9AA5-76A2E53C6D2B}/Port_2 Title=Action2
2188: AdvOrchUtil.CMsg: Class_Terminate()
2188: AdvOrchUtil.CMsg: Class_Terminate()
```

The output in Listing 13.2 shows that two different objects were constructed, as expected. The traces for the method calls show the port reference from each of the actions. Careful observers will notice that the GUID is different in Listing 13.2 and in Figure 13.5. This is true; this trace is from another run of the schedule. The number on the left is the process ID of the TestCOM+ App that generated the trace.

This concludes the first example. You should now have practical experience in creating a schedule, compiling, running, monitoring, and testing a schedule. You could also use the application event log, performance monitor and other system tools; however, we did not cover these here.

In the example, we used the AND Join and verified the behavior of the schedule. Though we used a single action in the concurrent pathways, this is not a necessity. We could have had a sequence of actions in the concurrent pathways, both incoming and outgoing. We develop this example next.

Using the OR Join Shape

Now we look at using the OR Join shape. The OR Join shape is used to synchronize concurrent business processes; see Chapter 9 for additional information. The example also demonstrates the use of the runtime object model used by the XLANG engine and use of the No Instantiation option for COM ports. You will also see a schedule dehydrating and rehydrating. Recall from Chapter 9 that when using the OR Join, there can be at most a single action in the concurrent pathway and that this action must be a "receive message" action. We will build a schedule that meets these requirements.

We can reuse `Concur1.skv` from the previous example along with the `AdvOrchUtil.CMsg` component developed for that schedule. This allows us to devote more time on the features of BizTalk Orchestration than on ancillary development. If you skipped the previous section, you should at least configure `AdvOrchUtil.CMsg` in COM+ so that it is properly registered. Save the `Concur1.skv` file as `Concur2.skv` and open it for editing. The next section describes the steps necessary to modify this schedule to use the OR Join. In the end, the schedule should look as shown in Figure 13.7

FIGURE 13.7
`Concur2.skv` *business process.*

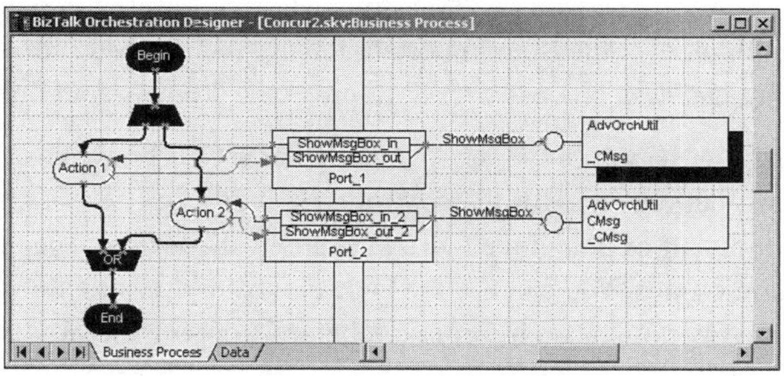

Modifying `Concur2.skv` to Use the OR Join

Perform the following changes to `Concur2.skv`. Double-click on the top COM port implementation and start the COM Component Binding Wizard. On the second page, select No Instantiation. On the third page, select the `_CMsg` interface exposed by the type library.

Next double-click the message communication between Action 1 and `Port_1`. The Method Communication Wizard starts. On the first page, switch to Wait for a Synchronous Method Call. In the text box below, enter a number greater than 180, say 200, denoting the time in seconds that the schedule can expect to wait for a message to arrive—in this case, an incoming method call. We will write a standalone Visual Basic application to make a call using this port. The schedule could be started and wait forever for the call to come in. By choosing a duration greater than 180 seconds, we are signaling the XLANG engine that it is okay to dehydrate the schedule and save system resources. Repeat this for the message communication between Action 2 and `Port_2`.

Double-click on the AND Join shape; you see the property setting for the Join. Change the Join type to OR. Note the comment displayed when you make the change: such a

Join can only be used in Fork flows containing a *single receive action*. The schedule is already modified to do this.

On the Data page, remove the links connecting the Port References message to other messages. If you forget to do this, you will get compilation errors. Note that we changed the schedule to receive messages. Even if you make connections to outgoing fields, the XLANG engine makes no attempt to transport the field values out from within the schedule.

Save and compile the schedule. You can start the XLANG Event Monitor and use it to run the schedule. You will notice that the schedule starts up and then a few seconds later gets dehydrated. This is as it should be. The schedule will now be around forever. You can convince yourself that this is so by rebooting the machine, shutting down the System Application or XLANG Scheduler COM+ applications by brute force, or inducing other failures you can think of. This is an important feature of XLANG schedules; they represent long-running business processes that are protected from system failures.

If you open the XLANG tab of the XLANG Scheduler COM+ application's property page, you see two buttons: one for the controlled shutdown of all XLANG applications, and the other for restart of dehydrated XLANG applications. See Chapter 11 for additional information on this. You can use the controlled shutdown to allow the XLANG engine to save any working state information before stopping the process. However, you can *ensure* proper failure handling by incorporating transactions in the schedule. Examples for both short-lived and long-lived transactions are developed in following sections. When you click the other button to restart dehydrated schedules, you will notice in the XLANG Event Monitor that the schedule briefly becomes active (the icon changes from a blue snowflake to a green circle).

At this point, let the started `Concur2.skx` schedule lay dehydrated as we work out an application to call methods on its ports. In fact, start another instance; we will use it later in the example. At this point, you should have two instances of `Concur2.skx` running, each waiting for a message to arrive. The message arrives only when a call is made into the ports bound to a COM implementation. Until that time, the schedules remain dehydrated. This is also an important feature of BizTalk Orchestration; such quiescent schedules consume only minimal system resources as they wait for further activity. In this example, either schedule will rehydrate and complete if it receives a single message on either port. Only a single message is needed because of the OR Join. Next, we develop the application to send this message.

Build CallConcur2.exe to Send Messages

The application used to send messages to Concur2.skx appears as shown in Figure 13.8.

FIGURE 13.8
CallConcur2.exe *application.*

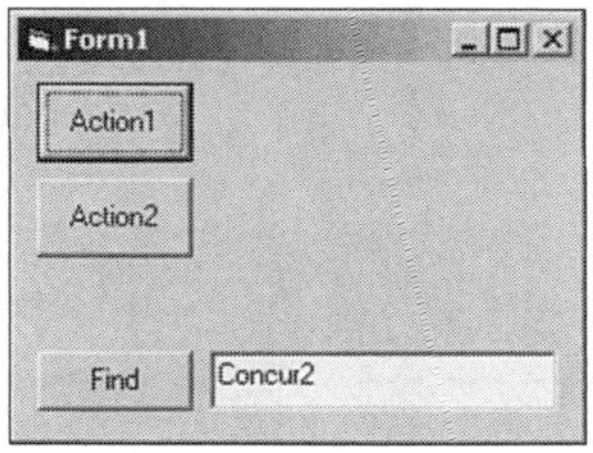

The two buttons, Action1 and Action2 in Figure 13.8, are each used to respectively call the ports Port_1 and Port_2 and send messages to them. The Find button at the bottom locates a started schedule having the module name specified in the text box next to it. The usage is to first find a schedule and then click an action button to make the call. Now, this scenario is a bit concocted for the purposes of an example. Usually, you will have the schedule or port moniker either provided to you at runtime as part of some document exchange, or retrieved from a database as part of some overall application.

Create a new Visual Basic project for an application CallConcur2.exe. Design the form to look like Figure 13.8. The names of the controls on the form are as shown in Table 13.1. The table also makes a note of events that you must add. The sample code is available on the publisher's Web site. You can follow along and build it all yourself, or you can get it from the Web site.

TABLE 13.1 Controls for CallConcur2

Type	*Caption or Text*	*Name*	*Notes*
Button	Action1	btnAction1	Add click event handler.
Button	Action2	btnAction2	Add click event handler.
Button	Find	btnFindSchedule	Add click event handler.
Text box	Concur2	txtModuleName	

To code the event handling code, you will need to reference certain COM type libraries. Add the references shown in Table 13.2 to the Visual Basic 6.0 project.

TABLE 13.2 References for `CallConcur2`

Reference	*DLL Name*	*Notes*
XLANG Scheduler System Manager	`SkedsMgr.dll`	Shows up as `SYSMGRLib` in the object browser
XLANG Scheduler Runtime Type Library	`SkedCore.dll`	Shows up as `COMRUNTIME` in the object browser.
`AdvOrchUtil`	`AdvOrchUtil.dll`	The component we wrote earlier in Listing 13.1.

Add the code shown in Listing 13.3 to the startup form in `CallConcur2`. We borrowed the tracing mechanism based on `OutputDebugString` from Listing 13.1. The other item to note is the declaration for `oSch`, which represents a schedule instance. We will set this variable later in the code to the schedule instance located by module name.

LISTING 13.3 Form1 Code for `CallConcur2`

```
Option Explicit

Private Declare Sub OutputDebugString Lib "kernel32"
➥Alias "OutputDebugStringA" (ByVal lpOutputString As String)

Dim oSch As COMRUNTIME.IWFWorkflowInstance

Private Sub Trace(sMsg As String)
    OutputDebugString "CallConcur2.exe: " & sMsg & vbCrLf
End Sub
```

Listing 13.4 shows how we locate the schedule instance.

LISTING 13.4 Find Button, Click Event Handler

```
Private Sub btnFindSchedule_Click()
    Dim oMgr As SYSMGRLib.SysMgr
    Dim oGrp As COMRUNTIME.IWFGroupAdmin
    Dim bFound As Boolean

    bFound = False
    Set oMgr = New SYSMGRLib.SysMgr
    For Each oGrp In oMgr
        For Each oSch In oGrp
            If oSch.ModuleName = txtModuleName.Text Then
                bFound = True
                Exit For
            End If
        Next oSch
```

LISTING 13.4 continued

```
        If bFound Then
            Exit For
        End If
    Next oGrp

    If bFound Then
        Trace "btnFindSchedule_Click(): " & oSch.FullyQualifiedName
    Else
        Trace "btnFindSchedule_Click(): Schedule " &
➥ txtModuleName & " not found"
        Set oSch = Nothing
    End If
End Sub
```

The description of the code in Listing 13.4 is as follows. First, we acquire a reference to the system manager on the local machine. We could just as well have used the moniker as follows:

```
Set oMgr = GetObject("sked://")
```

If we wanted the System Manager from another machine, we would include the machine name in the moniker. See Chapters 10 and 11 for more information on the structure and use of monikers in BizTalk Orchestration. Next, we iterate through each group manager on the machine and each schedule instance in the group manager. We try to match the `ModuleName` property with the contents of `txtModuleName`. If multiple schedules are running with the same module name, we will just find the first one we encounter.

If a schedule is not found, we reset the `oSch` reference to `Nothing`. In either case, we generate a trace.

Listing 13.5 shows the code required to call a port in the `Concur2` XLANG schedule instance. We have a private procedure that can be called by either action button in the form. The subroutine `CallPort` takes the name of the port as an argument.

LISTING 13.5 Calling a Schedule Port in `CallConcur2`

```
Private Sub CallPort(sPortName As String)
    Dim sMsg As String
    Dim sTitle As String

    sMsg = "Message" & sPortName
    sTitle = "Title" & sPortName

    If Not oSch Is Nothing Then
        Dim oPort As COMRUNTIME.IWFProxy
        Dim oComp As AdvOrchUtil.CMsg
```

LISTING 13.5 continued

```
        Set oPort = oSch.Port(sPortName)
        Set oComp = oPort
oComp.ShowMsgBox sMsg, sTitle
        Trace "CallPort(" & sPortName & "): " & "Post Call Msg=" &
➥ sMsg & " Title=" & sTitle
    End If
End Sub
```

In Listing 13.5, we attempt to call on the port only if the variable `oSch` is a valid reference to an instance of a running schedule. Two other variables are declared. The variable `oPort` is the COM proxy for the port available from the running schedule instance. We acquire this proxy using the `Port` property of the `oSch` schedule instance. If the port named in `sPortName` is not present, a runtime error occurs.

The other variable is `oComp` for the component for which a proxy is available. Note the type declaration for this component cannot be `IDispatch`, hence you couldn't have used a script component for this example. This restriction is because `Port` property of the schedule instance returns only an `IUnknown` interface. This interface can be queried for either the port proxy interface or the `IWFProxy` interface. The shaded statement queries the desired component interface from the `oPort` proxy and is the crucial step in this example. See Chapter 10 for more information on interfaces and proxies. Also see Visual Basic 6.0 documentation on how to program using COM components and the use of the `Set` statement.

The next statement makes the call to the `ShowMsgBox` method of the component. Recall that, in making the call, the interface is provided by a proxy for the COM component used in the port of the running schedule instance. When this call is made, the call is intercepted by the XLANG Scheduler Engine, the passed message fields are inducted into the data flows on the Data page, and the actual call to the component is made using the passed-in arguments. On return from the component, the call and the arguments are conveyed back to the original caller, which is the statement making the `ShowMsgBox` call in Listing 13.5. The returned values are traced by the next statement. See Chapter 10 for additional discussion on message flow in a schedule.

We wrap up the code listings by adding the remaining code shown in Listing 13.6 to the example.

LISTING 13.6 Click Event Handlers for Action Buttons

```
Private Sub btnAction1_Click()
    CallPort "Port_1"
End Sub

Private Sub btnAction2_Click()
```

LISTING 13.6 continued

```
    CallPort "Port_2"
End Sub
```

Listing 13.6 responds to the action button events by calling the `CallPort` private procedure to do the real work. Now, we are ready to see the schedule in action.

Sending Messages to `Concur2.skx` Running Instances

Save and compile the project. Start the XLANG Event Monitor, DbMon, and the Component Services console, if you haven't already done so.

> **Tip**
>
> Usually, it is also a good idea to keep an eye on the application and system event logs to detect any problems.

Start `CallConcur2.exe`. Two instances of the `Concur2` schedules should already be running. Click on the Find button. In the DbMon console, you will see a trace something like the following:

```
2156: CallConcur2.exe: btnFindSchedule_Click():sked://bztk.bztkdom.omicron.com
➥!XLANG
Scheduler/{FE4D6B18-AA46-4235-B306-8896E1334E07}
```

Now, click on the Action1 button. You will see a trace like the following:

```
2156: CallConcur2.exe: CallPort(Port_1): Post Call
➥ Msg=MessagePort_1 Title=TitlePort_1
```

You will also see the schedule rehydrate and complete. Two points are worth making here: The schedule completed after one of the two actions completed; this is what we expect. The trace message is coming from `CallConcur2.exe` only; there are no trace messages from the `AdvOrchUtil.CMsg` class, even though we ostensibly acquired a reference to this class and called a method on it, as shown in Listing 13.5. This is because of the No Instantiation option selected for the port. You see such traces in the next steps, when we use the other port that uses static instantiation.

Click Find again, this locates the other schedule. If you did not have the second schedule running, you get a runtime error. Now click Action2. You see a dialog box displayed by `AdvOrchUtil.CMsg` class and an instance activated in the Component Services console. The traces in the DbMon console are similar to the following:

```
888: AdvOrchUtil.CMsg: Class_Initialize()
888: AdvOrchUtil.CMsg: ShowMsgBox(): Msg=MessagePort_2 Title=TitlePort_2
2156: CallConcur2.exe: CallPort(Port_2): Post Call
➥ Msg=MessagePort_2 Title=TitlePort_2
888: AdvOrchUtil.CMsg: Class_Terminate()
```

The shaded lines appear after you dismiss the dialog box. At this point, the schedule also completes. Note the class activation and deactivation traces—an instance of the component was actually created.

If you were to look at the event history for one of these completed schedules, you would recognize the schedule execution events.

With an OR Join, only one of the two messages will surely occur before the schedule progresses beyond the Join. To use the passed-in messages, you must first detect whether the desired message exists, using the `__Exists__` system field. This is shown in Figures 13.9 and 13.10. This situation is briefly discussed next.

Business Process After the OR Join

The schedule `Concur3.skv`, shown in Figures 13.9 and 13.10, is an extension of the previous schedule `Concur2.skv`. The schedule shows how you can design a business process to follow the OR Join. The problem is that only one leg of the many possible paths terminating at the OR Join will have executed. So how do you design the subsequent schedule? The schedule `Concur3.skv` is available on the publisher's Web site.

Figure 13.9 shows that a Decision shape follows the OR Join. This shape checks for the existence of specific messages using rules. See Chapter 9 for more on Decision shapes and rules. The two rules used are as follows.

```
ShowMsgBox_in.[__Exists__]
ShowMsgBox_in_2.[__Exists__]
```

The rules check for the existence of specific incoming messages. If the message exists, the corresponding action that caused that message to be created must have occurred. It is left as an exercise for you to construct and try out this variation.

This concludes our discussion of concurrency, along with basic techniques of building, running, monitoring, and testing XLANG schedules. We also looked at creating and using COM components. The next section looks at transactions.

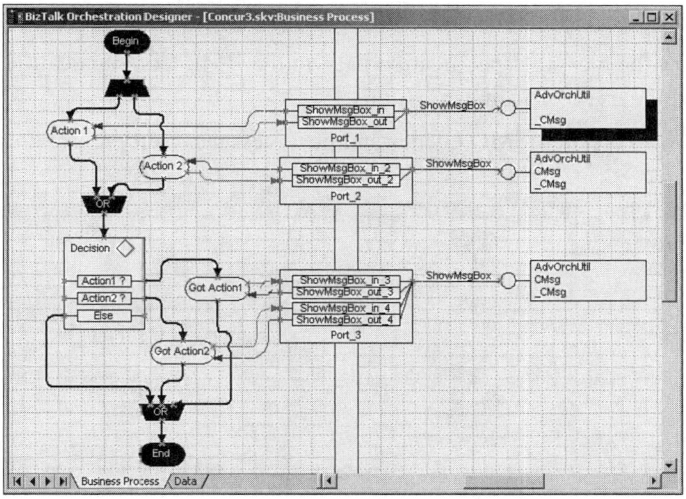

FIGURE 13.9
`Concur3.skv` *business process.*

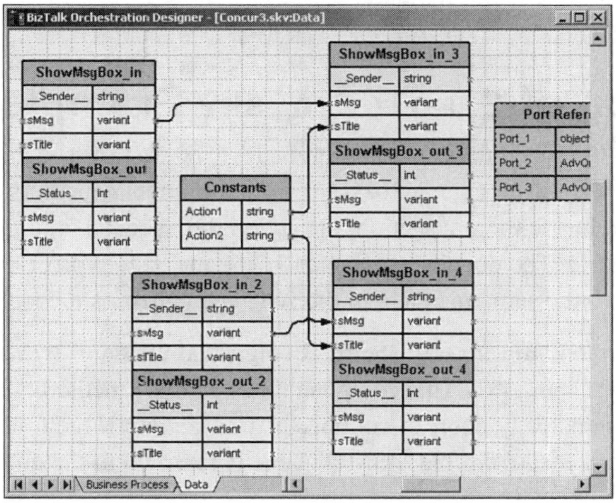

FIGURE 13.10
`Concur3.skv` *data page.*

DTC Style Transactions

The next example looks at a DTC style, short-lived, transaction. The schedule we will be working with looks as shown in Figure 13.11.

Figure 13.11 shows a schedule with a DTC style transaction. As you work through this example, you also see the following:

- How a COM+ configured component participates in a transaction
- How the transaction retries and the back-off timing mechanism works

- How the schedule manages state
- How the message specification page in the XML Communication Wizard is used and the use of XPath expressions
- How to create MSMQ queues and post messages to it programmatically

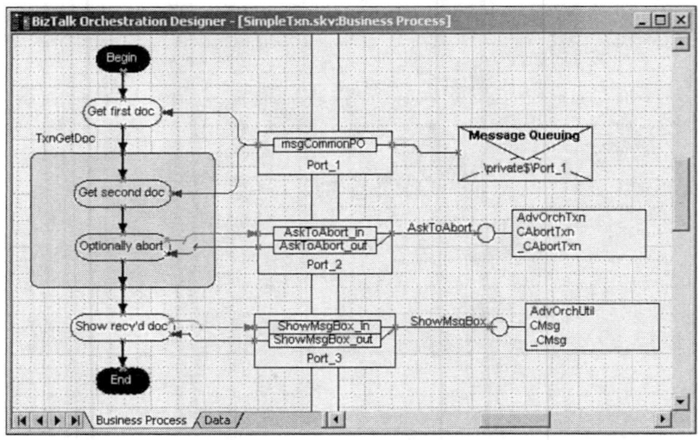

FIGURE 13.11
`SimpleTxn.skv` *business process.*

Description of `SimpleTxn.skv` Example

The first action in the schedule shown in Figure 13.11, `Get first doc`, reads a document from an MSMQ queue `.\private$\Port_1`. The flow then enters a transaction named `TxnGetDoc`. Inside the transaction, the action `Get second doc` reads another document from the queue. The documents each have the message type of `CommonPO`. Each message is read into the same message in the schedule called `msgCommonPO`.

The next action, called `Optionally abort`, is connected via `Port_2` to a component called `AdvOrchTxn.CAbortTxn`. This component has a single method that, when called, asks the user to interactively abort or commit the transaction. If the transaction is aborted, the message read from the MSMQ queue is returned to the queue.

The last action, called `Show recv'd doc`, actually displays the received document. It uses the component `AdvOrchUtil.CMsg` created in the previous section.

We will create a script to create the MSMQ queue and deliver documents into it. We will also create the component `AdvOrchTxn.CAbortTxn`. Both these activities are described in a later section. The next section describes the construction of the schedule itself.

The example shows how `TxnGetDoc` affects the behavior of the schedule and the messages flowing through it.

Building SimpleTxn.skv – Binding to Queue

First create the business process shown in Figure 13.11. This creates the actions, the short-lived transaction enclosing the two actions and the linear process path from the `Begin` to `End` shapes. We will set the specific properties of the transaction later. See Chapter 9 on how to build a business process.

Next, create the `Port_1` using the MSMQ queue port implementation. This is a static queue, common to all instances. The private queue name is Port_1. On the last page of the `Message Queuing Binding Wizard`, ensure that you select transactions required for the queue.

Now you can start the XML Communication Wizard by connecting the first action to Port_1. Choose to receive a message; allow for enough latency for the schedule to dehydrate, say 400 seconds. Name the message `msgCommonPO`. Choose to receive XML messages and specify the message type as `CommonPO`. On the last page of the wizard, also specify the document specification and enable document validation, as described later.

The document specification for `CommonPO` is provided with the product and is located at `\Program Files\Microsoft BizTalk Server\BizTalkServerRepository\DocSpecs\Microsoft\CommonPO.xml`. You can copy it over to the same directory as your schedule is in for ease of use. You also need a document instance of this specification; there is one handy at `\Program Files\Microsoft BizTalk Server\SDK\Messaging Samples\BTSAppIntegration\VB\Doc_CommonPO.xml`. Copy this file also into the current directory to make life easy later. You can see the structure of the document instance by viewing it in the Internet Explorer.

Figure 13.12 shows the last page of the XML Communication Wizard.

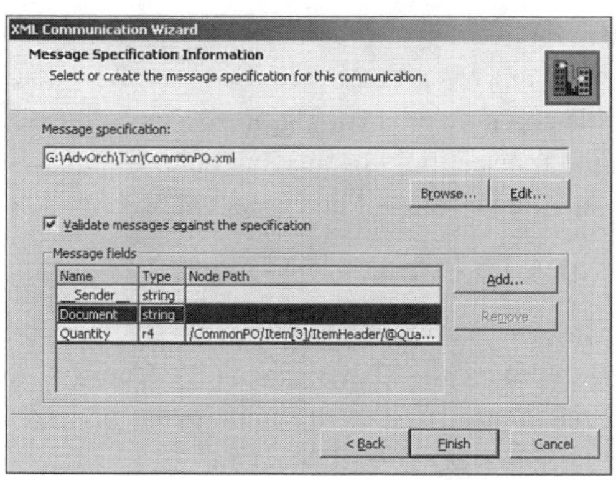

FIGURE 13.12
Message specification for `msgCommonPO` *in* `SimpleTxn.skv`.

By default, only two fields are created for an XML message. One is the system field `__Sender__`, which contains the authenticated identity of the sender in the form of an

SID, and the other is the `Document` field containing the entire document. We will need another field for this example. The value of this field is used to demonstrate how state is handled with transactions. You also see an example of how an XPath expression is used to add fields to messages on the Data page.

On this last page of the wizard, after specifying the `CommonPO.xml` document specification and selecting the Validate Messages Against the Specification check box, click the Add button. This brings up the Field Selection dialog box. The document schema is shown in a tree form. Traverse the nodes of the tree as indicated by the XPath expression `/CommonPO/Item/ItemHeader/@Quantity`. When you select the leaf node, `Quantity`, the Node Path and Field Name text boxes are populated. At this point, edit the XPath expression to read `/CommonPO/Item[3]/ItemHeader/@Quantity`. This XPath expression states that we are interested in the third `Item` in the document. Close the dialog box and complete this wizard step.

This additional field is named `Quantity`, and we use the value of this field to determine and show which document has been retained in the schedule.

> **Note**
>
> The message specification path shown in Figure 13.12 is the path during schedule development. This path will need to be modified for your machine. This also applies if you download the schedule from the publisher's Web site.

Configuring `TxnGetDoc` Transaction

Inside the transaction `TxnGetDoc`, shown in Figure 13.11, the second action makes a synchronous call to the method `AskToAbort` of the COM+ configured component `AdvOrchTxn.CAbortTxn`. This component is simple; it displays a message box and asks whether you want to abort the transaction. For this example, we always choose to abort the transaction. This component is developed in the next subsection.

The properties of the transaction are set as shown in Figure 13.13.

In Figure 13.13, note that Timeout is 60 seconds. If you do not respond to the dialog box in that time, the transaction automatically aborts. The Retry Count is 3, and the Backoff Time is 3 seconds. This means that the first retry should occur in 3 seconds, and the subsequent attempts should be successively at 9 (3 ** 2) and 27 (3 ** 3) seconds.

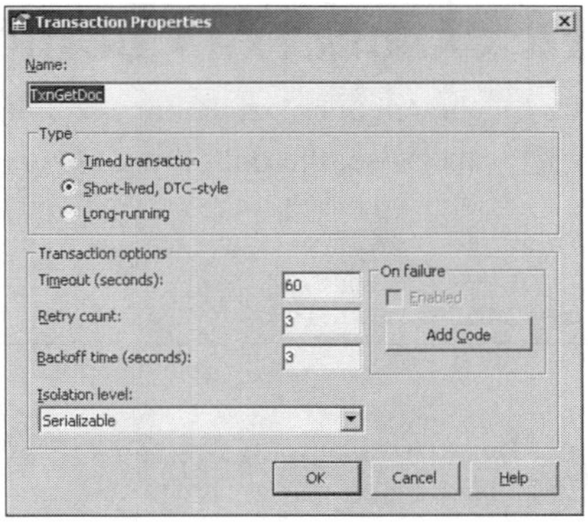

FIGURE 13.13
Properties of the transaction `TxnGetDoc`.

Building the Data page for `SimpleTxn.skv`

The last action of the schedule in Figure 13.11 makes a synchronous call to the method `ShowMsgBox` of the component `AdvOrchUtil.CMsg` developed in Listing 13.1. Using this call, we show the `Quantity` field of the `msgCommonPO` and the port reference for the `Port_1` MSMQ queue. The Data page appears as shown in Figure 13.14.

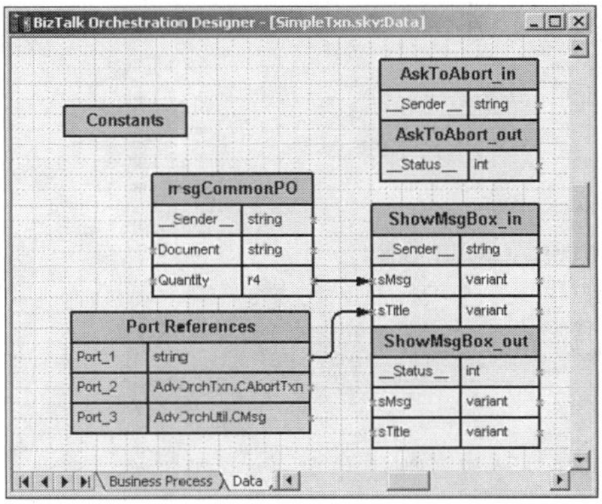

FIGURE 13.14
`SimpleTxn.skv` *data page.*

As Figure 13.14 shows, the Data page is simple. We will look at the value of `msgCommonPO.Quantity` shown by the message box. The port reference for an MSMQ queue is used for demonstration only. Note that the message `AskToAbort_*` has no fields other than the built-in system fields. The transaction is managed using built-in COM+ support. This is what we will look at next.

Building AdvOrchTxn.CAbortTxn Component

Listing 13.7 contains the entire code for the `AdvOrchTxn.CAbortTxn` class. There are a few embellishments from Listing 13.1; otherwise, the only thing new is the procedure `AskToAbort()`.

LISTING 13.7 Code for `AdvOrchTxn.CAbortTxn.cls`

```
Option Explicit

Private Declare Sub OutputDebugString Lib "kernel32" Alias
➥ "OutputDebugStringA" (ByVal lpOutputString As String)

Private Sub Trace(sMsg As String)
    Dim sNow As String
    sNow = FormatDateTime(Now(), vbLongTime)
    OutputDebugString sNow & ":AdvOrchTxn.CAbortTxn: " & sMsg & vbCrLf
End Sub

Private Sub Class_Initialize()
    Trace "Class_Initialize()"
End Sub

Private Sub Class_Terminate()
    Trace "Class_Terminate()"
End Sub

Sub AskToAbort()
    Dim oCtx As COMSVCSLib.ObjectContext
    Set oCtx = COMSVCSLib.GetObjectContext()
    If oCtx.IsInTransaction Then
        Dim bRet As VbMsgBoxResult
        bRet = MsgBox("Abort?", vbYesNo, "AdvOrchTxn.CAbortTxn.AskToAbort()")
        If bRet = vbYes Then
            oCtx.SetAbort
            Trace "AskToAbort(): Aborted!"
        Else
            oCtx.SetComplete
            Trace "AskToAbort(): SetComplete!"
        End If
    Else
        Trace "AskToAbort(): not in transaction"
    End If
End Sub
```

In the Listing 13.7, the `Trace` procedure is augmented to display a time stamp; this allows you to verify the backoff and retry mechanism.

To implement the procedure `AskToAbort`, we have to add a reference to the `COMSVCS.DLL`; this is listed as the COM+ Services Type Library under project references. Using this, we get a reference to the COM+ object context. Using this object context, we first check whether the component is being called in the context of a transaction. If it is, then we ask whether the user wants to abort or allow the transaction to commit. Finally, we either abort or commit the transaction and generate a trace for the action taken.

The class `CAbortTxn` is set to `UsesTransaction`. Compile the DLL and install it in a COM+ server application, say TestCOM+ App, discussed in Figure 13.4.

Script to Create and Send Messages to the Queue

Now we need a way to create and stuff the queue with two distinct messages but conform to the `CommonPO` document schema. The two documents should have a different value for the `Quantity` attribute of the third `Item`. Recall that we set the XPath expression to extract this item in the message field. This task of creating and sending the message is done using the `RunSimpleTxn.vbs` Visual Basic script shown in Listing 13.8.

LISTING 13.8 `RunSimpleTxn.vbs`

```
Option Explicit
On Error Resume Next

' Constants
Const sQueuePath = ".\private$\Port_1"
Const sDocName = "Doc_CommonPO.xml"
Const MQ_SEND_ACCESS            = 2
Const MQ_DENY_NONE                      = 0
Const MQ_SINGLE_MESSAGE         = 3

Dim oMQInfo, oQ
OpenMSMQQueue

Dim sPath, sFile
sPath = WScript.ScriptFullName
sPath = Mid(sPath, 1, InStrRev(sPath, "\"))
sFile = sPath & sDocName

Dim xmlDoc
Set xmlDoc = CreateObject("MSXML2.DOMDocument")
xmlDoc.setProperty "SelectionLanguage", "XPath"
xmlDoc.load sFile

Dim oMsg
```

LISTING 13.8 continued

```
Set oMsg = CreateObject("MSMQ.MSMQMessage")

xmlDoc.SelectSingleNode("//Item[3]/ItemHeader/@Quantity").text = "44"
oMsg.Body = xmlDoc.xml
oMsg.Label = "CommonPO"
oMsg.Send oQ, MQ_SINGLE_MESSAGE

xmlDoc.SelectSingleNode("//Item[3]/ItemHeader/@Quantity").text = "55"
oMsg.Body = xmlDoc.xml
oMsg.Label = "CommonPO"
oMsg.Send oQ, MQ_SINGLE_MESSAGE

oQ.Close

Sub OpenMSMQQueue
    On Error Resume Next

    Set oMQInfo = CreateObject("MSMQ.MSMQQueueInfo")
    oMQInfo.Label = ""
    oMQInfo.PathName = sQueuePath
    oMQInfo.Refresh
    if Len(oMQInfo.Label) = 0 then
        oMQInfo.Label = "BTS Unleashed: Adv Orchestration"
        oMQInfo.Create True, True ' transactional and world readable
    end if

    Set oQ = oMQInfo.Open(MQ_SEND_ACCESS, MQ_DENY_NONE)
End Sub
```

In Listing 13.8, skipping past the preamble of defining constants, the first action is opening the `.\private$\Port_1` queue to send messages. This is done by calling the procedure `OpenMSMQQueue`. The queue is created, if not found, and as a transactional queue that everyone can read from. This procedure sets the variable `oQ` as a reference to this queue.

The next four statements calculate the full path of the document instance to use to create the messages in the queue. You should have already copied the document instance to the current directory.

Prior to stuffing the queue with the message, we use the XML DOM to manipulate the value of the `Quantity` in the third `Item` to be `"44"` for the first document and `"55"` for the second document. Finally, we load an MSMQ message, `oMsg`, with the modified document and stuff it into the queue. Each document is also labeled `CommonPO`.

Running the SimpleTxn.skx Schedule

If you start the schedule first, without creating the queue, it will failfast with an event log entry for XLANG Scheduler, category `WFBinding`, stating that the queue `Port_1` is not present. You could start the schedule after manually creating the MSMQ queue and see the schedule dehydrate. Alternatively, you could run a subset of the `RunSimpleTxn.vbs` script from Listing 13.8, as shown in Listing 13.9.

LISTING 13.9 `CreateQueue.vbs`

```
Option Explicit
On Error Resume Next

' Constants
Const sQueuePath = ".\private$\Port_1"

Dim oMQInfo
Set oMQInfo = CreateObject("MSMQ.MSMQQueueInfo")
oMQInfo.Label = ""
oMQInfo.PathName = sQueuePath
oMQInfo.Refresh
if Len(oMQInfo.Label) = 0 then
    oMQInfo.Label = "BTS Unleashed: Adv Orchestration"
    oMQInfo.Create True, True ' transactional and world readable
end if
```

For this example, create the queue first by using the `CreateQueue.vbs` script from Listing 13.9.

You run a script by either using the right mouse menu and selecting Open with Command Prompt or running the script using the `CScript` or `WScript` engines. If you were to run the script `RunSimpleTxn.vbs` and look under the Private Queues in the Message Queuing management console, you would see the `port_1` queue. In the Queue Messages under this queue, you would also see the two messages present in the queue. The Message Queuing management console is available under the Computer Management and Services and Applications MMC snap-ins. However, we will run the `RunSimpleTxn.vbs` script only after starting the schedule, to deliver the messages to the queue.

So, the steps are to create the queue using `CreateQueue.vbs script, run the SimpleTxn.skx` schedule, and then send messages to the queue using `RunSimpleTxn.vbs` script.

Open the Component Services management console and view the node Transaction List under the Distributed Transaction Coordinator to see which transactions are flowing through the system. Also, start the XLANG Event Monitor and the DbMon debug monitor application. Run the schedule using the event monitor. Notice that the schedule soon dehydrates waiting for messages. Now run the `RunSimpleTxn.vbs` script.

You should see the schedule consume the messages in the queue. It also asks whether you want to abort the schedule; for this example, choose Yes. With the Retry Count set to 3, you will get three prompts. The resulting trace is shown in Figure 13.15. The trace contains all events; nothing is filtered out.

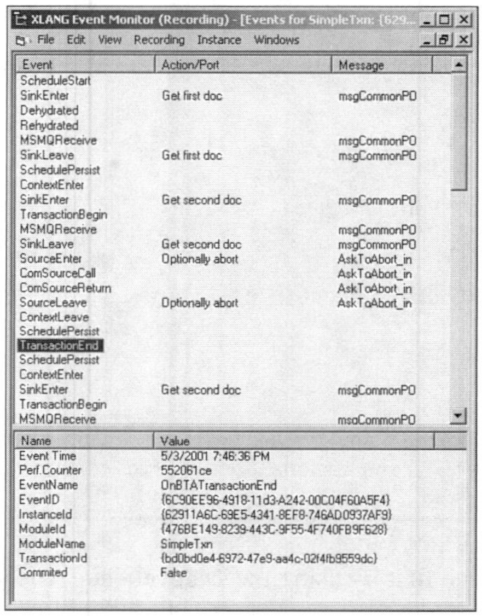

FIGURE 13.15
Schedule execution trace for `SimpleTxn.Skx`.

Looking at the events for the schedule `SimpleTxn.skx` in Figure 13.15, you can see that the schedule dehydrates soon after attempting to get the first document. When the script stuffs the queue with a document, the schedule is rehydrated by the engine. The event `MSMQReceive` denotes a message being read in by the schedule. The event `ContextEnter` denotes that the schedule is entering the transaction context. Just prior to this event, note that the schedule trace displays the `SchedulePersist` event. This denotes that the state of the schedule is checkpointed before attempting the transaction. The transaction is aborted. The highlighted event, `TransactionEnd`, shows that the transaction was in fact not committed (see the last line in the bottom pane).

Listing 13.10 displays the entire execution trace as seen in the DbMon console.

LISTING 13.10 DbMon Execution Trace for Schedule `SimpleTxn.skx`

```
580: 7:46:55 PM:AdvOrchTxn.CAbortTxn: Class_Initialize()
580: 7:46:59 PM:AdvOrchTxn.CAbortTxn: AskToAbort(): Aborted!
580: 7:46:59 PM:AdvOrchTxn.CAbortTxn: Class_Terminate()
```

LISTING 13.10 continued

```
580: 7:47:03 PM:AdvOrchTxn.CAbortTxn: Class_Initialize()
580: 7:47:05 PM:AdvOrchTxn.CAbortTxn: AskToAbort(): Aborted!
580: 7:47:05 PM:AdvOrchTxn.CAbortTxn: Class_Terminate()
580: 7:47:14 PM:AdvOrchTxn.CAbortTxn: Class_Initialize()
580: 7:47:27 PM:AdvOrchTxn.CAbortTxn: AskToAbort(): Aborted!
580: 7:47:27 PM:AdvOrchTxn.CAbortTxn: Class_Terminate()
580: 7:47:54 PM:AdvOrchTxn.CAbortTxn: Class_Initialize()
580: 7:47:55 PM:AdvOrchTxn.CAbortTxn: AskToAbort(): Aborted!
580: 7:47:55 PM:AdvOrchTxn.CAbortTxn: Class_Terminate()
580: AdvOrchUtil.CMsg: Class_Initialize()
580: AdvOrchUtil.CMsg: ShowMsgBox(): Msg=44
➥Title=bztk.bztkdom.omicron.com\private$\port_1
580: AdvOrchUtil.CMsg: Class_Terminate()
```

Listing 13.10 shows that each time the transaction is attempted, an instance of the class `AdvOrchTxn.CAbortTxn` is created. The trace shows this with the traces bracketed by the `Class_Initialize()` and `Class_Terminate()` trace statements. There are four sets of these, indicating that the class was instantiated four times. This is consistent with the three retries set up for the transaction. If you also look at the elapsed times between `Class_Terminate()` traces and following `Class_Initialize()` traces, you will note the 3, 9, and 27 second backoff time periods, as expected.

The remaining traces in Listing 13.10 show the content of the message box. Note, in particular, that only the first message (with the `Quantity` of 44) is successfully read. If you look into the pending messages in the queue `.\private$\Port_1`, you will see that the second message is still sitting in the queue. If, instead of aborting the transaction, you had chosen otherwise, this message would be retrieved from the queue and the message in the trace would have shown 55. The title portion of the message displays the port reference for an MSMQ queue.

In this example, we used the built-in support for transactions in COM+ and aborted the transaction that flowed from the XLANG schedule to the configured COM+ component `AdvOrchTxn.CAbortTxn`.

Using COM+ transaction services is not the only way transactions get aborted. Any of the following may also cause such an abort:

- When the process flow runs into an Abort shape inside a transaction.
- A port connected to a component is defined to abort a transaction if the component returns a failed `HRESULT`.
- A port connected to a messaging system is defined to abort a transaction if the message delivery or receipt fails.

- The XLANG Scheduler Engine may abort a transaction—for example, it may encounter an error, or one of the resource managers in a distributed transaction may be unable to proceed with the transaction.
- Pausing (suspending) a schedule may force the XLANG Scheduler Engine to abort transactions.
- The number of retries as available for the transaction have already been attempted.
- The time limit for the transaction to complete is exceeded.

Long-Lived and Nested Transactions

Long-lived and nested transactions extend the notion of transactions to application processes that can tolerate lower levels of isolation in return for transaction concurrency and throughput for the long-lived operations.

In the previous example shown in Figure 13.11, you could change the properties of the transaction shape `TxnGetDoc` (shown in Figure 13.13) from Short-Lived, DTC-Style to either Timed Transaction or Long-Running. Notice then that you can no longer specify the Isolation Level. If you attempt to run the resulting schedule, you will also notice that there is in fact no DTC style transaction flowing through to the `AdvOrchTxn.CAbortTxn` component—the schedule just completes. To abort a long-running (or a timed) transaction, you would typically use the Abort shape or return a nonzero `HRESULT` from a component connected to a COM port.

Look at the following example using nested and long-running transactions. In this example, you also see the On Failure of <*Transaction*> and Compensation for <*Transaction*> pages used. Note that the messaging process is not complicated. The contrived business process is to set up a cellular phone tower, shown in Figure 13.16.

In Figure 13.16, the outer, long-running, transaction is called Setup Cell Tower. There are three actions to perform: buy a pole, dig a hole, and set up the cell tower. This example uses the two COM components, `AdvOrchTxn.CAbortTxn` and `AdvOrchUtil.CMsg`, developed in previous examples. To construct the schedule, follow these steps:

1. Set down an Action shape and set the name property to `Buy pole`.
2. Drag a Transaction shape over the Action shape so that it completely encloses it. Double-click the Transaction shape and change the name to `BuyPole`. Set the retry count to zero. This is a short-lived transaction.
3. Repeat the steps 1 and 2 for the next action (named `Dig hole`) and its enclosing transaction (named `DigHole`).

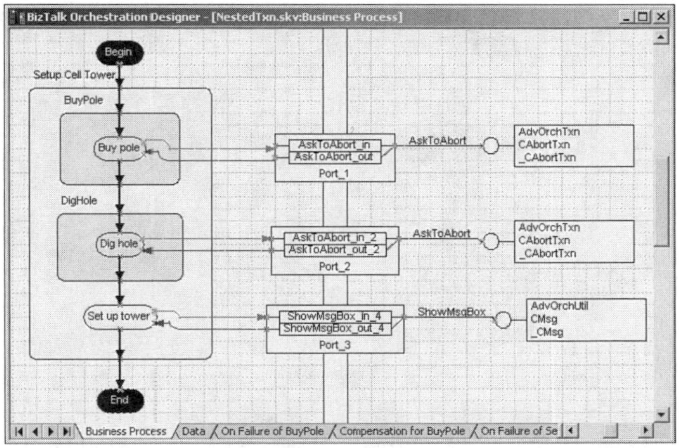

FIGURE 13.16
Business process for `NestedTxn.Skv`.

4. Add the last action shape and name it `Set up tower`.
5. Enclose the last action, added in step 4, and the other two transactions in an outer, long-lived, transaction, called `Setup Cell Tower`. To do this, drag the transaction shape onto the drawing surface, making sure that it does not overlap any other shape. Then, change the shape of the transaction rectangle into a thin, tall rectangle, positioned to the left of the other two transaction shapes. Make this rectangle tall enough to encompass the vertical range of the transaction and action shapes that you want to enclose. Finally, drag the rightmost vertical side of the rectangle over the shapes to enclose.
6. Open the properties of the `BuyPole` transaction. Click both the buttons to add code for failure and compensation.
7. Open the properties of the `DigHole` transaction. Click only to add code for failure. The reason compensation code is not defined is that, at least for our contrived example, if the `DigHole` transaction succeeds, the overall transaction will always succeed, and we never have to run a compensation for it.
8. Add the port implementations using code already developed. Refer to Listing 13.1 for the `AdvOrchUtil.CMsg` class and Listing 13.7 for the `AdvOrchTxn.CAbortTxn` class. Make sure that these classes are compiled and installed in a COM+ server application.
9. Join the actions with the respective implementations, as shown in Figure 13.16.

Before looking at the Data page, look at the failure and compensation pages. Figure 13.17 shows the On Failure of `BuyPole` page.

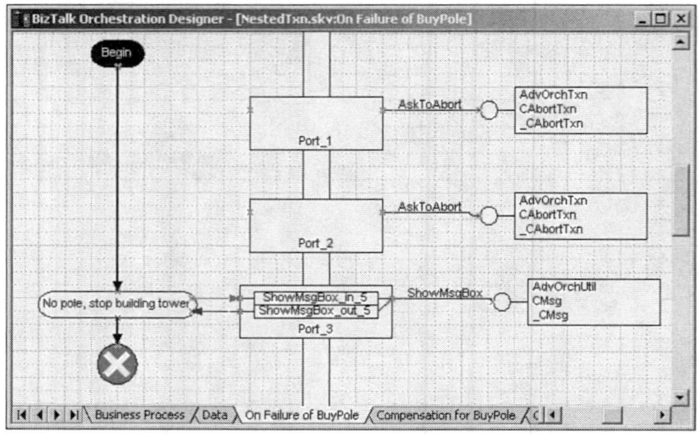

FIGURE 13.17
The On Failure of `BuyPole` *page in* `NestedTxn.skv`.

On the page shown in Figure 13.17, we perform the actions needed to handle the transaction failure for `BuyPole`, which for this example is to send a message to stop building the tower and, more importantly, aborting the enclosing (long-lived) transaction Setup Cell Tower. Recall that the actions on this page are executed in lieu of the actions inside the `BuyPole` transaction. Hence, the Abort shape aborts the outer transaction.

Next, look at Compensation for `BuyPole` page, shown in Figure 13.18.

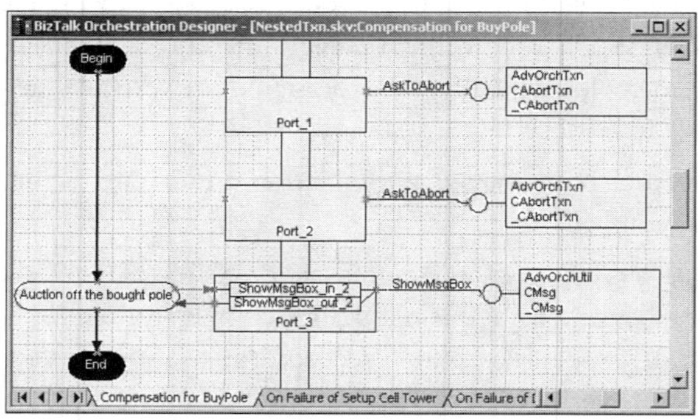

FIGURE 13.18
Compensation for `BuyPole` *page in* `NestedTxn.skv`.

The page shown in Figure 13.18 is executed when the outer transaction, Setup Cell Tower, fails, but the nested `BuyPole` transaction succeeded. Our compensatory action is to get rid of the bought pole as best as we can. The key point about compensation is that you cannot undo or abort something (such as a transaction) that has already happened in the real world; you can at best take corrective action.

Two other process pages are not shown: On Failure of Setup Cell Tower and On Failure of `DigHole`. These are similar to the ones being discussed here. When the outer transaction fails, we simply send a message to write up a status report for the failure of erecting a cell tower. When the `DigHole` transaction fails, we also cause the outer transaction to abort, just as we did in On Failure of `BuyPole`.

Now look at the Data page shown in Figure 13.19.

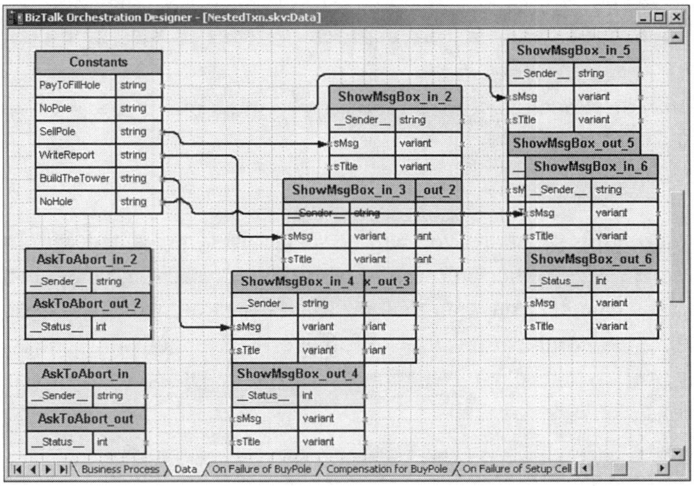

FIGURE 13.19
Data page for `NestedTxn.Skv`.

On the Data page, we add Constants strings to use with each of the messages. Six string constants are shown; however, one is not used. It would have been useful if we could have handled a compensation procedure for a hole already dug but one no longer necessary. The constants are as shown in Table 13.3.

TABLE 13.3 Strings in `NestedTxn.Skv`

Name	*Value*
`PayToFillHole`	Pay to fill the hole already dug! (This constant is not used in the schedule.)
`NoPole`	No pole. Stop setting up the tower!
`SellPole`	Auction off the bought pole!
`WriteReport`	Tower setup failed. Write project status report.
`BuildTheTower`	Build the tower!
`NoHole`	No hole. Stop setting up the tower!

Caution

Be careful with the messages that get the auto-numbered suffixes. The same suffixed message in your schedule may refer to a different port from the one shown in the figures. For example, `ShowMsgBox_in_2` may apply to `Port_3 in your schedule, whereas it applies to Port_1` in a schedule shown in this chapter.

To correctly reproduce the schedules, you must match the message and the port through which the message passes.

When you run this schedule, you will be successively presented with two dialog boxes. The first one asks whether you want to abort the transaction, which is `BuyPole`. The second one asks whether you want to abort the transaction, which is `DigHole`. You can try out the different combinations yourself; however, the interesting one is when you successfully buy a pole but fail to dig a hole for it. The DbMon trace for it is shown in Listing 13.11.

LISTING 13.11 DbMon Trace for `NestedTxn.skx`

```
2544: 2:37:57 PM:AdvOrchTxn.CAbortTxn: Class_Initialize()
2544: 2:37:59 PM:AdvOrchTxn.CAbortTxn: AskToAbort(): SetComplete!
2544: 2:37:59 PM:AdvOrchTxn.CAbortTxn: Class_Terminate()
2544: 2:37:59 PM:AdvOrchTxn.CAbortTxn: Class_Initialize()
2544: 2:38:00 PM:AdvOrchTxn.CAbortTxn: AskToAbort(): Aborted!
2544: 2:38:00 PM:AdvOrchTxn.CAbortTxn: Class_Terminate()
2544: AdvOrchUtil.CMsg: Class_Initialize()
2544: AdvOrchUtil.CMsg: ShowMsgBox(): Msg=No hole, Stop setting up tower! Title=

2544: AdvOrchUtil.CMsg: Class_Terminate()
2544: AdvOrchUtil.CMsg: Class_Initialize()
2544: AdvOrchUtil.CMsg: ShowMsgBox(): Msg=Auction off the bought pole! Title=
2544: AdvOrchUtil.CMsg: Class_Terminate()
2544: AdvOrchUtil.CMsg: Class_Initialize()
2544: AdvOrchUtil.CMsg: ShowMsgBox(): Msg=Tower setup failed.  Write project
➥status report! Title=
2544: AdvOrchUtil.CMsg: Class_Terminate()
```

Listing 13.11 shows that the first DTC style transaction to buy the pole is completed (trace `SetComplete!`), whereas the second one is aborted (trace `Aborted!`). When the second transaction is aborted, the On Failure of `DigHole` page is executed. This process sends a message declaring `"No hole, stop setting up tower!"`, and it aborts the outer Setup Cell Tower transaction. When the outer transaction is aborted, the compensation process starts. The Compensation for `BuyPole` page is executed. The process on this page sends the message to `"Auction off the bought pole!"`. After all the compensation processes have finished (there is only one in this example), the On Failure of Setup Cell Tower page for the outer transaction is executed. This sends the message to `"Write project status report!"`.

You could develop this example further by making both `BuyPole` and `DigHole` long-running transactions containing multiple steps with transactions that proceed concurrently. Such a long-lived process could occur over months, and the XLANG schedule would track this process just fine.

Long-running transactions sacrifice isolation; therefore, actions within a long running transaction may be exposed to inconsistent data. In our contrived example, if you don't take care of this in your application logic, the setup instructions may not match the hole you dug or the pole you bought. However, your installers just may be used to such state of affairs. See Chapter 9 for more information on transactions.

The next section investigates transactions and state with the iteration shape.

Iteration

We start our foray into usage of the While flowchart shape by building a basic example. We build the following schedule first, shown in Figure 13.20. This schedule is used to describe how iteration is accomplished. Later, we look at how transactions may be used with iterations, shown in Figure 13.22.

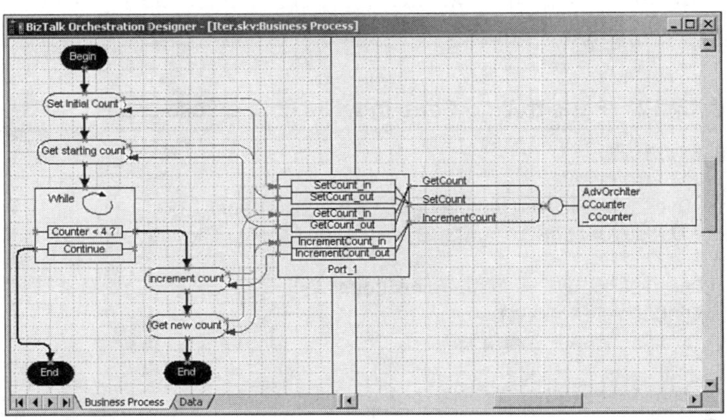

FIGURE 13.20
Business process for `Iter.skv`

Design of `Iter.skv` Sample

The operation of the `Iter.skv` schedule is as follows. It first sets an initial starting count, and then it counts up from 1 to 3. In this schedule, nothing else useful is done for the repeated flow. At the end, the schedule simply stops. The COM component to the right implements three methods used by the schedule. We need to build this new component `AdvOrchIter.CCounter` before building the schedule.

The component `AdvOrchIter.CCounter` serves as a counter with memory (state). Although a schedule manages the state of its messages, we cannot use this built-in state management in our own schedule logic; we must add a COM component. Adding a COM component has additional benefits; it provides granular control over the use of other COM+ services of transaction, security, and state management. For this counter, we also implement persistence support and demonstrate the use of persistence in schedules by the XLANG Scheduler Engine.

The component `AdvOrchIter.CCounter` supports three methods: `SetCount`, `IncrementCount`, and `GetCount`. Notice in Figure 13.20 that the call to `GetCount` occurs both before entering the body of the While and inside the body of the While. This is a common pattern you might see in the usage of the While shape. The rule inside the While must test a condition that changes during the operation of the schedule, and often this change is directly the result of actions in the body of the While shape.

Building `AdvOrchIter.CCounter` COM Component

To implement the component `AdvOrchIter.CCounter`, we start by identifying some basic code. The code you have already seen in other examples is shown as it applies to this class in Listing 13.12. This code is for generating trace messages and for class initialization and termination. Nothing conceptually new here.

LISTING 13.12 Basic tracing Code in `AdvOrchIter.CCounter`

```
Option Explicit

Private Declare Sub OutputDebugString Lib "kernel32"
➥Alias "OutputDebugStringA" (ByVal lpOutputString As String)

Const CCOUNTER_COUNT = "CCounter_Count"
Const DEF_CCOUNTER_COUNT = 0
Private m_nCount As Long

Private Sub Trace(sMsg As String)
    Dim sNow As String
    sNow = FormatDateTime(Now(), vbLongTime)
    OutputDebugString sNow & ":AdvOrchTxn.CCounter: " & sMsg & vbCrLf
End Sub
```

LISTING 13.12 continued

```
Private Sub Class_Initialize()
    Trace "Class_Initialize()"
    m_nCount = DEF_CCOUNTER_COUNT
End Sub

Private Sub Class_Terminate()
    Trace "Class_Terminate()"
End Sub
```

Listing 13.12 also contains some constants that we will use soon for implementing persistence. The `m_nCounter` variable embodies the entire (relevant) state of the class. In the Visual Basic project, change the class properties to `UsesTransaction` and `Persistable`. The operational part of the class is shown in Listing 13.13.

LISTING 13.13 Count Management in `AdvOrchIter.CCounter`

```
Function GetCount() As Long
    GetCount = m_nCount
    Trace "GetCount() = " & CStr(m_nCount)
End Function

Sub SetCount(ByVal nCount As Long)
    m_nCount = nCount
    Trace "SetCount(" & CStr(m_nCount) & ")"
End Sub

Sub IncrementCount()
    m_nCount = m_nCount + 1
    Trace "IncrementCount() = " & CStr(m_nCount)
End Sub
```


Listing 13.13 shows the implementation for the functions and methods of the class. When you make the class `Persistable`, you add three new event handlers for the class. You can select these in the procedures drop-down list in the Visual Basic IDE. The three events are `InitProperties`, `ReadProperties`, and `WriteProperties`. Implement these event handlers as shown in Listing 13.14.

LISTING 13.14 Persistence Support in `AdvOrchIter.CCounter`

```
Private Sub Class_InitProperties()
    Trace "Class_InitProperties()"
End Sub

' Implementation for IPersistStreamInit
```

LISTING 13.14 continued

```
Private Sub Class_ReadProperties(PropBag As PropertyBag)
    m_nCount = PropBag.ReadProperty(CCOUNTER_COUNT, DEF_CCOUNTER_COUNT)
    Trace "Class_ReadProperties(): m_nCount = " & CStr(m_nCount)
End Sub

' Implementation for IPersistStreamInit
Private Sub Class_WriteProperties(PropBag As PropertyBag)
    PropBag.WriteProperty CCOUNTER_COUNT, m_nCount, DEF_CCOUNTER_COUNT
    Trace "Class_WriteProperties(): m_nCount = " & CStr(m_nCount)
End Sub
```

As Listing 13.14 shows, appropriate tracing has been added. Notice also the use of the constants defined earlier. By defining the class as persistable and implementing the three required interfaces, Visual Basic 6.0 can provide an implementation for the `IPersistStream` interface for the class. This interface is used by the XLANG Scheduler Engine when it wants to persist the state of the COM component. See also Chapter 10 for more information on state management.

Now save and compile the Visual Basic project, making sure that you have turned on binary compatibility. Install the resulting DLL in a COM+ application. Now you can build the schedule shown previously in Figure 13.20.

Building the `Iter.skv` Schedule

Start by putting down the Action shapes and naming them as shown in Figure 13.20. In addition, put down the two End shapes. We will connect all shapes a bit later.

Drag a COM component implementation shape and drop it on the right. Create a static instance with the default port name of `Port_1`. On the third page of the wizard, select the registered component `AdvOrchUtil.CCounter`. The next wizard page shows the three methods exposed by this component; select all three. On the final page, make sure that the transactions are supported by the component and change the selection under the State Management Support drop-down to select Holds State, and Does Support Persistence.

Now, connect the actions on the left with the `Port_1` on the right. Draw the connection as shown in Figure 13.20 and select the corresponding method in the wizard. Note that the actions `Get starting count` and `Get new count` not only call the same method, `GetCount`, but also share the same message. This is important; without this sharing, the schedule will not function correctly.

By connecting the actions to the methods through `Port_1`, you also create messages on the Data page. Now we can construct the rule in the While shape to check for the counter value. Right-click the While shape and add a rule. Name the rule `Counter < 4 ?`, an arbitrary but descriptive string. The scripting expression for the rule is as follows:

```
GetCount_out.GetCount < 4
```

You may type in this expression or use the expression assistant to construct it. Now make the remaining connections as shown in the Figure 13.20. You may find the connector tool a handy mechanism for making connections quickly.

On the Data page there is only one connection of interest; this is to set the initial counter value from the constants in the schedule. This is shown in Figure 13.21. The constant is named `StartingCount`, of the type `i1`, and a value of one.

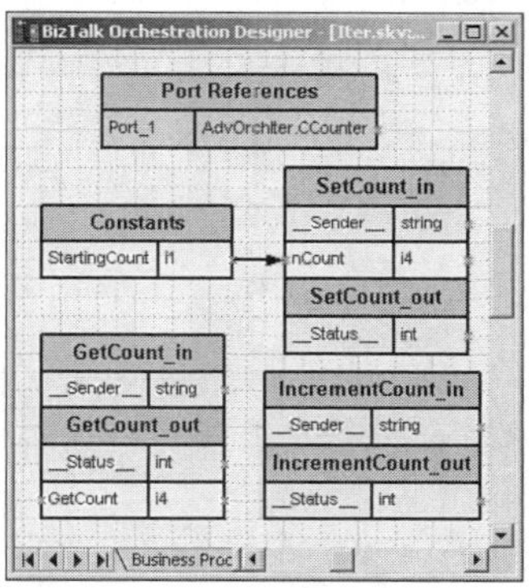

FIGURE 13.21
Data page for `Iter.skv`.

Running the `Iter.skx` Schedule

You can now run the schedule. Start up the XLANG Event Monitor, DbMon, and the Component Services administration console to see the running objects. Start the schedule using the event monitor. In the DbMon console, you should see something like Listing 13.15.

LISTING 13.15 DbMon Trace of Running `Iter.skx`

```
2152: 9:46:00 AM:AdvOrchTxn.CCounter: Class_Initialize()
2152: 9:46:00 AM:AdvOrchTxn.CCounter: Class_InitProperties()
2152: 9:46:00 AM:AdvOrchTxn.CCounter: SetCount(1)
2152: 9:46:00 AM:AdvOrchTxn.CCounter: GetCount() = 1
2152: 9:46:00 AM:AdvOrchTxn.CCounter: IncrementCount() = 2
2152: 9:46:00 AM:AdvOrchTxn.CCounter: GetCount() = 2
2152: 9:46:00 AM:AdvOrchTxn.CCounter: IncrementCount() = 3
2152: 9:46:00 AM:AdvOrchTxn.CCounter: GetCount() = 3
2152: 9:46:00 AM:AdvOrchTxn.CCounter: IncrementCount() = 4
2152: 9:46:00 AM:AdvOrchTxn.CCounter: GetCount() = 4
2152: 9:46:00 AM:AdvOrchTxn.CCounter: Class_Terminate()
```

The schedule runs to completion quickly. The persistence support is not used in this run. This demonstrates a simple use of the While shape. For the next step, to keep the narrative cross-references from becoming confusing, save the `Iter.skv` schedule as `Iter2.skv`. In this new schedule, we will introduce a transaction and look at how the persistence of COM components is used by the schedule.

Building `Iter2.skv` Schedule with a Transaction

Modify `Iter2.skv` to include a transaction `TxnWhile`, as shown in Figure 13.22. This is a short-lived transaction. Set the Retry Count to zero and enable code for on failure handling. An extra action, called `Abort ?` has been added inside the transaction, which calls the `AskToAbort` method of the `AdvOrchTxn.CAbortTxn` class, described previously in Listing 13.7.

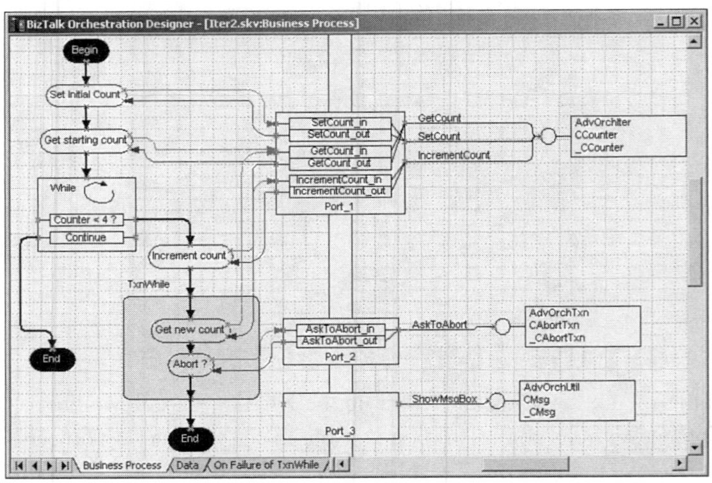

FIGURE 13.22
Business process for `Iter2.skv`.

When the transaction fails, the process in Figure 13.23 is run. It merely shows the value of the counter as captured in the `GetCount_in` message. The page uses the method `ShowMsgBox` of the `AdvOrchUtil.CMsg` class described in Listing 13.1.

Finally, the Data page associated with `Iter2.skv` is shown in Figure 13.24.

The Data page shown in Figure 13.24 is fairly simple. The starting count is loaded into the counter, and the currently read value of the counter is fed to the `ShowMsgBox` message. Note that, although the While loop iterates through counter values 1 to 3, the Actions in this example follow the call to the `IncrementCount` call; hence, we see counter values 2 through 4 in the schedule. Also, note that if you had included the incrementing step inside the transaction, the loop would never exit if the transaction kept failing—so don't do that!

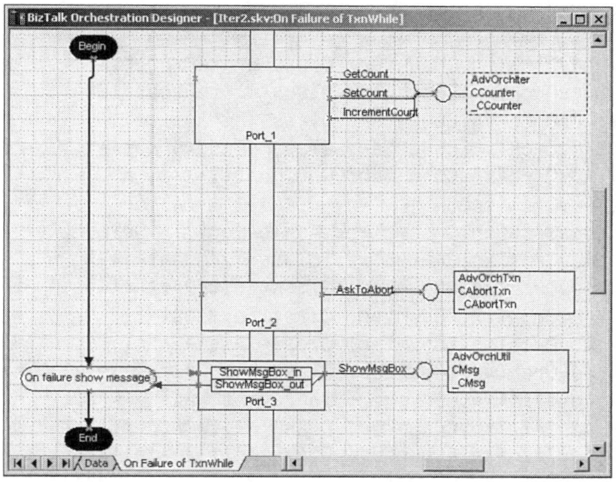

FIGURE 13.23
On Failure of `TxnWhile` *for* `Iter2.skv`.

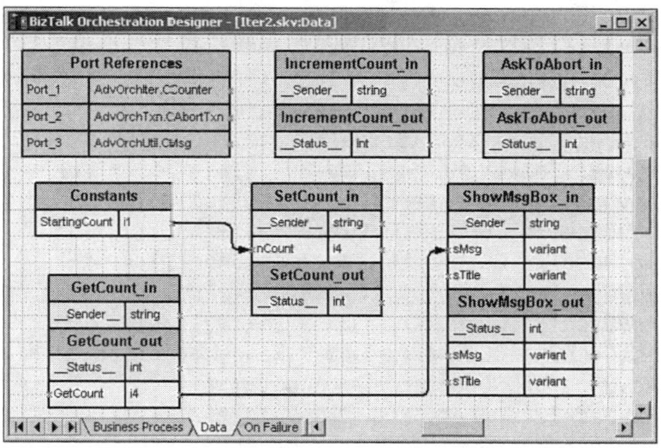

FIGURE 13.24
Data page for `Iter2.skv`.

When you run this example, you are prompted whether to abort the transaction on each iteration of the While loop. The trace in DbMon shown in Listing 13.16 is generated by aborting the second iteration of the loop. The shaded lines are for `Class_Initialize` of the counter and for the `GetCount` function call so that it is easier to navigate the trace output.

LISTING 13.16 DbMon Trace for `Iter2.skx` Without Preserving While State in Each Loop

```
2256: 3:29:17 PM:AdvOrchTxn.CCounter: Class_Initialize()
2256: 3:29:17 PM:AdvOrchTxn.CCounter: Class_InitProperties()
2256: 3:29:17 PM:AdvOrchTxn.CCounter: SetCount(1)
2256: 3:29:17 PM:AdvOrchTxn.CCounter: GetCount() = 1
2256: 3:29:17 PM:AdvOrchTxn.CCounter: IncrementCount() = 2
```

LISTING 13.16 continued

```
2256: 3:29:21 PM:AdvOrchTxn.CCounter: Class_WriteProperties(): m_nCount = 2
2256: 3:29:21 PM:AdvOrchTxn.CCounter: Class_WriteProperties(): m_nCount = 2
2256: 3:29:22 PM:AdvOrchTxn.CCounter: Class_Initialize()
2256: 3:29:22 PM:AdvOrchTxn.CCounter: Class_ReadProperties(): m_nCount = 2
2256: 3:29:23 PM:AdvOrchTxn.CCounter: GetCount() = 2
2256: 3:29:23 PM:AdvOrchTxn.CAbortTxn: Class_Initialize()
2256: 3:29:26 PM:AdvOrchTxn.CAbortTxn: AskToAbort(): SetComplete!
2256: 3:29:26 PM:AdvOrchTxn.CAbortTxn: Class_Terminate()
2256: 3:29:26 PM:AdvOrchTxn.CCounter: Class_WriteProperties(): m_nCount = 2
2256: 3:29:26 PM:AdvOrchTxn.CCounter: Class_Terminate()
2256: 3:29:26 PM:AdvOrchTxn.CCounter: Class_Initialize()
2256: 3:29:26 PM:AdvOrchTxn.CCounter: Class_ReadProperties(): m_nCount = 2
2256: 3:29:26 PM:AdvOrchTxn.CCounter: IncrementCount() = 3
2256: 3:29:27 PM:AdvOrchTxn.CCounter: Class_WriteProperties(): m_nCount = 3
2256: 3:29:27 PM:AdvOrchTxn.CCounter: Class_Initialize()
2256: 3:29:27 PM:AdvOrchTxn.CCounter: Class_ReadProperties(): m_nCount = 3
2256: 3:29:27 PM:AdvOrchTxn.CCounter: GetCount() = 3
2256: 3:29:27 PM:AdvOrchTxn.CAbortTxn: Class_Initialize()
2256: 3:29:28 PM:AdvOrchTxn.CAbortTxn: AskToAbort(): Aborted!
2256: 3:29:28 PM:AdvOrchTxn.CAbortTxn: Class_Terminate()
2256: 3:29:29 PM:AdvOrchTxn.CCounter: Class_Terminate()
2256: AdvOrchUtil.CMsg: Class_Initialize()
2256: AdvOrchUtil.CMsg: ShowMsgBox(): Msg=3 Title=
2256: 3:29:31 PM:AdvOrchTxn.CCounter: Class_Initialize()
2256: 3:29:31 PM:AdvOrchTxn.CCounter: Class_ReadProperties(): m_nCount = 3
2256: 3:29:31 PM:AdvOrchTxn.CCounter: IncrementCount() = 4
2256: 3:29:31 PM:AdvOrchTxn.CCounter: Class_WriteProperties(): m_nCount = 4
2256: 3:29:31 PM:AdvOrchTxn.CCounter: Class_Initialize()
2256: 3:29:31 PM:AdvOrchTxn.CCounter: Class_ReadProperties(): m_nCount = 4
2256: 3:29:31 PM:AdvOrchTxn.CCounter: GetCount() = 4
2256: 3:29:31 PM:AdvOrchTxn.CAbortTxn: Class_Initialize()
2256: 3:29:34 PM:AdvOrchTxn.CAbortTxn: AskToAbort(): SetComplete!
2256: 3:29:34 PM:AdvOrchTxn.CAbortTxn: Class_Terminate()
2256: 3:29:34 PM:AdvOrchTxn.CCounter: Class_Terminate()
2256: 3:29:34 PM:AdvOrchTxn.CCounter: Class_WriteProperties(): m_nCount = 4
2256: 3:29:34 PM:AdvOrchTxn.CCounter: Class_Terminate()
2256: 3:29:34 PM:AdvOrchTxn.CCounter: Class_Terminate()
2256: 3:29:34 PM:AdvOrchTxn.CCounter: Class_Terminate()
2256: AdvOrchUtil.CMsg: Class_Terminate()
```

The first call to `IncrementCount` denotes the start of the first iteration. The engine persists the state of the schedule and the counter prior to entering a transaction context. The process associated with the transaction starts from a known state; note the call to `Class_ReadProperties` just prior to every `GetCount` call. The outcome of a successful transaction is also committed to persistent store (Note the calls to `WriteProperties`).

The counter is a COM+ configured component; the XLANG engine manages the lifetimes of the counter component instances. An appropriate counter instance is utilized based on the calling context, and the state for that instance is restored using the persistence support provided by the component. In the trace, it is not possible to discern the instance identities—for example, it is not possible to match which `Class_Initialize` pairs up with which `Class_Terminate`.

At the point when the counter is at 3, the transaction in that (second) loop iteration is aborted (The trace line is bolded). This causes the execution of the failure process page and the display of the message from the `AdvOrchUtil.CMsg` class. After the transaction is aborted, the old counter value is re-read from the persisted value—as if that iteration never occurred. This demonstrates that supporting persistence in COM components is important, particularly if your schedule uses transactions.

This concludes the discussion of iteration. The next section examines dynamic ports.

Dynamic Ports

You have already had a chance to see what port references look like. Dynamic ports are ports resolved at runtime using port references. We will build XLANG schedules using port references for ports that use COM components or MSMQ queues. For more discussion of dynamic ports and port references, see Chapter 10.

The case for dynamic ports based on BizTalk Messaging Services (that is, dynamic channels) is covered in Chapter 16, "Correlation—Integrating BizTalk Server Messaging and Orchestration Services." In the case of dynamic channels, if you recall from Chapter 10, XLANG ports bound to BizTalk Messaging can be dynamic only when messages are sent out of the XLANG schedule. The port reference to resolve such a dynamic port at runtime is usually provided by a trading partner. Such a reference must contain adequate information for delivering messages from the XLANG schedule to BizTalk Messaging.

The following sections describe a schedule `DynCOM.skv`, which uses a dynamic port bound to a COM component and schedules `Request.skv` and `Response.skv`, which use a dynamic port bound to an MSMQ queue.

Design of `DynCOM.skv`

The next schedule described contains a dynamic port connected to a COM component. The schedule demonstrating this usage is shown in Figure 13.25. This schedule is called `DynCom.skv`.

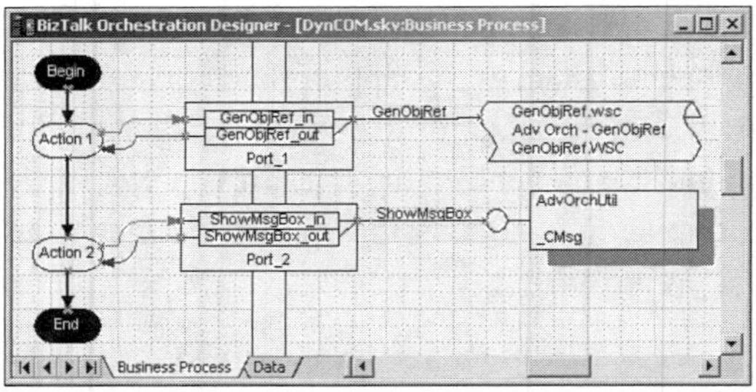

FIGURE 13.25
Business process for DynCOM.skv.

In Figure 13.25, Action 1 calls the script component `GenObjRef.WSC`. This component constructs the COM object required by the dynamic port `Port_2`. Action 2 uses the dynamic port—that is, it makes the method call on the component referenced by the dynamic port. However, the method call is actually performed on the object created by the script component, which provided the object reference to the dynamic port in the first place. Figure 13.26 shows the Data page corresponding to this schedule and how this reference is passed to the dynamic port.

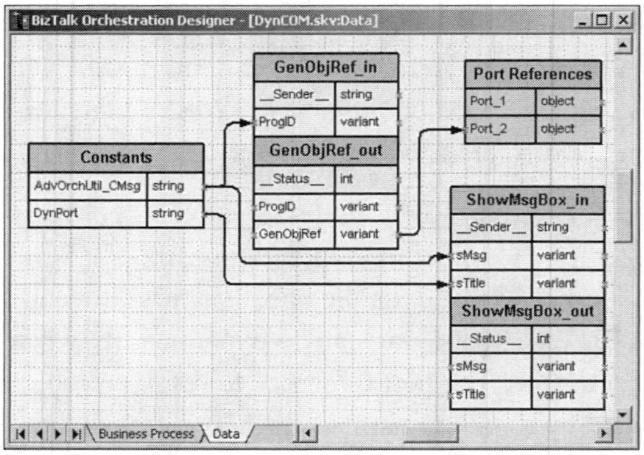

FIGURE 13.26
Data page for DynCOM.skv.

In Figure 13.26, the message pair `GenObjRef_*` is for the function implemented by the script component. This function takes a Prog ID for a component, constructs the component (see the "in" parameter), and returns the reference to it via the field `GenObjRef_out.GenObjRef (an "out" parameter)`. This returned reference is used to resolve the dynamic port `Port_2` by connecting the field to the `Port_2` port reference.

`Port_2` is bound to a dynamic instance of the class `AdvOrchUtil.CMsg` (refer to Listing 13.1). Action 2 calls the `ShowMsgBox` method of this class. The Prog ID provided to the script is `AdvOrchUtil.CMsg` (as it must, because of the type of the dynamic port) using the Constants message. The message box displayed contains this Prog ID and a descriptive title.

Implementing `DynCOM.skv`

As a first step to constructing the schedule, you need to build the script component. The script component is simple and is shown in Listing 13.17.

LISTING 13.17 Code for Script Component `GenObjRef.wsc`

```
<?xml version="1.0"?>
<component>

<?component error="true" debug="true"?>

<registration
    description="Adv Orch - GenObjRef"
    progid="GenObjRef.WSC"
    version="1.00"
    classid="{3FE40B9B-2F99-4643-BBA0-1907B776F90B}"
>
</registration>

<public>
    <method name="GenObjRef">
        <PARAMETER name="ProgID"/>
    </method>
</public>

<script language="VBScript">
<![CDATA[

function GenObjRef(sProgID)
    Set GenObjRef = CreateObject(sProgID)
end function

]]>
</script>

</component>
```


A script component uses the XML technology and the scripting engines to construct a COM component. In Listing 13.7, the script component has a ProgID of `GenObjRef.WSC` and an associated class GUID. The component has one public method, called `GenObjRef`. The implementation of the function is contained as a script inside the `CDATA` section of the XML document. The function creates and returns an object using the passed in ProgID. Use the `GenObjRef` script component to build the schedule shown in Figure 13.25. After creating the business process, you need to drop the script component implementation shape to the right of the separator bar. Follow through the wizard steps; specify the file path and ProgID for the script component. For `Port_2`, use the `_CMsg` interface of the `AdvOrchUtil` component developed in Listing 13.1. Choose a dynamic instantiation; other choices are as defaults.

> **Caution**
>
> If you use the sample from the publisher's Web site, remember to fix the path to the script component as appropriate on your machine. Also, make sure that you either build your COM components to conform to the type library of the sample or fix the references in your schedule to use your type library.

Make all the connections on the data page as shown in Figure 13.26. The constants are shown in Table 13.4.

TABLE 13.4 Strings in `DynCOM.Skv`

Name	*Value*
`AdvOrchUtil_CMsg`	AdvOrchUtil.CMsg
`DynPort`	Dynamic Port

Finally, compile the schedule.

Running `DynCOM.skx`

When you run this schedule, you get a dialog box. The corresponding trace is shown in Listing 13.18.

LISTING 13.18 DbMon Trace upon Running `DynCOM.skx`

```
2540: AdvOrchUtil.CMsg: Class_Initialize()
2540: AdvOrchUtil.CMsg: ShowMsgBox(): Msg=AdvOrchUtil.CMsg Title=Dynamic Port
2540: AdvOrchUtil.CMsg: Class_Terminate()
```

The dialog box has the title Dynamic Port and the message `AdvOrchUtil.CMsg` that was filled into the `ShowMsgBox_In` message on the data page. This message is displayed via the dynamic port `Port_2`.

This example showed the use of an interface as a port reference. You could also use a moniker, and it would work just as well. You must be careful, however, to provide a moniker that, when bound to a class instance, does in fact implement the interface expected by the dynamic port.

Building `Request.skv` and `Response.skv`

The next schedule shows the use of dynamic queues. Figure 13.27 shows a schedule called `Request.skv` that sends a document for processing to a queue known to all instances, named `.\private$\AdvOrchQueue`. Another schedule, `Response.skv` shown in Figure 13.29, sends a response back to the originating schedule instance. To receive this response, the `Request.skv` schedule uses a per-instance static queue shown as `.\private$\Pvt`. The last step in the schedule calls a method to show the content of the returned document. The known private queue, named `.\private$\AdvOrchQueue`, must be created by you and must be transactional for use with the schedule. The per-instance queue is created by the schedule instance when the schedule is run. The name of this per-instance queue is derived from the `.\private$\Pvt` prefix and a GUID suffix, generated at runtime.

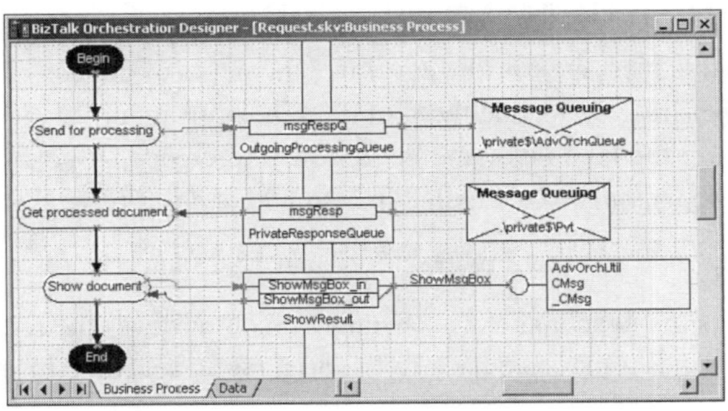

FIGURE 13.27
Business process for `Request.skv`.

When you connect the first action to send the outgoing message in 13.27, in the XML Communication Wizard, choose to Send Messages to the Queue as a String and also declare the message type as `RespQ`. The messages are picked up by the partner schedule using this message type. For the second action, choose to Receive String Messages from the Queue and pick up messages of the type `Resp`. The partner schedule sends messages of this type. Also, set the expected time that this schedule waits for the response to, say, 400 seconds, so that the schedule dehydrates when it is waiting.

To simplify the example, we are using non-XML documents. However, BizTalk internally still uses XML. For this, we must configure the Data page accordingly. This is shown in Figure 13.28.

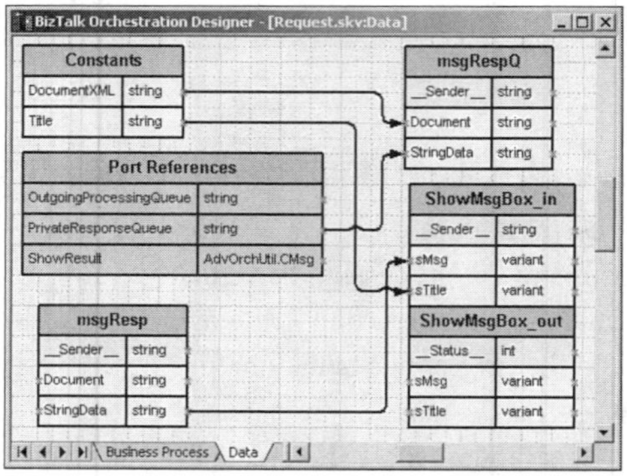

FIGURE 13.28
Data page for `Request.skv`.

When using non-XML messages, a special field, called `StringData` is added to those messages. If such non-XML messages are outgoing, then the `Document` field must be populated with the following XML envelope:

```
<?xml version="1.0" ?><StringData></StringData>
```

We use the Constants message for this envelope, the name of the constant used is `DocumentXML`. Other links show that the port reference for the private MSMQ queue is passed out in the `StringData` field, and the returned reference is shown in the message box. The title of the message box is filled in also with a descriptive string.

Build the `Request.skv` based on Figures 13.27 and 13.28 and the description here.

Figure 13.29 shows the `Response.skv` schedule, which retrieves the requests sent by `Request.skv` and sends a message back to the originating schedule instance.

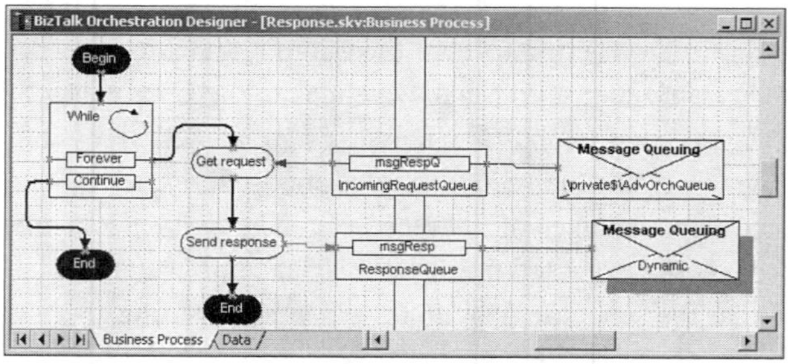

FIGURE 13.29
Business process for `Response.skv`.

The `Response.skv` schedule, shown in Figure 13.29, contains a While loop that runs forever. The rule named `Forever` contains the Visual Basic script expression of `True`. The body of the While loop reads messages from the `.\private$\AdvOrchQueue` queue and sends a response through the dynamic queue. By using the reference provided in the incoming message, the dynamic queue points back to the source schedule instance to send the response.

The settings in the incoming messages must match those for the outgoing messages in the sending schedule, `Request.skv`. Choose to receive non-XML messages of the type `RespQ`. Also set the receive latency high, say 500, so that the schedule dehydrates. The settings of the outgoing messages must match those for the queue in the `Request.skv` set up to receive the responses. Thus, choose to send non-XML messages of the type `Resp`.

The Data page for `Response.skv` is shown in Figure 13.30.

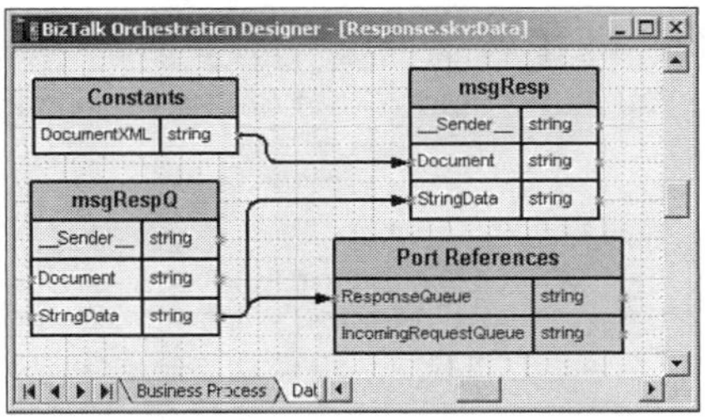

FIGURE 13.30
Data page for `Response.skv`.

For `Response.skv`, in Figure 13.30, you will need to again construct the XML wrapper for the non-XML document in the `StringData` field. The data flows show that the incoming `StringData` is used to resolve the dynamic queue and is returned to the sending schedule through the `msgResp` message. Thus, the message box in `Request.skx` will show the queue reference.

Build the schedules shown in Figure 13.27 and Figure 13.29. You will need to use the component `AdvOrchUtil.CMsg` developed in Listing 13.1. You will also have to manually create the private queue `.\private$\AdvOrchQueue` (as stated earlier).

Running `Request.skx` and `Response.skx`

To run this example, you will have to run `Response.skx` just once. If you have the XLANG Monitor running, you will see this looping schedule start up and promptly dehydrate waiting for requests. You can also start this schedule using the script `RunResponse.vbs` shown in Listing 13.19.

LISTING 13.19 Run the `Response.skx` Schedule: Script `RunResponse.vbs`

```
Option Explicit

Dim sPath, sResp
sPath = WScript.ScriptFullName
```

LISTING 13.19 continued

```
sPath = Mid(sPath, 1, InStrRev(sPath, "\"))
sResp = sPath & "Response.skx"

GetObject("sked:///" & sResp)
```

Listing 13.20 may be used to start three instances of the `Request.skx` schedule. In the XLANG Event monitor, you will see these schedules start up, dehydrate, restart, and then complete after you dismiss the dialog boxes. The dialog boxes shown contain the path of the per-instance queue created in each instance of the `Request.skx` started.

The `GetObject` call in either Listing 13.19 or Listing 13.20 uses a moniker for the schedule. The moniker used to start the schedules starts them on the local machine and in the default group manager.

LISTING 13.20 Run the `Request.skx` Schedule: Script `RunRequests.skx`

```
Option Explicit

Dim sPath, sReq
sPath = WScript.ScriptFullName
sPath = Mid(sPath, 1, InStrRev(sPath, "\"))
sReq = sPath & "Request.skx"

GetObject("sked:///" & sReq)
GetObject("sked:///" & sReq)
GetObject("sked:///" & sReq)
```

Listing 13.21 shows the output from the DbMon console when the two scripts `RunResponse.vbs` and `RunRequests.vbs` are run. Here you can also see what was shown in the dialog boxes.

LISTING 13.21 DbMon Output from Running the `RunRequests.vbs`

```
2556: AdvOrchUtil.CMsg: Class_Initialize()
2556: AdvOrchUtil.CMsg: Class_Initialize()
2556: AdvOrchUtil.CMsg: Class_Initialize()
2556: AdvOrchUtil.CMsg: ShowMsgBox(): Msg=bztk.bztkdom.omicron.com
➥\private$\pvt{a2702811-147a-4141-8bd9-ff34fa387050} Title=
➥Private queue port reference
2556: AdvOrchUtil.CMsg: ShowMsgBox(): Msg=bztk.bztkdom.omicron.com
➥\private$\pvt{65a3c661-3517-4ec3-976a-c6278615c681} Title=
➥Private queue port reference
2556: AdvOrchUtil.CMsg: ShowMsgBox(): Msg=bztk.bztkdom.omicron.com
➥\private$\pvt{3e9d56b6-f568-488b-8af4-1f9876177628} Title=
➥Private queue port reference
```

LISTING 13.21 continued

```
2556: AdvOrchUtil.CMsg: Class_Terminate()
2556: AdvOrchUtil.CMsg: Class_Terminate()
2556: AdvOrchUtil.CMsg: Class_Terminate()
```

In Listing 13.21, note the full port reference for the per-instance private queue for each of the schedule instances of the `Request.skv`. This per-instance and unique queue has the prefix `pvt` defined for it followed by a GUID string to generate the unique name. This port reference is the content of the `StringData` field in the schedules, and this port reference is used to resolve the dynamic queue in `Response.skv`.

Development, Runtime, and Deployment Considerations

This section provides general insights into designing, running, and deploying BizTalk Orchestrations. We look at aspects of robustness, scalability, and performance.

As a general guideline, to design a good BizTalk Orchestration Schedule, you must be able to factor your business process into the operations supported by BizTalk. By understanding the transaction support and error-handling characteristics of XLANG schedules, you can partition your business process into logical units that maintain the consistency and integrity of your business operations. You may also want to entertain the thought of modifying or re-engineering your business processes to truly automate them.

The following sections describe some things to keep in mind.

Robustness

You may recall that the messages in an XLANG schedule can carry COM interface handles around. Be careful when doing this because of what the XLANG engine could do when it dehydrates and rehydrates a schedule.

When a schedule is dehydrated, the XLANG engine calls the component to persist its state. When the schedule is later rehydrated, the engine constructs a new component and asks it to restore its state from the earlier persisted state. Now, if the component is implemented correctly, and the state is in fact restored correctly, and all is fine. The messages that contained the original COM interface are updated to contain the new interface; however, if another COM component had received this interface, it is no longer valid. This could occur if you passed the interface to the component as part of a message field. It is desirable that all your components support persistence or not hold any state.

Performance and Scalability

Here are some pointers to optimize performance of your schedules:

- Run the COM objects on the same server as the BizTalk Orchestration Persistence database. This eliminates the network latency to access the persisted state of the objects when the schedule is rehydrated. This means that, to achieve scalability, you should spread out related schedules and their objects on different servers each with its own persistence databases.
- Manage the dehydration of your schedules. Dehydrated schedules do not consume system resources other than the relatively inexpensive space in the database.
- Consider the trade-off of running COM+ packages in-process versus out-of-process. In-process deployment is faster; however, a failure in one application causes all applications in the failed process to fail.
- To support transactions, the XLANG Scheduler Engine checkpoints the state of the running schedule at the beginning and end of a transaction. This is an expensive operation. Batching work in a single transaction can alleviate this load; however, it might make error handling more complex.
- An XLANG schedule cannot dehydrate in the middle of an MSDTC transaction; however, these transactions are quick. Yet, try to lump multiple quick actions in a single short-lived transaction to conserve system resources.
- Try to decouple communicating applications by using asynchronous messaging. This enables a higher throughput at the expense of some latency. This is true in particular for long-running transactions and long-running business processes.
- Design COM components so that they finish their work quickly. If they must be time consuming, consider designing them so that they return synchronous calls quickly, but later the results of their work can be returned asynchronously.

If your XLANG schedules do not dehydrate, explore some of the following reasons:

- Pending actions, such as waiting to receive a message, have an associated acceptable latency. If this is greater than 180 seconds, then the schedule dehydrates immediately, barring other reasons not to.
- The schedule is not quiescent; not all actions in the schedule are in the same state. Unless forcibly dehydrated, a schedule dehydrates only when all actions that are ready to run must wait for an event—for example, a message to arrive.
- There are pending short-lived transactions.

- The state of a component bound to a port cannot be persisted. Such a port is called a *live port*. Although the state will be lost if the system crashes or there are other failures, the engine holds on to the port in the hope that the schedule will finish successfully.

Summary

This chapter covered examples of schedules that illustrate the use of concurrency, transactions, iteration, and dynamic ports. Along with these examples, we dived into techniques of designing, developing, running, testing, and monitoring the schedules. The examples also showed the use of document specifications in XLANG schedules and the use of XPath expressions to define fields in messages. Finally, the chapter covered practical considerations in designing and deploying your schedules.

CHAPTER 14

Integrating .NET

by Susie Adams

In This Chapter

Microsoft BizTalk Server Orchestration and BizTalk Messaging provide a robust set of tools and services that enable developers to automate business and data-exchange processes. These two services, the BizTalk Messaging Engine and XLANG Scheduler Engine, are built on a foundation consisting of COM and COM+, two Microsoft technologies that provide the services necessary to develop highly scalable distributed transactional applications. In July 2000, Microsoft officially announced Microsoft.NET, its next generation development platform and next generation component technology. This chapter discusses how to integrate and develop .NET Application Integration Components (AIC) and BizTalk Orchestration implementation objects.

The chapter begins with a brief conceptual discussion of .NET and the .NET Framework, then follows with a detailed description of the steps required to develop an application that implements a Bank debit and credit transaction using Visual Basic .NET, Visual Studio .NET, and BizTalk Orchestration. After we've created the .NET debit and credit classes, we will test them using a simple ASP.NET Web application and then compile and register them so that they can be accessed from a BizTalk Orchestration schedule. We will also construct a simple C# BizTalk Messaging AIC component that will consume an XML document and then save it to a local file directory.

Note

This chapter assumes a good working knowledge of BizTalk Orchestration and BizTalk Messaging, as covered in Chapter 4, "The BizTalk Editor"; Chapter 5, "The BizTalk Mapper"; Chapter 6, "Introduction to BizTalk Messaging"; Chapter 7, "Using the BizTalk Messaging Manager"; Chapter 9, "Introducing BizTalk Orchestration"; Chapter 10, "Using the BizTalk Orchestration Designer"; and Chapter 11, "XLANG Orchestration Engine," of this book. We also assume that you have been exposed, at least conceptually, to .NET as well as to COM and COM+ programming techniques.

An Overview of .NET

Before discussing how to integrate .NET into a BizTalk application, it's useful to have a conceptual understanding of .NET and the .NET Framework. The main goal of this section is to provide a high-level introduction to .NET and the new Microsoft development platform.

What Is .NET?

Over the last decade, the application development arena has undergone a host of transformations. We've seen the migration of large mainframe green screen applications to Win32 client server applications as well as the introduction and evolution of multitier Web application development. In the past several years, we've also seen the introduction of new and exciting technologies that focus on the integration of applications regardless of the platform and programming language they were developed with. Using Web Services, a technology based on standard transport protocols and data formats such as SOAP (Simple Object Access Protocol) and XML, we can now make platform-agnostic remote procedure calls (RPC) over the Web.

If you've ever tried to build a Web application, you're painfully aware of the complexities associated with stateless multitier Web development. Building these types of Web applications, although not rocket science, was and still is time consuming and tedious using traditional development tools. Microsoft .NET is Microsoft's next generation development platform designed to make standards-based Web and Win32 application development much simpler for the developer. It's a radical new way of looking at code development that allows developers to construct applications that can communicate using both traditional and standards-based transport protocols. Some of the new enhancements include the .NET Framework, Common Language Runtime (CLR), Web Services, ASP.NET, and ADO.NET. Visual Studio .NET has also been enhanced to include several new project types, a completely integrated, language-independent development environment, and a new programming language named C#.

By now, it's obvious that .NET introduces many new features, including new form factors, such as Web Forms and Win Forms, and new technologies, such as Web Services and ADO.NET, the next version of ADO. In fact, there are so many new enhancements that it would be impossible to cover them all in a single chapter. So in this chapter we are going to narrow the focus down to the concepts required to create a managed component. Specifically, this chapter introduces the Common Language Runtime (CLR), the .NET Framework, and .NET COM+ services now known as .NET Enterprise Services. Chapter 15, "Web Services and BizTalk Server," discusses .NET Web services.

The .NET Framework

At the foundation of .NET is the .NET Framework. The .NET Framework provides a standards-based, multilanguage environment for integrating existing applications with next generation applications and services. The .NET Framework consists of three main functional areas:

- The Common Language Runtime (CLR)
- .NET Framework Class Libraries
- ASP.NET

The CLR is designed to be a safe and secure managed environment, which means that the CLR automatically manages things such as the memory of an application, hence the term managed code, using a technique known as garbage collection. The runtime also supplies managed code with services such as cross-language integration, code access security, object lifetime management, and debugging and profiling support. Unlike traditional development environments, which require a developer to master multiple frameworks, the CLR also gives developers a single common execution model and object-oriented framework independent of the programming language they are developing in or operating system they are developing for. Figures 14.1 and 14.2 show a high-level diagram of the CLR services and .NET Framework class library.

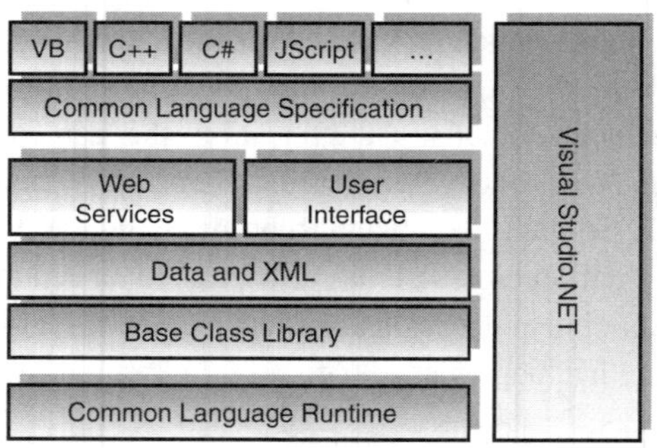

FIGURE 14.1
Common Language Runtime architecture diagram.

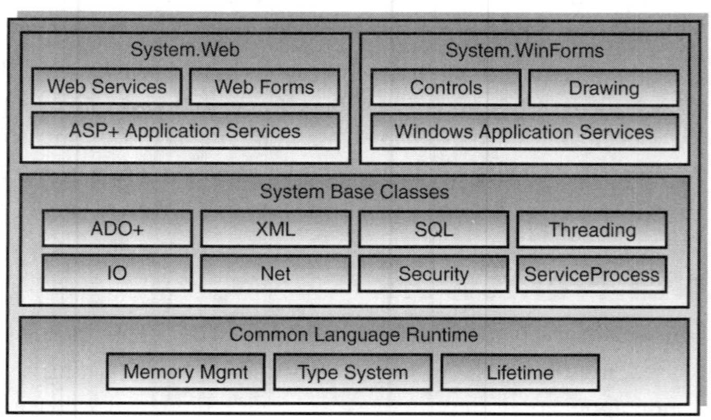

FIGURE 14.2
.NET Framework high-level architecture diagram.

To facilitate language and platform interoperability, a .NET language must adhere to two specifications: the Common Language Specification (CLS) and Common Type Specification (CTS). The CLS describes the visible features permitted in a public interface of a .NET class. The CTS defines the .NET types supported. Because the CLR manages the casting of types and marshalling of data between objects, conformance to these specifications by a .NET language permits developers to build applications that inherit objects from one another regardless of the language they are written in.

When compiling managed code, the compiler translates the .NET source code into something known as Microsoft intermediate language (MSIL), a CPU-independent set of instructions that can be converted into native code. At runtime, the MSIL code is converted into CPU-specific code by a just-in-time (JIT) compiler. The Microsoft `CLR` supplies one or more JIT compilers for each of the platforms it supports. This means that the same MSIL can be JIT compiled and executed on any supported platform. Currently, the CLR is supported on the Microsoft suite of operating system platforms including Windows 2000, 95, 98, and CE. It should also be noted that although the CLR appears to be developed exclusively for the Microsoft suite of operating systems, the list of supported platforms is expected to grow. The CLR specification has been made public and will most likely be ported by third-party organizations to additional operating system platforms in the near future. It is also possible for a developer to create a .NET-compatible language. To create a .NET compatible language, you must construct a language that complies with the CLS and CTS specifications as well as a precompiler that can omit MSIL code. You must also create a JIT compiler that can consume this MSIL code on each of the platforms you want to support. Currently, more than 15 third-party .NET languages are available, including COBOL, Perl, Python, and many more.

The deployment of a component module has also been greatly improved. A managed object's unit of deployment is an *assembly*. When managed code is compiled, it's converted into MSIL. An assembly is a self-contained unit (similar to a .DLL or .EXE), usually with a .DLL extension, that contains an object's MSIL, its metadata, and its references to any other files. The `assembly` also contains a *manifest*. The manifest enumerates the files contained in the assembly as well as the resources and required external references and/or files. This architecture eliminates the need for traditional type libraries and cumbersome registry entries and facilitates `XCOPY` deployment because an object's metadata is now self-contained. At runtime, the CLR locates and extracts the metadata from the file as needed as opposed to referencing type libraries and registry entries, eradicating DLL hell.

.NET and COM Interoperability

COM differs from the .NET Framework object model in many different areas. To facilitate the coexistence of managed and unmanaged code, the CLR provides two wrapper classes that hide the differences between both, allowing both managed and unmanaged clients to call one another's objects. Whenever your managed client calls a method on a COM object, the runtime creates a Runtime Callable wrapper (RCW). When a COM client references a method on a .NET object, the runtime creates a COM callable wrapper (CCW). Figure 14.3 depicts this process.

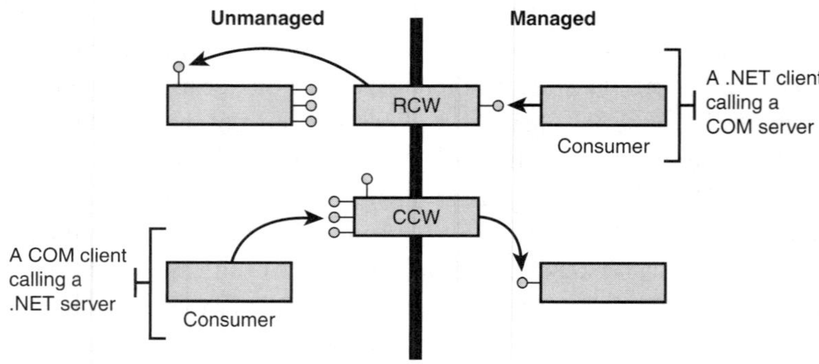

FIGURE 14.3
The COM wrapper overview.

The RCW and CCW wrappers act as proxies between the unmanaged COM code and managed .NET code. The wrappers marshal method arguments and method return values whenever the client and server have different representations of the data passed between them.

The CCW is an unmanaged COM object. It is not garbage-collected and is destroyed when the last client reference is released. After the CCW is destroyed, the managed object that it wraps is also marked for garbage collection. A few of the tasks the CCW is responsible for when a COM component references a managed .NET component include

- Managing the lifetime of the .NET component
- Creating and binding to the managed object
- Translating .NET exceptions into COM `HRESULT` values
- Synthesizing several COM interfaces (`IUnknown`, `IDispatch`, and so on) based on the object's type information
- Marshalling and translating data between the environments

The RCW is a managed object and is therefore garbage collected by the CLR. A few of its responsibilities include

- Managing the lifetime of the wrapped COM object
- Creating and binding to the underlying COM object
- Translating and marshalling data between environments
- Consuming COM interfaces and factoring the interfaces into a managed form
- Translating COM `HRESULT` values into .NET exceptions

To reference a method in a managed class from a COM client, you must first generate a COM type library for the managed object and then register it. There are several ways you can accomplish this in .NET. You can run the `type library export` command-line utility, `tlbexp.exe`, to generate a COM type library. However, it will only generate the type library; it will not register it. You could also run the `regasm.exe` command-line utility. This utility generates a type library and registers it for you automatically. Finally, you can configure Visual Studio .NET to complete both tasks automatically for you at build time by setting attributes in the properties page of a managed class.

Note

The command-line utilities for the .NET Framework are located in the `\program files\Microsoft.NET\FrameworkSDK\bin` directory on the Visual Studio .NET drive.

In our examples we will create and use both types of wrappers. We will use CCW wrappers in the Bank transaction example to reference the managed bank classes from a BizTalk Orchestration schedule, and both CCW and RCW to develop and reference a managed Application Integration Component (AIC) in the AIC example. We will also depend on Visual Studio .NET to do most of the registration work for us.

The `System.EnterpriseServices` Namespace

The CLR improves on and is a replacement for COM but not for COM+. COM+ is a runtime environment for objects that provides a set of services intended to make building scalable distributed systems easier by providing a significant portion of the underlying plumbing automatically for the developer. COM+ provides services such as database connection pooling, transaction management, object pooling, queued components, COM+ events, just-in-time activation, and several others so that a developer can focus on the development of the business logic as opposed to the underlying system services.

Like COM, the CLR relies on COM+ to provide runtime services to applications that require them; in fact, it's actually easier to configure COM+ services for the CLR environment than it is for COM. At first glance, you might think that these services are provided through the CLR-COM interoperability layer, which we discussed at length in the previous section. It is possible to use the CLR and associated interoperability wrappers to implement a COM component that uses COM+ services; however, a much more efficient programming model is available.

The CLR can supply COM+ services using an API managed through a namespace called the `System.EnterpriseServices`. All classes that want to implement COM+ services must extend the `ServicedComponent` class in that namespace as shown in the following code:

```
Imports System.EnterpriseServices
Namespace BankVB
   Public Class UpdateBankVB : Inherits ServicedComponent
      Public Function Credit() As Boolean
      ...
   End Class
End Namesace
```

> **Note**
>
> Namespaces are a new concept introduced by the .NET Framework that prevent ambiguity and simplify references when using large groups of class libraries. They also help organize objects defined in an assembly, a .NET component's unit of deployment. To learn more about namespaces and assemblies, refer to the appropriate .NET Framework documentation.

The inheritance from the `ServiceComponent` class notifies the CLR that instances of this class may require COM+ services. The CLR knows whether an instance of a class requires COM+ services by examining the use of embedded declarative attributes. The `System.EnterpriseServices` namespace defines a set of attributes that can be used to configure a class's COM+ runtime services.

In traditional COM development, a component's COM+ configuration information was stored in a database known as the COM+ catalog and configured at installation time using either the COM+ Microsoft Management Console (MMC) or a custom script that accessed the catalog directly. In the CLR world, the attributes don't take the place of the COM+ catalog; in fact, during registration, the attributes are evaluated and copied into the COM+ catalog. There is, however, one major distinction. When the CLR calls a managed component that requires COM+ services, it first evaluates the attributes in the code as opposed to the values in the COM+ catalog. Most of the COM+ attributes that we are accustomed to setting administratively are now set declaratively using code with a few exceptions in the role-based security arena. The following code displays how this is accomplished:

```
Imports System.EnterpriseServices
Namespace BankVB
   <Transaction(TransactionOption.Required)>, _
   Public Class UpdateBankVB : Inherits ServicedComponent
      Public Function Credit() As Boolean
      ...
   End Class
```

Many additional attributes facilitate the control of COM+ services; however, we are going to keep it simple and only focus on two in our example: the transaction and application name attributes. For additional information on the `System.EnterpriseServices` namespace, refer to the .NET Framework documentation.

After the appropriate configuration attributes are set, the .NET managed object configured class is ready to compile. The CLR COM+ integration layer requires that an assembly be strongly named if an object it contains implements the `ServicedComponent` interface. To strongly name an assembly, you must generate a strong name using the Strong Name command-line utility, `sn.exe`, or set the `Generate Strong Name` property in the properties page of the Visual Basic .NET file in Visual Studio .NET.

After the assembly is created, it's ready to deploy. To deploy a serviced component, you must run the `Services Installation` command line utility named `regsvcs.exe`. This utility registers the assembly as a COM component (just as if you had run `regasm.exe`), creates the COM type library (just as if you had run `tlbexp.exe`), and then deploys your configured classes to the COM+ catalog, setting the appropriate attributes based on the metadata contained within your configured classes. To enable the COM+ engine to locate your assembly at runtime, you must install the assembly into the Global Assembly Cache (GAC) using the `gacutil.exe` utility. We will walk through each of these steps in the Bank transaction and C# AIC examples later in this chapter.

Note

Remember that the unit of deployment for a managed object is an assembly that contains all the metadata required to run an object. To run an assembly, either a client must know its exact location or the assembly must be registered in the Global Assemble Cache (GAC). For additional information regarding the GAC, refer to the .NET Framework documentation.

Integrating .NET and BizTalk Server Orchestration Schedules

To illustrate how simple it is to execute a .NET managed object from a BizTalk Orchestration schedule, we are going to create a simple application that debits one bank account and credits a second. To guarantee the integrity of the application's data, we are going to add transactional support to both the BizTalk Orchestration schedule and the managed methods that update the Bank databases. The methods that require read-only access to a database will be marked as non-transactional. To execute the transfer transaction that is going to call the managed objects, we are going to construct a BizTalk Orchestration schedule that will serve as the bank transaction processing application. A completed `BankTransaction.skv` schedule is displayed in Figure 14.4. The first action in the schedule checks the balance of the account that is going to be debited to determine whether the account has sufficient funds to accommodate the transfer transaction. If the account has sufficient funds, the schedule will continue processing and call both the Debit and Credit methods in a managed Visual Basic .NET object. If the Debit or Credit transaction fails, the BizTalk Orchestration schedule will execute a compensating action notifying us, using a message box, of the failure. If the initial account does not have sufficient funds to accommodate the transaction, the schedule will again display a message box notifying us.

Note

Figure 14.4 shows the completed schedule, named `BankTransaction.skv` located in the `Schedules` directory under the `BTSDotNet` source code directory for this chapter. The complete source code for this chapter can be downloaded from the publisher's Web site.

The account data is maintained in two simple SQL Server 2000 databases named `Fidelity` and `BankofAmerica`. The following sections describe the steps required to set up the development environment, develop the .NET managed classes, register them, and then construct the BizTalk Orchestration schedule that will process an XML bank transaction.

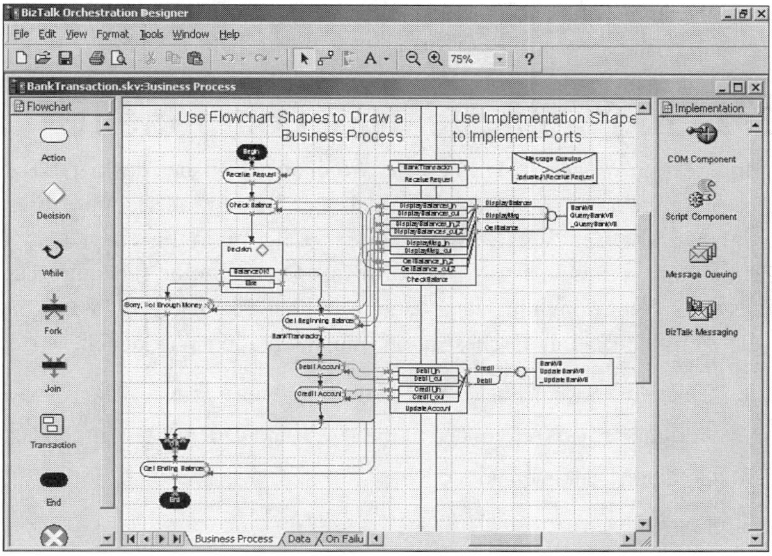

FIGURE 14.4
The completed bank BizTalk Orchestration schedule.

Setting Up the Development Environment

The development environment for this example requires an MSMQ private queue named `ReceiveRequest` and two SQL Server databases named `BankofAmerica` and `Fidelity`. The MSMQ private queue can be created by selecting the Start menu's Administrative Tools, Computer Management option. In the management console that appears, navigate to the `Services and Applications`, `Messaging`, `Private Queues` folder in the tree view. Right-click on Private Queues and select New. In the dialog that appears, enter the queue name as `ReceiveRequest`. Be aware that MSMQ queue names are case-sensitive and that the queue must be transactional.

> **Note**
>
> The source code and required setup files to create the MSMQ and databases can be found on the publisher's Web site in the `Setup` directory for this chapter.

The two database tables can be created by downloading the `CreateDBs.sql` script located on the publisher's Web site in the `Setup` directory for this chapter or manually using the SQL Server Enterprise Manager. The two database names are `Fidelity` and `BankofAmerica`. Each contains a single database table named `Accounts` with two fields, `AccountNo` and `Amount`, both integers. Each table should have a single record with the account number of 1 and an amount greater then 0. The SQL script will automatically create the databases and insert a single record in each.

Creating a Simple .NET Component

In this section we are going to create two managed Visual Basic .NET components. The classes we create are going to query, debit, and credit the account tables in the `Fidelity` and `BankofAmerica` SQL Server databases. Later on in this chapter, we are going to call the methods in these classes from a BizTalk Orchestration schedule. The following sections walk you through the steps required to build a managed component that can be selected in the BizTalk Orchestration Implementation Wizard. These steps are as follows:

1. Create the Visual Basic .NET project and class file.
2. Add the project references to the .NET and COM external objects.
3. Create the `QueryBankVB` class.
4. Create the `UpdateBankVB` class.
5. Set the Serviced Component and Interop attributes on the classes.
6. Compile and register the class(es), creating the appropriate COM type libraries and COM+ applications.

> **Note**
>
> There are several alternate ways to accomplish each of the preceding steps. In this chapter we will only explore a few of them. If you would like to learn more about building and deploying managed objects and CCWs, refer to the appropriate Microsoft .NET Framework documentation.

> **Note**
>
> The source code for the completed Bank transaction example can be downloaded from the publisher's Web site.

After we build the `BankVB.vb` managed object, we are going to create an ASP.NET application to test the methods in the classes.

Before we begin to create the managed Visual Basic .NET components, we should first discuss how to access the data in the SQL Server databases created in the setup for the Bank transaction example. The next section reviews the data access options available when developing .NET applications.

Understanding How to Access SQL Server Data

Most applications require some form of data access, and this chapter's bank transaction example is no exception. Before we begin to develop the .NET classes, we should discuss how we are going to access the data in the SQL Server databases created. If you are creating a .NET application, you generally have three data access choices: ADO.NET, ADO, and OLE DB. Typically, the newer data access technologies tend to reduce development time, simplify code, and provide much better performance. In an effort to direct the focus of this chapter toward BizTalk and .NET/COM interoperability issues, we decided to implement data access via ADO using a `RCW`.

The data for the Bank transaction example resides in two identical SQL Server 2000 databases, named `Fidelity` and `BankofAmerica`. Each database consists of one table named account with two fields, `AccountNo` and `Amount`. Figure 14.5 displays the account table structure.

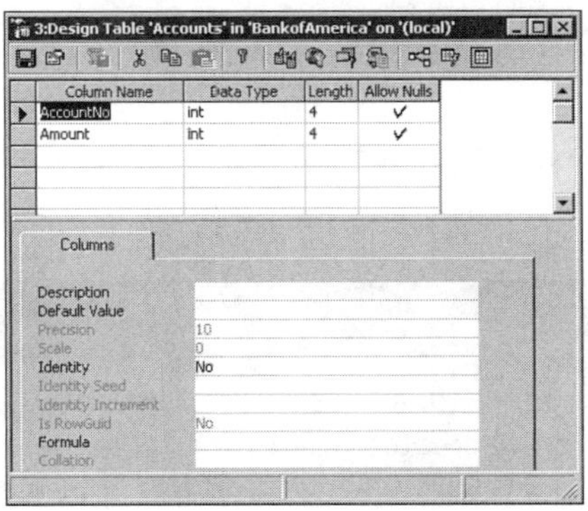

FIGURE 14.5
The bank databases account table.

Each table contains a single record with an account number of 1 and an amount of $500.

In the next section, we begin to develop our .NET managed classes.

Creating the Visual Basic .NET BankVB Project

To create the `BankVB` project and managed classes, open Visual Studio .NET and create a new Visual Basic .NET class library project named `BankVB`. Visual Studio .NET automatically creates a new class for you named `Class1.vb`. Select the `Class1.vb` file in the Solution Explorer and right-click. In the menu that appears, select the rename menu option and name the class `BankVB.vb`. Then select the `BankVB` solution in the Solution Explorer, right-click, and rename the solution `BTSDotNet`. Figure 14.6 shows the initial Visual Studio .NET project.

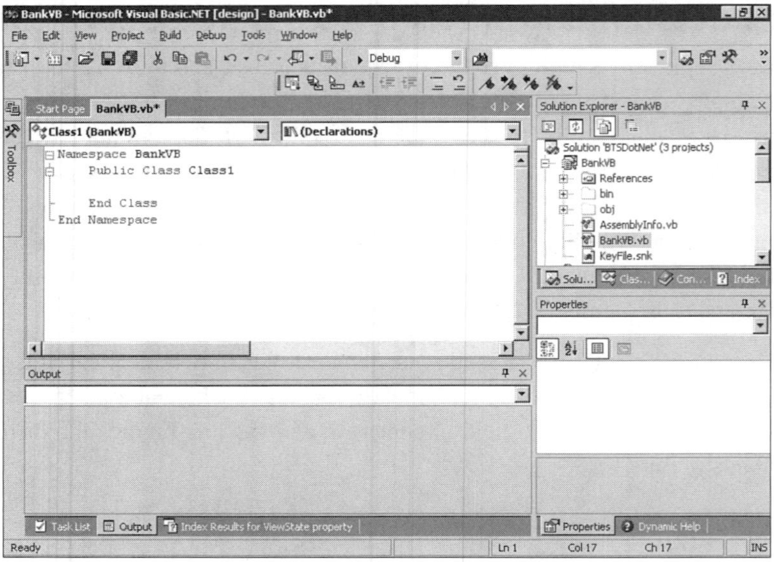

FIGURE 14.6
The `BTSDotNet` *Visual Studio .NET solution.*

The `BankVb.vb` file will contain two classes, `QueryBankVB` and `UpdateBankVB`, and a single Namespace, `BankVB`.

> **Note**
>
> Visual Basic .NET, unlike Visual Basic 6.0, allows you to have multiple classes in a single code file. In this example, we created a `.VB` file that contains two classes: one that's transactional, the UpdateBankVB class, and one that is not, the QueryBankVB class.

If you do not specify a namespace, Visual Basic .NET assumes the project name as its namespace. In this example, the namespace is going to be explicitly stated as `BankVB`. Listing 14.1 displays a code snippet that shows the structure of the methods in each class that we are going to create without their associated implementations.

LISTING 14.1 The `BankVB` Namespace

```
Namespace BankVB
    Public Class UpdateBankVB
        Public Function Credit(ByVal AccountNo As Integer, ByVal
➥AmountToCredit As Integer, ByVal myBank As String) As Boolean
        End Function
```

LISTING 14.1 continued

```
        Public Function Debit(ByVal AccountNo As Integer, ByVal
➥AmountToDebit As Integer, ByVal myBank As String) As Boolean
        End Function
    End Class

    Public Class QueryBankVB
        Public Function DisplayBalances(ByVal Bank1Account As
➥Integer, ByVal Bank1 As String, ByVal Bank2Account As Integer,
➥ByVal Bank2 As String) As String
        End Function

        Public Function DisplayMsg(ByVal sMessage As String)
        End Function

        Private Function GetBalance(ByVal AccountNo As Integer,
 ➥ByVal myBank As String) As String
        End Function
    End Class
End Namespace
```

Before we add the source code for the methods in both classes, we need to first set some configuration items on the project. The next section discusses how to accomplish this.

Setting Project References and Importing Namespaces

To call an external object, you must reference it explicitly in the Visual Studio .NET Explorer. In the `BankVB` project we reference three .NET namespaces and one unmanaged COM DLL to access the databases using ADO. To reference a namespace, you must add the namespace to the reference folder in the Visual Studio .NET Solution Explorer. To reference an unmanaged object, you must also add a reference, but to the COM object. When you add the reference to the `COM` object, the designer automatically creates an RCW for the unmanaged object and includes the assembly for that unmanaged object in the `bin` directory of the solution.

To add a reference to the `BankVB` solution, right-click on the references item in the Solution Explorer and select the `Add Reference` menu item. In the dialog that appears, select the .NET tab. The tab should display a list of .NET objects as shown in Figure 14.7.

The only namespace that needs to be exclusively added to the reference folder in the `BankVB` project is the `System.EnterpriseServices` namespace. The `System` namespace is referenced, by default, in Visual Studio .NET.

FIGURE 14.7
Adding namespace references.

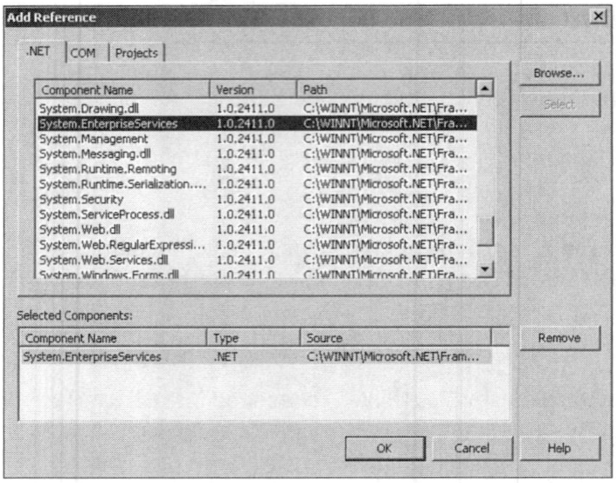

When calling objects in a referenced namespace, you can choose to either fully qualify each reference with the full namespace dot notation or simply add an imports statement prior to the namespace declaration in the managed code. In the `BankVB` example, we use the `Imports` directive. Three `Imports` statements need to be added to the top of the `BankVB.vb` file as displayed in the following code:

```
Imports System
Imports System.Runtime.InteropServices
Imports System.EnterpriseServices
```

The `System` namespace is the root namespace for all fundamental types in the .NET Framework. The `System.Runtime.InteropServices` namespace is a sub-namespace of the `System` namespace that allows you to reference the `COMVisible` attribute. Without the `COMVisible` attribute, which will be added later, you would be unable to view the class methods in the BizTalk Orchestration COM Implementation Wizard. The `System.EnterpriseServices` namespace supplies the managed code with access to the `COM+` API.

As stated earlier, we reference the SQL Server databases using ADO. To add the reference to the ADO COM object, again select the References item in the Solution Explorer and right-click. In the pop-up menu that appears, select the `Add New Reference` menu item. In the dialog that appears, select the COM tab. To reference the `ADO.dll` object, select the `Microsoft ActiveX Data Objects 2.6 Library`, as shown in Figure 14.8.

When you select OK, a message box appears asking whether you want to create a `Primary Interop Assembly` for this type library and have a wrapper automatically generated for you, as shown in Figure 14.9. Select `Yes` in this dialog.

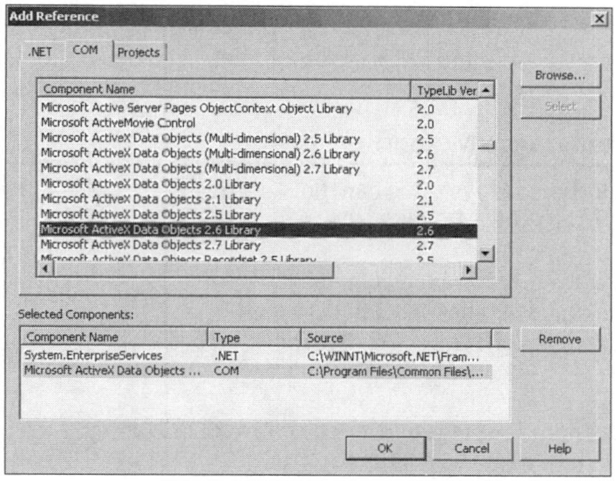

FIGURE 14.8
Adding a reference to ADO.

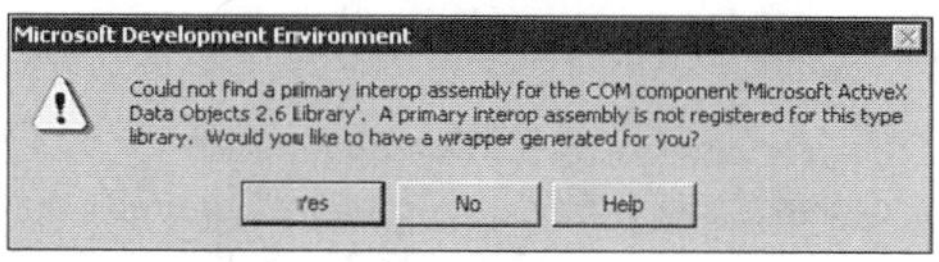

FIGURE 14.9
Creating the Primary Interop Assembly and wrapper.

Behind the scenes, Visual Studio .NET automatically creates the .NET Interop assembly for you and places it in the appropriate solution directory. The `ADO Interop` assembly object is copied to the `bin` directory of the `BankVB` project and is named `Interop.ADODB_2_6_.dll`. To view this file in your `Solution Explorer`, select the `Show All Files` button at the top of the `Solution Explorer`.

> **Note**
>
> You could have also created the `Interop` assembly and wrapper object manually by running the command-line utility `tlbimp.exe`.

We are now ready to add the source code for both the `QueryBankVB` and `UpdateBankVB` Visual Basic .NET classes. The following sections describe how to accomplish this.

Creating the `QueryBankVB` Class

The `QueryBankVB` class contains three methods: `DisplayBalances`, `DisplayMsg`, and `GetBalance`. The `GetBalance` method is the only method that requires access to the SQL Server databases and does nothing more than query the account table for the account balance. The `DisplayBalances` and `DisplayMsg` methods accept and supply arguments to a

Windows message box. To create the `QueryBankVB` class in the `BankVB.vb` file, add the code displayed in Listings 14.2 and 14.3 to the `BankVB.vb` file.

LISTING 14.2 The `GetBalance` Method

```
Public Function GetBalance(ByVal AccountNo As Integer,
➥ByVal myBank As String) As String

            Dim myConn As New ADODB.Connection()
            Dim myCommand As New ADODB.Command()
            Dim myConnectionString As String

            Try
                myConnectionString = "Provider=SQLOLEDB.1;
➥Persist Security Info=False;User ID=sa;Initial Catalog=" & myBank &
➥ ";Data Source=SUSIEA"

                myConn.Open(myConnectionString)

                myCommand.ActiveConnection = myConn
                myCommand.CommandType = ADODB.CommandTypeEnum.adCmdStoredProc
                myCommand.CommandText = "AccountBalance"

                myCommand.Parameters.Refresh()
                myCommand.Parameters("@AccountNo").Value = AccountNo

                myCommand.Execute()

                GetBalance = myCommand.Parameters("@AccountBalance").Value
            Catch ex As Exception
                MsgBox("Error: " & ex.ToString())
            Finally
                myCommand = Nothing
                myConn.Close()
                myConn = Nothing
            End Try
        End Function
```

The `GetBalance` method accepts two parameters, `myBank` and `AccountNo`, and returns the account balance. Each database in our example contains a stored procedure named `AccountBalance` that accepts one parameter, `AccountNo`, and returns a single parameter named `AccountBalance`. As you can see, the reference to the SQL Server database uses the familiar ADO object model. Also notice that we implement the new .NET error syntax called `Try, Catch, Finally`.

LISTING 14.3 The `DisplayBalances` and `DisplayMsg` Methods

```
Public Function DisplayBalances(ByVal Bank1Account As Integer,
➥ByVal Bank1 As String, ByVal Bank2Account As Integer,
```

LISTING 14.3 continued

```
➥ByVal Bank2 As String) As String
            Dim iBank1 As Integer
            Dim iBank2 As Integer

            iBank1 = GetBalance(1, Bank1)
            iBank2 = GetBalance(1, Bank2)
            DisplayBalances = Bank1 & ": " & CStr(iBank1) &
➥"     " & Bank2 & ": " & CStr(iBank2)
            DisplayMsg(DisplayBalances)
        End Function

        Public Function DisplayMsg(ByVal sMessage As String)
            MsgBox(sMessage)
        End Function
```

The `DisplayBalances` method accepts both the account number and bank name as arguments. It calls the `GetBalance` method displayed in Listing 14.2 to retrieve the balance of each account and then display the balance of each. The `DisplayMsg` method simply accepts a single string and supplies it as a parameter to the `MsgBox` function.

These three methods comprise the public class `QueryBankVB` that resides in the `BankVB` namespace. Due to their nontransactional read-only characteristics, the methods in this class do not require the COM+ services supplied by the `System.EnterpriseServices` namespace.

Creating the `UpdateBankVB` Class

In the Bank transfer transaction example, the `BankVB` namespace contains a second class named `UpdateBankVB`. The `UpdateBankVB` class contains two methods, `Debit` and `Credit`, that accept three parameters, `AccountNo`, `Amount`, and `Bank`. To create the `UpdateBankVB` class, open the `BankVB.vb` file in Visual Studio .NET and add the code displayed in Listings 14.4 and 14.5 to the end of the file.

LISTING 14.4 The `Credit` Method

```
Public Function Credit(ByVal AccountNo As Integer,
➥ByVal AmountToCredit As Integer, ByVal myBank As String) As Boolean
            Dim myConn As New ADODB.Connection()
            Dim myCommand As New ADODB.Command()
            Dim myConnectionString As String

            myConnectionString = "Provider=SQLOLEDB.1;
➥Persist Security Info=False;User ID=sa;Initial Catalog=" &
➥myBank & ";Data Source=Susiea"
```

LISTING 14.4 continued

```
        Try
            myConn.Open(myConnectionString)

            myCommand.ActiveConnection = myConn
            myCommand.CommandType = ADODB.CommandTypeEnum.adCmdStoredProc
            myCommand.CommandText = "Credit"
            myCommand.Parameters.Refresh()
            myCommand.Parameters("@AccountNo").Value = AccountNo
            myCommand.Parameters("@AmountToCredit").Value = AmountToCredit

            myCommand.Execute()

            Credit = CBool(myCommand.Parameters("@AccountBalance").Value)
            Credit = True

        Catch ex As Exception
            MsgBox("Error: " & ex.ToString())
            Credit = False
        Finally
            myCommand = Nothing
            myConn.Close()
            myConn = Nothing
        End Try
    End Function
```

Each of the `Bank` SQL Server databases contain two stored procedures named `Credit` and `Debit` that each accept two parameters, `AccountNo` and `AmountToCredit` or `AmountToDebit`, respectively. If the debit or credit is successful, the methods return a boolean value of `true`; if they are not successful, they return `false`. The code in each of these methods creates a connection to the database and then executes either the `Credit` or `Debit` stored procedure using the ADO object model. The `Debit` method is displayed in Listing 14.5.

LISTING 14.5 The `Debit` Method

```
Public Function Debit(ByVal AccountNo As Integer,
➥ByVal AmountToDebit As Integer, ByVal myBank As String) As Boolean
        Dim myConn As New ADODB.Connection()
        Dim myCommand As New ADODB.Command()
        Dim myConnectionString As String

        myConnectionString = "Provider=SQLOLEDB.1;
➥Persist Security Info=False;User ID=sa;Initial Catalog="
➥& myBank & ";Data Source=susiea"
```

LISTING 14.5 continued

```
        Try
            myConn.Open(myConnectionString)
            myCommand.ActiveConnection = myConn
            myCommand.CommandType = ADODB.CommandTypeEnum.adCmdStoredProc
            myCommand.CommandText = "Debit"

            myCommand.Parameters.Refresh()
            myCommand.Parameters("@AccountNo").Value = AccountNo
            myCommand.Parameters("@AmountToDebit").Value = AmountToDebit

            myCommand.Execute()

            Debit = CBocl(myCommand.Parameters("@AccountBalance").Value)
            Debit = True
        Catch ex As Exception
            MsgBox("Error: " & ex.ToString())
            Debit = False
        Finally
            myCommand = Nothing
            myConn.Close()
            myConn = Nothing
        End Try
    End Function
```

So, what happens if the credit method succeeds and the debit method fails within a single transfer transaction? If we leave the code as is, the credited account would be making money at the expense of the banking institution. To ensure that this doesn't occur, we need to do a few things. First we need to either write custom compensation logic to reverse the updates manually or we need to apply automatic transaction services using the COM+ services API provided in the `System.EnterpriseServices` namespace. COM+ automatic transactions guarantee that each method is capable of rolling back an update. To guarantee that both methods either succeed or fail, we must wrap the calls to both inside a transaction. In this case, we are going to use a BizTalk Orchestration schedule to call the methods, so when we build the schedule, we will need to add a transaction shape to wrap the method calls. In the `BankVB.vb` example, we depend on both the `System.EnterpriseServices` namespace and BizTalk Orchestration to automatically handle transaction management.

To incorporate COM+ services into our `BankVB` example, we need to add configuration attributes to the classes and project we just created. The next section describes how to accomplish this.

Setting Serviced Component and Interop Attributes

To implement a class that incorporates COM+ services, the class must derive from the `ServicedComponent` class. In the `BankVB.vb` example, the `UpdateBankVB` class inherits the `ServicedComponent` class using the following syntax:

```
Public Class UpdateBankVB : Inherits ServicedComponent
```

As discussed earlier, COM+ properties are specified as declarative attributes in the .NET world. In the `BankVB.vb` example, we are going to apply three attributes: `TransactionAttribute`, `AutoComplete`, and `ApplicationName`.

The `TransactionAttribute` provides the equivalent of the COM+ Explorer transactional support traditionally configured using the COM+ Microsoft Management Console (MMC). In the `BankVB.vb` example, we set the value of the attribute to `Required`. The `Transaction` attribute is set once per managed class.

The `AutoComplete` attribute instructs the runtime to automatically call the `SetAbort` function if the transaction encounters an exception and must be set on each method in the class. If an exception is not thrown, the `SetComplete` function is automatically called by the runtime.

The `ApplicationName` attribute is equivalent to the COM+ application name traditionally created in the COM+ Explorer and is specified once per namespace. To add these attributes, open the `BankVB.vb` file in Visual Studio .NET and add them as displayed in Listing 14.6. The `AutoComplete` and `Transaction` attributes should also be added to the `QueryBankVB` class.

LISTING 14.6 COM+ Serviced Component Declarative Attributes

```
Imports System
Imports System.Runtime.InteropServices
Imports System.EnterpriseServices

' - Registration details -
' Supply the COM+ application name.
<Assembly: ApplicationName("BankComponent")>

Namespace BankVB
    <Transaction(TransactionOption.Required)> _
    Public Class UpdateBankVB : Inherits ServicedComponent

        <AutoComplete()> _
        Public Function Credit(ByVal AccountNo As Integer,
➥ByVal AmountToCredit As Integer, ByVal myBank As String) As Boolean
            Dim myConn As New ADODB.Connection()
            Dim myCommand As New ADODB.Command()
...
```

Two additional attributes, `COMClass` and `COMVisible`, must be set to properly expose the managed class to an unmanaged COM object. `COMClass` accepts a GUID that uniquely identifies the COM type library generated for COM interoperability, and the `COMVisible` attribute ensures that the public managed methods are visible in the BizTalk `GUI` designers. Each managed class must be marked with a unique `COMClass` attribute and `GUID`, and the assembly must be marked as `COMVisible`. You can create the `GUID` by using the Visual Studio .NET tools, `CreateGUID` menu option. In the dialog that appears, select the Registry Format option and click Copy to copy it to the Clipboard as displayed in Figure 14.10. To add the attributes to the `BankVB.vb` file, open the file in Visual Studio .NET and add them as displayed in Listing 14.7.

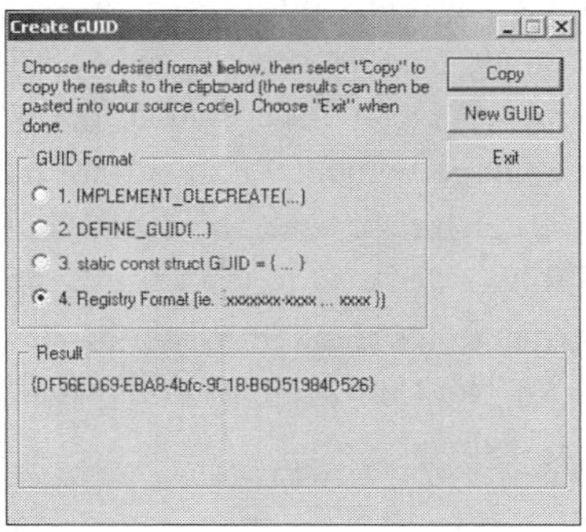

FIGURE 14.10
Generating a unique GUID.

LISTING 14.7 Additional COM Interop Attributes

```
Imports System
Imports System.Runtime.InteropServices
Imports System.EnterpriseServices

' - Registration details -
' Supply the COM+ application name.
<Assembly: ApplicationName("BankComponent")>

<Assembly: ComVisible(True)>
Namespace BankVB
    <Transaction(TransactionOption.Required), _
    ComClass("73297D71-DA59-43b6-9511-9743B379BF02")> _
    Public Class UpdateBankVB : Inherits ServicedComponent
        ' Define a local variable to store the DSN value.

        <AutoComplete()> _
        Public Function Credit(ByVal AccountNo As Integer,
➥ByVal AmountToCredit As Integer, ByVal myBank As String) As Boolean
            Dim myConn As New ADODB.Connection()
            Dim myCommand As New ADODB.Command()
```

Now that we have added the `COMClass` attributes to both classes and the `COMVisible` attribute to the `BankVB.vb` file, we need to compile and register the `BankVB` project. Before we can compile it, however, we need to set a few properties using the `Properties` dialog of the `BankVB` project in Visual Studio .NET. The following sections walk through each of the steps required to compile and register the `BankVB.vb` object in COM+.

Compiling and Registering the Component

In the Bank transaction example, we will call the managed Visual Basic .NET object from a COM client represented as a BizTalk Orchestration schedule. The BizTalk Orchestration schedule will instantiate the components from inside the context of a transaction. To call the managed object from a COM client that requires COM+ transaction services, you must first compile it and create a COM type library referencing the managed assembly. Because the managed object is also a serviced component that supports transactions, you also need to sign the managed object with a strong name key file prior to compiling it. Finally, we will need to register the assembly with COM+. To accomplish this, we need to add several additional attributes to the `BankVB.vb` file we have created, set some additional project properties in the `BankVB` Visual Studio .NET project, and execute a few command-line utilities. The following sections walk through each of the steps required to accomplish these tasks.

Creating a COM Type Library

To enable a COM client to call a managed component, the managed component must create and register a COM type library reflecting the metadata contained inside its assembly. There are several different ways to create and register a type library for a managed component. In previous sections of this chapter, we discussed the `tlbexp.exe` and `regasm.exe` command-line utilities that generate type libraries, the latter of which also automatically registers it as a COM object. In the `BankVB.vb` example, we will register the managed component using the configuration settings available in Visual Studio .NET.

To mark a managed object as COM-interoperable using Visual Studio .NET, select the `BankVB.vb` file in the Solution Explorer and right click. In the menu that appears, select the `Properties` option. Next, select the `Configuration Properties` folder's `Build` option and check the `Register for COM Interop` check box displayed in Figure 14.11. This instructs the Visual Studio designer to automatically generate and register a COM type library for your managed assembly.

Next, we need to sign the assembly with a strong name. To accomplish this, we add an `Assembly` attribute to the code we created. The following section describes how to accomplish this.

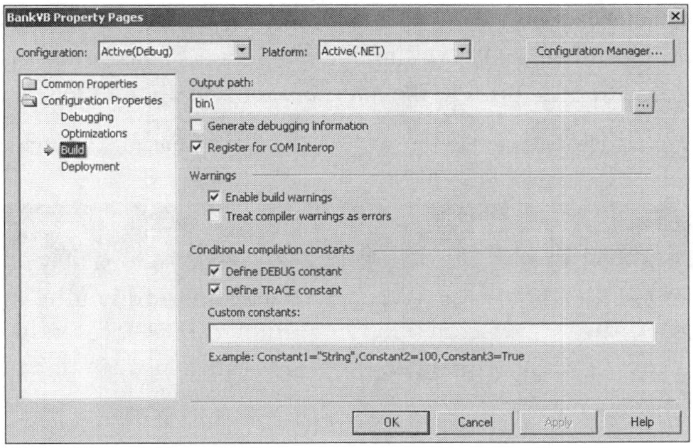

FIGURE 14.11
Marking an assembly for COM interop in Visual Studio .NET.

Creating a Strong-Named Assembly

As stated earlier, a serviced component must be strong-named. A strong name consists of the assembly simple text name, version number, and culture information, if provided, plus a public key and a digital signature. It is generated from an assembly file using the corresponding private key.

> **Note**
>
> After an assembly is created, you cannot sign it with a strong name. To create a strong-named assembly, you must sign it with a strong name when you create it.

There are two different ways to sign an assembly with a strong name:

- Using the `AL.exe` command-line Assembly Generation Tool
- Using declarative assembly attributes to insert the strong name information in your code

In the `BankVB.vb` example, we rely on an `Assembly` attribute in the source code. To mark an assembly as requiring a strong name using an attribute, you need to create a `.snk` key file and then add a reference to that key file to the `BankVb.vb` code. You can create the key file using the strong name `sn.exe` command-line utility. To accomplish this, navigate to the directory containing the utility and then enter the following text:

```
Sn -k BankVB.dll Bankvb.snk
```

This creates a key file named `Bankvb.snk`. After you create the file, add it to your `BankVB` solution; then select the `BankVB.vb` file in the Solution Explorer and open it. Next, add the following line of code prior to the namespace declaration in the `BankVB.vb` code.

```
<Assembly: AssemblyKeyFileAttribute("c:\btsdotnet\bankvb\Bankvb.snk")>
```

Note

The `AssemblyKeyFileAttribute` properties require a full pathname to the `.snk` key filename. The `sn.exe` command-line utility can be located in the `\Program Files\Microsoft Visual Studio .Net\FrameworkSDK\bin` directory.

We are now ready to build the `BankVB.vb` file. Select the `BankVB` project in the Solution Explorer and right-click. In the pop-up menu that appears, select the `Build` menu option. The assembly has now been signed with a strong name. Next, we need to register the assembly with COM+. The following section describes the steps required to accomplish this.

The next step is to compile your code. To compile `BankVB.vb`, select the Visual Studio .NET Build, Build menu option.

Registering a Managed Serviced Component with COM+

To register the managed component with COM+, you must run the `regsvcs.exe` command-line utility. The command-line utility accomplishes the following tasks:

- Loads and registers an assembly
- Generates, registers, and installs a type library into a specified COM+ 1.0 application
- Configures services that you have added programmatically to your class

To run the `regsvcs.exe` command-line utility, open a command prompt and navigate to the local directory where the `Bankvb.dll` assembly is located, and then type the following:

```
Regsvcs.exe Bankvb.dll
```

Note

Your assembly must be strong-named to run this utility. Serviced components can also be registered automatically by the CLR at runtime in certain situations. In our case, we are restricted to manual registration. If you want to learn more about registering serviced components, refer to the appropriate .NET Framework documentation.

The `regsvcs.exe` command-line utility is located in the `\WINDOWS\Microsoft.NET\Framework\v1.XXXX` directory. When you run the utility, ignore the warning in the command window that states that "The class '`BankVB.UpdateBankVB`' has no class interface, which means that late bound calls cannot take advantage of `AutoComplete` methods." This will have no effect on this example.

To verify that the managed object was added to the COM+ catalog, open the COM+ catalog by selecting the Start menu's Programs, Administrative Tools option and then select the Component Services option. If the component was registered successfully, you should see a COM+ application named `BankComponent` on the local system as shown in Figure 14.12.

FIGURE 14.12
The `BankComponent` *COM+ application.*

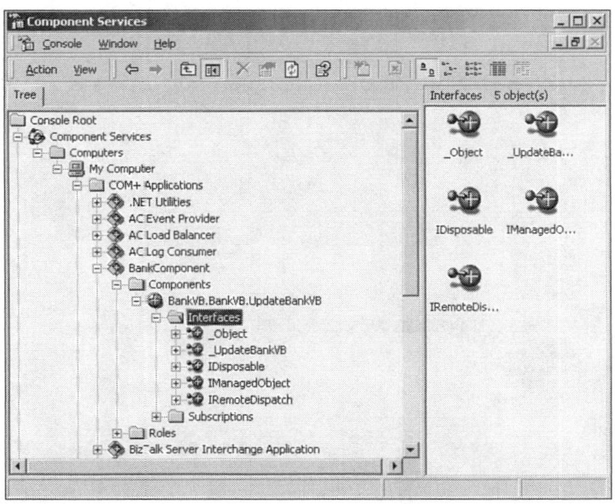

Now that the component has been registered, we can test its methods from a client application. In the following section, we will create a simple ASP.NET Web form to test the `QueryBankVB` and `UpdateBankVB` classes just created.

Creating a .NET Test Client

To test the `QueryBankVB` and `UpdateBankVB` classes, we will create a new ASP.NET project named `BankVBWebClient` and add it to the `BTSDotNet` Visual Studio .NET solution. To create the new project, open the `BTSDotNet` solution, select the solution name in the Solution Explorer, and right-click. In the pop-up menu that appears, select `Add`, New Project from the menu. In the dialog that appears, select Visual Basic Projects ASP.NET

Web Application and name the application `BankVBWebClient` off the root directory of your local Web server.

The application will consist of a single ASP.NET (`.aspx`) page named `BankVBClient.aspx`. When we created the new ASP.NET application, Visual Studio .NET automatically created a new Web form named `WebForm1.aspx`. To rename the form, select it in the Solution Explorer and right-click. In the pop-up menu that appears, select the rename menu option and name it `BankVBClient.aspx`.

Next, we need to add a reference to the managed `BankVB` object in the Visual Studio .NET Explorer `References` folder.

To add the reference to `BankVB`, select the `References` folder under the `BankVBWebClient` folder in the Solution Explorer and right-click. In the pop-up menu that appears, select the Add Reference menu item. In the dialog that appears, select the COM tab and navigate to and select the `BankVB` object as shown in Figure 14.13. Remember that the `BankVB` project was compiled with `COM` interoperability turned on, which now requires the `BankVBWebClient` project to reference the managed code using COM interoperability.

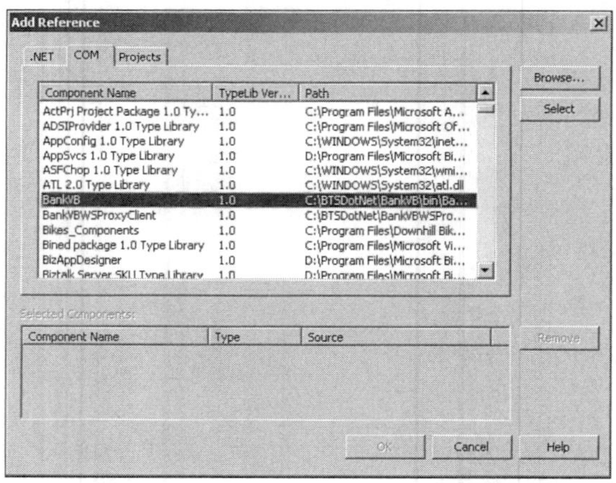

FIGURE 14.13
Adding the `BankVB` *COM reference.*

The `BankVBWebClient` Web form has several controls on it that allow you to enter the bank account names, numbers, and amount to transfer. The two buttons on the form take the data entered and execute the `GetBalance`, `Credit`, and `Debit` methods. Figure 14.14 shows the `BankVBWebClient.aspx` Web form.

Listing 14.8 displays the code behind the Get Balance VB Button.

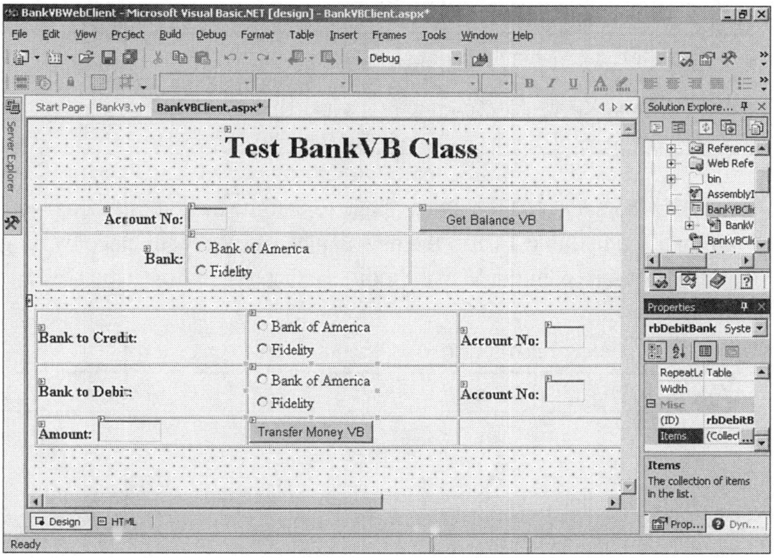

FIGURE 14.14
The `BankVBWebClient` *Web form.*

LISTING 14.8 The Balance Button Code

```
Private Sub btnBalance_Click(ByVal sender As System.Object,
➥ByVal e As System.EventArgs) Handles btnBalance.Click
        Dim oBank As New BankVB.QueryBankVB()

        Dim iReturn As Integer
        iReturn = oBank.GetBalance(txtBalanceAccountNo.Text,
➥rbBalanceBank.SelectedItem.Value)
        Response.Write("Return Value: " & iReturn)

    End Sub
```

Listing 14.9 shows the code behind the Transfer Money VB button.

LISTING 14.9 The Transfer Money Button Code

```
Private Sub btnTransfer_Click(ByVal sender As System.Object,
➥ByVal e As System.EventArgs) Handles btnTransfer.Click
        Dim oBank As New BankVB.BankVB.UpdateBankVB()

        Dim bReturn As Boolean
        bReturn = oBank.Credit(txtCreditAccount.Text,
➥txtTransferAmount.Text, rbCreditBank.SelectedItem.Value)
        Response.Write("Credit : " & bReturn)
```

LISTING 14.9 continued

```
        bReturn = oBank.Debit(txtDebitAccount.Text,
➥txtTransferAmount.Text, rbDebitBank.SelectedItem.Value)
        Response.Write("Debit : " & bReturn)
    End Sub
```

To modify the `BankVBClient.aspx` page to call the `BankVB` methods, add the Web Forms controls listed in Table 14.1 to the new `BankVBClient.aspx` page by dragging them from the Web Forms toolbox in the Visual Studio .NET Designer onto the Design view of the page.

TABLE 14.1 Web Forms Controls for `BankVBClient.aspx`

Control Type	*Name*	*Values*
Button	`BtnBalance`	
Button	`btnTransfer`	
Text Box	`txtBalanceAccountNo`	
Radio Button	`rbBalanceBank`	BankofAmerica, Fidelity
Radio Button	`rbCreditBank`	BankofAmerica, Fidelity
Radio Button	`rbDebitBank`	BankofAmerica, Fidelity
Text Box	`txtDebitAccount`	
Text Box	`txtCreditAccount`	
Labels(7)	n/a	Account No:, Bank:, Bank to Credit:, Bank to Debit:, Amount:, Account No:, Account No:

Next, add the two event routines displayed in Listings 14.8 and 14.9 to the application by double-clicking on each of the Web Form buttons in the Design page. Finally, compile and run the page by selecting the `BankVBWebClient` project in the Solution Explorer and right-clicking. In the pop-up menu that appears, select the `Build` menu option. On completion of the build, select the `BankVBClient.aspx` page in the Solution Explorer and right-click. In the pop-up menu that appears, select the `View in Browser` menu option. To execute the code, enter an Account No of 1 and amounts to transfer less than $500.

Creating the Bank Orchestration Schedule

Now that we've successfully created, registered, and tested the `BankVB.vb` managed code, we can begin to design and construct the BizTalk Orchestration schedule that will also call its methods. Earlier in the chapter, Figure 14.4 displayed a completed version of the `BankTransaction.skv` file.

> **Note**
>
> This section assumes that you are familiar with constructing and connecting actions in the left-hand side of BizTalk Orchestration Designer. The topics in this section focus on the implementation details specific to the managed objects.

But before we begin to build the schedule, we need to first construct a Transaction document. The Bank transaction schedule begins execution on the receipt of an XML file that contains the Bank names, accounts, and transfer amount. The XML file is dropped into a private MSMQ queue named `ReceiveRequest`. In the next section, we will discuss the structure of this document and how to create it.

The XML Bank Transaction Document

The bank schedule consumes a simple XML document that consists of the debit and credit bank names and their account numbers as well as the amount of money to transfer. Figure 14.15 shows an instance of the `BankTransInstance.xml` document.

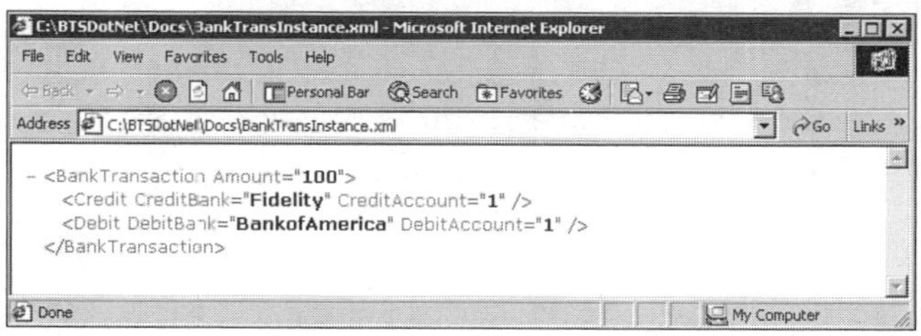

FIGURE 14.15
The XML bank transaction XML file.

To reference this document from the BizTalk Orchestration Schedule, we need to create a BizTalk `XDR` schema that defines the structure of the document using the BizTalk Editor. There are several ways to create the document. The easiest way is to create an instance of the XML document and then import it into BizTalk Editor. To accomplish this, open Notepad, copy the text from Figure 14.16 to the file, and then save it. Then open the BizTalk Editor; select the `Tools`, `Import` menu option; and choose the Well Formed XML Instance option. When the dialog appears, select the file you just created. You can also download the code from the publisher's Web site and import the `BankTransInstance.XML` document. The `BankTransaction.XML` BizTalk schema is displayed in Figure 14.16.

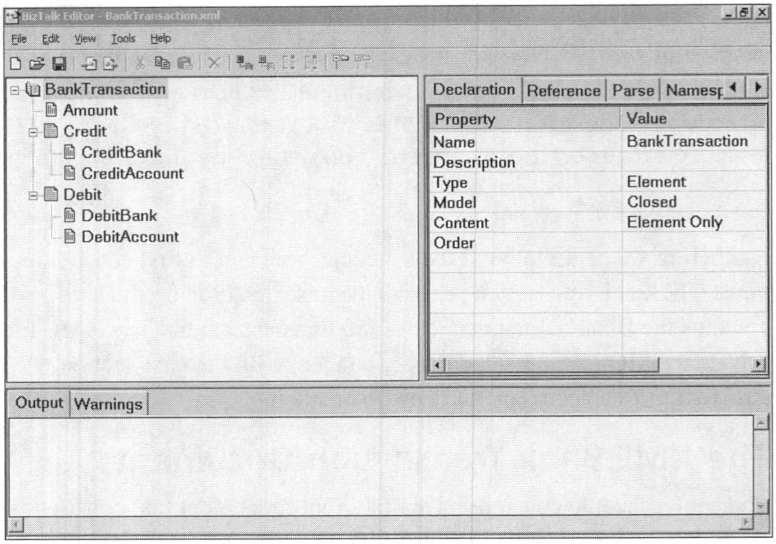

FIGURE 14.16
The XML bank transaction BizTalk schema.

> **Note**
>
> The `BankTransaction.skv` schedule file located in the `Schedules` directory of the source code on the publisher's Web site requires this document to live in the `\BTSDotNet\Docs` directory.

The BizTalk XDR schema will be referenced in the `BankTransaction.skv` schedule. Now that we have created the BizTalk schema, we are ready to begin to construct the `BankTransaction.skv` schedule.

Creating a New Orchestration Schedule

In this section, we are going to create a new schedule named `BankTransaction.skv`. The `BankTransaction.skv` schedule displayed in Figure 14.4 begins with the receipt of an XML bank transaction file from an MSMQ private queue named `ReceiveRequest`. The first action in the schedule, `ReceiveRequest`, is bound to the MSMQ queue that waits for an XML message of type `BankTransaction`. After the receipt of the XML document, the schedule verifies whether there is enough money in the account to be debited by calling the `GetBalance` method in the `QueryBankVB` class. Then a decision shape evaluates the return value from the method to determine whether it should continue processing the bank transaction.

If the account balance is sufficient, the schedule then executes the `Debit` and `Credit` methods in the `UpdateBankVB` class. Otherwise, it executes the `DisplayMsg` method in the `QueryBankVB` class. If for some reason the `Debit` or `Credit` method fails, we add a transaction shape to execute an On Failure action named `Error`. The `Error` action calls the `QueryBankVB DisplayMsg` method notifying us that the transaction failed. The On Failure of BankTransaction Orchestration tab is displayed in Figure 14.17.

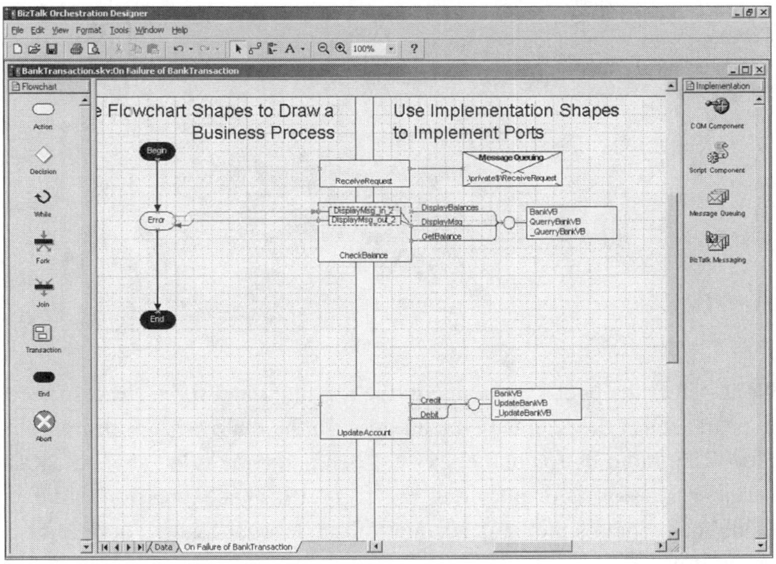

FIGURE 14.17
The compensating transaction.

The schedule contains seven actions bound to managed objects: `Check Balance`, `Get Beginning Balances`, `Get Ending Balances`, `Sorry Not Enough Money` J, `Debit Account`, `Credit Account`, and `Error`.

To create the `BankTransaction.skv` schedule, open the BizTalk Orchestration Designer and rename the schedule `BankTransaction.skv` by selecting the Save As menu option. Then add and connect the Actions, Decision, Fork, and End shapes to the left-hand side of the business process as displayed in Figure 14.4. Next, add a Message Queue implementation shape to the Designer for the `.\private$\ReceiveRequest` private queue and connect it to the Receive Request action. In the XML Communication Wizard dialog that appears when connecting to the Receive Request action, select the Receive option and click Next. In the `XML Communication Wizard` that appears, select the Rename Current Message radio button and name the message `BankTransaction`. In the XML Translation Information Wizard dialog that appears, select the Receive XML Message from the Queue radio button and click Next. In the Message Type Information dialog that appears, enter `BankTransaction` and click Next. In the Message Specification Information dialog, select the `BankTransaction.xml` BizTalk `XDR` schema you created and then click the Validate Message Against the Specification check box. Next, select the Add button and add the `Amount`, `CreditBank`, `CreditAccount`, `DebitBank`, and `DebitAccount` fields as displayed in Figure 14.18.

FIGURE 14.18
The XML Communication Wizard message specification.

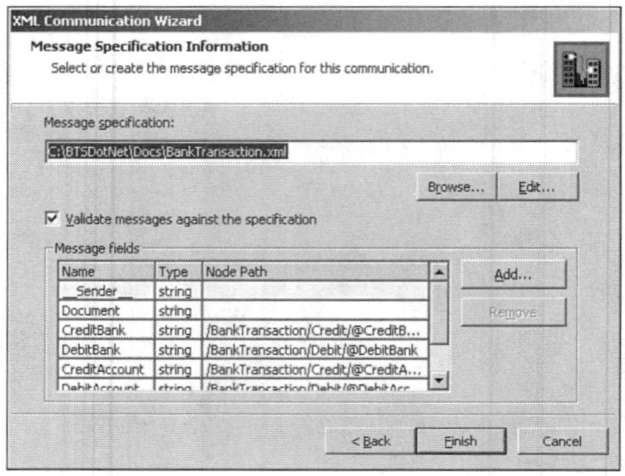

Next, select the `Decision` shape in the Designer and right-click. In the pop-up menu that appears, select the Add Rule menu item. In the dialog that appears, select the Create a New Rule radio button and click `OK`. Then name the rule `Balance OK!` and enter the script expression as displayed in Figure 14.19. This expression will evaluate a return value that contains the bank account of the account that is going to be debited by the transaction amount. If the account balance minus the transaction amount is greater than or equal to zero, the schedule will continue processing the transaction.

FIGURE 14.19
The Balance OK Decision shape rule.

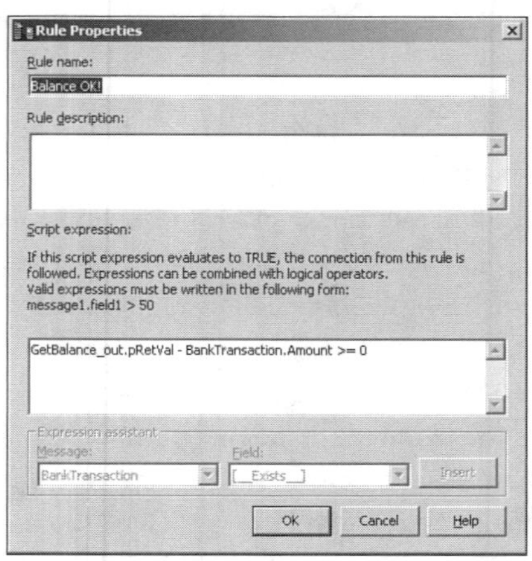

Note

The publisher's Web site contains a schedule named `BankTransactionStart.skv` that has been preconfigured with the initial steps to this point.

The next two sections discuss how to bind the remaining actions in the schedule to the appropriate methods in the managed object. We will also learn how to incorporate transaction management.

Referencing a .NET Managed Component

Referencing a managed object is as simple as referencing a standard unmanaged COM object. You simply drag the COM Component implementation object onto the designer and step through the wizard. Because we choose to register the managed `BankVB` object with COM, it appears just as if it were a regular COM object. Figure 14.20 shows the COM Component Binding Wizard Class Information page.

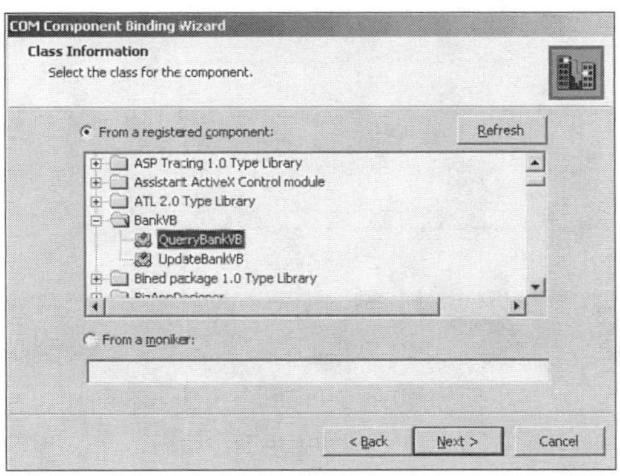

FIGURE 14.20
The COM Component Binding Wizard Class Information page.

Our schedule implements two instances of the managed `BankVB` object: one that is transactional, and one that is not. The nontransactional implementation exposes all methods in the `QueryBankVB` class, and the transaction implementation exposes all the methods in the `UpdateBankVB` class. When binding the object, you proceed through several wizard steps. The last step in the wizard, `Advanced Port Properties`, allows you to configure transaction settings for the object. The `QueryBankVB` class COM implementation object does not implement transaction support and does not enable a transaction to abort if an error is encountered.

To add the `BankVB` COM implementation objects to the schedule, drag the `COM` implementation shape onto the designer. In the COM Component Binding Wizard that appears, name the first port `CheckBalance` and click Next. In the Standard or Dynamic Communication dialog that appears, select the Static option and click Next. In the Class Information dialog that appears, select the `BankVB QueryBankVB` class and click Next. In the Interface Information dialog, select the `_QueryBankVB` interface and click Next. In the Method Information dialog that appears, select the Check All button and click Next. In the Advanced Port Properties dialog that appears, keep the default values and click Finish.

Now repeat the same steps to add the `UpdateBankVB` class, this time selecting the `BankVB UpdateBankVB` class in the Class Information dialog. In the Advanced Port properties dialog, set the properties as displayed in Figure 14.21.

FIGURE 14.21
The `UpdateBankVB` *Implementation Advanced Port Properties page.*

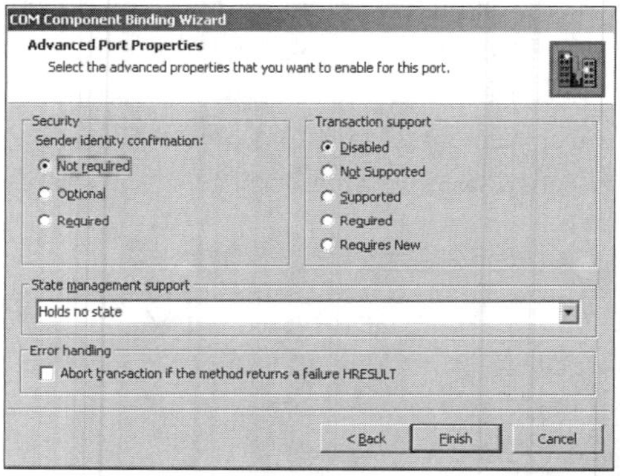

> **Note**
>
> The transaction attributes must be set on the `UpdateBankVB` implementation object to bind the object to actions contained in a BizTalk Orchestration transaction shape. You accomplish this by selecting the Required option in the Advanced Port Properties dialog for the COM object.

Next we need to bind each of the actions in the schedule to its appropriate method implementation in either the `QueryBankVB` object or the `UpdateBankVB` object. To begin, connect the Check Balance action to the `QueryBankVB` COM implementation shape. In the Method Communication Wizard that appears, select the Initiate a Synchronous Method Call option and click Next. In the Message Specification Information dialog that appears, select the `GetBalance` method and click Finish.

Next, connect the Get Beginning Balances action to the `QueryBankVB` implementation shape. In the Method Communication Wizard that appears, select the Initiate a

Synchronous Method Call option and click Next. In the Message Specification Information dialog that appears, select the `DisplayBalances` method and click `Finish`. The next action to bind is the `Sorry, Not Enough Money` J action. Connect this action to the `QueryBankVB` implementation object. In the Method Communication Wizard that appears, select the Initiate a Synchronous Method Call option and click Next. In the Message Specification Information dialog that appears, select the `DisplayMsg` method and click Finish. Now, connect the `Get Ending Balances` action to the `QueryBankVB` implementation object. In the Method Communication Wizard that appears, select the Initiate a Synchronous Method Call option and click Next. In the Message Specification Information dialog that appears, select the `DisplayBalances` method and click Finish. Finally, select the On Failure of `BankTransaction` tab in the BizTalk Orchestration Designer and connect the `Error` action to the `QueryBankVB` implementation object. In the Method Communication Wizard that appears, select the Initiate a Synchronous Method Call option and click Next. In the Message Specification Information dialog that appears, select the `DisplayMsg` method and click `Finish`.

Now we're ready to connect the `Debit` and `Credit` actions to the `UpdateBankVB` implementation object. Connect one at a time to the `UpdateBankVb` object. In the Method Communication Wizard that appears, select the Initiate a Synchronous Method Call option and then click Next. In the Message Specification Information dialog that appears, select the `Debit` method for the `Debit` action and the `Credit` method for the `Credit` action and click Finish. Each action in the schedule is now bound to its appropriate implementation object.

In the next section we will add transactional support to our BizTalk Orchestration schedule for both the `Credit` and `Debit` actions.

Incorporating Transaction Management

To ensure the integrity of the database, we created managed objects that implement the `System.EnterpriseServices` namespace's `ServicedComponent` interface. The `Credit` and `Debit` methods in the `UpdateBankVB` class both inherit from the `ServicedComponent` interface and implement attributes to ensure automatic transaction support. If we were to call each of the methods separately, they would both throw exceptions on failure and roll back any transaction-aware logic. In our case, we want to ensure that both actions succeed or fail as an atomic unit. To accomplish this, we wrap both actions, `Credit` and `Debit`, in a BizTalk Orchestration transaction.

To wrap the actions, drag the `Transaction` shape from the flowchart actions pane over both the `Credit` and `Debit` actions. Then select the transaction shape and right-click. In the pop-up menu that appears, select the Properties menu option to set its attributes. The `BankTransaction` attributes should be configured as displayed in Figure 14.22.

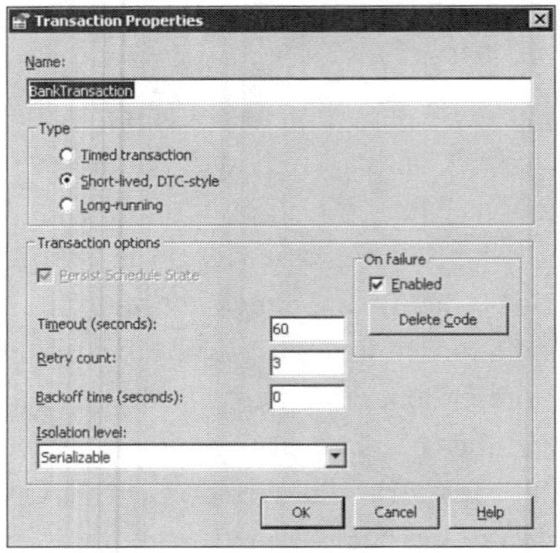

FIGURE 14.22
The bank transaction attributes.

The name of the transaction is `BankTransaction` and has a type of Short Lived, DTC `style`. Its retry count is set to three, and its `On Failure` check box is checked. If either the `Credit` or `Debit` method fails, the schedule will now redirect schedule processing to the first action, `Error`, in the On Failure of `BankTransaction` tab as displayed in Figure 14.17.

The message flow that occurs in the BizTalk Orchestration schedule is configured using the Data tab of the BizTalk Orchestration Designer. In the next section, we will discuss how to construct the data flow for the `BankTransaction.skv` schedule.

The Data Page

At this point, we assume that you have a good working knowledge of the importance of the BizTalk Orchestration data page. This page ensures that the messages flow between actions inside the schedule. The message fields should be connected to one another as detailed in Table 14.2.

TABLE 14.2 Orchestration Data Page Message Bindings

From Message Name	*From Field Name*	*To Message Name*	*To Field Name*
`BankTransaction`	`CreditBank`	`Credit_in`	`myBank`
`BankTransaction`	`CreditAccount`	`Credit_in`	`AccountNo`
`BankTransaction`	`DebitBank`	`Debit_in`	`myBank`
`BankTransaction`	`DebitAccount`	`Debit_in`	`AccountNo`
`BankTransaction`	`Amount`	`Credit_in`	`AmountToCredit`
`BankTransaction`	`Amount`	`Debit_in`	`AmountToDebit`
`BankTransaction`	`DebitBank`	`DisplayBalances_in_2`	`Bank1`
`BankTransaction`	`DebitAccount`	`DisplayBalances_in_2`	`Bank1Account`

TABLE 14.2 continued

From Message Name	*From Field Name*	*To Message Name*	*To Field Name*
BankTransaction	CreditBank	DisplayBalances_in_2	Bank2
BankTransaction	CreditAccount	DisplayBalances_in_2	Bank2Account
BankTransaction	DebitBank	DisplayBalances_in	Bank1
BankTransaction	DebitAccount	DisplayBalances_in	Bank1Account
BankTransaction	CreditBank	DisplayBalances_in	Bank2
BankTransaction	CreditAccount	DisplayBalances_in	Bank2Account
Constants	NotEnoughMoney	DisplayMsg_in	sMessage
Constants	TransactionFailed	DisplayMsg_in_2	sMessage
BankTransaction	DebitBank	GetBalance_in	myBank
BankTransaction	DebitAccount	GetBalance_in	AccountNo

Figure 14.23 displays the data page for the `BankTransaction` schedule.

FIGURE 14.23
The bank transaction data page.

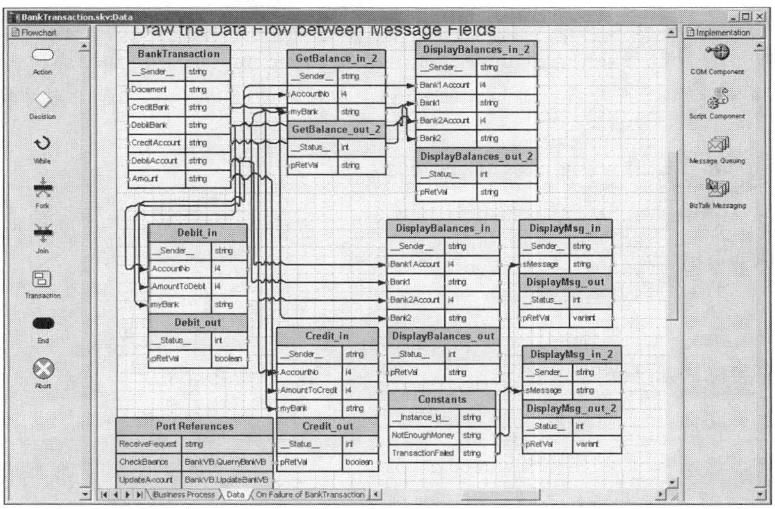

Note

The data page maintains two constant values, `NotEnoughMoney` and `TransactionFailed`, that contain the message text passed to the message box managed methods.

Compiling and Running the Schedule

We are now ready to compile and then run the schedule. To compile the schedule, select the File, Make XLANG `BankTransaction.skx File` menu option from the Orchestration designer menu. A dialog appears asking you to save the XLANG file to the local directory. To run the schedule, you will need to accomplish two tasks: drop an instance of the `BankTransaction.xml` file onto the `ReceiveRequest` MSMQ queue and start an instance of the `BankTransaction.skx` schedule.

> **Note**
>
> When compiling the schedule, you may encounter a Just-In-Time Debugging Runtime Exception error. If this occurs, select the No button and continue compiling. This error has no effect on the XLANG schedule creation.

The source code for this chapter located on the publisher's Web site contains two Visual Basic script files located in the `\BtsDotNet\Schedules` directory. The first, `processTrans.vbs`, starts an instance of the `BankTransaction` schedule and calls the second script. The second, `File2Queue.vbs`, submits an instance of the `BankTransaction.xml` file, located in the same directory, to the private MSMQ `ReceiveRequest` queue. Listings 14.10 and 14.11 display the Visual Basic script files.

LISTING 14.10 The `processTrans.vbs` File

```
dim objSked, strPath, WshShell

strPath = WScript.ScriptFullName
strPath = Mid(strPath, 1, InStrRev(strPath, "\"))

Set WshShell = WScript.CreateObject("WScript.Shell")
call WshShell.Run ("""" & strPath & "File2Queue.vbs"
➥& """ BankTransInstance.xml")
set objSked = GetObject("sked:///" & strPath & "BankTransaction.skx")
```

LISTING 14.11 The `File2Queue.vbs` File

```
'MSMQ constants

'Access modes
const MQ_RECEIVE_ACCESS        = 1
const MQ_SEND_ACCESS         = 2
const MQ_PEEK_ACCESS         = 32

'Sharing modes
```

LISTING 14.11 continued

```
const MQ_DENY_NONE          = 0
const MQ_DENY_RECEIVE_SHARE = 1

'Transaction Options
const MQ_NO_TRANSACTION       = 0
const MQ_MTS_TRANSACTION    = 1
const MQ_XA_TRANSACTION       = 2
const MQ_SINGLE_MESSAGE       = 3

'Queue Path
const QUEUE_PATH = ".\private$\ReceiveRequest"

dim qinfo, qSend, mSend, xmlDoc
dim sPath, sFile, sMesg, sInFileName

'Input file name
'sInFileName = WScript.Arguments(0)
sInFileName = "BankTransInstance.xml"

' Create the queue
set qinfo = CreateObject("MSMQ.MSMQQueueInfo")
qinfo.PathName = QUEUE_PATH

' Open queue with SEND access.
Set qSend = qinfo.Open(MQ_SEND_ACCESS, MQ_DENY_NONE)

' Put file into message.
sPath = WScript.ScriptFullName
sPath = Mid(sPath, 1, InStrRev(sPath, "\"))
sFile = sPath & sInFileName

set xmlDoc = CreateObject("MSXML.DOMDocument")
xmlDoc.load sFile

set mSend = CreateObject("MSMQ.MSMQMessage")
mSend.Body = xmlDoc.xml
mSend.Label = "BankTransaction"

' Send message to queue.
mSend.Send qSend, MQ_SINGLE_MESSAGE
msgbox "File """ & sInFileName & """ sent to queue """ &
➥QUEUE_PATH & """", vbOKOnly, "Basic BizTalk Example"

' Close queue.
qSend.Close
```

If the schedule runs correctly, a message box will appear notifying you of the beginning account balances or of insufficient funds to continue processing. If funds are available and both the `Debit` and `Credit` methods complete successfully, a second message box will appear notifying you of the updated balances.

Debugging Tips and Tricks

When building a BizTalk Orchestration schedule that references a managed object, we thought it might be useful to share a few debugging tips and tricks. First, when recompiling a managed object in Visual Studio .NET with the `Register for COM Interop` configuration setting on, you may need to either select the `Tools`, `Refresh Method Signatures` menu option to rebind the managed objects or manually re-associate your actions to the object and methods using the BizTalk Orchestration Designer COM `Component Implementation Wizard`. Although the signature of the object has not changed, the designer at times requires one or both of these steps.

Second, after a schedule instance is instantiated and has referenced a managed object, that object is locked and cannot be recompiled until all instances of the object are released. To release the object, you can do one or both of the following:

- Select the `Tools`, `Shut Down All Running XLANG Schedule Instances` menu option in the BizTalk Orchestration Designer.
- Open the COM+ Microsoft Management Console and select the XLANG Scheduler application. To shut down all running instances, right-click the application and choose `Shut Down`.

Creating a Managed AIC Component

Creating a managed Application Integration Component (AIC) is similar to creating a managed component called from a COM client. Chapter 17, "Application Integration Components," discussed two BizTalk Messaging COM AIC interfaces. The first implements the `IBTSAppIntegration` interface; the second implements the `IPipelineComponent` interface. The `IBTSAppIntegration` AIC consists of a lightweight model that requires a single interface and consists of a single method, `ProcessMessage`, as its entry point. The `ProcessMessage` public method accepts a single parameter, the document string. This section discusses and demonstrates the use of the `IBTSAppIntegration` interface in a managed C# component. In this section we are going to create a simple C# AIC that accepts an XML document and then persists it to a local file directory.

Creating the DotNetAIC C# AIC

Creating a managed .NET AIC isn't difficult; however, a few concepts are useful to know prior to tackling the task of developing one. First, all AIC `IBTSAppIntegration` components must reference the `BTSComponentsLIB.dll` COM DLL to implement the interface.

Because our AIC is managed by the CLR, it will need to reference the COM interface using a wrapper object called the Runtime Callable Wrapper (RCW). This type of wrapper object was used earlier in the chapter to reference the COM ADO DLL in the `BankVB` Visual Basic .NET component we created. The wrapper is automatically created for you in Visual Studio .NET when you add a reference to the DLL.

Second, when installing AICs, you must properly register them so that Microsoft BizTalk Server 2002 can identify them. The component must be registered with the category IDs for a pipeline component and for the specific type of pipeline component, in this case application integration. You can register the component manually using a registration file or by creating and installing the AIC in a COM+ application. In the C# AIC example, we register the managed object as a COM+ application using the `System.EnterpriseServices ServicedComponent` interface as we did earlier in the BankVB example.

The steps required to create, compile, and register the DotNetAIC C# AIC example in this section are listed below.

1. Create two strong name `.snk` key files using the `sn.exe` command-line utility.
2. Create an assembly for the `btscomplib.tlb` type library and sign it with a strong name key using the `tlbimp.exe` command-line utility.
3. Reference the `BTSComponentsLib` assembly and `System.EnterpriseServices` namespace in the project references.
4. Set the appropriate declarative attributes to assign the `EnterpriseServices` namespace attributes and COM class GUIDs.
5. Set the strong name key and register the `DotNetAIC` component for COM interop using the C# project properties dialog.
6. Compile or build the strong-named managed class.
7. Register the `DotNetAIC` object using the `regsvcs.exe` command-line utility to update the COM+ catalog.
8. Configure BizTalk Messaging to test the `DotNetAIC`.

In the following sections, we will walk through each of the preceding steps. After the component has been created, we will then test it using BizTalk Messaging. The test application will pick up a document from a local file directory and call a channel bound to a port that has a transport of type AIC.

Creating the C# Class Library

To create the new class library, add a new C# project named `DotNetAIC` to the `BTSDotNet` Visual Studio .NET solution we've been working with. To accomplish this, select the

BTSDotNet solution in the Solution Explorer and right-click. In the pop-up menu that appears, select Add, New Project from the menu and then select the `Visual C# Projects Class Library` project and name it `DotNetAIC`. Visual Studio .NET automatically creates a class file named `class1.cs` for you. This project will consist of a single class file named `DotNetAICtoFile.cs`. To rename `class1.cs`, select it in the Solution Explorer and right-click. In the pop-up menu that appears, select the `rename` menu option and rename the file to `DotNetAICtoFile.cs` as displayed in Figure 14.24.

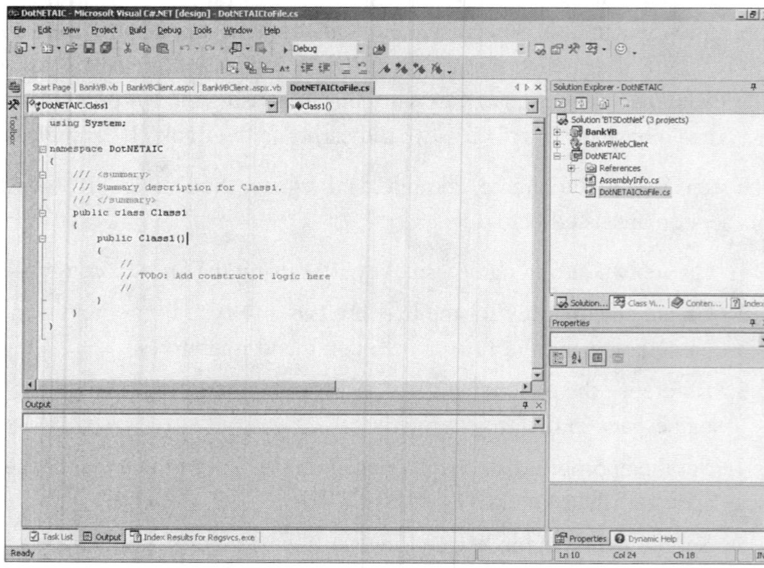

FIGURE 14.24
The `BTSDotNET` *solution with the C# AIC project.*

The C# AIC accepts a document from the BizTalk Server Messaging Engine as a string and then saves it as an XML document named `Output.xml` in a local file directory named `C:\btsdotnet\AICDeploy\Reply`.

Creating Strong Name Keys

The `DotNetAIC` class requires the use of two strong name key files. One will be used to sign the `BTSComponentsLIB` assembly, and the other will be used to sign the `DotNetAIC`. The `DotNetAIC` file must be signed to enable registration as a COM+ component. The `BTSComponentsLIB` assembly must be signed to be referenced from an assembly that is signed, in this case the DotNetAIC assembly. We are going to create the keys using the `sn.exe` command-line utility located in the `\Program Files\Microsoft Visual Studio .NET\FrameworkSDK\bin` directory of your local machine.

Note

To create the `.snk` files using this utility, you must either add this location to your system file path or specify full pathnames.

The two key files will be named `btstlb.snk` and `BTSNetAIC.snk`. To create them, type the following at the command prompt `sn -k btstlb.snk` and `sn -k BTSNetAIC.snk`. Then add the two files to the `DotNetAIC` project by dragging them into the Solution Explorer under the root of that project's folder.

Next we need to create and sign the `BTSComponentsLIB` assembly with the `btstlb.snk` that's been created.

Creating and Signing the `BTSComponentsLIB` Assembly with a Strong Name Key

To reference the COM type library from a C# project, we need to first wrap that object in a `RCW`. To create the wrapper, we will use the `tlbimp.exe` command-line utility located in the `\Program Files\Microsoft Visual Studio .NET\FrameworkSDK\bin` directory of your local machine. The `tlbimp.exe` utility also allows you to sign the assembly when you create it. To create and sign the assembly, open a command-line prompt and navigate to the `\Program Files\Microscft BizTalk Server` directory to locate the `btscomplib.tlb` type library file. Then type the following on the command-line prompt `tlbimp btscomplib.tlb /keyfile:(localfile path)\btstlb.snk`. This creates an assembly named `BTSComponentsLib.dll` that will be added in the next section as a reference in the `DotNetAIC` project.

Note

This line of script assumes that the .NET directory has been added to your file path. The source code on the publisher's Web site has copies of the command-line utilities in a subdirectory named `Utils`. There are also batch files created to assist with the command-line statements. It is sometimes easier to move these files into a single directory when running the utilities, as was done in the example on the publisher's Web site.

Adding References to the C# Project

The AIC managed component references three external objects: the `System.xml` and `System.EnterpriseServices` namespaces and the `RCW` named `BTSComponentsLIB.dll` that we just created. To add these references to the project, select the `References` folder in the `DotNETAIC` project and right-click. In the pop-up menu that appears, select the `Add Reference` menu item. Then navigate to the `.NET` tab and select the `System.xml` .NET and `System.EnterpriseServices` namespaces. Next, navigate to the `COM` tab and select the `BTSComponentsLIB.dll` file using the Browse button to navigate to and select the DLL from the directory you created in the previous section. Then add references to both in the source code using the `Using` statement as displayed in Listing 14.12.

Note

In C#, the `Using` statement is equivalent to the `Imports` statement and allows you to avoid fully qualifying methods in the namespace.

Creating the C# Business Logic

When creating a managed AIC, you must remember two important items. First, because AICs are instantiated by a COM+ application object named the BizTalk Messaging Engine, the managed AIC must be exposed as a COM object using a COM callable wrapper (CCW). Second, you must also ensure that the managed object is registered as a pipeline component. In the DotNetAIC example, we accomplish this by adding the appropriate COM+ declarative attributes to the DotNetAIC class file. We also implement inheritance from the `ServicedComponent` interface to enable the registry of the managed component as a COM+ application. In Listing 14.12, notice that the public class `AICtoFile` inherits from both the `ServicedComponent` and `IBTSAppIntegration` interfaces. Also notice a reference to the GUID attribute to ensure its uniqueness when registered with COM. You can create the GUID using the Create GUID tool in Visual Studio .NET.

Listing 14.12 shows the code for the C# AIC.

LISTING 14.12 The `DotNETAICtoFile.cs` File

```
using System;
using System.Runtime.InteropServices;
using System.EnterpriseServices;
using System.Xml;
using BTSComponentsLib;
```

LISTING 14.12 continued

```
hhh
namespace CSharpBTSAIC
{
    // Summary description for AICtoFile.

    // Guid attribute ensures same Guid is used for all
    // compilations, similar to binary compatibility in VB6
    [Guid("1AA73916-FB97-4049-B1AF-DF6BBB43CDB2")]
    // BTSInterop Inherits ServicedComponent and Implements
    // IBTSAppIntegration
    public class AICtoFile: ServicedComponent, IBTSAppIntegration
    {
        public AICtoFile()
        {
            //
            // TODO: Add constructor logic here
            //
        }

        // This means that the transaction governing the object
        // will automatically SetComplete() if the method call
        // returns normally. If the method call throws an exception,
        // the transaction will be aborted
        string IBTSAppIntegration.ProcessMessage(string strDocument)
        {
            // Write the Input XML to a file
            XmlDocument xmlDoc = new XmlDocument();
            xmlDoc.LoadXml(strDocument);
            xmlDoc.SelectSingleNode("BTSAICRoot/MessageText").InnerText =
➥"Message from AIC";
            xmlDoc.Save(@"C:\btsdotnet\AICDeploy\Reply\Output.XML");

            // Simply return the Input as Output
            return strDocument;
        }
    }
}
```

The `ProcessMessage` method's business logic creates a new instance of an XML document and then saves the contents of the input string `strDocument` to a file named `output.xml` file.

Note

To keep things simple, the pathname is hard-coded into the example.

To add the business logic to the `DotNetAIC.toFile.cs` files in the `DotNetAIC` C# project, open the `.cs` file in Visual Studio and add the source code displayed earlier in Listing 14.12.

Compiling and Registering the Component

To register a managed object with COM+, it must be signed with a strong name.

Earlier we created two `.snk` key files, one to sign the `BTSComponentLib.dll` file and the other to sign the `DotNetAIC` managed component. To accomplish this, we need to tell Visual Studio .NET that we want to compile this project for `COM interop` with a strong name key. First, select the project in the Visual Studio .NET Solution Explorer and right-click, selecting the `Properties` menu option. In the dialog that appears, select the `Common Properties` folder's `General` option and reference the key filename in the `Wrapper Assembly Key File` configuration setting as displayed in Figure 14.25.

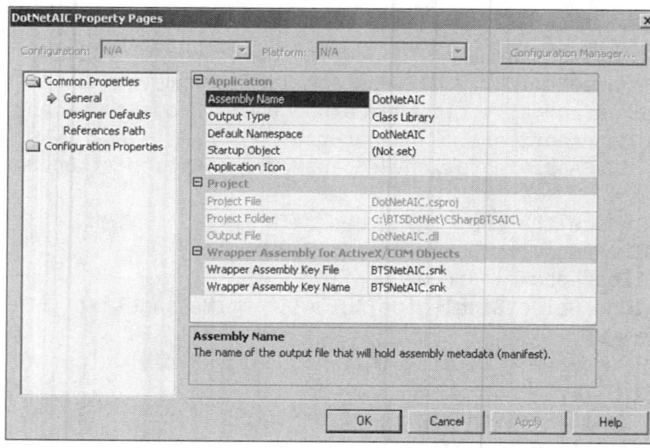

FIGURE 14.25 *Setting the C# .NET strong name key file properties.*

Next, navigate to the `Configuration` folder's `Build` menu option and set the `Register for COM Interop` value equal to `True` as displayed in Figure 14.26.

The `COM Interop` property creates the `CCW` and type library automatically for us when we compile the project. After the component is successfully compiled, run the .NET Framework command-line utility `regsvcs.exe` to create and register the object with COM+. To accomplish this, open the command window, navigate to the `\BTSDotNET\CSharpBTSAIC\bin\Debug` directory, and type `regsvcs dotnetaic.dll`. Then verify its registration by opening the COM+ MMC. If an application named `CSharpBTSAIC` is present, it has been successfully registered.

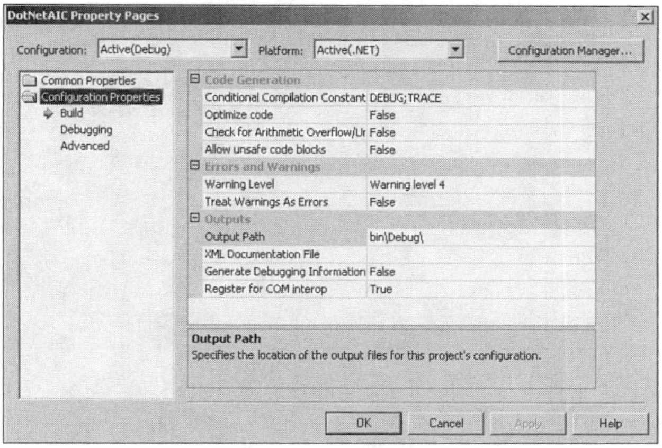

FIGURE 14.26
Setting the C# .NET COM Interop property.

> **Note**
>
> The .NET command-line utilities location is not usually found in your local system path. The utilities are located in the `c:\Program Files\Microsoft.NET\Framework SDK\bin` directory. You might need to include their location in your local path or fully qualify your references to the utilities.

BizTalk Messaging AIC Setup

To test the managed AIC, we are going to create a simple BizTalk Messaging example. The messaging example processes an XML document named `BTSAICInstance.xml` using a BizTalk Server file receive function. In the `DotNetAIC` example, we are going to create a new BizTalk Messaging organization named `DotNETAIC` and a new document named `BTSAIC`. The document specification will be stored in a `Web Dav` directory named `Bank`. The `BTSAIC.xml` document specification is displayed in Figure 14.27 in the BizTalk Editor.

To configure BizTalk Messaging, we need to complete the following steps. Each of these steps is described in detail later in this section.

1. Create an `XDR` schema using the BizTalk Editor and save it to a WebDav repository named `Bank`.
2. Create a new `Organization` named `DotNetAIC`.
3. Create a new `Port` to an `Organization` named `To BTS AIC` using the BizTalk Messaging Manager.

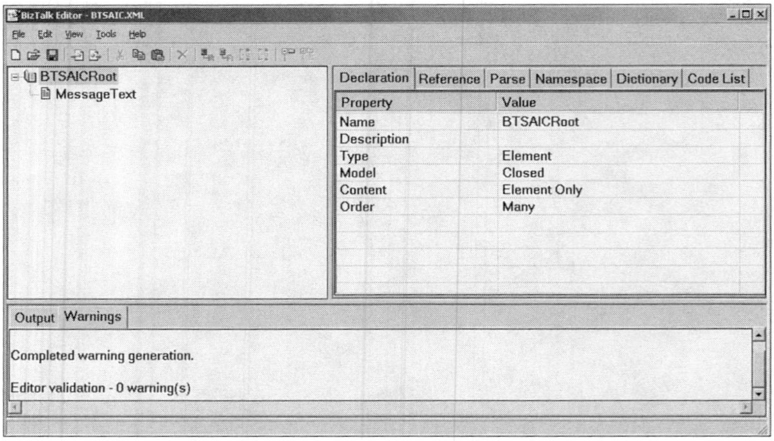

FIGURE 14.27
The `BTSAIC.XML` *BizTalk document.*

4. Bind the `Port` to a `Channel` from an `Organization` named `From AIC Test` that has inbound and outbound documents set to the `BTSAIC` document. The Port will have a transport of `AIC` that will reference the C# `DotNetAIC.dll` `AIC` created earlier.
5. Create a file receive function using the BizTalk Administration console that will pass `.xml` files to the `From AIC Test Channel`.
6. Test the AIC by dropping an instance of the `BTSAIC` document into the receive directory.

To configure BizTalk messaging, begin by creating the `BTSAIC.xml` BizTalk `XDR` schema using the BizTalk Editor and save it to a new WebDav folder named `Bank`. The schema can be created by hand or downloaded from the publisher's Web site. After you have created and saved the schema, open the BizTalk Messaging Manager and create a new document definition that references this schema in the repository and name the document `BTSAIC`. Then create a new `Organization` and name it `AIC Test`.

Next, create a new `Port` to an `Organization` and name it `To BTS AIC`. In the Messaging Port Wizard Destination Organization dialog that appears, select the AIC Test organization using the Browse button next to the Organization option. Then set the Primary transport type to AIC using the Browse button next to the Primary Transport Address option. In the dialog that appears, select AIC and then use the Browse button to select the `CSharpBTSAIC.AICtoFile` component. In the final wizard step, select Create a Channel for This Messaging Port and specify the From an Organization channel type.

Note

When you select the transport type of AIC, a dialog appears asking you to select a component from a list of registered AICs. If the C# component is not listed in the dialog, it has not been properly registered. To verify that it is registered, first check to see that the COM+ application exists. If it does, delete it manually using the COM+ MMC, recompile the managed object, and rerun the `regsvcs.exe` command-line utility.

The port will be bound to a channel named `From Test AIC` with the inbound and outbound documents set to the `BTSAIC` XML document created earlier.

In the New Channel Wizard that appears, name the Channel From `DOTNETAIC` and click Next. In the Source Organization dialog that appears, select the AIC Test organization and click Next. In the Inbound Document dialog that appears, select the `BTSAIC` document using the Browse button and click Next. Then select the `BTSAIC` document for the outbound document as well. The remainder of the wizard steps should keep the default settings.

The BizTalk file receive function will be configured to process all `.xml` files in the `\BTSDotNet\AICdeploy\Submit` directory. The channel also will be exclusively specified to `From DOTNET AIC` channel. To create the receive function, open the BizTalk Server Administration console and select the `Receive Functions` folder under the BizTalk Server Group and right-click. In the pop-up menu that appears, select the New File Receive Function menu option. In the Add a File Receive Function dialog that appears, name the function AIC Test, set the File `Types to Poll for` to `*.xml`, the Polling Location to `\BtsDotNet\AICDeploy\Submit`, and then click the Advanced button. In the Advanced Receive Function Options dialog that appears, select the From AIC Test channel in the Channel Name drop-down list and save the function.

To run the example, copy the `BTSAICInstance.xml` file from the `\BTSDotNet\Docs` directory to the `\BTSDotNET\AICDeploy\Submit` directory. The file receive function should pick up the file, executes the managed `AIC`, and then places the `Output.xml` file in the `\BTSDotNet\AICdeploy\Reply` subdirectory.

Note

The `BTSAICInstance.xml` document can be downloaded from the publisher's Web site or created using the BizTalk Editor.

> **Note**
>
> This example assumes a basic understanding of BizTalk Messaging. To learn more about BizTalk Messaging, refer to the chapters on BizTalk Messaging and/or the appropriate BizTalk Server documentation.

Summary

Microsoft's next-generation development platform is designed to make standards-based Web and Win32 application development much simpler for the Web developer. The many new enhancements included in the .NET Framework and CLR make what was once difficult in the Web development world much less complex. Although the new component technology is impressive and tempting to implement, its true value lies in its capability to communicate and coexist with existing applications and component technologies. Microsoft recognized this and provided built-in support for COM interop, making integration with existing applications such as BizTalk not only possible but easy to implement.

BizTalk Orchestration instantiates managed objects using a wrapper interface provided by the .NET runtime called the COM Callable wrapper. BizTalk Messaging supports the implementation of .NET-managed AICs using a wrapper object named the Runtime Callable wrapper. These wrapper interfaces hide the differences between the component technologies and allow both to communicate as if they were of the same type.

Although .NET may be new to some, you'll find the .NET Interop wrapper technology not only adequate but also an invaluable tool when developing BizTalk Server application integration solutions in the relatively near future.

CHAPTER 15

Web Services and BizTalk Server

By Susie Adams

In This Chapter

The term *.NET* introduces Microsoft's new application development platform with a revolutionary new vision. In the .NET vision, applications are constructed using multiple Web services that work together to provide data and business services for an application using standard Internet transport protocols and data formats. This concept of communication using industry standards as opposed to proprietary transports and data formats enables the integration of applications regardless of the language with which they were constructed or the platform for which they were developed. This chapter discusses the architecture and platform requirements of a Web Service and then demonstrates how to create and integrate a BizTalk Server 2002 Orchestration schedule with an ASP.NET Web Service.

Definition of a Web Service

Web Services enable the exchange of Extensible Markup Language (XML) data messages between heterogeneous systems using standard Internet protocols. From a developer's perspective, a Web Service is similar to a COM object. Both implement black-box functionality that can be consumed by remote clients that know nothing about their physical implementation details. The concept of remotely accessing data and application logic isn't new; doing so in a loosely coupled fashion, however, is. Traditional technology, such as DCOM, IIOP, and Java/RMI, require tight integration between the client and the server and use platform-specific binary data format implementations to communicate. These implementations require a particular component technology or object-calling convention, whereas Web services do not. The only assumption made between a Web Service client and the Web Service server is that recipients of the Web Service request understand the messages they receive. The client and server agree to a contract and then communicate by generating messages that honor the contract over a specified transport such as HTTP. The contract or service description consists of an XML document written in an XML grammar known as the *Web Service Description Language* (WSDL). WSDL defines the format of messages a Web Service understands and serves as an agreement that defines the behavior of a Web Service. As a result, programs written in any language, using any component model, and running on any operating system can access a Web Service provided that it is implemented using a standard Internet protocol and data transport format.

At first glance, this may seem like a new concept; however, developers have been implementing a poor man's version of this technique for years. For example, if you've ever written an Active Server Page (ASP) that accepts one or more values in its query string, executes some business logic, and then returns a data stream (XML or comma delimited) back to a client who then consumes it, you've written a Web Service. It's a technique I've used many times to integrate data from disparate systems and/or platforms.

Although Web Services are at the core of the Microsoft .NET vision, a Web Service isn't conceptually tied to a single vendor implementation. In fact, most major software vendors embrace the Web Services concept and employ a Web Services implementation of their own. The implementations are unique to each vendor's platform and programming language of choice; however, most are based on the standard Web Service data format and protocol specifications governed by the W3C standards organization.

The Microsoft .NET Web Services vision improves the implementation methods available to developers allowing them to write and consume business logic via standards-based protocols and data formats without having to worry about the underlying implementation plumbing. In the next section, we will discuss the basic technologies and associated data and transport protocol standards required to implement a .NET Web Service.

Web Service Technologies and Standards Specifications

Before you tackle the task of building a Web Service, it's a good idea to learn a little about the specifications and technologies you're likely to encounter. Several basic requirements must be addressed to define how a Web Service communicates, is located, and exchanges data. For example, a Web Service requires

- A standard way to represent data
- A common, extensible, service description language
- A common, extensible, message format
- A way to discover services located on a particular Web site
- A way to discover service providers

The two most obvious items involve the data message format and transport protocols used to send and receive Web Service messages. XML is the standard data format used to package and describe data. The Simple Object Access Protocol (SOAP) defines a lightweight protocol for data exchange using the HTTP protocol and has been chosen as the standard message format for communicating with Web Services. The SOAP specification defines both a set of rules describing how to use XML to represent Web Service messages and the conventions available to make remote procedure calls (RPC) using the SOAP message format, over the HTTP protocol.

The less obvious specifications have to do with the description and identification of Web Services. In the COM world, we typically describe a component using a type library. The type library provides the information clients need to communicate with the public methods of the COM object. In the Web Services world, we need a similar construct that defines a contract documenting and describing the messages a Web Service accepts and generates. This standard format is WSDL, better known as a Web Service contract. WSDL is an XML-based contract language developed jointly by Microsoft and IBM that describes the format of the messages a Web Service supports. The service description serves as an agreement that defines the behavior of a Web Service and instructs potential clients in how to interact with it.

Note

IBM and Microsoft have been working jointly on several versions of the Web Service contract specification including the Service Description Language (SDL) and the SOAP Contract Language (SDL). All previous contract languages are superceded by WSDL.

Finally, developers also need a way to discover Web Services. Two specifications facilitate this: the Discovery Protocol (Disco) and the Universal Description, Discovery, and Integration (UDDI) specifications. Disco defines a discovery document format that gives developers the capability to discover services at a known URL. UDDI allows Web Service providers to advertise the existence of their Web Services to consumers, similar conceptually to the Yellow Pages phone book.

Now that you have a basic understanding of the technology required to support a Web Service, we'll discuss the platform requirements required to deploy and run one.

Web Service Architecture

Figure 15.1 displays a classic architecture diagram for an application that implements a Web Service. If the diagram looks familiar, it is because it's similar to most n-tier Windows architectures. The major difference is the addition of a service called a Listener. Web Services are instantiated by a listener deployed on an HTTP Web server. The listener listens on a particular port for Web Service requests, parses and interprets the SOAP requests it receives, invokes the Web Services business logic, and then serializes and transports the SOAP response message back to the requestor.

Most major software vendors support an implementation of a SOAP server and an associated listener. As long as the Web Service vendor abides by the standards defined by the W3C, a client running on any platform written in any language is in theory able to send a SOAP request and receive a SOAP response from any SOAP server. Conceptually, this is a great idea; however, the current in-flux state of the Web Service protocol and data transport standards makes this a sometimes challenging implementation task. For example, the SOAP and WSDL specifications are still in W3C working groups awaiting ratification and recommendation by the W3C. Therefore, although most vendors support SOAP, the versions they support can differ, making it challenging, for example, to call an Apache Web Service from a Windows Visual Basic .NET client.

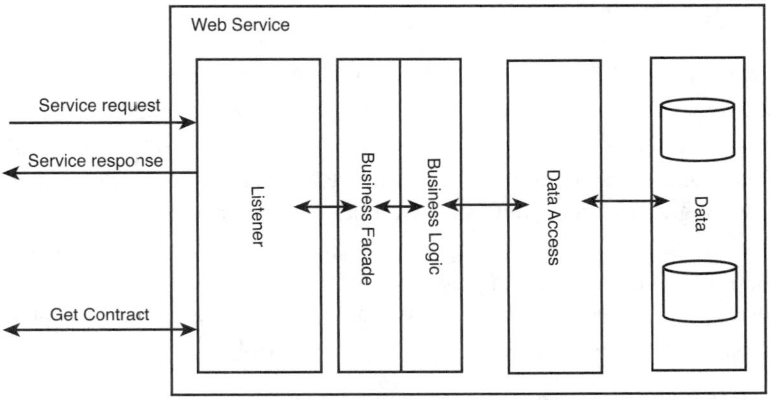

FIGURE 15.1
A classic Web Services architecture diagram.

To adequately support a Web Service, the platform that hosts the Web Service must provide a number of application services including

- Listening for incoming HTTP requests
- Performing security authentication and authorization checks
- Dispatching authorized requests to the correct service implementation
- Automatically recovering from service and system failures

Fortunately, these types of services are normally provided by the SOAP server implementation and operating system platform.

Microsoft has two Web Service implementation options, ASP.NET and the SOAP toolkit. The Microsoft SOAP toolkit is based on a COM implementation of a SOAP server and allows developers to create unmanaged Web Services in Visual Studio 6.0. This chapter focuses on the implementation of ASP.NET managed Web Services.

In Chapter 14, "Integrating .NET," we created a simple Bank Visual Basic .NET managed class that queried, credited, and debited an account table in two SQL Server databases. This chapter exposes the same business logic as an ASP.NET Web Service. But before tackling the task of building a Web Service, you need to first learn a little more about ASP.NET. The next section introduces Microsoft's ASP.NET Web Service architecture and Visual Studio .NET development environment, both of which we will later use to implement a Bank Web Service.

Overview of ASP.NET Web Services

ASP.NET Web Services are built on top of ASP.NET and use industry standard data formats and transport protocols that include SOAP, XML, and WSDL. The .NET platform gives ASP.NET Web Services the capability to take advantage of the platform's architectural enhancements; for example, all ASP.NET code is compiled rather than interpreted, allowing early binding and strong typing. ASP.NET is also just-in-time (`JIT`) compiled to native code at execution time, dramatically improving its execution speed compared to that of traditional ASP applications. ASP.NET Web Services' adherence to industry standards, such as SOAP, XML, and WSDL, allows clients from other platforms to seamlessly interoperate with and call an ASP.NET Web Service.

ASP.NET Web Services support client communication using three protocols: SOAP, `HTTP-GET`, and `HTTP-POST`. `HTTP-GET` and `HTTP-POST` support the passing of parameters in named value pairs. SOAP passes data to and from a Web Service using XML, allowing developers to define complex data types using XSD schemas.

As mentioned earlier, the system services required to implement a Web Service can become complex if not augmented by a vendor's implementation. Although not impossible to develop, most Web Service vendors normally hide this complexity from the developer. Microsoft's ASP.NET is no different; in fact, its feature set is robust, allowing developers to focus on the implementation details as opposed to underlying system services plumbing. In fact, developing a Web Service with Visual Studio .NET is as simple as building a standard class object. The development environment generates all the code required to communicate using HTTP and SOAP automatically.

An ASP.NET Web Service has a file extension of `.asmx` and can be created using Visual Studio .NET or any standard text editor. The simplest way to run and/or test an `.asmx` Web Service is to request its URL in a Web browser. When you request the `.asmx` file in a browser, the Web server returns a Web Service description page allowing you to test each of the Web Service methods.

You can also call an ASP.NET Web Service programmatically, both synchronously and asynchronously from a managed .NET client. To access a Web Service programmatically from a .NET client application, you add a Web reference to the Web Service project.

When you create a Web reference, Visual Studio .NET automatically creates and adds a Web Service proxy class for each Web Service to your project. The proxy class exposes the methods of the Web Service and handles the marshalling of data between the Web Service and your client application. Visual Studio .NET uses the Web Service service description language (WSDL) file to create the proxy class. This proxy class allows you to invoke the exposed methods of the Web Service just as you would any other method of a local component. If the Web Service is not accessible at development time, you can use the WSDL command-line tool (`Wsdl.exe`) to generate a Web Service client proxy class from a WSDL file manually.

The next section walks you through the steps required to expose the Visual Basic .NET managed classes created in Chapter 14 in the `BankVB.vb` object as Web Services.

Creating the Bank ASP.NET Web Service

This example demonstrates how to create two ASP.NET Visual Basic .NET Web Services that implement the Visual Basic .NET managed objects business logic created in Chapter 14.

Note

If you have not implemented Chapter 14's example, you may want to download Chapter 14's code from the publisher's Web site at this time. For more information regarding the `BankVB.vb` .NET example or for an overview of .NET, refer to Chapter 14.

The figures in this chapter depict a development environment that builds on Chapter 14's example. For simplicity, we added the two new Visual Studio .NET projects created in this chapter to the `BTSDotNet` solution created in Chapter 14.

We are going to walk through each of the following steps. After we complete the steps, we will modify the `Transaction.skv` BizTalk Orchestration schedule to implement the Web Services created.

1. Set up the development environment.
2. Create the `BankWS` ASP.NET Web Service project and add the `BankWS` and `UpdateBankWS` Web Services (`.asmx` files).

3. Add the business logic to the Web Service `.asxm` files defining the Web Service methods.
4. Add transaction attributes and the required assemblies to the .NET Web method code.
5. Test an ASP.NET Web Service from a browser.
6. Modify the `BankVBWebClient` ASP.NET project to test the Web Services from the `BankVBClient.aspx` ASP.NET Web form.

Setting Up the Development Environment

The development environment for this example requires an MSMQ private queue named ReceiveRequest and two SQL Server databases named BankofAmerica and Fidelity. The MSMQ private queue can be created by selecting the Start, Administrative Tools, Computer Management menu option. In the management console that appears, navigate to the Services and Applications, Message Queuing, Private Queues folder in the tree view. Right-click on Private Queues and select New. In the dialog that appears, enter the queue name as ReceiveRequest. Be aware that MSMQ queue names are case sensitive and that the queue must be transactional. Figure 15.2 shows the MSMQ receiverequest Properties dialog.

FIGURE 15.2
Creating the `ReceiveRequest` *MSMQ message queue.*

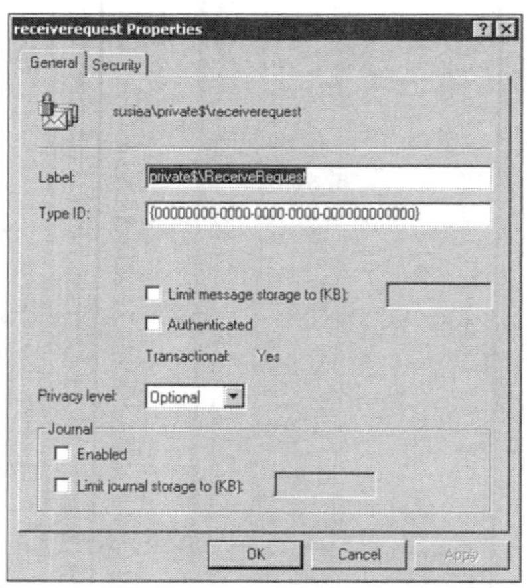

Note

The source code and required setup files to create the MSMQ and databases can be found on the publisher's Web site in the directory for this chapter.

The two database tables can be created by downloading the `CreateDBs.sql` script located on the publisher's Web site in the Setup directory for this chapter or manually by using the SQL Server Enterprise Manager. The two database names are `Fidelity` and `BankofAmerica`. Each contains a single database table named `Accounts` with two fields, `AccountNo` and `Amount`, both integers. Each table should have a single record with the account number of 1 and an amount greater than 0. The SQL script automatically creates the databases and inserts a single record in each `Account` table.

Creating a New Web Service Project

To add a new Visual Studio .NET Web Service project to the `BTSDotNet` solution, open the `BTSDotNet` solution and then right-click on it in the Solution Explorer. In the pop-up menu that appears, select Add, New Project from the menu. In the dialog that appears, select the Visual Basic ASP.NET Web Service project option and name it `BankWS` as displayed in Figure 15.3. You can also choose to create a new solution and add the Web Service project to it; however, the examples in this chapter assume that the solution is the `BTSDotNet` solution from Chapter 14.

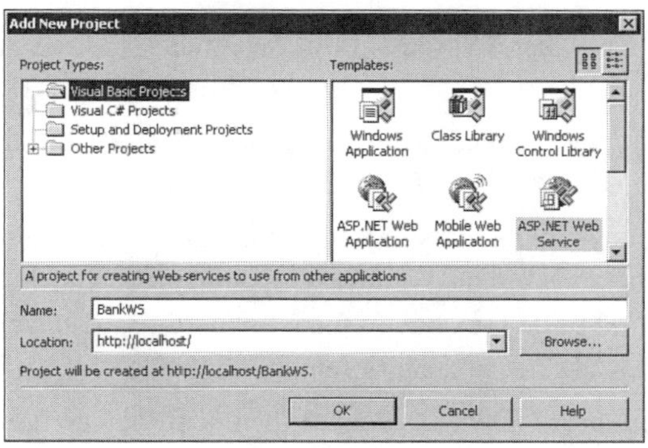

FIGURE 15.3
Adding a new Web Service to the `BTSDotNet` *solution.*

In the new `BankWS` Web service project that appears, select the `Service1.asmx` file and rename it `BankWS.asmx`. Then select the `BankWS` Web service project in the Solution Explorer and right-click. In the pop-up menu that appears, select Add, A Web Service. In the dialog that appears, name the service `UpdateBankWS` and save the project.

Adding the Business Logic and Defining the Web Service Methods

The `BankWS` and `UpdateBankWS` Web services are going to implement the same business logic as the `Bank.vb` Visual Basic .NET managed object created in Chapter 14. The `BankVB.vb` file contains two Visual Basic .NET classes, `QueryBankVB` and `UpdateBankVB`.

In the Web Services implementation of these classes, we are going to separate the classes into two distinct Web Service files. The `QueryBankVB` class code will become the `BankWS.asmx` Web Service, and the `UpdateBankVB` code will become `UpdateBankWS.asmx`.

As you begin to migrate the business logic into the Web Services files, you will notice a few subtle but important differences. First, the `BankVB` object was implemented as a .NET managed object and then later exposed via a COM wrapper to a BizTalk Orchestration schedule. To ensure that the object was registered properly with COM, we added a few attributes that will no longer be required in the Web Services implementation. Also notice that the `UpdateBankVB` class uses COM+ transactions. The Web Services version of this code supports transactions as well; however, the Web Services transaction model handles them in a slightly different manner. We will cover the transactional aspects of Web Services in the next section, "Adding Transaction Attributes and an Assembly to the Web Methods."

In the previous step, we created the two `.asmx` Web service files; in this step, we copy the business logic from the `BankVB.vb` file into each.

To begin, follow these steps:

1. Open the `BankWS.asmx` file and select the `Click here to switch to code` hyperlink.
2. Rename the default class named `Service1` to `QueryBankWS` and then open the `Bank.vb` file in the `BankVB` Visual Basic .NET project.
3. Navigate to the `QueryBankVB` class and copy the `DisplayBalances`, `DisplayMsg`, and `GetBalance` methods to the Windows Clipboard. Then, switch back to the `BankWS.asmx` file and paste the code in the Clipboard to the `QueryBankWS` class in between the public class declaration statements.
4. Although the methods are now members of the class, they are not yet publicly available as `WebMethods` in the Web Service. To expose the three methods as Web methods, place the attribute `<WebMethod()>` in front of each as displayed in Listing 15.1. We are not going to expose this class to a BizTalk Orchestration schedule using COM wrappers, so there is no need to add the `<ComClass("D995F48F-C075-426b-8D49-6B4E17CFF3F5")>` attribute as we did in the `BankVB` managed object.

Finally, we need to make one small modification to the business logic. Web Services are nonvisual objects and, therefore, do not have the capability to pop up message boxes. In the `BankVB` example in Chapter 14, we used the `DisplayMsg` method to display a message box containing the current account balance as the XML document moved through the schedule actions. The `DisplayBalances` method in the `BankVB` implementation calls the `DisplayMsg` method. To eliminate the message box call, comment out that line in the DisplayBalances method that calls the DisplayMsg method. You can leave the DisplayMsg method intact or delete it. In either case, it will not be exposed as a public method in our Web Service. In the section "Calling Web Service Methods from a BizTalk Orchestration Schedule," we will modify the BizTalk Orchestration schedule to accommodate the need to display the balance information without using this method in the Web Service. Listing 15.1 displays the code for the QueryBankWS class.

Note

You will also need to add a reference to the ADODB COM library as done in Chapter 14 to reference the ADO data access objects.

LISTING 15.1 The QueryBankWS.asmx File

```
Imports System.Web.Services

<WebService(Namespace:="http://tempuri.org/")> _
Public Class QueryBankWS
    Inherits System.Web.Services.WebService

    ' WEB SERVICE EXAMPLE
    ' The HelloWorld() example service returns the string Hello World.
    ' To build, uncomment the following lines then save and build the project.
    ' To test this web service, ensure that the .asmx file is the start page
    ' and press F5.
    '
    '<WebMethod()> Public Function HelloWorld() As String
    '    HelloWorld = "Hello World"
    ' End Function
    <WebMethod()> Public Function DisplayBalances(ByVal Bank1Account As Integer,
➥ByVal Bank1 As String, ByVal Bank2Account As Integer,
➥ByVal Bank2 As String) As String
  Dim iBank1 As Integer
  Dim iBank2 As Integer

  iBank1 = GetBalance(1, Bank1)
  iBank2 = GetBalance(1, Bank2)
  DisplayBalances = Bank1 & ": " & CStr(iBank1) & "     " &
➥Bank2 & ": " & CStr(iBank2)
  'DisplayMsg(DisplayBalances)
End Function


<WebMethod()> Public Function GetBalance(ByVal AccountNo As Integer,
➥ByVal myBank As String) As String
```

LISTING 15.1 continued

```
Dim myConn As New ADODB.Connection()
Dim myCommand As New ADODB.Command()
Dim myConnectionString As String

Try
            myConnectionString = "Provider=SQLOLEDB.1;
➥Persist Security Info=False;User ID=sa;Initial Catalog=" & myBank &
➥ ";Data Source=localhost"

            myConn.Open(myConnectionString)

            myCommand.ActiveConnection = myConn
            myCommand.CommandType = ADODB.CommandTypeEnum.adCmdStoredProc
            myCommand.CommandText = "AccountBalance"

            myCommand.Parameters.Refresh()
            myCommand.Parameters("@AccountNo").Value = AccountNo

            myCommand.Execute()

            GetBalance = myCommand.Parameters("@AccountBalance").Value
        Catch ex As Exception
            'MsgBox("Error: " & ex.ToString())
        Finally
            myCommand = Nothing
            myConn.Close()
            myConn = Nothing
        End Try
    End Function

End Class
```

Next, we need to add the business logic to the `UpdateBankWS.asmx` Web Service. To begin, select and open the `UpdateBankWS.asmx` file in Visual Studio .NET and select the `Click here to switch to code view` hyperlink. Then, open the `BankVB.vb` file and navigate to the `UpdateBankVB` public class and copy the `Debit` and `Credit` functions to the Windows Clipboard. Next, switch back to the `UpdateBankWS.asmx` file and copy the code in the Clipboard in between the public class declarations inside the file. The `BankVB.vb` implementation of this business logic implements the `Serviced Component` .NET interface allowing the `UpdateBankVB` class to participate in COM+ transactions. The Web Services model handles COM+ transactions a little differently, so for now delete the following attributes if you copied them:

```
<AutoComplete>
<Transaction(TransactionOption.Requires>
ComClass("73297D71-DA59-43b6-9511-9743B379BF02")>
```

Again, to expose the methods as Web methods, place the `<WebMethod()>` attribute in front of each of the methods. You also need to import two `System` namespaces, `System.WebServices` for the Web Services functionality, and `System.Enterprise Services` to allow the methods to participate in COM+ transactions. Listing 15.2 shows the code for `UpdateBankWS.asmx` Web Service.

LISTING 15.2 The `UpdateBankWS.asmx` File

```
Imports System.Web.Services
Imports System.EnterpriseServices


<WebService(Namespace:="http://tempuri.org/")> _
Public Class UpdateBankWS
    Inherits System.Web.Services.WebService

    ' WEB SERVICE EXAMPLE
    ' The HelloWorld() example service returns the string Hello World.
    ' To build, uncomment the following lines then save and build the project.
    ' To test this web service, ensure that the .asmx file is the start page
    ' and press F5.
    '
    '<WebMethod()> Public Function HelloWorld() As String
    '   HelloWorld = "Hello World"
    ' End Function
    <WebMethod(TransactionOption:=TransactionOption.RequiresNew)>
 ➥Public Function Credit(ByVal AccountNo As Integer,
➥ByVal AmountToCredit As Integer, ByVal myBank As String) As Boolean
Dim myConn As New ADODB.Connection()
Dim myCommand As New ADODB.Command()
Dim myConnectionString As String

myConnectionString = "Provider=SQLOLEDB.1;
➥Persist Security Info=False;User ID=sa;Initial Catalog=" &
➥myBank & ";Data Source=localhost"
Try
            myConn.Open(myConnectionString)

            myCommand.ActiveConnection = myConn
            myCommand.CommandType = ADODB.CommandTypeEnum.adCmdStoredProc
            myCommand.CommandText = "Credit"
            myCommand.Parameters.Refresh()
            myCommand.Parameters("@AccountNo").Value = AccountNo
            myCommand.Parameters("@AmountToCredit").Value = AmountToCredit

            myCommand.Execute()

            Credit = CBool(myCommand.Parameters("@AccountBalance").Value)
            Credit = True
```

LISTING 15.2 continued

```
        Catch ex As Exception
            'MsgBox("Error: " & ex.ToString())
            Credit = False
            'Throw New Exception("Database Error")
        Finally
            myCommand = Nothing
            myConn.Close()
            myConn = Nothing
        End Try
    End Function


    <WebMethod(TransactionOption:=TransactionOption.RequiresNew)>
 ➥Public Function Debit(ByVal AccountNo As Integer,
➥ByVal AmountToDebit As Integer, ByVal myBank As String) As Boolean
Dim myConn As New ADODB.Connection()
Dim myCommand As New ADODB.Command()
Dim myConnectionString As String

        myConnectionString = "Provider=SQLOLEDB.1;
➥Persist Security Info=False;User ID=sa;Initial Catalog=" &
➥myBank & ";Data Source=DevDays01"

Try
            myConn.Open(myConnectionString)
            myCommand.ActiveConnection = myConn
            myCommand.CommandType = ADODB.CommandTypeEnum.adCmdStoredProc
            myCommand.CommandText = "Debit"

            myCommand.Parameters.Refresh()
            myCommand.Parameters("@AccountNo").Value = AccountNo
            myCommand.Parameters("@AmountToDebit").Value = AmountToDebit

            myCommand.Execute()

            Debit = CBool(myCommand.Parameters("@AccountBalance").Value)
            Debit = True
        Catch ex As Exception
            'MsgBox("Error: " & ex.ToString())
            Debit = False
        Finally
            myCommand = Nothing
            myConn.Close()
            myConn = Nothing
        End Try
    End Function

End Class
```

Notice the addition of transaction properties on the `WebMethod` attributes. We will discuss these at length a little later in the chapter in the section "Adding Transaction Attributes and an Assembly to the Web Methods."

Now, save the files you've created and build the `BankWS` Web Service project. To save the files, select the `BankWS` Web Service project in the Visual Studio .NET Solution Explorer and then select File, Save from the menu. Next, select Build, `Build BankWS` from the menu. If `build` is successful, you see the message as displayed in Figure 15.4.

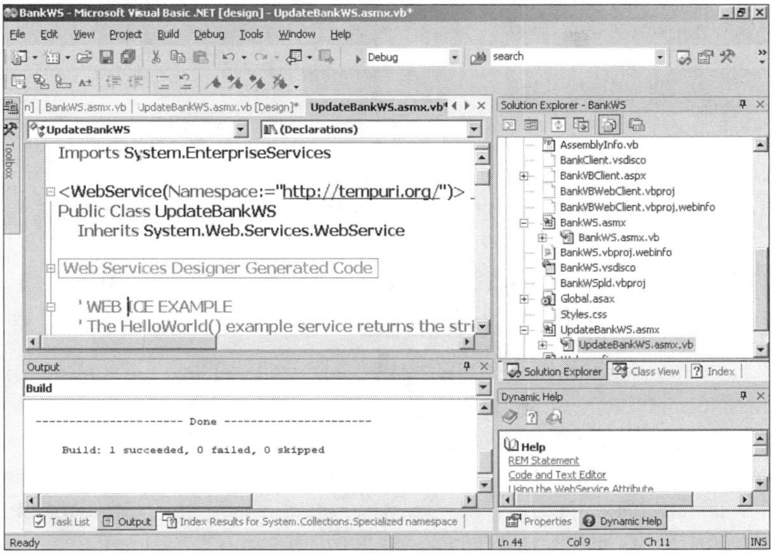

FIGURE 15.4
Building the `BankWS` *Visual Studio .NET Web Service.*

When you create a new Web Service project, it automatically creates a virtual directory at the destination you specified in the project's properties. When you build a Web Service, Visual Studio .NET automatically deploys it to that virtual directory. Deploying a Web Service involves copying the `.asmx` file and assemblies used by the Web Service that are not a part of the Microsoft .NET Framework to its virtual directory.

For example, the `BankWS` Web Service in this example lives in a virtual directory named `BankWS` off the root of the `localhost (susiea)` of the local machine. To verify this, you can open the Internet Services Manager management console by selecting the Start menu's, Programs, Administrative Tools option. Then, select the Internet Services Manager menu option. The `BankWS` virtual directory is displayed in the management console in Figure 15.5.

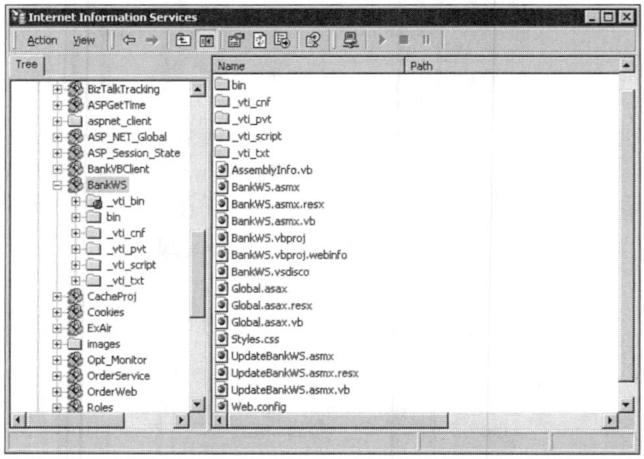

FIGURE 15.5
The Internet Services Manager Management Console.

In the next step, we will add the transaction attributes to the Web services.

Adding Transaction Attributes and an Assembly to the Web Methods

Transaction support in ASP.NET Web Services leverages the transaction support found in the common language runtime and is based on the COM+ Services model. You declare a Web Service's transactional behavior by setting the `TransactionOption` property in the `WebMethod` attribute. If an exception is thrown during a Web Service method, the transaction is automatically aborted; otherwise, the transaction is automatically committed. Due to the stateless nature of HTTP, Web Service methods can participate only as the root object in a transaction. Web Service methods, however, can invoke objects that participate in the same transaction if the object is marked to run within a COM+ transaction.

In our example, we call two Web methods from the context of a BizTalk Orchestration transaction, `Debit` and `Credit`, both of which are set with a `TransactionOption` property of `RequiresNew`. Because a Web Service can act only as the root object in a transaction, it will be instantiated in its own transactional context. So, for example, if the `Debit` action succeeds and the `Credit` action fails, the BizTalk Orchestration schedule will have to manually compensate for the failure by executing business logic to reverse the debit. This will require a slight modification to the BizTalk Orchestration schedule, `BankTransactionWS.skv`, and will be covered in the section "Calling Web Service Methods from a BizTalk Orchestration Schedule."

In our example, the only class that requires transaction support is the `UpdateBankWS.asmx` Web service's `UpdateBankWS` class. To add this support, add the following assembly and namespace references prior to the class declarations in the `UpdateBankWS.asmx` file as displayed in the following code:

```
Imports System.Web.Services
Imports System.EnterpriseServices

Public Class UpdateBankWS
    Inherits System.Web.Services.WebService
```

Next, add the `TransactionOption` property to the `WebMethod` attributes in both the `Credit` and `Debit` public Web methods as displayed here:

```
<WebMethod(TransactionOption:=TransactionOption.RequiresNew)>
➥Public Function Credit(ByVal AccountNo As Integer,
➥ByVal AmountToCredit As Integer, ByVal myBank As String) As Boolean
        Dim myConn As New ADODB.Connection()
        Dim myCommand As New ADODB.Command()


  <WebMethod(TransactionOption:=TransactionOption.RequiresNew)>
➥Public Function Debit(ByVal AccountNo As Integer,
➥ByVal AmountToDebit As Integer, ByVal myBank As String) As Boolean
        Dim myConn As New ADODB.Connection()
        Dim myCommand As New ADODB.Command()
```

Note

If the assembly is not referenced correctly, the transaction property will be highlighted as an error in the Visual Studio .NET development environment.

The Web Services code in this example is now complete and should be saved. In the next step, we build and then test the Web Services using the Web Services description page.

Testing an ASP.NET Web Service from a Browser

There are several ways to test a .NET Web Service. The easiest way is to reference its URL in a Web browser. The server, in response to this request, displays the Web Service's HTML description page. This page lists each method in the Web Service and provides a means for you to test the methods and see their XML responses.

Before you can test a Web Service, you must first build it. To build the `BankWS` Web Service project, select the `BankWS` project in the Visual Studio .NET Solution Explorer. Next, select Build, Build BankWS from the menu.

To test the two Web Services in this example, BankWS.asmx and UpdateBankWS.asmx, select each of them in the Visual Studio .NET Solution Explorer and right-click. In the pop-up menu that appears, select the View in Browser menu option. Because Visual Studio .NET contains a version of Internet Explorer, you will see the description page displayed within the Visual Studio .NET development environment. You can also choose to view the page outside the development environment by requesting the page's URL `http://localhost/BankWS/BankWS.asmx` or by entering the exact method you want to test using an `HTTP-GET` request. For example, you could enter this to test the BankWS service's GetBalance method:

```
http://localhost/BankWS/BankWS.asmx/GetBalance?AccountNo=1&myBank=BankofAmerica
```

> **Note**
>
> By default, ASP.NET Web Services support multiple protocols, including `HTTP-GET`, `HTTP-POST`, and `HTTP-SOAP`. To learn more about ASP.NET Web services please refer to the .NET Framework documentation.

Figure 15.6 shows the `QueryBankWS` Web Service test page.

FIGURE 15.6
The `QueryBankWS` *Web Service default test page.*

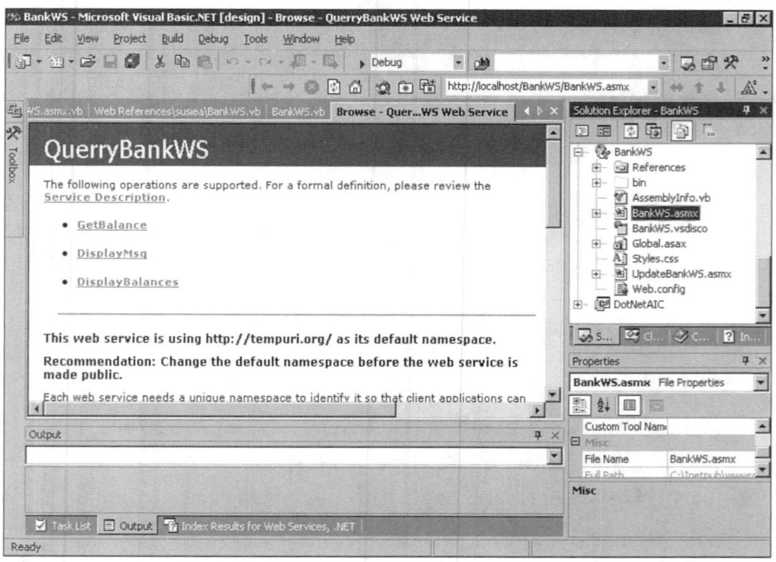

To invoke the `GetBalance` Web Service method, type an `AccountNo` equal to 1 and a `myBank` value equal to `BankofAmerica` and run the method. You should see the current balance of Account 1 from the `BankofAmerica` SQL Server database displayed as an XML response message.

Now that you've seen how easy it is to test a Web Service using a browser and the Web Services HTML description page, let's see how to do so programmatically.

Testing the Web Services from a Web Client

A compelling strength of the .NET Web Services model is its capability to mask the complexities of the Web Services architecture from the developer. In the previous section, you saw how easy it is to test a Web Service using HTTP and a standard Web browser. In the development environment, it's just as simple.

In Chapter 14, we created a simple ASP.NET Web form to test the `BankVB.vb` managed object. The Visual Studio .NET project is named `BankVBWebClient`, and the Web form is named `BankVBClient.aspx`. In this section, we modify the form by adding two buttons that will call the Web Services version of the business logic just created. Figure 15.7 shows the modified version of the Web form.

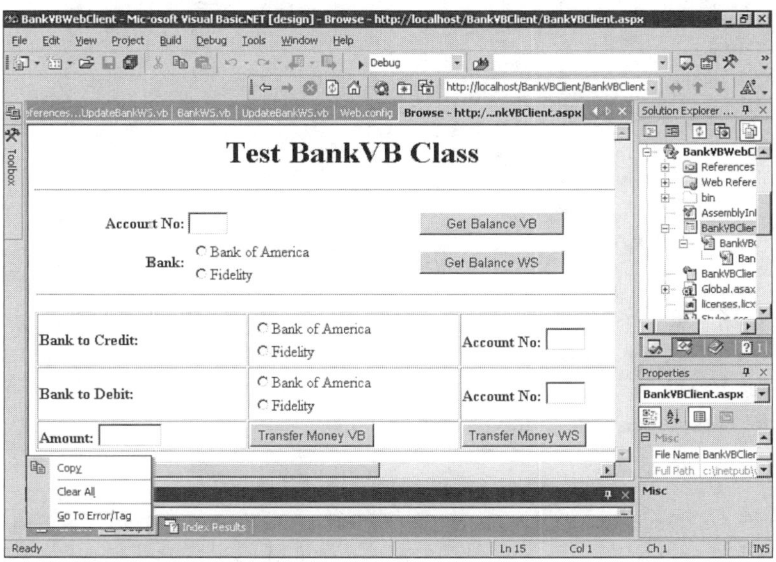

FIGURE 15.7
`BankVBClient.aspx` *Web form.*

> **Note**
>
> In ASP.NET, you have the capability to separate the business logic from the presentation layer using a concept called *code behind*. The business logic and

associated code for the `BankVBClient` example is located in a *code behind file* named `BankVBClient.aspx.vb`. Both the ASPX file and the code behind file are downloadable from the publisher's Web site.

The `Get Balance` buttons display the current value of the specific bank account in the upper left-hand corner of the page. The transfer buttons transfer the amount specified to the banks selected. You can create the test Web form from scratch or download the `BankVBClient.aspx` Web form and code behind files from the publisher's Web site. To create the example project, select the `BTSDotNet` solution in the Visual Studio .NET Solution Explorer and right-click. In the pop-up menu that appears, select Add, New Project. In the dialog that appears, select the ASP.NET Web Application option and name the Web application `BankVBWebClient` off the localhost root as displayed in Figure 15.8.

FIGURE 15.8
The Add Project dialog to add the `BankVBWebClient` *project.*

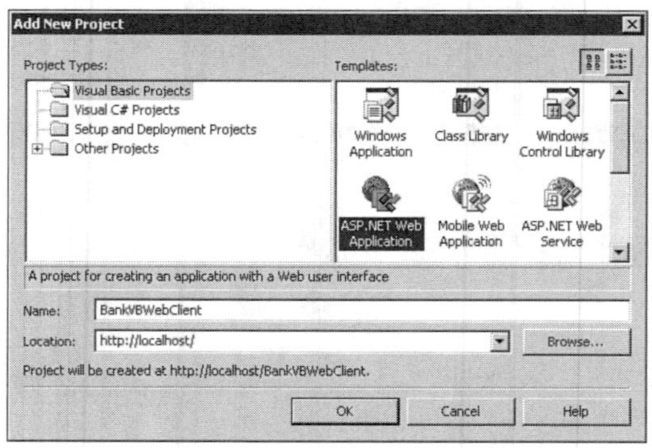

Next, you can either add a new ASP Web form manually or add the sample Web form located on the publisher's Web site. To keep things simple, we are going to assume that you have downloaded the sample code from the publisher's Web site and will be adding the completed code to the project.

To add the Web form to the new project follow these steps:

1. Select the `BankVBWebClient` project in the Solution Explorer and right-click. In the pop-up menu that appears, select the Add Existing Item menu option.
2. In the dialog that appears, navigate to the `BankVBWebClient.aspx` file and select Open.
3. Repeat the same steps, adding the code behind file named `BankVBWebClient.aspx.vb` to the project.

To reference a Web Service, you need to add a Web reference to the Visual Studio .NET project for the Web Service you want to instantiate. The Web reference creates a proxy class that defines methods that represent the actual methods exposed by the Web Service. At design time, the proxy class enables a developer to use statement completion in the Code Editor giving them the capability to code the instantiation of Web Service methods as if they were methods on a local object. The actual implementation of the methods in the proxy class consists of code to package and send SOAP requests and responses.

You create a proxy by adding a Web reference to the Web References folder in the Solution Explorer. You can also create a proxy manually using a the command-line utility `WSDL.exe`.

To create the Web reference in the `BankVBClient` Visual Studio .NET project, open the project in Visual Studio .NET and select the `References` folder in the Solution Explorer. In the dialog that appears, type your local computer name or `localhost` as the address in the address bar along with the complete path of the `.asmx` file, as shown in Figure 15.9, and press the Add Reference button.

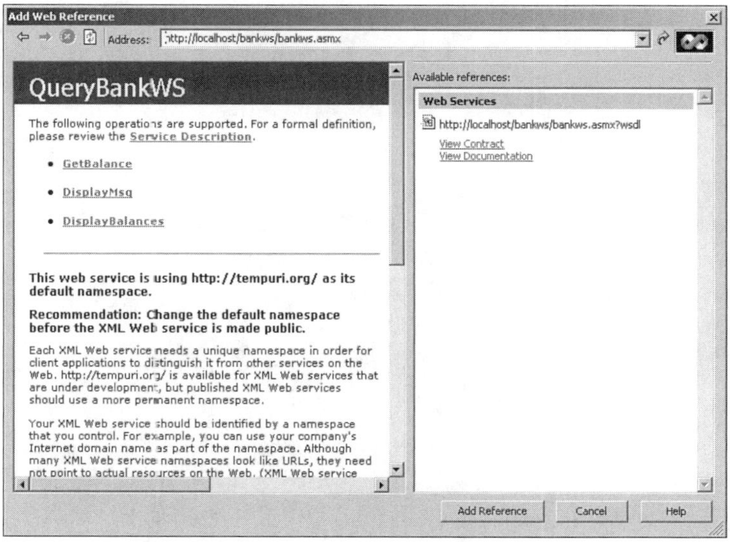

FIGURE 15.9
Adding a Web reference to the `BankVBClient` *ASP.NET project.*

A list of the Web Service's Web methods appears on the left-hand side of the dialog, and the available contracts appear in the right-hand side. In this example, there are two Web Services, `BankWS.asmx` and `UpdateBankWS.asmx`, that must be referenced. Figure 15.10 displays the `UpdateBankWS.asmx` Web Service Add Web Reference dialog.

Select the Add Reference button at the bottom of the dialog. The proxy code for the Web Services will be automatically generated and appended to the project for you. You need to repeat the same steps to add a Web reference to the `BankWS` service as well. The proxy code files are located in the `Web References` folder under the machine name you entered in the Add Web Reference dialog. In this example, we used `localhost` to reference both Web Services. Because we added two Web Services from the same location, the second service has a namespace of `localhost1`. The actual code for the proxy objects is located beneath the `Reference.map` files for each of the Web Services (see Figure 15.11).

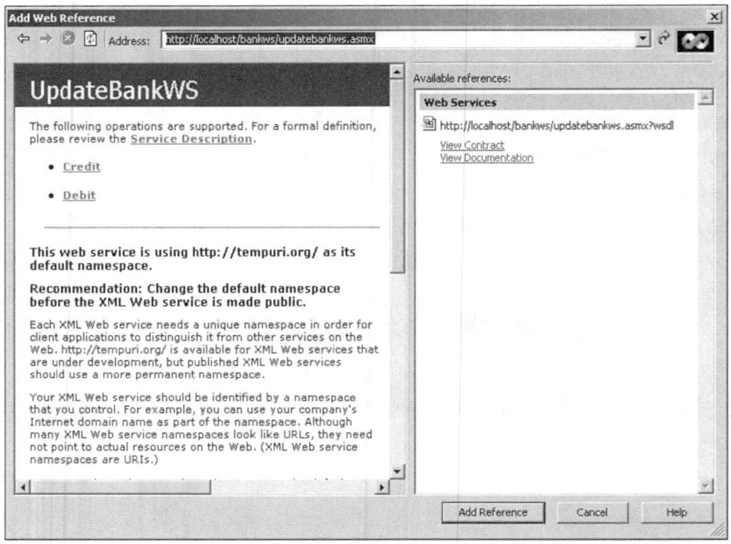

FIGURE 15.10
`UpdateBankWS.asmx` *Add Web Reference dialog.*

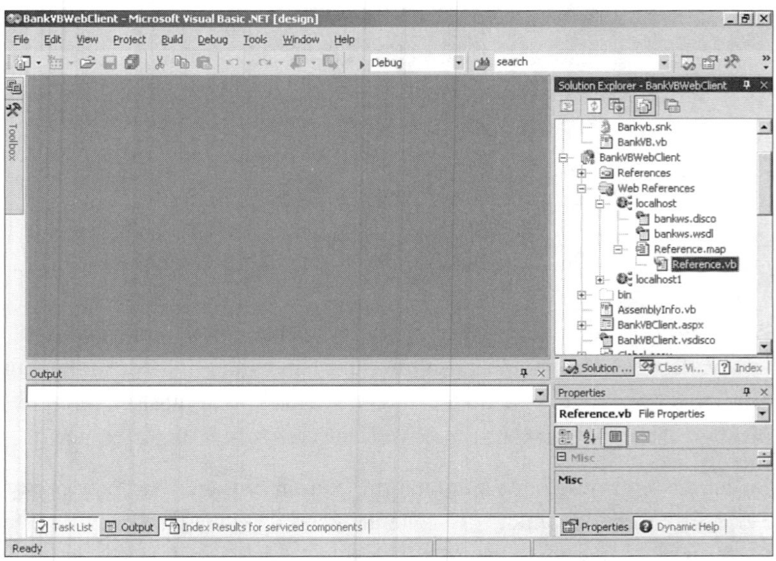

FIGURE 15.11
The Web Service proxy objects.

Listing 15.3 displays the code for the `BankWS` proxy object.

LISTING 15.3 The `Reference.vb` Proxy File

```
'------------------------------------------------------------------------------
' <autogenerated>
'     This code was generated by a tool.
'     Runtime Version: 1.0.3324.0
'
'     Changes to this file may cause incorrect behavior and will be lost if
'     the code is regenerated.
' </autogenerated>
'------------------------------------------------------------------------------

Option Strict Off
Option Explicit On

Imports System
Imports System.ComponentModel
Imports System.Diagnostics
Imports System.Web.Services
Imports System.Web.Services.Protocols
Imports System.Xml.Serialization

'
'This source code was auto-generated by Microsoft.VSDesigner,
➥Version 1.0.3324.0.
'
Namespace localhost

    '<remarks/>
    <System.Diagnostics.DebuggerStepThroughAttribute(),  _
     System.ComponentModel.DesignerCategoryAttribute("code"),  _
     System.Web.Services.WebServiceBindingAttribute(Name:="QueryBankWSSoap",
[Namespace]:="http://tempuri.org/")>  _
    Public Class QueryBankWS
        Inherits System.Web.Services.Protocols.SoapHttpClientProtocol

        '<remarks/>
        Public Sub New()
            MyBase.New
            Me.Url = "http://localhost/BankWS/BankWS.asmx"
        End Sub

        '<remarks/>
        <System.Web.Services.Protocols.SoapDocumentMethodAttribute(
➥"http://tempuri.org/DisplayBalances", RequestNamespace:=
➥"http://tempuri.org/", ResponseNamespace:="http://tempuri.org/",
Use:=System.Web.Services.Description.SoapBindingUse.Literal,
ParameterStyle:=System.Web.Services.Protocols.SoapParameterStyle.Wrapped)>  _
        Public Function DisplayBalances(ByVal Bank1Account As Integer,
```

LISTING 15.3 continued

```
➥ByVal Bank1 As String, ByVal Bank2Account As Integer,
➥ByVal Bank2 As String) As String
            Dim results() As Object = Me.Invoke("DisplayBalances",
➥New Object() {Bank1Account, Bank1, Bank2Account, Bank2})
      Return CType(results(0),String)
End Function

'<remarks/>
Public Function BeginDisplayBalances(ByVal Bank1Account As Integer,
➥ ByVal Bank1 As String, ByVal Bank2Account As Integer,
➥ByVal Bank2 As String, ByVal callback As System.AsyncCallback,
➥ByVal asyncState As Object) As System.IAsyncResult
            Return Me.BeginInvoke("DisplayBalances",
➥New Object() {Bank1Account, Bank1, Bank2Account, Bank2},
➥callback, asyncState)
End Function

'<remarks/>
Public Function EndDisplayBalances(ByVal asyncResult As
➥System.IAsyncResult) As String
      Dim results() As Object = Me.EndInvoke(asyncResult)
      Return CType(results(0),String)
End Function

'<remarks/>
<System.Web.Services.Protocols.SoapDocumentMethodAttribute(
➥"http://tempuri.org/DisplayMsg",
➥RequestNamespace:="http://tempuri.org/",
➥ResponseNamespace:="http://tempuri.org/",
➥Use:=System.Web.Services.Description.SoapBindingUse.Literal,
ParameterStyle:=System.Web.Services.Protocols.SoapParameterStyle.Wrapped)>  _
        Public Function DisplayMsg(ByVal sMessage As String) As String
            Dim results() As Object = Me.Invoke("DisplayMsg",
➥New Object() {sMessage})
      Return CType(results(0),String)
End Function

'<remarks/>
Public Function BeginDisplayMsg(ByVal sMessage As String,
➥ByVal callback As System.AsyncCallback, ByVal asyncState As Object)
➥As System.IasyncResult
      Return Me.BeginInvoke("DisplayMsg",
➥New Object() {sMessage}, callback, asyncState)
End Function

'<remarks/>
Public Function EndDisplayMsg(ByVal asyncResult As System.IAsyncResult)
➥ As String
      Dim results() As Object = Me.EndInvoke(asyncResult)
```

LISTING 15.3 continued

```
        Return CType(results(0),String)
End Function

'<remarks/>
<System.Web.Services.Protocols.SoapDocumentMethodAttribute(
➥"http://tempuri.org/GetBalance", RequestNamespace:="http://tempuri.org/",
ResponseNamespace:="http://tempuri.org/",
➥Use:=System.Web.Services.Description.SoapBindingUse.Literal,
ParameterStyle:=System.Web.Services.Protocols.SoapParameterStyle.Wrapped)>  _
        Public Function GetBalance(ByVal AccountNo As Integer,
➥ByVal myBank As String) As String
        Dim results() As Object = Me.Invoke("GetBalance",
➥New Object() {AccountNo, myBank})
        Return CType(results(0),String)
End Function

        '<remarks/>
        Public Function BeginGetBalance(ByVal AccountNo As Integer,
➥ByVal myBank As String, ByVal callback As System.AsyncCallback,
➥ByVal asyncState As Object) As
System.IAsyncResult
            Return Me.BeginInvoke("GetBalance", New Object() {AccountNo,
myBank},
➥callback, asyncState)
End Function

'<remarks/>
Public Function EndGetBalance(ByVal asyncResult As System.IAsyncResult)
➥As String
            Dim results() As Object = Me.EndInvoke(asyncResult)
            Return CType(results(0),String)
        End Function
    End Class
End Namespace
```

> **Note**
>
> Depending on which Web Service you choose in your first Web reference, the code may be generated slightly differently.

Although much of the generated proxy code is out of the scope of this chapter, there are a few things you will need to be aware of to reference the proxy object methods with which this chapter is concerned. First, the namespace that's created by Visual Studio .NET is by default set to the name of the Web Services host server, in this case `localhost` and `localhost1`. Second, each proxy class contains a public method for each of the Web

Service's public methods. To reference the proxy object in the `BankVBClient` application, you need to modify the code behind file for the `BankVBClient.aspx` file. The code behind file is named `BankVBClient.aspx.vb`. To accomplish this, open the `BankVBClient.aspx.vb` file by double-clicking on it in the Solution Explorer.

Caution

You must turn on the Show All Files option in the Solution Explorer to view this file in the tree view list. You can do this by selecting the Show All Files button located on top of the Solution Explorer.

Next, you need to create an instance of the proxy class and then access the methods of that class as you would the methods of any other class.

Note

The code has already been added for you in the sample code located on the publisher's Web site; however, the `imports` statement will need to be modified to reflect the name of your local server.

The `BankVBClient` Web form contains four buttons: two that implement the business logic in the `BankVB.vb` managed objects created in Chapter 14 and two that implement the Web Services just created. The code in Listing 15.4 was added to the `BalanceWS` and `TransferWS` buttons to call the Web Services methods.

LISTING 15.4 The `BankWS.vb` Proxy File Button Event Code

```
Private Sub btnBalance_Click(ByVal sender As System.Object,
➥ByVal e As System.EventArgs) Handles btnBalance.Click
        Dim oBank As New BankVB.BankVB.QueryBankVB()

        Dim iReturn As Integer
        iReturn = oBank.GetBalance(txtBalanceAccountNo.Text,
➥rbBalanceBank.SelectedItem.Value)
        Response.Write("Return Value: " & iReturn)

    End Sub

    Private Sub btnTransfer_Click(ByVal sender As System.Object,
➥ByVal e As System.EventArgs) Handles btnTransfer.Click
        Dim oBank As New BankVB.BankVB.UpdateBankVB()
```

LISTING 15.4 continued

```
        Dim bReturn As Boolean
        bReturn = oBank.Credit(txtCreditAccount.Text,
➥txtTransferAmount.Text, rbCreditBank.SelectedItem.Value)
        Response.Write("Credit : " & bReturn)

        bReturn = oBank.Debit(txtDebitAccount.Text,
➥txtTransferAmount.Text, rbDebitBank.SelectedItem.Value)
        Response.Write("Debit : " & bReturn)
    End Sub
    Private Sub btnBalanceWS_Click(ByVal sender As System.Object,
➥ByVal e As System.EventArgs) Handles Button3.Click, btnBalanceWS.Click
        Dim oBank As New localhost.QueryBankWS()
        Dim iReturn As Integer
        iReturn = oBank.GetBalance(txtBalanceAccountNo.Text,
➥rbBalanceBank.SelectedItem.Value)
        Response.Write("Return Value WS: " & iReturn)
    End Sub
    Private Sub btnTransferWS_Click(ByVal sender As System.Object,
➥ ByVal e As System.EventArgs) Handles btnTransfer.Click,
➥btnTransferWS.Click
       Dim oBank As New localhost1.UpdateBankWS()

       Dim bReturn As Boolear
       bReturn = oBank.Credit(txtCreditAccount.Text, txtTransferAmount.Text,
➥rbCreditBank.SelectedItem.Value)
       Response.Write("Credit : " & bReturn)

       bReturn = oBank.Debit(txtDebitAccount.Text, txtTransferAmount.Text,
➥rbDebitBank.SelectedItem.Value)
       Response.Write("Debit : " & bReturn)
   End Sub
```

The only difference between the `btnTransfer` and `btnGetbalance` buttons is the type of bank object they instantiate. For example, the `btnTransferWS_click` method creates an instance of the proxy object rather than an instance of the `BankVb` managed object created in Chapter 14.

To run the test Web form, select the `BankVBWebClient` project in the Solution Explorer and select Build, Build `BankVBWebClient` from the menu. When the project completes its build, select the `BankVBWebClient.aspx` file in the Solution Explorer and right-click. In the pop-up menu that appears, select the View in Browser menu option. Note the balance of account 1 in each bank, Bank of America and Fidelity, by selecting the `Get Balance WS` button. Then perform transfers by selecting the `Transfer WS` button. Both the `Get Balance` and `Get Balance WS` buttons should produce the same results.

To help you debug the Web Services code, the next section describes how to set up an ASP.NET project for debugging.

Debugging Tips and Tricks

To debug an ASP.NET Web Service, you must enable ASP.NET debugging in the Visual Basic application. To enable debugging, complete the following steps:

1. In Solution Explorer, select the Web Service ASP.NET project.
2. From the View menu, choose Property Pages.
3. In the project property pages dialog box, in the Configuration list box, choose Debug.
4. In the `Configuration Properties` folder, choose the Debugging category.
5. Under the `Debuggers` heading, select ASP.NET debugging.

Note

An ASP.NET project, by default, has debugging turned on.

The easiest way is to configure your Web Service project as the startup project of your solution by right-clicking on the project in the Solution Explorer. In the pop-up menu that appears, select `Set as StartUp Project`. Then select the `.asmx` file in the Solution Explorer, right-click, and set the file as the start page using the `Set As Start Page`. Next, set a break point in your Web Service file and then select `Debug, Start` from the menu or press F5.

You can also debug your Web Service by attaching to the ASP worker process. To debug your Web Service in this manner, browse an instance of it by selecting the `.asmx` file in the Solution Explorer and right-clicking. In the pop-up menu that appears, select the View in Browser menu option. The client application in this case is the Web Services description page. To debug the Web Service, set a break point in the Web Service code file and then select the Tools, Debug Processes menu option. In the dialog that appears, click the Show System Processes check box; then select the ASP.NET worker process named `aspnet_wp.exe` as displayed in Figure 15.12. To attach to the process, click the Attach button.

Then switch back to your Web Services description page and continue running the client. Your Web Service will now break on the breakpoint you set earlier.

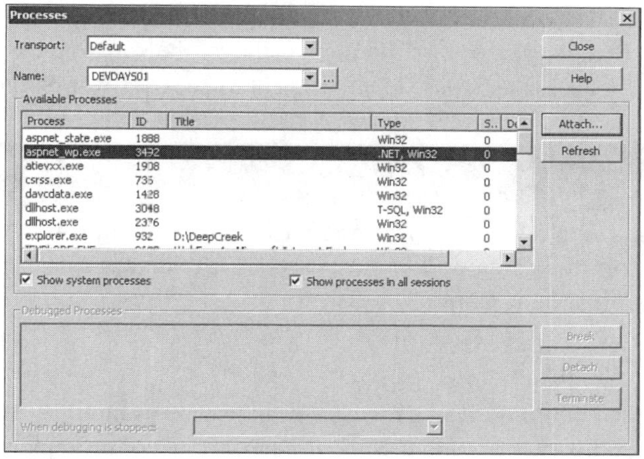

FIGURE 15.12
Attaching to the ASP.NET worker process.

> **Note**
>
> To learn more about debugging, refer to the appropriate ASP.NET Microsoft documentation.

Now that we have discussed how to create a .NET Web Service and test, it only seems natural to try and call the Web Services created from a BizTalk Orchestration schedule.

Calling Web Service Methods from a BizTalk Orchestration Schedule

Calling a Web Service from a BizTalk Orchestration schedule is similar to calling a managed component from a schedule. For example, in Chapter 14, we demonstrated how you can call a managed Visual Basic .NET object from a BizTalk Orchestration schedule by wrapping the object in a COM callable wrapper (CCW). Earlier in this chapter, the `BankVBWebClient` managed ASP.NET application was modified to call the Web Services version of the business logic. To accomplish this, we added a Web reference to the project, which automatically created two Visual Basic .NET proxy classes allowing us to call the Web Service methods as if they were local objects. Now in this chapter, we are going to discuss how to call a Web Service from an unmanaged client, the BizTalk Orchestration COM+ engine.

As mentioned earlier, ASP.NET Web Services support three protocols: `HTTP GET`, `HTTP POST`, and SOAP, each capable of remoting a call over the wire to a desired Web Service. By default, a proxy class uses the SOAP protocol to access a Web Service method.

> **Note**
>
> If for some reason a Web Service can be called only using the `HTTP-GET` or `HTTP-POST` protocols, the command-line utility `Wsdl.exe` is capable of generating the proxy classes for them manually.

We also discussed how easy it was to test a Web Service using `HTTP GET` or `POST` from a Web browser. In theory, we could use either a proxy class or a simple `HTTP` request to invoke a Web method from a BizTalk Orchestration schedule or unmanaged client application. To keep things simple, in this example, we are going to reuse the proxy Visual Basic .NET code generated by Visual Studio .NET in the `BankVBWebClient` ASP.NET application and expose it as a CCW.

In Chapter 14, we created a BizTalk Orchestration schedule named `BankTransaction.skv`. In this section, we are going to modify that schedule to call the Web method proxies. The Orchestration COM+ engine requires that all bound objects be COM based. To call the .NET proxies, they must first be wrapped in a CCW. Figure 15.13 displays the `BankTransaction.skv` schedule as it exists in Chapter 14.

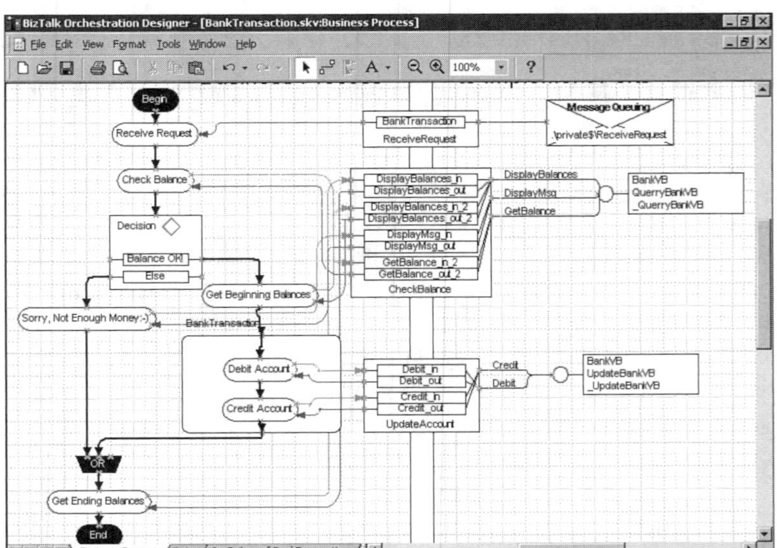

FIGURE 15.13
`BankTransaction.skv` *BizTalk Orchestration schedule.*

Figure 15.14 displays the `BankTransactionWS.skv` schedule with the modifications that are going to be made in this chapter.

FIGURE 15.14
`BankTransactionWS.skv` *BizTalk Orchestration schedule.*

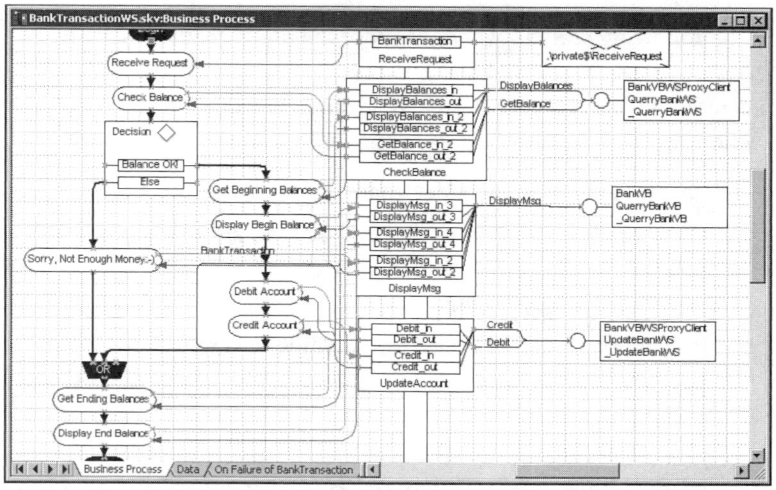

If you look closely at both schedules, you will notice that although they both produce similar technical results they differ slightly in how they process their underlying business logic. First, both schedules begin with the receipt of an XML request from a private MSMQ message queue named `ReceiveRequest`. The XML document named `BankTransaction.xml` contains the bank names, account numbers, and amount of money to transfer. After the XML document is received, it is parsed by the BizTalk orchestration Scheduler Engine and then passed to the next action, `Check Balance`. `Check Balance` calls the `GetBalance` method called the Visual Basic .NET `QueryBankVB` class created in Chapter 14. In the `BankTransactionWS.skv` file, we will call a proxy class named `BankVBWSProxyClient QueryBankWS` soon to be created in this chapter. Also note that the `Get Beginning Balance` and `Get Ending Balance` actions are also bound to that proxy object. The `Debit` and `Credit` actions are bound to a second new proxy object named `BankVBWSProxyClient UpdateBankWS` that will also be created in this chapter.

As also mentioned earlier, Web Services are nonvisual objects. In the new `BankTransactionWS.skv` schedule you will notice that there are two new actions, `Display Begin Balance` and `Display End Balance`, that call the `DisplayMsg` method of the `BankVB QueryBankVB` managed Visual Basic .NET class created in Chapter 14. The message boxes that appeared during the execution of the `BankTransaction.skv` schedule in Chapter 14 were originally called from within the `GetBalance` method of the Visual Basic .NET method. Remember, that when we created the Web Services version of this object, we commented out the line of code that instantiated the `DisplayMsg` method. So, to display a message box, these actions needed to be added and bound to the `DisplayMsg` method created in Chapter 14's object. This allows the schedule to continue to visually display the current account balances at runtime.

In the following section, we will expose the proxy methods created by Visual Studio .NET as COM objects and then modify the `Transaction.skv` file to call the proxy methods rather than the Visual Basic .NET `BankVB` methods created in Chapter 14. In the next section, we will walk through the following steps:

1. Set up the development environment.
2. Create a new Visual Basic .NET project to house the proxy objects and expose the objects and their methods using a CCW.
3. Create a new BizTalk Orchestration schedule named `BankTransactionWS.skv` from the Bank`Transaction.skv` file and modify it to call the new proxy methods.
4. Run the `BankTransactionWS.skv` file and follow its progress using the XLANG Schedule monitor.

Setting Up the Development Environment

The schedule in this example starts with a modified version of the `BankTransaction.skv` schedule in Chapter 14. This schedule can be created by modifying a downloaded version of the completed Chapter 14 schedule from the publisher's Web site or by manually adding the actions as shown in Figure 15.15.

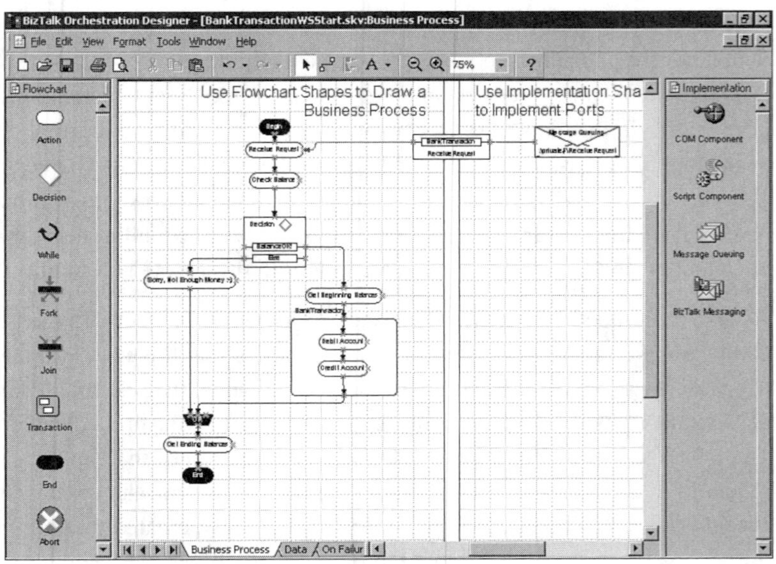

FIGURE 15.15
`BankTransactionWS.skv` *starting schedule.*

To modify the BankTransaction.skv schedule in Chapter 14, delete the component bindings not displayed in Figure 15.15 (all bindings except the MSMQ binding) and then choose Tools, Delete Unused Ports and Messages from the menu to clear the information associated with the old bindings in the Data page of the schedule. Then save the file as BankTransactionWS.skv.

> **Note**
>
> The BizTalk Orchestration piece of this chapter's example builds on the Web Service example in the first part of this chapter. If you have not yet created the MSMQ queue or SQL Server databases specified in Step 1 of the Web Services example, you must do so now.

Exposing the Web Service Proxies as COM Objects

In the BankVBWebClient ASP.NET project, we added a Web reference to access the Web Service methods. When the Web reference was added, it automatically generated two proxy objects named Reference.vb. These objects are located in the Web References folder of the BankVBWebClient project under the server names, localhost and localhost1, as displayed in Figure 15.16.

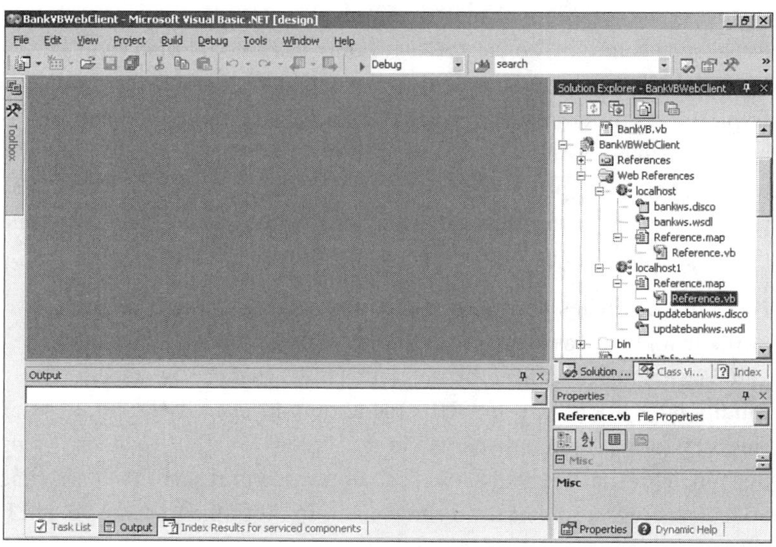

FIGURE 15.16
The Web Proxy Visual Basic .NET files for BankWS *and* UpdateBankWS *Web Services.*

To reference the proxy object methods from a BizTalk Orchestration schedule, you need to wrap them in a CCW. To accomplish this, we will create a new Visual Basic .NET project that includes the two proxy Visual Basic .NET files and then exposes them in a CCW. In this example, the new project is added to the `BTSDotNet` solution used in both Chapter 14 and this chapter.

To create the new project, select the `BTSDotNet` solution in Visual Studio .NET and right-click. In the pop-up menu that appears, select Add, New Project from the menu. In the dialog that appears, select the Visual Basic, Class Library option and name the project `BankVBWSProxyClient` as displayed in Figure 15.17.

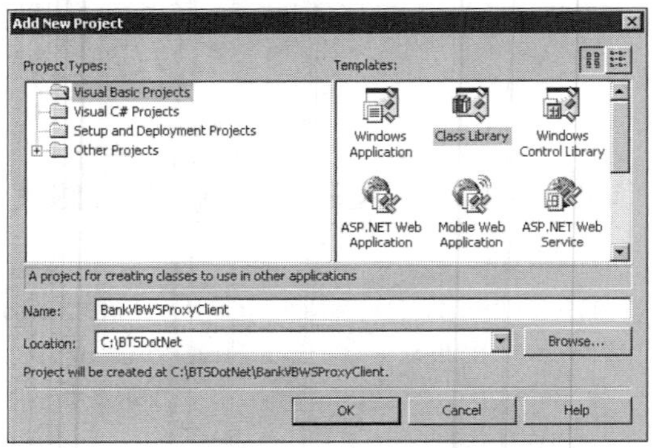

FIGURE 15.17
Adding a new Visual Basic .NET class project to the `BTSDotNet` *solution.*

Next, add the two proxy Visual Basic .NET class files to the new project by highlighting the proxy `.vb` objects one at a time in the Solution Explorer under the `Web References, Reference` folder in the `BankVBWebClient` project and then right-click to select the Copy menu option. Then navigate to the new `BankVBWSProxyClient` project in the Solution Explorer, right-click on the project, and select the Paste menu option. Because the files are both named `reference.vb`, we will need to rename them in the new project. Rename the `UpdateBankWS` proxy `reference.vb` file `UpdateBankWS.vb` and the `QueryBankWS` proxy `reference.vb` file `BankWS.vb`. The two proxy `.vb` files should now be located in the new Visual Basic .NET project as displayed in Figure 15.18.

Next, two attributes need to be added to each class: the `<Assembly (ComVisible=True)>` attribute and the `ComClass<("`*`your GUID`*`")>` attribute to the class. The `"`*`your GUID`*`"` value needs to be replaced by a unique GUID that can be generated using the Visual Studio .NET Tools, Create GUID menu option. The GUID should be generated using the Registry format option displayed in the dialog. Finally, you need to import the `System.Runtime.InteropServices` namespace to resolve the `ComClass` property just added. Listings 15.5 and 15.6 show code for both the `BankWS.vb` and `UpdateBankWS.vb` proxy files that show the addition of these attributes.

FIGURE 15.18
Adding the proxy Visual Basic .NET objects to the `BankVBWSProxy Client` *Visual Basic .NET project.*

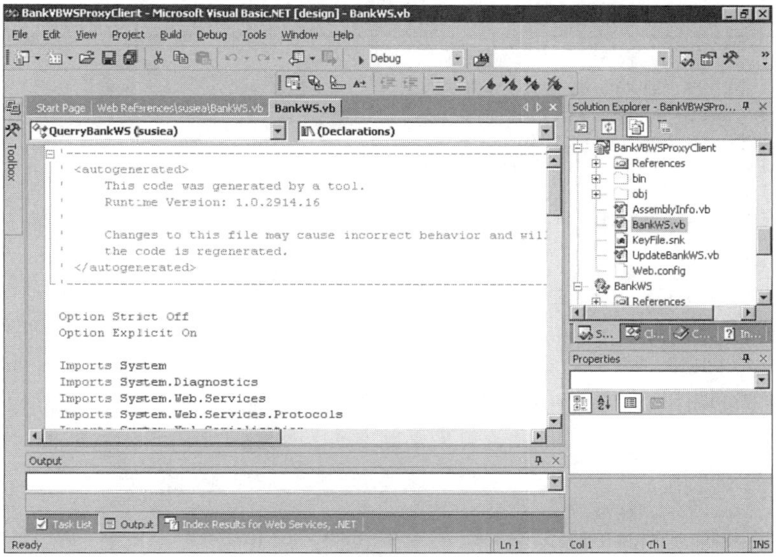

LISTING 15.5 The `BankWS.vb` Proxy File Code

```
Imports System
Imports System.ComponentModel
Imports System.Diagnostics
Imports System.Web.Services
Imports System.Web.Services.Protocols
Imports System.Xml.Serialization
Imports System.Runtime.InteropServices

'
'This source code was auto-generated by Microsoft.VSDesigner,
➥Version 1.0.3324.0.
'
<Assembly: ComVisible(True)>

Namespace localhost

    '<remarks/>
    <ComClass("54D193FA-C73C-4ba0-B972-506266673197"), _
    System.Diagnostics.DebuggerStepThroughAttribute(), _
     System.ComponentModel.DesignerCategoryAttribute("code"), _
     System.Web.Services.WebServiceBindingAttribute(Name:="QueryBankWSSoap",
[Namespace]:="http://tempuri.org/")> _
    Public Class QueryBankWS
        Inherits System.Web.Services.Protocols.SoapHttpClientProtocol
```

LISTING 15.6 The `UpdateBankWS.vb` Proxy File Code

```
Imports System
Imports System.ComponentModel
Imports System.Diagnostics
Imports System.Web.Services
Imports System.Web.Services.Protocols
Imports System.Xml.Serialization
Imports System.Runtime.InteropServices
'
'This source code was auto-generated by Microsoft.VSDesigner,
➥Version 1.0.3324.0.

'


<Assembly: ComVisible(True)>

Namespace localhost1

    '<remarks/>
    <ComClass("69F8E0A2-8EC4-4685-857C-93A1066D604A"), _
     System.Diagnostics.DebuggerStepThroughAttribute(), _
     System.ComponentModel.DesignerCategoryAttribute("code"), _
     System.Web.Services.WebServiceBindingAttribute(Name:="UpdateBankWSSoap",
[Namespace]:="http://tempuri.org/")> _
    Public Class UpdateBankWS
        Inherits System.Web.Services.Protocols.SoapHttpClientProtocol
```

Next, the project properties need to be modified to enable COM interoperability with the BizTalk Orchestration engine. To modify the project properties complete the following steps:

1. Select the `BankVBWSProxyClient` in the Solution Explorer and right-click.
2. In the pop-up menu that appears, select the Properties menu option.
3. In the dialog that appears, select the `Configuration Properties` folder and highlight the Build option.
4. Check the Register for COM Interop option. When the component is built, a COM interop wrapper will automatically be generated and registered in the Windows Registry.
5. Compile the project by selecting Build, Build `BankVBWSProxyClient` from the menu.

In the next section, we will bind the CCW just created in the `BankVBWSProxyClient` project to actions in a new schedule named `TransactionWS.skv`.

Modifying the BankTransactionWS.skv Orchestration Schedule

In the "Setting Up the Development Environment" subsection earlier in this section we discussed how to create a schedule that would serve as a starting point for the BankTransactionWS.skv Web Services BizTalk Orchestration example. The schedule is named BankTransactionWSStart.skv and was created by opening the Chapter 14 Transaction.skv schedule and deleting all bindings to the BankVB Visual Basic .NET COM implementation objects including the object itself. In this section, we will rebind the actions in the BankTransactionWSStart.skv schedule to the proxy classes in the BankVBWSProxyClient project just created.

The steps required to build the new BankTransactionWS.skv schedule are presented in the following list and will be addressed in detail in the following sections. The publisher's Web site has a series of schedules that you can download that follows along with each of these steps. The first schedule is named TransactionWSStart.skv.

1. Create two new actions named Display Begin Balance and Display End Balance and bind them to the BankVB DisplayMsg method in the schedule.
2. Bind the Check Balance, Get Beginning Balance, and Get Ending Balance actions to the BankVBWSProxyClient QueryBankWS classes DisplayBalances and GetBalances methods.
3. Bind the Credit and Debit actions to the BankVBWSProxyClient UpdateBankWS class methods Credit and Debit.
4. Modify the On Failure of Bank Transaction compensating transaction to roll back the Debit action on failure of the Credit action.

Creating Two New Actions to Display the Account Balances

As discussed earlier, Web Services by nature are nonvisual objects and as such do not have the capability to display a GUI message box. In Chapter 14's BankTransaction.skv file, we used the DisplayBalances method to retrieve the current account balance and then call the DisplayMsg method to display a GUI message box containing the account balances. During the creation of the Web Service implementation of this business logic, we commented out the call to the DisplayMsg method. To display a message box during the execution of the BankTransactionWS.skv schedule, we need to add two actions, Display Begin Balance and Display End Balance, to the schedule. These actions will be bound to the Visual Basic .NET DisplayMsg method in the BankVB.vb .NET object created in Chapter 14. The BankVB.vb object was compiled with the

Register for COM Interop option checked and is, therefore, accessible via a CCW in the schedule.

> **Note**
>
> The name of the method `DiplayBalances` in the Bank Web Service implementation is a little deceiving given that it no longer displays the balances. We kept the name the same to minimize the number of modifications to the `BankVB.vb` managed code.

To accomplish this, open the `BankTransactionWSStart.skv` file created in the "Setting Up the Development Environment" section earlier in this chapter. Select File, Save As from the menu and name the schedule `BankTransactionWS.skv`. Next, add two new actions to the schedule named `Display Begin Balance` and `Display End Balance`. The actions should be integrated into the schedule as displayed in Figure 15.19.

FIGURE 15.19

Adding the `Display Begin Balance` *and* `Display End Balance` *actions,*

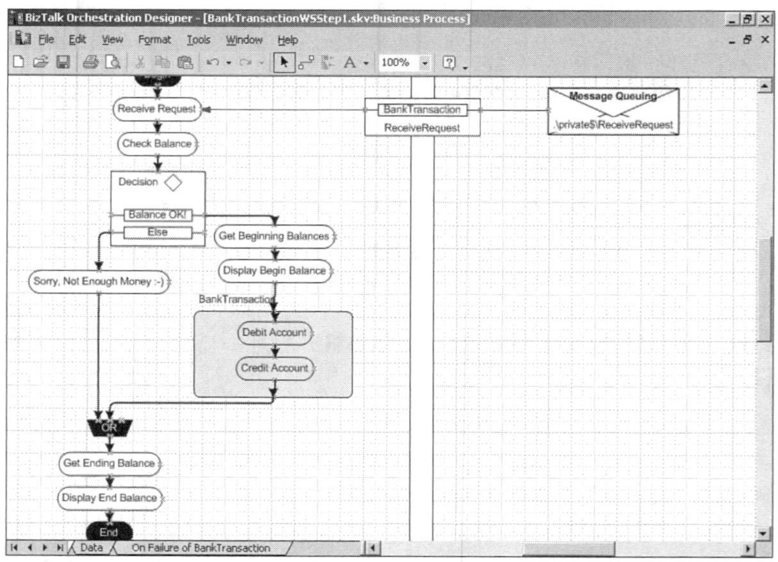

Now, we need to bind the actions to their implementation object, which in this case will be the `BankVB` managed object created in Chapter 14. To bind the `Display Begin Balance` to its implementation object, drag a COM object onto the implementation area. In the COM Component Binding Wizard dialog that appears, name the port `DisplayMsg` and select Next. In the Static or Dynamic Communication Wizard dialog, select Static and then click Next. In the Class Information step, navigate to the `BankVB QueryBankVB` object and select it as displayed in Figure 15.20.

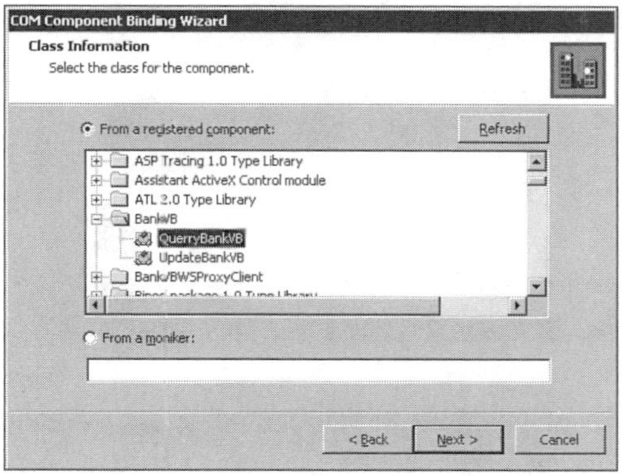

FIGURE 15.20
The Class Information step in the COM Component Binding Wizard.

Click Next and then in the Interface Information dialog that appears, select the `_QueryBankVB` option as displayed in Figure 15.21. The `QueryBankVB` interface contains the methods we are going to call from the schedule.

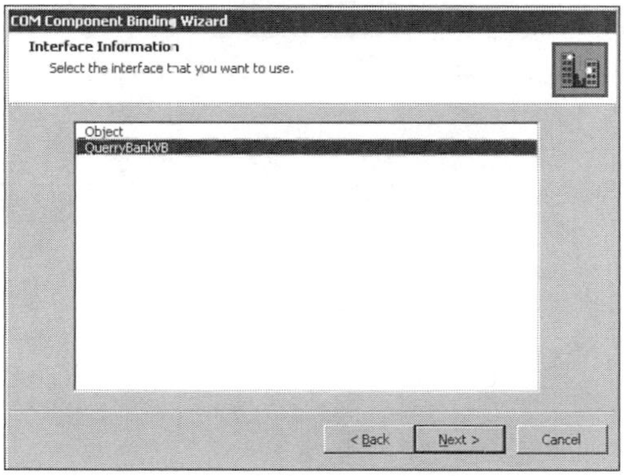

FIGURE 15.21
The Interface Information step in the COM Component Binding Wizard.

Click Next and then select the `DisplayMsg` check box in the Method Information dialog of the COM Component Binding Wizard and click Next (see Figure 15.22). In this case, we only need to use the `DisplayMsg` method.

In the Advanced Properties dialog that appears, keep the defaults and select Finish.

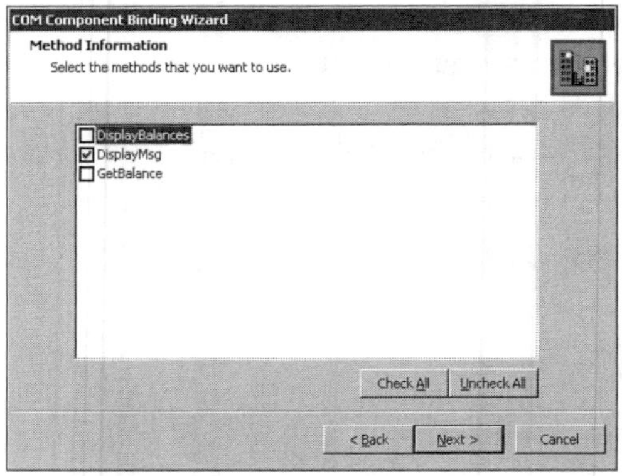

FIGURE 15.22
The Method Information step in the COM Component Binding Wizard.

Next, we need to bind the display actions to the methods in the `BankVB` implementation shape. To accomplish this, connect each action to the `DisplayMsg` port that's connected to the `BankVB` implementation object. A Communication Wizard appears when you attach each action. In the initial Communication Wizard step, select the Initiate Synchronous Method Call option and click Next. In the Message Information dialog that appears, select the Create a New Message option and then select Next. In the Message Specification Information dialog that appears, select the `DisplayMsg` method and then select Finish. Repeat the same steps for both the `Display End Balance` and `Display Begin Balance` actions. The `BankTransactionWS.skv` file appears as displayed in Figure 15.23.

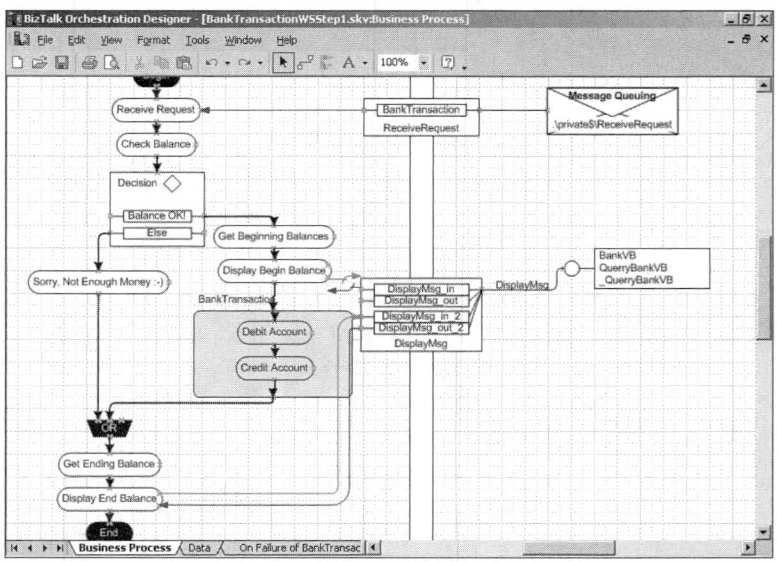

FIGURE 15.23
`BankTransactionWS.skv` *schedule after Step 1.*

Binding the `Check Balance`, `Get Beginning Balance`, and `Get Ending Balance` Actions

We are now ready to bind the Web Services to their appropriate actions. The first action to bind is the `Check Balance` action. This action calls the `DisplayBalances` method of the `BankVBWSProxyClient` proxy object `QueryBankWS` class. To begin, drag the COM implementation object onto the implementation area. In the COM Component Binding Wizard that appears, enter the name `GetBalances` as the port name and click Next. In the Static or Dynamic Communication wizard step, select Static and click Next. In the Class Information wizard step that appears, navigate to the `BankVBWSProxyClient` object and select the `QueryBankWS` class as displayed in Figure 15.24.

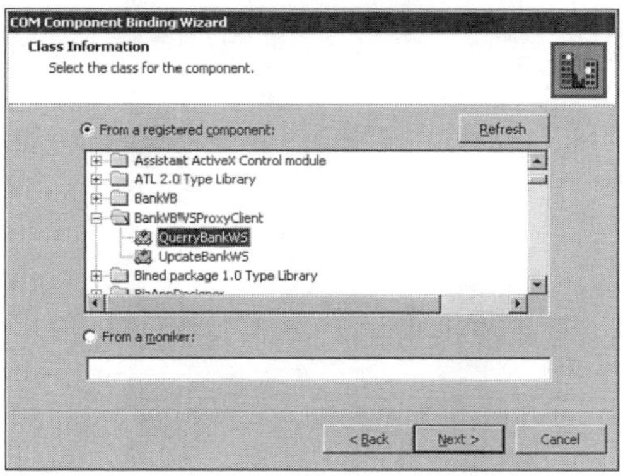

FIGURE 15.24
The Class Information dialog for the `QueryBankWS` *class.*

In the Interface Information dialog that appears, select the `_QueryBankWS` interface as shown in Figure 15.25 and then click Next.

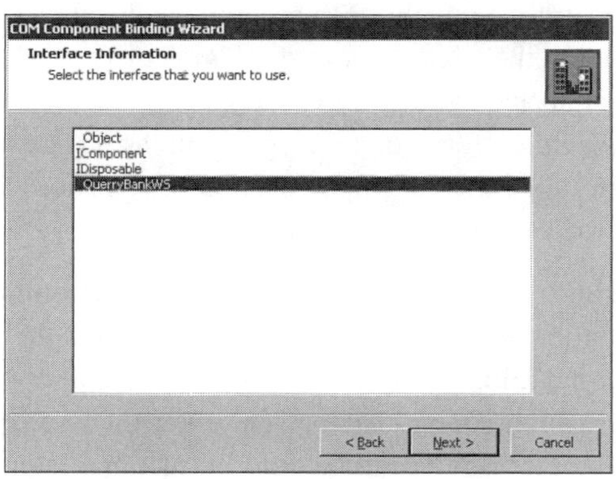

FIGURE 15.25
The Interface Information dialog for the `QueryBankWS` *class.*

In the Method Information dialog that appears, select the `DisplayBalances` and `GetBalance` methods as displayed in Figure 15.26.

Note

Remember, you do not need to check the `DisplayMsg` method in the Web Service. In this example, we are using the `DisplayMsg` method from the `BankVB` object created in Chapter 14.

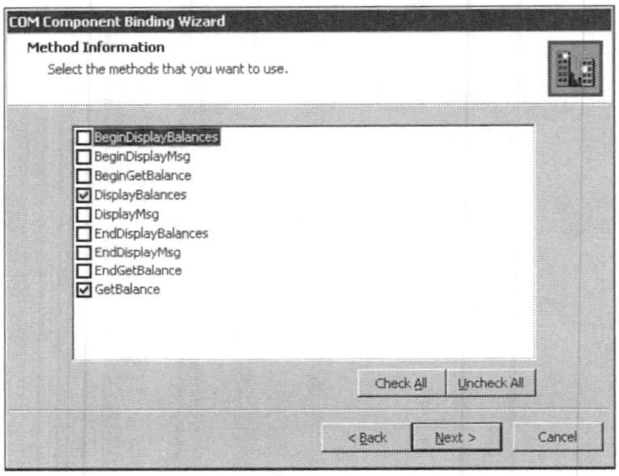

FIGURE 15.26
The Method Information dialog for the `QueryBankWS` *class.*

In the Advanced Port dialog that appears, keep the default values for all properties and click Finish.

Next, we need to bind the `Check Balance`, `Get End Balance`, and `Get Beginning Balance` actions to the appropriate methods in the `QueryBankWS` class. The `Check Balance` action calls the `GetBalance` method. To accomplish this, bind the action to the `GetBalances` port connected to the `QueryBankWS` class implementation object. In the Communication Wizard that appears, select Initiate a Synchronous Method Call option and click Next. In the Messaging Information dialog, select the Create a New Message Option and then click Next. In the Message Specification Information dialog that appears, select the GetBalance method as displayed in Figure 15.27 and then click Finish.

Next, we want to bind the `Get Beginning Balances` action to the same implementation object. Begin by connecting the action to the `GetBalances` port. In the Communication Wizard that appears, select the Initiate a Synchronous Method Call option and click Next. In the Message Information dialog that appears, select the Create a New Message option and click Next. In the Message Specification Information dialog that appears, select the `DisplayBalances` method as displayed in Figure 15.28 and click Finish.

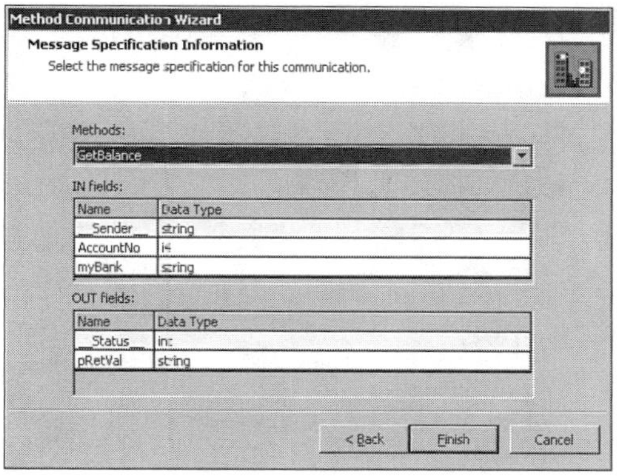

FIGURE 15.27
The Message Specification Information dialog for the `Check Balance` *action.*

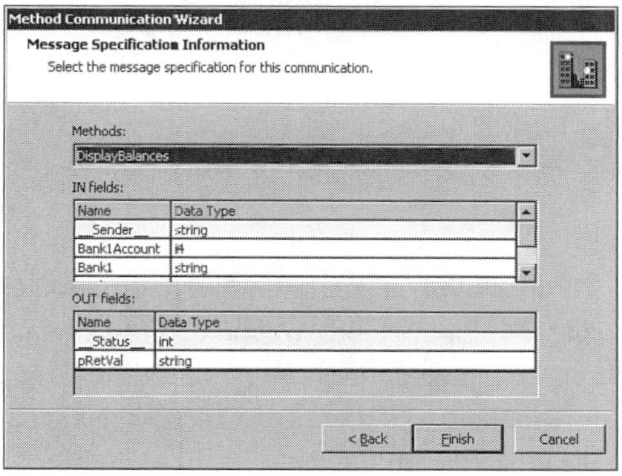

FIGURE 15.28
The Message Specification Information dialog for the `Get Beginning Balances` *action.*

The final action to bind is the `Get Ending Balances` action. To begin, connect the action to the `GetBalances` port as we did in the previous step. In the Communication Wizard that appears, select the Initiate a Synchronous Method Call option and click Next. In the Message Information dialog that appears, select the Create a New Message option and click Next. In the Message Specification Information dialog that appears, select the `DisplayBalances` method as we did in the `Get Beginning Balance` action and click Finish. At this point, all actions except the `Debit` and `Credit` actions in the `BankTransactionWS.skv` schedule should be connected to an implementation object as displayed in Figure 15.29.

Next, we need to address the data flow within the schedule. To begin, navigate to the Data page in the BizTalk Orchestration Designer. The schedule begins with the receipt of an XML file named `BankTransaction`. This file contains the names of the debit and credit banks, their account numbers, and the amount of money to transfer. The `BankTransaction` message is parsed by the BizTalk Orchestration COM+ engine and is available in the Data page.

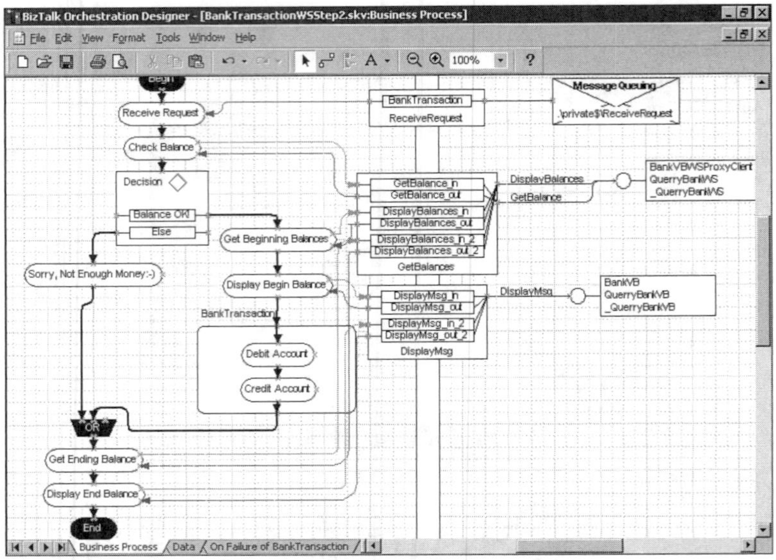

FIGURE 15.29
The completed Step 2 `TransactionWS.skv` *schedule.*

The first action that requires data input is the `Check Balance` action. The `Check Balance` action accepts the name of a bank and an account number and returns the current balance of the account. In this schedule, the input values are the debit bank name and the debit account number from the `BankTransaction` message. The return value is evaluated by the decision shape later in the schedule to determine whether the account has enough money to process the transaction. To set up the data flow, you need to connect the `BankTransaction` message's `DebitBank` and `DebitAccount` fields to the `GetBalance_in` message's `myBank` and `AccountNo` fields as shown in Figure 15.30.

Next, we need to set the data flow for the `Get Beginning Balance` and `Get Ending Balance` actions. The first action, `Get Beginning Balance`, calls the `DisplayBalances` method, which accepts the bank name and account number of both accounts and returns a string containing the balance of each. The `DisplayBalances` return value is then passed to the `DisplayMsg` method. To begin, connect the `BankTransaction` message's `DebitBank` and `DebitAccount` string fields to the `DisplayBalances_in` and `Display_Balances_in_2` `Bank1` and `Bank1Account` fields. Then repeat the same connections for the `CreditBank` and `CreditAccount` `BankTransaction` message strings, but this time connect them to the `Bank2` and `Bank2Account` fields as displayed in Figure 15.31. Next, connect the return value `pRetVal` of the `Display_Balances_in` message to the `DisplayMsg_in` `sMessage` field and the return value `pRetVal` of the `Display_Balances_ in_2` message to the `DisplayMsg_in_2` `sMessage` fields as shown in Figure 15.31.

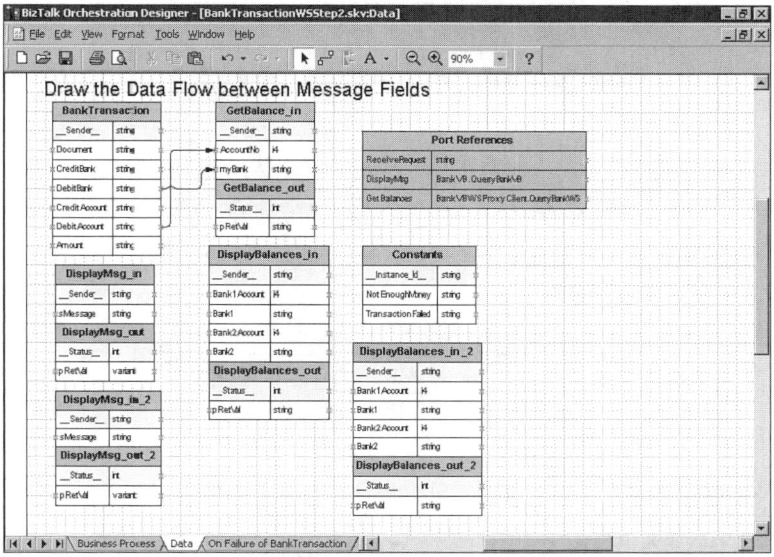

FIGURE 15.30
Binding the `BankTransaction` *message's* `DebitBank` *and* `AccountNo` *fields for* `Check Balance`.

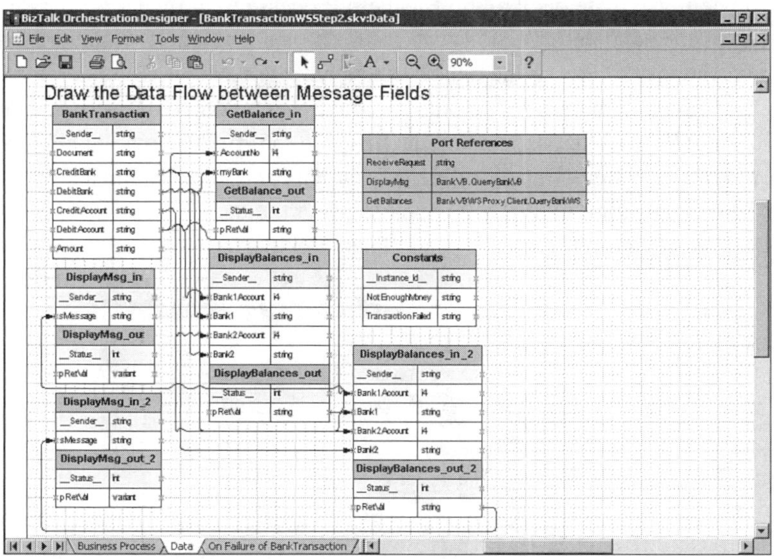

FIGURE 15.31
Binding the fields to display the begin and end balances.

The return value from the `Check Balance` action is evaluated in the `Balance OK!` decision shape. If the account has enough money, the transaction will continue; otherwise, a message box appears displaying an insufficient funds message. Figure 15.32 shows the properties for the decision shape.

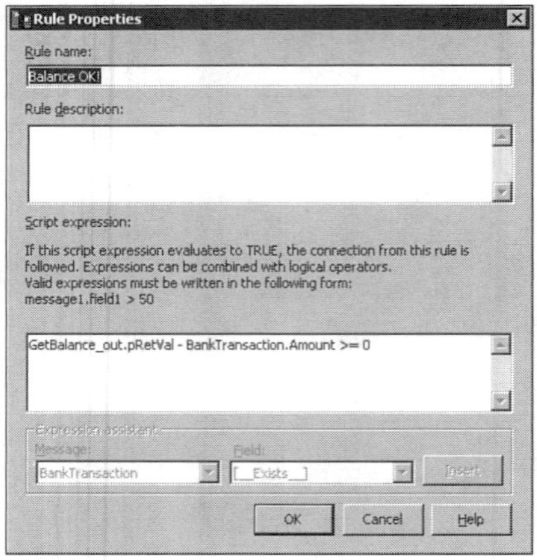

FIGURE 15.32
The `Balance OK!` *decision properties dialog.*

We are now ready to bind the `Credit` and `Debit` actions.

Binding the `Credit` and `Debit` Actions

To begin, navigate back to the Business Process tab in the `BankTransactionWS.skv` file. The `Credit` and `Debit` actions call methods on a new implementation object bound to the `UpdateBankWS` class of the `BankVBWSProxyClient` object. To create the object, drag the COM implementation shape onto the implementation area. In the COM Component Binding Wizard that appears, name the port `UpdateAccount` and click Next. In the Static or Dynamic Communication Wizard that appears, select Static and click Next. In the Class Information dialog that appears, select the `BankVBWSProxyClient UpdateBankWS` class as shown in Figure 15.33 and then click Next.

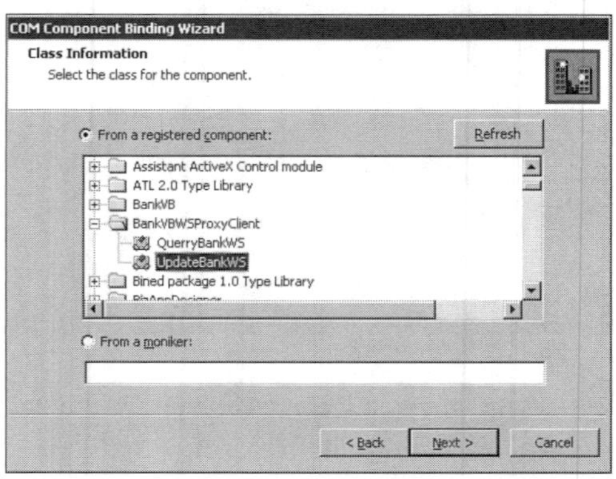

FIGURE 15.33
The Class Information dialog for `Debit` *and* `Credit` *actions.*

In the Interface Information dialog that appears, select the `_UpdateBankWS` interface as displayed in Figure 15.34 and then click Next. In the Method Information dialog that appears, select the `Credit` and `Debit` methods and then click Next.

FIGURE 15.34
The Interface Information dialog for `Debit` and `Credit` actions.

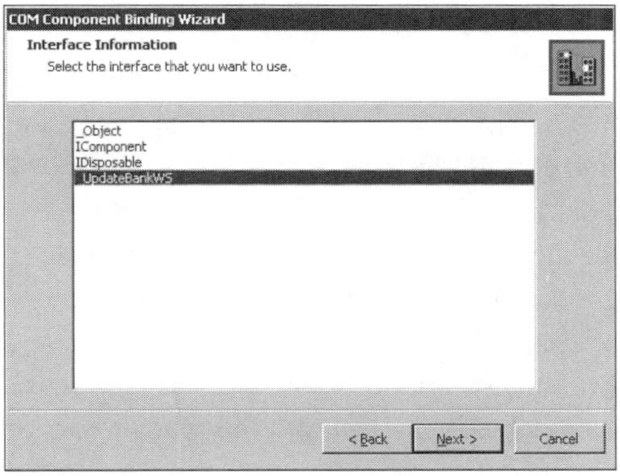

In the Advanced Port Properties dialog, set the Transaction Support to Supported and check the Abort Transaction if Method Returns a Failure HRESULT as shown in Figure 15.35 and then click Finish.

FIGURE 15.35
The Advanced Port Properties dialog for `Debit` and `Credit` actions.

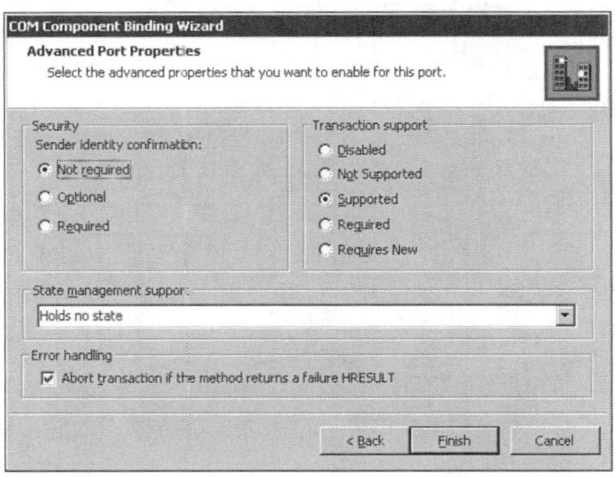

The transaction settings for this implementation shape must be set to Supports Transactions to be bound to an action that is included inside a BizTalk Orchestration transaction; for example, both the `Debit` and `Credit` actions are enclosed in a transaction named `BankTransaction`.

Next, we need to bind the `Debit` and `Credit` actions to the `Debit` and `Credit` methods in the `UpdateBankWS` class implementation shape. To begin, connect the `Credit Account` action to the `UpdateAccount` port shape. In the Communication Wizard that appears, select the Initiate a Synchronous Method Call option and click Next. In the Message Information dialog that appears, select the Create a New Message option and click Next. In the Message Specification Information dialog, select the `Credit` method and click Finish. Repeat the same steps for the `Debit` action, setting the Message Specification Information dialog method to the `Debit Account` method.

Next, we need to set the data flow for the actions we just bound. To begin, navigate to the Data page of the `BankTransactionWS.skv` schedule. The `Debit` and `Credit` methods expect three input parameters: account number, bank name, and amount to debit or credit. The values for these parameters are located in the input `BankTransaction` message. To set the data flow for these actions, connect the `BankTransaction` message's `DebitBank`, `DebitAccount`, and `Amount` fields to the `Debit_in` message's `myBank`, `AccountNo`, and `AmountToDebit` fields. Then connect the `BankTransaction` message's `CreditBank`, `CreditAccount`, and `Amount` fields to the `Credit_in` message's `myBank`, `AccountNo`, and `AmountToCredit` fields as displayed in Figure 15.36.

FIGURE 15.36
The data page at the completion of Step 3.

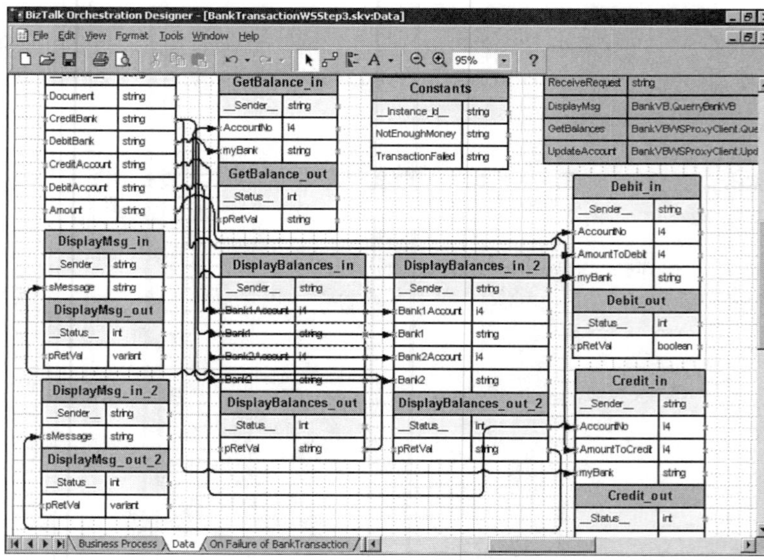

Modify the On Failure Processing

So what happens if the `Debit` or `Credit` action fails, or there is not enough money to debit? The easiest issue to address is a lack of sufficient funds in the debit account. If the `Debit` account's balance is less than the amount in the debit transaction, the transaction will not be processed, and an event will be triggered notifying us of this information. In this example, we check the current balance and then verify its value in the decision shape. If the balance is insufficient, a message box is triggered notifying us.

The decision shape and associated actions are already defined in the `BankTransactionWS.skv` schedule to accommodate this; however, we do need to complete the workflow by binding an action to a port and then modifying the Data page to accommodate the change. To complete the workflow, we need to bind the `Sorry, Not Enough Money!` action to the `DisplayMsg` port and set its input field values in the Data page. To begin, connect the `Sorry, Not Enough Money!` action to the `DisplayMsg` port. In the Communication Wizard that appears, select the Instantiate a Synchronous Method Call option and click Next. In the Message Information dialog, select the Create a New Message option and click Next. In the Message Specification Information dialog, select the `DisplayMsg` method and click Finish. Next, navigate to the Data tab. The new message is named `DisplayMsg_in_3`, and it accepts a constant from the Data tab as its only input. Connect the `NotEnoughMoney` string constant in the `Constants` message to the `sMessage` in field in the `DisplayMsg_in_3` message as displayed in Figure 15.37.

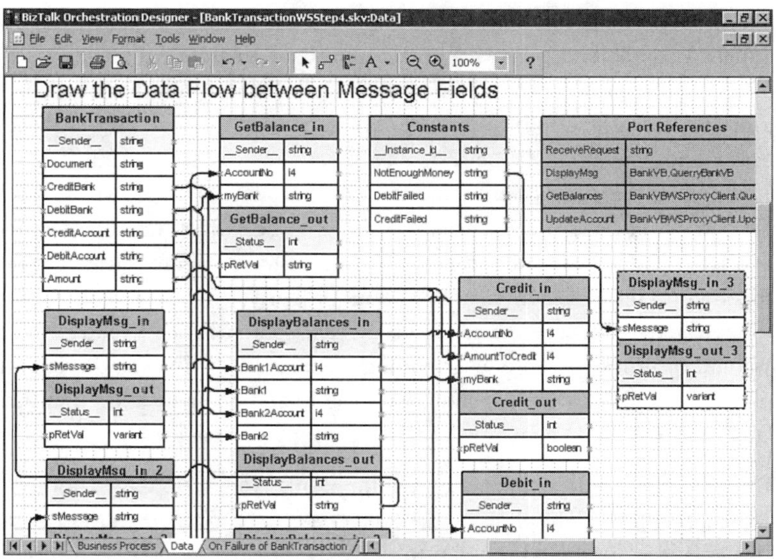

FIGURE 15.37
Connecting the Data page for the `Sorry Not Enough Money!` *action.*

Constants can be defined by selecting the `Constants` message in the Data tab and then right-clicking. In this example, we will use three constants: `NotEnoughMoney`, `DebitFailed`, and `CreditFailed`. The `BankTransaction.skv` schedule from Chapter 14 used a constant named `TransactionFailed`. In this example, we will use two distinct messages to notify us of the failure of the `Debit` or `Credit` action. To create the new constant, right-click on the `Constants` message and select the `Properties` pop-up menu option. In the `Constants Message Properties` dialog that appears, delete the `TransactionFailed` string and add two new constants named `DebitFailed` and `CreditFailed` as displayed in Figure 15.38. The messages can say anything you want.

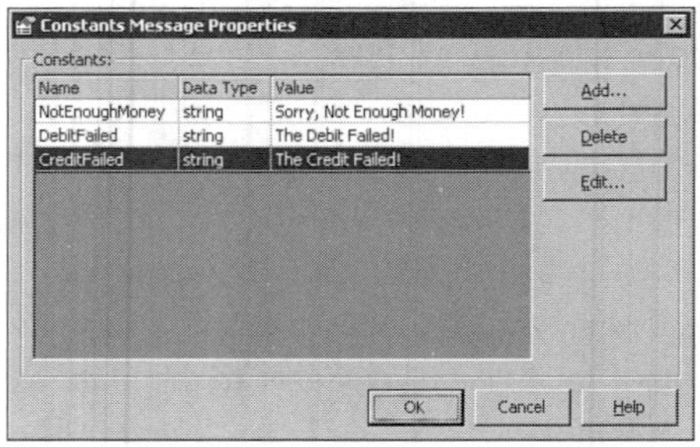

FIGURE 15.38
The `Constants` *message in the Data tab.*

Next, we need to configure the actions that will occur when either the `Debit` or `Credit` action fails. As mentioned earlier, the transactional capabilities of a Web Service are limited to its participation in the root level of a transaction. In this example, we are instantiating a Web method from within the context of an already existing transaction. This means that regardless of whether the BizTalk Orchestration transaction exists, a new transaction is going to be automatically generated for each Web Service call, in this case `Debit` and `Credit`. If the `Debit` succeeds and `Credit` fails, the `Debit` will not be rolled back unless it's done so programmatically because the business logic for each exists in the context of a separate transaction and does not affect the other's outcome. If an action in a BizTalk Orchestration transaction fails, all actions are retried the number of times specified in the transaction's retry count property. So, in the scenario just mentioned where the debit succeeds and the credit fails, both actions would be retried an equal amount of times—in essence, debiting the account X times and crediting an account 0 times. To eliminate this problem, we need to add compensation transaction logic to the On Failure of `BankTransaction` tab and set the transaction retry property value to 0.

To begin, we want to make sure that the Bank Transaction does not retry on failure. To accomplish this, right-click on the `BankTransaction` shape in the BizTalk Orchestration Designer and set the retry count to 0. Next, we need to modify the compensating transaction's workflow by adding some workflow actions to the On Failure of `BankTransaction` tab. To begin, navigate to the On Failure of `BankTransaction` tab and add five shapes to the designer: three action shapes, a decision shape, and a join shape. Next, configure them and name them as shown in Figure 15.39.

FIGURE 15.39
The On Failure of `BankTransaction` *tab.*

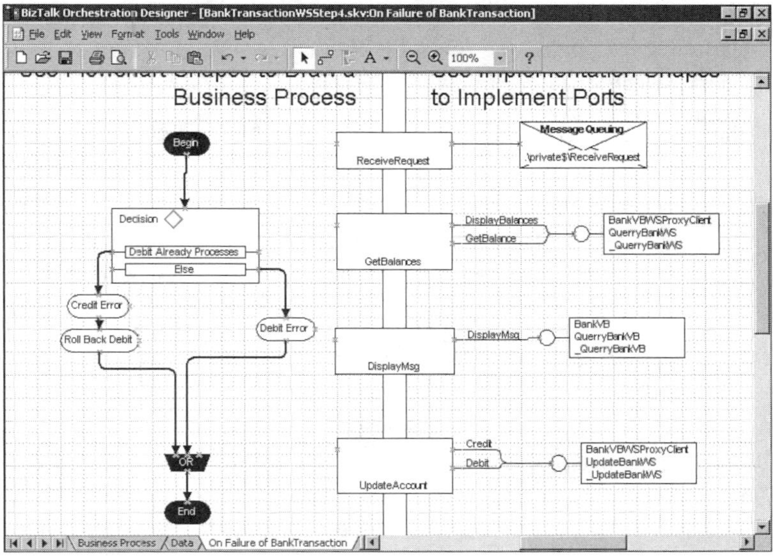

The three action shapes are named `Credit Failed`, `Debit Failed`, and `Roll Back Debit`. The decision shapes properties are configured as displayed in Figure 15.40.

FIGURE 15.40
The decision properties in the On Failure of `BankTransaction` *tab.*

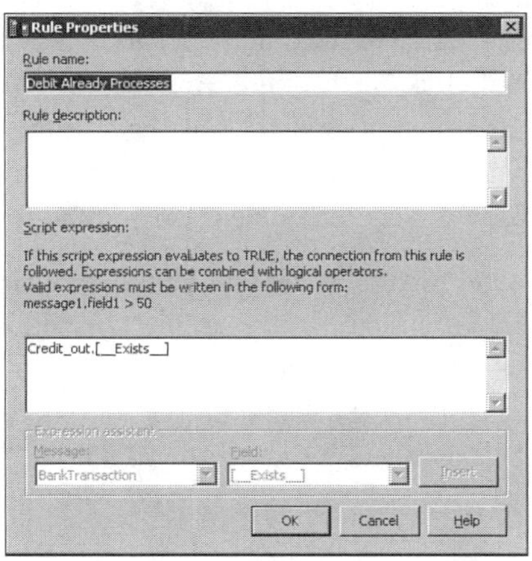

To configure the decision shape, right-click on the decision shape in the BizTalk Orchestration Designer and select the Add New Rule pop-up menu option. Next, add a new rule named `Debit Already Processed` to the criteria and set the script expression equal to the `Credit_out.[__Exists__]` value as displayed in Figure 15.40.

The join shape's properties also need to be configured. To configure the join shape, right-click on the join shape and select the Properties pop-up menu option. In the dialog that appears, select the OR option.

If the `Debit` succeeds and the `Credit` fails, the `Debit` action's business logic needs to be programmatically rolled back. The decision shape tests to see whether the `Credit_out` value exists. If it exists, the `Credit` action has failed; otherwise, the `Debit` action has failed and no additional processing is needed. If the `Credit` action fails, the account that was debited needs to be credited with the original debited account.

To accomplish this, you need to bind the actions you just added to their implementation objects. First, bind the `Credit Error` and `Debit Error` actions to the `DisplayMsg` port to enable the display a GUI message box notifying us of the error. Begin by selecting the `Credit Error` action and connecting it to the `DisplayMsg` port. In the Communication Wizard that appears, select the Initiate a Synchronous Method Call option and click Next. In the Message Information dialog that appears, select the Create a New Message Option and click Next. In the Message Information Specification dialog that appears, select the `DisplayMsg` method and click Finish. Repeat the same steps for the `Debit Error` action.

Next, we need to connect the `Roll Back Debit` action to the `UpdateAccount` ports `Credit` method. To begin, select the `Roll Back Debit` action and connect it to the `UpdateAccount` port. In the Communication Wizard that appears, select the Initiate Synchronous Method Call option and click Next. In the Message Information dialog that appears, select the Create a New Message Option and click Next. In the Message Specification Information dialog that appears, select the `Credit` method and click Finish. Next, we need to update the Data page to accommodate the data flow for the new actions.

The `Roll Back Debit` action is bound to an implementation object that supports transactions. To bind an action to an object with this property setting, the action must be enclosed within a transaction. To keep things simple, we are going to add a transaction shape to the designer that includes just the `Roll Back Debit` action. To accomplish this, drag the transaction shape onto the design pane over the top of the `Roll Back Debit` action as displayed in Figure 15.41.

The transaction shape requires that both the inbound and outbound connections be made to the shape itself as opposed to the first and last action in the shape. In this example, the `Error in Credit` action is directly connected to the `Roll Back Debit` action. To accommodate the transaction shape, connect the `Error in Credit` action directly to the transaction shape, the transaction shape to the `Roll Back Debit` action, the `Roll Back Debit` action back to the exit of the transaction shape, and then the exit of the transaction shape to the `OR` join shape as displayed in Figure 15.41.

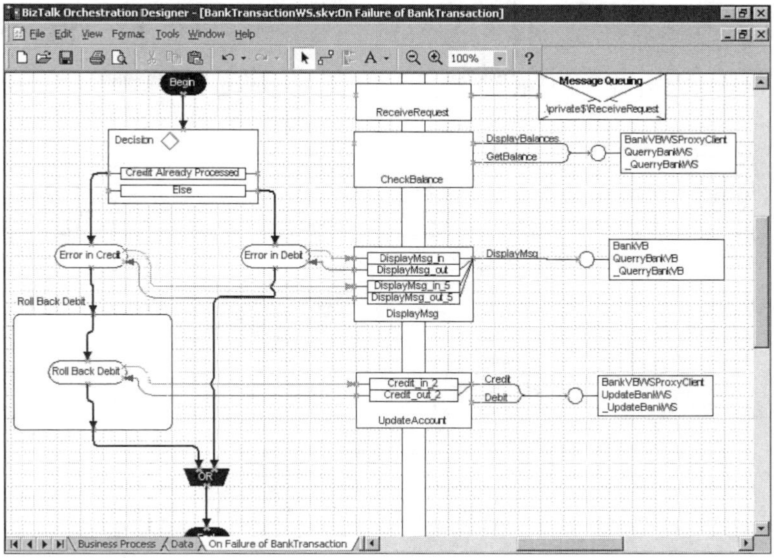

FIGURE 15.41
The On Failure of `BankTransaction` *tab at the completion of Step 4.*

To update the Data page, navigate to the Data tab in the BizTalk Orchestration Designer. As a result of our modification to the compensating transaction, there are three new messages in the Data page: `Display_msg_in_4`, `Display_msg_in_5`, and `Credit_in_2`. The display messages need to be bound to the `Constants` message's `DebitFailed` and `CreditFailed fields`. To accomplish this, select the `CreditFailed Constants` message and connect it to the `Display_msg_in_4 sMessage` field. Then select the `DebitFailed Constants` message and connect it to the `Display_msg_in_5 sMessage` field.

Next, we need to connect the `BankTransaction` message fields to the `Credit_in_2` to roll back the debit. To accomplish this, connect the `BankTransaction` message's `DebitBank`, `DebitAccount`, and `Amount` fields to the `Credit_in_2` message's `myBank`, `AccountNo`, and `AmountToCredit` fields as displayed in Figure 15.42.

The schedule is now complete and ready to compile. To compile the schedule, select File, Make XLANG `BankTransactionWS.skx` from the menu. A dialog appears telling you the status of the compile. When the compile is complete, an `.skx` file appears in the same directory as the `.skv` schedule file with which you've been working. In some installations, you may encounter a system error as displayed in Figure 15.43. If you receive this error, which may occur twice during a compile, select No each time.

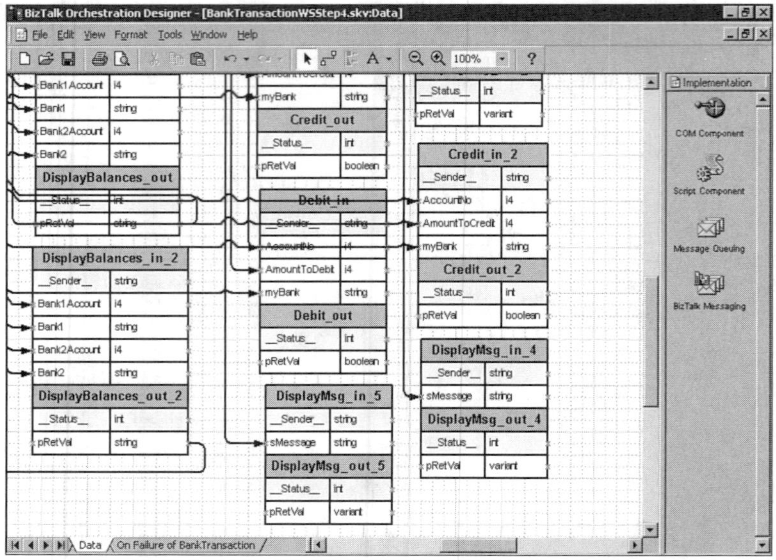

FIGURE 15.42
The Data tab at completion of Step 4.

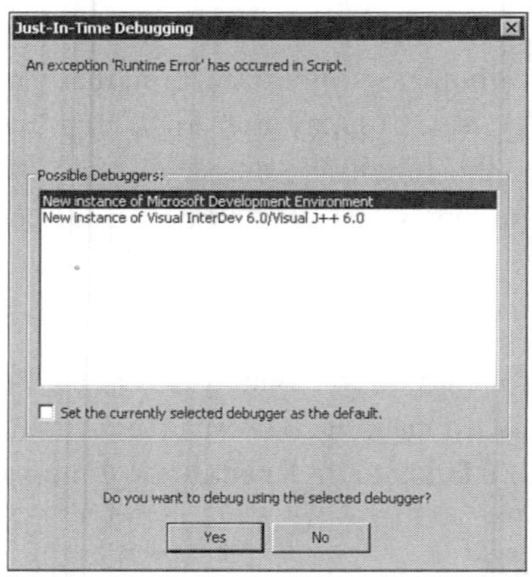

FIGURE 15.43
Just-in-time debugging error encountered while compiling.

Running the New `TransactionWS` Schedule

To run the schedule, you must place a `BankTransaction` XML file on the MSMQ private queue named `ReceiveRequest` and then start an instance of the `BankTransactionWS.skx` schedule. There are two `.vbs` script files to assist with this task. The first copies the contents of an XML file named `BankTransInstance.xml` to the private MSMQ queue named `ReceiveRequest`. The script file is named `File2Queue.vbs` and contains the code displayed in Listing 15.7.

LISTING 15.7 The `File2Queue.vbs` Script File

```
'************************************************************
'MSMQ constants

'Access modes
const MQ_RECEIVE_ACCESS          = 1
const MQ_SEND_ACCESS             = 2
const MQ_PEEK_ACCESS             = 32

'Sharing modes
const MQ_DENY_NONE                       = 0
const MQ_DENY_RECEIVE_SHARE = 1

'Transaction Options
const MQ_NO_TRANSACTION          = 0
const MQ_MTS_TRANSACTION= 1
const MQ_XA_TRANSACTION          = 2
const MQ_SINGLE_MESSAGE          = 3

'************************************************************
'Queue Path
const QUEUE_PATH = ".\private$\ReceiveRequest"

'************************************************************


dim qinfo, qSend, mSend, xmlDoc
dim sPath, sFile, sMesg, sInFileName

'Input file name
'sInFileName = WScript.Arguments(0)
sInFileName = "BankTransInstance.xml"

'************************************************************
' Create the queue
'************************************************************
set qinfo = CreateObject("MSMQ.MSMQQueueInfo")
qinfo.PathName = QUEUE_PATH

'************************************************************
' Open queue with SEND access.
'************************************************************
Set qSend = qinfo.Open(MQ_SEND_ACCESS, MQ_DENY_NONE)

'************************************************************
' Put file into message.
'************************************************************
```

LISTING 15.7 continued

```
sPath = WScript.ScriptFullName
sPath = Mid(sPath, 1, InStrRev(sPath, "\"))
sFile = sPath & sInFileName

set xmlDoc = CreateObject("MSXML.DOMDocument")
xmlDoc.load sFile

set mSend = CreateObject("MSMQ.MSMQMessage")
mSend.Body = xmlDoc.xml
mSend.Label = "BankTransaction"

'*************************************************************
' Send message to queue.
'*************************************************************
mSend.Send qSend, MQ_SINGLE_MESSAGE
msgbox "File """ & sInFileName & """ sent to queue """ &
➥QUEUE_PATH & """", vbOKOnly, "Basic BizTalk Example"

'*************************************************************
' Close queue.
'*************************************************************
qSend.Close
```

The second file is named `ProcessTransWS.vbs`. This script file calls the `File2Queue.vbs` file and then instantiates an instance of the `BankTransactionWS.skx` file using the BizTalk Orchestration Moniker syntax. The code for the `ProcessTransWS.vbs` file is displayed in Listing 15.8.

LISTING 15.8 The `ProcessTransWS.vbs` Script File

```
dim objSked, strPath, WshShell

strPath = WScript.ScriptFullName
strPath = Mid(strPath, 1, InStrRev(strPath, "\"))

Set WshShell = WScript.CreateObject("WScript.Shell")
call WshShell.Run ("""" & strPath & "File2Queue.vbs" &

""" BankTransInstance.xml")
set objSked = GetObject("sked:///" & strPath &

"BankTransactionWS.skx")
```

Summary

Web Services enable the exchange of XML data messages between heterogeneous systems using standard Internet protocols. In this chapter, we created two Web Services and then implemented them from a BizTalk Orchestration schedule. In the future, you will see BizTalk Orchestration schedules implemented as Web Services as well as schedules that call Web Services running on platforms other than Windows 2000. The implementation details may change over time but will most likely improve with the advancement of .NET technologies and the next release of Microsoft BizTalk Server.

CHAPTER 16

Correlation—Integrating BizTalk Server Messaging and Orchestration Services

By Akhtar Hossein

In This Chapter

In earlier chapters, we discussed in detail the functional capabilities of BizTalk Messaging and BizTalk Orchestration. You learned how to send a document to BizTalk Messaging, transform that document, and then finally route the processed document to an internal and/or external application. You also learned how to design and orchestrate a business process using the BizTalk Orchestration Designer. What we didn't discuss was business scenarios that require both categories of services—reliable document delivery and transformation as well as business process orchestration. This chapter focuses on business integration scenarios that require the integration of BizTalk Messaging and Orchestration services as well as long-running business processes that require the synchronization of schedule instances that have been previously dehydrated.

Why Is Correlation So Important?

The term *correlation* describes the process of returning a business message to a specific instance of a waiting schedule. So what types of solutions require correlation, and why do we need to be concerned about the correlation of schedule instances when a schedule rehydrates?

A true B2B (business-to-business) or EAI (enterprise application integration) scenario almost always involves several business processes, and each process may involve multiple steps and the exchange of multiple document types.

In a B2B scenario, consider the example of a marketplace (buyer) sending a purchase order to a seller organization for order fulfillment. Some of the business processes involved may be as follows:

1. After the order is received from the market site, the order needs to go through an internal business process. The business process involves checking accuracy of the order, approval of the order, determination of a seller from a list of subscribed sellers (say based on the lowest price) or even breaking down of an order to multiple product suppliers, notification to the consumer that the order has been received and sent for fulfillment, and, finally, sending the order to the seller and waiting for a response from the seller.
2. After the seller receives the order, the seller's internal business process kicks in. The business process involves order acknowledgement; determination of the best way to fulfill the order based on inventory, location of seller's warehouse, and ZIP Code of the consumer; and, finally, sending the order to the shipper organization and waiting for a response from the shipper.
3. After the shipper receives the order, the shipper's business process kicks in. The business process involves order acknowledgement, determination of shipping dates, mode of delivery and an ETA, and, finally, sending a response back to the seller.

4. After the seller's business process receives the response from the shipper (that may take a few hours to a few days), the seller's business process proceeds to completion by sending a response to the buyer.
5. Finally, when the buyer's business process receives the response from the seller (again, this may take a couple of hours to a couple of days), the buyer's business process proceeds to completion by updating the status of the order to the consumer.

In summary, you can see that at least three separate business processes (buyer, seller, and shipper) are involved in a simple supply chain scenario.

Similarly, in an EAI scenario, consider the example of the software company, where a new hire submits his information to an internal Account Management System application. Figure 16.1 refers to some of the steps involved in the business process:

FIGURE 16.1
Overview of an EAI scenario—Account Management System.

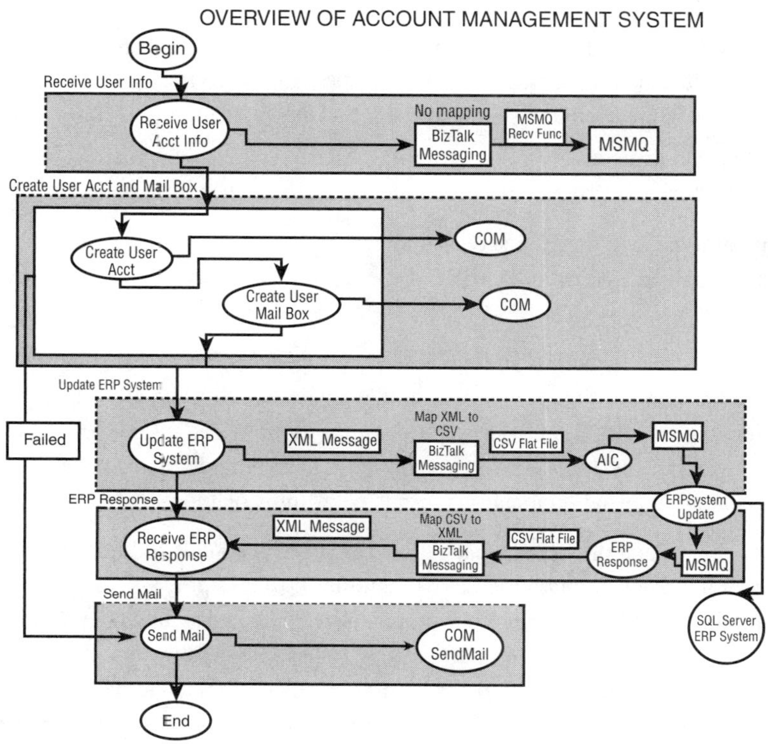

1. New hire submits information to the Account Management System (`AcctMngSys`).
2. The new hire information goes through an approval process.

3. A new account is created in the corporate network—for example, in Active Directory.
4. A mailbox is created for the new hire in the company's messaging system—for example, Exchange.
5. If steps 3 and 4 complete successfully, then update the company's ERP system—for example SAP—with the new hire information. This could be for payroll and benefits. At this point, the `AcctMngSys` business process waits for a response from the ERP system. This could take a few hours to a few days, depending on what the ERP system's business process does and whether human intervention is part of the process. The ERP system finally sends a response to the `AcctMngSys`.
6. The waiting `AcctMngSys` business process proceeds after the response from the ERP system is received. Depending on the response—success or failure—different actions are taken.
7. On a failed response from the ERP system, the `AcctMngSys`'s business process executes a compensating business process to undo the network account and the mailbox creation and sends an e-mail to the system administrator.
8. On a success response from the ERP system, the next action in the `AcctMngSys` business process is to send an e-mail to the new hire and his manager.

In summary, in the EAI scenario shown in Figure 16.1, at least three business processes are involved (`AcctMngSys`, ERP update, and optionally the compensating business process).

In many ways, there is little difference between B2B and EAI integration. Both involve executing one or more business processes, correlating the processes, and exchanging documents of different types (purchase order, invoice, acknowledgement, and response) between the systems across boundaries. These boundaries could be intranet, between disparate internal applications or business units, or Internet, between organizations.

As mentioned previously, each business process contains multiple steps, and one step may involve sending a message to another business process (orchestration schedule) in another application or another organization. The subsequent step in the originating business process may have to wait for a response message for hours, days, weeks, or months to continue and complete the remaining steps in the business process. The term *correlation* is used to describe the process of returning a business message to a specific instance of a waiting schedule.

In this chapter, you will learn how to correlate schedule instances and extend your knowledge of BizTalk Server Messaging and Orchestration to include the integration of BizTalk Messaging to an XLANG schedule. Specifically, you will learn how to

- Instantiate a schedule instance from BizTalk Messaging—that is, begin to execution a business process (an orchestration XLANG schedule) when a message arrives.
- Send a document from BizTalk Messaging to a running instance of orchestration via MSMQ—that is, correlate a message to a running instance of a schedule so that a business process waiting for a response can continue to completion.
- Integrate two business processes (implemented as two separate orchestrations) using BizTalk Messaging, where the processes are separated by an intranet or the Internet.

Building and Instantiating Schedules

The remainder of this chapter will walk you through four complete examples showing the integration of BizTalk Messaging and XLANG schedules and schedule correlation. The examples are for the EAI scenario described earlier in the chapter, essentially integration of two applications (Account Management System and ERP system) using schedule correlation. This will allow you to install and run these applications on a single machine. You can easily extend the examples to a B2B scenario on multiple machines with very little effort.

The four examples involve building five orchestration schedules. Each schedule is simply a revised version of the previous. The first demonstrates how to instantiate a schedule instance from BizTalk Messaging. The second example demonstrates HTTP-based correlation where both the applications have BizTalk Server. The third example demonstrates HTTP-based correlation where one of the applications has BizTalk Server and the other will be running on some non-Windows platform. The fourth and final example demonstrates non-HTTP-based correlation.

Installing the Examples on Your Machine

To work with the four example solutions in this chapter, you need to first install the examples. To do this, copy the `Chapter16` directory from the book's CD on to your hard drive. All examples have been configured as if installed on your hard drive in `c:\book\Chp16\...`. If for any reason you are unable to create and install in the directory as indicated, you will need to open up each of the orchestration schedule sample files and fix the path to your installed path. The examples also assume that you have a directory `c:\temp` in your hard drive, if you do not, you should create one at this time.

You can use the utility `BTConfAssistant.exe` to install all the BizTalk Messaging objects onto your machine. This utility, however, does not create the receive functions. The utility is provided as part of the BizTalk SDK in the directory `C:\Program Files\Microsoft BizTalk Server\SDK\Messaging Samples\BTConfigAssistant\EXE\` or in a similar directory where you have installed BizTalk Server. Invoke this utility from the directory specified. Select File, Import from the menu, and browse to the file in `..\Chp16\Installation Instructions\Example 1\BizTalkMessaging_Objects\BTConfig_Example1.xml`. This file contains all the BizTalk Messaging objects used in the first example in the chapter, with the exception of the receive functions. One disclaimer though: the `BTConfAssistant.exe` utility is supplied as a sample in the SDK and is not a part of the product. The BizTalk team does not guarantee its functionality. The source code for the utility is also provided in the SDK; you can choose to improve the utility.

Example 1: Instantiating a New Schedule Instance from BizTalk Messaging

A business process is generally started with the arrival of a business document.

This simple example shows you how to instantiate a new schedule in response to a message delivered by BizTalk Messaging. Figure 16.2 is the first block of the overall EAI scenario that described in Figure 16.1.

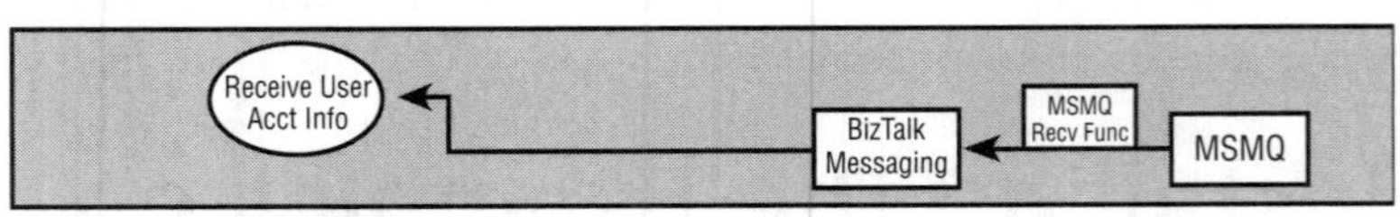

FIGURE 16.2

BizTalk Messaging instantiates a new instance of a BizTalk Orchestration Schedule. The blob "Receive User Acct Info" is part of the orchestration schedule.

Building Example 1

The following steps below walk you through Figure 16.2. The process begins when an XML message consisting of the new user information is dropped into a messaging queue. The message is picked up from the queue by a BizTalk MSMQ receive function. The receive function submits the message into BizTalk Messaging through a channel. The channel then passes the message to a port. The port creates a new instance of the XLANG schedule `AcctMngSys_16.skv` and then delivers this message to the newly created instance of the schedule. This kicks off the business process.

1. A Web-based application drops a message onto a private MSMQ queue.
2. The message is picked up from the queue using an MSMQ receive function and sent to BizTalk Messaging.
3. The message is delivered via a channel and BizTalk Messaging port.
4. The messaging port is configured to pass the message to a new instance of an orchestration schedule.
5. The schedule receives the message and executes the business process. The business process in this case consists of two actions. The first action merely receives the message, and the second action sends the message to a WSC scripting component. The component then displays a message box welcoming the new hire. The appearance of the message box is an indicator that a new instance of a schedule has been created and executed.

Note

The message box in this example is for testing purposes only. Message boxes require human intervention and would cause a schedule running in a production environment to stall until someone responded to the message box. However, this is a quick way to debug each of the actions in a schedule during the development phase. You can also use the XLANG Scheduler monitor to watch the execution of schedule instances.

Web Application—Account Management System

Before jumping to the business process, we will show you what triggers the business process. A simple Web application consisting of two Web pages—`default.htm` and CreateNewAccount.asp—starts the process. The two pages simply take the new user information, create an XML message, and drop the message into a local private queue. Figure 16.3 shows the `default.htm` page filled with a sample new hire information.

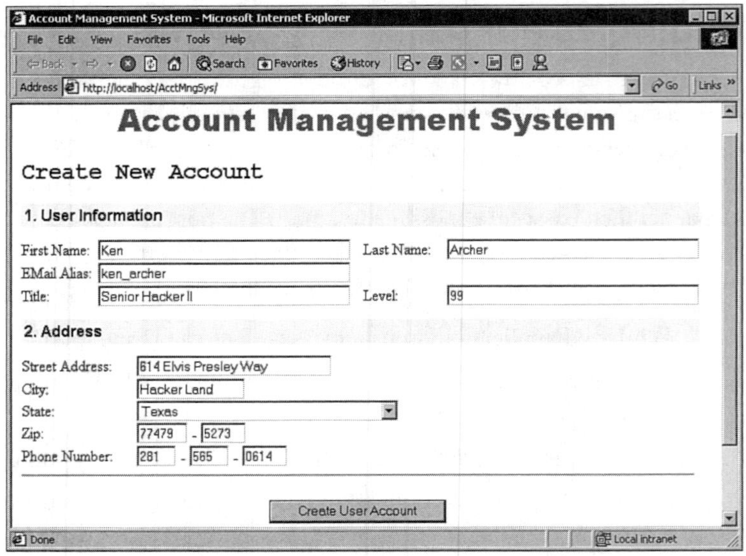

FIGURE 16.3
Simple Web application that drops the New Hire Account Info into the message queue. This triggers a business process.

Source code for the Web application is available in the `..\Chp16\AcctMngSys\WebApp\` directory. Of course, to run the `WebApp`, you will need to have Internet Information Server and configure a virtual directory to point to the `WebApp` directory where the `default.htm` and `CreateNewAccount.asp` files are. In addition to the Web application, you will create a private MSMQ queue called `ReceiveNewHire` on your machine to receive the New User Account Information.

To simplify the example, we have provided a VBScript called `File2Queue.vbs` (`..\Chp16\AcctMngSys\Source\` directory). The script takes a filename as the only command-line parameter. A sample test file called `AcctMngSys_NewHire.xml` is included in the source directory. The file in our case contains the New User Account Information in an XML format. The script will drop this file into the private queue `ReceiveNewHire`. You still have to remember to create the local private queue. In this example and in all other examples in this chapter, we will use the `File2Queue.vbs` script to start our process instead of the Web application.

Creating an Orchestration Schedule

The orchestration schedule in Figure 16.4 shows the business process. This section walks you through the important pieces of the schedule and shows you how BizTalk Messaging has been configured.

Figure 16.4 illustrates the orchestration schedule file `AcctMngSys_16.skv`. The schedule consists of two actions, `Receive Request` and `WelcomeNewHire`. The first action,

`Receive Request`, is bound to a BizTalk Messaging implementation shape using the orchestration binding port named `UserAcctInfo`. The second action, `WelcomeNewHire`, is bound to a Windows scripting component named `NewHireMsg.wsc` using the orchestration binding port named `DisplayMsgPort`. The file `NewHireMsg.wsc` can be found in the `..\Chp16\AcctMngSys\Source\` directory.

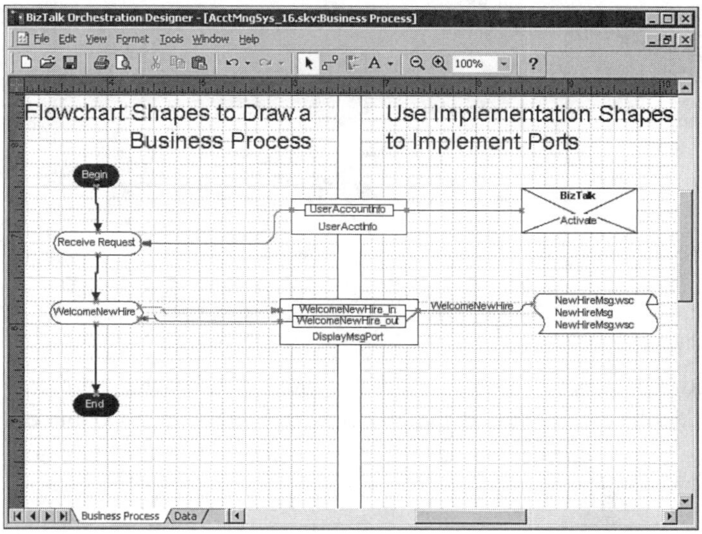

FIGURE 16.4
Snapshot of the orchestration schedule— `AcctMngSys_16.skv`.

The document or the XML message the schedule processes is defined by a schema named `UserAcctInfoXML.xml`. The process begins with the submission of an XML message that conforms to this schema to BizTalk Server Messaging. BizTalk Messaging receives the document and then passes it to an orchestration schedule instance. The schema was developed using the BizTalk Editor and stored in the WebDAV. The schema is shown in Figure 16.5, and a sample test message contained in the file `AcctMngSys_NewHire.xml` is shown in Listing 16.1.

LISTING 16.1 Sample XML Data File, `AcctMngSys_NewHire.xml`

```
<?xml version="1.0" ?>
<UserAcctInfo>
  <HEADER ReturnPort="" />
  <BODY><Name First="Ken" Last="Archer" Alias="ken_archer" />
     <Address Street="614 Elvis Presley Way" City="Hacker Land" State="Texas"
➥ ZipCode="77479-5273" />
     <Phone AreaCode="281" Number="565-9647" />
     <Level Code="99" Title="Senior Hacker II" />
  </BODY>
</UserAcctInfo>
```

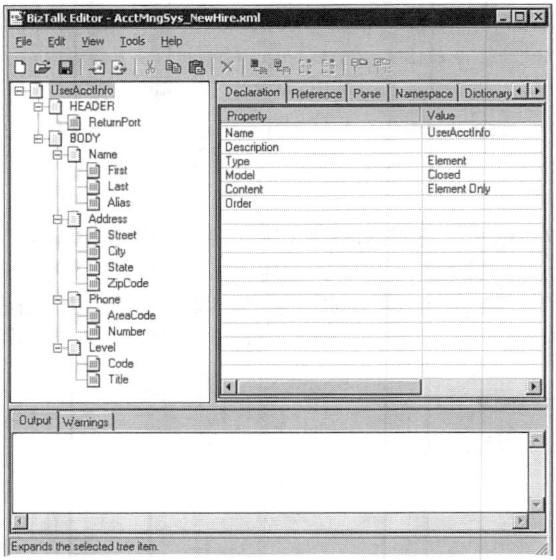

FIGURE 16.5
The schema file `UserAcctInfo.xml` *is shown in the BizTalk Editor.*

Let's now go back to Figure 16.4 and the orchestration schedule `AcctMngSys_16.skv`. Load the schedule into the BizTalk Orchestration Designer. Double-click on the BizTalk Messaging implementation shape. This starts up the BizTalk Messaging Binding Wizard as shown in Figure 16.6.

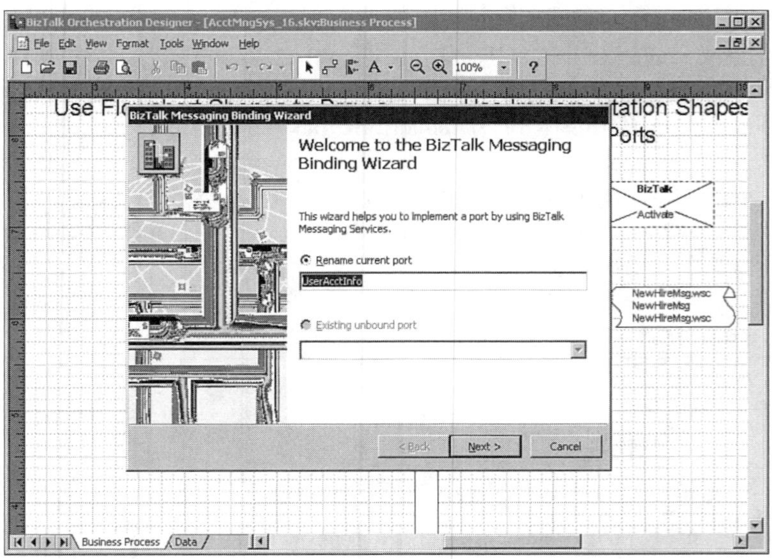

FIGURE 16.6
Binding the BizTalk Messaging implementation shape to an action on the schedule.

After you specify an appropriate name and click next, you get to the Communication Direction page as shown in Figure 16.7. Here you specify whether the schedule is receiving or sending a message. We have set it to receive the New Hire Account Info XML message.

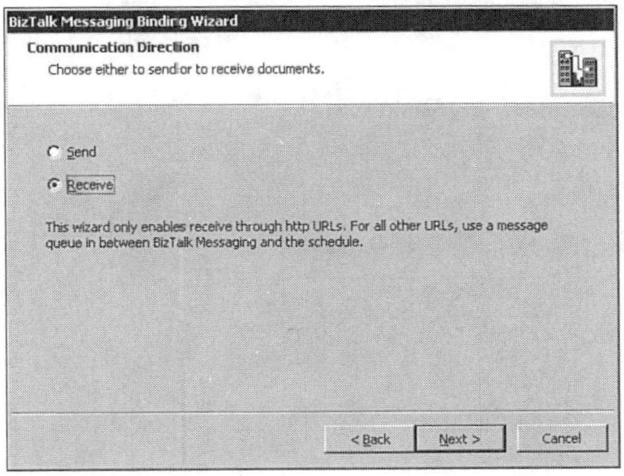

FIGURE 16.7
Selecting the direction of the message; either the schedule is receiving the message or sending the message.

The text on this page tells you that a dynamically created queue sits between the BizTalk Messaging and the schedule. We will discuss this further. Click Next to get to the, XLANG Schedule Activation Information page as shown in Figure 16.8.

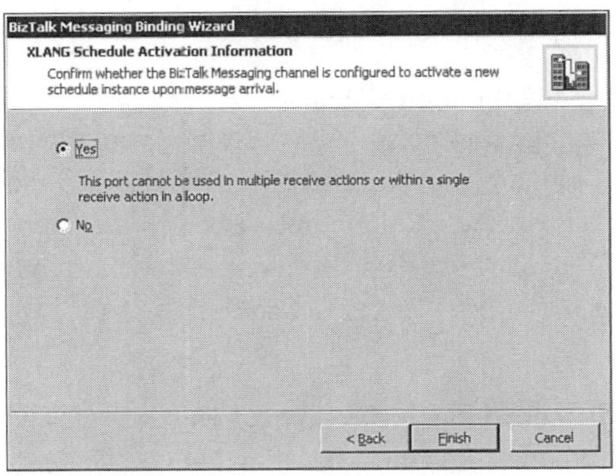

FIGURE 16.8
Determining the activation of the schedule. A Yes indicates that an instance of the schedule is created each time a new message is delivered.

Click Finish to close the BizTalk Messaging Binding Wizard. Do not close the XLANG schedule. Next double-click the arrow that enters into the first action `Receive Request`. The Welcome to the Communication Wizard pops up. Click Next four times to accept the defaults, until you are on the page Message Specification Information as shown in Figure 16.9. Here you select the specification for the incoming message. The XLANG engine will validate the incoming message against the specification because the Validate

Messages Against the Specification box is checked. Notice how we exposed the `First` and `Last` names attributes in the `UserAcctInfo` XML message. You can add fields by using the Add button and merely selecting the fields.

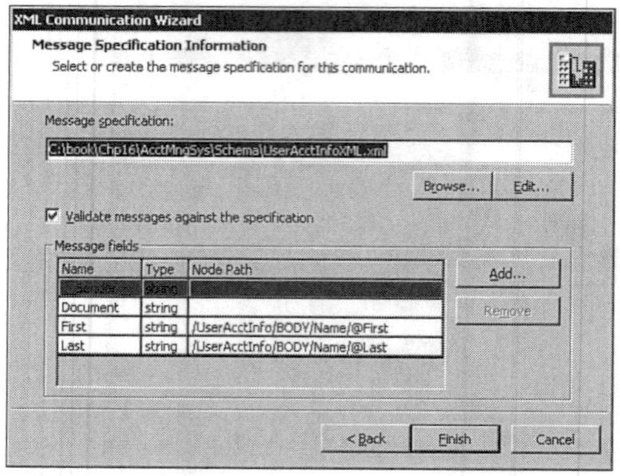

FIGURE 16.9
You select the specification for the message that the schedule action will receive.

Figure 16.9 shows a simple way of exposing the message contents in a schedule instance without having to programmatically load the document using the DOM. By simply pointing to the document schema using the wizard, you can quickly and easily expose pieces of information that you may need in certain steps of your schedule. The value of this becomes more important when the document schema is large. It eliminates the need for your components to load and parse the message manually to get to the needed attributes.

Now let's examine what is going on in the data page of the orchestration schedule. Figure 16.10 shows the data page for `AcctMngSys_16.skv`. From the incoming message, we are passing three pieces of data—the document (the whole message), the `First` attribute, and the `Last` attribute of the incoming message—to the appropriate parameters in the `WelcomeNewHire_in message`. The Port References block in the upper-left shows the implementation binding ports, `UserAcctInfo` and `DisplayMsgPort`, defined in the schedule.

The second action in the schedule in Figure 16.4 (`WelcomeNewHire`) is bound to a Windows scripting component. The scripting component is defined in the file `NewHireMsg.wsc`. The file is located in `.\Chp16\AcctMngSys\Source\` directory. Listing 16.2 shows the code for the component.

The component has a single method, `WelcomeNewHire()`, and takes three parameters `sMsg`, `sFirstName`, and `sLastName`. The method displays a message box containing the entire XML message, and the title of the message box shows the new hire first and last name concatenated together.

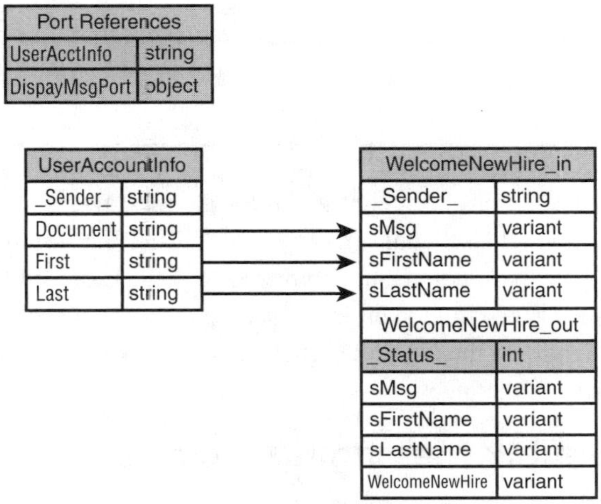

FIGURE 16.10
Data from the incoming message is flowed into the `WelcomeNewHire_in` *message parameters.*

LISTING 16.2 Code for the Scripting Component, `NewHireMsg.wsc`

```
<?xml version="1.0"?>
<component>

<?component error="true" debug="true"?>

<registration
    description="NewHireMsg"
    progid="NewHireMsg.wsc"
    version="1.00"
    classid="{9E7D4862-4B16-4fa1-ACF1-23CFB503F5F0}"
>
</registration>

<public>
    <method name="WelcomeNewHire">
        <PARAMETER name="sMsg"/>
        <PARAMETER name="sFirstName"/>
        <PARAMETER name="sLastName"/>
    </method>
</public>

<script language="VBScript">
<![CDATA[

function WelcomeNewHire(sMsg, sFirstName, sLastName)
    MsgBox CStr(sMsg), vbOKOnly, CStr(sFirstName & " " & sLastName)
    WelcomeNewHire = ""
end function
```

LISTING 16.2 continued

```
]]>
</script>
</component>
```

After the XLANG schedule has been configured for the messages and binding ports, the next step is to compile the schedule. You need to register the scripting component, `WelcomeNewHireMsg.wsc` before you can compile the schedule successfully. Use `Regsvr32.exe` to register the component in the same manner you register a COM component DLL. To compile the XLANG schedule to a `.skx` file, select File, Make `AcctMngSys_16.skx` from the menu.

Setting Up BizTalk Messaging Objects

We have completed the orchestration schedule that contains a BizTalk Messaging receive port that will instantiate an instance of the schedule on receipt of an incoming XML message. When the schedule receives the message, it displays a message box, showing the XML message and the name of the new hire in its title bar. In this section, we will configure BizTalk Messaging to call the orchestration schedule. Table 16.1 summarizes the BizTalk Messaging objects required.

TABLE 16.1 BizTalk Messaging Manager—Document Definition, Channel, and Port

Objects	*Options and Settings Chosen*	*Note*
Organization/ Application	Name: Home Organization Application: `NewHireApp`	Use the default Home Organization.
Document definition	Name: `NewHireInfo` Spec: UserAcctInfoXML.xml	The doc specification was created in the Editor. First copy this file to your WebDAV repository and then create the document definition.
Document Instance	Filename: AcctMngSysNewHire.xml	This is provided for you to test the app. If you want, you can create one in XML Notepad.
Port	Name: `NewHirePort` (To an Application) Destination Application: New XLANG Schedule Schedule Moniker: `AcctMngSys_16.skx` Schedule Port: `UserAcctInfo`	You must type the schedule port name exactly as it is in the orchestration drawing.

TABLE 16.1 continued

Objects	*Options and Settings Chosen*	*Note*
Channel	Name: `NewHireChannel` (From an Application) Application Name: `NewHireApp` InBoundDocument: `NewHireInfo` OutBoundDocument: `NewHireInfo` Mapping: No Document Logging: Check only, In Native Format Advanced Configuration: Take the Defaults	No mapping is required because the inbound doc spec is the same as outbound document spec.

> **Note**
>
> BizTalk Server uses the term *ports* in two places. In BizTalk Messaging Manager, a port refers to an abstract destination point where a message will be delivered after it has been transformed by the channel. In the BizTalk Orchestration Designer, a port refers to an abstract functionality (I like to call this an *implementation binding*), where it binds an action in the business process (orchestration schedule) to an implementation shape—for example, a COM component, MSMQ, BizTalk Messaging, or scripting component.

Figure 16.11 shows the completed BizTalk Messaging port. The port was created using the property settings shown in Table 16.1.

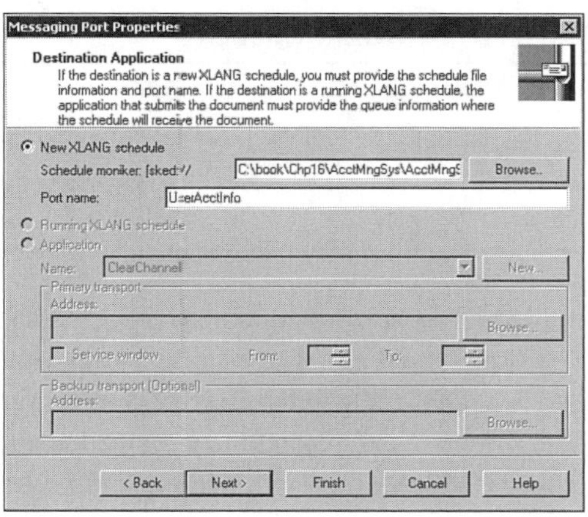

FIGURE 16.11
The messaging port `NewHirePort` *delivers the XML message to the XLANG schedule* `AcctMngSys_16.skx` *at the implementation binding port* `UserAcctInfo`.

This completes the destination where the message is going. Next, the channel defines where the message is coming from and the type of message being processed. Figure 16.12 shows the Source Application page of the Channel Wizard. Again, the channel was created using the property settings as shown in Table 16.1. Because the inbound and outbound document definitions are the same, `NewHireInfo`, mapping file is specified for the channel.

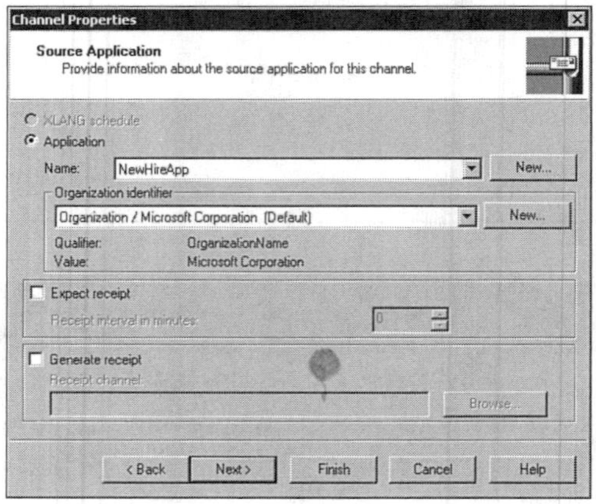

FIGURE 16.12
Source Application page of the channel, `NewHireChannel`.

Next we need a private transactional queue, where the VBScript `File2Queue.vbs` will drop the content of the sample data file `AcctMngSys_NewHire.xml`. Open up the Computer Management MMC Console and expand Services and Applications. Down the list is Message Queuing, expand Message Queuing to see the Private and Public Queues. Message Queuing is part of Windows 2000 and can be installed from the Windows 2000 Setup CD. Table 16.2 shows the properties of the private queue `ReceiveNewHire`.

TABLE 16.2 MSMQ—Create a Private MSMQ Queue

Objects	*Options and Settings Chosen*	*Note*
Queue	Name: `ReceiveNewHire` Type: Private Transaction: Yes	Transactional queue allows the message to be returned to the queue if there is an error and later retried.

Finally we need to create an MSMQ receive function to pick up messages from the queue. The receive function will pick up the message from the queue and deliver the message to the channel, `NewHireChannel`. Open the BizTalk Server Administration MMC and expand the BizTalk Server Group. Next expand the Receive Functions. Table 16.3 shows the property settings for the MSMQ receive function, `NewHireReceiveFunc`.

TABLE 16.3 BizTalk Server Administration—Create an MSMQ Receive Function

Objects	*Options and Settings Chosen*	*Note*
Receive function	Name: `NewHireReceiveFunc` Type: MSMQ Receive Function PollingLoc: `Direct=OS:.\private$\ReceiveNewHire` Advanced Tab: Openness: Not Open Channel Name: `NewHireChannel`	The Not Open in the Openness, indicates to BizTalk Server that the destination and source are explicitly specified.

Running Example 1

Let's begin with the fun part. We have just created an orchestration schedule and configured BizTalk Messaging to process and deliver a message to the schedule from an internal application. The `AcctMngSys` has a Web front-end, where a new hire enters his information. The Web application then submits the information on to an MSMQ queue. The MSMQ receive function picks up the message from the queue and then submits it to BizTalk Messaging, which in turn instantiates a business process, in our example the orchestration schedule. The orchestration schedule then displays the new hire info in a message box. In this example and the rest of the examples in this chapter, instead of the Web front-end, we have provided a VBScript (`File2Queue.vbs`) that drops the message to the queue. The script takes one parameter, the filename, which contains the XML file to submit. Listing 16.3 shows the script.

LISTING 16.3 Source Code for the VBScript, `File2Queue.vbs`

```
'**************************************************************
'MSMQ constants

'Access modes
const MQ_RECEIVE_ACCESS    = 1
const MQ_SEND_ACCESS        = 2
const MQ_PEEK_ACCESS        = 32

'Sharing modes
const MQ_DENY_NONE        = 0
const MQ_DENY_RECEIVE_SHARE      = 1

'Transaction Options
const MQ_NO_TRANSACTION    = 0
const MQ_MTS_TRANSACTION    = 1
const MQ_XA_TRANSACTION    = 2
const MQ_SINGLE_MESSAGE    = 3
```

LISTING 16.3 continued

```
'*************************************************************
'Queue Path
const QUEUE_PATH = ".\private$\ReceiveNewHire"

'*************************************************************

dim qinfo, qSend, mSend, xmlDoc
dim sPath, sFile, sMesg, sInFileName

'Input file name
sInFileName = WScript.Arguments(0)

'*************************************************************
' Create the queue
'*************************************************************
set qinfo = CreateObject("MSMQ.MSMQQueueInfo")
qinfo.PathName = QUEUE_PATH

'*************************************************************
' Open queue with SEND access.
'*************************************************************
Set qSend = qinfo.Open(MQ_SEND_ACCESS, MQ_DENY_NONE)

'*************************************************************
' Put file into message.
'*************************************************************
sPath = WScript.ScriptFullName
sPath = Mid(sPath, 1, InStrRev(sPath, "\"))
sFile = sPath & sInFileName

set xmlDoc = CreateObject("MSXML.DOMDocument")
xmlDoc.load sFile

set mSend = CreateObject("MSMQ.MSMQMessage")
mSend.Body = xmlDoc.xml
mSend.Label = "NewHireInfo"

'*************************************************************
' Send message to queue.
'*************************************************************
mSend.Send qSend, MQ_SINGLE_MESSAGE

if err <> 0 then
     msgbox "Error Submitting to queue.
➥Error = " & Cstr(err.Number) & ", Description = " & err.Description
Else
     msgbox "File """ & sInFileName & """ sent to queue """ &
➥QUEUE_PATH & """", vbOKOnly, "Account Management System"
End if
```

LISTING 16.3 continued

```
'**********************************************************
' Close queue.
'**********************************************************
qSend.Close
```

The script displays a message box on successful submission to the queue or notifies the user with a failure message if an error occurs. To begin, type the following on the command line to run this example:

```
File2Queue.vbs Test_NewHire.xml
```

If the message is correctly dropped into the queue, the message box in Figure 16.13 confirms that this has been successfully done.

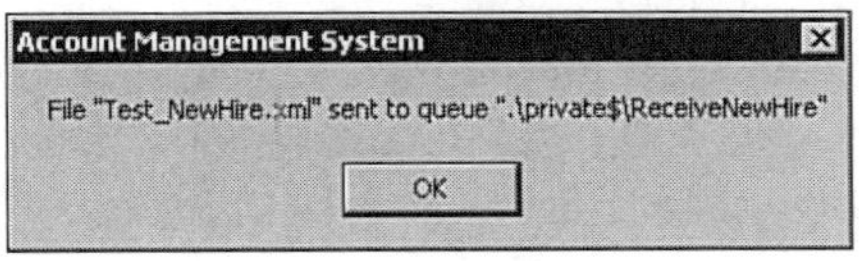

FIGURE 16.13
Message box confirms that the content of the XML file `AcctMngSys_NewHire.xml` *was successfully dropped into the queue,* `ReceiveNewHire`.

Click OK to acknowledge the message. Depending on whether you are running this for the first time, a few seconds will elapse before you see the second message box as in Figure 16.14. In the subsequent runs of the example, the message boxes may appear almost at the same time.

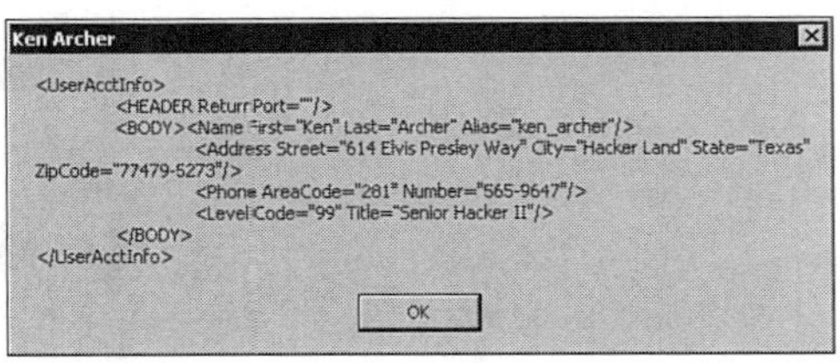

FIGURE 16.14
This message box confirms that the message has flown from the BizTalk Messaging port and into the XLANG schedule, entering through the first action, flowing into the second action, and finally invoking the scripting component.

The message box is displayed by the Windows scripting component, `NewHireMsg.wsc`. This component is associated with the second action in the schedule.

Why did we use MSMQ? The introduction of the queue in the architecture helps to totally decouple the Web front-end application from the BizTalk Server. Should the BizTalk Server be offline for any reason, nothing prevents the Web front-end from continuing to receive new hire information totally unaware of the final destination of the message. In addition, this allows BizTalk Server to be configured to process hundreds of these messages waiting in the queue at one time as a batch during some off-peak hours of the day. By making the queue transactional, we guarantee that either the whole process succeeds or the failed message is returned to the queue. The system is fault-tolerant and totally decoupled. We have achieved all this without writing a single line of code.

For similar reasons internally, BizTalk Messaging sends a message to the XLANG schedule through a dynamically created per-instance queue. This keeps the two applications totally decoupled. If you look at the Computer Management MMC and drill down to Message Queuing/Private Queues, you will notice a queue named `UserAcctInfo{GUID}`. Figure 16.15 shows the per-instance queue.

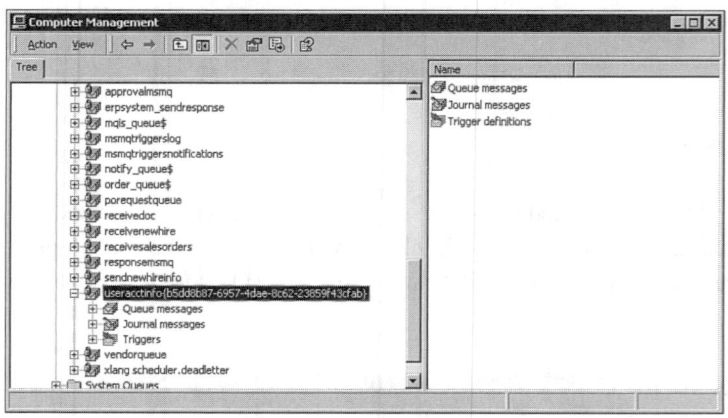

FIGURE 16.15
The per-instance queue generated by the XLANG Engine. The queue sits between the BizTalk Messaging and the XLANG schedule.

The prefix is the same as the port name of the implementation binding port in the BizTalk Orchestration Designer when hooking up the first action in the schedule to the BizTalk implementation. The GUID is dynamically generated. The port name combined with the GUID is the name of the queue that the XLANG Engine creates. The message queue is called a per-instance message queue because a unique message queue is created for each message transferred from BizTalk Messaging to the orchestration. After the schedule runs to completion, the per-instance message queue is removed. Figure 16.16 shows the Computer Management Console MMC after the schedule has run to completion.

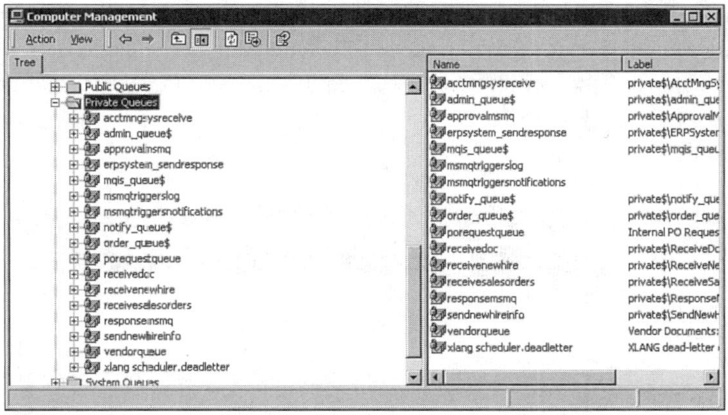

FIGURE 16.16
The per-instance queue is removed after the schedule has completed running.

Some people have found that the per-instance queue does not go away after the schedule has run to completion. The most common reason for the per-instance queue not going away can be attributed to some kind of error condition. However, in some rare cases, this has been blamed on COM+ and the XLANG Engine. Bizet, the code name for the next release of BizTalk Server, addresses this issue.

You may have noticed that when you ran the example for the first time, it took a little longer than when you ran it the second time. This is because the XLANG Engine reads the schedule from the disk when you run for the first time, compiles it, and stores the schedule in its internal representation. In subsequent runs, the XLANG Engine simply uses the compiled version. Thus, the first message passing through the system suffers a small performance hit.

Monitoring the Execution of an Orchestration Schedule

BizTalk Server provides an XLANG Monitoring tool, `XLANGMon.exe`, which you can find in the `..\Program Files\Microsoft BizTalk Server\SDK\XLANG Tools` directory. The tool referred to as XLANG Event Monitor by default only monitors a subset of the COM+ events generated by the orchestration engine. You can, however, choose to view additional events by choosing View, Events Filter from the menu and checking the COM and MSMQ binding check boxes.

Open the XLANG Event Monitor and choose View, Events Filter. Click the Check All button to monitor all the events and leave it running. From the command line, run the script `File2Queue.vbs AcctMngSys_NewHire.xml` that you ran previously. The script puts the message on the `ReceiveNewHire` queue and puts up a message box to notify that the message has been dropped. After the message has been picked up by BizTalk Messaging and passed to the orchestration schedule, at the same time a second message box is displayed showing the message and the name of the new hire on the title bar. Do not click OK yet. Figure 16.17 shows our schedule instance in the `Running` folder of the XLANG Event Monitor.

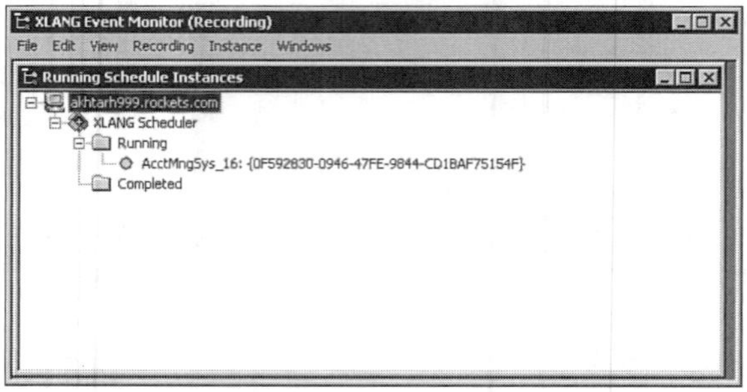

FIGURE 16.17
Monitoring running instance of a schedule in the XLANG Event Monitor.

Click OK on the message box. This completes the schedules, and the XLANG Event Monitor moves the entry from the `Running` to the `Completed` folder.

Some users have experienced problems with the XLANG Event Monitor. In some cases, schedule instances do not show up in the `Running` folder, or, when the schedule instance has completed, the instance does not move to the `Completed` folder. One way to get around this is to open two instances of the monitor. Schedule monitoring has improved dramatically in BizTalk Server 2002.

We learned in detail the integration of BizTalk Messaging to an orchestration schedule. We also looked at the benefits of the message queuing architecture and the per-instance queue concepts. Next we will dive deeper into schedule correlation.

Correlating to a Running Orchestration

In the previous section, you learned how BizTalk Server instantiates a new instance of a business process by delivering a message to the orchestration schedule. Our example showed that after the message was received it displayed the message in a message box. Although this established that the schedule was started, in a real-world scenario, this is the beginning of a business process and not the end. In general, most B2B or EAI business processes involve a minimum of two messages being exchanged:

- An outgoing message with a request
- An incoming message with a response

Returning to our `AcctMngSys` EAI application in Figure 16.1, we will look at the third and fourth block of the business process. The business process requires an update of the back-end ERP system. The schedule sends an update request to the ERP system and waits for a response. When the ERP system response finally arrives, the waiting schedule continues processing the remainder of the business process. The thing to note here is that the response from the ERP system may take hours, days, or weeks, especially if the ERP system is outsourced and lives in another organization.

This means that at any given time, hundreds of instances of a business process could be running on a single BizTalk Server. A new message arrives, a new instance of the schedule is created, and the schedule sends out a request to the ERP system and waits for a response before continuing to completion. This could turn into a resource management nightmare. Fortunately, BizTalk utilizes an XLANG persistence database and automatically *dehydrates* an orchestration schedule into this database, whenever the following sync action occurs:

- The schedule needs to wait for a response.
- The beginning of a transaction boundary occurs in the schedule.

By dehydrating the schedule in the database, the system ensures that it will survive a server shutdown. It also guarantees that the current state of the schedule is preserved even if long passages of time occur prior to the receipt of a response message. BizTalk Server automatically handles the hydration and rehydration of a schedule; however, one problem remains. We need to be able to match a response message to the instance of the schedule that originally sent the request. To achieve this, each instance of the orchestration schedule is persisted with its own GUID and is thus uniquely identifiable. This process of returning a message to a specific instance of a schedule is called *correlation*.

We will demonstrate three different ways of correlating a response message back to its appropriate running schedule instance. In Example 2 and 3, we will demonstrate HTTP-based correlation, and in Example 4 we will show non-HTTP-based correlation. The cases are

- Example 2, HHTP-based, with BizTalk Servers on both ends
- Example 3, HTTP-based, with BizTalk Server on one end and any external business process on the other end
- Example 4, Non-HTTP-based, with BizTalk Server on both ends

We will extend our `AcctMngSys` EAI example to illustrate each type of correlation. The two business processes involved are the `AcctMngSys` and the ERP system. The ERP system business process consists of a BizTalk Orchestration schedule and a COM component that inserts new hire information into a SQL Server database. Based on the success or failure, the COM component formats a response message. The message is then correlated to the running `AcctMngSys` schedule that originally requested the update. Figure 16.18 shows the scenario.

FIGURE 16.18
Overview of the `AcctMngSys` *and* `ERPSystem` *integration scenario.*

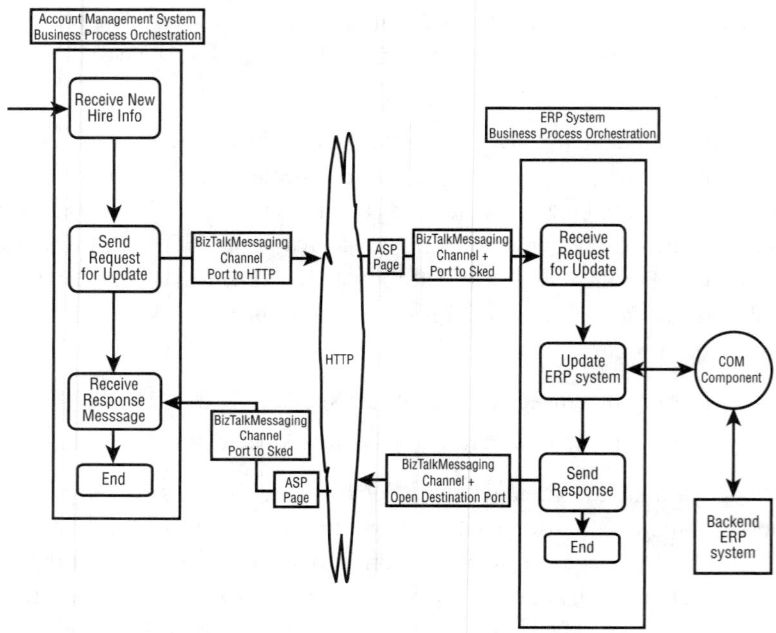

The following describes the steps used to accomplish this:

1. A new hire message, `UserAcctInfo`, is dropped into a private MSMQ queue.
2. A new schedule instance of the `AcctMngSys` business process receives the `UserAcctInfo` message.
3. The `AcctMngSys` orchestration schedule displays a message to indicate that the schedule has been activated. The next step in the orchestration sends out the message to BizTalk Messaging to deliver it to the ERP system business process. The message, `UserAcctInfo`, is then transferred using BizTalk Messaging to the ERP system business process. At this point, the `AcctMngSys` orchestration schedule instance waits for a response message.
4. BizTalk Messaging transfers the message, `UserAcctInfo`, to the ERP system business process.
5. The ERP system business process receives the message. The next step in the ERP system displays a message to indicate that the ERP system schedule has been activated. The third action calls a COM component to update the ERP system. Based

on this update operation, the component formats a response. The response message is then sent out via BizTalk Messaging. The ERP system business process ends at this point.

6. BizTalk Messaging transfers the response message between organization or application boundaries.
7. The `AcctMngSys` business process receives the response message and correlates the message back to the same instance of the schedule that sent out the `UserAcctInfo` message to the ERP system process. Finally, the `AcctMngSys` business process displays the response message indicating that the response, for which the schedule was waiting, has arrived, and the schedule runs to completion.

You have already done the first two steps of this example in the earlier scenario, dropping a file onto a message queue, picking up the message from the queue, and delivering the message to a new instance of a schedule. In this section, we will focus on the process of sending a message out and then correlating a response message back to an instance of the schedule that originally sent the message. We will start with the HHTP-based correlation example, where we have BizTalk servers on both endpoints.

Example 2: HTTP-Based Correlation Using Two BizTalk Servers

The process of schedule correlation differs based on the type of transport (HTTP or non-HTTP) selected to exchange messages between schedules. The BizTalk Messaging implementation shape in the BizTalk Orchestration Designer has built-in support for HTTP-based correlation.

Before we go into the specific scenario, let's see what is involved in HTTP-based correlation in general. Say that the two business processes are the `AcctMngSys` and the ERP system. The three keys steps are as follows:

1. Send the `UserAcctInfo` message out from the `AcctMngSys` business process.
2. Receive the `UserAcctInfo` in the ERP system process and send a response message.
3. Receive the response message back on the `AcctMngSys` business process and correlate the response back to the existing `AcctMngSys` process.

The following sections look at the details of each of these three steps. You need to understand what is involved without getting bogged down in the specifics of the example presented.

How HTTP Correlation Works Using Two BizTalk Servers

For schedule correlation to work correctly, two things must happen. First, there must be a unique identifier for each instance of the schedule, and, second, this unique identifier somehow needs to be sent to the destination application so that when the destination application is ready to send a response back, it can associate the unique identifier of the schedule instance with the response. Having said that, let's see how BizTalk achieves this. The XLANG Engine creates a GUID for each instance of the schedule. This is the unique identifier used. To send the unique identifier to the destination application, the GUID is included in one of the fields of the outgoing message itself. Of course, the source and the destination applications must agree and have the knowledge as to what field in the message is being used for this purpose.

For HTTP-based schedule correlation, three pieces of distinct information are sent to the destination application. The URL of the ASP page where the response message is to be posted, the name of the BizTalk Messaging channel that processes the response in the originating application, and, finally, the GUID or the unique identifier that identifies the schedule instance that originally sent the request. BizTalk Orchestration at runtime strings these three pieces of information and flows it into the designated field in the outgoing message agreed on both by the source and destination applications. In our examples, we are using the field `ReturnPort` in the `HEADER` section of the message for this purpose. This is shown in Figure 16.5. Let's look at the three pieces of information that are sent in the outgoing message. HTTP-based correlation is natively supported by BizTalk. All you need to do is on the data page of the orchestration flow the Response Port to the designated field in the message. In our case, it is the `ReturnPort`.

First let's look at the URL of the ASP page. This is the ASP page by the destination application to post the response. BizTalk provides a generic ASP page for this purpose. The ASP page is located in the `..\Chp16\AcctMngSys\WebApp\` directory. Listing 16.4 shows the content of the page.

LISTING 16.4 Source Code for the `ReceiveResponse.asp` Page

```
<%

'    ReceiveResponse.asp
'
'    Microsoft Biztalk Server 2000
'    Copyright  Microsoft Corporation, 1998-2000.  All rights reserved.
'
'    Description:
```

LISTING 16.4 continued

```
'    Sample Biztalk Server Receive Response page
'


   On Error Resume Next

    Dim interchange
    Dim SubmissionHandle
    Dim PostedDocument
    Dim ContentType
    Dim CharSet
    Dim EntityBody
    Dim Stream
    Dim StartPos
    Dim EndPos
    Dim queuepath
    dim channelname

    L_HTTPReqFailed_Text = "400 Request failed"
    queuepath = Request.QueryString("qpath")
    queuepath = "queue://Direct=OS:" & queuepath
    channelname = Request.QueryString("channel")

    Set interchange = Server.CreateObject( "BizTalk.Interchange" )

    ContentType = Request.ServerVariables( "CONTENT_TYPE" )

    '
    ' Determine request entity body character set (default to us-ascii)
    '
    CharSet = "us-ascii"
    StartPos = InStr( 1, ContentType, "CharSet=""", 1)
    If (StartPos > 0 ) then
        StartPos = StartPos + Len("CharSet=""")
        EndPos = InStr( StartPos, ContentType, """",1 )
        CharSet = Mid (ContentType, StartPos, EndPos - StartPos )
    End if

    '
    ' Check for multipart MIME message
    '
    PostedDocument = ""

    if ( ContentType = "" or Request.TotalBytes = 0) then
        '
        ' Content-Type is required as well as an entity body
        '
        Response.Status = "406 Not Acceptable"
        Response.Write "Content-type or Entity body is missing" & VbCrlf
        Response.Write "Message headers follow below:"  & VbCrlf
```

LISTING 16.4 continued

```
        Response.Write Request.ServerVariables("ALL_RAW") & VbCrlf
        Response.End
    else
        if ( InStr( 1,ContentType,"multipart/" ) > 0 ) then
            '
            ' MIME multipart message. Build MIME header
            '
            PostedDocument = "MIME-Version: 1.0" & vbCrLf & "Content-Type: " &
➥ContentType & vbCrLf & vbCrLf
            PostedDocument = PostedDocument &
➥"This is a multi-part message in MIME format." & vbCrLf
        End if

        '
        ' Get the post entity body
        '

         EntityBody = Request.BinaryRead (Request.TotalBytes )

        '
        ' Convert to UNICODE
        '
        Set Stream = Server.CreateObject("AdoDB.Stream")
        Stream.Type = 1        'adTypeBinary
        stream.Open
        Stream.Write EntityBody
        Stream.Position = 0
        Stream.Type = 2        'adTypeText
        Stream.Charset = CharSet
        PostedDocument = PostedDocument & Stream.ReadText
        Stream.Close
        Set Stream = Nothing

        '
        ' Submit document asynchronously to Biztalk Server
        '
        WriteDocumentToFile PostedDocument, 9999
        call interchange.submit (4,PostedDocument,,,,,queuepath,channelname)

        Set interchange = Nothing

        '
        ' indicate that the message has been received,
            ' but that processing may not be complete
'

        Response.Status = "202 Accepted"
        Response.End
    End if
```

LISTING 16.4 continued

```
   Sub CheckError(statement)

      If Err.Number <> 0 Then
               Response.write "Statement          : " & statement & vbCrLf _
                            & "  Err.Number        : " & CStr(Err.Number)
➥& vbCrLf _
                            & "  Err.Number (Hex) : " & CStr(Hex(Err.Number))
➥ & vbCrLf _
                            & "  Err.Description : " & Err.Description & vbCrLf

         Response.Status = L_HTTPReqFailed_Text
         Response.Write ("Fail")
      else
            Response.Write ("Success")

      End If
   End Sub

           Sub WriteDocumentToFile( strDoc, subHandle)
             Dim oFS
             Dim oTS
             Dim strFileName

             strFileName = "..\Chp16\AcctMngSys\WebApp\ERPResponse_"
➥& Cstr(subHandle) & ".xml"

             Set oFS = CreateObject("Scripting.FileSystemObject")
             Set oTS = oFS.CreateTextFile(strFileName, True)

             oTS.Write strDoc
             oTS.Close

             Set oTS = Nothing
             Set oFS = Nothing

           End Sub


%>
```

In Listing 16.4, the thing to note carefully is how the script extracts the queue path and the channel name from the query string. The channel name is self-explanatory; the queue path name contains the name of the XLANG port of the source application and the GUID of the XLANG instance. The XLANG port name combined with the XLANG GUID instance forms the name of the per-instance queue. Toward the middle of the script these two variables are used in the call to `IInterchange::Submit()`. `IInterchange::Submit()` is one of the ways to submit a document to BizTalk

Messaging. The file receive function, the MSMQ receive function, and the HTTP receive function are other ways to submit a document to BizTalk.

So far you have learned how to send the correlation information from the source XLANG application to the destination XLANG application. Next we will consider the way to send the response message back from the destination XLANG application to the correct XLANG schedule instance of the source application. To do this, in the destination XLANG schedule, in the data page of the orchestration, we simply flow the designated field in the message (`ReturnPort` in our case) to the XLANG port that delivers the message to a BizTalk Messaging. In the BizTalk Messaging in the destination application, we need to create an Open Destination Port. We will see this in more detail in the following examples.

In the next section, we will apply the general outline described here to the specifics of our example.

Pick Up `UserAcctInfo` Message and Deliver to a New `AcctMngSys` Business Process

You will find all the source code for this section in `..\Chp16\AcctMngSys`. The first two steps take the `UserAcctInfo` sample message `AcctMngSys_NewHire.xml` from the private MSMQ queue (`ReceiveNewHire`) and deliver the message via BizTalk Messaging to the `AcctMngSys` orchestration schedule, `AcctMngSys_16_2.skx`.

Table 16.4 specifies the BizTalk Messaging objects required in this step. Notice the private messaging queue in the receive function in the table. It is the same private queue earlier in Example 1.

TABLE 16.4 BizTalk Messaging Configuration

Objects	*Options and Settings Chosen*	*Note*
Organization/ Application	Name: Home Organization Application: `NewHireApp`	Use the default Home Organization.
Port	Name: AcctMngSys_ Receive`NewHireInfoPort` (To an application) Destination Application: New XLANG Schedule Schedule Moniker: `AcctMngSys_16_2.skx` Schedule Port: `UserAcctInfo`	You must type the schedule port name exactly as it is in the orchestration.

TABLE 16.4 continued

Objects	*Options and Settings Chosen*	*Note*
Channel	Name: `AcctMngSys_ReceiveNewHireInfoChannel` (from application) Application Name: NewHireApp InBoundDocument: `NewHireAccountInfo` OutBoundDocument: `NewHireAccountInfo` Mapping: No Document Logging: Check only, In Native Format Advanced Configuration: Take the Defaults	No mapping is required because the inbound doc spec is the same as outbound document spec. The Document Definition NewHireInfo was created earlier, we are simply using here
Receive function	Name: `AcctMngSys_ReceiveNewHireInfo` Type: MSMQ Receive Function PollingLoc: `Direct=OS:.\private$\ReceiveNewHire` Advanced Tab: Openness: Not Open Channel Name: AcctMngSys_ReceiveNewHireInfoChannel	The Not Open in the Openness indicates to BizTalk Server that the destination and source are explicitly specified. The Private Messaging Queue was created in Table 16.2.

We now have the plumbing set up to receive a message into the `AcctMngSys` orchestration schedule, `AcctMngSys_16_2.skx`. Let's take a look at the file `AcctMngSys_16_2.skx` in the BizTalk Orchestration Designer.

Receiving `UserAcctInfo` into BizTalk Orchestration, Sending `UserAcctInfo`, and Receiving Response Message

Load the schedule source file `AcctMngSys_16_2.skv` into the BizTalk Orchestration Designer. Figure 16.19 shows the schedule.

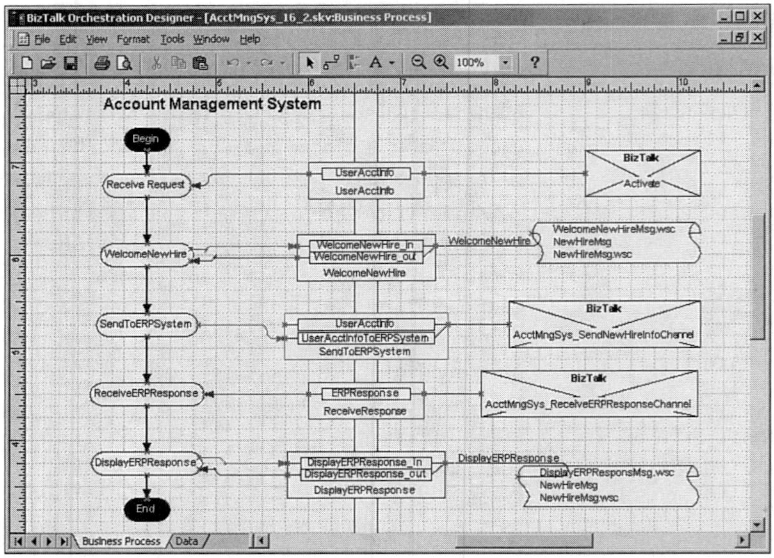

FIGURE 16.19
Orchestration schedule `AcctMngSys_16_2.skv`. *This represents the business process of the* `AcctMngSys` *application.*

We will look at each action in the schedule. BizTalk Messaging delivers the `AcctMngSys_NewHire.xml` to the XLANG schedule orchestration implementation binding port, `UserAcctInfo`, which is bound to the action Receive Request. In the BizTalk Messaging Binding Wizard for this action, the Schedule Activation is set to yes. This means that every time a message arrives, a new instance of the schedule is created and started. When this value is set to yes, the text "Activate" is added to the BizTalk Messaging implementation shape.

The second action, `WelcomeNewHire`, is bound to a Windows scripting host component, `WelcomeNewHireMsg.wsc`. The script component takes the `FirstName`, `LastName`, and the `Msg` as a whole as the three parameters. The script displays a message box, showing the message content in the body, and the title shows the new hire name.

```
Function WelcomeNewHire(sMsg, sFirstName, sLastName)
       MsgBox CStr(sMsg), vbOKOnly, CStr(sFirstName & " " & sLastName)
       WelcomeNewHire = ""
End function
```

In the third action, `SendToERPSystem`, the message is sent out to a BizTalk Messaging implementation shape. This is where the correlation action begins. Double-click on the BizTalk Messaging shape connected to the `SendToERPSystem` orchestration port. The BizTalk Messaging Binding Wizard pops up. Next traverse to the Static or Dynamic Channel Information page. You specify the name of a static channel through which the message will be sent out. The channel name is `AcctMngSys_SendNewHireInfoChannel`. We will define this channel in the next section. Figure 16.20 shows the wizard page, Static or Dynamic Channel Information.

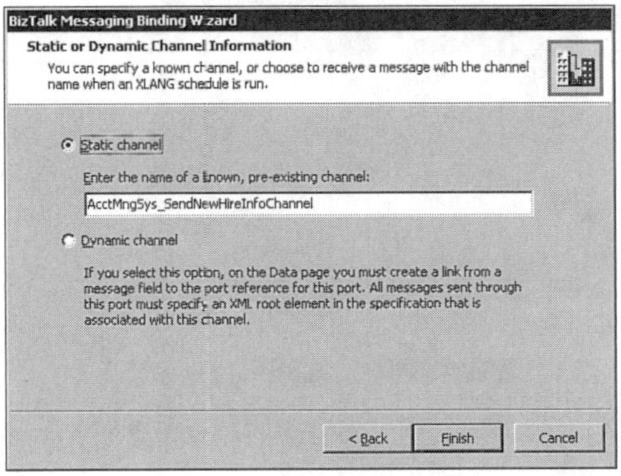

FIGURE 16.20
BizTalk Messaging Binding Wizard, Static or Dynamic Channel Information page.

After sending out the message to the `ERPSystem` business schedule, the `AcctMngSys` business process waits to receive the `ERPSystem` response message. At this point, BizTalk Server hydrates the schedule into the XLANG persistence database.

The response is received in the fourth action, `ReceiveERPResponse`. Double-click on the BizTalk Messaging shape connected to the `ReceiveResponse` orchestration port. The BizTalk Messaging Binding Wizard pops up. Click Next to move to the Communication Direction page shown in Figure 16.21. Note that the direction is set to receive. Click Next to go to the XLANG Schedule Activation Information page as shown in Figure 16.22. For this action, the value of the Schedule Activation is set to No. This means that when a response arrives at this port, no new schedule instance is created. Instead, the response message is correlated back to the existing and waiting schedule instance that originally sent out the `UserAcctInfo` message.

Again click Next to go to the Channel Information page as shown in Figure 16.23. You need to specify two things: the name of the BizTalk Messaging Channel (`AcctMngSys_ReceiveERPResponseChannel`) through which the response message from the `ERPSystem` will re-enter the schedule and the URL `http://localhost/AcctMngSys/ReceiveResponse.asp`) of the ASP page that will be used by the `ERPSystem` to send the response. The file `ReceiveResponse.asp` can be found in installation in `..\Chp16\AcctMngSys\WebApp\` directory.

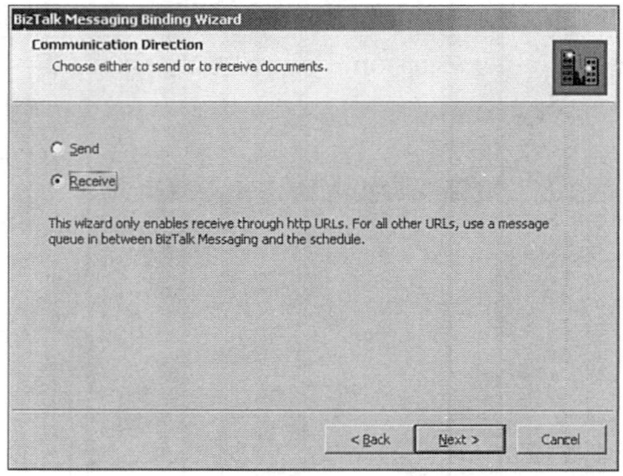

FIGURE 16.21
BizTalk Messaging Binding Wizard, Communication Direction page.

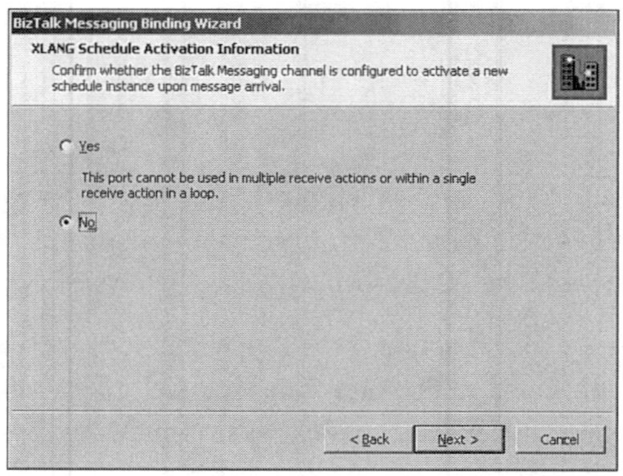

FIGURE 16.22
BizTalk Messaging Binding Wizard, XLANG Schedule Activation Information. Note that it is set to No.

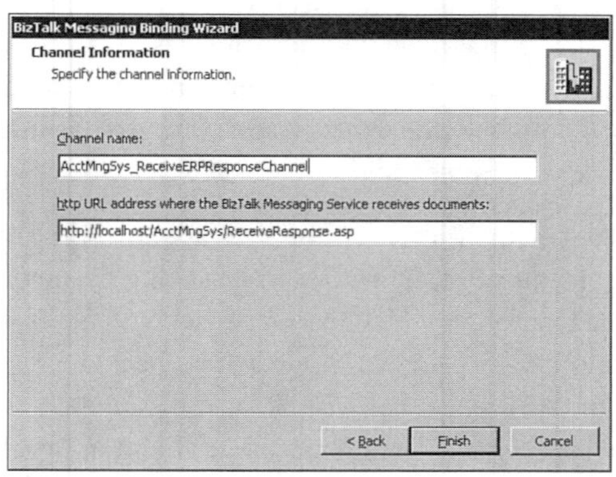

FIGURE 16.23
BizTalk Messaging Binding Wizard, Channel Information page. Note the ASP page URL and the channel name.

Note

Because we have configured both the `AcctMngSys` and the `ERPSystem` in the same computer, we are using *`localhost`* in the receive response URL path. To extend the example across machines or across an organization, you will need to substitute the *`localhost`* with appropriate machine name or domain name of the server.

The next action in the schedule, `DisplayERPResponse`, is bound to the same Windows scripting host component, `DisplayERPResponseMsg.wsc`. The component displays the `ERPResponse` in the body and the name of the new hire in the title.

Let's now examine what is going on in the data page of the schedule as shown in Figure 16.24.

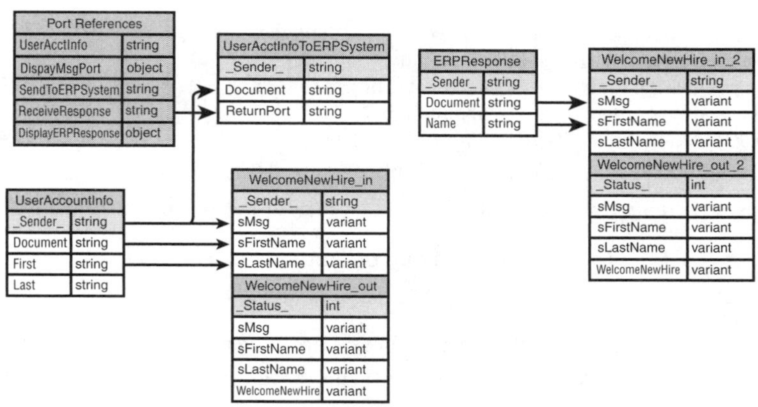

FIGURE 16.24
Data page of the orchestration schedule as in the `AcctMngSys_16_2.skv`.

The summary of the pieces in the data page are as follows:

Messages:

- `UserAcctInfo`—Incoming new hire account message to the `AcctMngSys` business process
- `UserAcctInfoToERPSystem`—Message that is sent to the `ERPSystem`
- `ERPResponse`—Message from the `ERPSystem`, as a result of the update made to the `ERPSystem`

Components:

- `WelcomeNewHireMsg.wsc`—Displays the new hire info that is going to be sent to the `ERPSystem`
- `DisplayERPResponseMsg.wsc`—Displays the response message, received from the `ERPSystem`

The inbound document in the `UserAcctInfo port` is passed to the `UserAcctInfoToERPSystem` port so that the contents of the document are sent to the `ERPSystem`. Next, the address of the schedule port, `ReceiveResponse`, is passed into the `ReturnPort` element of the outgoing message in the `UserAcctInfoToERPSystem Port`. This information in the `ReturnPort` is used to return a response message to the original instance of the `AcctMngSys` schedule. The `ReceiveResponse` port string contains the MSMQ private queue name of the queue that's created dynamically by the messaging engine on instantiation of the schedule as well as the channel name. The instance reference appears as follows:

```
http://localhost/acctmngsys/receiveresponse.asp?
➥channel=acctmngsys_receiveerpresponsechannel&
➥qpath=ComputerName.DomainName\\private$
➥\\acctmngsys_receiveerpresponsechannel
➥{c03f79c0-fad4-4843-af73-84dfb3e35ac0}
```

Three pieces of information are in the string: the URL to the `ReceiveResponse.asp` page, the channel name, and the queue path for the per-instance message queue:

- URL path—`http://localhost/acctmngsys/receiveresponse.asp`
- Channel name—`acctmngsys_receiveresponsechannel`
- Queue path—`MachineName.DomainName.com\private$\acctmngsys_receiveresponsechannel{c03f79c0-fad4-4843-af73-84dfb3e35ac0}`

In your machine, the GUID appended to the queue path will be different. When a message is returned to this per-instance message queue, it will correlate to the schedule. When the `ERPSystem` returns the response message back to this specific instance of the orchestration schedule, the system must use this `ReturnPort` information.

Finally, in the fifth action in the orchestration, `DisplayERPResponse` is bound to another Windows scripting host component. The component simply displays the response message received from the `ERPSystem`.

```
Function DisplayERPResponse(sMsg, sFirstName, sLastName)
      MsgBox CStr(sMsg), vbOKOnly, CStr(sFirstName & " " & sLastName)
      DisplayERPResponse = ""
End function
```

Sending the `UserAcctInfo` Message to the ERP System Using BizTalk Messaging Via HTTP

The action `SendToERPSystem` of the XLANG schedule delivers the outgoing message `UserAcctInfo` to the BizTalk Messaging channel, `AcctMngSys_SendNewHireInfoChannel`. The channel delivers the message to the BizTalk Messaging port that sends the message over the Internet using HTTP to the `ERPSystem` business process.

On the `ERPSystem` side of the exchange, the ASP page `ReceiveUserAccountInfo.asp` receives the message and delivers the message using BizTalk Messaging to the new orchestration schedule. We will cover the details of the `ReceiveUserAccountInfo.asp` page a little later when we talk about the `ERPSystem`. The following section sets up the required BizTalk Messaging objects to deliver the `NewHireInfomessage` to the `ERPSystem`.

In this section, you will configure BizTalk Messaging to set up a port for sending the message out via HTTP and then configure a channel to this port. Table 16.5 describes the steps required to accomplish this.

TABLE 16.5 BizTalk Messaging Objects Required to Send the `NewHireInfo` Message to the `ERPSystem`

Objects	*Options and Settings Chosen*	*Note*
Port	Name: `AcctMngSys_ToERPSystemPort` (To an Organization) Destination Organization: ERP System Primary Transport: HTTP Address: `http://LOCALHOST/ERPSystem/ReceiveUserAcctInfo.asp`	The port uses HTTP to send the `UserAccountInfo` message to the `ERPSystem`.
Channel	Name: `AcctMngSys_SendNewHireInfoChannel` (From an Application) Source Application: XLANG schedule InBoundDocument: `NewHireAccountInfo` OutBoundDocument: `NewHireAccountInfo` Mapping: No Document Logging: Check only, In Native Format Advanced Configuration: Take the defaults	No mapping is required because the Inbound doc spec is the same as Outbound document spec.

Receiving UserAcctInfo in the ERPSystem

Before we go into the ERPSystem business process, let's define the ERPSystem. This example simulates a real-world ERP system. You will need to create a virtual directory using the Internet Services Manger MMC. Name this directory as ERPSystem and map this to the physical directory ..\Chp16\ERPSystem\WebApp. In our example, the ERPSystem consists of the following:

- ReceiveUserAcctInfo.asp—To receive the UserAccountInfo message. The file is located in the ..\Chp16\ERPSystem\WebApp directory.
- Orchestration schedule—ERPSystem_16_2.skv, representing the business process of the ERPSystem. The file is located in the ..\Chp16\ERPSystem\ directory.
- COM component—ERPSystem.ERPSystemUpdate. The component simulates an ERPSystem by updating a table in the SQL Server. This is a good time to register the component in your machine, if you have not already done so. One way to do this is to host the component in a COM+ application. Create a new COM+ application called ERPSystem using the Component Services MMC; add the component into the COM+ application just created.
- BizTalk Messaging—A set of channel-port configurations to deliver the incoming message to the ERPSystem XLANG schedule and another set of channel-port configurations to send the response message back.

ReceiveUserAcctInfo.asp receives the incoming message and submits it to BizTalk Messaging, using the IInterchange object model's Submit() function. A section of the code is shown here:

```
channelname = "ERPSystem_ReceiveNewHireInfoChannel"
SubmissionHandle = interchange.submit (1,PostedDocument,,,,,,channelname)
```

The first parameter in the Submit() function is the BIZTALK_OPENNESS_TYPE. It is set to 1 to indicate BIZTALK_OPENNESS_TYPE_NOTOPEN. This means that the source and destination are completely defined. When you provide the ChannelName parameter, BizTalk explicitly knows which channel to send this document to. The second parameter is the document itself.

Let's take a look at the XLANG schedule for the ERPSystem business process. Open the file ERPSystem_16_2.skv. Figure 16.25 shows the schedule.

The schedule receives the UserAcctInfo message through the BizTalk Messaging port from the ERPSystem_ReceiveNewHireInfoChannel. This process is exactly the same as the previous the BizTalk Messaging implementation shape that activated the AcctMngSys business process. Note that the XLANG schedule activation is set to Yes for the BizTalk

Messaging binding shape because a new instance of the schedule is activated every time a message arrives at the port.

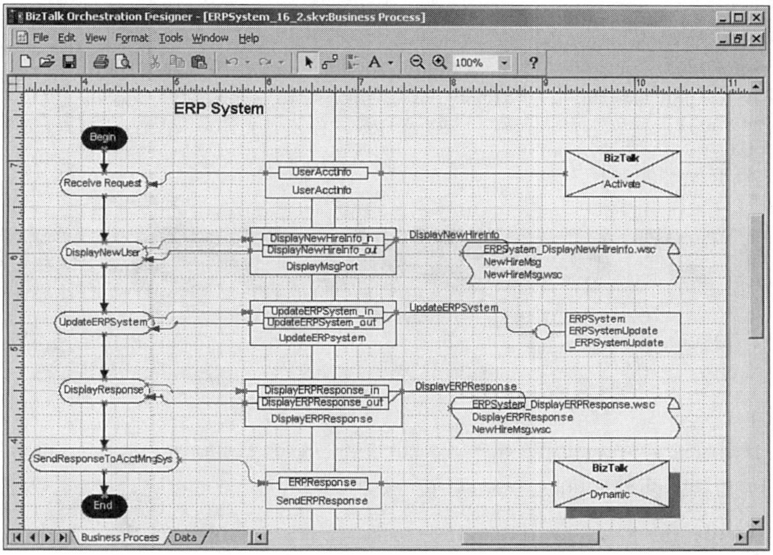

FIGURE 16.25
XLANG schedule `ERPSystem_16_2.skv`*. The schedule represents the* `ERPSystem` *business process.*

The message is then displayed using the `ERPSystem_DisplayNewHireInfo.wsc` scripting component.

The next action is bound to a COM component `ERPSystem.ERPSystemUpdate`. The component simulates an ERP system by inserting new hire information into a SQL Server table. To create the SQL database objects, use the scripts provided in `\Chp16\ERPSystem\SQLScript`. The component uses a DSN (Data Source Name), `"ERPSystem"`, to access this database. You will need to create a System DSN on your machine. Note to access the database the component code uses "sa" as the `userid` and a blank password. The component then formats a response message based on the schema `ERPResponse.xml` that contains the status of the insert operation into the SQL table.

An `ERPSystem` response message for a successful update may look like this:

```
<?xml version = "1.0"?>
<ERPResponse>
        <Employee Name="Ken Archer" Alias="ken_archer"/>
        <Response ResponseCode="0"
➥strDescription="Successfully Created New Hire Ken Archer."/>
</ERPResponse>
```

A response message for a failure to update may look like this:

```
<?xml version = "1.0"?>
<ERPResponse>
        <Employee Name="Ken Archer" Alias="ken_archer"/>
       <Response ResponseCode="0"
➥strDescription="[Microsoft][ODBC SQL Server Driver][SQL
Server]Violation of PRIMARY KEY constraint 'PK_UserAccountInfo'.
➥Cannot insert duplicate key in object
'UserAccountInfo'."/>
</ERPResponse>
```

Note

Source code for the `ERPSystem` component is located in `\Chp16\ERPSystem\Source\ERPSystem`.

The next action simply displays the `ERPSystem` response message using the `ERPSystem_DisplayERPResponse.wsc` scripting component.

Finally, the `ERPSystem` response message is sent out from the schedule through a dynamic BizTalk Messaging orchestration port. The use of the dynamic port ensures that the response message is correlated to the same instance of the `AcctMngSys` schedule that originally sent the `UserAcctInfo` message. In Figure 16.26, note that we do not explicitly supply the channel name; instead, we use a dynamic channel, and we will set this information in the data page of the schedule.

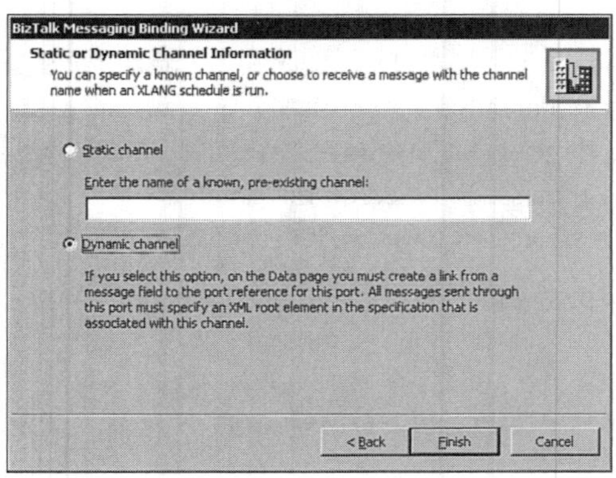

FIGURE 16.26
BizTalk Messaging Binding Wizard, Static or Dynamic Channel Information for sending the response from the `ERPSystem`.

Figure 16.27 shows the data page for the schedule `ERPSystem_16_2.skv`. The data page of the schedule is complex. The pieces in the data page are as follows:

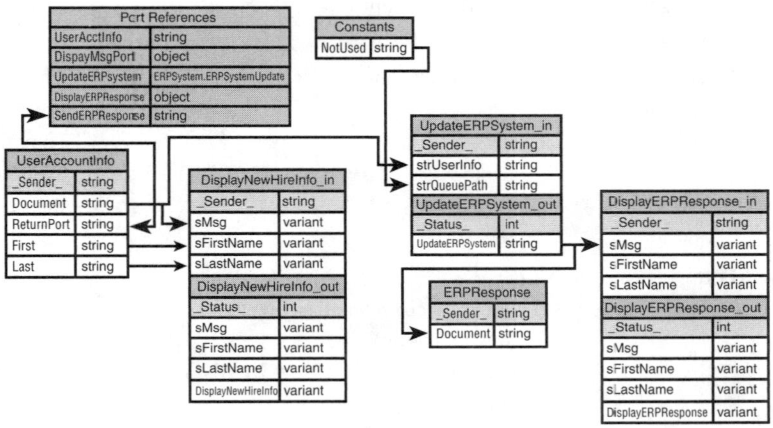

FIGURE 16.27
Data page for the schedule `ERPSystem_16_2.skv`.

The two messages that you should take note of in the Figure 16.27 are

- `UserAcctInfo`—The incoming message from the `AcctMngSys` business process
- `UpdateERPSystem_out`—The `ERPSystem` response message returned by the `ERPSystem` COM component

Messages sent to the two scripting components are

- `DisplayNewHireInfo_in`—The scripting component, `ERPSystem_DisplayNewHireInfo.wsc` receives this message.
- `DisplayERPResponse_in`—The scripting component, `ERPSystem_DisplayERPResponse.wsc` receives this message.

The most important part of the data flow is the flow of `HEADER@ReturnPort` from the `UserAcctInfo` message to the dynamic port `SendERPResponse`. This transfers the HTTP URL stored in the `UserAcctInfo` message to the dynamic port so that BizTalk knows which particular instance of the `AcctMngSys` business process to return the message.

The response message content returned by the `ERPSystem` component (`UpdateERPSystem_out`) is passed to the `ERPResponse` message.

Next, we will look at the BizTalk configuration needed for this section. Table 16.6 outlines the ports, channels, and document definition.

TABLE 16.6 ERPSystem BizTalk Messaging Configurations

Objects	*Options and Settings Chosen*	*Note*
Organization/ Application	Name: ERP_System	
Document definition	Name: ERPResponse	The doc specification was created in the Editor. First copy this file to your WebDAV repository and then create the document definition.
Port	Name: `ERPSystem_ReceiveNewHireInfoPort` (To an Application) Destination Application: New XLANG schedule Schedule Moniker: `ERPSystem_16_2.skx` Schedule Port: `UserAcctInfo`	You must type the schedule port name exactly as it is in the orchestration.
Channel	Name: `ERPSystem_ReceiveNewHireInfoChannel` (from Organization) Organization: Hacker's Den InBoundDocument: `NewHireAccountInfo` OutBoundDocument: `NewHireAccountInfo` Mapping: No Document Logging: Check only, In Native Format Advanced Configuration: Take the defaults	No mapping is required because the Inbound doc spec is the same as Outbound document spec. The document definition `NewHireAccountInfo` was created in the first example; we are simply reusing here.
Port	Name: `ERPSystem_SendResponsePort` (To an Organization) Destination Organization: Open Destination	This is an open destination port. Primary Transport does need to be set in open destination port. In the data page of the orchestration, we will flow the destination address from the incoming message.

TABLE 16.6 continued

Objects	*Options and Settings Chosen*	*Note*
Channel	Name: ERPResponse (from Application) Source Application: XLANG Schedule InBoundDocument: ERPResponse OutBoundDocument: ERPResponse Mapping: No Document Logging: Check only, In Native Format Advanced Configuration: Take the Defaults	No mapping is required because the Inbound doc spec is the same as the Outbound document spec. The ERPResponse document definition uses the schema in file ERPResponseXML_HTTP.xml.

Table 16.7 provides a list of SQL scripts to create the ERPSystem database in the SQL Server. Use the scripts to create the database, tables, and the stored procedure used in the example. You will also need to create a System DSN named ERPSystem.

TABLE 16.7 ERPSystem SQL Server Database

Objects	*Options and Settings Chosen*	*Note*
Database	Name: ERPSystem Table Name: UserAccountInfo SQL Script : create_table.sql Stored Procedure: erpsys_CreateUser SQL Script: create_sp.sql	Database scripts are in \Chp16\ERPSystem\SQLScript.
DSN	DSN Name: ERPSystem	DSN is used by the COM component to access the database. Note the component uses a userid "sa" and a blank password to access the database.

Note

The SendERPResponsePort in the orchestration schedule ERPSystem_16_2.skv as shown in Figure 16.26 delivers the ERP response message to a dynamic channel. The dynamic channel in BizTalk Messaging is always associated with open destination BizTalk Messaging ports. The open destination port sends the document to the URL as shown in the Listing 16.5. In our example, the ASP page is ReceiveResponse.asp.

We will now see what happens in the AcctMngSys system when the ASP page receives the response document.

Returning the ERPSystem Response Message to the Original Instance of the AcctMngSys Schedule

The response message is submitted to the standard ReceiveResponse.asp on the Accounting side, with the query string containing values for the channel name and the queue path sent by BizTalk messaging server on the ERP system. Once again the URL is shown here in Listing 16.5.

LISTING 16.5 Syntax for the URL Path for the Return Address

```
http://localhost/acctmngsys/receiveresponse.asp?
➥channel=acctmngsys_receiveerpresponsechannel&
➥qpath=MachineName.DomainName.com\\private$\\
➥acctmngsys_receiveerpresponsechannel{c03f79c0-fad4-4843-af73-84dfb3e35ac0}
```

The first thing that the ReceiveResponse.asp does is parse the document, channel name, and queue path from the query string. The script then takes the queue pathname from the query string, which is an MSMQ pathname syntax, and postfixes it with the string "queue://Direct=OS:." to translate it to MSMQ queue pathname syntax. The script then calls the IInterchange::Submit() function with the PostedDocument, channel name, and queue path, to submit the document to BizTalk Messaging. In our case, the channel name is AcctMngSys_ReceiveResponseChannel, as can be seen from the URL. Open ReceiveResponse.asp and examine the following code from the ASP file:

```
'Parse the query string for channel name and queue path
queuepath = Request.QueryString("qpath")
queuepath = "queue://Direct=OS:" & queuepath
channelname = Request.QueryString("channel")

'Create a BizTalk Interchange Object
Set interchange = Server.CreateObject( "BizTalk.Interchange" )

'Conde to convert the Posted Document to BSTR string
'
'Submit document asynchronously to Biztalk Server
'
 Call interchange.submit (4, PostedDocument,,,,, queuepath,channelname)
```

We will now configure BizTalk Messaging for the port-channel combination to receive this PostedDocument and deliver the document to the original schedule instance waiting for the response.

Table 16.8 shows you how to configure Messaging to return the ERPSystem response message to the original instance of the AcctMngSys schedule.

TABLE 16.8 AcctMngSys BizTalk Messaging Configuration to Receive the ERPSystem Response Message

Objects	*Options and Settings Chosen*	*Note*
Port	Name: AcctMngSys_ReceiveERPResponsePort (To an Application) Destination Application: Running XLANG Schedule	You do not specify anything other than Running XLANG Schedule for this port. The IInterchange::Submit() call in the ReceiveUserAcctInfo.asp provides the per-instance queue to return to. This correlates the ERPSystem response message to the running orchestration schedule.
Document Definition	Name: ERPSystemResponse_HTTP Document Specification: ERPResponseXML_HTTP.xml	The doc specification was created in the Editor. First copy this file to your WebDAV repository and then create the document definition.
Channel	Name: AcctMngSys_ReceiveERPResponseChannel (from Organization) Organization: ERP_System InBoundDocument: ERPSystemResponse_HTTP OutBoundDocument: ERPSystemResponse_HTTP ERPResponse Mapping: No Document Logging: Check only, In Native Format Advanced Configuration: Take the Defaults	No mapping is required because the Inbound doc spec is the same as Outbound document spec.

We are now ready to run the example and see how the response message is correlated to the running schedule.

Running the HTTP-Based Correlation with BizTalk on both Endpoints Example 2

To start the example, copy the File2Queue.vbs script and test Test_NewHire.xml to the `.\Chp16\AcctMngSys\Source` directory. Also make sure that all receive functions except the ones used in this example (AcctMngSys_ReceiveNewHireInfo) are disabled. Then type the following at the command prompt:

```
File2Queue.vbs AcctMngSys_NewHire.xml
```

The following steps list the sequence in which the message moves and the appropriate message boxes that appear.

> **Note**
>
> Steps 1 through 5 illustrate running the HTTP-based scenario, where BizTalk is at both ends of the business process.

1. On Submission of the `AcctMngSys_NewHire.xml` to the queue `ReceiveNewHire`, the pop-up message box is as shown in Figure 16.28.

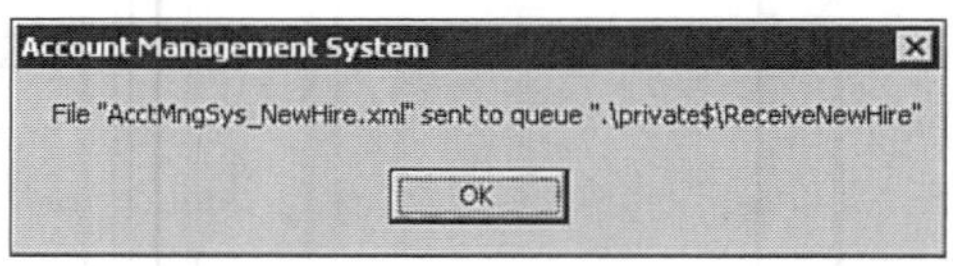

FIGURE 16.28
The message box that appears after submitting the `AcctMngSys_NewHire.xml` *to the queue* `ReceiveNewHire`.

2. On receipt of the `UserAccountInfo` into the `AcctMngSys_16_2.skx`, the pop-up message box is as shown in Figure 16.29.

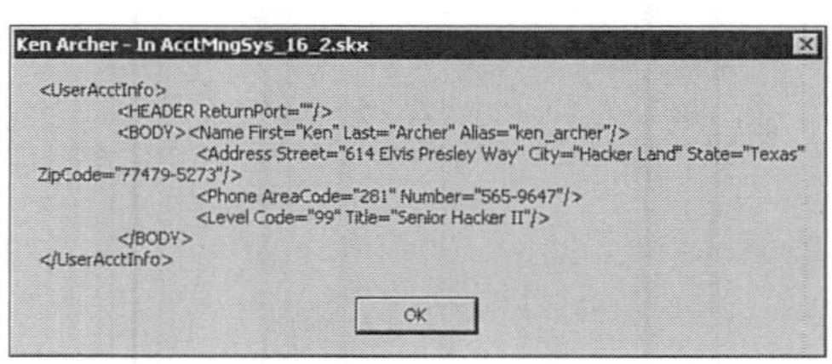

FIGURE 16.29
The message box on receipt of the `NewHireInfo` *in the* `AcctMngSys_16_2.skx` *business process.*

Note that the XLANG schedule name in the message box title is `AcctMngSys_16_2.skx`. In Figure 16.30, note the XLANG Monitor showing the schedule instance running.

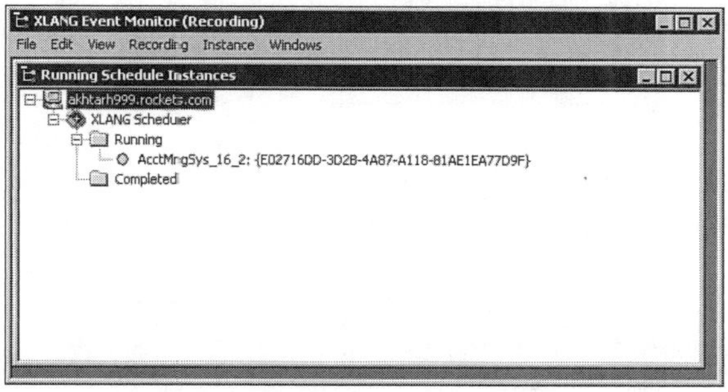

FIGURE 16.30
The XLANG Monitor showing the schedule instance for `AcctMngSys_16_2.skv`.

The Monitor displays the running instance of the schedule `AcctMngSys_16_2.skx`. Each instance of the schedule is identified by a GUID appended to the name of the schedule.

3. On receipt of the `UserAccountInfo` into the `ERPSystem_16_2.skx`, the pop-up message box is as shown in Figure 16.31.

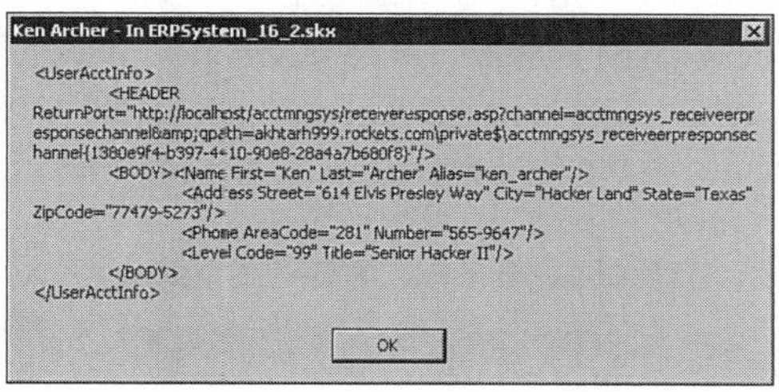

FIGURE 16.31
Note the message box title as `ERPSystem_16_2.skx`.

We are now in the `ERPSystem` business process. Figure 16.31 shows the message box showing the content of the `UserAccountInfo` message as received in the `ERPSystem` business process. Note that the `ReturnPort` attribute in the `HEADER` element is populated.

4. On completion of the `ERPSystem` update, the response message is displayed in the message box in Figure 16.32.

   Figure 16.32 displays the message box, showing the `ERPSystem` response message after the database update is completed. Note the attributes `ResponseCode` and `Description` in the response element of the message.

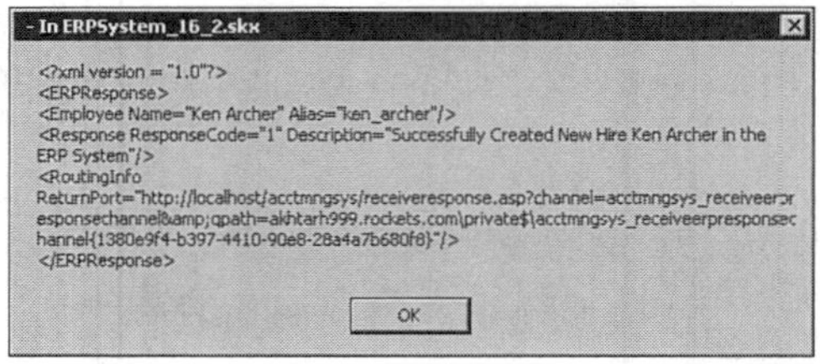

FIGURE 16.32
Content of the response message as returned by the `ERPSystem`.

We are still in the `ERPSystem`. The message box title again displays the schedule name. Figure 16.33 shows the update to the `ERPSystem` database.

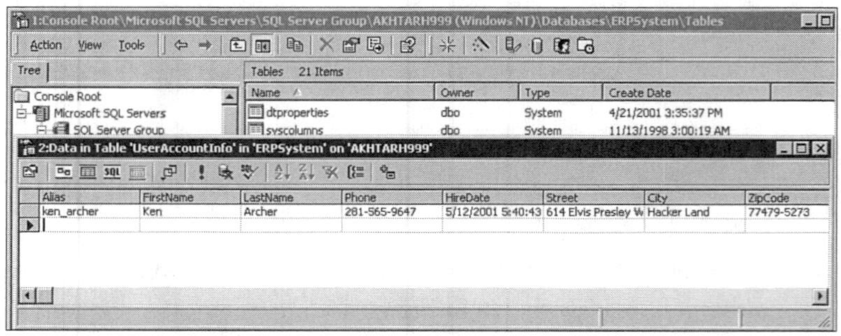

FIGURE 16.33
The `ERPSystem` *database after the new user is added to the system.*

Figure 16.34 shows the XLANG Monitor. The monitor displays two XLANG instances, one for the running and now waiting instance of the `AcctMngSys_16_2.skx` schedule and one instance of the `ERPSystem_16_2.skx` schedule.

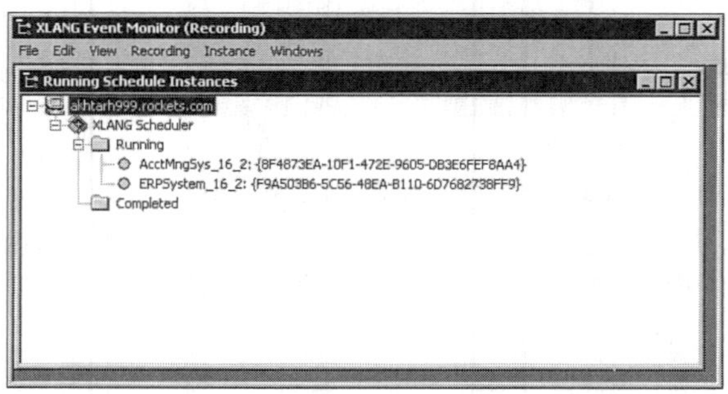

FIGURE 16.34
XLANG Monitor shows the running instances of `AcctMngSys_16_2.skv` *and* `ERPSystem_16_2.skv`. *Note that the instance of* `AcctMngSys_16_2.skv` *is waiting on the response.*

The final Step in the `ERPSystem` business process is to return the `ERPSystem` update response back to the source system.

5. Finally, on receipt of the `ERPSystem` response message back to the running `AcctMngSys_16_2.skv`, the pop-up message box is as shown in Figure 16.35.

FIGURE 16.35
The message box displaying the content of the `ERPSystem` *response as received in the* `AcctMngSys` *business process.*

This completes the schedule correlation that began by sending out the `NewHireInfo` message to the `ERPSystem`.

Note the title on the message box. We are back on the running instance of the `AcctMngSys_16_2.skx` schedule that originally sent the `UserAcctInfo` message to the `ERPSystem`.

The XLANG Monitor in Figure 16.36 now shows that only `AcctMngSys_16_2.skx` is running. The execution of the `ERPSystem_16_2.skx` schedule is now complete.

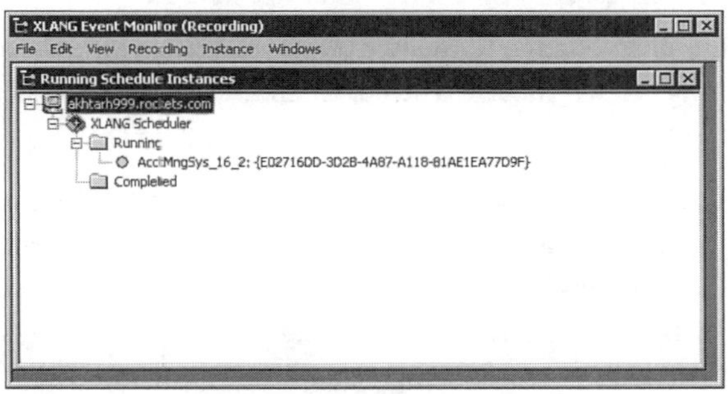

FIGURE 16.36
The XLANG Monitor displays the same instance of the schedule `AcctMngSys_16_2.skx` *that originally sent the message.*

Example 3: HTTP-Based Schedule Correlation, with BizTalk Server on One End and Any External Business Process on the Other End

This example illustrates a case of schedule correlation where BizTalk Server is at one end, and a non-BizTalk Server external process is at the other. Schedule correlation back to a BizTalk Server orchestration schedule does not require a BizTalk Server on the receiving end. A primary design goal of BizTalk Server was to allow interoperability with other environments not running BizTalk. Let's see how this is possible. The correlation information is passed as part of the message as seen in earlier examples. The message moves from the source schedule to the destination schedule with the correlation information contained in it. As long as the destination application can read and retain the information, the destination application will be able to correlate the response back to the source schedule instance.

This section shows an example of schedule correlation that interfaces with an external process not running BizTalk Server. Let's look at the generic steps involved in such a correlation.

The example assumes that there is no change in the `AcctMngSys` business process running on BizTalk Server. The ERP system business process is running on a different platform and technology other than BizTalk Server and therefore not using any orchestration schedule.

Understanding HTTP Correlation with a Non-BizTalk External Application

In this example, there is no change to the `AcctMngSys` application; however, for the `ERPSystem` application, we will not be using BizTalk Server at all. Instead, we will use an ASP page and a COM component to represent the `ERPSystem`.

In our next example, the `AcctMngSys` system is identical to the HTTP-based scenario with BizTalk Server at both ends. In this scenario, the only difference is that there is no BizTalk Server on the other end—that is, the `ERPSystem` is implemented as an external process not using BizTalk Server. To simplify things further, the `ERPSystem` will not have a business process. The `ERPSystem` is composed of the following components:

- `ReceiveUserAcctInfo2.asp`—The ASP page is the same as the `ReceiveUserAcctInfo.asp` with some modification. First, it extracts the `ReturnPort` address from the message body. The `ReturnPort` address will be used later to send a response back to the source system. Second, instead of submitting to BizTalk, the ASP page calls a COM component to implement a business process. There is no other change in the ASP page. The ASP page is located in the `..\Chp16\ERPSystem\WebApp` directory. We will visit the code in the ASP page in Listing 16.6 and Listing 16.7.
- The COM component with the `ProgID` of `ERPSystem2.ERPSystemUpdate2`—It is the same COM component used in the previous section. The only difference between the COM component `ERPSystem.dll` and `ERPSystem2.dll` is that we have

added a private function `SendERPResponseHTTP()` to the `ERPSystem2.dll` component. The component uses this function to directly post the ERP System response message to the `AcctMngSys` application. Internally, the function uses the `MSXML::HTTPPost()` method of the MSXML component. The source code for the COM component is in the `..\Chp16\ERPSystem\Source` directory. We will visit the code for the COM component `ERPSystem2.dll` in Listing 16.8 and Listing 16.9.

- `ERPSystem` database—There is no change to the database schema or the stored procedure used earlier. In fact, we will use the same database as in the other HTTP-based example.

The `ReceiveUserAcctInfo2.asp` is almost same the ASP page `ReceiveUserAcctInfo.asp` as shown in Listing 16.4. The only exception is that instead of submitting the document into the BizTalk Server in the `ERPSystem`, the code in `ReceiveUserAcctInfo2.asp` calls the COM component `ERPSystem2.dll`. Let's look at the code examples from the `ReceiveUserAcctInfo2.asp` page that differs from the ASP page, `ReceiveUserAcctInfo.asp`.

The following code section (shown in Listing 16.6) extracts the `ReturnPort` address attribute from the message `HEADER`. Remember that this is the address that will be used by the `ERPSystem` to send the response message back to the source system. The source system will use this information to correlate the response to the running `AcctMngSys` schedule.

LISTING 16.6 Code from the ASP Page `ReceiveUserAcctInfo2.asp`

```
'
'extract RetrunPort address from the message
'
Dim xmlDoc
Set xmlDoc = Server.CreateObject("MSXML2.DOMDocument")
xmlDoc.LoadXML PostedDocument

Dim strReturnPort
strReturnPort = xmlDoc.getElementsByTagName("HEADER").Item(0)
➥.getAttribute("ReturnPort")
Set xmlDoc = Nothing
```

Finally, the following section of code (shown in Listing 16.7) calls the COM component `ERPSystem2.ERPSystemUpdate2` to execute the business process. We will see how this component sends the `ERPSystem` response document back to the source system.

LISTING 16.7 Code from ASP Page `ReceiveUserAcctInfo2.asp`

```
'
' execute the business process
'
Dim erpSystem
Set erpSystem = Server.CreateObject( "ERPSystem2.ERPSystemUpdate2" )
erpSystem.UpdateERPSystem PostedDocument, strReturnPort
Set erpSystem = Nothing
```

Similarly, the COM component `ERPSystem2.ERPSystemUpdate2 (ERPSystem2.dll)` that is simulating the `ERPSystem` is identical to the one used in the HTTP-based scenario where BizTalk is on both ends of the interchange. Let's look at the method `UpdateERPSystem()`. The method takes two parameters, the `PostedDocument` and the `ReturnPort` address, as strings (see Listing 16.8).

LISTING 16.8 Code from the `ERPSystem2.dll` Component

```
Public Function UpdateERPSystem(ByVal strUserInfo As String,
➥ByVal strQueuePath As String) As String

Dim strLastName As String
Dim strFirstName As String
Dim strAlias As String
Dim strPhone As String
Dim strStreet As String
Dim strCity As String
Dim strZipCode As String
Dim strState As String
Dim strLevel As String
Dim strTitle As String
Dim strReturnPort As String
Dim status As Boolean
Dim strDescription As String
Dim strXMLResponse As String
Dim strResponse As String
Dim strQueueName As String
Dim strMsgLabel As String
Dim oTS As ADODB.Stream
Dim MsgText As String

On Error GoTo UpdateERPSystem_err

  MsgBox "Received UserAccountInfo in ERPSystem." & vbCrLf & _
         strUserInfo, , "ERPSytem"

  'Debug lines
  App.LogEvent "Message Received by the COM Componenet ERPSystem." &
➥vbNewLine & strUserInfo, vbLogEventTypeInformation
```

LISTING 16.8 continued

```
  SpitMsgToFile strUserInfo, "c:\temp\ERPSystemUpdate.xml"
  status = ExtractUserInfo(strUserInfo, strFirstName, strLastName,
➥strAlias, strPhone, strStreet, strCity,
➥strZipCode, strState, strLevel, strTitle, strReturnPort)

  status = InsertData(strLastName, strFirstName, strAlias,
➥strPhone, strStreet, strCity, strState, strZipCode, strLevel, strTitle,
strResponse)

  If status = True Then
    status = FormatSuccessResponse(strLastName, strFirstName,
➥strAlias, strPhone, strReturnPort, strResponse, strXMLResponse)
  Else
    status = FormatFailedResponse(strLastName, strFirstName,
➥strAlias, strPhone, strReturnPort, strResponse, strXMLResponse)
  End If

  If Not IsEmpty(strXMLResponse) Then
     SpitMsgToFile strXMLResponse, "c:\temp\ERPSystemResonse.xml"
  End If

     SendERPResponseHTTP strXMLResponse, strQueuePath

UpdateERPSystem_exit:
    MsgBox "ERPSystem Successfully Posted Response to AcctMngSys." & vbCrLf & _
           strXMLResponse, , "ERPSytem - " & strFirstName & " " & strLastName
    Exit Function

UpdateERPSystem_err:
    App.LogEvent "Error occured in the ERP System."
➥& vbNewLine & "Error = " & Err.Number & "Description = "
➥& Err.Description, vbLogEventTypeError
Err.Raise 999, Err.Source & ': UpdateERPSystem()", Err.Description
    Exit Function

End Function
```

The section of the code that is different from the one used in the earlier example is the call to the function `SendERPResponseHTTP()` toward the bottom of the public function, `UpdateERPSystem()`. The `SendERPResponseHTTP()` function does an HTTP Post of the `ERPSystem` response to the source system. The function uses the `ReturnPort` address (see Listing 16.9).

LISTING 16.9 Code from the `ERPSystem2.dll` Component

```
Private Function SendERPResponseHTTP(ByVal strMsg As String,
➥ByVal strReturnPort As String)
```

LISTING 16.9 continued

```
On Error GoTo SendERPResponseHTTP_err

Dim strResponseText As String
Dim strResponseBody As String

Dim oHTTP As MSXML2.XMLHTTP

    'Send the Message via HTTP to the RetrunPort.
➥If the ReturnPort is empty then flag error
    If Not IsEmpty(strReturnPort) Then

      Set oHTTP = CreateObject("Microsoft.XMLHTTP")
      oHTTP.Open "POST", strReturnPort, False
      oHTTP.setRequestHeader "Content-Type", "text/xml"
      oHTTP.Send strMsg

      strResponseText = oHTTP.responseText
      strResponseBody = oHTTP.responseBody

    Else
      Err.Raise 999, "SendERPResponseHTTP", "No HTTP URL found"
    End If


SendERPResponseHTTP_exit:

    Exit Function

SendERPResponseHTTP_err:
    App.LogEvent "Error = " & Err.Number & ", Description = "
➥& Err.Description, vbLogEventTypeError
    Err.Raise 999, Err.Source & ": SendERPResponseHTTP()", Err.Description
    Exit Function

End Function
```

Note

You can examine the full source code in the `\Chp16\ERPSytem\Source\ERPSystem2` directory. For the database component of the `ERPSystem`, refer to the earlier example.

There is only one change to the BizTalk Messaging configuration for the `AcctMngSys` application. The Messaging port, `AcctMngSys_ToERPSystemPort` points to the ASP page

ReceiveUserAcctInfo2.asp instead of pointing to ReceiveUserAcctInfo.asp as in the first HTTP example. This is shown in Table 16.9.

TABLE 16.9 Sending the Message to ERPSystem

Objects	*Options and Settings Chosen*	*Note*
Port	Name: AcctMngSys_ToERPSystemPort (To an Organization) Destination Organization: ERP_System Primary Transport: HTTP Address: http//localhost/ERPSystem/ReceiveUserAcctInfo2.asp	The port uses HTTP to send the UserAccountInfo message to the ERPSystem. You will make this change to run the Example 3 in this chapter—that is, HTTP-based correlation with BizTalk Server on one end and some other external System on the other end.

Running the HTTP-Based Correlation with BizTalk on One End Example 3

Make sure that you have made the change to the BizTalk Messaging port, AcctMngSys_ToERPSystemPort as instructed on Table 16.9. This is the only change required to run this example. To start the example, copy the File2Queue.vbs script and test Test_NewHire.xml to the .\Chp16\AcctMngSys\Source directory. Also make sure that all receive functions except the ones used in this example (AcctMngSys_ReceiveNewHireInfo) are disabled. Then type the following at the command prompt:

```
File2Queue.vbs AcctMngSys_NewHire.xml
```

The following steps list the sequence in which the message moves and the appropriate message boxes that pop up.

> **Note**
>
> Steps 1 through 5 illustrate running the HTTP-based scenario, where BizTalk is at one end, and an external process is at the other end.

1. The pop-up message box for submission of the AcctMngSys_NewHire.xml message to the queue ReceiveNewHire is the same as shown earlier in Figure 16.28.
2. On receipt of the UserAcctInfo into the AcctMngSys_16_2.skx, the pop-up message box is as shown earlier in Figure 16.29.

Note the XLANG schedule name in the message box title is `AcctMngSys_16_2.skx`. Similarly, the XLANG Monitor shows the running instance of the schedule as shown earlier in Figure 16.30.

3. On receipt of the `UserAcctInfo` message by the COM component `ERPSystem2.ERPSystemUpdate2 (ERPSystem2.dll)`, the pop-up message box is as shown in Figure 16.37.

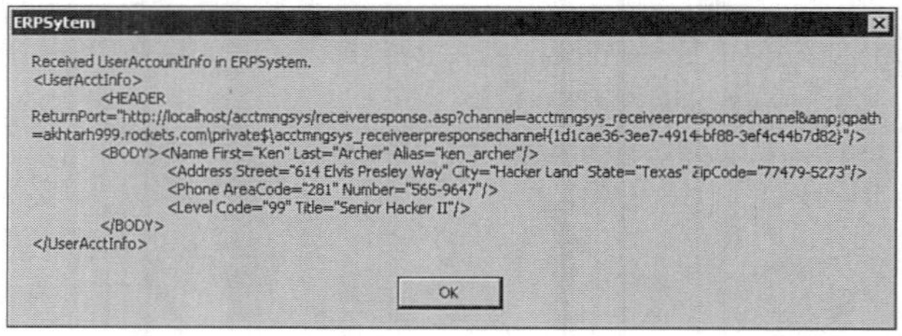

FIGURE 16.37
The message box displays the New Hire Information as received in the COM component simulating the `ERPSystem` *in the non BizTalk end of the HTTP-based correlation.*

Figure 16.37 shows the message box showing the content of the `UserAcctInfo` message as received in the `ERPSystem` business process. Because there is no BizTalk implementation at the `ERPSystem` for this example, there is no orchestration schedule. This message box is being displayed by the `ERPSystem` business component. Note that the `ReturnPort` attribute in the `HEADER` element is populated. Also the message box title is `ERPSystem`.

Bring up the XLANG Monitor again. Notice that the instance of the schedule `AcctMngSys_16_2.skv` is running and waiting for the response from the ERP system.

4. On completion of the `ERPSystem` update, the COM Component displays the response message in the message box as in Figure 16.38.

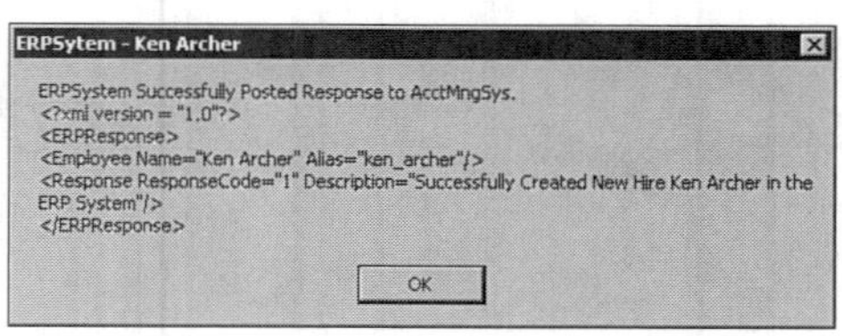

FIGURE 16.38
The message box, showing the `ERPSystem` *response message after the database update is completed.*

Note the attributes `ResponseCode` and `Description` in the response element of the message. We are still in the `ERPSystem`. The message box title again displays the `ERPSystem` application name.

The last step in the ERPSystem business process is to return the ERPSystem update response back to the source system.

5. Finally, on receipt of the ERPSystem response message back to the running AcctMngSys_16_2.skx, the pop-up message box is as shown in Figure 16.35. This is same as in our Example 2.

   This completes the schedule correlation that began by sending out the NewHireInfo message to the ERPSystem.

   Note the title on the message box. We are back to the running instance of the AcctMngSys_16_2.skx schedule that originally sent the UserAccountInfo message to the ERPSystem.

This concludes our example showing how to use HTTP-based correlation when you do not have BizTalk Server on the other end. You do not need BizTalk Server on both ends to do HTTP-based correlation. In the next section, we will see non-HTTP-based correlation.

Example 4: Non-HTTP-Based Correlation Using Two BizTalk Servers

Non-HTTP-based correlation is much more difficult to implement than HTTP-based correlation. The dynamic orchestration port (the port through which we send a message out of the orchestration schedule to the external entity) and the orchestration BizTalk Messaging receive ports (the ports through which we receive the response message back into the orchestration) support HTTP transports natively.

This is evident when you are required to enter a URL (for the return ASP page) in addition to the channel name in the BizTalk messaging orchestration receive port as shown previously in Figure 16.23. This simply means that there is built-in support for HTTP-based transport. For non-HTTP-based correlation, including MSMQ, SMTP, and file system-based transports, you will need to do this yourself.

We will take the same approach to illustrate the non-HTTP-based solution as we did in the case of HTTP-based correlation. The only difference between the two approaches will be the transport type used in the delivery of the document from one system to the other. The same three basic steps as used in the HTTP-based transport apply here:

1. The UserAcctInfo message is sent out from the AcctMngSys system to the ERPSystem.

2. The `ERPSystem` response is generated and sent back from the `ERPSystem` to the `AcctMngSys`.
3. The `ERPSystem` response message is correlated back to the running `AcctMngSys` orchestration schedule.

Understanding Non-HTTP Correlation Between Two BizTalk Servers

The non-HTTP-based correlation is much the same as the HTTP-based solution. In this case, instead of using HTTP as the mode of transport, we can use any one of the Messaging queue, SMTP, AIC, and file system. In our example, instead of using HTTP transport to send the `UserAcctInfo` message from the `AcctMngSys` to the `ERPSystem`, we will use MSMQ. Similarly, when sending the response from the `ERPSystem` back to the `AcctMngSys`, we will again use MSMQ.

We will illustrate the important differences between the HTTP-based and non-HTTP-based example. For the `AcctMngSys` business process, we will be using a slightly modified orchestration schedule, `AcctMngSys_16_3.skv`. The important thing to remember is to flow the address of the orchestration port (the port through which the schedule receives the response from the `ERPSystem`) into the physical message (`HEADER@ReturnPort`). This is done in the Data Page of the orchestration schedule.

The first step in schedule correlation is to pass the message containing the return address to the `ERPSystem`. In the schedule `AcctMngSys_16_3.skv`, this is done by passing the message to the BizTalk Messaging shape in the orchestration schedule. The BizTalk Messaging then uses the channel, `AcctMngSys_nonHTTP_SendToERPSystemChannel`, and a port to deliver the message to the `ERPSystem` using a messaging queue. Note that we could have directly used MSMQ Messaging shape in the orchestration to achieve this. However, we need a mechanism to transform the message queue format name to the pathname syntax (queue: `//DirectOS :`) in the return address. To do this, we will use mapping in the channel.

For the `ERPSystem` business process, we will be using a slightly modified orchestration schedule, `ERPSystem_16_3.skv`. To send the response from the orchestration schedule, we will use the BizTalk Messaging shape. The BizTalk Messaging implementation uses a static channel and a port to deliver the response to the `AcctMngSys` via a message queue.

Let us see how the response is correlated in the `AcctMngSys` application to the running instance of the `AcctMngSys_16_3.skv` schedule. Note that that this instance of the schedule is waiting for a response after having sent the `UserAcctInfo` to the `ERPSystem`. To do this, an MSMQ receive function picks up the message and submits it to BizTalk Messaging. BizTalk Messaging uses a channel and an open destination port to deliver the response message back to the running instance of the schedule. The process that BizTalk Messaging uses to determine the recipient of the response message is somewhat tricky. The schema file associated to the incoming response message identifies `HEADER@ReturnPort` as the Destination Value. We do this in the BizTalk Editor, using the Dictionary tab.

Building the Non-HTTP BizTalk-to-BizTalk Example

It is probably clear to you that many of the steps in the non-HTTP- and HTTP-based correlation are similar. The difference is in the transport used to deliver the message across the systems. For clarity, we will define the whole non-HTTP scenario as we did in the case of HTTP. The following sections walk through, in detail, the steps required to accomplish this.

Pick Up the `UserAcctInfo` Message Using BizTalk Messaging and Deliver the Message to the `AcctMngSys` Business Process

This step involves picking up the sample `AcctMngSys_NewHire.xml` and delivering it to the schedule `AcctMngSys_16_3.skx`.

We will first drop the `AcctMngSys_NewHire.xml` onto a message queue, `.\private$\ReceiveNewHire`, using `File2Queue.vbs`. The receive function, `AcctMngSys_nonHTTP_ReceiveNewHire`, monitors the queue. The receive function picks up the message and delivers it to the BizTalk Messaging channel, `AcctMngSys_nonHTTP_ReceiveNewHireInfoChannel`. The channel in turn delivers the message to the BizTalk Messaging port, `AcctMngSys_nonHTTP_ReceiveNewHireInfoPort`. Finally, the port delivers the message to a new instance of the schedule, `AcctMngSys_16_3.skx`.

Table 16.10 shows the BizTalk Messaging setup required for this.

TABLE 16.10 BizTalk Messaging Configuration for non-HTTP-Based Solution

Objects	*Options and Settings Chosen*	*Note*
Document definition	Name: `NewHireInfo` Spec: UserAcctInfoXML.xml	The doc specification was created in the Editor. First copy the file `UserAcctInfoXML.xml` to your WebDAV repository and then create the document definition.

TABLE 16.10 continued

Objects	*Options and Settings Chosen*	*Note*
Port	Name: `AcctMngSys_nonHTTP_ReceiveNewHireInfoPort` (To an Application) Destination Application: New XLANG Schedule Schedule Moniker: `AcctMngSys_16_3.skx` Port Name: `UserAcctInfo`	The port uses HTTP to send the `UserAccountInfo` message to the `ERPSystem`.
Channel	Name: `AcctMngSys_nonHTTP_ReceiveNewHireInfoChannel` (from Application) Source Application: `NewHireApp` InBoundDocument: `NewHireAccountInfo` OutBoundDocument: `NewHireAccountInfo` Mapping: No Document Logging: Check only, In Native Format Advanced Configuration: Take the Defaults	No mapping is required because the Inbound doc spec is the same as Outbound document spec.
Receive function	Name: `AcctMngSys_nonHTTP_ReceiveNewHire` Protocol: Message Queuing Polling Location: `Direct=OS:.\private$\ReceiveNewHire` Channel Name: AcctMngSys_nonHTTP_ReceiveNewHireInfoChannel	Note the syntax for the message queue.

Receiving the `UserAcctInfo` into the Schedule, Sending the `NewHireInfo` to the `ERPSystem`, and Finally Receiving the `ERPSystem` Response

Open the file `\Chp16\AcctMngSys\AcctMngSys_16_3.skv` in BizTalk Orchestration Designer. The schedule is shown in Figure 16.39.

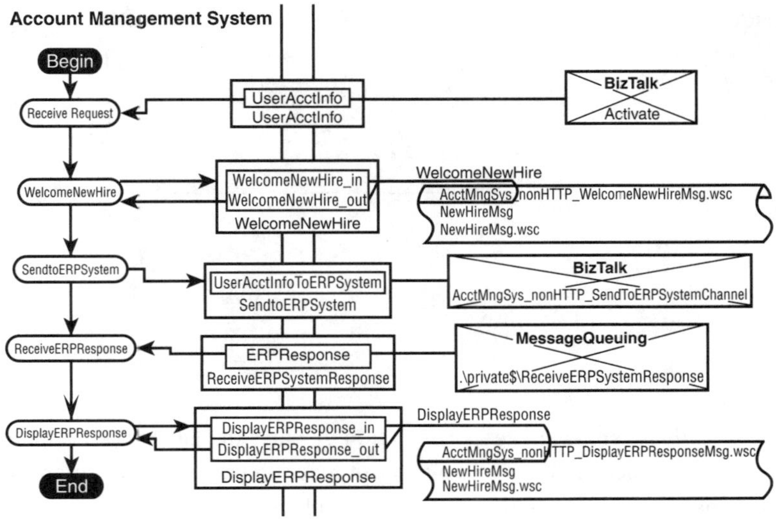

FIGURE 16.39
BizTalk Orchestration Schedule `AcctMngSys_16_3.skv`.

This is similar to the schedule for the HTTP-based example. The first action receives the `UserAcctInfo` XML message from the BizTalk Messaging. In the BizTalk Messaging Binding Wizard for receive request, the value of XLANG Schedule Activation is set to Yes. This means that each time a message arrives at the binding port, a new instance of the schedule is instantiated.

The second action, `WelcomeNewHire`, is bound to Windows scripting component. The component simply displays the content of the `UserAcctInfo` message in the body, and in the title it displays the name of the new hire and the schedule filename.

The next action, `SendToERPSystem`, sends the message out to the `ERPSystem` through the BizTalk Messaging binding port. In the BizTalk Messaging Binding Wizard for `SendToERPSystem`, we specify the BizTalk Messaging channel `AcctMngSys_nonHTTP_SendToERPSystemChannel`. This channel will be used by the schedule to send out the message.

After sending out the message to the `ERPSystem`, the schedule simply waits at the `ReceiveERPResponse` action. After a response is received at the binding port `ReceiveERPsystemResponse` in the message queue `.\private$\ReceiveERPSystemResponse`, the schedule instance continues to the next action. Note that in the Message Queue Binding Wizard for the `ReceiveERPSystemResponse`, the orchestration port is set to create a new queue for every instance, as shown in Figure 16.40.

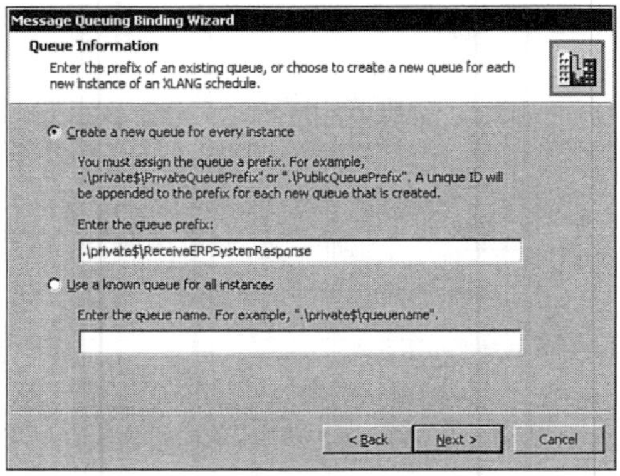

FIGURE 16.40
Message Queue Binding Wizard.

Finally, the `DisplayERPResponse` action displays the `ERPSystem` response message. The action is connected to a Windows scripting component. The component displays the response in the body, and in the title it displays the name of the new hire and the name of the schedule file.

Figure 16.41 shows the XLANG schedule data page.

Note that the port reference for `ReceiveERPSystemResponse` is passed into the physical message `UserAccountInfoToERPSystem`. This reference will be used later in the destination system to send the `ERPSystemResponse` message back. We are passing the `UserAcctInfo` message and the first and last names of the new hire to the `AcctMngSys_nonHTTP_DisplayERPResponsMsg.wsc` component. Similarly, to the `DisplayERPResponse.wsc` component, we are passing the `ERPResponse` message and the name of the new hire.

Sending the `UserAcctInfo` Message Through BizTalk Messaging to Another BizTalk Orchestration Schedule Via Non-HTTP Transport

The action `SendToERPsystem` in the XLANG schedule delivers the message to the BizTalk Messaging channel, `AcctMngSys_nonHTTP_SendToERPSystemChannel`. The channel in turn delivers the message to the BizTalk Messaging port, `AcctMngSys_nonHTTP_ToERPSystemPort`. The port is configured to deliver the message on to the queue `.\private$\SendNewHireInfo`. Finally, the `ERPSystem` imports the message into the `ERPSystem` using an MSMQ receive function, `AcctMngSys_nonHTTP_ReceiveNewHire`.

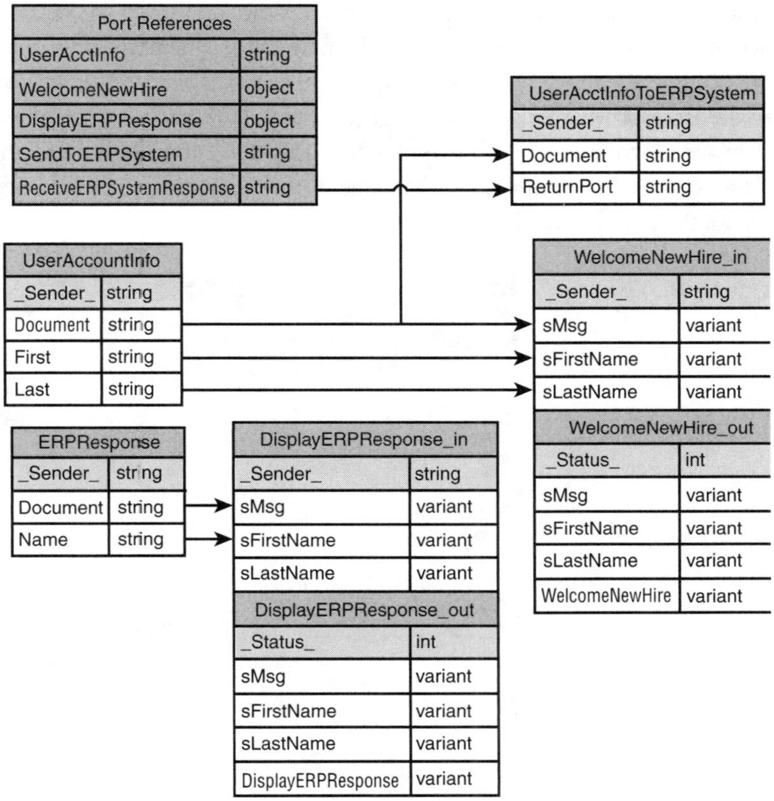

FIGURE 16.41
Data page of the `AcctMngSys` *business process.*

In the HTTP scenario, the channel simply delivered the message to the port, and the port posted the message via HTTP to the `ERPSystem`. In the non-HTTP example, the channel does a little more than that. In the channel, we apply a map to apply the MSMQ pathname to the MSMQ format name by prepending `queue://Direct=OS:` to the pathname. This is done to the field `HEADER@ReturnPort` in the `UserAcctInfo` message before the message is sent out to the `ERPSystem`.

You will recall that we did the same thing in the HTTP-based scenario, in the `ReceiveResponse.asp` page. The following code is from the `ReceiveResponse.asp` page to jog your memory:

```
queuepath = Request.QueryString("qpath")
queuepath = "queue://Direct=OS:" & queuepath
channelname = Request.QueryString("channel")
```

Now in the non-HTTP-based solution, there is no `ReceiveResponse.asp` page. We will accomplish the same process by using a map in the channel, before sending the document out to the `ERPSystem`. Open the map file, `UserAcctInfo_UserAcctInfo_Map.xml`, in the BizTalk Mapper. The source schema and the destination schema are the same, `UserAcctInfoXML.xml`. The mapping uses the string concatenate functoid to prepend the string `queue://Direct=OS:` to the value of the `HEADER@ReturnPort` field. Figure 16.42 shows the map in the Mapper.

FIGURE 16.42
Mapping.

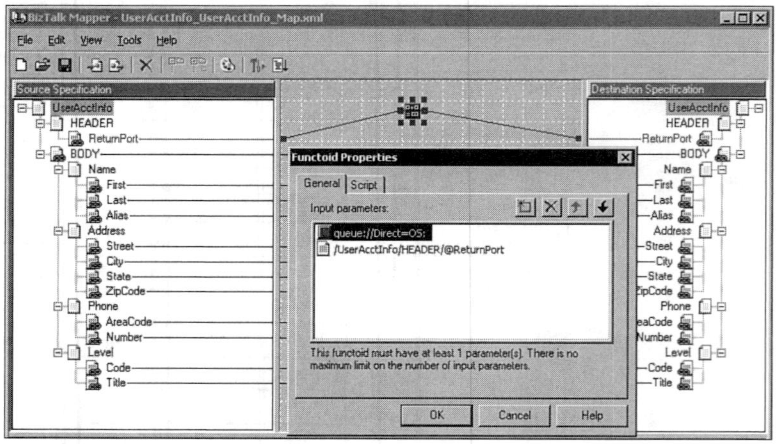

After the message is delivered to the MSMQ, the receive function in the `ERPSystem` picks up the message and delivers it to a channel and port. The port in the `ERPSystem` delivers the message to the `ERPSystem` business process orchestration schedule. In the case of the HTTP-based solution, the message was posted to the `ReceiveUserAcctInfo.asp` page on the `ERPSystem`. The ASP page then submitted the document to a channel and port and finally to the `ERPSystem` business process orchestration schedule.

Table 16.11 details the configuration required in BizTalk Messaging to send the `UserAcctInfo` message from the `AcctMngSys` schedule to the `ERPSystem`. Also listed is the receive function used to pick up the message at the `ERPSystem`, and the channel and port needed to deliver the message to the `ERPSystem` business process.

TABLE 16.11 BizTalk Configuration on AcctMngSys for Delivering the Message to the ERPSystem

Objects	*Options and Settings Chosen*	*Note*
Port	Name: AcctMngSys_nonHTTP_ToERPSystemPort (To an Organization) Destination Organization: ERP_System Primary Transport: Messaging Queuing Address: Direct=OS:.\private$\SendNewHireInfo	The port uses non-HTTP to send the UserAcctInfo message to the ERPSystem, using the MSMQ.
Channel	Name: AcctMngSys_nonHTTP_ SendToERPSystemChannel (from Application) Source Application: NewHireApp InBoundDocument: NewHireAccountInfo OutBoundDocument: NewHireAccountInfo Mapping: UserAcctInfo_ UserAcctInfo_Map.xml Document Logging: Check only, In Native Format Advanced Configuration: Take the Defaults	Mapping is used to prepend the string queue://Direct=OS: to the source field HEADER@ ReturnPort. We are using the string concatenate functoid in the Mapper. The map file is stored in the WebDAV.

Table 16.12 gives the detail of the BizTalk Messaging configuration required on the ERPSystem side to receive the message and deliver it to the ERPSystem business process.

TABLE 16.12 ERPSystem BizTalk Configuration on the ERPSystem

Objects	*Options and Settings Chosen*	*Note*
Port	Name: ERPSystem_nonHTTP_ ReceiveNewHireInfoPort (To an Application) Destination Application: New XLANG schedule Schedule Moniker: ERPSystem_16_3.skx Port Name: UserAcctInfo	For every message that arrives at this port, a new XLANG schedule is instantiated, and the message is delivered.

TABLE 16.12 continued

Objects	*Options and Settings Chosen*	*Note*
Channel	Name: `ERPSystem_nonHTTP_ReceiveNewHireChannel` (from Application) Source Application: `HRERPSystem` InBoundDocument: `NewHireAccountInfo` OutBoundDocument: `NewHireAccountInfo` Mapping: No Document Logging: Check only, In Native Format Advanced Configuration: Take the Defaults	No mapping is required because the Inbound doc spec is the same as Outbound document spec.
Receive function	Name: `ERPSystem_nonHTTP_ReceiveNewHireInfo` Protocol: Message Queuing Polling Location: `Direct=OS:.\private$\SendNewHireInfo` Channel Name: ERPSystem_nonHTTP_ReceiveNewHireChannel	Note the syntax for the message queue.

This completes the BizTalk Messaging configuration on the `ERPSystem` to deliver the message to the XLANG schedule, business process.

Receiving the `UserAcctInfo` Message and Sending the `ERPSystem` Response in BizTalk Orchestration

Now look at the XLANG schedule in the `ERPSystem`. Figure 16.43 shows the XLANG schedule `ERPSystem_16_3.skv`.

The schedule receives the message `UserAcctInfo` through the BizTalk Messaging binding port also called `UserAcctInfo` to a new instance of the XLANG schedule. This is the same way that the message was received into the schedule in the `AcctMngSys_16_3.skx`. Note that the XLANG Schedule Activation is set to Yes, which means that each time a message arrives at this port, a new schedule instance is created and the message delivered.

The next action in the schedule, `DisplayNewUser`, sends the message to a Windows scripting host component, which simply displays the message using a message box. The title of the message box shows the new hire name and the name of the schedule file.

FIGURE 16.43
`ERPSystem` *business process—* `ERPSystem_16_3.skv`.

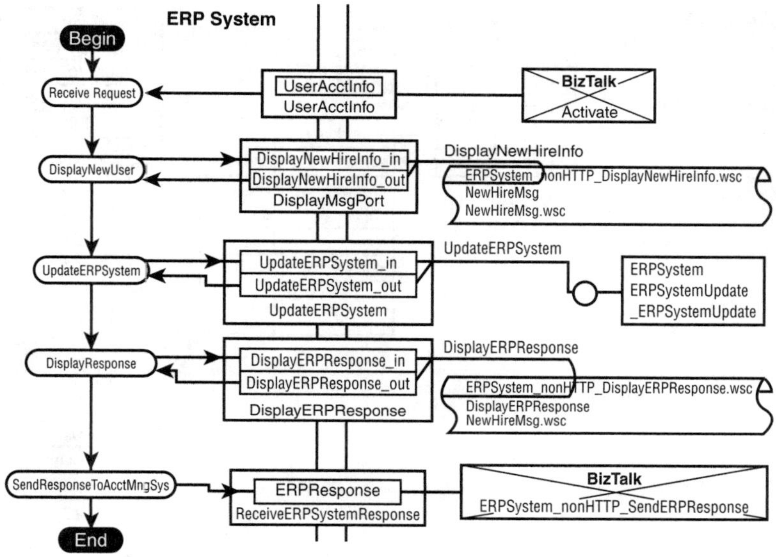

The third action in the schedule, `UpdateERPSystem`, sends the message to the same COM component as in the HTTP-based solution. The component simulates a real-world ERP system, such as the SAP R/3. Refer to the HTTP-based section earlier in this chapter to learn more on the functionality of this component. It is sufficient here to know that the COM component updates a SQL Server database with the new user information. The component then formats a response based on the status of the SQL Server update. The schema of the `ERPSystem` response message is defined in `ERPResponseXML_nonHTTP.xml`.

Open the data page of the schedule to see the data flow shown in Figure 16.44, specifically how the `ReturnPort` information is flowed into the COM component's message `UpdateERPSystem_in` (parameter `strQueuePath`). The component then includes this information as part of the response generated.

The next action, `DisplayResponse`, simply displays the response using the `WSH` component.

The final action in the schedule, `SendResponseToAcctMngSys`, sends the previous response message to the source business process. The response is sent out using the static BizTalk Messaging binding port, `SendERPSystemResponse`.

FIGURE 16.44
Data page for schedule `ERPSystem_16_3.skv`.

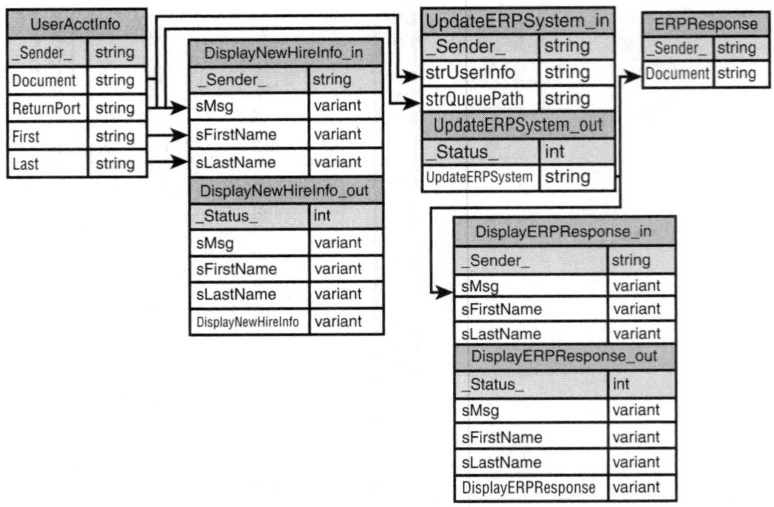

Returning the `ERPSystem` Response Message to the Source Schedule Instance of the `AcctMngSys`

The static BizTalk Messaging binding port, `SendERPSystemResponse`, delivers the message to the BizTalk Messaging channel `ERPSystem_nonHTTP_SendERPResponse`, which in turn delivers the message to the BizTalk Messaging port `ERPSystem_nonHTTP_SendResponsePort`. The port is configured to drop the message to the MSMQ queue `Direct=OS:.\private$\ERPSystem_SendResponse` for the source system to pick the response.

Look at Table 16.13 for the BizTalk Messaging configuration needed to accomplish this.

TABLE 16.13 `ERPSystem` BizTalk Messaging Configuration

Objects	*Options and Settings Chosen*	*Note*
Port	Name: `ERPSystem_nonHTTP_SendResponsePort` (To an Organization) Organization Name: Hacker's Den Transport Type: Message Queuing Address: Direct=OS:.\private$\ERPSystem_SendResponse	

TABLE 16.13 continued

Objects	*Options and Settings Chosen*	*Note*
Document Definition	Name: `ERPSystemResponse_nonHTTP` Spec: `ERPResponseXML_nonHTTP.xml`	Open the file `ERPResponseXML_nonHTTP.xml` in the BizTalk Editor and then store it into WebDAV.
Channel	Name: `ERPSystem_nonHTTP_SendERPResponse` (from Application) Source Application: `HRERPSystem` InBoundDocument: `ERPSystemResponse_nonHTTP` OutBoundDocument: `ERPSystemResponse_nonHTTP` Mapping: No Document Logging: Check only, In Native Format Advanced Configuration: Take the Defaults	No mapping is required because the Inbound doc spec is the same as Outbound document spec.

Finally, the next section explains the steps in correlating the `ERPSystem` response back to the instance of the source schedule that originally initiated the update of the `ERPSystem` for the new hire.

Returning the `ERPSystem` Response Message to the Original Instance of the `AcctMngSys` Business Process Schedule

After the `ERPSystem` drops the response to the messaging queue, the `ERPSystem` work is complete. Somehow the `AcctMngSys` must be able to get the response message and correlate the response message to the original instance of the schedule.

An MSMQ receive function on the `AcctMngSys` system picks up the response message and passes the message to BizTalk Messaging. A BizTalk Messaging channel pointing to an open destination messaging port delivers the message back to the original instance of the schedule. A point to note here is why the `ERPSystem` could not use an open destination port to deliver the message to the schedule. The reason is that the open destination port uses a private per-instance message queue, and private queues are not available on a remote machine.

Table 16.14 details the BizTalk Messaging configuration needed to accomplish this task.

TABLE 16.14 AcctMngSys BizTalk Messaging Configuration

Objects	*Options and Settings Chosen*	*Note*
Port	Name: AcctMngSys_nonHTTP_ReceiveERPResponsePort (To an Organization) Destination Organization: Open Destination	Note the Destination Organization is set to Open Destination. No Primary/Secondary Transport is defined.
Channel	Name: AcctMngSys_nonHTTP_ReceiveERPResponseChannel (from Application) Source Application: NewHireApp InBoundDocument: ERPSystemResponse_nonHTTP OutBoundDocument: ERPSystemResponse_nonHTTP Mapping: No Document Logging: Check only, In Native Format Advanced Configuration: Take the Defaults	No mapping is required because the Inbound doc spec is the same as Outbound document spec.
Receive function	Name: AcctMngSys_nonHTTP_ReceiveERPSystemResponse Protocol: Message Queuing Polling Location: Direct=OS:.\private$\ERPSystem_SendResponse Openness: Open Destination Channel Name: AcctMngSys_nonHTTP_ReceiveERPResponseChannel	Note the Openness is set to Open Destination. This means that the document is self-routing.

This completes the setup for receiving the ERPSystem response message and correlating this message to the original schedule instance that sent out the UserAcctInfo to the ERPSystem for update.

Running the non-HTTP-Based Correlation Example 4

To start the example, copy the File2Queue.vbs script and test AcctMngSys_NewHire.xml to the .\Chp16\AcctMngSys\Source directory. Also make sure that all receive functions except the ones used in this example (AcctMngSys_nonHTTP_ReceiveNewHire, AcctMngSys_nonHTTP_ReceiveERPSystemResponse, ERPSystem_nonHTP_ReceiveNewHireInfo) are disabled. Then type the following at the command prompt:

```
File2Queue.vbs    AcctMngSys_NewHire.xml
```

The following steps list the sequence in which the message moves and the appropriate message boxes that pop up.

Note

Steps 1 through 5 illustrate running the non-HTTP-based scenario.

1. Again, the pop-up message box on submission of the `UserAcctInfo message` to the queue `ReceiveNewHire` is the same as shown earlier in Figure 16.28.
2. On receipt of the `UserAcctInfo` into the `AcctMngSys_16_3.skx`, the pop-up message box is as shown in Figure 16.45.

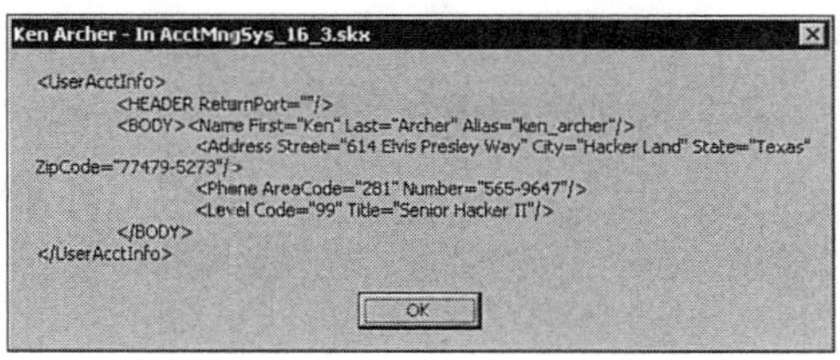

FIGURE 16.45
The message box on receipt of the `NewHireInfo` *in the* `AcctMngSys_16_3.skx` *business process.*

Note the XLANG schedule name in the message box title is `AcctMngSys_16_3.skx`. Also note the XLANG Monitor showing the schedule instance running in Figure 16.46.

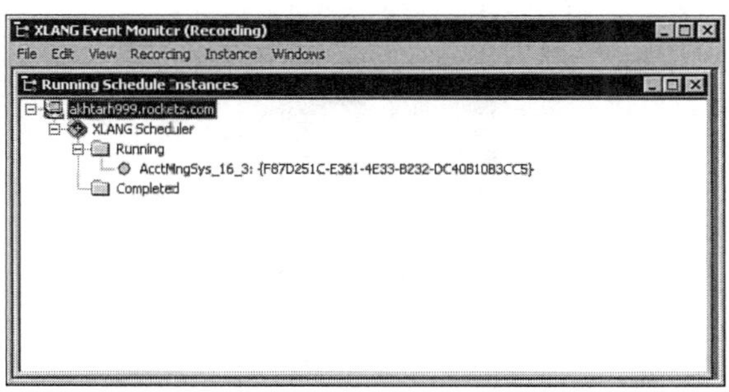

FIGURE 16.46
The XLANG Monitor displays the running instance of the schedule `AcctMngSys_16_3.skx`. *Each instance of the schedule is identified by a GUID appended to the name of the schedule.*

3. On receipt of the `UserAcctInfo` into the `ERPSystem_16_3.skx`, the pop-up message box is as shown in Figure 16.47.

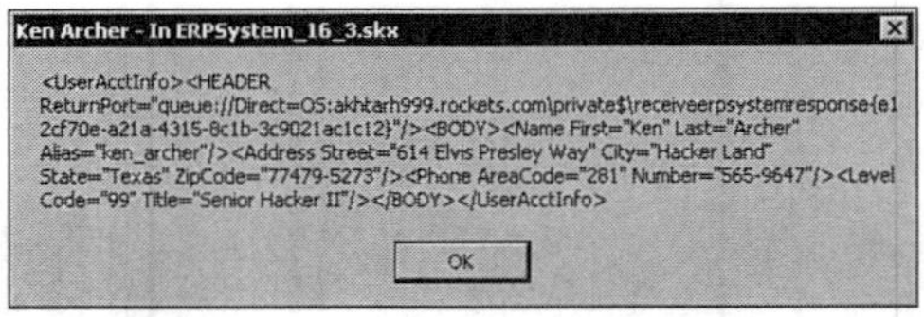

FIGURE 16.47
Note that the `ReturnPort` *attribute in the* `HEADER` *element is populated.*

We are now in the `ERPSystem` business process. Figure 16.47 shows the message box showing the content of the `UserAccountInfo` message as received in the `ERPSystem` business process.

Note the message box title is `ERPSystem_16_3.skx`. Also note XLANG Monitor in Figure 16.48 showing the two schedules running, one for the `AcctMngSys` and one for the `ERPSystem` business process.

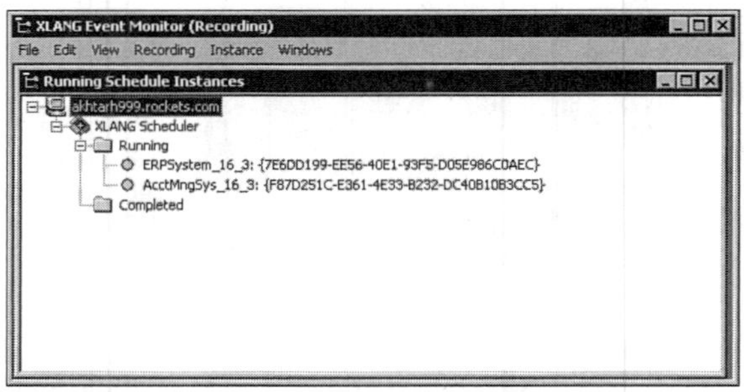

FIGURE 16.48
The `AcctMngSys` *and* `ERPSystem` *schedule instances running in the XLANG Monitor.*

4. On completion of the `ERPSystem` update, the response message is displayed in the message box shown in Figure 16.49.

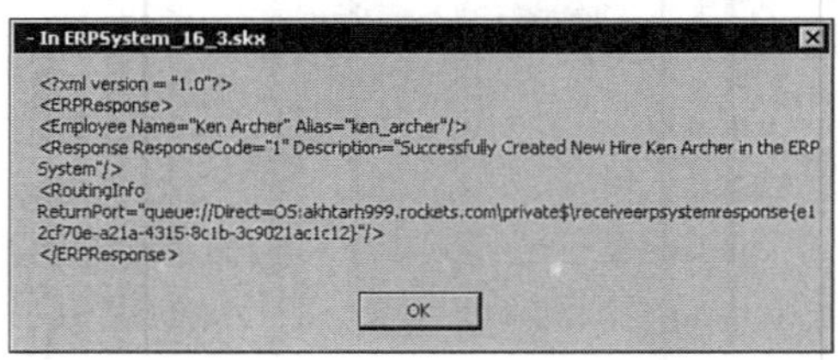

FIGURE 16.49
The message box shows the `ERPSystem` *response message after the database update is completed. Note the attributes* `ResponseCode` *and* `Description` *in the response element of the message.*

We are still in the `ERPSystem`. The message box title again displays the schedule name. The final step in the `ERPSystem` business process is to return the `ERPSystem` update response back to the source system.

5. Finally, on receipt of the `ERPSystem` response message back to the running `AcctMngSys_16_3.skx`, Figure 16.50 appears.

FIGURE 16.50
The message box displays the content of the `ERPSystem` *response as received in the* `AcctMngSys` *business process.*

This completes the schedule correlation that began by sending out the `NewHireInfo` message to the ERPSystem. Note the title on the message box. We are back on the running instance of the `AcctMngSys_16_3.skx` schedule that originally sent the `UserAccountInfo` message to the `ERPSystem`.

The XLANG Monitor in Figure 16.51 now shows that only `AcctMngSys_16_3.skx` is running. The execution of the `ERPSystem_16_3.skx` schedule is now complete.

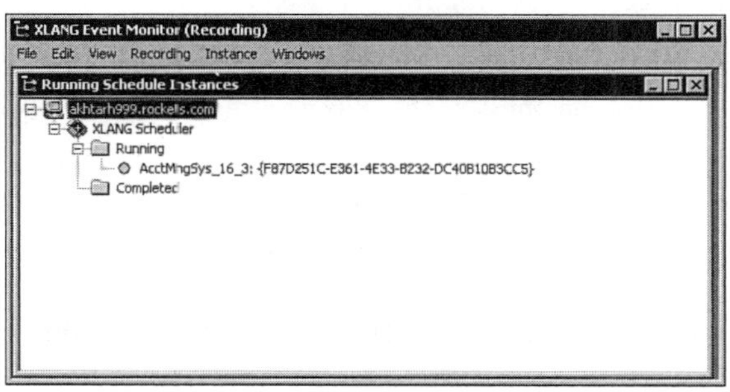

FIGURE 16.51
The XLANG Monitor displays the same instance of the schedule `AcctMngSys_16_3.skx` *that originally sent the message.*

Finally, when you click OK on the message box shown in Figure 16.50, the XLANG Monitor shows that the `AcctMngSys_16_3.skx` schedule has completed and no more schedule instances are running. This is shown in Figure 16.52.

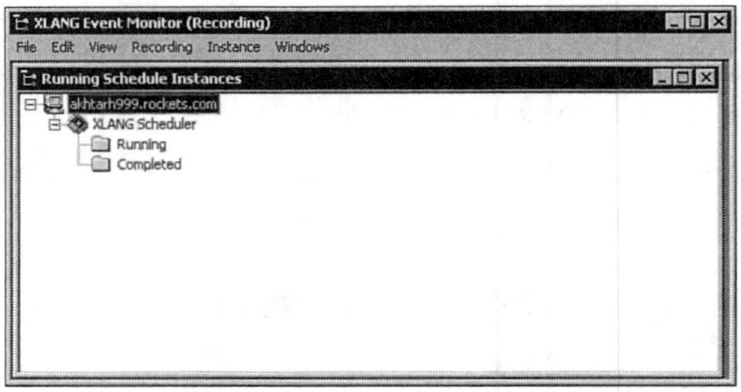

FIGURE 16.52
On completion of the `AcctMngSys` *business process, no instances of the schedule are running.*

Summary

We began this chapter with the focus on an organization's business process expressed in the BizTalk Orchestration Designer. BizTalk Messaging provides a mechanism to instantiate a new instance of the XLANG schedule when a message arrives at the port and then deliver this message to the business process. First we demonstrated this with a simple example. In a real business scenario, we are almost always required to integrate two or more business processes. A business process at some point sends out a message to a second business process and then waits for a response. The second business process then sends a response back to the source process. On receiving the response, the source business process proceeds to completion. This process of returning a response message back to the source schedule is called *correlation*.

Correlation in BizTalk Server is accomplished by using a return address in the body of the message. The destination business process must retain this return address and use this information to return the response back to the original schedule that sent the message in the first place. We demonstrated this by providing examples for both HTTP-based correlation and non-HTTP-based scenarios. The HTTP-based scenario showed an example where a BizTalk Server was on both the sending and receiving end. The second example demonstrated correlation with BizTalk Server on only the source end with a non-BizTalk external system.

Extending BizTalk Server

Part V

In This Part

CHAPTER 17

Application Integration Components

by Akhtar Hossein

In This Chapter

In previous chapters, you witnessed BizTalk Server's capability to integrate applications on heterogeneous systems, both within an organization and across organizational boundaries. We also discussed its capability to transform and route data between applications using proven Internet standards and technologies. As such, BizTalk can be considered an exciting and robust technology. However, an integration product wouldn't be complete without an interface or API that allowed developers to extend its capabilities.

Microsoft recognized this and gives developers the ability to extend BizTalk Server by writing custom modules and has built in extensibility in several areas, like the custom parsers, serializers, preprocessors, functoids, application integration components, and schema import modules. This chapter focuses on extending BizTalk Server by writing AICs (Application Integration Components). Other chapters in the book cover extensibility in other areas of the product.

This chapter examines how AICs play a role in application integration. You will learn to build, register, and deploy AICs. The chapter also focuses on types of AICs, when to choose one over the other, and how they interact with BizTalk Server.

Understanding Application Integration Components

AICs, commonly referred to as adapters or connectors, are COM components that extend the capability of BizTalk Server to integrate with external systems. They expose one or two programmatic interfaces that enable BizTalk Server to reference an AIC as an outbound transport. AICs are deployed at the BizTalk Messaging Port and are one of the transport types that BizTalk supports. Therefore, sometimes AICs are referred to as *transport adapters*.

Microsoft is working to provide adapters for ERP systems with many third parties, such as SAP, J. D. Edwards, and PeopleSoft, and marketplace vendors, such as Ariba, Commerce One, and Clarus. The Microsoft BizTalk Server team took the initiative to develop a few key adapters including one for SAP that will be sold as an add-on to BizTalk Server. The BizTalk SAP adapter is currently in Beta. To name a few others, Xceed Software provides an FTP adapter for BizTalk, and Travis, Inc., provides an adapter for Oracle Financial. To see the most current list of vendors and the BizTalk adapters they provide, go to the site `http://www.microsoft.com/biztalk/evaluation/adapters.asp`.

BizTalk Server provides three different ways to develop AICs, using the `IBTSAppIntegration`, `IPipelineComponent`, and the BizTalk Scriptor Component.

The `IPipelineComponent` and the Scriptor Component are the same mechanism used in Site Server Commerce Edition 3.0 Pipeline and in Commerce Server 2000 Pipelines.

When to Use AICs

So, when would you need to create an AIC? Well, you might need to write one or use a prebuilt AIC when you need to integrate with an external application system, such as SAP, or when you need to update data in an SQL database, such as SQL Server or Oracle. You may also need to write one when you integrate with a Web service. Each of these is depicted in Figure 17.1.

FIGURE 17.1
Using AIC to connect to various applications.

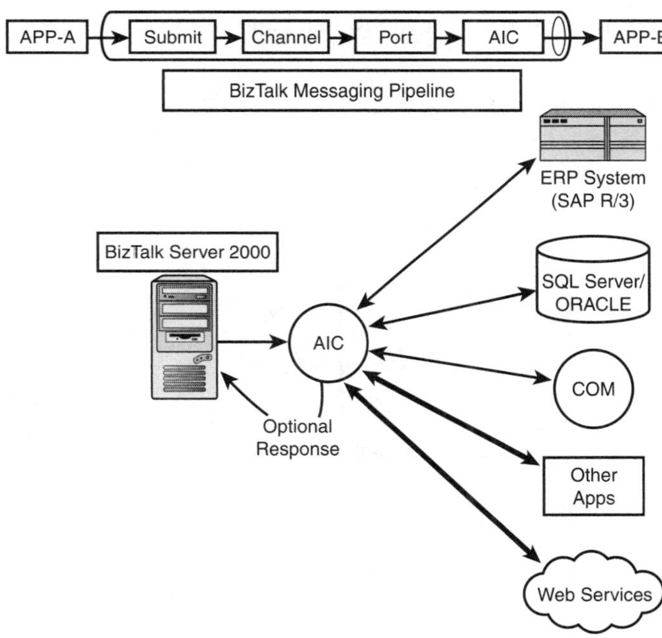

Figure 17.1 shows how an AIC on a BizTalk Messaging Port can be used to integrate to an ERP system (SAP R/3), databases, other COM components, or a Web service.

In BizTalk, messages can originate in one of two ways: BizTalk Messaging and BizTalk Orchestration. AICs are only required when integrating an application through a BizTalk Messaging transport. BizTalk Orchestration schedules do not require COM components attached to schedule actions to implement the special AIC interface. If you have implemented your business process using both messaging and orchestration services, you have the option of integrating external applications using either an AIC or standard COM component.

> **Note**
>
> Remember, you only need to implement the AIC when you are integrating with applications via BizTalk Messaging Port. In BizTalk Orchestration, when you use COM+ implementation shapes you do not need to implement any special COM interface in your COM components, such as the `IBTSAppIntegration` interface.

Typically, you write AICs in Enterprise Application Integration Scenarios, such as when you want to integrate Commerce One (BuySite) to your ERP system (SAP R/3). For example, the market site generates a purchase order (PO) and requires updating the ERP system and verifying that sufficient inventory and customer credit exists for the PO to be honored.

Figure 17.2 shows how AICs are used from a BizTalk Orchestration. In this example, a new user account is created in the Active Directory and then an Exchange Mailbox is created. The sequencing in Orchestration ensures that the new user is created first before creating the mailbox.

FIGURE 17.2
BizTalk Orchestration schedule using AICs to integrate applications.

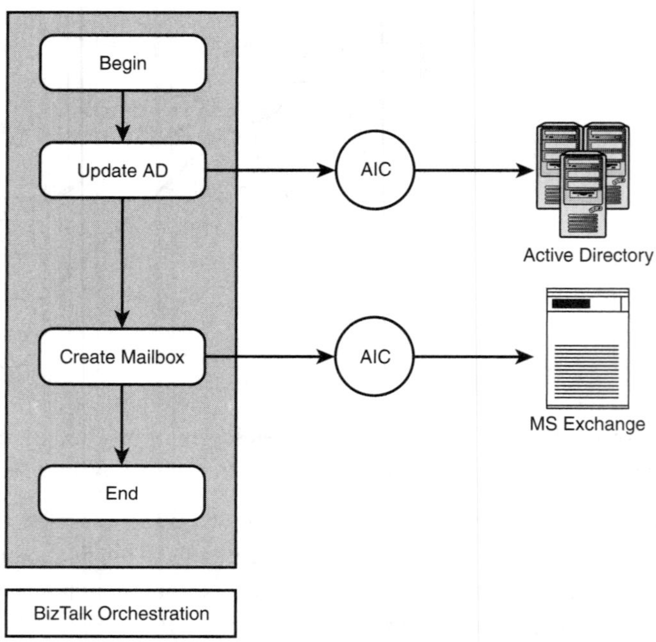

Types of AICs

As stated earlier, AICs are simply COM components that must implement at least one of the two COM interfaces:

- `IBTSAppIntegration`
- `IPipelineComponent`
- BizTalk Scriptor Component

`IBTSAppIntegration` components are compiled components designed for simplicity. You use this type of component when you do not need to configure the component at deployment or design-time to get different behaviors at runtime, depending on the configurations.

`IPipelineComponent` components are also compiled components; however, they allow the configuration of their behavior at design-time and then at the time of deployment. These components also have access to the BizTalk Messaging Interchange Metadata—for example, the organization name, application name, envelope information, and selection criteria, to name a few. The IPipelineComponent interface was originally introduced with the Site Server 3.0 Commerce Edition. So if you have worked with SSCE 3.0, you're probably familiar with these types of components. However, to get the capability to configure the component, the component must implement the `IPipelineComponentAdmin` interface in addition to the `IPipelineComponent` interface.

BizTalk Scriptor Components are interpreted components and are usually used for quick proof of concept and debugging purposes. Scriptor Components are written in VBScripts and have inherent performance issues. The advantage of Scriptor Components is that they are easy to write and modify.

In this chapter, we will first build a component using the `IBTSAppIntegration` interface. Then we will build that same component using the `IPipelineComponent` interface. We will also discuss when you should choose the `IPipelineComponent` interface over the simpler `IBTSAppIntegration` interface. Finally, we will build and implement a BizTalk Scriptor Component.

Steps in Setting Up AICs

Essentially you need to complete three steps to set up an AIC component:

1. Build the component.
2. Register the component
3. Deploy the component in BizTalk.

But before we begin building the component, it would be a good idea to select a scenario to implement.

Scenario—Simulating an Update to an ERP System Using SQL Server

If you are reading this book, we assume that you have installed or will install BizTalk Server on your machine to work or play with the examples in this book. You must have SQL Server 7.0 SP2 or SQL Server 2000 to install BizTalk Server. We will use SQL Server 2000 to set up the scenario.

Although we are simulating an actual ERP system using SQL Server, the same technique can be used to interface and update an ERP system such as SAP R/3.

Hackers Den is a fast-growing software company paid by software development companies to find security holes in their software products. Currently, its HR Department manually fills out a new employee form for every new employee that joins Hackers Den. The information on the form is manually keyed into an ERP system and then manually forwarded to the IT department where an e-mail account and exchange mailbox are created. This process takes a week or so to complete, leaving the new employee sitting at his desk, staring at his computer, and dreaming of his next hacking assignment. These days the hacking business is a little slow, so with cost cutting now a priority, the CEO of Hackers Den requested that the entire process be automated to eliminate 90 percent of the traditional keying costs.

In the new scenario, a new employee fills out his personal information using a Web-based application. The application formats the employee information into an XML document and then drops that document into a file system directory. BizTalk Server is configured to pick up the message and process it through a BizTalk channel bound to a port configured with a transport of type AIC. The AIC component's job is to take the message, extract the information in it, and update the SQL Server database ADO.

The script AcctMngSys.sql creates a database in SQL Server called AcctMngSys, a simple table called UserAcctInfo, and a stored procedure called ams_CreateUser. Figure 17.3 displays a snapshot of the UserAcctInfo table. Note that the Alias column is the Primary Key in the `UserAcctInfo` table. The SQL script to create the `AcctMngSys` database objects is located in `..\Chp17\SQL_Scripts`.

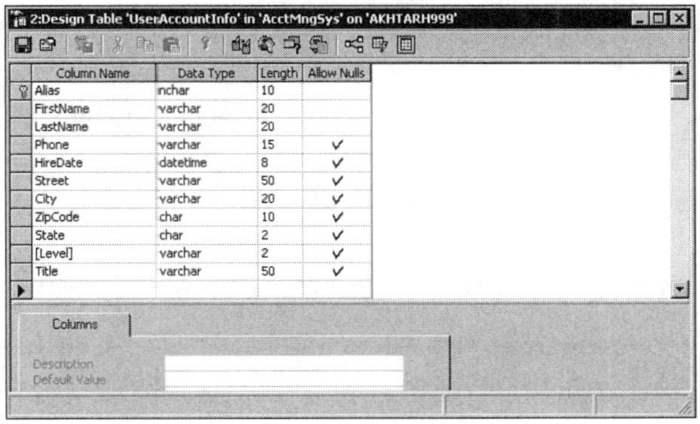

FIGURE 17.3
The `UserAccountInfo` *Table in the* `AcctMngSys` *database. Note the Alias column is the Primary Key.*

Now let's look at the Web application where the user fills out a New Hire form. This consists of `default.htm` and an ASP page `CreateNewAccount.asp`. These pages are located in the `..\Chp17\WebApp` directory. A snapshot of the WebApp is shown in Figure 17.4

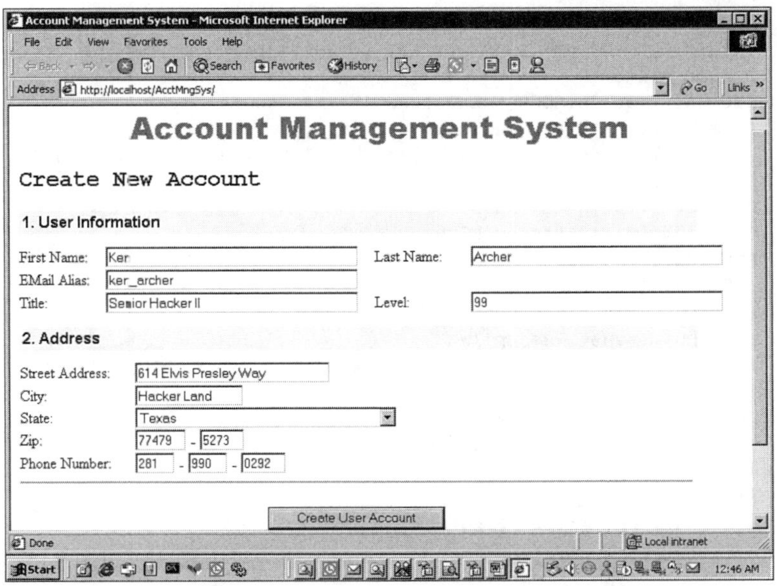

FIGURE 17.4
The WebApp that serves to take the New Hire info.

Deciding on a Schema for the Inbound Document

The Web application uses a simple XML message to send the information to the ERP system. The XML message is based on a schema named `AcctMngSys_NewHire.xml`.

You can find the schema file in the `..\Chp17\Schema` directory. Both the schema and an instance of the XML message are displayed in Listing 17.1.

Listing 17.1 shows the content of the schema file, as generated by BizTalk Editor. All XML documents that BizTalk processes must comply with this schema. Failure to comply causes validation failure, and your XML document lands in the Suspended Queue.

LISTING 17.1 XDR Schema of the New Hire Info XML Message created by BizTalk Editor.

```
<?xml version="1.0"?>
<!-- Generated by using BizTalk Editor on Sat, Sep 22 2001 12:25:16 PM -->
<!-- Microsoft Corporation (c) 2000 (http://www.microsoft.com) -->
<Schema name="UserAcctInfo" b:BizTalkServerEditorTool_Version="1.0"
 b:root_reference="UserAcctInfo" b:standard="XML"
 xmlns="urn:schemas-microsoft-com:xml-data"
 xmlns:b="urn:schemas-microsoft-com:BizTalkServer"
 xmlns:d="urn:schemas-microsoft-com:datatypes">
<b:SelectionFields/>

<ElementType name="UserAcctInfo" content="eltOnly" model="closed">
<b:RecordInfo/>
<element type="HEADER" maxOccurs="*" minOccurs="0"/>
<element type="BODY" maxOccurs="*" minOccurs="0"/>
</ElementType><ElementType name="Phone" content="textOnly" model="closed">
<b:RecordInfo/>
<AttributeType name="Number">
<b:FieldInfo/></AttributeType>
<AttributeType name="AreaCode">
<b:FieldInfo/></AttributeType>
<attribute type="AreaCode"/>
<attribute type="Number"/>
</ElementType><ElementType name="Name" content="textOnly" model="closed">
<b:RecordInfo/>
<AttributeType name="Last">
<b:FieldInfo/></AttributeType>
<AttributeType name="First">
<b:FieldInfo/></AttributeType>
<AttributeType name="Alias">
<b:FieldInfo/></AttributeType>
<attribute type="First"/>
<attribute type="Last"/>
<attribute type="Alias"/>
</ElementType><ElementType name="Level" content="textOnly" model="closed">
<b:RecordInfo/>
<AttributeType name="Title">
<b:FieldInfo/></AttributeType>
<AttributeType name="Code">
<b:FieldInfo/></AttributeType>
```

LISTING 17.1 continued

```
<attribute type="Code"/>
<attribute type="Title"/>
</ElementType><ElementType name="HEADER" content="textOnly" model="closed">
<b:RecordInfo/>
<AttributeType name="ReturnPort">
<b:FieldInfo/></AttributeType>
<attribute type="ReturnPort'/>
</ElementType><ElementType name="BODY" content="eltOnly" model="closed">
<b:RecordInfo/>
<element type="Name" maxOccurs="*" minOccurs="0"/>
<element type="Address" maxOccurs="*" minOccurs="0"/>
<element type="Phone" maxOccurs="*" minOccurs="0"/>
<element type="Level" maxOccurs="*" minOccurs="0"/>
</ElementType><ElementType name="Address" content="textOnly" model="closed">
<b:RecordInfo/>
<AttributeType name="ZipCode">
<b:FieldInfo/></AttributeType>
<AttributeType name="Street">
<b:FieldInfo/></AttributeType>
<AttributeType name="State">
<b:FieldInfo/></AttributeType>
<AttributeType name="City">
<b:FieldInfo/></AttributeType>
<attribute type="Street"/>
<attribute type="City"/>
<attribute type="State"/>
<attribute type="ZipCode"/>
</ElementType></Schema>
```

The best way to look at the content of the schema is to open the schema file in the BizTalk Editor.

Listing 17.2 is a sample XML instance of an XML document compliant to the schema. The sample shows New User Account Info.

LISTING 17.2 An XML Instance of the Message That Conforms to the Schema AcctMngSys_NewHire.xml

```
<?xml version="1.0" ?>
<UserAcctInfo>
  <HEADER ReturnPort=""/>
  <BODY><Name First="Ken" Last="Archer" Alias="ken_archer"/>
    <Address Street="614 Elvis Presley Way" City="Hacker Land" State="TX"
➥ZipCode="77479-5273"/>
<Phone AreaCode="281" Number="990-0292"/>
    <Level Code="99" Title="Senior Hacker II"/>
  </BODY>
</UserAcctInfo>
```

Deciding on a Schema for the Outbound Document

To keep the scenario simple, we will keep the outbound schema the same as the inbound. There will be no need to do any mapping in this case because we are not transforming the incoming message.

Transport Protocol

We must now determine the transport protocol to use to deliver the message to BizTalk Server and update the SQL Server database. In this case, we will use the file system directory as the receiving location and create a simple file receiving function in the BizTalk Administration Console to process the incoming messages. We will use the AIC transport on the outbound side to update the SQL database.

The advantage of the file system protocol is that it gives you the capability to decouple the Web application from the BizTalk server. Now the server can continue to receive requests for New Hire even when BizTalk Server is down or has been configured to process messages only at a certain time of the day. The file system has no limitation on the size of the message it can receive as opposed to the MSMQ transport, which has a size limitation of 2 MB for Unicode messages, and 4 MB for ASCII messages. Microsoft is working to eliminate this restriction in the next version of MSMQ.

Implementing the System

Because this chapter is dedicated to the discussion of Application Integration Components, we will not focus on the implementation of the Web application. It should be sufficient to know that the application drops the New Hire information as an XML file onto a local file system directory. When the message is dropped into the directory, a file receive function is triggered.

Note

To learn more on how to set up a file receive function, refer to the BizTalk Server Documentation online help.

The file receive function picks up the incoming `NewUserInfo` message and delivers it to a BizTalk Messaging Channel. The channel then passes the message on to a messaging port. Because the inbound and outbound documents are the same, no transformation is done in the channel. The port in this case points to an AIC. The AIC takes the XML message and uses ADO to update the SQL Server database. Figure 17.5 shows the sequence of events and the names of the channel, port, and AIC used by BizTalk Server Messaging.

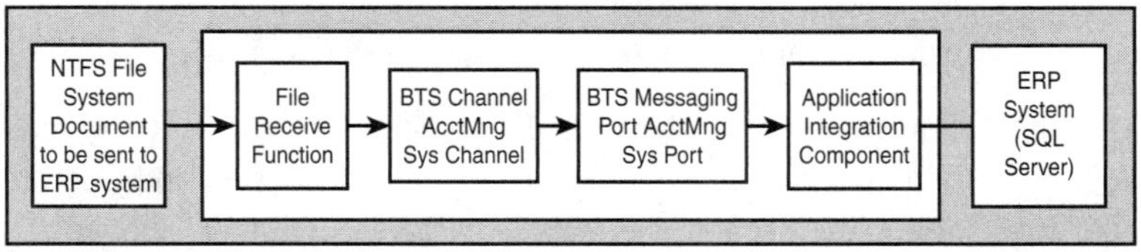

FIGURE 17.5
The sequence of processing steps and the names of the channel, port, and AIC Component used by BizTalk Server Messaging.

Building an AIC Component

As mentioned earlier, you can build an AIC component using the `IBTSAppIntegration` interface, the `IPipelineComponent` interface, or the BizTalk Scriptor Component. In the following sections, you will look at each one of them.

The `IBTSAppIntegration` interface is a simple COM interface that supports a single method called `ProcessMessage()`. `ProcessMessage()` has only one parameter, which is of type BSTR; BizTalk passes the interchange document to the AIC component using this parameter. The return parameter is also of type BSTR, where the method can optionally return a response if required. BizTalk publishes this interface using the type library file `btscomplib.tlb`. Table 17.1 shows detailed information on the interface.

TABLE 17.1 `IBTSAppIntegration`

Method	*Parameters/Type/Description*
`ProcessMessage ()`	The method processes a document and optionally returns a response. The BizTalk Server calls it via the port when it is ready to hand over the document.
Input	`bstrDocument` of type BSTR, containing the content of the document that is to be delivered.
Return	`pbstrResponseDocument` of type BSTR, containing an optional response document.

The AIC component we will build has the ProgID of `AcctMngSys.CreateUser`. The component extracts the information from the incoming XML message and then uses ADO to create the user in the SQL Server database.

Accessing XML Content

If you have handled XML documents in your code before, you're familiar with the XML Document Object Model (DOM). DOM objects parse and load an XML document from a string or a file into memory in a hierarchical tree structure. After the XML is loaded into the DOM object, you can use DOM APIs to traverse, sort, search, read, and/or update the values on any element or attribute in the document.

The DOM is not suitable for large XML documents because it requires the entire XML document to be loaded into memory prior to processing. In addition, the parsing process consumes large CPU cycles. The Simple API for XML (SAX) is more suitable for large XML documents, given that it is event-driven and does not require that the entire document be loaded into memory.

Because documents are not first loaded into memory, SAX can parse files of any size, making it both a fast and simple-to-use technology. SAX is also useful in situations where you want to build your own data structure representation of the XML contents.

Microsoft implements both DOM and SAX technologies in msxml3.dll. MSXML3.0 was released in November 2000.

In our AIC we will use the DOM to load the incoming XML document because the incoming XML messages are small in size and most XML developers are familiar with DOM. The New Hire information is then extracted and sent to SQL Server using ADO.

> **Note**
>
> To learn more about XML technology and the DOM object model, refer to Chapter 2, "XML and Related Technologies."

Developing the `AcctMngSys.CreateUser` AIC Using `IBTSAppIntegration`

The `AcctMngSys.CreateUser` AIC component implements `IBTSAppIntegration` interface and is developed in VB6. The VB Project file is AcctMngSys.vbp. The code processes the incoming New Hire user account information and then creates the user in the SQL Server database. The complete code is located at `..\Chp17\SourceCode\AIC_BTS\`.

To implement the AIC interface and reference ADO objects, you need to reference several libraries. To set these references, open the project file in Visual Basic, select the project in the project explorer, and then choose the Project menu's References option. Note, there are three references added to the project: one for Microsoft ActiveX Data Access Objects 2.5, one for Microsoft XML V3.0, and one for the Microsoft BizTalk Server Application Interface Component, as shown in Figure 17.6.

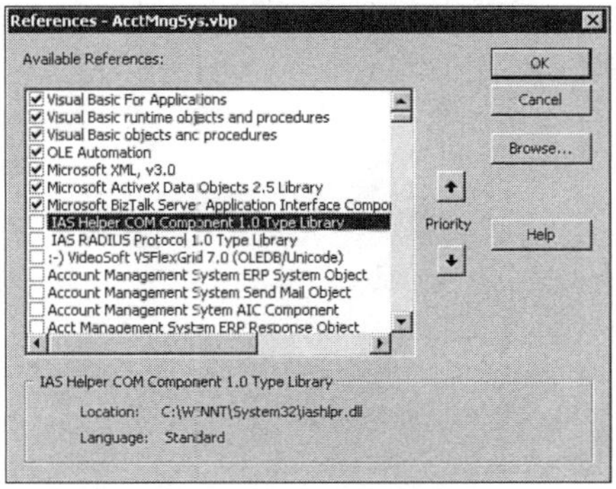

FIGURE 17.6
Project references for ADO, XML, and BTS application interface components.

The project contains a single class called `CreateUser` in the class file named `CreateUser.cls`. The `CreateUser` class implements the `IBTSAppIntegration` interface. We have kept the code simple. Essentially the code has two statements that call the following private functions:

`ExtractUserInfo()`	The function loads the XML message in a DOM object and then extracts different pieces of the User information.
`CreateUserAccount()`	The function creates an ADO object and calls a stored procedure `ams_CreateUeser`.

Now look at the code for these functions. First look at the method `ProcessMessage()` that the AIC exposes to accept the incoming message. Listing 17.3 shows the code for the function `ProcessMessage()`.

LISTING 17.3 The Code for Function `ProcessMessage()`

```
Option Explicit

'Implements the IBTSAppIntegration Interface
Implements IBTSAppIntegration

Private Function IBTSAppIntegration_ProcessMessage
➥(ByVal bstrDocument As String) As String
```

LISTING 17.3 continued

```
Dim strFirstName As String
Dim strLastName As String
Dim strAlias As String
Dim strPhone As String
Dim strStreet As String
Dim strCity As String
Dim strZipCode As String
Dim strState As String
Dim strLevel As String
Dim strTitle As String
Dim strPassword As String

Dim strResponse As String

On Error GoTo IBTSAppIntegration_ProcessMessage_err

 ExtractUserInfo bstrDocument, strFirstName, strLastName, strAlias, strPhone, _
                   strStreet, strCity, strZipCode, strState, _
                   strLevel, strTitle

 CreateUserAccount strFirstName, strLastName, strAlias, strPhone, _
                   strStreet, strCity, strZipCode, strState, _
                   strLevel, strTitle, strResponse

IBTSAppIntegration_ProcessMessage_exit:
  App.LogEvent "User Account Successfully Created for User = " &
➥strFirstName & " " & strLastName, vbLogEventTypeInformation
  Exit Function

IBTSAppIntegration_ProcessMessage_err:
  App.LogEvent "Failed to create User Account, for User = " &
➥strFirstName & " " & strLastName & vbNewLine & "Error = " &
➥Err.Number & " Description =" & Err.Description, vbLogEventTypeError
  Err.Raise Err.Number, Err.Source & ":CreateUserAcc", Err.Description
  Exit Function
End Function
```

The function `IBTSAppIntegration_ProcessMessage()` in the Listing 17.3 is the main function. The function uses many helper functions. The key is the error handling. In the event of an error, either in the helper functions or a system error, the execution jumps to the error handling code. The error handling code logs the error in the Event Log; more important is the code `Err.Raise()`. This signals to BizTalk Messaging that the transport AIC raised an error and the document submitted needs to be moved to the Suspended Queue.

Listing 17.4 is for the function `ExtractUserInfo()`.

LISTING 17.4 The Code for Function `ExtractUserInfo()`

```
Private Function ExtractUserInfo(ByVal strXML As String, _
                                 ByRef strFirstName As String, _
                                 ByRef strLastName As String, _
                                 ByRef strAlias As String, _
                                 ByRef strPhone As String, _
                                 ByRef strStreet As String, _
                                 ByRef strCity As String, _
                                 ByRef strZipCode As String, _
                                 ByRef strState As String, _
                                 ByRef strLevel As String, _
                                 ByRef strTitle As String)

Dim oXMLDom As MSXML2.DOMDocument
Dim oNode As IXMLDOMElement
Dim strAreaCode As String
Dim strNumber As String

On Error GoTo ExtractUserInfo_err

Set oXMLDom = CreateObject("MSXML2.DOMDocument")
oXMLDom.loadXML strXML

'Get the attribute values from the NAME Node of the XML Message
Set oNode = oXMLDom.getElementsByTagName("Name").Item(0)
strFirstName = oNode.getAttribute("First")
strLastName = oNode.getAttribute("Last")
strAlias = oNode.getAttribute("Alias")


'Get the attribute values from the ADDRESS Node of the XML Message
Set oNode = oXMLDom.getElementsByTagName("Address").Item(0)
strStreet = oNode.getAttribute("Street")
strCity = oNode.getAttribute("City")
strState = oNode.getAttribute("State")
strZipCode = oNode.getAttribute("ZipCode")

'Get the attribute values from the PHONE Node of the XML Message
Set oNode = oXMLDom.getElementsByTagName("Phone").Item(0)
strAreaCode = oNode.getAttribute("AreaCode")
strNumber = oNode.getAttribute("Number")
strPhone = strAreaCode & "-" & strNumber


'Get the attribute values from the LEVEL Node of the XML Message
Set oNode = oXMLDom.getElementsByTagName("Level").Item(0)
strLevel = oNode.getAttribute("Code")
strTitle = oNode.getAttribute("Title")
```

LISTING 17.4 continued

```
ExtractUserInfo_exit:
  Set oNode = Nothing
  Set oXMLDom = Nothing
  Exit Function

ExtractUserInfo_err:
  Set oNode = Nothing
  Set oXMLDom = Nothing

  Err.Raise 1000 + Err.Number, Err.Source & ":ExtractUserInfo", Err.Description
  Exit Function

End Function
```

The line, `Set oXMLDom = CreateObject("MSXML2.DOMDocument")` creates an instance of the DOM object. The second line `oXMLDom.loadXML strXML` loads the string `strXML` that contains the XML message sent to the AIC by BizTalk. The remaining lines of code get a reference to the first occurrence of Element *Name* and then retrieve the attribute values for First, Last, Alias and other elements.

Next look at what's happening in the function `CreateUserAccount()` (see Listing 17.5).

LISTING 17.5 The Code for Function `CreateUserAccount()`

```
Private Function CreateUserAccount(ByVal strLastName As String, _
                                   ByVal strFirstName As String, _
                                   ByVal strAlias As String, _
                                   ByVal strPhone As String, _
                                   ByVal strStreet As String, _
                                   ByVal strCity As String, _
                                   ByVal strZipCode As String, _
                                   ByVal strState As String, _
                                   ByVal strLevel As String, _
                                   ByVal strTitle As String, _
                                   ByRef strResponse) As Boolean

  Dim oCnn As ADODB.Connection
  Dim oCmd As ADODB.Command

On Error GoTo CreateUserAccount_err

  Set oCnn = CreateObject("ADODB.Connection")

  'Note the hard coded string for the DSN Name
  oCnn.ConnectionString = "DSN=AcctMngSys;UID=sa;PWD="
  oCnn.Open
```

LISTING 17.5 continued

```
  Set oCmd = CreateObject("ADODB.Command")
  oCmd.ActiveConnection = oCnn
  oCmd.CommandType = adCmdStoredProc
  oCmd.CommandText = "ams_createUser"

  oCmd.Parameters.Refresh

  With oCmd.Parameters
    .Item("@firstName").Value = strFirstName
    .Item("@lastName").Value = strLastName
    .Item("@alias").Value = strAlias
    .Item("@phone").Value = strPhone
    .Item("@street").Value = strStreet
    .Item("@city").Value = strCity
    .Item("@zipcode").Value = strZipCode
    .Item("@state").Value = strState
    .Item("@level").Value = strLevel
    .Item("@title").Value = strTitle
  End With

  oCmd.Execute

CreateUserAccount_exit:
  strResponse = "Successfully Created the User in the ERP System"
  CreateUserAccount = True
  Exit Function

CreateUserAccount_err:
  strResponse = Err.Description
  CreateUserAccount = False
  Exit Function


End Function
```

Note that `ConnectionString` is hard-coded in the line (`oCnn.ConnectionString = "`*`DSN=AcctMngSys;UID=sa;PWD=`*`"`) for the ADO connection object. This is a limitation of an `IBTSAppIntegration` AIC, in that it does not allow the component to be configured at the time of deployment. Of course, we could have put the `ConnectionString` into a Registry entry and read the Registry entry at runtime. You will see later how to overcome this limitation in `IPipelineComponent` AIC.

So now let's get back to the rest of the code in this function. The function sets up the Command object to call a stored procedure called `ams_createUser`. There are several advantages to using a stored procedure instead of creating a dynamic query to do this. First, stored procedures are precompiled in SQL Server and are much more efficient as well as faster. In addition, using a stored procedure allows the underlying database schema to change without affecting your application code. Writing a stored procedure in SQL Server is not that difficult. Of course, in this example we are using a simple stored procedure that inserts a record into a single table. Let's look at the stored procedure used in this example, as shown in Listing 17.6.

LISTING 17.6 SQL Script for the Stored Procedure `ams_CreateUser`

```
CREATE PROCEDURE [ams_CreateUser]
    @alias nchar(10),
    @firstName varchar (20),
    @lastName varchar(20),
    @phone varchar(15),
    @street varchar(50),
    @city varchar(20),
    @zipcode varchar(10),
    @state varchar(2),
    @level varchar(2),
    @title varchar(50)

AS

    INSERT INTO UserAccountInfo (Alias, LastName, FirstName,
➥Phone, HireDate, Street, City, ZipCode, State, [Level], Title)
    VALUES (@alias, @lastName, @firstName, @phone, GetDate(),
➥@street, @city, @zipcode, @state, @level, @title)
GO
```

Deployment of `IBTSAppIntegration` AIC

Deployment of `IBTSAppIntegration` is a two-step process:

1. Register the AIC.
2. Configure BizTalk Messaging to use the AIC.

Registering AIC Manually Using Regedit

After you have built and compiled the AcctMngSys.CreateUser into a DLL, the next step is to register the AcctMngSys.dll as an AIC component of type IBTSAppIntegration for it to be recognized by BizTalk Server Messaging as an AIC component.

As discussed earlier in this chapter, the underlying implementation of a BizTalk Server AIC is something known as a *pipeline*, a technology introduced in Microsoft Site Server Commerce Edition 3.0. If you are familiar with SSCE 3.0, you know that the product comes with a pipeline editor that allows users to add components to a staged pipeline. A

GUID Category ID identifies every pipeline, and another GUID Category ID identifies the different stages. In Site Server Commerce, a user can add a component to a shipping stage, subtotal stage, or check-out stage.

Similarly, BizTalk Messaging's underlying pipeline can be viewed to have a parsing stage, transformation stage, serialize stage, and transport stage. AICs implementing `IBTSAppIntegration` or `IPipelineComponent` interface are placed in the transport stage. BizTalk has a published GUID for the BizTalk Server AIC transport component. To be used as an AIC, you must identify the published GUID Category ID (*40FC6ED5-2438-11CF-A3DB-080036F12502*) in the component's Implemented Categories section in the Registry. This allows BizTalk Messaging to look through the Registry and discover the components that have implemented the IBTSAppIntegration or IPipelineComponent interface.

There are two ways you can register a component as an AIC to make it available to BizTalk Server. You can register it manually using regedit and/or a .reg file, or you can register it by adding it to a COM+ application.

Adding Registry Entries

When you compile your VB project for the IBTSAppIntegration component to build the AcctMngSys.dll, Visual Basic registers your component to create an unconfigured COM+ application. If you want to use an IBTSAppIntegration AIC developed by others, you can use the RegSvr32.exe utility to register the AIC Component. What VB or RegSvr32.exe utility does not do is add the additional Registry entries to make the component visible to BizTalk. To add these entries into the Registry, you first find the GUID CLSID of your AIC component and then add the two GUID Category IDs to the Implemented Key. You can create a .reg file as shown in Listing 17.7 and import it in the Registry editor.

LISTING 17.7 Registry Key entries for the Implemented Categories

```
REGEDIT4
HKEY_CLASSES_ROOT\CLSID\{<Your AIC Component CLSID>}\Implemented
Categories\{40FC6ED5-2438-11CF-A3DB-080036F12502}
```

Now to see the Registry entries that need to be added for our `AcctMngSys.CreateUser` AIC component with a CLSID of `{578B3C74-36D9-41FE-B0C4-18ABC3006E37}`, we can edit the Registry above, specifically for our example (see Listing 17.8).

LISTING 17.8 The Registry Entry Specific to the `CAcctMngSys.CreateUser` AIC Component

```
REGEDIT4
HKEY_CLASSES_ROOT\CLSID\{578B3C74-36D9-41FE-B0C4-18ABC3006E37}\Implemented
Categories\{40FC6ED5-2438-11CF-A3DB-080036F12502}
```

Again, your component's class ID will be different from what is in Listing 17.8. Figure 17.7 shows the `Regsvr32.exe` utility with the implemented categories for the AIC in the Registry.

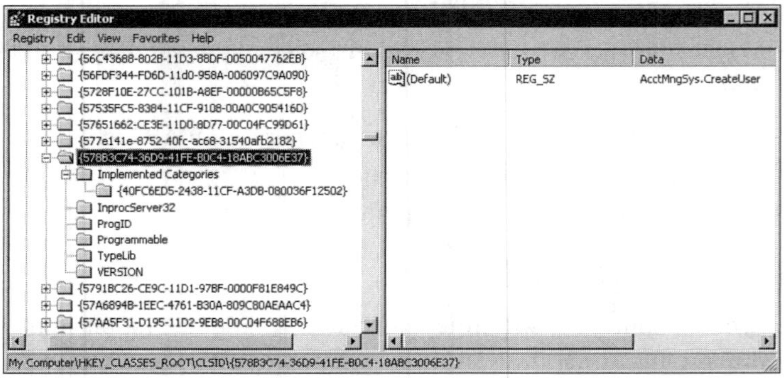

FIGURE 17.7
Implemented Categories key in the Windows Registry.

Registering AIC Using COM+ Application

Life has been easy since COM+ applications. Instead of using the regsvr32 utility to create an unconfigured COM+ application, you can create a configured COM+ application using the Windows Component Services MMC and install the component into the application. BizTalk Server UI will then be able to detect the Component, and there is no need to add the Registry entries.

Putting the component in the COM+ application makes it easy to debug your AIC at runtime. The way to do this is to set the Project Property `MTSTransactionMode` in the VB IDE to `NoTransaction` instead of the default `NotAnMTSObject`. Next you set your break points in your code and run the component by pressing F5. When BizTalk server delivers the message to your component, it triggers the VB debugger. To be able to debug in your familiar VB IDE makes it easier for you to fix problems in your AIC, unless of course you never have to debug code that you write. The VB Add-In for Component Services automatically refreshes your component in the COM+ application with the changes you make in the IDE.

Adding a Component in Windows 2000 Component Services

To install a component in a COM+ application, you need to first install a COM+ application in the Component Services. You can access the Component Services MMC by selecting the Start button and then selecting Programs, Administrative Tools, Component Services. Next expand My Computer, right-click on the COM+ Applications, and in the Action menu select New, Application. This opens up the COM Application Installation Wizard. Walk through the installation wizard to create a COM+ application. You could use a COM+ application that someone in your group has already created; however, it is better to create one separately for your application. This way you will not be constrained in configuring your application for security, identity, and other things.

After you have installed a COM+ application, it is easy to install a COM component, in this case the AIC into the COM+ application. Expand the COM+ application by double-clicking on it and then locate the COM+ application you just installed. Expand your application by double-clicking on it; this exposes Components and Roles. First double-click on the Components and then right-click on the components, New, Component. This opens a COM Component Install Wizard. Walk through the wizard to install your component.

If you are not familiar with COM+ applications in Windows 2000, it is a good time to become so. You can take advantage of declarative programming using COM+ applications, such as enabling security, impersonation, roles, and transactions without writing a single line of code inside your component. Visit `http://msdn.microsoft.com` and search for COM+ Application to learn more.

Adding AIC to BizTalk Messaging

Up to now we have built the AIC and have appropriately registered the AIC either using the RegSvr32 utility and manually adding the Category IDs, or by creating a COM+ application and installing the component into the application. The next step is to add the component to the BizTalk messaging port.

To complete the example, we will set up an organization including an application, a document definition, a channel, port, and a receive function. Finally, we will configure the component to the messaging port.

BizTalk Messaging Setup

In the BizTalk Messaging Manager, we will create an organization called Hackers Den and an internal application named NewHireApp. We will also create a document definition, port, channel, and a file receive function, as shown in Table 17.2.

Table 17.2 details the property settings for the BizTalk Messaging objects used in this example. Only those properties that you need to explicitly set are shown on the table. You can leave the other properties to their default settings. The section "Configuring the BizTalk Messaging Port" walks you through the port and the channels to make sure that you are on the right track.

Note

For details in creating the organization, document definition, port, channel, and receive function, refer to Chapter 6, "Introduction to BizTalk Messaging," and Chapter 7, "Using the BizTalk Messaging Manager."

TABLE 17.2 BizTalk Messaging Objects

BizTalk Objects	*Properties/Settings*
Home Organization	**Name**: Hackers Den
	Application: NewHireApp
Document definition	**Name**: NewHireInfo
	Schema File: `AcctMngSys_NewHire.xml`
Port	**Port To**: Application
	Name: CreateUser in SQL Server
	Application Name: NewHireApp
	Primary Transport: Application Integration Component
	Component Name: AcctMngSys.CreateUser
Channel	**From**: Application
	Name: NewHire Channel
	Application: NewHireApp
	Inbound Document: NewHireInfo
	Outbound Document: NewHireInfo
Receive function	**Type**: File receive function
	Name: NewHireRecvFunc
	Polling Location: c:\NewHire\input. This is the location where the Web application will drop the NewHire XML message. Make sure that the directory already exists. Create this directory if you do not already have one. This directory must have read-write permission. After the file is

TABLE 17.2 continued

BizTalk Objects	*Properties/Settings*
Receive function	picked up by the Receive function and stored in the BizTalk Work Queue, the file is deleted from the directory. BizTalk disables the Receive function if the directory is not accessible. **File Types**: *.xml. The wildcard "*" specifies that BizTalk will pick up any file dropped in this directory with an extension of xml. **Click on Advanced button and then select the channel name from the drop list** **Channel Name**: NewHire channel

We are using only one document definition, because our inbound and outbound documents are the same. Also there is no need for a mapping file because we are not doing any transformation in the channel.

Configuring the BizTalk Messaging Port

The following steps walk you through setting up the BizTalk Messaging Port and configuring it for adding the AIC component we developed. Open the BizTalk Messaging Manager and create a new port to an application, as specified in Table 17.2.

> **Note**
>
> We have created a COM+ application called Hackers Den, using the component services, and have added the AIC component. You can name your COM+ application anything you want. A server application runs your component in a separate process. Any ill-behaved component will not crash the callers.

1. Select the destination Application on Destination Application page. Figure 17.8 shows the Destination Application page of the Messaging Port Wizard.
2. To specify the primary transport type, click on the Browse button, as shown in Figure 17.9. This takes you to a page where you select the Transport Types.
3. From the Transport Type drop-down list, select Application Integration Component as shown in Figure 17.9.

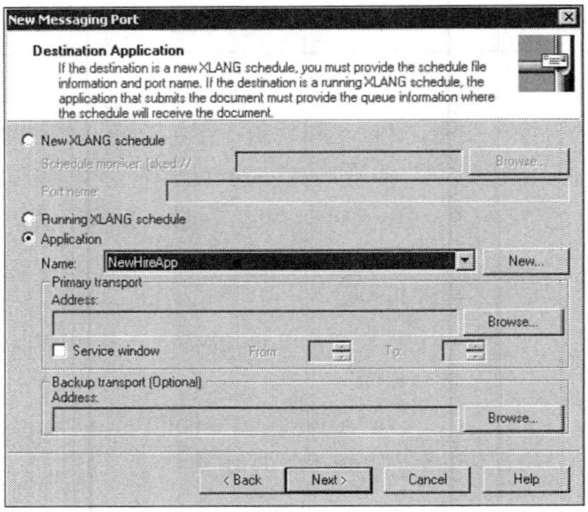

FIGURE 17.8
Selecting a destination application.

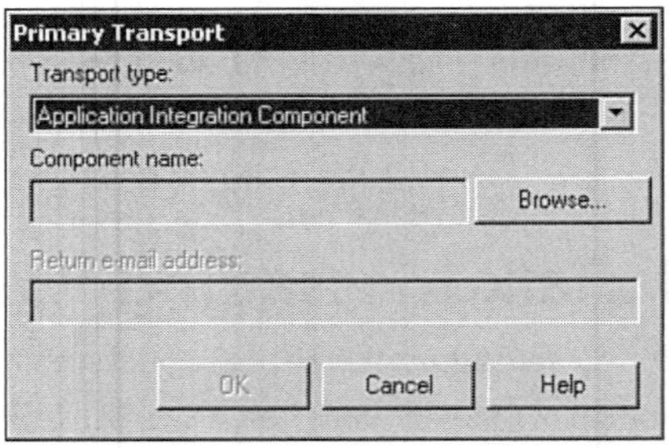

FIGURE 17.9
Selecting the Application Integration Component as the transport type.

4. Click the Browse button on the Primary Transport dialog as shown in Figure 17.9. At this point, the BizTalk UI scans the COM+ applications and determines the applications that have implemented IBTSAppIntegration interface. The next step is to specify which Application Integration Component will be attached to this port. Figure 17.10 shows the list of the AICs BizTalk has determined to have been registered in the machine.

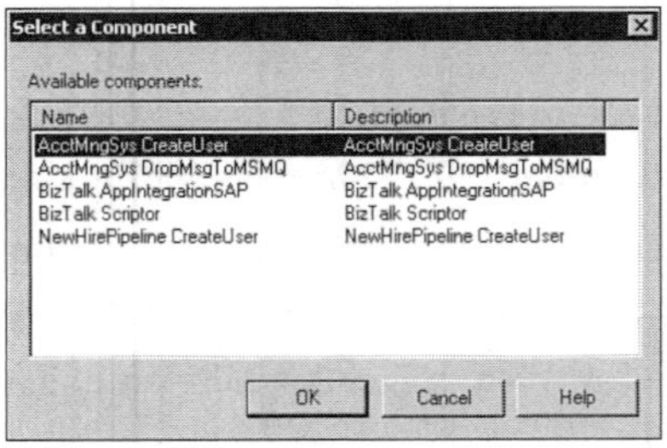

FIGURE 17.10
Selecting the `AcctMngSys.CreateUser` *AIC component.*

5. Select `AcctMngSys.CreateUser` AIC component from the list as shown in Figure 17.10. When you click OK, the AIC component will be attached to the port. The attached AIC now appears in the Primary Transport of the Messaging Port, as shown in Figure 17.11.

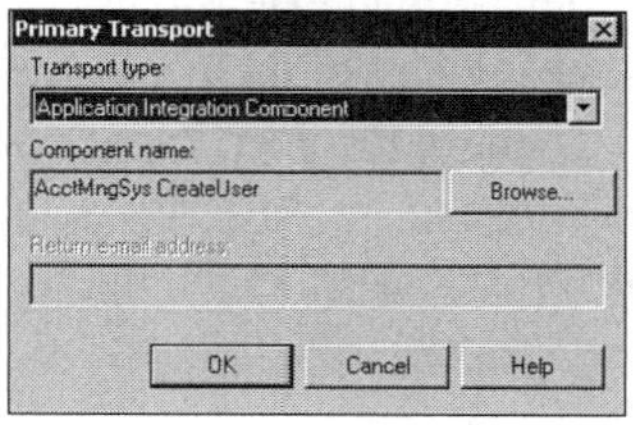

FIGURE 17.11
The Messaging Port now bound to the AIC Component `AcctMngSys.CreateUser`.

Tip

What could go wrong?

1. You do not see your AIC Component listed in Figure 17.9 or, worse, you see it listed more than once.

There are two possible reasons why you might not see your AIC. First, you forgot to register the component or to install the component in the COM+ application. Second, if you used regsvr32.exe to register the AIC component, you might have forgotten to add the Implemented Categories ID into the Registry for the component.

I strongly recommend that you install your AIC in the COM+ applications and not bother with the Registry. The topic was discussed to show you what goes on under the hood.

2. You can see and select the AIC component, but you get an error when you try to click Finish in the BizTalk Messaging Port Wizard.

This error occurs when the BizTalk Messaging Port attempts to bind the port to the AIC. You might have installed the AIC in the COM+ application and have decided to run the component as a specific user under the identity tab rather than the interactive user (this is by default). Either the username or the password is not valid. It is a good practice to install the AIC component as a specific user; this way your component will function even if no one is logged into the machine.

Running the `IBTSAppIntegration` AIC

The Web application front-end takes New Hire information, formats the information into an XML file, and drops the file onto file system directory `c:\NewHire\input`. Please create the directory when you are ready to run the example. A file receive function, `NewHireRecvFunc`, is configured to pick all files with an extension of *.xml from this location. The receive function then delivers the content of the file to the BizTalk channel, NewHire. The channel then delivers the document to the port, `CreateUser` in SQL Server. The port is configured to send the message to the AIC, `AcctMngSys.CreateUser`. The AIC creates a New User in the SQL Server. In our example, the SQL Server represents an ERP system.

When the application is run, it drops the `NewUserInfo.xml` file into the `c:\NewHire\input` folder. If everything is configured correctly, the New User is created in the SQL Server database.

For the AIC to work correctly, you need to set up a System DSN (Data Source Name) on your machine to access the database AcctMngSys. Recall in Listing 17.5 that the `Connection` string for the AIC was hard-coded as

```
oCnn.ConnectionString = "DSN=AcctMngSys;UID=sa;PWD="
```

Using the ODBC Data Source Administrator, create a system-level DSN to point to the `AcctMngSys` database. The system-level DSN allows all users of the system to use the DSN.

To test the application, run the Web application, as shown earlier in Figure 17.4, several times, each time changing the Alias field and other information. Remember the Alias field is the Primary Key and must be unique. To run the WebApp, you need to have Internet Information Server and need to configure a virtual directory using the Internet Service Manage MMC to point to the `..\Chp17\WebApp` directory where the `default.htm` and `CreateNewAccount.asp` files have been provided.

Alternatively, you can copy and drop the `Test_NewUserInfo.xml` file into the directory. This sample test file is provided in the directory `..\Chp17\input`.

Limitations

In summary, the IBTSAppIntegration AIC components interface is simple and easy to implement. However, it has a couple of limitations:

- There is no way to pass additional parameters to the AIC, other than the document content itself. Of course, we can extend the schema of the XML document and pass additional information to the `ProcessMessage()` method. You will recall that the `ConnectionString` in the component's `CreateUser()` function was hard-coded.

- The other limitation is that the IBTSAppIntegration components are not aware of the context of the document they are processing. For example, there is no way to know the source or destination organization or any of the tracking data.

We will soon see how IPipelineComponent can overcome these limitations.

To verify that the AIC component was successfully executed, open the SQL Server Enterprise Manager and expand the `AcctMngSys` database. You should see the New User entry in the `UserAccountInfo` table.

Creating AICs Using `IPipelineComponent` Interface

Microsoft, in its Site Server Commerce Edition 3.0, first introduced the IPipelineComponent interface. BizTalk Messaging is backward-compatible to the existing Site Server Pipeline components, through the IPipelineComponent interface. So if you have an existing `IpipelineComponent`, you can leverage those components in BizTalk Messaging as an AIC.

The `IPipelineComponent` AIC interface functionality has been enhanced by an additional interface called IPipelineComponentAdmin. This interface allows the component to be configured at the time it is deployed. It also allows the IPipelineComponent AICs to be configured differently per channel. Table 17.3 shows in detail the two interfaces `IPipelineComponent` and `IPipelineComponentAdmin`.

`IPipelineComponentAdmin` interface exposes two methods, `GetConfigData()` and `SetConfigData()`, as shown in Table 17.3, that give you the capability to configure the component at the time of deployment.

TABLE 17.3 `IPipelineComponentAdmin` Interface

Methods	*Parameters and Descriptions*
`GetConfigData() As Object`	This allows you to retrieve the component's private data members in a `CDictionary` Object. For example, the component has a private data member called `m_ConnectionString`. When you call the `GetConfigData`, the component returns a `CDictionary` object with a Name-Value pair for the `m_ConnectionString`.

TABLE 17.3 continued

Methods	*Parameters and Descriptions*
`SetConfigData(ByVal pDict As Object)`	This allows you to set private data members of the component, by sending a `CDictionary` object containing updated values. For example, you can update the value of the `m_ConnectionString` by sending to the component a `CDictionary` object containing the updated value.

The IPipelineComponent interface exposes two methods, Execute() and EnableDesign(), as shown in Table 17.4. The type library of this interface is published in the pipecomplib.tlb file and is located in \Program Files\Common Files\Microsoft Shared\Enterprise Servers\Commerce. The project references to include in a VB IDE for building an IPipelineComponent AIC are Microsoft Commerce 2000 Core Components Type Library and Commerce 2000 Default Pipeline Components Type Library. Now look at the IPipelineComponent interface.

TABLE 17.4 `IPipelineComponent` Interface

Methods	*Parameters and Descriptions*
`Execute(ByVal pdispOrder As Object, ByVal pdispContext As Object, ByVal lFlags As Long)`	The method processes the incoming document and optionally returns a response document if available. *`pdispOrder`* is a `CDictionary` object that contains the document to be processed and context data such as source and organization name. *`pdispContext`* is a required parameter in the method signature but is ignored by BizTalk Server. In Commerce Server, this parameter is used to pass context information to the component. *`lFlags`* is a reserved parameter.
`EnableDesign(ByVal fEnable As Long)`	This method is used at design mode when setting properties of the `pdispOrder` Dictionary object.

Comparing the `IBTSAppIntegration` and `IPipelineComponent`

The `IBTSAppIntegration` component method `ProcessMessage()` receives a single parameter that contains the document to process, whereas the pipeline component method

`Execute()` receives a CDictionary object. The dictionary contains a set of predefined name-value pairs and user-defined properties. One of the name-value pairs is the `working_data`, and the other is `responsefield`. The `working_data` contains the document to be processed. The component can optionally send a response back to BizTalk via the `responsefield`.

In addition to these two keys, the `pdispOrder` dictionary object contains several other keys that contain additional information on the processing context of the document, such as the source and destination organization names. Except for the `Responsefield` key, all others are input parameters. Table 17.5 lists the other keys in the `pdispOrder` dictionary object.

TABLE 17.5 `IPipelineComponent::Execute()` **Methods pDispOrder CDictionary key-value pair detail**

Key Name	*Description*
Working_data	Content of the document submitted to BizTalk.
Doc_type	Name of the root node of the incoming document.
Out_doc_doc_type	Name of the root node of the outgoing document.
Src_ID_Type	Source organization identifier—for example, organization name.
Src_ID_Value	Source organization identifier value—for example, Microsoft.
Nbr_bytes	The size in bytes of the document.
Tracking_ID	ID for tracking outbound document, stored in the DTA database.
In_doc_key	Incoming document key stored in DTA.
Document_Name	Inbound document definition.
In_doc_trcking_id	Tracking ID for inbound document, stored in DTA database.
Syntax	The document standard property, Flatfile, Custom XML.
Dest_ID_Type	Destination organization identifier—for example, organization name.
Dest_ID_Value	Destination organization identifier value—for example, Compaq.
Submission_id	Submission ID; this can be used to track document in the Suspended queue.
Id_interchange_key	Interchange key stored in the DTA database.

TABLE 17.5 continued

Key Name	*Description*
Responsefield	Optionally used to return to BizTalk a response document. Useful when document is submitted using `IBTSInterchange::SubmitSync()` and the transport in the port is Loop-Back.

Building `IPipelineComponent` AIC

One of the problems with the `IBTSAppIntegration` component is that it cannot be configured at the time of deployment. In our example we used a hard-coded connection string for accessing the SQL Server database. It would be great if the component could be configured at deployment. Of course, we could have stored the connection string in the Registry and modified the Registry to access different databases. In our example, the IPipelineComponent exposes the connection string as a configuration parameter.

Listing 17.9 shows you how to implement the functionality demonstrated earlier with little change to the code of the IBTSAppIntegration AIC component. This time we will construct the AIC by implementing the IPipelineComponent and IPipelineComponentAdmin interfaces. The pipeline component project is named NewHirePipeline.vbp. Open the project in VB. The project has a single class `CreateUser` implemented in `CreateUser.cls`. The source code can be found at `..\Chp17\SourceCode\AIC_Pipeline\`.

The `CreateUser` class implements the `IPipelineComponent` interface and the helper interface `IPipelineComponentAdmin`. Look at the two methods of `IPipelineComponentAdmin` interface in Listing 17.9

LISTING 17.9 Getting Configuration Data

```
Private Function IPipelineComponentAdmin_GetConfigData() As Object
   Dim oDic As CDictionary

   Set oDic = New CDictionary
   oDic.Value("ConnectionString") = m_ConnectionString
   Set IPipelineComponentAdmin_GetConfigData = oDic

End Function
```

The `GetConfigData()` method creates a `CDictionary` object. Line three creates a new key called `ConnectionString` and sets its value to the value of the private data member `m_ConnectionString`. Finally, the function returns the `oDic` object.

Listing 17.10 shows the `SetConfigData()` method of the IPipelineComponentAdmin interface.

LISTING 17.10 Setting the Configuration Data to Private Data Members

```
Private Sub IPipelineComponentAdmin_SetConfigData(ByVal pDict As Object)
  m_ConnectionString = CStr(pDict.Value("ConnectionString"))
End Sub
```

The `SetConfigData()` method is simply a reverse of `GetConfigData()`. The `Value` of the key `ConnectionString` from the dictionary object is assigned to the private data member `m_ConnectionString`.

In the private method `CreateUserAccount ()`, the code now, instead of using the hard-coded `ConnectionString`, gets the value from the private data member `m_ConnectionString`. Listing 17.11 illustrates this.

LISTING 17.11 Accessing the Private Data Member to Get the `ConnectionString`

```
Private Function CreateUserAccount(ByVal strLastName As String, _
                                   ByVal strFirstName As String, _
                                   ByVal strAlias As String, _
                                   ByVal strPhone As String, _
                                   ByVal strStreet As String, _
                                   ByVal strCity As String, _
                                   ByVal strZipCode As String, _
                                   ByVal strState As String, _
                                   ByVal strLevel As String, _
                                   ByVal strTitle As String, _
                                   ByRef strResponse) As Boolean

  Dim oCnn As ADODB.Connection
  Dim oCmd As ADODB.Command

On Error GoTo CreateUserAccount_err

  Set oCnn = CreateObject("ADODB.Connection")

  'Note the Connection string is not hard coded, but is set at design time
  'using the IPipelineComponentAdmin
  'methods GetConfigData() and SetConfigData()

  oCnn.ConnectionString = m_ConnectionString
  oCnn.Open

  Set oCmd = CreateObject("ADODB.Command")
  oCmd.ActiveConnection = oCnn
```

LISTING 17.11 continued

```
  oCmd.CommandType = adCmdStoredProc
  oCmd.CommandText = "ams_createUser"

  oCmd.Parameters.Refresh

  With oCmd.Parameters
    .Item("@firstName").Value = strFirstName
    .Item("@lastName").Value = strLastName
    .Item("@alias").Value = strAlias
    .Item("@phone").Value = strPhone
    .Item("@street").Value = strStreet
    .Item("@city").Value = strCity
    .Item("@zipcode").Value = strZipCode
    .Item("@state").Value = strState
    .Item("@level").Value = strLevel
    .Item("@title").Value = strTitle
  End With

  oCmd.Execute

CreateUserAccount_exit:
  strResponse = "Successfully Created the User in the ERP System"
  CreateUserAccount = True
  Exit Function

CreateUserAccount_err:
  strResponse = Err.Description
  CreateUserAccount = False
  Exit Function

  End Function
```

Even though we will not add any code to the `EnableDesign()` method of the IPipelineComponent interface, we must declare each of the methods that are part of the interface that we implement in a class. The Visual Basic 6.0 compiler enforces that the class implements all the pieces of the interface. You will get a Visual Basic Compile error if you leave this or any method out. This method is used by BizTalk to tell the component that it is running in the design mode. Listing 17.12 shows the empty function for `EnableDesign()`.

LISTING 17.12 Empty `EnableDesign()` Method

```
Private Sub IPipelineComponent_EnableDesign(ByVal fEnable As Long)

End Sub
```

Custom Property Pages for NewHirePipe.CreateUser Component

We must now provide a way for a user to configure the component's ConnectionString at design time. In Site Server 3.0 Commerce Edition, the pipeline component implemented yet another interface named IPipelineComponentUI to provide developers with the capability to build front-end UIs for pipeline components. BizTalk Server makes this process easier by providing the front-end to the GetConfigData() and SetConfigData() methods using two ASP pages.

The developers create two ASP pages and place them into a designated directory, ..\Program Files\Microsoft BizTalk Server\MessagingManager\pipeline. This enables BizTalk Messaging to automatically detect them at design time. You can create the ASP pages in Visual InterDev or simply in any text editor, like the universal notepad. There are some restrictions in the way the two ASP pages are named.

The two ASP pages must comply with following naming convention:

- *<ProjectName>*_*<ClassName>*.asp where *<ProjectName>* is the name of the project in VB project, and *<ClassName>* is the name of the class that implements IPipelineComponent and IpipelineComponentAdmin.
- *<ProjectName>*_*<ClassName>*_post.asp—The difference in the name of the two files is that in the second one, post is appended to it.

For our example, the ProgID of our AIC component is NewHirePipeline.CreateUser. So the two ASP property pages that we need to create are named NewHirePipeLine_Createuser.asp and NewHirePipeLine_CreateUser_post.asp. Both the pages have the standard includes for header and footer code. These includes are standard for all pipeline property pages.

In our example, the NewHirePipeline_Createuser.asp page looks like this:

```
<%@ LANGUAGE = VBScript %>
<!--#INCLUDE FILE="pe_edit_header.asp" -->

<%
        call InputText("ConnectionString")
%>
<!--#INCLUDE FILE="pe_edit_footer.asp" -->
```

As you can see, there are only three lines of code in the page; most of the work is done by the two include files pe_edit_header.asp and pe_edit_footer.asp. The only line I have added is the call InputText("ConnectionString"). This page prompts the user with a text box and a prompt of ConnectionString. The user input is then passed to the post page.

The ASP page `NewHirePipeline_CreateUser_post.asp` looks similar to the edit page.

```
<%@ LANGUAGE = VBScript %>
<!--#INCLUDE FILE="pe_global_edit.asp" -->

<%
        call GetInputText("ConnectionString", 0, bufsize_medium)
%>
<!--#INCLUDE FILE="pe_post_footer.asp" -->
```

The user-entered value for the `ConnectionString` is received here, and the include files have code sections to call `SetConfigData()` in the pipeline component.

> **Note**
>
> The ASP page `NewHirePipeline_Createuser.asp` is used to display the data to the user to set the configuration data of the AIC, in the Advanced button of the Channel Creation Wizard. The second ASP page `NewHirePipeline_CreateUser_post.asp` is called by the first, to take the user's updated configuration data and persist it in the channel.
>
> This is the same channel that delivers the data to the port. You can have multiple channels whose endpoints are the same port. Recall that the AIC is bound to the port. By configuring the AIC property for each channel, the configuration data is persisted as part of the channel. You are effectively using the same AIC with different configuration settings. Just think of the benefits in a real-world scenario—for example, Cyber Source's Tax Calculation AIC component.

The ASP page `NewHirePipeline_Createuser.asp` is used to display the data to the user to set the configuration data of the AIC in the Advanced button of the channel creation wizard. The second asp page `NewHirePipeline_CreateUser_post.asp` is called by the first, to take the user's updated configuration data and persist it in the channel.

This is the same channel that delivers the data to the port. You can have multiple channels whose end points are the same port. You recall that the AIC is bound to the port. By configuring the AIC property for each channel, the configuration data is persisted as part of the channel. You are effectively using the same AIC, with different configuration settings. Just think of the benefits in a real world scenario, for example Cyber Source's Tax Calculation AIC component.

Deploying `IPipelineComponent` AIC

Deploying the `IPipelineComponent` consists of two steps:

1. Registering
2. Configuring BizTalk Messaging Port and Channel

Registering `IPipelineComponent` AIC

Registering an `IPipelineComponent` is identical to registering the `IBTSAppIntegration` AIC component. You may choose to use the RegSvr32.exe utility to register and create an unconfigured COM+ application and then add the Category IDs using a Registry file. The choice is definitely yours; however, if you do not want to muck with the registry, the recommended way is to create a COM+ application using the Component Services and then install the IPipelineComponent into the application. Both methods of registration were discussed in the "Registering AIC Manually Using Regedit" section and "Registering AIC Using COM+ Application."

Configuring Messaging Port

To make it simple, we will use the BizTalk Messaging setup used for the `IBTSAppIntegration` AIC Component in Table 17.2. We will simply swap out the `IBTSAppIntegration` component with the `IPipelineComponent`.

This can be done by editing the messaging port `CreateUser` in SQL Server and selecting the `IPipelineComponent` AIC for the primary transport. Figure 17.12 shows the port is now configured for the `IPipelineComponent` AIC, `NewHirePipeline.CreateUser` component.

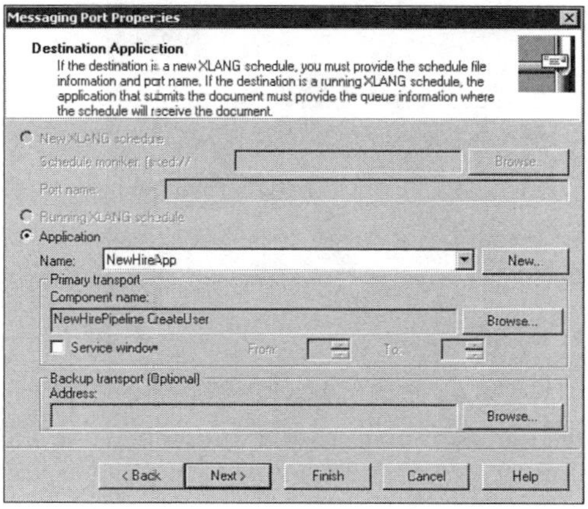

FIGURE 17.12
Binding the port to the Pipeline Component AIC.

We have completed adding the `IPipelineComponent` AIC to the messaging port, but we still have to configure the component to pass a valid value for the `ConnectionString` at design time.

Intuitively, you would think that the property pages for the component will be available somewhere on the port where we installed the AIC component. This is not the case; in fact, the property pages are accessible through the advanced configuration of the channel. Before configuring properties using the property pages, make sure that the ASP pages are in the appropriate BizTalk Server directory, `..\Program Files\Microsoft BizTalk Server\MessagingManager\pipeline`. The ASP property pages have been discussed in detail in the section "Custom Property Pages for `NewHirePipe.CreateUser` Component" of the chapter.

Recall from the earlier chapters that a single port can service multiple channels. By being able to set the property at the channel level, this allows us to set a unique set of properties for each document type or channel port combination.

Setting Component Properties in the Channel

The AIC component properties are set in the channel using the channel's Advanced Configuration page. Open the channel, NewHire Channel, for edit in the Hackers Den organization.

Navigate to the Advanced Configuration property page of the channel by clicking on the Next button. This is the last page on the Channel property. Figure 17.13 shows the Advanced Configuration page of the channel.

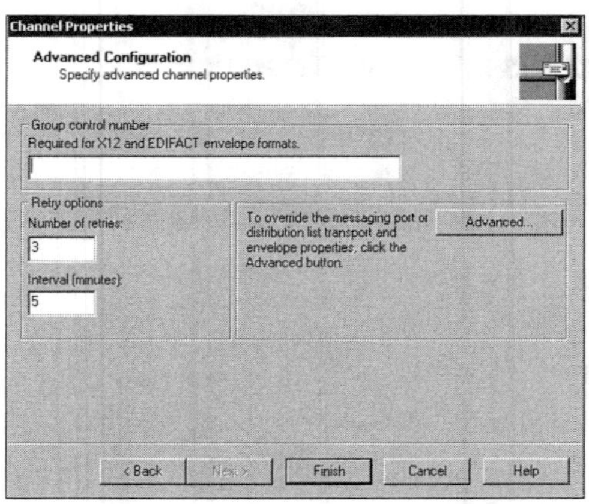

FIGURE 17.13
Advanced Configuration page to set channel properties.

Click on the Advanced button. This takes you to the Override Messaging Port Defaults dialog box, as shown in Figure 17.14. The dialog box shows the AIC component we assigned as the primary transport in the port.

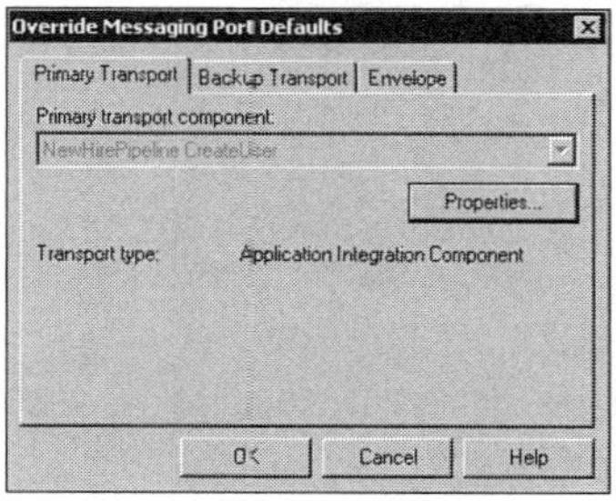

FIGURE 17.14
Overriding the default settings of the port.

When you click the Properties button on the Override Messaging Port Defaults dialog box, you will be executing the property page `NewHirePipeline_CreateUser.asp` that we created and placed in the BizTalk Server messaging pipeline directory.

In our example, the page displays the dialog box with a prompt for `ConnectionString`, as shown in Figure 17.15.

FIGURE 17.15
Channel Configuration page to configure the AIC Component.

This is where you provide the configuration information for the `IPipelineComponent` AIC at deployment time. We defined DSN using the ODBC Data Source Administrator in the section "Running IBTSAppIntegration AIC" earlier in the chapter. You will recall that the Connection string was hard-coded in the code (refer to Listing 17.5) for our `IBTSAppIntegration` AIC. In the case of `IpipelineComponent` AIC, we are providing the configuration for the Connection string at the time of deployment. Figure 17.15 provides the connection string.

Finally, for all those "codeholics," Listing 17.13 shows the code for the `Execute()` function and the rest of the code for the class `NewHirePipleline.CreateUser`.

LISTING 17.13 Code Listing for `CreateUser` Class that Implements `IPipelineComponent` and `IPipelineComponentAdmin`

```
Option Explicit

'the component implements IPipelineComponent and
'IPipelineComponentAdmin Interfaces
Implements IPipelineComponent
Implements IPipelineComponentAdmin

Private m_ConnectionString As String


Private Sub IPipelineComponent_EnableDesign(ByVal fEnable As Long)

End Sub

Private Function IPipelineComponent_Execute(ByVal pdispOrder As Object,
➥ByVal pdispContext As Object, ByVal lFlags As Long) As Long

Dim strFirstName As String
Dim strLastName As String
Dim strAlias As String
Dim strPhone As String
Dim strStreet As String
Dim strCity As String
Dim strZipCode As String
Dim strState As String
Dim strLevel As String
Dim strTitle As String
Dim strPassword As String

Dim bstrDocument As String
Dim strResponse As String


On Error GoTo IBTSAppIntegration_ProcessMessage_err

bstrDocument = pdispOrder.Value("working_data")

 ExtractUserInfo bstrDocument, strFirstName, strLastName, strAlias, strPhone, _
                  strStreet, strCity, strZipCode, strState, _
                  strLevel, strTitle


 CreateUserAccount strFirstName, strLastName, strAlias, strPhone, _
                  strStreet, strCity, strZipCode, strState, _
                  strLevel, strTitle, strResponse
```

LISTING 17.13 continued

```
IBTSAppIntegration_ProcessMessage_exit:
  App.LogEvent "User Account Successfully Created for User = " &
➥strFirstName & " " & strLastName, vbLogEventTypeInformation
  Exit Function

IBTSAppIntegration_ProcessMessage_err:
  App.LogEvent "Failed to create User Account, for User = " &
➥strFirstName & " " & strLastName & vbNewLine & "Error = " &
➥Err.Number & " Description =" & Err.Description, vbLogEventTypeError
  Err.Raise Err.Number, Err.Source & ":CreateUserAcctInAD", Err.Description
  Exit Function

End Function

Private Function ExtractUserInfo(ByVal strXML As String, _
                                 ByRef strFirstName As String, _
                                 ByRef strLastName As String, _
                                 ByRef strAlias As String, _
                                 ByRef strPhone As String, _
                                 ByRef strStreet As String, _
                                 ByRef strCity As String, _
                                 ByRef strZipCode As String, _
                                 ByRef strState As String, _
                                 ByRef strLevel As String, _
                                 ByRef strTitle As String)

Dim oXMLDom As MSXML2.DOMDocument
Dim oNode As IXMLDOMElement
Dim strAreaCode As String
Dim strNumber As String

On Error GoTo ExtractUserInfo_err

Set oXMLDom = CreateObject("MSXML2.DOMDocument")
oXMLDom.loadXML strXML

'Get the attribute values from the NAME Node of the XML Message
Set oNode = oXMLDom.getElementsByTagName("Name").Item(0)
strFirstName = oNode.getAttribute("First")
strLastName = oNode.getAttribute("Last")
strAlias = oNode.getAttribute("Alias")


'Get the attribute values from the ADDRESS Node of the XML Message
Set oNode = oXMLDom.getElementsByTagName("Address").Item(0)
strStreet = oNode.getAttribute("Street")
strCity = oNode.getAttribute("City")
strState = oNode.getAttribute("State")
strZipCode = oNode.getAttribute("ZipCode")
```

LISTING 17.13 continued

```
'Get the attribute values from the PHONE Node of the XML Message
Set oNode = oXMLDom.getElementsByTagName("Phone").Item(0)
strAreaCode = oNode.getAttribute("AreaCode")
strNumber = oNode.getAttribute("Number")
strPhone = strAreaCode & "-" & strNumber


'Get the attribute values from the LEVEL Node of the XML Message
Set oNode = oXMLDom.getElementsByTagName("Level").Item(0)
strLevel = oNode.getAttribute("Code")
strTitle = oNode.getAttribute("Title")

ExtractUserInfo_exit:
  Set oNode = Nothing
  Set oXMLDom = Nothing
  Exit Function

ExtractUserInfo_err:
  Set oNode = Nothing
  Set oXMLDom = Nothing

  Err.Raise 1000 + Err.Number, Err.Source & ":ExtractUserInfo", Err.Description
  Exit Function

End Function

Private Function CreateUserAccount(ByVal strLastName As String, _
                                   ByVal strFirstName As String, _
                                   ByVal strAlias As String, _
                                   ByVal strPhone As String, _
                                   ByVal strStreet As String, _
                                   ByVal strCity As String, _
                                   ByVal strZipCode As String, _
                                   ByVal strState As String, _
                                   ByVal strLevel As String, _
                                   ByVal strTitle As String, _
                                   ByRef strResponse) As Boolean

  Dim oCnn As ADODB.Connection
  Dim oCmd As ADODB.Command

On Error GoTo CreateUserAccount_err

  Set oCnn = CreateObject("ADODB.Connection")

  'Note the Connection string is not hard coded, but is set at design time
  'using the IPipelineComponentAdmin methods GetConfigData()
  'and SetConfigData()
```

LISTING 17.13 continued

```
  oCnn.ConnectionString = m_ConnectionString
  oCnn.Open

  Set oCmd = CreateObject("ADODB.Command")
  oCmd.ActiveConnection = oCnn
  oCmd.CommandType = adCmdStoredProc
  oCmd.CommandText = "ams_createUser"

  oCmd.Parameters.Refresh

  With oCmd.Parameters
    .Item("@firstName").Value = strFirstName
    .Item("@lastName").Value = strLastName
    .Item("@alias").Value = strAlias
    .Item("@phone").Value = strPhone
    .Item("@street").Value = strStreet
    .Item("@city").Value = strCity
    .Item("@zipcode").Value = strZipCode
    .Item("@state").Value = strState
    .Item("@level").Value = strLevel
    .Item("@title").Value = strTitle
  End With

  oCmd.Execute

CreateUserAccount_exit:
  strResponse = "Successfully Created the User in the ERP System"
  CreateUserAccount = True
  Exit Function

CreateUserAccount_err:
  strResponse = Err.Description
  CreateUserAccount = False
  Exit Function


End Function

Private Function IPipelineComponentAdmin_GetConfigData() As Object
   Dim oDic As CDictionary

   Set oDic = New CDictionary
   oDic.Value("ConnectionString") = m_ConnectionString
   Set IPipelineComponentAdmin_GetConfigData = oDic

End Function
```

LISTING 17.13 continued

```
Private Sub IPipelineComponentAdmin_SetConfigData(ByVal pDict As Object)
  m_ConnectionString = CStr(pDict.Value("ConnectionString"))
End Sub
```

Running the `IPipelineComponent` AIC

Once you have set up the property pages and configured the AIC as in Figure 17.15, you are ready to test. You will run this exactly the same way as you did IBTSAppIntegration AIC in the section "Running the IBTSAppIntegration AIC."

BizTalk Scriptor Component AIC

BizTalk Scriptor AICs provide a much simpler implementation of the underlying functionality of the `IPipelineComponent` interface. If you are familiar with Microsoft Site Server 3.0 Commerce Edition and have used the Commerce Server Pipelines, you will be familiar with the Pipeline Scriptor Component. BizTalk Server has borrowed this technology from the Commerce Server. The Scriptor components are written in VBScript or Jscript and as such are interpretive. From performance consideration, you will not use Scriptor AICs in production deployment. In addition to the performance, all variables are of type variants and sometimes present a problem when integrating with applications requiring certain data types.

BizTalk Scriptor Components are great for quick prototype and debugging purposes. Because these components are interpretive, you do not have to compile the component each time you make changes. In this section, you see how easy it is to build a Scriptor component. On top of that, there is nothing to register in this case. BizTalk Scriptor Component is provided out of the box and is registered at the time BizTalk is installed. The script that you write is hosted in this component.

Building and Deploying a BizTalk Scriptor AIC

In this section we will build and deploy a simple Scriptor AIC. The AIC takes the incoming message and logs the message to a file. We will configure the AIC for the log file at deployment. In this case, we will swap out the `IPipelineComponent` AIC with the Scriptor AIC. However, instead of inserting the `NewUserInfo` into the SQL Server database, the Scriptor AIC simply logs the file into a directory. The following steps install a Scriptor AIC:

1. Figure 17.16 shows the BizTalk Messaging Port and the list of Application Integration Components installed on my machine. Select the BizTalk Scriptor component from the list and click OK.

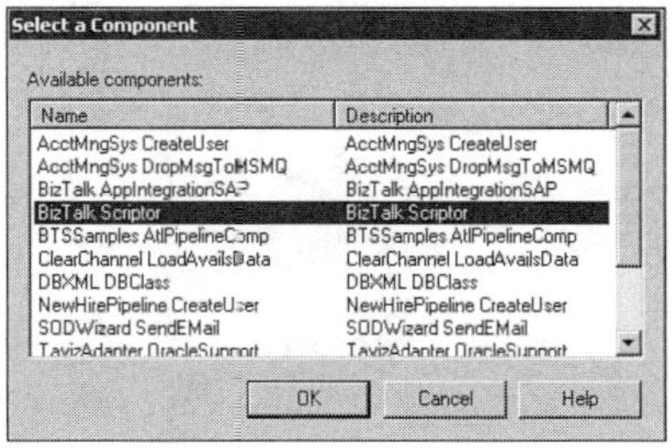

FIGURE 17.16
BizTalk Scriptor as an AIC.

2. Figure 17.17 shows the port bound to the Scriptor AIC. Click OK and click Finish to close the Messaging Fort Wizard.

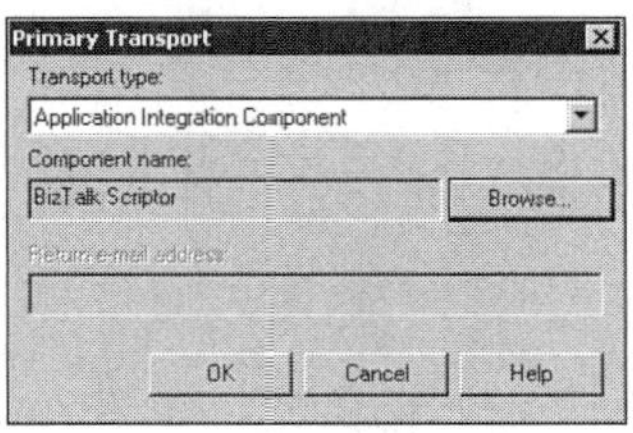

FIGURE 17.17
Port bound to the BizTalk Scriptor AIC.

3. Jump to the Advance configuration page of the channel and click on the Advanced button. Figure 17.18 shows the page Override Messaging Port Defaults. Click on the Properties button; the BizTalk Scriptor Properties dialog box appears (see Figure 17.19).

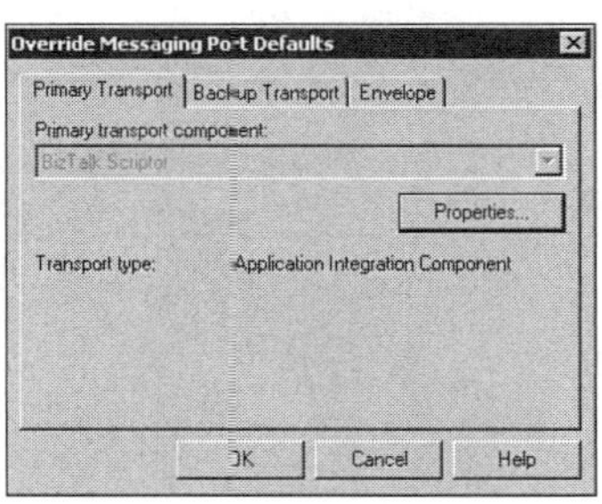

FIGURE 17.18
Advanced Channel Configuration—Override Messaging Port Defaults.

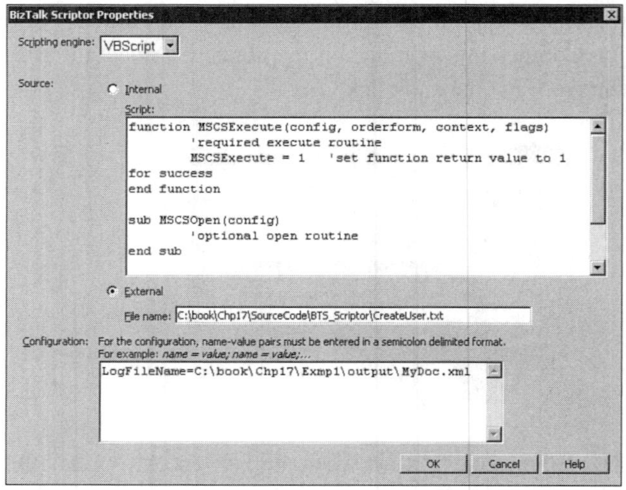

FIGURE 17.19
BizTalk Scriptor AIC property page.

- Selecting the Scripting Engine—You have two options VBScript or JScript. For our case, we will select VBScript.
- Configuration—In our case, we will specify the name of the log file we want the Scriptor AIC to write the content of the message to. The configuration information needs to be specified as a `Name=Value` pair, separated by “;". Name is important because the Scriptor AIC will be looking for a value for the Name specified. We have specified `LogFileName` as the Name and `..\Chp17\Exmp1\output\MyDoc.xml` as the Value.
- Script Source—The script can be internal or external. If you select external, you have to provide the full path to the file that contains the script. My personal preference is to have the script external. This allows me to use an editor of my choice, and in addition I can use source code control to track changes. Listing 17.14 shows the content of the script file `..\Chp17\SourceCode\BTS_Scriptor\CreateUser.txt`.

LISTING 17.14 Complete Source Code for Scriptor AIC

```
function MSCSExecute(config, orderform, context, flags)

On Error Resume Next

  Dim oFileSysObj, oTextStreamObj
  Dim strLogFileName
  Dim strDocument
```

LISTING 17.14 continued

```
  'get the log file name from the config Dictionary
  strLogFileName = config.value("LogFileName")

  'Create a file to write the in coming document
  Set oFileSysObj = CreateObject("Scripting.FileSystemObject")
  Set oTextStreamObj = oFileSysObj.OpenTextFile(strLogFileName, 2, True)

 if Err.Number = 0 then
   'get the in coming document from the orderform dictionary. The key that
   'has the document is working_data

   strDocument = Cstr(orderform.Value("working_data"))

   'Finally write the document
   call oTextStreamObj.Write(strDocument)

   oTextStreamObj.Close
   Set oTextStreamObj = Nothing
   Set oFileSysObj = Nothing

   'indicate success
   MSCSExecute = 1

 else

   'indicate failure
   MSCSExecute = 0
   Set oTextStreamObj = Nothing
   Set oFileSysObj = Nothing

 end if

end function

sub MSCSOpen(config)
    'optional open routine
end sub

sub MSCSClose()
    'optional close routine
end sub
```

We will briefly discuss the Scriptor AIC code here.

The function `MSCSExecute()` has four parameters. They are all dictionary objects except the flag. The third parameter MTS context is not available to the Scriptor component, and the flag is for backward compatibility. The first parameter `config` holds all the configuration information and the second parameter `orderform` holds most of the data, such as the working_data (the message itself), Document_Name, tracking_id, and others.

The line of code `strLogFileName = config.value("LogFileName")` extracts the value of the `LogFileName` key from the `config` dictionary object. The `LogFileName` is then used to create a file using the `Scripting.FileSystemObject`. Next we get the actual message from the `orderform` object in the line `strDocument = Cstr(orderform.Value("working_data"))`.

The rest of the code writes the content of the message to the log file. Note the return value of the function `MSCSExecute()`. A return value of 0 is failure, and a return value of 1 indicates success. If you return 0 from this function, BizTalk Server detects this as a failure in the port and forces the document into the Suspended Queue.

The functions `MSCSOpen()` and `MSCSClose()` are optional and are not required for BizTalk Scriptor AIC.

Summary

This chapter explained in great detail how to extend the BizTalk Messaging plumbing to deliver messages to any business process or application.

You have learned how Application Integration Components bound to a messaging port can extend the reach of BizTalk Server to legacy applications. In Chapters 7 and 8 you learned a great deal about the BizTalk Messaging Manager and how to create document definitions, ports, and channels. This chapter showed how BizTalk Messaging provides support and plumbing to extend BizTalk Server by writing Application Integration Components. You learned three ways to develop an AIC—starting from the simple AICs implementing the `IBTSAppIntegration` interface to more complex AICs using the `IPipelineComponent` and `IPipelineComponentAdmin` interfaces. The `IBTSAppIntegration` AICs are lightweight and simple and suitable for most cases; the `IPipelineComponent` AICs provide the flexibility of configuring the component differently for specific channels. Finally, we discussed briefly BizTalk Scriptor Component AICs, which are great for testing, debugging, and prototyping purposes. In the following chapter, you will learn how to extend BizTalk functionality using Custom Serializers, Parsers, and Functoids.

CHAPTER 18

Creating Custom Serializers, Parsers, and Functoids

By Bill Martschenko

In This Chapter

In this chapter, we will extend how BizTalk handles data, one of BizTalk's cornerstones. In addition to a flexible design time for business processes, BizTalk offers unprecedented flexibility for rapid integration.

Our focus for extension, here, is the point where data flows between partner organizations and internal business processes. This flow of data falls in the purview of BizTalk Messaging Services. In contrast, the flow of data within a business process is handled by BizTalk Orchestration Services or by a custom application. See Chapter 12, "Advanced BizTalk Messaging," and Chapter 13, "Advanced BizTalk Orchestration," for more details on the design-time environment for BizTalk Orchestration.

The BizTalk *channel* is the element within BizTalk Messaging Services that defines the data flow extended in this chapter. See Chapter 6, "Introduction to BizTalk Messaging," and Chapter 7, "Using the BizTalk Messaging Manager," for more details on BizTalk Messaging.

The channel has two important areas for extension. First, custom data formats need to enter and exit channels. That is, custom data formats need to be exchanged between businesses and internal applications. Second, data transformation within the channel needs to incorporate custom business logic.

Specifically, we will use COM in this chapter to extend channels with *parsers*, *serializers*, and *functoids*. Parsers recognize custom data formats, serializers render custom formats, and functoids perform custom transformation.

Why have custom handling of business data? We live in a world diverse in its data. This diversity is in lock step with business diversity. Every business has its own needs, and although standards help, the number of standards itself is overwhelming.

This chapter will help if you have data in a format different from those natively recognized in BizTalk. BizTalk currently recognizes XML, EDIFACT, X12, and flat files that are comma-delimited or position-based.

This chapter will also help if you have custom data transformations for use in BizTalk Mapper.

> **Note**
>
> For more background on BizTalk's data handling capabilities, look to the following chapters: Chapter 4, "The BizTalk Editor," specifies the format of data; Chapter 5, "The BizTalk Mapper," covers data reformatting using the BizTalk Mapper; and Chapter 8, "Document Tracking," covers the tracking of data.
>
> For another type of channel extension, see Chapter 17, "Application Integration Components."

We will begin with a series of examples to reveal the architecture for extending channels. Next, we will design and implement an extension for functoids. The majority of the chapter covers the design and implementation of parsers and serializers for custom business data formats.

Channel Extensibility by Example

Before jumping into code, we need to lay a foundation. We will build an intuition using examples and then identify an extensible architecture for a channel. With the architecture in place, alternatives to creating extensions become clear. These alternatives serve to clarify our understanding by showing other ways to achieve the same result.

Scenario: Accepting Custom Data from a Business Partner

A financial broker needs to send its stream of transactions for trades through our fictitious company, illustrated in Figure 18.1. Presumably, we will do something useful with them. They use the financial standard for trades, the Financial Information Exchange (FIX) messaging standard. FIX is a compact, binary message format; it is not XML. See `http://www.fixprotocol.org` for details, though no FIX expertise is required for this chapter.

FIGURE 18.1
Scenario for accepting custom business data.

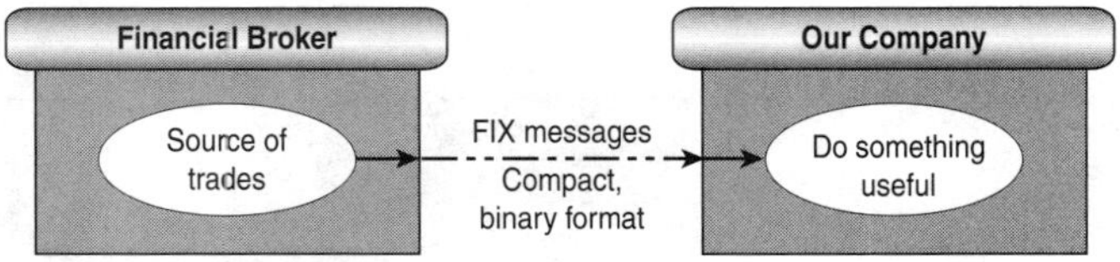

It is useful to see what happens when we try to send the stream of FIX messages into BizTalk. The point that we fail is precisely the point where we will build an extension.

A standard setup, using BizTalk terminology in italics, is as follows:

- The *Home Organization* is our company.
- A new *organization* represents the financial broker in the diagram.
- A new *channel* represents the stream of FIX messages, the dashed line in the diagram, from the financial broker. We need a *receive function* to accept an external data feed and route data to our *channel*.

- A new *port* serves as the endpoint for the *channel*. The *port* delivers the data to an internal process per the rightmost solid line in the diagram.
- An *XLANG schedule* handles the FIX data as an internal process within the *Home Organization*, per the rightmost oval in the diagram.

Working through the setup, we trip creating the channel. The channel requires a document definition for data entering the channel and another document definition for data leaving the channel to arrive at the corresponding port.

The problem is that the document definition must be for a supported format: XML, EDIFACT, X12, comma-delimited, or position-based flat file.

Ultimately, the data arriving to the XLANG schedule must be in XML. A mechanism for parsing the inbound FIX format into XML is required. We will use the `IBizTalkParserComponent` interface later in this chapter for this purpose.

Scenario: Producing Custom Data for a Business Partner

Extending the first scenario, Figure 18.2 shows a financial broker that sends us trade data and expects us to be a link in a chain. Trade data is to be routed through us. We perform our really useful function and then continue the trade data on its route to another financial broker, possibly modifying the trade data as we go. In this scenario, we must format FIX data.

FIGURE 18.2
Scenario for producing custom business data.

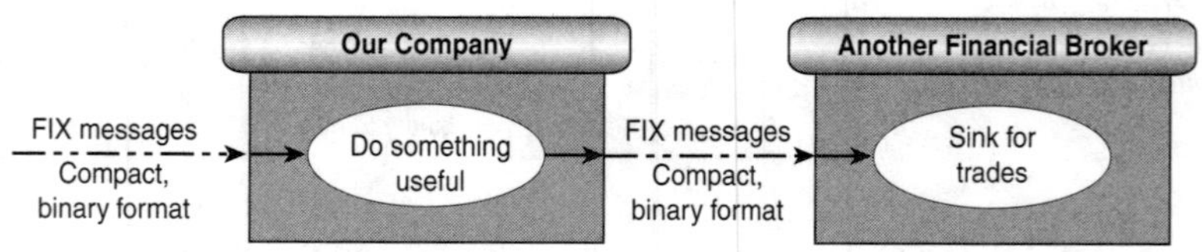

A standard setup, using BizTalk terminology in italics, is as follows:

- A new *organization* represents the second financial broker.
- A new *channel* receives output from the *XLANG schedule*.
- A new *port* serves as the endpoint for the new *channel*. The port delivers the data to the new *organization*.

We trip in this setup for the same reason in the first scenario. Document definitions for data entering and exiting the new channel must be available. The definition for the data outbound to the second financial broker is not possible because it uses the nonsupported FIX format.

A mechanism for serializing the outbound FIX format is required. We will use the `IBizTalkSerializerComponent` interface later in this chapter for this purpose.

Scenario: Using Business Logic to Transform Data

The trade information needs classification before the XLANG schedule processes it internally. By *classification*, we mean analyzing the data to calculate a value from some predetermined category, such as `HighPriority`, `Normal`, and `LowPriority`. Classification and ranking are common functions requiring rules specific to a business.

The classification will help simplify the decision nodes on the BizTalk Orchestration diagram, illustrated in Figure 18.3. A single decision node can select among all possible classification values, similar to a C++ `switch` statement or a VB `select case` statement.

FIGURE 18.3
A Decision node on a BizTalk Orchestration diagram.

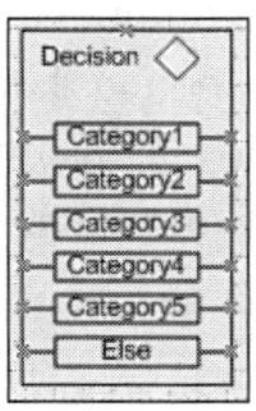

Using BizTalk maps, we can apply our business rules in the channel. The order is important. The data arrives in the channel using a format defined by an external organization. The data leaves the channel in a format needed internally by a BizTalk Orchestration schedule.

In general, BizTalk maps allow for a flexible data transformation within the channel. This transformation connects an external interface with a trading partner to an internal interface of a business process. The internal interface becomes more important when multiple channels provide the data in different formats such as from different trading partners. A map in each channel can normalize to comply with a single internal interface.

A mechanism for applying business rules in maps is required. We will use the `IFunctoid` interface later in this chapter for this purpose.

General Scenario

In general, the three preceding scenarios reveal the need for the channel to have an extensible structure. Figure 18.4 diagrams the composite scenario.

FIGURE 18.4
General scenario for the BizTalk channel.

1. Inbound document as XML, EDI, flat file, or custom format including binary.
2. Optional parsing interface IBizTalkParserComponent.
3. XML result of parsing step.
4. Optional transformation using business rules via interface IFunctoid.
5. XML result of transformation step.
6. Optional serialization interface IBizTalkSerializerComponent.
7. Outbound document as XML, EDI, flat file, or custom format including binary.

The channel supports two data formats, one inbound and one outbound. A transformation between the two formats can occur inside the channel. The inbound data can have a custom parser to recognize its format. The outbound data can have a custom serializer to render its format. The transformation from inbound format to outbound format can use custom business logic.

Depending on the setup for the channel, the inbound data and outbound data represent public or private interfaces. *Public* means visible to a trading partner; *private* means visible to internal applications only. Table 18.1 gives three channel setups.

TABLE 18.1 Channel Usage

Channel Setup		*Type of Interface*	
From	*To*	*for Inbound Data*	*for Outbound Data*
Trading partner	Internal application	Public	Private
Internal application	Trading partner	Private	Public
Internal application	Internal application	Private	Private

When a channel flows data from a trading partner to an internal business process, the inbound data represents a public interface, and the outbound data represents a private interface.

Conversely, when a channel flows data from an internal business process to a trading partner, the inbound data represents a private interface, and the outbound data represents a public interface.

Alternatives to the Extensibility Model

With the extensibility model in place, it is useful to consider programmatic alternatives. These alternatives clarify our understanding by offering other ways to achieve the same result.

The most straightforward alternative to parsing the inbound flow is to intercede before the data arrives at the channel. In the case where data arrives from a trading partner, we need to change the receive function. For example, if we use a queue-based receive function, then whatever code we have posting messages to the queue can parse before posting. Likewise, serialization can occur after data leaves the channel.

The drawback to this approach is a lack of integration. BizTalk has document tracking features for data inside the channel. BizTalk offers a closed environment where a trading partner can submit data in its format directly into a BizTalk channel. This closed environment has other advantages such as reliable delivery and auto-restart. Any componentry inserted between the trading partner and BizTalk poses risks to integrity.

BizTalk provides an integrated alternative to parsing. A receive function can have a preprocessor. An example use is to decompress data before submitting to BizTalk. For more on preprocessors, find the interface `IBTSCustomProcess` in the product documentation.

The drawback to the preprocessor becomes clear when we design a parser later in this chapter. For example, the preprocessor offers simple data conversion, whereas the parser can structure data into groups.

Considering functoids, there is a functionally equivalent alternative. The `Scripting` functoid allows an arbitrary script to be used. Later in this chapter, we will see that `IFunctoid` too must use script in its implementation.

The drawback to the `Scripting` functoid is usability. With `IFunctoid`, we can integrate into the user interface of BizTalk Mapper. The `Scripting` functoid contains the script as a property, which means that reuse requires cut-and-paste.

A second alternative to a custom functoid is available if there is also the custom parsing step. We can eliminate the functoid entirely by performing all custom transformations in the parsing step.

The advantage is performance. Functoids must be script, which means that BizTalk must load a scripting engine as well as execute a slower code set.

The disadvantage is a loss of modularity by mixing public and private interfaces, per Table 18.1. For example, suppose that one trading partner submits the binary FIX format and another submits with another format. The classification functoid from the earlier scenario now has two implementations. One implementation is in the FIX-to-XML parser. The other implementation is in the parser yielding XML from the other financial format. Performance versus modularity is a common trade-off.

Functoid Design

In this section, we will design a custom functoid that we will implement in the next section. To this point, the discussion has centered on architecture of the BizTalk channel and example scenarios for functoids. The important take-home points were that a functoid operates within a BizTalk channel to provide custom business logic in transforming business data. This transformation plays a key role in bridging between public and private interfaces.

A functoid is relatively easy to design and requires two main specifications:

- Functionality—Interface with data elements in channel's map and provide the desired computation
- BizTalk Mapper integration—User interface images and classification

Functionality

A functoid is a single function though which the COM interface `IFunctoid` implements one or more functoids. Each functoid accepts input parameters and must have a return value. The number of input parameters can be variable. There are no output parameters. All input parameters and the return value must be a simple type insertable into XML such as a string, number, or boolean.

The first step is deciding the function signature. As designers, we must avoid the usual practice of placing the burden of constructing the inputs on the caller. It must be possible for the user to drag the function input directly from the XML data or from the output of another functoid. There is a limited capability to format or calculate input parameters.

For a general-purpose functoid, such as a formatter, the function signature is largely independent of the XML format in the channel. For a business-specific functoid, such as a classifier, the function signature might need to account for the XML schema for the data inside the channel.

Example: `Selector`, a General-Purpose Functoid

The functoid `Selector` is similar to the C++ `operator ?:` and the VB `iif` function. The similarity is that you can write a single expression that will evaluate to one of n subexpressions based on a single value, termed the selector.

Example usage:

```
Selector(true, "A", "B") returns "A"
Selector(false, "A", "B") returns "B"
Selector(1, "A", "B", "C", "D") returns "A"
Selector(4, "A", "B", "C", "D") returns "D"
```

In general, there are n+1 arguments, for n >= 0. The first argument, the selector, is a boolean value or an integer index. The last n arguments are a list of possible return values. The first argument can be a nonintegral number, in which case the floor of the number is used. The first argument can be a string representation of a number.

```
Selector( s, v1, …, vn )
        = v1 if s = true or "true" (case insensitive)
        = v2 if s = false or "false" (case insensitive)
        = vs if s is an integer and 1 <= s <= n
        = empty string "", otherwise
```

Example: `TradeClassifier`, a Business-Specific Functoid

A functoid `TradeClassifier` expects data specific to a FIX message. It accepts a set of data items from the trade data and returns a classification “A”, “B”, “C”, or “D”. The meaning of these classification levels is specific to an internal business process. We do not get more descriptive here to retain the focus on the mechanism rather than the financial trade example. If it helps, substitute meaningful category names.

We will not actually implement this functoid. The `Selector` functoid will suffice for showing the coding techniques.

BizTalk Mapper Integration

Integration with the BizTalk Mapper tool requires an icon, a display name, ToolTips, a tab on which to place the functoid, and a set of constraints for connecting the functoid to other diagram elements.

To integrate seamlessly, exercise care to match the icon design and naming conventions. Table 18.2 provides the list of tabs from the Functoid Palette with a sample item from each. Each tab has a single color for the icon background. The one exception is the Advanced tab. Icons are 16×16 pixels, though no guidelines are documented for the number of colors.

TABLE 18.2 BizTalk Mapper Functoid Tabs with Sample Items

Tab	*Icon RGB Color*	*Functoid*	*ToolTip*
String	`(156,48,49)`	Uppercase	Converts a text item to uppercase characters.
Mathematical	`(49,154,156)`	Multiplication	Multiplies one number by another number.
Logical	`(0,130,0)`	Logical OR	Returns the logical OR of parameters.
Date/Time	`(0,0,156)`	Time	Returns the current time.
Conversion	`(156,0,156)`	Hexadecimal	Returns a hexadecimal value when given a decimal number.
Scientific	`(99,101,0)`	Cosine	Returns the cosine of a number.
Cumulative	`(255,48,99)`	Cumulative Sum	Sums all values for the connected field by iterating over its parent record.
Database	`(0,101,255)`	Database Lookup	Searches a database for a specific value, retrieves the record that contains the value, and stores it in an ADO record set.
Advanced	`(206,154,0)`	Scripting	Enables customized functionality based on a script that you provide.
	`(132,0,132)`	Looping	Creates multiple output records by iterating over each input record.

The number and names of tabs are fixed. Note that BizTalk 2002 recommends that no custom functoids be added to the Database tab. Use the Advanced tab for any new database-related functoids.

Functoid Implementation

In this section, we will implement the `Selector` functoid design from the preceding section using C++ and ATL. For alternative implementation technologies, check the BizTalk product samples. They provide functoids in Visual Basic and C#.

The implementation in this section comprises the following items:

- A script implementing the `Selector()` functionality
- A COM coclass implementing `IFunctoid`

It is reasonable to ask why there is a mixture of COM and script. Script is not sufficient. BizTalk Mapper needs additional metadata for how to incorporate the functoid onto the mapper's diagram surface. BizTalk Mapper also uses COM categories to catalog available functoids.

We cannot eliminate the script entirely in favor of a COM object either. BizTalk Mapper pastes the script into an XSLT transformation. Although XSLT transformations could access COM objects, BizTalk Mapper favors scripting.

Script Implementation

BizTalk Mapper supports VBScript and JScript. Listing 18.1 has the JScript implementation of the `Selector` functoid. The ATL implementation will contain a function that returns this script as a string later in the chapter.

LISTING 18.1 JScript Implementation for `Selector`

```
function Selector ( j, val1, val2 )
{
    try
    {
        // Normalize the various forms of the input to an integer
        switch (j.constructor) // let's check the type
        {
           case Number:  // make sure any number is integer
                j = Math.floor(j); // e.g., use 1 if have 1.1
                break;
           case Boolean: // use 1 for true and 2 for false
                j = j ? 1 : 2;
                break;
           case String: // string could hold bool or number
                switch (j.toUpperCase())
                {
                     case "TRUE": j = 1; break;
                     case "FALSE": j = 2; break;
                     default: j = Math.floor(parseInt(j)); break;
                }
                break;
           default:
                j = 0; // flag error with invalid index
                break;
        }

        // return the selected value, if any
    return eval('val' + j);
    }
    catch ( x )
```

LISTING 18.1 continued

```
    {
    }
    return ""; // error return
}
```

The implementation starts by checking the type of the first argument. The task is to normalize any noninteger into an integer index. Per the design specification earlier, boolean values use index 1 for true and index 2 for false. In the case of a string, we look for a boolean or number in the string.

This implementation assumes three parameters. In general, there can be many parameters. Later, we will implement a method on `IFunctoid` to return the script given a specific number of parameters. The script modification is only in the function's parameter list. Simple inspection will reveal how simple this extension is.

ATL Shell Implementation

The first step in the COM implementation of the functoid is making an ATL shell. The shell will contain a fully compilable C++ project with a sample implementation for `IFunctoid`. We assume the latest release of Visual Studio 6, which is SP5.

First, install a custom ATL Object Wizard in two simple steps. Locate the folder `ATL Object Wizards` in the sample code accompanying this book. In that folder is a `.reg` file and a folder named `BizTalk Unleashed`. Merge the Registry settings file by right-clicking it and selecting Merge or by double-clicking the file. Next, copy the entire `BizTalk Unleashed` folder to the Visual C++ template folder, typically at `C:\Program Files\Microsoft Visual Studio\Common\MSDev98\Template\ATL`. The result should place a `BizTalk Unleashed` folder directly under the `Common\MSDDev98\Template\ATL` folder. This step actually installs three ATL Object Wizards. The other two are needed later in this chapter.

The next step is to create an empty ATL project. Launch Visual Studio 6. Select File, New from the menu and select ATL COM App Wizard from the Projects tab. Enter **`SelectorFunctoid`** in the Project Name edit box and fill in the Location edit box to some suitable directory. Click OK. Click Finish on the next screen and then click OK on the next.

Next, run the ATL Object Wizard as follows. Select Insert, New ATL Object from the menu. Select BizTalk Unleashed in the Category list box and Custom Functoid in the Objects list box as shown in Figure 18.5. Click Next. Enter **`Selector`** in the Short Name list box. Change the `ProgID` to `BizTalkUnleashed.SelectorFunctoid`. Click OK.

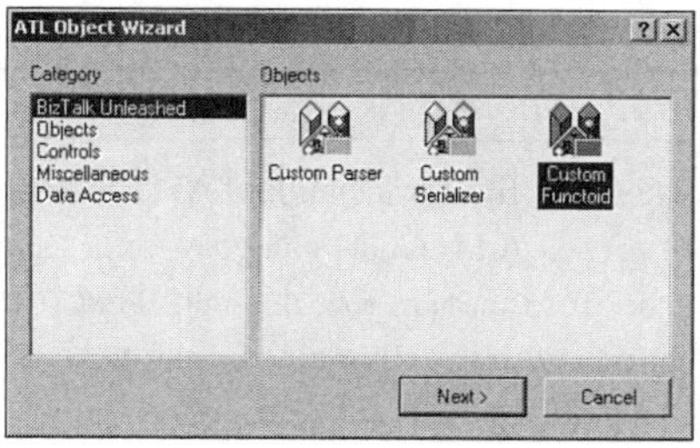

FIGURE 18.5
ATL Object Wizard for a custom functoid

Tip

If there are no choices for BizTalk Unleashed and Custom Functoid, then the install of the ATL Object Wizard did not complete. Retry and confirm each step.

The custom functoid implementation in ATL is complete. We will examine and extend the implementation in the section "Adding Custom Functionality."

Before compiling, confirm that the include directory for the BizTalk SDK is available to your project. Select Tools, Options from the menu. On the Directories tab, select Include Files in the Show Directories For list box. Add the BizTalk SDK include path, typically found at `C:\Program Files\Microsoft BizTalk Server\SDK\Include`. Click OK.

Also, confirm that C++ Exception Handling is enabled for your project. Select Project, Settings from the menu. Select All Configurations in the Settings For list box. Select C++ Language in the Category combo box on the C++ tab. Check Enable Exception Handling and click OK.

Build the project by selecting Build, Rebuild All from the menu. The build should complete with no errors, and the COM registration of the new functoid should succeed.

To test, launch the BizTalk Mapper. Open any map. To use a stock map, select File, Retrieve from WebDAV and select any of the standard ones Microsoft provides. Show the Functoid Palette by selecting View, Functoid Palette from the menu. On the tool window for the palette, navigate to the last tab, labeled Advanced. There should be two blank functoids.

Understanding the ATL Shell Implementation

Table 18.3 shows the actions that the ATL Object Wizard took on our project. Note that the sample files with this chapter match the names of the files in the table. The description of each file varies somewhat because the sample files are the complete implementation rather than the starter files generated by the wizard.

TABLE 18.3 ATL Object Wizard Actions for Functoids

Project File	*Wizard Action*
`Selector.h`	Created this file for a standard ATL declaration of a coclass, `CSelector`. Adds COM category map, `IFunctoidImpl.h`, `IFunctoidDispatchImpl`, `DECLARE_FUNCTOID_MAP()`, and two functions with the signature format `BSTR f(long)`.
`Selector.cpp`	Created this file for a standard implementation of the coclass `CSelector`. Adds the `BEGIN_FUNCTOID_MAP` macro and two functions with the signature format `BSTR f(long)`.
`SelectorFunctoid.idl`	Added to this project IDL file. Uses `IFunctoid` from the import of the BizTalk SDK file `functoid.idl`.
`Selector.rgs`	Created this file for standard COM registration.
`IFunctoidImpl.h`	Helper code provided by the wizard. Contains functoid map macros and the ATL-compliant class `IFunctoidDispatchImpl`.
`Functoid.bmp`	16×16 image used for the Functoid Palette in BizTalk Mapper.
`FunctoidBlanks.bmp`	Vector of 16×16 images. Each one matches the background color and 3D shading of the BizTalk Mapper built-in functoids. Helps create images matching the Mapper's color scheme.
`Resource.h` `SelectorFunctoid.rc`	Updated for the two bitmaps and a Registry resource.

We will explore the implementation in full detail as we add functionality specific to the `Selector` example designed earlier. For now, we will build an intuition by examining elements that directly correspond to the BizTalk Mapper GUI.

The wizard uses a map-based implementation commonly found in ATL. The idea is to use metadata to drive an interface implementation. To define the metadata, macros give a human readable format. These macros usually populate internal data structures of the class. For example, the functoid map in Listing 18.2 shows the metadata for two custom functoids.

LISTING 18.2 Functoid Map (`Selector.cpp`)

```
BEGIN_FUNCTOID_MAP(CSelector, _VERSION, FUNCTOID_FIRST_USER_FUNCID)
   BEGIN_FUNCTOID(L"Selector #1", FUNC_CATEGORY_UNKNOWN)
        FUNCTOID_TOOLTIP(L"Custom functoid with exactly 3 input params.")
        FUNCTOID_BITMAP(IDB_FUNCTOID_SELECTOR)
        FUNCTOID_OUT(CONNECT_TYPE_ALL)
```

LISTING 18.2 continued

```
        FUNCTOID_IN(CONNECT_TYPE_ALL_EXCEPT_RECORD)
        FUNCTOID_IN(CONNECT_TYPE_ALL_EXCEPT_RECORD)
        FUNCTOID_IN(CONNECT_TYPE_ALL_EXCEPT_RECORD)
        FUNCTOID_IMPL(SCRIPT_CATEGORY_JSCRIPT, GetFunctoidImpl1)
    END_FUNCTOID
    BEGIN_FUNCTOID(L"Selector #2", FUNC_CATEGORY_UNKNOWN)
        FUNCTOID_TOOLTIP(L"Custom functoid with at least 1 input param.")
        FUNCTOID_BITMAP(IDB_FUNCTOID_SELECTOR)
        FUNCTOID_OUT(CONNECT_TYPE_ALL)
        FUNCTOID_IN(CONNECT_TYPE_ALL_EXCEPT_RECORD)
        FUNCTOID_IN_OPTIONAL(CONNECT_TYPE_ALL_EXCEPT_RECORD)
        FUNCTOID_IMPL(SCRIPT_CATEGORY_VBSCRIPT, GetFunctoidImpl2)
    END_FUNCTOID
END_FUNCTOID_MAP
```

To visualize how some of the metadata gets used, return to BizTalk Mapper. On the Advanced tab of the Functoid Palette are two custom functoids with blank icons, as shown in Figure 18.6. Each one corresponds to a `BEGIN_FUNCTOID/END_FUNCTOID` pair in the map. The exact position of the blank icons might vary from Figure 18.6.

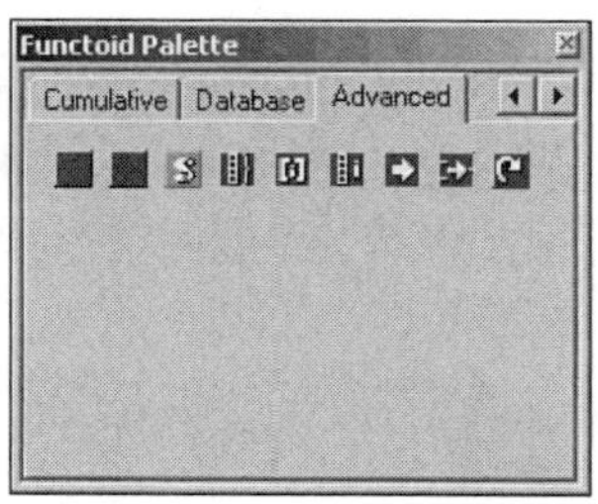

FIGURE 18.6
Two new functoids on the Advanced tab.

Hover the mouse above one of the blank icons on the palette until a ToolTip appears as in Figure 18.7. It has the form "name: description". Notice that the names and descriptions in BizTalk Mapper appear in the `BEGIN_FUNCTOID` and `FUNCTOID_TOOLTIP` macros shown in Listing 18.2.

Both functoids have the same blank image. The `FUNCTOID_BITMAP` macros shown previously also have the same `IDB_FUNCTOID_SELECTOR` resource ID. Check the project resources to find that the bitmap matches the image in BizTalk Mapper.

In BizTalk Mapper, drop the first functoid onto the Mapper surface. Double-click it on the Mapper surface to show a property sheet. On the General tab, notice that exactly three parameters are allowed. Manually add three constants, as in Figure 18.8. In the previous macros, the first functoid also has exactly three `FUNCTOID_IN` macros.

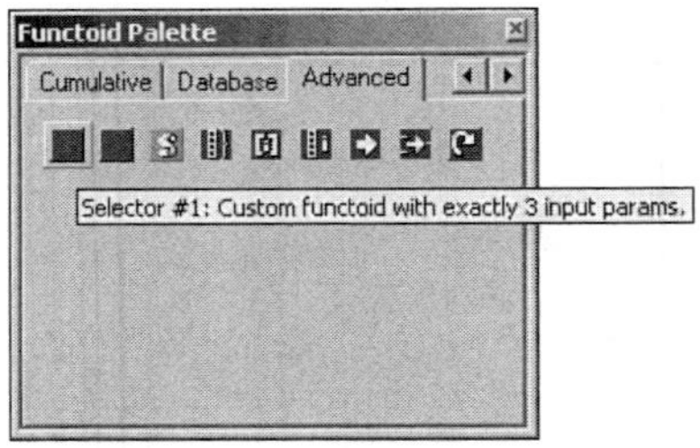

FIGURE 18.7
Functoid ToolTip.

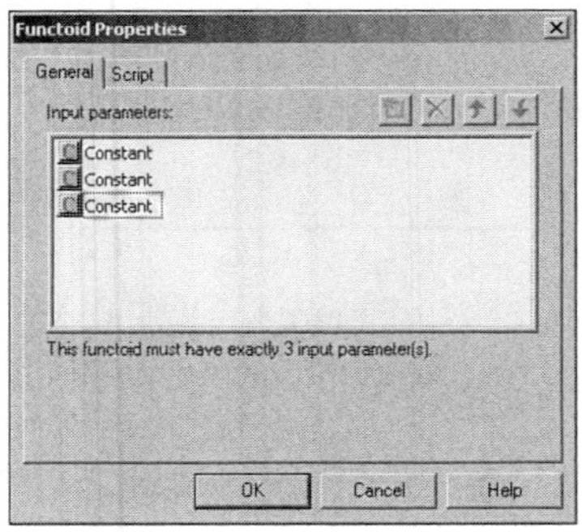

FIGURE 18.8
Functoid with exactly three input parameters.

Back in BizTalk Mapper, the Script tab has the JScript implementation shown in Figure 18.9. In the previous macros, the `FUNCTOID_IMPL` macro identifies JScript as the language and gives the name of the `CSelector` member function that calculates and returns JScript as a string.

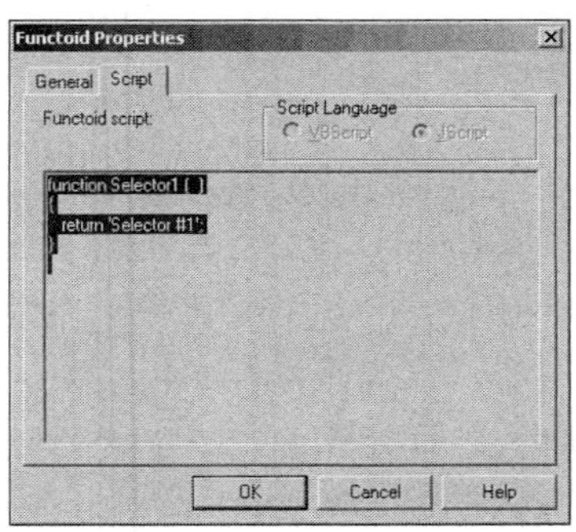

FIGURE 18.9
Functoid script implementation.

Repeat the steps for the second functoid. The differences here are the use of VBScript and a variable number of input parameters. In the previous macros for the second functoid, the `FUNCTOID_IMPL` macro references VBScript and a second `CSelector` member function. There is also only one `FUNCTOID_IN` macro for the one required input parameter. The macro `FUNCTOID_IN_OPTIONAL` flags that any number of additional parameters is valid.

Adding Custom Functionality

We are ready to add the specifics of the `Selector` functoid to the implementation. In the process, we will examine the map-based implementation in detail.

BEGIN_FUNCTOID_MAP / END_FUNCTOID_MAP

These two macros delimit the start and end of the functoid map.

```
BEGIN_FUNCTOID_MAP(CSelector, _VERSION, FUNCTOID_FIRST_USER_FUNCID)
...
END_FUNCTOID_MAP
```

`BEGIN_FUNCTOID_MAP` has three arguments. The first argument is the name of the C++ class implementing the COM coclass. The second argument is the integer version to report to BizTalk Mapper. The last argument is the `FUNCID` for the first functoid in the map.

Each functoid must have a unique id, or `FUNCID`. BizTalk reserves IDs 0 to 1000 so that the first available ID for user-defined functoids is 1001, the value of `FUNCTOID_FIRST_USER_ID`. `IFunctoidDispatchImpl` assigns `FUNCIDs` F, F+1, F+2, and so on to each of the functoids in the map where F is the last argument to `BEGIN_FUNCTOID_MAP`.

No changes are required here for the `Selector` implementation.

BEGIN_FUNCTOID/END_FUNCTOID

These two macros delimit the start and end of each functoid within the map. Use one pair of these macros for each functoid in an ATL implementation. The ATL Object Wizard produces two pairs. These macros must appear between the `BEGIN_FUNCTOID_MAP/END_FUNCTOID_MAP` pair.

The `Selector` implementation needs just one functoid. Delete the first one in the map because the second one better fits our remaining needs. To do so, delete from the first `BEGIN_FUNCTOID` to its matching `END_FUNCTOID`. Also, change the first parameter of the remaining `BEGIN_FUNCTOID` to `"Selector"`.

```
BEGIN_FUNCTOID(L"Selector", FUNC_CATEGORY_UNKNOWN)
...
END_FUNCTOID
```

`BEGIN_FUNCTOID` has two arguments. The first argument is the name BizTalk Mapper should use for the functoid in the GUI. This value must be a `wchar_t` based string.

The second argument is the function category. BizTalk Mapper uses the category to determine which tab on the Functoid Palette should contain the custom functoid. The value `FUNC_CATEGORY_UNKOWN` means the Advanced tab. Table 18.4 shows the categories assigned to each tab on the Functoid Palette. BizTalk does not allow you to create new tabs. For reference, the table also has what functoids BizTalk provides by default in each category.

TABLE 18.4 Functoid Categories on Tool Palette

Tab	*Category Value*	*BizTalk Functoids*
String	`FUNC_CATEGORY_STRING`	Find, Left, Lowercase, Right, Length, Extract, Concatenate, Left Trim, Right Trim, Uppercase
Mathematical	`FUNC_CATEGORY_MATH`	Absolute Value, Integer, Max, Min, Modulo, Round, Square Root, Add, Subtract, Multiply, Divide
Logical	`FUNC_CATEGORY_BOOLEAN`	Greater, GreaterEqual, Less, LessEqual, Equal, NotEqual, IsString, IsDate, IsNumeric, Or, And, Existence
Date/Time	`FUNC_CATEGORY_DATETIME_FMT`	Add Days, Date, Time, Date and Time
Conversion	`FUNC_CATEGORY_DATACONV`	ASCII from Char, Char from ASCII, Hex, Octal
Scientific	`FUNC_CATEGORY_SCIENTIFIC`	Arc Tangent, Cosine, Sine, Tangent, Natural Exp, Natural Log, Exp, Log, X^Y, X Log Y
Cumulative	`FUNC_CATEGORY_CUMULATIVE`	Sum, Average, Group Min, Group Max, Group Concatenate
Database	* `FUNC_CATEGORY_DBLOOKUP`	Database Lookup, Error Return
	* `FUNC_CATEGORY_DBEXTRACT`	Value Extractor
Advanced	`FUNC_CATEGORY_SCRIPTER`	Scripting
	`FUNC_CATEGORY_INDEX`	Index
	`FUNC_CATEGORY_UNKNOWN`	(none)
	** `FUNC_CATEGORY_COUNT`	Record Count
	** `FUNC_CATEGORY_VALUE_MAPPING`	Value Mapping, Value Mapping Flattening
	** `FUNC_CATEGORY_LOOPING`	Looping
	** `FUNC_CATEGORY_ITERATION`	Iteration

** BizTalk 2002 recommends not using the Database tab.*

*** Not supported in BizTalk 2002.*

These category values are from the enum `FUNC_CATEGORY` from the BizTalk SDK.

FUNCTOID_TOOLTIP

This macro specifies the ToolTip for BizTalk Mapper to use for a functoid. This macro must appear between a BEGIN_FUNCTOID/END_FUNCTOID pair exactly once.

The Selector implementation needs to adjust the ToolTip from the generic one produced by the ATL Object Wizard. Change the macro to read as follows:

```
FUNCTOID_TOOLTIP(L"Select one value from a list of values.")
```

FUNCTOID_TOOLTIP has one argument, and it must be a wchar_t based string. The ToolTip is typically a one-line description. Refer to Table 18.2 for a list of sample ToolTips used by BizTalk.

FUNCTOID_BITMAP

This macro specifies the resource ID of an image for a functoid. BizTalk Mapper will use the image on the Functoid Palette. This macro must appear between a BEGIN_FUNCTOID/END_FUNCTOID pair exactly once.

The Selector implementation does not need to modify this entry:

```
FUNCTOID_BITMAP(IDB_FUNCTOID_SELECTOR)
```

The resource ID IDB_FUNCTOID_SELECTOR refers to a blank image. The image is 16×16 and matches the color scheme of the icons on the Advanced tab.

There are no requirements in the BizTalk documentation for matching the color scheme of images used by BizTalk. If you elect to follow the color scheme, the image FunctoidBlanks.bmp provides blanks for all tabs used in BizTalk Mapper. The ATL Object Wizard adds this image for convenience. Each blank follows the background color and 3D shading colors used by BizTalk Mapper. Refer to Table 18.2 for a list of the RGB colors of each tab.

FUNCTOID_IN and FUNCTOID_IN_OPTIONAL

These macros specify input parameters for a functoid. These macros must appear between a BEGIN_FUNCTOID/END_FUNCTOID pair.

FUNCTOID_IN works in concert with FUNCTOID_IN_OPTIONAL. Use FUNCTOID_IN to specify required input parameters. Use FUNCTOID_IN_OPTIONAL to specify that a variable number of parameters is allowed. For example, if a functoid has exactly two parameters, use FUNCTOID_IN twice. If a functoid has at least two parameters, then use FUNCTOID_IN twice and FUNCTOID_IN_OPTIONAL once.

The `Selector` implementation has one or more input parameters. The ATL Object Wizard output is exactly what we require.

```
FUNCTOID_IN(CONNECT_TYPE_ALL_EXCEPT_RECORD)
FUNCTOID_IN_OPTIONAL(CONNECT_TYPE_ALL_EXCEPT_RECORD)
```

Both macros have a single input parameter. It is the bitwise-or of a set of connection flags. Each flag specifies to BizTalk Mapper a diagram element that is valid to connect to the functoid as the input parameter. The value `CONNECT_TYPE_ALL_EXCEPT_RECORD` means that any diagram element can serve as the input to the functoid except the non-leaf nodes, also known as *records*, in the source document.

`FUNCTOID_IN_OPTIONAL` works the same as `FUNCTOID_IN` except that it specifies one set of connection flags for all optional parameters. Note that the BizTalk SDK does not require that all optional parameters have the same flags. Rather, the map-based implementation provided by this book has the limitation for simplicity.

In general, BizTalk Mapper must decide whether a line may connect two elements on the diagram. Each element carries a set of connection flags. A connection is allowed if there is a non-empty intersection between the two sets of flags. These lines specify the flow of information through input and output parameters.

Table 18.5 shows which diagram elements each connection flag specifies.

TABLE 18.5 Diagram Elements for Each Connection Flag

Connection Flag	*Diagram Elements Specified*
`CONNECT_TYPE_NONE`	No element.
`CONNECT_TYPE_FIELD`	Leaf nodes in the document specification. In XML, leaf nodes are attributes and tags with no subtags.
`CONNECT_TYPE_RECORD`	Non-leaf nodes in the document specification. In XML, non-leaf nodes are tags that have subtags. Using this connection flag is meaningful only if the XML tag can have both subtags and values, such as text. This connection type for an input parameter, for example, means to input the tag's values, not its subtags.
`CONNECT_TYPE_RECORD_WITH_CONTENT`	Similar to `CONNECT_TYPE_RECORD`. The exact difference is not documented.

TABLE 18.5 continued

Connection Flag	*Diagram Elements Specified*
CONNECT_TYPE_XXX where XXX = STRING, MATH, SCIENTIFIC, DATACONV, DATETIME_FMT, BOOLEAN, SCRIPTER, COUNT, INDEX, CUMULATIVE, VALUE_MAPPING, LOOPING, ITERATION, DBLOOKUP, DBEXTRACT	Output from a functoid in category FUNC_CATEGORY_XXX. Example: CONNECT_TYPE_FUNC_STRING corresponds to output from functoid category FUNC_CATEGORY_STRING.
CONNECT_TYPE_ALL	All elements on the diagram.
CONNECT_TYPE_ALL_EXCEPT_RECORD	All elements on the diagram except non-leaf nodes.

These category values are from the enum `CONNECTION_TYPE` from the BizTalk SDK.

For example, to restrict an input parameter to accept data from leaf nodes in the document, mathematical functoids, and scientific functoids, use the bitwise-or of `CONNECT_TYPE_FIELD`, `CONNECT_TYPE_FUNC_MATH`, and `CONNECT_TYPE_SCIENTIFIC`. No other element will be allowed to connect to the functoid.

FUNCTOID_OUT

This macro specifies the output parameter for a functoid. A functoid must have exactly one output parameter.

`FUNCTOID_OUT` works identically to `FUNCTOID_IN` except that exactly one occurrence of `FUNCTOID_OUT` is required.

The `Selector` implementation uses the `FUNCTOID_OUT` macro provided by the ATL Object Wizard.

```
FUNCTOID_OUT(CONNECT_TYPE_ALL)
```

This macro means that connecting the output of the functoid to another element is not restricted at all by this functoid.

FUNCTOID_IMPL

This macro specifies the script-based implementation for the functoid. This macro must appear between a `BEGIN_FUNCTOID`/`END_FUNCTOID` pair exactly once.

The `Selector` implementation needs to adjust the script from the generic one produced by the ATL Object Wizard. Change the macro to read as follows:

```
FUNCTOID_IMPL(SCRIPT_CATEGORY_JSCRIPT, GetSelectorImpl)
```

FUNCTOID_IMPL has two arguments. The first argument specifies the type of script. Use the value SCRIPT_CATEGORY_JSCRIPT or SCRIPT_CATEGORY_VBSCRIPT from the enum SCRIPT_CATEGORY in the BizTalk SDK. That enum also has the value SCRIPT_CATEGORY_XSLSCRIPT, which is currently not supported.

The second argument is a member function of CSelector. Strictly speaking, it is a member function of the class name passed as the first argument to the BEGIN_FUNCTOID_MAP macro. To complete this change started previously, rename the member function CSelector::GetFunctoidImpl1 to CSelector::GetSelectorImpl in both the .h file and .cpp file. At the same time, delete the member function CSelector::GetFunctoidImpl2; it is no longer needed.

The signature of the function needs to be BSTR CSelector::GetSelectorImpl(long). The parameter to this function will be the number of actual parameters specified on the diagram for the functoid. The GetSelectorImpl() function can use that number to calculate a script specific to that number and return a string allocated by SysAllocString().

The JScript implementation appears earlier in the section "Script Implementation" and is incorporated in Listing 18.3. To complete the Selector implementation, replace the body of CSelector::GetSelectorImpl() with the JScript. Notice that the implementation uses the nParameters argument to format how many parameters the JScript function should take. Rebuild the project.

LISTING 18.3 Implementation of CSelector::GetSelectorImpl() (Selector.cpp)

```
BSTR CSelector::GetSelectorImpl ( long nParameters )
{
   // format function signature :  function Selector (j, val1, ..., valn)
   wchar_t wsz[4096];
   wcscpy(wsz, L"function Selector ( ");
   if (nParameters > 0) ::wcscat(wsz, L"j");
   for ( int i = 1;  i < nParameters;  ++ i )
      swprintf(wsz+::wcslen(wsz), L", val%d", i);
   wcscat(wsz, L" )\r\n");

   // append function body
   wcscat(wsz,
      L"{\n"
      L"    try\n"
      L"    {\n"
      L"        // Normalize the various forms of the input to an integer\n"
      L"        switch (j.constructor) // let's check the type\n"
      L"        {\n"
      L"            case Number:  // make sure any number is integer\n"
      L"                j = Math.floor(j); // e.g., use 1 if have 1.1\n"
```

LISTING 18.3 continued

```
        L"                  break;\n"
        L"              case Boolean: // use 1 for true and 2 for false\n"
        L"                  j = j ? 1 : 2;\n"
        L"                  break; \n"
        L"              case String: // string could hold bool or number\n"
        L"                  switch (j.toUpperCase()) \n"
        L"                  {\n"
        L"                      case \"TRUE\":  j = 1; break;\n"
        L"                      case \"FALSE\": j = 2; break;\n"
        L"                      default: j = Math.floor(parseInt(j)); break;\n"
        L"                   }\n'
        L"                   break;\n"
        L"              default:  \n"
        L"                  j = 0; // flag error with invalid index\n"
        L"                  break;\n"
        L"          }\n"
        L"          \n"
        L"          // return the selected value, if any\n"
        L"          return eval('val' + j);\n"
        L"      }\n"
        L"      catch ( x )\n"
        L"      {\n"
        L"      }\n"
        L"      return \"\"; // error return\n"
        L"}\n");
    return SysAllocString(wsz);
}
```

Debugging the Functoid

Debugging the functoid is a simple matter of running BizTalk Mapper under the debugger. Return to the Visual C++ IDE that has the project for the custom functoid. Select Project, Settings from the menu and select the Debug tab on the property page that opens. Select a debug configuration in the Settings For combo box. Enter the full path to `BIZMAP1.EXE` in the Executable for Debug Session edit box. The full path is typically `C:\Program Files\Microsoft BizTalk Server\XML Tools\BizMap1.EXE`. Click OK.

Start the Visual Studio debugger for the functoid project, and BizTalk Mapper launches. Breakpoints will fire inside the functoid component as you create a map and exercise the functoid.

Bear in mind that debugging the functoid does not actually debug the functoid's script. The debugger steps through the COM component. Debugging the script must be done separately outside the Visual C++ IDE.

Parser Design

In this section, we will design a custom parser that we will implement in the next section. To this point, we have covered the architecture of the BizTalk channel in which custom functoids, parsers, and serializers have a role. The preceding section implemented a custom functoid that assumes the data in the channel is already in an XML format. The next two sections will produce that XML format.

A parser operates generally as follows. It accepts from BizTalk a stream of data representing the raw data posted to the channel. The parser inspects the stream to identify whether it is in a format the parser can handle. If so, the parser decides whether the stream contains groups of documents or just a flat sequence of documents. The parser converts the raw format into documents and imposes grouping and document order.

A parser design requires the following specifications:

- Format of the non-XML data entering the channel
- Format of the XML data output by the parser
- Support for batching
- Support for correlation receipts
- Integration with document tracking

Format of Non-XML Data Entering the Channel

Data entering the channel is a non-XML format. For example, the FIX format for financial data mentioned earlier uses a `tag=value(delimiter)tag=value(delimiter)tag=value` format. For simplicity of demonstration, we will use an HTML form post that has the same structure. Here, the delimiter is the `&` symbol. The parser for this chapter will recognize four tag-value pairs.

```
broker=Alpha%20Financials&stock=ABC&quantity=10&minimum-price=5.00
```

To easily construct a document of this format, a simple HTML form suffices. The HTML form will submit a document directly into the BizTalk channel using a BizTalk HTTP receive function.

The non-XML format must have some identifiable signature. BizTalk will ask our parser to decide whether a block of data is in a format it recognizes. In practice, we will have to examine the data directly to find a suitable signature. For simplicity in our example, an efficient method for identification is a prefix. Our parser will expect the following prefix on the data:

```
schema=biztalk-unleashed-custom-parser-ch18
```

In general, BizTalk has an ordered sequence of parsers registered. Stock parsers ship for XML, EDIFACT, X12, and flat files. Whenever BizTalk receives a document, it passes an `IStream` for it to each of the parsers until one of them accepts. BizTalk then asks that parser to parse the document.

Format of XML Data Output by the Parser

The output of the parser is XML. Recall that a BizTalk channel has a document definition for inbound XML data. The parser output must match this definition.

The document definition for the custom parser in this chapter appears in Listing 18.4.

LISTING 18.4 XML Schema for Our Custom Parser (`BrokerItemSchema.xml`)

```
<xdr:Schema name="broker-item"
            xmlns:xdr="urn:schemas-microsoft-com:xml-data"
            xmlns:dt="urn:schemas-microsoft-com:datatypes">
   <xdr:ElementType name="broker"    content="textOnly" model="closed"
➥ dt:type="string"/>
   <xdr:ElementType name="stock"     content="textOnly" model="closed"
➥ dt:type="string"/>
   <xdr:ElementType name="quantity"  content="textOnly" model="closed"
➥ dt:type="int"/>
   <xdr:ElementType name="min-price" content="textOnly" model="closed"
➥ dt:type="number"/>
   <xdr:ElementType name="broker-item" content="eltOnly" model="closed">
      <xdr:element type="broker"    maxOccurs="1" minOccurs="0" />
      <xdr:element type="stock"     maxOccurs="1" minOccurs="0" />
      <xdr:element type="quantity"  maxOccurs="1" minOccurs="0" />
      <xdr:element type="min-price" maxOccurs="1" minOccurs="0" />
   </xdr:ElementType>
</xdr:Schema>
```

The non-XML data given earlier is repeated here for reference.

```
broker=Alpha%20Financials&stock=ABC&quantity=10&minimum-price=5.00
```

The corresponding XML document meeting the document definition in Listing 18.4 appears in Listing 18.5.

LISTING 18.5 Sample XML for Our Custom Parser (`SampleBrokerItem.xml`)

```
<broker-item>
   <broker>Alpha Financials</broker>
   <stock>ABC</stock>
   <quantity>10</quantity>
   <min-price>5.00</min-price>
</broker-item>
```

An important design consideration is whether to make the document definition public. If it is made public, then there is an immediate benefit. The channel can accept both XML and non-XML versions for the document. For example, there is an emerging XML standard for FIX financial data format called FIXML. With a parser that outputs FIXML, the BizTalk channel can accept both FIX and FIXML documents. This setup allows old clients to submit FIX and newer clients to submit FIXML. No additional work is required.

Support for Batching

Batching is a common method for submitting data. The parser design must accommodate batching. In general, the parser receives an *interchange*. An interchange is a BizTalk term for a sequence of documents or a sequence of *document groups*. A document group is itself a sequence of documents related by some grouping criteria such as the source of the document. Groups cannot contain groups. If the parser does not support batching, then it handles a document sequence of length one:

Document Sequence: D_1, D_2, D_3

Group Sequence: $G_1 (D_{11}, D_{12}, D_{13}), G_2 (D_{21}, D_{22}), G_3 (D_{31}, D_{32}, D_{33}, D_{34})$

BizTalk asks the parser whether it supports groups. If so, BizTalk asks the parser for group boundaries and allows group-level information to be identified.

Documents can appear in the input in any order, and documents from different groups can interleave. However, the unparsed form of a document must be contiguous in the input. Note that empty groups and empty document sequences are not allowed.

The parser in this chapter supports batching with document groups. Recall that each document is a single form post. Multiple form posts will be submitted at one time. Listing 18.6 has an example batch submission.

LISTING 18.6 Sample Batch Submission (`SampleBatchSubmit.txt`)

```
schema=biztalk-unleashed-custom-parser-ch18
broker=Delta&stock=ABC&quantity=1000&min-price=25.00
broker=Beta&stock=JKL&quantity=1500&min-price=35.00
broker=Alpha&stock=DEF&quantity=2500&min-price=20.00
broker=Beta&stock=WXYZ&quantity=2500&min-price=100.00
broker=Delta&stock=STUV&quantity=50&min-price=35.00
```

Grouping is done on the `broker` tag. This example has three groups: Delta, Beta, and Alpha. The Delta and Beta groups have two documents, and the Alpha group has one document.

Support for Correlation Receipts

The parser has the option of participating in BizTalk's mechanism for issuing receipts for documents received. For XML-based documents, BizTalk can automatically generate receipts using its guaranteed messaging feature. For other documents, such as those received by a channel with a custom parser, a separate BizTalk channel is required for sending receipts.

To set up a receipt channel, create a new channel and provide document definitions and a map between them. BizTalk has a standard definition for the inbound receipt although the document definition for the outbound receipt format must adhere to the expectations of the receiver of the receipt, such as a trading partner. The final step is to create a COM component that implements the interface `IBizTalkCorrelation`. BizTalk asks the custom parser for the COM `ProgID` of this COM component.

The parser in this chapter will not issue receipts.

Integration with Document Tracking

The parser has the option of integrating with BizTalk's Document Tracking feature. BizTalk provides an HTML application, `http://localhost/BizTalkTracking`. Replace `localhost` with the name of the appropriate machine on your network.

Document Tracking can log all inbound and outbound documents for a channel in both the XML and non-XML formats. User-defined fields can be tracked explicitly. Tracking setup is done on a per-channel basis in the BizTalk Messaging Manager.

The parser in this book will not explore document tracking.

Parser Implementation

In this section, we implement the parser design from the preceding section using C++ and ATL. Unlike the functoid implementation earlier, there is not a method for implementing the parser using Visual Basic. The COM interface uses types, such as `IStream`, not accessible from Visual Basic.

The parser implementation comprises the following items:

- BizTalk channel configuration
- A COM coclass implementing `IBizTalkParserComponent`

The COM coclass provides the following:

- Identification—Given a data stream, test whether it is the input format for the parser.
- Properties—Get organization identifiers, codepages, and other properties.
- Group separation—Identify grouping boundaries.
- Document separation—Identify document boundaries.

We will use an HTML application for a test harness.

Configuring a Channel for a Custom Parser

Adapting the diagram in Figure 18.4, Figure 18.10 shows the channel we will configure.

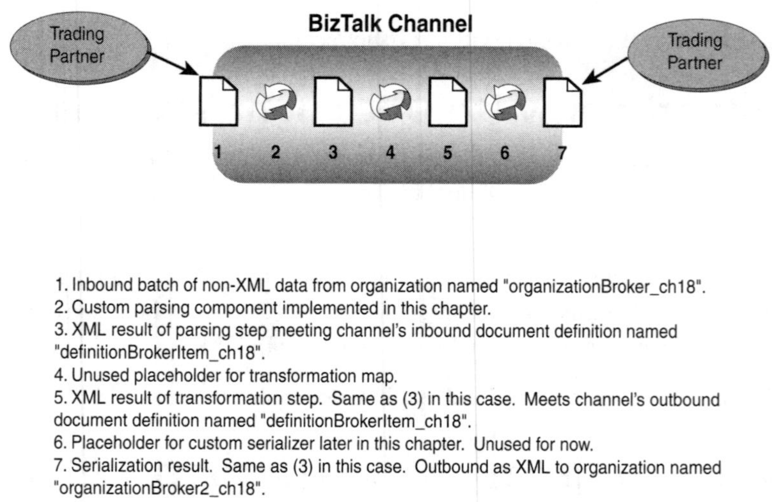

FIGURE 18.10 *Channel configuration for our custom parser.*

Start the BizTalk Messaging Manager.

Create an organization to represent the broker that submits the data. xSelect File, New, Organization from the menu and name it `organizationBroker_ch18`. In the comment field, use `This organization submits batch data in a non-XML format via an http form post monitored by a BizTalk http receive function`. Click OK.

Create a second organization named `organizationBroker2_ch18` with the comments `This organization receives items posted by the original broker.`

Create a document definition for the XML we will generate in the parser. Select File, New, Document Definition and name it `definitionBrokerItem_ch18`. Check the

Document Specification check box and select the file BrokerItemSchema.xml from this chapter's sample files. You will need to copy this file to the BizTalk's WebDAV Repository first. This Repository is typically at C:\Program Files\Microsoft BizTalk Server\BizTalkServerRepository\DocSpecs.

Next, create an e-mail port to the second organization. First we have to identify the SMTP host. Start BizTalk Server Administration. Open the node Microsoft BizTalk Server 2002, right-click BizTalk Server Group node, and select Properties. On the General tab, enter the name of a machine on your network that will be the SMTP host for sending e-mail. Any machine with IIS installed can be the SMTP host using the Virtual SMTP Server feature, even if the machine is not connected to a network. Click OK.

To create the e-mail port, or file port, select File, New, Messaging Port, To An Organization from the menu in the Messaging Manager, and name it portBroker2_ch18 with the comments This port delivers by e-mail or file to the second broker. Click Next. Browse for the organization named organizationBroker2_ch18 created previously. Browse for the Primary Transport and select SMTP or File. For SMTP, enter mailto:yourname@yourdomain.com in both the Address and Return e-mail address boxes. For File, enter an output filename with %tracking_id% embedded in it to guarantee a unique file. Click OK. Click Next. Click Next again accepting all defaults for Envelope Information. Check the Create a Channel for This Messaging Port check box and select From an Organization for the channel type. Click Finish.

The New Channel Wizard will now auto-launch. Name the new channel channelBroker_ch18 with comments This channel accepts an inbound batch of documents from a broker organization via an HTTP Receive Function. Click Next. Select the Open Source radio button. Click Next. Browse for the inbound document definition definitionBrokerItem_ch18 created previously. Click Next. Browse for the same output document definition definitionBrokerItem_ch18. Click Next. Click Next again, accepting all defaults for the Document Logging page. Click Finish, accepting all defaults for the Advanced Configuration page.

If you selected an e-mail port in the preceding steps, you must also enable e-mail relaying. By default, the Virtual SMTP Server will not allow e-mail to relay to external domains such as yahoo.com. Start Internet Services Manager from Administrative Tools. Open the node for the machine selected as the SMTP host earlier. Right-click Default SMTP Virtual Server and select Properties. On the Access tab, click the Relay button. Make sure that the domain for your e-mail address is included. A simple way is to select the All Except the List Below radio button and use an empty list. Click OK and then click OK again.

Caution

A caveat about the e-mail port is worth mentioning. During debugging, the system became unstable with exceptions in `MSCIS.EXE` before the first method in the parser component was invoked. Switching to the file port during debugging resolved the issue. Outside the debugger, using the e-mail port worked reliably.

Configuring a Test Harness for the Custom Parser

For a test harness, we need an HTML application and an HTTP receive function. The HTML application performs an HTTP Post, and the HTTP receive function routes the posted data to the channel with our custom parser.

Figure 18.11 shows the test harness supplied with this chapter. It allows us to queue items and submit them in one batch.

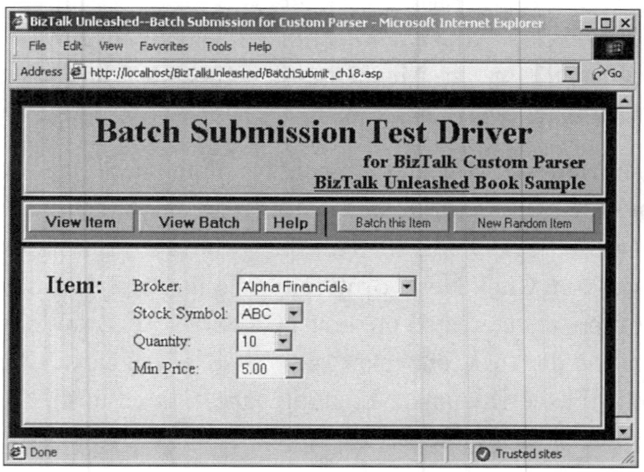

FIGURE 18.11
Sample test harness.

To install this test harness, first create a virtual directory in IIS or select an existing one for testing purposes. To create one, launch Internet Services Manager. Open the node for your computer, right-click Default Web Site, and select New, Virtual Directory from the menu. Follow the wizard's instructions. When the wizard asks for an alias, use `BizTalkUnleashed`. The virtual directory must include Execute permissions. After the directory is created, right-click its node and select Properties. On the Virtual Directory tab, select High (Isolated) from the Application Protection combo box. Click OK. This protection setting is only necessary to match the rest of the following steps. The following steps assume `http://localhost/BizTalkUnleashed/` as the virtual directory.

Copy two files into the virtual directory. From the chapter samples, copy `batchsubmit_ch18.asp`. From the BizTalk install, copy `BizTalkHTTPReceive.dll`, typically found in `C:\Program Files\Microsoft BizTalk Server\HTTP Receive`.

To configure the HTTP receive function, start BizTalk Server Administration. Open the node Microsoft BizTalk Server 2002, open the BizTalk Server Group node, and select Receive Functions. Select Action, New, HTTP Receive Function from the menu. In the dialog that opens, set the name to `receiveBatchSubmit_ch18` and the comment to `This HTTP Receive Function accepts a batch submission of non-XML data and forwards it to a channel with a custom parser`. Set the Server and Virtual Directory to match the virtual directory we created previously. For example, the virtual directory entry might read `/BizTalkUnleashed/BizTalkHTTPReceive.dll`. Check the check box for returning a correlation token. Select an asynchronous submission to BizTalk. Click the Advanced button. Choose Open Source in the Openness combo box. Specify the inbound channel as `channelBroker_ch18` that we created previously. Click OK. Then click OK again.

The final step is to grant the HTTP receive function permission to access BizTalk in the context of IIS. Launch Component Services in Administrative Tools (on the Control Panel). Open the path `Component Services\Computers\My Computer\COM+ Applications`, right-click the node for your virtual directory, and select Properties. For example, the name might be `IIS-{Default Web Site//Root/BizTalkUnleashed}`. We created this COM+ application implicitly when we selected High (Isolated) for the Application Protection setting for our virtual directory. On the Identity tab, fill in the user ID and password for the BizTalk Service account created during installation and click OK. Click Yes when a warning dialog pops up double-checking that you know what you are doing. To discover the user ID for the BizTalk Service account, launch Services from Administrative Tools. Open the Services (local) node and select the entry for BizTalk Messaging Service. The user ID needed here is in the column Log On As.

To confirm that the test harness is configured properly, launch `http://localhost/BizTalkUnleashed/batchsubmit_ch18.asp`. Click the View Batch button. Click the Add Sample button. Notice that each item in the batch is in the HTTP Form Post syntax per the format in the Parser Design section earlier in this chapter. Figure 18.12 shows the results.

Click the Submit Batch button to post over HTTP the entire batch to the HTTP receive function we configured previously. Our configuration is ready if we get a message box showing a correlation identifier for the submission. The message will have an XML format as in Figure 18.13.

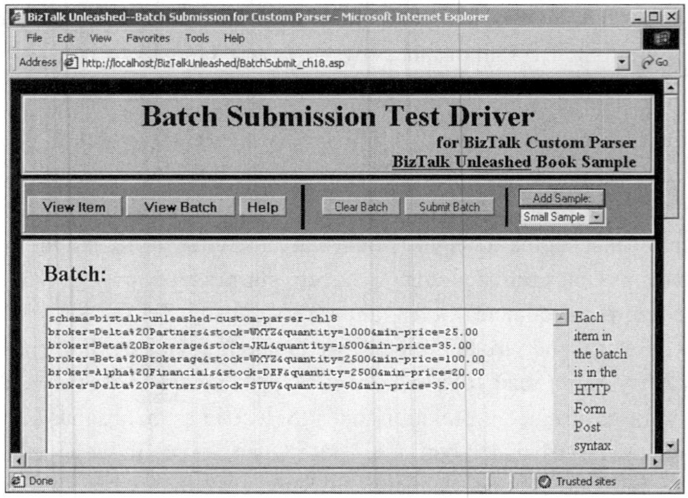

FIGURE 18.12
Test driver before submit.

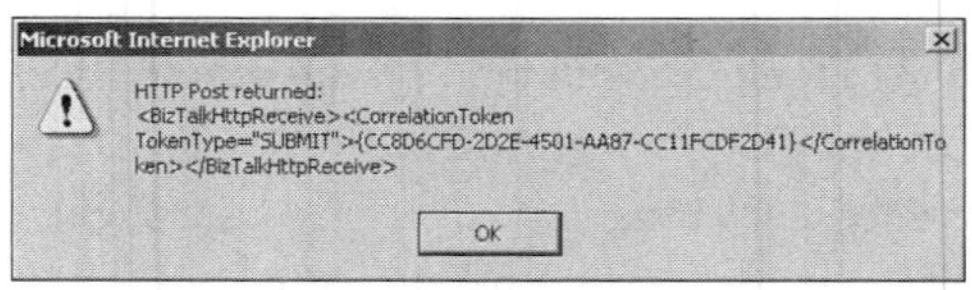

FIGURE 18.13
Message indicating successful batch submit.

No parser is installed yet so the submission should fail inside BizTalk. To confirm, launch BizTalk Server Administration, and open the paths `\Event Viewer (local)\Application` and `\Microsoft BizTalk Server 2002\BizTalk Server Group\Queues\Suspended Queue`. The document state shows as Parsing, and the error description shows as Parsing Failure. To see the document data, right-click the item in the Suspended Queue and select View Interchange. Figure 18.14 shows the results.

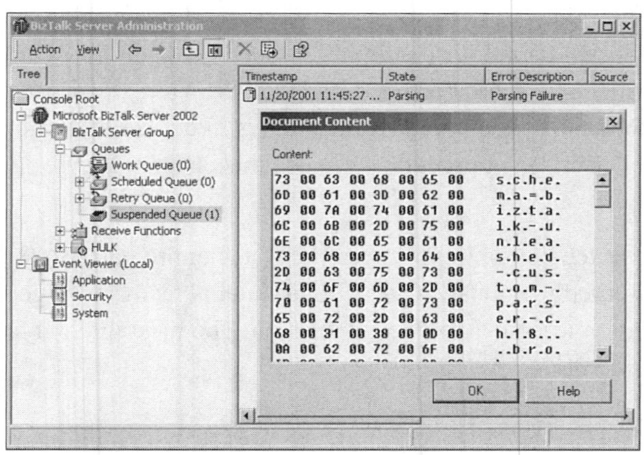

FIGURE 18.14
Parsing failure is expected at this point.

In the event log, there is an error entry. Double-click it to see a description that no parser could recognize the data.

To test the e-mail port or file port for the channel's outbound data, we need to post a valid XML document to the channel. To do so, return to the test driver. Replace the contents of the text box for the batch data with XML satisfying the schema assigned to this channel, such as in Listing 18.5 previously in this chapter in the section "Format of XML Data Output by the Parser." The XML from Listing 18.5 is repeated here for reference:

```
<broker-item>
   <broker>Alpha Financials</broker>
   <stock>ABC</stock>
   <quantity>10</quantity>
   <min-price>5.00</min-price>
</broker-item>
```

Click Submit Batch again. The document should pass the validation test for the schema and pass through the channel arriving by e-mail or file depending on the port selection earlier. If you selected an e-mail port, an e-mail with the XML submitted should appear in your inbox. If your network connection is down, you can still confirm by checking the directory that holds queued e-mail messages. Typically, this directory is `C:\Inetpub\Mailroot\Queue`. Other directories under `Mailroot` could also contain the message if there is an SMTP configuration problem. If no message is found, then check BizTalk Server Administration for an item in the Suspend or Retry queue.

ATL Shell Implementation

The first step in the COM implementation of the parser is making an ATL shell. The shell will contain a fully compilable C++ project with a sample implementation for `IBizTalkParserComponent`. We assume the latest release of Visual Studio 6, which is SP5.

> **Note**
>
> A custom ATL Object Wizard should be available at this point. If you skipped ahead, then briefly return to the section "ATL Shell Implementation" for custom functoids. Follow the instructions for installing the ATL Object Wizards and return here.

Create an empty ATL project in Visual Studio 6 as follows. Select File, New from the menu and select ATL COM App Wizard from the Projects tab. Enter `FormPostBatchParser` in the Project Name edit box and fill in the Location edit box to some suitable directory. Click OK. Click Finish on the next screen and then click OK on the next.

Next, run the ATL Object Wizard as follows. Select Insert, New ATL Object from the menu. Select BizTalk Unleashed in the Category list box and Custom Parser in the Objects list box as shown in Figure 18.15. Click Next. Enter `FormPostParser` in the Short Name list box. Change the `ProgID` to `BizTalkUnleashed.FormPostBatchParser`. Click OK.

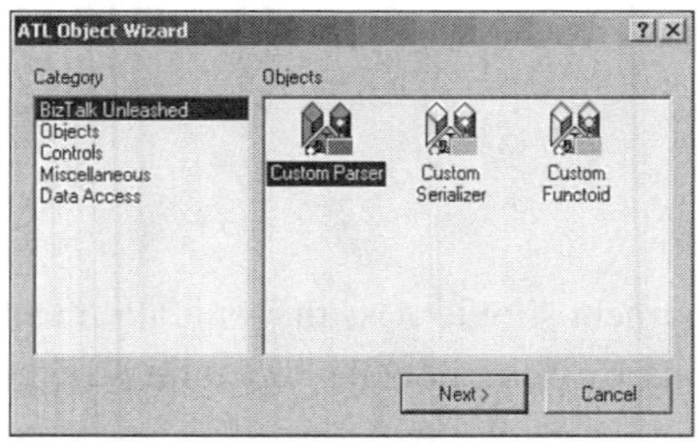

FIGURE 18.15
ATL Object Wizard for a custom parser.

> **Note**
>
> If there are no choices for BizTalk Unleashed and Custom Parser, then the install of the ATL Object Wizards did not complete. Please retry and confirm each step.

Table 18.6 shows the actions the ATL Object Wizard took on our project. Note that the sample files with this chapter match the names of the files in this table. The description of each file varies somewhat because the sample files are the complete implementation rather than the starter files generated by the wizard.

TABLE 18.6 ATL Object Wizard Actions for Parsers

Project File	*Wizard Action*
`FormPostParser.h`	Created this file for a standard ATL declaration of a coclass, `CFormPostParser`. Adds COM category map, BizTalk SDK includes, and `IBizTalkParserComponent`.
`FormPostParser.cpp`	Created this file for a standard implementation of the coclass `CFormPostParser`. Adds interface stubs with `ATLTRACE` statements including custom tracers.
`FormPostBatchParser.idl`	Added to this project IDL file. From BizTalk SDK file `BTSParserComps.idl`, uses `IBizTalkParserComponent`.

TABLE 18.6 continued

Project File	*Wizard Action*
`FormPostParser.rgs`	Created this file for standard COM registration.
`Resource.h`	Updated for the Registry resource.
`FormPostBatchParser.rc`	

The ATL Object Wizard forces `ThreadingModel=Both` regardless of the threading model selection in the wizard. Although this setting is not documented in BizTalk, the stock parsers shipped by BizTalk all have `ThreadingModel=Both`.

A shell implementation in ATL for the custom parser is complete. We will examine and extend the implementation later in the section "Adding Custom Functionality."

Before compiling, confirm that the include directory for the BizTalk SDK is available to your project. Select Tools, Options from the menu. On the Directories tab, select Include Files in the Show Directories For list box. Add the BizTalk SDK include path, typically found at `C:\Program Files\Microsoft BizTalk Server\SDK\Include`. Click OK.

Also, confirm that C++ Exception Handling is enabled for your project. Select Project, Settings from the menu. Select All Configurations in the Settings For list box. Select C++ Language in the Category combo box on the C++ tab. Check Enable Exception Handling and click OK.

Build the project by selecting Build, Rebuild All from the menu. The build should complete with no errors, and the COM registration of the new parser should succeed.

To see that BizTalk recognizes the new parser, start BizTalk Server Administration. Open the node Microsoft BizTalk Server 2002. Right-click BizTalk Server Group and select Properties. On the Parsers tab, there is the list of standard parsers provided by BizTalk. Click the Refresh button, and our new parser should appear, similar to Figure 18.16. Move our parser to the top of the list using the up arrow button. BizTalk will now call our parser first when it needs to identify and parse a data stream.

Tip

If the parser did not appear in the Parsers tab, then double-check that the registration succeeded during the build. BizTalk locates our component by checking the registration of all COM components. It looks for components with a specific COM category. Our ATL implementation provides that category using ATL's category map in `FormPostParser.h`.

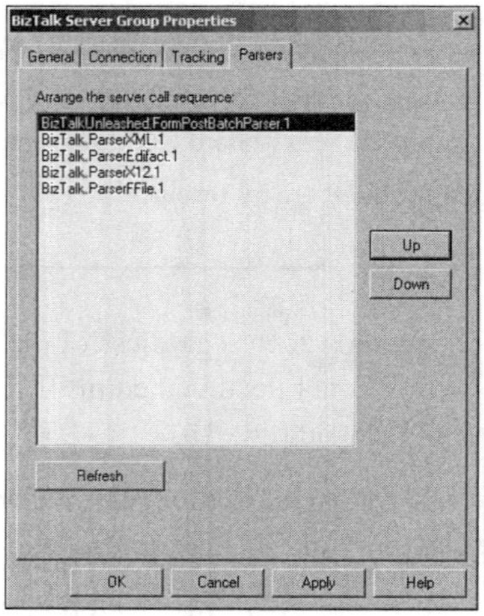

FIGURE 18.16
Parsers recognized by BizTalk.

Adding Custom Functionality

We are ready to add the specifics of the form post batch parser to the implementation. The completed parser is in the sample files. Unlike the custom functoid section, we will not incrementally change the ATL Object Wizard output. Rather, we will examine each function in the implementation in detail.

Interface Overview

The `IBizTalkParserComponent` interface has seven functions, as shown in Table 18.7.

TABLE 18.7 Functions in `IBizTalkParserComponent`

Interchange Level	`ProbeInterchangeFormat()`	Test whether an interchange can be handled by the parser.
	`GetInterchangeDetails()`	Accept interchange information from BizTalk.
Group Level	`GroupsExist()`	Test whether groups are in the interchange.
	`GetGroupDetails()`	Identify pre-group parsing information.
	`GetGroupSize()`	Identify post-group parsing information.
Document Level	`GetNextDocument()`	Parse one document.
	`GetNativeDocumentOffsets()`	Identify post-document parsing information.

BizTalk calls `ProbeInterchangeFormat()` to test whether a stream of bytes is an interchange supported by the parser. If so, BizTalk calls `GetInterchangeDetails()` to pass information to the parser and calls `GroupsExist()` to learn whether there are groups in the interchange.

If no groups are present, BizTalk parses the document sequence in the interchange by repeatedly calling the two document level functions. Specifically, for each document, BizTalk calls `GetNextDocument()` and `GetNativeDocumentOffsets()` in succession.

If groups are present, BizTalk repeats the document parsing sequence for each group. To start a group, BizTalk calls `GetGroupDetails()`. After the last document in a group, BizTalk calls `GetGroupSize()`.

IBizTalkParserComponent::ProbeInterchangeFormat()

`ProbeInterchangeFormat()` tests the format of a stream of data. The function returns `S_OK` if the data is an interchange the parser can handle and `S_FALSE` otherwise.

Listing 18.7 is a concise form of our sample parser's implementation. The sample source code with this chapter has a full version with documentation, tracking, and error checking.

LISTING 18.7 Concise Implementation of `ProbeInterchangeFormat()` (FormPostParser.cpp)

```
HRESULT CFormPostParser::ProbeInterchangeFormat ([in] IStream * pstm,
➥[in] BOOL bFromFile, [in] BSTR bstrEnvName, [in] IStream * pstmReceipt,
➥[out] BSTR * pbstrFormat)
{
   const wchar_t S[] = L"schema=biztalk-unleashed-custom-parser-ch18";
   const size_t N = sizeof S - 2; size_t nPeeked = 0;
   wchar_t * buf = (wchar_t*) peekStream(pstm, N, nPeeked);
   bool bOk = buf && (nPeeked == N) && !memcmp(buf, S, N);
   delete[] (BYTE*)buf;
   *pbstrFormat = bOk ? SysAllocString(L"custom") : 0;
   if (bOk) this->m_spstmData = pstm;
   return bOk ? S_OK : S_FALSE;
}
/*  This function peeks the first N bytes from the stream which it assumes
    is wchar_t data.  If N bytes are available, it compares against an
    expected prefix, named S in the code.  It returns S_FALSE if the prefix
    is not found.  Otherwise, it addrefs the given IStream, retains a copy in
    class member m_spstmData, sets output parameter pbstrFormat to "custom",
    and returns S_OK.  Care is taken to not change the current
position in the
    stream.
*/
```

The first three parameters are derived from `IInterchange::Submit()` and `IInterchange::SubmitSync()`, which are the only two means for an interchange to enter BizTalk.

`IInterchange` accepts data as a `BSTR` or a file reference. BizTalk builds an `IStream` interface to the data to pass as `pstm` to our parser. This `IStream` is read-only and only has members `Read()`, `Stat()`, and `Seek()` implemented. If a BSTR was passed to `IInterchange`, then `bFromFile` is `FALSE`, and `pstm` is a stream of Unicode data from the string. If a file was passed to `IInterchange`, then `bFromFile` is `TRUE`, and `pstm` is a stream from the file that the parser must know how to interpret. In the sample code in Listing 18.7, we assume `wchar_t` data for clarity.

The custom parser must retain a reference-counted copy of the given `IStream` if it returns `S_OK`. In the sample code in Listing 18.7, we retain it in a data member of type `CComPtr<IStream>` whose assignment operator does an implicit `addref`. Subsequent method calls on this interface will need access to the stream.

The parameter `bstrEnvName` is the optional envelope parameter passed to `IInterchange::Submit()` or `IInterchange::SubmitSync()`. Acquire `IBizTalkEnvelope` from the `IBizTalkConfig` interface to access envelopes by name. In our sample parser, we do not use envelopes.

The parameter `pstmReceipt` is a stream "that contains the receipt document" according to the BizTalk documentation. Little else is described. This parameter is not used in this sample.

The output parameter `pbstrFormat` is set to the document format, if `S_OK` is returned, and set to null otherwise. This value needs to match the value allowed for `IBizTalkEnvelope::Format` and `IBizTalkDocument::Type`. Valid values are `x12`, `edifact`, `custom xml`, `custom`, `flatfile`, and `reliable`. Case sensitivity is not specified in the documentation. We use `custom` in our example.

IBizTalkParserComponent::GetInterchangeDetails()

`GetInterchangeDetails()` receives information from BizTalk about the source and destination organizations for the interchange being parsed.

Listing 18.8 is the vacuous implementation used in our sample parser.

LISTING 18.8 Concise Implementation of `GetInterchangeDetails()` (`FormPostParser.cpp`)

```
HRESULT CFormPostParser::GetInterchangeDetails ([in] IDictionary * pdict)
{
   return S_OK;
```

LISTING 18.8 continued

```
}
/*  This function simply returns S_OK.  The sample parser does not need to
    extract information about this interchange from the given dictionary.
*/
```

The single parameter is a dictionary, a set of name-value pairs. Names are not case sensitive for `IDictionary`. BizTalk specifies that the minimum set of name-value pairs at this point for the dictionary is per Table 18.8.

TABLE 18.8 Minimum Dictionary Contents

Name	*Value*
`src_id_type`	Source organization qualifier (a number)
`src_id_value`	Source organization value
`dest_id_type`	Destination organization qualifier (a number)
`dest_id_value`	Destination organization value

Recall that an organization has one or more identifiers. Each identifier has a name, such as "telephone number", a qualifier, and a value, such as "800-555-1212". The qualifier is a number and is used to refer to an organization identifier by number rather than by string. For example, in BizTalk, the number 12 is the qualifier corresponding to the name "telephone number". The qualifier number is also known as type for the organization identifier. At runtime, BizTalk tracks just the type and value, per Table 18.8.

In practice, however, testing our parser with a file receive function yielded the dictionary settings in Table 18.9. Note that we used a file receive function instead of an HTTP receive function for debugging purposes. The section "Debugging the Parser" later in this chapter describes this switch.

TABLE 18.9 Actual Dictionary Contents

Name	*Value*
`Src_ID_Type`	`OrganizationName`
`Tracking_ID`	`{316D42A9-769F-404C-9F52-8D6BFE7049C8}`
`Src_filepath`	`e:\temp\CustomParserBatchReceive`
`Document_Name`	`definitionBrokerItem_ch18`

TABLE 18.9 continued

Name	*Value*
submission_id	{C87F22B6-703C-414A-A762-4C95F7FC05A3}
Src_filename	batch.txt
Dest_ID_Type	OrganizationName

Our use of a file receive function is indicated by the entries for `src_filepath` and `src_filename`. Note that entry for `Document_Name` is the name of the inbound document definition for our channel configured earlier in the chapter.

IBizTalkParserComponent::GroupsExist()

`GroupsExist()` flags whether the interchange contains document groups. If so, the functions `GetGroupDetails()` and `GetGroupSize()` will be called. BizTalk calls `GroupsExist()` after calling `ProbeInterchangeFormat()` and before parsing begins.

Recall that an interchange can be a single document, a sequence of documents, or a sequence of groups. A group itself contains a sequence of documents.

Listing 18.9 is a concise form of our sample parser's implementation. The sample source code with this chapter has a full version with documentation, tracking, and error checking.

LISTING 18.9 Concise Implementation of `GroupsExist()` (`FormPostParser.cpp`)

```
HRESULT CFormPostParser::GroupsExist ([out] BOOL * pbGroupsExist)
{
   *pbGroupsExist = TRUE;
   return S_OK;
}
/*  This function flags that groups exist and returns S_OK.
*/
```

The parser with this chapter always has groups. To conditionally support groups, the stream passed into `ProbeInterchangeFormat()` must be inspected.

IBizTalkParserComponent::GetGroupDetails()

`GetGroupDetails()` specifies for the next group in the interchange details to add to the BizTalk Tracking Database. BizTalk calls this function only if `GroupsExist()` flags that groups exist. If no groups exist, this function can return `E_NOTIMPL`. BizTalk calls this function once before each group is processed by the parser. As such, this function can also perform any internal pre-group handling.

Listing 18.10 is a concise form of our sample parser's implementation. The sample source code with this chapter has a full version with documentation, tracking, and error checking.

LISTING 18.10 Concise Implementation of `GetGroupDetails()` (`FormPostParser.cpp`)

```
HRESULT CFormPostParser::GetGroupDetails ([in] IDictionary *pdict)
{
   if (! m_pwchStream)
   {
      m_pwchStream = (wchar_t*)loadStream(m_spstmData);
      for ( wchar_t * s = wcstok(m_pwchStream, L"\r\n");  s;
➥s = wcstok(0, L"\r\n") )
      {
         wchar_t * x = wcschr(s, L'&'); // find first '&' delimiter in line
         if (! x) continue; // skip non-document lines like the schema line
         *x = '\0'; // null-terminate at the '&'
         m_docs.push_back(s); // add to an std::vector<wchar_t*>
      }
      std::sort(m_docs.begin(), m_docs.end(), lesspwsz()); // sort w/ wcscmp()
      m_docpos = m_docs.begin();
   }
   return S_OK;
}
/*  This function skips recording information for the BizTalk Tracking
    Database.  It performs first time initialization by loading the
    interchange stream into class member m_pwchStream, a wchar_t buffer.
    The main loop separates newline-delimited documents.  Each document is a
    single line and is &-delimited.  The first & in each line is replaced with
    an embedded null character.  The modified document line is then added to
    an std::vector<wchar_t*> class member, m_docs.  After the loop, m_docs is
    sorted using wcscmp() and STL via the STL comparator lesspwsz:  struct
    lesspwsz { bool operator() (const wchar_t * x, const wchar_t * y) const {
    return wcscmp(x, y) < 0; } };  Sorting is on everything to the left of the
    embedded null in each line.  After the embedded null is more document data
    that itself is null terminated.  That data is parsed in GetNextDocument().
    The first document in the vector is recorded in class member m_docpos.
    This function returns S_OK.
*/
```

Our custom parser uses this function for first time initialization. It is called before each group is parsed, which also means that it is called before any parsing takes place.

The comments with the code in Listing 18.10 describe the mechanics. Here is an image of what takes place. It first loads the entire stream, such as the following, into a character buffer:

```
schema=biztalk-unleashed-custom-parser-ch18\r\n
broker=Delta&stock=ABC&quantity=1000&min-price=25.00\r\n
broker=Beta&stock=JKL&quantity=1500&min-price=35.00\r\n
broker=Alpha&stock=DEF&quantity=2500&min-price=20.00\r\n
broker=Beta&stock=WXYZ&quantity=2500&min-price=100.00\r\n
broker=Delta&stock=STUV&quantity=50&min-price=35.00\r\n
```

Next, it inserts each newline-delimited document into an array of type `std::vector<wchar_t*>`. The one-line document has an embedded null where the first "&" symbol appeared:

```
broker=Delta\0stock=ABC&quantity=1000&min-price=25.00\0
broker=Beta\0stock=JKL&quantity=1500&min-price=35.00\0
broker=Alpha\0stock=DEF&quantity=2500&min-price=20.00\0
broker=Beta\0stock=WXYZ&quantity=2500&min-price=100.00\0
broker=Delta\0stock=STUV&quantity=50&min-price=35.00\0
```

This technique isolates the `broker` field. Sorting the lines in the array using `wcscmp()` effectively groups the documents by the `broker` field.

```
broker=Alpha\0stock=DEF&quantity=2500&min-price=20.00\0
broker=Beta\0stock=JKL&quantity=1500&min-price=35.00\0
broker=Beta\0stock=WXYZ&quantity=2500&min-price=100.00\0
broker=Delta\0stock=ABC&quantity=1000&min-price=25.00\0
broker=Delta\0stock=STUV&quantity=50&min-price=35.00\0
```

The `GetNextDocument()` function will be able to progress through the sorted array, detecting group boundaries as it goes.

Note that, in our parser, we chose to organize the data into groups. In a simpler scenario, a group would be contiguous in the interchange data stream. In the case where groups are contiguous, there might be explicit group delimiters and group-level attributes available to parse.

Our sample parser elected not to set values for the BizTalk Tracking Database. To do so, set the `IDictionary` parameter according to the article "Supporting the Tracking Database with Parser and Serializer Components" in the BizTalk help file. This article enumerates dozens of name-value pairs that BizTalk will transfer from an `IDictionary` into the tracking database.

IBizTalkParserComponent::GetGroupSize()

`GetGroupSize()` specifies the size of the last group parsed and whether there are any more groups to parse. BizTalk calls this function only if `GroupsExist()` flags that groups exist. If no groups exist, this function can return `E_NOTIMPL`. BizTalk calls this function once after each group is processed by the parser. As such, this function can also perform any internal post-group handling.

Listing 18.11 is a concise form of our sample parser's implementation. The sample source code with this chapter has a full version with documentation, tracking, and error checking.

LISTING 18.11 Concise Implementation of `GetGroupSize()` (`FormPostParser.cpp`)

```
HRESULT CFormPostParser::GetGroupSize ([out] long * pnGroupSize,
➥[out] BOOL * pbLastGroup)
{
   *pbLastGroup = (m_docpos == m_docs.end()) ? TRUE : FALSE;
   *pnGroupSize = 0;
   for ( int i0 = m_docpos - m_docs.begin() - 1, i = i0;
➥(i >= 0) && (0 == wcscmp(m_docs[i], m_docs[i0]));  — i )
      *pnGroupSize += docSize(m_docs[i]);
   return S_OK;
}
/*  This function examines class member m_docpos.  It is given that m_docpos-1
    is the position of the last document parsed.  m_docpos is either
    m_docs.end() or the first document of the next group.  *pbLastGroup is set
    to whether it is the end position.  *pnGroupSize is calculated by walking
    the m_docs array backward starting with the last document parsed, at
    m_docpos-1, and stopping at the first document of the group.  Recall that
    two documents are in the same group if wcscmp() returns zero for them.
    Inside th loop *pnGroupSize is incremented by the size of the document
    using the helper function docSize().  The function returns S_OK.
*/
```


The value stored in output parameter `pnGroupSize` will appear in the BizTalk Server Tracking Database.

The comments with the code in Listing 18.11 describe the mechanics. Table 18.10 has an image of what takes place. On entry to the function, class member `m_docpos` points to one position beyond the last document parsed. That last document was also the last document of a group. Here is a sample with three groups showing the possible values for `m_docpos`.

TABLE 18.10 Group Iteration Using `m_docpos`

m_docpos	m_docs array
	`[0] = broker=Alpha\0stock=DEF&quantity=2500& min-price=20.00\0`
⟹	`[1] = broker=Beta\0stock=JKL&quantity=1500& min-price=35.00\0`
	`[2] = broker=Beta\0stock=WXYZ&quantity=2500& min-price=100.00\0`

TABLE 18.10 Group Iteration Using `m_docpos`

`m_docpos`	`m_docs array`
⟹	`[3] = broker=Delta\0stock=ABC&quantity=1000& min-price=25.00\0`
	`[4] = broker=Delta\0stock=STUV&quantity=50& min-price=35.00\0`
⟹	(end position)

The first position for `m_docpos` is just after the Alpha group. The second position is just after the Beta group. The final position is just after the Delta group.

IBizTalkParserComponent::GetNextDocument()

`GetNextDocument()` parses the next document in the interchange and converts it to XML. It handles the case where the document is actually a receipt, and it provides for the proper correlation of receipts. This function also flags whether this document is the last one in the entire interchange or the last one in the current group.

Listing 18.12 is a concise form of our sample parser's implementation. The sample source code with this chapter has a full version with documentation, tracking, and error checking.

LISTING 18.12 Concise Implementation of `GetNextDocument()` (`FormPostParser.cpp`)

```
HRESULT CFormPostParser:: GetNextDocument ([in] IDictionary * pdict,
➥[in] BSTR bstrName, [out] BOOL * pbValid, [out] BOOL * pbLast,
➥[out] enum GeneratedReceiptLevel * pnReceipt,
➥[out] BOOL * pbReceipt, [out] BSTR * pbstrCorr)
{
   *pbReceipt = FALSE;  *pnReceipt = NoReceiptGenerated;  *pbstrCorr = 0;
   int n;  std::wstring f, v;  wchar_t s[4096];  wcscat(s, L"<broker-item>");
   for ( wchar_t * doc = *m_docpos;  *doc;  doc += n )
   {  // (*m_docpos) has form: broker=xxx\0field1=v1&...&fieldn=vn\0
      n = parseFormPostField(doc, f, v); // returns number of chars parsed
      swprintf(s+wcslen(s), L"<%s>%s</%s>", f.c_str(), xmlEscape(v).c_str(),
➥f.c_str());
      if ((doc[n] == L'&') || (doc == *m_docpos))
         n++; // skip '&' or embedded null
   }
   wcscat(s, L"</broker-item>");
   pdict->put_Value(L"working_data", CComVariant(s));
   *pbValid = TRUE;
   *pbLast = (BOOL)((++m_docpos  == m_docs.end()) ||
➥wcscmp(*m_docpos, *(m_docpos -1)));
   return S_OK;
}
/*  This function initializes the three output parameters for dealing with
    receipts to indicate no support for receipts.  Next it constructs the
    <broker-item/> XML from of the next document in the interchange.
```

LISTING 18.12 continued

```
    *m_docpos is that document and the main loop walks the &-delimited fields
    in it.  One special case is that the first field is delimited by an
    embedded null rather than &.  The helper function parseFormPostField() is
    called inside the loop to extract the next field-value pair and return the
    number of characters parsed.  That number is used to advance the loop
    index variable.  The field-value pair is stored in the XML document by
    adding a tag with the same name as field.  Helper function xmlEscape()
    ensure that the tag's value is well-formed XML.  After the loop, the XML
    document is closed and stored in the IDictionary parameter.  Output
    parameter *pbValid is set to TRUE.  Class member m_docpos is advanced to
    the next document.  *pbLast is set as TRUE if there are no more documents
    or the next document is in a new group.  Otherwise, it is set to FALSE.
    The test for the new group is done by comparing the next document with the
    one just parsed.  Recall that two documents are in the same group if
    wcscmp()returns 0 for them.  The function returns S_OK.
*/
```

Input parameter `pdict` is the dictionary for the document. In our custom parser, the fields in Table 18.11 were in the dictionary. Note that these fields are the same ones in the dictionary passed to `GetInterchangeDetails()` except for the `syntax` field.

TABLE 18.11 Dictionary Contents in Sample Parser

Name	*Value*
Src_ID_Type	OrganizationName
Tracking_ID	{316D42A9-769F-404C-9F52-8D6BFE7049C8}
src_filepath	e:\temp\CustomParserBatchReceive
Document_Name	definitionBrokerItem_ch18
submission_id	{C87F22B6-703C-414A-A762-4C95F7FC05A3}
src_filename	batch.txt syntax custom
Dest_ID_Type	OrganizationName

On output, the dictionary field `working_data` is to hold the XML form of the document as a string.

Input parameter `bstrName` is the name of the document definition for data in the channel. In our custom parser, the value was set to `definitionBrokerItem_ch18`, which is also the field `Document_Name` in the dictionary. Acquire `IBizTalkDocument` from the `IBizTalkConfig` interface to access document definitions by name if schema information is needed.

Error handling is done with output parameter `pbValid` rather than the `HRESULT` return value. Returning a negative `HRESULT` such as `E_FAIL` aborts the rest of the documents in the interchange. Set `*pbValid=TRUE` if a valid document was parsed. Otherwise, set `*pbValid=FALSE`, advance the stream position to the start of the next document, set `working_data` in the dictionary to the invalid content for the administrator to review, and return `S_OK`.

Output parameter `pbLast` flags whether this document is the last one in the interchange or the last one in the current group.

The comments with the code in Listing 18.12 describe the mechanics. Here is an image of what takes place. On entry to the function, class member `m_docpos` points to the next document to parse. There is a simple mapping of the `tag=value` syntax to the `<tag>value</tag>` syntax.

```
*m_docpos = broker=Beta\0stock=JKL&quantity=1500&min-price=35.00\0

"working_data" field for IDictionary:
    <broker-item>
        <broker>Beta</broker>
        <stock>JKL</stock>
        <quantity>1500</quantity>
        <min-price>35.00</min-price>
    </broker-item>
```

The last three output parameters, `pnReceipt`, `pbReceipt`, and `pbstrCorr`, are for handling receipts. Our sample parser does not support receipts. In the event that a receipt enters the channel instead of a document, the parser must detect the receipt. A detected receipt is converted to XML and placed in the dictionary. Output parameter `*pbReceipt` is set to `TRUE` to flag that the document is really a receipt. Output parameter `*pbstrCorr` is set to the `ProgID` of a custom COM component that implements `IBizTalkCorrelation`. For details on correlating receipts, see the article "Creating Receipt Correlator Components" in the BizTalk documentation.

IBizTalkParserComponent::GetNativeDocumentOffsets()

`GetNativeDocumentOffsets()` calculates size and position information for the native, unparsed form of the document in the interchange stream. BizTalk Tracking uses this information to log the unparsed data.

Listing 18.13 is a concise form of our sample parser's implementation. The sample source code with this chapter has a full version with documentation, tracking, and error checking.

LISTING 18.13 Concise Implementation of `GetNativeDocumentOffsets()` (`FormPostParser.cpp`)

```
HRESULT CFormPostParser:: GetNativeDocumentOffsets ([out] BOOL *
➥pbSizeFromXMLDoc, [out] LARGE_INTEGER * pnOffset, [out] long * pnSize)
```

LISTING 18.13 continued

```
{
   *pbSizeFromXMLDoc = FALSE; // false means we calculate size and offset
   const wchar_t * d = *(m_docpos - 1); // d points to last document parsed
   pnOffset->QuadPart = (char*)d - (char*)m_pwchStream;
   *pnSize = docSize;
   return S_OK;
}
/*  This function flags that it will calculate size and offset by setting
    *pbSizeFromXMLDoc=FALSE.  The start of the last document is inferred from
    m_docpos which has already been advanced to the next document.  Hence,
    *(m_docpos-1) is the last document.  The offset from the start of the
    stream is simple a pointer difference, just subtract class member
    m_pwchStream.  Helper function docSize() calculates the length of the
    document.  The function returns S_OK.
*/
```

Set output parameter `*pbSizeFromXMLDoc=TRUE` and BizTalk will calculate size and offset information. In this case, the other two parameters are not used.

To calculate the size and offset, set `*pbSizeFromXMLDoc=FALSE`. Set `*pnOffset` to the offset within the interchange data to the first byte of the document. This offset can be passed to `IStream::Seek()`. Set `*pnSize` to the total number of bytes the document occupies in the stream.

In our custom parser, we calculate the offset using class member `m_pwchStream`. Remember that `m_pwchStream` is a copy of stream contents. We get the pointer to the last document and subtract `m_pwchStream` using pointer arithmetic to get the stream offset. The size of the document is handled by the helper function `docSize()`, which is given in Listing 18.14.

LISTING 18.14 Implementation of Helper Function `docSize()` (`FormPostParser.cpp`)

```
size_t docSize ( const wchar_t * d ) // return size in bytes
{  // d has the form:  broker=xxx\0field1=val1&...&fieldn=valn\0
   //    There is an embedded null so wcslen() must be called twice.
   size_t n = wcslen + 1; // tally 1st field + embedded null following it
   n += wcslen(d+n); // tally remaining fields after embedded null
   return n * (sizeof wchar_t);
}
```

Debugging the Parser

To simplify debugging, we use a file receive function. Our HTTP receive function runs inside `DLLHOST.EXE`, which is more difficult to debug.

To configure the file receive function, start BizTalk Server Administration. Open the node Microsoft BizTalk Server 2002, open the BizTalk Server Group node, and select Receive Functions. Select Action, New, File Receive Function from the menu. In the dialog that opens, set the name to `receiveFileSubmit_ch18` and the comment to `This File Receive Function is used to debug the custom parser`. Enter `*.txt` in the File Types to Poll For edit box. Enter a path in the Polling Location edit box such as `C:\Temp\CustomParserBatchReceive`. Make sure that the directory exists. Click the Advanced button. Choose Open Source in the Openness combo box. Specify the inbound channel as `channelBroker_ch18`. Click OK. Then click OK again.

Return to the Visual C++ IDE that has the project for the custom parser. Select Project, Settings from the menu and select the Debug tab on the property page that opens. Select a debug configuration in the Settings For combo box. Enter the full path to `MSCIS.EXE` in the Executable for Debug Session edit box. The full path is typically `C:\Program Files\Microsoft BizTalk Server\MSCIS.EXE`. Click OK.

`MSCIS.EXE` is the service for BizTalk Messaging Services. Stop this service as follows. Start BizTalk Server Administration. Open Microsoft BizTalk Server 2002 and then BizTalk Server Group. Select the node that is the name of your computer. Right-click and select Stop.

Start the Visual Studio debugger for the parser project, and the service now restarts in the context of the debugger. Breakpoints will fire inside the parser component when data enters the channel.

To place data in the channel, copy a file ending in `.txt` into the directory monitored by the file receive function. Be sure that the file is stored in a Unicode format. The parser only understands Unicode for simplicity. There is a chapter sample file, `SampleBatchSubmit.txt`, for this purpose.

Tip

`NOTEPAD.EXE` has an option for saving in Unicode.

During the debugging process, BizTalk automatically disables the file receive function if there are any failures. Be sure to re-enable by monitoring the properties for the file receive function in BizTalk Server Administration.

Tip

Interchanges that are not completely handled can remain queued for handling. The result is that after debugging for a while there may be many interchanges that immediately get replayed against your component. To avoid interference, manually empty the Work Queue as follows. In BizTalk Server Administration, open `\Microsoft BizTalk Server 2002\BizTalk Server Group\Queues\Work Queue`. Right-click any queue items and select All Tasks, Move to Suspended Queue from the menu. Items in the Suspended Queue can be deleted by right-clicking them and selecting Delete.

Be advised that the `MSCIS.EXE` process will keep our parser's DLL loaded, thereby locking it. To rebuild the DLL, `MSCIS.EXE` must not be running. By default, this process autostarts at boot time and has options to restart a fixed number of times. You can either modify these settings or forcibly end the process. If you accept the risks for forcibly ending, right-click the entry for `MSCIS.EXE` in the Task Manager and select Debug. When the debugger attaches to the process, use the debugger to end the process. Using Task Manager directly to end the process will not work.

To shut down `MSCIS.EXE` cleanly, launch Services from Administrative Tools found in the Control Panel. Under the node `Services (local)`, double-click the entry for the BizTalk Messaging Service. On the General tab, change the Startup Type to Manual. On the Recovery tab, select Take No Action for all three combo boxes. Restart the computer.

`DLLHOST.EXE` also keeps our parser's DLL loaded if you use the HTTP receive function. To shut down the `DLLHOST.EXE` cleanly, open Internet Information Services from Administrative Tools. Open the node with the machine with the HTTP receive function, right-click the virtual directory for the HTTP receive function and select Properties. On the Virtual Directory tab, click the Unload button. Click OK.

Tip

Remember to restart the `MSCIS.EXE` service when debugging is done. To restart, just reverse the steps given previously for stopping the service including any modifications to the options for auto-starting and auto-restarting.

Serializer Design

In this section, we will design a custom serializer that we will implement in the next section. To this point, we have covered the architecture of the BizTalk channel in which custom functoids, parsers, and serializers have a role. The preceding few sections implemented a custom functoid and custom parser. The test driver for the custom parser accepted non-XML data and input XML data to the channel. In a real application, the XML data would exit the channel and provide input to an application such as an XLANG schedule. In our sample, the resultant XML exited the channel by e-mail or by file. In this section and the next, non-XML data will exit the channel.

A serializer operates generally as follows. It accepts from BizTalk a stream into which to place output. BizTalk hands the serializer a series of documents to be added to the output stream. BizTalk then allows the serializer to impose a grouping on the documents already output. First, BizTalk asks the serializer how many, if any, groups there are. Next, it asks which documents are in which group.

A serializer design requires the following specifications:

- Format of the XML data in the channel
- Format of the data, possibly non-XML, output by the serializer
- Support for grouping

Format of XML Data in the Channel

The format of the data in the channel is already specified with the document definition, `definitionBroker_ch18`. That format is output by our parser. In our case, the format of the XML data in the channel does not change. In general, however, the XML format can change using a map. The result is that the inbound XML format is not always the outbound format.

Repeated here is an example document output by the parser:

```
<broker-item>
   <broker>Alpha Financials</broker>
   <stock>ABC</stock>
   <quantity>10</quantity>
   <min-price>5.00</min-price>
</broker-item>
```

Format of Data Output by the Serializer

The output of the serializer has no restrictions. In particular, it does not have to be XML. Examples are spreadsheets, PDF files, proprietary binary files, or industry standard specifications such as the message format in the financial protocol FIX.

For simplicity, we will choose a binary format that is easy to confirm, an image. Figure 18.17 shows the image for the XML data shown previously.

FIGURE 18.17
Sample image output for serializer.

The image serves as a visual receipt for the information that entered the channel. It is easy to validate that the information entering the channel made it into the binary format.

The image leaving the channel will arrive by file or e-mail depending on the port configuration chosen earlier.

Support for Grouping

BizTalk does not currently support grouping. However, the API allows for its future use, and we will examine that API in the implementation. For our design, however, we are forced to select no grouping even though we had grouping in the interchanges submitted to the channel.

Serializer Implementation

In this section, we will implement the serializer design from the preceding section using C++ and ATL. Unlike the functoid implementation earlier, there is not a method for implementing the serializer using Visual Basic. The COM interface uses types, such as `IStream`, not accessible from Visual Basic.

The implementation comprises the following items:

- BizTalk envelope, port, and channel configuration
- A COM coclass implementing `IBizTalkSerializerComponent`

The COM coclass provides the following:

- Serialization—Conversion of XML to the output format
- Group separation—Identify grouping boundaries
- Sizing—Identify sizes of documents, groups, and the interchange

For a test harness, we will use the same HTML application used to test the parser.

Configuring an Envelope, Port, and Channel for a Custom Serializer

Figure 18.18 shows the channel we will configure. Most of the configuration is in place. We will focus on steps six and seven in the following discussion.

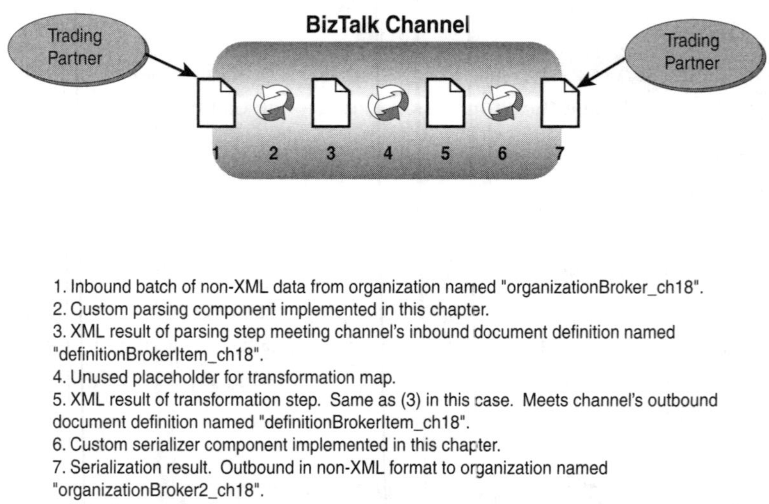

FIGURE 18.18
Channel configuration for our custom serializer.

To update the configuration from our parser, start the BizTalk Messaging Manager.

> **Note**
>
> If you skipped ahead, briefly return to the section "Configuring a Channel for a Custom Parser." Follow the configuration steps and then return here.

Create an envelope for the custom data format our serializer will produce as follows. Select File, New, Envelope from the menu and name it `envelopeBroker2_ch18`. Choose

CUSTOM in the Envelope Format combo box because our format is binary. Leave the Envelope Specification check box unchecked. Click OK.

Next, we will modify our port, portBroker2_ch18, and channel, channelBroker_ch18. The port needs a reference to our new envelope, and the channel needs a reference to our new serializer component.

Trying to change either one results in an error message simply because of mutual dependencies. To break the dependency, delete the channel; we will re-create it.

After deleting the channel, locate the port portBroker2_ch18. Double-click it to edit. Click Next twice to get to the Envelope Information page. In the Envelope Information combo box, select the envelope just created, envelopeBroker2_ch18. Click Finish.

Now, we will re-create the channel. Right-click the port and select New Channel, From an Organization from the menu. As before, name the new channel channelBroker_ch18 with comments This channel accepts an inbound batch of documents from a broker organization via an HTTP Receive Function. Click Next. Select the Open Source radio button. Click Next. Browse for the inbound document definition definitionBrokerItem_ch18. Click Next. Browse for the same output document definition definitionBrokerItem_ch18. Click Next. Click Next again. On the Advanced Configuration page, click the Advanced button. On the Envelope tab, examine the combo box Serializer Component. When we build our serializer component, it will show up here, as shown in Figure 18.19. For now, click OK without selecting a serializer. Click Finish.

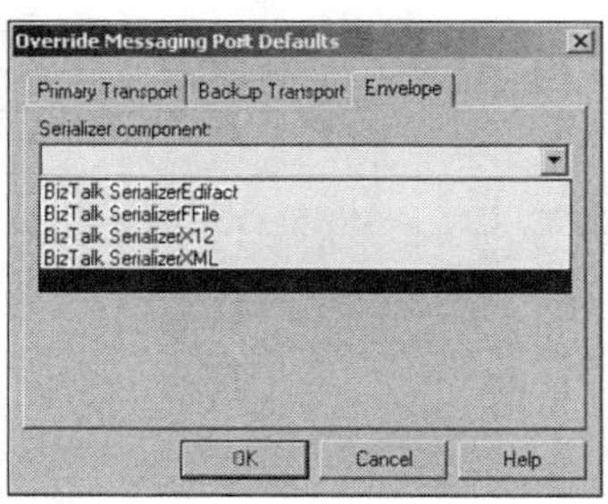

FIGURE 18.19
Serializers registered with BizTalk.

Configuring a Test Harness for the Custom Serializer

For a test harness, we will use the same HTML application and an HTTP receive function used for testing the parser.

> **Note**
>
> If you skipped ahead, briefly return to the section "Configuring a Test Harness for the Custom Parser." Follow the configuration steps and then return here.

If you are using a file port rather than an e-mail port for the test harness, we need to specify an output file that ends in `.bmp` instead of `.xml`. To do so, launch the BizTalk Messaging Manager. Locate the port `portBroker2_ch18`, and double-click it to edit. Click Next. Click the Browse button for the Primary Transport. Update the filename and click OK. Click Finish.

To confirm that the test harness is configured properly, launch `http://localhost/BizTalkUnleashed/batchsubmit_ch18.asp` as we did for the parser. Click the View Batch button. Click the Add Sample button. Click the Submit Batch button to post over HTTP the entire batch to the HTTP receive function.

No serializer is installed yet, so the submission should fail inside BizTalk after the parsing step. To confirm, launch BizTalk Server Administration and open the paths `\Event Viewer (local)\Application` and `\Microsoft BizTalk Server 2002\BizTalk Server Group\Queues\Suspended Queue`. The document state shows as `Serializing`, and the error description shows as `Serializing Failure`. To see the document data, right-click the item in the Suspended Queue and select View Document. Figure 18.20 shows the results.

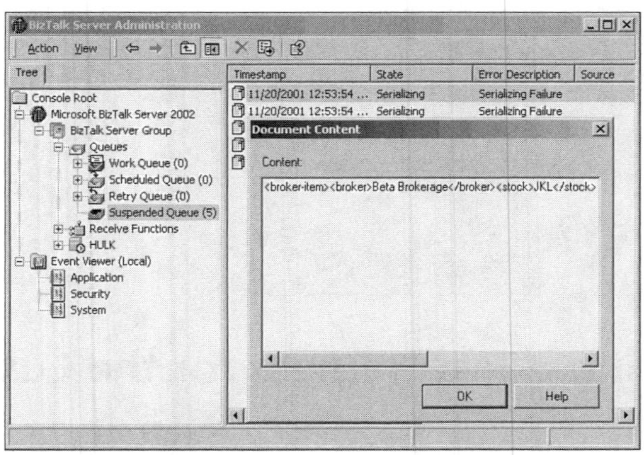

FIGURE 18.20
Serializing failure is expected at this point.

In the event log, there is an error entry. Double-click it to see a description that the server could not finish processing our message port, `portBroker2_ch18`.

ATL Shell Implementation

The first step in the COM implementation of the serializer is making an ATL shell. The shell will contain a fully compilable C++ project with a sample implementation for `IBizTalkSerializerComponent`. We assume the latest release of Visual Studio 6, which is SP5.

> **Note**
>
> A custom ATL Object Wizard should be available at this point. If you skipped ahead, then briefly return to the section "ATL Shell Implementation" for custom functoids. Follow the instructions for installing the ATL Object Wizards and return here.

Create an empty ATL project in Visual Studio 6 as follows. Select File, New from the menu and select ATL COM App Wizard from the Projects tab. Enter `FormPostBatchSerializer` in the Project Name edit box and fill in the Location edit box to some suitable directory. Click OK. Click Finish on the next screen and then click OK on the next.

Next, run the ATL Object Wizard as follows. Select Insert, New ATL Object from the menu. Select BizTalk Unleashed in the Category list box and Custom Serializer in the Objects list box, as shown in Figure 18.21. Click Next. Enter `FormPostSerializer` in the Short Name list box. Change the `ProgID` to `BizTalkUnleashed.FormPostBatchSerializer`. Click OK.

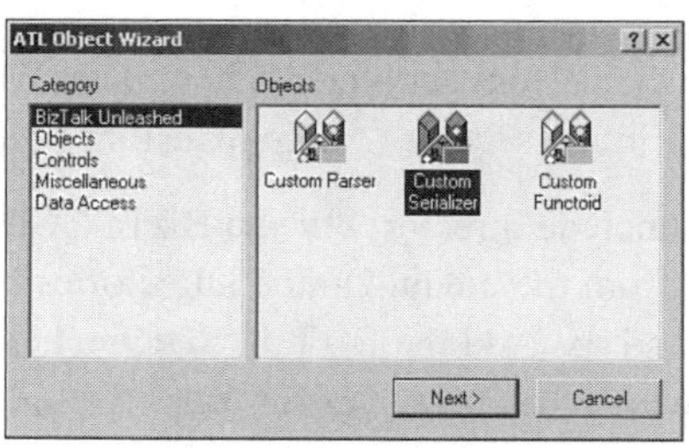

FIGURE 18.21
ATL Object Wizard for a custom serializer.

> **Note**
>
> If there are no choices for BizTalk Unleashed and Custom Serializer, then the install of the ATL Object Wizards did not complete. Please retry and confirm each step.

Table 18.12 shows the actions the ATL Object Wizard took on our project. Note that the sample files with this chapter match the names of the files in this table. The description of each file varies somewhat because the samples files are the complete implementation rather than the starter files generated by the wizard.

TABLE 18.12 ATL Object Wizard Actions for Serializers

Project File	*Wizard Action*
`FormPostSerializer.h`	Created this file for a standard ATL declaration of a coclass, `CFormPostSerializer`. Adds COM category map, BizTalk SDK includes, and `IBizTalkSerializerComponent`.
`FormPostSerializer.cpp`	Created this file for a standard implementation of the coclass `CFormPostSerializer`. Adds interface stubs with `ATLTRACE` statements including custom tracers.
`FormPostBatchSerializer.idl`	Added to this project IDL file. From BizTalk SDK file `BTSSerializerComps.idl`, uses `IBizTalkSerializerComponent`.
`FormPostSerializer.rgs`	Created this file for standard COM registration. `Resource.h`
`FormPostBatchSerializer.rc`	Updated for the Registry resource.

The ATL Object Wizard forces `ThreadingModel=Both` regardless of the threading model selection in the wizard. Although this setting is not documented in BizTalk, the stock serializers shipped by BizTalk all have `ThreadingModel=Both`.

A shell implementation in ATL for the custom serializer is complete. We will examine and extend the implementation later in the section "Adding Custom Functionality."

Before compiling, confirm that the include directory for the BizTalk SDK is available to your project. Select Tools, Options from the menu. On the Directories tab, select Include Files in the Show Directories For list box. Add the BizTalk SDK include path, typically found at `C:\Program Files\Microsoft BizTalk Server\SDK\Include`. Click OK.

Also, confirm that C++ Exception Handling is enabled for your project. Select Project, Settings from the menu. Select All Configurations in the Settings For list box. Select C++ Language in the Category combo box on the C++ tab. Check Enable Exception Handling and click OK.

Build the project by selecting Build, Rebuild All from the menu. The build should complete with no errors, and the COM registration of the new serializer should succeed.

To see that BizTalk recognizes the new serializer, start BizTalk Messaging Manager. Locate the channel named `channelBroker_ch18`. Double-click to edit it. Click the Next button five times to get to the Advanced Configuration page. Click the Advanced button. On the Envelope tab, open the combo box Serializer Component to see whether our component is there. Figure 18.22 shows an expected list. Go ahead and select our component and click OK. Click Finish.

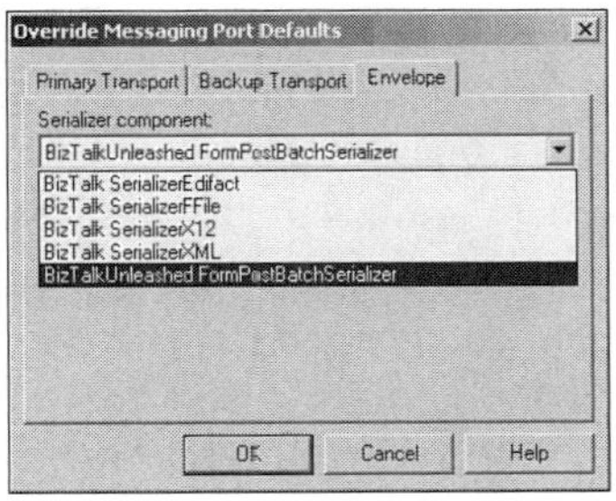

FIGURE 18.22
BizTalk recognizes our new serializer.

> **Tip**
>
> If the serializer did not appear in the combo box, then double-check that the registration succeeded during the build. BizTalk locates our component by checking the registration of all COM components. It looks for components with a specific COM category. Our ATL implementation provides that category using ATL's category map in `FornPostSerializer.h`.

Adding Custom Functionality

We are ready to add the specifics of the form post serializer to the implementation. The completed serializer is in the sample files. Unlike the custom functoid section, we will not incrementally change the ATL Object Wizard output. Rather, we will examine each function in the implementation in detail.

Interface Overview

The `IBizTalkSerializerComponent` interface has five functions, as shown in Table 18.13.

TABLE 18.13 Functions in `IBizTalkSerializerComponent`

Interchange Level	`Init()`	Initialize the serializer.
	`GetInterchangeInfo()`	Get tracking and grouping information.
Group Level	`GetGroupInfo()`	Get information for tracking a group.

TABLE 18.13 continued

Document Level	`AddDocument()`	Serialize one document.
	`GetDocInfo()`	Get information for tracking a document.

BizTalk calls `Init()` to pass an output stream to the parser and to indicate how many documents are to be serialized in the interchange. BizTalk then calls `AddDocument()` successively, once for each document in the interchange. At this point, no grouping information has been specified. BizTalk next calls `GetInterchangeInfo()` to get a tracking ID for the interchange and to get the number of groups the serializer will impose on the set of documents already serialized. If zero groups are specified, then BizTalk calls `GetDocInfo()` for each document already serialized to get offset and size within the output stream. Alternatively, if groups are specified, then BizTalk calls `GetGroupInfo()` to get offset and sizing information for the first group. `GetGroupInfo()` also outputs how many documents are in the first group. BizTalk then calls `GetDocInfo()` repeatedly for the number of documents specified in the group. BizTalk repeats this `GetGroupInfo()`/`GetDocInfo()` usage for the remaining groups.

BizTalk, however, only uses a subset of the serializer interface in the BizTalk 2002 release. The `Init()` function always specifies one for the number of documents in the interchange. The `GetInterchangeInfo()` may only return zero or one for the number of groups. With a maximum of one document and one group in an interchange, grouping is not meaningful. The grouping API is a placeholder for a future release.

IBizTalkSerializerComponent::Init()

`Init()` receives the output stream that the serializer will use. It also receives the number of documents it will serialize into that stream. For the BizTalk 2002 release, this number will always be one.

Listing 18.15 is a concise form of our sample serializer's implementation. The sample source code with this chapter has a full version with documentation, tracking, and error checking.

LISTING 18.15 Concise Implementation of `Init()` (`FormPostSerializer.cpp`)

```
HRESULT CFormPostSerializer::Init([in] BSTR bstrSrcQual, [in] BSTR bstrSrcID,
➥[in] BSTR bstrDestQual, [in] BSTR bstrDestID, [in] long nEnvID,
➥[in] IDictionary * pdictDelims, [in] IStream * pstmOut, [in] long nDocs,
➥[in] long nPortID)
{
   this->m_spstmOutput = pstmOut;
   return S_OK;
}
```

LISTING 18.15 continued

```
/*  This function addrefs the given IStream, retains a copy in class member
    m_spstmOutput., and returns S_OK.  None of the other input parameters are
➥needed.
*/
```

The parameters `bstrSrcQual`, `bstrSrcID`, `bstrDestQual`, and `bstrDestID` give the qualifiers and identifiers for the source and target organizations. Use these parameters for organization-specific handling.

Parameter `nPortID` identifies the port to which the channel using the custom serializer is connected. This port has an envelope whose identifier is given by `nEnvID`. The envelope for a port is set using the BizTalk Messaging Manager. On the same property page for setting the envelope is a property for an optional set of delimiters to use during serialization. These delimiters are passed into this function using the dictionary parameter `pdictDelims`.

The parameter `pstmOut` is the stream into which the serializer is to write all output. This `IStream` interface is write-only, and only has members `Write()` and `Stat()` implemented. The custom serializer must retain a reference-counted copy of the given `IStream` if it returns `S_OK`. In the sample code in Listing 18.15, we retain it in a data member of type `CComPtr<IStream>` whose assignment operator does an implicit `addref`. Subsequent method calls on this interface will need access to the stream.

The parameter `nDocs` is always one in BizTalk 2002. In a future release, it will specify the number of documents in the interchange.

IBizTalkSerializerComponent::AddDocument()

`AddDocument()` formats one document in the output format and writes it to the stream that was passed into the `Init()` function.

Listing 18.16 is a concise form of our sample serializer's implementation. The sample source code with this chapter has a full version with documentation, tracking, and error checking.

LISTING 18.16 Concise Implementation of `AddDocument()` (`FormPostSerializer.cpp`)

```
HRESULT CFormPostSerializer::AddDocument([in] long nDocHandle,
➥[in] IDictionary * pdict, [in] BSTR bstrTrackID, [in] long nChannelID)
{
   CComVariant vaKey(L"working_data"), vaDoc;
   pdict->get_Value(vaKey.bstrVal, &vaDoc);  vaDoc.ChangeType(VT_BSTR);
```

18 SERIALIZERS, PARSERS, AND FUNCTOIDS

LISTING 18.16 continued

```
    CComPtr<XMLDOM::IXMLDOMDocument2> spxml;  VARIANT_BOOL bLoaded;
    spxml.CoCreateInstance(__uuidof(XMLDOM::DOMDocument30));
    spxml->loadXML(vaDoc.bstrVal, &bLoaded);
    CComVariant vaB = xmllookup(spxml, L"//broker", VT_BSTR, L"???");
    CComVariant vaS = xmllookup(spxml, L"//stock", VT_BSTR, L"???");
    CComVariant vaQ = xmllookup(spxml, L"//quantity", VT_I4, 0L);
    CComVariant vaP = xmllookup(spxml, L"//min-price", VT_R4, 0.0f);
    time_t tm = time(0); TCHAR sz[1024];
    _stprintf(sz, _T("Stock Trade Receipt\n\n     %ls\n")
                  _T("Broker:  %ls\nStock:  %ls\n\n%d share%s at $%0.2f"),
              tasctime(localtime(&tm)), vaB.bstrVal, vaS.bstrVal, vaQ.lVal,
              (vaQ.lVal == 1) ? _T("") : _T("s"), vaP.fltVal);
    CComPtr<IPicture> sppict = makeReceiptBitmap(sz);
    sppict->SaveAsFile(m_spstmOutput, TRUE, &m_nDocSize);
    m_nDocHandle = nDocHandle;
    return S_OK;
}
/*  This function gets the XML document as text from the transport dictionary
    under the key "working_data".  Next, it instantiates a new XML DOM and
    loads the XML text.  It then extracts the broker, stock, quantity, and
    price fields using the helper function xmllookup().  That function takes
    an XML DOM, an XPath expression to a value, a variant type for the return
    value, and a default value.  The fields are formatted into a text string
    that is then rendered onto a bitmap using the function
    makeReceiptBitmap().  The bitmap is contained in an IPicture which is used
    to save to the output stream, m_spstmOutput.  The number of bytes written
    and the document handle are recorded in class members m_nDocSize and
    m_nDocHandle, respectively, for future use by GetDocInfo().  This function
    returns S_OK.
*/
```

Input parameter `bstrTrackID` provides the identifier used in the tracking database for this document. Input parameter `nChannelID` is the identifier of the channel using this serializer. Our sample serializer does not need either of these parameters.

Input parameter `pdict` is the transport dictionary that contains the XML document to be serialized. The document appears under the dictionary key `working_data`. Remember that dictionary keys are not case sensitive.

Our sample parser extracts the XML document and renders an image in the bitmap format shown earlier in the section Format of Data Output by the Serializer.

Input parameter `nDocHandle` is an integer handle used by BizTalk to uniquely identify this document. This handle is valid only for the life of this serializer instance.

`GetDocInfo()` requires us to map each document handle originally passed into `AddDocument()` to two values: the size and offset of the document in the output stream.

We use a simplified implementation because there will only be one document. In our implementation, the offset always will be zero. We record just a single handle and size in data members `m_nDocHandle` and `m_nDocSize`, respectively.

IBizTalkSerializerComponent::GetInterchangeInfo()

`GetInterchangeInfo()` returns information about the entire interchange after all documents have been serialized.

Listing 18.17 is a concise form of our sample serializer's implementation. The sample source code with this chapter has a full version with documentation, tracking, and error checking.

LISTING 18.17 Concise Implementation of `GetInterchangeInfo()` (`FormPostSerializer.cpp`)

```
HRESULT CFormPostSerializer::GetInterchangeInfo([out] BSTR * pbstrID,
➥[out] long * pnNumGroups)
{
   GUID guid; wchar_t wszGuid[128];
   CoCreateGuid(&guid);  StringFromGuid2(guid, wszGuid, sizeof wszGuid);
   *pbstrID = CComBSTR(wszGuid).Detach();
   *pnNumGroups = 0;
   return S_OK;
}
/*  This function sets output parameter *pbstrID to a new guid, sets the
    number of groups for the interchange to zero, and returns S_OK.
*/
```


Set output parameter `*pbstrID` to a new ID to be used for the interchange in the tracking database. Our sample serializer allocates a new GUID and converts it to a string.

Set output parameter `*pnNumGroups` to the number of groups in the interchange. For BizTalk 2002, this value must be zero or one. Our sample serializer sets it to zero.

IBizTalkSerializerComponent::GetGroupInfo()

`GetGroupInfo()` returns information about one group for the tracking database.

Listing 18.18 is a concise form of our sample serializer's implementation. The sample source code with this chapter has a full version with documentation, tracking, and error checking.

LISTING 18.18 Concise Implementation of `GetGroupInfo()` (`FormPostSerializer.cpp`)

```
HRESULT CFormPostSerializer::GetGroupInfo([out] long * pnNumDocs,
➥[out] LARGE_INTEGER * pnOffset, [out] long * pnGroupLen)
```

LISTING 18.18 continued

```
{
   return E_UNEXPECTED;
}
/*  This function returns E_UNEXPECTED because groups are not supported and
    this function should not be called.
*/
```

Set output parameter `*pnNumDocs` to the number of documents in the group. This value must be one because only one document per interchange is supported in BizTalk 2002.

Set output parameter `*pnOffset` to the offset of the start of the group in the output stream. Given that only one group is allowed, this offset must be zero.

Set output parameter `*pnGroupLen` to the total number of bytes in all documents in the group. Given that only one document is allowed, this value is also the size of the one document.

Our sample serializer does not support groups, so it returns `E_UNEXPECTED`.

IBizTalkSerializerComponent::GetDocInfo()

`GetDocInfo()` returns information about one document for the tracking database.

Listing 18.19 is a concise form of our sample serializer's implementation. The sample source code with this chapter has a full version with documentation, tracking, and error checking.

LISTING 18.19 Concise Implementation of `GetDocInfo()` (`FormPostSerializer.cpp`)

```
HRESULT CFormPostSerializer::GetDocInfo([out] long * pnHandle,
➥[out] BOOL * pbSizeFromXMLDoc, [out] LARGE_INTEGER * pnOffset,
➥[out] long * pnLen)
{
   *pnHandle = m_nDocHandle;
   *pnLen = m_nDocSize;
   *pnOffset->QuadPart = 0;
   *pbSizeFromXMLDoc = FALSE;
   return S_OK;
}
/*  This function sets output parameters to the handle and size to the values
    recorded by AddDocument().  The offset is set to 0 because there is only
    one document.  The boolean output parameter is set to false to flag that
    size and offset are set by this function.  This function returns S_OK.
*/
```

Set output parameter `*pnHandle` to the handle the next document in the current group. Given that only one document is allowed in the interchange, the handle is the value passed to the one call to `AddDocument()`. Our sample serializer uses the value recorded in data member `m_nDocHandle`.

Set output parameter `*pbSizeFromXMLDoc=TRUE` and BizTalk will calculate the size and offset of the document in the output stream. In this case, the last two parameters are not used.

To calculate the size and offset, set `*pbSizeFromXMLDoc=FALSE`. Set `*pnOffset` to the offset within the stream. This value must be zero because only one document is allowed. Set `*pnLen` to the total number of bytes the document occupies in the stream.

Our sample serializer sets `*pbSizeFromXMLDoc=FALSE`. It sets the offset to zero and uses data member `m_nDocSize` for `*pnLen`. Method `AddDocument()` set the value of `m_nDocSize` earlier.

Debugging the Serializer

Debugging the serializer follows the same steps for debugging the parser.

Summarizing these steps, we will use a file receive function to simplify setting breakpoints. The Visual C++ project sets the debugging process to be `MSCIS.EXE`. The BizTalk Messaging service, `MSCIS.EXE`, needs to be stopped and set to manual start without any restart options. Launch `MSCIS.EXE` in the debugger and drop a Unicode text file into the folder monitored by the file receive function. Watch out for automatic disabling of the file receive function if errors occur. `MSCIS.EXE` and `DLLHOST.EXE` will hold onto our DLL preventing a rebuild. Shutting down these processes is sometimes necessary. Remember that documents will sometimes automatically resubmit themselves from the Work Queue, which is managed in BizTalk Server Administration. After debugging, remember to reinstate `MSCIS.EXE` settings modified during debugging such as auto-start.

In addition, there are specific debugging considerations for the serializer. Consider submitting an exchange with a single document in it during early testing. BizTalk will run the serializer simultaneously on each parsed document. The result is a difficult debugging walk-through for the code. BizTalk will instantiate the serializer component once for each document and use the instances simultaneously. Note that each serializer instance will handle exactly one document, so race conditions within a component should not occur. Of course, a race condition can occur if you rely on global state. Be careful about functions in the C runtime library that maintain state between calls such as `strtok()`. We did not face this problem during parsing because parsing a single stream is inherently a singular task.

> **Note**
>
> Our custom serialization component should already be configured for use by the channel. If you skipped ahead, briefly return to Figure 18.22. Follow the instructions for selecting our serializer and return here.

Summary

In this chapter, we implemented three extensions to the BizTalk channel. Parsers accept custom data formats and produce XML for standard BizTalk consumption. Functoids transform XML data within the channel and can include custom business logic. Serializers output custom data formats from the XML flowing out of the channel.

We started with an overall architecture of the channel to see where programmatic extension was possible. For each extension, we began with the design considerations before getting to the implementation.

Implementation was in ATL, and we covered the steps necessary to configure and debug our extensions. For a test harness, we used an HTML application that took advantage of BizTalk's capabilities for an HTTP receive function. We also used BizTalk's SMTP capabilities to connect output from a channel directly to e-mail.

At this point, you should feel comfortable in molding the BizTalk channel architecture to meet the custom data needs of your business.

> **Coding Takeaways**
>
> The samples in this chapter were specifically designed to get you started building channel extensions. A number of programming takeaways were designed for reuse in your next project.
>
> There are three ATL Object Wizards for jump-starting new parsers, new functoids, and new serializers. The wizard for the functoid includes a familiar map-driven implementation similar to ATL's map-driven philosophy.
>
> Another takeaway is the HTML application used for the test driver. It shows by example how to use an HTML form post to submit information to BizTalk. It even shows how to queue a series of posts and submit them in one batch using the COM interface `IXMLHTTPRequest`. This HTML application also uses a modular technique for building a toolbar-driven GUI. Each major subpage is dynamically shown in much the same way that a `CView` is dynamically shown in a Microsoft Foundation Classes (MFC) application. Just follow the pattern and you can add your new views with toolbar support.

CHAPTER 19

The BizTalk Messaging Configuration Object Model

By Rick Pearson

IN THIS CHAPTER

If you've already read the chapters on BizTalk Messaging or played with BizTalk Messaging Manager on your own, you've probably come to the conclusion that large-scale administration of BizTalk Messaging is cumbersome through BizTalk Messaging Manager.

BizTalk Messaging Manager provides no support for the exchange of object configurations, automated creation of messaging objects, or a simple process by which objects can be refreshed. The BizTalk Messaging Configuration object model enables you to automate the creation, modification, and removal of BizTalk Messaging objects.

In this chapter, we will discuss the manipulation of the BizTalk Messaging system through the use of the BizTalk Messaging Configuration object model.

BizTalk Messaging Overview

Before discussing the BizTalk Messaging Configuration object model, it is useful to have a conceptual understanding of BizTalk Messaging. This section provides a high-level overview of BizTalk Messaging. Refer to Chapter 6, "Introduction to BizTalk Messaging," and Chapter 12, "Advanced BizTalk Messaging," for an in-depth discussion of BizTalk Messaging.

BizTalk Messaging

BizTalk Messaging is a set of services that provide a mechanism for routing documents in an enterprise environment. These services allow you to define how documents are received, processed, and delivered. In addition, you can specify settings for data mapping, integrity, security, document tracking, and receipt generation. In short, think of BizTalk Messaging as the glue that ties many disparate systems together in an enterprise messaging environment.

Configuration Objects Versus BizTalk Messaging Objects

This chapter refers to two types of objects:

- BizTalk Messaging objects
- BizTalk Messaging Configuration objects

BizTalk Messaging objects are the actual objects stored in the BizTalk Messaging database. BizTalk Messaging Configuration objects are the COM objects exposed by the BizTalk Messaging Configuration object model. Configuration objects are used to create, inspect, modify, and remove BizTalk Messaging objects in the database.

Figure 19.1 shows the relationships established by BizTalk Messaging objects. This UML-style diagram uses solid lines terminated with a diamond arrow to indicate associations between objects. The arrow direction indicates which object makes the association. For example, ports establish associations with envelopes. The numbers at either end indicate how many associations can be made. For example, a port may specify up to one envelope, whereas an envelope may have any number of ports (including none) that refer to it.

FIGURE 19.1
BizTalk Messaging object relationships.

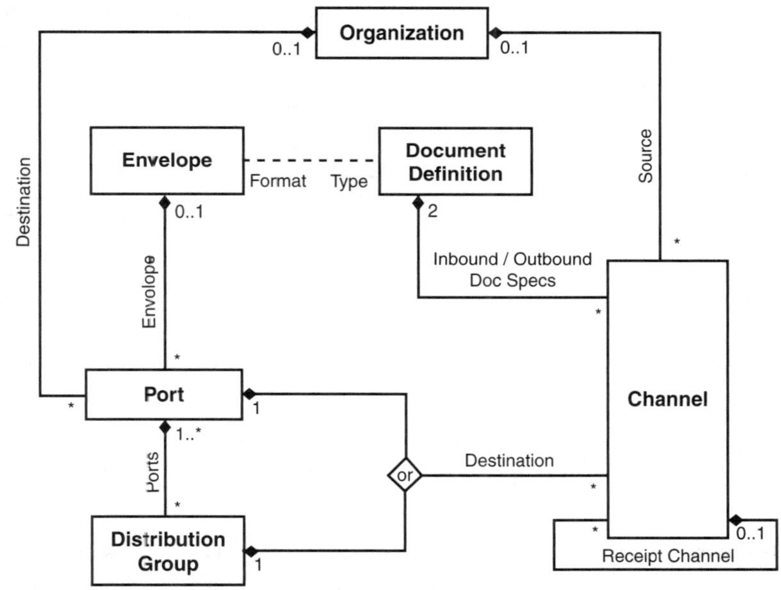

Figure 19.2 shows the relationships established by the BizTalk Messaging Configuration object model. Notice that the associations shown in Figure 19.1 are still in place in the Configuration object model.

Figure 19.2 shows three types of relationships:

- Inheritance—Indicated by a dotted arrow from the derived interface to the base interface
- Dependency—Indicated by a dashed arrow from an object to the object it uses
- Association—Indicated by a solid arrow (terminated with a diamond) from the object that makes an association to the object that is associated

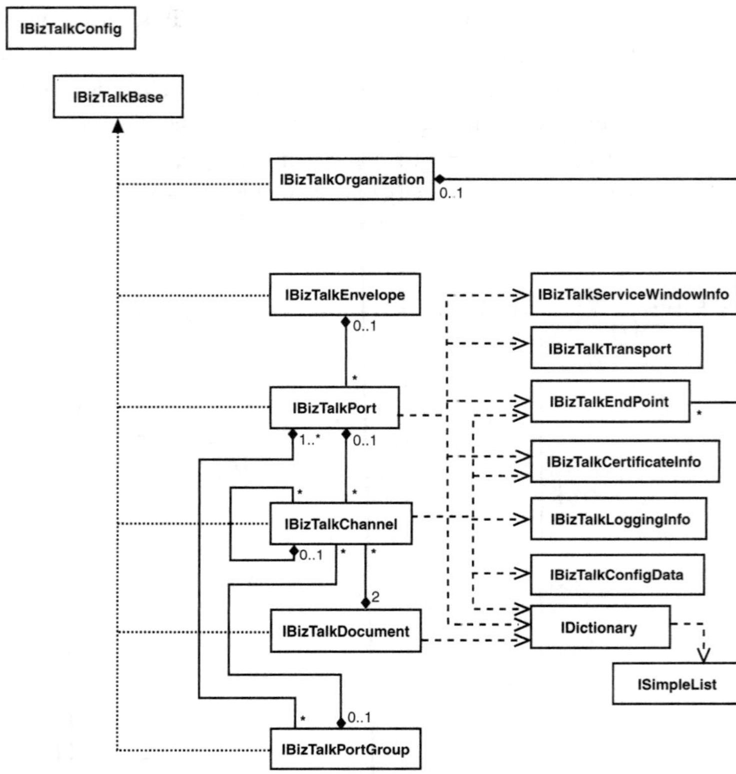

FIGURE 19.2
BizTalk Messaging Configuration object relationships.

If Figure 19.2 looks a little confusing, don't worry. We will discuss each of the major Configuration objects later in this chapter. At that time, we'll break down this diagram to include only those parts that pertain to a particular object and include the properties and methods that establish or report these relationships.

Referential Integrity

The term *referential integrity* means that one BizTalk Messaging object cannot be deleted while another BizTalk Messaging object maintains a reference to it. An object that maintains a reference to another object is said to have a *referential dependency* on that object.

There are two approaches to removing referential dependencies. The first approach is to change which BizTalk Messaging object is referenced within the referring object. For instance, you could change the inbound document specification referenced by a channel object. This is not always possible, though, because many references cannot be changed after the object is created. That leads to the second approach, which is to delete the referring object altogether.

To avoid problems when removing BizTalk Messaging objects, remove them in the opposite order of creation. BizTalk Server recommends that BizTalk Messaging objects be created in the following order:

- Organizations
- Document specifications
- Envelopes
- Ports
- Channels
- Distribution lists

When deleting BizTalk Messaging objects, remember that organizations, document specifications, envelopes, and ports could have any number of referential dependencies in place and that all object references must be removed before the object itself can be removed.

Caution

Entities such as XLANG schedules and document submission scripts may refer to BizTalk Messaging objects. BizTalk Server does not check for these types of dependencies when a BizTalk Messaging object is removed. In addition, a running XLANG schedule that refers to a BizTalk Messaging object prevents that object from being removed from the BizTalk Messaging database.

Security

During installation, Microsoft BizTalk Server 2002 creates a Windows 2000 User Group named BizTalk Server Administrators. To access any of the objects in the BizTalk Messaging Configuration object model, a script or application must be run in the context of a user account that is a member of the BizTalk Server Administrators group. An access denied error (0x80070005) is returned when the user account is not a member of this group.

A scenario where this error occurs but the cause is not obvious is when the BizTalk Messaging Configuration object model is accessed through Web Services or a Web page running under Internet Information Services (IIS). The default user account for anonymous access in IIS is `IUSR_`*`MACHINE`*, where *`MACHINE`* is typically the network name for your computer. It is, of course, highly recommended that you secure all BizTalk

Messaging Configuration access through Web-based applications; however, for testing, you could make the `IUSER_MACHINE` account a member of the BizTalk Server Administrators group.

Documentation

Microsoft BizTalk Server 2002 ships with two types of documentation: online help and samples. The online help contains everything from conceptual overviews and tutorials to bare metal explanations of BizTalk Messaging. This includes the Configuration object model reference, which is located under "BizTalk Server 2002 Developer Solutions/BizTalk Server Reference/Messaging Services Reference."

In addition to the online help, BizTalk Server 2002 ships with many useful BizTalk Messaging samples. The samples are located in the `Microsoft BizTalk Server\SDK\Messaging Samples` directory. Most of the samples do not pertain directly to the Configuration object model; however, they still contain useful sample code in the form of setup scripts.

The setup scripts create and configure the necessary BizTalk Messaging objects required to run the associated sample. Most of the scripts were generated using a legacy tool named BizPort. You'll see odd variable names such as `lOrg110047` (formed by concatenating "l" for long, "Org" for a BizTalk Messaging organization, and the organization handle value) and related functions such as `Create_lOrg110047`. That being said, the setup scripts are still useful, especially when you consider what the sample itself is doing. For example, you can use the `config.vbs` script in the BizTalk `ServerAppIntegrate` sample as a guide for configuring BizTalk Messaging for Application Integration Components (AIC).

One sample that applies specifically to BizTalk Messaging Configuration is `BTConfigAssistant`. The `BTConfigAssistant` sample allows users to select and export BizTalk Messaging objects in the form of a configuration VBScript. The sample itself is a direct consumer of the Configuration object model.

A word of caution to those using the `BTConfigAssistant` sample to reproduce BizTalk Messaging configurations on other BizTalk servers. The `BTConfigAssistant` sample is not supported by Microsoft and doesn't always work as intended. In fact, the functionality of this sample may be superceded by the SEED Wizard. In other words, use `BTConfigAssistant` as an example for code that consumes the BizTalk Messaging Configuration object model.

For the hard-core programmers, the `DistributionList` sample includes usage of the object model in C++. The properties and methods exposed by the object model are no different for C++, but the sample does include all the messy COM overhead code required in C++.

One last code resource is the `Microsoft BizTalk Server\SDK\Include` directory. Here you will find the `idl` and header files for the BizTalk Messaging Configuration object model as well as other BizTalk Server object models.

BizTalk Messaging Configuration Interfaces

The BizTalk Messaging Configuration object model enables programmers and administrators to manipulate and manage the BizTalk Messaging system in a programmatic fashion. This section discusses the interfaces in the Configuration object model as well as provides example code that demonstrates interface usage.

The sample code in this section is designed for Visual Basic/Visual Basic Script. The Visual Basic language was chosen for the sake of clarity and brevity. If you want to see sample C++ code, refer to the `DistributionList` sample that ships with BizTalk Server 2002.

Configuration Object Model Overview

The functionality exposed by the BizTalk Messaging Configuration object model closely replicates the functionality available in BizTalk Messaging Manager. This is no accident because BizTalk Messaging Manager is built directly on top of the Configuration object model. We're going to use this to our advantage as we learn the BizTalk Messaging Configuration object model by relating the properties and methods of each object to concepts we've already learned in BizTalk Messaging.

Table 19.1 lists the interfaces and associated objects exposed by the BizTalk Messaging Configuration object model.

TABLE 19.1 BizTalk Messaging Configuration Interfaces and Objects

Interface	*Implemented By*
`IBizTalkBase`	`BizTalkChannel`, `BizTalkDocument`, `BizTalkEnvelope`, `BizTalkOrgnization`, `BizTalkPort`, `BizTalkPortGroup`
`IBizTalkCertificateInfo`	`BizTalkCertificateInfo`
`IBizTalkChannel`	`BizTalkChannel`
`IBizTalkConfig`	`BizTalkConfig`

TABLE 19.1 continued

Interface	*Implemented By*
`IBizTalkConfigData`	`BizTalkConfigData`
`IBizTalkDocument`	`BizTalkDocument`
`IBizTalkEndPoint`	`BizTalkEndPoint`
`IBizTalkEnvelope`	`BizTalkEnvelope`
`IBizTalkLoggingInfo`	`BizTalkLoggingInfo`
`IBizTalkOrganization`	`BizTalkOrganization`
`IBizTalkPort`	`BizTalkPort`
`IBizTalkPortGroup`	`BizTalkPortGroup`
`IBizTalkServiceWindowInfo`	`BizTalkServiceWindowInfo`
`IBizTalkTransportInfo`	`BizTalkTransportInfo`
`IDictionary`	`Dictionary`
`ISimpleList`	`SimpleList`

> **Note**
>
> The BizTalk Messaging Configuration interfaces and objects are implemented in `BizTalkObjectModel.dll`.

`IBizTalkConfig` Interface

Programmatic access to the BizTalk Messaging system begins with the `IBizTalkConfig` interface. Through its methods, `IBizTalkConfig` acts as an object factory for the main BizTalk Messaging Configuration objects. The `IBizTalkConfig` properties serve as a central source for information about existing BizTalk Messaging objects. Table 19.2 lists the properties and methods exposed by the `IBizTalkConfig` interface.

TABLE 19.2 `IBizTalkConfig` Properties and Methods

Name	*Type*	*Description*
`Certificates`	Property	ADO recordset containing the list of certificates registered with BizTalk Server
`Channels`	Property	ADO recordset containing information about all BizTalk Messaging channels in the database
`CreateChannel`	Method	Creates and returns a new `BizTalkChannel` object

TABLE 19.2 continued

Name	*Type*	*Description*
`CreateDocument`	Method	Creates and returns a new `BizTalkDocument` object
`CreateEnvelope`	Method	Creates and returns a new `BizTalkEnvelope` object
`CreateOrganization`	Method	Creates and returns a new `BizTalkOrganization` object
`CreatePort`	Method	Creates and returns a new `BizTalkPort` object
`CreatePortGroup`	Method	Creates and returns a new `BizTalkPortGroup` object
`Documents`	Property	ADO recordset containing information about all BizTalk Messaging document definitions in the database
`Envelopes`	Property	ADO recordset containing information about all BizTalk Messaging envelopes in the database
`Organizations`	Property	ADO recordset containing information about all BizTalk Messaging organizations in the database
`PortGroups`	Property	ADO recordset containing information about all BizTalk Messaging distribution lists in the database
`Ports`	Property	ADO recordset containing information about all BizTalk Messaging ports in the database

The following sections discuss these properties and methods in greater detail.

Creating New BizTalk Messaging Configuration Objects

`IBizTalkConfig` exposes six methods for creating new BizTalk Messaging Configuration objects. Listing 19.1 shows these methods and their syntax.

LISTING 19.1 Sample Configuration Object Creation Code

```
Set BT = CreateObject("BizTalk.BizTalkConfig")
Set org = BT.CreateOrganization
Set doc = BT.CreateDocument
Set env = BT.CreateEnvelope
Set port = BT.CreatePort
Set channel = BT.CreateChannel
Set group = BT.CreatePortGroup
```

Note

The `IBizTalkConfig Create` methods (`CreateChannel`, `CreateDocument`, and so on) only create instances of Configuration objects. You'll learn how to create BizTalk Messaging objects in the database in the next section.

Inspecting Existing BizTalk Messaging Objects

`IBizTalkConfig` exposes six properties that return ADO recordsets containing information about the BizTalk Messaging objects currently configured in the database. Listing 19.2 shows these properties and their syntax.

LISTING 19.2 `IBizTalkConfig` BizTalk Messaging Object ADO Recordset Properties

```
Set BT = CreateObject("BizTalk.BizTalkConfig")
Set channel_rs = BT.Channels
Set doc_rs = BT.Documents
Set env_rs = BT.Envelopes
Set org_rs = BT.Organizations
Set group_rs = BT.PortGroups
Set port_rs = BT.Ports
```

Table 19.3 shows the fields returned by the ADO recordset properties.

TABLE 19.3 ADO Recordset Fields

Field	*Description*
`id`	Indicates the internal handle for the object
`name`	Indicates the name of the object
`datemodified`	Indicates the date and time of the last update
`format`	Indicates the envelope format (`Envelopes` property only)
`defaultflag`	Indicates the default organization—0 for false, –1 for true (`Organizations` property only)

Certificates

Certificates are used to authenticate and secure exchanges on nonsecured networks. Microsoft BizTalk Server relies heavily on the security provided by certificates. Public-key encryption is supported for all documents handled by BizTalk Server.

The `IBizTalkConfig` interface allows you to search the contents of a certificate store using the `Certificates` property. Table 19.4 shows the ADO recordset fields returned by the `Certificates` property.

TABLE 19.4 `Certificates` ADO Recordset Fields

Field	Description
`name`	Specifies the certificate name
`reference`	Specifies a reference to the certificate in the certificate store
`store`	Specifies the certificate store
`usage`	Specifies the how the certificate can be used

Listing 19.3 demonstrates usage of the `Certificates` property.

LISTING 19.3 Usage of the `IBizTalkConfig` Certificates Property

```
Set BT = CreateObject("BizTalk.BizTalkConfig")
Set rs = BT.Certificates(BIZTALK_STORE_TYPE_BIZTALK,
➥BIZTALK_USAGE_TYPE_ENCRYPTION, "")

Do While Not rs.EOF
    MsgBox "Name: " & rs("name") & vbCRLF & _
           "Reference: " & rs("reference") & vbCRLF & _
           "Store: " & rs("store") & vbCRLF & _
           "Usage: " & rs("usage")
    rs.MoveNext
Loop
```

Note that the `Certificates` property is not a traditional property in that it takes several parameters. Those parameters in order are a `BIZTALK_STORE_TYPE` enumeration value, a `BIZTALK_USAGE_TYPE` enumeration value, and a prefix filter string to further refine your search.

Tables 19.5 and 19.6 show the possible values for the `BIZTALK_STORE_TYPE` and `BIZTALK_USAGE_TYPE` enumerations.

TABLE 19.5 `BIZTALK_STORE_TYPE` Enumeration Values

Name	Description
`BIZTALK_STORE_TYPE_MY`	Store for certificates authorized only by your organization
`BIZTALK_STORE_TYPE_BIZTALK`	Dedicated BizTalk Server store

TABLE 19.6 `BIZTALK_USAGE_TYPE` **Enumeration Values**

Name	*Description*
`BIZTALK_USAGE_TYPE_ENCRYPTION`	Certificate is used for encryption.
`BIZTALK_USAGE_TYPE_SIGNATURE`	Certificate is used for signature.
`BIZTALK_USAGE_TYPE_BOTH`	Certificate is used for encryption and signature.

`IBizTalkBase` Interface

The `IBizTalkBase` interface, as its name suggests, exposes common properties and methods of the six primary BizTalk Messaging Configuration objects:

- `BizTalkChannel`
- `BizTalkDocument`
- `BizTalkEnvelope`
- `BizTalkOrganization`
- `BizTalkPort`
- `BizTalkPortGroup`

Table 19.7 lists the properties and methods of the `IBizTalkBase` interface.

TABLE 19.7 `IBizTalkBase` **Properties and Methods**

Name	*Type*	*Description*
`Clear`	Method	Clears the object in memory
`Create`	Method	Creates a new BizTalk Messaging object in the database
`DateModified`	Property	Date and time the object was created or saved
`Handle`	Property	BizTalk Messaging object handle
`Load`	Method	Loads an object from the database by its handle
`LoadByName`	Method	Loads an object from the database by its name
`Name`	Property	Name of the object
`Remove`	Method	Removes the object from the database
`Save`	Method	Saves the object to the database

Figure 19.3 shows the hierarchical relationship between `IBizTalkBase` and the six primary Configuration interfaces.

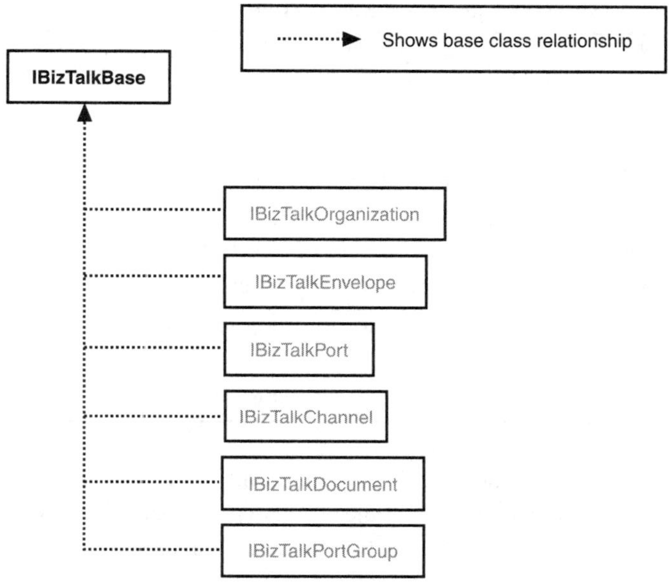

FIGURE 19.3
`IBizTalkBase` *interface UML diagram.*

Creating New BizTalk Messaging Objects

BizTalk Messaging objects are created in the database by calling the `Create` method. Before calling `Create`, you must name the object:

```
Org.Name = "BizTalk Unleashed Organization"
Org.Create
```

> **Note**
>
> Some Configuration objects such as `BizTalkPort` and `BizTalkChannel` have additional prerequisites before calling the `Create` method.

BizTalk Server places two restrictions on object names:

- The name must be at least one character and can be no more than 64 characters.
- The name, which is not case sensitive, must be unique across the database for the object type.

In addition, BizTalk Server reserved several names for BizTalk Messaging objects. Table 19.8 shows the names reserved by BizTalk Server 2002 and their associated object type.

TABLE 19.8 Reserved Object Names in BizTalk Server 2002

Reserved Name	*Object Type*
Reliable Message Acknowledgement Port	Port
Reliable Message Acknowledgement Channel	Channel
BizTalk Canonical Receipt	Document definition
Reliable Messaging Acknowledgement	Document definition
Reliable Messaging Acknowledgement SMTP from Address	Organization identifier
Home Organization	Organization

When new objects are created in the database, BizTalk Server generates and assigns a unique internal handle value to the object. This value is static for the life of the object on this server. After calling `Create`, the `Handle` and `DateModified` properties are updated to reflect the new object information.

Note

The `DateModified` property returns a string with the coordinate universal time (UTC) in the format *yyyy-mm-dd hh:mm:ss.*

Caution

The BizTalk Server 2002 documentation warns that when creating or saving an object that refers to an XML document specification outside your local domain, you may receive an error. If an error occurs, you will need to download and configure the WinHTTP proxy utility from the Microsoft MSDN Web site.

Modifying BizTalk Messaging Objects

To change any of the settings for an existing BizTalk Messaging object, you must first load the object into memory. `IBizTalkBase` provides two methods for doing just that, `Load` and `LoadByName`. The following sample code demonstrates how to use these methods:

```
Org.Load hOrg   ' where hOrg is the handle to an organization
Org.LoadByName "BizTalk Unleashed Organization"
```

After loading the object, you can make the necessary changes through the properties and methods of the Configuration object. Call the `Save` method to store your changes back to the database. The following code sample demonstrates an update to an organization in the database:

```
Org.LoadByName "BizTalk Unleashed Organization"
Org.Name = "New BizTalk Unleashed Organization"
Org.CreateAlias "My Alias", False, "Qualifier", "Value"
Org.Save
```

After you call `Save`, the `DateModified` property is updated to reflect the new date and time.

Caution

Changing the name of an existing BizTalk Messaging object could adversely affect scripts and schedules that refer to the object by name.

Removing BizTalk Messaging Objects

To remove an object from the BizTalk Messaging database, first load the object into memory and then call `Remove` to delete the object from the database. For example:

```
Org.LoadByName "New BizTalk Unleashed Organization"
Org.Remove
```

Caution

The `Remove` method will fail when called for a BizTalk Messaging object that is referred to by another BizTalk Messaging object or a running XLANG schedule. This is known as referential integrity. BizTalk Server enforces referential integrity in the BizTalk Messaging database.

`IBizTalkBase` Example

Listing 19.4 shows a simple example illustrating the use of the `IBizTalkBase` properties and methods. Because a `BizTalkBase` object cannot be instantiated directly, a surrogate `BizTalkOrganization` object is used.

Tip

You can see the effects of this code in real-time through BizTalk Messaging Manager. Make sure that you refresh the search after each step.

LISTING 19.4 Visual Basic Code Illustrating the `BizTalkBase` Properties and Methods

```
' Step 1 - Create an organization configuration object
Set BT = CreateObject("BizTalk.BizTalkConfig")
Set org = BT.CreateOrganization()

' Step 2 - Name the organization and create it in the database
org.Name = "BizTalk Unleashed Organization"
hOrg = org.Create()
MsgBox "New object created, Handle = " & org.Handle & ", DateModified = " &
➥org.DateModified & "."

' Step 3 - Load our Organization by handle
org.Clear
org.Load hOrg
MsgBox org.Name & " loaded."

' Step 4 - Change the organization's name and save it back to the database
org.Name = "BizTalk Unleashed Sample Organization"
org.Save
MsgBox org.Name & " saved."

' Step 5 - Clear the config object and load our organization by name
org.Clear
org.LoadByName "BizTalk Unleashed Sample Organization"
MsgBox org.Name & " loaded."

' Step 6 - Remove our new organization from the database
org.Remove
MsgBox org.Name & " removed."
```

Note

The code (`19newListing04.vbs`) in Listing 19.4 is also available for download at the Sams Publishing Web site.

`IBizTalkOrganization` Interface

The `IBizTalkOrganization` interface exposes properties and methods that manage BizTalk Messaging organizations. Organizations represent trading partners with which you exchange documents. The Home Organization represents your business and may contain specific applications where inbound documents are routed. Table 19.9 shows the properties and methods of the `IBizTalkOrganization` interface.

TABLE 19.9 `IBizTalkOrganization` Properties and Methods

Name	*Type*	*Description*
`Aliases`	Property	ADO recordset containing information about all aliases for the organization
`Applications`	Property	ADO recordset containing information about all applications in the organization
`Comments`	Property	User comments about the organization
`CreateAlias`	Method	Creates an alias
`CreateApplication`	Method	Creates an application
`GetDefaultAlias`	Method	Returns the handle to the default alias
`IsDefault`	Property	Flag indicating whether the organization is default
`LoadAlias`	Method	Loads an alias into memory
`LoadApplication`	Method	Loads an application into memory
`RemoveAlias`	Method	Removes an alias
`RemoveApplication`	Method	Removes an application
`SaveAlias`	Method	Saves an alias
`SaveApplication`	Method	Saves an application

In addition to the properties and methods shown in Table 19.9, `BizTalkOrganization` objects also implement the properties and methods of `IBizTalkBase` shown in Table 19.7.

Note

BizTalk Messaging Manager refers to the default organization as the Home Organization. The home organization cannot be deleted from the BizTalk Messaging database.

Figure 19.4 shows a UML-style diagram illustrating the relationship between `IBizTalkOrganization` and `IBizTalkBase`.

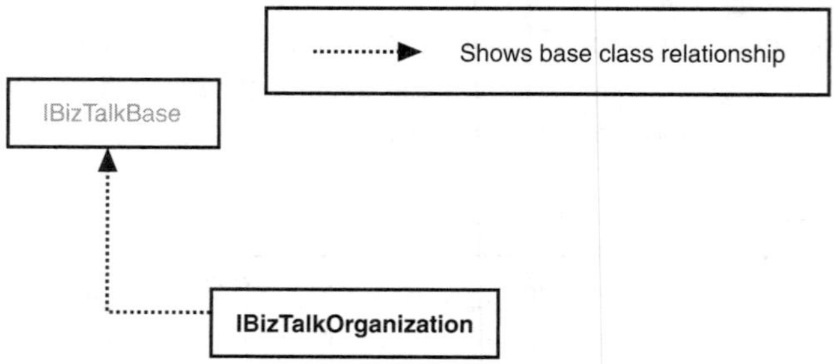

FIGURE 19.4
`IBizTalkOrganization` *interface UML diagram.*

The following sections discuss the properties and methods of the `IBizTalkOrganization` interface.

Aliases

Aliases are otherwise known as *identifiers* in BizTalk Messaging Manager. They specify qualifier-value pairs that uniquely identify an organization and consist of four properties:

- A handle that uniquely identifies the alias across the BizTalk Messaging database. Alias handles are assigned by BizTalk Server when the alias is created.
- A name unique across the organization object.
- An qualifier-value pair unique across the BizTalk Messaging database.
- A Boolean flag to indicate whether the alias is default.

Multiple aliases can be specified for a single organization; however, each alias name must be unique for the given organization. Alias qualifier-value pairs must be unique across all organizations in the database.

When new organizations are created, BizTalk Server automatically generates an alias with the name "Organization" and the qualifier-value pair, `"OrganizationName"-<name of organization>`. When an organization name is changed, BizTalk Server automatically updates the value in this qualifier-value pair to reflect the new organization name. Use the `CreateAlias`, `LoadAlias`, `SaveAlias`, and `RemoveAlias` methods to manipulate the current list of aliases for an organization. Listing 19.5 shows sample code that uses these methods. The handle value (100034) is made up for illustration purposes.

LISTING 19.5 Sample Code for Manipulating Organization Aliases

```
org.CreateAlias "My Alias Name", False, "Alias Qualifier", "Alias Value"

Dim name, def, qual, val
org.LoadAlias 100034, name, def, qual, val

val = "New Alias Value"
org.SaveAlias 100034, name, def, qual, val

org.RemoveAlias 100034
```

You cannot remove auto-generated aliases, default aliases, or aliases referred to by BizTalk Messaging channels and/or ports.

Note

After creating, saving, or removing an alias from a `BizTalkOrganization` object, you must call the `Create` or `Save` method to persist the new alias settings in the database.

The `Aliases` property returns an ADO recordset containing the current list of aliases in the organization. Table 19.10 shows the fields returned for each record.

TABLE 19.10 `Aliases` Property ADO Recordest Fields

Field	*Description*
`id`	Specifies the alias handle
`name`	Specifies the alias name
`defaultflag`	Specifies whether the alias is default (0 for false, –1 for true)
`qualifier`	Specifies the identifier in the alias identifier-value pair
`value`	Specifies the value in the alias identifier-value pair

Listing 19.6 shows example usage of the `Aliases` property.

LISTING 19.6 Sample Code Illustrating the `IBizTalkOrganization` `Aliases` Property

```
Set BT = CreateObject("BizTalk.BizTalkConfig")
Set org = BT.CreateOrganization
org.LoadByName "Home Organization"
Set rs = org.Aliases

Do While Not rs.EOF
    MsgBox "ID: " & rs("id") & vbCRLF & _
           "Name: " & rs("name") & vbCrLf & _
           "Default: " & rs("defaultflag") & vbCRLF & _
           "Qualifier: " & rs("qualifier") & vbCrLf &_
           "Value: " & rs("value")
    rs.MoveNext
Loop
```

Applications

Applications in the Home Organization identify actual internal applications within your business. They do not, however, enable the flow of documents through BizTalk Messaging to the internal applications. Instead, they serve as placeholders to indicate a document destination. The actual configuration that enables the flow of documents to an application is specified by the transport properties of a messaging port.

BizTalk Messaging Manager only allows applications to be created in the Home Organization. The Configuration object model, however, does not enforce this rule. Therefore, any applications created in nondefault organizations cannot be manipulated in BizTalk Messaging Manager. Although creating applications outside the Home Organization is generally not recommended, it is possible to access and manipulate them through the Configuration object model.

Note

An application name must be unique within its organization.

Use the `CreateApplication`, `LoadApplication`, `SaveApplication`, and `RemoveApplication` methods to manipulate the current list of applications for an organization. Listing 19.7 shows sample code that uses these methods. Once again the handle value (100034) is made up for illustration purposes.

LISTING 19.7 Sample Code for Manipulating Applications

```
org.CreateApplication "My Application Name"

Dim name
org.LoadApplication 100034, name

name = "New Application Name"
org.SaveApplication 100034, name

org.RemoveApplication 100034
```

An application cannot be removed if a BizTalk Messaging port or channel refers to it.

> **Note**
>
> After creating, saving, or removing an application from the Home Organization, you must call the `Create` or `Save` method on the associated `BizTalkOrganization` object to persist the new application settings in the database.

The `Applications` property returns an ADO recordset containing the current list of applications in the organization. Table 19.11 shows the fields returned for each record.

TABLE 19.11 `Applications` Property ADO Recordset Fields

Field	*Description*
`id`	The application handle
`name`	The application name

`IBizTalkOrganization` Example

Listing 19.8 demonstrates the creation of a new partner organization named Joe's Crab Shack.

LISTING 19.8 Sample Script Demonstrating the Creation of a New Organization

```
' Create a new organization
Set BT = CreateObject("BizTalk.BizTalkConfig")
Set org = BT.CreateOrganization
org.Name = "Joe's Crab Shack"
org.Create
```

LISTING 19.8 continued

```
' Create an alias for the organization
org.CreateAlias "Best Crabcakes in Maryland", False, "Awards", "Best Crabcakes"
org.Save

' Add a new application to the home organization
org.Clear
org.LoadByName "Home Organization"
org.CreateApplication "Restaurant Reviews"
org.CreateApplication "My Application"
org.Save
```

IBizTalkDocument Interface

The `IBizTalkDocument` interface provides properties and methods for managing BizTalk Messaging document definitions. Document definitions represent specific types of documents handled by BizTalk Server. They consist of a BizTalk Server-specific XML document specification schema, which describes the content and format of the document. Table 19.12 shows the properties and methods of the `IBizTalkDocument` interface.

TABLE 19.12 `IBizTalkDocument` Properties and Methods

Name	*Type*	*Description*
`Content`	Property	Content of the document definition specified by `Reference`
`LoadByPropertySet`	Method	Loads the document definition based on the specified `PropertySet Dictionary` object
`NameSpace`	Property	String that resolves naming conflicts in the document
`PropertySet`	Property	`Dictionary` object containing the selection criteria for extracting information from an EDI document
`Reference`	Property	WebDAV URL specifying the document specification file
`TrackFields`	Property	`Dictionary` object containing the custom fields that Tracking uses to track documents based on this specification
`Type`	Property	Document specification type
`Version`	Property	Version of the document standard

In addition to the properties and methods shown in Table 19.12, `BizTalkDocument` objects also implement the properties and methods of `IBizTalkBase`, shown in Table 19.7.

Figure 19.5 shows a UML-style diagram illustrating the relationships between `IBizTalkDocument` and various Configuration interfaces.

FIGURE 19.5
`IBizTalkDocument` *interface UML diagram.*

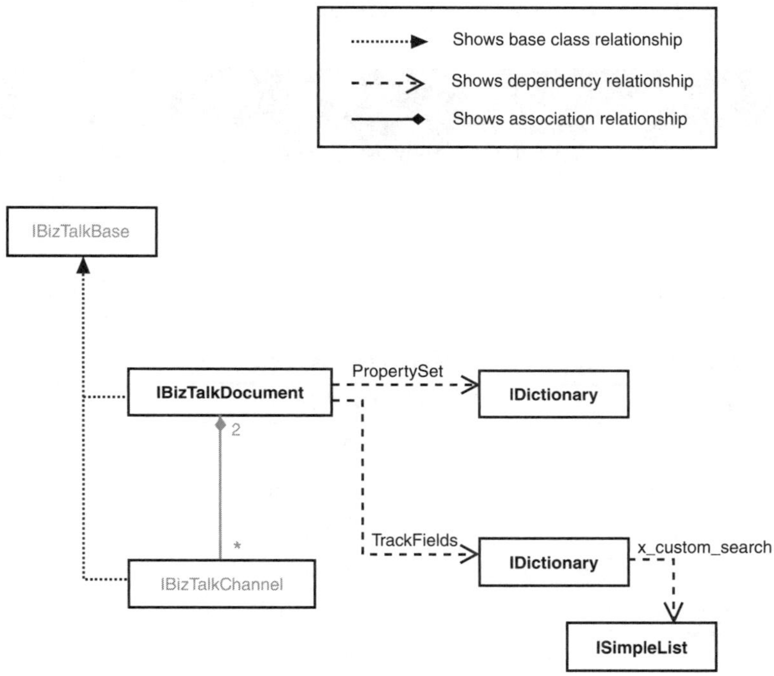

Document Specification

The document specification for a `BizTalkDocument` object is set by specifying the full WedDAV URL for the document specification file in the `Reference` property. For example:

```
doc.Reference = "http://machine/BizTalkServerRepository/DocSpecs/
➥Microsoft/CommonPO.xml"
```

When a document definition is created or saved using the `Create` or `Save` methods, the `Content`, `NameSpace`, `Type`, and `Version` properties are updated to reflect the new document specification. When `Reference` is empty, these properties are cleared.

Global Tracking

Document tracking data designates fields within the document specification that you want to log to the Tracking database. The `TrackFields` property is used to specify tracking data for a `BizTalkDocument` object. `TrackFields` returns a `Dictionary` object containing the custom fields that Tracking uses to track documents based on this specification. Tracking fields apply only to inbound documents in a channel. Any tracking data specified for an outbound document is ignored by BizTalk Server.

Note

A valid document definition must be specified in the `Reference` property before setting any tracking data.

Table 19.13 shows the predefined `Dictionary` fields used by Tracking.

TABLE 19.13 Predefined Tracking Fields

Field Name	*Field Type*
`i_value1`	Integer value
`i_value2`	Integer value
`r_value1`	Real value
`r_value2`	Real value
`d_value1`	Date value
`d_value2`	Date value
`s_value1`	String value
`s_value2`	String value
`x_custom_search`	List of additional tracking fields

The fields in the dictionary must contain valid XPath values that identify the fields to be tracked. Listing 19.9 shows some example XPath expressions. The XPath expressions were derived from the `CommonPO.xml` document specification that ships with BizTalk Server.

LISTING 19.9 Sample XPath Tracking Fields

```
doc.TrackFields.r_value1 = "/CommonPO/SpecialCharge/@Amount"
doc.TrackFields.r_value2 = "/CommonPO/Currency/@ExchangeRate"
```

LISTING 19.9 continued

```
doc.TrackFields.s_value1 = "/CommonPO/TermsOfSale/@PaymentMethod"
doc.TrackFields.s_value2 = "/CommonPO/CarrierDetail/@Routing"

doc.TrackFields.i_value1 = "/CommonPO/TermsOfSale/@NetDays"
doc.TrackFields.i_value2 = "/CommonPO/TermsOfSale/@DiscountDaysDue"

doc.TrackFields.d_value1 = "/CommonPO/Item/DateReference/@Date"
doc.TrackFields.d_value2 = /CommonPO/POHeader/@CreationDate
```

If additional fields are required, the `x_custom_search` field can be used. `x_custom_search` returns a `SimpleList` to which fields can be added or removed using the `ISimpleList.Add` and `ISimpleList.Remove` methods. Listing 19.10 shows sample code for the `x_custom_search` `Dictionary` field.

LISTING 19.10 Sample Code for Custom Tracking Fields

```
doc.TrackFields.x_custom_search.Add "/CommonPO/Total/@LineItemTotal"
doc.TrackFields.x_custom_search.Add "/CommonPO/Total/@QuantityTotal"
doc.TrackFields.x_custom_search.Add "/CommonPO/Total/@POTotal"

doc.TrackFields.x_custom_search.Remove "/CommonPO/POHeader/@Purpose"
doc.TrackFields.x_custom_search.Remove /CommonPO/POHeader/@Type
```

Selection Criteria

Selection criteria are a set of unique name-value pairs used to process EDI documents. The `PropertySet` property is used to specify selection criteria for a `BizTalkDocument` object. `PropertySet` returns a `Dictionary` object with the EDI selection criteria for the document specification. Selection criteria is required for X12 and EDIFACT type document definitions.

> **Note**
>
> A valid document definition must be specified by the `Reference` property before setting any selection criteria.

Tables 19.14 and 19.15 show the required and optional header elements that must be specified for EDI document specifications.

TABLE 19.14 Required X12 Header Elements

Field Name	*Required*	*GS Element*
functional_identifier	Yes	GS01
application_sender_code	Yes	GS02
application_receiver_code	Yes	GS03
standards_version	Yes	GS08

TABLE 19.15 EDIFACT Header Elements

Field Name	*Required*	*UNH Element*	*UNG Element*
functional_identifier	Yes	S009, 0065	0038
application_sender_code	No	not used	S006, 0040
application_receiver_code	No	not used	S007, 0044
standards_version_type	Yes	S009, 0052	S008, 0052
standards_version_value	Yes	S009, 0054	S008, 0054

`IBizTalkDocument` Example

Listing 19.11 shows sample code that creates a new document definition named Restaurant Reviewer based on the `CommonPartnerProfile.xml` document specification that ships with BizTalk Server. Before running this code on your machine, you need to change *`machine`* in the Reference WebDAV URL to the network name of the machine where your BizTalk Server is installed.

LISTING 19.11 Sample Code to Create a New Document

```
' Create a new document specification
Set BT = CreateObject("BizTalk.BizTalkConfig")
Set doc = BT.CreateDocument
doc.Name = "Restaurant Reviewer"
doc.Reference = "http://machine/BizTalkServerRepository/DocSpecs/Microsoft/
➥CommonPartnerProfile.xml"
doc.Create

' Add tracking fields
doc.TrackFields.s_value1 = "/CommonPartnerProfile/Name/@Text"
doc.TrackFields.s_value2 = "/CommonPartnerProfile/Location/@AgencyCode"
doc.Save
```

Tip

After running this script, you can review the changes in BizTalk Messaging Manager.

`IBizTalkEnvelope` Interface

The `IBizTalkEnvelope` interface provides properties and methods for managing BizTalk Messaging envelopes. An envelope encapsulates electronic business data for transport into and out of BizTalk Server. Conceptually, it consists of a header and sometimes a footer and provides BizTalk Server with the necessary information to open inbound interchanges and create outbound documents.

The BizTalk Messaging envelope itself consists of a format type, which in turn may require an envelope specification. Table 19.16 shows the properties of the `IBizTalkEnvelope` interface.

TABLE 19.16 `IBizTalkEnvelope` Properties

Name	*Type*	*Description*
`Content`	Property	Content of the envelope specification indicated by `Reference`
`Format`	Property	Specifies the envelope format
`NameSpace`	Property	String that resolves naming conflicts in the document
`Reference`	Property	WebDAV URL specifying the envelope specification file
`Version`	Property	Version of the envelope format specification

In addition to the properties and methods shown in Table 19.16, `BizTalkEnvelope` objects also implement the properties and methods of `IBizTalkBase`, shown in Table 19.7.

Figure 19.6 shows a UML-style diagram illustrating the relationships between `IBizTalkEnvelope` and various Configuration interfaces.

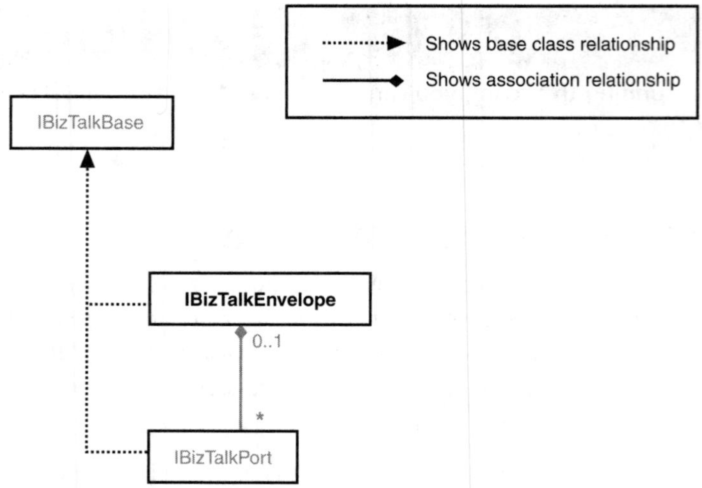

FIGURE 19.6
`IBizTalkEnvelope` *interface UML diagram.*

Envelope Format

An envelope format is specified through the `Format` property. `Format` takes one of the following strings:

- `x12`
- `edifact`
- `custom xml`
- `flatfile`
- `custom`
- `reliable`

Specifying anything other than one of these strings results in a runtime error when `Save` or `Create` is called. If this occurs, the previously specified format is not changed. The following code sample shows correct and incorrect format specification strings:

```
env.Format = "edifact"    ' OK
env.Format = "EDIFACT"    ' OK
env.Format = "flatfile"   ' OK
env.Format = "flat file"  ' Error
```

Notice that the format string is not case sensitive.

Note

Custom formats require that a custom parser and/or serializer be registered with BizTalk Server. Refer to Chapter 18, "Creating Custom Seriliazers, Parsers, and Functoids," for more information about creating custom parsers and serializers.

Envelope Specification

The conditionally required envelope specification is specified through the `Reference` property. `Reference` takes a string containing the full WebDAV URL for the envelope specification file. `X12`, `EDIFACT`, and reliable are well-known formats to BizTalk Server and as such do not need a specification file. The system goes so far as to throw a runtime error when `Reference` is set for one of these formats. Listing 19.12 shows correct and incorrect usage of the `Reference` property for an EDI envelope.

LISTING 19.12 Correct and Incorrect Usage of the `Reference` Property for EDI Envelopes

```
' Incorrect:
Set BT = CreateObject("BizTalk.BizTalkConfig")
Set env = BT.CreateEnvelope
env.Name = "BizTalk Unleashed Envelope"
env.Format = "x12"
env.Reference = "http://machine/BizTalkServerRepository/DocSpecs/Envelope.xml"
env.Create ' Runtime error!

' Correct:
Set BT = CreateObject("BizTalk.BizTalkConfig")
Set env = BT.CreateEnvelope
env.Name = "BizTalk Unleashed Envelope"
env.Format = "x12"
env.Create
```

When an envelope is created or saved using the `Create` or `Save` methods, the `Content`, `NameSpace`, and `Version` properties are updated to reflect the new envelope specification. If `Reference` is empty, these properties are cleared to their default values.

`IBizTalkEnvelope` Example

Listing 19.13 shows an example that creates an envelope based on the Simple SOAP Envelope document specification that ships with BizTalk Server 2002.

LISTING 19.13 Sample Code to Create a New Envelope

```
Set BT = CreateObject("BizTalk.BizTalkConfig")
Set env = BT.CreateEnvelope
env.Name = "Simple Soap Envelope"
env.Format = "custom xml"
env.Reference = "http://machine/BizTalkServerRepository/DocSpecs/Microsoft/
➥Simple SOAP Envelope.xml"
env.Create
```

IBizTalkPort Interface

The `IBizTalkPort` interface provides properties and methods for managing BizTalk Messaging ports. A BizTalk Messaging port defines the one-way transfer of a document between organizations and applications. Table 19.17 shows the properties and methods of the `IBizTalkPort` interface.

TABLE 19.17 `IBizTalkPort` Properties and Methods

Name	*Type*	*Description*
`Channels`	Property	ADO recordset containing information about all channels that refer to this port
`Comments`	Property	User comments about the port
`ControlNumberValue`	Property	Interchange control number
`Delimiters`	Property	`Dictionary` object containing all delimiters used in the document specification
`DestinationEndPoint`	Property	`BizTalkEndPoint` object containing information about the destination
`EncodingType`	Property	`BIZTALK_ENCODING_TYPE` enumeration value that indicates the document encoding type
`EncryptionCertificateInfo`	Property	`BizTalkCertificateInfo` object containing information about the certificate that encrypts the document
`EncryptionType`	Property	`BIZTALK_ENCRYPTION_TYPE` enumeration value that indicates the document encryption type
`Envelope`	Property	Handle to the associated envelope
`PrimaryTransport`	Property	`BizTalkTransportInfo` object containing information about the primary transport
`SecondaryTransport`	Property	`BizTalkTransportInfo` object containing information about the secondary transport

TABLE 19.17 continued

Name	*Type*	*Description*
`ServiceWindowTransport`	Property	`BizTalkServiceWindowInfo` object containing information about the service window
`SignatureType`	Property	`BIZTALK_SIGNATURE_TYPE` enumeration value that indicates the type of digital signing and verification

In addition to the properties and methods shown in Table 19.17, `BizTalkPort` objects also implement the properties and methods of `IBizTalkBase` shown in Table 19.7.

Figure 19.7 shows a UML-style diagram illustrating the relationships between `IBizTalkPort` and various Configuration interfaces.

FIGURE 19.7
`IBizTalkPort` *interface UML diagram.*

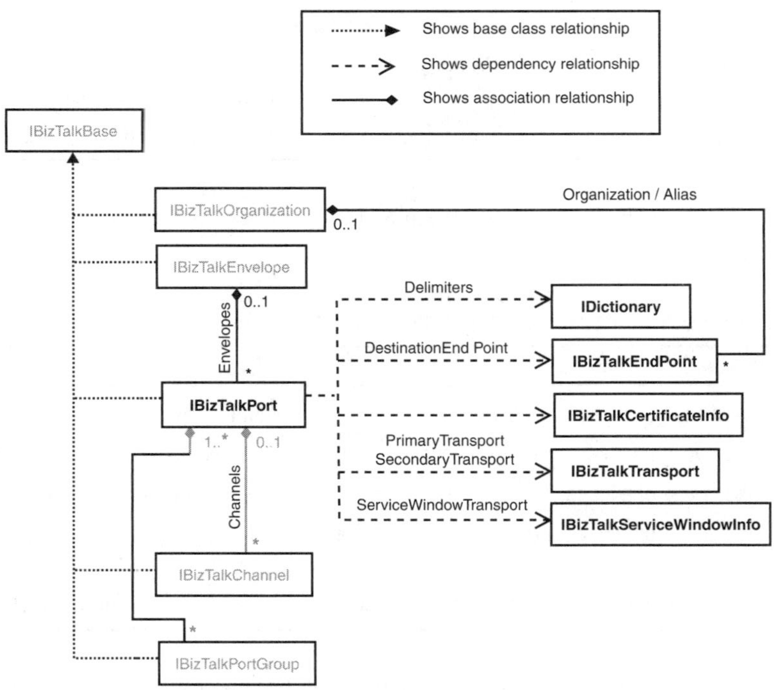

Destination

Messaging port destinations specify where the messaging port delivers documents. Destinations can be organizations, XLANG schedules, or applications in the Home Organization. A messaging port destination is specified through the `DestinationEndPoint` property of the `IBizTalkPort` interface. `DestinationEndPoint` returns an instance of an object that implements the `IBizTalkEndPoint` interface. Table 19.18 shows the properties of the `IBizTalkEndPoint` interface.

TABLE 19.18 `IBizTalkEndPoint` Properties

Name	*Type*	*Description*
`Alias`	Property	Handle to the organization alias for the destination organization
`Application`	Property	Handle to the associated application in the destination organization
`Openness`	Property	`BIZTALK_OPENNESS_TYPE_EX` enumeration value that indicates the openness of the destination
`Organization`	Property	Handle to the destination organization

Table 19.19 shows the possible enumeration values for the `Openness` property of the `IBizTalkEndPoint` interface.

TABLE 19.19 `BIZTALK_OPENNESS_TYPE_EX` Enumeration Values

Name	*Description*
`BIZTALK_OPENNESS_TYPE_EX_NOTOPEN`	Not open.
`BIZTALK_OPENNESS_TYPE_EX_SOURCE`	Source organization is open.
`BIZTALK_OPENNESS_TYPE_EX_DESTINATION`	Destination organization is open.
`BIZTALK_OPENNESS_TYPE_EX_FROMWORKFLOW`	Document is received from an XLANG schedule.
`BIZTALK_OPENNESS_TYPE_EX_TOWORKFLOW`	Document is sent to an XLANG schedule.

The `Alias` and `Organization` properties can both be used for specifying a destination organization. It is not necessary to specify an alias and an organization, though; one or the other will suffice.

Note

The `Openness` property cannot be changed after a messaging port is created.

The following "Destination:" sections discuss the various messaging port destination types and the implications of using each type.

Destination: Organization

For destinations to organizations, the messaging port may specify a specific partner organization or leave the destination open, creating an open messaging port. Open messaging ports expect the destination information to be supplied at runtime through fields in the document or parameters passed during submission.

Before configuring a messaging port to an organization, the organization must be added to the BizTalk Messaging database. Listing 19.14 demonstrates the required settings for the `DestinationEndPoint` property to configure a messaging port to a specific partner organization.

LISTING 19.14 `DestinationEndPoint` Settings for a Partner Organization

```
org.LoadByName "Joe's Crab Shack"
port.DestinationEndPoint.Organization = org.Handle
port.DestinationEndPoint.Openness = BIZTALK_OPENNESS_TYPE_EX_NOTOPEN
```

Listing 19.15 demonstrates the required settings for the `DestinationEndPoint` property to configure an open messaging port.

LISTING 19.15 `DestinationEndPoint` Settings for an Open Messaging Port

```
port.DestinationEndPoint.Openness = BIZTALK_OPENNESS_TYPE_EX_DESTINATION
```

When creating open messaging ports, you must abide by the following constraints:

- `PrimaryTransport.Type` must be set to `BIZTALK_OPENNESS_TYPE_OPENDESTINATION`.
- `EncryptionType` cannot be set.
- The messaging port cannot be included in a distribution group.

Destination: XLANG Schedule

Messaging ports to XLANG schedules can be configured to activate a new XLANG schedule or deliver documents to a running XLANG schedule. Listing 19.16 demonstrates the required settings for the `DestinationEndPoint` property to configure a messaging port to activate an XLANG schedule.

LISTING 19.16 `DestinationEndPoint` Settings for a Messaging Port to a New XLANG Schedule

```
org.LoadByName "Home Organization"
port.DestinationEndPoint.Organization = org.Handle
port.DestinationEndPoint.Openness = BIZTALK_OPENNESS_TYPE_EX_TOWORKFLOW
```

Listing 19.17 demonstrates the required settings for the `DestinationEndPoint` property to configure a messaging port to a running XLANG schedule.

LISTING 19.17 `DestinationEndPoint` Settings for a Messaging Port to a Running XLANG Schedule

```
port.DestinationEndPoint.Openness = BIZTALK_OPENNESS_TYPE_EX_TOWORKFLOW
```

Notice that a destination to a running XLANG schedule does not require that an organization be specified. Information that identifies running XLANG schedules is passed in document fields as parameters during document submission.

Destination: Application

Before configuring a messaging port destination to an application, the application must be added to the Home Organization. Listing 19.18 demonstrates the required settings for the `DestinationEndPoint` property to configure a messaging port to an application.

LISTING 19.18 `DestinationEndPoint` Settings for a Messaging Port to an Application

```
org.LoadByName "Home Organization"
Set rs = org.Applications
AppHandle = 0

Do While Not rs.EOF
    If (rs("name") = "My Application") Then
        AppHandle = rs("id")
        Exit Do
    End If
    rs.MoveNext
Loop
```

LISTING 19.18 continued

```
port.DestinationEndPoint.Organization = org.Handle
port.DestinationEndPoint.Application = AppHandle
port.DestinationEndPoint.Openness = BIZTALK_OPENNESS_TYPE_EX_NOTOPEN
```

Transport

Messaging port transports specify the transport service that will be used to transport documents as well as the specific address to which documents are sent. Messaging port transports are specified through the `PrimaryTransport` and `SecondaryTransport` properties of the `IBizTalkPort` interface. Both properties return an instance of an object that implements the `IBizTalkTransportInfo` interface. Table 19.20 shows the properties of the `IBizTalkTransportInfo` interface.

TABLE 19.20 `IBizTalkTransportInfo` Properties

Name	*Type*	*Description*
`Address`	Property	Destination address
`Parameter`	Property	Specifies additional information as required by `Type` and `Address`
`Type`	Property	`BIZTALK_TRANSPORT_TYPE` enumeration value that indicates the type of transport component to use

Transport Type

The transport type is specified through the `Type` property of the `IBizTalkTransportInfo` interface. Table 19.21 shows the transport type enumeration values.

TABLE 19.21 `BIZTALK_TRANSPORT_TYPE` Enumeration Values

Name	*Description*
`BIZTALK_TRANSPORT_TYPE_APPINTEGRATION`	Application Integration Component
`BIZTALK_TRANSPORT_TYPE_FILE`	File
`BIZTALK_TRANSPORT_TYPE_HTTP`	Hypertext Transport (HTTP)
`BIZTALK_TRANSPORT_TYPE_HTTPS`	Secure Hypertext Transport (HTTPS)
`BIZTALK_TRANSPORT_TYPE_LOOPBACK`	Specifies that the submitted document is processed and returned as the response document
`BIZTALK_TRANSPORT_TYPE_MSMQ`	Microsoft Message Queuing (MSMQ)

TABLE 19.21 continued

Name	*Description*
BIZTALK_TRANSPORT_TYPE_NONE	No transport component
BIZTALK_TRANSPORT_TYPE_OPENDESTINATION	Open messaging port
BIZTALK_TRANSPORT_TYPE_ORCHESTRATIONACTIVATION	Specifies that the document activates a new XLANG schedule instance
BIZTALK_TRANSPORT_TYPE_SMTP	Simple Mail Transfer (SMTP)

Transport type is closely tied to—and even constrained by—the destination type of the associated messaging port. For example, open messaging ports must specify `BIZTALK_TRANSPORT_TYPE_OPENDESTINATION` as their primary transport type.

Messaging ports that activate new XLANG schedules must set their primary transport type to `BIZTALK_TRANSPORT_TYPE_ORCHESTRATIONACTIVATION`.

Transport Address

The transport address indicates the destination of the document and is specified through the `Address` property of the `IBizTalkEndPoint` interface. Table 19.22 shows the transport types that require an associated address as well as the address prefix required by the type.

TABLE 19.22 Transport Types That Require an Address Parameter

Transport Types	*Prefix (if any)*
BIZTALK_TRANSPORT_TYPE_APPINTEGRATION	
BIZTALK_TRANSPORT_TYPE_FILE	file://
BIZTALK_TRANSPORT_TYPE_HTTP	http://
BIZTALK_TRANSPORT_TYPE_HTTPS	https://
BIZTALK_TRANSPORT_TYPE_MSMQ	
BIZTALK_TRANSPORT_TYPE_ORCHESTRATIONACTIVATION	
BIZTALK_TRANSPORT_TYPE_SMTP	mailto:

Listing 19.19 shows example usage of the `Type` and `Address` properties for each available transport type in BizTalk Server.

LISTING 19.19 Sample Transport Types and Addresses

```
port.PrimaryTransport.Type = BIZTALK_TRANSPORT_TYPE_APPINTEGRATION
port.PrimaryTransport.Address = "{11111111-1111-1111-1111-111111111111}"

port.PrimaryTransport.Type = BIZTALK_TRANSPORT_TYPE_FILE
port.PrimaryTransport.Address = "file://C:\BizTalk Unleashed\Test.xml"

port.PrimaryTransport.Type = BIZTALK_TRANSPORT_TYPE_HTTP
port.PrimaryTransport.Address = "http://www.samspublishing.com"

port.PrimaryTransport.Type = BIZTALK_TRANSPORT_TYPE_HTTPS
port.PrimaryTransport.Address = " https://www.samspublishing.com "

' Does not require Address
port.PrimaryTransport.Type = BIZTALK_TRANSPORT_TYPE_LOOPBACK

port.PrimaryTransport.Type = BIZTALK_TRANSPORT_TYPE_MSMQ
port.PrimaryTransport.Address = "DIRECT=OS:.\private$\myqueue"

' Does not require Address
port.PrimaryTransport.Type = BIZTALK_TRANSPORT_TYPE_NONE

' Does not require Address
port.PrimaryTransport.Type = BIZTALK_TRANSPORT_TYPE_OPENDESTINATION

port.PrimaryTransport.Type = BIZTALK_TRANSPORT_TYPE_ORCHESTRATIONACTIVATION
port.PrimaryTransport.Address = "C:\BizTalk Unleashed\test.skx"

port.PrimaryTransport.Type = BIZTALK_TRANSPORT_TYPE_SMTP
port.PrimaryTransport.Address = mailto:info@microsoft.com
```

For the most part, there are no surprises in the sample addresses listed here. One exception may be the address for `BIZTALK_TRANSPORT_TYPE_APPINTEGRATION`. The `APPINTEGRATION` address specifies the `CLSID` of a registered COM+ AIC component.

Additional Transport Data

Some transport types require additional information beyond the transport address. Additional data is specified through the `Parameter` property of the `IBizTalkTransportInfo` interface. Table 19.23 shows which transport types require more information and what that information is.

TABLE 19.23 Additional Transport Information

Transport	*Parameter*
SMTP	Return e-mail address of the associated source
Schedule Activation	BizTalk Orchestration port in the schedule to be activated

Service Window

A service window indicates the valid time range as hours in the day for transmitting documents. A service window is specified through the `ServiceWindowTransport` property of the `IBizTalkPort` interface. `ServiceWindowTransport` returns an instance of an object that implements the `IBizTalkServiceWindowInfo` interface. Table 19.24 shows the properties of the `IBizTalkServiceWindowInfo` interface.

TABLE 19.24 `IBizTalkServiceWindowInfo` Properties and Methods

Name	*Type*	*Description*
`FromTime`	Property	Specifies the earliest hour of any day that the interchange can be transmitted
`IsEnabled`	Property	Specifies whether the service window is enabled
`ToTime`	Property	Specifies the latest hour of any day that the interchange can be transmitted

When setting a service window, you must specify a valid time range using the `FromTime` and `ToTime` properties of `BizTalkServiceWindowInfo`. Service window times must contain a value between 0 and 23 indicating the hour of the day. BizTalk Server does not provide support for fractional hours or minutes. Listing 19.20 shows sample code that uses the `ServiceWindowTransport` property.

LISTING 19.20 `ServiceWindowTransport` Property Sample Code

```
' 7am to 7pm
port.ServiceWindowTransport.FromTime  = 7
port.ServiceWindowTransport.ToTime    = 19
port.ServiceWindowTransport.IsEnabled = True
```

The following sections will build on the samples started in the "Destination" section to include transport information.

Destination: Organization (ver HTTPS/HTTP)

Listing 19.21 demonstrates the required destination and transport settings to configure a messaging port to an organization over HTTPS (primary) and HTTP (secondary).

LISTING 19.21 Transport Settings for a Messaging Port to an Organization over HTTP and HTTPS

```
org.LoadByName "Joe's Crab Shack"
port.DestinationEndPoint.Organization = org.Handle
port.DestinationEndPoint.Openness = BIZTALK_OPENNESS_TYPE_EX_NOTOPEN
port.PrimaryTransport.Type = BIZTALK_TRANSPORT_TYPE_HTTPS
port.PrimaryTransport.Address = "https://secure.joescrabs.com"
port.SecondaryTransport.Type = BIZTALK_TRANSPORT_TYPE_HTTP
port.SecondaryTransport.Address = http://www.joescrabs.com
```

Destination: Organization (over SMTP)

Listing 19.22 demonstrates the required destination and transport settings to configure a messaging port to an organization over SMTP.

LISTING 19.22 Transport Settings for a Messaging Port to an Organization over SMTP

```
org.LoadByName "Joe's Crab Shack"
port.DestinationEndPoint.Organization = org.Handle
port.DestinationEndPoint.Openness = BIZTALK_OPENNESS_TYPE_EX_NOTOPEN
port.PrimaryTransport.Type = BIZTALK_TRANSPORT_TYPE_SMTP
port.PrimaryTransport.Address = "mailto:joe@joescrabs.com"
port.PrimaryTransport.Parameter = mailto:me@mycompany.com
```


Destination: Open Destination

Listing 19.23 demonstrates the required destination and transport settings to configure an open messaging port.

LISTING 19.23 Transport Settings for an Open Messaging Port

```
port.DestinationEndPoint.Openness = BIZTALK_OPENNESS_TYPE_EX_DESTINATION
port.PrimaryTransport.Type = BIZTALK_TRANSPORT_TYPE_OPENDESTINATION
```

Destination: New XLANG Schedule

Listing 19.24 demonstrates the required destination and transport settings to configure a messaging port to activate a new XLANG schedule.

LISTING 19.24 Transport Settings for a Messaging Port to Activate a New XLANG Schedule

```
org.LoadByName "Home Organization"
port.DestinationEndPoint.Organization = org.Handle
port.DestinationEndPoint.Openness = BIZTALK_OPENNESS_TYPE_EX_TOWORKFLOW
port.PrimaryTransport.Type = BIZTALK_TRANSPORT_TYPE_ORCHESTRATIONACTIVATION
port.PrimaryTransport.Address = "C:\BizTalk\Schedules\MySchedule.skd"
port.PrimaryTransport.Parameter = "start_port"
```

Destination: Running XLANG Schedule

Listing 19.25 demonstrates the required destination and transport settings to configure a messaging port to a running XLANG schedule.

LISTING 19.25 Transport Settings for a Messaging Port to a Running XLANG Schedule

```
port.DestinationEndPoint.Openness = BIZTALK_OPENNESS_TYPE_EX_TOWORKFLOW
port.PrimaryTransport.Type = BIZTALK_TRANSPORT_TYPE_OPENDESTINATION
```

Destination: Application (AIC)

Listing 19.26 demonstrates the required destination and transport settings to configure a messaging port to an Application Integration Component (AIC).

LISTING 19.26 Transport Settings for a Messaging Port to an AIC

```
org.LoadByName "Home Organization"
Set rs = org.Applications
AppHandle = 0

Do While Not rs.EOF
    If (rs("name") = "My Application") Then
        AppHandle = rs("id")
        Exit Do
    End If
    rs.MoveNext
Loop

port.DestinationEndPoint.Organization = org.Handle
port.DestinationEndPoint.Application = AppHandle
port.DestinationEndPoint.Openness = BIZTALK_OPENNESS_TYPE_EX_NOTOPEN
port.PrimaryTransport.Type = BIZTALK_TRANSPORT_TYPE_APPINTEGRATION
port.PrimaryTransport.Address = "{23A4973A-EF2F-11D2-BF2C-00C04F682DE1}"
```

Destination: Application (ASP)

Listing 19.27 demonstrates the required destination and transport settings to configure a messaging port to an ASP page.

LISTING 19.27 Transport Settings for a Messaging Port to an ASP Page

```
org.LoadByName "Home Organization"
Set rs = org.Applications
AppHandle = 0

Do While Not rs.EOF
    If (rs("name") = "My Application") Then
        AppHandle = rs("id")
        Exit Do
    End If
    rs.MoveNext
Loop

port.DestinationEndPoint.Organization = org.Handle
port.DestinationEndPoint.Application = AppHandle
port.DestinationEndPoint.Openness = BIZTALK_OPENNESS_TYPE_EX_NOTOPEN
port.PrimaryTransport.Type = BIZTALK_TRANSPORT_TYPE_HTTP
port.PrimaryTransport.Address = http://www.mycompany.com/submit_review.asp
```

Envelope

An envelope consists of a header and sometimes a footer and provides BizTalk Server with the necessary information to open inbound documents and interchanges and to create outbound documents. When BizTalk Server processes an outbound document, the properties of the messaging port envelope are used to create an interchange by encapsulating the document. Envelopes are associated with messaging ports through the `Envelope` property of the `IBizTalkPort` interface.

```
env.LoadFromHandle "Simple SOAP Envelope"
port.Envelope = env.Handle
```

Associating an envelope to a port is optional. If you do choose to use an envelope, the format of the envelope must agree with the format of the document that it contains. The document format is determined by the outbound document specification of the associated channel.

Control Number

An interchange control number is used to identify and track documents processed by the messaging port. You must specify an interchange control number when the associated envelope uses an X12 or EDIFACT format. The interchange control number is specified through the ControlNumberValue property of the IBizTalkPort interface. The value must be between 1 and 999999999.

```
port.ControlNumberValue = 42
```

Delimiters

Delimiters specify which characters are used to separate data within the envelope and documents of an interchange. You must specify a delimiter when the associated envelope uses an X12 or EDIFACT format. Delimiter lists are set through the Delimiters property of the IBizTalkPort interface. A delimiter returns a Dictionary object. Table 19.25 shows the required delimiter identifiers for X12 and EDIFACT envelopes.

TABLE 19.25 Required Delimiter Identifiers for X12 and EDIFACT Envelopes

Delimiter	*X12*	*EDIFACT*
Record_delim	Yes	Yes
Field_delim	Yes	Yes
Subfield_delim	Yes	Yes
Escape_char	No	Yes

Note

Envelopes using a custom format may also require a delimiter list.

Security

The security settings in a messaging port apply to the messaging port as well as all associated channels. If different channels need different security arrangements, you must create separate messaging ports for each channel.

Encoding

The messaging port encoding type is specified through the EncodingType property of the IBizTalkPort interface. EncodingType takes one of the BIZTALK_ENCODING_TYPE enumeration values shown in Table 19.26.

```
port.EncodingType = BIZTALK_ENCODING_TYPE_MIME
```

TABLE 19.26 BIZTALK_ENCODING_TYPE Enumeration Values

Name	Description
BIZTALK_ENCODING_TYPE_NONE	No encoding
BIZTALK_ENCODING_TYPE_MIME	Multipurpose Internet Mail Extensions (MIME)
BIZTALK_ENCODING_TYPE_CUSTOM	Custom encoding

Specifying a custom encoding type implies that a custom encoding component is specified in the associated BizTalk Messaging channel.

Encryption

The messaging encryption type is specified through the `EncryptionType` property of the `IBizTalkPort` interface. `EncryptionType` takes one of the `BIZTALK_ENCRYPTION_TYPE` enumeration values shown in Table 19.27.

```
port.EncryptionType = BIZTALK_ENCRYPTION_TYPE_SMIME
```

TABLE 19.27 BIZTALK_ENCRYPTION_TYPE Enumeration Values

Name	Description
BIZTALK_ENCRYPTION_TYPE_NONE	No encryption
BIZTALK_ENCRYPTION_TYPE_CUSTOM	Custom encryption
BIZTALK_ENCRYPTION_TYPE_SMIME	Secure Multipurpose Internet Mail Extensions (S/MIME) encryption

> **Note**
>
> Open messaging ports cannot use encryption. For open messaging ports, set the encryption type to `BIZTALK_ENCRYPTION_TYPE_NONE`.

Specifying a custom encryption type implies that a custom encryption component is specified in the associated BizTalk Messaging channel.

Encryption Certificate

The `EncryptionCertificateInfo` property returns an instance of an object that implements the `IBizTalkCertificateInfo` interface. The `BizTalkCertificateInfo` object contains information about the certificate that encrypts the document. Table 19.28 shows the properties of the `IBizTalkCertificateInfo` interface.

TABLE 19.28 IBizTalkCertificateInfo Properties

Name	*Type*	*Description*
Name	Property	Certificate name
Reference	Property	Reference to the certificate in the certificate store
Store	Property	BIZTALK_STORE_TYPE enumeration indicating which store holds the certificate
Usage	Property	BIZTALK_USAGE_TYPE enumeration indicating the type of use for the certificate

Note

The EncryptionCertificateInfo property is required when EncryptionType is set to BIZTALK_ENCRYPTION_TYPE_SMIME.

The Reference and Store properties of the IBizTalkCertificateInfo interface together specify a unique certificate from the certificate store. The certificate reference can be obtained from the Certificates property of the IBizTalkConfig interface. The Store property takes one of the BIZTALK_STORE_TYPE enumeration values listed in Table 19.29.

TABLE 19.29 BIZTALK_STORE_TYPE Enumeration Values

Name	*Description*
BIZTALK_STORE_TYPE_MY	Specifies the store that contains certificates authorized by your organization only
BIZTALK_STORE_TYPE_BIZTALK	Specifies the dedicated BizTalk Server 2002 store

The read-only Name and Usage properties of IBizTalkCertificateInfo reflect the certificate specified by the Reference and Store properties. Name contains the string name of the certificate, whereas Usage contains one of the BIZTALK_USAGE_TYPE enumeration values shown in Table 19.30.

TABLE 19.30 `BIZTALK_USAGE_TYPE` Enumeration Values

Name	*Description*
`BIZTALK_USAGE_TYPE_ENCRYPTION`	Specifies an encryption certificate
`BIZTALK_USAGE_TYPE_SIGNATURE`	Specifies a signature certificate
`BIZTALK_USAGE_TYPE_BOTH`	Specifies an encryption and signature certificate

For more information about certificates, refer to the "`IBizTalkConfig` Interface" section earlier in this chapter.

Signature Type

The `SignatureType` property specifies the type of digital signing and verification and accepts one of the `BIZTALK_SIGNATURE_TYPE` enumeration values shown in Table 19.31.

```
port.SignatureType = BIZTALK_SIGNATURE_TYPE_SMIME
```

TABLE 19.31 `BIZTALK_SIGNATURE_TYPE` Enumeration Values

Name	*Description*
`BIZTALK_SIGNATURE_TYPE_NONE`	No signature
`BIZTALK_SIGNATURE_TYPE_CUSTOM`	Custom signature
`BIZTALK_SIGNATURE_TYPE_SMIME`	S/MIME signature

Note

Custom encoding, encryption, and signatures are only available through the BizTalk Messaging Configuration object model.

IBizTalkPort Example

Listing 19.28 shows example code that creates two types of messaging ports.

LISTING 19.28 Sample Code for Messaging Port Creation

```
' Create the config objects
Set BT = CreateObject("BizTalk.BizTalkConfig")
set org = BT.CreateOrganization
Set port = BT.CreatePort

' Find the Review application handle
org.LoadByName "Home Organization"
```

LISTING 19.28 continued

```
Set rs = org.Applications
AppHandle = 0

Do While Not rs.EOF
    If (rs("name") = "Restaurant Reviews") Then
        AppHandle = rs("id")
        Exit Do
    End If
    rs.MoveNext
Loop

' Create a messaging port to the review request ASP page
port.Name = "Restaurant Review Requests"
port.Comments = "Messaging port for receiving requests to review a restaurant"
port.DestinationEndPoint.Organization = org.Handle
port.DestinationEndPoint.Application = AppHandle
port.DestinationEndPoint.Openness = 'BIZTALK_OPENNESS_TYPE_EX_NOTOPEN
port.PrimaryTransport.Type = 'BIZTALK_TRANSPORT_TYPE_HTTP
port.PrimaryTransport.Address = "http://www.mycompany.com/submit_review.asp"
port.Create

' Reset the objects
org.Clear
port.Clear

' Load Joe's orgnaization
org.LoadByName "Joe's Crab Shack"

' Create a messaging port to send reviews to Joe's
port.Name = "Joe's Review Results"
port.Comments = "Messaging port to send a review back to Joe"
port.DestinationEndPoint.Organization = org.Handle
port.DestinationEndPoint.Openness = 'BIZTALK_OPENNESS_TYPE_EX_NOTOPEN
port.PrimaryTransport.Type =' BIZTALK_TRANSPORT_TYPE_SMTP
port.PrimaryTransport.Address = "mailto:joe@joescrabs.com"
port.PrimaryTransport.Parameter = "mailto:me@mycompany.com"
port.Create
```

Note

The code (`19newListing28.vbs`) in Listing 19.28 is also available for download at the Sams Publishing Web site.

`IBizTalkChannel` Interface

The `IBizTalkChannel` interface provides properties and methods for managing BizTalk Messaging channels. A BizTalk Messaging channel configures BizTalk Messaging Services to process the documents that it receives. Table 19.32 shows the properties and methods of the `IBizTalkChannel` interface.

TABLE 19.32 `IBizTalkChannel` Properties and Methods

Name	*Type*	*Description*
`Comments`	Property	User comments about the channel
`ControlNumberValue`	Property	Interchange control number
`DecryptionCertificateInfo`	Property	`BizTalkCertificateInfo` object containing information about the certificate tat decrypts the input document
`ExpectReceiptTimeout`	Property	Time, in minutes, in which to expect a receipt before treating the document as expired
`Expression`	Property	Equations for filtering the documents
`GetConfigComponent`	Method	Gets the CLSID of the component associated with the messaging port
`GetConfigData`	Method	Gets the configuration associated with the specified messaging port
`InputDocument`	Property	Handle to the input document definition
`IsReceiptChannel`	Property	Flag to indicate whether channel is a receipt channel
`LoggingInfo`	Property	`BizTalkLoggingInfo` object containing information about logging
`MapContent`	Property	Contents of the map specified by `MapReference`
`MapReference`	Property	WebDAV URL specifying a document map
`OutputDocument`	Property	Handle to the output document definition
`Port`	Property	Handle to the associated messaging port
`PortGroup`	Property	Handle to the associated distribution group

TABLE 19.32 continued

Name	*Type*	*Description*
`ReceiptChannel`	Property	Handle to the receipt channel for this channel
`RetryCount`	Property	Number of times to retry a document submission when there is an error
`RetryInterval`	Property	Interval, in minutes, between resubmission attempts
`SetConfigComponent`	Method	Sets the CLSID of the component associated with the messaging port
`SetConfigData`	Method	Sets the configuration associated with the specified messaging port
`SignatureCertificateInfo`	Property	`BizTalkCertificateInfo` object containing information about the certificate that signs the output document
`SourceEndPoint`	Property	`BizTalkEndPoint` object containing information about the document source
`TrackFields`	Property	`Dictionary` object that stores additional tracking fields
`VerifySignatureCertificateInfo`	Property	`BizTalkCertificateInfo` object containing information about the certificate that verifies the signature of the input document

In addition to the properties and methods shown in Table 19.32, `BizTalkChannel` objects also implement the properties and methods of `IBizTalkBase` shown in Table 19.7.

Figure 19.8 shows a UML diagram illustrating the relationships between `IBizTalkChannel` and various Configuration interfaces.

Source and Destination

A channel source specifies where source documents come from. Just like messaging port destinations, channel sources can be organizations, XLANG schedules, or applications in the Home Organization. The channel source is specified through the `SourceEndPoint` property of the `IBizTalkChannel` interface. `SourceEndPoint` returns an instance of an object that implements the `IBizTalkEndPoint` interface. Refer to Table 19.18 for a list of `IBizTalkEndPoint` properties.

FIGURE 19.8
`IBizTalkChannel` *interface UML diagram.*

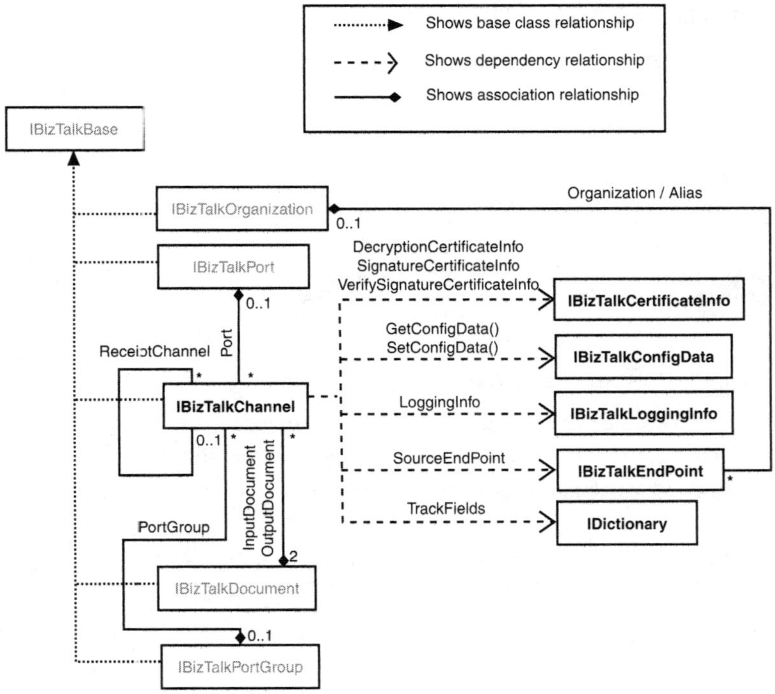

Source: Organization

For source organizations, the channel may specify a partner organization or leave the source open, creating an open channel. Before configuring a channel from an organization, the organization must be added to the BizTalk Messaging database. Listing 19.29 demonstrates how to configure the `SourceEndPoint` property for a channel from a specific partner organization.

LISTING 19.29 `SourceEndPoint` Settings for a Channel from an Organization

```
org.LoadByName "Joe's Crab Shack"
channel.SourceEndPoint.Organization = org.Handle
channel.SourceEndPoint.Openness = BIZTALK_OPENNESS_TYPE_EX_NOTOPEN
```

Listing 19.30 demonstrates how to configure the `SourceEndPoint` property to create an open channel from an organization.

LISTING 19.30 `SourceEndPoint` Settings for an Open Channel from an Organization

```
channel.SourceEndPoint.Openness = BIZTALK_OPENNESS_TYPE_EX_SOURCE
```

Source: XLANG Schedule

Channels from XLANG schedules are by definition open. Listing 19.31 demonstrates how to configure the `SourceEndPoint` property for an open channel from an internal XLANG schedule.

LISTING 19.31 `SourceEndPoint` Settings for a Channel from an XLANG Schedule

```
org.LoadByName "Home Organization"
channel.SourceEndPoint.Organization = org.Handle
channel.SourceEndPoint.Openness = BIZTALK_OPENNESS_TYPE_EX_FROMWORKFLOW
```

Source: Application

Before configuring a channel source from an application, the application must be added to the Home Organization. Listing 19.32 demonstrates how to configure the `SourceEndPoint` property for a channel from an internal application.

LISTING 19.32 `SourceEndPoint` Settings for a Channel from an Application

```
org.LoadByName "Home Organization"
Set rs = org.Applications
AppHandle = 0

Do While Not rs.EOF
    If (rs("name") = "My Application") Then
        AppHandle = rs("id")
        Exit Do
    End If
    rs.MoveNext
Loop

channel.SourceEndPoint.Organization = org.Handle
channel.SourceEndPoint.Application = AppHandle
channel.SourceEndPoint.Openness = BIZTALK_OPENNESS_TYPE_EX_NOTOPEN
```

Destination

Channels are always associated with a specific messaging port or distribution list. The messaging port or ports within the distribution list specify the document destination. To associate a messaging port or distribution list with a channel, use the `Port` or `PortGroup` properties of the `IBizTalkChannel` interface. The following code demonstrates these properties:

```
port.LoadByName "Restaurant Review Requests"
channel.Port = port.Handle
```

or

```
portgroup.LoadByName "My Port Group"
channel.PortGroup = portgroup.Handle
```

One of these properties must be set when creating a new channel. In addition, the properties are mutually exclusive. After a BizTalk Messaging channel is created in the database, the port or distribution list association cannot be changed.

Valid Source-Destination Combinations

BizTalk Server 2002 supports a limited number of channel (source) and messaging port (destination) combinations. In the following list of valid combinations, *internal application* refers to an application listed in the Home Organization or an XLANG schedule:

- Trading partner to an internal application
- Internal application to a trading partner
- Internal application to internal application
- Internal application to distribution list
- Internal application to open destination
- Open source to internal application
- Trading partner to trading partner (where your BizTalk Server serves as an intermediary)

Note

BizTalk Server 2002 does not support an open-source channel to an open destination port combination.

Inbound and Outbound Document Definitions

Document definitions enable a channel to translate documents between their native formats and an intermediate XML format. With the inbound document in the intermediate format, the channel can map, filter, and log document fields. Input and output document specifications are specified through the `InputDocument` and `OutputDocument` properties of the `IBizTalkChannel` interface. For example:

```
doc.LoadByName "Restaurant Reviewer"
channel.InputDocument = doc.Handle
channel.OutputDocument = doc.Handle
```

Both properties are required when creating a new BizTalk Messaging channel, and neither can be changed after the channel is created. In the preceding sample, the inbound and outbound document definitions are the same. The implication is that a document map is not needed.

> **Caution**
>
> If the channel is an open channel—that is `SourceEndPoint.Type` is set to `BIZTALK_OPENNESS_TYPE_SOURCE` or `BIZTALK_OPENNESS_TYPE_FROMWORKFLOW`—then the `OutputDocument` property cannot specify an X12 or EDIFACT specification.

Control Number

If the envelope format of the associated messaging port is X12 or EDIFACT, then an interchange control number must be specified. Custom envelope formats sometimes require an interchange control number as well. Use the `ControlNumberValue` property of the `IBizTalkChannel` interface to specify a control number. Interchange control values are between 1 and 999999999.

Decrypting and Verifying Inbound Documents

Inbound document decryption certificates and digital signature verification certificates are specified through the `DecryptionCertificateInfo` and `VerifySignatureCertificateInfo` properties of the `IBizTalkChannel` interface, respectively. Both properties return an instance of an object that implements the `IBizTalkCertificateInfo` interface.

Refer to Table 19.28 for a list of `IBizTalkCertificateInfo` properties.

Signing Outbound Documents

Outbound documents can be signed by BizTalk Server using a digital signature certificate. To specify a signature certificate, use the `SignatureCertificateInfo` property of the `IBizTalkChannel` interface. This property returns an instance of an object that implements the `IBizTalkCertificateInfo` interface.

Refer to Table 19.28 for a list of `IBizTalkCertificateInfo` properties.

Mapping

Sometimes the format of the inbound document specification does not match the format of the outbound document specification. When this occurs, a map is needed to translate the inbound document into the format of the outbound document. Maps are created using BizTalk Mapper and are specified in the `IBizTalkChannel` interface through the `MapReference` property. `MapReference` takes a string containing the full WebDAV URL of the associated map file. For example:

```
channel.MapReference =
http://somemachine/BizTalkServerRepository/Maps/map.xml
```

Tracking

Document definitions can specify fields within the document that are logged to the Tracking database. Channels can override the fields specified by the document definition with a set of channel-specific tracking fields. When this occurs, the channel-specified fields are logged in lieu of the global tracking fields defined by the document specification.

> **Note**
>
> Tracking applies only to inbound documents.

To specify tracking fields in a channel, use the `TrackFields` property of the `IBizTalkChannel` interface. `TrackFields` returns an instance of the `Dictionary` object. Listing 19.33 shows sample code with XLANG tracking fields.

Refer to the "`IBizTalkDocument` Interface" section earlier in this chapter for more information about tracking fields.

LISTING 19.33 Sample XPath Tracking Fields

```
channel.TrackFields.r_value1 = "/CommonPO/SpecialCharge/@Amount"
channel.TrackFields.r_value2 = "/CommonPO/Currency/@ExchangeRate"

channel.TrackFields.s_value1 = "/CommonPO/TermsOfSale/@PaymentMethod"
channel.TrackFields.s_value2 = "/CommonPO/CarrierDetail/@Routing"

channel.TrackFields.i_value1 = "/CommonPO/TermsOfSale/@NetDays"
channel.TrackFields.i_value2 = "/CommonPO/TermsOfSale/@DiscountDaysDue"

channel.TrackFields.d_value1 = "/CommonPO/Item/DateReference/@Date"
channel.TrackFields.d_value2 = "/CommonPO/POHeader/@CreationDate"

channel.TrackFields.x_custom_search.Add "/CommonPO/Total/@LineItemTotal"
channel.TrackFields.x_custom_search.Add "/CommonPO/Total/@QuantityTotal"
channel.TrackFields.x_custom_search.Add /CommonPO/Total/@POTotal
```


Filtering

A channel filter provides a mechanism for determining when a channel should be invoked. When BizTalk Server receives a document, the filtering expression is evaluated against the values of the specified fields in that document. If the expression evaluates to true, the channel is invoked. If the expression evaluates to false, the channel is not invoked.

Use the `Expression` property of the `IBizTalkChannel` interface to specify a filtering expression.

Logging

BizTalk Server allows channels to specify whether and how inbound and outbound documents are logged. To configure logging options, use the `LoggingInfo` property of the `IBizTalkChannel` interface. `LoggingInfo` returns an instance of an object that implements the `IBizTalkLoggingInfo` interface. Table 19.33 shows the properties on the `IBizTalkLoggingInfo` interface.

TABLE 19.33 `IBizTalkLoggingInfo` Properties

Name	*Type*	*Description*
`LogNativeInputDocument`	Property	Flag to indicate whether the input document is logged in its native format
`LogNativeOutputDocument`	Property	Flag to indicate whether the output document is logged in its native format
`LogXMLInputDocument`	Property	Flag to indicate whether the XML input document is logged
`LogXMLOutputDocument`	Property	Flag to indicate whether the XML output document is logged

Overriding Messaging Port Defaults

BizTalk Server allows channels to override certain messaging port properties associated with the transport; the document serializer; and custom encoding, encryption, and signature verification. This functionality is exposed in the Configuration object model through the following `IBizTalkChannel` methods:

- `GetConfigComponent`
- `GetConfigData`
- `SetConfigComponent`
- `SetConfigData`

Each of these methods takes as a parameter a `BIZTALK_CONFIGDATA_TYPE` enumeration value. The value indicates the messaging data being requested or changed. Table 19.34 shows the `BIZTALK_CONFIGDATA_TYPE` enumeration values.

TABLE 19.34 `BIZTALK_CONFIGDATA_TYPE` Enumeration Values

Name	*Description*
`BIZTALK_CONFIGDATA_TYPE_PRIMARYTRANSPORT`	Configure the primary transport
`BIZTALK_CONFIGDATA_TYPE_SECONDARYTRANSPORT`	Configure the secondary transport

TABLE 19.34 continued

Name	*Description*
BIZTALK_CONFIGDATA_TYPE_ENCRYPTION	Configure the encryption certificate
BIZTALK_CONFIGDATA_TYPE_ENCODING	Configure the encoding type
BIZTALK_CONFIGDATA_TYPE_SIGNATURE	Configure the signature verification
BIZTALK_CONFIGDATA_TYPE_SERIALIZER	Configure the serializer

The `GetConfigComponent` method returns the CLSID of the associated component for the specified `BIZTALK_CONFIGDATA_TYPE` enumeration value.

The `SetConfigComponent` method sets the CLSID of the component associated with the messaging port. This method is used to specify components that implement custom encryption, encoding, or signature verification. `SetConfigComponent` is also used to specify a custom serializer when the messaging port envelope is set to the custom format. You cannot change the transport components associated with the messaging port.

The `GetConfigData` method returns a `Dictionary` object containing values specific to the configuration component returned by `GetConfigComponent()`. It is not necessary to get the CLSID of the configuration component before calling `GetConfigData()`.

Note

Changes made through the `SetConfigData` method apply only to the channel where those changes were made.

Transport Properties

Transport components are associated with messaging ports based on the transport type of the associated primary or secondary transport. The `GetDataComponent` method returns the CLSID of the associated transport component. Table 19.35 shows the transport components that ship with BizTalk Server 2002.

TABLE 19.35 BizTalk Server 2002 Transport Components

Transport Type	*ProgID for Transport Component*
File	BizTalk.SendLocalFile
HTTP/HTTPS	BizTalk.SendHTTPX
MSMQ	BizTalk.SendMSMQ

TABLE 19.35 continued

Transport Type	*ProgID for Transport Component*
SMTP	`BizTalk.SendSMTP`
Orchestration activation	`BizTalk.BPOActivation`

The transport component for AIC transports is the Application Integration Component itself.

A channel cannot override which transport component is associated by the messaging port. What can be changed are specific properties of the transport component. The following sections discuss the transport types that can be customized through the `GetConfigData` and `SetConfigData` methods.

HTTP/HTTPS

The settings associated with an HTTP/HTTPS transport on a messaging port only specify the destination URL. When the destination URL requires login information or BizTalk Server requires a proxy server (because the server itself sits behind a firewall), the configuration data in the associated channel must be used. Table 19.36 shows the dictionary fields used by the HTTP/HTTPS transport component.

TABLE 19.36 Dictionary Fields for HTTP/HTTPS Transport Customization

Field Name	*Description*
`ClientCert`	Reference to the certificate used for HTTPS transports
`ContentType`	Content-Type HTTP/HTTPS header value
`MaxRedirects`	Maximum number of redirects allowed
`Password`	Password for the specified destination URL
`ProxyName`	URL of the proxy server
`ProxyPassword`	Proxy server password
`ProxyPort`	Port to use on the proxy server
`ProxyUserName`	Proxy server login name
`RequestTimeout`	Request timeout value in seconds
`URL`	Destination URL, indicates the address of the transport specified in the messaging port (cannot be changed)
`UseProxy`	Specifies whether to use a proxy server (-1 for True, 0 for False)
`UserName`	Login name for the specified destination URL

SMTP

The settings associated with an SMTP transport on a messaging port specify only the destination and return e-mail addresses. The `SetConfigData` method allows a channel to specify SMTP server information, additional e-mail header values, and character sets. Table 19.37 shows the dictionary fields used by the SMTP transport component.

TABLE 19.37 Dictionary Fields for SMTP Transport Customization

Field Name	*Description*
`CC`	Additional e-mail addresses to forward the document to
`CharSet`	Character set
`From`	Return e-mail address, must be prefixed with `mailto:`
`SMTPAuthenticate`	Type of authentication to use (0 for no authentication, 1 for basic authentication, 2 for NTLM authentication)
`SMTPHost`	SMTP server
`SMTPSendPassword`	SMTP server password
`SMTPSendUserName`	SMTP server login name
`Subject`	E-mail subject line
`To`	Destination e-mail address, indicates the address of the transport specified in the messaging port (cannot be changed)

File

The settings associated with a File transport on a messaging port specify only the destination file. The `SetConfigData` method allows a channel to specify how the file should be written and to specify a Windows username and password. Table 19.38 shows the dictionary fields used by the File transport component.

TABLE 19.38 Dictionary Fields for File Transport Customization

Field Name	*Description*
`CopyMode`	Indicates how the file should be written (0 to overwrite an existing file, 1 to append to an existing file, 2 to create a new file)
`FileName`	Destination filename, indicates the address of the transport specified in the messaging port (cannot be changed)
`Password`	Windows login password
`Username`	Windows login username

MSMQ

The settings associated with an MSMQ transport on a messaging port specify only the destination queue. The `SetConfigData` method allows a channel to specify specific MSMQ properties. Table 19.39 shows the dictionary fields used by the MSMQ transport component.

TABLE 19.39 Dictionary Fields for MSMQ Transport Customization

Field Name	*Description*
`AuthLevel`	Indicates whether the message needs to be authenticated (0 for no authentication, 1 to always authenticate, 2 for MSMQ 1.0 signature, 3 for MSMQ 2.0 signature)
`Delivery`	Delivery method (0 to indicate message resides in memory only, 1 to back up message until it is delivered)
`Journal`	Journal (0 for none, 1 for the Dead Letter queue)
`MessageLabel`	Message label
`Password`	Windows login password
`Priority`	Message priority (integer from 0 to 7, where higher values indicate higher priority)
`QueueName`	Destination queue, indicates the address of the transport specified in the messaging port (cannot be changed)
`Transactional`	Indicates whether message is transactional (0 for non-transactional, 1 for COM+ transactions, 2 for Single Message transactions)
`Username`	Windows login username

Orchestration Activation

Table 19.40 shows the dictionary fields used by the orchestration activation transport component.

TABLE 19.40 Dictionary Fields for MSMQ Transport Customization

Field Name	*Description*
`Port`	Destination orchestration port within the specified schedule
`SkedFile`	Destination schedule, indicates the address of the transport specified in the messaging port (cannot be changed)

Application Integration Components

AIC components can specify their own dictionary fields as needed. There are no standard fields for AIC components. Refer to the AIC documentation for a list of appropriate dictionary fields.

Serializer Properties

Serializers are associated with messaging ports based on the format of an associated envelope. Use the `SetDataComponent` method to specify a custom serializer. Table 19.41 shows the serializers that ship with BizTalk Server 2002.

TABLE 19.41 BizTalk Server 2002 Serializers

Envelope Format	*ProgID for Serializer*
custom xml	`BizTalk.SerializerXML`
edifact	`BizTalk.SerializerEdifact`
flatfile	`BizTalk.SerializerFFile`
reliable	`BizTalk.Scriptor`
x12	`BizTalk.SerializerX12`

The EDIFACT and X12 document serializers expose `Dictionary` objects for customizing the serialization process via the `GetConfigData` method. Tables 19.42 and 19.43 show the dictionary fields for the built-in EDI serializers.

TABLE 19.42 Dictionary Fields for EDIFACT Serializer Customization

Field Name	*Description*
`SerializerEdifact_AckRequest`	Acknowledgement request
`SerializerEdifact_AgreementID`	Interchange agreement identifier
`SerializerEdifact_ApplicationRef`	Application reference
`SerializerEdifact_ProcPriCode`	Processing priority code
`SerializerEdifact_RecipientIntID`	Interchange Recipient internal identification
`SerializerEdifact_RecipientIntSubID`	Interchange recipient internal subidentification
`SerializerEdifact_RecipentRefPwd`	Recipent reference and password
`SerializerEdifact_RecipientRefPwdQual`	Recipient reference and password qualifier
`SerializerEdifact_SenderIntID`	Interchange sender internal identification

TABLE 19.42 continued

Field Name	*Description*
`SerializerEdifact_SenderIntSubID`	Interchange sender internal subidentification
`SerializerEdifact_SyntaxID`	Syntax identifier, can be one of the following strings: UNOA, UNOB, UNOC, UNOD, UNOE, UNOF, UNOG, UNOH, UNOI, UNOJ, UNOK
`SerializerEdifact_TestInd`	Test indicator
`SerializerEdifact_UNACtrl`	UNA Control, 0 to indicate "Send UNA only when required" and 1 to indicate "Send UNA always"

TABLE 19.43 Dictionary Fields for EDIFACT Serializer Customization

Field Name	*Description*
`SerializerX12_AckRequired`	Acknowledgement required (0 for no, 1 for yes)
`SerializerX12_AuthInfo`	Authorization information
`SerializerX12_AuthInfoQual`	Authorization information qualifier
`SerializerX12_CtrlStdID`	Interchange control standards identifier
`SerializerX12_CtrlVerNum`	Interchange control number version
`SerializerX12_SecInfo`	Security information
`SerializerX12_SecInfoQual`	Security Information qualifier
`SerializerX12_UseInd`	Usage indicator

Encryption, Encoding, and Signature

Custom encryption, encoding, and signature verification requires that components that implement the custom functionality be specified through the `SetConfigComponent` method of the `IBizTalkChannel` interface. In addition, these custom components may expose customization options via a `Dictionary` object returned from `GetConfigData`.

`IBizTalkPortGroup` Interface

The `IBizTalkPortGroup` interface provides properties and methods for managing BizTalk Messaging distribution lists. A BizTalk Messaging distribution list is a group of BizTalk Messaging ports that enable BizTalk Server to deliver a single document to multiple destinations with a one-document submission. Table 19.44 shows the properties and methods of the `IBizTalkPortGroup` interface.

TABLE 19.44 `IBizTalkPortGroup` Properties and Methods

Name	*Type*	*Description*
`AddPort`	Method	Adds a port to the distribution list
`Channels`	Property	ADO recordset containing information about all associated channels
`Ports`	Property	ADO recordset containing information about all ports in the port group
`RemovePort`	Method	Removes a port from the distribution list

In addition to the properties and methods shown in Table 19.44, `BizTalkPortGroup` objects also implement the properties and methods of `IBizTalkBase` shown in Table 19.7.

Figure 19.9 shows a UML-style diagram illustrating the relationships between `IBizTalkPortGroup` and various Configuration interfaces.

FIGURE 19.9
`IBizTalkPortGroup` *interface UML diagram.*

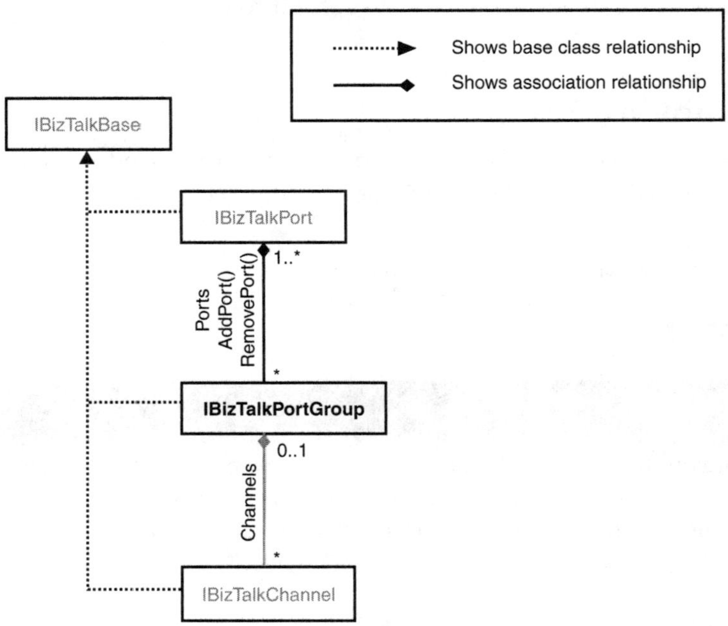

Adding Ports

BizTalk Server enforces two rules when adding ports to a distribution list:

- The messaging port `Openness` property must be set to `BIZTALK_OPENNESS_TYPE_EX_NOTOPEN`.
- Duplicate ports cannot be added to the same distribution list.

Use the `AddPort` method of the `IBizTalkPortGroup` interface to add a port to the distribution list. The following sample code demonstrates how to add a port to a distribution list:

```
port.LoadByName "Restaurant Review Requests"
group.AddPort = port.Handle
group.Save
```

Note

After adding or removing ports from a `BizTalkPortGroup` object, you must call Save or Create to persist the new port list to the database.

Removing Ports

Use the `RemovePort` method of the `IBizTalkPortGroup` interface to remove a messaging port from a distribution list. The following sample code demonstrates how to remove a port from a distribution list:

```
port.LoadByName "Restaurant Review Requests"
group.RemovePort = port.Handle
group.Save
```

Note

Distribution lists are required by BizTalk Server to contain at least one associated messaging port. As such, the last port in a distribution list cannot be removed. Instead, you must remove the entire distribution list.

Refresh Sample

A common annoyance that crops up while managing BizTalk Messaging is the complexity of refreshing a messaging object. For example, when an underlying envelope specification file is changed, the BizTalk Messaging envelope object must reset the document reference to effect the change in BizTalk Messaging. This sounds simple enough at first glance, but trying to change a document reference in an envelope associated with a port object proves impossible without first removing the reference. Now imagine changing the underlying document specification and refreshing the corresponding envelope where tens or hundreds of ports refer to it. This is an excellent opportunity to put the BizTalk Messaging Configuration object model to work.

Listing 19.34 contains VBScript code to refresh envelopes by first removing all port references, refreshing the envelope document, and finally reestablishing the envelope references. The code is fairly straightforward and dispenses with the usual UI niceties.

Note

The code in Listing 19.34 is also available for download at the Sams Publishing Web site.

LISTING 19.34 Sample Code to Refresh an Envelope Messaging Object

```
On Error Resume Next : Err.Clear

' Create config objects
Set BT = CreateObject("BizTalk.BizTalkConfig")
Set env = BT.CreateEnvelope
Set port = BT.CreatePort

' Get Envelope name
env_name = InputBox("Enter the name of the envelope to refresh:")

' Try to load envelope
env.LoadByName env_name

If (Err.Num = 0) Then

    ' Find all ports that reference this envelope
    Set rs = BT.Ports

    Dim port_handles(0)

    Do While Not rs.EOF

        ' Load the port
        port.Load rs("id")

        ' Check if port references the envelope
        If port.Envelope = env.Handle Then
```

LISTING 19.34 continued

```
            ' Store the port handle
            size = UBound(port_handles)
            Redim Preserve port_handles(size + 1)
            port_handles(size) = port.Handle

            MsgBox "Storing " & port.Name & " reference to " & env.Name

            ' Clear the envelope reference
            port.Envelope = ""
            port.Save

        End If

        port.Clear

        rs.MoveNext

    Loop

    ' Refresh envelope specification
    ref = env.Reference
    env.Reference = ""
    env.Save
    env.Reference = ref

    ' Restore envelope references in ports
    For Each h In port_handles

        port.Load h

            MsgBox "Restoring reference to " & env.Name & " in " & port.Name

        port.Envelope = env.Handle
        port.Save
        port.Clear

    Next

    MsgBox "Envelope specification refreshed."

Else

    MsgBox "Unable to load specified envelope."

End If
```

The principles used in this sample can be applied to other messaging objects that need refreshing as well.

Summary

The BizTalk Messaging Configuration object model is an essential tool in BizTalk Messaging management. This chapter discussed some of the limitations of large-scale BizTalk Messaging administration using the BizTalk Messaging Manager. It also introduced and discussed the components of the BizTalk Configuration object model. Samples demonstrated property usage for different situations.

In the end, the BizTalk Messaging Configuration object model is a powerful tool that gives BizTalk administrators and developers the ability to automate the complicated and the mundane in BizTalk Messaging management.

BizTalk Server Administration

PART VI

IN THIS PART

CHAPTER 20

Installing BizTalk Server

by Kevin Price

IN THIS CHAPTER

Installing any software package should be as simple as double-clicking an icon and simply clicking Next until you click Finish. This chapter provides information regarding the preliminary steps to make installing BizTalk Server just that easy. In this chapter, you will learn:

- Hardware requirements and recommendations for installing BizTalk Server
- Software requirements and installation techniques for supporting software of BizTalk Server
- How to install Microsoft BizTalk Server 2002 and client tools

Hardware Requirements and Recommendations

To install BizTalk Server or its associated tools successfully, ideally you would begin with a computer. Assuming that you at least have a shell of a computer inside this shell, the following minimum hardware requirements are recommended by Microsoft to support BizTalk Server:

- Intel Pentium 300 processor or equivalent
- 128 megabytes (MB) of RAM
- 6-gigabyte (GB) hard disk
- CD-ROM drive
- Network adapter card
- VGA or Super VGA monitor/VGA or SVGA display card
- Microsoft Mouse or compatible pointing device

Although software requirements are listed later in this chapter, it is important to recognize that BizTalk Server requires the Windows 2000 operating system. The minimum recommended hardware requirements for Windows 2000 Server operating system are as follows:

- 133-MHz Intel Pentium or higher processor
- 256 megabytes (MB) of RAM
- VGA or Super VGA monitor/VGA or SVGA display card
- Keyboard
- Mouse or other pointing device (optional)
- CD-ROM or DVD drive

- High-density 3.5-inch disk drive
- 6-gigabyte (GB) hard disk

Because the installation of BizTalk not only requires hardware but software as well, we will also look at the minimum hardware requirements for the supporting software required by BizTalk.

BizTalk Server requires a valid installation of Microsoft SQL Server, Version 7.0 (SP2) or better. At the time of this writing, SQL Server 2000 has been released. The minimum recommended hardware requirements for SQL Server 2000 are as follows:

- Intel or compatible Pentium 166 MHz or higher
- Memory (RAM) 1 Enterprise Edition: 64 MB minimum, 128 MB or more recommended—highly recommended
- Hard disk space 250 MB typical installation
- Monitor VGA or higher resolution
- 800 × 600 or higher resolution required for the SQL Server graphical tools
- Pointing device Microsoft mouse or compatible
- CD-ROM drive required

In addition to the items just listed, BizTalk Server's Orchestration Designer also requires installation of Microsoft Visio 2000 (SR-1).

BizTalk Server can be deployed on a single standalone server or as a BizTalk Server Group, which consists of multiple BizTalk Servers processing data from a single SQL Server database. The first scenario that follows is based on an installation of BizTalk Server 2002 and SQL Server 2000 on the same machine. This configuration is usually adequate for development machines as well as lightweight sites (fewer than 1000 documents or transactions per day). The second configuration represents a more robust implementation that takes advantage of BizTalk Server's capability to be scaled up and out for large enterprise configurations.

An example recommended configuration for a single-server configuration—that is, a single machine running Windows 2000 Server, BizTalk Server 2002, SQL Server 2000, and Visio—would be as follows:

- Two (2) Intel Pentium III™ or compatible processors, 500 MHz or higher
- 1024 megabytes (MB) of RAM
- 18.1 gigabyte (GB) SCSI hard drive
- Network interface card
- SVGA video card/SVGA compatible monitor

- Keyboard
- Mouse or other pointing device
- CD-ROM or DVD drive
- High-density 3.5-inch disk drive

Scaling up and scaling out of course requires more expensive hardware. The designs recommended here are based on deployments of BizTalk Server 2002 in the real world. The following list demonstrates a suggested BizTalk Server hardware configuration for a machine running only Windows 2000, Visio, and BizTalk Server:

- Intel Pentium III or compatible processor, 500 MHz or higher
- 512 megabytes (MB) of RAM
- 18.1 gigabyte (GB) SCSI hard drive, RAID 5
- (2) Network interface cards
- SVGA video card/SVGA compatible monitor
- Keyboard
- Mouse or other pointing device
- CD-ROM or DVD drive
- High-density 3.5-inch disk drive

These configurations are intended to represent basic, realistic minimum configurations to successfully install and use Microsoft BizTalk Server 2002. Additional information on scalability and optimizations is available in the BizTalk Server documentation.

Software Requirements

Now that the hardware has been put together, it's time to add some software. Because most software packages start with the operating system, that's where we will start. This section covers what is necessary to support BizTalk Server. It is not within the scope of this book to go into detail regarding the installation of Windows 2000 Server, SQL Server 2000, or Visio 2000 (SR-1A); however, all configuration parameters needed to successfully install BizTalk Server are outlined in this chapter.

Note

BizTalk Server also requires the installation of MSXML Version 3.0. If this is not already installed, BizTalk will install it for you.

Preparing Windows 2000 Server for BizTalk Server

Assuming that you have Windows 2000 Server or Advanced Server installed and your network and any necessary devices configured, the following describes the additional Windows components necessary to install BizTalk Server.

> **Note**
>
> Remember that these components, as well as all supporting software, need to be installed prior to installing BizTalk Server.

Installing Service Pack 1

At the time of this writing, BizTalk Server requires that Windows 2000 Service Pack 1 be installed prior to attempting to install BizTalk Server.

To install Windows 2000 Service Pack 1, either download the service pack from `http://www.microsoft.com/windows2000` or order the CD. After you have the distribution media (download or CD), follow the appropriate instructions to install the service pack.

> **Note**
>
> The default version of the service pack does not use 128-bit encryption. To upgrade your service pack installation to use 128-bit encryption, you must download an additional file from Microsoft.

Installing Message Queuing

Message Queuing is an essential part of how BizTalk Server exchanges information with other machines. This component of Windows can be found on the Windows 2000 Server installation CD. The following steps outline how to add Message Queuing components to your Windows 2000 Server installation:

1. Click the Start button, point to Settings, and click Control Panel.
2. Double-click Add/Remove Programs.
3. The Add/Remove Programs dialog box appears.
4. Click the Add/Remove Windows Components icon.
5. The Windows Components Wizard opens.

6. In the Components list, select the Message Queuing Services check box and click Next.
7. On the Message Queuing Type page, accept all defaults and click Next.
8. Click the Finish button to close the wizard.

Installing Internet Information Services (IIS)

Because all these transactions are occurring over the Internet or an intranet, you need to install a Web server. Windows 2000 Server and Advanced Server provide one out-of-the-box named Internet Information Services 5.0.

IIS installs by default on Windows 2000; however, should you discover that it has not been installed, the following steps outline how to install IIS on your Windows 2000 Server:

1. Click the Start button, point to Settings, and click Control Panel.
2. Double-click Add/Remove Programs.
3. The Add/Remove Programs dialog box appears.
4. Click the Add/Remove Windows Components icon.
5. The Windows Components Wizard opens.
6. In the Components list, select the Internet Information Services (IIS) check box and click Next.
7. Click the Finish button to close the wizard.

Caution

After completing the installation of IIS on your server, you must disable authoring on the default Web site the BizTalk Server will use. To do this, go into the properties page for the default Web site and clear the Enable Authoring check box on the Server Extensions tab.

Creating a Service Account

Ideally, BizTalk Server should be installed to run under a Service Account—that is, an account that has specific rights and does not require a specific user to be logged in to allow services to start. This is similar to the "system" user, with limited rights. The following steps list how to create a service account for BizTalk Server to execute under:

1. Log on as Administrator or an account with Administrator rights.
2. On the Start menu, point to Settings, click Control Panel, double-click Administrative Tools, and then double-click Computer Management. Or, right-click My Computer and select Manage.
3. The Computer Management dialog box appears as shown in Figure 20.1

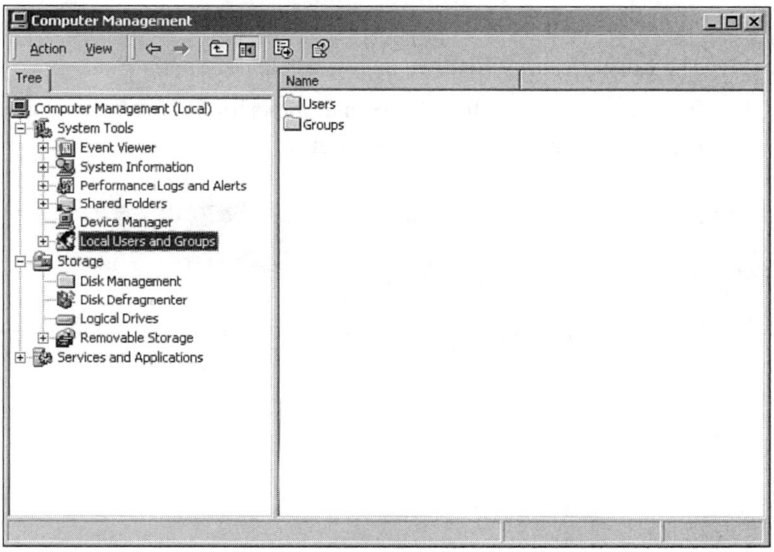

FIGURE 20.1
Computer Management dialog.

4. In the console tree, click the expand indicator (+) for System Tools and click Local Users and Groups.
5. Click Users, right-click anywhere in the details pane, and then click New User.
6. The New User dialog box appears (see Figure 20.2).

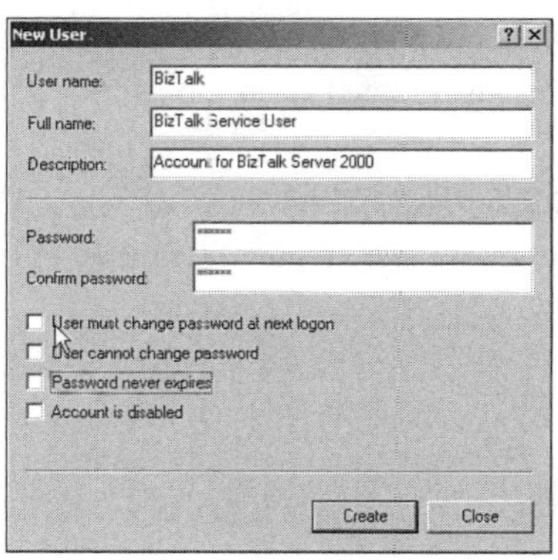

FIGURE 20.2
New User dialog.

7. In the User Name box, type a name for the service account. In the Password box, type a password and then type the same password in the Confirm Password box.
8. Clear the User Must Change Password at Next Logon check box as shown in Figure 20.2, click Create, and then click Close.
9. Close the Computer Management window.
10. On the Start menu, point to Settings, click Control Panel, double-click Administrative Tools, and then double-click Local Security Policy.
11. The Local Security Settings dialog box appears.
12. In the console tree, click the expand indicator (+) for Local Policies and click User Rights Assignment, as shown in Figure 20.3.

FIGURE 20.3
Local Security Settings dialog.

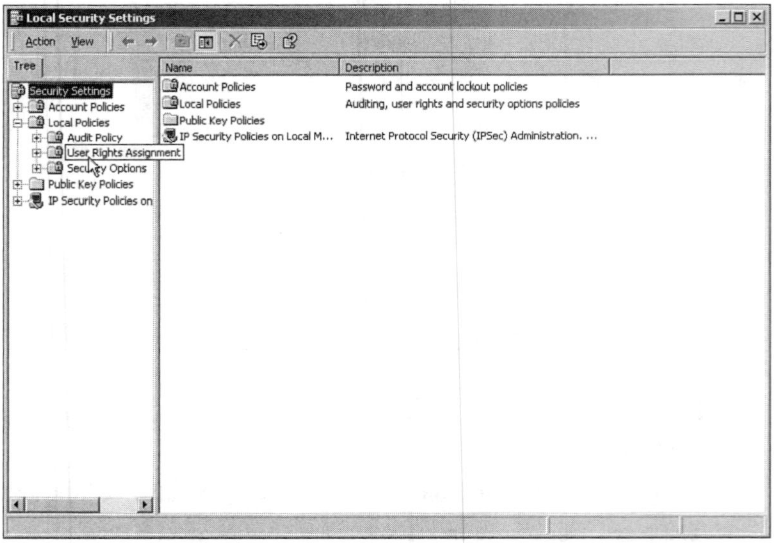

13. In the details pane, double-click Act as Part of the Operating System and click Add. Click the account name you just created from the list box, click Add, and then click OK. See Figure 20.4.
14. In the details pane, double-click Log on as Service, as shown in Figure 20.5, and click Add. Click the account name you just created from the list box, click Add, and then click OK twice.

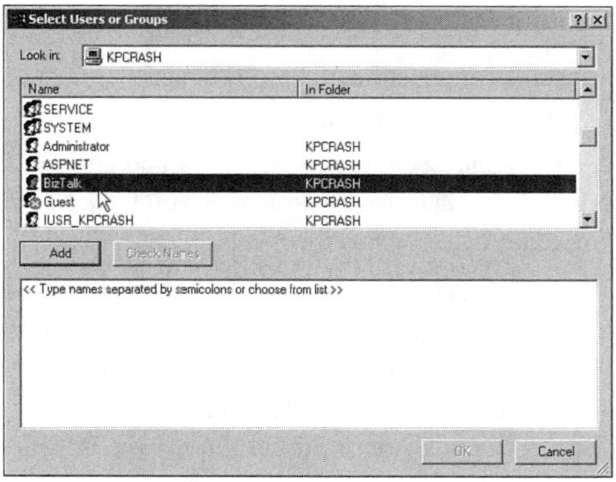

FIGURE 20.4
Select Users or Groups dialog.

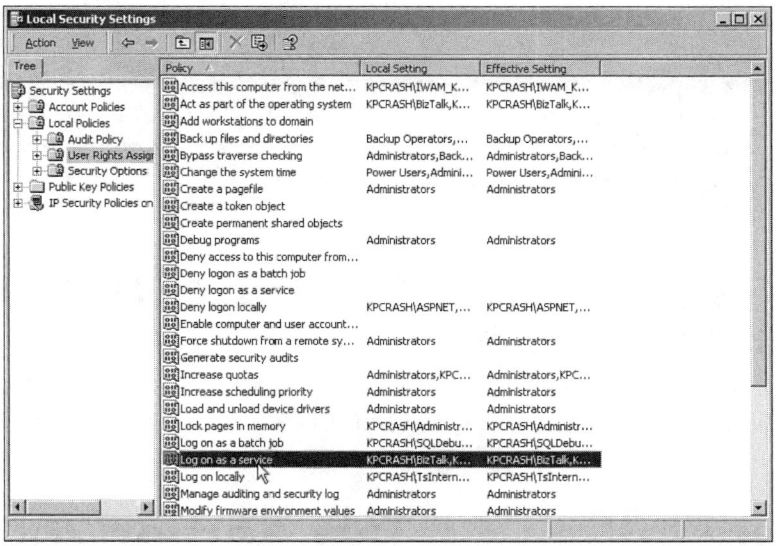

FIGURE 20.5
Selecting Log on as Service.

Installing Microsoft SQL Server 2000

When you install BizTalk Server, the installation creates the databases that BizTalk needs. For this to be successful, two things must be in place. SQL Server 7.0 with Service Pack 2 or SQL Server 2000 must be installed and running at the time of install.

When installing SQL Server to accommodate BizTalk Server, keep the following in mind:

- The SQL Server installation must be at least Typical.
- If you are using SQL Server 7.0, Service Pack 2 for SQL Server 7.0 must be installed. To check this, open SQL Query Analyzer and connect to your database. In the query window, type `SELECT @@VERSION`. If you have Service Pack 2 installed, you should get `7.00.842` as the result.
- Make sure that the default network library is set to TCP/IP. To do this, in SQL Server 7.0, click Start, click Programs, click Microsoft SQL Server, and click Client Network Utility. If you have SQL Server 7.0, on the General tab, in the Default Network Library list, click TCP/IP. If you have SQL Server 2000, on the Network Libraries tab, in the Network Library list, click TCP/IP.
- In SQL Server 2000, mixed-mode authentication must be enabled.

> **Caution**
>
> Mixed-mode authentication must be enabled for BizTalk to work successfully. The authentication mode property is available through the properties window of a selected server in SQL Enterprise Manager.

Installing Microsoft Visio 2000 (SR-1A), Enterprise Edition

The final piece to install prior to launching the BizTalk Server installation program is Visio. To do this, insert the CD into the CD-ROM drive. Run the setup program and follow the onscreen directions.

Installing BizTalk Server 2002

Now that you have all the supporting software installed, in the correct order and configured correctly, it's time to put in the BizTalk Server 2002 CD and launch the setup program. A screen-by-screen instruction set for installing BizTalk Server follows. Assuming that all the preceding instructions have been adhered to, the installation will go smoothly. If any of the required prerequisite components are not installed, the installation will fail.

After you have either inserted the CD or double-clicked the BizTalk Server installation MSI file, the Setup Wizard begins (see Figure 20.6).

FIGURE 20.6
BizTalk Server 2002 Setup Wizard.

The next screen, as shown in Figure 20.7, is the always-present license agreement. You must accept this agreement for installation to continue.

FIGURE 20.7
License agreement.

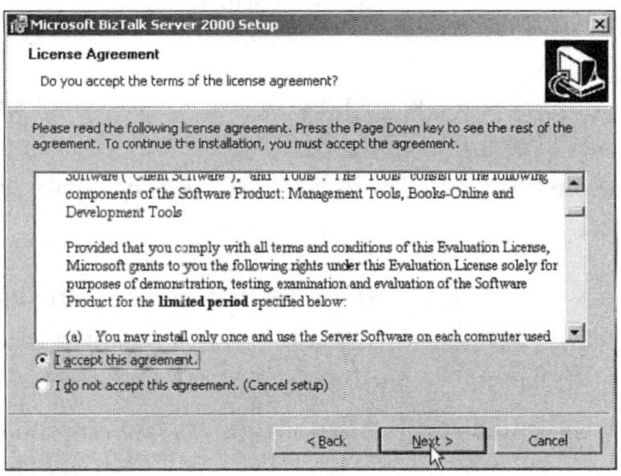

The following screen requires that you enter some user information. Make sure to select the Anyone Who Uses This Computer option (see Figure 20.8).

FIGURE 20.8
Customer information.

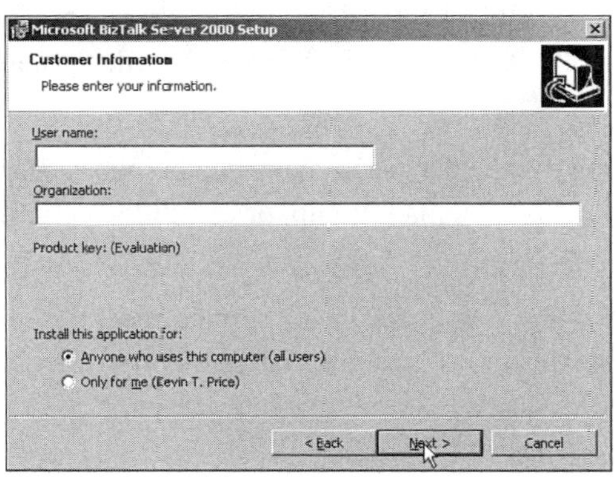

The next dialog, as shown in Figure 20.9, allows you to change the installation directory for BizTalk. Installing BizTalk to a partition other than your C: drive is fine, as long as you have administrative rights to that partition.

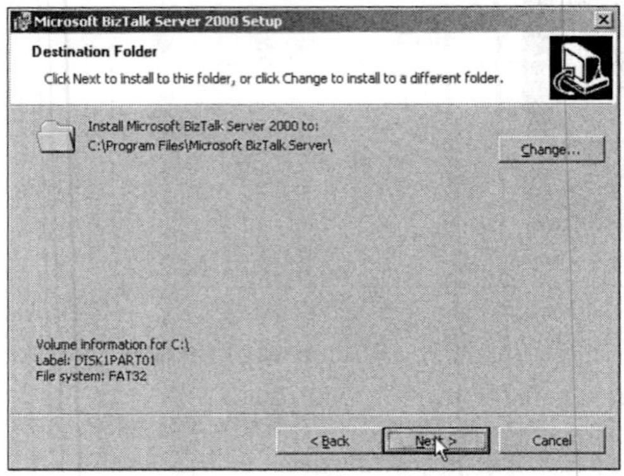

FIGURE 20.9
Destination Folder dialog.

After you select the installation directory, you are prompted to select the installation type. To remain efficient for development purposes, select the Complete option, as shown in Figure 20.10, to have the install program copy everything possible from the CD to the hard drive.

As with many Microsoft servers, BizTalk Server has the option to install just the administrative tools as well. The tools installation enables you to perform a complete installation of the BizTalk Server 2002 tools, including BizTalk Orchestration Designer, BizTalk Document Tracking, BizTalk Editor, and BizTalk Mapper. The BizTalk Server 2002 parser, serializer, correlation, and runtime binaries are not installed. The tools will run on the following operating systems:

- Microsoft Windows 2000 Server
- Microsoft Windows 2000 Advanced Server
- Microsoft Windows 2000 Professional with the NTFS file system and Service Pack 1

The next screen prompts you to create a group that can administer BizTalk Server. You can change this to an existing local/domain group, or accept the default as shown in Figure 20.11.

Following the administrative group selection is the service account selection. Based on the previous instructions, set this to use that account (see Figure 20.12).

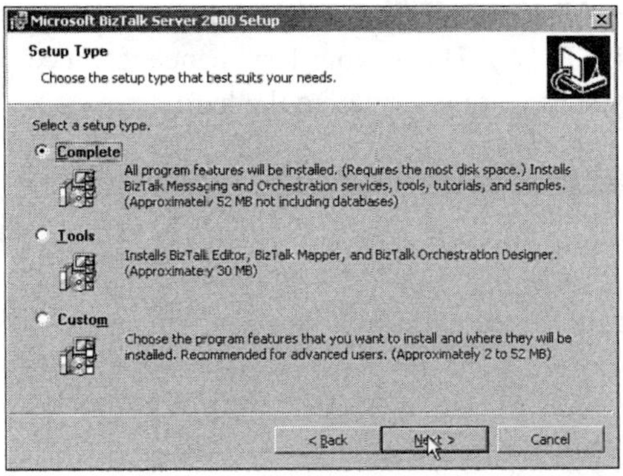

FIGURE 20.10
Setup Type dialog.

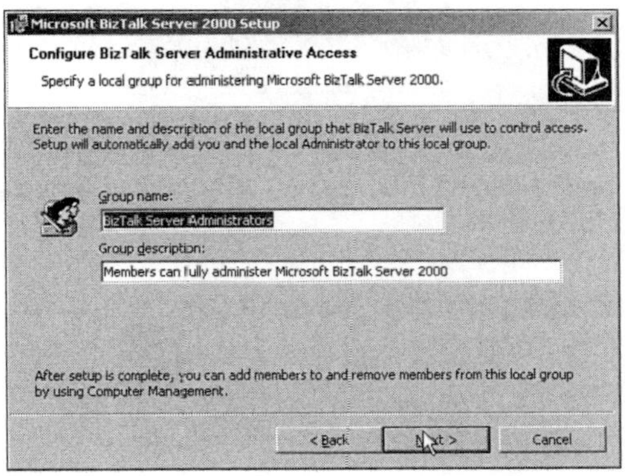

FIGURE 20.11
Configure BizTalk Server Administrative Access dialog.

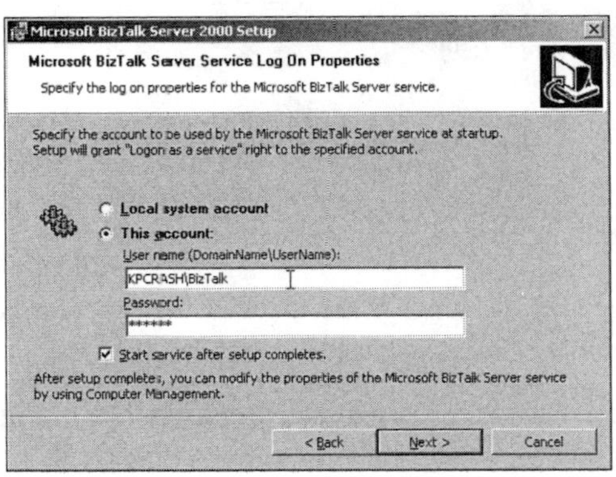

FIGURE 20.12
Service Logon Properties dialog.

The next screen, as shown in Figure 20.13, displays your selected install information and a warning about having Visio installed. If you have Visio installed, you can ignore this warning. If you do not have Visio installed, now would be a good time to cancel installation and install Visio 2000 (SR-1A). This is your last chance to cancel installing BizTalk Server before files actually start getting written to the hard drive.

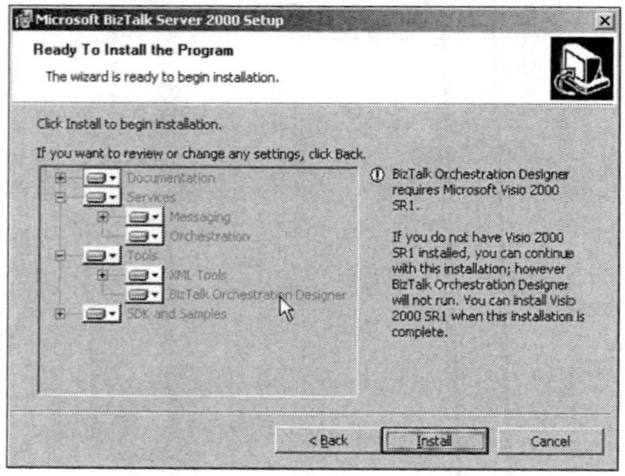

FIGURE 20.13
Ready to Install dialog.

A series of progress bars appears as BizTalk Server 2002 is installed, as shown in Figure 20.14.

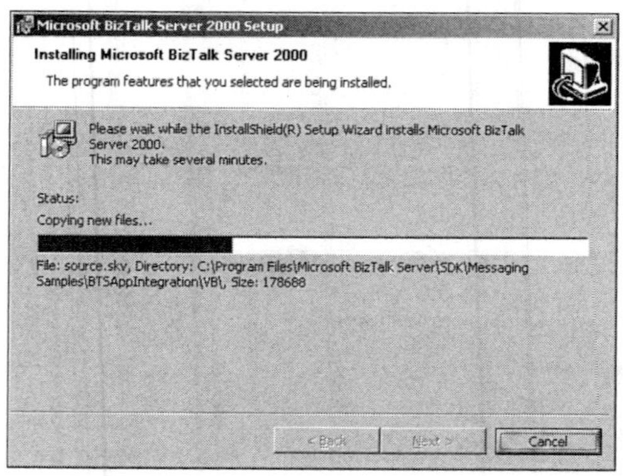

FIGURE 20.14
Installation status dialog.

After BizTalk Server is installed, it launches the database setup wizards. The first of these is the Messaging Database Setup Wizard (see Figure 20.15).

In the configuration dialog for the Messaging database, as shown in Figure 20.16, make sure that the SQL Server login parameters are correct and click Next.

The next screen prompts you to either create a new BizTalk Server group to store the BizTalk Server database servers or add it to an existing group. Because this example is based on an initial install, accept the default, as shown in Figure 20.17.

FIGURE 20.15
Messaging Database Setup Wizard dialog.

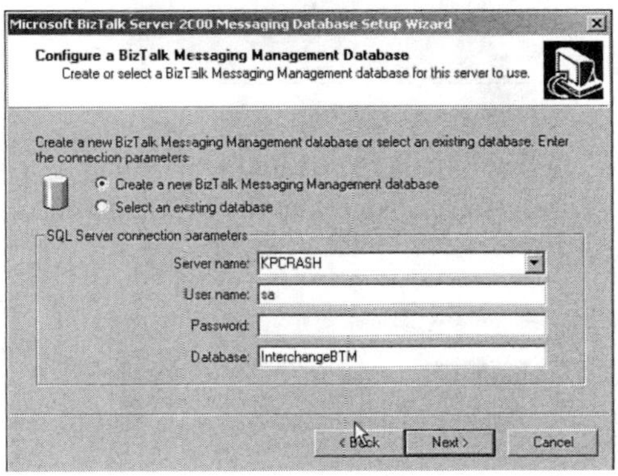

FIGURE 20.16
Configure a BizTalk Messaging Management Database dialog.

Should you want to add BizTalk Server to an existing group, keep in mind that you must have administrative rights on the central BizTalk Server. Also, you need to have an account to use to set up the now Shared Queue database. Assuming you have these accounts, use the Select an Existing BizTalk Server Group dialog and select a name from the Group Name list.

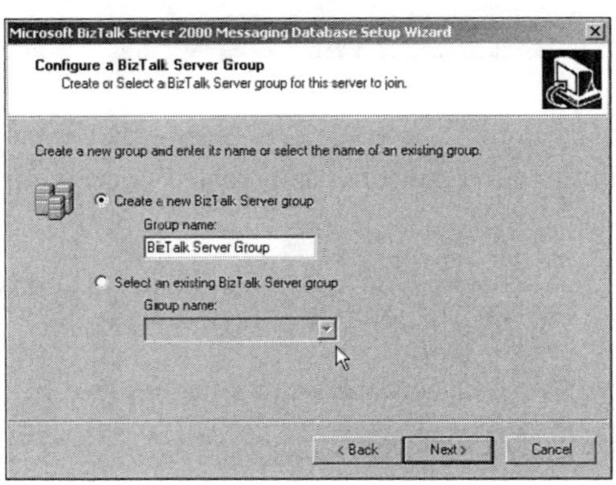

FIGURE 20.17
Configuring a BizTalk Server Group dialog.

The next database to be created is the Tracking database (see Figure 20.18). As stated before, make sure that the SQL Server login parameters are correct and then click Next.

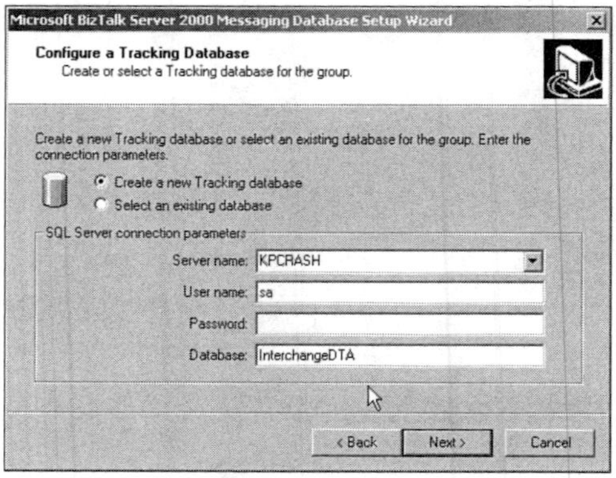

FIGURE 20.18
Configure a Tracking Database dialog.

The final part of the messaging database is the Shared Queue database (see Figure 20.19). Again, in this dialog, simply make sure that the SQL Server login credentials are correct and then click Next.

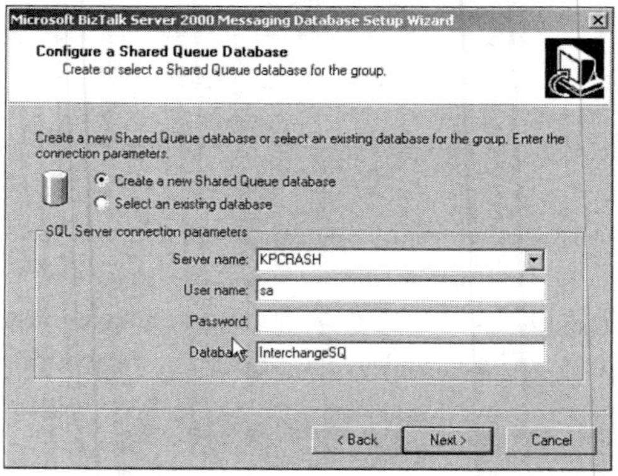

FIGURE 20.19
Configure a Shared Queue Database dialog.

After the Shared Queue configuration is complete, you see a dialog (as shown in Figure 20.20) confirming all the information collected and created in generating the BizTalk Server Group.

When complete, you see a dialog letting you know that the installation and configuration of the messaging database is complete, as shown in Figure 20.21.

Next, the Orchestration Persistence Database Wizard launches (see Figure 20.22). This is similar to the Messaging Database Setup Wizard.

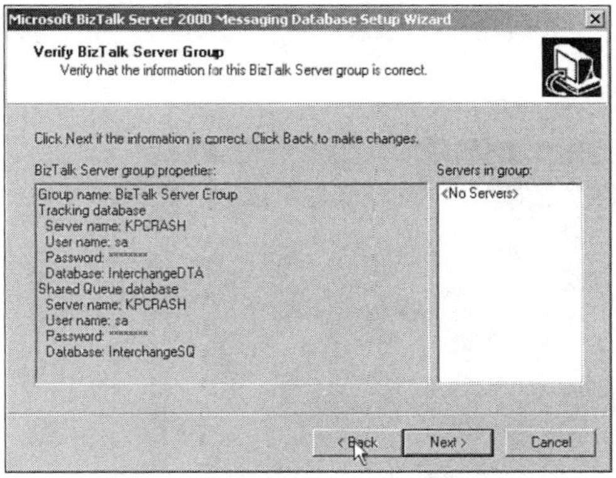

FIGURE 20.20
Messaging Database Setup Wizard dialog.

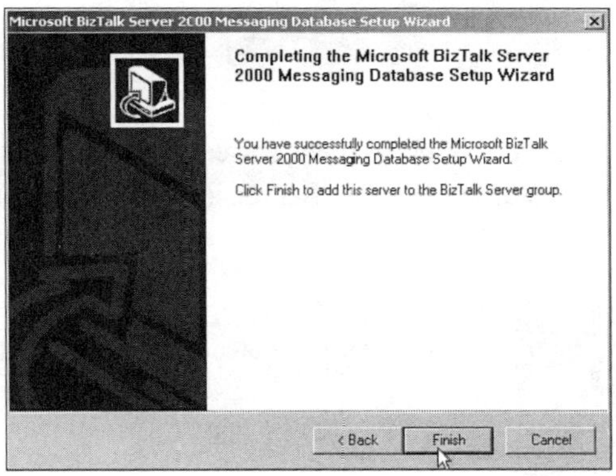

FIGURE 20.21
Messaging Database Setup Wizard Complete dialog.

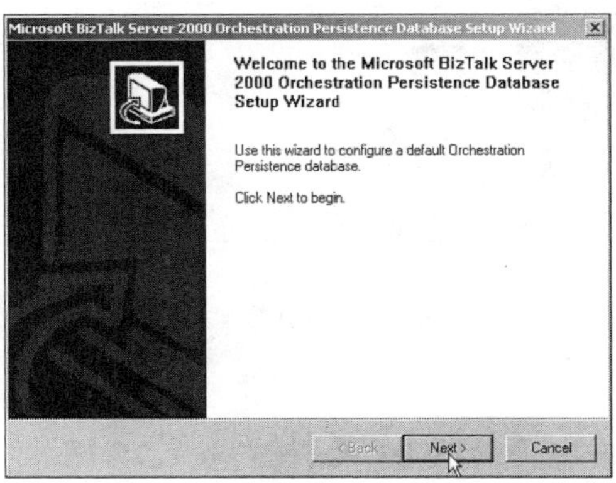

FIGURE 20.22
Orchestration Persistence Database Setup Wizard dialog.

On the following screen, as shown in Figure 20.23, you are given the option of selecting a different server to install the Orchestration Persistence database. This is recommended on systems that will require high-performance. For this example, though, keep everything on one machine.

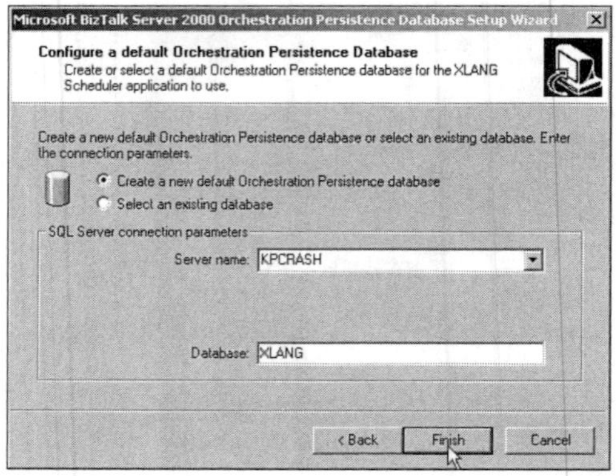

FIGURE 20.23
Orchestration Persistence Database Configuration dialog.

Finally, after the Orchestration Persistence database creation is complete, you get a confirmation dialog notifying you that the BizTalk Server installation is complete (see Figure 20.24).

FIGURE 20.24
BizTalk Server Installation Wizard Complete dialog.

Click Finish to complete the installation. Microsoft BizTalk Server 2002 is now installed on your server.

Installing BizTalk Server Client Tools

The BizTalk Server Client Tools can be installed on a workstation or other server to allow for remote management of different BizTalk Servers. The main difference between installing the server and installing the tools is that during the install, you select Tools Only on the installation type selection screen.

Note

To dramatically increase the performance of BizTalk Orchestration Services, in Windows Explorer, browse to `Program Files\Common Files\System\ado` and then double-click `adofre15.reg`, or right-click the file and select Merge. In the confirmation dialog box, click Yes; then click OK. This procedure changes the ADO threading model from Apartment Threaded to Both and may affect other applications that use ADO.

Summary

In this chapter, you learned how to prepare your server for BizTalk Server 2002 installation, as well as how to install BizTalk Server 2002. For more specific installation instructions, Chapter 21, "Performance Analysis and Tuning," discusses performance tuning and deployment options.

CHAPTER 21

Performance Analysis and Tuning

By Clifford R. Cannon

In This Chapter

A small- to medium-sized BizTalk Server installation can work effectively on a single server machine without particular attention to performance tuning, using the default configuration. However, as the number and size of documents to be processed increase, so does the need for performance analysis and tuning as part of the development and deployment plan.

Because BizTalk Server uses SQL Server intensively to store complete documents and state information before, during, and after document processing, you must become familiar with how BizTalk uses databases to optimize the distribution of the workload. In larger installations, performance optimization often involves placing BizTalk Server and SQL Server on separate machines, so each machine can use all its resources for its part of the total task. Two of the databases, the Shared Queue and the Document Tracking databases, can be used so intensively in a high-traffic BizTalk installation that each database should be placed on its own dedicated SQL Server machine.

In addition to deploying separate servers for BizTalk and SQL Server, multiple BizTalk Server machines can be combined into a unified group of servers, all of which can take documents from the same message-processing queue and thereby balance the processing load across all machines in the group. To specialize the BizTalk servers even further, some machines in a server group can be dedicated to document-receive functions only, whereas other machines only process documents from the Shared Queue but do not receive document submissions from message senders.

While separating different BizTalk functions across multiple server machines, of course you will also want to scale the hardware of each machine for the desired performance. The speed and number of processors, size of physical memory, speed and layout of disk drives, and speed and configuration of network interfaces can significantly affect performance. In many cases, scaling the server hardware alone will increase the performance of a single-server installation enough to avoid the need to distribute the workload across several machines.

Finally, during system testing and after deployment, BizTalk Server provides many performance counters you can use with Windows System Monitor to measure and tune the performance of your BizTalk installation. Other Windows tools, such as the Defragmenter and the Alerter, can maintain your installations performance at optimum levels and can notify administrators of system problems as—or even before—they occur.

Separating Database Servers from BizTalk Servers

One powerful option for increasing the performance of a BizTalk installation is to use dedicated SQL Server machines, separate from the BizTalk Server machines. To design a multiple-server configuration, you need to understand how BizTalk Server uses databases and how the document-processing workload is distributed among those databases.

Databases Used by BizTalk Server

Four types of databases are used by BizTalk Server, with differing degrees of 1-to-N or M-to-N relationship allowed between database instances and BizTalk Server instances:

- Messaging Management database (default name `InterchangeBTM`)—Defines all BizTalk Messaging objects for a BizTalk server group. Must be shared by all BizTalk servers in the same group. (Server groups are explained in next section of this chapter.)
- Shared Queue database (default name `InterchangeSQ`)—Persists all received documents until successfully processed. Contains Scheduled, Work, Retry, and Suspended queues for a BizTalk server group. Shared by all BizTalk servers in the same group.
- Document Tracking database (default name `InterchangeDTA`)—Contains copies of incoming and outgoing documents along with selected data fields and time stamps for tracking document flow. Also shared by all BizTalk servers in the same group.
- Orchestration Persistence database (default name XLANG)—Used to store state data for BizTalk Orchestration schedules (which may need to run for days or weeks before completing). This can be a separate database for each individual BizTalk server or can be shared among servers in any combination.

Recommended Division of Database Workload

For low-volume BizTalk Server installations (or for a development system), it is permissible to host BizTalk Server and all the SQL Server databases on a single machine. However, the recommended configuration for a production BizTalk installation includes at least *three* server machines: one BizTalk Server machine and two SQL Server machines. (Web services and mail services for HTTP [Hypertext Transfer Protocol] and SMTP [Simple Mail Transfer Protocol] document transport generally should be hosted on additional separate machines.)

The reason for two separate SQL Server machines is that the Shared Queue database is heavily read and written by the BizTalk servers. All documents received are written to the Shared Queue database, and all documents to be processed are read from there. Similarly, full copies of both received and sent documents are written to the Document Tracking database. To avoid the database services competing with each other for resources, or competing with BizTalk services, each of these two databases should be located on its own separate SQL Server machine.

The performance requirements for the other two BizTalk Server databases are not so stringent. The Messaging Management database is written to only during development or administration (creating or deploying Messaging objects, defining BizTalk server groups, and configuring individual BizTalk servers). During operations, Messaging Management information is cached on individual servers and is read from the database only to refresh the cache (every 50 seconds by default). Because the Messaging Management database is written so infrequently—and therefore does not often write to its transaction log—it can be conveniently hosted on the same machine that hosts the Document Tracking database.

Depending on the number, complexity, and duration of your BizTalk Orchestration schedules, the Orchestration Persistence database will experience a low to moderate amount of database traffic. Unlike the other three BizTalk database types, this database can be configured separately for each individual BizTalk server. It makes the most sense initially to host the Orchestration Persistence database on the same machine as the Shared Queue database and to use the same database for all BizTalk servers in the server group. If you expect a large workload, or if performance evaluation reveals the need (see “Monitoring BizTalk Server for Performance” later in this chapter), you can install additional SQL Server machine(s) to host Orchestration Persistence.

Grouping BizTalk Servers for Performance

In addition to using separate database server machines, you can further increase the performance of a BizTalk installation by using multiple BizTalk Server machines, organized into a *server group*. All the machines in a server group share the same Messaging Management database and can share the processing workload for the same types of documents, through the same channels and ports. Also, to maximize the total throughput of a BizTalk server group, some servers can be configured to execute receive functions only (doing no document processing), whereas other servers can be configured exclusively for document processing.

BizTalk Server Groups

How are individual BizTalk servers combined into a server group, and how does each server know to which group it belongs? To begin with, a BizTalk Messaging Management database stores server group properties and membership—in addition to its function of defining organizations, ports, channels, and other BizTalk Messaging objects. Actually, one Messaging Management database can be used by more than one server group. However, keep in mind that there is only one namespace for the BizTalk Messaging objects defined in a Messaging Management database. Therefore, if you share a database among server groups, you must take care to avoid name collisions between objects used by different server groups.

The binding between BizTalk servers and databases—and vice versa—is by name, not by SID, GUID, or some other immutable identifier. Hence the bindings are easy to reconfigure. A Messaging Management database contains the names of one or more BizTalk server groups, and the names of the member servers of each group. Conversely, when a server is added to a server group (whether during installation or afterward), values under the registry key `HKEY_LOCAL_MACHINE\SOFTWARE\Microsoft\BizTalk Server\1.0\Administration\` are set to tell the BizTalk server how to connect to its Messaging Management database. Thus there is a two-way linkage between individual servers and the Messaging Management database that defines its server group.

The registry linkage is also the reason that you can run BizTalk Server Administration on any server in the group and see the same server groups, servers, and configuration properties. If you start BizTalk Server Administration, right-click Microsoft BizTalk Server 2002, and choose Properties, you will see the server name and database name (from the Administration registry key) that connect the BizTalk server to its Messaging Management database. All other properties of the server and of its server group are contained within the database, not in the registry. We'll now examine the relationship of server groups and individual servers, and see how the grouped servers cooperate to increase the performance of BizTalk Server document processing.

Creating BizTalk Server Groups

For the first BizTalk server you install, you must create a new Messaging Management database and a new server group (see Figure 21.1). During subsequent installations on the same network, you have the option of creating a new server group or joining an existing group. The first step to joining a group of servers is to choose the existing Messaging Management database (see Figure 21.2). Then you have the chance to join an existing server group at a later stage in the installation.

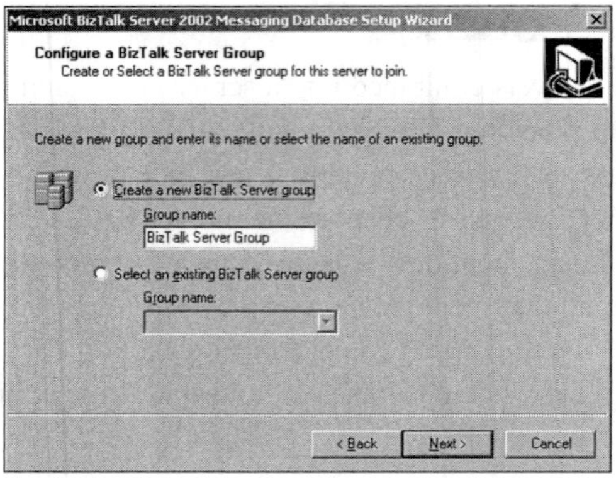

FIGURE 21.1
Creating a new server group during installation.

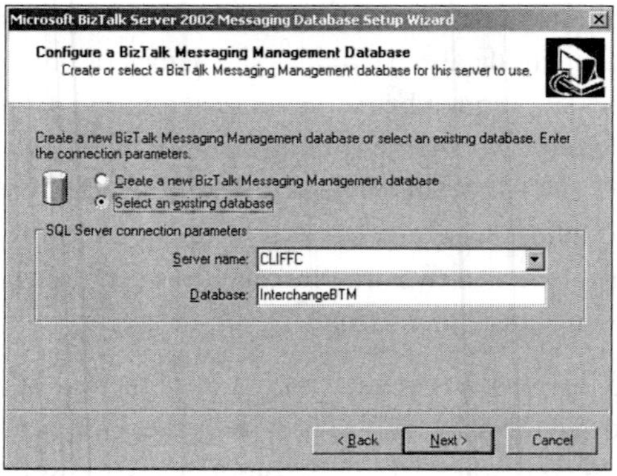

FIGURE 21.2
Choosing an existing database during installation.

It is also possible to add a BizTalk server to a server group after installation. Simply open BizTalk Server Administration; expand to the desired server group; right-click; and choose New, Server. Type in the name of the server to add (see Figure 21.3); sorry, there is no drop-down list of available servers. BizTalk Server must already be installed, and the BizTalk Messaging Service must be running, to add an existing server to a server group.

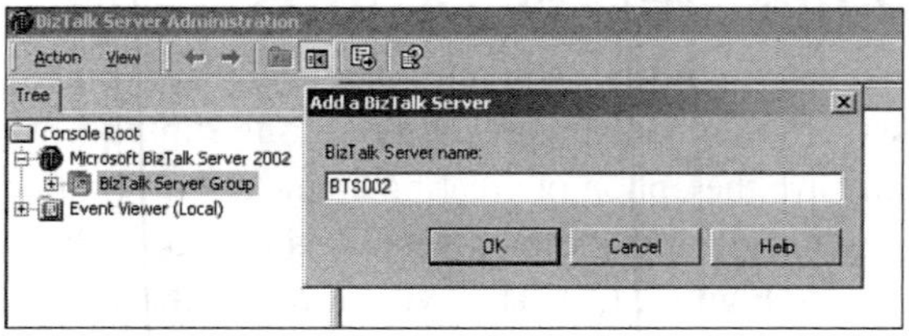

FIGURE 21.3
Adding a BizTalk server to a server group.

When you want to remove a BizTalk server from a server group, you must first right-click the server name and choose Stop to stop the BizTalk Messaging service on that machine. Then, to return any unfinished documents to the Work Queue so that another server in the group can process them, again right-click the name of the stopped server and choose All Tasks, Free Interchanges. You can then Delete the stopped server from the server group.

Properties of a BizTalk Server Group

In Figure 21.4, we open BizTalk Server Administration to examine the properties of the server group. Notice that all servers in the group use the same SMTP server and the same reply-URL for reliable messaging. Also, the refresh interval for Messaging Management objects is configured here for all servers in the group. If you are in production and are making only infrequent changes to Messaging Management, you could reduce the database load slightly by increasing the refresh interval to 5 or 10 minutes.

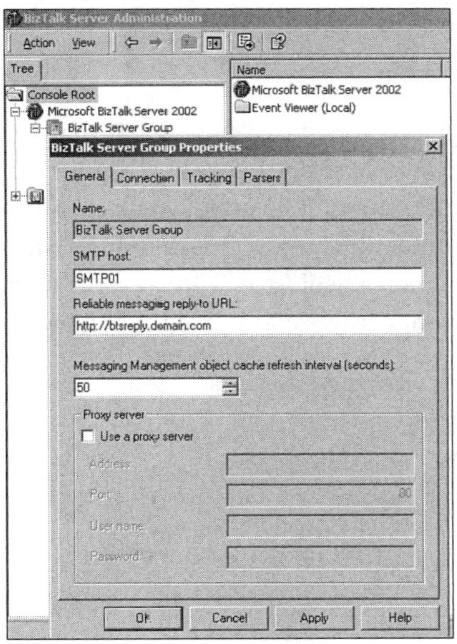

FIGURE 21.4
Server group properties, General tab.

In Figure 21.5 you see, as already noted, that the Tracking and Shared Queue databases are configured for the entire server group, not for individual servers. Therefore, all documents processed by servers in the server group are tracked in a single database. Even more important for performance scaling, any BizTalk server in the group can process documents stored in the Shared Queue database. In effect, grouping provides a simple form of load balancing across all the BizTalk servers in the group because each server will query for more documents to process whenever it becomes idle. This is an effective way to increase the total capacity of a BizTalk installation and is perhaps the most important reason for the existence of BizTalk server groups.

FIGURE 21.5
Server group properties, Connection tab.

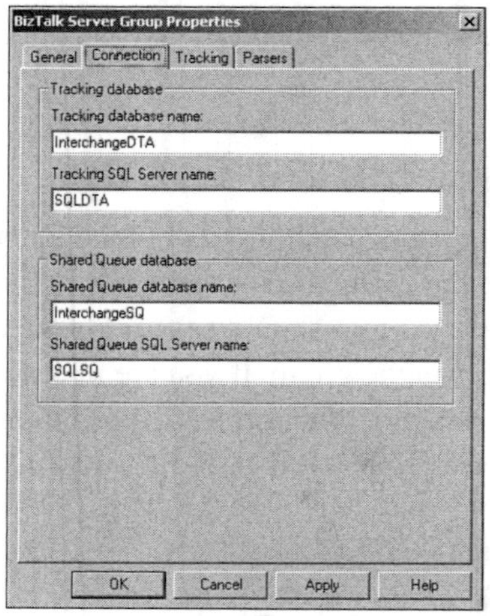

Figure 21.6 illustrates the server group properties Tracking tab. On a production server in a high-traffic installation, you can disable all document tracking for the server group to improve database and network performance. If possible, you may want to use the Document Tracking database to troubleshoot messaging and processing problems. If necessary, host the tracking database on a dedicated SQL server and upgrade the server's processor, memory, disk, and network hardware as needed to achieve the required performance.

FIGURE 21.6
Server group properties, Tracking tab.

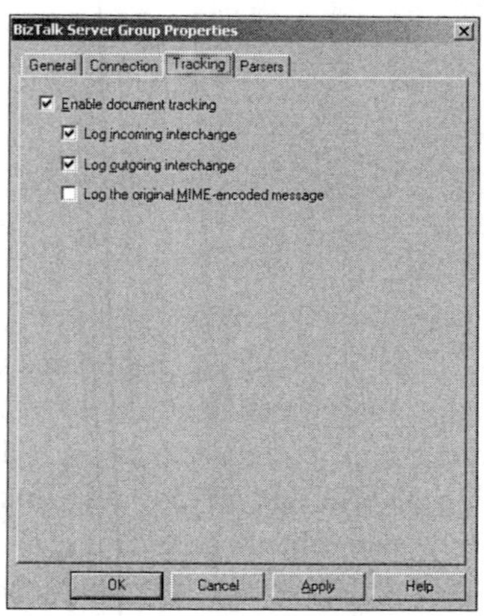

Figure 21.7 is the server group properties Parsers tab. Recall that BizTalk attempts to identify a document whose specification is not declared by the submission method. To do so, BizTalk must attempt to parse the document according to one of the known formats: XML, EDIFACT, ANSI X12, or flat file. To minimize time spent parsing unknown documents (and therefore improving performance), the call sequence on this tab should be configured to reflect the expected proportion of received document formats.

FIGURE 21.7
Server group properties, Parsers tab.

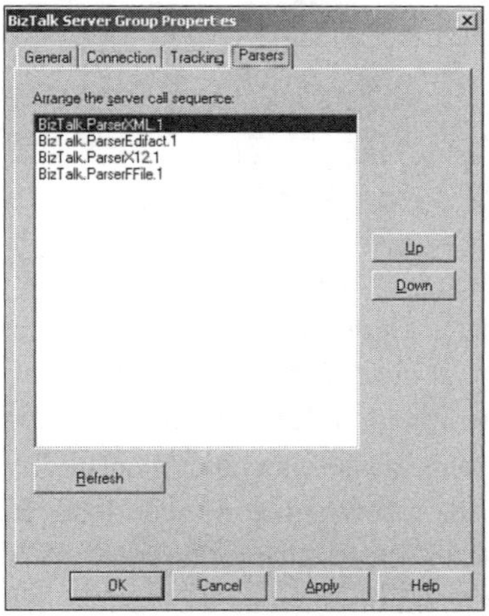

In a large-scale BizTalk installation, such as a national government department receiving documents from millions of submitters, it may make sense to create a separate server group for each parser type, placing that parser first in the call sequence for its dedicated server group.

Properties of an Individual BizTalk Server

The Properties dialog for an individual BizTalk server (see Figure 21.8) is far simpler than that for a server group. The more important properties are the check box for work-item processing and the number of worker threads per processor. Oddly, the default number of worker threads is 4, but the recommended number is from 15 to 20. Hence this is one property you should be sure to manually configure on all BizTalk servers.

If you have several BizTalk servers in the server group, you have the option to separate the servers into *document-receive* servers and *document-processing* servers. Any individual server for which you uncheck the Participate in Work-Item Processing box will not query the Shared Queue database for documents and can dedicate all its resources to executing receive functions. Conversely, you can configure all the receive functions for the server group to run on document-receive BizTalk servers, so no resources on document-processing servers are used for initially receiving documents.

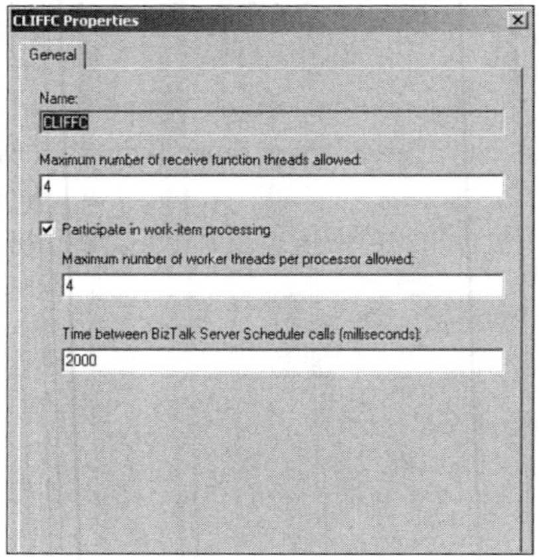

FIGURE 21.8
Properties of an individual BizTalk server.

Easy to miss, but very important, is that each defined receive function runs on *only one server* in the BizTalk server group. The choice of server is specified on the Advanced tab on the Properties dialog of each receive function. Receive functions should be carefully distributed among the servers in the group. If there are document-receive servers in the group, they will fulfill the majority of the receive function workload. But some receive functions can still be configured to run on document-processing servers if it makes sense to do so. The performance monitoring techniques detailed in "Monitoring BizTalk Server for Performance," later in this chapter, will help you determine the optimal distribution of servers to execute receive functions.

The less-important properties of an individual BizTalk server are the number of receive function threads and the Shared Queue polling interval. Leave both these at their default values unless you have definite evidence (from performance monitoring) of delays that might be cured by changing their values.

Scaling Server Hardware for Performance

You have already seen how to divide the labor of a BizTalk installation among multiple SQL Server and multiple BizTalk Server machines. This section describes the options for scaling the hardware of individual servers and the network that connects them. "Monitoring BizTalk Server for Performance," later in this chapter, explains how to monitor the actual performance realized and modify the workload division and server hardware to eliminate any remaining bottlenecks.

Scaling Server Processors

Both BizTalk Server and SQL Server support multiprocessing, so the performance of both can benefit from including multiple fast processors in your system design. However, counting both hardware costs and per-processor software licensing costs, it may be more effective to create N single-processor servers rather than one N-processor server in which all the processors share single memory, disk, and network subsystems. In either case, it is important to choose processors for the BizTalk servers that have at least 1 MB of Level 2 cache—2 MB is better. The large cache is needed for efficient execution of the BizTalk Parser, and overall performance may suffer considerably if smaller caches are used.

Scaling Server Memory

Both BizTalk servers and SQL servers should have at least 512 MB of physical memory. More is better; money spent on extra memory generally has a greater effect on performance than that spent on greater processing power.

An important additional factor on machines running SQL Server is that, using the default installation memory settings, processing large result sets will use 100 percent of physical memory. That causes the operating system itself to page out, and because SQL Server itself relies on operating system services, the result is page thrashing so severe that the machine may become completely unresponsive for several minutes. Setting the maximum memory allowed for the SQL Server process (see Figure 21.9) to about 75 percent of the physical memory size appears to eliminate this problem completely—actually improving the overall performance of the database server.

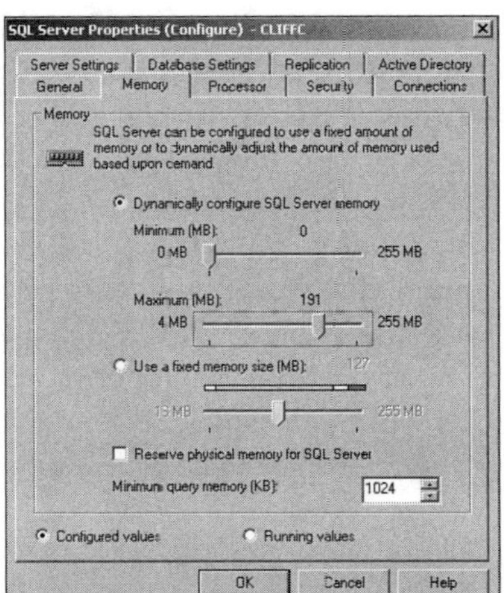

FIGURE 21.9
Setting maximum SQL Server memory.

Scaling Disk Storage

Disk performance is most critical for the database servers in a BizTalk installation. The BizTalk servers themselves mostly communicate with database servers over the network and do not heavily tax their local disk storage (except file-receive servers, and even then the disk systems are usually much faster than the local network connection). Standard recommendations to optimize a SQL server to host a single database include at least three separate physical disk systems per server:

- One disk for the operating system and paging file (assuming that memory is large enough that paging is minimized)
- One disk for the database transaction log (mostly sequential write, so heads move very little)
- One disk for the database data file(s) (random access, separate from the operating system and transaction log disks so that all seeks are used for database read and write only)

To attain the full benefit of multiple disk systems, you must also include a multichannel disk controller capable of performing separate data transfers on all the disk systems simultaneously.

High-availability for a SQL server is usually achieved by mirroring the system/paging volume and the transaction-log volume, and using hardware RAID-5 (Redundant Array of Inexpensive Devices with parity) for the data volume. However, because of the high volume of database activity in BizTalk Server, RAID-5 is not recommended for the servers hosting the Shared Queue and Document Tracking databases. The reason is that, although a single failed drive does not impair the performance of a RAID-5 array, replacing a failed drive does considerably reduce performance of the array. During the recovery process, the entire content of all the drives in the array must be read to initialize the replacement drive with parity data. All the seeks required to read that data are interfering with the seeks required to read and write data for the database file on the running server. Therefore, for a database server in a BizTalk Server installation, the recommended technologies for the database file volume are RAID-0 (disk striping for performance, but no parity) or RAID-10 (a mirrored pair of RAID-0 volumes). At a minimum, if you choose to use RAID-5 on a database server, you may need to wait for off-peak hours to replace a failed drive in the array, accepting a slight risk of complete server failure (availability risk) to avoid the higher risk that you will fall behind in document processing (performance risk).

Scaling Network Hardware

The performance of a multiserver BizTalk Server installation is heavily dependent on efficient network communication among all the servers. Web servers are submitting documents; BizTalk servers are sending documents to the Tracking database, reading documents from the Shared Queue database, and sending processed documents on to their recipients. In a high-volume installation, a single 100-Mbps network segment may not be sufficient to carry all the traffic.

One solution is to include two or even three NICs (Network Interface Cards) in the BizTalk servers and create several physically separate network segments to allow simultaneous traffic between several pairs of servers. For example, one segment could be dedicated to connecting BizTalk servers to the Shared Queue database server, whereas another segment could be used only for connections to the Document Tracking database server. A third segment could be used for receiving and sending documents.

Another way to increase the effective bandwidth of the local network is to use smart switches in place of simple network hubs. Ordinary hubs broadcast all packets received to all machines on the network, so only one machine can "talk" at a time. Smart switches examine the packet to see which machine is the intended destination and forward the packet only on the wire connected to that destination machine. Therefore several machines can send at one time—the switch may even be able to buffer simultaneous messages to the same destination—and the network bandwidth is effectively increased to several times its rated speed of 100 Mbps.

Finally, faster technologies such as 1000 Mbps fiber-optic cables can be employed to connect some or all of the servers in the BizTalk Server installation. Such networks normally include smart switches as a standard feature, so the effective capacity can be 20–30 times greater than a simple-hub 100 Mbps network. Some high volume BizTalk Server installations may justify the use of this expensive but powerful technology.

Monitoring BizTalk Server for Performance

You will already have designed your BizTalk Server installation as detailed earlier in this chapter, separating the database servers, grouping the BizTalk servers, and scaling the computer and network hardware to meet the performance requirements of your expected workload. Now, to verify that you have provided adequate resources at every point and to identify any remaining bottlenecks, you can employ the Windows System Monitor to chart and log the performance of your servers and communications. Also, to avoid performance degradation in the disk subsystems, you can degfragment the disk volumes periodically and send alerts for inadequate free space on any disk volume.

Windows System Monitor

Several sets of performance counters are useful for monitoring performance of a BizTalk Server installation. We'll go through the setup of one counter set in detail, a combination useful for evaluating disk performance. Then we'll list the other counter sets and how to evaluate and apply each of them.

Open Windows System Monitor by choosing Start, Programs, Administrative Tools, Performance. Then follow these steps:

1. Expand Performance Logs and Alerts, right-click Counter Logs, choose New Log Settings, enter a name such as DiskLog for the counter set, and click Add (see Figure 21.10).

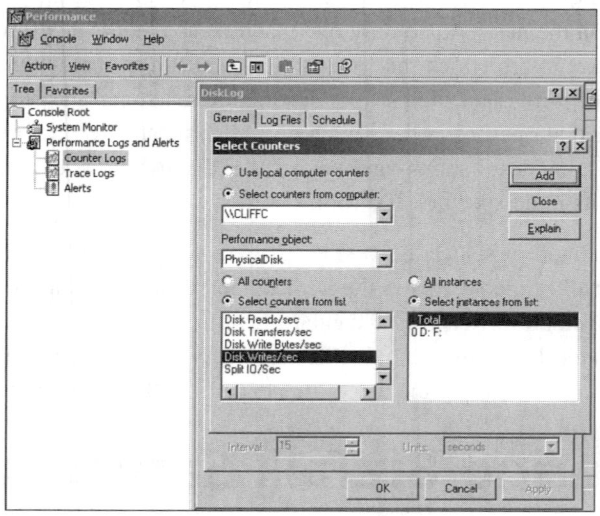

FIGURE 21.10
Choosing `PhysicalDisk` *counters to log performance.*

2. Choose Performance Object: PhysicalDisk and Add in turn the counters % Disk Time, Current Disk Queue Length, Disk Reads/sec, and Disk Writes/sec (select the _Total instance for each, or, if you have multiple physical drives, select each physical drive as a separate instance).
3. Click Close after adding all the counters.
4. For long-term logging, a sample interval of 1 minute should be adequate.

5. On the Log Files tab (see Figure 21.11), specify the location, filename, and suffix (serial number or date+time) for storing the log data. You also have the option to store the data as a comma-separated or tab-separated file to make it easier to import into Excel or another application for later analysis.

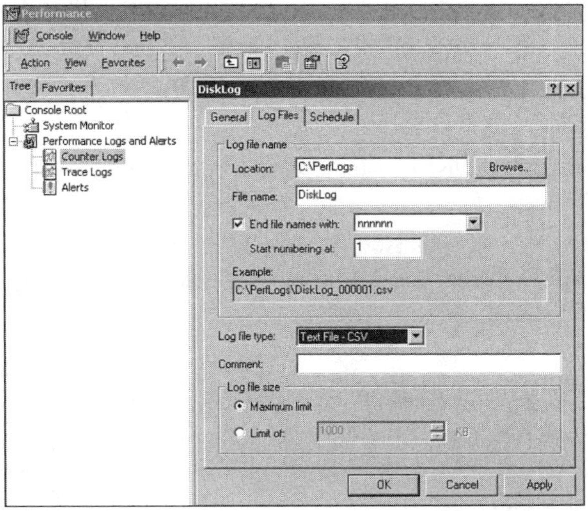

FIGURE 21.11
Specifying performance log filename and type.

6. On the Schedule tab, select Start Log Manually and click OK to save the counter set and log-file definition for later use.
7. To log data for the counter set, select Counter Logs in the left pane, right-click the name (for example, `DiskLog`) in the right pane, and choose Start (see Figure 21.12).

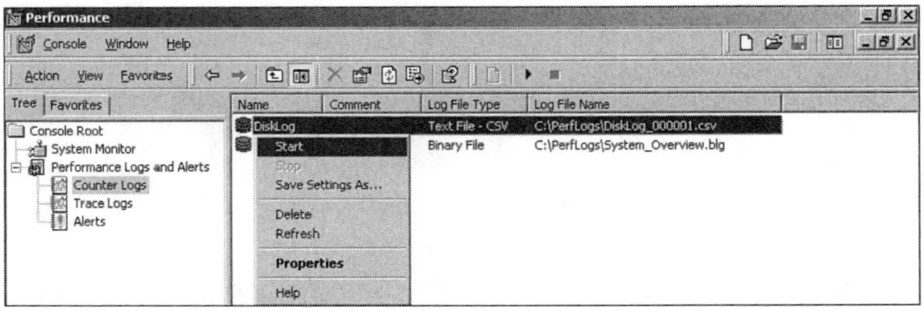

FIGURE 21.12
Manually starting a performance counter log.

8. To change the sample interval or to schedule the log to start and stop at scheduled times, right-click the name and choose Properties.
9. When you have sampled for the desired period, again right-click the name and choose Stop.

To chart the data collected in the log, select System Monitor in the left pane, right-click in the right pane, choose Properties, and click the Source tab. Then follow these steps:

1. Select Log File and Browse to the most recent serial number or date+time of the desired log file.
2. Click Time Range and use the slider to select the starting and ending times for display, if desired.
3. Click the Data tab and click Add. Select all Performance Counters (if more than one), select All Counters, and All Instances; click Add. Click Close and click OK (see Figure 21.13).

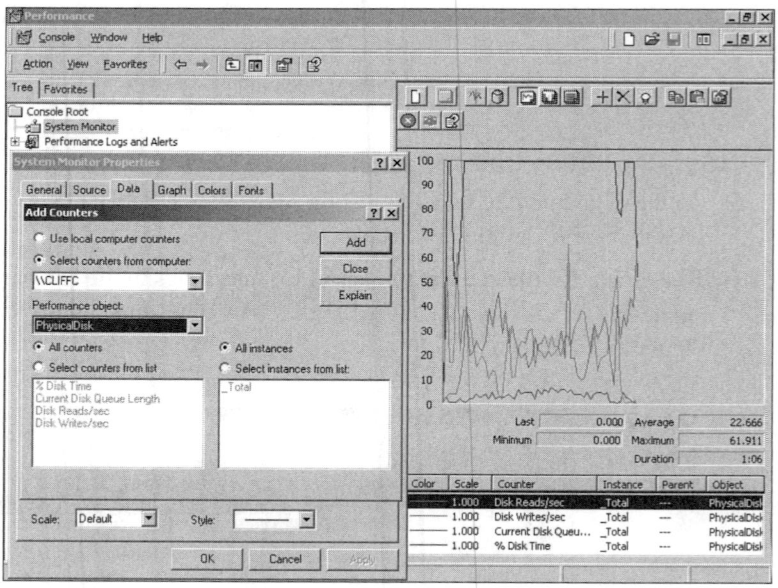

FIGURE 21.13
Charting data from a counter log file.

The chart now displays the data from the sampled log file. To rescale any of the counters to make the results easier to interpret, right-click the right pane, choose Properties, click the Data tab, select the desired counter, and choose a new Scale from the drop-down list.

Counter Sets for Evaluating Performance

To evaluate disk performance (useful on all servers in your BizTalk installation), follow these guidelines:

- PhysicalDisk\% Disk Time—Should be below 100 percent. If above, add more physical drives, use faster drives or faster disk controllers, or split the workload between two machines (for example, move a database to another server, or add an additional file-receiving server and move some of the receive functions to that server).
- PhysicalDisk\Current Disk Queue Length—Should be less than two times the number of drive spindles (each drive in a RAID array counts as a spindle). If above, add more physical drives, use faster drives or faster disk controllers, or divide the workload between multiple servers.
- PhysicalDisk\Disk Reads/sec and Disk Writes/sec—Sum should be well under the maximum capacity of the drive (determined from manufacturer's documentation or estimated by dividing drive RPM by 60 to calculate revolutions per second). If above, use same remedies as in the preceding items.

To evaluate processor and memory performance (on all servers), monitor the following:

- Memory\Available Bytes—Should be above 10 MB. If not, add more physical memory or lower maximum memory setting for SQL Server.
- Memory\Page Reads/sec and Pages Input/sec—Should be well below 100, usually below 20. If not, add more physical memory or lower maximum memory setting for SQL Server.
- Processor\%Processor Time—Should be under 100 percent except for brief periods. If not, add faster processors, add more processors, or divide workload among more servers.
- System\Processor Queue Length—Should be less than two times number of processors. If not, add faster processors, add more processors, or divide workload among servers.

To evaluate network performance (all servers), monitor the following:

- Network Interface\Bytes Total/sec—Should be under 30 percent of rated speed of network segment. If not, install a faster network connection.
- Network Interface\Output Queue Length—Should average well under 1, usually under 0.1. If not, network collisions are slowing communication. Add more network segments (with multiple adapters per server) or install smart switches to increase effective network capacity.

To evaluate Web server performance (for HTTP transport services), monitor the following:

- Web Service\Get Requests/sec and Post Requests/sec—Sum indicates number of documents being received via HTTP for submission to BizTalk Server.
- Active Server Pages\Requests Queued and Request Wait Time—Should be near zero except for brief periods. If not, distribute workload among additional Web servers.
- Process\Private Bytes (select `inetinfo` instance)—Steady increase indicates memory leak, possibly in a COM+ component, that will eventually crash the Web server.

To evaluate Message Queue server performance, monitor the following:

- MSMQ Service\Incoming Messages/sec, Total messages in all queues, and Total bytes in all queues—Allow monitoring of workload on queue servers. Limits depend on server memory, disk, and network capacity. Monitor to establish initial baseline and revisit periodically to detect large deviations that may warn of developing problems.
- MSMQ Queue\Messages in queue and Bytes in queue (select individual instances)—Use to monitor activity on individual queues. Establish initial baseline; monitor periodically for variations.

To evaluate BizTalk Server performance, monitor the following:

- BizTalk Server\Synchronous Submissions/sec and Asynchronous Submissions/sec—Rate of submissions by `Interchange` object method calls. Note that one submission may contain multiple documents. However, on pass-through systems (with no document processing), these counters are the only measure of inbound performance.
- BizTalk Server\Documents Received/sec—Rate at which documents are being received—both documents that are added to the Work Queue in the Shared Queue database and documents that fail parsing and are added to the Suspended Queue.
- BizTalk Server\Documents Processed/sec—Rate at which a document-processing server is pulling documents from the Work Queue. Does not include documents that failed parsing.
- System\Context Switches/sec—A high number on a BizTalk Server indicates too many input/output tasks on the same machine or too many work-item processing threads. On a document-receive server, redistribute some receive functions to other server(s). On receive-and-processing servers, redistribute some or all receive

functions to another server. On document-processing servers, reduce number of work-item processing threads.

Windows Defragmenter

Often overlooked in optimization of servers, fragmentation of disk files can cause significant loss of performance as the read/write heads make extra movements that would be unnecessary if all the files were contiguous on disk. Conversely, running the Windows Defragmenter regularly (or using third-party tools that allow automatic, scheduled defragmentation) can maintain efficient operation of the disk storage subsystem.

To check disk volumes for fragmentation, right-click My Computer (in Windows Explorer or on the Desktop), choose Manage, expand Storage, and select Disk Defragmenter (see Figure 21.14). Select a volume and click Analyze. The program will suggest whether the volume needs to be defragmented, but you can make your own choice whether to proceed and click Defragment if you choose. Defragmentation is more effective and will complete more quickly, when the volume is not being heavily used. However, it is possible, and safe, to defragment at any time.

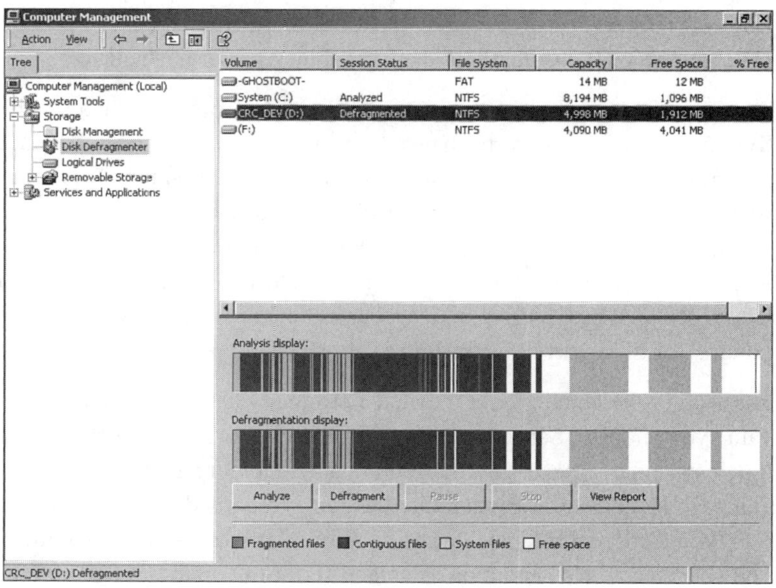

FIGURE 21.14
Windows Defragmenter display.

Windows Alerts

An important cause of file fragmentation is running out of free space on a disk volume. When there is no single piece of contiguous free space large enough to contain a file, multiple smaller pieces (possibly far from each other on the physical disk) must be used. As a rule of thumb, an NTFS volume suffers increased fragmentation when its free space falls below about 15 percent. You probably already knew that it is not a good idea to stuff your disk volumes to capacity, to avoid unexpectedly running completely out of space. Now avoiding fragmentation offers another reason to keep your disks well below the "full" mark, to keep them performing efficiently for both read and write operations. You may have volumes right now that are below 15 percent, even below 10 percent or 5 percent, free space. If you open the Windows Defragmenter and Analyze those volumes, you will probably find them to be highly fragmented—and their performance has probably been reduced as a result.

For any BizTalk Server or SQL server machine, a Windows Alert should be created for each disk volume on the machine to notify an administrator when the free space falls below 15 percent. (You may want to set the threshold higher, 20 percent or 25 percent, to allow time to respond before free space falls well below 15 percent.) First to activate the LogicalDisk performance counters, choose Start, Run, `cmd /k diskperf -YV`, and click OK. Restart Windows to allow the logical disk performance driver to be installed.

To create a free-space alert, again right-click My Computer, choose Manage, expand System Tools, expand Performance Logs and Alerts, right-click Alerts, choose New Alert Settings, enter a name for the alert, and click the Add button. There may be a delay the first time you click Add as all the available performance counters are being discovered and listed. On the Select Counters dialog (see Figure 21.15), choose Performance Object: LogicalDisk, select counter % Free Space, select All Instances, click Add, and click Close. (Note: The C:\ drive may appear as `HardDiskVolumeN`, as may any special boot volume for third-party disk imaging software.)

For each of the counters, set the alert to trigger when the value is under 15 (or higher value you choose). Sampling every 10 minutes provides a timely alert without imposing much system overhead. On the Action tab (see Figure 21.16), you can specify how the alert will be delivered. By default, the alert is recorded in the Application Log. In addition, you can specify a machine to be notified (via net send) when the alert occurs. And you can execute a program or command script to e-mail or page system operators to respond when the alert occurs.

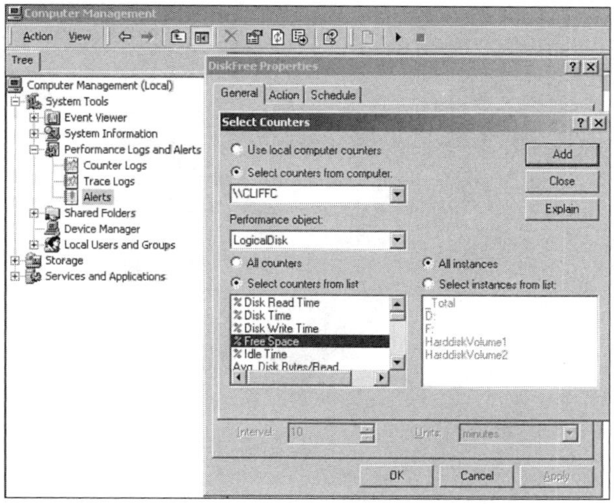

FIGURE 21.15
Choosing counters to monitor disk free space.

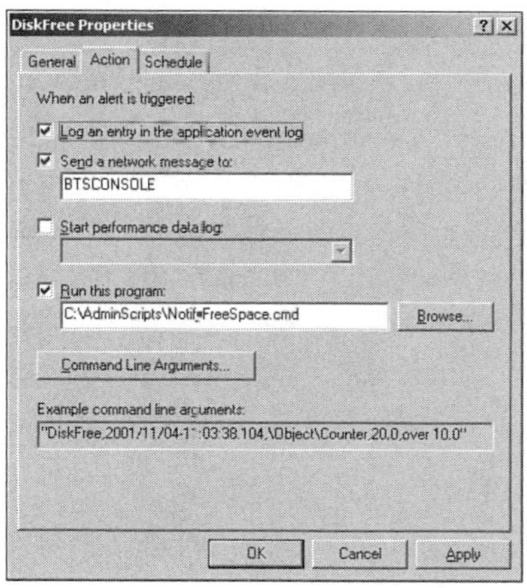

FIGURE 21.16
Specifying actions when alert is triggered.

Summary

BizTalk Server by its distributed design provides many possibilities for performance optimization. Not only can you separate the BizTalk servers from the SQL servers on different machines, you can also combine multiple BizTalk servers into server groups for parallel messaging and processing of documents. Furthermore, you can specialize BizTalk servers into separate message-receiving and document-processing machines. Of course, the power of the server hardware can also be increased, and there are specific recommendations for the level of server and network hardware to use in a BizTalk Server installation. Finally, you can use performance monitoring and other tools to verify and ensure that the designed performance is maintained over time.

CHAPTER 22

Security

by Kevin Price

IN THIS CHAPTER

Security is often the most overlooked aspect of any application development effort. In fact, the mere thought of having to implement security usually makes most developers cringe. In reality, security in any application, not just Internet applications, is usually relatively easy to implement. BizTalk Server is no exception. BizTalk Server enables the secure exchange of data via the standard security features found in Windows 2000 Server and SQL Server: public-key infrastructure, COM+, Crypto API, and Kerberos. This chapter covers some security basics and then specifically exploits BizTalk Server's capability to securely exchange data with business partners. Specifically, this chapter will:

- Introduce basic Internet security terms
- Explain how to use the different security options available in BizTalk Server, as well as programming in general
- Use certificates to verify identities between BizTalk Servers

Caution

This chapter is meant only as a guide and is not designed to be a comprehensive resource for implementing Internet security. Several books and Web sites are dedicated to this. Visit `http://www.microsoft.com/technet/security` for more information on this topic.

To begin, let's discuss some basic security terminology in relation to the technology used on the Internet today as well as the security features found in Windows 2000, SQL Server, IIS 5.0, and BizTalk Server 2002.

Understanding Security Basics

To begin, you should become familiar with a few terms. Understanding these concepts is the first step toward understanding just how easy it is to secure your applications.

Table 22.1 shows some basic security terms and what they mean.

TABLE 22.1 Basic Terms and Definitions for Security

Term	*Definition*
Algorithm	A mathematical equation determining how a message is encrypted or decrypted.
Encryption	The process of scrambling information to make it unreadable or unusable.

TABLE 22.1 continued

Term	*Definition*
Certificate	A "key" that identifies you or carries a public key for secure communications.
Key	Keys are basically passwords. In most cases there is a public key and a private key. A private key allows encryption/decryption in the event a public key is lost or fails.
Hash	A hash is a signature created when content is processed through a certain algorithm, such as MD5.
Authentication	The process of verifying a user's identity on a computer or network system.
Secure Socket Layer (SSL)	A protocol that encrypts and decrypts data exchanged between the application and server using session-specific data.

Algorithms

As stated, an algorithm is the math behind the security. In most cases, the math is being performed on bytes, or arrays of bytes, that make up the data you see on a computer screen. In a simple example, using the numeric ASCII and/or hexadecimal values of characters you can totally change the data a user sees. Listing 22.1 shows a basic algorithm written in Visual Basic 6.0. This sample takes the ASCII value of a character and performs a simple Xor operation against the ASCII value of a character from the password. When the operation is run in reverse, of course, you get your original text back.

LISTING 22.1 Basic Encryption/Decryption Algorithm

```
Public Sub DoCrypt(sPassword as String, sMsgToCrypt as String)
    On Error Goto ErrorHandler
    Dim iLen as Integer, lCode as Long, i as Integer
    iLen = 1
    For i = 1 to Len(sMsgToCrypt)
        lCods = Asc(Mid(sPassword, iLen, 1))
        iLen = iLen + 1
        If iLen > Len(sPassword) Then
            iLen = 1
        End If
        Mid(sMsgToCrypt, i, 1) = Chr(Asc(Mid(sMsgToCrypt, i, 1)) Xor lCode)
    Next
    Exit Sub
    ErrorHandler:
        MsgBox "Error in doCrypt", vbOkOnly
End Sub
```

The code sample listed will not necessarily work by itself. This is the case with many algorithms as the data being passed to them must often be formatted in some manner or converted to a more basic data type. For example, the Microsoft CryptoAPI requires that most data be converted to the BYTE data type prior to sending it through an encryption algorithm. These algorithms then work by creating or using existing byte arrays to comprise an encrypted message or file.

Sometimes algorithms are written to purposely create a hash that cannot be reversed. This type of hash is useful when you do not want to preserve the original value of the hashed data. In this case an application process would compare a hash as opposed to the data it was created from.

> **Note**
>
> Sniffing is the process of monitoring network packets to gather information. Hackers use this technique to try and capture authentication or sensitive data that can be used to perform illegal acts or gain unauthorized access to systems. Unfortunately, sniffing is common, even in the best scenario. Therefore, it is highly recommended that all sensitive or proprietary data be encrypted prior to transport.

Encryption

Encryption is always the favorite topic around the dinner table isn't it? You spend long hours with the family talking about rearranging letters, numbers, and other characters with unrecognizable trash for the purposes of thwarting hackers and other prying eyes, right? I'm guessing the answer to this question is no; however, encryption is an important—if not the most important—technology available to a developer when securing an application's data. Imagine that a hacker gets through your $40,000 firewall system, figures out that your network administrator password is "password," and discovers that your administrator password on your SQL Server is "sa"—the encrypted content is still not usable.

For example, if your phone number was stored in a database as (111) 555-1212, and a hacker saw it, it would be pretty easy for them to call you or use your phone for purposes other than what you intended. On the other hand, if your phone number appeared in a hacked database or other file as `DKGYD1D3IVdCVEDOCOFE0C3bDI` or `8BBEC5B8B51C98E731B09B211564F89ABB4701EA`, they would probably have a difficult time figuring out how to dial it. Achieving this is not difficult; it is just a matter of remembering to do it. According to a report from the SANS Institute (http://www.sans.org), of companies that were willing to admit a security breach, $337,000,000 worth of information was lost during the year 2000 alone. That is a lot more expensive than the extra disk space would cost to support the storage of encrypted strings in a database.

Note

The amount of space encrypted strings consume depends on the size of the string, as well as the encryption algorithm. The sample algorithm illustrated previously creates a string that is twice as long as the original, whereas the MD5 hash creates a 32-byte string that cannot be decrypted every time. The main deciding factor between a hash and using encryption is whether you need to decode/decrypt the information. Most hashes are designed to not be decrypted, but to be used to create a unique signature for comparison purposes.

BizTalk Server 2002 can process both binary and text-based flat files. This section focuses on the encryption of flat files using string manipulation techniques. Binary encryption is covered in the discussion on Microsoft's Crypto API later on in this chapter.

Listing 22.2 uses the previously listed algorithm to encrypt and decrypt text. The difference here is that although the encryption technique is still simple, the password is now complex. I'm not talking about the typical more-than-eight characters, mixed case and alphanumeric password variety. I am referring to the capability of an application to store the key, a hash of the key, the encrypted key, or an encrypted hash of a key, that you would otherwise never remember, resulting in a much more effective encryption algorithm. A key used in the phone number example might look like this: `748989904949515053535454575764679969697170727274757776787981808311148585878 61`. It also could look like the key in the first example hash.

LISTING 22.2 Simple Encryption and Decryption Routines

```
Dim sPassword as String, sMsgToCrypt as String, sHex as String
'The above code would need be in the declarations section
Public Function EncryptText(sPass as String, sTextToCrypt as String) as String
    sPassword = sPass
    sMsgToCrypt = sTextToCrypt
    Call DoCrypt(sPassword, sMsgToCrypt)
    Dim sChar as String, i as Integer
    sHex = ""
    'Convert the encrypted text to hex  so that it can be stored as a String
For i = 1 to Len(sMsgToCrypt)
        sChar = Hex(Asc(Mid(sMsgToCrypt, i, 1)))
```

LISTING 22.2 continued

```
        If Len(sChar) = 1 Then sChar = "0" + sChar
        sHex = sHex + sChar
    Next
    sHex = Format(Len(sHex), "000") + sHex
    EncryptText = sHex
End Function

Public Function DecryptText(sPass as String, sTextToCrypt as String) as String
'Watch closely for the reversal here
    sHex = sTextToCrypt
    sPassword = sPass
    sHex = Mid(sHex, 4, Val(Left(sHex, 3)))
    sMsgToCrypt = ""
    Dim i as Integer, sTemp as String
    For i = 1 to Len(sHex) Step 2
        sTemp = Mid(sHex, I, 2)
        sMsgToCrypt = sMsgToCrypt + Chr(Val("&H" + sTemp))
    Next
    Call DoCrypt(sPassword, sMsgToCrypt)
    DecryptText = sMsgToCrypt
End Function
```

Now, you're probably wondering just how secure this encryption method really is given that you now have access to the algorithm and the code. Can't we do anything we want now? Well, not quite. If you can figure out the key I used to encrypt the phone number, let me know. You see, without the key, the code and algorithm are useless. Granted, this probably isn't the most difficult hash to crack, but it definitely beats not having one at all by a long shot.

> **Note**
>
> The complete code for this project is available for download from the publisher's Web site.

Encryption in BizTalk Server 2002 can be provided through adding code, like the previous samples, to custom serializers and parsers or through functionality built into the Message Queuing Service. For example, when you specify a port to use for messaging, you can select an encryption method to use as well. Although the BizTalk documentation discusses the use of hardware accelerator cards for encryption/decryption, you can also use custom COM+ objects as application integration components or as preprocessing components to encrypt/decrypt data. Certain levels of encryption are also available through the new Encrypted File System on Windows 2000.

Certificates

By definition, certificates are public keys issued by a certificate authority and placed in certificate stores accessed by computers when needed by a user, application, or machine. Every machine has a unique certificate store, just as each certificate issued by a certificate authority to each different user is unique.

Microsoft Windows 2000, as well as NT, can act as a certificate authority. This provides the capability to create your certificates to be used for secure communications. Certain authorities are public and known to software manufacturers so that their certificates are usually accepted by default, such as Verisign. Because you may not be a "trusted root" authority by default, users usually would be prompted to accept any certificate issued by you. Machines can be set to automatically accept or deny certificates based on machine policies.

Certificates are exchanged between machines to establish or verify identity. This is done through an electronic exchange of information between machines of a protocol such as HTTP (Hypertext Transfer Protocol). When one machine receives a certificate from another machine, it checks a *certificate store* to see whether the certificate was issued by a valid certificate authority. If the certificate is okay, the information in that certificate is verified against the original issuer of the certificate, and based on that response, a server (or client) can accept or deny access.

Listing 22.3 shows a sample certificate request. After a certificate authority has processed the request, a certificate is generated and installed on the machine that needs to use it. Once installed, this certificate travels back and forth between machines that need this information for security validation.

LISTING 22.3 Sample Certificate Request


```
.-----BEGIN NEW CERTIFICATE REQUEST-----
EIIBnjCCAQcCAQAwXjELMAkGA1UEBhMCVVMxCzAJBgNVBAgTAnZhMREwDwYDVQQH
EwhzdGVybGluZzELMAkGA1UEChMCaTMxDDAKBgNVBAsTA2RldjEUMBIGA1UEAxML
aTNzb2x1dGlvbnMwgZ8wDQYJKoZIhvcNAQEBBQADgY0AMIGJAoGBAKajbKOvI71N
J6PfiMuuW4GEaFa2SRPo7YtGXSx2cfLgbrT077yAxbfl23EPnrvx92iRwT7ParOg
YaCAaWaANJmtfgJjFJtRwMh7mPJsNg6WoTQEFo2BZnZarDuvWkvpZXdTfsEY5jiw
MXgscOyNiAGew3o/7seWnEMO30YDgRjZAgMBAAGgADANBgkqhkiG9w0BAQQFAAOB
gQCS4gsoIPh/sKxwmPMwbC5nRRnrTYEQECtI59f1p5mMAs4WZ6KWAMGTyrPSJjvt
02C2M9F8TREWUg3SpQ4vx7EluWPKJR/JN4Cex3Ng+zV8/IDW6oP2vUYQMNPlIOGs
gjMIjzUhRlBNIDvu/ScMDWhqSUiAAW3LOZ93J4GTJZuyxw==
-----END NEW CERTIFICATE REQUEST-----
```


Based on the complexity of this listing, you probably already realize that requests aren't usually hand typed by someone. Many tools are available, including what is available through Windows 2000 Server to assist with the automated generation of certificate requests, including the Certificate Request Wizard in Internet Information Services.

Describing the many types of certificates available and what they all do would be well outside even the scope of this book. If you are thinking about implementing certificate technology with BizTalk, BizTalk recommends that you use machine certificates. A machine certificate is one that is issued as either a client or server certificate, or both. It is accessible from any valid logon on a machine—so no screaming about lack of administrator rights when trying to use one.

The use of certificates in BizTalk Server is essential to its capability to maintain secure communications between servers. In some cases, you may not personally know the person or company on the other side of the world that you are exchanging vital company financial records with. In this situation, certificates are meant to serve as a type of "reference" to assure you that the other party can be trusted. This further adds to the justification of BizTalk's recommendation to use computer certificates. Client certificates are unique to the person who issued them, so their credentials may require their password to access the certificate. BizTalk has to use the credentials of the entity to which the certificate is issued. Unless BizTalk Server 2002 can always run as that person, the certificate is not accessible. Running every service on the machine as a specific user is not generally recommended.

Keys

Keys are essential to security in all aspects. Even for a task as simple as locking your car, a key is necessary to unlock the door of that car, electronically or otherwise. Developing a key strategy can make implementation of security far more successful. A simple key strategy may include using a random number generator to create a key that is used to hash data. The important thing to remember is not to use keys that are easily figured out.

Keys usually come in two flavors, public and private. At times, it may require both keys to unlock data, such as any transaction in BizTalk. This way, you can distribute your public key for distributed information while maintaining your private key for localized data. A private key is used in conjunction with a public key to encrypt/decrypt data or verify identity. Public keys are shared between machines and/or software packages, whereas private keys are specific to a user or machine. This exchange can be seen when entering a Web site over SSL. A certificate is sent from your browser verifying that you are indeed coming from your specific machine. The Web site looks at this certificate, sends that information to the certificate authority (CA), and waits for a response. When it gets that response, it decides whether to let you in.

Hashes

I know what you're thinking, and no I haven't found one yet that rivals a visit to Amsterdam. Many times you will hear something referred to as an "MD5 Hash" or a "SHA-1 Hash." This simply relates to the algorithm used to generate encrypted or hashed data. Listing 22.4 shows the same data hashed through different algorithms. If you want more information related to a specific algorithm, check with the creator's Web site (`http://www.rsa.com`).

LISTING 22.4 Sample Hashes

```
Using a Key of 818fd4f63c1eb02e2dbac2bffb18fb5dc3114846
and a text string of Microsoft BizTalk Server Unleashed:
MD2 = 7966B5DF5DA085CDC5730523FE7E94AA4EF21367
MD4 = 110CA589C9ABF812DC12A9622304858D
MD5 = E687DE039C39C7020EE4CF5A5AD48159
SHA-1 = 7966B5DF5DA085CDC5730523FE7E94AA4EF21367
```


Note

Usually "one-way" hashes are more secure because they cannot be reversed. MD5 hashes, for example, cannot be reversed. Most hashes are one-way only. Information that can be changed and reversed is usually referred to as encrypted or encoded.

Authentication

Authentication is the process by which a user, program, or machine is validated for identity. Authentication is usually the first step in preventing a malicious attack on your data. Authentication forces your application to maintain the correct identity of all users at all times. Windows 2000 has added a time stamp to its authentication process to prevent what is known as a *replay attack*. This is where a hacker uses some device, hardware or software, to record or sniff network activity and then plays the recording back against a system or application to try and gain access. In Internet applications, responsible use of session timeout properties on a Web server, as well as use of SSL, can prevent unauthorized users from gaining access to information.

Authorization on the other hand relies on authentication and then uses an Access Control List (ACL) to establish permissions and rights for a user. More detail on Windows 2000 authentication methods is in the section titled "Windows 2000 Security Basics" later in this chapter.

It is recommended that you avoid the use of a plain-text authentication method at all times. This method of authentication is commonly found in Web applications that have clear text authentication turned on or in applications that store unencrypted usernames and passwords in a database. If someone is smart enough to hack into your database, she can certainly write a query to relate a user ID to a user's name, address, and credit card number. Again, even using the simple techniques previously listed can save you much embarrassment in the event of a security breach. Having at least something to answer with is far better than having to answer the question of how the data was left unprotected.

Authentication is the main method of security in Message Queuing Services. Although Message Queuing can accept certificates, it uses a logon procedure based on Windows 2000 authentication schemes before allowing anyone or anything to see the contents of the queue.

Secure Sockets Layer (SSL)

Now that you have an understanding of **some** of the finer points of security technology, let's take a look at an example of how several of them fit together. The Secure Sockets Layer protocol is a combination of public key exchange and symmetric key exchange. This means that because symmetric key encryption is faster than public key encryption, mostly due to the algorithms used, after a session is established using your public key, the server's public key symmetric key encryption/decryption starts to make data processing more efficient. Symmetric key encryption is also called *secret key* encryption. This is almost exactly the same as private key encryption. Using two private keys allows for faster operations because the algorithms and the keys, or information used in the certificate, are smaller.

SSL is fully supported by BizTalk Server 2002 and does provide for the secure communication of data over a wire; however, it's probably not enough for most of your application deployments. Consider the items discussed in previous sections of this chapter. Just because the data is encrypted during the transfer does not mean that it is encrypted at any other time during the lifetime of that data.

SSL currently supports at least the following algorithms:

- Triple DES
- DES
- RC2
- RC4

For an excellent article explaining all the steps associated with an SSL exchange, search the Microsoft Knowledge Base for article Q257591.

Windows 2000 Security Basics

Windows 2000 introduced many new security features. Many of these are merely enhancements to existing infrastructure. Some of the more recent developments in application use are Internet related. Considering that most companies, including Microsoft, didn't know that the Internet existed prior to NT Service Pack 3, Microsoft has done a lot of work to close the gaps in OS security while maintaining a user-friendly means by which to implement these features.

Some of the newer features include

- Encrypting File System
- SmartCard Authentication
- Active Directory Services
- Kerberos and Fortezza support
- Public Key Infrastructure (PKI)

BizTalk Server 2002's security is truly dependent on the Windows 2000 infrastructure. Understanding Windows 2000 security is key to protecting your information. What follows is a best practices guide, more than a how-to guide, to help make your servers as secure as possible using features available in Windows 2000.

Perhaps the most recommended task is setting up services such as BizTalk Server 2002 to run under a separate local system account. This is demonstrated in the section "Setting Up BizTalk Security" later in the chapter. This provides protection in two ways. First, because it is a machine account, it is doubtful that anyone really needs to distribute the password or log in with that account from across the network. The second is that if you set up services to run under a user account, if that user logs out, the services stop running. After you have created this account, it is important to give it the correct privileges to allow it to act as a service account.

Creating a Service Account on Windows 2000

To create a service account on Windows 2000, perform the following steps:

1. Log on as Administrator, or a member of the Administrators group.
2. Right-click My Computer and select Manage. This opens the Computer Management Console.

3. If it is not already expanded, click the (+) to expand System Tools and click Local Users and Groups. Note that this cannot be done on a machine designated as a domain controller that is using Active Directory Services. If you are using Active Directory, you must create the user first in the Active Directory Users and Computers management console and then proceed with step 8.
4. Select Users; a list of all the local users currently on the system appears. Right-click anywhere on the details side of the console and select New User.
5. Enter a username for the account as well as the password. The password must be entered twice to confirm, hence the Confirm Password text box requires you to enter the password again.
6. Be sure to clear the User Must Change Password at Next Login check box. Then click Create and click Close.
7. Close the Computer Management Console.
8. From the Start menu, select Administrative Tools and then Local Security Policy.
9. In the Local Security Policy Console, click the (+) to expand Local Policies and click User Rights Assignment.
10. From the details pane, right-click Act as Part of the Operating System and select Security. Click Add to add the account you created in steps 1–6; then click OK twice.
11. Repeat steps 9 and 10 using the Log On as a Service policy.

Reassigning BizTalk Context Account

If you have already installed BizTalk and did not have this account created prior to installation or have not yet assigned BizTalk to run under a service account, the following steps guide you through reassigning the context under which BizTalk runs:

1. From the Start menu, select Administrative Tools and then Services.
2. From the detail pane, right-click BizTalk Messaging Service and select Properties.
3. Click the Logon tab; then from that tab, click the This Account radio button.
4. Click the Browse button. This opens an Accounts dialog box for you to select which account to use.
5. In the Password box, type the same password you used when creating the account—yes, twice to confirm—and then click OK.
6. A message box appears indicating success; click OK.
7. Restart the computer to ensure the new context. Just restarting the service may not flush out any instances of the service that are currently in memory.

Caution

It is essential that a service account be used when using certificates with BizTalk Server 2002 and that BizTalk runs under that account.

Keep in mind that if you use, or you intend to use, the new Encrypting File System the data is not encrypted during any transfer. To protect your data, you must use SSL, IPSec (Internet Protocol Security), or some other means of security. However, by setting BizTalk to the service account, that account can be used to encrypt/decrypt files on a machine. The only issue that may arise is if an account other than BizTalk needs to access a file.

The new SmartCard authentication that Windows 2000 uses is really an extension of the Public Key Infrastructure (PKI). This is an exchange of certificate information for purposes of validating identity prior to release of information. With the new Active Directory Services, Windows 2000 provides a means by which to monitor security on an object level. This means that you can actually assign rights to parts of an object on the system—for example, you could assign rights to one group that can only see usernames on the network, whereas another group can see all the information related to users in the Active Directory database.

Internet Information Server Security Basics

Out of the box, Internet Information Server (IIS) 5.0 is not set up for maximum security but rather maximum usability. To start with, authoring is enabled. This is intentional, to work with Front Page Server Extensions, but causes problems with installing BizTalk Server 2002 as well as raising security risks if not needed, but left unattended. Maintaining the number of security bulletins and hot fixes needed for IIS could almost be a full-time job; however, tools are becoming available that help notify administrators that risks have been discovered and the steps to rectify them. IIS is necessary in the use of BizTalk because BizTalk does not contain its own Web server.

Disabling Authoring in IIS 5.0

This section demonstrates the steps to disable authoring in IIS 5.0. This is required by BizTalk Server 2002 to avoid issues saving settings to the BizTalk Server Repository. The following are step-by-step instructions for how to disable authoring in IIS 5.0:

1. From the Start menu, select Administrative Tools and then Internet Services Manager.
2. Click the (+) beside the name of the local IIS server.
3. Right-click Default Web Site and select Properties.
4. Click the Server Extensions tab and make sure that the Enable Authoring check box is clear.

IIS now supports such authentication methods as *digest authentication*, which is preferred by many because it never actually transmits a username or password, rather a hash of the two to a server for validation. Through use of a special certificate, available to banks and other financial institutions, IIS 5 can also use server-gated cryptography. This allows financial institutions to exchange information with 128-bit encryption. There are many business cases for use of BizTalk Server 2002 to communicate with financial institutions. Microsoft also added several wizards to the existing management tools to assist with permissions and certificate management on the server.

One unique feature of IIS 5 is the capability to encode your Active Server Page (ASP) scripts. This is designed not as a complete security solution but as an aide to protect developers from having their scripts copied and pasted for use in other sites that may not have permission to do so. When created, the script is standard ASCII text; however, the code is made unreadable by an encoding scheme determined by the developer. Scripts are decoded at runtime by their specific engine. This is currently available for both VBScript and Jscript Versions 5.0. There are many considerations in using script encoding including—surprise—browser incompatibilities, so when considering your options, consider your audience.

Setting Up BizTalk Security

Based on all the information discussed, you should have a general understanding of the basic settings to establish as preliminary steps for securing BizTalk Server 2002. Setting up the machine account and disabling authoring should actually be performed prior to installation if possible. BizTalk Server 2002 security relies heavily on what is available in Windows 2000, certain aspects of which rely heavily on the use of certificates and certificate stores to encrypt and decrypt information as well as validate a user's identity.

This section covers in detail how to use certificates with BizTalk Server 2002 as well as other minor settings to SQL Server 2000. Before reading further, it is recommended that you read Chapter 20, "Installing BizTalk Server," in this book. Without having BizTalk installed correctly, including correct configuration of SQL Server, the rest of this is meaningless.

BizTalk Server 2002 uses three basic certificate stores:

- Personal—This is where your computer's certificates are stored.
- BizTalk—This store is used to hold your trading partner's certificates.
- Trusted root certification authorities—All certification paths are located in this store.

Note

Keep in mind that all these stores must be located on the same computer. Also, when a certificate is issued, it may not be placed in the correct store by default because Windows 2000 assumes that all certificates are for the user by default. Because BizTalk does not use the user certificate store, it cannot access the certificate and thus cannot process a document with that certificate.

Almost all these actions require you to be an administrator in the BizTalk Server 2002 Administrators Group and/or have administrative rights on the machine that BizTalk Server 2002 is running. The next section covers certain basics of certificate management. The instructions outlined are created on the assumption that Microsoft Certificate Server is installed on a machine that you have access to.

Creating a Certificate Manager

The following steps are necessary for creating a Certificate Manager for a local machine. We demonstrate this first because it is essential to have a way to manage certificates before trying to request, receive, import, and export them. Using a Certificate Manager is the way to move, delete, and generally manage certificates.

1. On the Start menu, click Run and type mmc.
2. On the Console menu, as shown in Figure 22.1, click Add/Remove Snap-in.
3. Click Add.
4. Click Certificates and click Add.
5. Click Computer account, click Next, and then click Finish.
6. In the Add Standalone Snap-In dialog box, click Certificates and click Add.
7. Click Computer account, click Next, click Finish, click Close, and then click OK to close the dialog boxes.

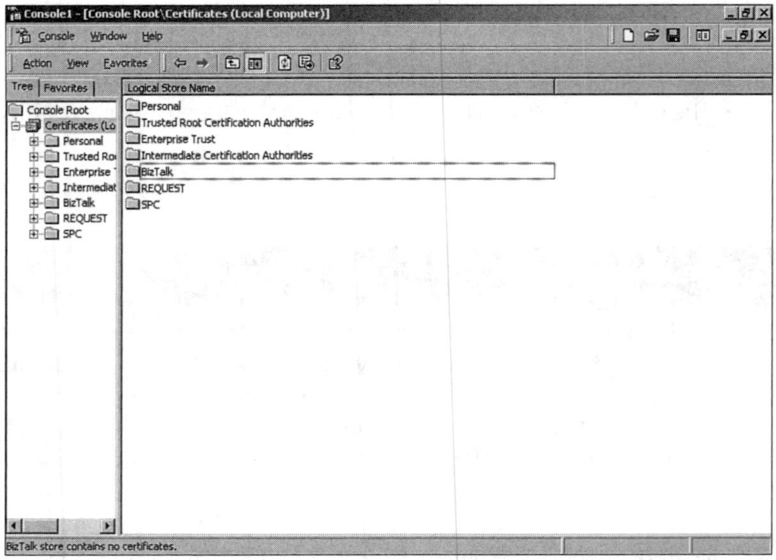

FIGURE 22.1
The Certificate Manager console.

Now that there is a way to manage all these certificates, you can request a new one from a certification authority. The remaining exercises use Windows 2000 Certificate Services. Ideally, these requests would be done over SSL, even on an internal network.

How to Request a Certificate from Microsoft Certificate Services

The following steps are necessary to request a certificate for use with BizTalk Server 2002:

1. Open Internet Explorer and navigate to `http://<yourw2kcertificateservername>/certsrv`.
2. Select Request a Certificate and click Next.
3. On the Choose Request Type page, select Advanced Request and click Next.
4. The next page is Advanced Certificate Requests, as shown in Figure 22.2. On this page, select Submit a Certificate Request to this CA Using a Form and click Next.
5. You now see all the options pertaining to your request. For Certificate Template, select User. Under Key Options, for CSP select Microsoft Base Cryptographic Provider v1.0. This is the default. Select Both for the Key Usage option. For Key Size, click the hyperlink to set the key size to 1024. The default settings should be that Create New Key Set is selected and the Hash Algorithm is SHA-1. If not, select these items appropriately.

6. Under Additional Options, check the Save This Request to a PKCS #10 File box. This causes a text box to display for you to enter the filename. Don't worry about the extension; one is not really necessary. Enter a path and filename that is accessible on that machine and click Save.

FIGURE 22.2
Advanced certificate requests.

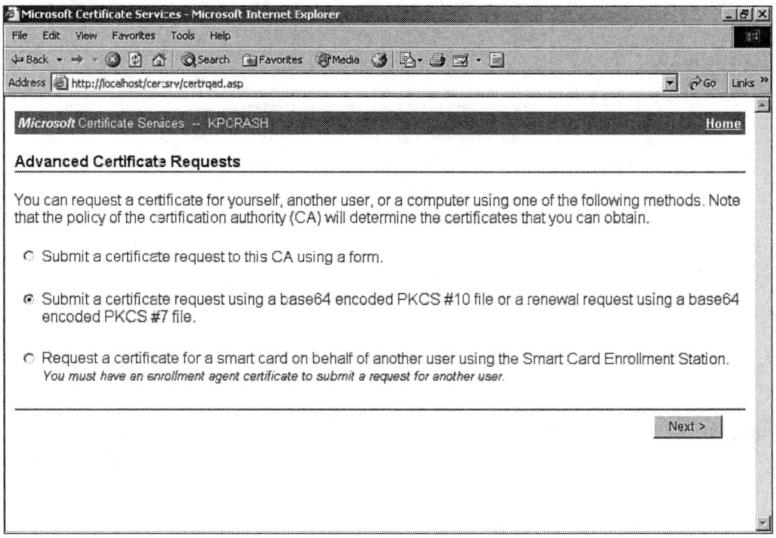

7. You are asked whether you want to save the request to the filename you specified; click Yes.
8. After the file is generated, you see a message box; click OK.
9. Repeat steps 1–3.
10. Because you are requesting a server certificate, select Submit a Certificate Request Using a Base64 Encoded PKCS #10 File or a Renewal Request Using a Base64 Encoded PKCS #7 File and click Next.
11. On the Submit a Saved Request page, as shown in Figure 22.3, you can either click the Browse link to insert the file saved in step 7, or you can open that file in a text editor and copy and paste the content into the Saved Request text box.
12. For Certificate Template, make sure that you select User; otherwise, your request will be denied. You can create certificates for any template, they just have to match.
13. If your certificate is approved, you see the Certificate Issued page. Click Download CA Certificate (as shown in Figure 22.4) and save the file to your hard drive.

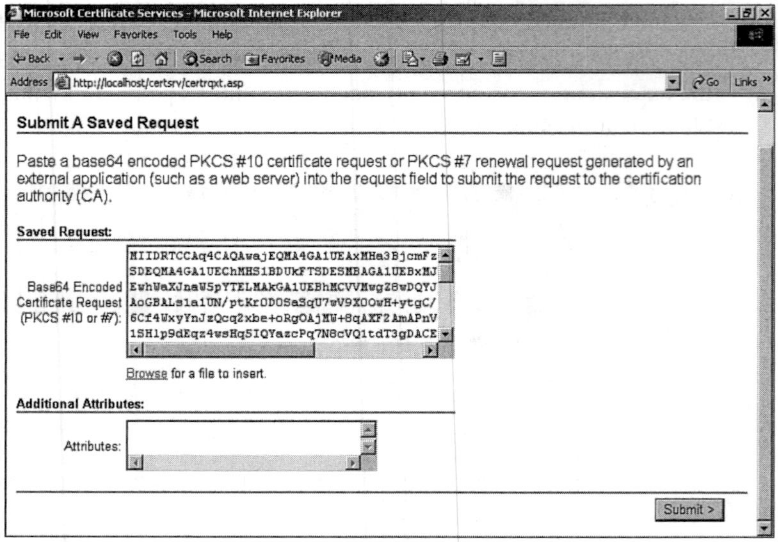

FIGURE 22.3
Submitting a saved request.

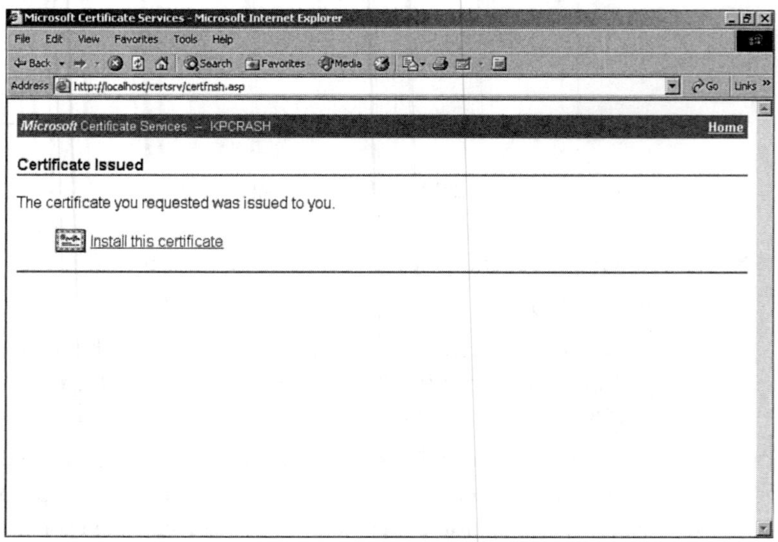

FIGURE 22.4
Download Certificate page.

Tip

Remember, by default all certificates are installed to your personal store unless otherwise directed. If presented with the option to install a certificate or download it, opt for download. After you have the certificate, you can install it in the correct store using the Certificate Manager discussed earlier.

How to Check Status of and Install Certificates

The following outlines the steps necessary to retrieve and install the certificate:

Note

This section is provided because not all Certificate Authorities are set up to automatically approve requests. Contact your system administrator should you have questions regarding how certificates are processed in your organization.

1. Open Internet Explorer and navigate to a known certificate server running Windows 2000 Certificate Server that is authorized to issue certificates. See your system administrator for information on this. The URL would look similar to `http://`*`yourserver`*`/certsrv`.
2. Select Check on a Pending Certificate and click Next.
3. On the next page, under Please Select the Certificate Request That You Want to Check, click the certificate that you want to check. This list may only include certificates that you have requested.
4. Unless your certificate was denied, proceed. If it was denied, contact your system administrator to find out why. Also at this point, you can select to delete your request.
5. Click Download CA Certificate or Install this Certificate.

Caution

DO not use cut and paste operations to move your certificates between stores. Doing so may destroy your private key, thus making the certificate useless.

How to Export a Certificate

This section shows you how to export a certificate. This is especially useful for certificates that may have been received to the wrong store or when you need to send your certificate to someone for identification. Follow these steps:

1. Open the Certificate Manager (created earlier).
2. Click the (+) to expand Certificates (Local Computer).
3. Click the (+) to expand the store that currently holds the certificates you want to move—that is, Personal—and click the Certificates folder under the selected store.
4. Select the certificate you want to move by clicking it once.
5. Right-click the certificate and select All Tasks and then click Export. This launches the Certificate Export Wizard. Click Next to get through the first screen.
6. On the Export Private Key dialog box, click Yes, Export the Private key. Then click Next.
7. The Export File Format dialog box contains options for the export format. Under Select the Format You Want to Use, select the appropriate option. For this example, select Personal Information Exchange and check the Enable Strong Protection (Requires IE 5.0, NT 4.0 SP4 or Above) check box. Then click Next.
8. If you have selected to not delete the private key after successful export, you are prompted for a password. If this certificate is going to be used by BizTalk, use the same password as you did when creating the service account for BizTalk to run. Then click Next.
9. Beside the File Name box, click Browse.
10. After deciding on a location for the file and a filename, make sure that the extension you give it matches the options selected in step 7.
11. Click Next; then click Finish. If a message box appears, click OK.

How to Import Certificates Using the Certificate Manager

This section, regarding certificate management, demonstrates how to import certificates using the Certificate Manager for BizTalk Server 2002 to be able to communicate in a secure fashion.

After exporting a certificate, it must be imported to the correct store. Follow these steps to make this happen:

1. Open the Certificate Manager.
2. Click the (+) to expand Certificates (Local Computer).
3. Right-click the BizTalk store, select All Tasks, and then select Import. This launches the Certificate Import Wizard.
4. Click Next to get through the first screen.
5. On the File to Import screen, click Browse and locate the certificate file that you want to import. You may have to change the filter in the Open dialog box so that you can see the specific type of file you want to import. After selecting the file, click Next.
6. Make sure that, on the Certificate Store screen, Place All Certificates in the Following Store is selected and BizTalk is in the Certificate Store text box. If it is not, click Browse and select BizTalk from the Select Certificate Store dialog box before continuing.
7. Click Next; then click Finish. If a message box is displayed, click OK.

Note

Should you decide to cluster BizTalk Server 2002, you will have to install all the certificates that a client might access on every computer in the cluster. This is currently a manual process of copying the certificate to each machine and installing it as outlined in this section.

Now that you have mastered certificate management, it's time to use it. Perhaps one of the first challenges you will face with this is importing a trading partner's public key. Keeping this in mind, and maintaining the configuration steps outlined previously, BizTalk Server 2002 is now ready to encrypt outgoing documents, decrypt incoming documents, and sign outgoing messages as needed.

Note

BizTalk Server 2002 supports SHA-1 and MD5 as signature algorithms. SHA-1 is the default. You cannot change this through the BizTalk Messaging Manager; you must change this through the BizTalk Messaging Configuration Object Model. This rule applies to all differences in default algorithms and supported algorithms used with BizTalk messaging.

When it comes to encryption algorithms, BizTalk Server 2002 defaults to RC2 (40-bit); however, RC2 (128-bit), RC4 (40 and 128-bit), DES (56-bit), and 3DES (112-bit and 168-bit) are supported. To use these in your application, it may be necessary to install the High-Encryption Pack for Windows 2000 Server, Service Pack 1 from Microsoft.

Before you begin, here is an example of using certificates. Consider this: before any data is sent using HTTP, the BizTalk Server 2002 Administrator has to send a copy, via export, of the client certificate to a specific trading partner. This partner imports the certificate to its BizTalk certificate store, and the servers can communicate securely.

Summary

This chapter demonstrated ways to make your BizTalk Server 2002 machine and data secure. Although no security measure alone is absolutely foolproof, the combination of techniques described in this chapter should help to provide confidence in the fact that you are taking a proactive stand on the topic of information security. In addition to the information contained in this chapter, numerous additional resources are available on the Internet and in print should this create an interest for you in cryptography as a means of security.

CHAPTER 23

Deploying BizTalk Server—Application Center 2000 Integration

By Tom Lake

In This Chapter

Prior to the release of BizTalk Server 2002 the migration of BizTalk Server applications from development, staging and then production was a challenging and somewhat tedious process. With the release of BizTalk Server 2002 and the integration of Application Center 2000 services, the method of deploying configurations has been greatly improved. In this chapter, you will learn:

- About using Application Center 2000 with BizTalk Server 2002
- How to install the new BizTalk drivers for Application Center 2000
- How to create an Application Center cluster
- How to add new members to your Application Center cluster
- Which BizTalk resources can be deployed
- Steps required before deploying BizTalk configurations to minimize post deployment changes
- How to create an Application Center application with BizTalk resources
- Steps to deploy an Application Center application
- Post deployment modifications that may need to be made
- How to use Application Center 2000 to delete BizTalk resources on a remote server
- Redeploying BizTalk resources after making changes
- How to use Application Center 2000 via the command line
- Sample configuration to deploy with Application Center 2000

Application Center 2000 and BizTalk Server 2002

Application Center 2000 is a Microsoft .NET Enterprise Server that simplifies the deployment of resources to remote servers. It is designed to make it easy to scale a Web farm and ensure that your applications are highly available. Application Center 2000 provides built-in support for deploying COM+ applications, data sources, file system paths, Registry keys, Web sites and virtual directories. Starting with the release of Service Pack 1, Application Center has also added support for pluggable replication drivers, the BizTalk driver being the first of these.

The Application Center 2000 pluggable replication driver supports deployment of ports (including all objects bound to the port, such as channels), port groups, receive functions, and custom counters. Using the built-in replication drivers, you can now replicate most of a BizTalk configuration with a few easy steps.

With Application Center 2000, you create *applications*, which are logical groupings of related resources, and then deploy those applications to one or more clusters. Application Center clusters are similar to BizTalk server groups. A BizTalk server group is a grouping of servers that all point to the same database, whereas an Application Center cluster is a grouping of computers with one of the computers being the controller.

BizTalk resources should only be deployed to the cluster controller. With Application Center 2000, the cluster controller is responsible for making sure that all the member computers of the cluster are kept up-to-date with the resources listed in the applications that have been created on that Application Center cluster. All the BizTalk-specific resources, when deployed, go to the central database for that BizTalk server group, and do not need to be replicated to each of the members.

Installing BizTalk drivers for Application Center 2000

It is recommended that you first install Application Center 2000 followed by Service Pack 1 and then install BizTalk Server 2002. However, if you installed BizTalk Server 2002 before installing Application Center 2000 and Service Pack 1, you will need to go to the `AppCenter` folder located in the BizTalk installation directory:

```
\Program Files\Microsoft BizTalk Server\AppCenter
```

It will contain two files, `AcBtsEnm.dll` and `rdrvbts.dll`, and a folder named `Images`. After installing Application Center 2000, copy the two DLLs into the directory where you installed Application Center 2000 and register them:

```
\Program Files\Microsoft Application Center
```

```
regsvr32 <Path>AcBtsEnm.dll
```

Next copy the files in the `Images` folder into the following location:

```
\Program Files\Microsoft Application Center\Admin\Images\
```

If you installed Application Center 2000 followed by BizTalk Server 2002, but have not yet installed Service Pack 1 for Application Center 2000, go to the `Application Center 2000 SP1` folder on the root of your BizTalk Server 2002 CD. Copy `ACSP1Setup.exe` to your local hard drive and then double-click the file to install Service Pack 1. Make sure that you have the Application Center 2000 CD handy because you will be asked for it during the installation of the Service Pack.

After Application Center 2000 and Service Pack 1 are installed, you will need to create an Application Center cluster. Make sure that the SQL Server that the BizTalk server group is pointing to is the controller of the Application Center cluster, as shown in Figure 23.1, or that it is remote to both the BizTalk server group and the Application Center cluster. If the SQL Server is not the controller, but is a member of the cluster, you will receive an error when you attempt to deploy any BizTalk configurations.

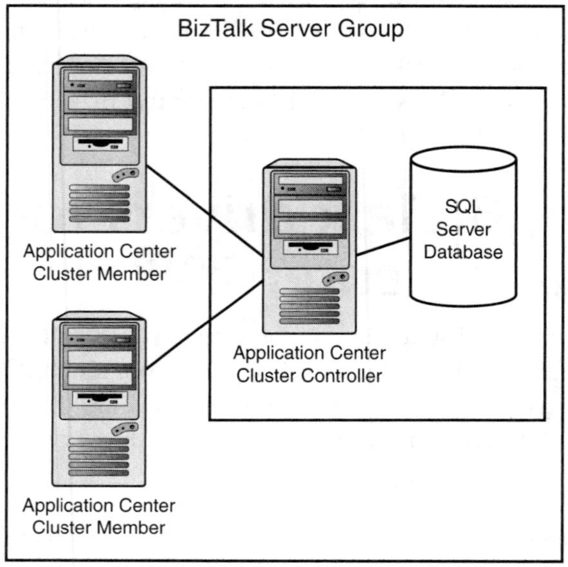

FIGURE 23.1
BizTalk server group and Application Center cluster diagram.

All the members of your BizTalk server group need to have Application Center 2000 with Service Pack 1 installed, and all the members need to be members of the Application Center cluster.

Creating an Application Center Cluster

The first step in creating an Application Center cluster is to go to the computer that will be your controller. It is best to use the computer that has your SQL server, assuming that you are not using a remote database. If you are using a remote database, go to any of the computers in your BizTalk server group. Then follow these steps:

1. Start Application Center 2000. Go to Start, Programs, Administrative Tools, and click on Application Center.

2. Right-click on the Application Center node, and click on Connect.
3. In Server Name text box, on the Connect to Server dialog, enter **`localhost`**, as shown in Figure 23.2. Make sure that Manage Cluster for the Specified Server is selected and Connect As is unchecked, and click OK.

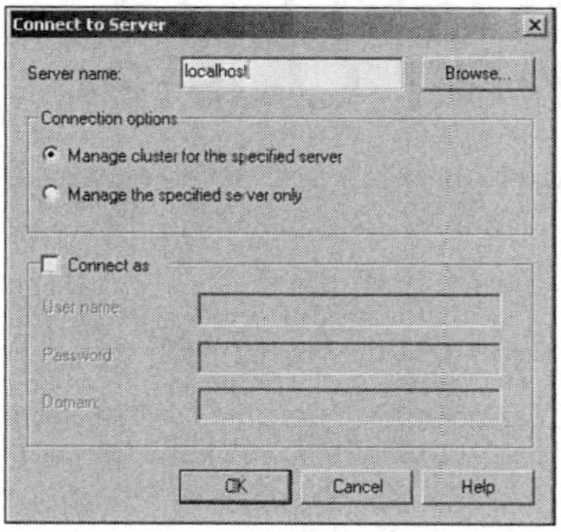

FIGURE 23.2
The Connect to Server dialog.

4. On the New Server dialog, make sure that the Create a New Cluster option is selected, and click OK. At this point, the New Cluster Wizard starts.
5. Click Next on the Welcome to the New Cluster Wizard page.
6. On the Cluster Name and Description page, shown in Figure 23.3, enter a name and description for the cluster being created, and click Next.

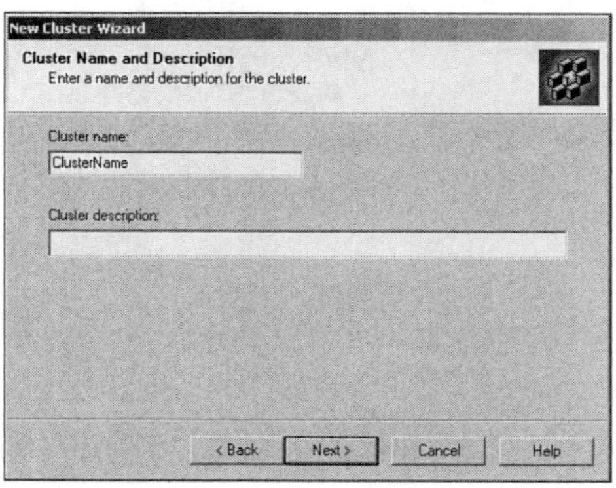

FIGURE 23.3
The New Cluster Wizard dialog.

7. Make sure that General/Web cluster is selected on the Cluster Type page, and click Next.
8. On the Load Balancing page, select the appropriate option and click Next. If you are not using load balancing, make sure that you select None.

9. If you want to have e-mails sent when the cluster encounters a failure, enter your e-mail address and the name of your server, and click Next.
10. Finally, on the Completing the New Cluster Wizard page, click Finish.

Adding New Members to an Application Center Cluster

After you have created your Application Center cluster, if you have a BizTalk server group with multiple computers in it, you will need to add each of them to the Application Center cluster. Make sure that you do this for both the source and target BizTalk server groups. To add new members to the cluster, follow these steps:

1. Start Application Center 2000. Go to Start, Programs, Administrative Tools, and click on Application Center.
2. Expand the Application Center node followed by the cluster that you want to add the member to.
3. Right-click on the Members node and expand the menu under All Tasks. Click on Add Cluster Member, as shown in Figure 23.4. At this point, the Add Cluster Member Wizard starts.

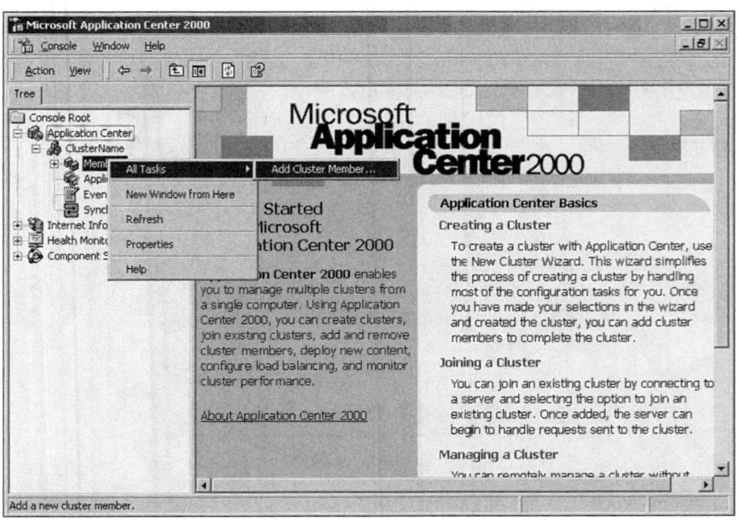

FIGURE 23.4
The Add Cluster Member menu.

4. On the Welcome to the Add Cluster Member Wizard page, click Next.
5. Enter the Server Name, User Name, Password, and Domain for the member to be added to the cluster on the Name and Credentials page, as shown in Figure 23.5. The User information that is entered must be an Administrator for the BizTalk Administrators Group on the server being added.

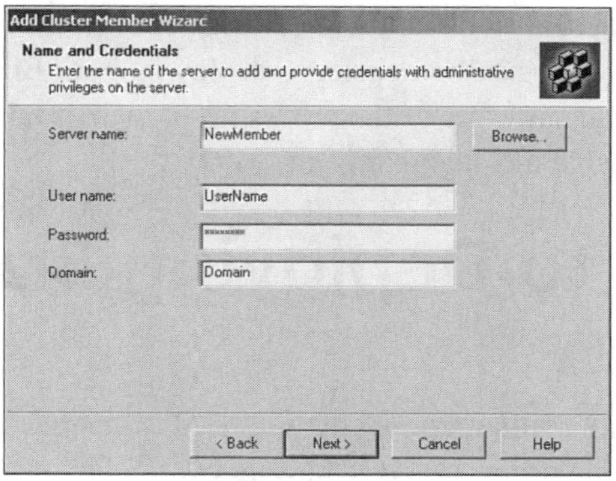

FIGURE 23.5
Name and Credentials page.

6. You can leave Automatically Synchronize This Cluster Member checked, or you can uncheck it on the Cluster Member Options page.

> **Note**
>
> BizTalk resources are never synchronized because they are stored in a central database for the BizTalk server group.

7. Finally, click Finish on the Completing the Add Cluster Member Wizard page.

Which BizTalk Resources Can Be Deployed?

The new drivers written for BizTalk support the replication of BizTalk ports, port groups, receive functions, and custom counters. When choosing ports, or port groups, the driver will determine all channels, document definitions, and envelopes bound to that port and will replicate all of them for you. Any unbound BizTalk artifact, such as an envelope or a document, that may need to be deployed must be configured manually on the target computer.

Using the built-in replication drivers for Application Center 2000, you can also deploy other resources used in a BizTalk configuration. For example, if you are using any Application Integration Components (AICs), you can add them to a COM+ application. File drop locations for receive functions and schedules can be replicated with the File System Paths driver, and virtual directories used with HTTP receive functions can be deployed with the Web Sites and Virtual Directories driver.

At this time, there is no support for replication of certificates or MSMQs. To handle these, you need to manually configure them prior to deploying your BizTalk configuration. Also, you need to set manually any of the properties of the BizTalk server group, such as SMTP host and Reliable messaging reply, to URL.

Steps Prior to Deploying BizTalk Resources

Prior to deploying the BizTalk configuration, you will need to ensure that if you are using certificates, MSMQs, file drops, or AICs they are configured on the target server. Those resources that can be deployed using Application Center 2000, such as file drops and AICs, create an Application Center application containing those resources and deploy them before you deploy the BizTalk resources. If the BizTalk configuration was deployed before the external resources are present, you may find that those BizTalk resources are not created or that the deployment fails all together.

Creating an Application Center 2000 Application

After you make sure that all the dependencies for your BizTalk configuration are in place, it is time to create an Application Center application with your BizTalk resources. Follow these steps:

1. Start Application Center. Go to Start, Programs, Administrative Tools, and click on Application Center.
2. Expand the Application Center node followed by the cluster that you want to add the application to. Then select Applications.
3. Click on New in the Applications pane, and the Create a New Application dialog appears as shown in Figure 23.6.

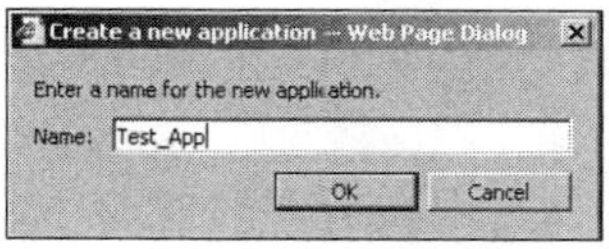

FIGURE 23.6
The Create a New Application dialog.

4. In the Name box, enter the name of the new Application Center application and click OK.
5. Select the application that you just created, and in the Contents pane, select BizTalk from the Resource Type list, as shown in Figure 23.7; then click Add. The Add Resource dialog appears.

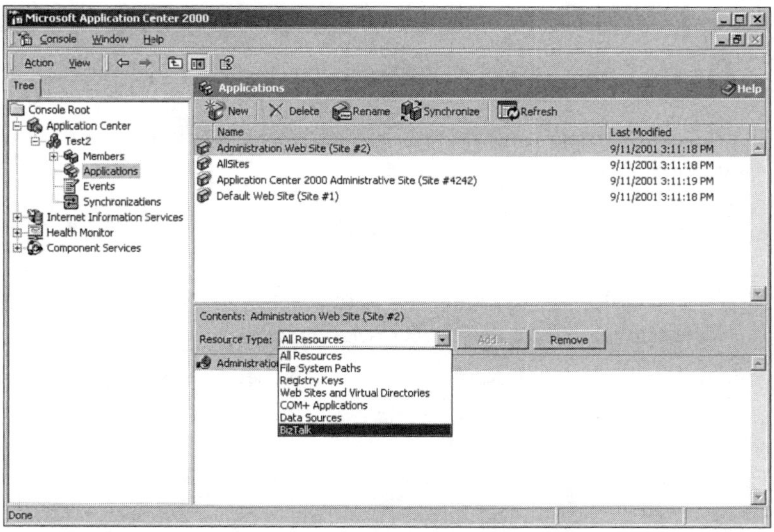

FIGURE 23.7
The Application Center 2000 Resource Type list.

6. To add all of a BizTalk resource type, select the resource type, as shown in Figure 23.8 and click Add. To select individual resources, double-click the resource type, to enumerate all of that resource type, select the resource to be added, and click Add.

If your BizTalk configuration contains schedules or HTTP receive functions, you can include them with your other BizTalk resources. For schedules, use File System Paths. With the HTTP receive functions, you can include the virtual directory that is needed by selecting the Web Sites and Virtual Directories resource type, and adding the appropriate virtual directory.

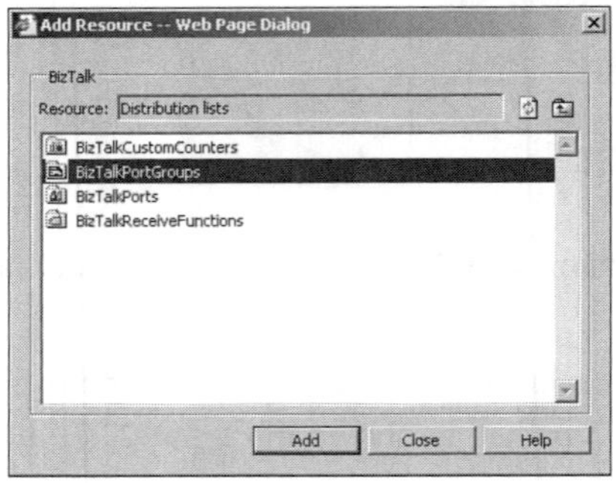

FIGURE 23.8
The Add Resource dialog.

Deploying an Application Center 2000 Application

The following steps walk you through the procedure of deploying your newly created Application Center application.

1. Start Application Center. Go to Start, Programs, Administrative Tools and click on Application Center.
2. Expand the Application Center node followed by the cluster that you want to add the application to; then select Applications.
3. Right-click on the Application node and select New Deployment, as shown in Figure 23.9.

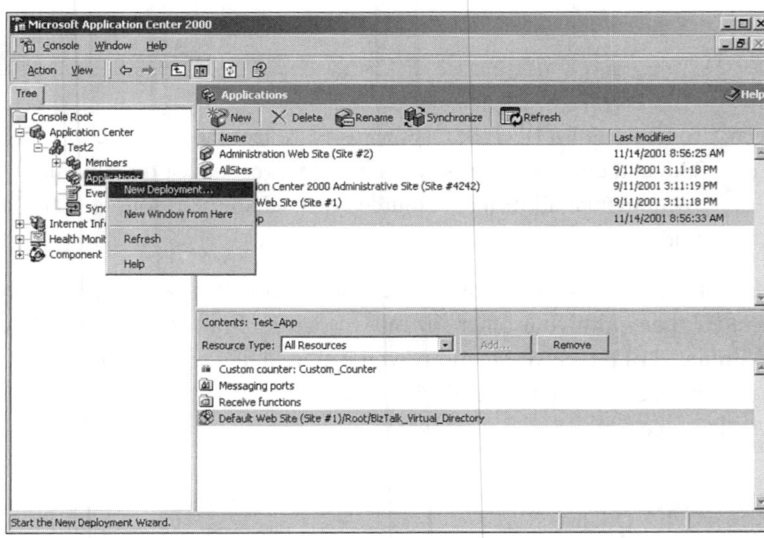

FIGURE 23.9
The Application Center node pop-up menu.

4. On the Deployment Target Options page, enter the name for your deployment, or leave the default, select Deploy Content Outside the Current Cluster, and click Next, as shown in Figure 23.10.

FIGURE 23.10
The Deployment Target Options dialog.

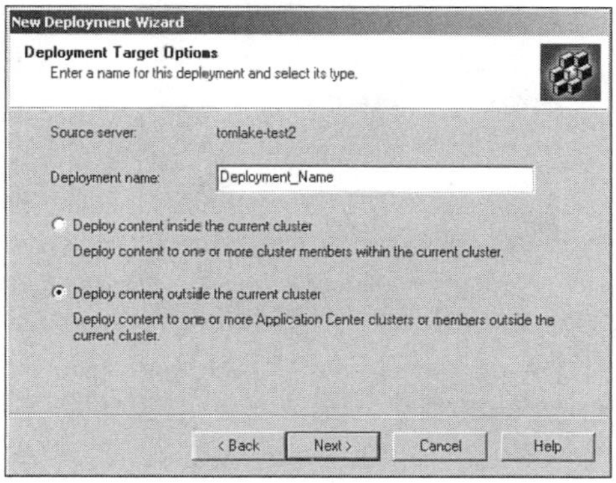

5. On the Deployment Target Authentication page, enter the credentials for a user that has Administrative privileges on the target server.
6. On the Deployment Target page, enter the name of the computer that the configuration is being deployed to and click Add. Keep adding servers until all that you are deploying to have been added. Keep in mind that you will only need to deploy the application to the cluster controller and not to all the member computers in the cluster.
7. On the Deployment Content Page, select Deploy One or More Applications, or Deploy All Applications and Related Cluster Configurations, as shown in Figure 23.11. If you choose to deploy one or more applications, select the first application to deploy from the list. If you need to deploy more than one, hold down Ctrl and select each application you want to deploy. After all the applications have been selected, click Next.
8. On the Deployment Options page, select the appropriate options and click Next.

Note

For deployment of ports, port groups, receive functions, and custom counters, these options have no effect. If you are using Application Center 2000 to deploy schedules and/or file drops, you might choose to have Deploy Folder and File Permissions (NTFS Only) checked. For AICs, you will need to check Deploy COM+ Applications.

9. On the Completing the New Deployment Wizard page, click Finish.

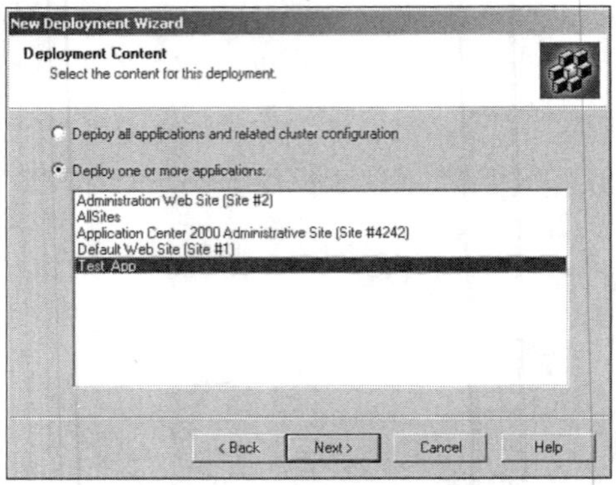

FIGURE 23.11
The Deployment Content dialog.

Post Deployment

After the deployment is complete, you might need to make some changes to all the ports that have machine-specific HTTP or HTTPS and to the receive functions that have user-names and passwords entered.

If you have any ports that have HTTP or HTTPS primary or backup transport addresses, and they need to point to the local server, you may need to change the server with a simple Visual Basic Script. The VB Script defined in Listing 23.1 can be used to update the Port Primary Transport Address for a deployed configuration to the local server.

LISTING 23.1 Script to Change the Server Referenced in Port Transport Address (ChangePortServer.vbs)

```
Function GetEnvVariable(ItemName)
     'ItemName e.g.: USERNAME, COMPUTERNAME, etc.
     Dim shell, env
     set shell = WScript.CreateObject("WScript.Shell")
     set env = shell.Environment("Process")

     GetEnvVariable = env.Item(ItemName)

     set shell = Nothing
     set env = Nothing
End Function

dim strServer

strServer = GetEnvVariable("ComputerName")

Set BT = CreateObject("BizTalk.BizTalkConfig")
```

LISTING 23.1 continued

```
set port = BT.CreatePort

port.LoadByName "Port_To_Org_1"
port.PrimaryTransport.Address = "http://"&strServer& _
    "/BizTalk_Virtual_Directory/BizTalkHTTPReceive.dll"
port.Save

Set port = nothing
Set BT = nothing
```

> **Note**
>
> ChangePortServer.vbs is available for download from the publisher's Web site.

If you have any receive functions that have usernames and passwords, you will need to open the receive function in the BizTalk Server Administration tool, uncheck Disable Receive Function, and enter the correct password. The reason for this is because receive function passwords are write-only, so the password cannot be replicated.

Deleting BizTalk Resources with Application Center 2000

When replicating any of the built-in resources with Application Center 2000 to delete them on the target server, you need to have an Application Center application that contains them on the source server. Next, you remove the resource on the source server, leaving it in the application. Finally, you deploy the application to the remote server. Application Center 2000 makes sure that the target server is the same as the source. If you have a folder containing no files on the source and the target has several files in it, when you deploy the empty folder, the files in the folder on the target will be deleted. This is because Application Center 2000 works on the premise that the target is a clone of the source.

With BizTalk, cloning would be a problem. If you deployed all the BizTalk ports to a target server, and that server has any ports that are not on the source, they would be removed. The BizTalk drivers work differently. To delete BizTalk resources, you need to create an Application Center application that contains the resources to be deleted. You will need to select the specific resource by name, not just deploy the collection of that resource type, like if you deployed all the ports. Create the application before deleting the physical resource, but do not deploy it. Next delete the resources on the source cluster, leaving them in the application, and then deploy the application, which contains the resources to be deleted, to the target servers. When Application Center 2000 sees that the resource to be deployed is on the target and not the source, the resource will be removed.

Redeploying BizTalk Resources After Making Changes

After deploying your BizTalk configuration, you might find the need to make changes to the source configuration, which will also need to be deployed. The only change that cannot be replicated is changing the path to a document definition. The BizTalk object model restricts any document that has been bound to a channel from having the path to its schema modified. Any other changes to a BizTalk configuration can be deployed by creating an Application Center application with those resources and deploying it to the target server.

Should you need to make a change to the path of a document, you will be able to make the change on the source and target, it will just take a little bit of planning. First create an application containing all the ports bound to channels using the document you need to modify. Next, delete all the channels bound to the document and the associated ports. Now deploy the application created so that the configurations will be deleted on the target computers.

With the object model restrictions being removed, with the deletion of the channels, you can now modify the path to the document without any problems. After making all the necessary changes, rebuild all the ports and channels using the documents. If the ports are the same name, just redeploy the application used to delete the configurations, and all your changes will be on the remote server, or just create a new application containing the ports to be deployed.

Application Center Using Command Line

It is also possible to generate a command file that creates your Application Center application, adds the appropriate resources, and finally deploys the application to your target servers. The command file described in Listing 23.2 adds all of each type of the BizTalk resource to an application and deploys it to a target server.

LISTING 23.2 Sample Command File to Create Application with BizTalk Resources (`Test_App.cmd`)

```
AC APPLICATION /CREATE /NAME:Test_App

AC APPLICATION /ADDRESOURCE /NAME:Test_App /RESOURCETYPE:BizTalk /
➥RESOURCEPATH:BizTalkPorts

AC APPLICATION /ADDRESOURCE /NAME:Test_App /RESOURCETYPE:BizTalk /
➥RESOURCEPATH:BizTalkReceiveFunctions

AC APPLICATION /ADDRESOURCE /NAME:Test_App /RESOURCETYPE:BizTalk /
➥RESOURCEPATH:BizTalkCustomCounters \Custom_Counter

AC APPLICATION /ADDRESOURCE /NAME:Test_App /RESOURCETYPE:IIS
/RESOURCEPATH:/LM/w3svc/1/Root/BizTalk_Virtual_Directory

AC DEPLOY /START /TARGETS:TargetServerName /TARGETUSER:Domain/UserName /
➥TargetPassword:Password /AppName:Test_App /Wait
```

> **Note**
>
> Using `/Wait`, for `AC DEPLOY /START`, is optional; however, if it is used, the deployment will be done synchronously, and control will not be returned until synchronization completes. Also you can include the Password in your command file or enter *, and you will be prompted for the password.
>
> `Test_App.cmd` is available for download from the publisher's Web site.

To add a specific BizTalk resource, you use the same syntax that you do to add all of that particular resource and add `\Resource_name`. If any spaces are in the name of the resource, put quotation marks around the `/RESOURCEPATH` parameter.

```
AC APPLICATION /ADDRESOURCE /NAME:Test_App /RESOURCETYPE:BizTalk "/
➥RESOURCEPATH:BizTalkPorts\Port with spaces"
```

Sample Configuration to Deploy with Application Center 2000

The code in Listing 23.3 creates a BizTalk server configuration with a custom counter, two ports, two receive functions, and a virtual directory, which is used by one of the ports and the receive functions. To deploy the configuration, use the command file in Listing 23.2.

LISTING 23.3 Sample BizTalk Configuration

```
Const HTTPTType_File = 1

Const ADMIN_PROTOCOL_TYPE_FILE = 1
Const HTTP = 3

Const RECVSVC_NAMESPACE = "MicrosoftBizTalkServer_ReceiveFunction"
Const SERVER_NAMESPACE = "MicrosoftBizTalkServer_SERVER"

Const wbemChangeFlagCreateOnly = 2

Dim strServerName, strGroupName
Dim g_objService, l_bAdminUtilInitialized
Dim sPath, BT
Dim org, doc, env, port, chan, dl

Function GetEnvVar(strName)

    On Error Resume Next

    Dim wshShell, wshSysEnv

    Set wshShell = WScript.CreateObject ("WScript.Shell")
    Set wshSysEnv = wshShell.Environment("PROCESS")

    GetEnvVar = wshSysEnv(strName)

End Function

Function InitAdminUtil()
    If (l_bAdminUtilInitialized = 1) Then  Exit Function

    Set g_objLocator = CreateObject("WbemScripting.SWbemLocator")
    Set g_objService = g_objLocator.ConnectServer(".", _
            "root\MicrosoftBiztalkServer")
    l_bAdminUtilInitialized = 1
End Function

Function CleanupAdminUtil()
    If (l_bAdminUtilInitialized = 0) Then  Exit Function

    Set g_objService = Nothing
    Set g_objLocator = Nothing

    l_bAdminUtilInitialized = 0
End Function

Function GetServerByName(inServerName)
    Set GetServerByName = Nothing
    Set GetServerByName = g_objService.Get(SERVER_NAMESPACE & ".NAME=""" & _
```

LISTING 23.3 continued

```
        inServerName & """")
End Function

Function GetBTSGroupName(strServer)
    Dim objServer, bOnTheFly

    If (l_bAdminUtilInitialized = 0) Then
        InitAdminUtil
        bOnTheFly = True
    End If

    Set objServer = GetServerByName(strServer)
    GetBTSGroupName = objServer.GroupName

    Set objServer = Nothing

    If (bOnTheFly) Then
        CleanupAdminUtil
    End If
End Function

Sub CreateVirtualDirectory(directoryName, _
        directoryPath)
    On Error Resume Next
    Dim webObj
    Dim root
    Dim virtualDir

    Set webObj = GetObject("IIS://localhost/w3svc/1")
    Set root = webObj.GetObject("IIsWebVirtualDir", "Root")

    'If virtual directory exist, then delete it.

    Call root.Delete("IIsWebVirtualDir", directoryName)

    Err.Clear

    Set virtualDir = root.Create("IIsWebVirtualDir", _
            directoryName)
    virtualDir.AccessRead = True
    virtualDir.AccessWrite = True
    virtualDir.AccessExecute = True
    virtualDir.AccessScript = True
    virtualDir.Path = directoryPath
    virtualDir.AppIsolated = 0
    virtualDir.EnableDirBrowsing = True
    virtualDir.SetInfo
```

LISTING 23.3 continued

```
    Err.Clear
    Set webObj = Nothing
End Sub

Sub CreateWebApplication(directoryName)
    On Error Resume Next
    Dim webObj
    Dim INPROC
    Dim OUTPROC

    Const POOLED = 2

    INPROC = True
    OUTPROC = False

    Set webObj = GetObject("IIS://localhost/w3svc/1/ROOT/" & directoryName)
    'Create an application out-of-process.
    webObj.AppCreate OUTPROC
    Set webObj = Nothing

End Sub

Public Sub SetIsolation(directoryName)
    On Error Resume Next
    Dim webObj
    Dim virtualDir

    Set webObj = GetObject("IIS://localhost/w3svc/1/Root/" & directoryName)
    webObj.AppIsolated = 0
    webObj.SetInfo
    Set webObj = Nothing
End Sub

Function CreateReceiveFunction(strRecvSvcName, _
            strGroupName, _
            strProcessingServer, _
            strFileMask, _
            fProtocolType, _
            strPollingLoc, _
            strPassword, _
            strUsername, _
            strDocumentName, _
            strSourceID, _
            strSourceQualifier, _
            strDestinationID, _
            strDestinationQualifier, _
            lOpenness, _
            lPassthrough, _
            strChannelName, _
```

LISTING 23.3 continued

```
            fDisabled, _
            strEnvelopeName, _
            strPreProcessor, _
            fHttpTransportType, _
            strTransportURL, _
            bReturnToken, _
            strReturnContentType)


    Dim objBTSRecvSvc 'As SWbemObject
    Dim objBTSRecvSvcInstance 'As SWbemObject

    On Error Resume Next
    CreateReceiveFunction = True
    Set g_objLocator = CreateObject ("WbemScripting.SWbemLocator")
    Set g_objService = g_objLocator.ConnectServer(".", _
           "root\MicrosoftBiztalkServer")
    Set objBTSRecvSvc = g_objService.Get(RECVSVC_NAMESPACE)
    Set objBTSRecvSvcInstance = objBTSRecvSvc.SpawnInstance_
    objBTSRecvSvcInstance.Name = strRecvSvcName
    objBTSRecvSvcInstance.groupName = strGroupName
    objBTSRecvSvcInstance.FilenameMask = strFileMask
    objBTSRecvSvcInstance.ProcessingServer = strProcessingServer
    objBTSRecvSvcInstance.ProtocolType = fProtocolType
    objBTSRecvSvcInstance.PollingLocation = strPollingLoc
    objBTSRecvSvcInstance.password = strPassword
    objBTSRecvSvcInstance.UserName = strUsername
    objBTSRecvSvcInstance.DocumentName = strDocumentName
    objBTSRecvSvcInstance.SourceID = strSourceID
    objBTSRecvSvcInstance.SourceQualifier = strSourceQualifier
    objBTSRecvSvcInstance.DestinationID = strDestinationID
    objBTSRecvSvcInstance.DestinationQualifier = strDestinationQualifier
    objBTSRecvSvcInstance.envelopeName = strEnvelopeName
    objBTSRecvSvcInstance.DisableReceiveFunction = fDisabled
    objBTSRecvSvcInstance.PreProcessor = strPreProcessor
    If fProtocolType = http Then
        objBTSRecvSvcInstance.HttpReturnCorrelationToken = bReturnToken
        objBTSRecvSvcInstance.HttpReturnContentType = strReturnContentType
        objBTSRecvSvcInstance.HttpTransportType = fHttpTransportType
        objBTSRecvSvcInstance.TransportURL = strTransportURL
    End If
    If lOpenness <> 0 Then
        objBTSRecvSvcInstance.OpennessFlag = lOpenness
    End If

    If lPassthrough <> 0 Then
        objBTSRecvSvcInstance.IsPassThrough = lPassthrough
    End If
```

LISTING 23.3 continued

```
    If strChannelName <> "" Then
       objBTSRecvSvcInstance.channelName = strChannelName
    End If

    objBTSRecvSvcInstance.Put_ (wbemChangeFlagCreateOnly)
    If err <> 0 Then
        CreateReceiveFunction = False
    End If
End Function

Function CreateCustomCounter(strName, _
            strDescription, _
            strCaption, _            strSrcOrgName, _
            strSrcOrgQualifier, _
            strSrcOrgQualifierValue, _
            strDestOrgName, _
            strDestOrgQualifier, _
            strDestOrgQualifierValue, _
            strDocType, _
            intInterval, _
            inGroupName, _
            strSettingID)

    Set CCFact = GetObject("Winmgmts:{impersonationlevel=impersonate}"& _
            "!root/MicrosoftBizTalkServer").Get("MSBTS_CustomCounterSetting")
    Set CustCountSetting = CCFact.SpawnInstance_

    CreateCustomCounter = True

    CustCountSetting.Name = strName
    CustCountSetting.Description = strDescription
    CustCountSetting.Caption = strCaption
    CustCountSetting.SrcOrgName = strSrcOrgName
    CustCountSetting.DestOrgName = strDestOrgName
    CustCountSetting.DocType = strDocType
    CustCountSetting.TimeInterval = intInterval ' In seconds
    CustCountSetting.GroupName = inGroupName
    CustCountSetting.SettingID = strSettingID

    If ("" = CustCountSetting.GroupName) Then
        Exit Function
    End If

    Set objObjectPath = CustCountSetting.Put_(wbemChangeFlagCreateOnly)

    If (IsEmpty(objObjectPath)) Then
        CreateCustomCounter = False
    End If
End Function
```

LISTING 23.3 continued

```
Function GetAliasID(ByVal strOrgName, _
            ByVal strAliasName, _
            ByVal strAliasQual, _
            strAliasValue)

Dim config, Organization, RS

    On Error Resume Next

    Set config = CreateObject("BizTalk.BizTalkConfig")
    Set Organization = config.CreateOrganization

    Call Organization.LoadByName(strOrgName)

    Set RS = Organization.Aliases

    While Not RS.EOF
        If RS("Name") = strAliasName And RS("qualifier") = strAliasQual And _
            RS("value") = strAliasValue Then
            GetAliasID = RS("id")
        End If
        RS.MoveNext
    Wend

    Set Organization = Nothing
    Set config = Nothing

End Function

Sub CreateBizTalkConfig()

'Create BizTalk Configuration
Set BT = CreateObject("BizTalk.BizTalkConfig")

' Create Orgs

Set org = BT.CreateOrganization

org.clear
org.name = "Dest_Org"
Org110001 = org.Create
Alias120001 = GetAliasID ("Dest_Org", "Organization", "OrganizationName", _
    "Dest_Org")


org.clear
org.name = "Source_Org"
Org110002 = org.Create
```

LISTING 23.3 continued

```
Alias120002 = GetAliasID ("Source_Org", "Organization", "OrganizationName", _
    "Source_Org")

Set org = nothing

' Create Docs

set doc = BT.CreateDocument

doc.clear
doc.name = "Common_PO"
Set doc.PropertySet = CreateObject("Commerce.Dictionary")
doc.reference = "http://"&strServerName& _
    "/biztalkserverrepository/docspecs/Microsoft/CommonPO.xml"
Doc140001 = doc.create

doc.clear
doc.name = "Common_Invoice"
Set doc.PropertySet = CreateObject("Commerce.Dictionary")
doc.reference = "http://"&strServerName& _
    "/biztalkserverrepository/docspecs/Microsoft/CommonInvoice.xml"
Doc140002 = doc.create

Set doc = nothing

' Create Ports

set port = BT.CreatePort

port.clear
port.name = "Port_To_Org_1"
port.DestinationEndpoint.Alias = Alias120001
port.DestinationEndpoint.Application = App0
port.DestinationEndpoint.Openness = 1
port.DestinationEndpoint.Organization = Org110001
port.EncodingType = 1
port.PrimaryTransport.Address = "file://C:\Port_To_Org_1-%tracking_id%.xml"
port.PrimaryTransport.Parameter = ""
port.PrimaryTransport.Type = 256
port.SecondaryTransport.Address = ""
port.SecondaryTransport.Parameter = ""
port.SecondaryTransport.Type = 1
Port160001 = port.create

port.clear
port.name = "Port_To_Org_2"
port.DestinationEndpoint.Alias = Alias120002
port.DestinationEndpoint.Application = App0
port.DestinationEndpoint.Openness = 1
```

LISTING 23.3 continued

```
port.DestinationEndpoint.Orgarization = Org110002
port.EncodingType = 1
port.PrimaryTransport.Address = "file://C:\Port_To_Org_2-%tracking_id%.edi"
port.PrimaryTransport.Parameter = ""
port.PrimaryTransport.Type = 256
port.SecondaryTransport.Address = ""
port.SecondaryTransport.Parameter = ""
port.SecondaryTransport.Type = 1
Port160002 = port.create

set port = nothing

' Create Channels

set chan = BT.CreateChannel

chan.clear
chan.Name = "Channel_From_Org_1"
chan.InputDocument = Doc140001
chan.IsReceiptChannel = False
chan.LoggingInfo.LogNativeInputDocument = True
chan.LoggingInfo.LogNativeOutputDocument = False
chan.LoggingInfo.LogXMLInputDocument = True
chan.LoggingInfo.LogXMLOutputDocument = False
chan.OutputDocument = Doc140001
chan.port = Port160001
chan.ReceiptChannel = Chan0
chan.RetryCount = 3
chan.RetryInterval = 5
chan.SourceEndpoint.Alias = Alias120001
chan.SourceEndpoint.Openness = 1
chan.SourceEndpoint.Organization = Org110001
Chan180001 = chan.Create

chan.clear
chan.Name = "Channel_From_Org_2"
chan.InputDocument = Doc140002
chan.IsReceiptChannel = False
chan.LoggingInfo.LogNativeInputDocument = True
chan.LoggingInfo.LogNativeOutputDocument = False
chan.LoggingInfo.LogXMLInputDocument = False
chan.LoggingInfo.LogXMLOutputDocument = False
chan.OutputDocument = Doc140002
chan.port = Port160002
chan.ReceiptChannel = Chan0
chan.RetryCount = 3
chan.RetryInterval = 5
chan.SourceEndpoint.Alias = Alias120002
chan.SourceEndpoint.Openness = 1
```

LISTING 23.3 continued

```
chan.SourceEndpoint.Organization = Org110002
Chan180002 = chan.Create

set chan = nothing

Set BT = nothing

End Sub

'Get variable values
strServerName = GetEnvVar("COMPUTERNAME")
strGroupName = GetBTSGroupName(strServerName)
sPath = GetEnvVar("ProgramFiles")  & "\Microsoft BizTalk Server\HTTP Receive"

'Create Virtual Directory
Call CreateVirtualDirectory("BizTalk_Virtual_Directory", sPath)
Call CreateWebApplication("BizTalk_Virtual_Directory")
Call SetIsolation("BizTalk_Virtual_Directory")

'Create Receive Functions
Call CreateReceiveFunction("Receive_Function_1", strGroupName, strServerName, _
    "*.edi", ADMIN_PROTOCOL_TYPE_FILE, "C:\", "", "",  "",  "", "", "", "", _
    0, 0, "Channel_From_Org_1", false, "", "", "", "", "", "")
Call CreateReceiveFunction("Receive_Function_2", strGroupName, strServerName, _
    "*.x12", ADMIN_PROTOCOL_TYPE_FILE, "C:\", "", "", "",  "", "", "", "", 0, _
    0, "Channel_From_Org_2", false, "", "", "", "", "", "")
Call CreateReceiveFunction("HTTP_Receive_File", strGroupName, strServerName, _
    "*.*", HTTP, "/BizTalk_Virtual_Directory/BizTalkHTTPReceive.dll?file1", _
    "", "", "", "", "", "", "", 0, 0, "", false, "", "", HTTPTType_File, _
    "\\Sample\%guid%.xml", True, "")

'Create Custom Counter
Call CreateCustomCounter("Custom_Counter", "Description", "Caption", _
    "Source Org", "", "", "Dest Org", "", "", "Testing", 10000, strGroupName, _
    "SettingID")

Set g_objService = nothing

'Create BizTalk Configuration
Call CreateBizTalkConfig

MsgBox "Done"
```

Note

This is not a working configuration. It is only intended to demonstrate how to deploy a BizTalk configuration.

`Sample_Config.vbs` is available for download from the publisher's Web site.

Summary

With the new replication driver that has been written to deploy BizTalk Server 2002 resources, using Application Center 2000 SP1, moving a BizTalk configuration from development to staging and finally on to production has become much simpler. Now you can create one Application Center application with all your needed BizTalk resources, select which server to deploy to, and everything is replicated to the target server or cluster of servers.

Line of Business Adapters and Industry Toolkits

PART VII

IN THIS PART

CHAPTER 24

The Microsoft BizTalk Accelerator for HIPAA

By Robert Oikawa

This chapter covers the Microsoft BizTalk Accelerator for HIPAA version 1.0. Topics to be covered in the first part of this chapter include a high-level overview of the healthcare insurance industry, review of the basic terminology of HIPAA to establish context for use, and a brief overview of the basic concepts of X12 messaging needed to understand the product features and use. Example solution architectures using the BizTalk Accelerator for HIPAA will be reviewed at a high level, followed by detailed presentation of the key features of the Accelerator for HIPAA, and how it differs from BizTalk Server 2002. Practical exercises are then presented to demonstrate how to configure the BizTalk Accelerator for HIPAA to perform simple EDI-to-XML and XML-to-EDI messaging using the HIPAA 837 Institutional Claim transaction, how to configure a 997 receipt for use in HIPAA solution architectures, and how to built a custom EDI preprocessor using Microsoft Visual Basic 6.0 for examination of X12N EDI header information.

Healthcare Insurance and HIPAA

This section contains a brief review of the basic concepts and terminology of the healthcare insurance industry and HIPAA (Health Insurance Portability and Accountability Act of 1996), which is needed to effectively use the Microsoft BizTalk Accelerator for HIPAA. Readers with experience in these areas may want to jump ahead to the section "What Is the Microsoft BizTalk Accelerator for HIPAA?" to begin learning immediately about product features.

The Business of Healthcare Insurance

The chief purpose of healthcare insurance is to protect people against the financial impact and consequences of accidents and disease. In the United States this is accomplished by a complex system of private insurance companies and government agencies, but in some countries around the world it is provided largely if not entirely through government agencies. Many of the basic concepts in this chapter will be applicable to healthcare systems outside the United States because of the universal need for efficient industry standards-based electronic information exchange to control costs and improve quality.

The basic business processes of the healthcare insurance industry are built around creating benefits offerings, selling policies (that is, contracts) to consumers or purchasing groups for delivery of those benefits offerings, collecting premium payments, and investing those premiums over time. When policy subscribers have healthcare or accident-related events requiring services, payments are made to the providers of those services (for example, physicians and hospitals). Insurance companies are successful when they are able to spread the burden of financing the care rendered for a few across the premiums collected from the large population. More recently, the industry as a whole has become much more interested in management of this financial risk and has evolved procedures for more closely monitoring use of expensive resources to control costs.

Many healthcare organizations recognize the benefits of electronic data exchange, but the lack of a single, universally adopted industry standard has resulted in proliferation of many proprietary data formats and has limited the potential benefits of automation within the industry. Although the healthcare insurance industry was an early adopter of computer technology for automation of internal data processing, it has only recently adopted Electronic Data Interchange (EDI) standards for cross-organization business, lagging behind other industries such as transportation, retail, and manufacturing.

What Is HIPAA?

HIPAA is comprehensive U.S. Federal legislation whose primary purpose is to ensure that workers and their families do not lose healthcare insurance benefits when they change or lose their jobs. The following discussion introduces some basic terms and concepts of the healthcare insurance industry and HIPAA as background for learning about the features of the Microsoft BizTalk Accelerator for HIPAA solution.

This brief summary should not to be used as a substitute for direct study of the HIPAA regulations and the X12N Implementation Guides, and should not be used as a basis for determining whether a given implementation meets HIPAA compliance as defined by the regulations. It is strongly recommended that the services of a qualified HIPAA and EDI consultant be retained when planning and deploying solutions with the Microsoft BizTalk Accelerator for HIPAA if the appropriate levels of skill in EDI implementation and understanding of HIPAA are not available within the implementation team. The HIPAA regulations may be found at `http://aspe.os.dhhs.gov/admnsimp/`. The latest version of the Implementation Guides may be found at `http://www.wpc-edi.com/hipaa/HIPAA_40.asp`.

Administrative Simplification

The Administrative Simplification section of HIPAA is a separate piece of legislation intended to reduce the cost and complexity of administrating healthcare by using standardized electronic interchanges among the various entities involved in healthcare business transactions. It provides support for the overall HIPAA legislation by establishing standards for electronic data exchange within the healthcare industry. Only widespread implementation of such standards will make possible true portability of the administrative and clinical information needed for continuity of benefits and care.

Covered Entities

The Administrative Simplification regulations of HIPAA apply to three classes of entities:

- Providers
- Payers
- Clearinghouses

Providers are organizations or individuals that deliver healthcare services for patients or members enrolled in healthcare plans, or who hold individual health insurance policies. Examples of providers are physicians, nurses, clinics, hospitals, diagnostic laboratories, and long-term care facilities.

Payers are typically insurance organizations or governmental agencies that finance the delivery of healthcare services. They enroll members, collect premium payments from individual subscribers or from sponsoring organizations such as employers, and administrate the payment of providers for services delivered. Examples of payers are insurance companies, health plans, State Medicaid agencies, and Health Maintenance Organizations (HMOs).

Clearinghouses are entities that provide value-added connectivity, data formatting, validation, transformation, and routing services to facilitate information transfer between providers and payers.

The HIPAA Administrative Simplification regulations may under certain circumstances also apply to third-party business associates who are performing services on behalf of the three covered entities.

> **Note**
>
> Discussion of the precise definitions and applicability of these regulations to third-party entities is outside the scope of this chapter.

There are four parts of the Administrative Simplification regulations:

- National Provider Identifiers
- Security
- Privacy
- Transactions

The discussion will be limited in this chapter to the area of transactions. For a detailed discussion of Microsoft BizTalk Server 2000 security configuration, see Chapter 22 "Security." Visit the U.S. Department of Health and Human Services Web site to read the Proposed and Final Rules and for more information on HIPAA Administrative Simplification at `http://aspe.os.dhhs.gov/admnsimp/`.

Transactions

The HIPAA legislation specifies a set of transactions that must be used by covered entities when exchanging electronic information. These transactions are specified by the ANSI ASC X12N version 4010 Implementation Guides published by Washington Publishing Company. Table 24.1 contains a list of the names and descriptions of the transactions.

TABLE 24.1 ASC X12N HIPAA Transactions

Transaction	*Name*	*Typical Use*
270	Eligibility, Coverage or Benefit Inquiry	Determine whether a payer has a particular subscriber on file and the eligibility or benefits information for the subscriber and dependents
271	Eligibility, Coverage or Benefit Information	Response to 270 request
276	Health Care Claim Status Request	Request the status of an individual claim (use with 277)
277	Health Care Claim Status Notification	Return status of an individual claim, notification of claim status, or request for further information about a claim
278	Health Care Services Review—Request for Review	Requests for Admission Precertification, referral review, health-care services certification review, certification appeals
278	Health Care Services Review—Response to Request for Review	Response to 278 request
820	Payment Order/Remittance Advice	Initiation of electronic payments for premium with or without remittance details
834	Benefit Enrollment and Maintenance	Transfer of enrollment information and maintenance information (changes and dis-enrollments) from sponsors to payers, plan administrators, or third-party plan administrators

TABLE 24.1 continued

Transaction	*Name*	*Typical Use*
835	Health Care Claim Payment/Advice	Claim payment and/or Explanation of Benefits (EOB) remittance advice
837	Health Care Claim: Institutional	Submission of claims from hospitals and other institutional providers
837	Health Care Claim: Professional	Submission of claims from providers such as physicians for professional services
837	Health Care Claim: Dental	Submission of claims for dental services

These transaction standards must be implemented by all covered entities by no later than Oct 16, 2002. Small health plans whose annual receipts are not greater than $5 million have one additional year to achieve compliance.

The specified transaction set will be updated at regular intervals according to the regulations. Changes expected in the near future include additional transaction standards (for example, the forthcoming Healthcare Claim attachment transaction) and adoption of newer versions of the standard itself (for example, the forthcoming change to the version 4050 ASC X12N standard).

The precise specifications defining how the transactions must be implemented are contained in the ANSI ASC X12N HIPAA Implementation Guides published by Washington Publishing Company and available for free download after registration at `http://www.wpc-edi.com/hipaa/HIPAA_40.asp`. Gaining familiarity with the contents of these guides and developing experience in reading and interpreting them is strongly recommended before attempting to design or implement solutions for HIPAA scenarios. Table 24.2 contains a list of the Transaction Guides and the specific transaction sets.

TABLE 24.2 ASC X12N HIPAA Transaction Guides

Transaction Set	*Guide ID*	*Guide Name*
270/271	004010X092	Health Care Eligibility/Benefit Inquiry and Information Response
276/277	004010X093	Health Care Claim Status Request and Response
278	004020X094	Health Care Services Review—Request for Review and Response
820	004010X061	Payroll Deducted and Other Group Premium Payment for Insurance Products

TABLE 24.2 continued

Transaction Set	*Guide ID*	*Guide Name*
834	004010X095	Benefit Enrollment and Maintenance
835	004010X091	Health Care Claim Payment/Advice
837	004010X096	Health Care Claim: Institutional
837	004010X097	Health Care Claim: Dental
837	004010X098	Health Care Claim: Professional

These guides are the definitive standard for implementation and represent the criteria by which an organization will be judged from a compliance perspective in the area of transactions. They contain precise definitions of all terms, data types, X12N syntax, data structures, situational rules, and examples of use for each transaction.

Using the HIPAA Transaction Set

Covered entities will use the HIPAA Transaction sets to automate essential core business processes. Four common scenarios for use are presented in this section:

- Enrollment
- Eligibility
- Authorization
- Claims processing

Note that these simple scenarios do not represent the only ways that the HIPAA transaction sets may be used within the healthcare industry. Many real-world scenarios combine different transactions to solve end-to-end business workflows. For more information on how to use the X12N Transaction sets in healthcare, see Health Care EDI Transactions: A Business Primer, published by Washington Publishing Company, located at `http://www.wpc-edi.com/models/PrimerHome.html`. Also, the first section (entitled "1. Purpose and Business Overview) within each ANSI ASC X12 HIPAA Implementation Guide describes the purposes for which the transaction may be used and provides examples illustrating proper use.

Enrollment

Enrollment is a core business process within payer organizations and large sponsors. As part of the hiring process, new employees will typically select a particular health plan and benefits package associated with a policy held by the employer, who acts as the sponsor of the plan. The Human Resources Benefits group of the sponsor may manage the demographic and policy benefits information within an Enterprise Resource Planning

(ERP) system, or it may be outsourced to a third-party administrative party. Payers may use the ASC X12N 834 Benefit Enrollment and maintenance transaction to accept membership list transfers from plan sponsors such as employers who maintain this information in electronic form. Membership lists may also be transferred from the payer to other third-party administrative organizations such as pharmacy benefits administrators using the 834 transaction set. Figure 24.1 shows how the 834 Enrollment transaction may be used in the enrollment scenario.

FIGURE 24.1
Enrollment and the 834.

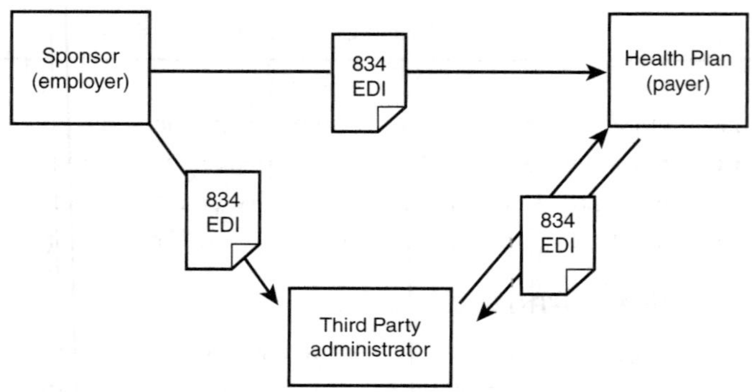

Eligibility Verification

Eligibility verification is the process of determining whether an individual requesting medical services has applicable coverage (benefits) under the terms of a given healthcare plan. It will be most frequently initiated by providers (physicians, hospitals, diagnostic laboratories) who want to determine in advance of a patient visit whether they will be paid by the insurance company for services to be delivered. The ASC X12N 270 Health Care Eligibility/Benefit Inquiry transaction contains the "request" sent to the payer. This transaction may be used in "real-time" mode, being initiated from a clinic or diagnostic laboratory where a response is expected in a short amount of time as with a credit card verification. Alternatively, it may be used in a periodic scheduled update mode where local application data stores receive updated benefits and eligibility information on a daily, weekly, or monthly basis. The response is contained in the ASC X12N 271 Health Care Eligibility/Benefit Information transaction. Figure 24.2 shows how the 270 and 271 transaction set may be used in the eligibility scenario.

FIGURE 24.2
Eligibility and the 270/271.

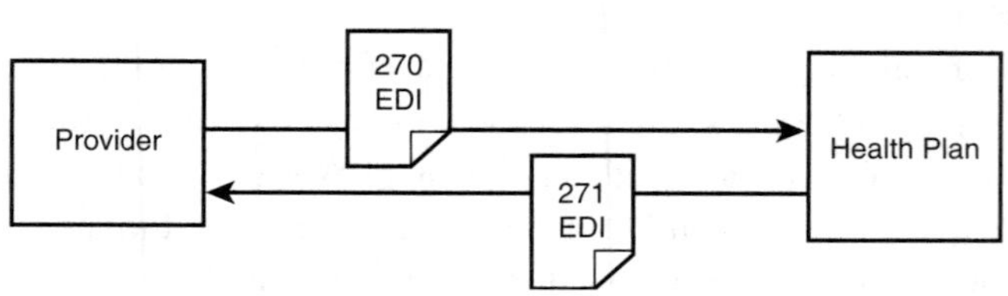

Authorization

Providers and payers use the authorization process to monitor and provide a measure of control over the use of expensive services such as specialty consultations, hospital procedures, and diagnostic testing. The ASC X12N 278 Health Care Services Review transaction set may be used in either "real-time" or batch mode to automate the authorization process depending on the business requirements. Figure 24.3 shows how the 278 transaction may be used in the authorization scenario.

FIGURE 24.3
Authorization and the 278.

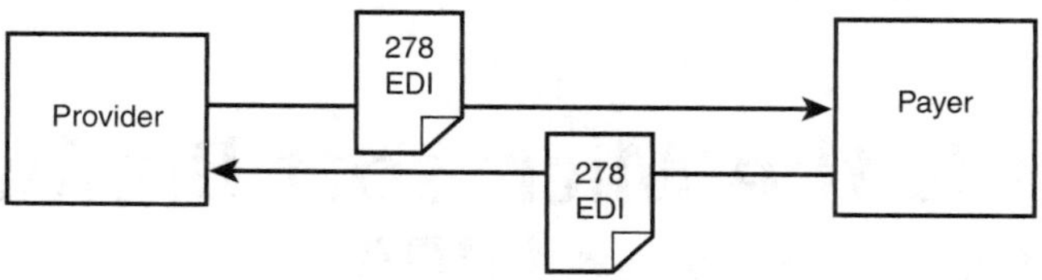

Claims

The claims process is typically initiated by a provider organization (hospital, clinic, physician, diagnostic laboratory) by preparation of a bill (claim) to a payer for services delivered for a given patient. The ASC X12N 837 Health Care Claim transaction comes in three variants for submitting bills electronically to payers under HIPAA depending on the kind of services being delivered. The three transactions are as follows:

- 837 Health Care Claim: Professional
- 837 Health Care Claim: Institutional
- 837 Health Care Claim: Dental

The 837 Professional Claim (often denoted as the 837P) is typically used by physicians, the 837 Institutional Claim (837I) is used by hospitals and chronic care facilities, and the 837 Dental Claim (837D) is used by dental offices.

The ASC X12N 835 Health Care Claim Payment/Advice transaction provides the provider who submitted the 837 with the summary of the financial transaction. This includes items of financial interest such as the amount paid, the amount not paid, any adjustments, and so forth. This statement is often referred to as the Explanation of Benefits (EOB).

The ASC X12N 276 Request for Health Care Claim Status and the ASC X12N 277 Health Care Claim Status Response may be used by providers and payers to determine the processing status of a previously submitted claim.

Figure 24.4 shows how the 835, 837, 276, and 277 transactions may be used within the claims processing scenario.

FIGURE 24.4
Claims processing and the 837, 835, 276, and 277 transactions.

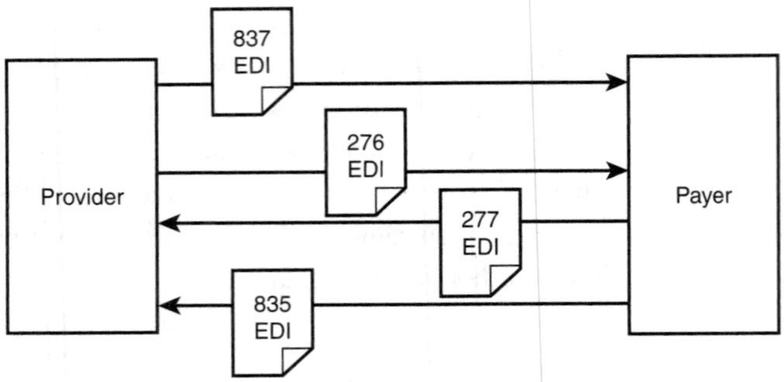

What Is the Microsoft BizTalk Accelerator for HIPAA?

The Microsoft BizTalk Accelerator for HIPAA is a set of components added to Microsoft BizTalk Server 2002 that provide specialized support for processing the 12 ASC X12N EDI transactions mandated by the HIPAA Transaction Rule. One of the major design goals for this product was to enable developers to accelerate the speed of delivery for HIPAA EDI solutions by reducing the difficulty of implementing parsers and schema for the complex X12N EDI document formats, thus giving rise to the descriptive term *Accelerator*.

The ease with which X12N EDI can be converted to and from XML or other non-EDI data formats by using this product, which has all the same capabilities as the base Microsoft BizTalk Server 2002, will assist IT professionals with rapid integration of existing Line-of-Business systems within and between healthcare organizations. Developers will benefit from the same highly extensible programming model and their experience using BizTalk Server 2002 to create new "HIPAA Transaction-aware" applications and business solutions without having to hand-code support for the complex and arcane X12N EDI transaction sets.

The Microsoft BizTalk Accelerator for HIPAA version 1.0 consists of the following components:

- BizTalk Accelerator for HIPAA parser
- HIPAA-specific document specifications
- BizTalk Editor HIPAA document validation component
- HIPAA transaction set guide
- Claims processing sample

Each of these components is described in detail in the following sections.

BizTalk Accelerator for HIPAA Parser

The BizTalk Accelerator for HIPAA parser transforms inbound EDI X12N files into the canonical internal XML format used by BizTalk Server, and it functions in the same manner as the XML, EDIFACT, X12, and flat file parsing components that are part of the base BizTalk Server 2002 product.

In the default installation configuration for the BizTalk Accelerator for HIPAA, this parser component (`BizTalk.ParserHipaaX12.1`) is placed higher in the call order than the standard X12 parser (`BizTalk.ParserX12.1`). Parser call order is an important factor in tuning server performance, and highest performance in parsing inbound X12N HIPAA EDI transactions will occur when the `BizTalk.ParserHIPAAX12.1` component is listed first in the server call sequence. Never place the HIPAA parser lower than the standard X12 parser because this may result in unexpected parsing behavior. In general, the Accelerator for HIPAA parser can handle any X12 EDI document parsing responsibilities that the standard BizTalk X12 parser can perform.

Submitting EDI documents to this parser is accomplished by using the standard Microsoft BizTalk Server mechanisms, and parser selection is handled automatically. Programmatic submission to Microsoft BizTalk Server is via the `IInterchange::Submit` or `IInterchange::SubmitSync` COM interfaces or via use of the file receive, http receive, or MSMQ receive functions described elsewhere in this book. No interfaces for directly programming against the parser component are supported by Microsoft.

Custom Data Types

Although not a capability specific to the BizTalk Accelerator for HIPAA parser (it is also seen in the X12 parser), there is built-in support for working with data types that do not have exact counterparts in XML. Two X12 data types that are not found within XML are

- Implied decimal
- Time

Implied Decimal

The implied decimal data type uses the notation N*x* where *x* is a positive integer ranging in value from 0 through 9 that denotes the number of digits to the right of the decimal point. This data type is called an implied decimal because the decimal point is not inserted in the X12 data. Thus an EDI data element of type N2 containing the value 300 has a numeric value of 3, and it will appear as 3.00 in the output XML. A value of 3 in XML will appear as 300 when mapped to an N2 data type in EDI. At runtime, the BizTalk Accelerator for HIPAA parser in combination with the BizTalk Server serializer automatically adds the appropriate decimal point and zero padding when mapping between XML and EDI implied decimals. Table 24.3 illustrates how the X12 implied decimal appears in X12 data and how the BizTalk Accelerator for HIPAA treats it within XML.

TABLE 24.3 X12 Implied Decimal Data Type

X12 Data Type	*X12 Data*	*XML Data*
N0	300	300
N1	300	30.0
N2	300	3.00
N3	300	0.300
N4	300	0.3000

Time

The X12 standard supports a time data type with the format HHMMSSDD where HH ranges between 00 and 23, MM ranges between 00 and 59, SS ranges between 00 and 59, and DD ranges between 00 and 99. The BizTalk Accelerator for HIPAA parser automatically converts the EDI time data type to a string in XML, and the BizTalk serializer converts strings in the HHMMSSDD format to the appropriate EDI time data type. Table 24.4 illustrates how the BizTalk Accelerator for HIPAA treats the X12 time data type.

TABLE 24.4 X12 Time Data Type

X12 Format	*X12 Data*	*XML String*	*Value*
HHMMSSDD	10314555	10314555	10:31:45:55—i.e. 31 minutes, 45.55 seconds past 10 AM
HHMMSSD	1031455	1031455	10:31:45:5
HHMMSS	103145	103145	10:31:45
HHMM	1031	1031	10:31

You will have to convert the XML string representation of time to any application-specific representation of time using custom code.

One-to-Many Parsing

Certain X12N EDI documents such as the 834, 835, and 837 may have valid X12 structures that allow them to bundle together many transactions into a single larger transaction. This feature allows healthcare EDI systems to bundle many individual business transactions together and submit them as a single larger batch. However, these larger documents are often broken down on receipt into individual transactions for processing on an individual level. Figure 24.5 demonstrates the different modes of parsing behavior available with the BizTalk Accelerator for HIPAA.

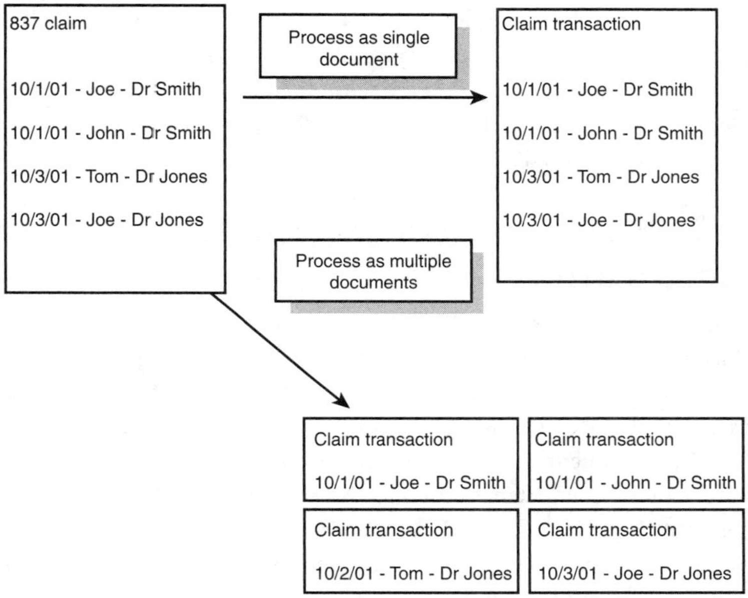

FIGURE 24.5
One-to-many parsing.

The Microsoft BizTalk Accelerator for HIPAA parser is capable of supporting either mode of behavior. Selection between the two different parsing behaviors ("single" versus "multiple") is accomplished by using different BizTalk Accelerator for HIPAA document schemas (see discussion on BizTalk Accelerator for HIPAA Document Specifications).

Triggers

Although X12 and XML both support construction of hierarchical structured documents, the transformation between the two is not without some irregularities. For instance, X12 permits under certain circumstances for segments with similar content and identical structures to be sent without mandating a specific delivery order. The "meaning" of the contents can only be inferred by examining the contents of a data field within the segment. When two identically named nodes at a sibling level would result from this X12 construction when expressed in XML, no valid XDR schema can represent the XML structure. To overcome this restriction, the BizTalk Accelerator for HIPAA parser uses the concept of a *trigger field* which is an attribute-value pair placed within the XDR schema that allows the parser to resolve ambiguous data structures in X12 and assign them to the correct elements and attributes within the XML document.

The NM1 segment provides an example of such a circumstance. Within X12 documents, an NM1 segment typically represents an organization or individual name. In healthcare insurance transactions, there are references to many different kinds of physicians—for example, referring physicians, attending physicians, or admitting physicians. When an NM1 segment arrives, the parser cannot unequivocally know which kind of provider is being referred to by the simple appearance of the NM1 data element. It must therefore examine the contents of a specific field in the NM1 segment and decide based on the code within the trigger field which part of the XML data structure should receive the contents of this particular NM1 segment.

BizTalk Accelerator for HIPAA Document Specifications

The nine ANSI ASC X12N HIPAA Implementation Guides published by Washington Publishing Company specify the precise physical document structure required for each X12N transaction. The BizTalk Accelerator for HIPAA Document Specifications are XML Data Reduced (XDR) schemas for each of the 12 X12N transaction set documents. These BizTalk document specifications schemas are programmatically generated directly from the publishing database used by Washington Publishing Company to prepare the Implementation Guides. As XDR schemas, these document specifications carry all the structural and data type information needed for the BizTalk Accelerator for HIPAA to validate the structure of an incoming X12N HIPAA EDI document and transform it into the canonical XML format used by the BizTalk Server Messaging Services. Figure 24.6 shows the BizTalk Editor containing a BizTalk HIPAA transaction schema, in this case the 837 Institutional Claim.

FIGURE 24.6
837 Institutional Claim schema loaded into the BizTalk Editor.

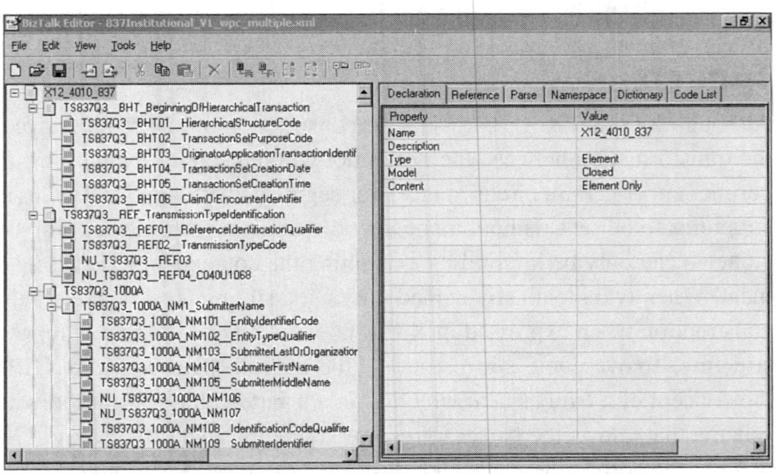

Although the tag names in these schemas may seem somewhat verbose, they are designed for clarity and have the same naming conventions as the corresponding sections within the ANSI ASC X12N HIPAA Implementation Guides.

The BizTalk HIPAA document specifications also contain enumerated data element values specified in the Implementation Guides. Some large code sets must be licensed separately from their respective publishers for use in production implementations such as the CPT-4 and ICD-9CM codes, but other code sets are available within the guides, and these may be viewed as enumerations on the Code List tab within the BizTalk Editor. Figure 24.7 shows an enumerated code set used within the 837 transaction. See the Appendices of the ANSI ASC X12N HIPAA Transaction Implementation Guides for a list and description of the External Code Sources used by each transaction.

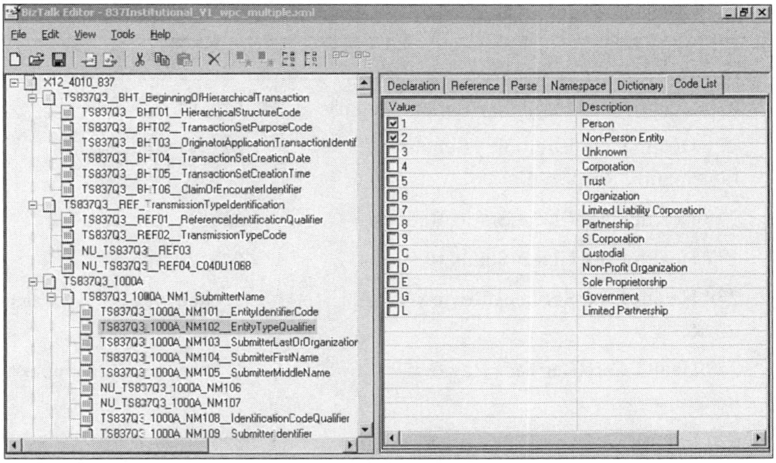

FIGURE 24.7
Enumerated code set within the BizTalk Editor.

Syntax notes from the Implementation Guides may also be viewed using the BizTalk Editor. Syntax notes are explanatory notes added by the X12N committees to provide clarification of the meaning of the published text. These syntax notes can be invaluable in understanding how to interpret a specific EDI data set and the situational logic within the schemas. Figure 24.8 shows a syntax note for the 837 Institutional Claim schema within the BizTalk Editor.

Microsoft will make updated versions of these document schemas available when new versions of the Implementation Guides are published by Washington Publishing Company. Any modification of these document specifications may result in deviation from the specifications contained within the Implementation Guides. Such actions risk noncompliance with the HIPAA regulations and therefore should be undertaken only with extreme caution!

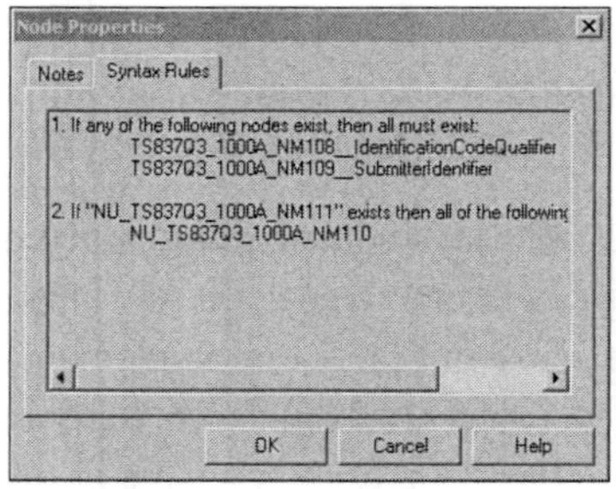

FIGURE 24.8
BizTalk HIPAA schema syntax note.

Table 24.5 lists the XML document schemas installed with the Microsoft BizTalk Accelerator for HIPAA version 1.0.

TABLE 24.5 BizTalk HIPAA Document Schema

X12N Transaction	*Filename of XDR Schema*
270 Health Care Eligibility/Benefit Inquiry	`270_V1_wpc.xml`
271 Health Care Eligibility/Benefit Information Response	`271_V1_wpc.xml`
276 Health Care Claim Status Request	`276_V1_wpc.xml`
277 Health Care Claim Status Response	`277_V1_wpc.xml`
278 Health Care Services Review—Request for Review	`278Request_V1_wpc.xml`
278 Health Care Services Review—Response	`278Response_V1_wpc.xml`
820 Payroll Deducted and Other Group Premium Payment for Insurance Products	`820_V1_wpc.xml`
834 Benefit Enrollment and Maintenance	`834_V1_wpc_multiple.xml`
834 Benefit Enrollment and Maintenance	`834_V1_wpc_single.xml`
835 Health Care Payment/Advice	`835_V1_wpc_multiple.xml`
835 Health Care Payment/Advice	`835_V1_wpc_multiple.xml`
837 Health Care Claim Dental	`837Dental_V1_wpc_multiple.xml`
837 Health Care Claim Dental	`837Dental_V1_wpc_single.xml`
837 Health Care Claim Institutional	`837Institutional_V1_wpc_multiple.xml`
837 Health Care Claim Institutional	`837Institutional_V1_wpc_single.xml`
837 Health Care Claim Professional	`837Professional_V1_wpc_multiple.xml`
837 Health Care Claim Professional	`837Professional_V1_wpc_single.xml`

Note that there are two versions of the 278 Health Care Services Review Transaction. Use the `278Request_V1_wpc.xml` version of the 278 when working with the Request for Services Review, and use the `278Response_V1_wpc.xml` when working with the Response. This dual format is a result of the structure and intended use of the 278 EDI document. See the ANSI X12N Implementation Guide for the 278 for more details on the structural differences and use.

The 834, 835, and 837 series of transactions also have two versions of XDR schema. These documents may often contain multiple smaller transactions within them. Depending on the business requirements, these documents may need to be treated as a single large document, or they may need to parsed into a series of smaller documents, one for each individual transaction. The Microsoft BizTalk Accelerator for HIPAA parser supports both modes of action by providing two different schema for evaluating inbound EDI documents of this type. Use the version containing "single" in the filename to force the parser to treat the document as a single transaction on parsing, and use the version containing "multiple" to force the parser to break up the document into a series of individual transactions. Figure 24.9 demonstrates the different parsing behaviors of the BizTalk Accelerator for HIPAA parser invoked by using different XML document schemas.

For more information on the structure of the HIPAA document schemas, see "How to Interpret the Schemas" within the Microsoft BizTalk Accelerator for HIPAA Transaction Set Schema Guide.

FIGURE 24.9
Parsing behavior using "single" and "multiple" versions of XML schema.

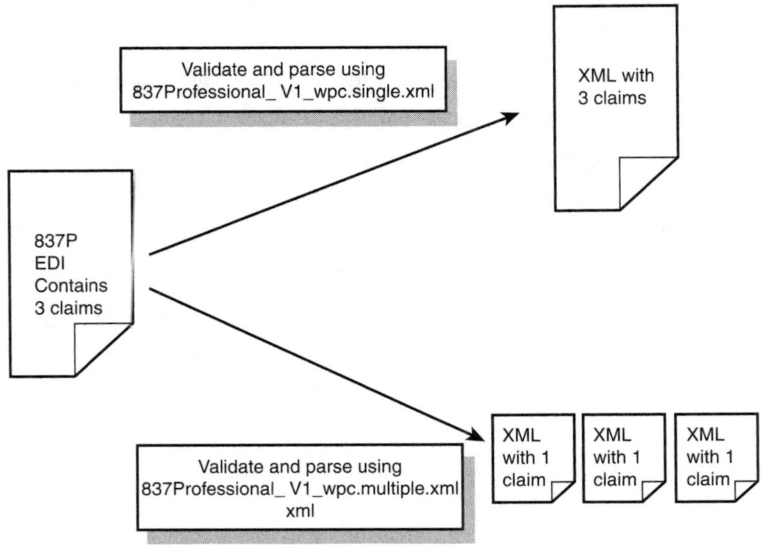

BizTalk Editor

The BizTalk Editor tool is used to create and manage the XML document specifications for inbound and outbound documents processed by BizTalk Server. The version of the Editor that accompanies the BizTalk Accelerator for HIPAA has a few additional features that enable it to be used for debugging and testing purposes and specific support for the X12 custom data types used in the HIPAA transaction standards.

If you examine a BizTalk HIPAA document schema using the BizTalk Editor, you will see for some of the document elements a new trigger field property located on the Parse tab. Do not change the setting of this property or attempt to edit these schemas because it may result in parsing behavior not in compliance with the Implementation Guide specifications.

A new validation component (`HIPAAvalidatedoc.dll`) is installed as part of the BizTalk Accelerator for HIPAA to permit the BizTalk Editor to validate instances of HIPAA EDI documents interactively during development and testing. Follow these steps to use this feature:

1. Use the BizTalk Editor to create a document schema from the HIPAA templates for the transaction set validation.
2. Open the EDI document using Notepad. Remove the EDI headers (ISA-GS-ST) and EDI trailers (SE-GE-IEA) from the EDI document, leaving behind only the data. Be sure to remove any extraneous trailing characters, but do not remove the trailing segment delimiter (may be a carriage return).
3. Save the document instance.
4. Load the HIPAA schema that you want to use into the BizTalk Editor.
5. In the editor, choose Tools, Validate Instance from the main menu.
6. Observe the Warnings and Output panes within the BizTalk Editor. If the EDI document validates against the schema, then you will see the canonical XML document structure corresponding to the EDI document displayed within the Output pane.

Figure 24.10 shows the data taken from an 837 Institutional Claim and validated against the 837 Institutional Claim document specification using the BizTalk Editor.

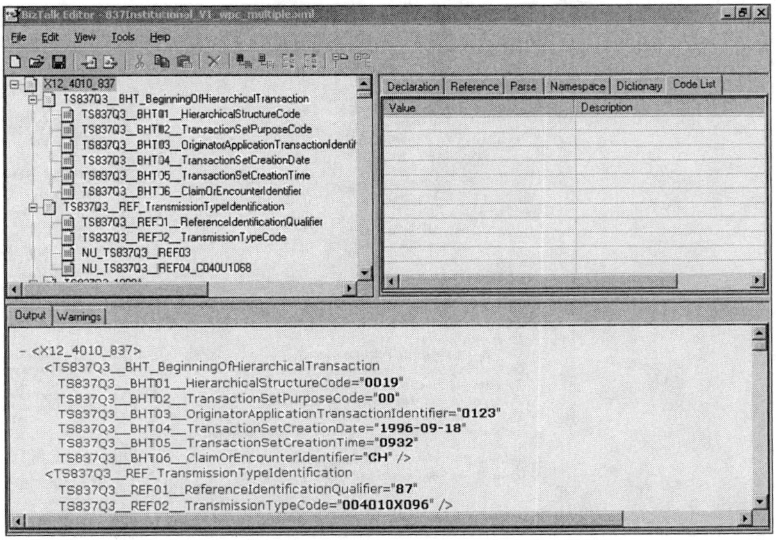

FIGURE 24.10
Using the BizTalk Editor to validate an EDI instance.

Microsoft BizTalk HIPAA Transaction Set Schemas Guide

The Microsoft BizTalk HIPAA Transaction Set Schemas Guide is a compiled HTML file installed with the BizTalk Accelerator for HIPAA. This document provides a subset of information from the Implementation Guides that will be of interest to developers. Documentation linking the HIPAA Implementation Guides with the XML tag element and attribute names used within the HIPAA document schemas is helpful in debugging parsing failures because these element and attribute tag names are recorded in both the Editor when validating an instance of an EDI document or within the event log during runtime.

Figure 24.11 shows the contents of the Microsoft BizTalk Accelerator for HIPAA Transaction Set Schemas Guide. Although this document covers all 12 of the X12N HIPAA transactions, it should not be considered a substitute for the HIPAA Implementation Guides, but rather a helpful compendium of information linking specific implementation features of the Microsoft BizTalk Accelerator for HIPAA such as XML schema tag names with the relevant sections in the ANSI ASC X12N HIPAA Implementation Guides. The Implementation Guides remain the official standard for judging compliance with HIPAA regulations.

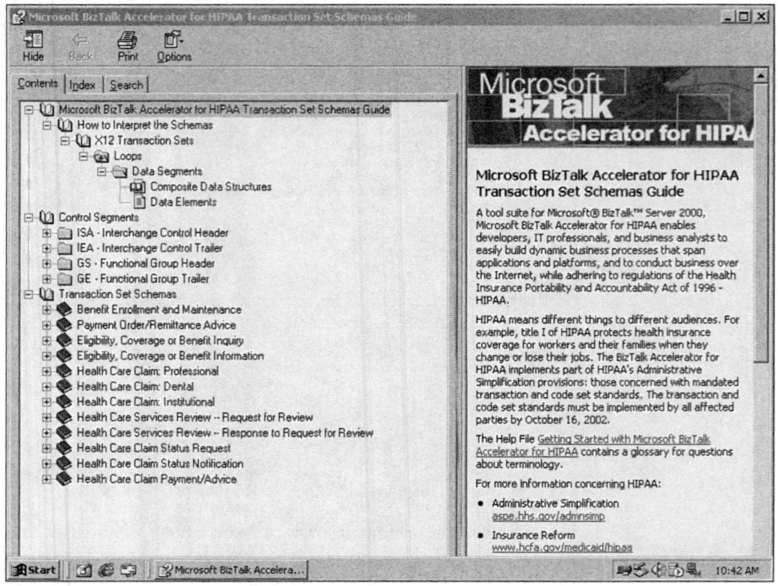

FIGURE 24.11
BizTalk HIPAA transaction set reference guide.

Debugging steps for errors arising from parsing of HIPAA EDI documents are as follows:

1. Identify the parsing error in the Event Log or the description in the Suspended queue.
2. Enter the XML tag name reported by the parser error handler into the Search text box within the HIPAA Transaction Set Reference Guide.
3. Click on the Search button to locate where the XML tag name occurs in the transaction set reference guide.
4. Review the information in the transaction set reference guide and refer to the appropriate ANSI ASC X12N HIPAA Implementation Guide for more details.

Claims Processing Sample

The claims processing sample is installed with the Microsoft BizTalk Accelerator for HIPAA. The setup file can be found in the `\Program Files\Microsoft BizTalk Accelerator for HIPAA\Samples\Claims Processing\Setup` directory. The Claims Processing sample illustrates a simple example of the claims processing process end-to-end using the Microsoft BizTalk Accelerator for HIPAA and BizTalk Orchestration with custom COM components. This sample can be configured at installation to demonstrate either a provider perspective of the claims process or the payer perspective of the claims process. See the Microsoft BizTalk Accelerator for HIPAA online help for more information on installing and running this sample as well as design documentation.

Using the BizTalk Accelerator for HIPAA

The BizTalk Accelerator for HIPAA is designed to provide support for the X12N HIPAA EDI document transactions used within the healthcare industry and covered under the HIPAA regulations. Real-world implementations have a high degree of variability around the specific details of mapping the X12N HIPAA transaction data sets to legacy system data, but they all tend to build around fundamental architectural designs reflecting the nature of core healthcare insurance business processes.

Solution Architecture

Four example architectures are presented in this section, demonstrating how the Microsoft BizTalk Accelerator for HIPAA can be deployed to build real-world solutions.

Enrollment Scenario

To support a typical sponsor-based enrollment scenario, Microsoft BizTalk Accelerator for HIPAA can be deployed as shown in Figure 24.12.

FIGURE 24.12
Example enrollment scenario.

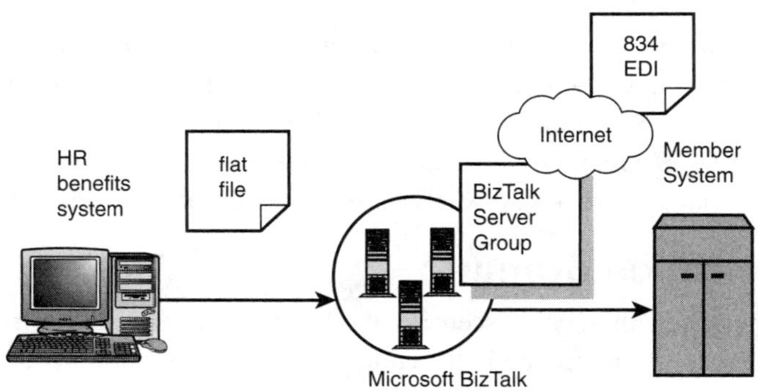

In this scenario, demographics and benefits information is exported from the sponsor HR benefits system using a flat file format, transported to the payer, and then transformed using the BizTalk Accelerator for HIPAA to an 834 Enrollment transaction. The 834 EDI document is then submitted to the Membership system located at the payer to provide the update to the membership list.

The solution described in this scenario is not required at the present for all employers under the current HIPAA regulations because employers acting as sponsors are not classified as "covered entities." However, the solution can offer clear benefits for employers and payers by reducing the costs of benefits administration and by providing an easy way to convert the many different formats for data to be transferred from sponsors into a single format for entry into the core membership systems.

Eligibility Scenario

To verify eligibility, the Microsoft BizTalk Accelerator for HIPAA can be deployed as shown in Figure 24.13 at a provider organization to allow a practice management system to perform eligibility inquiries directly to a payer system.

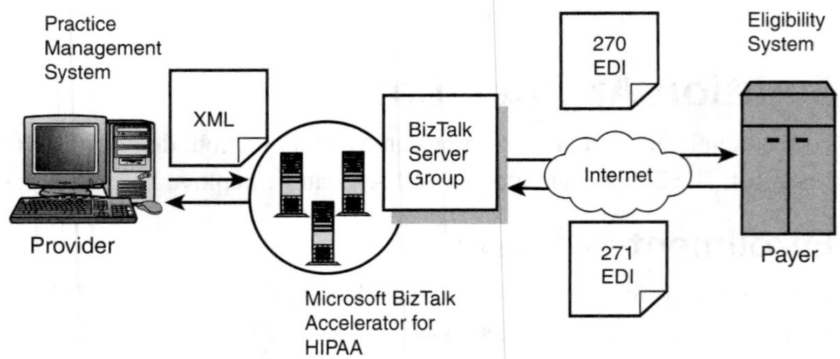

FIGURE 24.13
Example eligibility scenario.

In this eligibility scenario, a practice management system located at a large clinic is configured to send eligibility requests and receive eligibility information via an XML data structure. Using the BizTalk Accelerator for HIPAA, these XML transactions can be converted into EDI 270 requests and submitted to the payer system. The EDI 271 response can then be converted back into XML and loaded into the practice management system.

Authorization Scenario

To implement an authorization scenario, the Microsoft BizTalk Accelerator for HIPAA can be deployed at a payer site in the configuration shown in Figure 24.14.

In this authorization scenario, a payer wants to add support for online authorization of referrals for physician practices that have practice management systems that support the 278 EDI transaction. The BizTalk Accelerator for HIPAA can be deployed at the health plan to provide the needed 278 transaction support integrating to the legacy benefits system using exchange of flat files.

Claims Scenario

A claims scenario might deploy two Microsoft BizTalk Accelerators for HIPAA as shown in Figure 24.15.

FIGURE 24.14
Example authorization scenario.

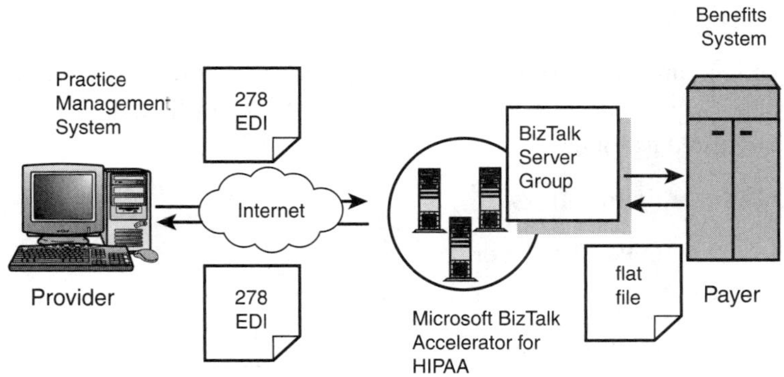

FIGURE 24.15
Example claims processing scenario.

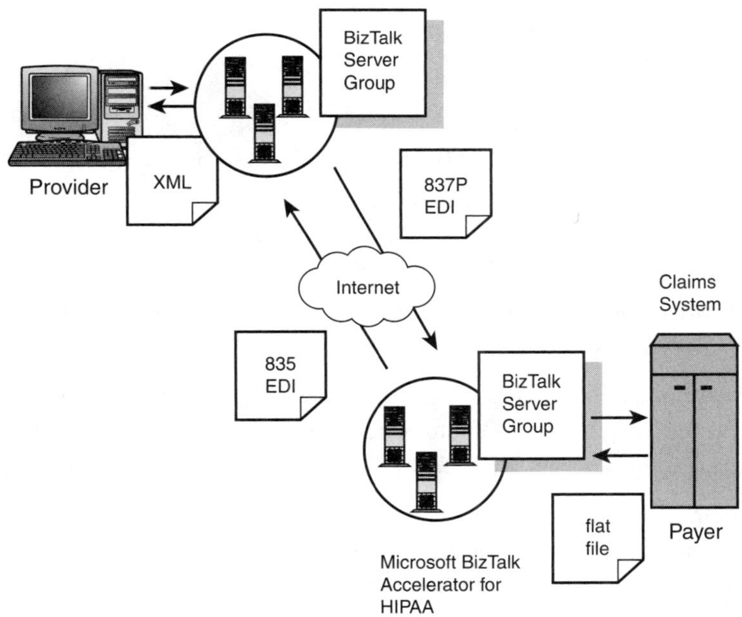

In this claims processing scenario, the practice management system and the claims system both use the Microsoft BizTalk Accelerator for HIPAA to provide support for HIPAA EDI using the 837 transaction to submit claims and the 835 transaction to return the remittance advice.

Installation

The minimum hardware and software requirements for installation of the Microsoft BizTalk Accelerator for HIPAA are similar to those for Microsoft BizTalk Server 2002 and are listed as follows:

Hardware (minimum)

- 300 MHz Pentium III or better
- 128 MB RAM (256 MB recommended)
- 6 GB hard drive
- CD-ROM drive
- SVGA or VGA monitor
- Mouse or pointing device

Software

- Microsoft Windows 2000 Server or Advanced Server with Service Pack 2
- Microsoft BizTalk Server 2000, any version, with BizTalk Server 2000 Service Pack 1a, or Microsoft BizTalk Server 2002, any version, with the BizTalk Accelerator for HIPAA Service Pack 1
- Microsoft SQL Server 7.0 with Service Pack 3, or Microsoft SQL Server 2000 with Service Pack 2

For development machines running Microsoft SQL Server 7.0 or SQL Server 2000 and Visual Studio 6.0, it is helpful to increase the RAM to at least 256 MB. To use the Orchestration Designer, Visio 2000 SR1, or Visio 2002 must be also be installed.

If you are running on BizTalk Server 2000, you must be sure to run the SQL database update scripts after installing BizTalk Server 2000 SP1a. These scripts should be applied to SQL 7.0-based installations as well as SQL 2000-based installations of BizTalk Server. The two scripts to run are

- `ControlNumbers.sql`
- `CleanQueuesPatch.sql`

These may both be found in the `\Program Files\Microsoft BizTalk Server\Setup` folder. Run the `ControlNumbers.sql` script against the BizTalk Messaging Management database and run the `CleanQueuesPatch.sql` script against the BizTalk Shared Queue database. Follow the detailed installation instructions in the Readme file for BizTalk Server 2000 SP1A to ensure that the SQL database updates are performed correctly when using BizTalk Server 2000.

If you are installing the BizTalk Accelerator for HIPAA 1.0 on BizTalk Server 2002, then you do not need to install BizTalk Server 2000 SP1A or run the two SQL scripts. You must instead apply the BizTalk Accelerator for HIPAA SP1 to ensure proper operation.

Working with the 837 Institutional Claim Transaction

In this section, you will use the BizTalk Editor, BizTalk Messaging Manager, BizTalk Server Administrator, and a sample 837 Institutional Claim to explore the features of the Accelerator for HIPAA.

X12 EDI Review

The X12 EDI standards are developed by the consensus activity of voluntary industry participants using a standardized process to be generic and cross-industry. The X12N standards are a subset of the generic X12 standards and represent the insurance industry specific requirements. The ANSI ASC X12N HIPAA Implementation Guides specify these requirements in precise detail.

It is therefore important to have a solid understanding of X12 EDI messaging before attempting to use the Microsoft BizTalk Accelerator for HIPAA. This section contains a brief survey of the basic X12 concepts and terminology necessary to understand the features and operation of the product.

X12 Data Types

Data types defined by X12 are listed in Table 24.6 along with a brief description of notation and some examples of use.

TABLE 24.6 X12 Data Types

Data Type	*Description*	*Nomenclature Used in Implementation Guides*	*Example*
Alphanumeric	String of alphanumeric characters	AN	123 Somewhere St.
Binary	Any sequence of 8-bit bytes	B	
Numeric (implied decimal)	Decimal number with implied decimal	N*x* where *x* is a digit from 0 to 9 indicating the number of places to the right of the decimal point	1234

TABLE 24.6 continued

Data Type	*Description*	*Nomenclature Used in Implementation Guides*	*Example*
Decimal	Explicit decimal value	R	12.34
Identifier	Coded value, usually alphanumeric	ID	A123543
Date	YYYYMMDD	DT	20011003
Time	HHMMSS	TM	143020

X12 Delimiters

Three levels of delimiters are used within X12N to separate individual data elements and to build the structure of the EDI document. These delimiters are as follows:

- Data segment
- Data element
- Component

The smallest unit for data defined within X12 is the data element. Some data elements in X12N may be composed of smaller related fields called components. Data segments are composed of one or more data elements that group together elements with related meaning. Keep in mind that the use of the term *element* within X12 is not the same as the use of the same term within XML. The HIPAA Transaction Implementation Guides do not require that implementations use a specific set of delimiters. In general, delimiter sets are negotiated within individual trading partner agreements. The list of potential delimiters available may be found in the appendix of the HIPAA Implementation Guides. The BizTalk Accelerator for HIPAA offers a choice of any arbitrary set of valid X12 delimiters. In the sample data that ships with the product that is used in the hands-on exercises in this chapter, the delimiter set is listed in Table 24.7. Using the carriage return as the segment delimiter has the advantage of displaying one segment per line when viewing an EDI file within Notepad or a standard text editor.

TABLE 24.7 Example Delimiter Set

Delimiter	*Hex value*	*Character*
Component	3A	:
Data element	2A	*
Segment	0D	<carriage return>

See the ANSI ASC X12N HIPAA Implementation Guides for more detailed information on how the delimiters are used within the individual transactions.

X12 Document Structure and Loops

The structure of EDI documents dates back to a time when transmission speeds on networks were slow and costs were priced on a per-byte basis. The format of EDI therefore is designed to be efficient and compact. Unlike XML, however, EDI documents were not designed to be user readable. X12 EDI documents are capable of representing hierarchical data structures by using a system of embedded pointers within the character stream. The ANSI ASC X12N HIPAA Implementation Guides provide numerous examples where such structures are implemented within the HIPAA transactions and provide detailed guidance specifying under what circumstances parent-child relationships may be used.

In X12 terminology, a *loop* is a data structure analogous to a branch in an XML hierarchical data structure. Loops contain a sequence of segments that contain logically related information. For instance, a commonly found loop within a typical X12 document is a Name and Address loop. Loops may contain child loops, leading to a complex hierarchical structure whose form is not clearly evident from examining the EDI data in a standard text editor. Figure 24.16 depicts schematically what the structure of an X12 EDI document may look like when it has multiple loops with parent-child relationships.

FIGURE 24.16
Example X12 document structure.

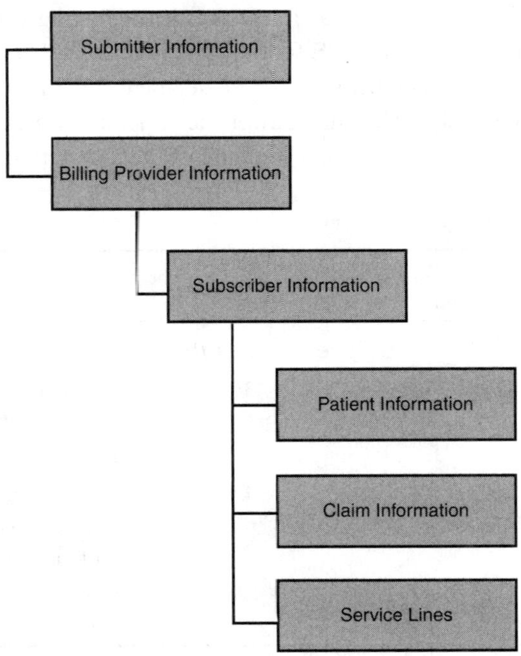

Not every field, record, and subcomponent will be used in every transaction. Because many data elements and indeed entire segments are optional under the standard, there is no unequivocal answer to the question "how big is a HIPAA transaction?" The presence of looping structures within X12 implies that under certain conditions an X12N HIPAA transaction can become extremely large (several megabytes). In the final analysis, the size of any given X12N HIPAA transaction will be determined by the business requirements driving its use.

Examination of the HIPAA transaction document schema within the BizTalk Editor reveals visually how rich in content these transaction sets documents are. The ANSI ASC X12N HIPAA Implementation Guides provide the details for how specific individual elements should be used, the potential for looping structures, what kind of data types are supported, enumeration of specified code list values, field lengths, and the situational logic for use of optional field values. An example of situational logic specifying the circumstances under which an element is required is cited here from the syntax notes of the 837 Institutional Claim for Loop 2402—Attending Physician Name:

- If either NM108 or NM109 is present, then the other is required.
- If NM111 is present, then NM220 is required.

Transaction Set Header and Trailer

Each transaction is surrounded by a transaction set header beginning with ST and ending with a transaction set trailer denoted by SE followed by two fields that contain the number of segments (records) contained between the SE segment and ST segment, and a transaction control number. Table 24.8 summarizes the structure of the transaction set header (ST), and Table 24.9 summarizes the structure of the transaction set trailer (SE).

TABLE 24.8 Transaction Set Header (ST)

Name	*Data Element*	*Attributes*		*Comments*
		Type	*Length*	
Transaction Set Identifier Code	ST01	ID	3/3	The transaction number (for example, 270, or 271, 276, and so on)
Transaction Set Control number	ST02	AN	4/9	Unique number assigned by the originator within the transaction set functional group. Must match the value in the SE02 field.

TABLE 24.9 Transaction Set Trailer (SE)

Name	*Data Element*	*Attributes*		*Comments*
		Type	*Length*	
Number of Included Segments	SE01	N0	1/10	Total number of segments in the transaction including the ST and SE segments
Transaction Set Control Number	SE02	AN	4/9	Must match the value in the ST02 field.

For more detailed information on the structure and use of the transaction set header and trailer, search for the terms "TRANSACTION SET HEADER" and "TRANSACTION SET TRAILER" within the ANSI ASC X12N HIPAA Transaction Implementation Guides.

Control Segments

X12 EDI control segments are headers and trailers placed before and after the transaction set headers delimited by the ST-to-SE segments. Control segments add information needed for addressing, security, and transaction versioning. The two control segments defined in the ANSI ASC X12N HIPAA Implementation Guides are as follows:

- Functional Group Header and Trailer(GS/GE)
- Interchange Control Header and Trailer (ISA/IEA)

TABLE 24.10 Functional Group Header (GS)

Name	*Data Element*	*Attributes*		*Comments*
		Type	*Length*	
Functional ID Code	GS01	ID	2/2	See Functional ID values in Table 24.11.
Application Sender's Code	GS02	AN	2/15	Mutually agreed on in trading partner agreement.
Application Receiver's Code	GS03	AN	2/15	Mutually agreed on in trading partner agreement.
Date	GS04	DT	8/8	CCYYMMDD.
Time	GS05	TM	4/8	HHMM, HHMMSS, HHMMSSD, or HHMMSSDD.

TABLE 24.10 continued

Name	*Data Element*	*Attributes*		*Comments*
		Type	*Length*	
Group Control Number	GS06	N0	1/9	Nine digits assigned by sender.
Responsible Agency Code	GS07	ID	1/2	X is the only permitted code and refers to the Accredited Standards Committee X12.
Version/Release/ Industry Identifier Code	GS08	AN	1/12	See Table 24.12

The Functional Group Header is used to wrap groups of transactions of the same class (that is, 270 or 835 or 837 and so on). The type of the transaction within the functional group is specified within the GS01 field. Table 24.11 contains the definitions for the two-letter Functional ID codes. The GS06 field contains the Group Control Number, which is generated from a one- to nine- digit number specified when an EDI port is configured (Group Control Number seed value) and incremented after each transmission of a document through the port. Additional information in the Functional Group Header includes date and time stamps, and routing and addressing information used by BizTalk Server during channel selection.

The Application Sender's code (GS02) and the Application Receiver's Code (GS03) are used to identify specific internal applications used by trading partners. They provide an additional level of granularity for addressing beyond the organizational identifier information contained within the Interchange Header. The precise values of these codes are determined by mutual agreement between trading partners, and they will be defined within the trading partner agreement.

TABLE 24.11 Functional Code Identifiers

Transaction	*Code in GS01*
270	HS
271	HB
276	HR
277	HN

TABLE 24.11 continued

Transaction	*Code in GS01*
278	HI
820	RA
834	BE
837 Institutional	HC
837 Professional	HC
837 Dental	HC

The Functional Group Header also contains version information for the transaction sets within the GS08 field. Table 24.12 contains the list of codes for each transaction type.

TABLE 24.12 Version/Release/Industry Identifier Codes

Transaction	*Code in GS08*
270	004010X092
271	004010X092
276	004010X093
277	004010X093
278	004010X094
820	004010X061
834	004010X095
837 Institutional	004010X096
837 Dental	004010X097
837 Professional	004010X098

The Functional Group Trailer (GE) is simple in structure but contains important information used for tracking and auditing data integrity. The GE01 field contains the transaction set count within the functional group and must equal the number of ST-to-SE blocks. The GE02 element contains the Group Control Number and must be identical to the value contained in GS06. Table 24.13 contains a summary description of the structure of the Functional Group Trailer.

TABLE 24.13 Functional Group Trailer (GE)

Name	*Data Element*	*Attributes*		*Comments*
		Type	*Length*	
Number of Transaction Sets Included	GE01	N0	1/6	Number of ST-SE documents in this group
Group Control Number	GE02	N0	1/9	Must be identical to GS06

The Interchange Control Header (ISA) is used to wrap a series of Functional Groups, thus allowing EDI documents to combine different types of transactions into a single transmission. The Interchange Control Header contains the major addressing information for the EDI document in the Interchange Identifiers and Identifier Qualifiers. X12 does not depend on a single method for determining a unique identity for a sending or receiving organization, but instead has evolved a flexible method for using named attribute-value pairs. Attributes of an organization that uniquely identify an organization are called *Organizational Qualifiers*.

Table 24.14 lists eight qualifiers using various identification numbers assigned by government agencies and industry organizations along with their encoding defined within the HIPAA Implementation Guides. Thus, if the value of the Interchange ID Qualifier in ISA05 is set to 01, then the Interchange Sender ID value corresponding to it in ISA06 must be a DUNS (Data Universal Numbering System) number. If the value of ISA05 is set to 30, then ISA06 must contain the sending organization's Federal tax ID number. If the value of ISA05 is set to ZZ, then this indicates that the value of ISA06 is set to a custom value agreed on by individual trading partners.

TABLE 24.14 Interchange Identifier Qualifier Codes for Use in ISA05 and ISA06

Code	*Meaning*
01	DUNS number
14	DUNS plus suffix
20	Health Industry Number (HIN)
27	Carrier Identification Number assigned by HCFA
28	Fiscal Intermediary Identification Number as Assigned by HCFA
29	Medicare Provider and Supplier Identification as assigned by HCFA

TABLE 24.14 continued

Code	*Meaning*
30	U.S. Federal Tax ID number
33	National Association of Insurance Commissioners Company Code (NAIC)
ZZ	Mutually agreed on code defined by trading partners

The Interchange Control Header also contains a nine-digit tracking number, the Interchange Control Number, in ISA13. This tracking number is generated by the sending organization and incremented between document interchanges. Table 24.15 contains a summary description of the structure of the Interchange Control Header.

TABLE 24.15 Interchange Control Header (ISA)

Name	*Data Element*	*Attributes*		*Comments*
		Type	*Length*	
Authorization Information Qualifier	ISA01	ID	2/2	See Implementation Guide
Authorization Information	ISA02	AN	10/10	See Implementation Guide
Security Information Qualifier	ISA03	ID	2/2	See Implementation Guide
Security Information	ISA04	AN	10/10	See Implementation Guide
Interchange ID Qualifier	ISA05	ID	2/2	Source Organization Qualifier (see Table 24.14)
Interchange Sender ID	ISA06	AN	15/15	Source Organization Value
Interchange ID Qualifier	ISA07	ID	2/2	Destination Organization Qualifier (see Table 24.14)
Interchange Receiver ID	ISA08	AN	15/15	Destination Organization Value
Interchange Date	ISA09	DT	6/6	YYMMDD format
Interchange Time	ISA10	TM	4/4	HHMM format

TABLE 24.15 continued

Name	*Data Element*	*Attributes*		*Comments*
		Type	*Length*	
Interchange Control Standards Identifier	ISA11	ID	1/1	U = U.S EDI Community of ASC X12, TDCC, and UCS
Interchange Control Version Number	ISA12	ID	5/5	00401 = Draft Standards for Trial Use Approved for publication by ASC X12 procedures review board
Interchange Control Number	ISA13	N0	9/9	Nine-digit number assigned by sender
Acknowledgement Requested	ISA14	ID	1/1	Request to send TA1
Usage Indicator	ISA15	ID	1/1	P=production, T=testing
Component Element Separator	ISA16		1/1	By agreement with trading partner

The Interchange Control Trailer (IEA) has a similar structure as the Functional Group Trailer. It contains the Interchange Control Number, which must match the contents of the ISA13 element, and a count of the enclosed Functional Groups, each delimited by a GS-to-GE block. Table 24.16 summarizes the description of the structure of the Interchange Control Trailer.

TABLE 24.16 Interchange Control Trailer (IEA)

Name	*Data Element*	*Attributes*		*Comments*
		Type	*Length*	
Number of Included Functional Groups	IEA01	N0	1/5	Number of GS-GE functional groups in this interchange
Interchange Control Number	IEA02	N0	9/9	Must match ISA13

Using the control header structures X12 documents can be combined to support a heterogeneous batch structure—that is, X12N permits mixing of transactions of different types within the same document.

The general structure of such a combination X12N EDI document is depicted in Figure 24.17.

FIGURE 24.17
X12 EDI document header structure.

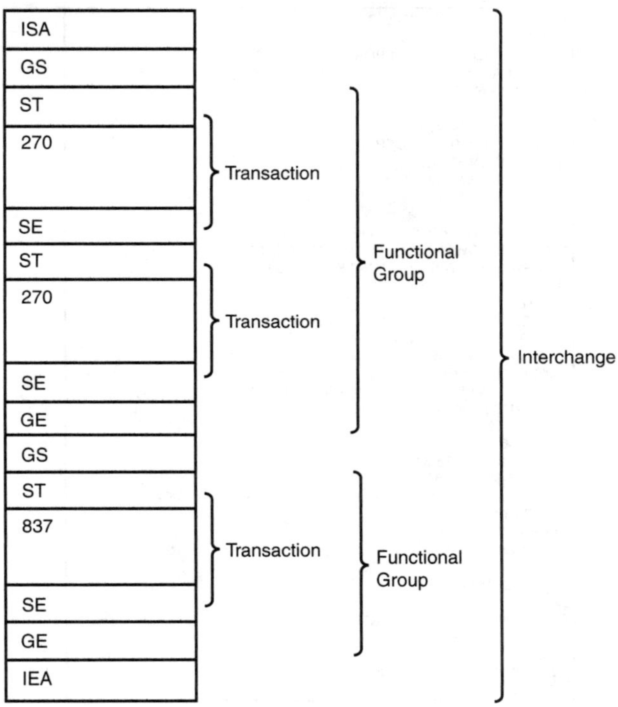

Figure 24.18 shows a real-world example of an EDI document demonstrating this structure.

For more detail on control segments, see the ANSI ASC X12N HIPAA Implementation Guides for each transaction, Appendix B.1 Control Segments.

Routing and Addressing

Microsoft BizTalk Server uses the following information to select the correct channel for processing a document:

- Source qualifier
- Source value
- Destination qualifier
- Destination value
- Document type

FIGURE 24.18
Structure of the 837 Institutional Claim.

ISA*00* *00 *30*12-3456789 *ZZ*9876543-21 *000104*1820*U*00401*000000001*0*T*:	Interchange Control Segment Header
GS*HC*HOSP CLAIM*PAYER ADJ DEPT*20000104*1820*1*X*004010X096	Functional Group Header
ST*837*987654	Transaction Header
BHT*0019*00*0123*19960918*0932*CH REF*87*004010X096 NM1*41*2*CONTOSO HOSPITAL*****46*00120 PER*IC*DAVID CAMPBELL *TE*9005555555 NM1*40*2*PAYER NAME*****46*12345 HL*1**20*1 PRV*BI*ZZ*203BA0200N NM1*85*2*CONTOSO HOSPITAL*****XX*330127 N3*1234 MAIN STREET N4*SEATTLE*WA*56789 REF*G2*987654080 HL*2*1*22*1 SBR*P**GROUP/POLICY NUMBER******CI NM1*IL*1*BROWN*ROBERT****MI*123-45-0001 NM1*PR*2*PAYER NAME*****PI*0043599999 HL*3*2*23*0 PAT*01 NM1*QC*1*BROWN*JO****MI*123-45-0002 N3*789 SECOND AVENUE N4*SEATTLE*WA*56789 DMG*D8*19400930*F CLM*756048Q*89.93***14:A:1*Y*A*Y*Y*********Y DTP*434*D8*20000104 CL1*3*1 HI*BK:366.9 HI*BF:401.9*BF:794.31 HI*BQ:15.3:D8:19960911 HI*BH:A1:D8:19261111*BH:A2:D8:19911101*BH:B1:D8:19261111*BH:B2:D 8:19870101 HI*BE:A2:::15.31 HI* BG:09 NM1*71*1*FUNK*DON****XX*B99937 PRV*AT*ZZ*363LP0200N LX*1 SV2*305*HC:85025*13.39*UN*1 DTP*472*D8*20000104 LX*2 SV2*730*HC:93005*76.54*UN*3 DTP*472*D8*20000104	Transaction body
SE*40*987654	Transaction Trailer
GE*1*1	Functional Group Trailer
IEA*1*000000001	Interchange Control Segment Trailer

When receiving inbound EDI documents with the Accelerator for HIPAA, the channel selection information is found within the document control segments and compared with the settings of the available channels. The EDI document is then processed by all BizTalk channels having matching settings for these properties. Unlike XML, all valid X12 EDI documents are essentially capable of self-routing behavior within BizTalk Server because they must contain data within the EDI headers for the document type, and source and destination qualifiers and values.

Table 24.17 summarizes the channel selection information and where it is located within a BizTalk Server configuration and the EDI document headers. The inbound documents contain source organization, destination organization, and document name information within the Interchange Control Segment Header (ISA) and the Functional Group Header (GS). These values are used to identify messaging port-channel combinations that will process the EDI document based on the values of their source and destination organization settings, and the values of the document definition selection criteria for the inbound document definition.

TABLE 24.17 EDI Documents and BizTalk Channel Selection

	Control Header data	*is compared with BizTalk Configuration settings*	*located in*
Source qualifier	ISA05	Source Organization identifier qualifier	Channel properties
Source value	ISA06	Source Organization identifier value	
Destination qualifier	ISA07	Destination Organization qualifier	
Destination value	ISA08	Destination Organization value	
Document type information	GS01	`functional_identifier`	Inbound document definition selection criteria
	GS02	`application_sender_code`	
	GS03	`application_receiver_code`	
	GS08	`standards_version`	

When BizTalk Server outputs an EDI document, it adds an EDI envelope to the content transformed from the internal canonical XML format and then places the organization information from the channel settings and the outbound document definition selection criteria into the appropriate ISA and GS data elements. Table 24.18 summarizes the location of the addressing information within the EDI headers and where the configuration location is within BizTalk Server for outbound document transport. The values for the source and destination organization identifiers and values are taken from the port and channel configuration and the document type information taken from the outbound document definition selection criteria. The values are then used to construct the appropriate Interchange Control Segment (ISA) and Functional Group (GS) header information on the outbound document.

TABLE 24.18 Outbound EDI Document Addressing

	Control Segment Data in	*is copied from the BizTalk Server configuration information*	*located in*
Source qualifier	ISA05	Source Organization identifier qualifier	Channel properties
Source value	ISA06	Source Organization identifier value	
Destination qualifier	ISA07	Destination Organization qualifier	
Destination value	ISA08	Destination Organization value	
Document type information	GS01	`functional_identifier`	Outbound document definition selection criteria
	GS02	`application_sender_code`	
	GS03	`application_receiver_code`	
	GS08	`standards_version`	

Configuring BizTalk Server Accelerator for HIPAA for EDI

This section contains some basic guidelines for configuring the BizTalk Accelerator for HIPAA to perform basic EDI messaging using HIPAA X12N transaction sets.

Creating Organizations

When creating BizTalk organizations for use in HIPAA EDI settings, be sure to add the appropriate identifiers and set the default value appropriately. When you add a new custom identifier to a BizTalk organization, the name of the identifier is not important, so using "ID" or "MyCustomID" is fine because it provides a user-friendly descriptive value visible in the BizTalk Messaging Manager user interface.

The qualifier, however, has special meaning within HIPAA EDI. "ZZ" is far from being an arbitrary string selection for the qualifier, but rather, it signifies that the values for the identifier have been mutually agreed on for use by trading partners. If you select a standard identifier, you can select the type of identifier from the drop-down list in the Identifier Properties dialog box (see Figure 24.19). Although more than 40 standard identifiers are in the drop-down list (including the mutually defined ZZ Qualifier), the HIPAA Implementation Guides specify which Interchange Qualifier codes are valid. Refer to Table 24.14 for a list of acceptable qualifier codes and their meaning. Each organization will already have an assigned standard identification code such as a Federal Taxpayer ID. The specific qualifier and values should be included in the trading partner agreement.

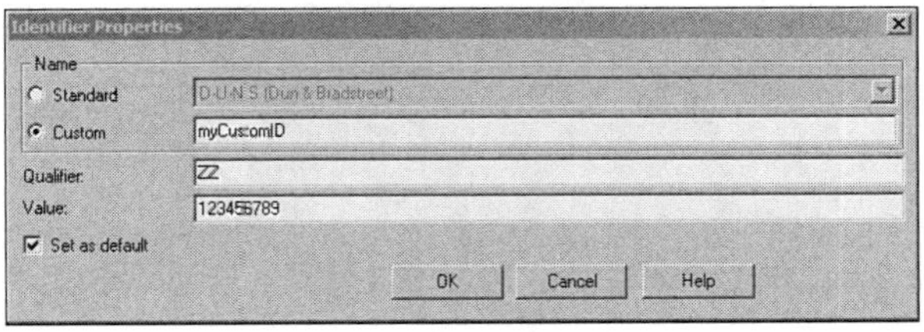

FIGURE 24.19
Organizational identifiers within the BizTalk Messaging Manager.

Creating Document Schemas

The BizTalk Server Accelerator for HIPAA installs XML document schemas for the HIPAA transaction set as read-only templates and does not automatically create document schemas in the BizTalk Server WebDAV repository. Use the BizTalk Editor to create an XML document schema for each HIPAA EDI document that will be processed. It is helpful to preserve the name of the underlying XML template file to ensure that the correct schema will be used when creating BizTalk document definitions and map files. The schema templates can be found by selecting the HIPAA template in the New Document Specification dialog box that appears, as shown in Figure 24.20, after clicking File, New on the main menu of the BizTalk Editor.

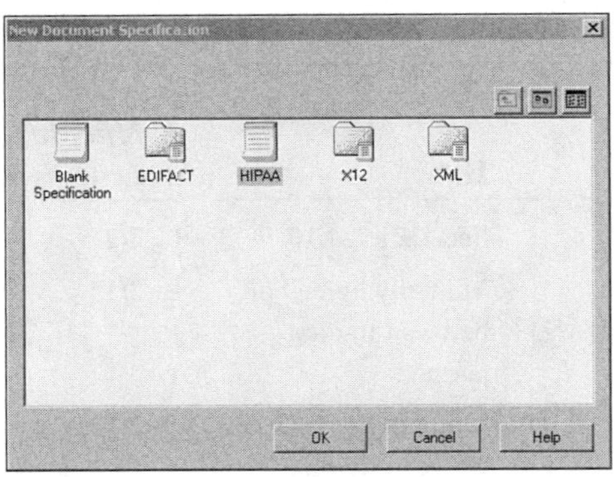

FIGURE 24.20
BizTalk Editor New Document Specification dialog.

Creating Document Definitions

When creating a document definition for HIPAA EDI documents, remember to add the document selection criteria name-value pairs using the Selection Criteria tab on the Document Definition Properties dialog within the BizTalk Messaging Manager, as shown in Figure 24.21.

FIGURE 24.21
Document selection criteria.

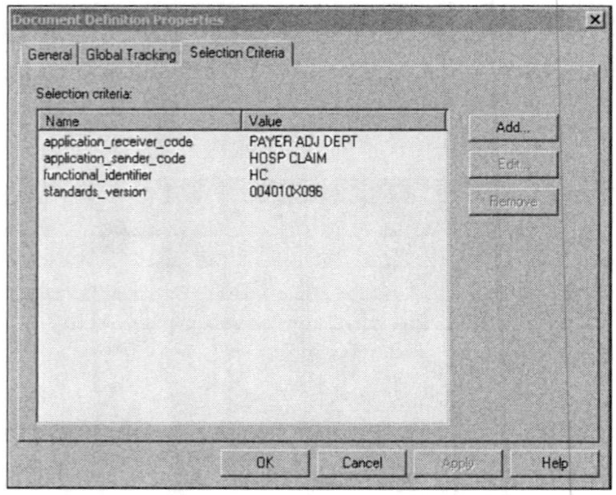

The document selection criteria specified by the value of `application_sender_code` and `application_receiver_code` are a means for routing documents among specific applications inside an organization. The value of `application_sender_code` and `application_receiver code` are mutually agreed on between trading partners and may include embedded spaces but must adhere to the size restrictions listed in Table 24.19. The `functional_identifier` is a two-character string assigned to a specific ASC X12N transaction and listed in Table 24.11, and the `standards_version` is a code that refers to the version identifier codes used by X12 to identify the insurance industry specific implementation standards listed in Table 24.12.

TABLE 24.19 Document Selection Criteria Requirements

Name	*Value*	*Min/Max Length*	*Associated Data Element*
`functional_identifier`	See Table 24.10	2/2	GS01
`application_sender_code`	Mutually agreed on between trading partners	2/15	GS02
`application_receiver_code`	Mutually agreed on between trading partners	2/15	GS03
`standards_version`	See Table 24.11	1/12	GS08

Configuring Ports for Outbound Transport

When creating ports for delivery of HIPAA EDI documents, you need to configure some settings within the BizTalk Messaging Port Wizard Envelope Information page, as shown in Figure 24.22. Configure the port to

- Use an X12 envelope
- Use delimiter values to be applied to the outbound document
- Use an Interchange control number seed value
- Use the correct organizational identifier (qualifier and value)

The X12 envelope adds the correct EDI header and trailer structure to the EDI document, and the delimiter settings determine what characters will be used to separate data segments, elements, and components within the document body. The Interchange control number seed is a numeric value incremented with each document transmitted through this messaging port. The organization identifier settings specify the Destination Organization for this messaging port and provide the destination information for the Interchange Control Segment fields ISA07 and ISA08.

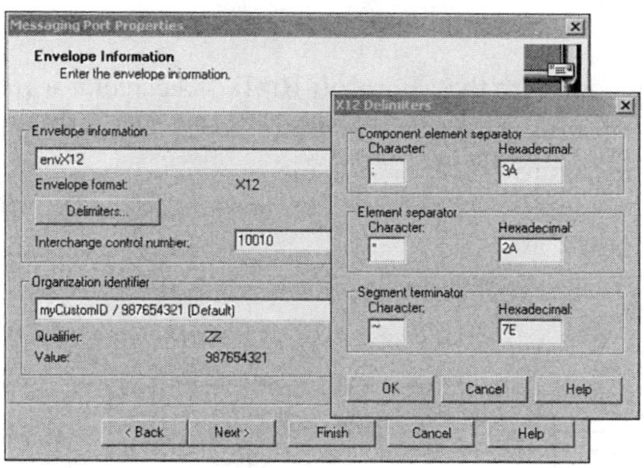

FIGURE 24.22
Messaging Port Properties – Envelope Information.

Creating Channels for Inbound Processing

When creating channels for processing HIPAA EDI documents, you will need to do the following:

1. Use the correct organizational identifier (qualifier and value).
2. Select the correct EDI document definitions.
3. Set the Group Control Number.

The Group Control Number is set using the Advanced Configuration page on the BizTalk Channel Wizard, shown in Figure 24.23.

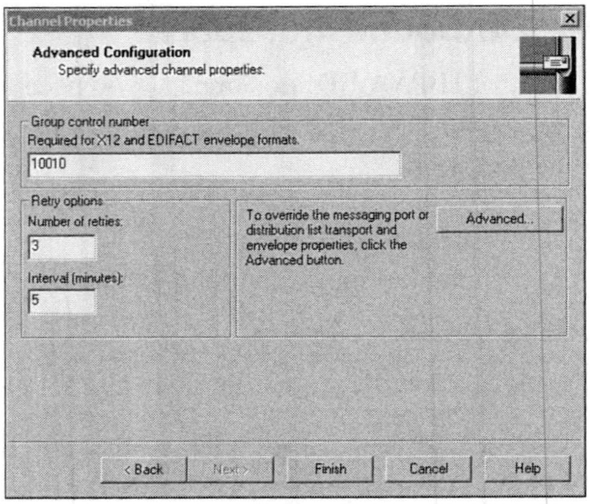

FIGURE 24.23
The Advanced Configuration Channel Properties Dialog.

Receive Functions

No special configuration is required for using receive functions with the BizTalk Accelerator for HIPAA. Keep in mind, however, the 2 MB UNICODE file size limit for MSMQ when designing solutions that may involve large EDI transactions.

EDI to XML

In this section, you will configure the Microsoft BizTalk Accelerator for HIPAA to receive an EDI 835 transaction and transform it into XML. You will implement the configuration depicted in Figure 24.24.

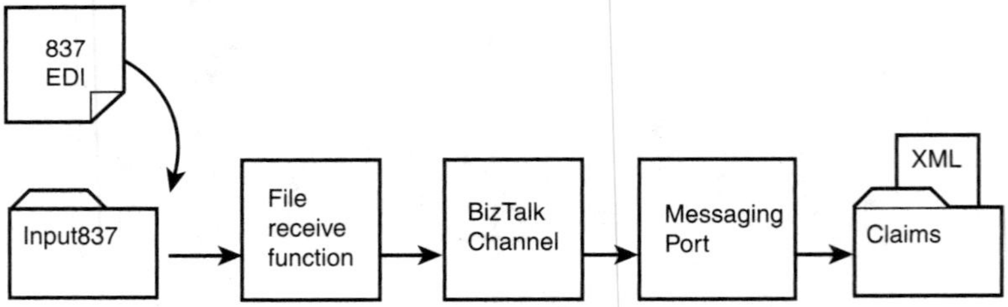

FIGURE 24.24
Converting EDI to XML.

This configuration simulates the delivery from a provider organization (in this case a hospital) of an 837 Institutional Claim to a payer organization by using file folders and file receive functions and transport. The goal is to submit an EDI 837 and transform it into an XML document that might be used to interface with an internal claims processing application at the payer.

Modify the Home Organization

Using the BizTalk Messaging Manager, modify the Home Organization so that it has the properties listed in Table 24.20.

TABLE 24.20 Home Organization Settings

Property	*Setting*
Name	Payer
Applications	Claims
Custom Organization Identifier Name	`MyCustomID`
Custom Organization Identifier Qualifier	ZZ
Custom Organization Identifier Value	9876543-21
Set as Default	Yes

In this demonstration, you will use the mutually agreed on Identifier Qualifier code ZZ and assign it a fictional value. In a real implementation, this value would be part of the trading party agreement. Because the ultimate destination within the Home Organization is the claims processing application, you will create a single BizTalk organization application named Claims.

Add a BizTalk Organization

Using the BizTalk Messaging Manager, add a new organization with the properties listed in Table 24.21. This organization will be the source of the EDI 837 Institutional Claim.

TABLE 24.21 Source Organization Properties

Property	*Setting*
Name	Hospital
Applications	None
Custom Organization Identifier Name	Federal Tax ID number
Custom Organization Identifier Qualifier	30
Custom Organization Identifier Value	12-3456789
Set as Default	Yes

Here you use a different identification method for the source organization involving the Federal Tax ID number in contrast to the ZZ identifier used for the Home Organization.

Create a HIPAA Transaction Document Specification

Using the BizTalk Editor, create a new document specification using the `837Institutional_V1_wpc_single.xml` template. Store this schema in the WebDAV repository as `837Institutional_V1_wpc_single.xml`.

Create an EDI Document Definition

Using the BizTalk Messaging Manager, create a document definition for the 837 Institutional (single) document schema. Modify the document selection properties so that it has the properties listed in Table 24.22.

TABLE 24.22 837 Institutional Claim Document Schema

Property	*Value*
Document definition name	`837_Institutional_Single`
Document specification	`837Institutional_V1_wpc_single.xml`

Add the document selection criteria properties listed in Table 24.23 to the document definition.

TABLE 24.23 Document Selection Criteria

Property	*Value*
`functional_identifier`	HC
`application_sender_code`	HOSP CLAIM
`application_receiver_code`	PAYER ADJ DEPT
`standards_version`	004010X096

The functional_identifier and standards version codes are selected from Tables 24.11 and 24.12 to correspond to the 837 Institutional Claim, version 4010. The application sender and receiver codes are mutually agreed on definitions and, in a real implementation, would need to be specified in the trading partner agreement.

Create a BizTalk Messaging Port

Create a folder `c:\Claims`. Using the BizTalk Messaging Manager, create a new messaging port to an application with the properties listed in Table 24.24.

TABLE 24.24 BizTalk Messaging Port Configuration

Property	*Value*
Name	`port_Hospital_to_Payer`
Destination application	Claims
Primary Transport type	File
Target address	`C:\Claims\837I%tracking_id%.xml`
Envelope	None
Encoding, encryption, and digital signature	Not required

This port uses file transport to deliver the outbound XML transformation of the 837 EDI document into a folder named `Claims`. You may need to modify the folder path to suit your computer configuration.

Create a BizTalk Channel

Using the BizTalk Messaging Manager, create a new channel from an organization with the properties listed in Table 24.25.

TABLE 24.25 BizTalk Channel Configuration

Property	*Value*
Port	`port_Hospital_to_Payer`
Name	`ch_837_Institutional_Hospital_to_Payer`
Source Organization	Hospital
Organization Identifier Name	Federal Tax ID number
Organization Identifier Qualifier	30
Organization Identifier Value	12-3456789
Inbound Document Definition	`837_Institutional_Single`
Outbound Document Definition	`837_Institutional_Single`
Document Logging	Not required
Group Control Number	101000

This channel configuration is the simplest way to convert an inbound X12N EDI document to XML. Use of the BizTalk HIPAA document schema and the same document definition for both inbound and outbound documents causes this channel to transform the inbound EDI into an XML document that fits the XML specification. No mapping is necessary to create this XML representation.

Create a File Receive Function

Create a folder `c:\Input837` that you will use to submit an 837 EDI document to the Microsoft BizTalk Accelerator for HIPAA. Using the BizTalk Administrator, create a new file receive function with the properties listed in Table 24.26.

TABLE 24.26 File Receive Function Configuration

Property	*Value*
Name	`Receive837`
File types to poll for	`*.txt`
Polling location	`C:\Input837`
Channel Name	`ch_837_Institutional_Hospital_to_Payer`

This file receive function simulates the transmission of the 837 Institutional Claim from the hospital to the payer organization where it is submitted to the BizTalk Server Accelerator for HIPAA for transformation into XML.

Receive EDI and Transform to XML

In this section, you will demonstrate submitting an EDI 837 to the BizTalk Accelerator for HIPAA and observe the subsequent transformation into XML. You will use a sample 837 Institutional Claim file as the input.

1. Locate the 837 Institutional Claim sample file `\Program Files\Microsoft BizTalk Accelerator for HIPAA\Samples\Claims Processing\TestData\837I.txt` that is installed with the Claims Processing Sample.
2. Open it using Notepad and look at the contents of the various headers and loop segments.
3. Place a copy of this file in the `c:\Input837` folder.
4. Observe the `c:\Claims` folder for the appearance of an XML file containing the transformation of the 837 EDI file contents.

Figure 24.25 shows the output XML file.

XML to EDI

In this section you will configure the Microsoft BizTalk Accelerator for HIPAA to convert XML to EDI. You will implement the configuration depicted in Figure 24.26.

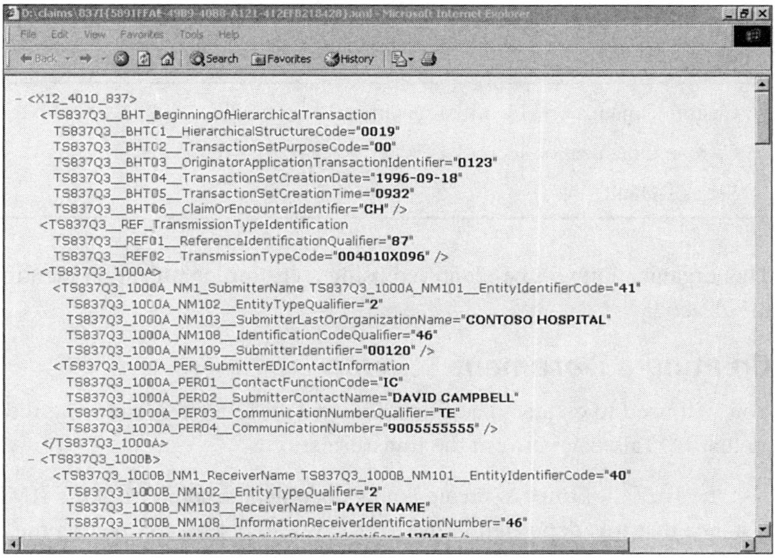

FIGURE 24.25
837 Institutional claim as XML.

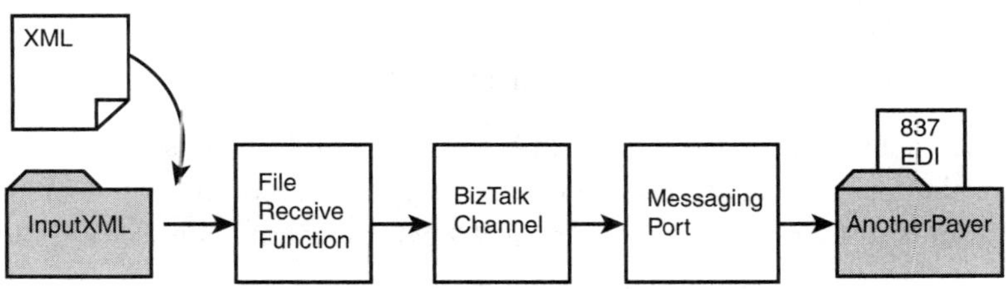

FIGURE 24.26
Converting XML to EDI.

For this demonstration, you will transform the XML document output from the previous EDI-to-XML scenario back into EDI and simulate sending it to another payer organization.

Creating Another Organization

Using the BizTalk Messaging Manager, create a new organization with the properties listed in Table 24.27.

TABLE 24.27 BizTalk Organization Configuration

Property	*Setting*
Name	AnotherPayer
Applications	None
Custom Organization Identifier Name	`myCustomID`

TABLE 24.27 continued

Property	*Setting*
Custom Organization Identifier Qualifier	ZZ
Custom Organization Identifier Value	987654321
Set as Default	yes

This organization will be identified using a custom organization identifier qualifier and the ZZ code.

Creating a Document Schema

You will need to create an additional document schema referencing the XML document so that BizTalk can perform the transformation.

Use the BizTalk Editor to create a new document schema from the XML document instance that was deposited in the `c:\Claims` folder by completing the following steps:

1. Choose Tools, Import, Well-Formed XML Instance to import the XML document instance.
2. Save the XML document schema to WebDAV under the name `sch_837_XML.xml`.

You cannot use the BizTalk HIPAA Transaction document schema for the 837 Institutional Claim because it describes the structure of the EDI document and does not describe the structure of the canonical XML transformation of the EDI document.

Creating a Document Definition

Use the BizTalk Messaging Manager to create a new document definition for this XML document with the properties listed in Table 24.28.

TABLE 24.28 XML Document Definition

Property	*Value*
Name	`837_Institutional_XML`
Document Specification	`sch_837_XML.xml`

Create a BizTalk Messaging Port

Create a folder `c:\AnotherPayer`. Using the BizTalk Messaging Manager, create a new messaging port to an organization with the properties listed in Table 24.29.

TABLE 24.29 BizTalk Messaging Port Configuration

Property	*Value*
Name	`port_Claims_to_AnotherPayer`
Destination organization	`AnotherPayer`
Primary Transport type	file
Target Address	`c:\AnotherPayer\837EDI%tracking_id%.txt`
Envelope	X12 (create a new X12 Envelope if one does not exist already)
Encoding, encryption and digital signature	Not required
Component Element Separator	: (3A)
Element Separator	* (2A)
Segment Terminator	~ (7E)
Interchange Control Number	100001
Organization Identifier Name	`myCustomID`
Organization Identifier Qualifier	ZZ
Organization Identifier Value	987654321

This BizTalk messaging port must be configured to deliver the outbound EDI document, so you must configure the appropriate envelope, delimiter, and Interchange Control Number seed values. In this part of the demonstration, you will use a different segment terminator (~) than was used in the original EDI 837 file (carriage return). You will also need to use an X12 envelope. You may create one from within the Messaging Port Wizard or by using the BizTalk Messaging Manager.

Create a BizTalk Channel

Using the BizTalk Messaging Manager, create a new channel from an application with the properties listed in Table 24.30.

TABLE 24.30 BizTalk Channel Configuration

Property	*Value*
Port	`port_Claims_to_AnotherPayer`
Name	`ch_837_Institutional_Claims_to_AnotherPayer`
Source Application	Claims
Organization Identifier Name	`MyCustomID`

TABLE 24.30 continued

Property	*Value*
Organization Identifier Qualifier	ZZ
Organization Identifier Value	9876543-21
Inbound Document Definition	`837_Institutional_Single`
Outbound Document Definition	`837_Institutional_Single`
Document Logging	Not required
Group Control Number	111111

This channel configuration represents the simplest and easiest way to transform XML into the EDI. By using the canonical XML document structure used by BizTalk Server to represent the 837 Institutional Claim data, there is no need for a mapping file. However, if you were attempting to use any other XML data structure as input, you would need to create a document specification for the XML document instance and create a mapping file between the XML document specification and the BizTalk HIPAA transaction document schema for the 837 Institutional Claim. This can be a tedious process owing to the complexity of the 837, and the Implementation Guides are specific regarding what elements must be present within the outbound EDI document for it to be within the HIPAA regulations.

Washington Publishing Company has developed a special mapping tool for tackling this gap analysis and remediation process for mapping between legacy file formats and the BizTalk Accelerator for HIPAA document schema that can create BizTalk Server compatible mapping files. It is highly recommended that you strongly consider use of this tool for best results during the mapping process. For more information on the OnlyConnect™ gap analysis and mapping tool, visit `http://www.wpc-edi.com`.

Create a File Receive Function

Just as in the previous part of the demonstration, you will use file folders and a file receive function to simulate document transmission to BizTalk Server. For the XML-to-EDI exercise, create a folder named `c:\InputXML` that you will use to submit an 837 EDI document to the BizTalk Accelerator for HIPAA. Using the BizTalk Administrator, create a new file receive function having the properties listed in Table 24.31.

TABLE 24.31 File Receive Function Configuration

Property	*Value*
Name	`ReceiveXML`
File types to poll for	`*.txt`

TABLE 24.31 continued

Property	*Value*
Polling location	`C:\InputXML`
Channel Name	`ch_837_Institutional_Claims_to_AnotherPayer`

Receive XML and Transform to EDI

In this section you will demonstrate submitting an XML document containing claims information to the BizTalk Accelerator for HIPAA and subsequent transformation into an EDI 837 Institutional Claim. You will use an XML document instance with canonical BizTalk structure for the 837 Institutional Claim as the input.

1. Locate the `837I{tracking guid}.xml` file that appeared in the `c:\Claims` folder when you received the inbound EDI file.
2. Place a copy of this file in the `c:\InputXML` folder.
3. Observe the `c:\AnotherPayer` folder for the appearance of a text file containing the 837 Institutional Claim.

Figure 24.27 shows the output of the 837 Institutional Claim.

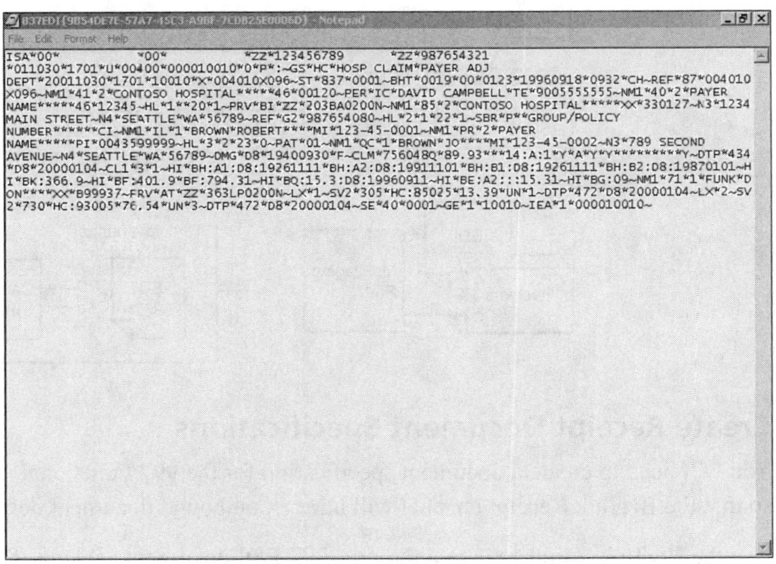

FIGURE 24.27
837 Institutional Claim.

Notice that the segment terminator has been set in this EDI file to the tilde character (~) instead of the carriage return appearing in the original 837 (refer to Figure 24.18).

Configuring Receipts Using the 997

Although not mandated by the HIPAA Transaction Standards, the use of the 997 Functional Acknowledgement is generally accepted to be an industry EDI best practice. The Microsoft BizTalk Accelerator for HIPAA provides support for configuring production and return of 997 Functional Acknowledgements.

The mechanism for receipt production builds on the core receipt functionality of BizTalk Server. Internally, information related to delivery such as date, time, and document type is stored in an internal data structure known as the canonical receipt. The BizTalk Accelerator for HIPAA installs a special map file to produce a valid X12N 997 Functional Acknowledgement from the internal canonical receipt information. For more on how BizTalk Server produces receipts, see the Microsoft BizTalk Server 2002 Online help.

In this section you will modify the EDI-to-XML configuration you created earlier so that it will send an 997 EDI Functional Acknowledgement on receipt of the 837 Institutional Claim.

Figure 24.28 shows the modified configuration.

FIGURE 24.28
997 Functional Acknowledgements.

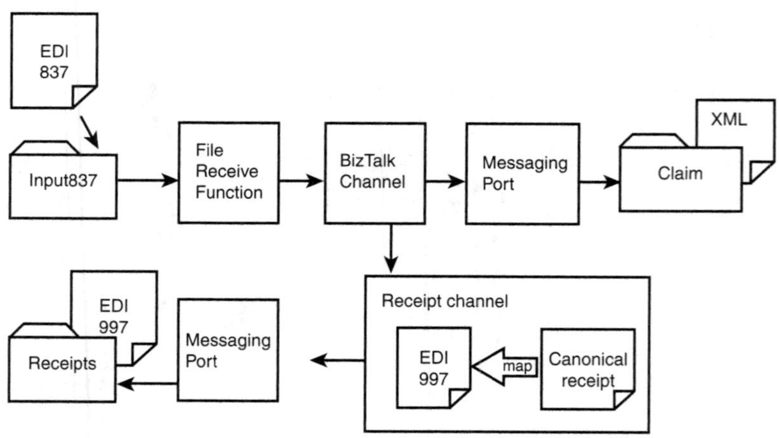

Create Receipt Document Specifications

You will need to create a document specification for the 997 Functional Acknowledgement so that the BizTalk Receipt channel will have an outbound document definition.

Use the BizTalk Editor to create the new 997 EDI document schema. The template for the 997 may be found in the X12 template folder within the New Document Specification dialog box (refer to Figure 24.20). It will be found as the file

997schema.xml contained within the 4010 folder, which is inside the X12 folder. Store this schema in WebDAV under the name 997schema.xml.

Create a second new XML document schema for the BizTalk canonical receipt. The document schema template for the BizTalk canonical receipt is found in the XML folder in the New Document Specification dialog box and has the name CanonicalReceipt.xml. Store this document schema in the WebDAV repository under the name sch_CanonicalXMLReceipt.xml.

Document Definitions

You will need to create document definitions for use when you configure the BizTalk Receipt channel. Use the BizTalk Messaging Manager to create a new document definition with the properties listed in Table 24.32.

TABLE 24.32 Document Definition for 997 Functional Acknowledgement

Property	*Value*
Name	997EDI
Document specification	997schema.xml

Because this is an X12 EDI document, you will need to add the document selection properties listed in Table 24.33.

TABLE 24.33 Document Selection Properties for the 997

Property	*Value*
functional_identifier	AK
application_sender_code	PAYER ADJ DEPT
application_receiver_code	HOSP CLAIM
standards_version	004010X091

You must set the functional_identifier to AK and the standards_version to 004010X091 to indicate that this is a 997 Functional Acknowledgement. These two values are specified within the appendix of each of the ANSI ASC X12N HIPAA Transaction Guides in the section "B.2 Functional Acknowledgement Transaction Set, 997."

Now create a document definition for the XML canonical receipt using the properties listed in Table 24.34.

TABLE 24.34 Document Definition for XML Canonical Receipt

Property	*Value*
Name	XML Canonical Receipt
Document Specification	`sch_CanonicalXMLReceipt.xml`

Receipt Port and Channel

BizTalk Server 2002 uses the same message channel-and-port mechanisms for configuring delivery of receipts as for delivery of the outbound documents. To demonstrate 997 Functional Acknowledgement delivery, you will need to create the receipt port and a receipt channel. In this section, you will step though configuration of an existing channel for receiving EDI 837 transactions to produce 997 Functional Acknowledgments and deliver them to a file folder.

First, create a folder named `c:\Receipts`. This will simulate the delivery point for the 997 in the provider (hospital) organization. Next, create a messaging port to an organization using the properties listed in Table 24.35 to deliver the 997.

TABLE 24.35 Receipt Delivery Port Configuration

Property	*Value*
Name	`port_997_to_Hospital`
Type	To an organization
Destination Organization	Hospital
Primary Transport Type	File
Target Address	`c:\Receipts\997EDI%tracking_id%.txt`
Envelope	X12
Component Element Separator	: (3A)
Element Separator	* (2A)
Segment Terminator	~ (7E)
Interchange Control Number	110001
Organization Identifier Name	Federal Tax ID number
Organization Identifier Qualifier	30
Organization Identifier Value	12-3456789
Encoding, encryption and digital signature	Not required

Receipt ports are simply standard BizTalk messaging ports configured for delivery of EDI documents. Accordingly, you will need to supply envelope and delimiter information.

Using the BizTalk Messaging Manager, create a new channel with the properties listed in Table 24.36.

TABLE 24.36 Receipt Channel Configuration

Property	*Value*
Port	`port_997_to_Hospital`
Type	From an Application
Name	ch_997_Receipt_to_Hospital
This is a Receipt Channel	Yes
Source Application	Claims
Organization Identifier Name	`MyCustomID`
Organization Identifier Qualifier	ZZ
Organization Identifier Value	9876543-21
Inbound Document Definition	XML Canonical Receipt
Outbound Document Definition	997EDI
Map Inbound Document to Outbound Document	Yes
Map Reference	Located in WebDAV repository within the `\Microsoft\HIPAA` folder. File name is `HipaaCanonicalReceiptTo4010-997.xml`
Document Logging	Not required
Group Control Number	10001

The configuration of the receipt channel requires you to specify the map file between the XML canonical receipt and the 997 Functional Acknowledgement.

Updating the Channel

In this section you will use the BizTalk Messaging Manager to update the EDI-to-XML configuration you created earlier so that it will send a 997 Functional Acknowledgement on receipt of the 837 Institutional Claim.

1. Open the channel named `ch_837_Institutional_Hospital_to_Payer`, which processes inbound 837 Institutional Claims.
2. Set the Generate Receipt Property by checking the check box on the Source Organization property page of the Channel Wizard.

3. Click on the Browse button and select ch_997_Receipt_to_Hospital from the list of Receipt Channels.
4. Save the changes to the channel.

Demonstrating Receipt Generation

To demonstrate the generation and delivery of a 997 Functional Acknowledgement, you will submit an 837 Institutional Claim to the EDI-to-XML configuration you modified.

1. Place a copy of the EDI837 Institutional claim in the `c:\Input837` folder.
2. Verify that the XML claim data appears in the `c:\Claims` folder and a 997 EDI receipt appears in the `c:\Receipts` folder.

Figure 24.29 shows the 997 Functional Acknowledgement.

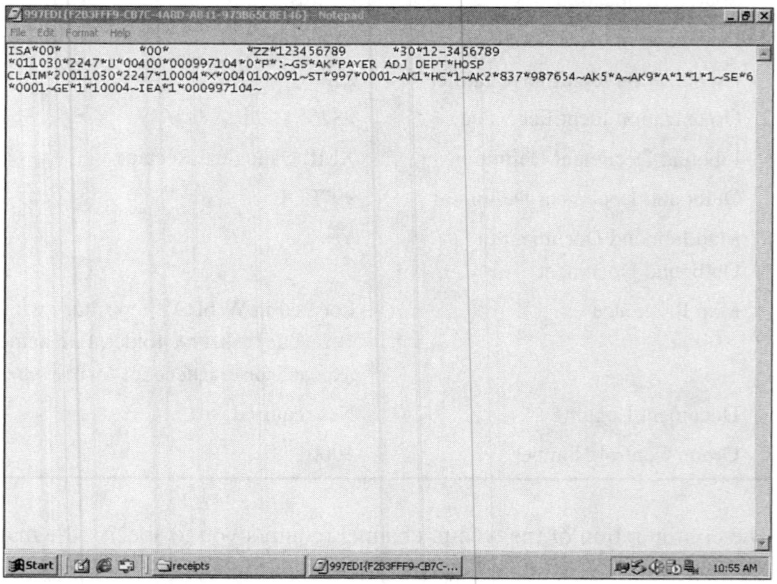

FIGURE 24.29
997 Functional Acknowledgement.

Using Preprocessors

Preprocessors are a powerful feature of the Microsoft BizTalk Server programming model that permits you to extend the product by adding custom processing functionality that occurs before the document reaches the BizTalk parser components. In this section you will learn about how preprocessors work, you will see what kinds of typical uses they have, and you will use Microsoft Visual Basic 6.0 to build and install a sample custom preprocessor for working with EDI transactions.

What Is a Preprocessor?

A preprocessor is a COM component that can be installed into BizTalk Server (and the BizTalk Accelerator for HIPAA) to provide additional document processing after a document is picked up by a receive function, but before it is submitted to the server for parsing and channel selection. Figure 24.30 shows this process for a file receive function.

FIGURE 24.30
BizTalk preprocessor architecture.

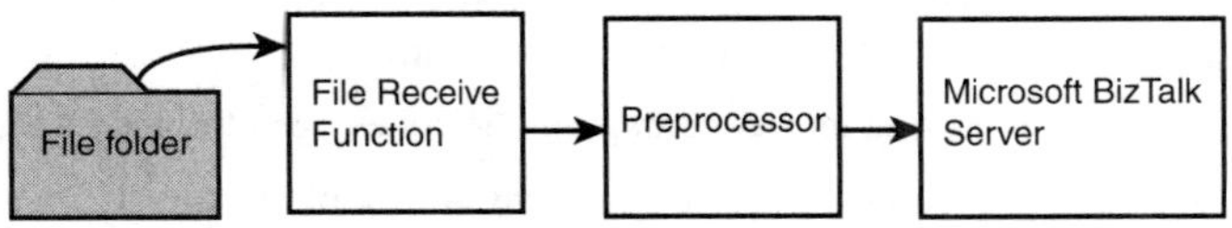

Some examples of additional processing that can be carried out by using a preprocessor are

- Data decompression
- Decoding or decryption
- Modification of header or document contents
- Parsing
- Custom receipt generation (such as TA1)
- Custom logging or tracking

How Do Preprocessors Work?

Preprocessors are COM components that implement the `IBTSCustomProcess` interface. This interface has only two methods, `Execute` and `SetContext`. The `Execute` method implements the custom work to be performed on the inbound document by the preprocessor.

Table 24.37 contains the method signatures for Visual Basic and C++ versions of the `Execute` method

TABLE 24.37 `IBTSCustomProcess::Execute` Method

Visual Basic	*C++*
`Sub IBTSCustomProcess_Execute`	`HRESULT Execute(`
`(ByVal vDataIn,`	`VARIANT vDataIn,`
`ByVal nCodePageIn as Long,`	`Long nCodePageIn,`
`ByVal bIsFilePath as Boolean,`	`VARIANT_BOOL bIsFIlePath,`
`ByRef nCodePageOut,`	`VARIANT* nCodePageOut,`
`ByRef vDataOut)`	`VARIANT* vDataOut`
	`);`

Table 24.38 defines the parameters for this method.

TABLE 24.38 Parameters for `IBTSCustomProcess::Execute`

Name	*Description*
`VdataIn`	Variant containing the input data. If read from a file receive function, `vDataIn` contains the file path. If read from a message queue, `vDataIn` may be either a BSTR or an array.
`nCodePageIn`	Long integer containing the code page of the input data.
`bIsFilePath`	Variant Boolean indicating source of the data. If `bIsFilePath` is true, then `vDataIn` contains a file path.
`nCodePageOut`	Pointer to a `VARIANT` containing the output data code set.
`vDataOut`	Pointer to a `VARIANT` containing the data to be sent to BizTalk Server.

The `SetContext` method provides a means for the preprocessor to retrieve information from the BizTalk Server regarding the document processing by the channel after submission. Table 24.39 shows the method signatures in Visual Basic and C++ versions.

TABLE 24.39 `IBTSCustomProcess::SetContext` Method

Visual Basic	*C++*

`IBTSCustomProcess_SetContext(`
`ByVal pCtx as`
`IBTSCustomProcessContext)`
	`HRESULT SetContext(`
	`IBTSCustomProcessContext* pCtx`
	`);`

The `IBTSCustomProcess_SetContext` method returns a read-only `IBTSCustomProcessContext` object that contains information on the document and channel that ultimately receives the document from the preprocessor. Table 24.40 lists the properties available for use within the preprocessor.

TABLE 24.40 `IBTSCustomProcessContext` Object Properties

Property Name	*Data Type*	*Description*
`ChannelName`	BSTR	Name of the channel that processed the document
`DestID`	BSTR	Value of the destination organization qualifier
`DestQualifier`	BSTR	Destination organization qualifier
`DocName`	BSTR	Name of the document
`EnvelopeName`	BSTR	Name of the envelope

TABLE 24.40 continued

Property Name	*Data Type*	*Description*
`Openness`	Long	`BIZTALK_OPENNESS_TYPE` enumeration
`PassThrough`	Long	0=not passthrough, non-zero value = pass-through submission mode
`SourceID`	BSTR	Value of the source organization qualifier
`SourceQualifier`	BSTR	Source organization qualifier

The events that occur when a file receive function is configured to use a preprocessor are as follows:

1. File arrives in folder monitored by file receive function.
2. File receive function notifies BizTalk Server that a file has arrived.
3. BizTalk Server calls the `IBTSCustomProcess_Execute` method passing the file path to the component as a parameter.
4. Within the `Execute` method, custom code is invoked to load the file from the folder and any work done to the file contents.
5. The file contents is passed to BizTalk Server as if it had been received by the file receive function.

The `IBTSCustomProcess_SetContext` method can be invoked by the preprocessor component to return channel and document information.

Using a Preprocessor in an EDI Scenario

When the BizTalk Accelerator for HIPAA receives a document, it removes the EDI headers (ISA, GS, ST) and trailers (IEA, GE,S E) before submitting the document for parsing and processing by a channel. The information contained in the headers is not stored within the document tracking database. The information if there is a need for keeping track of any of the information contained within the EDI headers for auditing or tracking purposes, a custom preprocessor must be used. In the following sections you will implement a custom preprocessor that will demonstrate how to access the contents of the Interchange Control Segment Header (ISA) to illustrate the flexibility of the programming model. Virtually any functionality that you may require within your solution can be implemented within the `Execute` method programmatically.

The Visual Basic Custom Preprocessor Sample

Microsoft BizTalk Server 2002 includes as part of the Software Development Kit (SDK) Visual Basic and Visual C++ samples for creating a preprocessor. The preprocessor projects are located in the `\Program Files\Microsoft BizTalk Server\SDK\Messaging Samples` folder. In this section we will modify the Visual Basic sample to read the EDI header information contained in the ISA segment.

Follow these steps to create and install a custom BizTalk preprocessor for use with the BizTalk Accelerator for HIPAA:

1. Open the `CustomVBPreprocessor` project in `\Program Files\Microsoft BizTalk Server\SDK\Messaging Samples\VBCustPreProcessor using Microsoft` Visual Basic 6.0.
2. Examine the `CustomProcess` class module.
3. Locate the `IBTSCustomProcess_Execute` procedure.
4. Substitute the following code for this subprocedure call:

```
Sub IBTSCustomProcess_Execute(ByVal vDataIn, ByVal nCodePageIn as Long,
➥ByVal bIsFilePath As Boolean, ByRef nCodePageOut, ByRef vDataOut)

'vDataIn contains the path of the file in the receive function
'vDataOut is a string that contains the entire file contents
'    which will be passed back to BizTalk Server
'add project reference to Microsoft Scripting Runtime
'add project reference to Microsoft BizTalk Server
     'Application Interface Components 1.0 Type Library

nCodePageOut = nCodePageIn

If bIsFilePath Then
    Dim objFSO As FileSystemObject
    Dim objText As TextStream
    Set objFSO = New FileSystemObject
    Set objText = objFSO.OpenTextFile(vDataIn, ForReading)

    Dim str837 As String
    Dim strISA As String

    str837 = objText.ReadAll
    objText.Close
    Set objText = Nothing
    strISA = Left(str837, 105)
    vDataOut = str837

    Dim objTextOut As TextStream
    Set objTextOut = objFSO.OpenTextFile("c:\ISA.txt", ForWriting, True)
    objTextOut.Write (strISA)
    objTextOut.Close

    Set objTextOut = Nothing
    Set objFSO = Nothing
End If

End Sub
```

5. Add a Visual Basic project reference to the Microsoft Scripting Runtime.
6. Add a Visual Basic project reference to the Microsoft BizTalk Server Application Interface Components 1.0 Type Library.
7. Build an ActiveX EXE component using the binary compatibility project setting.
8. Install this component onto your system.
9. Obtain the CLSID from the Registry by using `Regedit.exe` or `Regedt32.exe` and searching the `HKEY_CLASSES_ROOT` hive for your component. For the sample project, it will be named VBCustomPreProcessor.CustomProcess.
10. Run the following Registry script to install the component into BizTalk Server:

```
Windows Registry Editor Version 5.00
[HKEY_CLASSES_ROOT\CLSID\{<your preprocessor guid>}\Implemented Categories\
➥{20E8080F-F624-4401-A203-9D99CF18A6D9}]
```

You can find a copy of the registry script (`VBCustPreProcessor.reg`) in the directory containing the Visual Basic custom preprocessor sample project. Copy the CLSID for your component from the registry and paste it into the script. Be extremely careful when working with the registry as changes are reflected immediately and cannot be undone!

After running this script you will be able to see the component listed in the Preprocessors drop-down list in the Service tab in the `Receive837` file receive function you created earlier for the EDI-to-XML demonstration.

Test your preprocessor by submitting the `837I.txt` sample claim. Look for the file named ISA.txt in the `c:\` directory and examine the contents using Notepad. This file was constructed by the preprocessor from the ISA segment contents and is shown in Figure 24.31.

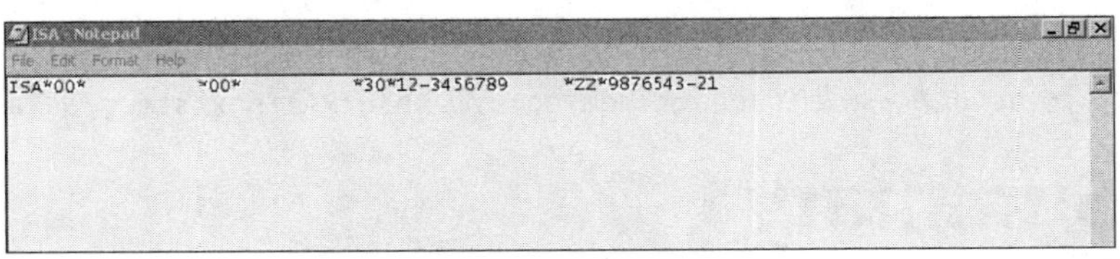

FIGURE 24.31
Contents of the ISA control segment header.

For More Information

For more information on the Health Insurance Portability and Accountability Act of 1996, visit the following Web sites:

- `http://www.hcfa.gov/hipaa/hipaahm.htm`
- `http://aspe.os.dhhs.gov/admnsimp/`

For more information on the business background of healthcare insurance, see

- Microsoft Encarta 2002, Article "Medical Insurance."
- *The Health Insurance Primer*. An Introduction To How Health Insurance Works, by The Health Insurance Association of America, 2000, Health Insurance Association of America, Washington, D.C.(ISBN 1-879143-51-8).
- *Health Insurance Nuts and Bolts*. An Introduction to Health Insurance Operations, by The Health Insurance Association of America, 2001. Health Insurance Association of America, Washington, D.C. (ISBN 1-879143-49-6).

For more information on the HIPAA transaction sets, see the ANSI ASC X12N HIPAA Implementation Guides. These guides are available from Washington Publishing Company for free download after registration at `http://www.wpc-edi.com/hipaa/hipaa_40.asp`. See also

- *HIPAA Compliance Solutions*, by Steve Bass, Lisa Miller, and Bryan Nylin, 2001. Microsoft Press, Redmond, Washington (ISBN 0-7356-1496-2).

For additional expert training and consulting services regarding HIPAA and X12N EDI concepts, contact

- Washington Publishing Company, `http://www.wpc-edi.com`. (PMB 161, 5284 Randolph Road, Rockville, MD 20852-2116, 301-949-9740).

For the latest information on the Microsoft BizTalk Accelerator for HIPAA solution, visit

- http://www.microsoft.com/solutions/HIPAA/default.asp.

To contact Microsoft Consulting Services or to locate a Microsoft Partner with experience in designing and deploying Microsoft BizTalk Accelerator for HIPAA solutions, visit

- `http://www.microsoft.com/solutions/HIPAA/nextsteps/default.asp`

Summary

In this chapter, you learned about the basic functionality of the Microsoft BizTalk Accelerator for HIPAA. You reviewed common scenarios for deployment, learned the basics of X12 EDI messaging, and gained experience in configuring the Accelerator for HIPAA to perform EDI to XML conversions and XML to EDI conversions. You also learned how to create custom EDI preprocessors for evaluating EDI header information.

CHAPTER 25

Microsoft BizTalk Server Accelerator for RosettaNet

By Cuneyt Havlioglu

In This Chapter

Microsoft BizTalk Server Accelerator for RosettaNet provides a flexible path to reducing the cost and business impact of building a RosettaNet Implementation Framework (RNIF) presence. The powerful combination of easy-to-use tools, robust business-to-business (B2B) support, and wide-sweeping application integration components allows organizations to quickly reduce the costs of managing their supply chain.

After briefly introducing the RosettaNet standards, this chapter describes the BizTalk Accelerator for RosettaNet architecture and shows a transaction process implementation using the Accelerator.

This chapter assumes that you have general BizTalk Server knowledge. This chapter describes the Accelerator but does not go into the details of RosettaNet standards or BizTalk Server related areas.

We assume that you have a general understanding of RosettaNet standards and the Accelerator for RosettaNet. The Accelerator for RosettaNet comes with a well-described step-by-step tutorial. We will not repeat those steps here, but rather give you a broad understanding of how the Accelerator plugs on top of BizTalk Server and everything works together. You are encouraged to complete the Accelerator for RosettaNet product tutorial before continuing because most references in this chapter will be in conjunction with the tutorial. This will give you a full sense of understanding.

To keep the story intact throughout this chapter, a single scenario is used for all examples. The assumption is that we are the Home Organization. The Destination Organization is our partner. We want to implement a 3A8 Partner Interface Process (PIP) with this partner, where we, the Home Organization will have the initiator role.

What Is RosettaNet?

RosettaNet is a nonprofit consortium of more than 400 of the world's leading Information Technology, electronic components, semiconductor manufacturing, and solution provider companies working to create, implement, and promote open e-business process standards.

RosettaNet consortium defines the RNIF, a general information exchange standard. RNIF describes how a message should be exchanged in an end-to-end partner scenario. Currently, two versions of RNIF are available: RNIF 1.1 and RNIF 2.0. These frameworks differ from each other in many ways and are not compatible.

The Accelerator for RosettaNet was built for RNIF 1.1. As this chapter is being written, the next version of Accelerator for RosettaNet is under development, and it will provide support for RNIF 2.0.

The RosettaNet consortium also defines the Partner Interface Processes (PIPs). A PIP describes all details of a certain business operation flow, including the transaction flow, document schemas, rules, and restrictions.

As a whole, RNIF and PIPs construct a standard process definition for the electronic sharing of business information.

For detailed technical and related information on the RosettaNet consortium visit `RosettaNet.org`.

BizTalk Accelerator for RosettaNet and RNIF

RNIF describes a messaging framework, where different types of documents can be exchanged in a reliable manner. It provides a business flow without getting involved with the details of the transaction documents themselves. For this reason, so far RNIF has received strong acceptance by different industries, such as the electronics supplier and chemical industries. Perhaps the biggest reason for this acceptance is the speed and accuracy of automatic document exchange, hence the savings it can bring over to manual processing.

With its rich and flexible feature-set, BizTalk Server provides a perfect bed for RNIF. Accelerator for RosettaNet, a vertical add-on to BizTalk Server, makes a reliable platform for implementing RNIF solutions. Accelerator for RosettaNet includes the following:

- Messaging components
  - Custom parser, serializer, and signer for RNIF 1.1 messages
- Patterns for implementation of any PIP
- Utilities
  - Messaging Configuration Wizard, which facilitates and automates the process of creating new BizTalk messaging interfaces for a new partner relation
  - PIP Schema Manager, for incorporating new document schemas into the Accelerator
  - PIP XLANG Schedule Tester, an end-to-end process testing tool
  - PIP Administrator, for creating and managing overall partners and process flow
- Software Development Kit, for tailoring the solution to fit the custom needs.
- Detailed documentation of the solution object model and user guide

Before going into the details of the Accelerator, it is important to understand the RNIF and the underlying messaging structure. For that, the best resource is the RosettaNet organization Web site; `www.rosettanet.org`. Following is a relatively quick introduction.

RosettaNet Message Object

RNIF 1.1 describes the RosettaNet object as the entity being transferred from one partner to another on the transport layer. Figure 25.1 illustrates the structure of the RosettaNet object.

FIGURE 25.1
RosettaNet message object.

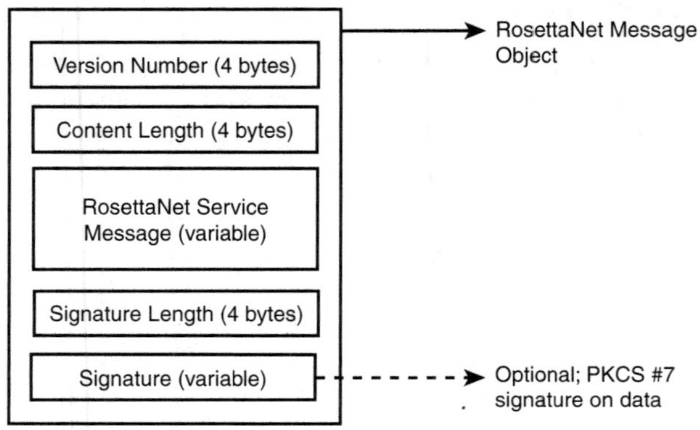

Version number indicates the RNIF version. Content length is the length of the RosettaNet Service Message. The RosettaNet Service Message is a multipart/related MIME message entity. It has three parts, namely the Preamble, Service Header, and the Service Content. Signature length is the signature length in bytes. Signature is (if it exists) PKCS #7 signature on the RosettaNet Service Message field. If there is no signature, then this field will be empty.

RosettaNet Service Message is a Multipart/Related MIME entity of the type Application/x-RosettaNet. Figure 25.2 illustrates its structure.

FIGURE 25.2
RosettaNet Service Message structure.

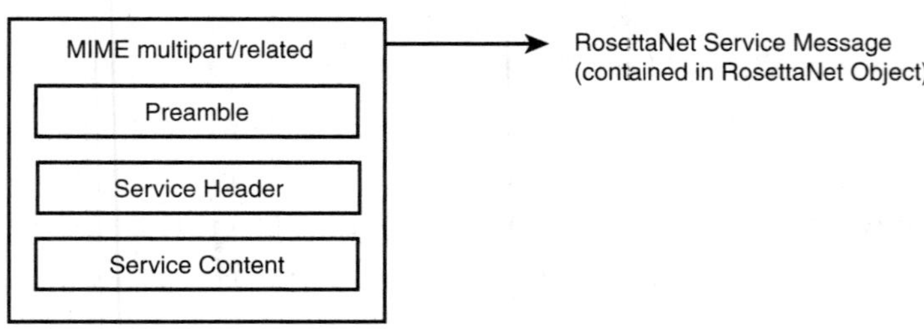

The Preamble, Service Header, and Service Content parts have the following content type information (see Table 25.1):

TABLE 25.1 RosettaNet Service Message Parts

Part	*Content Type*
Preamble	Application/XML; `RNSubType=preamble-header`
Service Header	Application/XML; `RNSubType=service-header`
Service Content	Application/XML; `RNSubType=service-content`

Architecture and Message Flow

Accelerator for RosettaNet is a vertical solution platform built as an add-on to BizTalk Server. As its name suggests, it is designed to speed up the process of getting a company to interact with RNIF transactions. At a high overview, Accelerator for RosettaNet consists of three main parts:

- Executable platform components
- Tools and utilities
- Software Development Kit (SDK)

The executable components are the parts that provide the RNIF existence. For example, the parser, which consumes incoming messages, is part of this group.

Tools and utilities are designed to help the user create and manage Trading Partner Agreements.

SDK provides the source code of the Accelerator as a sample, and it also exposes some of the object model. The SDK makes it easy to reuse the Accelerator features, so to answer custom needs of a spoke if necessary. Most of the time, the end user will not have to use the SDK.

This chapter does not go into the details of the tools, utilities, and the SDK. Accelerator for RosettaNet product documentation is a sufficient reference for those areas. We will, however, do a general architectural and implementation walkthrough. Figure 25.3 illustrates the overall design architecture of Accelerator for RosettaNet.

An inbound message comes through the transport level and finds its way to the Line of Business application at the back-end. The following subsections will describe exactly how this flow works.

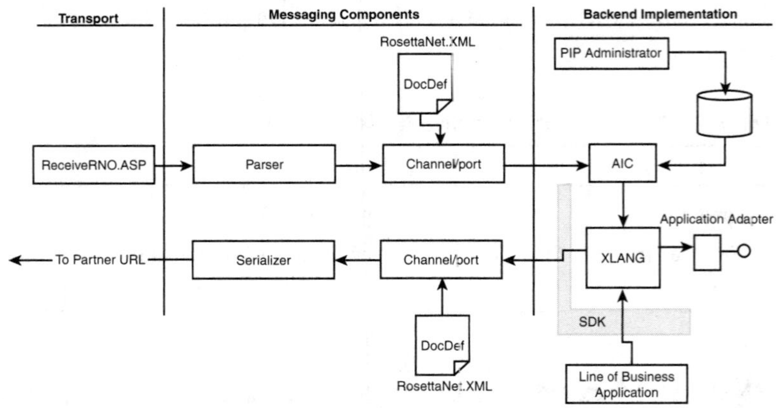

FIGURE 25.3
Accelerator for RosettaNet overall architecture.

Transport (`ReceiveRNO.ASP`)

`ReceiveRNO` is the HTTP front-end to receive inbound messages. This is where Accelerator for RosettaNet expects to receive messages from trading partners. Outbound messages are transferred by BizTalk messaging services. `ReceiveRNO.ASP` briefly checks the content type, whether it is `application/x-rosettanet-agent` or not. If so, it submits the HTTP request to BizTalk Server with the following code:

```
EntityBody = Request.BinaryRead (Request.TotalBytes )
SubmissionHandle = interchange.Submit(1, EntityBody)
```

Notice how the code reads the message as binary and submits the body to `BizTalk.Interchange` object.

`ReceiveRNO.ASP` comes with Accelerator for RosettaNet. During the installation, it does not get copied to the default IIS (Internet Information System) Web root location. You will need to manually copy it to the location where it will be available to outside partners to submit messages. If ASP access security is an issue, then this ASP page can be placed outside a firewall, and inbound messages can be forwarded from the ASP code into the secure network.

Listing 25.1 lists `ReceiveRNO.ASP` code. As you see, it is not that much code, and it is easy to modify.

LISTING 25.1 `ReceiveRNO.ASP`

```
<%
    copyright information

    declarations
```

LISTING 25.1 continued

```
   Set interchange = CreateObject( "BizTalk.Interchange" )

    ContentType = Request.ServerVariables( "CONTENT_TYPE" )

    if ( ContentType = "" or Request.TotalBytes = 0) then
        '
        ' Content-Type is required as well as an entity body
        '
        Response.Status = "406 Not Acceptable"
        Response.Write "Content-type or Entity body is missing" & VbCrlf
        Response.Write "Message headers follow below:"  & VbCrlf
        Response.Write Request.ServerVariables("ALL_RAW") & VbCrlf
        Response.End
    else
        if ( 0 = InStr( 1, ContentType, "application/x-rosettanet-agent", _
➥vbTextCompare) ) then
            Response.Status = "406 Not Acceptable"
            Response.Write "BizTalk Server RosettaNet ASP receiver _
➥rejected the document." & VbCrlf
            Response.Write "Content-type must contain _
➥application/x-rosettanet-agent" & VbCrlf
            Response.Write "Message headers follow below:"  & VbCrlf
            Response.Write Request.ServerVariables("ALL_RAW") & VbCrlf
            Response.End
        else
            EntityBody = Request.BinaryRead (Request.TotalBytes )

            SubmissionHandle = interchange.Submit(1, EntityBody)
            Set interchange = Nothing

            Response.Status = "200 OK"
            Response.End
        end if
    End if
%>
```

ASP page makes sure that the Content Type is 'application/x-rosettanet-agent' and submits the document to BizTalk Server using the Submit method using the BizTalk. Interchange interface.

RNIF 1.1 mandates using HTTP Post for message transfer. You may choose to implement your own function to receive HTTP requests (perhaps in front of a firewall using some other technology than ASP). Regardless of how you will implement this transport layer, submission to BizTalk will need to happen through BizTalk.Interchange interface as shown in Listing 25.1.

Messaging Components

After the message is submitted by `ReceiveRNO.ASP` or by any other component, BizTalk Server tries to identify the message by submitting it one-by-one to all available parsers. Accelerator for RosettaNet adds the RosettaNet Object Parser (`RNIF1_1Support.RNOParser.1`) to the pool of BizTalk Server parsers during setup. The RosettaNet Object Parser recognizes the RosettaNet object and converts the message into its XML form.

Tip

After the Accelerator for RosettaNet setup, move the RosettaNet Object Parser to the top of the parsers list. This makes the server ping RosettaNet Object Parser before other parsers and hence it will identify the document faster.

RosettaNet Object Parser converts the inbound message into its XML form. Accelerator for RosettaNet uses the XML structure shown in Listing 25.2 to represent RosettaNet messages internally.

LISTING 25.2 XML Representation of a RosettaNet Message

```
<RosettaNet>
        <Preamble>
           .Preamble part comes here.
        <ServiceHeader>
           .Service Header part comes here.
        <ServiceContent>
           .Service Content part comes here.
</RosettaNet>
```

After converting the message into its XML form, the parser then passes the message to the BizTalk pipeline along with some other information such as the sender and receiver DUNS (Data Universal Numbering System) numbers. With this information, BizTalk Server locates the correct channel and therefore the port for the message.

Channels

Before continuing to describe how the message continues to flow through the channels, let's have a look at what type of channels are created by the Accelerator.

We will create a new agreement between our Home Organization and a Destination Organization. For this we will use the Messaging Configuration Wizard. The script generated by Messaging Configuration Wizard will create five channels as shown in Table 25.2. Two of these channels are inbound channels—one for signed messages and one for unsigned. Three channels are for outbound—one for signed, one for unsigned, and one for failure.

For each channel, a generic document definition will be used. In other words, these document definitions are used by all similar channels. So for example, if we were to create another agreement between Home Organization and partner B, the same document definitions would be used there as well. There is one important aspect to note here. All these document definitions refer to the same schema called *Universal Message Schema* (`RosettaNet.XML`). Universal Message Schema embraces all implemented PIP action document definitions. See the "Content Validation" section later in the chapter for more information on the Universal Message Schema.

TABLE 25.2 Channels Created Between Home and Destination Organizations

Default Channel Name	*Document Definition*	*Port*	*Direction*
Destination to Home PIPMgr	`RosettaNetMessage_inbound_nonsigned`	Home PIPMgr in	Inbound
Destination to HomePIPMgr Signed	`RosettaNetMessage_inbound_signed`	Home PIPMgr in	Inbound
Home to Destination failure	`RosettaNetMessage_outbound_failure`	Destination failure out	Outbound
Home to Destination signed	`RosettaNetMessage_outbound_signed_action`	Destination signed out	Outbound
Home to Destination unsigned	`RosettaNetMessage_outbound_nonsigned_action`	Destination unsigned out	Outbound

Tip

After you use the Messaging Configuration Wizard, it is a good idea to browse the channels and ports using the BizTalk Messaging Manager. One by one, open and observe the settings of the channels created automatically.

Going back to our message flow, after it is parsed and submitted to BizTalk Server, the inbound message will be matched to one of these channels. Whether the message is signed or not, its source, destination and document structure are the three factors used to identify the correct channel. The corresponding channel moves the message to its assigned port without applying any modification to the message it self. In other words, the inbound document and outbound document definitions in a given channel are always set up the same.

Messaging Ports

The script generated by the Messaging Configuration Wizard will create necessary messaging ports. As shown in Table 25.2, four different ports are created for the relation we created between the Home and Destination Organizations. Table 25.3 shows the direction and primary transport settings of these ports.

TABLE 25.3 Ports Created Between Home and Destination Organizations

Port Name	*Direction*	*Primary Transport*
Home PIPMgr in	Inbound	Application Integration Component (`PIPAdapterSDK CPIPAdapterManager`)
Destination failure out	Outbound	Destination failure URL
Destination signed out	Outbound	Destination default URL
Destination unsigned out	Outbound	Destination default URL

All inbound messages are directed to the Accelerator for RosettaNet Application Integration Component (AIC). AIC will do the right matchup and direct the inbound message to the correct BizTalk Orchestration schedule. All outbound messages are directed to a URL (HTTP or File URL). The Messaging Configuration Wizard prompts the user for these URLs.

Note

The Messaging Configuration Wizard is a tool to collect the correct information for creating channels, ports, and related messaging components and settings for a partner relation. Later in this chapter, we will explain how this tool creates these components. Even though creating these messaging components is automated, it is important to know what is going on behind the scenes. This way, you can always go back to the BizTalk Messaging Manager to change the messaging components' settings.

Application Integration Component (AIC)

After the message is passed to the AIC, the AIC checks for the characteristics of the message and finds the correct BizTalk Orchestration schedule for it. This information is in the database created by the PIP Administrator tool.

> **Note**
>
> The Accelerator for RosettaNet setup lets you choose the name and location of this database during installation. By default, the Accelerator for RosettaNet uses the same database server that the BizTalk Server databases were created on.

If the message is the first document in a process, then the AIC initiates a new BizTalk Orchestration and passes along the message. However, if the message is a response, then the AIC correlates this message to an already existing BizTalk Orchestration, hydrates the BizTalk Orchestration if necessary, and passes the message along.

BizTalk Orchestration

BizTalk Orchestration provides the framework integrity by performing actions such as holding a state, automatically generating acknowledgements, and initiating retries. Accelerator for RosettaNet comes with four ready-to-use BizTalk Orchestration templates. For more information on this, refer to the "Orchestration Templates" section later in this chapter.

After the message is passed to the BizTalk Orchestration, the flow automatically sends acknowledgements, does some minor checks, and provides the necessary hook-up with the back-end system. Back-end integration is provided with an application adapter, which is a simple COM interface.

Application Adapter

An application adapter is a COM interface that gets plugged into a BizTalk Orchestration schedule. The application adapter is the gateway between the BizTalk Orchestration schedule and your back-end system. An adapter must implement one of the following interfaces depending on its role as being the initiator or the responder:

- `IPIPInitiatorApplication`
- `IPIPResponderApplication`

The definitions of these interfaces are exposed through the following type library:

```
Microsoft BizTalk Server Accelerator for RosettaNet PIP
➥Application Interfaces 1.0 Type Library
```

You will use the methods exposed by these interfaces to respond to messages and even customize the handling of some important transaction events.

Line of Business Application

Line of Business Application represents the back-end system. Throughout this chapter, we will refer to this application as the *initiator* or *responder* application as the context suggests. In either case, the application uses the Accelerator for RosettaNet SDK to communicate through the system. Later in this chapter, we will examine how an initiator or responder application uses the Accelerator for RosettaNet SDK. At the most basic description, an initiator application sends a message over to its partner organization; a responder application receives the message and responds back to the initiator.

Orchestration Templates

RNIF describes two types of processes: *transactions* and *notifications*. Transactions hold a request and a response and the corresponding acknowledgements. Notifications, however, consist of only a single message and the following acknowledgement. Considering that each implementation has an initiator and a responder side, we end up with four types of BizTalk Orchestration:

- Notification initiator
- Notification responder
- Transaction initiator
- Transaction responder

Accelerator for RosettaNet provides BizTalk Orchestration templates for all these process types. Figures 25.4, 25.5, 25.6, and 25.7 illustrate the general flow of each BizTalk Orchestration. Each of these BizTalk Orchestrations is tailored to fit into the description its name suggests. BizTalk Orchestration templates are located under the Accelerator for RosettaNet installation folder in the `PIP SDK\PIP Patterns` folder.

FIGURE 25.4
Notification initiator.

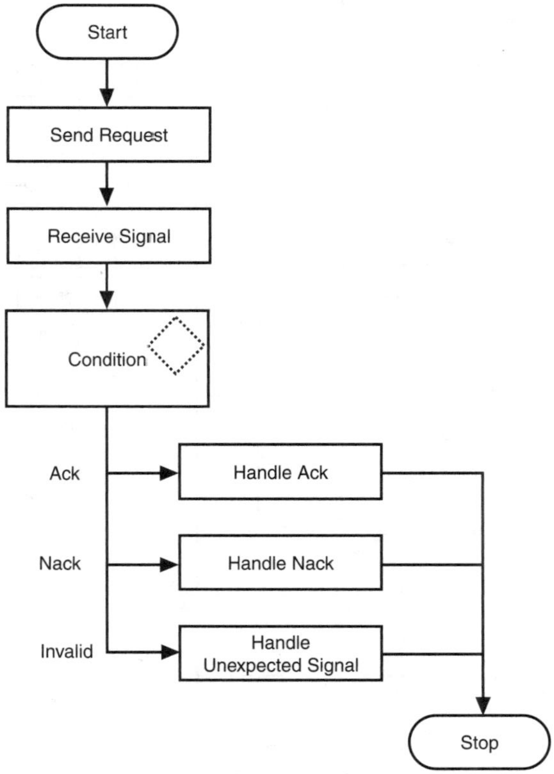

FIGURE 25.5
Notification responder.

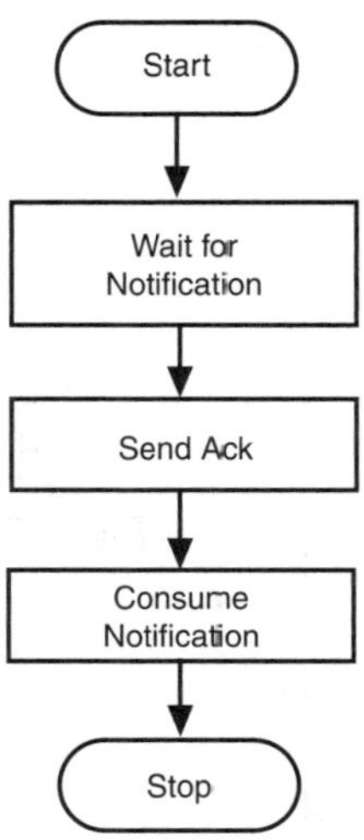

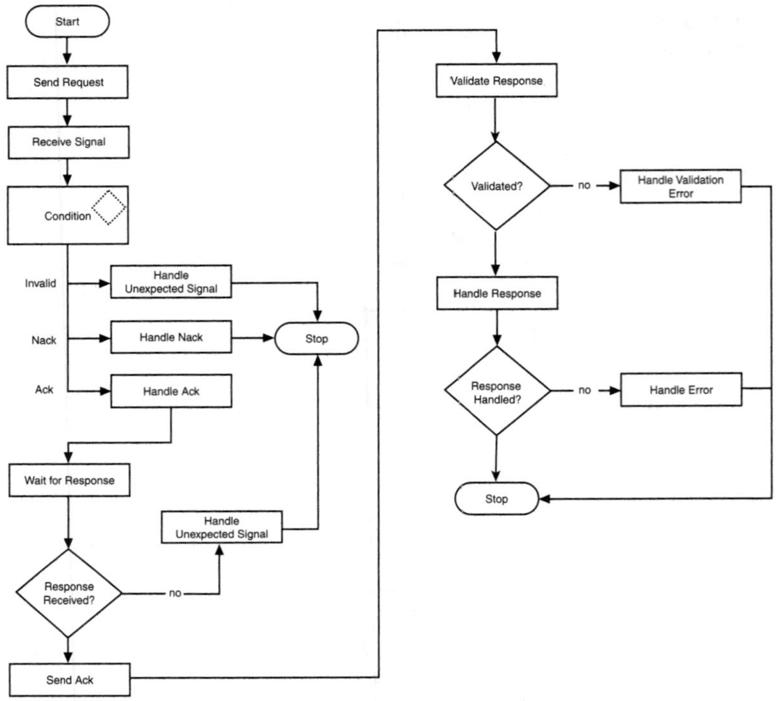

FIGURE 25.6
Transaction initiator.

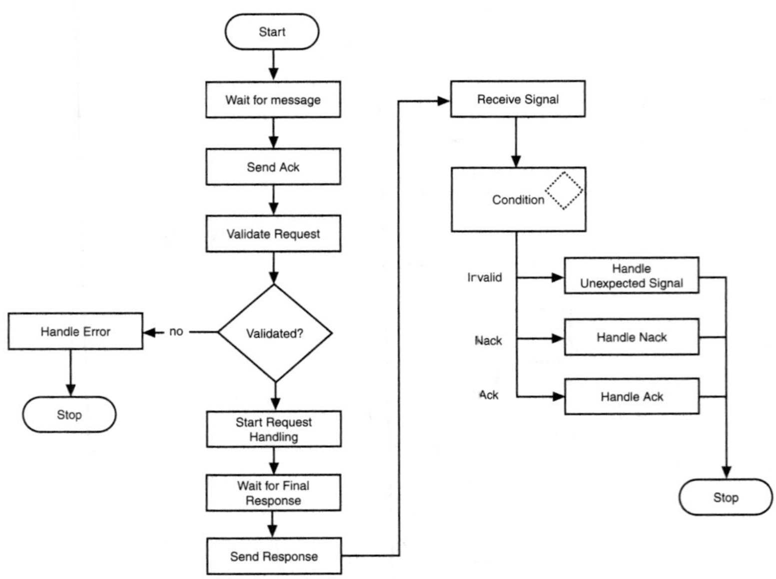

FIGURE 25.7
Transaction responder.

Messaging Configuration Wizard

As mentioned before, Accelerator for RosettaNet comes with four tools to facilitate the implementation of RNIF existence. PIP Administrator, PIP Schema Manager, Messaging Configuration Wizard, and PIP XLANG Schedule Tester.

All these utilities are easy to use, and they are explained in detail in the product documentation. However, the Messaging Configuration Wizard has particular importance.

The Messaging Configuration Wizard collects all necessary information for creating the necessary BizTalk Messaging components. When completed, it generates a Visual Basic Script file. Running this script file creates the mentioned components in return. In a case where many copies of these components need to be created, such a process can be easily automated by cloning the script created by the wizard.

In the simplest terms, the mentioned script creates the following:

- Initiator and responder organizations
- Ports for transferring messages
- Channels for routing messaging

The script generated by the Messaging Component Wizard uses the `BizTalkConfig` interface of the BizTalk class. This interface inherits from `IDispatch`.

```
Set BTConfig = CreateObject("BizTalk.BizTalkConfig")
```

The `IBizTalkConfig` interface exposes the following methods for organization, port, and channel creation:

```
IBizTalkConfig::CreateOrganization
IBizTalkConfig::CreatePort
IBizTalkConfig::CreateChannel
```

These methods make it easy to automatically create and modify numerous messaging components.

Implementing a New PIP

Accelerator for RosettaNet documentation includes an end-to-end tutorial explaining PIP implementation. This chapter does not repeat the tutorial included in the product documentation. Instead, we will concentrate on the logical flow of a message within Accelerator for RosettaNet and how all components relate to each other. Also, the product tutorial assumes that the corresponding document schemas (DTDs) have already been downloaded (from `www.rosettanet.org`) and applied to the consolidated message schema. Later in this chapter we will describe how to apply a schema to the consolidated schema. In this section, we will describe what differs if you want to implement a completely new PIP.

Overview of Implementing a New PIP

Assume that we will implement the PIP 3A8: Request Purchase Order Change process, between the Home Organization and Destination Organization, where Home Organization has the initiator role.

To make it easier to understand what needs to be implemented, let's have a look at the PIP implementation overview as shown in Figure 25.8. This figure illustrates the flow of a message from initiator, to responder, and back to initiator. With this overview, it is clear that for either side we have to think of the following six factors: LOB, XLANG schedule, application adapter, PIP registration, channels and ports, and the Universal Message Schema.

FIGURE 25.8
PIP implementation overview.

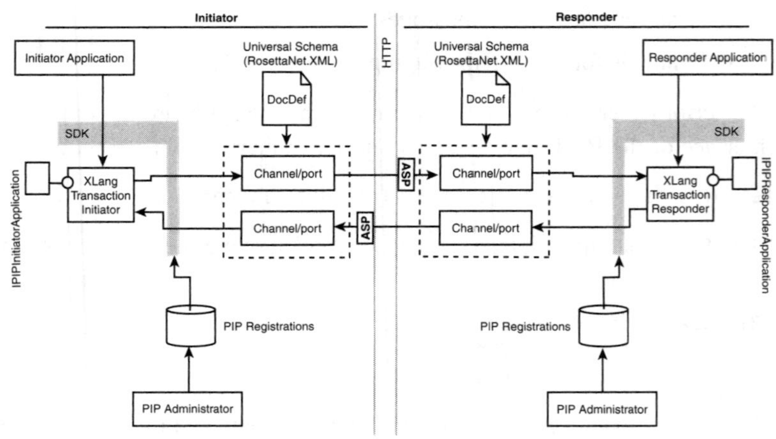

To implement this process, Home Organization, the initiator role, needs to complete the following six steps:

1. Create the 3A8 document schema. First, download PIP 3A8 Request DTD and convert it into a consolidated schema. Then merge the consolidated schema to the Universal Message Schema (RosettaNet.XML). The Accelerator for RosettaNet uses the Universal Message Schema to verify all inbound and outbound messages. This is the reason why we need to merge the DTD information into the Universal Message Schema. RosettaNet.XML is located at the default BizTalk WebDAV repository.

2. Implement the initiator application, which initiates the process and sends the request message.
3. Implement the initiator adapter, which will be plugged into the 3A8 Initiator Orchestration, to serve as the main gateway between the back-end system and the PIP.
4. Create a new BizTalk Orchestration schedule for 3A8 using the Transaction Initiator template and plug in the adapter created in the previous step to this BizTalk Orchestration.
5. Using the PIP Administrator utility, register the BizTalk Orchestration schedule created in step 4.
6. If this is the first process interface between the Home and Destination Organizations, then run the Messaging Configuration Wizard and create the necessary messaging components.

To implement this process, the Destination Organization, the responder role, also needs to do the exact same steps as Home Organization, but with some minor differences:

1. Create the 3A8 document schema. First, download PIP 3A8 Response DTD and convert it into a consolidated schema. Then merge the consolidated schema to the Universal Message Schema (RosettaNet.XML).
2. Implement the responder application, which picks up and processes the message received by the responder orchestration.
3. Implement the responder adapter, which will be plugged into the 3A8 responder BizTalk Orchestration schedule, to serve as the main gateway between the back-end system and the PIP.
4. Create a new BizTalk Orchestration schedule for 3A8 by creating a new copy of the Transaction Responder template and plug in the adapter created in step 3 to this BizTalk Orchestration.
5. Using the PIP Administrator utility, register the BizTalk Orchestration schedule created in step 4.
6. If this is the first process interface between the Home and Destination Organizations, then run the Messaging Configuration Wizard and create the necessary messaging components.

Implementing the Initiator

Now we will go into the details of how to implement the initiator side. In our example, Home Organization is the initiator and would like to implement the 3A8 process with Destination Organization.

Creating the Schema

To initiate the process, as described in the PIP 3A8 specification, the Home Organization needs to perform the Purchase Order Change Request Action. This corresponds to sending a Purchase Order Change Request document to the Destination Organization. We first need to create the document schema for this action. Following steps describe how to do that:

1. Import the DTD for 3A8 Purchase Order Change Request into the BizTalk Schema Editor and save it as a *.XML file (make sure that the encoding selection is UTF-8).
   You can download the DTD files for and PIP actions from `www.rosettanet.org`. Let's assume that you named the file `3A8Request.XML`.

   This will convert the DTD into a BizTalk schema. Note that, through this conversion, Schema Editor will ignore the DTD groups and condition statements.

2. Using the PIP Schema Manager tool, create the 3A8 consolidated message. Use the following settings:

Document specification to merge from	`3A8Request.XML`
Document specification to merge to	`<A4RN installation folder>\PIP SDK\SDK Repository\DocSpecs\ConsolidatedMessage.xml`
Output file	`*.XML` Let's assume that you name this `3A8ConsolidatedMessage.XML`
Operation type	From imported RosettaNet DTD XML schema to Consolidated RosettaNet Message

3. Using the PIP Schema Manager again, now merge `3A8ConsolidatedMessage.XML` to the Universal Message schema. Use the following settings:

Document specification to merge from	`3A8ConsolidatedMessage.XML`
Document specification to merge to	`<A4RN installation folder>\PIP SDK\SDK Repository\DocSpecs\RosettaNetMessage.xml` (By default, setup installs this `RosettaNetMessage.XML` file as the global schema and stores it in the BizTalk WebDav schema repository, which is by default located at `<BizTalk installation folder>\BizTalkServerRepository`)

Output file	`*.XML` Let's assume that you name this `NewRosettaNetMessage.XML`
Operation type	From Consolidated RosettaNet Message to BizTalk Messaging RosettaNet Universal Message

4. To update the Universal Message schema, save `NewRosettaNetMessage.XML` to the BizTalk WebDav schema repository as `RosettaNet.XML`. It is important that you name this file `RosettaNet.XML` because all other related messaging components are already configured for this name, and they will complain if it doesn't exist in the WebDav repository.

Implementing the Initiator Application

To deliver the request message, the initiator application makes two calls to the `CPIPAdapterManager` interface of the PIPAdapterSDK component:

```
CPIPAdapterManager::StartActivity
CPIPAdapterManager::DeliverInitiationMessage
```

Listing 25.3 shows a simplified piece of code showing the general structure of the initiator application.

LISTING 25.3 Initiator Application

```
Dim PIPAdapterManager As PIPAdapterSDK.CPIPAdapterManager
    Dim strFlowID, strDocument As String


    Set PIPAdapterManager = CreateObject("PIPAdapterSDK.CPIPAdapterManager")

    'Initiate orchestration
    strFlowID = PIPAdapterManager.StartActivity( _
        "3A8", "Purchase Order Change Request", _
        "Request", "Production", _
        "Purchase Order Change Request", _
        False, _
           GenerateUniqueID(), _
        GetDUNSNumber('Home'), GetDUNSNumber('Destination'), _
        strDocument)

    'strFlowID is now a moniker to the orchestration instance

    'strDocument includes skeletal consolidate message with Preamble and
    'Service Header elements filled. Service Content is left empty
```

LISTING 25.3 continued

```
    '>>> fill the Service Content in strDocument

    'Deliver Message
    PIPAdapterManager.DeliverInitiationMessage strFlowID, _
➥"NoCertificate", strDocument

    Set PIPAdapterManager = Nothing
```

The `StartActivity` method call initiates a BizTalk Orchestration and returns the BizTalk Orchestration moniker to `strFlowId`. We will use this moniker to hold the correspondence to the BizTalk Orchestration. The `StartActivity` method call will also fill the `strDocument` variable with a skeletal *consolidated message*. A consolidated message is an XML message stream consisting of three main elements of a RosettaNet message: namely, Preamble, Service Header, and Service Content. The `StartActivity` method fills the Preamble and Service Content sections automatically, but leaves the Service Content empty. We need to fill the Service Content section in the code. When the Service Content section is completed, the initiator application calls `DeliverInitiationMessage`. At this call, `strDocument` is the message to be sent. The `strFlowID` parameter corresponds to the previously initiated BizTalk Orchestration so that the SDK knows where to pass the message.

Implementing the Initiator Adapter

For the initiator adapter, you need to implement the `IPIPInitiatorApplication` interface. You will need to reference to the following type library to have this interface known by Visual Basic:

```
Microsoft BizTalk Server Accelerator for RosettaNet PIP Application Interfaces
        1.0 Type Library
```

This interface exposes nine methods. Listing 25.4 shows the skeleton of an example code using Visual Basic. The method parameters are not shown in this example.

LISTING 25.4 `IPIPInitiatorApplication` Interface Implementation

```
Implements IPIPInitiatorApplication

Private Sub IPIPInitiatorApplication_HandleError(parameters)
End Sub

Private Sub IPIPInitiatorApplication_HandleResponseMessage(parameters)
End Sub

Private Sub IPIPInitiatorApplication_HandleRNException(parameters)
End Sub
```

LISTING 25.4 continued

```
Private Sub IPIPInitiatorApplication_HandleRNReceiptAcknowledgementException_
➥(parameters)
End Sub

Private Sub IPIPInitiatorApplication_HandleRNReceiptAcknowledgment(parameters)
End Sub

Private Sub IPIPInitiatorApplication_HandleUnexpectedResponse(parameters)
End Sub

Private Sub IPIPInitiatorApplication_HandleUnexpectedSignal(parameters)
End Sub

Private Sub IPIPInitiatorApplication_InitializeRequestMessage(parameters)
End Sub

Private Sub IPIPInitiatorApplication_ValidateResponseMessage()
End Sub
```

`IPIPInitiatorApplication` provides a single interface to the BizTalk Orchestration schedule to interact with the back-end Line of Business application.

At the minimum, the interface must implement the `HandleResponseMessage` method. After the response comes back from the Destination Organization, the BizTalk Orchestration calls this method and passes along the response message. At this point, you may ask how the Destination Organization sends the message back. It should not really matter how the Destination Organization does this. The only thing we need to know is that the response comes through our transport layer (ReceiveRNO.ASP), then goes through the messaging components, and eventually finds its way to the Initiator Adaptor. `HandleResponseMessage` is the place where you need to capture the response. The example shown in Listing 25.5 saves the response message as `ResponseMessage.XML` into the application working folder.

LISTING 25.5 `HandleResponseMessage` Implementation Example

```
Private Sub IPIPInitiatorApplication_HandleResponseMessage(p_strFlowID _
➥As String, _
p_strRequestMessage As String, _
          p_strResponseMessage As String, _
          p_strErrDesc As String)
    Dim XMLDOM As New DOMDocument

    'load the response into XMLDOM
    XMLDOM.loadXML p_strResponseMessage
```

LISTING 25.5 continued

```
    'save the response into the applicatio folder
    XMLDOM.save "ResponseMessage.XML"
End Sub
```

As such, you will need to implement all other methods—for example, `HandleRNException` to catch exceptions, `ValidateResponseMessage` if you want to do an extra validation on the response message before passing it to your backend system, or `HandleRNReceiptAcknowledgement` to get a handle to the acknowledge signal sent by the Destination Organization.

Initiator Orchestration

3A8 is a transaction type process—in other words, it defines a request and the corresponding response message. Therefore, for the initiator side, we should use a Transaction Initiator type of BizTalk Orchestration.

BizTalk Orchestration templates are located under the Accelerator for RosettaNet installation folder, in the `PIP SDK\PIP Patterns` folder. To create a new BizTalk Orchestration for 3A8 initiator, do the following:

1. Create a copy of the `TransactionInitiator.SKV` file and rename it `3A8Initiator.SKV`.
2. Open `3A8Initiator.SKV` and change the stub adapter with your adapter.

(You can find a detailed description of these steps in Accelerator for RosettaNet documentation in the Binding the Application Adapter to the XLANG Schedule page.)

3. Find the `PIPApplicationInterfacesLib.StubInitiatorApplication` shape and double-click on it. This starts the COM Component Binding Wizard. Follow the steps in the wizard.
4. In the Class Information page, choose From a Registered Component and select the initiator adapter you created earlier.
5. Make sure that you select all methods in the Method Information page.
6. Finish the wizard.

Bind the schedule to `SendRNMessage` method as follows:

1. Find `SendRequestPort`. This port sends its messages to MSMQ. However, we want it to send its messages to `SendRNMessage` component.
2. Move the incoming messages of `SendRequestPort` to `RNSendPort`:
    - `SentRequestMessage` to `SendRNMessage_in`
    - `SentAckMessage` to `SendRNMessage_in_2`

Change the data page so that it reflects the change we have just made:

1. Go to `RNSendPort`.
2. For each pipe, right-click on it and select Show on Data Page.
3. When the data page appears, move the data flow arrows from
   - `SentRequestMessage` to `SendRNMessage_in`
   - `SentAckMessage` to `SendRNMessage_in_2`

Save the file and compile it into an executable XLANG schedule by selecting File, Make from the menu.

Register the BizTalk Orchestration Schedule

Next step is to let the Accelerator for RosettaNet know about this new BizTalk Orchestration schedule, so that when it needs to send a 3A8 request message, it will know which BizTalk Orchestration schedule to use. For that, we will use PIP Administrator.

Start PIP Administrator and select the Register New XLANG Schedule action. Complete the registration with the entries as shown in Table 25.4.

TABLE 25.4 Entries for the Initiator XLANG Schedule Registration

XLANG Schedule	Browse to the BizTalk Orchestration you created in the previous step.
Global Process Indicator Code	Type **3A8**.
Global Process Code	Type **Request Purchase Order Change**.
Global Business Action Code	Type **Purchase Order Change Request**.
Initiating Role Executes This Schedule	Because this is the initiator role, select this check box.

> **Note**
>
> Global Process Code and Global Business Action Code values given here are as interpreted from the currently published PIP 3A8 – Request Purchase Order Change R01.0100B specification. These values represent the corresponding elements in the RosettaNet message. To prevent interoperability glitches, it would be recommended for the Home Organization to first agree with the Destination Organization on the values of these fields. Not everybody interprets the specifications in the same way.

Messaging Components

The Messaging Configuration Wizard is a useful tool for automatically creating all necessary messaging components. For each partner pair, the wizard just needs to be run once.

To create the necessary channels, ports, organization definitions, and related settings between the Home and Destination Organizations, you will need to provide the information shown in Table 25.5.

TABLE 25.5 Messaging Settings for Home to Destination Relation

Source Organization	
Name	Home If this organization does not exist, a new organization record will be created for Home.
DUNS Number	Type in the DUNS Number of Home Organization. If the Home Organization already has a DUNS number, then it will be displayed here. Otherwise, the number you entered will be assigned to the Home Organization as the DUNS number.
Certificate	Select the certificate for Home Organization. The certificate must be previously loaded on BizTalk Server. Refer to BizTalk Server documentation for how to load a certificate.
Destination Organization	
Name	Destination If this organization does not exist, a new organization record will be created for the destination.
DUNS Number	Type in the DUNS Number of Destination Organization. Just as in the Home Organization, if the Destination Organization already has a DUNS number, then it will be displayed here. Otherwise, the number you entered will be assigned to the Home Organization as the DUNS number.
URL Default Message / Signal	This is the URL Destination expects the regular messages and signals to arrive. If the Destination Organization uses the Accelerator for RosettaNet, then this URL would point to their ReceiveRNO.ASP page.

TABLE 25.5 continued

Destination Organization	
URL Failure Notification	This is the URL the Destination expects to receive failure notifications Using a different URL path for failure is a good practice, because if the main URL is broken, then it is likely that the failure notification URL is still active. This URL also points to ReceiveRNO.ASP, preferablly on another physical HTTP server.
Channels and Ports	This page shows you the channels and ports that will be created for communication between the Home and Destination organizations. Review the names of the channels and ports and click Next.
VB Script File	The wizard will generate a VBScript file. This script will be used to create the mentioned organizations, channels and ports. Review the name and location of the script to be created and finish the wizard.

After the wizard is complete, running it creates all necessary messaging components for the Home and Destination Organizations to talk to each other. Basically, this script creates the channels and ports as described earlier in Table 25.1.

Implementing the Responder

As described earlier in the "Overview of Implementing a new PIP" section, the responder implementation requires the same steps as the initiator implementation but with some minor differences. The differences are due to the fact that responder needs to wait for a document and then send a response. In conjunction, the back-end integration also needs to be slightly different.

Creating the Schema

To respond to a 3A8 request, the Destination Organization needs to perform the Purchase Order Change Confirmation Action. This action corresponds to replying with a Purchase Order Confirmation Request document. For that, a 3A8 response consolidated schema needs to be created and merged into the Universal Message Schema.

The necessary steps for doing this are exactly the same with what we did for the initiator. We will not repeat the steps here. The only difference is the DTD file that is being merged.

For the responder side, we will be using the DTD for 3A8 Purchase Order Confirmation Request document. As are all PIP DTDs, this one is also available for download from `RosettaNet.org`.

Implementing the Responder Adapter

The responder application adapter must implement the `IPIPResponderApplication` interface. You will need a reference to the following type library to have this interface known by VB:

```
Microsoft BizTalk Server Accelerator for RosettaNet PIP Application Interfaces
        1.0 Type Library
```

This interface exposes six methods. Listing 25.6 shows the skeleton of an example using Visual Basic. The method parameters are not shown in this example.

LISTING 25.6 `IPIPResponderApplication` Interface Implementation

```
Implements IPIPResponderApplication

Private Sub IPIPResponderApplication_HandleError(parameters)
End Sub

Private Sub IPIPResponderApplication_HandleRNReceiptAcknowledgementException _
➥(parameters)
End Sub

Private Sub IPIPResponderApplication_HandleRNReceiptAcknowledgment(parameters)
End Sub

Private Sub IPIPResponderApplication_HandleUnexpectedSignal(parameters)
End Sub

Private Sub IPIPResponderApplication_StartRequestHandling(parameters)
End Sub

Private Sub IPIPResponderApplication_ValidateRequestMessage(parameters)
End Sub
```

At a minimum, the interface must implement the `HandleResponseMessage` method. BizTalk Orchestration calls this method and passes along the response message. This is the place where you need to capture the message. Listing 25.7 shows an example of how to do that. In this example, we save the `p_strFlowID`, `p_strRequestMessage`, and `p_strSkeletalResponseMessage` parameters.

- `p_strFlowID` is the moniker to the responder schedule, which invoked this method. The responder application will have to use this moniker when replying back.
- `p_strRequestMessage` is the incoming message in its XML form.
- `p_strSkeletalResponseMessage` is a RosettaNet Message XML stream with the Preamble and Service Header already filled in for you. The Service Content area is left blank.

The responder application needs to pick up these three files, generate a response message, and deliver it back to the BizTalk Orchestration with the `p_strFlowID` unique moniker.

In this chapter, we are not going into the gory details of how to implement the rest of the methods exposed with this interface. It is straightforward. You will have to implement all these methods for a correct implementation.

LISTING 25.7 Handling Requests in the Responder Adapter

```
Private Sub IPIPResponderApplication_StartRequestHandling _
➥(p_strFlowID As String, _
p_strRequestMessage As String, _
          p_strSkeletalResponseMessage As String, _
          p_strErrDesc As String)

       StrToFile "<FlowID>" & p_strFlowID & "</FlowID>", "FlowID.XML"
    StrToFile p_strRequestMessage, "RequestMessage.xml"
    StrToFile p_strSkeletalResponseMessage, "SkeletalResponseMessage.xml"
End Sub

Private Sub StrToFile(strStr as String, strFName as String)
    save strStr as strFName
End Sub
```

Implementing the Responder Application

The responder application needs to pick up the three files dropped by the responder adapter, generate a valid response document, and deliver it back to the responder BizTalk Orchestration.

To deliver the response message back to the BizTalk Orchestration, the responder application makes one method call `CPIPAdapterManager` interface of the `PIPAdapterSDK` component:

`CPIPAdapterManager::DeliverResponseMessage`

Listing 25.8 is an example of a simple response application. The Preamble and Service Header nodes of the skeletal message were already completed automatically by Accelerator for RosettaNet at the time the responder adapter saved the `SkeletalResponseMessage.XML`. The application needs to fill the Service Content and call the `DeliverResponseMessage` method to send the response back.

To fill the Service Content, though, you will have to do some coding. One recommendation would be having a template 3A8 Service Content ready. You can then paste this template into the skeletal message and then fill in the XML element values as you want.

LISTING 25.8 Response Application Example

```
Private Sub cmdDeliverResponse_Click(Index As Integer)
    Dim XMLDOM As New DOMDocument
    Dim PIPAdapterManager As PIPAdapterSDK.CPIPAdapterManager
    Dim FlowID As String
    Dim SkeletalMessage As String

    Set PIPAdapterManager = CreateObject("PIPAdapterSDK.CPIPAdapterManager")

    XMLDOM.async = False

    'get the flow ID
    XMLDOM.Load "FlowID.xml"
    FlowID = XMLDOM.documentElement.Text

    'get the skeletal message
    XMLDOM.Load "SkeletalResponseMessage.xml"
    SkeletalMessage = XMLDOM.xml

    Fill in the Service Content node of the skeletal message

    Call PIPAdapterManager.DeliverResponseMessage(FlowID, SkeletalMessage)

    Set PIPAdapterManager = Nothing
    Set XMLDOM = Nothing
End Sub
```

Responder Orchestration

As discussed before, 3A8 is a Transaction type process. Therefore, for the responder side, we will be using a Transaction Responder type of BizTalk Orchestration here.

Create a copy of the `TransactionResponder.SKV` file and rename it `3A8Responder.SKV`. Just as we did for the initiator BizTalk Orchestration, change the stub adapter with your adapter.

Bind the schedule to `SendRNMessage` method. This procedure is little bit different from the initiator. The difference is the name of the MSMQ port.

1. Find the `RNMsgOutAck` port. This port sends its messages to MSMQ. Change this to the `SendRNMessage` method.
2. Move the incoming messages of `SendRequestPort` to `RNSendPort`
    - `RosettaNetMessageAck` to `SendRNMessage_in`
    - `SentResponseMessage` to `SendRNMessage_in_2`

Change the data page so that it reflects the change we have just made:

1. Go to `RNSendPort`.
2. For each pipe, right-click and select Show on Data Page.
3. When the data page appears, move the data flow arrows from
    - `RosettaNetMessageAck` to `SendRNMessage_in`
    - `SentResponseMessage` to `SendRNMessage_in_2`

Save the file and compile it into an executable XLANG schedule by selecting File, Make from the menu.

Register the orchestration

The next step is to register the 3A8 responder BizTalk Orchestration using the PIP Administrator utility.

Start the PIP Administrator and select Register New XLANG Schedule action. Complete the registration with the entries as shown in Table 25.6.

TABLE 25.6 Entries for the Initiator XLANG Schedule Registration

XLANG Schedule	Browse to the BizTalk Orchestration you created in the previous step.
Global Process Indicator Code	Type **3A8**.
Global Process Code	Type **Request Purchase Order Change**.

TABLE 25.6 continued

Global Business Action Code	Type **Purchase Order Change Request**. This indicates the request code that we are replying to.
Initiating Role Executes This Schedule	This is the responder side. So leave this not checked.

Messaging Components

We will need to run the Messaging Configuration Wizard once again, this time to create the messaging components where the Destination Organization is the source organization. We will select Destination as the source organization and Home as the destination organization. Complete the wizard and run the script generated. The script creates the channels and ports listed in Table 25.7—just like the initiator side, but this time in the opposite direction.

TABLE 25.7 Messaging Settings for Destination to Home Relation

Default Channel Name	*Document Definition*	*Port*
Home to Destination PIPMgr	`RosettaNetMessage_inbound_nonsigned`	Destination PIPMgr in
Home to Destination PIPMgr Signed	`RosettaNetMessage_inbound_signed`	Destination PIPMgr in
Destination to Home failure	`RosettaNetMessage_outbound_failure`	Home failure out
Destination to Home signed	`RosettaNetMessage_outbound_signed_action`	Home signed out
Destination to Home unsigned	`RosettaNetMessage_outbound_nonsigned_action`	Home unsigned out

Sending and Receiving Signals

Accelerator for RosettaNet handles signals automatically from within the BizTalk Orchestrations. As examined earlier, both initiator and responder adapter interfaces include methods for handling acknowledgements. There are three obvious questions here:

- Timing—How does the Accelerator for RosettaNet know when to send them?
- Message composition—How do the signal messages get composed?
- Messaging—How are the signals sent?

The Accelerator for RosettaNet uses BizTalk Orchestration schedules to handle message flow and state. When a message is received, the BizTalk Orchestration schedule describes how to send an acknowledgement. For example, have a look at the beginning of a Transaction Responder orchestration in Figure 25.9. After the activation message arrives, the schedule calls the `CreateReceiptAcknowledgementMessage` method. This method takes the inbound message and runs it through the `RNMsgToAckAll.xml` map to generate the corresponding acknowledgement message. This map and all others are installed to the following location:

```
<Accelerator for RosettaNet installation folder>\PIP SDK\SDK Repository\Maps
```

FIGURE 25.9
Transaction Responder schedule.

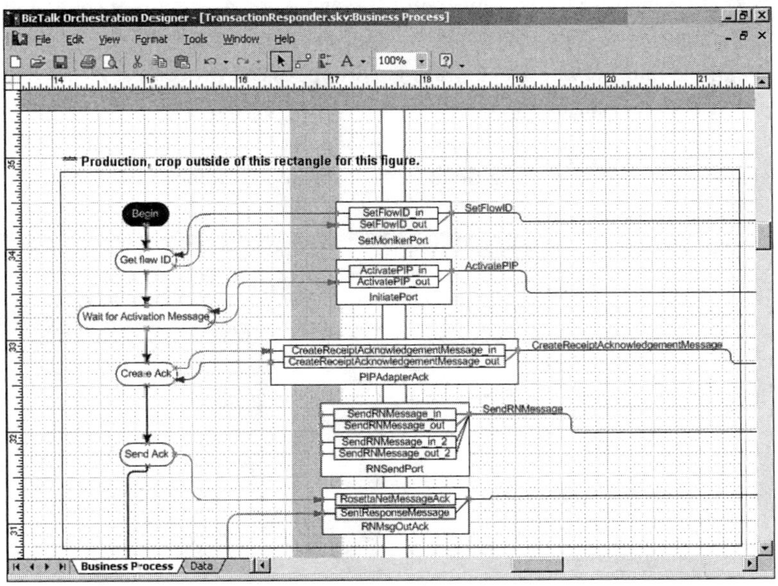

Just like this example, there are several other places in the BizTalk Orchestration schedule where `CPIPAdapter` gets called to create a signal message. All these calls will use the maps located in the location given previously. Therefore, if a signal pattern needs to change, modifying the corresponding map in the said repository will be sufficient.

After the signal message is built, the BizTalk Orchestration schedule asks the `CPIPAdapter` to send it. This will be done by a normal Submit call to BizTalk Server. Just as with any other message, BizTalk Server will match the signal message to one of the channels. In this case, the channel will be one of the signal channels created by the Messaging Configuration Wizard. The channel will receive and forward the signal message to the corresponding partner URL.

This is a fairly easy process, and you do not really have to modify anything about it. Knowing how the signals are sent is a good piece of information, though.

Content Validation

The Accelerator for RosettaNet uses a Universal Message schema for validating all messages going through its channels. This Universal Message schema contains document validation information for Service Content of all PIP action documents and Preamble and Service Header parts.

Figure 25.10 shows how the Universal Message Schema looks like when opened with BizTalk Schema Editor. Universal Message is a single `<RosettaNet>` node, which has three sub nodes `<Preamble>`, `<Service Header>`, and `<Service Content>`. The Preamble and Service Header are generic between processes. However, Service Content varies between different actions. For that reason, the Service Content node includes several subnodes, each describing the service content of a particular document, literally the DTD of the corresponding document described by `RosettaNet.org`.

FIGURE 25.10
Universal Message Schema (`RosettaNet.XML`).

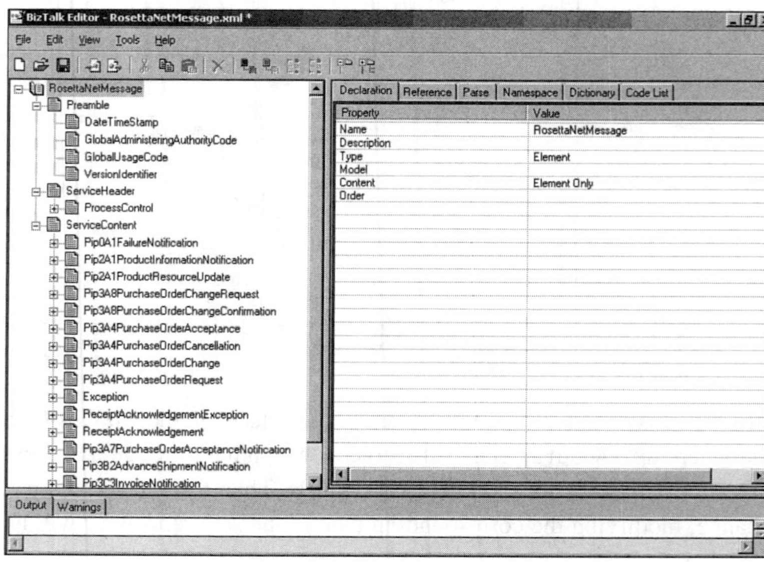

This approach has advantages and disadvantages. Perhaps the biggest advantage is the capability to use only one schema for all actions. On the other hand, there is one disadvantage, which is a result of merging all Service Content DTDs into one big schema—that is, losing validation strength as you add more document schemas into the Universal

Message Schema. The reason is simple. In a BizTalk document schema definition, each element is represented by a single top-level node, such as:

```
<ElementType name="myelement" content="eltOnly" model="closed">
  <b:RecordInfo />
  <element type="FreeFormText" maxOccurs="1" minOccurs="1" />
</ElementType>
```

The `Element Type` name must be unique in the schema. This means that `myelement` cannot be used in more than one document in a different way. All documents using `myelement` will have to use it as described in the preceding example.

CIDX Chem eStandards

Chem eStandards are XML-based interchange document standards endorsed by the Chemical Industry Data Exchange (CIDX) organization. CIDX intended Chem eStandards for introducing an eBusiness automation into the chemical industry world. Chem eStandards describe the document schemas, but they inherit the enveloping and security standards from RNIF version 1.1.

For a Chem eStandards implementation, adopting RNIF means, being able to read and generate documents packaged in an RNIF-compliant envelope, which is multipart related MIME format.

The Accelerator for RosettaNet, with its open architecture, is a ready-to-use platform for implementing Chem eStandards communications.

The current version of Accelerator for RosettaNet can accept and deliver Chem eStandards messages. At the time of this writing, a CIDX Chem eStandards SDK is under development, and it will be available for download as you are reading this chapter. Refer to `www.microsoft.com/biztalk` for details.

For more information on CIDX, refer to `www.CIDX.org`.

Accelerator for RosettaNet Version 2.0

At the time of this writing, the Accelerator for RosettaNet version 2.0 is under development. As an upgrade to the version discussed throughout this chapter, version 2.0 brings a lot of new features:

- Simultaneous support for RNIF 1.1 and RNIF 2.0.
- Easy Trading Partner Agreement creation. While staying compatible with the current implementation, Version 2.0 will simplify the PIP implementation. All PIPs published so far by `RosettaNet.Org` will be implemented out of the box. This means that you don't need to worry about how the PIP works. The only work you will need to do is provide the integration with the back-end system.
- With version 2.0, it will be possible to conduct synchronous or asynchronous processes.
- Version 2.0 will fully incorporate and support the CIDX Chem eStandards SDK.
- Version 2.0 will use generic schedules for all same type transactions. This means that you will not have to create a new schedule for each process implementation.

Summary

As an add-on to BizTalk Server, BizTalk Accelerator for RosettaNet provides out-of-the-box RNIF presence, allowing reliable RosettaNet and CIDX Chem eStandards message exchange.

The Accelerator for RosettaNet should not be considered a closed solution. As a result of being an add-on to BizTalk Server, it is possible to integrate Accelerator for RosettaNet with the legacy back-end systems, which are already being supported by various BizTalk adapters and plug-ins.

As of this writing, the accelerator supports RNIF 1.1; however, we expect version 2.0 to support both RNIF 1.1 and RNIF 2.0 simultaneously.

Updated accelerator information can be obtained from the Microsoft BizTalk Web site at `www.microsoft.com/biztalk/accelerators/`.

Appendixes

In This Part

APPENDIX A

Understanding XML Schemas

At the heart of a BizTalk specification is something known as *XML schema*. At the highest level, XML schemas provide a means for defining the structure, content, and semantics of XML documents. To make this more meaningful, take a look at Listing A.1, a typical XML document.

LISTING A.1 An XML Document—`Transactions.xml`

```
<?xml version="1.0"?>
<Transactions location="Federal Credit Union" type="checking">
 <Transaction id="ABCD-01234" date="02/02/2001">
  <Amount currency="usd">-41.50</Amount>
  <Type>ATM Withdrawal</Type>
  <Facility>ATM # VA555555</Facility>
  <Location>
   <Name>VA55555 Jans Grocery</Name>
   <Address>555 Main Street</Address>
  </Location>
 </Transaction>
<Transaction id="ABCD-00123" date="02/01/2001">
  <Amount currency="usd">-23.99</Amount>
  <Type>POS Withdrawal</Type>
  <Facility>POS # A3457CD CGI</Facility>
  <Location>
   <Name>Joes Pizza Parlor</Name>
   <Address>560 Main Street</Address>
  </Location>
 </Transaction>
</Transactions>
```

This XML instance describes a number of banking transactions processed through a financial institution. A schema can be used to define this document so that others—for example, a trading partner or paying customer—can enable their applications to process this document correctly. Several different schema languages are available—XDR, XSD, and DTDs to name three. Listing A.2 displays the XML Data Reduced version of the schema for this file.

LISTING A.2 The Transaction XML XDR Schema

```
<?xml version="1.0"?>
<!-- Generated by using BizTalk Editor on Sat, Nov 17 2001 06:00:49 PM -->
<!-- Copyright  Microsoft Corporation. All rights reserved. -->
<Schema xmlns="urn:schemas-microsoft-com:xml-data" name='Transaction"
➥xmlns:d="urn:schemas-microsoft-com:datatypes">
➥<ElementType name="Type" content="textOnly" model="closed"
➥d:type="string">
</ElementType><ElementType name="Transaction" content="eltOnly" model="closed">
<element type="Amount" maxOccurs="1" minOccurs="0"/>
```

LISTING A.2 continued

```
<element type="Type" maxOccurs="1" minOccurs="0"/>
<element type="Facility" maxOccurs="1" minOccurs="0"/>
<element type="Location" maxOccurs="1" minOccurs="1"/>
</ElementType><ElementType name="Name" content="textOnly" model="closed"
➥d:type="string">
</ElementType><ElementType name="Location" content="eltOnly" model="closed">
<element type="Name" maxOccurs="1" minOccurs="0"/>
<element type="Address" maxOccurs="1" minOccurs="0"/>
</ElementType><ElementType name="Facility" content="textOnly" model="closed"
➥ d:type="string">
</ElementType><ElementType name="Amount" content="textOnly" model="closed"
➥ d:type="float">
</ElementType><ElementType name="Address" content="textOnly" model="closed"
➥d:type="string">
</ElementType></Schema>
```

Listing A.3 displays the XSD schema describing the same XML transaction document.

LISTING A.3 The Transaction XML XSD Schema

```
<?xml version="1.0" encoding="UTF-16"?>
<!--
  [XDR-XSD] This schema automatically updated from an IE5-compatible
➥XDR schema to W3C
  XML Schema by xdr-xsd-converter.xslt 1.5, available from Microsoft.
  See http://msdn.microsoft.com/xml.

  Note: if a local copy of XMLSchema.dtd and datatypes.dtd are not
  available, use the official location of
➥"http://www.w3.org/2000/10/XMLSchema.dtd"
  for the system id.
-->
<xs:schema version="1.0" xmlns:xs="http://www.w3.org/2001/XMLSchema">
    <xs:annotation>
        <xs:documentation>Schema name: Transaction</xs:documentation>
    </xs:annotation>
    <!-- [XDR-XSD] "Type" element  -->
    <xs:element name="Type" type="xs:string">
    </xs:element>
    <!-- [XDR-XSD] "Transaction" element  -->
    <xs:element name="Transaction">
        <xs:complexType>
            <xs:choice minOccurs="0" maxOccurs="unbounded">
                <xs:element ref="Amount" minOccurs="0"/>
                <xs:element ref="Type" minOccurs="0"/>
                <xs:element ref="Facility" minOccurs="0"/>
                <xs:element ref="Location"/>
```

LISTING A.3 continued

```
            </xs:choice>
        </xs:complexType>
    </xs:element>
    <!-- [XDR-XSD] "Name" element  -->
    <xs:element name="Name" type="xs:string">
    </xs:element>
    <!-- [XDR-XSD] "Location" element  -->
    <xs:element name="Location">
        <xs:complexType>
            <xs:choice minOccurs="0" maxOccurs="unbounded">
                <xs:element ref="Name" minOccurs="0"/>
                <xs:element ref="Address" minOccurs="0'/>
            </xs:choice>
        </xs:complexType>
    </xs:element>
    <!-- [XDR-XSD] "Facility" element  -->
    <xs:element name="Facility" type="xs:string">
    </xs:element>
    <!-- [XDR-XSD] "Amount" element  -->
    <xs:element name="Amount" type="xs:float">
    </xs:element>
    <!-- [XDR-XSD] "Address" element  -->
    <xs:element name="Address" type="xs:string">
    </xs:element>
    <!-- [XDR-XSD] XDR datatype derivations -->
</xs:schema>
```

Note

BizTalk Server currently supports a subset of the recently ratified XML Schema language (XSD) named XML Data Reduced (XDR). It is important to understand that there is a fundamental difference between *XML schemas* and the *XML Schema* language. XML schemas define the structure of an XML document using an XML Schema language. The XSD Schema language (XSD) will be supported in future versions of BizTalk Server. Presently, Microsoft BizTalk Server supports XSD documents using an XDR to XSD command-line utility.

Before we begin to discuss the technical specifics of XML schema languages let's take a look at the history behind them.

History of XML Schemas

In Chapter 2, "XML and Related Technologies," you learned that XML is a subset of SGML. SGML uses something known as a Document Type Definition (DTD), for defining the structure of an SGML application language.

A DTD defines the semantics of an application language—that is, the names of elements and attributes and the markup's structure—and the hierarchy of those elements within the document. For instance, an HTML DTD dictates that the `<HTML>` element (or tag) must come first in an HTML document, followed by a `<HEAD>` tag, and then a `<BODY>` tag. You can also gather from the DTD that inside the `<HEAD>` element may be a `<META>` tag with certain attributes, such as a `name` attribute for defining certain properties of the document or an `http-equiv` attribute for gathering information for the HTTP response headers.

A DTD also references items called *entities*. An entity's primary purpose is to incorporate additional internal and external characters into the document with greater ease and efficiency. For instance, if you didn't want to type your company name over and over in your XML document, you could create an entity reference to it in your schema. Therefore, you might need to type in only the initials to your company name, but when the XML is parsed, the entire name will be printed. Entity references are delimited by the ampersand (&) and semicolon (;).

XML schemas take DTDs to another level. Like DTDs, they do a great job at defining the structure and semantics of XML documents, but they also allow for the added benefit of defining data types and namespaces. We will discuss each of these in addition to some other advantages that XML schemas have over DTDs and then discuss some other schema languages to give you an overall idea of their similarities and differences. HTML defines the static display of text, and XML defines the data itself.

DTD versus XDR Schemas

DTDs validate XML data formats as do XML schemas, which include XDR and XSD. This section covers DTD versus XDR schemas in detail.

DTD

First look at the DTD, as shown in Listing A.4.

LISTING A.4 An XML DTD

```
<?xml version='1.0' encoding='UTF-8' ?>
<!ELEMENT Transactions (Transaction+)>
<!ATTLIST Transactions  location CDATA  #REQUIRED
                         type     CDATA  #REQUIRED >
<!ELEMENT Transaction (Amount , Type , Facility , Location)>
<!ATTLIST Transaction  date CDATA  #REQUIRED
                       id   CDATA  #REQUIRED >
<!ELEMENT Amount (#PCDATA)*>
<!ATTLIST Amount  currency  (usd )  #REQUIRED >
<!ELEMENT Type (#PCDATA)*>
<!ELEMENT Facility (#PCDATA)*>
<!ELEMENT Location (Name , Address)>
<!ELEMENT Name (#PCDATA)*>
<!ELEMENT Address (#PCDATA)*>
```

The first line in the DTD is an XML *processing instruction*. This tells the application that it is dealing with an XML 1.0 DTD, rather than an SGML DTD, and that the characters are encoded in 8-bit Unicode.

The second line dictates that the first element in the document must be a `<Transactions>` element and that one or more `<Transaction>` tags will follow it. The plus (+) sign in the second line is the operator that determines the number of elements allowed in a particular node list. A *node list* is a record of the number of elements meeting a certain criteria. For instance, the length of the node list for `<Transaction>` elements in our XML instance is 2 (or 1, on a zero-based scale, for those programmers who will hold me to that). This is because there are two `<Transaction>` nodes in the document. If we add another `<Transaction>` element to the document, the length will be three.

The third and fourth lines define attributes that belong to the `<Transactions>` element. In this case, you have two attributes, named `location` and `type`. Both are required, and each consists of `CDATA`, or Character Data, which means that the characters in the attributes will be ignored by the XML parser and treated as normal text.

The fifth through the fourteenth lines convey much of the same to the XML application as the second, third, and fourth lines. The application, in this case, should expect a `<Transaction>` element with an `<Amount>` child node, a `<Type>` child node, a `<Facility>` child node, and a `<Location>` child node. Each of the child nodes contains `PCDATA`—Parsed Character Data, which means that the XML parser will search the text for things such as additional elements and any possible entity references.

XDR

At this point, you should be grasping how a DTD defines the element and attribute names in an XML document, as well as the markup's structure. Now look at Listing A.5, which shows how the same XML is defined using XDR.

LISTING A.5 An XML Schema Using the XDR Language—`Transactions.xdr`

```
<?xml version = "1.0" encoding = "UTF-8"?>
<Schema name = "Transaction.xdr"
xmlns = "urn:schemas-microsoft-com:xml-data"
xmlns:dt = "urn:schemas-microsoft-com:datatypes">
<ElementType name = "Transactions" content = "eltOnly" order = "seq" model =_
➥ "closed">
   <AttributeType name = "location" dt:type = "string" required = "yes"/>
   <AttributeType name = "type" dt:type = "string" required = "yes"/>
    <attribute type = "location"/>
    <attribute type = "type"/>
   <element type = "Transaction" minOccurs = "1" maxOccurs = "*"/>
 </ElementType>
 <ElementType name = "Transaction" content = "eltOnly" order = "seq"_
➥ model = "closed">
  <AttributeType name = "date" dt:type = "string" required = "yes"/>
  <AttributeType name = "id" dt:type = "string" required = "yes"/>
   <attribute type = "date"/>
   <attribute type = "id"/>
   <element type = "Amount"/>
   <element type = "Type"/>
   <element type = "Facility"/>
   <element type = "Location"/>
 </ElementType>
 <ElementType name = "Amount" content = "textOnly" dt:type = "fixed.14.4"_
➥ model = "closed">
  <AttributeType name = "currency" dt:type = "string" dt:value = "usd "_
➥ required = "yes"/>
   <attribute type = "currency"/>
 </ElementType>
 <ElementType name = "Type" order = "many" model = "closed"/>
 <ElementType name = "Facility" order = "many" model = "closed"/>
 <ElementType name = "Location" content = "eltOnly" order = "seq" model_
➥ = "closed">
  <element type = "Name"/>
   <element type = "Address"/>
</ElementType>
 <ElementType name = "Name" order = "many" model = "closed"/>
 <ElementType name = "Address" order = "many" model = "closed"/>
</Schema>
```

The first thing you might notice is that the XDR version is longer than the DTD and that the XDR version is written using the XML syntax. You will soon see that this extra robustness—and the decision to use XML as the syntax of choice—adds enough benefits to make it worth its heavy verbiage.

The first line of Listing A.5 is exactly the same as the first line in the DTD version, and the purpose of the processing instruction is similar as well.

The second line of Listing A.5 is where the similarity ends. Except for the fact that the XDR schema is going to define the structure of the XML documents—as the DTD did—the XDR language allows us to be much more definitive as to the data that will be encapsulated in the XML.

The following code from Listing A.5 represents the document element of the schema and the namespaces that will be used:

```
<Schema name = "Transaction.xdr"
  xmlns = "urn:schemas-microsoft-com:xml-data"
  xmlns:dt = "urn:schemas-microsoft-com:datatypes">
```

Every XML document requires a *document element*, and in this case, the schema's document element is the `<Schema>` element. The `name` attribute is of little importance, but it should be known that it can help to identify the schema's name to an application. The `xmlns` attributes are namespace identifiers and allow the processor to know what to do with particular pieces of the XML document. In this case, the default namespace is the *Uniform Resource Name* (URN), a unique identifier tied programmatically to the XDR schema.

Note

It is probably important to pause for a moment and discuss what namespaces actually represent. A *namespace* provides a simple method for qualifying element and attribute names used in [XML] documents by associating them with namespaces identified by URI references. This means that a namespace is a way to ensure that the elements and attributes that you are using in your XML are unique.

In `xmlns = "urn:schemas-microsoft-com:xml-data"`, the default namespace is set to the namespace for XDR. Therefore, each of the elements in the schema will be unique to XDR, unless otherwise directed to use another namespace. The fourth line of Listing A.5 defines another namespace, and this one is for the specification that defines how the

XML (within the scope of the XDR language) uses data types. As you work with XML, you will learn that any element or attribute prefixed with a `dt:` will be referenced to a particular data type.

Before diving much deeper into the XDR schema language, you can use Table A.1 as a guide through the rest of this section.

TABLE A.1 XML Schema Elements

Schema Element	*Description*
`attribute`	Refers to a declared attribute type that can appear within the scope of the named `ElementType` element
`AttributeType`	Defines an attribute type for use within the `Schema` element
`datatype`	Specifies the data type for the `ElementType` or `AttributeType` element
`description`	Provides documentation about an `ElementType` or `AttributeType` element
`element`	Refers to a declared element type that can appear within the scope of the named `ElementType` element
`ElementType`	Defines an element type for use within the `Schema` element
`group`	Organizes content into a group to specify a sequence
`Schema`	Identifies the start of a schema definition

The following lines of code from Listing A.5 define the `Transactions` element—that is, the `<Transactions>` tag.

```
 <ElementType name = "Transactions" content = "eltOnly" order = "seq"
➥model = "closed">
   <AttributeType name = "location" dt:type = "string" required = "yes"/>
   <AttributeType name = "type" dt:type = "string" required = "yes"/>
    <attribute type = "location"/>
    <attribute type = "type"/>
   <element type = "Transaction" minOccurs = "1" maxOccurs = "*"/>
</ElementType>
```

The `<ElementType>` Element

In the lines

```
<ElementType name = "Transactions"
 content = "eltOnly" order = "seq" model = "closed">
```

the properties of an XML element are defined by the `<ElementType>`. The element type is used to describe the specific details of a particular tag in an XML document, which in this case happens to be the `<Transactions>` tag. The name of the tag is defined by the `name` attribute. The tag name in this case will be `"Transactions"`, as shown in Listing A.6.

> **Note**
>
> The words "tag" and "element" are used synonymously throughout this appendix.

LISTING A.6 Constructs of an `<ElementType>`

```
<ElementType
  name="idref"
  content="{empty | textOnly | eltOnly | mixed}"
  dt:type="datatype"
  model="{open | closed}"
  order="{one | seq | many}">
```

Next, because the `content` attribute is set to `eltOnly`, the inclusion of text is disallowed between the opening and closing `<Transactions> </Transactions>` tags. In other words, according to the content model, putting the words "Here is some text" between the `<Transactions>` tags is *invalid*, but adding other elements—for example, the `<Transaction>` tag—to the element list is completely valid. Table A.2 shows some other properties of the content attribute.

TABLE A.2 Content Attribute Values in `<ElementType>`

Value	*Description*
`empty`	The element cannot contain content.
`textOnly`	The element can contain only text, not elements. If the `model` attribute is set to "open," the element can contain text and other unnamed elements.
`eltOnly`	The element can contain only the specified elements. It cannot contain any free text.
`Mixed`	The element can contain both elements and attributes.

The `order` and `model` attributes are also vital to the classification of the element type. The `order` attribute specifies how the elements will be sequenced within the context of this element. For instance, think of HTML. The order is important within the context of the <HTML> element because <HEAD> must go before <BODY>. However, within the context of the <P> tag, the order is not as pressing with regards to certain elements. For example, a <DIV> tag might come before a <P> tag, under which there's another <P> tag. There is no set order in which they must occur under the <BODY> element—that is, the order is set to "many." Table A.3 shows possible attribute values for the element <ElementType>.

TABLE A.3 Order Attribute Values in <ElementType>

Value	*Description*
one	Permits only one of a set of elements. For a document to correctly validate when the one attribute is specified, the model attribute for the ElementType must be specified as "closed."
seq	Requires the elements to appear in the specified sequence.
many	Permits the elements to appear (or not appear) in any order. If you specify many for the order attribute, maxOccurs values are no longer relevant during validation.

The model attribute is necessary for controlling the extensibility of the document. Remember, we are working with XML here, which means that extensibility is the key. A document can be expanded at the whim of the developer because XML models are "open" by default. However, if the model is "closed," then a developer is not allowed to add custom elements to the model. In the case of our transactions document, a developer would not be allowed to add any elements under the <Transactions> tag because the model is closed.

The <AttributeType> Element

The attribute types of the <Transactions> element are defined in Listing A.7. The <AttributeType> element defines the properties of attributes.

LISTING A.7 Constructs of an <AttributeType>

```
<AttributeType
    default="default-value"
    dt:type="primitive-type"
    dt:values="enumerated-values"
    name="idref"
    required="{yes | no}">
```

In the attribute type, you can identify the `default` value of the attribute. For example, if you wanted to create a schema for an XML document describing apple trees, you could set the default value for the `color` attribute to "red." However, it is important to remember that the default value must be legal for that attribute instance, according to its data type.

The attribute's data type values may be classified using `dt:type` (remember that the `dt:` namespace identifier corresponds to Microsoft's implementation of XML data types). As you can see, in Listing A.7, the data types have been set to the type `"string"`. Here, we could set a default value for the attribute to either `"bank"`, or `"checking"`, or whatever else would make sense in light of the application. Note that if you use the `"enumerator"` data type, then the enumerated values must go into the `dt:value` attribute, with the default value being listed first.

The final property to remember is the `required` attribute. Fairly self-explanatory, this attribute specifies whether the attribute must exist in the selected element.

The `<attribute>` Element

The following code lines contain the `<attribute>` element:

```
<attribute type = "location"/>
<attribute type = "type"/>
```

This element refers to a declared attribute type that can appear within the scope of the named `<ElementType>` element. In other words, you build an attribute definition with the `<AttributeType>` and effectively "place" it at one or more locations throughout the schema by using the `<attribute>` element.

You reference an attribute type within the attribute element by using the `type` property. For instance

```
<attribute type = "location"/>
```

references the attribute type in

```
<AttributeType name = "location" dt:type = "string" required = "yes"/>
```

because the value of its type property is `"location"`. In a sense, the `<AttributeType>` element is the real representation of the actual attribute, and the `<attribute>` element is the pointer.

There are two other properties for the `<attribute>` element, the `value` property and the `required` property. The `value` property represents a default value for the attribute that supersedes the default value set in the `<AttributeType>` element.

The `required` property simply states whether the attribute is required in the XML document. Two things to keep in mind with regard to the `required` property are that when the required attribute is set to `"yes"` and the default attribute specifies a default value, the supplied default value must always be the value, and documents containing other attribute values are invalid. When the `required` attribute is set to `"yes"` and no default is specified, each element whose type is declared to have the attribute must supply its value.

The <element> Element

The following code line introduces the `<element>` element:

```
<element type = "Transaction" minOccurs = "1" maxOccurs = "*"/>
```

Much like the `<attribute>` element you just learned about, the `<element>` is simply a pointer to the `<ElementType>` and tells the parser where a particular element needs to be within the XML document. In the preceding code line, the parser knows that the `<Transaction>` element is required under the `<Transactions>` node. This is also referred to as being *nested* within a particular node. The value of the `type` property is a pointer to the element type. Therefore, when you see

```
<element type = "Transaction" minOccurs = "1" maxOccurs = "*"/>
```

it is pointing to the following `<ElementType>`:

```
<ElementType name = "Transaction" content = "eltOnly" order = "seq"_
➥ model = "closed">
```

So, all you need is one `<ElementType>` for all your `<element>` declarations, as long as you want them to inherit their properties from that particular `<ElementType>`.

Only two other properties belong to the `<element>`. The `minOccurs` and the `maxOccurs` properties. The values of these attributes can be `"0"`, `"1"`, or `"*"`. The asterisk represents more than one. This means that an element can be used in a number of different ways, as you can see in Table A.4.

TABLE A.4 `MinOccurs` and `MaxOccurs` Attribute Values in `<element>`

`minOccurs : maxOccurs`	*Description*
1 : *	1 or more times
0 : *	0 or more times
0 : 1	0 or 1 time
1 : 1	Only 1 time

If you have been able to stick with me so far, you are going to have a much better understanding of how the BizTalk Editor works because many of the values you fill in on the Editor will correspond directly to the elements that we've just reviewed. However, we have covered only a portion of what a complete BizTalk specification represents. After we discuss a few other variations of XML schema languages, we will move on to a thorough discussion of the BizTalk specification and how it uses XDR.

Note

If you aren't completely satisfied with this introduction to XDR, visit the Microsoft MSDN site at `http://msdn.microsoft.com/library/psdk/xmlsdk/xmls5gkl.htm`. You will find it helpful in learning more about XML-Data Reduced and other XML-related technologies.

Even though it is highly recommended that our focus should remain on XDR and the W3C XML Schema language (XSD), we want to share a few other languages with you to illustrate the diverse nature from which schemas have evolved.

Other XML Schema Languages

Here is a short list of some other popular languages (including DTD, XDR, and XML Schema).

- W3C XML Schema—A W3C language specification, the XML Schema language is designed to express shared vocabularies and allow machines to carry out rules made by people. They provide a means for defining the structure, content, and semantics of XML documents. XML Schema has an advantage over previous forms of validation—for example, DTD—because of added extensibility (built on the XML syntax), namespaces, and data type functionality. For more information on W3C XML Schema, visit `http://www.w3.org/XML/Schema`.
- XDR (XML-Data Reduced) as defined by Microsoft—XDR was Microsoft's early adoption schema language. It was designed so that developers could begin learning how to use XML schemas in their applications. Microsoft has—from the beginning—stated that it would evolve all its applications to incorporate the W3C's schema language—that is, XML Schema—when it became a Recommendation. It is great to see that Microsoft is living up to its promise. XML Schema appears to be making its way onto the .NET platform, so don't be afraid to play around with XDR, but get ready for XML Schema.

- DTD—The Document Type Definition (DTD) has been around for quite some time, but if my history lessons serve me correctly, it was officially ratified in 1986, when SGML became an official ISO Standard. Although still useful and still popular among XML architects and markup specialists, DTDs are limited when it comes to defining business documents in XML. Primarily because XML schemas enable developers to define data types and easily extend their schemas—whereas DTDs do not—you will not likely see DTDs too often in the EAI or B2B application realm.
- JIS RELAX—RELAX is a much more modest XML grammar for describing XML documents than the XML Schema language. RELAX is a combination of DTD features and rich data types of XML Schema represented in the XML syntax. For the most part, RELAX can be thought of as a great transition mechanism for making the move from DTDs to XML Schema, prior to the XML Schema language becoming a Recommendation.
- Schematron—This language differs in concept from other schema languages because it is not based on grammars but on finding tree patterns in the parsed document. XSLT and XPath are used to discover context nodes and evaluate them for validity against other schema, if necessary. For more information on Schematron, visit `http://www.ascc.net/xml/resource/schematron/schematron.html`.
- Document Structure Descriptions (DSD)—A grammar-based language, DSD uses CSS-like functionality for validating XML documents. DSD allows a kind of simple path expressions for getting context-dependent validation, inspired by W3C CSS selectors. In this it provides more than W3C XML Schema but much less than Schematron, which is not constrained to the ancestor tree. For more information on DSD, visit `http://www.brics.dk/DSD/`.

APPENDIX B

BizTalk Editor Configuration Properties

IN THIS APPENDIX

This appendix takes a closer look at the BizTalk Editor, its visual properties and menus. The BizTalk Editor can be opened by navigating to the Microsoft BizTalk Server 2002 group under the `Start/Programs` folder on your desktop.

Menu Functions

In the upper-left corner, you will find the common Windows menu displayed. There are five different menu items:

- File
- Edit
- View
- Tools
- Help

The following sections describe the capabilities of each of these menu items in more detail.

The File Menu and WebDav

The File menu includes the New, Open, Close, Save, Save As, Exit, and Recent Files menu options. In addition to these basic menu options, you will also find two of the more esoteric looking options, Retrieve from WebDAV and Store to WebDAV.

WebDav (Web Distributed Authoring and Versioning) is a set of extensions to the HTTP 1.1 protocol that allows users to collaboratively edit and manage files on remote servers. It does this by exposing a hierarchical file storage media, such as a file system, over an HTTP connection. WebDav locks files when they are "busy" being accessed over the Web so that they cannot be overwritten accidentally by other users. Therefore, by using the retrieve and store capabilities of the BizTalk Editor interface, developers can easily protect their intellectual assets—that is, BizTalk specifications—using the WebDav server of their choice. By default, BizTalk Server uses your installation directory—for example, `\Program Files`—plus `\Microsoft BizTalk Server \BizTalkServerRepository \DocSpecs` as the root for your WebDav server. From there, it is as simple as storing and retrieving your document specifications to and from the WebDav directory of choice.

The Edit Menu

The Edit menu also contains some recognizable options including Cut, Copy, Paste, and Delete. However, some new options will require some serious inquiry. The New/Insert Record and New/Insert Field options seem ordinary, but there are quite a few details that a schema architect needs to consider before choosing to use either of them.

As mentioned earlier in Appendix A, "Understanding XML Schemas," XML is made up primarily of *elements* and *attributes*. Elements typically contain either other elements, in which case they are known as *parent elements*, or text and sometimes a mixture of both. Attributes on the other hand never contain other attributes or elements but always encapsulate some form of data or basic text. For instance


```
<Document_Element>
 <Element>My element might contain lots of text
   and other <OtherElement>elements</OtherElement>.
   But an attribute will only contain <A attribute="some kind of value"> some
   kind of value</A>.
 </Element>
</Document_Element>
```

Records

Microsoft lets you differentiate between *container elements* and *value elements* through the use of *records* and *fields*. A record can be thought of as a container element that encapsulates other records or fields; this feature is great for defining the structure of any document, not just XML. Here is an example:

```
<Record1> <!-- Comment: Contains Record2 -->
<Record2> <!-- Comment: Contains Field_Elements -->
  <Field_Element>This is a field element</Field_Element>
  <Record3 field_attribute="data">This is a
      record element, with a field attribute</Record3>
</Record2>
</Record1>
```

It is important to note that records can contain attributes. In fact, an easy rule to remember is that an element with anything other than text is a record. If you add an attribute to an element, it's a record. If you add a child element to an element, it's a record. The only way you can have a field in BizTalk is if you have either an element with text only or an attribute. And an attribute always represents a field. You will notice when building a BizTalk specification with the BizTalk Editor that choosing records over fields gives you different options regarding what you can do with the data, so it's important that you understand these concepts thoroughly. Table B.1 makes this more clear.

TABLE B.1 Records and Fields

	Has attributes	*Has elements*	*Has text*
No attributes	None	Record (element)	Field (element)
No elements	Field (element or is an attribute)	None	Field (element or is an attribute)
No text	Record	Record (element)	None

NOTE: Remember that a record cannot have text, and a field cannot contain elements.

Fields

As just discussed, a field can be an element or an attribute, but its primary responsibility is to handle data. Whereas a record is responsible for handling attributes and other elements, a field is responsible for describing data and text explicitly. Here are two examples of fields in an XML instance (wrapped inside a record):

```
<Record field="This is a field within a record element">
  <Field>This is a field within a record element, too</Field>
</Record>
```

This will become much more clear as we develop some of our specifications later in the chapter, so let's move along to discuss some of the other menu options.

The View Menu

The first six options of the View menu are simply links to the different tabs in the right window pane of the BizTalk Editor. The same goes for the Output and Warnings options. These will each be discussed later in this appendix. Here we will discuss an *invalid character map*. You can block a character or a range of characters from being passed through BizTalk Server by using *invalid character ranges* in the destination specification. Whenever BizTalk Server attempts to process a character specified in the Invalid Character Ranges dialog box, processing stops and an error message appears.

You can also expand and collapse the element tree in the left pane using the Expand Tree Items option and the Collapse Tree Items option.

The Tools Menu

The Tools menu probably contains the most unique options inside the BizTalk Editor. They are

- Validate Specification
- Validate Instance

- Create XML Instance
- Create Native Instance
- Import
- Export XDR Schema
- Export XSD Schema
- Options

The Validate Specification option simply allows you to validate the current specification. Any warnings will be displayed in the Warnings tab at the bottom of the Editor.

The Validate Instance option opens a Validate Document Instance window for you to choose an XML document instance you want to validate the schema against. In fact, you can use the validate instance to validate any type of document specification not just XML. You can validate against CSV, EDI, and so on. Just select the document you want to validate against, and the Warnings tab displays the status of the validation process. If there is an error, you will typically be told where it occurred in the document—that is, line number and position—and which node was at fault for the inconsistency.

Creating an XML instance in accordance with the schema or specification that you are designing is performed by choosing Tools, Create XML Instance from the menu. When you select this option, a Create Document Instance As window opens, allowing you to save a valid instance. If the document specification is describing a document type other than XML, you also have the ability to generate a native instance of the document by selecting Tools, `Create Native Instance` from the menu. Both these features give developers the ability to test their specifications prior to the completion of the application.

The Import option is a great tool for creating BizTalk specifications from current documents. When importing a document into BizTalk Editor, it must be one of the following formats:

- Well-formed XML instance
- Document type definition
- XDR schema

Tip

Importing an XML instance into BizTalk Editor is useful, but it is not generally the best way to create a specification. This is because many generalities might be missed when importing an instance, as opposed to importing a DTD or XDR schema. Remember, schemas have a lot of metadata (detailed information) about the XML document, that the XML itself cannot reveal—that is, data type.

> Also, it is possible to only put one element under a record, in an XML instance, when you want the specification to allow for more than one element in the record. If the Editor only sees one element, it's going to assume that you are going to want to limit the specification in the same manner. However, that being said, importing well-formed XML instances is a simple way to get started on developing a specification and almost always beats building one from scratch!

Importing a DTD gives you the added benefit of using someone's in-depth knowledge of the required document structure and putting it to use in your specification. A DTD cannot be developed without a thorough understanding of the document and its structure, so using a DTD is a great way to get a jump on building your specification. The only thing you need to add are the details that DTDs can't account for, such as namespaces and data types.

Perhaps the easiest way to go about developing your BizTalk specification is to import an XDR schema that someone has already built. From there, all you need to do is allow the Editor to append the necessary BizTalk-specific elements to the XDR, and you're ready to go.

If you want to create a valid XDR schema from the schema being viewed in the BizTalk Editor, you can use the Export XDR Schema option to extract all the BizTalk-specific elements from the specification and export only the XDR version. You also have the ability to export an XSD schema by using the Export XSD Schema option. These options are useful when you need to share your schema with business partners, or within your own organization, so that they can share information with you in a compatible format.

> **Note**
>
> There is also a utility called the SampleImporter in the `.\Program Files\Microsoft BizTalk Server\SDK\Messaging Samples\SampleImporter` directory that helps you create a BizTalk Editor specification from a CSV instance.

The Options menu allows you to choose to add fields as elements rather than as attributes by default. This is nothing fancy, but helpful to those you don't want to switch to an element every time they create a new field.

The Help Menu

Finally, there is the Help menu. The Help menu is nothing new to many of you, but if you choose the Microsoft BizTalk Server 2002 Help option, you will find a useful interface with sections on "Getting Started," tutorials, administration, application development, and even an interface reference for those interested in building custom components for BizTalk Server.

Left "Folder" Pane

The left pane of the BizTalk Editor displays the specification as a collapsible tree. You can identify the differences between records and fields by the type of icons displayed. Also, each node displays its respective node name.

By clicking on the nodes, you can expand or collapse the node tree, relative to the current node selected and view its properties in the right pane. If you right-click on the nodes, a menu appears that allows you to insert new records and fields, rename nodes, and delete nodes, among other things.

Right "Tab" Pane

The right pane in the BizTalk Editor is perhaps the most complex-looking section of all, but don't let its looks intimidate you. All you do here is manipulate the XML document that represents the BizTalk specification. If you understand what each of the nodes in the BizTalk specification represents and know what task you want to perform, building the specification will be a trivial task.

The right pane is split into six different tabs. Each represents a subset of the BizTalk specification. They are

- Declaration
- Reference
- Parse
- Namespace
- Dictionary
- Code List

Tip

It may be a bit baffling at first trying to figure out how to clear values from the various tabs. To do this, right-click on the property you want to reset and select Clear Property from the context menu.

The Declaration Tab

The Declaration tab's primary role is to define the name of the node, specify what type of node it is—that is, whether it is an element or an attribute—provide a description of the node, and define many of the constraints that will exist within the schema.

Tables B.2, B.3, and B.4 describe the properties of the node, depending on whether it is a root node (or document element), a record, or a field. You will get to know these properties better when you build a BizTalk specification.

Note

If you change the Name value on the Declaration tab, the name of the root node in the specification tree automatically changes to match it. In a newly created specification, changing the Name value on the Declaration tab also changes the Schema Name value on the Reference tab. However, because it is possible to have a schema name that is different from the root node name, changing the Schema Name value has no effect on the Name value or the root node name in the specification tree. After the Schema Name value has been edited, however, changing the Name value or the root node name has no effect on the Schema Name value.

TABLE B.2 Declaration Tab: Root Node Properties

Property	*Value*
Name	The name of the root node.
Description	The description of the specification.
Type	The type of record.
Model	Closed. Indicates that the data contained in the document instance and the specification structure match. Open. Indicates that the data in the document instance does not totally adhere to the structure of the specification.

TABLE B.2 continued

Property	*Value*
	If this property value is left blank, the default value is Open.
Content	Element Only. Indicates that the root node can contain only elements. This is the automatic default when the root contains a child record.
	Empty. Indicates that the root node cannot contain subelements.
	Text Only. Indicates that the root node can contain text and not subelements.
	Note:
	BizTalk Editor does not support elements that contain mixed content (text information as well as subelements).
Order	Select one of the following values:
	One. Indicates that one and only one of the constituent elements can appear.
	Sequence. Indicates that the constituent elements must appear in the order specified.
	Many. Indicates that zero or more of the constituent elements can appear, in any order or combination.

TABLE B.3 Declaration Tab: Record Properties

Property	*Value*
Name	The name of the record.
Description	The description of the record.
Type	The type of record.
Model	Closed. Indicates that the data contained in the document instance and the specification structure match.
	Open. Indicates that the data in the document instance and the specification structure do not match.
	If this property value is left blank, the default value is Open.
Content	Element Only. Indicates that the record can contain only elements. This is the automatic default for any record that contains a child record.

Table B.3 continued

Property	*Value*
	Empty. Indicates that the record cannot contain subelements.
	Text Only. Indicates that the record can contain text and not subelements.
	Mixed. Indicates that the record can contain text and elements.
Order	Select one of the following values:
	One. Indicates that one and only one of the constituent elements can appear.
	Sequence. Indicates that the constituent elements must appear in the order specified.
	Many. Indicates that zero or more of the constituent elements can appear, in any order or combination.
Cycle Count	Type the number of cycles you want to be available below the base record. For more information, see Cyclical References in the BizTalk Server documentation.
	Note:
	This property field appears only if you have created a cyclical reference.

Table B.4 Declaration Tab: Field Properties

Property	*Value*
Name	The name of the field.
Description	The description of the field.
Type	Select one of the following values:
	Element
	Attribute
Model	Closed. Indicates that the data contained in the document instance and the specification structure match.
	Open. Indicates that the data in the document instance and the specification structure do not match.

TABLE B.4 continued

Property	*Value*
	Note: If this property value is left blank, the default value is Open. The Model property is available only for a field with its Type value set to Element.
Content	Text Only. Indicates that the record can contain text and not subelements. **Note:** The Content property is available only for a field with its Type value set to Element. Text Only is the only value available for the Content property of a field.
Data Type	A valid data type. **Important:** If the Standard property value on the Reference tab is set to X12, EDIFACT, or Custom, you can assign a Custom Data Type value on the Parse tab. If you specify a Custom Data Type value, the value in the Data Type field is automatically changed to match the selection that you specified for the Custom Data Type value. If you already have a value specified in the Custom Data Type field and then specify a value in the Data Type field on the Declaration tab, the value specified in the Custom Data Type field is cleared. In a specification, if you create a field with the Data Type property set to IDREF or IDREFS, you must create another field in that specification with the Data Type set to ID. To select a field for tracking or for use in a channel filtering expression in BizTalk Messaging Manager, you must assign a data type to that field in the specification. More information on tracking can be found in Chapter 3, "Overview of BizTalk Server."
Data Type Values	If you select Enumeration in the Data Type list, the data type values "a b c" appear by default in the Data Type Values box. You can replace the default values with custom values separated by spaces.

TABLE B.4 continued

Property	Value
	If you are working with an X12 or EDIFACT document and include codes associated with a particular field, those codes automatically appear in the Data Type Values box, and Enumeration automatically appears in the Data Type box.
Minimum Length	The minimum number of characters that the field can contain. **Note:** The Minimum Length property can be set only for fields with the following Data Type values: String, Number, Binary (base64), and Binary (hex).
Maximum Length	The maximum number of characters that the field can contain. **Note:** The Maximum Length property can be set only for fields with the following Data Type values: String, Number, Binary (base64), and Binary (hex).
Default Value	The value that is provided if the incoming document instance does not contain the field. **Note:** The Default Value property appears only in specifications when the Standard property (on the Reference tab for the root node) is set to XML, and the Type property (on the Declaration tab for the field) is set to Attribute.

The Reference Tab

The Reference tab handles most of the metadata that deals with the purpose of the document directly. You will notice in Tables B.5, B.6, and B.7 that almost all the properties are related to the document element, and only a few are applicable to records and fields. However, the few properties that do involve the record and field nodes are fairly important. For instance, in a record, the Reference tab allows you to define the minimum and maximum number of times the node can occur as a child under a parent node. You also define whether the field is required and, if it is a positional flatfile, where the start and end positions are for this particular field.

TABLE B.5 Reference Tab: Root Node Properties

Property	*Value*
Specification Name	The name of the specification. This name corresponds to the value of the `<Schema>` tag in the specification.
Standard	Select one of the following values: XML for creating a specification based on Extensible Markup Language (XML). X12 for creating a specification based on X12. EDIFACT for creating a specification based on EDIFACT. Custom for creating a specification based on flat file, or for creating a custom specification to be parsed with a custom parser.
Standards Version	The standards version, such as X12 version 4010, on which the specification is based.
Document Type	The document type, such as 850, on which the specification is based.
Version	The version number of the document standard on which the specification is based.
Default Record	Character Delimiter used as Delimiter node for which the Delimiter Type on the Parse tab is set to Default Record Delimiter. **Note:** This property field displays only if the Standard field on the Reference tab (for the root node) is set to Custom.
Default Field Delimiter	Type or select a character to be used as the delimiter within any node for which the Delimiter Type on the Parse tab is set to Default Field Delimiter. **Note:** This property field displays only if the Standard field on the Reference tab (for the root node) is set to Custom.
Default Subfield Delimiter	Type or select a character that will be used as the delimiter within any node for which the Delimiter Type on the Parse tab is set to Default Subfield Delimiter. **Note:** This property field displays only if the Standard field on the Reference tab (for the root node) is set to Custom.

Table B.5 continued

Property	*Value*
Default Escape Character	Type or select a character that will be used as the escape character within any node for which the Escape Type on the Parse tab is set to Default Escape Delimiter. **Note:** This property field displays only if the Standard field on the Reference tab (for the root node) is set to Custom.
Code Page	Choose one of the following values: Arabic (1256) Baltic (1257) Central-European (1250) Cyrillic (1251) Greek (1253) Hebrew (1255) Japanese-Shift-JIS (932) Korean (949) Little-Endian-UTF16 (1200) Simplified-Chinese-GBK (936) Thai (874) Traditional-Chinese-Big5 (950) Turkish (1254) Vietnamese (1258) Western-European (1252) **Note:** This property field displays only if the Standard field on the Reference tab (for the root node) is set to Custom. UTF7 (65000) and UTF8 (65001) are not supported by BizTalk Server. If the Code Page value is left blank, the default value is Western-European (1252).

TABLE B.5 continued

Property	*Value*
Receipt	Choose one of the following options: Yes. Indicates that the specification is to be used as an inbound receipt document. A correlator component (X12, EDIFACT, or CUSTOM) is expected to correlate the receipt document to the outbound document that it acknowledges (in other words, something previously sent to the sender of the receipt). No. Indicates that the specification is not to be used as an inbound receipt document. **Notes:** If the receipt value is left blank, the default value is No. For specifications based on the `CanonicalReceipt` and for specifications to which the `CanonicalReceipt` is mapped (both are used in the scenario of generating an outbound receipt), the Receipt property should be set to No.
Envelope	Choose one of the following options: Yes. Indicates that the specification is an interchange specification. No. Indicates that the specification is not an interchange specification. More information about envelopes is available in Chapter 5, "The BizTalk Mapper."
Target Namespace	If you have a BizTalk Framework instance and have specified a namespace in the instance, you must enter the corresponding namespace used in the instance. **Note:** If you use "x-schema" in the target namespace value of an instance, you might cause a test failure when you test the instance in BizTalk Mapper.

TABLE B.6 Reference Tab: Record Properties

Property	*Value*
Minimum Occurrences	The minimum number of times a record can occur in its position within the node hierarchy. Possible values are 0 or 1. **Note:** If this property value is left blank, the default value is 1.
Maximum Occurrences	The maximum number of times a record can occur in its position within the node hierarchy. Possible values are 1 and *. **Note:** If you type an asterisk (*), the record is considered to be a looping record. If this specification is used in BizTalk Mapper, it compiles this record as a loop. If you type 1, BizTalk Mapper does not consider this record to be a looping record. If this property value is left blank, the default value is 1.

TABLE B.7 Reference Tab: Field Properties

Property	*Value*
Required	Choose one of the following options: Yes. Indicates that the field is required. No. Indicates that the field is not required. If this property value is left blank, the default value is No.
Start Position	A number that indicates the starting position of the field in the record. **Note:** This property field displays only if the structure of the parent record is positional.
End Position	A number that indicates the ending position of the field in the record. **Note:** This property field displays only if the structure of the parent record is positional.

> **Note**
>
> For positional file schemas, you can just put the length of the field and then right-click on the record node and select the Calculate Field Positions menu option.

The Parse Tab

The Parse tab contains the properties described in Tables B.8 through B.13. The available properties depend on the standard (`X12`, `EDIFACT`, or `Custom`) and on the structure property that you use. By default, new specifications based on a blank specification have a standard property of XML. For each property, enter a value as needed. The primary role of this tab is for setting delimiter information, as well as instructions for controlling the parsing of the messages.

> **Note**
>
> No parsing properties are required for XML documents.

TABLE B.8 Parse Tab: Root Node or Record Properties

Property	*Value*
Structure	This value automatically defaults to Delimited for the root node. **Note:** If the Standard property value is set to `X12` or `EDIFACT` on the Reference tab for the root node of a specification, you cannot edit the Structure property value on the Parse tab for the root node or any record. If you want to edit the Structure property value, you must change the standard to `CUSTOM`.
Source Tag Identifier	The name of the source tag identifier. This is the tag name used to match the record with the data. **Note:** For a non-XML file, such as a flat file, you can type a Source Tag Identifier property to identify any tag that might exist in the original file. The Source Tag Identifier property is case sensitive.

TABLE B.8 continued

Property	*Value*
Field Order	Select one of the following options: Prefix. A prefix delimiter appears before each component, and each member of a component in a series. For example, where * is the delimiter: *a*a*b*c. Postfix. A postfix delimiter appears after each component and each member of a component in a series. For example, where * is the delimiter: a*a*b*c*. Infix. An infix delimiter appears between components and members of components in a series. For example, where * is the delimiter: a*a*b*c. This is the inherent field order for all EDI documents. **Note:** If the Field Order value is left blank, the default value is Prefix.
Delimiter Type	Select one of the following options to choose a delimiter for the child nodes directly below the current node: Default Record Delimiter. Indicates that the delimiter is the value of the Default Record Delimiter property, which is defined in the document instance. Default Field Delimiter. Indicates that the delimiter is the value of the Default Field Delimiter property, which is defined in the document instance. Default Subfield Delimiter. Indicates that the delimiter is the value of the Default Subfield Delimiter property, which is defined in the document instance.
Escape Type (Also known as an escape character)	Select the following option to indicate that you want an escape character for the child nodes directly below the current node: Default Escape Character. Indicates that the escape character is a value defined in the document instance. An escape character is useful if you have a character in your field data that is also used as the delimiter character for the field's parent node. For example, if your field data is *Browne,Peter,1231,yes*

TABLE B.8 continued

Property	*Value*
	and you have chosen a comma as the delimiter value of the node that contains the field, BizTalk Editor interprets the comma after "Browne" to be a delimiter, even if you intend for it to be part of the field data. A solution for this is to place an escape character directly preceding the delimiter character that you want to include in the field data. For example, if your escape character is specified as a backslash, you can place a backslash directly preceding a delimiter character as in the following example: *Browne\,Peter,1231,yes* The comma after the backslash is interpreted by BizTalk Editor as field data rather than a delimiter character. Using the preceding example, the field data would be Browne, Peter **Note:** The Escape Type property is not available for `X12` specifications.
Append New Line	Select one of the following options: Yes. Indicates that when the serializer reaches the record delimiter, the serializer automatically appends a new line (LF,0x0A). No. Indicates that when the serializer reaches the record delimiter, the serializer continues on the same line for the following record. **Note:** If the Append New Line value is left blank, the default value is No.
Skip Carriage Return	Select one of the following options: Yes. Tells the parser to skip the carriage return (CR) value after a delimiter. No. Tells the parser not to skip the CR value after a delimiter. **Note:** If the Skip Carriage Return value is left blank, the default value is Yes.

Table B.8 continued

Property	*Value*
Skip Line Feed	Select one of the following options: Yes. Tells the parser to skip the line feed (LF) value after a delimiter. No. Tells the parser not to skip the LF value after a delimiter. **Note:** If the Skip Line Feed value is left blank, the default value is Yes.
Ignore Record Count	Select one of the following options: Yes. Tells the parser or the serializer not to count this record when counting the total number of records in the specification. No. Tells the parser or the serializer to count this record when counting the total number of records in the specification. **Notes:** When a document instance is submitted to BizTalk Server, if the number of records in the document instance does not match the calculated number of records in the specification, a parsing failure results. If the Ignore Record Count value is left blank, the default value is Yes.

Standard: ***X12 or EDIFACT***

Table B.9 Parse Tab: Field Properties

Property	*Value*
Custom Data Type	Select one of the following options: String (AN). AN is for alphanumeric fields. Binary Hexadecimal (B). B is for binary fields. Date (CY). CY is for four-digit date fields. Number (D0-D4). D0 through D4 (inclusive) are for decimal fields. The single-digit number represents the number of digits to the right of the decimal.

TABLE B.9 continued

Property	*Value*
	Date (DT). DT is for date fields. String (ID). ID is for identification fields. Number (N). N is for integer fields. Number (N0-9). N0 through N9 (inclusive) are for implied decimal fields (the decimal character does not appear in the data). The single-digit number represents the number of digits to the right of the decimal. Number (R). R is for real number fields. Number (R0-R9). R0 through R9 (inclusive) are for real number fields. The single-digit number represents the number of digits to the right of the decimal. Time (TM). TM is for time fields. **Important:** If you specify a Custom Data Type value, the value in the Data Type field on the Declaration tab is automatically changed to match the selection that you specified for the Custom Data Type value. For example, if you change the Custom Data Type on the Parse tab to Date (CY), the Data Type value on the Declaration tab automatically changes to Date. If you specify a value in the Data Type field on the Declaration tab, the value specified in the Custom Data Type field is cleared. **Notes:** If you specify Date (DT), Date (CY), or Time (TM) for the Custom Data Type property, you must also set a value for the Custom Date/Time Format property. All these custom data type values are supported in specifications with the Standard property set to X12. For specifications with the Standard property set to EDIFACT, the supported custom data type values are String (AN) and Number (N).
Custom Date/Time	If you set Date (DT), Date (CY), Format character for (TM) as the Custom Data Type property, click an option in the list.

TABLE B.9 continued

Property	*Value*
	Notes:
	This property field is available only if the Custom Data Type is set to Date (DT), Date (CY), or Time (TM).
Justification	Select one of the following options:
	Left. Aligns data to the left in positional files when the data is less than the maximum field length. Also aligns data to the left in delimited files when the amount of data is less than the minimum length requirement.
	Right. Aligns data to the right in positional files.
	Notes:
	If the Justification value is left blank, the default value is Left.
Pad Character	Type a character to pad the field. You can choose any character for a pad character, including a space or a zero.
Wrap Character	Type a character to enclose field data. This property is useful if you have a character in your field data that is also used as the delimiter value for the field's parent node. For example, if your field data is
	Browne,Peter,1231,yes
	and you have chosen a comma as the delimiter value of the node that contains the field, BizTalk Editor interprets the comma after "Browne" to be a delimiter, even if you intend for it to be part of the field data. A solution for this is to define a value for the wrap character property and then enclose the field data in the wrap character. For example, you can set the wrap character property to double quotation marks for the first field and then type your field data as in the following example:
	"Browne,Peter",1231,yes
	The comma between the double quotation marks is interpreted by BizTalk Editor to be field data rather than a delimiter value.
	Notes:
	If your field data includes characters that are also used as the wrap character, you must enclose those characters in another set of wrap characters.

TABLE B.9 continued

Property	*Value*
	For example, with the wrap character value set to double quotation marks, *"Browne,Peter ""Pete"""* is parsed by BizTalk Editor to appear as *Browne,Peter "Pete"* If the field data in an input document instance includes the line feed character followed directly by the carriage return character, the corresponding field data in the output document instance includes only the line feed character, even if both are enclosed in a set of wrap characters.
Minimum Length with Pad Character	The minimum length of a field in an output document instance, including pad characters. **Notes:** This property is available only if the pad character is set for that field. If the Minimum Length property on the Declaration tab is set for the field, the Minimum Length with Pad Character property must be greater than or equal to the value of the Minimum Length property. If the Minimum Length property is not set, the Minimum Length with Pad Character property must be greater than or equal to one.

Standard: ***Custom***

Structure Property: ***Delimited***

TABLE B.10 Parse Tab: Root Node or Record Properties

Property	*Value*
Structure	Select the following option for the Root Node property: Delimited. Indicates that the root node is based on a delimited file structure. Records can be individually based on delimited or positional file structures. Select one of the following options for Record properties: Delimited. Indicates that the record is based on a delimited file structure. Descendant records can be individually based on delimited or positional file structures.

TABLE B.10 continued

Property	*Value*
	Positional. Indicates that the record is based on a positional file structure. Positional records cannot have child records. **Note:** For a document to be both delimited and positional, the root node must have its Structure property set to Delimited. You can then set the Structure property for individual records to Positional or Delimited, as necessary. If you change from one structure to another, a message box appears. Click Yes to confirm the structure change. Some new properties might appear, and some existing properties might be removed. If you right-click the Structure property value field of a positional record and click Clear Property, BizTalk Editor interprets the structure of the record as delimited. Some new properties might appear, and some existing properties might be removed. When the Standard property for a document is set to Custom, by default the Structure property for the root node and all records is blank. If you leave the Structure property blank, its value is Delimited.
Source Tag Identifier	The name of the source tag identifier. This is the tag name that is used to match the record with the data. **Note:** For a non-XML file, such as a flat file, you can type a Source Tag Identifier property to identify any tag that might exist in the original file. The Source Tag Identifier property is case sensitive.
Field Order	Select one of the following options: Prefix. A prefix delimiter appears before each component, and each member of a component, in a series. For example, where * is the delimiter: *a*a*b*c. Postfix. A postfix delimiter appears after each component, and each member of a component, in a series. For example, where * is the delimiter: a*a*b*c*.

TABLE B.10 continued

Property	*Value*
	Infix. An infix delimiter appears between components, and members of components, in a series. For example, where * is the delimiter: a*a*b*c. This is the inherent field order for all electronic data interchange (EDI) documents. **Note** If the field order value is left blank, the default value is Prefix.
Delimiter Type	Select one of the following options to choose a delimiter for the child nodes directly below the current node: Character. Allows you to designate a delimiter value on the Parse tab. If you select Character, you must specify a delimiter value. Default Record Delimiter. Indicates that the delimiter is the value of the Default Record Delimiter property, on the Reference tab for the root node. Default Field Delimiter. Indicates that the delimiter is the value of the Default Field Delimiter property, on the Reference tab for the root node. Default Subfield Delimiter. Indicates that the delimiter is the value of the Default Subfield Delimiter property, on the Reference tab for the root node.
Delimiter Value	Type or select a character value for the delimiter. To specify a delimiter value, you must first set the Delimiter Type to Character on the Parse tab.
Escape Type (Also known as an escape character)	Select one of the following options to choose a release character for the child nodes directly below the current node: Character. Allows you to designate an escape character value on the Parse tab. If you select Character, you must specify an escape value. Default Escape Character. Indicates that the escape character is the value of the Default Escape Delimiter property, on the Reference tab for the root node.

TABLE B.10 continued

Property	*Value*
	An escape character is useful if you have a character in your field data that is also used as the delimiter character for the field's parent node. For example, if your field data is *Browne,Peter,1231,yes* and you have chosen a comma as the delimiter value of the node that contains the field, BizTalk Editor interprets the comma after "Browne" to be a delimiter, even if you intend for it to be part of the field data. A solution for this is to place an escape character directly preceding the delimiter character that you want to include in the field data. For example, if your escape character is specified as a backslash, you can place a backslash directly preceding a delimiter character as in the following example: *Browne\,Peter,1231,yes* The comma after the backslash is interpreted by BizTalk Editor as field data rather than a delimiter character.
Escape Value	Type or select a character value for the escape character. To specify an escape character value, you must first set the Escape Type to Character on the Parse tab.
Append New Line	Select one of the following options: Yes. Indicates that when the parser reaches the record delimiter, the parser must move to the next line and begin with the following record on that line. No. Indicates that when the parser reaches the record delimiter, the parser must continue on the same line for the following record. **Note:** If the Append New Line value is left blank, the default value is No.
Skip Carriage Return	Select one of the following options: Yes. Tells the parser to skip the carriage return (CR) value after a delimiter. No. Tells the parser not to skip the CR value after a delimiter.

TABLE B.10 continued

Property	*Value*
	Note: If the Skip Carriage Return value is left blank, the default value is Yes.
Skip Line Feed	Select one of the following options: Yes. Tells the parser to skip the line feed (LF) value after a delimiter. No. Tells the parser not to skip the LF value after a delimiter. **Note:** If the Skip Line Feed value is left blank, the default value is Yes.
Ignore Record Count	Select one of the following options: Yes. Tells the parser or the serializer not to count this record when counting the total number of records in the specification. No. Tells the parser or the serializer to count this record when counting the total number of records in the specification. **Note:** When a document instance is submitted to BizTalk Server, if the number of records in the document instance does not match the calculated number of records in the specification, a parsing failure results. If the Ignore Record Count value is left blank, the default value is Yes.

Standard: ***Custom***

Structure Property: ***Delimited***

TABLE B.11 Parse Tab: Field Properties

Property	*Value*
Custom Data Type	Select one of the following options: String (AN). AN is for alphanumeric fields. Binary Hexadecimal (B). B is for binary fields. Date (CY). CY is for four-digit date fields. Number (D0-D4). D0 through D4 (inclusive) are for decimal fields. The single-digit number represents the number of digits to the right of the decimal. Date (DT). DT is for date fields. String (ID). ID is for identification fields. Number (N). N is for integer fields. Number (N0-9). N0 through N9 (inclusive) are for implied decimal fields (the decimal character does not appear in the data). The single-digit number represents the number of digits to the right of the decimal. Number (R). R is for real number fields. Number (R0-R9). R0 through R9 (inclusive) are for real number fields. The single-digit number represents the number of digits to the right of the decimal. Time (TM). TM is for time fields. **Important:** If you specify a Custom Data Type value, the value in the Data Type field on the Declaration tab is automatically changed to match the selection that you specified for the Custom Data Type value. For example, if you change the Custom Data Type on the Parse tab to Date (CY), the Data Type value on the Declaration tab automatically changes to Date. If you specify a value in the Data Type field on the Declaration tab, the value specified in the Custom Data Type field is cleared. **Note:** If you specify Date (DT), Date (CY), or Time (TM) for the Custom Data Type property, you must also set a value for the Custom Date/Time Format property.

TABLE B.11 continued

Property	*Value*
Custom Date/Time	If you set Date (DT), Date (CY), Formator Time (TM) as the Custom Data Type property, click an option in the list. **Note:** This property field is available only if the Custom Data Type is set to Date (DT), Date (CY), or Time (TM).
Justification	Select one of the following options: Left. Aligns data to the left in positional files when the data is less than the maximum field length. This also aligns data to the left in delimited files when the amount of data is less than the minimum length requirement. Right. Aligns data to the right in positional files. **Note:** If no value is selected for the Justification property, data is aligned to the left by default. If the Justification value is left blank, the default value is Left.
Pad Character	Type or select a character to pad the field. You can choose any character for a pad character, including a space or a zero.
Wrap Character	Type a character to enclose field data. This property is useful if you have a character in your field data that is also used as the delimiter value for the field's parent node. For example, if your field data is *Browne,Peter,1231,yes* and you have chosen a comma as the delimiter value of the node that contains the field, BizTalk Editor interprets the comma after "Browne" to be a delimiter, even if you intend for it to be part of the field data. The solution to this is to define a value for the wrap character property and then enclose the field data in the wrap character. For example, you can set the wrap character property to double quotation marks for the first field and then type your field data as in the following example: *"Browne,Peter",1231,yes*

TABLE B.11 continued

Property	*Value*
	The comma between the double quotation marks is interpreted by BizTalk Editor to be field data rather than a delimiter value. **Note:** If you have characters in your field data that are also used as the wrap character, you must enclose those characters in another set of wrap characters. For example, with the wrap character value set to double quotation marks, *"Browne,Peter ""Pete"""* is parsed by BizTalk Editor to appear as *Browne,Peter "Pete".* If the field data in an input document instance includes the line feed character followed directly by the carriage return character, the corresponding field data in the output document instance includes only the line feed character, even if both are enclosed in a set of wrap characters.
Minimum Length with Pad Character	The minimum length of a field in an output document instance, including pad characters. **Note:** This property can be set for a field only if the pad character is set for that field. If the Minimum Length property on the Declaration tab is set for the field, the Minimum Length with Pad Character property must be greater than or equal to the value of the Minimum Length property. If the Minimum Length property is not set, the Minimum Length with Pad Character property must be greater than or equal to one.

Standard: ***Custom***

Structure Property: ***Positional***

TABLE B.12 Parse Tab: Root Node or Record Properties

Property	*Value*
Structure	Select the following option for the Root Node property: Positional. Indicates that the root node is based on a positional file structure. **Note:** A document with a positional root node can have no records. If you right-click the Structure property value field of a positional root node and click Clear Property, BizTalk Editor interprets the structure of the root node as delimited. Some new properties might appear, and some existing properties might be removed. When the Standard property for a document is set to Custom, by default the Structure property for the root node and all records is blank. If you leave the Structure property blank, its value is Delimited.
Source Tag Identifier	The name of the source tag identifier. This is the tag name that is used to match the record with the data. **Note:** For a non-XML file, such as a flat file, you can type a Source Tag Identifier property to identify any tag that might exist in the original file. The Source Tag Identifier property is case sensitive.
Source Tag Position	A number that refers to the position of the beginning of the tag in a positional record.
Append Newline	Select one of the following options: Yes. Indicates that when the parser reaches the record delimiter, the parser must move to the next line and begin with the following record on that line. No. Indicates that when the parser reaches the record delimiter, the parser must continue on the same line for the following record. **Note:** If the Append New Line value is left blank, the default value is No.

TABLE B.12 continued

Property	*Value*
Skip Carriage Return	Select one of the following options: Yes. Tells the parser to skip the carriage return (CR) value after a delimiter. No. Tells the parser not to skip the CR value after a delimiter. **Note:** If the Skip Carriage Return value is left blank, the default value is Yes.
Skip Line Feed	Select one of the following options: Yes. Tells the parser to skip the line feed (LF) value after a delimiter. No. Tells the parser not to skip the LF value after a delimiter. **Note:** If the Skip Line Feed value is left blank, the default value is Yes.
Ignore Record Count	Select one of the following options: Yes. Tells the parser or the serializer not to count this record when counting the total number of records in the specification. No. Tells the parser or the serializer to count this record when counting the total number of records in the specification. **Note:** When a document instance is submitted to BizTalk Server, if the number of records in the document instance does not match the calculated number of records in the specification, a parsing failure results. If the Ignore Record Count value is left blank, the default value is Yes.

Standard: ***Custom***

Structure Property: ***Positional***

TABLE B.13 Parse Tab: Field Properties

Property	*Value*
Custom Data Type	Select one of the following options: String (AN). AN is for alphanumeric fields. Binary Hexadecimal (B). B is for binary fields. Date (CY). CY is for four-digit date fields. Number (D0-D4). D0 through D4 (inclusive) are for decimal fields. The single-digit number represents the number of digits to the right of the decimal. Date (DT). DT is for date fields. String (ID). ID is for identification fields. Number (N). N is for integer fields. Number (N0-9). N0 through N9 (inclusive) are for implied decimal fields (the decimal character does not appear in the data). The single-digit number represents the number of digits to the right of the decimal. Number (R). R is for real number fields. Number (R0-R9). R0 through R9 (inclusive) are for real number fields. The single-digit number represents the number of digits to the right of the decimal. Time (TM). TM is for time fields. **Important:** If you specify a Custom Data Type value, the value in the Data Type field on the Declaration tab is automatically changed to match the selection that you specified for the Custom Data Type value. For example, if you change the Custom Data Type on the Parse tab to Date (CY), the Data Type value on the Declaration tab automatically changes to Date. If you specify a value in the Data Type field on the Declaration tab, the value specified in the Custom Data Type field is cleared. **Note:** If you specify Date (DT), Date (CY), or Time (TM) for the Custom Data Type property, you must also set a value for the Custom Date/Time Format property.

TABLE B.13 continued

Property	*Value*
Custom Date/Time Format	If you set Date (DT), Date (CY), or Time (TM) as the Custom Data Type property, click an option in the list. **Note:** This property field is active only if the Custom Data Type is set to Date (DT), Date (CY), or Time (TM).
Justification	Select one of the following options: Left. Aligns data to the left in positional files when the data is less than the maximum field length. Also aligns data to the left in delimited files when the amount of data is less than the minimum length requirement. Right. Aligns data to the right in positional files. **Note:** If the Justification value is left blank, the default value is Left.
Pad Character	Type a character to be used to pad the field. You can choose any character for a pad character, including a space or a zero.

The Namespace Tab

The purpose of the Namespace tab is to serve as a place to declare namespace *prefixes* and *URNs* (*Uniform Resource Name*). BizTalk defines three namespaces `automatically`, because they are the building blocks of the specification. There is one for XDR, another for BizTalk-specific tags, and one more to define data types. Table B.14 outlines these namespaces.

TABLE B.14 Default Namespaces in BizTalk Editor

Prefix	*Namespace*
`(default)`	`urn:schemas-microsoft-com:xml-data`
`b`	`urn:schemas-microsoft-com:BizTalkServer`
`d`	`urn:schemas-microsoft-com:datatypes`

To add a new namespace, right-click on the editable section and choose Add from the context menu.

The Dictionary Tab

In a typical messaging application, information about where a business document needs to be routed to will be hard-coded into the application. However, sometimes this information will not be available, and the business documents themselves must be able to provide this information. At times, the routing information might need to be added to the routing header manually; but if this information is already in the data document, the BizTalk Editor can help you extract that information and insert it into the routing header. The Dictionary tab allows the XML architect to tell BizTalk where to look for routing information in the data document.

When you view this tab, you will notice six predefined properties. The first one worth noting is the Document Container Node property. This property represents the data document—or business document—as a whole. The idea is that you wrap this document with BizTalk-specific routing information and then after it is delivered to its final destination, the routing information will be stripped away, and the business document will be parsed—that is, processed—accordingly.

The rest of the properties relate to explicit fields within the document, as outlined in Tables B.15 and B.16.

TABLE B.15 Dictionary Tab: Root Node or Record Properties

Property	*Node Path*
Document Container Node	In an envelope schema, the document node indicates the record that contains the document.

TABLE B.16 Dictionary Tab: Field Properties

Property	*Node Path*
Document Name	Displays the path to the field of a document instance that contains the document name.
Source Type	Displays the path to the field of a document instance that contains the source type.
Source Value	Displays the path to the field of a document instance that contains the source value.
Destination Type	Displays the path to the field of a document instance that contains the destination type.
Destination Value	Displays the path to the field of a document instance that contains the destination value.

Now that you have seen all the properties and what their particular purposes are, you need to use a language called XPath to point to the fields in the data document. XPath is, in part, a query language that can be used to point to nodes within an XML document. An XPath statement will be placed in the Node Path column to locate the field required for that particular property.

Note

You can learn more about XPath in Appendix A, "Understanding XML Schemas."

The Code List Tab

The Code List tab is used for EDI-related specifications (X12 and EDIFACT) that require special codes to be attached to fields in the business document. Not all fields in a specification based on X12 or EDIFACT have codes associated with them. The codes that are valid for particular fields will be displayed when applicable and are associated with a field if the check box in the Value field is selected. A description of the codes will be displayed in the Description column as well.

Note

An association is displayed on the Declarations tab when you associate a code with a field on the Code List tab, and the data type automatically will be set to Enumeration. The enumeration value will be the code list numbers you selected on the Code List tab.

Bottom "Output" Pane

The bottom pane serves two purposes. One is to show the output (or the result) of a process, such as the validation of an XML instance. The other is to show any warnings that might occur while running through a parsing procedure. This window can assist BizTalk developers in finding out where their schemas are "breaking" and why.

INDEX

A

C

Q–R

S

X–Z